# REFERENCE ONLY

D1348552

# A DICTIONARY
# OF IRISH LAW

(A Sourcebook)

Also by Henry Murdoch:

Invention and the Irish Patent System (1971) — published by the Administrative Research Bureau, Dublin University.

Working Women, An International Survey (1984) — Chapter on Ireland — published by John Wiley & Sons, London.

Building Society Law in Ireland — A Guide (1989) — published by Topaz Publications, Dublin.

Cover: Design Council, 22 Crofton Road,
Dun Laoghaire,
Co Dublin

# A DICTIONARY

# OF

# IRISH LAW

(A Sourcebook)

by

**Henry Murdoch**

BE, C.Eng, F.IEI, MBA.
**Barrister**

WITH A FOREWORD BY

The Hon. Thomas A. Finlay
Chief Justice

Topaz Publications, Dublin 1988 and 1993

First published in 1988 by Topaz Publications, 10 Haddington Lawn, Glenageary, Co Dublin.

Computer typeset and printed in Ireland by Dublin University Press Limited, 17 Gilford Road, Sandymount, Dublin 4.

| First Edition | November 1988 |
| Reprinted | December 1988 |
| Reprinted | March 1990 |
| Reprinted | September 1992 |
| Braille Edition | May 1989 |
| Second Edition | September 1993 |

*British Library Cataloguing in Publication Data.*
Murdoch, Henry,
 A dictionary of Irish law.
 1. Ireland (Republic). Law
 344.17

ISBN   0 9514032 3 0 (hardback)
ISBN   0 9514032 4 9 (paperback)

Professional advice should be obtained before acting on the information contained in this book.

To my father who in his 89th year has given me tremendous encouragement and sound advice and to my wife Davida and my children Maeve and Breffni, who continue to accept this dictionary as a member of the family.

v

## FOREWORD TO FIRST EDITION

A dictionary of law is and has always been an intensely useful book. A dictionary of Irish law, the first as far as I am aware in anything like modern times, is particularly welcome.

This dictionary provides an excellent tool in the hands of lawyers both experienced and those less experienced as well. It will, I am certain, also provide an extremely convenient, if not indispensable, piece of equipment to persons of other disciplines who have, from time to time or consistently, recourse to the law or concern with the law or with legal documents.

The author has been most painstaking in the compilation of this dictionary and has been extremely conscientious in the accuracy of the information which he has provided. It seems to me a particularly attractive feature that this dictionary should bring the law up to a date so close to the time of its publication.

I warmly welcome this book and I have no doubt that it will attain the success and make the contribution to the understanding and administration of Irish law which it clearly deserves to do.

The 3rd day of November 1988.

Thomas A. Finlay
Chief Justice,
Four Courts,
Dublin 7.

## PREFACE TO FIRST EDITION (1988)

I have written this book because, despite the development of our own legal system over the last sixty six years, there is no reference book available which gives to the reader a definition of the principal words and phrases which are encountered in Irish law. This book seeks to fill that gap by providing in one volume a definition of these key words, giving in most instances the legal source of such definition, whether statutory or judicial, and a brief introduction to the relevant law.

The book is designed primarily for busy practising lawyers, whether barrister or solicitor, who want an aide memoire or an introduction to an area of law with which they are not immediately familiar, and which will either fulfil their needs there and then, or point the correct direction for further information.

However, I hope that the book will prove useful also to the growing number of persons who are directly involved in or who encounter the law in their work, study, or otherwise eg students, company secretaries, accountants, auctioneers, bankers, journalists, engineers, architects, medical personnel, the Gardai, local and national politicians, trade union officials, employers and managers, and those involved in the public service, insurance, trade associations, or in law enforcement generally and of course the general public.

The book is extensively cross-referenced to increase its usefulness. ......Reference is made to the growing number of books on Irish law which can be consulted for further information. Included also are references to books on UK law where they are of relevance to Ireland and to those legal maxims in Latin which are in everyday use or which capture the essence or historical basis of our law.

I have endeavoured to cover all areas of law; however, because of limitations on the size of one volume, difficult choices had to be made on what to include and exclude. Inevitably, there may be omissions which some readers may consider should not have been made; these, and any errors which may have crept into the text, I would appreciate having pointed out to me.

I am most grateful to The Hon Thomas A. Finlay, Chief Justice, for so kindly writing the Foreword. His encouraging words have made the writing of this book all the more worthwhile.

I would also like to express my gratitude: to my colleagues in the Law Library, particularly Kieran Fleck BL and Vincent Landy SC; to the staff of the Central Office in the Four Courts; to the staff of the libraries of Trinity College Dublin, of Kings Inns, and of the Law Library, particularly Jennefer Aston and Pat Redmond; to Brendan Murphy for expert advice on my computer requirements; to Doreen McBride, Edie McGarry and Nuala Smith for the data input which was done with considerable skill; and to Michael Burke of Topaz Publications and Sarah Kelly and Peter Allman of Dublin University Press for translating the manuscript from "floppy discs" to a book.

I particularly thank my father and my family to whom this book is dedicated.

The measure of success of this dictionary will be the extent to which it is used by those who buy it and the extent to which they find it helpful in such use. I hope it will be successful on both counts.

## PREFACE TO SECOND EDITION (1993)

In the five years since the first edition, there has been substantial change in the law, particularly relating to companies, competition, product liability, insurance, building societies, patents, the environment, planning, local government, elections, judicial separation, part-time workers, safety at work, unfair dismissals, evidence, crime, sexual offences, sentence review, court jurisdiction and limitation of actions.

There also has been the implementation of the Single Market in Europe and the moves towards European Union with the Maastricht Treaty 1992 which will have increasing significance for Ireland over the next decade. In addition to the 150 statutes enacted since 1988, there also has been considerable clarification and development of the law through judicial decisions in all our courts.

There has been a virtual explosion in the last five years in the number of legal texts on various aspects of Irish law and a welcome expansion in the reporting of judicial decisions (eg the Irish Times Law Reports and the Irish Criminal Law Reports), all of which improve access of the professional and the layperson to information.

I have endeavoured to reflect all these changes in this revised, updated and expanded dictionary which is intended primarily to be a sourcebook and a signpost to the law. I have improved the cross-referencing between entries. I have also included references to all statute law enacted since the last edition and the 1,000 or so important cases reported since then, in most of these cases identifying the level of court in the reference.

I have had tremendous encouragement, support and assistance from a very large number of persons, particularly members of the judiciary, the legal profession and public officials in updating the dictionary. I would like to extend my thanks to all and to hope that the second edition adequately reflects their contributions. I am also indebted to the library staff of Trinity College Dublin, to the staff of the Bills Office in Leinster House and the Government Publications Office, to the Bar Council of Ireland, and to Dublin University Press who as usual have done a first class job in computer typesetting and printing.

The mammoth task of typing the second edition was undertaken by my wife Davida; I thank her, my children Maeve and Breffni, and my father, without whose assistance, forbearance and support this publication would not have been possible.

I have endeavoured to state the law as accurately as possible on the sources available to me on 24th August 1993.

10 Haddington Lawn
Glenageary
Co Dublin.                                                24th August 1993

# GUIDE TO DICTIONARY

Consider this typical entry in conjunction with the notes below:

> **partnership.**[1] The relationship existing between two or more persons carrying on business in common with a view to profit: Partnership Act 1890 s.1.[2] There are rules for determining if a partnership exists (ibid s.2)[3] ....... There are two kinds of partnership, the ordinary partnership and the limited partnership (qv).[4] .......[Text: Keane (1); Lindley UK].[5] See Macken v Revenue Commissioners (1962) IR 302.[6] See also RSC O.46 rr.3-4.[7] See FIRM.[8]

1. The entries are in alphabetical order in bold print. There may be further entries based on the key word eg **partnership, dissolution of; partnership, liability in;** and **partnership, number to form.**

2. A reference is usually given to the statutory basis for an entry with the section (s.) of the Act identified. Where there is reference to draft legislation, the particular Bill under consideration by the Oireachtas at the time of writing, is identified eg Road Traffic Bill 1993, Criminal Justice (Public Order) Bill 1993, Matrimonial Home Bill 1993. Care should be taken to compare the exact wording of these Bills, if and as enacted, with the wording in this dictionary, as the text of Bills is frequently changed during the course of their passage through the Dail and Seanad. Note also that an Act or a section of an Act may require a Commencement Order to bring the Act or the Section into force eg by 1993, many sections of the Child Care Act 1991 had not been brought into force.

3. Any further references to the last mentioned source are identified by *ibid*.

4. *(qv)* after a word or series of words indicates that there is a separate entry in the dictionary for that word or for the series of words. In the example, there is a separate entry under *limited partnership*.

5. Where a major topic of law is dealt with, for which there is a good text book available which could be usefully consulted for further information, it is identified by the surname of the author after [Text:]. If *UK* appears after the author's name, it indicates that the book deals with the law of the United Kingdom but is of relevance to Irish Law. A list of authors and their texts is in Appendix 3.

6. Reference is made in many entries to the more significant or interesting case law which could be usefully consulted eg (1991 HC) ITLR (21 Jan); the date refers to the date of the Law Report and not the date the case was decided; in some instances the level of court eg HC (High Court) is indicated after the date. The list of Law Reports and abbreviations is in Appendix 1.

7. Reference is also made in some entries to other sources eg the Rules of the Superior Courts (RSC) and the Order (O) and Rules (rr) applicable. A list of abbreviations is included below.

8. The final reference in capital letters directs the reader to another relevant or associated entry in the dictionary eg in this case to FIRM.

9. In many entries a reference is made to a function or power of a Minister but his Department is not indicated in view of the changes which take place from time to time in the allocation of these Departments to different Ministers.

10. Throughout the Dictionary, the male includes the female unless the context suggests otherwise.

## ABBREVIATIONS

| | | |
|---|---|---|
| AG | = | Attorney General |
| app | = | appendix |
| art | = | article |
| CC | = | Circuit Court |
| CCA | = | Court of Criminal Appeal |
| CCC | = | Central Criminal Court |
| C of A in NI | = | Court of Appeal in Northern Ireland |
| DC | = | District Court |
| DCR | = | District Court Rules 1948 (as amended) |
| DPP | = | Director of Public Prosecutions |
| EC Pub | = | European Communities Publication |
| Gov Pub | = | Government Publications |
| HC | = | High Court |
| ibid | = | referring to the same source |
| LG(PD) | = | Local Government (Planning and Development) |
| LRC | = | Law Reform Commission |
| No | = | Number |
| O | = | Order Number |
| para | = | paragraph |
| r | = | rule |
| rr | = | rules |
| RCC | = | Circuit Court Rules 1950 (as amended) |
| RSC | = | Rules of the Superior Courts 1986 |
| regs | = | regulations |
| s | = | section |
| SC | = | Supreme Court |
| SCC | = | Special Criminal Court |
| sch | = | schedule |
| SGSS | = | Sale of Goods and Supply of Services |
| SI | = | Statutory Instrument |
| SR O | = | Statutory Rules and Orders |
| ss | = | sections |

1922 Constitution = The Constitution of the Irish Free State (Saorstat Eireann) which came into operation on 6th December 1922.

1937 Constitution = The Constitution of Ireland enacted by the People on 1st July 1937 and which came into operation on 29th December 1937.

See Appendix 1 for abbreviations of Law Reports.
   Appendix 2 for Reports of Law Reform Commission.
   Appendix 3 for Text — Bibliography.

# A

**a coelo usque ad centrum.** [From heaven to the centre of the earth]. In principle, the extent of the ownership of property. See AIRSPACE, INTERFERENCE WITH; CUJUS EST SOLUM.

**a fortiori (rationale).** [Much more; with or for a stronger reason]. See Shelly v Mahon and DPP (1990) ITLR (23 Jul).

**a mensa et thoro.** [From board and bed]. See DIVORCE A MENSA ET THORO.

**a posteriori.** [From the effect to the cause]. Inductive reasoning.

**a priori.** [From the cause to the effect]. Deductive reasoning.

**a tempore cujus contrarii memoria non existet.** [From a time of which there is no memory to the contrary]. See TIME IMMEMORIAL.

**a verbis legis non est recedendum.** [You must not vary the words of a statute]. See LEGISLATION, INTERPRETATION OF.

**a vinculo matrimonii.** [From the bond of matrimony]. See DIVORCE

**A & B.** See CONTRIBUTORY; TRADE MARK, REGISTERED.

**ab antiquo.** [From old times].

**ab extra.** [From outside].

**ab initio.** [From the beginning]. See TRESPASSER AB INITIO. MARRIAGE, NULLITY OF.

**ab intestato.** [From an intestate]. Succession *ab intestato* is succession to property of a person who has not disposed of it by will. See INTESTATE SUCCESSION.

**abandoned house.** A house which has been abandoned by the person to whom a housing authority has made a housing loan and which has been or is in danger of being trespassed upon or damaged; the housing authority is empowered to take whatever measures it considers necessary to secure and protect the house:: Housing (Miscellaneous Provisions) Act 1992 s.12.

**abandonment.** The relinquishment or surrender of an interest, claim or thing. (1) A person will not be held to have surrendered or abandoned his constitutional rights unless it is shown that he is aware of what the rights are and of what he is doing, and that the action he has taken is such as could reasonably lead to the clear and unambiguous inference that such was his intention: G v An Bord Uchtala (1980) IR 80. (2) An easement (qv) may be lost by abandonment; evidence of abandonment must be supported by evidence of conduct or intention adverse to the exercise of the right: Carroll v Sheridan (1984) ILRM 451; O'Gara v Murray (1989) 7 ILT Dig 82. (3) In marine insurance where there is a constructive total loss (qv), the insured may abandon the subject matter insured to the insurer or underwriter by giving notice of abandonment to him within a reasonable time. The insured then becomes entitled to the insurance moneys and the insurer or underwriter to the subject matter insured. See Marine Insurance Act 1906 ss.60-62. (4) For abandonment of parental rights, see ADOPTION. (5) For abandonment of children, see CRUELTY TO CHILDREN; FOS-TER-CHILD; WELFARE OF CHILDREN.

**abandonment of claim.** A plaintiff in District or Circuit Court proceedings may abandon any part of his claim in order to bring the claim within the jurisdiction of the court; such abandonment must be stated in the civil process or civil bill, as the case may be: DCR r.141; RCC O.5 r.6(c), O.9 r.4.

**abatement.** A reduction, allowance or rebate. An abatement *pro rata* refers to the proportionate reduction of the amount of each of a number of debts or claims eg where a fund or estate is insufficient to meet them all in full. See DAMAGES; DISABILITY PENSION.

**abatement of action.** A suspension or termination of proceedings in an action: RSC O.17 rr.12-13. A cause or matter is not abated by reason of death or bankruptcy if the cause of action survives: RSC O.17 r.1. See DEATH, EFFECT OF.

**abatement of legacy.** The reduction of a legacy due to an insufficiency of assets in the testator's estate. *Specific* legacies (qv) take priority over *general* legacies (qv) and are liable to abatement only if the assets are otherwise insufficient for the payment of debts. *Demonstrative* legacies (qv) only abate if the fund out of which payment is directed is insufficient or if otherwise the assets of the estate are insufficient to pay debts. *General* legacies abate proportionally between themselves except where a legacy has been given in payment of a debt. See Succession Act 1965 s.46, first schedule. See ADMINISTRATION OF ESTATES; LEGACY.

**abatement of nuisance.** The right to remove or put an end to a nuisance (qv), as an alternative to taking an action. If a nuisance can only be abated by entry on the land of another, the person abating must give notice to the occupier of the lands on which it exists, except in the case of emergency. If no entry is required (eg to cut overhanging branches of a tree), no notice is required. Generally abatement is a remedy that the law does not favour. See SANITARY AUTHORITIES AND NUISANCE.

**abattoir.** Any premises used for or in connection with the slaughter of animals whose meat is intended for human consumption and does not include a place situate on some farms: Abattoirs Act 1988. Abattoirs and knackeries are required to be licensed annually; local authorities are responsible for veterinary control of the premises; and all meat intended for human consumption must be stamped with a health mark. The purpose of the 1988 Act is to provide the same standard at slaughtering premises as apply at export meat plants. See Abattoirs Act 1988 (Veterinary Examination) Regulations 1992 (SI No 89 of 1992); Abattoir (Health Mark) Regulations 1992 (SI No 90 of 1992).

**abbreviated accounts.** Accounts of a company other than as part of the full accounts; abbreviated accounts must be distinguished from the full accounts filed with the Registrar of Companies: Companies Amendment Act 1986 s.19.

**abbutals.** The bounds of land; the parts where it abuts on other lands.

**abdication.** Voluntary renunciation of an office or responsibility.

**abduction.** The wrongful taking away of a person. It was an offence, without lawful authority or excuse to take out of the possession and against the will of any person having lawful care of her, an unmarried girl under the age of eighteen years with the intent that she would have unlawful sexual intercourse with men or a particular man: Criminal Law Amendment Act 1855 s.7 repealed by Criminal Justice Act 1951. See The People (Attorney General) v McCormack

(1944) Frewen 55. See LRC 12 of 1985. See also CHILD ABDUCTION; FALSE IMPRISONMENT; KIDNAPPING.

**abearance.** Behaviour.

**abet.** To aid in the commission of a crime. See AIDER AND ABETTER.

**abeyance.** The condition of an inheritance which has no present owner; an estate is in abeyance when there is no person in whom it can vest.

**abjuration.** Renounciation by oath (qv).

**abode.** Habitation or place of residence. A man's residence, where he lives with his family and sleeps at night, is always his place of abode in the full sense of that expression: R v Hammond (1852) 17 QB 772. The *place of abode* test for residence in the State for tax purposes in respect of Irish persons working abroad has been abolished: Finance Act 1987 s.4. Under that test, an Irish person working abroad was deemed to be resident in the State for tax purposes if he maintained a place of abode in the State and returned, even for a short period, during the tax year. Now such a person may visit his home and transfer his savings to the State without being subject to Irish taxation.

Possession by a person, when not in his place of abode, of any article intended to be used in a larceny or burglary, is an offence: Larceny Act 1990 s.2. Place of abode in similar UK legislation has been held to be a site in which the accused intends to reside: R v Bundy (1992) 2 All ER 382. See DOMICILE.

**abominable crime.** The expression used to describe the felonies of sodomy (qv) and bestiality (qv): Offences Against the Person Act 1861 s.61. See BUGGERY.

**abortion.** A miscarriage or the premature expulsion of the contents of the womb before the term of gestation is completed. It is a felony (qv) to procure an abortion by means of any poison (qv), noxious substance, instrument or any other thing. It is also an offence for a woman, who is actually pregnant at the time, to procure or attempt to procure an abortion. See The People (Attorney General) v Coleman (1945) IR 237; Offences Against the Person Act 1861 s.58.

However, it has been held that termination of pregnancy is permissible under the Constitution where it is established as a matter of probability that there is a real and substantial risk to the life, as distinct from the health, of the mother, which can be avoided by the termination of her pregnancy: AG v X (1992 SC) ILRM 401; 1937 Constitution art.40(3)(3). See Kingston & Whelan in 10 ILT & SJ (1992) 93.

It has also been held that activities in assisting pregnant women within the jurisdiction to travel abroad to obtain abortions by referral to a clinic; by making of their travel arrangements, or by informing them of the identity and location of and method of communication with a specified clinic or clinics are unlawful, having regard to the provisions of the 1937 Constitution, art.40(3)(3): AG at the relation of the Society for the Protection of Unborn Children (Ireland) Ltd v Open Door Counselling Ltd and Dublin Wellwoman Centre Ltd (1988 SC) IR 593. The European Court of Human Rights has held that the injunction granted by the Supreme Court against these defendants violated their rights to receive and impart information: Open Door Counselling Ltd & Ors v Ireland — see ILSI Gazette (1992 Dec) 395.

An interlocutory injunction was granted by the Supreme Court to prevent publication and distribution of information relating to abortion: SPUC v Grogan (1990) ILRM 350. The High Court referred to the European Court of Justice the question as to whether there is a right to give information about abortion clinics outside the State: SPUC v Grogan (1989) IR 753. The European Court held that medical termination of pregnancy, performed in accordance with the law of the State in which it is carried out, constitutes a *service* within the meaning of the Treaty of Rome 1957 art.60; however, it also held that it is not contrary to Community law for a member State where medical termination of pregnancy is forbidden, to prohibit the distribution of information about the identity and location of clinics in another member State where voluntary termination of pregnancy is lawfully carried out: SPUC v Grogan (ECJ) (1992) ILRM 461.

However in 1992, an amendment to the Constitution provided that art.40(3)(3)

shall not limit freedom to obtain or make available, in the State, subject to such conditions as may be laid down by law, information relating to services lawfully available in another State: Fourteenth Amendment to the Constitution Act 1992. There is a prohibition on the EC Treaties affecting the application in Ireland of Article 40(3)(3) of the Constitution: Maastrict Treaty 1992 (Abortion Protocol).

The Medical Council issued guidelines on abortion in March 1993, stating that — "Situations arise in medical practice where the life and/or health of the mother or of the unborn, or both, are endangered. In these situations, it is imperative ethically that doctors shall endeavour to preserve life and health" ...."it is unethical always to withhold treatment beneficial to a pregnant woman, by reason of her pregnancy".

In 1992, the people by referendum rejected the Twelfth Amendment to the Constitution, which would have provided: "It shall be unlawful to terminate the life of an unborn unless such termination is necessary to save the life, as distinct from the health, of the mother where there is an illness or disorder of the mother, giving rise to a real and substantial risk to her life, not being a risk of self-destruction": Referendum (Amendment) (No 2) Act 1992. See also Health (Family Planning) Act 1979 s.10. See PRIVATE PROSECUTION; MURDER; LIFE, RIGHT TO; SERVICES, PROVISION OF.

**abridged time bill.** See BILL, ABRIDGED TIME.

**abrogate.** To repeal, cancel, annul or abolish.

**abscond.** To go away secretly or to hide from the jurisdiction of the court. It may amount to an act of bankruptcy: Bankruptcy Act 1988 s.7(1)(c). An absconding debtor may be arrested by order of the court (ibid s.9). An absconding bankrupt may also be arrested (ibid s.23). It is an offence for a debtor to abscond with property to the value of £500 or more with the intent to defraud his creditors (ibid s.124). See BAIL; BANKRUPTCY, ACT OF.

**absence.** (1) Non appearance by a party to a summons (qv) or a subpoena (qv). (2) Absence of a spouse for seven years may be a conclusive defence to a charge of bigamy (qv). (3) A person may be presumed to be dead if not heard of for seven years. (4) Where a defendant fails to appear in the District Court on the date specified in a valid summons duly served on him, the judge may proceed, in the absence of the defendant, to hear and determine the charge described in the summons or may adjourn the hearing to a later date and may secure the attendance of the defendant by warrant or otherwise: DPP v Roche (1988 SC) ILRM 39. In relation to the absence of the prosecutor, see DPP v Gill (1980) IR 263. See DEATH, PRESUMPTION OF; JUDGMENT IN DEFAULT OF APPEARANCE.

**absent without leave.** The offence committed by a person, subject to military law, who absents himself without authority eg leaving his unit or formation or the place where his duty requires him to be: Defence Act 1954 s.137.

**absenteeism.** Absence without sufficient cause or in breach of a term or condition of employment may be a ground for dismissal from employment. Chronic absenteeism of a prison officer has been found to justify his dismissal: Lang v Minister for Justice (1993 HC) — Irish Times 8/7/1993. See also Ruane v Barrett (1990) ELR 28; Rigney v Offaly Co Council (1990) ELR 38; Hynes v GEC Distributors (1992 EAT) ELR 95. See UNFAIR DISMISSAL.

**absente reo.** [The defendant being absent].

**absoluta sententia expositore non indiget.** [When you have plain words capable of only one interpretation, no explanation of them is required]. See LEGISLATION, INTERPRETATION OF.

**absolute.** Complete and without conditions. An order of a court is absolute when it is complete and of full force and effect eg a garnishee order (qv) absolute. Contrast with NISI.

**absolute liability.** See STRICT LIABILITY.

**absolve.** To free from liability or guilt.

**absque impetitione vasti.** [Without impeachment of waste (qv)].

**absque tali causa.** [Without the alleged cause].

**abstract of title.** A chronological statement of the instruments and events under which a person is entitled to land showing the links to his title. A vendor of land is bound to deliver an abstract

to the purchaser, at the vendor's expense. See REQUISITIONS ON TITLE.

**abundans cautela non nocet.** [There is no harm done by great caution]. In order to ensure that there is no doubt, there is often expressed (eg in a contract) that which would otherwise be implied.

**abuse.** Words of insult, invective or vituperation; they do not generally afford a ground for defamation (qv): Thorley v Kerry (1812) 4 Taunt 355. See also M'Gregor v Gregory (1843) 11 M & W 287. See VULGAR ABUSE.

**abuse of dominant position.** See DOMINANT POSITION, ABUSE OF.

**abuse of monopoly right.** Formerly, the grounds upon which an application could be made to the Controller of Patents for a licence under a patent or for an endorsement of the patent *licences of right* (qv): Patents Act 1964 s.39. Although the 1964 Act has been repealed, a similar measure exists under the Patents Act 1992 s.70; the term "abuse of monopoly right" however is not used. See LICENCES OF RIGHT.

**abuse of process.** A tort (qv) based on damage caused by use of a legal process for some purpose other than that for which it was designed. See Cavern Systems Dublin Ltd v Clontarf Residents Association (1984) ILRM 24. Also the defence to an action on the grounds that the action is frivolous, vexatious or is seeking to have litigated again a question already decided against the intending plaintiff. See Kelly v Ireland (1986) ILRM 318; In re Bula Ltd (in receivership) (1988) SC; Olympia Productions Ltd v Cameron Mackintosh (1992 HC) ITLR (3 Feb). See RSC O.19 r.19.

The adding of a party to proceedings in order to oust the jurisdiction of the English courts is technically an abuse of the processes of the court: Jurisdiction of Courts and Enforcement of Judgments Act 1988; Gannon v B & I Steam Packet Co Ltd and Landliner Travel (1993 SC) ITLR (25 Jan) and 11 ILT Dig (1993) 144. See BARRATRY; ISSUE ESTOPPEL; MALICIOUS PROSECUTION; OPPRESSIVE PROCEEDINGS.

**Ab; Abr.** Abridgment.

**ac etiam.** [And also].

**acceleration clause.** A clause in a contract where a debtor repays sums of money in instalments whereby the whole balance becomes due immediately upon failure to pay any of the instalments. Such a clause will be upheld but will be policed carefully by the courts. See Protector Loan Co v Grice (1880) 5 QBD 529; UTD Ltd v Patterson (1973) NI 142. See PENALTY.

**acceptance.** The act of assenting to an offer. Acceptance of an offer to create a contract, may be by words or by conduct. It must generally be communicated to the offeror and must be absolute and unqualified and must be made while the offer is in force, or before it has lapsed or been revoked or rejected. If the offer is one which is capable of being accepted by being acted upon, no communication to the offeror is necessary, unless stipulated for in the offer itself: Carlill v Carbolic Smoke Ball Co (1893) QB 256.

Where an acceptance (or offer) is couched in general terms and the parties contemplate the execution of a further contract between them, if the terms of such further contract were in existence and known to the parties, the offer and acceptance will be inclusive of the fuller terms. If the terms of the fuller contract were merely in contemplation, then the acceptance is too general to constitute a contract. See Lowis v Wilson (1949) IR 347; Felthouse v Bindley (1862) 31 LJCP 204. See WRITING, CONTRACTS REQUIRING.

**acceptance of bill.** Signing a bill of exchange by the *drawee* in such a way as to signify acceptance of liability to pay the sum of money stated in the bill: Bills of Exchange Act 1882 ss.17-19. Acceptance may be a *general* acceptance which is an acceptance without qualification or a *qualified* acceptance which can be *conditional, partial, local,* qualified as to *time* or qualified as to *parties.* Acceptance for honour *supra protest* is acceptance of a bill in order to safeguard the drawee's good name (ibid ss.65-68). See Hazylake Fashions Ltd v Bank of Ireland (1989) ILRM 698. See BILL OF EXCHANGE.

**acceptance of goods.** A buyer is deemed to have accepted goods when he intimates to the seller that he has accepted them, or, subject to the buyer's right of examining the goods, when the goods have been delivered to him and he does any act in relation to them which is inconsistent with the ownership of the seller or when, without good and sufficient reason, he retains the goods without intimating to the seller that he has rejected them: Sale of Goods Act 1893 s.35; SGSS Act 1980 s.20. See Gill v Heiton Co Ltd (1943) Ir Jur Rep 67.

**acceptance of service.** Acceptance in writing of a summons (qv) by a solicitor on behalf of a defendant, undertaking to enter an appearance on his behalf: RSC O.9(1). See SUMMONS, SERVICE OF.

**acceptance supra protest.** [Acceptance for honour]. See ACCEPTANCE OF BILL.

**access.** Every place at which any person has at any time to work must be made and kept in a safe condition and in addition there must, so far as reasonably practical, be provided and maintained safe means of *access* to and *egress* from every such place: Factories Act 1955 s.37 as amended by Safety in Industry Act 1980 s.12. This duty applies not only to an employer but also to an occupier in whose premises a person works who is not an employee of the occupier: Dunne v Honeywell Control (1991 HC) 9 ILT Dig 147. See Daly v Avonmore Creameries Ltd (1984) IR 131; Kielty v Ascon Ltd (1969) IR 122. See also Safety, Health and Welfare at Work Act 1989 s.6(2)(b).

**access to children.** See CHILD, ACCESS TO; CHILD, CUSTODY OF; CHILD IN CARE.

**access to courts.** There is a constitutional right of access to the courts. "It is the right of the citizens under the Constitution to have access to the Courts for the resolution of justiciable controversies": Bula Mines Ltd v Tara Mines Ltd (No 1) (1987 HC) IR 85 at 92. Access to the courts may be curtailed by statute to the extent that the leave of the court may be required as a precondition to bringing a claim (eg proceedings under the Mental Treatment Act 1945 s.260). Such statutory limitation on right of access must be strictly construed: Murphy v Greene (1991 SC) ILRM 404.

It has not been definitively decided whether the levies imposed by the State on litigants (by way of stamp duty on legal documents and other charges) constitutes an unconstitutional restriction on the citizen's right of access to the courts: MacGairbhith v AG (1991) 2 IR 412. See also Boddie v Connecticut

(1971) 401 US 371; Calor Teoranta v Colgan (1990 SC) in 8ILT & SJ (1990) 255.

**access to information.** See INFORMATION, ACCESS TO.

**access to road.** See MOTORWAY; PUBLIC ROAD.

**access to solicitor.** See SOLICITOR, ACCESS TO.

**accession.** The process by which property belonging to a person becomes the property of another by reason of its having been affixed or annexed to the property of that other. See FIXTURES.

**accessory.** A person involved in the commission of an offence otherwise than as principal. An accessory *before the fact* is a person who, being absent at the time of the felony, assists, procures, counsels, commands or instigates another to commit it: The People (DPP) v Madden (1977) IR 336; People (DPP) v Egan (1990 SC) ILRM 780. An accessory *after the fact* is a person who, although not present at the crime, knowing that a felony has been committed, subsequently shelters one of the felons in such a way to enable him to evade justice; active assistance to the felon is required; mere passive connivance would be the misdemeanour of *misprision of felony* (qv). See DPP v Diemling (1993 CCA) 11 ILT Dig 185. See Accessories and Abettors Act 1861. See FELONY.

**accident.** An unlooked for mishap or an untoward event which is not expected or designed: Fenton v Thorley Co (1903) AC 443. Compensation for an *occupational* accident is available through the scheme pursuant to the Social Welfare (Consolidation) Act 1981 ss.36-70.

Accident insurance policies usually provide cover for *injury by accident* or *injury caused by accidental means*. If a deliberate act on the part of the assured brings about an injury which is an unexpected and unforeseeable result of that action, his injury is caused by accident.

A person may be appointed by the Minister to report upon the nature and causes of an accident at sea: Merchant Shipping Act 1894 s.728; where the Minister subsequently establishes a formal inquiry pursuant to s.466, a person represented at that inquiry is entitled to a copy of the report only if he establishes

a right to the production of the report: Haussman v Minister for the Marine (1991 HC) ILRM 383. See NO FAULT COMPENSATION; PERSONAL INJURIES; SAFETY AT WORK; TRIBUNALS OF INQUIRY.

**accident, inevitable.** See INEVITABLE ACCIDENT.

**accident, reporting of.** (1) Where injury is caused to person or property in a public place and a vehicle is involved in the occurrence of the injury, whether the use of the vehicle was or was not the cause of the injury, various provisions apply regarding stopping the vehicle, keeping the vehicle at or near the place of the occurrence for a reasonable period, and giving appropriate information to a garda or to a person entitled to demand the information: Road Traffic Act 1961 s.106 as amended by the Schedule to the Road Traffic Act 1968.

(2) An accident at a place of work must be reported to the Health and Safety Authority (i) in the case of a death, by the quickest practicable means, with the name of the deceased, brief particulars and the location of the accident, and (ii) by way of written report in the approved form of the death, injury, condition, accident, or dangerous occurrence: Safety Health and Welfare at Work (General Application) Regulations 1993 (SI No 44 of 1993), reg.59. The accident must be reported if the person dies or is prevented from performing his normal work for more than three consecutive days or if he requires treatment from a registered medical practitioner or treatment in a hospital as an in-patient or out-patient.

**accidental omission.** There are provisions in many statutes which ensure that proceedings or acts are not invalidated by the "accidental omission" to do something eg omission to send a notice to a person entitled to receive one — Building Societies Act 1989 ss.68(6), 74(8), 75(6).

**accommodation.** See HOMELESS PERSON.

**accommodation party.** A person who has signed a bill of exchange (qv) as drawer, acceptor or indorser, without receiving value therefor and for the purpose of lending his name to some other person. An accommodation party is liable on a bill to a *holder for value* (qv), and it is immaterial when such holder took the bill, whether he knew such party to be an accommodation party of not: Bills of Exchange Act 1882 s.28.

**accomplice.** A person associated with another, whether as *principal* (qv) or *accessory* (qv) in the commission of an offence. The evidence of an accomplice is admissible but the judge must warn the jury of the danger of acting on the uncorroborated evidence of an accomplice. It is for the judge to decide whether a witness is an accomplice and the jury must accept his ruling. See People v Carney and Mulcahy (1955) IR 324; DPP v Murtagh (1990) 8 ILT Dig 158; DPP v Diemling (1993 CCA) 11 ILT Dig 185. See WITNESS, COMPETENCE OF.

**accord and satisfaction.** The purchase of a release (qv) from an obligation (whether arising under contract or tort) by means of any valuable consideration (qv), not being the actual performance of the obligation itself; the *accord* is the agreement by which the obligation is discharged; the *satisfaction* is the consideration which makes the agreement operative: British Russian Gazette v Associated Newspapers (1933) 2 KB 616. If A owes B £100 for work done and B accepts a bicycle in full settlement, there is accord and satisfaction. If the satisfaction is executory (qv) and the other party has completely performed his part of the contract, it is ineffective unless under seal or there is consideration eg in the case where A has delivered corn to B and B has yet to pay for the goods, a promise by A not to sue B is ineffective unless under seal or consideration is given by B.

No satisfaction is needed for the renunciation of a debt owed to the holder of a bill of exchange or promissory note: Bills of Exchange Act 1882 s.62.

**account payee.** The addition of the words *account payee* on a cheque is an instruction to the collecting banker to collect only for the payee's account. The words put the bank on enquiry and it is negligence on the part of the banker should adequate enquiry not be made: Home Property Co of London v London County and Westminster Bank (1915) 84 LJ KB 1846.

**account, settled.** A statement in writing of the account between two parties, one of whom is under a duty to account to the other, which both of them have agreed to and accepted as correct. It is a defence to a claim for an account. See In re Webb (1894) 1 Ch 83.

**account stated.** An agreed balance between parties resulting from a series of transactions. An account stated with an infant is generally void: Infants Relief Act 1874 s.1. See Joseph Evan Co v Heathcote (1918) 1 KB 434.

**accountant.** As regards claims in negligence and/or breach of contract against accountants, see Sisk v Flynn (1986) ILRM 128; Golden Vale Co-operative Creameries v Barrett (1987) HC; Allied Pharmaceutical Distributors Ltd v Robert J Kidney Co (1991) 2 IR 8. See also AUDITOR; COMPANY, REGISTERED; PARTNERSHIP; PARTNERSHIP, NUMBER TO FORM.

**accounting, false.** See FALSE ACCOUNTING.

**accounting principles.** The principles governing the amounts to be included in the accounts of a company: Companies Amendment Act 1986 s.5; eg the company is presumed to be carrying on as a going concern (qv); the accounting policies are to be applied consistently from one year to the next; only realised profits at the balance sheet date are to be included in the profit and loss account; and all income and charges relating to the financial year are to be included in the accounts irrespective of the date of payment. If there are special reasons for departing from these accounting principles, the directors of the company must state the particulars and reasons for departure in a note to the accounts (ibid s.6). See also Building Societies Act 1989 s.77(8)(c).

**accounts.** Every company must keep proper books of accounts that (a) correctly record and explain the transactions of the company, (b) will at any time enable the financial position of the company to be determined with reasonable accuracy, (c) will enable any balance sheet, profit and loss account or income and expenditure account to comply with the Companies Acts, and (d) will enable the accounts to be readily and properly audited: Companies Act 1990 s.202.

Copies of the balance sheet, the profit and loss account and of the directors' and auditors' report must be sent to every shareholder and debenture holder and laid before the annual general meeting: Companies Act 1963 ss.148 and 159. The particular format of accounts to be used is specified in s.4 of the Companies Amendment Act 1986; a *small company* and a *medium sized company* are exempted from many of the requirements of preparing and publishing a full set of accounts (ibid ss.10-12). A criminal offence may be committed by a director for failing to keep proper books of accounts (ibid 1990 Act s.202(10)), or by officers where the company is wound up (ibid s.203). Also an officer may be ordered by the court to be personally liable for the debts of the company where proper books of accounts have not been kept (ibid s.204). See Healy v Healy Homes Ltd (1973) IR 309; Sinnot v O'Connor (1991 SC) 9ILT Dig 266. See also Building Societies Act 1989 ss.76-77. See MacCann in 9ILT & SJ (1991) 177. [Text: Kelleher; Power]. See ACCOUNTING PRINCIPLES; BALANCE SHEET; FALSE ACCOUNTING; PROFIT & LOSS; SMALL COMPANY; MEDIUM SIZED COMPANY.

**accredit.** To furnish a diplomatic agent with papers, called credentials or letters of credit, which certify his public character. See AMBASSADOR.

**accumulation.** The process whereby there is a continual increase in principal by the investment of interest as it accrues. A person may not direct the accumulation of interest for any period longer than:- the life of the settlor, or 21 years from the settlor's death, or the minority of any person living at the death of the settlor, or the minority of the person entitled to the income: Accumulations Act 1800 (principles followed in Ireland) and 1892. A direction to accumulate for a period longer than the *perpetuity* period is void; but where the period is longer than the Acts allow but not longer than the perpetuity period, the direction is merely void in so far as it exceeds the former. See PERPETUITIES, RULE AGAINST.

**accusare nemo se debet; accusare nemo se debet nisi coram Deo.** [No one is bound to accuse himself except to God]. See INCRIMINATE.

**accusatorial procedure.** The legal procedure in common law (qv) countries whereby the responsibility of collecting and presenting evidence lies generally with the party who seeks to introduce that evidence. Contrast with INQUISITORIAL PROCEDURE.

**accused.** A person charged with an offence.

**accused, disclosure of name of.** See PUBLIC JUSTICE.

**acknowledgment.** Avowal or assent to. As regards a will, if it is not signed by the testator in the presence of witnesses, he must acknowledge his signature in their presence: Succession Act 1965 s.78. As regards a right of action on a debt, an acknowledgment of the debt by the person liable, will result in the right of action being deemed to have accrued on and not before, the date of the acknowledgment: Statute of Limitations 1957 s.56. See Smith v Ireland (1983) ILRM 300.

**acquiescence.** Consent which is expressed or implied from conduct. Acquiesence to the infringement of a right will normally result in the loss of equitable relief. See LACHES.

**acquifer.** Any stratum or combination of strata that stores or transmits groundwater: LG (Water Pollution) (Amendment) Act 1990 s.2. See WATER POLLUTION.

**acquired rights, employees.** The rights of employees which are safeguarded in the event of transfers of undertakings, businesses or parts of businesses. It includes obligations under the redundancy payments scheme. See Premier Motors (Medway) Ltd v Total Oil of Great Britain Ltd (1983) IRLR 471. See EEC Council Directive 77/187; SI No 306 of 1980. See Barry in 8ILT & SJ (1991) 138. See REDUNDANCY; TRANSFER OF EMPLOYMENT.

**acquittal.** Discharge from prosecution following a verdict of not guilty or a successful plea in bar (qv). It has been held that a verdict of not guilty in respect of criminal charges is a certificate of a person's uninterrupted innocence: McCarthy v Garda Commissioner (1992 HC) ELR 50 (under appeal). There is generally no appeal against acquittal. When an accused is acquitted by the majority verdict of a jury, the fact that it was a majority verdict must not be disclosed: Criminal Justice Act 1984 s.25(4). See APPEAL; AUTRE FOIS ACQUIT; AUTREFOIS CONVICT.

**acquittance.** A written acknowledgment of the payment of a sum of money.

**acronym, deceptive.** See DECEPTIVE ACRONYM.

**Act.** Legislation which has passed, or deemed to have been passed by both Houses of the Oireachtas (qv) and has been signed by the President of Ireland (qv). The elements in an Act include: number eg No 27 of 1965; long title, which describes the purpose of the Act; short title, by which the Act may be cited; interpretation clause with definitions; commencement clause, which specifies when or how the Act will come into operation; transitional provisions; repealing clause; and schedules. See BILL; PASSING OF ACT; REPEAL; STATUTE LAW.

**act of bankruptcy.** See BANKRUPTCY, ACT OF.

**Act of God.** An event which happens independently of human intervention and due to natural causes (eg storm, earthquake, extraordinary rainfall, unusually bad weather at sea) which could not be foreseen and which could not be guarded against. It is a good defence in torts of strict liability (qv). See Pandorf v Hamilton (1886) 17 QBD 675. See INEVITABLE ACCIDENT.

**act of law.** The effect of the operation of law rather than as a result of the act of parties eg the legal right of a spouse in succession to property.

**acta exteriora indicant interiora secreta.** [External actions show internal secrets]. The maxim that intention may be inferred from a person's acts. See INFERENCE.

**acting capacity.** The appointment of a person in an acting capacity may give rise to a *legitimate expectation* of receiving a benefit or privilege which the court will protect: Duggan & Ors v An Taoiseach (1989 HC) ILRM 710. See EXPECTATION, LEGITIMATE.

**actio personalis moritur cum persona.** [A personal action dies with the person]. Formerly, a personal representative could not sue or be sued in respect of a tort committed against or by the deceased. However since 1961, all causes of action survive for the benefit of a deceased's estate and also against the estate, other than excepted causes eg defamation, seduction: Civil Liability Act 1961 ss.6-10. See DEATH, EFFECT OF.

**action.** A civil proceeding commenced by summons or in such other manner as may be prescribed by the rules of court eg an administration action regarding a grant of representation. See CIVIL PROCEEDINGS.

**actions, consolidation of.** See CONSOLIDATION OF ACTIONS.

**active trust.** A trust (qv) which requires the trustee to perform active duties eg collecting rents and transferring the proceeds to the beneficiaries. Contrast with BARE TRUST.

**actuary.** A person who is an expert on mortality and insurance statistics. The evidence of an actuary is not only desirable but is necessary to enable a jury to arrive at anything like a reasonably accurate figure for damages for *future loss of earnings*: Long v O'Brien & Cronin Ltd (1972) SC. Any insurer which has its head office in the State and which has an authorisation to undertake life assurance, is required to appoint an actuary: Insurance Act 1989 s.34. The Minister is empowered to prescribe the qualifications and experience of such actuary. For qualifications for appointment as an actuary to an occupational pensions scheme, see Pensions Act 1990 s.51. See also Sexton v O'Keeffe (1966) IR 204.

**actuarial value.** The equivalant cash value of a benefit, calculated in a manner as specified: Pensions Act 1990 s.2.

**actus Dei nemini facit injuriam.** [The act of God prejudices no one]. See ACT OF GOD.

**actus legis nemini facit injuriam.** [The act of the law injures no one].

**actus non facit reum, nisi mens sit rea.** [An act does not of itself constitute guilt unless the mind is guilty]. A cardinal maxim of criminal law. See Fowler v Padget (1798) 7 TR 509. See ACTUS REUS; MENS REA.

**actus reus.** The elements of an offence excluding those which concern the mind of the accused; it consists of some act, or some omission, forbidden by law. The act must have been done voluntarily, and must be directly attributable to the accused and not to another person. See Haughton v Smith (1973) 3 All ER 1109. See MENS REA.

**ad arbitrium.** [At will].

**ad avizandum.** [To be deliberated upon].

**ad colligenda bona.** [To collect the goods]. A grant of administration of the

9

estate of a deceased which is of a perishable or precarious nature, for the purpose of collecting and preserving it, but not for distributing it.

**ad diem.** [On the appointed day].

**ad eundem.** [To the same class].

**ad hoc.** [For this purpose].

**ad idem.** [Of the same mind]. A contract, to be binding requires that there is *consensus ad idem* ie agreement as to the same thing: Raffles v Wichelhaus (1864) 2 H & C 906. See CONTRACT.

**ad interim.** [In the meantime].

**ad litem.** [For the suit]. (1) A *guardian ad litem* may be appointed by the court to defend an action on behalf of a minor (qv) or a person of unsound mind: RSC O.13 r.1; O.15 r.35; O.52 r.17(6,7); O.63 r.1(3); In re Midland Health Board (1988) ILRM 251. In care proceedings and proceedings regarding children in the care of a health board, the court may apppoint a *guardian ad litem* for the child: Child Care Act 1991 s.26.

(2) A grant of *administration ad litem* may be made where it is necessary to appoint a personal representative to substantiate legal proceedings by or against an estate; it is a form of limited grant: Succession Act 1965 s.27(1).

**ad medium filum viae (aquae).** [To the middle line of the road (stream)]. The normal boundary of lands separated by a road or a river. For example, see Geraghty v Rohan Industrial Estates Ltd (1988) IR 419. See PUBLIC ROAD.

**ad referendum.** [To further consideration].

**ad rem.** [To the point].

**ad sectam; ads.** [At the suit of].

**ad summam.** [In conclusion].

**ad valorem.** [According to the value]. An ad valorem tax is one which is proportionate to the value of the article taxed. See STAMP DUTIES.

**adaptation.** The *adaptation* of a work is an act restricted by the copyright in a literary, dramatic or musical work: Copyright Act 1963 s.8(6). *Adaptation* means in relation to a literary or dramatic work (a) a translation, (b) a version of the work in which the story or action is conveyed wholly or mainly by means of pictures or (c) in the case of a dramatic work, a version in which it is converted into a non-dramatic work and vice-versa (ibid s.8(7)). In relation to a musical

work, *adaptation* means an arrangement or transcription of the work (ibid s.8(7)(b)). See COPYRIGHT.

**added defendant.** See DEFENDANT.

**additional evidence.** See FRESH EVIDENCE.

**address.** The President of Ireland may, after consultation with the Council of State (qv), communicate with the Houses of the Oireachtas by message or address on any matter of national or public importance: 1937 Constitution, art.7. Each such message or address must have received the approval of the government. Two such addresses have been made, in 1969 by President de Valera to commemorate the 50th anniversary of the first Dail, and in 1992 by President Robinson on the topic "The Irish Identity in Europe".

**address, mode of.** See MODE OF ADDRESS.

**adduce.** To present or bring forward eg evidence in support of some proposition or statement already made in the course of a proceedings.

**ademption.** The complete or partial extinction or withholding of a legacy by some act of the testator during his life eg sale of the object comprising a *specific* legacy. Where a father or other person *in loco parentis* provides a *portion* by way of legacy in his will and subsequently provides a like or greater sum by a settlement on the marriage of that child, there is a presumption that the legacy is adeemed. See Re Nolan (1923) 58 ILTR 13.

**adhesion, contract of.** See CONTRACT OF ADHESION.

**adjective law.** The part of law dealing with practice and procedure in the courts as distinct from the actual law. See SUBSTANTIVE LAW.

**adjournment.** The postponement or suspension of the hearing of a trial to a future time or day; a judge may, if he thinks it expedient for the interest of justice, postpone or adjourn a trial for such time and upon such terms, as he thinks fit: RSC O.36 r.34; RCC O.30 r.11. An adjournment *sine die* is a postponement for an indefinite time. An adjournment of a plaintiff's action in the District Court may be made pending the determination of the defendant's action in the High Court on the same issues: Gay O'Driscoll Ltd v Kotsonouris (1987) IR 265. See also DCR r.147 as substituted by DCR 1955 r.6. See Doyle v Hearne (1988) ILRM 318; Butler v Ruane (1989) ILRM 159.

**adjudication.** Formal judgment or decision of a court eg the order declaring a debtor to be a bankrupt. See In re McNeela (1987) HC. See BANKRUPTCY, ADJUDICATION OF.

**adjustment.** The operation of ascertaining and settling the amount which an assured is entitled to receive under a policy of marine insurance, and of fixing the proportion which each underwriter (qv) is liable to pay. See AVERAGE.

**administration, grant of.** See LETTERS OF ADMINISTRATION.

**administration, revocation of.** The revoking, cancelling or recalling of a grant of letters of administration (qv) which the High Court is empowered to do. See Succession Act 1965 ss.27(2) and 35.

**administration of company.** See COURT PROTECTION OF COMPANY.

**administration of estates.** The collection of the assets of a deceased person, payment of debts and distribution of the surplus to the persons beneficially entitled by the personal representatives (qv) of the deceased.

Where the estate is insolvent ie the assets are insufficient for the payment of debts, the debts are paid as follows:

1. The funeral, testamentary and administration expenses.

2. As in bankruptcy. As from 1st January 1989, the estates of persons who die insolvent are wound up in bankruptcy: Bankruptcy Act 1988 ss.115-122.

Where the estate is solvent, the order in which the assets of the deceased are applied in payment of debts (subject to directions in the will and to charges on the property) is as follows:

1. Property undisposed of by will, subject to the retention of a fund sufficient to meet pecuniary legacies.

2. Property not specifically devised or bequeathed but included in a residuary gift.

3. Property specifically appropriated for payment of debts.

4. Property charged with payment of debts.

5. Fund retained to meet pecuniary legacies (qv).

6. Property specifically devised or bequeathed.

7. Property appointed by will under a general power.

8. Assets are applied in accordance with the value of devise or bequest at the death of the deceased.

See Succession Act 1965 s.46, first schedule; Bankruptcy Act 1988 s.138. See INSOLVENT ESTATE; LETTERS OF ADMINISTRATION; PENAL SUM; PENDENTE LITE; PROBATE; PROBATE TAX; WILL.

**administration of justice.** See JUSTICE.

**administration suit.** An application requesting the court to administer the estate of a deceased where problems or disputes have arisen in the course of administration as between creditors, beneficiaries or personal representatives. It is instituted by a special summons in the High Court or by equity civil bill in the Circuit Court. See RSC O.5 r.2(4)(a); O.15 r.8; RCC O.34. [Text: Scanlon].

**administrative law.** The law relating to the organisation, powers and duties of administrative authorities eg public and local authorities. [Text: Hogan & Morgan; Stout].

**administrative tribunals.** Tribunals concerned with administrative law or matters concerning large numbers of persons or concerns, where questions arise involving the conferring of rights, or the restriction or loss of rights of individuals. It has been held that when a court is reviewing (eg by judicial review (qv)) a decision of an administrative tribunal, the decision may be set aside where the decision plainly and unambiguously flies in the face of fundamental reason and common sense; the court may not substitute its own decision for that of the tribunal: Stroker v Doherty (1991 SC) 1 IR 23. Allegations of criminal conduct may be aired before administrative tribunals or before inquiries which have a statutory basis: Keady v Garda Commissioner (1992 SC) ILRM 312. See also Matthews v Irish Coursing Club (1992 HC) ITLR (30 Mar). See TRIBUNALS.

**administrator/ administratrix.** A person (male/female) appointed to manage the property of another. (1) The person to whom the grant of administration of the estate of a deceased person is made. An administrator of an estate has the same rights and liabilities as if he were the executor of the deceased: Succession Act 1965 s.27. He is required to enter into a bond called an *administration bond*: RSC O.79 rr.29-32; RSC App Q Part 11. An attorney, acting under a power of attorney, or a guardian, may be an administrator: RSC O.79 rr.23 and 25.

(2) An administrator may be appointed to take over management of the business of an insurer: Insurance (No 2) Act 1983. See EXECUTOR; LETTERS OF ADMINISTRATION; ADMINISTRATOR OF INSURER; PROBATE TAX.

**administrator of insurer.** The taking over of the management of an insurer, on an order for administration made by the High Court, if the court considers (a) that the insurer has made inadequate provision for its debts or that the rights and interests of policy holders are being prejudiced or that the insurer is unable to comply with EC insurance regulations and (b) that administration would be in the public interest.

The administrator so appointed is required to carry on the business as a going concern with a view to placing it on a sound commercial and financial footing. There is provision for contribution from other insurers to an Insurance Compensation Fund and payment from that fund to the administrator. See Insurance (No 2) Act 1983; In re PMPA Insurance Co (1986) ILRM 524 and (1988) ILRM 109. [Text: Forde (9)].

**administrator pendente lite.** See PENDENTE LITE.

**admiralty action.** Proceedings for the determination of: a claim for the sale of a ship or any share therein; or a claim to prohibit any dealing with a ship or any share therein; or in respect of a mortgage of, or charge on, a ship or any share therein; or a claim arising out of bottomry (qv) or in the nature, or arising out, of pilotage or arising out of a general average act; or a claim for the forfeiture of any ship or her tackle. The High Court has jurisdiction in admiralty matters. The Cork Circuit Court traditionally had limited admiralty jurisdiction but its jurisdiction is now abolished: Jurisdiction of Courts (Maritime Conventions) Act 1989 s.14. See Motokov v Fermoyle Investments Ltd (1985) HC. See RSC O.64. See AVERAGE; CHARGE ON SHIP; COLLISION OF SHIP; DETENTION OF SHIP; MALICIOUS DAMAGE.

**admissibility of evidence.** Evidence may be received by a court only if it is both relevant and admissible. In general, all evidence relevant to *facts in issue* is admissible. Certain evidence is inadmissible eg evidence of privileged communications without the waiver of the person in whose favour the privilege exists. The admissibility of evidence is decided by the judge; the jury must be absent during arguments as to admissibility: The State v Treanor (1924) 2 IR 193; The People v Murray (1971) CCA; The People v O'Brien (1969) CCA. See EVIDENCE; EVIDENCE AND CONSTITUTIONAL RIGHTS; FACT IN ISSUE; PRIVILEGE, EVIDENTIAL; TRIBUNALS OF INQUIRY; VOIRE DIRE.

**admission.** An acknowledgement of fact, oral written or inferred from conduct, made by or on behalf of a party to a proceeding, which is admissible as against the party making it, as proof of the facts admitted. The admission may be formal or informal. A *formal* admission of a fact may arise in pleadings eg matters not denied in the defence are taken as admitted, or in answer to interrogatories (qv). An *informal* admission may arise by express or implied statement, by silence or by conduct, or in various documents such as wills, account books, or maps. Informal admissions are admissible if made by the parties themselves, their privies, partners or agents, and hearsay (qv) evidence of the admission may be admissible.

In criminal proceedings, admissions may be made by plea of guilt, by a statement of facts by the accused, or by a confession (qv). Silence after a legal caution is not an admission. See Attorney General v Durnan (1934) IR 308. Provision is made for the formal admission in criminal proceedings of matters not in dispute in order to dispense with the need for formal proofs: Criminal Justice Act 1984 s.22.

In bankruptcy matters, a person who on examination, admits that he is indebted to a bankrupt or has property belonging to him, may be ordered by the court to pay it or deliver it to the Official Assignee (qv): Bankruptcy Act 1988 s.22.

**admit, notice to.** See NOTICE TO ADMIT.

**adoptable powers.** Powers which must,

in order to be exercised by a body, be "adopted" by the body eg see Building Societies Act 1989 ss.2(1) and 36.

**adopted child.** See CHILD, ADOPTED.

**adoption.** The process by which the rights and duties of the natural parents of a child are extinguished by the making of an *adoption order*, while the equivalent rights and duties become vested in the adoptive parents to whom the child then stands in all respects as if born to them in lawful wedlock: Adoption Act 1952. There are specific requirements relating to the *consent* which is required before an adoption order may be made. A child must be under 18 years of age to be adopted: Adoption Act 1988 s.6. See also Adoption Act 1964; Adoption Act 1974; Adoption Rules 1984 (SI No 134 of 1984); Adoption Rules 1988 (SI No 304 of 1988); Adoption Rules 1990 (SI No 170 of 1990).

The categories of children who may be legally adopted has been extended, to include, in certain restricted and exceptional circumstances, children whose parents are married to each other and are, or where one parent is, alive: Adoption Act 1988. Such adoption is allowed only where the parents of a child have failed in their duty towards the child and the failure is likely to continue and it constitutes an *abandonment of their parental rights*. These provisions are not repugnant to the Constitution: Reference pursuant to Art 26 of the Constitution In re Adoption (No 2) Bill 1987 (1989 SC) IR 656. Also, it has been held that the 1988 applied to a child, born abroad of foreign parents, who is in the State: (1993 SC) — Irish Times 9/3/1993. Health boards are required to provide a service for the adoption of children: Child Care Act 1991 s.6. See Woulfe in 6ILT & SJ (1988) 271. See also Rules of the Superior Courts (No1) 1990 (SI No 97 of 1990). [Text: O'Halloran; Shatter]. See ADOPTION, CONSENT TO; CHILD, ADOPTED.

**adoption, application for.** Applications from persons for an adoption order are made to the Adoption Board (qv). An applicant must be ordinarily resident in the State, must be of good moral character, must have sufficient means to support the child and be a suitable person to have parental rights and duties:

Adoption Act 1952 s.13(1). In addition the applicant, or applicants, must be: a married couple living together; or the natural mother; or the natural father; or a relative of the child; or a widow, or a widower: Adoption Act 1991 s.10(1).

Applicants must be at least 21 years of age, except where the applicants are a married couple and one of them is the mother, father or relative of the child when it suffices if one of them is 21 years of age (ibid 1991 Act s.10(5)). An adoption order must not be made where the applicant is married unless the applicant's spouse has consented, except in the case of divorce a mensa et thoro, judicial separation, separation by deed, or desertion (ibid s.10(4)). See Adoption Acts 1952, 1964, 1974; Adoption Rules 1984 (SI No 134 of 1984).

**adoption, consent to.** An adoption order cannot be made by the Adoption Board (qv) unless the consent of the natural mother or guardian (qv) or other person having control over the child, is given: Adoption Act 1952 s.14(1). The consent must be in writing and can be withdrawn before the adoption order is made; the consent must be a fully informed, free and willing surrender or abandonment of the consentor's rights: G v An Bord Uchtala (1980) IR 32. A consent is invalid if given before the child is six weeks old, or if given at any time before three months of the adoption application: Adoption Act 1974 s.8.

In cases of religious differences, an adoption order cannot be made unless every person whose consent is necessary knows the religion of the applicants: 1974 Act s.4; M v An Bord Uchtala (1975) IR 86. The Adoption Board (qv) may dispense with consent if it is satisfied that the person whose consent is required is mentally unfit or is unable to be found.

Where a child is placed for adoption and the appropriate person fails, neglects or refuses consent or withdraws a consent already given, the applicant for the adoption order may apply to the High Court for an order authorising the Adoption Board to dispense with such consent: Adoption Act 1974 s.3. See G v An Bord Uchtala (1980) IR 32; McC v An Bord Uchtala (1982) ILRM 159. See ADOPTION.

**adoption, foreign.** An adoption of a child which was effected outside the State under and in accordance with the law of the place where it was effected: Adoption Act 1991 s.1. A foreign adoption is deemed, unless contrary to public policy, to have been effected by a valid Irish adoption order (ibid ss.2-5). Certain conditions must be satisfied eg that the adoption outside the State has essentially the same legal effect as an Irish adoption, that the required consents have been obtained, and that payment or reward has not been made in consideration of the adoption (ibid s.1). For adoptions effected after commencement of the 1991 Act, the child must be under 18 years of age (ibid s.1). An Bord Uachtala (Adoption Board (qv)) must maintain a Register of Foreign Adoptions (ibid ss.6-7). See Report on the Recognition of Foreign Adoption Decrees (LRC 29 — 1989).

**Adoption Board.** The board set up for the purpose of making adoption orders (qv) and consisting of a chairman and eight ordinary members appointed by the government (qv): Adoption Act 1952 s.8 as amended by Adoption Act 1991 s.11. The chairman must be a judge of the Supreme, High, Circuit or District Courts, or a barrister or solicitor of at least ten years standing. An adoption society or a health board which wishes to process adoptions must be registered with the Adoption Board. An adoption society is not required to carry out its statutory tasks through its own servants or agents: JP & SP v O'G (1991 SC) ITLR (24 Jun). Persons who wish to adopt a child must apply to the Board, which may at its discretion grant or refuse the application. When considering an adoption application, the Board must regard the welfare of the child as the first and paramount consideration: Adoption Act 1974. See also SI No 327 of 1982.

**adoptive leave.** The government in 1993 announced its intention to introduce legislation to provide entitlement to adoptive leave to female employees who adopt a child.

**adult.** A person who attains *full age*. See AGE OF MAJORITY.

**adultery.** An act of voluntary sexual intercourse which takes place during the subsistence of a valid marriage with a person of the opposite sex who is not the spouse. It is a ground for a decree of judicial separation (qv), but may not be relied upon solely by an applicant for a decree, where the spouses have lived with each other for more than a year after the adultery became known to the applicant; the court may also refuse a decree where the respondent proves the adultery was committed with the connivance (qv) of the applicant: Judicial Separation and Family Law Reform Act 1989 ss.2(1)(a), 4(1) and 44(2). See JUDICIAL SEPARATION; CONNIVANCE; DIVORCE A MENSA ET THORO; RECRIMINATION.

**advancement, child.** A gift intended to make permanent provision for a child and includes advancement by way of portion or settlement: Succession Act 1965 s.63. Includes some permanent provision for the child of a deceased for the purpose of establishing the child in a profession, vocation, trade or business or a marriage portion (qv) or payments made for the education of a child to a standard higher than that provided for other children of the deceased (ibid s.63(3)). Children must bring into hotchpot (qv) any money or property they received from the deceased in his lifetime by way of advancement if they wish to share in the distribution of the estate. See Succession Act 1965 s.63. See DOUBLE PORTIONS, RULE AGAINST; RESULTING TRUST.

**adversary procedure.** Accusatory procedure (qv).

**adverse possession, title by.** See LONG POSSESSION, TITLE BY.

**adverse witness.** A witness, adverse to the party calling him, who may be cross-examined by that party with the leave of the court. See HOSTILE WITNESS.

**advertisement.** (1) For the purposes of planning legislation, means any word, letter, model, balloon, kite, poster, notice, device or representation employed for the purpose of advertisement, announcement or direction: LG(P&D) Act 1963 s.2(1). Advertisement structure means any structure which is a hoarding, scaffold, framework, poll, standard, device, or sign (whether illuminated or not) and which is used or intended for use for exhibiting advertisements. See 1963 Act s.54 and LG(P&D) Regulations

1977, third schedule, Part II (SI No 65 of 1977).

(2) The publisher of an advertisement can be compelled to disclose the name and address of the person or his agent who procured the publication of an advertisement in relation to the supply or provision of any goods, services, living accommodation or facilities. See Consumer Information Act 1978 s.13; Restrictive Practices (Amendment) Act 1987 s.30. Advertisement in this context includes a catalogue, a circular and a price list (ibid 1978 Act s.l).

(3) An advertisement is also defined as a paid-for communication addressed to the public or a section of it, the purpose being to influence the opinions or behaviour of those to whom it is addressed: Advertising Standards Authority for Ireland — Code of Advertising Standards — art.19.

(4) Advertisements relating to employment must not contravene the Employment Equality Act 1977 s.8 ie they must not indicate an intention to discriminate on the grounds of sex. The Act does not apply where the sex of the person is an occupational qualification (ibid s.17). Discrimination previously justified on the grounds of privacy or decency (ibid s.17(c) and (d)) has since been repealed: EC (Employment Equality Regulations 1982 (SI No 302 of 1982) and EEA v Cork Examiner (1991) ELR 6. See also Tipperary Sub-Contracting Ltd and Nenagh Guardian v EEA — EE 6/1993. See Flynn in 11 ILT and SJ (1993) 157.

(5) Solicitors are now permitted to advertise the services they offer: Solicitors Advertising Regulations 1988 (SI No 344 of 1988).

See also Indecent Advertisements Act 1889; Tobacco Products (Control of Advertising, Sponsorship and Sales) Promotion Act 1978 s.1; Building Societies Act 1989 s.42(3)(a). See ANNUAL PERCENTAGE CHARGE; DISCRIMINATION; MEDICAL PREPARATIONS; PLANNING PERMISSION; SIGN.

**advertisement, misleading.** An advertisement in relation to the supply or provision in the course or for the purpose of a trade, business or profession, of goods, services or facilities which is likely to mislead and thereby cause loss, damage or injury to members of the public to a material degree. It is an offence for a person to publish, or cause to be published, such an advertisement. Any person, including the Director of Consumer Affairs, may obtain an order from the High Court prohibiting the publication of such an advertisement. See Consumer Information Act 1978 s.8; European Communities (Misleading Advertising) Regulations 1988 (SI No 134 of 1988).

**advertisement, radio and television.** The total daily time for advertising on independent radio and tv services must not exceed (a) 15 per cent of the total daily broadcasting time and (b) ten minutes in any hour (ibid s.10(4)). The limits on RTE were 7.5 percent of daily transmission time and five minutes in any hour: Broadcasting Act 1990 s.3. They are now such periods as are approved by the Minister: Broadcasting Authority (Amdt) Act 1993 s.2. There is a prohibition on the broadcast of any advertisement which is directed towards any religious or political end or which has any relation to an industrial dispute: Radio and Television Act 1988 ss.10(3) and 18. See SOUND BROADCASTING SERVICE.

**advertising order.** An order which the Minister may make to compel inclusion of particular information in an advertisement of goods, services, living accommodation or facilities. It is an offence to publish an advertisement which fails to comply with the order. See Consumer Information Act 1978 s.ll.

**advice on proofs.** The directions given by counsel, at the close of pleading and prior to the trial of an action, as to the documents to be produced at the trial, the witnesses who are to be called and the notices which are to be served eg a notice to admit (qv).

**advocate.** A person who pleads the cause of another in court eg a barrister (qv) or solicitor (qv). Formerly an advocate was a member of the College of Advocates which was abolished by the Court of Probate Act 1857. [Text: Finlay(2); Napley (UK)].

**aedificatum solo, solo cedit.** [That which is built upon land becomes part of the land]. See FIXTURES.

**aequitas sequitur legem.** [Equity follows the law]. See EQUITY, MAXIMS OF.

**affidavit.** A written (or printed bookwise)

statement in the name of a person, called the *deponent*, by whom it is sworn: RSC O.40. It includes a *declaration* in the case of persons for the time being allowed by law to declare instead of swearing: Interpretation Act 1937 s.12 sch. An affidavit must be drawn up in the first person (ibid RSC r.8) and must be confined to such facts as the deponent is able of his own knowledge to prove, and must state his means of knowledge thereof (ibid r.4), except on *interlocutory* motions, on which statements as to his belief, with the grounds thereof, may be admitted (ibid r.4 and Bula Ltd v Tara Mines Ltd (1991 HC) 9ILT Dig 128) which permitted hearsay material in an interlocutory application.

The facts relied upon must, in the absence of special procedures, be clearly deposed to in the affidavit itself and not by reference to any other written document: Murphy v Greene (1991 SC) ILRM 404. The court may order the attendance for cross-examination of a person making an affidavit (ibid RSC r.1). Also, in proceedings commenced by summary summons and special summons, a party is entitled to cross-examine a deponent who has made an affidavit filed on behalf of the opposite party: RSC O.37 r.2; O.38 r.3. See also RCC O.22. See also Arbitration Act 1954 s.22(1)(c). See ARGUMENTATIVE AFFIDAVIT; DECLARATION BY DECEASED; JURAT; SUMMONS, HIGH COURT; THIRD PARTY NOTICE.

**affidavit of discovery.** See DISCOVERY OF DOCUMENTS.

**affidavit of service.** An affidavit which states when, where, and how, and by whom, delivery of a document (eg a summons) was effected and in the case of delivery to any person, which states that the deponent was, at the time of such delivery, acquainted with the appearance of such person: RSC O.40 r.9. See also RCC O.22 r.15, O.10 r.7. See SUMMONS, SERVICE OF.

**affiliation order.** An order of the court which provided for the payment of a periodical or lump sum of money by the father of an illegitimate child as a contribution towards the maintenance of that child: Illegitimate Children (Affiliation Orders) Act 1930 s.2; Status of Children Act 1987 s.25. Formerly, the onus was on the applicant mother to prove to the satisfaction of the court that the person she alleged to be, was, the father; she had to give evidence herself and she had to produce corroborative evidence in support; and proceedings had to be brought within specified time limits (ibid 1930 Act s.2(2); Family Law (Maintenance of Spouses and Children) Act 1976 s.28(1)(b)).

Now, however, a person may apply for a *maintenance order* (qv) for the support of a child whose parents are not married to each other, at any time during the child's dependency, and the court will have regard to the circumstances as if the application was one relating to a legitimate child; if there is any dispute as to paternity or parentage, the issue will be decided on the balance of probability, prior to any maintenance order being made: Status of Children Act 1987 ss.15-25. See RB v HR (1990 CC) as reported in 8ILT & SJ (1990) 295. See DEPENDENT CHILD; PARENTAGE, DECLARATION OF.

**affinity.** Relationship by marriage. The relationship between a husband and his wife's blood relations, and between a wife and her husband's blood relations. There is no affinity between a person and the relations by marriage of his or her spouse. See CONSANGUINITY; MARRIAGE.

**affirm.** (1) To elect to be bound by a voidable contract. (2) To make a solemn declaration instead of an oath. See AFFIRMATION; VOIDABLE.

**affirmanti non neganti incumbit probatio.** [The burden of proof is on him who affirms, not on him who denies]. See PROOF.

**affirmation.** A solemn declaration which a person may make instead of taking an oath, where the person states that he has no religious belief or that an oath is contrary to his religious belief: Oaths Act 1888. See Report on Oaths and Affirmations (LRC 34 — 1990). See OATH.

**affirmative order.** An order made pursuant to a statute, a draft of which must be laid before each House of the Oireachtas and be approved by each such House eg an order conferring additional functions on An Foras Aiseanna Saothair: Labour Services Act 1987 s.5(3).

**affray.** The common law misdemeanour

consisting of the fighting of two or more persons in a public place and of such a nature as might frighten reasonable people. In England it has been held that it need not be in a public place and that one person acting alone may cause an affray: Button v DPP (1965) 3 All ER 587; Taylor v DPP (1973) 2 All ER 1108.

Under proposed draft legislation, the common law offence will be abolished: Criminal Justice (Public Order) Bill 1993 s.17(4). It is proposed that where (a) two or more persons at any place use or threaten to use violence towards each other, and (b) the violence so used or threatened by one of those persons is unlawful, and (c) the conduct of those persons taken together is such as would cause a person of reasonable firmness present at that place to fear for his or another person's safety, then, each such person who uses or threatens to use unlawful violence will commit the offence of *affray* (ibid s.17(1)). The place may be a public place, a private place or both. See RIOT; VIOLENT DISORDER.

**affreightment.** A contract made by bill of lading (qv) or charterparty (qv), whereby a shipowner agrees to carry goods in his ship for reward. See FREIGHT.

**aftercare.** The assistance which a health board (qv) is empowered to provide for a child who leaves the care of the board, where the board is satisfied as to his need for assistance: Child Care Act 1991 s.45. The aftercare may be provided until the person is 21 years of age, or beyond that age until the completion of the course of education in which he is engaged. See Health Act 1953 ss.55(4) and (5) which is repealed on the commencement of this new legislation. See CARE ORDER; WELFARE OF CHILDREN.

**after-acquired property.** Property which is acquired by or devolves on a bankrupt before the discharge or annulment of the adjudication order by which he was declared a bankrupt. Such property vests in the Official Assignee (qv) if and when he claims it, except for damages recovered or recoverable by the bankrupt for personal injury or loss suffered by him: Bankruptcy Act 1988 ss.3 and 44(5). It is an offence for a bankrupt to fail to disclose to the Official Assignee any after-acquired property

(ibid s.127).

**A.G.** Attorney General (qv).

**age.** A person attains a particular age expressed in years on the commencement of the relevant anniversary of the date of his birth; this applies for the purpose of any rule of law or statutory provision, deed, will or other instrument: Age of Majority Act 1985 s.4. A person born on the 29th February attains a particular age on the 29th February in leap years and on 1st March in other years: R v Roxby (Inhabitants) 109 ER 370 (1829). At common law a person attained a particular age at the first moment of the day preceding the relevant anniversary of his birth.

**age for employment.** See UNFAIR DISMISSAL; YOUNG PERSON.

**age limit.** The age at which a person is required by statute or by contract to cease to perform some function or to hold office eg trustees of a Trustee Savings Bank are required to retire at age 70 although there is no statutory age limit for company directors. Employees in the private and public sectors are generally required by their contract of employment to retire at age 65. See Trustee Savings Bank Act 1989 s.18.

**age of consent.** See CONSENT, AGE OF.

**age of majority.** The age at which a person attains *full age* ie when he attains the age of eighteen years, or, in case he marries before attaining that age, upon his marriage: Age of Majority Act 1985 s.2. The age of majority for all purposes of the Taxes Acts is also 18, except in the case of incapacitated children, where it remains 21 years: Finance Act 1986 s.112.

**age of minor.** When a *minor* sues as plaintiff, a certified extract from the register of births must be produced and proved on his behalf at the trial or hearing or on an application to have a proposed settlement approved by the court: RSC O.66 r.1.

In child care proceedings, the true age of a person to whom an application relates is deemed to be the age presumed or declared by the court following due inquiry, unless the contrary is proved: Child Care Act 1991 s.32. See MINOR.

**agency.** See AGENT.

**agent.** A person who is employed for the purpose of bringing his principal (qv) into contractual relations with third parties. An agent does not make contracts on his own behalf and consequently it is not necessary that he should have full contractual capacity. When the agent has brought his principal into contractual relations with another, he drops out and the principal sues or is sued on the contract.

An agent may be a universal agent, a general agent or a special agent. A *universal* agent has authority to act for the principal in all matters eg under a universal power of attorney (qv). A *general* agent has authority to act in transactions of a class eg a solicitor, a managing director of a company; the scope of authority is that usually possessed by such agents. A *special* agent is one who is appointed for a particular purpose and his authority is limited to that purpose eg an auctioneer. An act done by an agent within the scope of his authority, binds his principal.

Agency may arise: (a) by express agreement, verbal or in writing, and will be limited by that agreement; (b) by implication or by conduct eg when a husband and wife are living together, the wife is presumed to have his authority to pledge his credit for necessaries suitable to their style of living; (c) by necessity (qv); (d) by ratification (qv) eg where a principal confirms and adopts a contract made by an agent who at the time of its making had no or insufficient authority.

An agency can be terminated by act of the parties (by agreement or by revocation) and by operation of law (death, bankruptcy or insanity of the principal or agent). See Yonge v Toynbee (1910) 1 KB 215. [Text: Bowstead UK]. See COMMISSION; DELEGATUS NON POTEST DELEGARE.

**agent, duties of.** An agent is required to use diligence and to display any special skill he may profess or be required to have. He must account for such property of his principal as comes into his hands. He must make no profit beyond his commission and may not become a principal against his own employer. He cannot enter into a transaction where his duty and his personal interest conflict, unless he makes a full disclosure. Also he must not delegate his authority unless

justified by usage of the particular trade, by necessity or where the act is purely ministerial. See Chariot Inns Ltd v Assicurazioni Generali SPA (1981) ILRM 173.

**agent, gratuitous.** An agent who gives his services without any express or implied promise of remuneration. He is required to exercise the degree of care and skill which may reasonably be expected from him in all the circumstances of the case: Chandhry v Prabhakar (1988) 3 All ER 718 as discussed by Gill in 7ILT & SJ (1989) 132.

**agent, insurance.** See INSURANCE AGENT.

**agent, payment to.** See PAYMENT TO AGENT.

**agent of necessity.** Agency of necessity arises where the law confers on a person the authority to act for and bind another (his principal) without requiring the consent of the principal. This may arise when (a) the agent is unable to communicate with his principal and (b) he acts under a definite commercial necessity and (c) he acts bona fide in the interest of his principal eg the master of a ship may contract and bind the owner in an emergency: Couturier v Hastie (1852) 5 HLC 673. See also Walsh v Bord Iascaigh Mhara (1981) IR 470.

**agent provocateur.** A person who entices another to commit an express breach of the law which he might not otherwise have committed and then proceeds to inform against him in respect of such offence. The evidence of a witness who acts as an agent provocateur in order to obtain the evidence tendered, may be accepted and evaluated on its merits, without as a matter of law requiring to be corroborated: Dental Board v O'Callaghan (1969) IR 181. For UK consideration of agent provocateur, see R v Mealey and Sheridan (1975) 60 Cr App R 150; R v Sang (1979) 3 WLR 263. See ENTRAPMENT.

**aggravated assault.** An assault which is aggravated in respect of violence, not by reason of indecency: R v Baker (1876) 46 LJ Ex 75. Assaults are divided into basic assaults aggravated either by the harm thereby done, the nature of the intent of the accused, the status of the victim, or the circumstances of the commission: Charlton in "Offences Against the Person" (1992) para 6.02.

An *aggravated assault* was formerly an assault on a male child of 14 years of age or under or on any female which was of such an *aggravated nature* that it could not be sufficiently punished as a common assault: Offences Against the Person Act 1861 s.43, repealed by the Criminal Justice Act 1951. For arrest powers for any aggravated assault, see Dublin Police Act 1842 s.28. See ASSAULT.

**aggravated burglary.** See BURGLARY, AGGRAVATED.

**aggravated larceny.** See LARCENY, AGGRAVATED.

**aggravated murder.** See MURDER, AGGRAVATED.

**aggravated sexual assault.** See SEXUAL ASSAULT.

**aggravation of damages.** Matters which may tend to increase the amount of damages in a defamation (qv) action eg failure of a plea of justification (qv); the conduct of the defendant in repeating the defamation, in refusing to apologise, or in persisting in a charge known to be unfounded; or an inappropriate mode of publication. "Aggravated damages are given for conduct which shocks the plaintiff, exemplary damages (qv) for conduct which shocks the jury": Salmond on Torts as cited in McIntyre v Lewis & Dolan (1991 SC) ITLR (22 Apr). See Kennedy v Hearne (1988 HC & SC) ILRM 52 and 531. See DAMAGES.

**agistment.** A licence to graze livestock on the land of another. The person on whose land the livestock graze is called the *agister*; he is a bailee (qv) for reward.

**agm.** See ANNUAL GENERAL MEETING.

**agnates.** Relations through males ie on the father's side, eg a father's son, brother or sister. See COGNATES.

**agreement.** A declared concurrence of will of two or more persons which affects or alters their rights and duties. For *agreement to sell* see Uniacke v Cassidy Electrical Supply Company (1981) HC. See CONTRACT; RETENTION OF TITLE; SALE OF GOODS.

**agreement, closed shop.** See CLOSED SHOP.

**agreement, collective.** See COLLECTIVE AGREEMENT.

**agricultural land.** See INTENSIVE AGRICULTURE; VALUATION.

**agricultural land, leasing of.** Provisions to facilitate the leasing of agricultural land are contained in the Land Act 1984.

**agricultural society.** A society where the number of the society's members is not less than 50 and all or a majority of its members are persons who are mainly engaged in, and derive the principal part of their income, from husbandry; the Minister may give a certificate that a society is to be treated as an agricultural society: Finance Act 1978 s.18(1). The trading profits of such a society from certain transactions are exempt from corporation tax. For *agricultural co-operative society* see Industrial & Provident Societies Act 1978 s.4.

**aid and abet.** See AIDER AND ABETTER.

**aider and abetter.** A principal in the second degree. *The kernal of the matter is the establishing of an activity on the part of the accused from which his intentions may be inferred and the effect of which is to assist the principal (in the first degree) in the commission of the crime proved to have been committed by the principal*: The People (DPP) v Madden (1977) IR 336. It is sufficient if the prosecution can show that the accused knew the nature of the crime intended; it is not necessary for the prosecution to show that the accused knew the means to be employed by the principal offender: DPP v Egan (1989 CCA) ITLR (27 Nov). See PROSTITUTE; SUICIDE.

**aiel.** A grandfather.

**air law.** The body of law dealing with the flight and operation of aircraft which is derived from common law, statutes and international agreements. The State is a party to the Chicago Agreements incorporating the Chicago Convention 1944, International Air Services (*two freedoms*) Agreement 1944 and the International Air Transport (*five freedoms*) Agreement 1944; the Warsaw Convention 1929 and the Hague Protocol 1955; the Guadalajara Convention 1961; the Paris Agreements of 1956, 1960 and 1967; the Brussels Protocols of 1970; 1978; 1981; the Tokyo Convention 1963; the Hague Convention 1970 (unlawful seizure of aircraft); the Montreal Convention 1971 (unlawful acts against aviation safety). See Air Navigation and Transport Acts 1936-1975; Air Navigation (Eurocontrol) Act 1983; Air Companies Act 1983; Air Transport Act 1986.

Further provisions for the promotion

of security and safety of civil aviation and airports is contained in the Air Navigation and Transport Act 1988. See also RSC O.111. [Text: Forde (5); Shawcross & Beaumont UK]. See FALSE ALARM; INTERCEPTION OF AIRCRAFT; IRISH AVIATION AUTHORITY; PREINSPECTION.

**air piracy/hijacking.** Colloquial expression describing a range of offences involving the unlawful seizure or endangering the safety of an aircraft. See Air Navigation and Transport Act 1988 s.51.

**air pollution.** A condition of the atmosphere in which a *pollutant* (qv) is present in such a quantity as to be liable to (a) be injurious to public health or (b) have a deleterious effect on flora or fauna or damage property or (c) impair or interfere with amenities or with the environment: Air Pollution Act 1987 s.4. The occupier of any premises, other than a private dwelling, must use the *best practicable means* to limit and, if possible, to prevent an *emission* from such premises; the occupier must not cause or permit an emission from such premises in such a quantity, or in such a manner, as to be a nuisance (ibid s.24).

The Minister may, by regulation, prohibit either absolutely, or subject to exception, such emissions as may be specified or any substance which may cause air pollution (ibid s.23). Local authorities have power to require measures to be taken to prevent or limit air pollution (ibid s.26) and to declare or limit air pollution (ibid s.26) and to declare an area to be a *special control area* (ibid ss.39-45). The Minister may issue directions specifying the *best practical means* for preventing or limiting emissions (ibid s.5(3)) and may make regulations (ibid s.10). Contravention of any provision of the Act or of any regulation or any notice served under the Act is an offence (ibid s.11).

There is provision for the licensing of industrial plant (ibid ss.30-38 as amended by Environmental Protection Agency Act 1992 s.18(2) and third schedule); for the specification of air quality standards and of emission limit values (ibid 1987 Act ss.50-51); for the production of air quality management plans (ibid s.46) and for monitoring of air quality and emissions (ibid s.54).

In 1992 provision was made for civil remedies for air pollution by way of injunctive relief and damages, similar to that available under water pollution legislation (ibid 1987 Act ss.28A and 28B inserted by 1992 Act s.18(2) and third schedule, para 4). See also SI 201, 243, 244 of 1987; 265 of 1988, and 167 of 1989. See also Hanrahan v Merck Sharpe & Dohme (Ire) Ltd (1988 SC) ILRM 629; Cork County Council v Angus Fire Chemicals Ltd (1991 HC) ILRM 173. [Text: Duggan].

**air quality standard.** The standard prescribed by the Minister: Air Pollution Act 1987 s.50. See AIR POLLUTION.

**aircraft, unlawful seizure of.** The Convention for the Suppression of Unlawful Seizure of Aircraft done at The Hague on 16th December 1970, is given effect in the State by the Air Navigation and Transport Act 1973. See AVIATION, UNLAWFUL ACTS AGAINST.

**airspace, interference with.** The owner of land is entitled to ownership and possession of a column of air above the surface. However, liability is avoided in respect of trespass or nuisance *by reason only of the flight of aircraft over any property at a height above the ground, which having regard to wind, weather, and all the circumstances of the case is reasonable, or the ordinary incidents of the flight*: Air Navigation and Transport Act 1936 s.55. Strict liability is provided for, where there is material damage or loss (ibid s.21(1)).

**alcohol, consumption of.** Consumption of alcohol by an employee during working hours may be a ground for dismissal. See Lawless v RTV National Vision Ltd (1990) ELR 46. See DRUNKEN DRIVING; DRUNKENESS; INTOXICATED.

**alcohol strength.** Bottles and cans containing a beverage with more than 1.2 per cent of alcohol are required to carry a label showing the actual alcoholic strength by volume: European Communities (Labelling, Presentation and Advertising of Foodstuffs) (Amendment) Regulations 1988 (SI No 202 of 1988).

**alcohol test.** See BLOOD SPECIMEN.

**alderman.** The name borrowed from the anglo-saxon *ealdorman* (literally, an elder); an alderman is a member of the council which governs the municipal affairs of a borough (qv).

**aleatory contract.** A wagering contract

(qv).

**alias; alias dictus.** [Otherwise called]. A false name; a second or assumed name.

**alibi.** [Elsewhere]. A defence of an accused that at the time of the commission of the offence, with which he is charged, he was elsewhere. Notice of intention to raise an alibi in a trial on indictment (qv) must be given to the prosecution: Criminal Justice Act 1984 s.20.

Failure by an employer to conduct a full and fair inquiry into an employee's alibi, may lead to the employee's dismissal being held to be procedurally unfair: Burke v Form Print Ltd (1992 EAT) ELR 163. See WITNESS.

**alien.** A person who is not a citizen. There is substantial control given to the Minister over aliens eg to prohibit or restrict their entry or exit; to exclude or deport them; to require or prohibit residence in a particular area; and to regulate registration, travel and employment within the State: Aliens Act 1935. However, only a grave and substantial reason associated with the common good would justify the removal of a family (constituted of alien parents and children who are Irish citizens) against its will outside the State: Fajujono v Minister for Justice (1990 SC) ILRM 234. There is freedom of movement for workers within the EC under the Treaty of Rome 1957, art.48. See also European Communities (Aliens) Orders 1977 to 1985; Air Navigation and Transport (Preinspection) Act 1986. See Shum v Ireland (1986) ILRM 593; Osheku v Ireland (1987) ILRM 330; Ji Jao Lau v Ireland (1993 HC) ILRM 64; ANM (an infant) v An Bord Uchtala (1992 HC) ILRM 569. See ASYLUM, CLAIM FOR; CITIZENSHIP; DEPORTATION; EUROPEAN ECONOMIC COMMUNITY.

**alienate.** To exercise the power of disposing of or transferring property.

**alienation.** The power of an owner or tenant in property to dispose or transfer his interest. Alienation may be *voluntary* eg by conveyance or will; it may be *involuntary* eg sale by the court on the application of a judgment mortgagee. As regards covenants in leases against alienation, see Landlord and Tenant (Amendment) Act 1980 s.66. See INALIENABILITY.

**alienato rei preferturi juri accres-**

**cendi.** [The law favours the alienation rather than the accumulation of property]. See INALIENABILITY.

**alieni juris.** [Of another's right]. Term used to refer to a person subject to the authority of another eg a minor (qv). Contrast with SUI JURIS.

**alimentary trust.** A protective trust (qv).

**alimony.** An allowance paid by a husband to his wife for her support in circumstances where they were judicially separated; the amount was determined by the court on consideration of the circumstances. It was called *alimony pendente lite* where ordered to be paid pending the court proceedings for the judicial separation, and *permanent alimony* when finally determined by the judge on making the judicial decree. A capital sum could not be awarded by a judge by way of alimony, since alimony was, by nature a periodic payment which was subject to increase or decrease according to the income of the party paying it, or even to complete termination: MB v RB (1989) IR 412 and Woulfe in 7 ILT & SJ (1989) 296.

The Judicial Separation and Family Law Act 1989 introduced new provisions for judicial separation and the maintenance of spouses; any alimony order made prior to the 1989 Act is deemed to be a *periodical payments order* under s.14(1)(a) and consequently can be varied (ibid s.43). Provision is also made for alimony pending suit as such orders can still be made in nullity petitions (ibid s.25). See also Defence Act 1954 s.98(1)(h) as amended by the 1989 Act s.27. See DIVORCE A MENSA ET THORO; MAINTENANCE ORDER.

**alio intuitu.** With a motive other than the ostensible and proper one.

**aliquis non debetesse judex in propria causa quia non potest esse judex et pars.** [No man ought to be a judge in his own cause, because he cannot act as a judge and at the same time be a party]. See NATURAL JUSTICE.

**aliter.** [Otherwise].

**aliud est celare, aliud tacere.** [Silence is not the same thing as concealment]. However, active concealment may be equivalent to a positive statement that the fact does not exist and may amount to the tort of deceit (qv). See Delany v Keogh (1905) IR 267.

**aliunde.** [From elsewhere]. From another place or person.

**allegation.** A statement or assertion of fact in proceedings made by a party thereto; it particularly refers to a statement or charge which is not yet proven.

**allegiance.** In a monarchy, the natural and legal obedience which a subject owes to the monarch. A citizen of Ireland owes the fundamental political duties of fidelity to the nation and loyalty to the State: 1937 Constitution, art.9(2). See TREASON.

**allocation.** The appropriation (qv) of a fund to particular persons or purposes.

**allocatur.** [It is allowed].

**allocutus.** The demand of a court to a person found guilty by jury of treason (qv) or of a felony (qv), asking whether he has cause to show why judgment should not be pronounced against him.

**allonge.** [Make longer]. A piece of paper attached to a bill of exchange (qv) as a continuation sheet for endorsements where there is no further room for them on the bill: Bills of Exchange Act 1882 s.32(1). The last endorsement on the actual bill should be made partly on the bill and partly on the allonge.

**alloted capital.** See CAPITAL.

**allotment, land.** A piece of land, containing not more than one-quarter of a statute acre, let or intended to be let for cultivation by an individual for the production of vegetables mainly for the consumption of himself and his family: Acquisition of Land (Allotments) Act 1926 s.1 and Acquisition of Land (Allotments) (Amendment) Act 1934. For recovery of possession of an allotment, see the 1926 Act s.14 (1).

**allotment, shares.** The appropriation to a person of a certain number of shares in a company. Shares are said to have been alloted when a person acquires the unconditional right to be included in the company's register of members in respect of those shares: Companies Amendment Act 1983 s.2(2). A *public limited company* (plc) may not allot shares as fully or partly paid up otherwise than in cash unless the consideration for the allotment has been valued by an expert (ibid s.30). Also a *plc* may not allot shares unless at least one quarter of their nominal value, together with any premium on them, is

immediately payable to the company (ibid s.28); in other companies, at least five per cent of the shares' nominal value must be payable on application: Companies Act 1963 ss.53(3) and 55, as amended by 1983 Act, first schedule. A *return of allotments* must be made to the Registrar of Companies: 1963 Act s.58 as amended by the 1982 Act s.19; 1983 Act ss.31(2) and 55(1)(g).

Directors may not issue shares without express authority being given by the articles of association or by a resolution in general meeting. Such authority may be given for a specific allotment or generally and must state the maximum amount of shares which may be issued; if authority is given by the articles it cannot last for more than five years: 1983 Act s.20. It is a criminal offence for a *private company* to offer shares or debentures in the company or to allot them for that purpose (ibid s.21). See also Building Societies Act 1989 s.106(7). See PRE-EMPTION; SHARES; UNDERSUBSCRIBED; VALUATION REPORT.

**allowance to bankrupt.** The High Court may make to the bankrupt out of his estate such allowances as the court thinks proper in the special circumstances of the case: Bankruptcy Act 1988 s.71. On adjudication as a bankrupt, the bankrupt is entitled to retain such articles such as clothing, household furniture, bedding, tools or equipment of his trade or occupation or other like necessaries as he may select, not exceeding in value £2500, or such further amount as the court may allow (ibid s.45). See BANK-RUPTCY.

**alluvion.** Land imperceptibly gained from the sea or a river by the washing up of sand and soil so as to form *terra firma*. See Hindson v Ashby (1896) 2 Ch 1. See AVULSION.

**alteration.** A material alteration to an instrument without the consent of the other party, generally invalidates it, except as against the person making the alteration eg the alteration of the date of a bill of exchange to accelerate payment, invalidates it. An alteration in a deed (qv) is presumed to have been made before or at the time of execution. Alterations, obliterations or interlineations in a will (qv) are presumed to have been made after execution and are invalid unless they existed in the will prior to its execution or, if made afterwards, unless they have been executed and attested or unless they have been rendered valid by re-execution of the will or by a codicil: Succession Act 1965 s.86; Myles, Margaret Ismay, deceased (1993 HC) ILRM 36; RSC O.79 rr.10-11; O.80 rr.12-13. It is a rebuttable presumption: In the goods of Benn (1938) IR 313. See In re Rudd (1945) IR 180; Lombard & Ulster Banking v Bank of Ireland (1987) HC. See DOCU-MENTS, PRESUMPTIONS AS TO; WILL, REVOCA-TION OF.

**alternative, pleading in the.** Including in pleadings (qv) of two or more inconsistent sets of material facts and claiming relief thereunder in the alternative.

**alternative directors.** Substitute directors. See Irish Civil Service Building Society v Registrar of Building Societies (1985) IR 167.

**alternative disputes resolution.** Refers to systems for the resolution of disputes without recourse to formal legal proceedings eg arbitration (qv). A new service was established by the Law Society in 1991 to help solve disputes between companies; the firm "Commercial Disputes Resolution" offers a neutral person to assist in finding a mutually acceptable solution to business disputes. In the UK, some 80% of cases referred to disputes resolution are settled without recourse to legal proceedings. See also MacGreevy Keane Mediation, Dublin. See SMALL CLAIM.

**alternative employment.** There is an obligation on an employer to look for an alternative to redundancy: O'Connor v Power Securities Ltd UD 344/89 as reported by Barry in 8ILT & SJ (1990) 108.

**alternative verdict.** A person charged with a complete offence may be convicted of an attempt to commit the offence, if commission of the complete offence is not proved: Criminal Procedure Act 1851 s.9. A court may substitute verdicts in other cases as enacted eg a verdict of handling of stolen property may be made where an accused has been charged with stealing or vice versa: Larceny Act 1990 s.8. The power to substitute verdicts is a matter of substantive jurisdiction and

is not available to the Special Criminal Court: DPP v Rice (1979) IR 15. Also a person indicted for rape can be convicted of lesser offences eg if found guilty of rape under section 4, or of aggravated sexual assault, or of sexual assault: Criminal Law (Rape) (Amendment) Act 1990 s.8; or of attempted rape: DPP v Riordan (1992 CCA) ITLR (30 Nov). See VERDICT.

**allurement and children.** See OCCUPIER'S LIABILITY TO CHILDREN.

**amalgamation.** The combination of two or more companies or bodies. See Companies Act 1963 ss.201-203 and 260; Trade Union Act 1975 s.15; Building Societies Act 1989 s.95; Trustee Savings Bank 1989 ss.47-48; Industrial Relations Act 1990 s.22. See MERGER/TAKE OVER.

**ambassador.** Head of a diplomatic mission, representing his country, accredited to the Head of State in which he resides. See Diplomatic Relations and Immunities Acts 1967 and 1976. See DIPLOMATIC PRIVILEGE.

**ambiguitas verborum patens nulla verificatione excluditur.** [A patent ambiguity in the words of a written instrument cannot be cleared up by evidence extrinsic to the instrument]. See AMBIGUITY.

**ambiguity.** Uncertain meaning. A *patent* ambiguity is one which is apparent on the face of an instrument eg a blank space in a deed. It cannot generally be resolved by oral evidence: Watcham v AG for E Africa (1919) AC 533. A *latent* ambiguity is one not apparent on the face of the instrument (eg *my car I leave to my nephew Patrick* where the testator had two nephews of that name) may be resolved by oral evidence. Extrinsic evidence (qv) is admissible to assist the court in construing ambiguity in a will: In re Estate of Egan (1990) 8ILT Dig 108; Rowe v Law (1978) IR 55. See CONSTRUCTION SUIT; CONTRA PROFERENTEM; EQUIVOCATION; UNAMBIGUOUS.

**ambulatoria est voluntas defuncti usque ad vitae supremum exitum.** [The will of a deceased person is ambulatory until the latest moment of death]. See WILL, REVOCATION OF.

**ambulatory.** Capable of being revoked. A person's will is ambulatory until death. See Vynior's case (1609) 8 Co Rep 81b. See CHATTEL MORTGAGE; WILL.

**ameliorating waste.** See WASTE.

**amendment.** The correction of a defect (eg an error or omission) in a summons or pleadings. See PLEADINGS, AMENDMENT OF; SLIP RULE; SUMMONS, AMENDMENT OF.

**amends, offer of.** See OFFER OF AMENDS.

**amenity, loss of.** The loss of a faculty (eg an eye or a leg) which may entitle a plaintiff to compensation. See Roche v Kelly & Co (1969) IR 100. See DAMAGES; PAIN AND SUFFERING.

**amenity order, special.** See SPECIAL AMENITY ORDER.

**amicus curiae.** [A friend of the court].

**amnesty.** The pardoning of certain past offences by enactment of the Houses of the Oireachtas; usually such amnesties are for taxation offences, conditional on the offender making a full disclosure by a specified date eg see Finance Acts 1988 s.72 and 1991 s.120; Waiver of Certain Tax, Interest and Penalties Act 1993. See CHINESE WALL.

**amortisation.** Provision for the payment of a debt by means of a sinking fund.

**amusement machine.** A machine which (a) is constructed or adapted for play of a game, and (b) the player pays to play the machine, and (c) the outcome of the game is determined by the action of the machine, and (d) when played successfully, affords the player an opportunity to play again without paying: Finance Act 1992 s.120. Every amusement machine made available for play must be licensed and there must be a permit for the public place concerned (ibid ss.120-129). See also Finance Act 1993 s.70.

**ancestor.** A relative from whom descent can be traced through the father or mother; the person prior to 1961 to whose property an heir succeeded on intestacy. See SUCCESSION.

**ancient document.** A document which is at least 30 years old and produced from proper custody. Execution of such a document does not have to be proved. See DOCUMENTS, PRESUMPTION AS TO.

**ancient lights.** The right to light which becomes absolute after 20 years of actual uninterrupted enjoyment of access to it, unless enjoyed by written consent: Prescription Act 1859 s.3. See LIGHT, RIGHT TO.

**ancient monuments.** See NATIONAL MONUMENTS.

**ancipitus usus.** [Of doubtful use].

**and.** In a particular case, it was held that the word "and" had to be given a conjunctive rather than a disjunctive meaning; it was not permissible to construe "and" as if it were the word "or": Duggan v Dublin Corporation (1991 SC) ILRM 330 and Malicious Injuries Act 1981 s.6(1).

**and company; & Co.** The words marked on a cheque between two parallel traverse lines which have the effect of making the cheque payable only through a bank or building society: Bills of Exchange Act 1882 s.79(2) and Building Societies Act 1989 s.126. See CHEQUE, LIABILITY ON.

**angling.** Angling is to be construed as angling with rod and line: Fisheries (Consolidation) Act 1959 s.3(1). See TROUT.

**Anglo-Irish Agreement.** The agreement entered into in 1985 by the governments of Ireland and the United Kingdom and lodged with the United Nations. It is an interstate treaty governed by the ordinary rules of international law ie the Vienna Convention on the Law of Treaties of 1969. The Agreement recognises the requirement for majority consent within Northern Ireland for any change in its status, establishes an intergovernmental ministerial conference and secretariate, sets out the role of the conference in respect of security, policing, prison policy, law enforcement and extradition. The Agreement has been held not to be repugnant to the 1937 Constitution. See Crotty v An Taoiseach (1987) ILRM 400; McGimpsey v AG and Ireland (1990 SC) ILRM 440. The Agreement constitutes a recognition of the de facto situation in Northern Irelend but does so expressly without abandoning the constitutional claim to the integration of the national territory (qv): McGimpsey case. See also Ex p. Molyneux (1986) 1WLR 331. [Text: Hadden & Boyle].

**animal remedy.** Any substance or combination of substances for the purpose of (a) treating, preventing or modifying disease in animals, (b) making a medical or surgical diagnosis in animals, or (c) restoring, correcting or modifying physiological functions in animals: Animal Remedies Act 1993 s.1(1). A *prohibited animal remedy* is an animal remedy or ingredient for which a licence, authorisation or direction is required and has not been issued or has not been complied with (ibid s.1(1)).

Provision has been made in the 1993 Act for (a) the regulation of the availability, possession and use of animal remedies and for the prescription of maximum permitted residues of animal remedies in foods of animal origin, (b) the control of animals, and food derived from animals, to which animal remedies are administered, and (c) the inspection and testing of substances, animals and food of animal origin.

**animals.** Reasonable care must be taken by the owner, or controller, of animals which are brought onto the highway, to prevent them causing injury or damage: Furlong v Curran (1959) Ir Jur Rep 30. An owner of an animal which causes damage may be liable for (a) negligence: Howard v Bergin O'Connor & Co (1925) 2 IR 110; (b) public nuisance: Cunningham v Whelan (1918) 52 ILTR 67; (c) private nuisance: O'Gorman v O'Gorman (1903) 2 IR 573, (d) trespass and (e) under the rule in Ryland v Fletcher (qqv).

Under the *scienter* (qv) action, the keeper of an animal is strictly liable if the animal which causes the damage is wild *(fera natura)*, or if, being a tame or domesticated animal *(mansueta natura)*, it had a vicious propensity known to the keeper. Formerly, no liability attached to the owner of domestic animals which strayed onto the highway and caused damage: Searle v Wallbank (1947) AC 341; Gillick v O'Reilly (1984) ILRM 402.

However, the Animals Act 1985 s.2(1) abolishes so much of the rules of the common law relating to liability for negligence as excludes or restricts the duty which a person might owe to others to take such care as is reasonable to see that damage is not caused by an animal straying onto a public road. There is an exemption for animals straying from unfenced land in certain circumstances (ibid s.2(2)).

It has been held that s.2(1) created a res ipsa loquitor (qv) presumption and that it was necessary for the landowner to prove that he exercised reasonable care: McCaffrey v Lundy (1988) 6ILT & SJ 245 as approved in O'Reilly v Lavelle (1990) 2 IR 372. See also Protection of Animals kept for Farming Purposes Act 1984; Malicious Damage Act 1861 ss.40-41 as amended by Criminal Damage Act 1991 s.14(2)(b). See LRC 2 of 1982. See SCIENTER; DOGS; RYLAND V FLETCHER, RULE IN; STRICT LIABILITY; HOUSEHOLD CHATTELS; VIDEO RECORDING.

**animus.** [Intention].

**animus cancellandi.** [The intention of cancelling].

**animus dedicandi.** [The intention of dedicating]. The owner of land beside a public road is presumed to be the owner of the soil of up to half of the road, having dedicated it to the public. See DEDICATION; PUBLIC ROAD.

**animus et factum.** [The combination of the intention with the act].

**animus furandi.** [The intention of stealing]. See LARCENY.

**animus manendi.** [The intention of remaining. An essential element in domicile (qv).

**animus possidendi.** [The intention of possessing]. See Dundalk UDC v Conway (1987) HC.

**animus quo.** [The intention with which].

**animus revertendi.** [The intention of returning].

**animus revocandi.** [The intention of revoking] eg a will.

**animus testandi.** [The intention of making a will]. See WILL.

**anni nubiles.** The marriageable age of a female. It is now the same age as that of male ie 16 years of age, although parental consent is required up to 21 years of age: Marriage Act 1972. See MARRIAGE.

**annotation.** Addition of notes eg annotation of a stature usually consists of notes about each section or group of sections of an Act, explaining the reason for the section, giving the background to the previous law both statutory and judicial, giving definitions of key words, giving any important links with other sections, and indicating if the section has been brought into force by a statutory instrument if applicable. See Sweet & Maxwell — Irish Current Law Statutes Annotated — 1984 to date.

**annual general meeting; agm.** Every company must hold an annual general meeting every year and not more than fifteen months may elapse between these meetings: Companies Act 1963 s.131. The principal business to be transacted at an agm is consideration of the audited accounts and the directors' and auditors' reports, the election of directors, appointment of auditors and fixing their remuneration, and declaring a dividend (ibid Table A, art 53). The agm must be held in the State unless the articles of association do not require the meeting to be so held. See also Building Societies Act 1989 s.67. [Text: Shaw & Smith UK]. See EXTRAORDINARY GENERAL MEETING; POLL; PROXY; QUORUM; RESOLUTION; VOTING AT MEETINGS.

**annual leave.** The period of annual holidays, in addition to public holidays (qv), to which employees are entitled by contract or by statute. The statutory entitlement is to three weeks holidays for each leave year (1st April to 31st March), with *pro rata* entitlements for less than a year, provided the employee has worked at least 120 hours in a calendar month (110 hours if the employee is under 18 years of age) or at least 1400 hours in the leave year (1300 hours if under 18 years). *Wet time* (qv) up to 40 hours in a month may count as hours worked. Regular part-time workers (qv) are entitled to 6 hours paid leave for every 100 hours worked: Worker Protection (Regular Part-Time Employees) Act 1991 s.4.

Provision is made for an unbroken period of a certain length of leave; two working weeks in the case of full-time employees. In a particular case, it was held that dismissal was too severe a penalty for an employee taking holidays against the wishes of management: Conroy v Iggy Madden Transport Ltd (1991 EAT) ELR 29. Pay for annual leave must be given to the employee in advance of that leave. See Holiday (Employees) Act 1973. See WORKING TIME DIRECTIVE.

**annual percentage charge; APR.** The true cost of credit to consumers which must be shown in any advertisement which refers to the availability and the cost of credit: Consumer Information (Consumer Credit) Order 1987 (SI No 319 of 1987). The APR must be shown by way of example if no other means is practicable. Where the advertisement relates to the provision of goods or services, the cash price payable under the credit agreement and the number and amount of instalments must also be indicated. Similar provisions relating to APR apply to any notice or leaflet displayed at a place where a cash loan can be obtained or a credit purchase made. The order does not apply to loans involving free credit. The exclusion of its applicability to banks licensed under the Central Bank Act 1971 has been repealed: Consumer Information Act 1978 s.23; Restrictive Practices (Amdt) Act 1987 s.3. The cost of house and mortgage protection insurance is not to be included in calculating the APR for the purpose of advertising the service provided by building societies: Director of Consumer Affairs v Irish Permanent Building Society (1990 HC) ILRM 743.

**annual return.** See REGISTRAR OF COMPANIES.

**annual value.** The estimate of the net annual value of every tenement or rateable hereditament: Valuation (Ireland) Act 1852. See VALUATION.

**annuity.** An annual payment of a certain sum of money; it may be perpetual or be for the life of the annuitant or be statutory. An annuity given by a will is a *pecuniary* legacy (qv) payable by instalments. If an annuity is charged on land, it amounts to a rent-charge (qv): Revenue Commissioners v Malone (1951) IR 269. There are *statutory annuities* which are charged on land in repayment of sums advanced to tenant farmers under the Land Purchase Acts eg Land Law Acts 1923 s.9; 1931 ss.4 and 7; 1953 s.4. Such annuities are burdens (qv) which affect registered land whether they are registered or not: Registration of Title Act 1964 s.72.

**annuity mortgage.** A mortgage (qv) wherein the principal sum advanced by the mortgagee (lender) is intended to be repaid by the mortgagor (borrower) in regular, usually monthly, instalments which comprise both principal and interest on the principal outstanding. Contrast with ENDOWMENT MORTGAGE.

**annulment.** (1) The declaration that judicial proceedings or their outcome are no longer of legal effect eg the annulment of adjudication of a person as a bankrupt: RSC O.76 rr.45 107.

(2) The annulment of an act of the EC

Council or Commission on appeal to the European Court of Justice (qv) on the grounds of lack of jurisdiction, or violation of an essential procedural matter, or infringment of the Treaty of Rome, or misuse of powers: Treaty of Rome 1957, arts.173-174.

**annulment of bankruptcy.** See BANK-RUPTCY, ANNULMENT OF.

**annulment of marriage.** See MARRIAGE, NULLITY OF; CHURCH ANNULMENT.

**annulment order.** See COMPULSORY PUR-CHASE ORDER.

**anonymous and pseudonymous works.** Where a literary, dramatic or musical work, or an artistic work other than a photograph, is first published anonymously or pseudonymously, copy-right in such works subsists for 50 years from the end of the year in which the work was first published: Copyright Act 1963 s.15. However, if during that period it is possible for a person without previous knowledge of the facts to ascertain the identity of the author by reasonable enquiry, the copyright will subsist until 50 years from the end of the year in which the author died (ibid s.15(2)). See COPYRIGHT.

**answer.** The reply to interrogatories (qv).

**ante litem motam.** [Before litigation was in contemplation]. See DECLARATION BY DECEASED.

**antecedent negotiations.** In relation to a hire-purchase agreement, means any negotiations or arrangements with the hirer whereby he was induced to make the agreement or which otherwise pro-moted the transaction to which the agreement relates: SGSS Act 1980 s.35. Where goods are let under a hire-purchase agreement to a hirer *dealing as consumer* (qv), the person by whom antecedent negotiations were conducted will be deemed to be a party to the agreement and that person and the owner, shall, *jointly and severally*, be answerable to the hirer for breach of the agreement and for any misrepresentations made by that person with respect to the goods in the course of the antecedent negotiations (ibid s.32). This provision extends liability to those persons such as dealers, salesmen or shopkeepers who carry out antecedent negotiations.

**ante-date.** The date which a document bears which is a date before the date on which it was drawn. A bill of exchange (qv) is not invalid by reason only that it is ante-dated: Bills of Exchange Act 1882 s.13(2). See POST-DATE.

**antenatus.** A child born before the marriage of his parents.

**ante-nuptial.** Before marriage.

**anticipatory breach.** The repudiation of a contract before the time for perform-ance is due. The other party is not bound to wait until the actual time for performance has arrived, but may im-mediately treat the contract as discharged and sue for damages: Hochster v De La Tour (1853) 2 E & B 678; Leeson v North British Oil & Candle Co (1874) 8 IRCL 309.

**anti-discrimination.** See DISCRIMINA-TION.

**anton piller order.** A form of mandatory injunction (qv), normally granted *ex parte* without notice to the defendant, which requires the defendant to permit the plaintiff or his agents to enter his premises, to inspect documents or other articles and remove any that belong to the plaintiff. Its object is to prevent the defendant from removing or destroying pirated or stolen material before the action comes to trial: Anton Piller K G v Manufacturing Process Ltd (1976) Ch 55; Rank Film Distributers Ltd v Video Information Centre (1982) AC 380; Bimeda Chemical Co v Brennan & Ruddy (1989 HC). This form of injunc-tion has been granted by our courts but has not yet been considered by the Supreme Court.

A form of statutory Anton Piller order is available on application by the owner of the copyright (eg of a video-recording) to the District Court which can authorise a garda to seize without warrant infring-ing copies of the work: Copyright (Amendment) Act 1987 s.2.

**apartment.** See FLAT.

**apices juris non sunt jura.** [Legal principles must not be carried to their most extreme consequences, regardless of equity and good sense]. See EQUITY.

**apology.** In a defamation (qv) action, an offer of apology from the defendant for having defamed the plaintiff was no defence at common law. However, an offer of apology is now admissible in mitigation of damages: Defamation Act 1961 s.17. In cases of *unintentional* defamation, an offer of amends may be made, which if rejected, is a good defence to defamation proceedings (ibid s.21).

In a summary trial in the district court, a suggestion to an an accused that the judge might apply the Probation of Offenders Act 1907 if the accused apologised for his actions, did not interfere with the accused's right to fair procedures: Kelly v O'Sullivan (1991 HC) 9 ILT Dig 127. See MITIGATION OF DAMAGES; OFFER OF AMENDS; PROBATION OF OFFENDERS.

**apparent authority.** See PRINCIPAL.

**appeal.** The transference of a case from an inferior to a higher tribunal in the hope of reversing or modifying the decision of the former: Edlesten v LCC (1918) 1 KB 81. Where an appeal is provided for, generally only one appeal is allowable.

The Supreme Court has appelate jurisdiction from decisions of the High Court, unless otherwise prescribed by law: 1937 Constitution art.34(4)(3); Minister for Justice v Wang Zhu Jie (1991 SC) ILRM 823. An appeal lies to the High Court from an order of the Circuit Court in a civil matter by way of a re-hearing (qv) and the decision is generally not appealable: Courts of Justice Act 1936 ss.38–39.

Up to 1993, the State had no right of appeal against the alleged insufficiency of a punishment in a criminal matter. However, an appeal lay to the Supreme Court against the acquittal by direction of a trial judge in the Central Criminal Court: The People (DPP) v O'Shea (1982) IR 384. Now, a review of an unduly lenient sentence has been provided for: Criminal Justice Act 1993 s.2.

Matters occurring to a plaintiff after the making of a High Court order cannot provide grounds for an appeal to the Supreme Court: Dalton v Minister for Finance (1989 SC) ILRM 519. See RSC O.87; RCC O.15 r.7; O.43; O.44. For recommendations on the review of criminal cases where persons have exhausted normal appeals procedures, see Report of Committee ("Martin Committee") to Enquire into certain Aspects of Criminal Procedure (1990). See COURT; FRESH EVIDENCE; MISCARRIAGE; REVIEW OF SENTENCE; STAY; TIME, COURT RULES.

**appearance, entry of.** The formal step taken by a defendant to a court action, after being served with a summons, which in the High Court, must be made within eight days of such service, exclusive of the day of service, unless the court orders otherwise; except that a defendant in proceedings commenced by *special* summons may enter an appearance at any time: RSC O.12. The time limit for entering an appearance in the Circuit Court is ten days: RCC O.12 r.2. Notice of *intention to defend* a civil process in the District Court is required: DCR r.153; DCR (1963) r.5.

Failure of an employer to enter an appearance to a claim of unfair dismissal to the Employment Appeals Tribunal (qv) does not prevent the Circuit Court from hearing an appeal from the employer against the decision of the Tribunal: Mulvey v Kennedy & Fox (1989) 7ILT & SJ 28.

**appellant.** A person who appeals. See APPEAL.

**appellate jurisdiction.** See JURISDICTION.

**appendant.** Annexed to a hereditament. See POWER OF APPOINTMENT.

**application of assets.** See ADMINISTRATION OF ESTATES.

**apply.** When a court follows a previous decision in a current case, it is said to *apply* the previous decision. See RATIO DICIDENDI; DISTINGUISHING A CASE.

**appointment, power of.** See POWER OF APPOINTMENT.

**apportionment.** Division into parts which are proportionate to the interests and rights of the parties. See Howe v Lord Dartmouth (1802) 7 Ves 137. See AVERAGE CLAUSE.

**appraisement.** The valuation of goods or property; in particular the valuation of goods seized in execution, or by distraint, or by order of the court. A person who is authorised to conduct auctions may act as an *appraiser* within the meaning of the Appraisers Act 1806 without being licensed under that Act: Finance Act 1950 s.8. See AUCTIONEER.

**appraiser.** A valuer; a person who makes an appraisement. See AUCTIONEER.

**apprentice.** A person who binds himself for a definite time to serve and learn from an employer who undertakes to teach his trade or calling. An apprentice is also a person employed by way of apprenticeship in a *designated industrial* *activity*: Industrial Training Act 1967 s.2(1). "In order to establish the relation of apprentice and master there must be a binding agreement on the part of the apprentice to serve for a definite period and, on the part of the master, a reciprocal agreement to teach the apprentice his trade or calling: Sister Dolores v Minister for Social Welfare (1960) 2 IR 77 at p.92.

A *minor's* contract of apprenticeship is binding on him if it is substantially to his advantage. *Statutory apprenticeship* means an apprenticeship in a designated industrial activity within the meaning of the Industrial Training Act 1967. The Unfair Dismissals Act 1977 does not apply to a dismissal of a statutory apprentice if it takes place within 6 months of commencement of the apprenticeship or within one month of its completion (s.4 and Unfair Dismissals (Amdt) Act 1993 s.14). There is no longer a preference given to the payment of apprentice fees from the property of a bankrupt: Bankruptcy Act 1988 s.81. An Foras Aiseanna Saothair (FAS) may make rules relating to the employment, education and training of statutory apprentices: Labour Services Act 1987; Industrial Training Act 1967 ss.27-36. FAS has made rules to underpin a new standards based system of apprenticeship being introduced in 1993/1994. (SI No 236 of 1993)

The power of the District Court to order an apprentice to perform his duties has been abolished: Age of Majority Act 1985 s.8(c). An apprentice is regarded as an employee for all provisions of the Safety, Health and Welfare at Work Act 1990 (ibid s.2(1)). An apprentice who was dismissed for altering the date on a medical certificate, which he later admitted, was ordered to be re-engaged: Parsons v Liffey Marine Ltd (1992 EAT) ELR 136. See Doyle v White City Stadium (1935) KB 110; Dempsey v Grant Shopfitting Ltd (1990) ELR 43; Redmond v EG Tew 1971 Ltd (1992 EAT) ELR 7. See WILFUL NEGLECT.

**appreticii ad legem.** [Apprentices to the law].

**approbate.** To approve as valid; to sanction authoritatively. See AMN v JPC (1988) ILRM 170; JM and GM v An Bord Uchtala (1988) ILRM 203.

Where there is no true consent to a marriage, there can be no question of approbation: DB v O'R (1991 SC) ILRM 160.

**approbate and reprobate.** Term used to describe that a person is not allowed to take a benefit under an instrument and to disclaim the liabilities imposed by the same instrument. See Codrington v Codrington (1875) 45 LJ Ch 660. See ELECTION.

**appropriation.** Making a thing the property of a person. The setting apart of goods or moneys out of a larger quantity as the property of a particular person eg appropriating goods to a contract.

(1) Appropriation by a personal representative is the application of the property of the deceased in its actual condition towards satisfaction of any share in the estate: Succession Act 1965 s.55; also H v O [1978] IR 194. Where the estate includes the family dwelling, the surviving spouse may require the personal representative to appropriate the dwelling and household chattels (ibid s.56; also Hamilton v Armstrong [1984] ILRM 306; H v H [1978] IR 194).

(2) Appropriation of payments made in respect of hire-purchase agreements is provided for by the Hire-Purchase Act 1946 s.10 as amended by the SGSS Act 1980 s.18.

(3) Where, in pursuance of a contract for the sale of goods, the seller delivers the goods to the buyer or to a carrier or other bailee (whether named by the buyer or not) for the purpose of transmission to the buyer, and does not reserve the right of disposal, he is deemed to have unconditionally appropriated the goods to the contract: Sale of Goods Act 1893 s.18 r.5(2).

(4) For appropriation by the Official Assignee (qv) of a bankrupt's income, see Bankruptcy Act 1988 s.65. See DISPOSAL OF GOODS; GOODS, PROPERTY IN.

**Appropriation Act.** This is an Act of the Oireachtas which is passed annually to enable the Government to pay out of the Central Fund the amounts needed to defray the charges for the public service during the year in which the Act is passed into law. The Oireachtas in voting money to a body by means of the Appropriation Act does not empower

29

the body to carry out works which are not authorised by its statutory constitution: Howard & Ors v Commissioners of Public Works (1993 HC) — Irish Times 13/2/1993.

**approval, sale on.** When goods are delivered to a buyer *on approval,* or *sale and return,* the property therein passes to the buyer when he signifies his approval or acceptance to the seller, or does any other act adopting the transaction. If he does not signify his approval or acceptance but retains the goods without giving notice of rejection, the property therein passes to him on the expiration of the time fixed for the return of the goods, or, if no time has been fixed, on the expiration of a reasonable time. What is a reasonable time is a question of fact. See Sale of Goods Act 1893 s.18 r.4.

**appurtenant.** Belonging to; necessary to the enjoyment of a thing; annexed to a hereditament eg a right of way. See WAY, RIGHT OF.

**APR.** [Annual Percentage Charge (qv)].

**aqua cedit solo.** [Water passes with the soil]. Ownership of water generally goes with the ownership of the soil beneath the water. See Tennant v Clancy (1988) ILRM 214. See RIPARIAN.

**aquaculture.** The culture of any species of fish, aquatic invertebrate animal of whatever habitat or aquatic form of any food which is suitable for the nutrition of fish: Fisheries Act 1980 s.54(19). The designation by the Minister of an area for which licences to engage in aquaculture may be granted, may be set aside by the High Court: Courtney v Minister for the Marine (1989 HC) ILRM 605.

**arbitration.** The determination of disputes by the decision of one or more persons called *arbitrators.* Differences between arbitrators are decided by an *umpire.* An agreement to refer a dispute to arbitration is called an *arbitration agreement* (qv). Most contracts of insurance, partnership agreements, travel and building contracts, include an *arbitration clause* requiring that disputes be determined by an arbitrator. The decision of an arbitrator is called an *award.*

If legal proceedings are instituted in contravention of an arbitration agreement or clause, they may be *stayed* by either party, but only after an appearance has been entered and before delivering pleadings or taking any other *steps in the proceedings*: Arbitration Act 1980 s.5. Any court before which an action has been commenced has the power to stay proceedings: Mitchell v Budget Travel Ltd (1990 SC) ILRM 739.

A stay will not be placed on proceedings by a consumer where the damages recoverable in arbitration are limited under an arbitration clause unless (a) the consumer's attention was specifically drawn to the arbitration term prior to contract and (b) the arbitration term is fair and reasonable: McCarthy v Joe Walsh Tours Ltd (1991 HC) ILRM 813, also reported in (1991) 9ILT & SJ 92.

An arbitrator has power to proceed despite the absence of a party where that party has been refused an adjournment: Grangeford Structures Ltd v SH Ltd (1990 SC) ILRM 277. See also Williams v Artane Service Station Ltd (1991 HC) ITLR (14 Oct). An award of an arbitrator carries interest in the same manner as a judgment (qv) unless the award expressly provides otherwise: Arbitration Act 1954 s.34. It has been held in England that this provision does not apply to an arbitration under the Acquisition of Land (Assessment of Compensation) Act 1919: All Soul's College v Middlesex County Council 54 TLR 677.

The High Court has jurisdiction to set aside an arbitration award if there is an error in law on its face: Church General Insurance Co v Connolly (1981) HC. However, an arbitrator's decision on a point of law referred to him will not be set aside or remitted to him by a court by reason of the fact that it might be established to be erroneous: McStay v Assicurazioni Generali SPA & Moore (1991 SC) ILRM 237. See also Stanbridge v Healy (1985) ILRM 290; Hogan v Saint Kevins Co (1986) IR 80; Childers Heights Housing v Molderings (1987) ILRM 47. See Quinn in 9ILT & SJ (1991) 218. See RSC O.56. [Text: Stewart; Bernstein UK; Russell UK]. See STEP IN PROCEEDINGS; CONTRACT OF EMPLOYMENT.

**arbitration agreement.** A written agreement to refer present or future differences to arbitration whether an arbitrator is named therein or not: Arbitration Act

1954 s.2(1); an agreement in writing (including an agreement contained in an exchange of letters or telegrams) to submit to arbitration present or future differences capable of settlement by arbitration: Arbitration Act 1980 s.2. The Court has a discretion to order that an arbitration agreement ceases to have effect where an allegation of fraud is made: Administralia Asigurarilor de Stat v Insurance Corp of Ireland (1990) 8 ILT Dig 190 and Arbitration Act 1954 s.39. See also Sweeney v Mulcahy (1993 HC) ILRM 289.

**archaeological area.** An area which the Commissioners of Public Works in Ireland consider to be of archaeological importance but does not include the area of a registered *historic monument* (qv): National Monuments (Amendment) Act 1987 s.1(1). The degree of protection afforded by legislation to an archaeological area is less than that afforded to an historic monument. See also NATIONAL MONUMENT; WRECK.

**architect's certificate.** In a particular case, the court refused to stay a judgment sought by a building contractor for monies due on an architect's interim certificate, notwithstanding a counter-claim for damages for defective work: Rohan Construction Ltd v Antigen Ltd (1989 HC) ILRM 783. See FINAL CERTIFICATE; RIAI CONTRACT.

**architecture.** See ARTISTIC WORK; SAFETY AT WORK.

**archives.** See NATIONAL ARCHIVES.

**arguendo.** [In the course of argument].

**argumentative affidavit.** An affidavit (qv) which unnecessarily sets forth argumentative matter ie arguments as to the bearing of facts; the costs of such an affidavit will not be allowed: RSC 0.40 r.4.

**argumentum ab inconvenienti plurimum valet in lege.** [An argument based on inconvenience is of great weight in the law].

**armchair principle.** The principle by which the court (in order to determine what was meant by the words used by a testator in his will) could *sit in the testator's armchair* and take account of all the circumstances surrounding the testator when he made his will: Boyes v Cook (1880) 14 Ch D 53; Fitzgerald v Ryan (1899) 2 IR 637; In re Hall (1944)

IR 54. Extrinsic evidence is admissible to show the intention of a testator and to assist in the construction of, or to explain any contradiction in, a will: Succession Act 1965 s.90. See EVIDENCE, EXTRINSIC.

**armed rebellion.** See NATIONAL EMERGENCY.

**arms length, at.** Removed from personal influence. *Articles of association* of a company usually require that a director is not to vote in respect of any contract in which he is interested, directly or indirectly. By statute, a director is required to disclose the nature of his interest in any contract between himself and the company; however a general notice by the director will suffice stating that he is a member of a specified company or firm and that he is to be regarded as interested in any contract entered into by the company thereafter with that company or firm: Companies Act 1963 s.194, as amended by the Companies Act 1990 s.47. See also Finance Act 1991 s.31(1); Roads Act 1993 ss.37 and 40. See CONFLICT OF INTEREST; COUNCILLOR, DISCLOSURE OF INTEREST; UNDUE INFLUENCE.

**army personnel, dismissal of.** See GARDA, DISMISSAL OF.

**arraignment.** The beginning of a criminal trial whereby the prisoner is called to the bar by naming him, the *indictment* (qv) is read to him and he is asked whether he is guilty or not.

**arrangement.** See ARRANGING DEBTOR; SCHEME OF ARRANGEMENT.

**arrangement and reconstruction.** See RECONSTRUCTION OF COMPANY.

**arranging debtor.** A debtor who has been granted an *order for protection* by the High Court: Bankruptcy Act 1988 ss.3 and 87- 109. The debtor, seeking to affect an *arrangement* with his creditors under the control of the court, presents a petition setting out the reason for his inability to pay his debts and requests that his person and property be protected (ibid s.87). An order for protection enables the debtor to continue to trade but he must not dispose of his property save in the ordinary course of trade (ibid s.88).

The arranging debtor is required to file a *statement of affairs* containing his proposal for the future payment or *compromise* of his debts (ibid s.91), which, if approved by three-fifths in number and value of the creditors voting at a private sitting of the court, and if approved by the court, will be binding on all persons who were creditors at the date of the petition and who had notice of the sitting (ibid s.92). A creditor whose debt is less than £100 is not entitled to vote (ibid s.92(2)).

The arranging debtor's proposal may provide for vesting of his property in the Official Assignee (qv) either as security of the offer or for the purpose of having the property realised and distributed by the Official Assignee (ibid s.93). There is also provision for granting a *certificate* to an arranging debtor which will operate as a discharge to him from the claims of creditors who received notice of the arrangement (ibid s.98). The court may, if it thinks fit, *adjudicate* an arranging debtor as bankrupt (ibid ss.105-106).

The court may refuse to grant protection to a debtor who is a member of a partnership, unless all the partners join in a petition (ibid s.87(3) and Re Love (1889) 23 LR Ir 365). For procedure re an order for protection, see SI No 79 of 1989 Part XXIII. See RECEIVER OF BANKRUPT'S PROPERTY.

**arrears.** Money not paid at the due date.

**arrest.** To deprive a person of his liberty by some lawful authority in order to compel his appearance to answer a criminal charge or as a method of execution. No person may be arrested (with or without a warrant) save for the purpose of bringing that person before a court at the earliest reasonable opportunity; arrest is simply a process of ensuring the attendance at court of the person so arrested: Walsh J in The People v Shaw (1982) IR 1.

An arresting garda is entitled to use such force as is necessary to ensure that the arrest is maintained: Dowman v Ireland (1986) ILRM 111. It is lawful for a person to be arrested immediately at the cessation of an arrest under s.30 of the Offences Against the State Act 1939: Finucane v McMahon (1989) 7ILT Dig 322. See ARREST WITHOUT WARRANT; CIVIL ARREST; ESCAPE.

**arrest, resisting.** It is an offence to resist a lawful arrest: Offences Against the

Person Act 1861 s.38. An unlawful arrest can be resisted but only with force which is reasonable; the use of lethal force will normally constitute manslaughter (qv): The People v White (1947) IR 247.

**arrest of judgment.** An accused at any time after conviction and before sentence may move the court to *arrest judgment* (eg for want of sufficient certainty in the indictment which has not been amended), which, if granted, has the effect of an acquittal (qv) but it does not bar a fresh indictment (qv).

**arrest without warrant.** There are wide powers given to various persons by statute to arrest another without a warrant, eg an officer of excise is entitled to arrest a person found in a place where illegal distillation is in progress: Illicit Distillation (Ireland) Act 1831 s.19; a pawnbroker is entitled to arrest a person offering to him stolen or lost property: Pawnbrokers Act 1964 s.35; an aircraft commander can arrest a person where he has reason to believe that the person has committed a serious offence aboard an aircraft: Air Navigation and Transport Act 1973 s.7; any person is entitled to arrest another on reasonable suspicion of a contravention of official secrets: Official Secrets Act 1963 s.15; a garda has wide powers of arrest eg when he is of the opinion that the person has committed the offence of dangerous driving and has caused death or serious bodily harm: Road Traffic Act 1961 s.53(6); also where he has reasonable grounds for believing that a person is committing or has committed certain specified offences: Transport Act 1987 s.11. A garda in making an arrest does not have to use technical or precise language; provided the arrested person knows in substance why he is being arrested, the arrest is valid: DPP (Cloughley) v Mooney (1993 HC) ILRM 214. See also Criminal Damage Act 1991 s.12; Criminal Justice (Sexual Offences) Act 1993 s.13. For extensive list see Text. [Text: Ryan & Magee, Appendix G]. See INCAPABLE; UNLAWFUL ARREST.

**arson.** The offence of *damaging property by fire* which must be charged as *arson*; the common law offence of arson has been abolished: Criminal Damage Act 1991 ss.2(4) and 14(1). Arson is now the offence of damaging by fire, without lawful excuse, any property belonging to another intending to damage it or being *reckless* as to whether it would be damaged (ibid s.2(1)).

It also includes damage by fire to property, whether belonging to the accused or another, where there is an intention by the damage to endanger the life of another or being *reckless* as to whether the life of another would be thereby endangered (ibid s.2(2)). It also includes damage by fire of any property with intent to defraud (ibid s.2(3)). A person is *reckless* if he has foreseen the particular kind of damage that in fact was done might be done and yet has gone on to take the risk of it (ibid s.2(6)). See Attorney General v Kyle (1933) IR 15. See CRIMINAL DAMAGE TO PROPERTY.

**articles.** Clauses in a document eg articles in the 1937 Constitution of Ireland.

**articles of association.** See ASSOCIATION, ARTICLES OF.

**artificial insemination.** Introduction of semen into the uterus by other than natural means; a child is legitimate when born to a married couple as a result of artificial insemination whereby the husband's semen is used. The position is unclear if the husband's semen is used in his widow after his death eg from a sperm bank. A child is illegitimate (now — *a child whose parents are not married to each other*: Status of Children Act 1987) when born as a result of insemination by a third party donor or born to a surrogate mother. See Law Reform Commission: Report on Illegitimacy 1982 (LRC 4 of 1982).

As regards the control and practice of artificial insemination of cattle, sheep, goats, swine and horses, see Live Stock (Artificial Insemination) Act 1947. [Text: Shatter]. See ADOPTION; EMBRYO IMPLANTATION; SURROGATE MOTHER.

**artificial person.** A body which is invested by law with a personality having rights and duties eg a corporation (qv) or company (qv).

**artist, tax exemption of.** The exemption which may be claimed by a writer, dramatist, musical composer, painter, or sculptor, from income tax which would otherwise be payable on profits, arising from the publication, production or sale of original and creative works falling under the following headings: (a) a book or other writing; (b) a play; (c) a musical composition; (d) a painting or other like picture; or (e) a sculpture: Finance Act 1969 s.2. The exemption may be claimed only by a individual resident in the State, who is not resident in any other country as well, and only in respect of profits from works which have cultural or artistic merit.

It has been held that to qualify for the artist's tax exemption, a work must (a) be an original and creative work and (b) be determined by the Revenue Commissioners to be a work which actually has, in their opinion, cultural or artistic merit, or alternatively, to be a work generally recognised as having cultural or artistic merit: Healy v Inspector of Taxes (1986) HC.

There is now a right of appeal to the Appeal Commissioners: 1969 Act s.2 as amended by the Finance Act 1989 s.5. There is also an exemption from capital gains tax in respect of the disposal of certain items which have been loaned for public display for at least 6 years before their disposal; items qualifying are: a work of art, picture, print, book, manuscript, sculpture, or jewellery, with a market value of not less than £25,000 at the date of loan: Finance Act 1991 s.43.

**artistic work.** For the purposes of copyright protection, *artistic work* means a work of any of the following descriptions (a) paintings, drawings, sculptures, engravings and photographs; (b) works of architecture, being either buildings or models for buildings and (c) works of artistic craftsmanship: Copyright Act 1963 s.9(1). *Engraving* includes any etching, lithograph, woodcut, print or similar work not being a photograph; *sculpture* includes any cast or model made for the purpose of sculpture (ibid s.2(1)). See COPYRIGHT.

**arts.** Painting, sculpture, architecture, music, the drama, cinema, literature, design in industry and the fine arts and applied arts generally: Arts Acts 1951 and 1973. The Arts Council is a body corporate with perpetual succession, established pursuant to these Acts, to stimulate and promote public interest in the arts; to promote the knowledge, appreciation and practice of the arts; to assist in improving the standard of the arts; and to advise the government on artistic matters.

Local authorities have power to provide, or assist in the provision of a concert hall, theatre or opera house: Local Government Act 1960 s.1. They can also assist the promotion of public interest in the arts, with money or in kind or by the provision of services or facilities: Arts Act 1973 s.12.

**asbestos.** A number of regulations, which give effect to Council Directive 87/217/ EEC, govern the prevention and reduction of environmental pollution by asbestos eg SI No 28 of 1990 — which prescribes emission limit values for the use of asbestos and determines sampling and analysis methods; SI No 30 of 1990 — which provides for the transport and deposit of asbestos waste; SI No 31 of 1990 — which provides for the general obligation to prevent the entry of asbestos to waters, for measures to be applied to certain industrial plant using asbestos, and for the monitoring of discharges. See also Environmental Protection Agency Act 1992, second schedule. See TOXIC WASTE.

**ascertained goods.** See UNASCERTAINED GOODS.

**asportation.** The *carrying away* with intention to steal, which is an essential element in the offence of larceny (qv).

**assault.** The common law misdemeanour consisting of an unlawful attempt to do with violence a corporal wrong to another person; a *battery* is such a wrong actually done in an angry, revengeful, rude or insolent manner. For punishment, see Offences Against the Person Act 1861 ss.42 and 47; Criminal Justice Act 1951 s.11, as proposed to be amended by the draft Criminal Justice (Public Order) Bill 1993 s.11. For tort of assault, see TRESPASS TO THE PERSON.

A variety of assaults have been made statutory offences eg shooting or attempting to shoot, or wounding with intent to do grievous bodily harm; inflicting bodily injury with or without a weapon; attempting to choke a person in order to commit any indictable offence (ibid 1861 Act ss.18-21; Criminal Law (Jurisdiction) Act 1976 schedule). These offences are sometimes referred to as *aggravated assault* because they are more serious

than a common assault, but they are not defined as "aggravated" in the legislation.

Under the 1993 Bill, it is proposed that it will be an offence to assault a person with intent to cause bodily harm or to commit an indictable offence (ibid 1993 Bill s.19). See also AGGRAVATED ASSAULT; BODILY HARM, GRIEVOUS; COMMON ASSAULT; PEACE OFFICER; ROBBERY; SEXUAL ASSAULT.

**assault, indecent.** Any indecent touching of a female by a male or by another female, without her consent, is an offence and is punishable: Criminal Law (Rape) Act 1981 s.10. An indecent assault on a male person either by another male or by a female is an offence: ibid 1981 Act s.10 and Offences Against the Person Act 1861 s.62. On a count for indecent assault, a person may be convicted of common assault: R v Bostock (1893) 17 Cox's CC 700. The offence of indecent assault upon a male or female person is now known as *sexual assault* and is a felony: Criminal Law (Rape) (Amendment) Act 1990 s.2. See Doolan v DPP (1993 HC) ILRM 387. See SEXUAL ASSAULT.

**assault in tort.** See TRESPASS TO THE PERSON.

**assault with intent to rob.** See ROBBERY.

**assay.** The testing of the quality of an article. See HALLMARKING.

**assay office.** The office controlled by the Company of Goldsmiths of Dublin. See GOLDSMITHS OF DUBLIN; HALLMARKING.

**Assembly, European.** See EUROPEAN PARLIAMENT.

**assembly, freedom of.** The State guarantees, subject to public order and morality, liberty for the exercise of the right of citizens to assemble peaceably and without arms: 1937 Constitution, art.40(6)(1)(ii). Provision may be made by law, however, to prevent or control meetings calculated to cause a breach of the peace or to be a danger or nuisance to the general public and to prevent or control meetings in the vicinity of either Houses of the Oireachtas (qv). It is an offence to hold a meeting or procession in any public place within one-half mile of the Oireachtas in certain specified circumstances: Offences Against the State Act 1939 s.28. See TRESPASS TO PROPERTY; NUISANCE, PUBLIC.

**assembly, riotous.** See RIOTOUS ASSEMBLY.

**assembly, unlawful.** See UNLAWFUL AS-

SEMBLY.

**assent.** Agreement. The instrument or act whereby a personal representative effectuates a testamentary disposition by transferring the subject matter of the disposition to the person entitled to it. An assent to unregistered land must be in writing and to registered land must comply with s.61 of the Registration of Title Act 1964. See Succession Act 1965 ss.53-54.

**assessment.** The act of determining, apportioning or valuing eg assessment of damages, assessment of tax.

**assessor.** (1) A person who investigates and assesses the amount of loss on behalf of an insurer.

(2) A person who assists the court in relation to scientific or technical matters. Trials with assessors take place in such manner and upon such terms as the court directs: RSC O.36 r.41. In any admiralty (qv) action, the judge may appoint assessors either at the instance of any party or where he deems it requisite for the due administration of justice: RSC O.64 r.39. A court holding a formal investigation into a shipping casualty is assisted by a nautical engineering assessor: Merchant Shipping Act 1894 ss.466 and 467; Shipping Casualties and Appeals and Re-hearing Rules 1907. The court may call in the aid of an assessor to assist it in any action for infringement or revocation of a patent: Patents Act 1992 s.95; Farbwerke Hoechst AG v Intercontinental Pharmaceuticals (Eire) (1968) FSR 187. See also Martin v Irish Industrial Benefit Society (1960) Ir Jur Rep 42.

Under proposed draft legislation, there is provision for the President of the High Court to act as *judicial assessor* to the presidential returning officer in relation to ruling on the validity of a nomination as a candidate for a presidential election; the returning officer must have regard to the opinion of the assessor: Presidential Elections Bill 1993 s.23. See TRIBUNALS OF INQUIRY.

**asset valuation.** Fixed assets in a company must be valued at cost (or their valuation in the company's books) less the aggregate sum provided for or written off in respect of their depreciation: Companies Act 1963, sixth schedule, reg 5; also see Companies Amendment Act

1983 s.45. This rule does not apply inter alia to goodwill, patents, trademarks, investments whose values are shown, and assets the replacement of which is provided for in a specified manner.

A company may treat as a realised profit any difference between the sum set aside for depreciation of a fixed asset which has been revalued and the amount of the unrealised profit thereby discovered: Companies Amendment Act 1983 s.45(6).

Where development costs are shown as an asset in the accounts, they must be properly written off: Companies Amendment Act 1986 s.20; they must be regarded as realised losses for the purposes of s.45 and s.47 of the 1983 Act. See also 1986 Act s.3(1). See SURPLUS ASSETS; VALUATION REPORT.

**assets.** Property available for the payment of debts. *Real* assets are real property and *personal* assets are personal property. Property is also classified as *legal* assets and *equitable* assets. The estate of a deceased person, both legal and equitable, together with estate disposed by will in pursuance of a general power, are assets for payment of debts, liabilities and any legal right (qv). See Succession Act 1965 s.45. See SURPLUS ASSETS.

**assets, marshalling of.** See MARSHALLING.

**assign.** To transfer property; an assignee (qv).

**assignatus utitur jure auctoris.** [An assignee is clothed with the right of his principal].

**assignee.** The person to whom an assignment is made. See OFFICIAL ASSIGNEE.

**assignment of contract.** Generally liabilities under a contract cannot be assigned without the consent of the other party to the contract. Liabilities can be assigned by *novation* (qv). Some contractual rights in a contract cannot be assigned eg those involving contracts of service (qv) and some others require to meet statutory requirements eg transfer of shares in a company.

Other rights may be assigned in a number of ways: (a) by operation of law eg death passes the rights and liabilities of the deceased to his personal representatives (qv); bankruptcy passes all rights and liabilities to the Official Assignee in bankruptcy; (b) under equity, but the assignee takes *subject to equities* and (c) under the Judicature Act 1877 which carries the advantage that the assignee can sue in his own name; the assignment must be absolute, in writing with notice also in writing to the debtor and the assignee still takes *subject to equities*.

The assignment of insurance contracts is generally limited to those of life insurance, which is effected either by an endorsement on the policy itself or by a separate document, and gives to the assignee the right to sue thereon in his own name. See also Marine Insurance Act 1906 ss.15 and 50.

**assignment of lease.** The transfer of the total interest of the lessee under a lease (qv) to a new lessee. The *assignee* or new lessee takes subject to all the rights and liabilities of the former lessee. See Deasy's Act 1860 ss.9, 12,13; Landlord and Tenant (Amendment) Act 1980 s.66. See SUB-LETTING.

**assignment of trade mark.** See TRADE MARK, ASSIGNMENT OF.

**assignor.** A person who assigns or transfers property to another.

**assisa cadera.** [A non-suit].

**assize.** [A sitting or session]. Formerly, there were courts of assize. See GRAND JURY.

**associated trade mark.** A trade mark which is identical with another trade mark in the name of the same proprietor in respect of the same goods or description of goods, or so nearly resembles it as to be likely to deceive or cause confusion if used by a person other than the proprietor: Trade Marks Act 1963 s.31(2). Such trade marks may be required by the Controller (qv) of Trade Marks at any time to be entered on the register as *associated* trade marks and this operates to prevent such marks from being assigned or transferred except as a whole (ibid s.31(1)). See The Steel Nut and Joseph Hampton Ltd (1964) Supp OJ No 956 p.23.

**association, articles of.** The regulations by which a company is to be governed and managed. The articles must be printed, divided into paragraphs numbered sequentially, be stamped in the same way as a deed and be signed by each subscriber to the *memorandum of association* and attested: Companies Act 1963 ss.11–15. This Act contains a model set of articles in Table A, which apply to any company limited by shares unless excluded or modified in duly registered articles (ibid s.13). A model set of articles for companies limited by guarantee and not having a share capital is contained in Table C, which applies to such a company registered after 1982 unless excluded or modified in duly registered articles: Companies Amendment Act 1982 s.14.

Articles of companies that are listed in the Stock Exchange are required to contain provisions on matters such as transfers of securities, share certificates, dividends, directors, accounts, rights, notices, redeemable shares, capital structure, voting entitlements and proxies: s.9 ch.1 of Rules in Listing Agreement. A company may by special resolution alter or add to its articles of association: Companies Act 1963 s.15 and Companies Amendment Act 1983 s.20(3). See also Building Societies Act 1989 s.102(2). See ASSOCIATION, MEMORANDUM OF.

**association, freedom of.** The State guarantees, subject to public order and morality, liberty for the exercise of the right of citizens to form associations and unions: 1937 Constitution, art 40(6)(1)(iii). The Garda Siochana may have to accept limitations in their right to form associations and unions which other citizens would not have to accept: Aughey v Ireland (1986) ILRM 207. See Smartt in ISLR (1993) 116. See DEFENCE FORCES; TRADE UNION.

**association, memorandum of.** A document which regulates a company's external activities and which must be drawn up on the formation of a company. Any seven or more persons associated for any lawful purpose may by subscribing their names to a memorandum of association and otherwise complying with the statutory requirements as to registration, form an incorporated company, with or without *limited liability;* two or more persons are only required where the company to be formed is to be a *private* company: Companies Act 1963 s.5(1). The memorandum must be printed, stamped as a deed, signed by each subscriber, witnessed and attested (ibid s.7). It must state the company's name and the objects of the company (ibid s.6 as amended by 1983 Act, first schedule, para.2). The memorandum of a company limited by shares or by guarantee must state that the liability of its members is limited.

Where the company is *limited by guarantee,* the memorandum must state that each member undertakes to contribute to the assets of the company in the event of its being wound up (ibid 1963 Act s.6(3)). If the company has a share capital, the memorandum must state its amount and each subscriber must write opposite to his name the number of shares he takes (ibid s.6(4)). The memorandum cannot be varied by the company itself except in specified circumstances (ibid s.9).

The memorandum must be delivered to the Registrar of Companies and be accompanied by a statement specifying the situation of the company's registered office and the names of the first secretary and first directors: Companies Amendment Act 1982 s.3 as amended by 1983 Act, second schedule. See ASSOCIATION, ARTICLES OF; NAME OF COMPANY; BUSINESS NAME; ULTRA VIRES.

**association clause.** The clause in a memorandum of association of a company in which the subscribers state that they desire to be formed into a company and agree to take the number of shares set opposite their names. See ASSOCIATION, MEMORANDUM OF.

**assumpsit.** [He has undertaken].

**assurance.** (1) The documentary evidence of the transfer of land. See In re Ray (1896) 1 Ch 468. (2) Insurance (qv).

**assured.** Insured (qv).

**asylum.** A refuge; a place of refuge and relative security; originally a place of safety from pursuit and later a place for reception and treatment of the insane. See POLITICAL OFFENCE; PSYCHIATRIC CENTRE.

**asylum, claim for.** A claim by a person from a foreign country to remain in the State. An alien claiming asylum must be given an adequate opportunity to put forward representations to show why his application should be acceded to; there is an obligation to follow fair procedures in dealing with the question of the removal of the applicant from the jurisdiction: Fakih v Minister for Justice (1993 HC) ILRM 274.

Member States of the European Union

(qv) are required to regard asylum policy as a matter of common interest: Maastricht Treaty 1992 art.K.1 and Declaration. See ALIEN; COMMON POLICIES; EXTRADITION; REFUGEE.

**ats; ad sectam.** [At the suit of].

**attachiamenta bonorum.** Distress (qv) of a person's goods and chattels for debt.

**attachment.** (1) An order which directs that a person be brought before the court to answer the contempt (qv) in respect of which the order is issued eg the failure of a witness without lawful excuse to attend court having been served with a sub-poena (qv) and having been paid or offered a reasonable sum for his expenses. See RSC O.44 r.1; RCC O.36.

(2) The attachment of debts by way of garnishee (qv). Attachment by way of garnishee proceedings or receiver by way of equitable execution can apply only to *present* debts due to a judgment debtor and cannot apply to *future* earnings; consequently attachment of a sum owing from the annual wages of an employee is not possible: Shalvey v Telecom Eireann (1992 HC) reported in ILSI Gaz (March 1993).

(3) The enforcement of a direction to pay money. An *attachment of earnings order* is an order applied for by the person for whose benefit *maintenance* (qv) is to be paid; it is directed to the maintenance debtor's employer who is bound to make such periodical deductions from the debtor's earnings as specified by the order and to pay them over to the District Court clerk: Family Law (Maintenance of Spouses and Children) Act 1976 Act s.10. There is a *normal deduction rate* and a *protected earnings rate* (ibid s.11). A redundancy lump sum payment may not be so attached: Byrne v Byrne (76 Gazette of ILSI p.26). See COMMITTAL, ORDER OF; COMPENSATION ORDER.

**attachment of funds.** The Revenue Commissioners are empowered, with effect from 1st October 1988, to attach amounts owed by a third party to a tax defaulter: Finance Act 1988 s.73. Such attachment will not apply to amounts due in respect of wages and salaries.

**attempt.** The offence which arises from a proximate act towards the carrying out of an indictable (qv) offence; an act remotely leading to the commission of the offence will not be considered as an attempt to commit it. *An attempt consists of an act done by the accused with a specific intent to commit a particular crime; .. it must go beyond mere preparation and must be a direct movement towards the commission after the preparations have been made*: The People (Attorney General) v Thornton (1952) IR 91.

There cannot be a conviction for the substantive offence and a conviction for an attempt to commit the same offence: The People (Attorney General) v Dermody (1956) IR 307. An attempt is a misdemeanour (qv) at common law; it has been made a felony (qv) for some crimes eg attempted murder. See also Attorney General v Richmond (1935) Frewen 28; The People (Attorney General) v England (1947) CCA; Devereaux v Kotsonouris (1992 HC) ILRM 140. See ALTERNATIVE VERDICT.

**attest.** To witness any act or event eg the signature or execution of a document or a will. If a document is required by law to be attested, it cannot be used as evidence until an attesting witness has proved its execution. If no such witness is alive, or procurable, it must be proved that the attestation of one attesting witness is in his handwriting and that the signature of the executing party is in his handwriting. In a document at least 30 years old produced from proper custody, the signature is presumed to be genuine. See DOCUMENTS, PRESUMPTION AS TO.

**attestation clause.** The statement in a deed or will or other document that it has been duly executed in the presence of witnesses eg in a will the attestation clause is sometimes in the following form: *signed by the testator as his last will and testament in the presence of us who at his request and in his presence and in the presence of each other hereunto sign our names as witnesses.*

**attorney.** (1) A person appointed by another person to act in his place. (2) Prior to the Judicature Act 1873, there were attorneys as well as solicitors, the attorneys being those who conducted proceedings on behalf of clients in the common law courts, and solicitors, those who conducted them in the chancery courts. The 1873 Act abolished attorneys and made them all *solicitors of the supreme*

*court.* [Text: Hogan & Osborough]. See POWER OF ATTORNEY.

**Attorney General.** The adviser to the government on all matters of law and legal opinion, who is appointed by the President of Ireland on the nomination of the Taoiseach: 1937 Constitution, art.30. He also has the function of guardian of the public interest, which he exercises for the community independently of government, as *parens patriae* (qv), when he takes action to ensure that the law is enforced eg to vindicate and defend the right to life of the unborn: AG v Open Door Counselling Ltd (1988) IR 393; AG v X (1992 SC) ILRM 401. The nature of his office charges him with the duty to enforce the Constitution: AG v Tribunal of Inquiry into the Beef Industry (1993 SC) ILRM 81.

The AG is not a member of the government and must retire from office on the resignation of the Taoiseach but may continue to carry out his duties until a successor to the Taoiseach has been appointed. He may be given additional functions and duties by law eg he is responsible for enforcing charitable trusts. [Text: Casey]. See CRIMINAL INFORMATION; DIRECTOR OF PUBLIC PROSECUTIONS; PARENS PATRIAE; RELATOR.

**Attorney General's Scheme.** The scheme to provide legal representation for persons who need it but cannot afford it and which is not covered by civil or criminal aid ie (a) habeas corpus applications; (b) bail motions; (c) judicial reviews of certiorari, mandamus or prohibition; (d) applications under s.50 of the Extradition Act 1965. An application must be made to the court at the commencement of the proceedings for a recommendation to the Attorney General that the scheme be applied. See Application of Michael Woods (1970) IR 154. See ILSI Gazette (Apr 1992) 97. See LEGAL AID.

**attorney, power of.** See POWER OF ATTORNEY.

**attornment.** (1) An acknowledgement by a person in occupation of land to be the tenant of the owner thereof. A mortgage may contain an *attornment clause* whereby the mortgagor attorns himself tenant of the mortgagee so that possession of the land may be obtained by way of ejectment (qv). See Deasy's Act 1860 s.94; Ulster

Bank v Woolsey (1890) 24 ILTR 65.

(2) The acknowledgement by a third person that he holds the seller's goods on behalf of the buyer: Sale of Goods Act 1893 s.29(3). Delivery of the goods to the buyer is not deemed to take place until this acknowledgement is made. See BAILMENT.

**auction sales.** A sale by auction is complete when the auctioneer announces its completion by the fall of a hammer or in other customary manner; until such announcement any bidder may retract his bid. A sale by auction may be notified to be subject to a *reserve* or *upset price* and a right to bid may also be reserved expressly by or on behalf of the seller. Where a sale by auction is not so notified, it is not lawful for the seller to bid himself or to employ any person (a *puffer*) to bid, or for the auctioneer knowingly to take any bid from the seller or any such person; a sale contravening this rule may be treated as fraudulent by the buyer. An *upset price* includes a price specifically named as the sum from which bidding may start.

Where goods are put up for sale by auction in lots, each lot is prima facie deemed to be the subject of a separate contract of sale. In a *dutch auction* the property is put up at an excessive price and is offered at decreasing prices until someone closes. See Sale of Goods Act 1893 s.58. [Text: Mahon; Murdoch UK]. See SALE OF LAND.

**auctioneer.** A person who conducts sales by auction to the highest bidder. A person may not carry on or hold himself out or represent himself as carrying on the business of auctioneer except under and in accordance with a licence and no person may conduct an auction except with a licence or permit: Auctioneers and House Agents Act 1947 s.6. An auctioneer's licence is granted by the Revenue Commissioners on application accompanied by a *certificate of qualifications*, a certificate of maintenance by the applicant of a deposit in the High Court, and the excise duty payable (ibid s.8). A certificate of qualifications is obtained on application to a judge of the district court(ibid s.11; Auctioneers and House Agents Act 1967 s.12). An auctioneer must keep a *client account* (ibid s.5) and there are provisions governing proceed-

ings in relation to deposits and banking accounts and bankruptcy (ibid ss.7- 11).

The auctioneer is the agent of the seller, but becomes an agent of the buyer and seller for the purposes of providing a memorandum (qv) under the Sale of Goods Act 1893 and the Statute of Frauds. For the authority of an auctioneer as agent of the seller, see Law v Roberts & Co (1964) IR 292. Any agreement in a contract relating to the sale, lease, or letting of property which makes the purchaser, lessee or tenant liable to pay the fees or expense of an auctioneer or house agent is void: Auctioneers and House Agents Act 1973 s.2. See also Attorney General v Manorhamilton Co-operative Livestock Mart Ltd (1966) IR 192; Ballyowen Castle Homes v Collins (1986) HC. [Text: Mahon]. See APPRAISEMENT; BANKRUPTCY, ACT OF; COMMISSION; DEPOSIT; TAX CLEARANCE CERTIFICATE.

**auctioneering service.** Any business to which the Auctioneers and House Agents Act 1947 relates, including the business of a house agent (qv) within the meaning of that Act: Building Societies Act 1989 s.32(6)(a). A building society is, under certain circumstances, empowered to provide an *auctioneering service* and other *services relating to land* (ibid s.32(1)).

**audi alteram partem.** [Hear the other side]. One of the principles of *natural justice* (qv) that no judicial or quasi-judicial decision may be taken without giving the party affected an opportunity of stating his case and being heard in his own defence. See The State (Ingle) v O'Brien (1975) 109 ILTR 7; The State (Gleeson) v Minister for Defence (1976) IR 280; Garvey v Ireland (1981) IR 75; The State (IPU) v Employment Appeals Tribunal (1986) ILRM 36; Hourigan v Supt Kelly (1991 HC).

**audience, right of.** The right to appear and conduct proceedings in court. Barristers (qv), and solicitors (qv) have such a right in all the courts. See LOCUS STANDI.

**audit.** A detailed inspection of the accounts of a body, usually by a person who is not employed by that body. See AUDITOR, COMPANY; AUDITOR, LOCAL AUTHORITY; ENVIRONMENTAL AUDIT.

**auditor, company.** Every company must appoint an auditor or auditors at each annual general meeting; in default of appointment, the Minister may appoint. The auditor must be a member of a body of accountants recognised by the Minister and hold a valid practising certificate from such a body. The auditor may not be a body corporate or a close family relative of, or a partner of, or in the employment of, an officer of the company: Companies Act 1990 s.187.

The primary duty of the auditor is to ascertain and state the true financial position of the company by an examination of its books. The auditor must report to the members of the accounts examined by him and on every balance sheet and profit and loss account; the report must contain certain specified information: 1990 Act s.193. The auditor is under a general duty to carry out the audit with professional integrity (ibid s.193(6)) and to serve notice on the company if he forms the opinion that proper books of accounts are not being kept (ibid s.194).

It is the duty of the auditor not only to report on the annual accounts but also to state whether the directors' annual report is consistent with the contents of the audited accounts, and if he considers them inconsistent, he must give particulars of the inconsistency: Companies Amendment Act 1986 s.15.

An auditor's appointment lapses when he resigns, becomes ineligible to hold office or is removed from office or is replaced. An auditor, who is proposed to be removed, is entitled to have representations sent out before the meeting at which he is to be removed: Companies Act 1963 s.161 as amended by 1990 Act s.184.

When an auditor resigns during his term of office, he must report to the members any circumstances connected with it which should be brought to their notice (ibid 1990 Act s.185).

See Companies Act 1990 (Auditors) Regulations 1992 (SI No 259 of 1992). See also Building Societies Act 1989 ss.83-88; Pensions Act 1990 ss.2 and 56 as amended by Social Welfare Act 1993 ss.42 and 47. See In re Kingston Cotton Mills (No 2) (1896) 2 Ch 279; Hedley Byrne v Heller (1964) AC 465; JEB Fastners Ltd v Marks Bloom Co (1983) 1 All ER 583; Sisk v Flynn (1986)

ILRM 128. See Companies Act 1963 s.160 et seq as amended; Companies Act 1990 ss.182-201. See Eight Directive on Company Law — O J No L 126/20 (1984). See O'Ceidigh in ILSI Gazette (Apr 1992) 101. See ACCOUNTS; DISQUALIFICATION ORDER.

**auditor, local government.** An auditor appointed by the Minster to investigate the accounts of a local authority: Local Government Act 1946 s.68. His duties include to examine into the matter of every account which is audited by him; to disallow all payments, charges and allowances which are contrary to law or which he deems to be unfounded; to *surcharge* (qv) any such payments upon the person making, or authorising the making of, the illegal payment: Local Government (Ireland) Act 1871 s.12 as amended by the Local Government (Ireland) Act 1902 ss.19-20. The auditor in carrying out the audit, is discharging a function of a judicial nature and is bound by the principles of *natural justice* (qv) and the doctrine of *res judicata* (qv). He is empowered to take evidence on oath and to require production of documents: 1946 Act s.86. See R (Butler) v Browne (1909) 2 IR 333.

Previously, the accounts of a health board (qv) were required to be audited by a local government auditor appointed by the Minister: Health Act 1970 ss.28-29. They are now audited by the Comptroller and Auditor General (qv): Comptroller and Auditor General (Amdt) Act 1993 s.6. See FUNCTUS OFFICIO; SURCHARGE.

**authentic instrument.** A document which has been formally drawn up or registered as an authentic instrument and is enforceable in one contracting state of the EC must, in another contracting state, have an order for its enforcement issued there, on application made in accordance with specified procedures, unless enforcement is contrary to public policy in the state in which enforcement is sought: Jurisdiction of Courts and Enforcement of Judgments (European Communities) Act 1988, first schedule, art.50.

**authenticate.** To make valid and effective by proof or by appropriate formalities as required by law.

**author.** Copyright continues generally for

the lifetime of the author of original work and for a period of fifty years from the end of the year in which he died: Copyright Act 1963 ss.8(4) and 9(5). There is also tax exemption in respect of profits arising from original and creative works. See ARTIST, TAX EXEMPTION OF; COPYRIGHT; JOINT AUTHORSHIP; LITERARY WORK; MANUSCRIPT; ORIGINAL; PERFORMERS' PROTECTION; PHOTOGRAPH; PROPRIETOR OF NEW DESIGN; UNIVERSAL COPYRIGHT CONVENTION..

**authorised trade union.** See TRADE UNION, AUTHORISED.

**authority.** (1) The rights invested in a person or body by another allowing performance of an act. (2) A body exercising such rights eg a planning authority. (3) A decided case, judgment, textbook of repute or statute cited as a statement of the law. See AGENCY; ATTORNEY, POWER OF; DELEGATED LEGISLATION; STATE AUTHORITY.

**authority, apparent.** See PRINCIPAL.

**authority, customary.** See CUSTOMARY AUTHORITY.

**authorship, false attributation of.** A person who falsely attributes authorship in relation to literary, dramatic, musical or artistic works may be sued for a breach of statutory duty: Copyright Act 1963 s.54. It is not a criminal offence. See Moore v News of the World (1972) 1 QB 441.

**authorship, joint.** See JOINT AUTHORSHIP.

**automated teller machine card; ATM.** See CASH CARD.

**automatism.** In England, has been held to mean an act which is generally not punishable which is done by the muscles without any control by the mind, such as a spasm, a reflex action or a convulsion, or an act done by a person who is not conscious of what he is doing, such as an act done whilst suffering from concussion or whilst sleepwalking: Bratty v AG for Northern Ireland (1963) AC 386. See Donohue v Coyle (1953-1954) Ir Jur Rep 30. See IRRESISTIBLE IMPULSE.

**autopsy.** See POST-MORTEM.

**autre droit, in.** [In the right of another]. An executor or trustee holds property in right of the persons entitled thereto.

**autre vie.** [The life of another]. See LIFE ESTATE.

**autrefois acquit.** [Formerly acquitted]. A special *plea in bar* to a criminal prosecution that the accused has already been tried for the same offence before a court of competent jurisdiction and has been acquitted after a trial on the merits. An acquittal by direction of the judge on an insufficient indictment will not support a plea of autrefois acquit, nor will an *acquittal* arising from a conviction being quashed on certiorari (qv) proceedings: The People (Attorney General) v Marchel O'Brien (1963) IR 92; State (Tynan) v Keane (1968) IR 348. See The State (Keeney) v O'Malley (1986) ILRM 31.

However, where a conviction is quashed on certiorari where there has been a breach of the fundamental tenets of constitutional justice, the defendant may plead autrefois acquit: Sweeney v District Judge Brophy (1993 SC) ILRM 449. See DOUBLE-JEOPARDY; AUTREFOIS CONVICT; GARDA, DISCIPLINE OF.

**autrefois convict.** [Formerly convicted]. A special *plea in bar* by which the accused alleges that he has already been tried and convicted for the same offence by a court of competent jurisdiction. For reference to, see Singh v Ruane (1990 HC) ILRM 62. See AUTREFOIS ACQUIT.

**aver.** To allege or affirm, in pleadings (qv).

**average.** Apportionment of loss. In carriage of goods by sea, average can be *general* or *particular*. *General* average is the general loss which is caused by an act voluntarily incurred eg where goods are thrown overboard in a storm to save the ship and the rest of the cargo; the loss is borne rateably by all those interested: Marine Insurance Act 1906 s.66. *Particular* average arises where the damage is not caused for the general benefit eg damage to goods by ingress of sea water; in which case the loss remains where it falls. See AVERAGE CLAUSE.

**average clause.** A term in a contract of insurance under which there is an apportionment of the loss between the insured and the insurer having regard to the extent to which the risk has been under-insured, eg in property insurance where the property is of greater value than the sum insured, the insured is in effect his own insurer of the difference and must bear a rateable share of any loss.

**averia.** Cattle.

**averment.** An allegation or affirmation in pleadings (qv). See INVESTIGATION OF COMPANY.

**aviation.** See AIR LAW.

**aviation, unlawful acts against.** The Convention for the Suppression of Unlawful Acts against the Safety of Civil Aviation, done at Montreal on 23rd September 1971, is given effect in the State by the Air Navigation and Transport Act 1975. See AIRCRAFT, UNLAWFUL SEIZURE OF.

**avoid.** To make void. A person is said to avoid a contract when he repudiates it and sets up, as a defence in legal proceedings taken to enforce it, some defect which prevents it being enforceable.

**avoidance.** Setting aside; making null and void. See TAX AVOIDANCE.

**avow.** To admit or confess.

**avulsion.** Land torn off by an inundation or current of water from property to which it originally was joined, and gained by the land of another; also where a river or stream, flowing between two properties, changes course and thereby cuts off part of one property and joins it to the other property. Despite the separation, the property of the part separated continues in the ownership of the original owner. See ALLUVION.

**award.** The finding or decision of an arbitrator. Unless a contrary intention is expressed therein, every arbitration agreement (qv) is deemed to contain a provision that the award will be final and binding: Arbitration Act 1954 s.27. Also unless an award otherwise directs, it carries interest as from the date of the award and at the same rate as a judgment debt (ibid s.34). The High Court has jurisdiction to set aside an arbitration award if there is an error in law on its face: Church & General Insurance Co v Connolly (1981) HC. See also McStay v Assicurazioni General Spa (1991 SC) ILRM 237. See ARBITRATION; FUNCTUS OFFICIO; INTEREST ON JUDGMENTS.

# B

**baby, wrong.** Damages of £35,000 were awarded to a mother who was given the wrong baby while in hospital: Broomfield v Midland Health Board (1990 HC) — Irish Times 20/11/1990.

**back injury.** See MANUAL HANDLING OF LOADS.

**backing of warrants.** See RENDITION.

**back-up data.** Data kept only for the purpose of replacing other data in the event of their being lost, destroyed or damaged: Data Protection Act 1988 s.1(1). Back-up data, which is necessarily inaccurate between updatings is exempted from the obligation to be accurate and up-to-date (ibid s.2(4)). See DATA PROTECTION.

**bad.** Wrong in law; unsound; ineffectual; inoperative; void.

**bad debt.** A debt which seemingly cannot be recovered by a creditor. A trading debt is allowed to be written off as bad in the period in which it is irrecoverable. Debts previously written off as bad must, to the extent recovered in a subsequent period of account, be credited as a trading receipt.

As regard bad debts in respect of rental income, see Income Tax Act 1967 s.90.

**bad reputation.** See CHARACTER, EVIDENCE OF.

**bail.** The setting at liberty of an accused person upon others becoming sureties for the accused at the trial. The accused is bailed into the custody of the sureties who must ensure the attendance of the accused at the trial or be liable to the State for the sums secured in the event of his non-appearance. The fundamental test in deciding whether to grant bail or not is the probability of the accused evading justice if released, either by the accused absconding, or interfering with witnesses, or by destroying, concealing or otherwise interfering with physical evidence: The People v O'Callaghan (1966) IR 501. The likelyhood that the accused may commit offences while awaiting trial is not an acceptable criterion for refusing bail: DPP v Ryan (1989 SC) ITLR (27 Feb). It has been held that the test for granting bail in extradition cases should not be different from that in ordinary criminal cases: The People (Attorney General) v Gilliland (1986) ILRM 357. A new offence of *failure to surrender to bail* has been created by the Criminal Justice Act 1984 s.13. See also Childrens Act 1908 s.94

as amended by Childrens Act 1941 s.24. See RSC O.84 rr.15-17; DCR r.60. See PREVENTATIVE DETENTION; STATION BAIL.

**bail, offences committed while on.** Courts are now required to pass a *consecutive* sentence for an offence committed by a person while on bail (qv) awaiting trial for a previous offence: Criminal Jurisdiction Act 1984 s.11. See also Family Law (Protection of Spouses & Children) Act 1981 s.8.

**bailee.** A person to whom the possession of goods is entrusted by the owner (the *bailor*) but not with the intention of transferring ownership. The bailee must re-deliver the bail to the bailor on the determination of the bailment, unless he has a lien (qv) on the chattel.

Where a bailment is solely for the benefit of the bailor eg a gratuitous deposit, the bailee is liable only for gross negligence. Where the bailment is entirely for the benefit of the bailee eg a gratuitous loan, then the bailee is liable for slight negligence eg the omission of the care a vigilant person takes in his own goods. Where the bailment is for the mutual benefit of bailor and bailee eg hire for reward, the bailee is liable for ordinary negligence eg failure to take the care that an ordinary man would; the onus is on the bailee of the goods to show that loss did not occur through lack of reasonable care on his part: Sheehy v Faughan (1991 HC) ILRM 719.

When a bailee does an act so repugnant to the bailment as to show disclaimer, the bailment is automatically determined eg bailee selling a chattel hired under a hire-purchase agreement. Also if the bailee departs from the terms of the bailment, he will be liable for any loss or damage to the chattels due to such deviation: Lilley v Doubleday (1881) 7 QBD 510. A bailee is liable to account for any increase in profits accrued in respect of the chattel bailed eg a cow calving. Also a bailee must pay the ordinary expenses of maintaining the chattel and is estopped from denying the bailor's title. See BAILMENT; INTERPLEADER; TREASURE TROVE.

**bailiff.** A person employed by a sheriff (qv) to serve and execute writs and orders. A bailiff may plead the Statute of Limitations against a person benefi-cially entitled to a share in the estate of a deceased person: Succession Act 1965 s.124 overruling Rice v Begley (1920) 1 IR 243.

**bailiwick.** The area under the jurisdiction of a sheriff (qv) or bailiff (qv).

**bailment.** The delivery of goods to another on the condition express or implied, that they shall be restored to the bailor, or according to his directions, as soon as the purpose for which they are bailed is answered: Coggs v Bernard (1703) 2 Ld Ray 909. The act of delivery is called a *bailment*, the person making the delivery is called a *bailor* and the person to whom it is made is called the *bailee*.

There are three classes of gratuitous bailment: (a) depositum (deposit) — delivery of goods to be taken care of by the bailee who receives no reward for his services; special kinds of deposit include *involuntary bailment* and *bailee by finding*; (b) mandatum (mandate) — delivery of goods to a bailee to do something to them or to carry them from place to place, with the bailee not receiving any reward; (c) commodatum (loan for use) — a gratuitous loan for the bailee's benefit.

There are two classes of bailment for valuable consideration: (a) vadium, pledge or pawn — delivery of goods to another as security for money borrowed by the bailor — see PAWNBROKER; (b) locatio conductio — delivery of goods for reward eg locatio rei — goods hired for reward; locatio operis faciendi — goods to be carried or something to be done to them (eg repair) for reward; and locatio custodiae — goods deposited for reward.

Delivery may be *actual* (by handing over the article), *constructive* (by delivery of some instrument of dominion over the goods eg a key to a warehouse) or by *attornment* (qv). See Webb & Webb v Ireland (1988) IR 353. The mere permission to deposit cargo on the premises of Harbour Commissioners does not impute the necessary degree of control to create a bailment: Doherty Timber Ltd v Drogheda Harbour Commissioners (1993 HC) ILRM 401. See BAILEE; BAILOR; CONVERSION; DETINUE; APPROPRIATION; HIRE- PURCHASE.

**bailment, involuntary.** See INVOLUNTARY

BAILMENT.

**bailment by finding.** See FINDING, BAILMENT BY.

**bailor.** A person who entrusts goods to another, called the bailee (qv). In a gratuitous loan of goods for the use of the bailee, the bailor must disclose defects of which he knows which would make the goods dangerous or unprofitable to the bailee. In bailment for hire and reward, the bailor must use reasonable care to ensure that the goods are reasonably fit for the purpose intended. See Reed v Dean (1949) 1 KB 188. See BAILMENT.

**balance.** That which remains after something has been taken out of a fund: In re Burke Irwin's Trusts (1918) I IR 350.

**balance of convenience.** The test used by the court in deciding whether to grant an *interlocutory* injunction; it will grant such an injunction when the plaintiff has established a fair question to be tried, and the balance of convenience lies in granting the injunction, and where the recoverable damages would be an inadequate remedy. Where an interlocutory injunction is refused, the court may order the defendant to lodge certain monies in a bank account (eg income from an alleged breach of copyright) to meet any claim which the plaintiff might establish at the hearing of the action eg see Paramount Pictures Corp v Cablelink Ltd (1991 HC) 1 IR 521. See Campus Oil Ltd v Minister for Industry & Commerce (No 2) (1983) IR 88; Mantruck Services Ltd & Manton v Ballinlough Electrical (1991 SC) ITLR (23 Dec). See INJUNCTION.

**balance of probability.** The concept in the law of evidence whereby a party, upon whom the burden of proving some matter rests, is entitled to a decision in his favour in that issue if he establishes the proof of the matter in the balance of probabilities. It is the normal standard of proof in civil proceedings. It applies in civil cases alleging breach of EC competition provisions: Masterfoods Ltd t/a Mars v HB Ice Cream Ltd (1992 HC) ITLR (5 Oct). It also applies to disciplinary hearings resulting in the dismissal of an employee: Georgopoulus v Beaumont Hospital Board (1993 HC) — Irish Times 10/7/93. It is often explained to juries in court as *Which*

story would you believe; which story is the more likely?.

A lapse of 23 years in a negligence action between the date of injury and the hearing of the action, does not change the onus of proof from the "balance of probability" to "beyond reasonable doubt": Maitland v Swan & Sligo Co Council (1992 HC) ITLR (6 Jul). See SEE Co Ltd v Public Lighting Services (1988 SC) ILRM 677. See BEYOND REASONABLE DOUBT; RECTIFICATION; STANDARD OF PROOF.

**balance sheet.** The account required to be prepared by a company which shows its overall financial position at the end of the accounting period eg what its issued and actual capital is, what reserves it has, and its assets and liabilities: Companies Act 1963, sixth schedule, regs 2-11. Banks, discount houses and assurance companies are exempted from many of the requirements (ibid regs 23-26). The balance sheet must also give a true and fair view of the state of affairs of the company at the end of its financial year: Companies Amendment Act 1986 s.3. See also Building Societies Act 1989 ss.77 and 81. See ACCOUNTS.

**ballot.** Any system of secret voting. Voting in elections to Dail Eireann, Seanad Eireann and for the President of Ireland must be by *secret* ballot, which has been held to mean secret to the voter: McMahon v Attorney General (1972) IR 69. The ballot paper of a voter at a Dail election must be in a specified form: Electoral Act 1992 s.88 and fourth schedule. Candidates or their agents must not handle ballot papers during the counting of votes (ibid s.117). Breach of secrecy of a ballot is an offence (ibid s.137). A person cannot be required in legal proceedings to state how and for whom he voted (ibid s.162).

The selection of persons empannelled as jurors to serve on a particular jury is made by balloting in open court: Juries Act 1976 s.15. See also Building Societies Act 1989 ss.50-51; proposed draft Presidential Elections Bill 1993 ss.36-44, 48-51, 60;. See also ELECTION; SPOILT VOTE; STRIKE.

**Bangeman wave.** The expression used to describe the waving by EC nationals of their unopened passports to gain entry to another EC State, named after Martin

Bangeman, EC Internal Market Commissioner, who proposed it in 1992; introduced in Ireland on 1st March 1993.

**banishment.** Formerly, the compulsory quitting and expulsion from the realm.

**bank.** A financial institution engaged in the acceptance of deposits of money, the granting of credits by loan or overdraft or otherwise, and engaged in other financial transactions such as the collection and payment of cheques and other money transmission services, the discounting of bills and the dealing in foreign exchange. As regards bills of exchange (qv), a *banker* includes (a) a body of persons, whether incorporated or not, which carries on the business of banking, (b) a building society, (c) ACC Bank plc (d) ICC Bank plc: Bills of Exchange Act 1882 s.2 as amended by ICC Bank Act 1992 s.7.

*Banking business*, for which a licence is required from the Central Bank, includes the business of accepting deposits payable on demand or on notice or at a fixed or determinable future date: Central Bank Act 1971 s.2 (as amended by the Central Bank Act 1989 s.29(a)). No company, association or partnership consisting of more than ten persons may be formed for the purpose of carrying on the business of banking unless it is registered as a company or is formed in pursuance of some other statute: Companies Act 1963 s.372.

A person must not carry on a banking business or hold himself out or represent himself as a banker unless he is the holder of a licence and maintains a deposit in the Central Bank: Central Bank Act 1971 s.7 (as amended by the Central Bank Act 1989 s.30). Consumer protection in the Consumer Information Act 1978 applies to licensed banks (ibid s.23; Restrictive Practices (Amdt) Act 1987 s.3).

The Registrar of Companies is required to notify the Central Bank of the delivery to him of any memorandum of association or articles of any company, which would in his opinion, be holding itself out as a banker or have one of its objects the carrying out of banking business, and he may not issue a certificate of incorporation to such a company unless the Central Bank indicates its willingness to issue a licence to the company or to exempt it: Central Bank Act 1971 s.15.

It is prohibited for a building society, an industrial and provident society, a friendly society, a credit union, an investment trust company or in a unit trust scheme (qv), to use in its name or description any of the words *bank, banker* or *banking* (ibid s.14). See also Central Bank Acts 1942 to 1989. [Text: Forde (5); McGann; Holden UK; Paget UK]. See BANKER; CREDIT INSTITUTION; OMBUDSMAN FOR THE CREDIT INSTITUTIONS.

**bank holiday.** Formerly a day on which banks were closed by statute: Bank Holidays Acts now repealed by the Central Bank Act 1989 s.4 and schedule. A bank holiday is now, in effect, a public holiday as defined in the Holiday (Employees) Act 1973. Public holidays are Christmas Day, St Stephen's Day, 1st January (New Year's Day — SI No 341 of 1974), St Patrick's Day, Easter Monday, the first Monday in June and August, the last Monday in October (SI No 193 of 1977), and the first Monday in May with effect from 1994 (SI No 91 of 1993).

A public holiday is a *non-business* day, as are Saturdays and Sundays; a bill of exchange (qv) which is due and payable on a non-business day, is payable on the next succeeding business day: Central Bank Act 1989 s.132. Special provision is made for a Saturday where the drawee of the bill is a banker and the drawee is normally open for business on that day.

A person is not compellable to make any payment or do any act on a public holiday which he would not be compellable to make or do on Christmas Day or Good Friday by virtue of any rule of law (ibid s.135).

**banker, duty of care.** The relationship between a banker and a customer who pays money into the bank is the ordinary relation between debtor and creditor, with a super-added obligation, arising out of the custom of bankers, to honour the customer's drafts: Joachimson v Swiss Bank Corporation (1912) 3 KB 110.

A banker owes a duty to pay all cheques properly drawn on the customer's account, provided the account is in credit or within an agreed overdraft limit. The duty and authority of a banker to pay a cheque drawn on him is terminated by a *countermand* from the customer, or by notice of death or mental disorder of the customer, or notice of the presentation of a bankruptcy petition in respect of the customer, or notice of presentation of a petition to wind-up a company customer. It has been held that the correction by a bank of an error in its procedures on a short notice to the plaintiff company, did not constitute a breach of the duty of care owed to the company: Hazylake Fashions Ltd v Bank of Ireland (1989 HC) ILRM 698. See also Reade v Royal Bank of Ireland (1922) 2 IR 46; Dublin Port & Docks Board v Bank of Ireland (1976) IR 118; Towey v Ulster Bank Ltd (1987) ILRM 142; Banco Ambrosiano v Ansbacher & Co (1987) ILRM 669. See BANKERS' BOOKS; CHEQUE; CHEQUE, DISHONOUR OF; BILL OF EXCHANGE; PARTNERSHIP, NUMBER TO FORM.

**banker and confidentiality.** The relationship between banker and customer is a confidential one, subject to certain statutory exceptions. A court may make an order authorising a party to legal proceedings, to inspect, and take copies of, entries in the books of a bank: Bankers' Books Evidence Act 1879 s.7; RSC O.31 r.17; O.63 r.1(17). A court may also order a *financial institution* to reveal the affairs of a customer and has power to freeze the account of a customer who is a taxpayer: Finance Act 1983 s.18. A financial institution is broadly defined to include a licensed bank, building society, friendly society, credit union, and industrial and provident society (ibid s.18(1)). Also, in certain circumstances, the Revenue Commissioners can now obtain from financial institutions, without court order, details of the accounts and certain auxilliary financial information on a taxpayer who is a resident of the State: Waiver of Certain Tax, Interest and Penalties Act 1993 s.13.

The Director of Consumer Affairs is empowered to examine the accounts maintained by a *financial institution* on the order of the High Court, which may so order if satisfied that it is reasonable to do so and is satisfied that the exigencies of the common good so warrant: Restrictive Practices (Amendment) Act 1987 s.41. *Financial institution* in this context is also widely defined in the Act to include licensed banks, building societies, industrial and provident societies, friendly societies and credit unions (ibid s.41(4)(b)).

A court or judge is empowered to authorise a garda to inspect and take copies of any entries in a banker's book for the purposes of investigation of an indictable offence, where the court or judge is satisfied that there are reasonable grounds for believing that such an offence has been committed and that there is material in the possession of the bank which is likely to be of substantial value to the investigation: Bankers' Books Evidence Act 1879 s.7A, as inserted by the Central Bank Act 1989 s.131(c). See ATTACHMENT; INVESTIGATION OF COMPANY.

**bankers' books.** A copy of an entry in a banker's book is prima facie evidence of the contents of the entry and of the matters recorded therein, on the copy being proved to be correct: Bankers' Books Evidence Act 1879 ss.3-5. See also Bankers' Books Evidence (Amendment) Act 1959; RSC O.31 r.17; O.63 r.1(17).

This provision is now extended to the books of a building society, of ACC Bank plc, and of ICC Bank plc: Building Societies Act 1989 s.126(1); ACC Bank Act 1992 s.10; ICC Bank Act 1992 s.7.

The definition of bankers' books and records which may be admissible in evidence in court proceedings has been extended to include computerised and other modern day recording media: Central Bank Act 1989 s.126.

**bankers' draft.** An order for the payment of money drawn by a bank upon itself. Payment on such a draft is certain; however an injunction may be granted to restrain a bank from honouring its own draft where there is evidence that such honouring would aid and abet a fraudulent transaction: Murphy v Allied Irish Banks and Deele Fuels (1988) HC. See also Building Societies Act 1989 s.29(2)(q).

**bankrupt.** A debtor who has been adjudicated a bankrupt by the High Court. See AFTER-ACQUIRED PROPERTY; FRAUDULENT DEBTOR; RECEIVER OF BANKRUPT'S PROPERTY.

**bankrupt, duties of.** A bankrupt is

required to deliver up to the Official Assignee (qv) his property and his books and accounts and other papers: Bankruptcy Act 1988 s.19. The bankrupt is required to make a *statement of affairs* in the prescribed form, to disclose any *after-acquired property* (qv), and to notify the Official Assignee of any change in his name or address (ibid ss.19, 20, and 127). He cannot refuse to answer any question put to him on examination by the court on the ground that his answers might incriminate him (ibid s.21(4)). For arrest of bankrupt and committal to prison, see 1988 Act ss.23-25. For format of statement of affairs, see SI No 79 of 1989 Part XX. See STATUTORY SITTING.

**bankruptcy.** *Bankruptcy is a law for the benefit and the relief of creditors and their debtors, in cases where the latter are unable or unwilling to pay their debts:* In re Reiman (1874) 20 Fed Cas 490. Its objective is to secure an equitable distribution of the property of the bankrupt: In re Boyd (1885-86) 15 LR Ir.

A person is *adjudicated* a bankrupt on the petition of the debtor himself or more usually on the petition of the creditor when the debtor has committed an *act of bankruptcy*. However, without becoming a bankrupt, a debtor may seek the protection of the court while he makes an *arrangement* with his creditors. This he does by petitioning the court to protect his property and person at the suit of creditors, until such time as he submits an offer of composition (qv). See ARRANGING DEBTOR.

New legislation to revise, update and consolidate bankruptcy law came into force on 1st January 1989, modelled on legislation drafted by the Bankruptcy Law Committee, which was established in 1962 and reported in 1972: Bankruptcy Act 1988 which repeals the Acts of 1857, 1872 and 1889. Under the 1988 Act the unpaid debt which constitutes an act of bankruptcy is £1500 (ibid s.8(1)); the new legislation also provides for discharge of a bankrupt after 12 years in certain circumstances (ibid s.85); the Official Assignee (qv) is given primary responsibility in bankruptcy administration similar to a *liquidator* of a company; bankruptcy law is more closely aligned to the law on the winding up of companies, particularly in regard to disclaimer of *onerous property* (qv), *fraudulent preferences* (qv) and *preferential payments* (qv); the jurisdiction of the Cork Circuit Court in bankruptcy is abolished; and provision is made for the winding up in bankruptcy of the estates of persons dying insolvent. See Lynch in 7ILT & SJ (1989) 138 and 300. [Text: Forde (4); Holohan & Sanfey; Robb; Gov Pub (2)]. See BANKRUPTCY, ACT OF; BANKRUPTCY, PETITION FOR; INSOLVENT ESTATE; SUBSEQUENT BANKRUPTCY; WINDING UP BY TRUSTEE.

**bankruptcy, act of.** A debtor commits an *act of bankruptcy* if: (a) he conveys his property to a trustee for the benefit of his creditors generally; or (b) he makes a fraudulent conveyance of his property; or (c) he conveys his property or creates a charge on it which would be void as a fraudulent preference (qv) if he were adjudicated bankrupt; or (d) he leaves the State or departs from his dwelling-house or otherwise absents himself or evades his creditors; or (e) he files in court a declaration of insolvency; or (f) if his goods have been seized under an order of the court or a return of no goods is made; or (g) if he fails to pay the sum referred to in a *bankruptcy summons* (qv) within 14 days after service or fails to compound for it to the satisfaction of the creditor: Bankruptcy Act 1988 s.7.

A transaction by a debtor is void as against the Official Assignee (qv) where it is entered into after an act of bankruptcy is committed and within three months of adjudication, if it is a sale at a substantial undervalue (ibid s.58).

In addition, a banker and an auctioneer are deemed to have committed an act of bankruptcy in the circumstances as provided for under the Central Bank Act 1971 s.28(1) and the Auctioneers and House Agents Act 1967 ss.11(3) and 11(4) respectively. See BANKRUPTCY SUMMONS; DEBTOR'S SUMMONS.

**bankruptcy, adjudication of.** The adjudication by the court that a debtor is bankrupt where the court is satisfied that the requirements of the petition therefor are satisfied: Bankruptcy Act 1988 ss.14-15. A person adjudged bankrupt, may show cause against the validity of the adjudication and it may be annulled: RSC 0.76 r.45; ibid 1988 Act s.16.

Following adjudication, the bankrupt is required to surrender and conform and to make a full and true disclosure and discovery of his estate (ibid s.19). A *composition* (qv) with creditors at this stage is still a possibility. On adjudication as a bankrupt, all the debtor's property, real and personal, present and future, vested and contingent, vests in the Official Assignee (qv) (ibid s.44). However, property of which a bankrupt is a trustee does not so vest, although bankruptcy will be a good ground for his removal as a trustee (ibid s.44(4)(a)).

The creditors may appoint a creditor's assignee to act with the Official Assignee in realising the estate, by sale, public auction or private treaty; however from 1989, the role of the creditor's assignee is diminished and he no longer has a shared function with the Official Assignee in relation to the property of the bankrupt (ibid ss.18 and 44). Following distribution to the creditors, the bankrupt could previously in certain circumstances, obtain a *certificate of conformity* from the court and this released him from all debts due at the date of bankruptcy and discharged him as a bankrupt: Bankruptcy Ireland (Amendment) Act 1872 s.56. From 1989, the certificate of conformity has been abolished; instead a certificate of *discharge* or *annulment* under the seal of the court may be issued (ibid 1988 Act s.85(7)). For procedure for an order of adjudication, see SI No 79 of 1989 Part VII. See ARRANGING DEBTOR; BANKRUPTCY, ANNULMENT OF; STATUTORY SITTING.

**bankruptcy, annulment of.** The order of annulment of adjudication which a bankrupt is entitled to, where he has shown cause against the validity of the adjudication or in any other case where, in the opinion of the High Court, he should not have been adjudicated bankrupt: Bankruptcy Act 1988 s.85(5); In re M'G 11 ILTR 93. An *order of annulment* will provide for any property then vested in the Official Assignee (qv) to be revested in the bankrupt and this will be deemed to be a conveyance, assignment or transfer, which may be registered where appropriate (ibid s.85(6)).

**bankruptcy, discharge from.** A bankrupt is entitled to a discharge from bankruptcy: (a) where the adjudication took place before 1 January 1960; or (b) where provision has been made for the payment of all expenses as well as the preferential payments and he has either paid one pound in the pound or he has the consent of all his creditors; or (c) where he has made a *composition* (qv) after bankruptcy and lodged with the Official Assignee (qv) cash or securities to meet the composition; or (d) where in the opinion of the High Court, his estate has been fully realised and certain specified conditions have been complied with eg where either 50 pence or more in the pound has been paid or the bankruptcy has subsisted for twelve years: Bankruptcy Act 1988 s.85.

An *order of discharge* is provided for any property then vested in the Official Assignee to be revested in the bankrupt and this is deemed to be a conveyance, assignment, or transfer, which may be registered where appropriate (ibid s.85(6)). See also ibid s.41. For procedural rules and forms, see SI 79 of 1989 Part XXXI. See UNDISCHARGED BANKRUPT.

**bankruptcy, effect of.** See UNDISCHARGED BANKRUPT.

**bankruptcy, petition for.** The petition which may be brought by a debtor or by a creditor for an *adjudication of bankruptcy* of the debtor. When a debtor cannot pay his debts, he may bring a *petition* to the High Court to be adjudged a bankrupt, if he can show that his assets are sufficient to produce a sum of £1,500: RSC 0.76 r.37; Bankruptcy Act 1988 s.11(3). More usually the petition is brought by a creditor after the debtor has committed an *act of bankruptcy*. The minimum debt to ground a petition by a creditor is £1,500; the period within which an act of bankruptcy is available for the purpose of obtaining an adjudication is three months; and the debtor must be domiciled or have resided or carried on business in the State within a year before the presentation of the petition (ibid s.11). For format and procedure for petition, see RSC (No 3) 1989 (SI No 79 of 1989) Part VI. See BANKRUPTCY, ACT OF.

**bankruptcy inspector.** The new title given to the former Court Messenger: Bankruptcy Act 1988 ss.3 and 60(2) and

(3). A bankruptcy inspector has power, acting under warrant from the High Court, to seize property of a bankrupt and for that purpose to enter and break open any house or place belonging to the bankrupt where any of his property is believed to be (ibid ss.27-29). He has a duty to take an inventory and report on the bankrupt's property; to seize property of the bankrupt pursuant to a warrant issued by the court; and to take possession of an *arranging debtor's* (qv) property (ibid s.62). It is an offence to obstruct an inspector (ibid s.128).

**bankruptcy summons.** A summons which may be granted by the court to a creditor who proves that a *liquidated* debt of £1,500 or more is due to him by the person against whom the summons is sought and a notice in the prescribed form, requiring payment of the debt, has been served on the debtor: Bankruptcy Act 1988 s.8(1). Failure to comply with a bankruptcy summons within fourteen days after service can constitute an *act of bankruptcy* (ibid s.7(1)(g)). The court must dismiss the summons on the application of the debtor, who disputes the debt, if satisfied that an issue would arise for trial (ibid s.8(5)). For format and service of bankruptcy summons, see RSC (No 3) of 1989 (SI No 79 of 1989) Part III. See DEBTOR'S SUMMONS.

**banns.** The proclamation in church in the form of a public notice of an intended marriage (qv).

**bar.** (1) A partition across a court of justice; only senior counsel, solicitors (as officers of the court) and the parties are allowed within the bar. Being *called to the Bar* means being admitted by the Chief Justice in the Supreme Court to practice as a barrister. *The Bar* is the collective name for the professional body of barristers.

(2) Any open bar or any part of a licensed premises exclusively or mainly used for the sale and consumption of intoxicating liquor and includes any counter or barrier across which drink is or can be served to the public: Intoxicating Liquor Act 1988 s.2(1). A restaurant in respect of which a special restaurant licence has been granted must not contain a bar (ibid s.16). It is an offence for the holder of a licence of any licensed premises to allow a person under

the age of 15 years to be present on the premises unless accompanied by a parent or guardian (ibid s.34); other restrictions apply to persons under 18 years of age during extended hours or on an off-licensed premises (ibid ss.35-36).

(3) To bar a right is to destroy or end it eg a debt being barred by the Statute of Limitations. (4) An impediment. See DISBAR; INTOXICATING LIQUOR; LIMITATION OF ACTIONS.

**Bar Council.** The council, elected by members of the Law Library (qv), which deals with matters affecting the profession of barristers, eg etiquette and professional practice; relationship with the solicitors' profession and with the State and its civil service departments. The Law Library is situated in the Four Courts in Dublin; membership of the Library and practice at the Bar have become virtually synonymous. See BARRISTER.

**bar, plea in.** See PLEA.

**bare licence.** A mere licence. A bare licensee is a person who has permission, which is not supported by consideration (qv), to enter land or premises for his own purposes, so as not to be a trespasser. A bare licence is always revocable. See LICENCE.

**bare trust.** A trust (qv) which merely requires the trustee to hold property on trust with no duty in relation thereto except to convey it when required. See Christie v Ovington (1875) 1 Ch D 279. See Companies Act 1990 s.55(1)(a). Contrast with ACTIVE TRUST.

**bargain.** A contract; an agreement.

**barking, excessive.** See DOGS.

**barratry.** The common law misdemeanour (qv) of inciting, promoting or maintaining a false or groundless action. It is very rarely prosecuted. Barratry also includes every wrongful act wilfully committed by the master or crew to the prejudice of the owner, or as the case may be, the charterer: Marine Insurance Act 1906, first schedule, art.11.

**barring order.** An order preventing one spouse from entering the family home even if that spouse is the owner thereof, either wholly or in part: Family Law (Maintenance of Spouses and Children) Act 1976 s.2. The court may make such an order if it is of the opinion that there are reasonable grounds for believing that the safety and welfare of the other spouse, or of any child of the family, so requires it.

A barring order may prohibit a spouse from using or threatening to use violence against, molesting or putting in fear the other spouse or any child of the family: Family Law (Protection of Spouses and Children) Act 1981 s.2(2). See O'B v O'B (1984) ILRM 1. A barring order may be made after an application for or on granting a decree of judicial separation (qv): Judicial Separation and Family Law Reform Act 1989 ss.11(a) and 16(e). See EXCLUSION ORDER. [Text: Duncan & Scully].

**barring the entail.** The conversion by the tenant in tail of an estate tail into a fee simple. The former methods of achieving such a conversion were *suffering a recovery* or *levying a fine.* Since 1833 it is achieved by a *disentailing deed.* The Official Assignee (qv) in bankruptcy is empowered to bar the entail: Bankruptcy Act 1988 s.64. See FEE TAIL.

**barrister.** Counsel; a member of the Honourable Society of King's Inns who has been called to the Bar. A practising barrister is one who holds himself out as willing to appear in court or to give legal advice and services to his client for reward. He has a right of audience in every court. As a member of the Law Library, a barrister intending to practise must spend 12 months as a pupil (called a *devil*) of an experienced barrister (called a *master*). After some years as a *junior counsel,* the barrister may take *silk* and become a *senior counsel* by applying to and obtaining the approval of the government.

A barrister is paid a fee, comprising a *brief* fee (qv) and a *refresher* fee (qv) where appropriate. The Taxing Master may review a barrister's fees; he is required to decide whether a reasonably prudent solicitor acting in a reasonable way would have offered such a fee: Smyth v Tunney (1991 HC) 10 ILT Dig (1992) 267. A barrister may not sue for his fees, which are deemed to be in the nature of an *honorarium*: Wells v Wells (1914) P 157.

Law books purchased by a barrister are "plant" within the meaning of Income Tax Act 1967 s.241(1) and qualify for wear and tear allowance: Breathnach v McC (1984) IR 340.

The Minister is empowered to specify by regulation, provided such regulation is approved by both Houses of the Oireachtas (qv), the maximum number of counsel in respect of whom costs may be allowed, on *taxation* by a Taxing Master, for payment by another party to certain actions eg actions which claim damages in respect of personal injuries caused by negligence, nuisance or breach of duty: Courts Act 1988 s.5. See also SI No 58 of 1979; SI No 197 of 1981.

It had been held in England that a barrister was immune from actions for negligence in the performance of his professional duties (Rondel v Worsley [1969] 1 AC191) but that situation changed in relation to claims in negligence in pre-trial work: Saif Ali v Sydney Mitchell & Co (1980) AC 198.

A Professional Conduct Tribunal with lay representation, has been established by the Bar Council to consider complaints against barristers, whether from solicitors, members of the public or others. A range of penalties may be imposed, including fines and a recommendation to the Benchers of King's Inns that a barrister be disbarred. There is provision for appeal to the Barristers' Professional Conduct Appeals Board. The first case heard by the Tribunal and the Appeal Board was in 1993, when a barrister was found to have breached proper professional standards and was directed to pay £500 to the Bar Benevolent Fund. See ILSI Gazette (Apr 1992) 98. See FRIEND, MY; LITIGATION; TAXATION OF COSTS.

**barter.** The practice of exchanging goods for goods or services. See Simpson v Connolly (1953) 1 WLR 911. See Miller in 10 ILT & SJ (1992) 13.

**base fee.** A particular kind of determinable *fee simple;* it continues only so long as the original grantor or any heirs of his body are alive and there is a remainder (qv) or reversion (qv) after it. A base fee arises where a tenant in tail attempts to convey a fee simple without *barring the entail* or when the tenant in tail disentails without the consent of the *protector of the settlement* (qv). A base fee may be enlarged into a fee simple by a fresh disentailing deed by the former tenant in tail, or by the passage of time under the Statute of Limitations 1957, or by the owner of the base fee becoming the owner of the remainder or reversion in the fee simple immediately following the base fee.

**bastard.** A person born out of wedlock; an illegitimate person; now referred to as a person *whose parents are not married to each other.* See CHILD, ILLEGITIMATE; EVIDENCE TENDING TO BASTARDISE CHILDREN.

**baths, public.** A sanitary authority (qv) is empowered to provide and maintain: public baths; public swimming baths or public bathing places; conveniences for bathers; or public wash-houses: Local Government (Sanitary Services) Act 1948 s.5 and 35. In addition, the authority is entitled to make charges for their use, to employ life-guards, to arrange for the giving of instructions in swimming and life-saving, and to make bye-laws (ibid ss.36-41).

**battery in crime.** See ASSAULT.

**battery in tort.** See TRESPASS TO THE PERSON.

**bawdy house.** A brothel (qv).

**beach.** See BATHS, PUBLIC.

**beach material.** Sand, clay, gravel, shingle, stones, rocks and mineral substances on the surface of the seashore (qv): Foreshore Act 1933 s.1. The Minister is empowered to grant a licence allowing a person to remove any beach material from, or disturb any beach material, in a foreshore (ibid s.3 as amended by Foreshore Amendment Act 1992 s.2). The Minister is also empowered by order to prohibit the removal of beach material from, or disturbance of beach material in, an area of seashore where he is of the opinion that such removal or disturbance had effected or is likely to affect any flora or fauna, or any amenities or public rights, or cause injury to land or any building, wall, pier or other structure (ibid 1933 Act s.6 amended by 1992 Act s.3).

The High Court is empowered to prohibit continuance of contraventions of a licence, prohibitory order or notice, on the application of the Minister, a local authority or any other person (ibid 1992 Act s.5). Also application may be made to other courts (eg District — £5,000; Circuit — £30,000; High — no limit) to order a person to refrain from or cease removal or disturbance, or to

mitigate or remedy any effects, or to reimburse the applicant for the costs in investigating, mitigating or remedying the effects of such removal or disturbance (ibid 1992 Act s.6). See FORESHORE.

**bear.** The term used to describe a person who sells stocks and shares before owning them, in the expectation that he will be able to buy in later when the price has fallen, and thereby make a profit. Contrast with BULL. See SHARES.

**bearer bill.** A bill of exchange payable to bearer, or on which the only or last endorsement is an *endorsement in blank.* An *endorsement in blank* arises where the endorser merely signs his own name, or one which is payable to a fictitious or non-existent person. See Bills of Exchange Act 1882 ss.8(3) and 34. See ORDER BILL; BILL OF EXCHANGE.

**bed and breakfast.** Colloquial expression describing an arrangement whereby the owner of shares in a company sells and repurchases sufficient shares to realise a capital gain which is within his annual capital gains tax allowance. The shares are sold and bought back at the same price. Where shares have increased in value from the price they were originally bought at, this "bed and breakfast" transaction enables the investor to retain his shareholding while increasing the base cost at which a future disposal of the shares will be reckoned for capital gains tax purposes. See CAPITAL GAINS TAX.

**beget.** Procreate. There is a constitutional right to beget children within marriage, guaranteed by Article 40 of the Constitution, which is suspended and placed in abeyance when one spouse is lawfully imprisoned: Murray & Murray v Ireland & AG (1991 SC) ILRM 465.

**begin, right to.** See RIGHT TO BEGIN.

**Bell Houses clause.** A clause in the objects of a company which permits the company, or the board of directors, to extend its activities into another business which would benefit the company's main business. There must be an honestly held belief that the extension will benefit the company: Bell Houses Ltd v City Wall Properties Ltd (1966) 2 QB 656. See MacCann in 10 ILT & SJ (1992) 81.

**below cost selling.** The selling, or advertising for sale, of grocery goods (including alcoholic beverages) below cost price; such selling or advertising is prohibited: Restrictive Practices (Groceries) Order 1987 (SI No 142 of 1987); Restrictive Practices (Confirmation of Order) Act 1987. The Order also contains provisions in relation to the withholding of supply of grocery goods, and the boycotting of any person in relation to grocery goods; it also prohibits the payment or receipt of *hello money* (qv). See also Director of Consumer Affairs v Dunnes Stores (1988 HC) and (1992 HC). A building society is prohibited from providing certain services at below cost eg services relating to land: Building Societies Act 1989 ss.31(12)(a) and 32(5)(a).

**bench.** The judges in a court of law. Being *raised to the Bench* means being appointed a judge.

**bench warrant.** An order of the court for the immediate arrest of a person eg for failure to surrender to bail. See Criminal Justice Act 1984 s.13(4) and (5). See WARRANT.

**Benchers.** The governing body of the Bar of Ireland. See KINGS INNS, THE HONOURABLE SOCIETY OF.

**beneficial interest.** The interest of a beneficial owner (qv) or beneficiary as contrasted with the estate or interest of a nominal or legal owner such as a trustee.

**beneficial owner.** The person who enjoys or who is entitled to the benefit of property ie on his own right rather than on behalf of someone else. See INVESTIGATION OF COMPANY; REGISTER OF MEMBERS; TRUE PERSON.

**beneficiary.** A person for whose benefit property is held by a trustee or executor; a *cestui que trust*; a person who receives a gift under a will.

**beneficiary, remedies of.** Where a trustee departs from the terms of the trust or is in breach of duties imposed by statute or by equity, the beneficiary of the trust may, in a suitable case, obtain an order for account, an injunction, damages, and a tracing order (qqv). See TRUSTEE, DUTY OF; TRACING.

**benefit-in-kind.** A colloquial phrase usually referring to the value which the law places on a benefit accruing to a person eg an employee's access to a company car for private use. The taxation of the benefit of the availability of a company car for private use has been held not to be unconstitutional: Browne & Ors v Attorney General (1991 HC) 2 IR 58.

**benignae faciendae sunt interpretationes et veba intentioni debent inservire.** [Liberal interpretation should be the rule, and the words should be made to carry out the intention]. See CONSTRUCTION, RULES OF; LEGISLATION, INTERPRETATION OF.

**Benjamin order.** An order of the court authorising the distribution of an estate on certain presumptions eg that certain beneficiaries are dead, where there is difficulty for the personal representative (qv) to so determine: In re Benjamin, Neville v Benjamin (1902) 1 Ch 723 applied by Baker v Cohn-Vossen (1986) ILRM 175.

**bequeath.** To give personal property by will eg a legacy.

**bequest.** A gift of personal property by will; a legacy. A *residuary bequest* is a gift of the residue of the testator's personal estate. A *specific bequest* is a gift of property of a certain kind eg *my large diamond ring*. See LEGACY.

**Berne Copyright Union.** The copyright Convention which was signed at Berne in 1886. Most countries in the world, including Ireland, are members but not the USA or the former USSR. Under the Union, an author is given in countries other than the country of origin, not only the rights which are given by these countries' domestic laws but also the rights granted by the Union. Unlike the Universal Copyright Convention, there are no formalities required to be performed to obtain protection under the Union; the minimum term of protection is greater (generally 50 years); and the scope of protection is laid down in greater detail and is more extensive. Works published in any country of the Berne Union or of the Universal Copyright Convention are given the same protection in Ireland as if the works were first published within the State: Copyright (Foreign Countries) Order 1978 (SI Nos 132 and 133 of 1978). [Text: Copinger UK; Laddie UK]. See UNIVERSAL COPYRIGHT CONVENTION.

**best available technology.** The Environmental Protection Agency must not grant a licence for an *activity* unless it is satisfied that the best *available technology not entailing excessive costs* will be used to prevent or eliminate or, where that is not practicable, to limit, abate or reduce an emission from the activity: Environmental Protection Agency Act 1992 ss.83(3)(f) and 5. An activity includes any process or action involving a genetically modified organism (ibid s.5(6)).

**best evidence rule.** The rule that requires that the best and most direct evidence of a fact be adduced, or its absence accounted for eg the best evidence of the contents of a letter is its production in court. See DPP v O'Donoghue (1992 HC) 10 ILT Dig 74. See DOCUMENTARY EVIDENCE; EVIDENCE, PRIMARY.

**bestiality.** The crime of buggery (qv) committed with an animal. See Offences Against the Person Act 1861 ss.61–62 which are repealed by the Criminal Law (Sexual Offences) Act 1993 save in so far as they apply to buggery or attempted buggery with animals.

**bet.** A wager. Criminal prosecution for recovery of duty payable on a bet requires an order to be made by the Revenue Commissioners prior to commencement of the prosecution: Inland Revenue Regulations Act 1890 s.21(1) and DPP v Cunningham (1989) IR 481. The recovery of excise duty on a bet is a criminal matter within the meaning of the Prosecution of Offences Act 1974: DPP v Boyle (1993 HC) ILRM 128. It is an offence to accept a bet in premises which are not registered or to evade betting duty: Finance Act 1984 s.76. See also Finance Act 1989 s.42. See BOOK-MAKER; REVENUE OFFENCE; WAGERING CONTRACT.

**betaghs.** A class of unfree tenant found on Norman-Irish manors, drawn from the native Irish population, who owed labour services rather than rent, and were bound to the soil. See Mac Niochaill (1966) 1 Ir Jur (ns) 292.

**beware of dog sign.** A Circuit Court judge is reported to have said that a defendant's *Beware of Dog* sign had "no bearing in law": Martin J in O'Sullivan v Delahunty (1988 CC) — Irish Times 19/9/1988. See GUARD DOG; SCIENTER.

**beyond reasonable doubt.** The concept in the law of evidence whereby an accused is entitled to an acquittal if the prosecution has not established his guilt beyond reasonable doubt. Contrast with BALANCE OF PROBABILITY. See INFERENCE; STANDARD OF PROOF.

**bid.** An offer to buy at a stated price something which is being sold by auction. See AUCTION SALES.

**bigamy.** An offence committed by a person who has been previously married and has not since been legally divorced, and who goes through a legally recognised ceremony of marriage with another person, while the original spouse is still living: Offences Against the Person Act 1861 s.57. It is a conclusive defence to show that the accused's original spouse had been continually absent from the accused during the seven years preceding the second marriage and had never been heard of by the accused meanwhile. See R v Tolson (1889) 23 QBD 168. See DIVORCE.

**bill.** (1) An account sent by a creditor to a debtor. (2) A written instrument eg a bill of exchange (qv). (3) A draft legislative proposal, which when passed, or deemed to have been passed, by both Houses of the Oireachtas (qv), becomes an Act when signed by the President of Ireland: 1937 Constitution, art.13(3). A bill may be a *private* bill (eg referring to a particular person or town) or a *public* bill (applying to the State). A bill may also be classified as an *ordinary* bill, a *money* bill or an *abridged-time* bill, or a bill to amend the Constitution (qqv). A bill becomes law from the date of signature by the President unless a contrary intention appears; many Acts, or sections thereof, do not become operational until activated by a designated Minister. See ACT; BILL, ABRIDGED-TIME; BILL, MONEY; BILL, ORDINARY; CONSTITUTION, BILL TO AMEND; EXPLANATORY MEMORANDUM; PRESIDENT OF IRELAND; PETITION; PRIVATE MEMBER'S BILL.

**bill, abridged-time.** A bill, which the Taoiseach certifies in writing is, in the opinion of the government, urgent and immediately necessary for the preservation of the public peace and security: 1937 Constitution, art.24. The time for consideration of such a bill by the Seanad will be abridged, if Dail Eireann so resolves and if the President of Ireland, after consultation with the Council of

c

State (qv), concurs. Such legislation may remain in force for only ninety days unless both Houses prolong the period by resolution.

**bill, money.** A bill which contains only provisions dealing with all or any of the following matters, namely, the imposition, repeal, remission, alteration or regulation of taxation; the imposition for the payment of debt or other financial purposes of charges on public moneys or the variation or repeal of any such charges; supply; the appropriation, receipt, custody, issue or audit of accounts of public money; the raising or guarantee of any loan or the payment thereof; matters subordinate and incidental to these matters or any of them: 1937 Constitution, art.22(1)(1). A money bill can be initiated in Dail Eireann only; the Seanad cannot amend or reject such a bill although it may make recommendations thereon, which the Dail may accept or reject. An example of a money bill, certified as such, is the bill which was enacted as the Tourist Traffic Act 1987.

**bill, ordinary.** A bill other than a money bill or an abridged-time bill. An ordinary bill which is passed by Dail Eireann and sent to Seanad Eireann and which is either rejected by the Seanad, or passed by the Seanad with amendments to which the Dail does not agree, or is neither passed (with or without amendments) nor rejected by the Seanad within 90 days from first being sent to the Seanad, will be deemed to have been passed by both Houses of the Oireachtas (qv) if the Dail so resolves within 180 days after the expiration of the 90 day period: 1937 Constitution, art.23.

**bill, stages of.** A bill is normally initiated by a Minister of the government in either Dail Eireann or Seanad Eireann, except that a money bill must be initiated in the Dail. The 1st stage of the bill is its introduction. During the 2nd stage, the general principles of the bill are debated. At the 3rd or *committee* stage, each section of the bill is considered and at the 4th or *report* stage, accepted amendments are incorporated, leading to the 5th or *final* stage when the bill is passed and sent for consideration to the other House. It is subsequently signed by the President of Ireland and is promulgated by notice in Iris Oifigiuil (qv). Bills, when enacted, are numbered in the order and year in which they are signed and promulgated as the law eg No 7 of 1988 is the 7th bill to become law in 1988. See BILL; COMMENCEMENT; MONEY; PRESIDENT OF IRELAND.

**bill of costs.** A statement of account furnished by a solicitor to his client setting out in detail the work done on behalf of the client, and showing the amount charged for each item, including disbursements. A solicitor cannot sue for payment for one month after delivery of such bill: Attorneys and Solicitors (Ireland) Act 1849 ss.2 and 6; State (Shatter) v de Valera (1986) ILRM 3. See COSTS AND CRIMINAL PROCEEDINGS; COSTS IN CIVIL PROCEEDINGS; TAXATION OF COSTS.

**bill of exchange.** A form of negotiable instrument. An unconditional order in writing, addressed by one person to another, signed by the person giving it, requiring the person to whom it is addressed to pay on demand, or at a fixed or determinable future time, a sum certain in money, to, or to the order of, a specified person, or to bearer: Bills of Exchange Act 1882 s.3(1).

The person who gives the order to pay is the *drawer*; the person to whom the order to pay is made is the *drawee* and becomes the *acceptor* by writing his name across the face of the bill. The person to whom the payment is to be made is the *payee*; the payee must be named or indicated with reasonable certainty (ibid s.7(1)). If the payee is a fictitious or non-existing person, the bill may be treated as payable to bearer (ibid s.7(3)). A non-existent person is one whom the drawer did not know existed when he signed, whereas a fictitious person is one who does exist but was not the person intended by the drawer to receive payment: Clutton v Attenborough (1897) AC 90; Bank of England v Vagliano (1891) AC 107. See Building Societies Act 1989 s.126. See also Gill in 7 ILT & SJ (1989) 88. [Text: Byles UK; Paget UK; Richardson UK]. See NEGOTIABLE INSTRUMENT; CHEQUE; ENDORSEMENT.

**bill of exchange, acceptance of.** See ACCEPTANCE OF BILL.

**bill of exchange, discharge of.** See DISCHARGE OF BILL.

**bill of exchange, dishonour of.** See

DISHONOUR OF BILL.

**bill of exchange, payment of.** A bill of exchange is *payable on demand* if it is expressed to be payable on demand, or at sight, or on presentation, or where no time for payment is expressed, or where it is accepted or endorsed when overdue: Bills of Exchange Act 1882 s.10. A bill which is not payable on demand must be payable at a fixed or determinable future time; ie it must be payable at a fixed period after date or sight, or on, or at a fixed period after, the occurrence of a specified event which is certain to happen, though the time of happening may be uncertain (ibid s.11).

**bill of lading.** A document, used in foreign trade, signed and delivered by the master of a ship to the shipper on goods being shipped. The bill of lading specifies the name of the master, the port and destination of the ship, the goods, the consignee and the rate of freight. Copies are kept by the master, the shipper and the consignee. It is a document of title transferable by endorsement and delivery, giving the holder the right to sue thereon but it is not a fully negotiable instrument (qv), in that the transferee obtains no better title than the transferor has. See Vita Food Products v Unus Shipping Co (1939) AC 277. See Merchant Shipping Act 1947 s.13, second schedule.

**bill of sale.** A document given with respect to the transfer of chattels used in cases where possession is not intended to be given. There are two types of bills of sale: (a) *absolute,* purporting to be a complete transfer of the chattels by way of sale, gift or settlement and (b) by way of *mortgage,* where there is a transfer for the purpose of creating a security, subject to a proviso for redemption on repayment of the money secured. Every bill of sale must be attested and registered within seven days of execution and must set forth the consideration for which it was given. A bill of sale of stock (whether including or not including any other chattels) is void and incapable of being registered under bill of sale legislation: Agricultural Credit Act 1978 s.36. Bills of Sale are now almost obsolete. See Johnson v Diprose (1893) 1 QB 512. See Bills of Sale (Ireland) Act 1879 and 1883; Central Bank Act 1971 s.36. [Text: Forde

(5)].

**bill to amend constitution.** See CONSTITUTION, BILL TO AMEND.

**binding to the peace.** An order, which may be made by a judge, binding a person to the peace or to good behaviour or to both the peace and good behaviour and requiring him to enter into a *recognizance* in that behalf: Courts (Supplemental Provisions) Act 1961 s.54. See Halpin v Rice (1901) 1 IR 593. See PROBATION.

**biotechnological invention.** See MICROORGANISM.

**birching.** See WHIPPING.

**bird watching.** See HUNT.

**birds, wild.** See WILD BIRDS, PROTECTED.

**birth, concealment of.** See CONCEALMENT OF BIRTH.

**birth, home.** See MIDWIFE.

**birth, registration of.** The recording of full details of the birth and parentage of a child at the request of either parent or of the *occupier of the house* (eg usually an employee of a hospital) or other qualified informant: Births and Deaths Registration (Ireland) Acts 1863 and 1880. Registration of the parents of a child whose parents are not married to each other at the time of birth or at any time during the previous ten months, is now governed by the Status of Children Act 1987 ss.48-49, amending the 1880 Act. In such cases, the father's name may be registered: (a) on the joint request of both parents, as heretofore; (b) on the request of either parent supported by a declaration by that parent and a statutory declaration from the other parent as to the *paternity* of the child, or at the written request of either parent supported by an appropriate court order; (c) where the child is born to a married woman and a man other than her husband, on the request where the woman, her husband and the father all consent (implementing S v S (1983) IR 68) or on court order where her husband is unavailable or refuses to consent; (d) on re-registration where no father's name has been entered on the register in the circumstances set out above.

The Minister is empowered to make regulations dealing with the registration and re-registration of the birth of a person who has obtained a *declaration of parentage* (ibid s.48) and has made such regulations: Registration of Births Regulations 1988 (SI No 123 of 1988).

Birth certificates are issued by Oifig an tArd-Chlaraitheora, the superintendent registrars, and the local registrars. Two forms are available, the *full* certificate which is a true copy of the entry in the register, and the *short* certificate on which is shown only the name, surname, sex, date of birth, and district of registration. See also Births and Deaths Registration Acts 1863 to 1972. See FOETAL DEATH; PARENT; PATERNITY, PRESUMP- TION OF; PARENTAGE, DECLARATION OF.

**BL.** Barrister-at-Law. See BARRISTER.

**black leg.** Generally understood to mean a person who continues, or attempts, to continue to work during a strike (qv).

**blacklist.** Generally understood to mean a list of persons or firms or companies with whom no dealings are to be made. See BELOW COST SELLING; BOYCOTT; UNFAIR PRACTICES.

**blackmail.** Popular name for offences involving extortion by menaces. See EXTORTION BY MENACES.

**blank cheque.** See FEE.

**blank transfer.** The transfer of fully paid shares in a company which need not specify the name of the transferee to be effective. See Stock Transfer Act 1963. See SHARES, EQUITABLE MORTGAGE OF.

**Blaskets.** The island group near Dingle in the Kerry Gaeltacht, the largest island of which is An Blascaod Mor. Provision has been made for the preservation of this island as a cultural centre and national park: An Blascaod Mor National Historic Park Act 1989. See Gaeltacht Areas Order 1956 (SI No 245 of 1956).

**blasphemy.** The crime which consists of indecent and offensive attacks on Christianity, or the Scriptures, or sacred persons or objects calculated to outrage the feelings of the community. The Constitution declares that the publication or utterance of blasphemous matter is an offence which shall be punishable in accordance with law: 1937 Constitution, art. 40(6)(1)(i). The mere denial of Christian teaching is not sufficient to constitute the offence. See also Defamation Act 1961 s.13.

It is an offence to be guilty of riotous, violent or indecent behaviour in a chapel or churchyard or burial ground, or to molest, disturb, vex or trouble a preacher or clergyman celebrating any sacrament or divine service or rite: Ecclesiastical Courts Jurisdiction Act 1860 s.2.

**blood relationship.** The quality or relationship which enables a person to take by descent, being descended from one or more common ancestors. A person is said to be of the *whole blood* to another where they are both descended from the same pair of ancestors eg two sisters who have the same father and mother. A person is said to be of the *half-blood* to another when they are descended from one common ancestor only eg two brothers who have the same father but different mothers. In an intestacy, relatives of the half-blood share equally with relatives of the whole blood in the same degree. See Succession Act 1965 ss.71- 72. See BLOOD TEST; NEXT-OF-KIN; PAREN- TAGE, DECLARATION OF.

**blood specimen.** The specimen of blood which certain persons in a garda station are required to permit a designated registered medical practitioner to take from them; it is an offence to refuse and fail to comply with this requirement: Road Traffic (Amendment) Act 1978 ss.13-14; Medical Practitioners (Amend- ment) Act 1993 ss.4-5. A quantity of the specimen must be offered to the person (ibid 1978 Act s.21(2)). Failure to allow a person access to a solicitor prior to obtaining a blood specimen does not render the evidence so obtained as inadmissible: Walshe v O'Buachalla (1991 HC) 9ILT Dig 226. See Director of Public Prosecutions v Smyth (1987) ILRM 570; Connolly v Sweeney (1988) ILRM 35.

Under proposed draft legislation, cer- tain other persons will be obliged to give a breath, blood or urine specimen following arrest eg persons arrested for dangerous driving or for taking a vehicle without authority: Road Traffic Bill 1993 s.13. For power of a garda to have a blood sample taken in relation to other offences, see BODILY SAMPLE. See also BLOOD TEST; DESIGNATED; DRUNKEN DRIVING; URINE SAMPLE.

**blood test.** A test made with the object of ascertaining inheritable characteristics to assist the court in determining the question of *parentage*: Status of Children Act 1987 s.37. Statutory procedures for obtaining and giving blood test evidence in questions of parentage, arising in civil proceedings, are provided for in the 1987 Act ss.37-43. Where an application is brought for an order directing that blood tests be used to determine parentage, judicial discretion is required to be exercised on matters touching on the welfare of the children: ibid s.38 and JPD v MG (1991 SC) ILRM 217. Where a person fails to comply with a direction by the court for the use of such blood tests, the court may draw whatever inferences it considers proper from the refusal (ibid 1987 Act s.42). See District Court (Status of Children Act 1987) Rules 1988 (SI No 152 of 1988); Blood Tests (Parentage) Regulations 1988 (SI No 215 of 1988). See GENETIC FINGERPRINTING; PARENTAGE, DECLARATION OF.

**blot on title.** A defect in title (qv) to land.

**blue chip.** Generally understood to mean the shares (qv) of a well established company which is highly regarded as an investment.

**board meeting.** A meeting of the directors (qv) of a company (qv) at which decisions are made by majority vote, with the chairman having a casting vote. See Companies Act 1963, Table A, arts. 100 etc. See CHAIRMAN; MANAGING DIRECTOR; MINUTES.

**board of conservators.** See WATER POLLUTION.

**board of directors.** See DIRECTORS; RECKLESS TRADING.

**boarding out.** An arrangement by which a person becomes a resident in another person's private dwelling. A health board is empowered to board out a person with his consent, in a private dwelling and may pay for all or part of the cost; this applies to a person who, in the opinion of the board, ought having regard to his means and circumstances, be boarded out: Health (Nursing Homes) Act 1990 s.10. See FOSTER CHILD.

**boards of guardians.** Formerly, the bodies consisting of justices of the peace (qv) and members elected by ratepayers, with responsibility in their area, called the *Union*, for superintending the poor relief system, including workhouses, the provision and maintenance of sewers and the enforcement of laws relating to public health generally, in addition to being the custodians of burial grounds and the construction of public water works, all of which were performed under the general supervision of the Poor Law Commissioners and later of the Local Government Board: Poor Relief (Ireland) Act 1838; Local Government Board (Ireland) Act 1872. The functions of the board of guardians were transferred initially to *rural district councils* (qv) which were themselves later abolished.

**bodily harm, grievous.** It is a felony (qv) unlawfully and maliciously to *wound* or cause *grievous* bodily harm to any person or to shoot at him with intent to maim, disfigure or disable or do any other grievous bodily harm, or to resist arrest: Offences Against the Person Act 1861 s.18. To constitute *wounding*, the continuity of the skin must be broken; bodily harm is *grievous* where the injury is serious although not necessarily a permanent one: People (Attorney General) v Messitt (1974) IR 406. *Maliciously* means having an intention to do the particular kind of harm; ill-will to the injured party is not required. An unlawful wounding or causing grievous bodily harm, without intent, is a misdemeanour (ibid 1861 Act s.20). See ASSAULT; POISON; BURGLARY.

**bodily integrity, right to.** There is a constitutional right to bodily integrity: Ryan v Attorney General (1965) IR 294; The State (Richardson) v Governor of Mountjoy (1980) HC.

**bodily sample.** A sample of blood, hair, pubic hair, urine, saliva, nail or of any material found under a nail; a swab from a body orifice or a genital region or any other part of the body; a dental impression; a footprint or similar impression: Criminal Justice (Forensic Evidence) Act 1990 s.2.

A garda may take, or cause to be taken, such a bodily sample for the purpose of forensic testing from a person who is in custody under the provisions of s.30 of the Offences Against the State Act 1939 or s.4 of the Criminal Justice Act 1984 or in certain circumstances if the person is in prison (ibid ss.2(1) and 2(2)) — see DETENTION; OFFENCES AGAINST THE STATE).

This new power enables the Gardai to avail of developments in DNA (qv) profiling. Authorisation from a garda, not below the rank of superintendent, to take a bodily sample is required; the consent in writing of the person is also required if the sample is an intimate one (ibid s.2(4)).

The court in determining whether a person is guilty of an offence may draw such inference as appears proper from a refusal to consent to taking a sample but cannot convict solely on the inference drawn (ibid s.3). There are particular protections for young persons regarding consent and inferences from a refusal (ibid ss.2(10) and 3(4)). See SI No 130 of 1992. See BLOOD SPECIMEN; DNA; GENETIC FINGERPRINTING.

**body.** See DISSECTION.

**body corporate.** A succession or collection of persons having in the estimation of the law an existence and rights and duties distinct from the individual persons who form it from time to time eg a company registered under the Companies Acts, a local authority, a body established by charter. See CORPORATION.

**bona fide.** In good faith; honestly; without fraud, collusion, or participation in wrongdoing.

**bona vacantia.** Goods without an apparent owner in which no one claims a property but the State eg shipwreck, treasure trove. The right of the State to forfeiture by way of bono vacantia in respect of personalty on an intestacy, has been replaced by the right of the State as ultimate intestate successor: Succession Act 1965 s. 73. See TREASURE TROVE.

**bond.** (1) An agreement under seal whereby the *obligor* binds himself to the *obligee* to perform or refrain from an action. A *simple bond* is one without condition. A *common money bond* is one given to secure payment of money. (2) An interest bearing document, securing long term debt, usually issued by government or corporations. See Building Societies Act 1989 s.30. See EXCHEQUER BILLS; LAND BOND; PERFORMANCE BOND.

**bond, engineering contract.** Generally an agreement under seal whereby a *surety* and a *contractor* are jointly and severally bound unto an *employer* for the payment of a specified sum; it usually arises where the employer and the contractor have entered into a contract for the construction completion and maintenance of certain works and provides that in default of such contract the surety shall satisfy and discharge the damages sustained by the employer up to the amount of the bond. [Text: Kilty (1); Abrahamson UK].

**bond washing.** The term sometimes used to describe a transaction which has as its purpose the avoidance of tax by the sale and re-purchase of stocks, shares and other securities. The anti- avoidance rules governing such transactions are contained in the Income Tax Act 1967 ss.367-370 (purchase and sale *ex div* of securities); 1967 Act ss.371-372 (purchase of shares by share dealers and exempted persons); 1967 Act s.449 (transfer of right to receive interest etc from securities); Finance Act 1984 s.29 (sale of government securities cum div); Finance Act 1991 s.27 (sale of government securities ex div). Life assurance companies are relieved of the computational requirements imposed by Finance Act 1984 s.29, but are chargeable to corporation tax in respect of gains: Finance Act 1993 ss.21 and 11. [Text: Judge]. See TAX AVOIDANCE.

**bonded goods.** Dutiable goods in respect of which a bond has been given to pay the duty. See Patrick Monahan (Drogheda) Ltd v O'Connell (1987) HC.

**bonded warehouse.** A secure place approved by the Revenue Commissioners for the deposit of dutiable goods upon which duty has not been paid.

**bonus shares.** Shares in a company which are distributed free to existing members arising from the capitalisation by the company of undistributed profits in its reserves which are otherwise available for distribution as dividends. Sums capitalised in this way must be applied on behalf of the members who would have been entitled to receive the same if the same had been distributed by way of dividend and in the same proportions: Companies Act 1963, Table A, art 130. See also ibid arts 130A and 131; Companies Amendment Act 1983, first schedule, reg 24(f). Contrast with RIGHTS ISSUE.

**book and library.** The publisher of any book first published in the State must, within one month after publication deliver, at his own expense, one copy of the book to the National Library of Ireland, to Trinity College Dublin, to Dublin City University, to the University of Limerick, to the British Museum (now, the British Library) and four copies to the National University of Ireland: Copyright Act 1963 s.56; Dublin City University Act 1989 s.6; University of Limerick Act 1989 s.7.

**book debts.** Any charges on the book debts of a company must be registered: Companies Act 1963 s.99 as amended by the Companies Act 1990 s.122. The Acts do not define a book debt. The assignment of possible future refund from an insurance premium does not amount to a book debt: In re Brian Tucker (1989) 7 ILT Dig 259. See also In re Keenan Bros Ltd (1985) IR 40; In re Wogan's (Drogheda) Ltd (1993 SC) 11 ILT Dig 67. See Fealy in 11 ILT & SJ (1993) 133. See CHARGE, REGISTRATION OF.

**book of evidence.** The statements of evidence to be given at the trial of an accused and the list of the exhibits (qv); in a criminal trial by jury, the book of evidence must be served by the State on the accused: Criminal Procedure Act 1967 s.6. There is no requirement for the accused to disclose his defence except where he intends to raise the defence of *alibi* (qv). In an appeal, the book of evidence must not be given to the Court of Criminal Appeal (qv) as it may contain matters, highly prejudicial to the accused, which were not put in evidence at the trial: DPP v McKeever (1992 CCA) ITLR (24 Aug). See Gilligan v Director of Public Prosecutions (1987) HC; The People (DPP) v McGinley (1987 CCA) IR 342; The State (Daly) v Ruane (1988) ILRM 117. See also Criminal Evidence Act 1992 s.15(1). See DISCLOSURE IN CRIMINAL PROCEEDINGS.

**bookmaker, licensed.** A person (not being a body corporate or an unincorporated body of persons) who is the holder of a bookmaker's licence: Betting Act 1931 s.1. No person may carry on business or act as a bookmaker or hold himself out or represent himself as a bookmaker or a licensed bookmaker unless he holds a bookmaker's licence (ibid s.2). A person to whom a *certificate of fitness* has been given may apply to the Revenue Commissioners for a licence (ibid s.7); a person ordinarily resident in the State applies to a superintendent of the Garda Siochana for such certificate

(ibid s.4). An appeal against the refusal to issue a licence lies to the District Court which has a discretion to permit an objector to appear: Cashman v Clifford (1989) IR 121. See also The State (Ledwidge) v Bray D J (1944) IR 486; The State (Bambury) v Walsh (1977) HC; McDonnell v Reid (1987 HC) IR 51. See also Finance Act 1984 s.77. See TAX CLEARANCE CERTIFICATE; WAGERING CONTRACT.

**Bord Pleanala, An.** [The Planning Board]. The board consisting of a chairman and five ordinary members which hears and determines appeals made to it against the decision of a planning authority (qv) in relation to planning permission for the *development* of land: LG(P&D) Act 1976 ss.2 and 3 and LG(P&D) Act 1983 s.5. The chairman is appointed by the government (ibid 1983 Act s.5). The board has a duty to ensure that appeals are disposed of as expeditiously as may be and that there are no unavoidable delays; an objective of 4 months is specified for dealing with appeals: LG (P&D) Act 1992 s.2.

Any person may appeal to the board against the decision of a planning authority: LG (P&D) Act 1963 s.26(5) as amended by the 1992 Act s.3. The appeal must be made within one month beginning on the day of giving of the decision (ibid 1963 Act s.26(5)(f)). A person appealing to the board is entitled to rely on the date entered in the statutory register as the date upon which planning permission was granted, even though that entry is incorrect: Foley v Dublin Corporation (1990) HC — Irish Times 26/10/90.

The appeal must state in full the grounds of the appeal and the reasons, considerations and arguments on which they are based (ibid 1992 Act s.4), and any request for an oral hearing must be made at the outset of the appeal process (ibid 1992 Act s.12). Other parties to the appeal have one month to comment on the appeal (ibid 1992 Act ss.7-8).

The board must determine the application as if it had been made to them in the first instance and their decision operates to annul the decision of the planning authority (ibid 1963 Act s.26(5)(b)), except in the case of an appeal against conditions proposed to be attached to a planning permission or approval in which case the board may confine itself to considering the conditions only, rather than the original application *de novo* (ibid 1992 Act s.15). The Board in determining an appeal may take into account matters not raised by the parties to the appeal (ibid 1992 Act s.13).

The board has an absolute discretion as to whether they will hold an oral hearing (ibid 1992 Act s.12). Oral hearings are normally conducted by a person appointed by the board, who is known as an *inspector,* who is required to make a written report to the board which must include a recommendation on the matter (ibid 1976 Act s.23).

The board has other functions eg to confirm or annul a purchase notice (qv). See Killiney and Ballybrack Development Association v Minister for Local Government (1974) HC; Geraghty v Minister for Local Government (1976) IR 153; O'Keefe v An Bord Pleanala and Radio Tara (1992 SC) ILRM 237. See Kimber in 11 ILT & SJ (1993) 17. See PLANNING APPEAL, PROCEDURE.

**Bord Uchtala, An.** [The Adoption Board (qv)].

**border.** The abolition of certain intra-Community border controls from the creation of the Single Market is given legal effect by the European Communities (Abolition of Intra-Community Border Controls) Regulations 1993 (SI No 3 of 1993). See DUTY FREE; NORTHERN IRELAND.

**borough.** A town originally incorporated by royal charter with a common seal, the right to hold lands and to contract and to sue in the name of the *Mayor (or Lord Mayor), Aldermen and Burgesses of the Borough of* ..... The boroughs of Dublin, Cork, Limerick and Waterford were originally established by royal charter; their corporate existence was confirmed as were their titles: Municipal Corporations (Ireland) Act 1840 s.12. Each of these boroughs is deemed to be an administrative county of itself, called a *county borough,* with the powers and duties of county councils: Local Government (Ireland) Act 1898 s.21.

The county borough councils of Dublin, Limerick and Waterford are each known as the *city council* and that of Cork, the

*borough council*: Cork City Management Act 1929 s.1; Local Government (Dublin) Act 1930; Limerick City Management Act 1934; Waterford City Management Act 1939. Additional boroughs were created for Dun Laoghaire and Galway by the Local Government Act 1930 s.3 and Local Government (Galway) Act 1937 respectively; Galway achieved the status of a county borough by virtue of the Local Government (Reorganisation) Act 1985. See ALDERMAN; LORD MAYOR; LOCAL GOVERNMENT, REORGANISATION OF.

**borrowing.** A company may borrow money if expressly or impliedly authorised to do so by its *memorandum of association;* a trading company has an implied power to borrow as being incidental to the carrying on of its business. See In re Bansha Woolen Mills (1887) 21 LR Ir 181; Northern Bank Finance Corp v Quinn (1979) HC.

A building society with an "authorisation" may raise funds to be used for the objects of the society, by borrowing money: Building Societies Act 1989 s.18. [Text: Burgess UK].

**borstal.** See REFORMATORY SCHOOLS.

**bottomry.** A pledge of a ship and its freight as security for a loan of a sum of money. It is virtually obsolete in admiralty law. See ADMIRALTY ACTION.

**boundary alteration.** The boundary of any county, county or other borough, committee district, urban district or town may be altered by order of the Minister: Local Government Act 1991 s.31. There is provision in particular circumstances for an independent *boundary committee,* whose report the Minister must have regard to in making an order. A proposal from a local authority for a boundary alteration must be furnished to each local authority affected by the proposal; a decision subsequently to apply to the Minister for the making of an order is a reserved function (qv) of the authority (ibid s.29). See URBAN DISTRICT COUNCILS.

**boycott.** A concerted refusal to have anything to do with another person or his goods or services, so called after Captain Boycott in the land aggitation of the 1880's. An injunction may be obtained to restrain a boycott of a company: Talbot (Ireland) Ltd v Merrigan (1981) SC. There are provisions governing the boycotting of any person in relation to grocery goods: Restrictive Practices (Groceries) Order 1987 (SI No 142 of 1987) and Restrictive Practices (Confirmation of Order) Act 1987. See BELOW COST SELLING.

**brain death.** The term used in other jurisdictions to describe the death of a person when that person's brain has died, even though other organs of that person's body continue to function with mechanical or other assistance. In this State the concept of *brain death* has not been judicially determined or defined by statute, although one High Court judge has indicated that it was likely that the concept would be accepted by the courts if appropriate expert testimony established the validity of the criteria: Mr Justice Costello (1987). See also Costello J in "The Terminally Ill — The Law's Concerns": 21 Ir Jur (1986) 35. For position in UK law, see Airedale National Health Service Trust v Bland: The Times Law Report UK — 10th December 1992.

**breach.** The invasion or violation of a right, duty or law.

**breach of confidence.** See CONFIDENCE, BREACH OF; CONFIDENTIAL COMMUNICATIONS; TRADE SECRETS.

**breach of contract.** The refusal or failure by a party to a contract to fulfil an obligation imposed by the contract. The breach may occur: (a) by repudiation of his liability to perform; (b) by his own act disabling himself from performing the contract; or (c) by failing to fulfil all his obligations during his performance of the contract.

Breach entitles the injured party to bring an action for damages. It may also entitle him to treat the contract as discharged if the breach is of the entire contract or is of some term which is so vital that it goes to the root of the contract. See ANTICIPATORY BREACH; FUNDAMENTAL BREACH; REPUDIATORY BREACH.

**breach of duty.** See DUTY OF CARE.

**breach of promise.** An agreement between two persons to marry each other has no effect as a contract and no action may be brought in the State for a breach of such agreement, whatever the law applicable to the agreement: Family Law Act 1981 s.2. However, where one party has incurred expenditure of a substantial nature on behalf of the other party, the court may make such order as appears to it just and equitable in the circumstances (ibid s.7). See Courts Act 1991 s.13. See LRC 1 of 1981. See ENGAGED COUPLE.

**breach of statutory duty.** See STATUTORY DUTY.

**breach of the peace.** Minor offences against the public peace which are common law misdemeanours eg affray (qv), challenge to fight, and creating a public nuisance. Any act likely to cause reasonable alarm and apprehension to members of the public is a breach of the peace: Attorney General v Cunningham (1932) IR 28. See BINDING TO THE PEACE.

**breach of trust.** Some improper act, neglect or default of a trustee of which he is personally guilty; the measure of liability is the loss caused to the trust property: Trustee Act 1893 s.24. The trustee must replace misappropriated trust property with interest at 4%; if he has traded with the trust funds, the beneficiary can claim interest at 5% or the profits actually made.

In determining liability of a trustee for breach of trust, the court distinguishes between a breach of his duties, wherein utmost diligence is required (*exacta diligentia*), and a breach of a discretion, wherein he must act honestly and use the diligence of a prudent person.

A trustee is only liable for his own acts, but he must not sit passive while co-trustees commit a breach of trust. There are certain circumstances where one trustee must indemnify his co-trustees. A beneficiary may be required to indemnify a trustee where the breach takes place at the instigation of the beneficiary: Trustee Act 1893 s.45; Anketell Jones v Fitzgerald (1931) 65 ILTR 185. Property acquired in breach of a trust can become subject to the trust: Hortensius Ltd v Bishop (Trustees of TSB, Dublin) (1989 HC) ILRM 294.

A *certificate of conformity* issued to a bankrupt trustee does not relieve him of liability for a breach of trust. See Statute of Limitations 1957 ss.2(2), 43-44 and 71-72.

A "breach of trust" by an employee has been held to warrant his dismissal: Nolan v Assured Performance International Ltd (1990) ELR 172. See BENEFI-

CIARY, REMEDIES OF; FRAUDULENT CONVERSION; PLEADINGS; TRUST.

**break clause.** A clause in a lease, usually for a fixed term, conferring on the tenant an option to determine the lease before expiration of the term. Usually the option is made subject to various conditions eg that the tenant has complied with the terms of the lease up to the time of exercise of the option, or perhaps be confined to the happening of specified events (Watters v Creagh (1958) 92 ILTR 196). A break clause may also give the landlord a right to terminate a lease early eg in the event that the landlord gets planning permission for a development. [Text: Wylie (4)].

**breathalyser.** See BREATH ANALYSIS.

**breath analysis.** The analysis which a garda is permitted to carry out when he is of the opinion that a person in charge of a mechanically propelled vehicle in a public place has consumed intoxicating liquor; he is permitted to require the person to provide a specimen of his breath by exhaling into an apparatus for indicating (a) the concentration of alcohol in breath or blood or (b) the presence of alcohol in breath: Road Traffic (Amendment) Act 1978 s.12-15. Refusal or failure to comply forthwith with the requirement is an offence.

It is a good defence to that charge if no evidence is adduced to show that the garda had formed the necessary opinion, but it is not a defence to a charge of exceeding the limit: DPP v Brady (1991 HC) 1 IR 337. However, where the garda had a reasonable and genuine opinion, which is adduced in evidence, it is no defence to show that his opinion was wrong eg that the vehicle was not a "mechanically propelled vehicle": DPP v Breheny (1993 SC) ITLR (31 May). Also the garda, in requiring a person to submit to a breath test, does not have an obligation to inform the person of the particular statutory provision he is invoking: DPP v Gaughran (1993 HC) ILRM 472. See also Director of Public Prosecutions v Joyce (1985) ILRM 206; Dougal v Mahon (1989) 7 ILT Dig 229.

Under proposed draft legislation, (a) a new maximum permissible alcohol level of 35 microgrammes of alcohol per 100 millilitres of breath is to be introduced, (b) a person will be required to remain with a garda for up to an hour until a breath testing apparatus becomes available, (c) the category of persons obliged to give a breath specimen will be extended to include those arrested for dangerous driving or for taking a vehicle without authority, and (d) persons will be required to give two breath specimens: Road Traffic Bill 1993 ss.10, 12, 13. See DRUNKEN DRIVING; PUBLIC PLACE; ROAD TRAFFIC CHECKS; SANCTUARY.

**Brehon Laws.** The laws of Ireland which developed from before 250 AD until the 17th century when the common law (qv) of England was established throughout Ireland by proclamation of James I in 1606. The Brehon Laws were the laws of the clan (tribe), under the control of *brehons*, an hereditory caste of lawyers. The laws survived despite the arrival of the Danes in 790 AD and the Norman conquest. The Anglo-Norman nobles, who took the place of the Irish chieftains, chose to accommodate themselves to the lex loci, except in the Pale (a small district, the extent of which varied with the fortunes of war and rarely exceeded four of the present Leinster counties). Under the Brehon system, land belonged to the clan, although the private ownership of copyright was recognised in the celebrated case of Abbot Finnian v Columba (561 AD) with the famous maxim: *le gach bain a bainin, le gach leabhar a leabhran* — *to every cow its calf, to every book its copy*. See also Foyle and Bann Fisheries Ltd v Attorney General (1949) 83 ILTR 29. [Text: Ginnel; Kelly; Hogan & Osborough].

**brevi manu.** [A short cut].

**brewer, private.** A brewer of beer, not being a brewer for sale within the meaning of the Inland Revenue Act 1880 s.19. A private brewer is not required to take out a brewer's licence; the beer brewed is not liable to excise duty provided it is solely for his own domestic use: Finance Act 1989 s.51. It is an offence for a private brewer to brew beer otherwise than for his own domestic use or for any person to offer such beer for sale.

**bribe.** See SECRET PROFIT.

**bribery and corruption.** It is an indictable misdemeanor at common law corruptly to solicit, promise, give, receive or agree to receive a bribe (ie a reward) in order that any public official should either (a) act contrary to a duty he has to do something in which the public has an interest, or (b) show favour in the discharge of his duty and function. The offer of a bribe is an offence even though it is not accepted. See Prevention of Sale of Offices Act 1809; Public Bodies Corrupt Practices Act 1889; Prevention of Corruption Act 1906; Prevention of Corruption Act 1916. It is an offence to give valuable consideration to induce a voter to vote at a Dail election: Electoral Act 1992 s.135. See SECRET PROFIT.

**bridewell.** A prison.

**bridge.** The maintenance and construction of bridges is part of the duty of a local authority: Local Government Act 1925 ss.1 and 24. In certain cases, a local authority may require the consent of the Minister, by way of a *bridge order* eg where the rights of navigation may be affected or where a contribution to the expense from an adjoining local authority may be appropriate: Local Government Act 1946 s.48; Local Government Act 1955 s.40. See CIE v Carroll and Wexford County Council (1986) ILRM 312.

The National Roads Authority is empowered to direct a roads authority to make an application to the Minister for a bridge order under the 1946 Act: Roads Act 1993 s.20(1)(b). See also Roads Act 1993 s.51(7). See NAVIGATION, RIGHT TO.

**bridging loan.** Generally a short-term advance made by a bank to a customer pending his receipt of funds from another source or by a building society to a member pending completion of his mortgage. See Building Societies Act 1989 s.23. See UNSECURED LOANS.

**brief.** A concise statement. The written instructions furnished by a solicitor (qv) to a barrister (qv) to enable him to represent the client in legal proceedings. It usually contains a narrative of the facts; copies of material documents and correspondence; and the formal pleadings. Formerly, it was the practice for a solicitor to mark a fee on the brief. It has been held that this practice, which has fallen into disuse, had the merit that the solicitor focussed on the question of the appropriate fee for counsel, but that it was not the court's function to revive

the practice: Smyth v Tunney (1992 HC) 10 ILT Dig 267.

**British citizen.** A person who under the Act of the British Parliament entitled the British Nationality Act 1981 is an British citizen: Electoral Act 1992 s.8(7). Such a citizen is entitled to be registered as a Dail elector if resident in Ireland and has reached 18 years of age. The Minister is empowered to amend the definition of British citizen to accommodate any changes in British legislation governing citizenship (ibid s.8(4)(b)). See DAIL ELECTION.

**British statute.** An Act of the Parliament of the late United Kingdom of Great Britain and Ireland: Interpretation Act 1937, schedule, para 3. See LEGISLATION, CONSTITUTIONALITY OF; SAORSTAT EIREANN; STATUTE LAW.

**broadcast.** A broadcast by wireless telegraphy of communications, sounds, signs or visual images or signals, whether such are actually received or not: Broadcasting and Wireless Telegraphy Act 1988 s.1. It is an offence to make a broadcast from any premises or vehicle in the State unless made pursuant to and in accordance with a licence (ibid s.3).

It is also an offence to provide accommodation, equipment or programme material for unlicensed broadcasts, or to advertise by means of, or take part in broadcasts; the Minister is empowered to prohibit the provision of telephone or electricity services to premises in which illegal broadcasts are made (ibid 1988 Act). There is also a prohibition on the interception of services supplied by a licensee: Broadcasting Act 1990 ss.9 to 15.

Public sector broadcasting on radio and television is carried out by Radio Telefis Eireann and is regulated by the Broadcasting Authority Acts 1960 to 1979 and the Broadcasting Act 1990. Private sector broadcasting is carried out by sound broadcasting contractors under the Independent Radio and Television Commission (IRTC) pursuant to the 1988 and 1990 Acts. The 1988 Act provides also for a private sector national television service under contract to the IRTC.

The High Court decided not to interfere with a decision by RTE to refuse to accept an advertisement for a book of short stories written by the president of Sinn Fein: Brandon Books v RTE (1993 HC) — Irish Times 17/7/1993. See EQUALITY BEFORE THE LAW; INDEPENDENT TELEVISION PROGRAMME; RADIO AND TELEVISION COMMISSION.

**Broadcasting Complaints Commission.** The Commission established in 1976 to investigate and decide on complaints made to it by the public, provided the complaints fall within specified categories. The Commission has limited powers to provide relief. It must draw attention in its annual report, which is laid before the Houses of the Oireachtas, to any decision it has made which has not been accepted. RTE is required to broadcast the Commission's decisions where these decisions find in favour of the complainant, unless the Commission considers it inappropriate so to do. See Broadcasting Authority Act 1960 s.18 as inserted by the Broadcasting Authority (Amendment) Act 1976 s.4 and the Broadcasting Act 1990 s.8. The Minister may, by regulation, direct complaints in respect of independent radio and television to the Commission (Radio and Television Act 1988 ss.11 and 18) and has done so (SI No 329 of 1992).

**broker.** A merchantile agent for the purchase and sale of stocks and shares, goods, insurance policies etc. He is an agent primarily to establish privity of contract between two other parties. A broker cannot sue or be sued on a contract unless he signs a written memorandum with his own name. See INSURANCE BRO ᴀR; AGENT.

**brokerage.** Payment or commission paid to a broker for his services.

**brothel.** A place resorted to by persons of both sexes for the purposes of prostitution: Singleton v Ellison (1895) 1 QB 607. It is an offence to keep or manage a brothel, or to permit a premises to be used as a brothel: Criminal Justice (Sexual Offences) Act 1993 s.11. A search warrant may be issued by the District Court where there are reasonable grounds for suspecting that a premises is a brothel; a garda may demand the name and address of every person found on the premises during the search: Criminal Law Amendment Act 1935 s.19 amended by 1993 Act s.12, and 1993 Act s.13.

See also Childrens Act 1908 s.16 as amended by Criminal Law Amendment Act 1935 s.11. See DPP v Murphy (1993 CC) — Irish Times 6/2/1993.

**Brussels Convention.** Generally understood to mean the EC Convention on Jurisdiction and Enforcement of Judgments in Civil and Commercial Matters, given effect to by the Jurisdiction of Courts and Enforcement of Judgments (European Communities) Act 1988. See JURISDICTION; DEFENDANTS, JOINT; EXCLUSIVE JURISDICTION; FOREIGN JUDGMENTS, ENFORCEMENT OF; TORT.

**brutum fulmen.** [An empty threat]. See THREAT.

**budget.** An estimate of government expenditure and revenue for the ensuing year presented to Dail Eireann by the Minister for Finance. It includes proposals for taxes which are necessary to raise the revenue required. These proposals, if accepted, are enacted as the Finance Act for that year. See 1937 Constitution, art.28(4)(3). See FINANCIAL RESOLUTION.

**budgetry rules.** Rules in the economic area to ensure the monetary stability of the EC, which become progressively applicable as the member States move towards *economic and monetary union* (qv): Treaty of Rome 1957 arts.104-104c as replaced by Maastricht Treaty 1992 art.G(D)(25). The basic rules are: (a) no monetary financing eg by way of overdraft arrangements between governments and their central bank; (b) no bail-outs eg the EC will not step in to rescue a member State which defaults in its debt; (c) avoidance of excessive government deficits eg criteria are laid down (ibid art.104c and the Protocol on the Excessive Deficit Procedure). Non-compliance with the budgetry rules may lead to the imposition of sanctions.

**bug.** See PRIVACY.

**buggery.** Intercourse by penetration *per anum* upon a man, a woman, or an animal. It was a common law offence, the penalties for which were provided by the Offences against the Person Act 1861 ss.61-63. The European Court of Human Rights held in 1988 that the existence of legislation in Ireland penalising certain homosexual acts carried out in private by consenting adult males constituted a breach of rights under

Article 8 of the European Convention on Human Rights: Norris v Ireland (1988) EHRR. See also Attorney General v Troy 84 ILTR 193; Norris v Attorney General (1984 SC) IR 36.

In 1993, the crime of buggery between adult persons was abolished: Criminal Law (Sexual Offences) Act 1993 s.2. However, a person is guilty of an offence who commits or attempts to commit an act of buggery with a person under 17 years of age or a person who is mentally impaired of any age (unless married to the person) — (ibid ss.3 and 5). Also the crime of buggery with an animal (bestiality) has been retained. See BESTIALITY; MENTALLY IMPAIRED; SOLICIT.

**builder, duty of.** A builder owes a duty of care in relation to hidden defects not discoverable by the kind of examination he could expect a purchaser to make; he also has a duty to avoid dangerous defects and to avoid defects in the quality of the work: Ward v McMaster (1985) IR 29. Damages awarded may include economic loss, including the cost of alternative accommodation and a sum for inconvenience and discomfort. See Quill in 10 ILT & SJ (1992) 185 and 202.

**building, dangerous.** See FIRE SAFETY NOTICE; DANGEROUS STRUCTURE.

**building bye-laws.** The bye-laws which sanitary authorities were empowered to make with respect:- to the structure and description of the substances used in buildings; to the sites and foundations of houses, buildings and other erections; to the sufficiency of space; and to the drainage: Public Health (Ireland) Act 1878 s.41. Building bye-laws have been replaced by building regulations: Building Control Act 1990 s.22 (except para 1 of s.41 of the Public Health (Ireland) Act 1878). See BUILDING REGULATIONS.

**building contract.** See RIAI CONTRACT.

**building control.** See Fagan and Furlong in ILSI Gazette (May 1992) 137. See BUILDING BYE-LAWS; BUILDING REGULATIONS.

**building law.** See [Text: Keane D]. See ENGINEERING LAW.

**building construction.** In an action for infringement of copyright in respect of the construction of a building or any structure, no injunction may be made to prevent the building being completed after its construction has begun, or to require the building, in so far as it is constructed, to be demolished: Copyright Act 1963 s.22(5).

**building lease.** A lease of land, situated in an urban area, or else demised for a term of at least 20 years, on which permanent buildings, which were not merely ancillary and subsidiary improvements, were erected by the lessee at the time of erection or under an agreement for the grant of the lease on their erection: Landlord and Tenant (Reversionary Leases) Act 1958 s.4; Southern Health Board v Reeves Smith (1980) IR 26. A building lease (although not now referred to as such), entitled to acquire the fee simple, is entitled to a reversionary lease (qv): Landlord and Tenant (Amendment) Act 1980 s.30. See PROPRIETARY LEASE.

**building regulations.** The regulations which the Minister is empowered to make in relation to: (a) the design and construction of buildings, (b) material alterations or extensions of buildings; (c) the provision of services, fittings and equipment in, or in connection with, buildings, (d) buildings where a material change in use takes place: Building Control Act 1990 s.3. The purposes for which building regulations may be made include not only public health and safety but also provisions for the special needs of disabled persons, energy conservation, the efficient use of resources and the encouragement of good building practice.

Every building to which building regulations apply must be designed and constructed in accordance with the regulations (ibid s.3(5)). Certain local authorities are the building control authorities (ibid s.2) with powers to grant dispensations or relaxations of the regulations (ibid s.4), to inspect buildings (ibid s.11) and to serve *enforcement notices* (ibid s.8). There is provision for self regulation by way of *certificates of compliance* (ibid s.6(2)(a)(i)). A *fire safety certificate* from the building control authority is required in respect of buildings of a prescribed class (ibid s.6(2)(a)(ii)) and also a *certificate of approval* (ibid s.6(2)(a)(iii)) which indicates the opinion of the authority of compliance with the regulations. See Building Regulations 1991 (SI No 396 of 1991); Building Control Regulations

1991 (SI No 305 of 1991); Building Control (Amdt) Regulations 1993 (SI No 190 of 1993). The first conviction under the new regulations in believed to be Dublin Corporation v McCann (1993 DC) — Irish Times 9/8/1993. See BUILDING BYE-LAWS.

**building society.** A building society incorporated or deemed to be incorporated under the Building Societies Act 1989 (ibid s.2(1)). Originally, a building society was a body established with the sole purpose of raising funds for making loans to its members to enable them to build a home. Now, while a building society must have one of its objects the raising of funds for making *housing loans* (qv), it may also engage in a wide range of financial and other services, provided it *adopts* the power to do so and obtains the approval of the Central Bank eg auctioneering, conveyancing, financial, and services relating to land. Societies are *mutual* societies but they may de-mutualise by converting to a public limited company.

A building society is a body corporate (with the name contained in its memo-randum and rules) having perpetual succession and a seal (qv) and the power to hold land (ibid s.10(6)). A society must have a board of directors of at least 3 directors, a chairman, a chief executive and a secretary (ibid ss.48 and 49). [Text: Murdoch (2); Ovey & Waters (UK); Wartzburg & Mills (UK)]. See BANKER AND CONFIDENTIALITY; CONVERSION; CONVEYANCING SERVICES; CREDIT INSTITUTION; DERIVATIVE ACTION; INSURANCE; LINKING SERVICES; MORTGAGEE, RIGHT OF; OMBUDSMAN FOR THE CREDIT INSTITUTIONS; PRIOR MORTGAGE; REDEMPTION FEE; SAVINGS PROTECTION SCHEME; SHARE; TIERED INTEREST RATE; VALUATION REPORT.

**bull.** The term used to describe a person who buys stocks or shares with the intention of selling them at a higher price before the time for taking delivery of the shares. See BEAR.

**bulls, control of.** It is unlawful for a person to have in his possession an unregistered bull unless authorised by permit; a bull is an entire male of the bovine species over the the age of nine months. See Control of Bulls for Breeding Act 1985. See also SI Nos 333 and 334 of 1986; SI No 166 of 1990.

**Bunreacht na hEireann.** [Constitution of Ireland (qv)].

**burden.** An encumbrance or liability affecting the ownership of land. The title of a registered owner of *registered land* is subject to (a) the burdens which appear on the register as affecting the land: Registration of Title Act 1964 s.69; (b) the burdens, though not registered, which affect all registered land (ibid s.72); (c) unregistered rights, which are enforceable personally against the registered owner who created them and against a volunteer (qv) transferee from the registered owner, but are not enforceable against a registered transferee for value.

The ownership of registered burdens is itself registered in the *register of leaseholds* where the burden is a lease, and in the *subsidiary register* for other burdens; except that a charge (qv) is usually registered in the register of the land on which the charge is a burden. See CAUTION; INHIBITIONS.

**burden of proof.** The obligation of proving facts. The obligation, in the sense of establishing a case, generally rests on the party who asserts the affirmative of the issue and it does not shift, being fixed at the beginning of the case eg in a criminal case, the burden of proving the guilt of the accused rests on the prosecution; in a negligence case, the onus of proving negligence rests on the plaintiff and of proving contributory negligence (qv) rests on the defendant.

The burden of proof, in the sense of adducing evidence, rests on the party who would fail if no evidence at all, or no more evidence, as the case may be, were given on either side. This burden will rest on the party substantially asserting the affirmative of the issue at the start of the case, but as evidence is presented, the burden may shift con-stantly throughout the case. The burden may shift because of the evidence, but also because of presumptions (qv) of the law, or statutory requirements which sometimes put proof of authority, consent or lawful excuse on the accused (eg Larceny Act 1916; Road Traffic Act 1961 s. 38) or which put the onus of proof on the defendant (eg on an employer to justify a dismissal: Unfair Dismissal Act 1977). See also Abbey

Films v Attorney General (1981) IR 158. See PROOF; RES IPSA LOQUITUR.

**burgess.** Formerly, a special class of urban tenant who owed suit to the *hundred*, a court composed of fellow burgesses. Formerly, the council of any borough was empowered to elect any person, except a convicted felon, to be an honorary burgess of such borough: Municipal Privileges (Ireland) Act 1896 ss.11-12; LG (Repeal of Enactments) Act 1956 s.1, sch. The 1896 Act is now repealed and the power is replaced with a power to confer a *civic honour*: Local Government Act 1991 ss.4, 48 and sch. See Lyons v Fitzgerald (1825) Sm & Bat 405. See BOROUGH; CIVIC HONOUR.

**burglary.** The offence committed by a person who enters any *building* or part of a building as a trespasser and with intent to steal, or to inflict grievous bodily harm, or to rape or to do unlawful damage to the building: Criminal Law (Jurisdiction) Act 1976 s.6. It is also a burglary where the person having entered the building, steals or attempts to steal anything in the building, or inflicts or attempts to inflict on any person therein any grievous bodily harm. *Building* includes an inhabited vehicle or vessel. See NIGHT; POSSESSION AND CRIME

**burglary, aggravated.** The offence committed by a person who commits any burglary (qv) and at the time he *has with him* any firearm or imitation firearm or any *weapon of offence* or any explosive: Larceny Act 1916 s.23B as inserted by the Criminal Law (Jurisdiction) Act 1976 s.7. A knife is an offensive weapon: The People (Attorney General) v O'Brien (1969) (CCA) 103 ILTR 109. The physical presence of the accused on or about the premises at which the burglary occurred is not required for him to be treated as a principal offender: DPP v O'Reilly (1991 HC) 1 IR 77.

**burial grounds.** Land used for the burial of persons which may be vested in the legal incumbent of the parish or in the sanitary authority of the district as the *burial board* for such district: Representative Church Body v Crawford and Crawford v Bradley 74 ILTR 49; Public Health (Ireland) Act 1878 ss.160, 161, 174, 175. There are restrictions on the places in which a body may be buried; it is an offence to bury a body in a place which is not a burial ground: Local Government (Sanitary Services) Act 1948 s.44. Joint burial boards can be set up (ibid ss.12-13) and they have power to acquire land compulsorily: Local Government (Sanitary Services) (Joint Burial Boards) Act 1952. The Minister is empowered to make regulations in relation to the disposal of human remains otherwise than by burial eg by cremation (ibid 1948 Act s.47). Also a health board may arrange for the burial of a person who dies in an institution from an infectious disease: Health Act 1947 s.39 and Infectious Diseases Regulations 1981 art.12 (SI No 390 of 1981). See McCarthy v Johnson (1989 SC) ILRM 706. See EXHUMATION.

**bus.** See OMNIBUS.

**business.** (1) "Almost anything which is an occupation as distinguished from a pleasure — anything which is an occupation or duty which requires attention as a business": Rolls v Miller (1884) 27 Ch D 88 followed in AE v Revenue Commissioners (1984) ILRM 301. (2) Any trade, profession or vocation: Finance Act 1989 s.86. [Text: Sheeran].

**business associate.** A person who provides relevant services to a building society eg conveyancing, advertising, public relations: Building Societies Act 1989 s.60. There are disclosure requirements regarding the fees paid to a business associate who is also an officer of the society.

**business development scheme.** The scheme whereby *qualified individuals* may claim tax relief for amounts subscribed for *eligible shares* in a *qualifying company*, which shares have been issued for the purpose of raising money for a *qualifying trade*: Finance Acts 1984 ss.11-27; 1986 s.13; 1987 ss.8-12; 1988 s.7. The shares must be new ordinary shares and they must not, for a period of five years from issue, carry any *preferential* right to receive dividends or to share in the company's assets on its winding up, or to be redeemed.

The shares must also be retained by the individual for more than five years from the date of issue. Extensions and restrictions on the scheme were made by Finance Acts — 1989 s.9; 1990 s.10; 1991 ss.14-17; 1993 ss.25-27. [Text:

Judge].

**business efficacy test.** The test which may imply a term in a contract so as to give the contract the efficacy which both parties must have intended. See The Moorcock (1889) 14 PD 64; Tridax (Ireland) Ltd v Irish Grain Board Ltd (1984) IR 1.

**business name.** The name or style under which any business is carried on, and in relation to a newspaper, includes the title of the newspaper: Registration of Business Names Act 1963 s.2. This Act requires registration of such name in the case of (1) every individual or body corporate carrying on business under a name which does not consist of his true surname or corporate name respectively, and (2) every person carrying on business of publishing a newspaper (ibid s.3).

The Minister may refuse to permit the registration of any name which in his opinion is undesireable (ibid s.14). The certificate of registration must be exhibited in a conspicuous position (ibid s.8). An index of business names is maintained at the Companies Office at Dublin Castle which may be inspected by any person (ibid ss.13 and 16). See SI No 100 of 1987; RSC O.100.

It is an offence for a bankrupt (qv) or an arranging debtor (qv), without disclosure, to engage in any trade or business under a different name to that under which he was adjudicated a bankrupt or was granted protection: Bankruptcy Act 1988 s.129(b). See NAME OF COMPANY; NAME, CHANGE OF.

**business tenant.** The tenant of a *tenement* (qv). The rights of *business* tenants have been extended as regards alienation of their interest, as to improvement and change of use of the leased premises, as to acquiring a new tenancy and to compensation for disturbance and improvements: Landlord and Tenant (Amendment) Act 1980.

The tenant of a tenement has a right, subject to certain exceptions, to a new tenancy: (a) where the tenement was for three years continuously occupied by the tenant or his predecessors in title and bona fide used wholly or partly for the purpose of carrying on a *business*; a temporary break may be disregarded by the court if it considers it reasonable so to do; or (b) where the tenement was for

the previous 20 years continuously in the occupation of the tenant or of his predecessors in title; or (c) where improvements have been made on the tenement that they account for not less than half of the letting value of the tenement (ibid s.13(1)).

*Business* includes trade, profession or business, whether or not carried on for gain or reward, and any activity for providing cultural, social or sporting services, for the public service, or for carrying out the functions of local authorities, health boards and harbour authorities.

An indirect attempt to avoid the provisions of the 1980 Act will fail: Bank of Ireland v Fitzmaurice (1989) ILRM 452. The 1980 Act is restricted in its application to certain tenements in the Custom House Docks Area: Landlord and Tenant (Amendment) Act 1989. It also does not apply to a house leased under a shared ownership lease (qv) or to a house let by voluntary housing bodies: Housing (Miscellaneous Provisions) Act 1992 s.32. See also Gatien Motor Co Ltd v The Continental Oil Co of Ireland (1979) IR 406; Irish Shell v John Costello Ltd (1981) ILRM 66; OHS Ltd v Green Property Co Ltd (1986) ILRM 451; Mealiffe v Walsh (1987) ILRM 301. See IMPROVEMENTS, COMPENSATION FOR; DISTURBANCE, COMPENSATION FOR.

**busway.** A public road (qv) or proposed public road specified to be a busway in a *busway scheme* approved by the Minister: Roads Act 1993 s.2(1) and 44. There is a prohibition on the use of a busway by pedestrians or pedal cyclists, and persons must not permit animals to be on a busway (ibid s.44(4)). There is no right of direct access to a busway from land adjoining it and no such right may be granted (ibid s.44(2)); this includes a prohibition on the granting of planning permission which would involve direct access (ibid s.46). The Minister may prescribe the classes of vehicles which may use a busway (ibid s.44(3)).

A road authority may submit a busway scheme to the Minister, having first notified the public and affected land owners/occupiers (ibid s.48). The Minister, before approving a scheme, must cause a public local inquiry to be held, must consider any objections, and the report and recommendations of the person conducting the inquiry (ibid s.49). The road authority is required to prepare an environmental impact statement on the construction of the busway (ibid s.50).

Similar provisions apply regarding compulsory purchase, compensation for disturbance and loss, and alternative access for adjoining landowners/occupiers as for a motorway scheme. See MOTORWAY.

**buyer.** A person who buys or agrees to buy goods: Sale of Goods Act 1893 s.62. The remedies available to a buyer include damages for non delivery of the goods, an order for specific performance of the contract, and damages for breach of warranty (ibid ss.51-53). Certain statements purporting to restrict the rights of buyers are prohibited: SGSS Act 1980 s.11.

**bye-election.** An election of a member of Dail Eireann (qv) to fill a vacancy occasioned by a person having ceased to be a member of the Dail otherwise than in consequence of a dissolution: Electoral Act 1992 s.2(1). A writ for a bye-election must be issued by the Clerk of the Dail to the returning officer when he has been directed to do so by the Chairman of the Dail; the Chairman must do so when directed by the Dail (ibid s.39(2)). A member of the Dail, while still holding his seat, cannot be a candidate at a bye-election (ibid s.43).

The High Court has refused to order that bye-elections be held to fill two vacant Dail seats as to do so would be to interfere in the functions of the executive: Grimes v Ireland (1993 HC) — Irish Times 27/6/1993. See SEPARATION OF POWERS.

**bye-law.** *An ordinance affecting the public or some portion of the public imposed by some authority clothed with statutory powers, ordering something to be done or not to be done and accompanied by some sanction or penalty for its non- observance ... it has the force of law within the sphere of its legitimate operation*: Kruse v Johnson (1898) 2 QB 91. A bye-law must be reasonable: Dun Laoghaire Corporation v Brock (1952) Ir Jur Rep 37. It must not be repugnant to the general law; it can add to that law but cannot make lawful an act already made

unlawful or vice versa. Local authorities are empowered to make bye-laws under a number of statutes eg Municipal Corporations (Ireland) Act 1840 ss.125-127; Local Government (Ireland) Act 1898 s.16; Public Health (Ireland) Act 1878 s.41. Bye-laws may be deemed to be statutory instruments (qv): Statutory Instruments Act 1947 ss.1(1), 2(1)(b)(v) and (c)(i). Some bye-laws must be laid before the Oireachtas eg those made under Blascaod Mor National Historic Park Act 1989. See BUILDING BYE-LAWS.

# C

©. [Copyright]. The symbol which some foreign countries require to be on all published copies of a work, accompanied by the name of the copyright proprietor and the year date of first publication, in order to provide copyright protection to that work. For books, the copyright notice must appear on the title page or verso thereof. For periodicals, the notice must appear on the title page, the first page of text, or under the title heading. It is a requirement of the Universal Copyright Convention (qv).

**cabinet.** Popularly understood to mean the government (qv) but not named as such in the 1937 Constitution. The government is the executive organ of the State. See AG v The Sole Member of the Beef Tribunal (1993 SC) ILRM 81. See COLLECTIVE RESPONSIBILITY; CONFIDENCE, BREACH OF.

**cabotage.** [Coasting-trade]. A *cabotage authorisation* allows a haulier to carry goods from one point to another within any of the other eleven member states of the EC; applicants must hold an *international road freight carrier's licence* as provided for by the Road Transport Act 1986. See CARRIER'S LICENCE.

**cadit quaestio.** [The matter admits of no further argument].

**caeteris paribus.** [Other things being equal]. See CETERIS PARIBUS.

**caeterorum.** [Rest]. A *grant caeterorum* is a grant of representation in respect of the rest of the property of a deceased made to the person so entitled, where a grant of part only of the estate (*save and* *except*) has already been made. See PROBATE.

**call.** A demand on the holder of partly paid-up shares in a company for payment of the balance or part thereof. Companies whose articles of association so provide are allowed to differentiate between shareholders in the amounts of, and times for, paying calls, and to accept payments of unpaid amounts although they have not been called up: Companies Act 1963 s.66. See also: ibid Table A, art 15; RSC 0.74 rr 92-94. See Blackstaff Flax Spinning Weaving Co v Cameron (1899) 1 IR 252. See OPTION.

**call to the Bar.** The formal ceremony whereby a member of the Honourable Society of King's Inns is admitted to take his place in court and to practice. See BARRISTER.

**camera, in.** See IN CAMERA.

**camping.** The occupier of land cannot use it or permit it to be used for camping, on more than eighteen consecutive days, or thirty-six days within a period of twelve consecutive months, without a licence from the sanitary authority and in accordance with the terms of that licence: Local Government (Sanitary Services) Act 1948 s.34.

**canals.** Ownership and responsibility for the Grand Canal and Royal Canal was transferred from CIE to the Commissioners for Public Works by the Canals Act 1986. It is the duty of the Commissioners to undertake the care, management and maintenance of the canals. The Commissioners are empowered to make bye-laws (qv) (ibid s.7 and SI No 247 of 1988).

**cancellation.** The act of nullifying or invalidating an instrument eg by drawing lines across it with the intention of depriving it of its effect. For cancellation of a will, see WILL, REVOCATION OF.

**candour, lack of.** See CERTIORARI.

**cannabis.** The flowering or fruiting tops of any plant of the genus cannabis from which the resin has not been extracted, by whatever name they may be designated; *cannabis resin* means the separated resin, whether crude or purified obtained from any plant of the genus cannabis: Misuse of Drugs Act 1977 s.1; any plant of the genus *cannabis* or any part of such plant: Misuse of Drugs Act 1984 s.2. Every person who cultivates opium poppy or a plant of the genus cannabis, except in accordance with a licence issued in that behalf by the Minister, is guilty of an offence (ibid s.17). See also s.19. See DRUGS, MISUSE OF.

**canon.** A rule of canon or ecclesiastical law. Sometimes used to mean a rule of the ordinary law eg the canons of descent; canons of construction.

**canon law.** The basic law of the Roman Catholic Church. It was codified in 1917 under Benedict XV. As regards the incardination (qv) of a curate under Canon 114 of the 1917 Code, the powers of a curate are not inherent in his office: Buckley v Cathal Daly (1991 NI HC) ITLR (7 Jan). See FOREIGN LAW.

**canons of descent.** See DESCENT.

**canvassing.** It is an offence to canvass voters at an election in any place within 100 meters of a polling station; included in the prohibition is loitering or congregating with other persons, displaying or distributing election literature, inducing an elector to vote or not to vote, or using any loudspeaker or public address system: Electoral Act 1992 s.147. In certain circumstances it is an offence for an employee of a building society to solicit support for a candidate for election as a director of the society: Building Societies Act 1989 s.51(8).

**capacity of child in criminal law.** See DOLI INCAPAX.

**capacity to contract.** The legal competency, power or fitness to enter and be bound by a contract. Generally a *minor* (qv) lacks contractual capacity. However an infant (ie a minor) or a person who by reason of mental incapacity or drunkeness is incompetent to contract, must pay a reasonable price for *necessaries* which are sold and delivered to him. Necessaries means goods suitable to the condition in life of such minor or other person, and to his actual requirements at the time of sale and delivery. See Sale of Goods Act 1893 s.2. See Ryder v Wombwell (1867) LR 4 Ex 32; Davies v Beynon-Harris (1931) 47 TLR 424; Coutts & Co v Browne-Lecky (1947) KB 104. See MINOR; INSANE PERSON; DRUNKEN PERSON.

**capias.** [That you take].

**capita.** [Heads]. See PER CAPITA.

**capital.** The capital of a company is the amount of principal with which the company is formed to carry on business. The memorandum of association (qv) of a limited company with a share capital must state the amount of the share capital and the division of it into shares of a fixed amount: Companies Act 1963 s.6(4). This share capital is said to be the *nominal* or *authorised* capital ie the aggregate par value of shares the company is authorised to issue to its members. The *issued* or *allotted* capital is the total amount of capital issued in shares to members. It is prohibited to allot shares at less than their par value. Frequently, shares are issued at a premium (qv).

The *paid up* capital of a company is the amount in money or money's worth which has been paid to the company in return for shares allotted by it; it is the aggregate of the shares that have been allotted together with the total of any premiums paid on them. The *called-up* capital is the amount paid to a company where it does not require the entire amount to be paid over to it immediately; the *uncalled* capital is the remainder of such partly paid shares. The *reserve* capital is the portion of the uncalled capital which the company has by special resolution determined will not be called up except in the event of the company being wound up. *Working* capital is understood to mean the amount of money necessary for the company to trade or carry on business.

A public limited company (plc) must have a minimum authorised capital of £30,000: Companies (Amendment) Act 1983 ss.5(2), 17(1), 19(1). See REDUCTION OF CAPITAL; SHARES; UNDERSUBSCRIBED.

**capital, serious loss of.** Where the *net assets* of a registered company, public or private, are half or less of the amount of the company's called-up share capital; net assets are aggregate assets less total liabilities. When this fact is known to a director, there is an obligation within 28 days to convene an extraordinary general meeting of the company for the purpose of considering whether any, and if so what, measures are to be taken to deal with the situation. See Companies (Amendment) Act 1983 s.40.

**capital acquisitions tax; CAT.** A tax on gifts *inter vivos* (ie taken during the donor's lifetime) and on *inheritances* (ie taken following the disponer's death):

Capital Acquisitions Tax Act 1976 as amended by annual Finance Acts.

There are tax free *threshold amounts* which vary depending on the relationship between the donee (or successor) and the donor (or disponer) eg the highest class threshold applies in the case of a spouse or child. Inheritances, but not gifts, taken by one spouse from another on or after 30th January 1985 are exempt from CAT.

There are specific provisions for *deserving* nephews and nieces, for successive gifts in one or more than one class, and relief for agricultural property. The value of gifts or inheritances comprising property outside the State may be liable for CAT. Future interests (qv) are liable to CAT only when the person becomes entitled to possession of the gift or inheritance. The value of a limited interest (eg a life interest) is calculated from actuarial tables. [Text: Bale & Condon].

**capital at risk.** As regards life insurance, the amount payable on death less the mathematical reserve in respect of the relevant contracts: European Communities (Life Assurance) Regulations 1984 (SI No 57 of 1984).

**capital gains tax.** A tax payable on the gains made on the disposal of an asset: Capital Gains Tax Act 1975; Capital Gains Tax (Amendment) Act 1978; as amended by annual Finance Acts. Disposal includes sales, gifts and the transfer of assets into a *settlement*. Some gains are exempt eg the sale of a private residence, including grounds of up to one acre, which has been used as the main residence throughout the period of ownership.

There is provision for *indexation*, ie an adjustment is made for inflation as measured by the *consumer price index* in calculating the chargeable gain. There are also special reliefs eg on the disposal of a business or farm within the family or on retirement. The sale of shares of the same class in a company are deemed to be on a *first in first out* basis, ie the shares held longest are deemed to be the ones sold. Capital gains tax has been brought within the self-assessment system: Finance Act 1991 ss.45-53. See Multiplier (1993–1994) Regulations 1993 (SI No 184 of 1993). [Text: Appleby &

Roche]. See BED AND BREAKFAST; VALUA-TION.

**capital liberalisation.** The prohibition on restrictions on the movement of capital and payments between member States of the EC: Treaty of Rome 1957 arts.73a-73h inserted by Maastricht Treaty 1992 art.G(D)(15). Capital liberalisation also affects movement of capital and payments between member States and third countries as from 1 January 1994. The rights of member States however are not prejudiced in relation to taxation, to prudential supervision of financial institutions, or to issues of public policy or public security. See EXCHANGE CONTROL.

**capital money.** Money arising by way of exercise of the powers given by the Settled Land Acts 1882 and 1890. See SETTLEMENT.

**capital murder.** Formerly was the murder of a member of the Garda Siochana or a prison officer acting in the course of his duty; or murder done in the course or furtherance of specified offences created by The Offences Against the State Act 1939; or murder committed within the State for a political motive of the head of a foreign State or of a member of its government or of its diplomatic officer; or the commission by a person subject to military law of a number of offences created by the Defence Act 1954: Criminal Justice Act 1964 s.1. Now, with the abolition of the death penalty, capital murder is replaced by the offence of *aggravated murder*: Criminal Justice Act 1990 s.3.

The death penalty was mandatory in a conviction of capital murder: 1964 Act s.3(2). See also The People (DPP) v Murray (1977) IR 360. See MURDER; MURDER, AGGRAVATED; PARDON.

**capital punishment.** Death by hanging (qv). Commutation or remission of capital punishment is vested solely in the President of Ireland: 1937 Constitution art 13.6. However, the death penalty has now been abolished. See DEATH PENALTY; HANGING.

**capital reconstruction.** Changes to the share capital clause of the memorandum of association may be made in general meeting by a company, provided that the articles of association (qv) authorise the changes: Companies Act 1963 ss.68-70. It may increase its share capital by the issue of new shares; consolidate its shares into ones of larger amounts; convert any paid up shares into stock; reconvert stock into shares; and subdivide any of its shares into smaller amounts.

However a proposed reduction of capital must be approved by special resolution of the members, by creditors and by the court (ibid ss.72-77 as amended by the Companies Act 1990 s.231(c); RSC 0.75 r.17). Accounting rules have been prescribed to prohibit paying dividends from capital: Companies (Amendment) Act 1983, Part 1V, ss.45-51 as amended by Companies Acts 1986 s.20 and 1990 s.232(d).

Any limited company having a share capital is prohibited from acquiring its own shares, whether by purchase, subscription or otherwise; there are some important exceptions eg redemption of preference shares or redeemable shares, forfeiture of shares, or authorised capital reduction (ibid 1983 Act s.41 as amended by 1990 Act s.232(a)). Also a limited company may acquire its own fully paid shares otherwise than for valuable consideration (ibid 1983 Act s.41(2)). See In re Irish Provident Assurance Co (1913) IR 352. See CLASS RIGHTS; REDEEMABLE SHARES; REDUCTION OF CAPITAL; SHARES; STOCK; SURPLUS ASSETS.

**caption.** The formal heading of a legal instrument.

**carat.** A measure to denote the fineness of gold; pure gold is said to be 24 carats fine. See HALLMARKING.

**caravan.** Any structure designed or adapted for human habitation which is capable of being moved from one place to another, whether by towing or transport on a vehicle or trailer, and includes a motor vehicle so designed or adapted and a mobile home, but does not include a tent: Housing Act 1988 s.13 (b). A housing authority is empowered to provide, improve, manage and control sites for caravans used by persons belonging to the class of persons who traditionally pursue or have pursued a nomadic way of life ie travellers (ibid s.13).

It is an offence to place a caravan on a public road, without lawful authority or consent, for the purposes of advertising, the sale of goods, the provision of services, or other similar purpose; the caravan may be removed by an authorised person: Roads Act 1993 s.71. See also TRAVELLER.

**carcinogens.** Employers are required to carry out an assessment of the risks to workers' health posed by the use of carcinogens in the workplace and to take steps to reduce or eliminate such risks: Council Directive 90/394/EEC implemented by Safety, Health and Welfare at Work (Carcinogens) Regulations 1993 (SI No 80 of 1993).

**care, duty of.** See DUTY OF CARE.

**care of child.** See CHILD, CARE OF.

**care order.** An order which the District Court is empowered to make, committing a child (qv) to the care of a health board (qv) for so long as he remains a child or for such shorter period as the court may determine: Child Care Act 1991 s.18. The effect of a *care order* is to suspend the parent's right to custody of the child and to place him in the control of the health board as if it were his parent (ibid s.18(3)(a)). A health board has a duty to apply for a care order or supervision order (qv) in respect of a child who requires care or protection (ibid s.16).

The court may make a care order when it is satisfied that the child requires care or protection which he is unlikely to receive unless a care order is made and that: (a) the child has been or is being assaulted, ill-treated, neglected or sexually abused, or (b) the child's health, development or welfare has been or is being avoidably impaired or neglected, or (c) the child's health, development or welfare is likely to be avoidable impaired or neglected (ibid s.18(1)).

The court is required to have regard to the rights and duties of the parents, whether under the 1937 Constitution or otherwise, but must regard the welfare of the child as the first and paramount consideration and must give due consideration, in so far as is practical, to the wishes of the child (ibid s.24). A care order ceases to have effect where the child becomes adopted (ibid s.44(2)). There is also provision for the court to make an *interim care order* (ibid s.17), an *emergency care order* (ibid s.13) or a *supervision order* (qv). See AFTERCARE; CHILD, EMERGENCY CARE OF; CHILD, CARE OF; WARD OF COURT; WELFARE OF CHILDREN.

**careless driving.** The offence committed by a person who drives a vehicle in a public place (qv) without due care and attention: Road Traffic Act 1961 s.52 as substituted by Road Traffic Act 1968 s.50. Where a person is tried on indictment (qv) or summarily for the offence of *dangerous driving* (qv) and the jury (or the court in a summary trial) is of the opinion that he was not guilty of that offence, he may be found guilty of the offence of careless driving. An acquittal on a charge of dangerous driving affords a *plea in bar* to a charge of careless driving, arising out of the same facts: Attorney General v Power (1964) IR 458. Endorsement on the defendant's licence is mandatory in the event of a third conviction: DPP v O'Brien (1989) 7ILT Dig 260. See also The People (Attorney General) v O'Neill (1964) Ir Jur Rep 1; The Queen v Megaw (1993 C of A NI) ITLR (1 Feb).

**carer.** A person who resides with and provides full-time care and attention to a *relevant pensioner*, ie a person who is so incapacitated as to require full-time care and attention: Social Welfare Acts 1990 s.17, 1991 s.8 and 1992 s.36. An allowance is payable to a carer.

**caretaker.** A person who has been put into possession of any lands or premises by the owner thereof and who agrees to give up possession when requested by the landlord. So long as the relationship of caretaker exists, the caretaker cannot acquire a title under the Statute of Limitations: Musgrave v McAvey (1907) 41 ILTR 230. A caretaker is estopped from disputing or disclaiming his landlord's title: Gowrie Park Utility Society Ltd v Fitzgerald (1963) IR 436. See also Deasy's Act 1860 s.86.

**carnal knowledge, unlawful.** The offence of sexual intercourse with a female under the age of fifteen years which is a felony (qv); or with a female over the age of fifteen and under the age of seventeen, which is a misdemeanour: Criminal Law Amendment Act 1935 ss.1-3. These offences are *statutory rape* in that intercourse is essential to constitute the offence but the element of consent is removed. There cannot be a conviction of rape and unlawful carnal knowledge in relation to the same incident: The People (Attorney General) v Dermody (1956) IR 307.

To prove carnal knowledge it is not necessary "to prove the actual emission of seed in order to constitute a carnal knowledge, but the carnal knowledge shall be deemed complete upon proof of penetration only": Offences against the Person Act 1861 s.63. It is also an offence for a person to have *sexual intercourse* with a person who is mentally impaired (qv); sexual intercourse is construed as a reference to carnal knowledge as defined in the 1861 Act s.63: Criminal Law (Sexual Offences) Act 1993 ss.1(3) and 5(1). See SEXUAL INTERCOURSE; SEXUAL OFFENCES.

**carriage by rail.** See LIABILITY, STATUTORY EXEMPTION FROM; CMR.

**carriage by sea.** Liability for carriage of passengers and goods by sea is governed by the common law rules as amended by the Merchant Shipping Act 1894. Liability is limited by the tonnage of the ship (ibid s.503) and the shipowner escapes liability in certain other cases eg in respect of gold, silver, watches or jewels lost by robbery where their value has not been declared (ibid. s.502). See PASSENGER BOAT; PASSENGER SHIP; CARRIER.

**carriage contracts.** See LIABILITY, STATUTORY EXEMPTION FROM.

**carriage of goods.** See CMR.

**carriage of passengers.** See INTERNATIONAL CARRIAGE OF PASSENGERS.

**carrier.** A person who carries goods for reward. A carrier is either a *private* carrier (a bailee for reward) or a *common* carrier (qv). A licence is not required for a person to carry his own goods, or to deliver goods supplied by him to a customer in the course of his business, or to deliver goods repaired, cleaned, laundered or dyed by him. See Dangerous Substances Act 1972 s.51. [Text: Chitty UK; Clarke UK]. See CARRIER'S LICENCE.

**carrier, common.** A person who holds himself out to the public, expressly or by conduct, as ready and willing to carry all goods of a certain kind, offered to him for carriage to and from specified places for reward. At common law, a common carrier is bound to carry between the places he professes to carry, all goods offered to him in respect of which he professes to carry; to deliver the goods within a reasonable time; to

be an insurer of the goods entrusted to him while *in transit* except caused by an Act of God, the consignor's fault, or an inherent defect in the goods carried. The carrier has a lien (qv) on the goods carried for the cost of carriage.

A common carrier by land is not liable for loss or injury to certain articles contained in a package delivered to him for carriage when the value of the package exceeds £10 unless the nature and value is declared and any increased charge paid which the carrier may demand: Carriers Act 1830 s.1; Transport Act 1944 s.87(1) sch.9. The articles specified include gold or silver articles, precious stones, jewellery, clocks, bank notes or securities, stamps, maps, title deeds, engravings, pictures, glass, china or furs. A carrier may make a special contract with the consignor (ibid s.6). See Belfast Ropework Co v Bushell (1918) 1 KB 210. See CARRIER'S LICENCE; CONSIGNMENT.

**carrier, delivery of goods to.** Delivery of goods to a carrier, whether named by the buyer or not, for the purpose of transmission to the buyer, is prima facie deemed to be delivery of the goods to the buyer: Sale of Goods Act 1893 s.32. If the carrier is the agent of the seller, delivery to the carrier is not deemed to be delivery to the buyer. The seller is obligated to make a contract with the carrier on behalf of the buyer as may be reasonable having regard to the nature of the goods and the other circumstances of the case; if the seller omits to do so and the goods are lost or damaged in the course of transit, the buyer may decline to treat delivery to the carrier as a delivery to himself, or hold the seller responsible in damages (ibid s.32(2)). See Michel Freres Societe Anonyme v Kilkenny Woolen Mills Ltd (1959) IR 157; Spicer-Cowan Ireland Ltd v Play Print Ltd (1980) HC.

**carrier, private.** A carrier who is not a common carrier (qv) ie he does not hold himself out as ready and willing to carry for all persons without discrimination, either all goods or certain classes of goods; he is free to enter into such transactions as he so wishes. He is liable at common law for his negligence. See Barnfield v Goole and Sheffield Transport Co (1910) 2 KB 94. See also

Transport Act 1958 s.8(8); SI No 133 of 1974 reg.3; Transport (Reorganisation of Coras Iompair Eireann) Act 1986. See CARRIER'S LICENCE; PASSENGER ROAD SERVICE.

**carrier's licence.** A merchandise licence which is required to carry on a merchandise road transport business; a national road freight licence or an international road freight licence: Road Transport Act 1986 s.1. This Act had as its objective the removal of all *quantity* control on licences over a two year period, after which time, licences for road haulage operations will be available for all applicants who satisfy the *quality* requirements of the European Communities (Merchandise Road Transport) Regulations 1977 (SI No 386 of 1977). See Twomey v Minister for Transport (1989) 7 ILT Dig 24.

A *national* licence qualifies the holder to carry on a merchandise road transport business in the State with such vehicles as may be specified in the licence; an *international* licence similarly qualifies the holder for business either inside or outside the State (ibid 1986 Act s.4).

A merchandise licence may be revoked by the Minister but in so doing he must have regard for the requirements of natural justice (ibid s.5). Carriage of goods is permitted in hired, rented or leased vehicles provided they are so hired without a driver (ibid s.9). There is provision for the appointment of transport officers by the Minister (ibid ss.15-16). See European Communities (Merchandise Road Transport) Regulations 1988 (SI No 180 & 211 of 1988). See EC Directive 74/ 561/EEC. See also Road Transport Acts 1933–1978. See CABOTAGE.

**carrier's lien.** The common law lien (qv) by which a carrier is entitled to keep possession of the goods consigned until he has been paid the *freight* owing to him for their carriage: Skinner v Upshaw (1702) 2 Ld Raym 752.

**carry over.** The postponement of the completion of a contract to buy or sell shares from one account period of the Stock Exchange (qv) to the other.

**cartel.** An association with the objective on maintaining higher prices for goods than would otherwise obtain. See DOMINANT POSITION, ABUSE OF; UNFAIR PRACTICES.

**case stated.** A statement of the facts in a case submitted for the opinion of a higher court, clearly identifying the point of law upon which opinion is sought. It is consultative in that the lower court seeks the assistance of the higher court. A Circuit Court judge may refer any question of law to the Supreme Court by way of case stated and may adjourn the pronouncement of his judgment or order pending the determination of such case stated: Courts of Justice Act 1947 s.16; Doyle v Hearne (1988) ILRM 318. See also Irish Refining plc v Commissioner of Valuations (1990) 1 IR 568. A case may be stated on a question of law by the High Court to the Supreme Court: Courts of Justice Act 1936.

A case may be stated on a question of law from the District Court to the High Court, before or after the determination of the proceedings in the District Court: Courts (Supplemental Provisions) Act 1961 ss.51-52. No appeal is allowed to the Supreme Court except by leave of the High Court: ibid s.52(2) and Minister for Justice v Wang Zhu Jie (1991 SC) ILRM 823. A judge of the District Court must not refuse to state a case where the application is made to him by or under the direction of a Minister, the Director of Public Prosecutions, or the Revenue Commissioners; the only ground for refusing in other cases is where he is of opinion that the application is frivolous: Summary Jurisdiction Act 1857 s.4; DCR r.202; Sport Arena Ltd v O'Reilly (1987 HC) IR 185. Service in relation to a case stated on the solicitor who acted for a party in the District Court may be sufficient: Crowley v McVeigh (1989) IR 73. Also, the court has jurisdiction to enlarge the time limit fixed for transmission of a case stated to the High Court but only in appropriate circumstances: DPP v Regan (1993 HC) ILRM 335. See also RSC O.59, O.62 r.1 and O.122 r.7. [Text: Collins & O'Reilly]. See SUPREME COURT; PRELIMINARY RULINGS; VALUATION.

**cash.** Cash that is *legal tender* (qv): Payment of Wages Act 1991 s.1(1).

**cash card.** A card issued by a bank or building society to a person having an address in the State by means of which cash may be obtained in the State by the person from an automated teller machine: Finance Act 1992 s.203 as amended by Finance Act 1993 s.102. Stamp duty is payable in respect of cash cards.

**casting vote.** The second and deciding vote which a chairman may have power to give when there is an equality of votes. See CHAIRMAN; FOSS V HARBOTTLE, RULE IN.

**casual trading.** Selling goods by retail at a place (including a public road) to which the public have access as of right or at any other place that is a *casual trading area*: Casual Trading Act 1980 s.2. It does not include a number of selling transactions eg selling by auction, selling of fish by whom they were caught, selling of agricultural or horticultural produce (including livestock) by the producer thereof or his servants or agents, selling of newspapers, or selling for charitable purposes (ibid s.2(2)).

It is an offence for a person to engage in casual trading in (a) a *casual trading area* unless he holds a casual trading *licence* and a casual trading *permit* or (b) an area other than a casual trading area unless he holds a casual trading licence or (c) in a functional area of a local authority other than a casual trading area where there is a casual trading area in that functional area (ibid s.3).

The Minister cannot grant a casual trading licence to a person who has been convicted of two or more offences under the Act (ibid s.4(6)); where there is a conviction-free period of five years, one conviction after such period is not sufficient to bring s.4(6) into operation; this section has been found not to be repugnant to the Constitution: Hand v Dublin Corporation (1991 SC) ILRM 556.

A local authority has power to designate casual trading areas (ibid s.7). See Skibbereen UDC v Quill (1986) IR 123 ILRM 170; Comerford v O'Malley (1987) ILRM 595; Lyons v Corporation of Kilkenny (1987 HC); Crosby v Delap (1992 HC) ILRM 564. Contrast with OCCASIONAL TRADING.

**casus belli.** [A case for war]. An event which is used to justify a war.

**casus omissus.** [An omitted case]. A matter which has not been, but should have been provided for by statute or by statutory rule or regulation.

**catalogue.** See ADVERTISEMENT.

**catching bargain.** See UNCONSCIONABLE BARGAIN.

**cattle trespass.** See ANIMALS.

**causa causans.** The immediate cause; the last link in the chain of causation. The real effective cause of damage: Pandorf v Hamilton (1886) 17 QBD 675. Causa causans is to be distinguished from *causa sina qua non* which means some preceding link but for which the causa causans could not have become operative — see Kehoe & Haythornwaite v Cullimore (1991 CC) as reported by Boyle in 10 ILT & SJ (1992) 50. See also Fitzsimmons v Bord Telecom and ESB (1991 HC) ILRM 277. See CAUSATION.

**causa mortis.** [Because of death]. See DONATIO MORTIS CAUSA.

**causa proxima non remota spectatur.** [The immediate, not the remote cause is to be considered]. See CAUSATION.

**causa remota.** [The remote cause]. See NOVUS ACTUS INTERVENIENS.

**causa sine qua non.** See CAUSA CAUSANS

**causation.** The relation of cause and effect. A defendant in an action in tort is liable only if the chain of causation between himself and the plaintiff is unbroken. See NOVUS ACTUS INTERVENIENS.

**cause.** Includes any action, suit or other original proceeding between a plaintiff and defendant and any criminal proceedings: RSC O.125 r.1.

**cause of action.** The facts which give rise to a right of action in a court of law. Every fact which is material to be proved to entitle the plaintiff to succeed, and every fact which the defendant would have a right to traverse: Cooke v Gill (1873) LR 8 CP 107.

A cause of action runs from the time a wrongful act is committed when the act is actionable *per se* without proof of damage eg as in libel; however when the wrong is not actionable without actual damage (eg as in negligence (qv)), the cause of action is not complete until that damage happens, eg time runs when a provable personal injury, capable of attracting compensation, occurs to the plaintiff: Hegarty v O'Loughran (1990 SC) ITLR (2 Apr). However, in personal injuries cases the three year limitation period, within which an action may be taken, now runs from the date of accrual of the cause of action or from the *date of knowledge* if later: Statute of Limitations (Amendment) Act 1991. The *date of knowledge* is the date the person first had knowledge that he had been "injured" and that the injury had been significant: ibid s.3(1) and Maitland v Swan & Sligo County Council (1992 HC) ITLR (6 Jul). "Injured" is synonymous with "harmed". See also Liability of Defective Products Act 1991 s.7(4). See DEATH, EFFECT OF; DISCOVERABILITY TEST; LIMITATION OF ACTIONS; UNSOUND MIND.

**cause of action estoppel.** See RES JUDICATA.

**causes books.** The books in the Central Office (qv) in which all proceedings commenced by originating summons, issued out of the office, must be entered. See RSC O.5 r.7.

**caution.** A warning.

(1) An entry in the register of the Land Registry to protect unregistered rights on registered land from being defeated by the registration of a subsequent transferee for value: Registration of Title Act 1964 ss.97-98. It is a requisition to the Registrar requiring notice to be given to the *cautioner* before registration of any dealing by the registered owner of specified land.

(2) The *judge's rules* (qv) provide that when a police officer has made up his mind to charge a person with a crime, he should first caution such person before asking any questions or any further questions as the case may be. The caution to a prisoner when he is formally charged should be in the following words: *Do you wish to say anything in answer to the charge? You are not obliged to say anything unless you wish to do so, but whatever you say will be taken down in writing and may be given in evidence.* See BURDEN.

**caveat.** A warning. An entry made in the books of the offices of a registry or court to prevent a certain step being taken without previous notice to the person entering the caveat (who is called the *caveator*). Any person having, or claiming, an interest in the estate of a deceased person may enter a caveat at the Probate Office and so prevent a grant of representation issuing in respect of that estate without reference to him. See RSC O.79 rr.41-51; O.80 rr.48-55.

**caveat actor.** [Let the doer beware].

**caveat emptor.** [Let the buyer beware]. At common law, a buyer was expected to look after his own interest. However statute law now imposes *implied conditions* (qv) and *warranties* (qv) to protect the buyer in many instances eg where the seller acts in the course of a business and also where the buyer deals as consumer. See Wallis v Russell (1902) 2 IR 585. See CONSUMER, DEALING AS; PRODUCT LIABILITY.

**CAV.** See CUR ADV VULT.

**caveat venditor.** [Let the seller beware].

**Ceann Comhairle.** The chairman of Dail Eireann elected from its members: 1937 Constitution, art.15(9)(1). Provision may be made by law for the outgoing Ceann Comhairle to be deemed to be elected at the ensuing general election without actually contesting the election (ibid art.16(6)). Such provision has been made by the Electoral Act 1992 s.36. See also 1992 Act s.63.

**censorship.** The prohibition on exhibiting in public, cinematograph pictures which have not been certified as fit for such exhibition by the *official censor;* the prohibition on publishing material which is indecent or obscene or which advocates abortion (qv); the prohibition on the sale of indecent pictures. See Irish Planning Association v Judge Ryan (1979) IR 295. Provision has been made for the appointment of assistant censors and for the refund of fees in the event that an appeal is successful: Censorship of Films (Amendment) Act 1992. See also Censorship of Films Acts 1923 — 1970; Censorship of Publications Acts 1929 — 1967; Health (Family Planning) Act 1979 s.12(3). See VIDEO RECORDING.

**censorship of books.** The Censorship of Publication Board has power to prohibit the sale and distribution in the State of books which it has examined and where the Board is of opinion that the books are indecent or obscene: Censorship of Publications Act 1946 ss.6 and 7; Health (Family Planning) Act 1979 s.12.

**census.** (1) The enumeration of the inhabitants of the State. The last census of population was taken in 1991 (SI No 62 of 1991). Provision has been made to permit access to the records of a census of population after 100 years: Statistics Act 1993 s.35. (2) Compilation of statistics in relation to any specified matter eg census of production (SI No 81 of 1993). See STATISTICS.

**Central Bank.** The Bank established to be the principal currency authority in the State and with regulatory functions in relation to banks, building societies and investment companies: Central Bank Acts 1942 to 1989; Building Societies Act 1989. The Bank is conducted and managed by a board of directors consisting of a Governor (qv) and other directors: Central Bank Act 1942 s.5 as amended by the Central Bank Act 1989 s.14. See EUROPEAN CENTRAL BANK; GOVERNOR OF CENTRAL BANK.

**Central Criminal Court.** See HIGH COURT.

**central office.** The administrative office, situated in the Four Courts (qv), established by the Courts (Supplemental Provisions) Act 1961 s.55(1), eighth schedule.

**centrebinding.** The practice which took its name from the case In re Centrebind Ltd (1967) 1 WLR 377 whereby a liquidator (qv) appointed at a shareholders' meeting could dissipate the assets of the company prior to the creditors' meeting eg by selling the assets of the company at a very low price to another company closely connected to the existing shareholders. The practice has been countered by limitations put on the liquidator's powers to dispose of assets in the period prior to a creditors' meeting: Companies Act 1990 s.131.

**certificate.** A statement in writing by a person with a public or official status, concerning some matter within his own knowledge or authority. See DOCUMENTARY EVIDENCE.

**certificate of conformity.** See BANKRUPTCY, PETITION FOR.

**certificate of fitness.** See BOOKMAKER, LICENSED.

**certification trade mark.** A particular type of trade mark which is registrable under Part A (qv) of the register of trade marks where the mark is adapted in relation to any goods to distinguish in the course of trade, goods *certified* by any person (in respect of origin, material, mode of manufacture, quality, accuracy or other characteristic), from goods not so certified, provided that the mark may not be so registrable in the name of a

person who carries on a trade in goods of the kind certified: Trade Marks Act 1963 s.45. It differs from an ordinary trade mark, which is intended to identify the goods of a particular trader from those of his competitors.

**certified copy.** A copy of a public document, signed and certified as a true copy by the officer to whose custody the original is entrusted, and admissible as evidence when the original would be admissible. Attested copies of all documents filed in the High Court are admissible in evidence in all causes and matters and between all persons and parties to the same extent as the originals would be admissible: RSC O.39 r.3. See DOCUMENTARY EVIDENCE.

**certified trade union.** See TRADE UNION, CERTIFIED.

**certiorari.** An order of the High Court *granted in exercise of its general superintending and corrective jurisdiction over orders of inferior courts for the purpose of bringing up orders for review*: The State (Hunt) v C J Midland Circuit (1934) IR 196. The grounds for an order of certiorari include where there is: want or excess of jurisdiction; error apparent on the face of an order of an inferior court; disregard for the essentials of justice; bias or disqualification of the court or tribunal; fraud: R (Martin) v Mahony (1910) 2 IR 695; Lennon v Clifford (1993 HC) ILRM 77. Certiorari is also the appropriate remedy where a court or tribunal apparently acts within jurisdiction but where the proceedings are so fundamentally flawed as to deprive an accused of a trial in due course of law: Sweeney v District Judge Brophy (1993 SC) ILRM 449.

Certiorari however must not be used as a method of appealing decisions of inferior courts: The State (Daly) v Ruane (1988) ILRM 117. It is also not available to correct an error in respect of the discrepancy between a written order and an oral order of a court: The State (Wilson) v D J Nealon (1987) ILRM 118. However, it may be available where there is an adequate remedy which has been inadequately prosecuted: Duff v D J Mangan & Judge Gleeson (1993 SC) ITLR (14 Jun).

An order of certiorari is frequently used to review and to quash decisions of bodies which, or of persons who, have exceeded their legal powers. Delay or lack of candour does not, of itself, disentitle a person to an order of certiorari where it can be shown that a public wrong has been done to him and that the wrong continues to mark his life: The State (Furey) v Minister for Justice and Attorney General (1988) ILRM 89. See also The State (Gleeson) v Minister for Defence (1976) IR 280; The State (Keeney) v O'Malley (1986) ILRM 31; McGirl v McArdle (1989) IR 596; O'Neill v Iarnrod Eireann (1991 SC) ELR 1; Matthews v Irish Coursing Club (1992 HC) ITLR (30 Mar); Bannon v Employment Appeals Tribunal (1992 HC) ELR 203. See CONVICTION; JUDICIAL REVIEW; STATE SIDE ORDERS.

**certitudine indigent sunt referenda.** [Subsequent words, added for the purpose of certainty, are to be referred to preceding words which need certainty].

**certum est quod certum reddi potest.** [That which is capable of being made certain is to be treated as certain]. See Duncombe v Brighton Club and Norfolk Hotel Company (1875) LR 10 QB 371.

**cess.** See GRAND JURY.

**cessante causa, cessat effectus.** [When the cause ceases, the effect ceases].

**cessante ratione legis, cessat ipsa lex.** [When the reason of the law ceases, the law itself ceases]. This maxim may apply to common law, but not generally to statute law.

**cessante statu primitivio cessat derivativus.** [The original estate ceasing, that which derived from it ceases].

**cessat executio.** [Suspending execution].

**cessate grant.** A grant of administration of a deceased's estate which is given to a minor, named as an executor, on attaining his majority; it has the effect of terminating the powers of an administrator *durante minore aetate* (qv).

**cesser.** Ending or determination. Where an executor renounces probate, there is cesser of his right to prove the will.

**cestui que trust.** [He for whom is the trust]. A beneficiary of a trust.

**cestui que use.** See USE.

**cestui que vie.** The person for whose lifetime another holds an estate or interest in land. See LIFE ESTATE.

**cestuis que trust.** Beneficiaries of a trust (qv).

**ceteris paribus.** [Other things being equal].

**cf.** Compare.

**chain of representation.** See EXECUTORSHIP BY REPRESENTATION.

**chain of title.** The instruments which show the successive conveyances from the original source to the present owner. See MARKETABLE TITLE.

**chairman.** Person who regulates the proceedings of a meeting. At a general meeting of a company, the chairman has the duty of ensuring that the business before the meeting is properly conducted. His rulings on points of order and related matters are deemed prima facie to be correct (see John v Rees [1970] Ch 345). He normally has a casting vote where there is an equality of votes: Companies Act 1963, Table A, art 61. It has been held that the casting vote of a chairman who has been invalidly appointed is void: Clark v Workman (1920) 1 IR 107.

**challenge to jurors.** See JUROR, CHALLENGE TO.

**chambers.** The rooms of judges. A judge sitting in chambers can exercise the full jurisdiction of the court. Some statutes require proceedings to be in chambers for reasons of confidentiality eg proceedings regarding the legal right of a testator's spouse; making provision for children; and excluding persons from succession as being unworthy to succeed: Succession Act 1965 ss.119 and 122. See PUBLIC JUSTICE.

**champerty.** The maintenance and finance by a person, not necessarily a solicitor, of an action or litigation in order to make a gain; it is a common law misdemeanour (qv). Where a person undertakes actively to assist in the recovery of shares of an estate to which other persons are entitled, an agreement whereby the former will receive a percentage of the shares of the latter savours of champerty and is void: McElroy (t/a Irish Genealogical Services) v Flynn (1990 HC) ITLR (17 Sep). It is not illegal, however, for solicitors taking action on behalf of persons of little or no means to charge a solicitor/client fee estimated at 10% of the monies recoverable, particularly where the solicitor had paid all the expenses in relation to the case out of his own pocket: *obiter* *dictum* in Kennedy v Nolan (1990 HC) ITLR (23 Oct). See also Rees v De Bernardy (1896) 2 Ch 437. See CONTINGENCY FEE; NO FOAL NO FEE.

**chancery.** The court of chancery was a court of *equity* (qv), presided over by the Lord Chancellor, which was merged in the High Court by the Judicature Act 1873.

**chance-medley.** The killing of an aggressor in self-defence in the course of a sudden brawl or quarrel. It has been held in England that the doctrine of chance-medley has no longer any place in the law of *homicide* and that each case must now be decided on the principles of self-defence (qv) or provocation (qv): R v Semini (1949) 1 KB 405.

**change of parties.** The change permitted in the parties to an action after proceedings have commenced eg because of death or bankruptcy or where there is misjoinder (qv) or non-joinder (qv). See RSC O.17 r.4; RSC O.15.

**change of user.** See PLANNING PERMISSION.

**character.** Reputation and disposition: Selvey v DPP (1970) AC 304.

**character, evidence of.** Evidence as to the character of a person is generally inadmissible in proceedings, unless character is in issue or is relevant. In civil cases, the character of the plaintiff is in issue in defamation (qv) cases eg where the defence claims justification (qv). In criminal cases, evidence of the good character of the accused is always relevant and admissible. Evidence of the bad character of the accused is admissible in the following instances: (a) where the accused seeks to establish his good character, the prosecution may rebut it by giving evidence of his bad character including previous convictions, and (b) an accused person, who gives evidence, may be cross-examined as to his bad character and previous convictions in specified circumstances: Criminal Justice (Evidence) Act 1924 s.1(f).

However, claims that the gardai fabricated a confession by the accused does not put his character in issue: DPP v McGrail (1990 CCA) ITLR (19 Feb). Also evidence of bad reputation should never found a view that an accused had been guilty of offences: DPP v Martin (1991 CCA) ITLR (4 Nov).

The character of the person prosecuting may be relevant in rape and similar offences eg Criminal Law (Rape) Act 1981 s.3 as amended by the Criminal Law (Rape) Amdt Act 1990 s.13. The character of a witness is always relevant as to his credit (qv). See Attorney General v O'Leary (1926) IR 445; Attorney General v O'Sullivan (1930) IR 552. See Newman in ISLR (1993) 96. See CONVICTION, EVIDENCE OF; CROSS-EXAMINATION.

**character or quality of goods.** Words which have no direct reference to the character or quality of goods, may be registered as a trade mark (qv) under Part A (qv) of the register. See Fry-Cadbury (Ireland) Ltd v Synott (1935) IR 7OO; Bulmers Ltd v Showerings Ltd (1962) IR 189.

**charge.** (1) A criminal accusation. (2) A judge's instructions to a jury. (3) A form of security for the payment of a debt or performance of an obligation. A charge created by a company may be *fixed* or *floating*. A charge by a public company on its own shares is void, apart from certain exceptions: Companies (Amendment) Act 1983 s.44. [Text: Forde (1); Keane (1); Ussher; Gough UK]. See LIEN; FIXED CHARGE; FLOATING CHARGE; CHARGE, REGISTRATION OF; SURCHARGE.

**charge, registration of.** The systems which exist to register charges on a person's property to enable others to determine the assets which are mortgaged. The systems often impute notice of the existence and the content of the charges registered. Special procedures exist for registering mortgages on land, mortgages on ships, farmers' chattel mortgages, and company charges. See Registration of Title Act 1964; Mercantile Marine Act 1955 s.50; Agricultural Credit Act 1978 s.26.

As regards companies, a wide category of charges must be registered at the Registry of Companies within 21 days of their creation. A registered charge takes priority over an unregistered one, even if the owner of the registered charge knew of the other's existence, and an unregistered charge cannot be enforced in a liquidation; there is provision, however, for the court to extend the time for registration. See Companies Act 1963 ss.99-106.

A company is required to register

charges it creates on ships or aircraft or any part of an aircraft: Companies Act 1990 s.122 amending s.99 of the 1963 Act. Also the Minister may by regulation amend the list of charges requiring registration.

As regards the registration of charges created by a foreign company where the property comprised in the charge is situate in Ireland, see Courtney in ILSI Gazette (May 1992) 151.

See also Bank of Ireland Finance v Daly Ltd (1978) IR 79; In re Telford Motors Ltd (1978) HC. See BOOK DEBTS; CHARGE ON LAND; FIXED CHARGE; FLOATING CHARGE; SEARCHES.

**charge, take in.** The creation of a public road by resolution of a local authority. See PUBLIC ROAD.

**charge card.** A card issued by a promoter to an individual having an address in the State by means of which goods, services or cash may be obtained by the individual, and amounts in respect of the goods, services or cash may be charged to the individual's account: Finance (No 2) Act 1981 s.17(2)(a).

**charge d'affaires.** The subordinate head of a diplomatic mission accredited to the Minister for Foreign Affairs. If the sending state accredits the head of mission to more than one state, it may establish a diplomatic mission headed by a charge d'affaires *ad interim* in each state where the head of mission has not his permanent seat: Diplomatic Relations and Immunities Act 1967, first schedule, art.5(2). See DIPLOMATIC PRIVILEGE.

**charge on land.** A charge which the registered owner of land can create to secure an advance of money; the charge must be registered as a charge on the land and the chargeant must be registered as the owner of the charge. The registered owner of the charge has all the powers of a mortgagee (qv) by deed within the meaning of the Conveyancing Acts: Registration of Title Act 1964 s.62.

It has been held that a provision in a deed of charge permitting the registered owner to take possession in the event of certain defaults of the chargor need not be registered on the folio separately from the deed of charge: Gale & Gale v First National Building Society (1985) IR 609.

The deposit of a certificate of charge, or of a land certificate (qv) has the same effect as the deposit of title deeds of unregistered land. Money charged on land in the State must be construed, unless otherwise described, as being in the currency of the State: Northern Bank v Edwards (1986) ILRM 167. See DEPOSIT OF TITLE DEEDS.

**charge on public funds.** The terms of any international agreement involving a charge on public funds, must be approved by Dail Eireann, otherwise the State is not bound thereby: 1937 Constitution, art.29(5)(2). See The State (McCaud) v Governor of Mountjoy Prison (1986) ILRM 129; The State (Gilliland) v Govenor of Mountjoy Prison (1987) ILRM 278. For example, see Multilateral Investment Guarantee Agency Act 1988.

**charge on ship.** A charge on a ship in the form of a legal mortgage must comply with the requirements of the Merchantile Marine Act 1955. A yacht is not a ship in this context: In re South Coast Boatyard, Barbour v Burke (1980) SC. See CHARGE, REGISTRATION OF.

**charge to jury.** See SUMMING UP.

**charging order.** An order of the court made on the application of a judgment-creditor to charge the amount of his judgment upon stocks (qv) or shares (qv) belonging to the judgment-debtor, or upon his interest in funds in court, which application is made ex-parte and grounded on an affidavit of facts: RSC O.46 r.1. An order of the court may be obtained subsequently, by motion on notice to the defendant, to have the stocks and shares transferred to the sheriff (qv) to be realised to satisfy the judgment debt (ibid r.2). See also RSC O.77 rr.84 and 95. See STOP ORDER.

**charitable devise or bequest.** Where a will contains a charitable devise or bequest, the Commissioners of Charitable Donations and Bequests (qv) may, in their discretion, require the personal representative (a) to deliver to them evidence to show that the gift has been transferred to the charity or the trustees of the charity are aware of the gift, or (b) to publish such particulars of the gift as the Commissioners (the *Board*) may require: Charities Act 1973 s.16. The probate officer is required to notify the Commissioners as to all charitable gifts in wills entered in the probate office (qv).

**charitable gift.** A gift for charitable purposes: Charities Act 1961. See CHAR-ITIES.

**charitable trust.** See CHARITIES.

**charities.** Trusts (qv) in favour of legally *charitable objects*. Such trusts, unlike private trusts, are not subject to the rule against perpetuities (qv) and they do not fail for uncertainty.

A charity must confer a benefit on the public or on a sufficiently wide section of the public. Charitable objects are classified into four main divisions: Income Tax Special Purposes Commissioners v Pemsel (1891) AC 531; Barrington's Hospital v Commissioner of Valuations (1957) IR 299. These are (a) relief of poverty — a public element is essential; (b) advancement of education — contrast University College Cork v Commissioner of Valuations (1911) 2 IR 593 and Wesley College v Commissioner of Valuations (1984) ILRM 17; (c) advancement of religion — *religion* includes all religions tolerated by law; a gift for Masses is a charitable purpose: O'Hanlon v Cardinal Logue (1906) 1 IR 247; Halpin v Hannon (1948) ILTR 75; In re Greene (1914) 1 IR 242; (d) other charitable purposes — the gift must not only be for the benefit of the community but must be beneficial in a way the law regards as charitable eg National Anti-vivisection Society v IRC (1948) AC 31; In re MacCarthy's Will Trust (1958) IR 311.

The general administration of charities is the responsibility of the Commissioners of Charitable Donations and Bequests for Ireland (qv), a statutory body, appointed by the government. See Charities Acts 1961 and 1973. See Report of the Committee ("Costello Committee") on Fundraising Activities for Charitable and other Purposes (1990). [Text: Delaney; Keane (2); Kiely; Snell UK]. See CY-PRES.

**charter.** A deed; a constitution; an instrument from the State (formerly the Crown) conferring rights and privileges. See COMPANY, CHARTERED.

**chartered company.** See COMPANY, CHAR-TERED.

**charterparty.** A contract between a shipowner and a charterer whereby the shipowner lets the ship to the charterer for the conveyance of goods. The contract must be in writing but need not be sealed. The charterparty may operate as a demise or lease of the ship with or without the services of the master and crew. A *time* charterer of a ship has an interest in the ship which he can enforce against a purchaser of the ship with notice of the charterparty: Strathcona v Dominion Coal Co (1926) AC 108; Port Line Ltd v Ben Line Steamers Ltd (1958) QB 146. See DEMURRAGE.

**chattel mortgage.** When used without qualification, it means an instrument under seal made between a recognised borrower of the one part and a recognised lender of the other part which is (a) a floating chattel mortgage, or (b) a specific chattel mortgage, or (c) both a floating and specific chattel mortgage: Agricultural Credit Act 1978 s.23(1). A *floating chattel mortgage* is an instrument under seal whereby the borrower charges stock from time to time on the borrower's land with the payment of any money advanced or to be advanced to the borrower. A *specific chattel mortgage* is one which charges specific stock (wherever situate). A register of chattel mortgages must be kept and maintained in every Circuit Court office (ibid s.26).

A registered specific chattel mortgage operates and has the effect of prohibiting the mortgagor from selling or otherwise transferring ownership or possession of the stock without giving notice in writing to the mortgagee, and of prohibiting the mortgagor from selling at less than a fair and reasonable price (ibid s.27). A registered floating chattel mortgage creates an ambulatory and shifting charge on all stock the property of the mortgagor from time to time on the land to which the chattel mortgage relates (ibid s.30). Priority of chattel mortgages is in accordance to the times at which they are respectively registered (ibid s.34). See also Chattel Mortgages (Registration) Order 1928 (SR & O No 40 of 1928). [Text: Forde (5)]. See BILL OF SALE.

**chattels.** Generally property other than freehold. *Chattels real* are leasehold and other interests in land which are less than freehold. *Chattels personal* are movable tangible articles of property eg goods (qv) and choses in possession (qv). See CHOSE; HOUSEHOLD CHATTELS.

**cheating.** The offence of winning of any

money or valuable thing by any fraud or unlawful device or ill-practice in (a) playing at or with cards, dice, tables or other game, (b) bearing a part in stakes, wagers or adventures, (c) bettings on the sides or hands of persons who play, or (d) wagering on the event of any game, pastime or exercise. Cheating may be deemed to be an obtaining of money by false pretences (qv). See Gaming and Lotteries Act 1956 s.11.

It has been held that a charge of plagiarism by a university student is a charge of cheating; the principles of natural justice must apply to the hearing of such a charge: Flanagan v University College Dublin (1989 HC) 7 ILT Dig 23. See GAMING.

**cheque.** A bill of exchange (qv) drawn on a banker, payable on demand: Bills of Exchange Act 1882 s.73. The person making the cheque is the *drawer* and the person to whom it is payable is the *payee*. When a cheque bears across its face the words *and Company*, or any abbreviation thereof, between two parallel traverse lines, it is said to be *crossed generally*, and when it bears across its face the name of a banker, it is said to be *crossed specially* (ibid s.76). A generally crossed cheque can be paid only through a bank and a specially crossed cheque only through the bank so specified. A cheque which is crossed *not negotiable* cannot give to the transferee a better title than the holder of the cheque had (ibid s.81).

It is not open to a drawer of a cheque to question the value of his own cheque; the endorsement by the defendant of a cheque to the plaintiff amounted to an absolute discharge of any indebtedness: Private Motorists Provident Society v Moore (1988 HC) ILRM 526. See also Cheques Act 1959; Building Societies Act 1989 ss.29(2)(f) and 126. [Text: McGann; Paget UK; Richardson UK]. See ACCOUNT PAYEE; DAYS OF GRACE; ENDORSEMENT.

**cheque, blank.** See FEE.

**cheque, countermand of payment.** Revocation by the drawer of the authority to pay a cheque. *Stopping* a cheque is dishonour by non-payment: Gaynor v McDyer (1968) IR 295. A cheque in general is a conditional payment which suspends but does not extinguish a debt;

the debt revives if the cheque is countermanded. A banker is liable if he wrongly pays a countermanded cheque. See Bills of Exchange Act 1882 s.75. See Reade v Royal Bank of Ireland (1922) 2 IR 22. See Doyle in 9ILT & SJ (1991) 255. See DISHONOUR OF BILL.

**cheque, dishonour of.** The refusal by the drawee of a cheque (eg a bank) to accept the cheque or having accepted it fails to pay it: Bills of Exchange Act 1882 s.47. With the exception of claims arising on cheques not presented for payment within a reasonable time (ibid s.74) or on specially crossed cheques (ibid s.79(2)) or on cheques marked good by the paying bank, the general principle is that a payee named in a cheque has no right of action against the bank on which the cheque is drawn if the cheque is dishonoured: Dublin Port & Docks Board v Bank of Ireland (1976) IR 118. However, this is subject to qualification if the bank, without lawful justification, embarks on a course of conduct which is calculated to deceive the payee in a manner which may result in financial loss to such payee: TE Potterton Ltd v Northern Bank Ltd (1993 HC) ILRM 225. See BANKER, DUTY OF CARE.

**cheque, drawing of.** Drawing a cheque implies three statements — (a) that the drawer has an account with that bank, (b) that he has authority to draw on it for that amount, and (c) that the cheque, as drawn, is a valid order for that amount (ie that the present state of affairs is such that, in the ordinary course of events, the cheque will on its future presentation be duly honoured). The drawing of a cheque by a company does not itself operate as a disposition of the funds in the accounts of a company; the disposition occurs when the cheque is paid: In re Ashmark Ltd (in liquidation) v Nitra Ltd (1990 HC) ITLR (5 Mar).

**cheque, issue.** A cheque is *issued* at the time of its first delivery complete in form to the person who takes it as a holder: Bills of Exchange Act 1882 s.2.

**cheque, liability on.** A banker who pays a cheque drawn on him in good faith and in the ordinary course of business, is not liable to the true owner if an endorsement is forged: Bills of Exchange Act 1882 s.60. Also, where a banker pays the holder of a cheque, in good faith and without notice that the holder's title is defective, the payment is valid and the banker is entitled to debit the customer's account (ibid s.59).

In order to obviate the long established practice by which bankers refused to pay a cheque unless it was endorsed at the bank by the party presenting it, the law was changed in 1959 to provide that *where a banker in good faith and in the ordinary course of business pays a cheque drawn on him which is not endorsed, or is irregularly endorsed, he does not in doing so, incur any liability by reason only of the absence of, or irregularity in, endorsement, and he is deemed to have paid it in due course*: Cheques Act 1959 s.1.

A collecting banker is protected from liability to the true owner of a cheque where the banker receives payment of the cheque for a *customer*, who has no title, or a defective title to the cheque, provided the banker acts in good faith and without negligence: Cheques Act 1959 s.4. A collecting banker is also protected if he becomes a *holder for value* (qv) or an *holder in due course* (qv).

**cheque, stopping of.** See CHEQUE, COUNTERMAND OF PAYMENT.

**cheque, overdue.** A cheque which has been in circulation for an unreasonable time. It can only be negotiated subject to any defect of title affecting it at its maturity. See Bills of Exchange Act 1882 s.36(2) and(3). See MATURITY.

**cheque, post-dated.** A cheque which bears a date subsequent to the actual date on which it was drawn, and issued before the date it bears. A cheque is not invalid by reason only that it is post-dated: Bills of Exchange Act 1882 s.13(2). See Royal Bank of Scotland v Tottenham (1894) 71 LT 168.

**cheque, presentation by notification.** Provision has been made for presentation for payment by a collecting banker of a cheque *by notification* to the drawee banker of the *essential features of the cheque* other than by its physical presentation: Bills of Exchange Act 1882 s.45A, as inserted by the Central Bank Act 1989 s.132(c). Presentation by notification includes presentation by the transmission of an electronic message.

A cheque paid on presentation by notification is deemed to have been paid in the *ordinary course of business* but this does not relieve the collecting banker or the drawee banker from the liability they would have been subject to if the cheque had been physically presented for payment. The drawee banker can request the physical presentation of the cheque and this does not constitute *dishonour* of the cheque for non-payment.

The *essential features of the cheque* include: the serial number, the identification code number of the drawee banker, the account number of the drawer of the cheque, and the amount of the cheque.

**cheque, stale.** A cheque which is *out of date* ie one bearing a date of twelve (or, in some cases, six) months prior to presentation. See London County Banking Co v Groome (1881) 8 QBD 288.

**cheque card.** A card issued by a bank (or building society) and presented with a cheque to a supplier of goods or services, who as a consequence is assured of payment by the bank to a stated maximum amount. The drawer of the cheque represents that he has authority from the bank to use the card so as to oblige the bank to honour the cheque. See Metropolitan Police Comr v Charles (1977) AC 177.

**Chief Justice.** The president of the Supreme Court (qv); he is also ex officio an additional judge of the High Court (qv): 1937 Constitution, art.34(4)(2); Courts (Establishment and Constitution) Act 1961 ss.1(2) and 2(3). The Chief Justice is an ex-officio member of the Council of State (qv) and of the Presidential Commission (qv). He is empowered to appoint notaries public and commissioners to administer oaths.

Where the Chief Justice is of opinion that the conduct of a judge of the District Court has been such as to bring the administration of justice into disrepute, he may interview the judge privately and inform him of such opinion (ibid s.10(4)). If the Chief Justice is unable owing to illness or any other reason to transact the business of his office, his powers may be exercised by the President of the High Court (ibid s.10(2)).

The Chief Justices since the establishment of the State have been: The Hon Thomas A Finlay (1985 to present): Thomas F O'Higgins (1974-1985); William O'Brien Fitzgerald (1973-1974);

Cearbhall O'Dalaigh (1961-1972); Conor A Maguire (1946-1961); Timothy Sullivan (1936-1946); Hugh Kennedy (1925-1936). See JUDGES; NOTARY PUBLIC.

**chief office.** A building society is required to have an office in the State (to be known as its chief office) to which all communications and notices (qv) may be addressed: Building Societies Act 1989 s.15. See BUILDING SOCIETY.

**child.** A person under the age of 18 years other than a person who is or has been married: Child Care Act 1991 s.2(1). See AGE; MINOR.

**child abduction.** Measures have been introduced to secure the return of a child who has been removed to any *Contracting State* in defiance of a court order or against the wishes of a parent with custody rights: Child Abduction and Enforcement of Custody Orders Act 1991. A child for the purposes of the Conventions, given force by this Act, is a person under 16 years of age.

The Department of Justice will initiate steps to trace a child who has been abducted into the State and seek a child's return where a child has been abducted from the State. The Department will assist the wronged party in seeking return of the child. Applicants are entitled to legal aid and no charge is imposed for the services. However, a child will not be returned to another jurisdiction where there would be a grave risk that the child would be exposed to physical or psychological harm: ibid Hague Convention 1980 art.13 (b) and RG v BG (1993 HC) ITLR (1 Feb). Such a risk must be weighty and in regard to sychological harm, it must be substantial and not trivial: CK v CK (1993 HC) ILRM 534. See also Northampton County Council v ABF and MBF (1982) ILRM 164; Kent Co Council v CS (1984) ILRM 292. See Appointment of Central Authorities Order 1993 (SI No 121 of 1993). See Corrigan in 9ILT & SJ (1991) 273 & 10ILT & SJ (1992) 4. See CHILDREN, CUSTODY OF.

**child, access to.** The right of the non-custodial parent to see and share the company of children of the family. Access to children is a basic right of parents but it may be lost by the misbehaviour of a parent. The courts will usually grant the right to access to take place at particular times.

A health board is required to facilitate reasonable access to a child in its care by his parents, any person acting in loco parentis, or any other person who has a bona fide interest in the child; the court may make an order refusing to allow a named person access to such a child in order to safeguard or promote the child's welfare: Child Care Act 1991 s.37. See also Guardianship of Infants Act 1964 s.11 and Judicial Separation and Family Reform Act 1989 s.11(b). See CARE ORDER; CHILD, CUSTODY OF; GUARDIAN.

**child, adopted.** A child in respect of whom an *adoption order* has been made. In general, adoption is restricted to orphans and children whose parents are not married to each other; such children must be at least six weeks old and if over the age of seven years be consulted, and must be under the age of eighteen years (previously 21). In 1988, the categories of children who could be adopted was extended and the age was reduced to under eighteen years: Adoption Act 1988.

An adopted child has the same property and succession rights after the making of an adoption order as a child of the adopter or adopters born in lawful wedlock: Adoption Act 1952 s.26; Succession Act 1965 s.110; this does not infringe the rights under the Constitution of natural born children of a marriage: The State (Nicolaou) v An Bord Uchtala (1966) IR 567. A reference in a will or other disposition is to be interpreted as including a child adopted subsequent to the making of the will or disposition: Status of Children Act 1987 s.27(4).

This provision reverses the previous law in that regard by providing that an adopted person, unless a contrary intention appears, is entitled to take under a disposition in the same manner as he would have been entitled to take if, at the date of the adoption order, he had been born in lawful wedlock to the person or persons who adopted him. See ISSUE; ADOPTION.

**child, advancement.** See ADVANCEMENT, CHILD.

**child, begetting of.** See BEGET.

**child, born out of wedlock.** See CHILD, ILLEGITIMATE.

**child, care of.** See AFTERCARE; CARE ORDER; CHILD, EMERGENCY CARE OF; MOOT; WARD OF COURT; WELFARE OF CHILDREN .

**child, emergency care of.** An emergency care order placing a child in the care of the health board for eight or lesser days may be made by a judge of the District Court on application of the health board if he is of opinion that there is a reasonable cause to believe that (a) there is an immediate and serious risk to the health or welfare of the child, or (b) there is likely to be such risk if the child is removed from the place where he is for the time being: Child Care Act 1991 s.13.

A garda may enter, by force if need be, a house or other place and remove a child to safety if he has reasonable grounds for believing that (a) there is an immediate and serious risk to the health or welfare of the child and (b) it would not be sufficient to await the making of an application for an emergency care order (ibid s.12). An appeal from an emergency care order does not stay the order (ibid s.13(5)). It is not necessary to name the child in an application or order if such name is unknown (ibid s.13(6)). A health board may also obtain a *care order* or *interim* care order. See CARE ORDER; FOSTER-CHILD; WELFARE OF CHILDREN.

**child, cruelty to.** See CRUELTY TO CHILDREN.

**child, custody of.** In deciding on the question of custody and access to children, the courts must have regard to their welfare as the first and paramount consideration; welfare comprises their religious and moral, intellectual, physical and social welfare: S v S (1992 SC) ILRM 732, Judicial Separation & Family Law Reform Act 1989 s.3 and Guardianship of Infants Act 1964 s.11.

It has been held that an unmarried mother has a constitutional right to the custody and control of her child: G v An Bord Uchtala (1980) IR 32. It has also been held not to be unconstitutional to allow the adoption of an illegitimate child without the consent of the father: The State (Nicolaou) v An Bord Uchtala (1966) IR 567. All matters concerning the guardianship and custody of children must be decided on the basis of the welfare of the child and to the constitu-

tional principle that parents have equal rights to, and are joint guardians of their children: Guardianship of Infants Act 1964 ss.3 and 6.

In disputes relating to the custody of children, in general, young children will be given into the custody of their mother; parents or a parent will be given custody as against a stranger or the State: (ibid s.10). However, see ibid S v S (1992 SC) ILRM 732 where custody was given to the father.

Previously, in relation to an illegitimate child, the natural mother had a constitutional right to the custody of the child, while the natural father could apply to the court for an order for custody of the child (ibid s.6(4) and 11(4); this latter provision is now replaced with like provisions for the father of a child who has not married the mother and has not been appointed guardian: Status of Children Act 1987 s.13. See also In re O'Brien (1954) IR 1; The State (McP) v G (1965) HC; B v B (1975) IR 54.

Where a court grants a decree of judicial separation, it may declare either spouse to be unfit to have custody of any dependent child of the family; if that spouse is the parent of the child, he will not, on the death of the other spouse, be entitled as of right to the custody of that child: Judicial Separation and Family Law Reform Act 1989 s.41. See also ibid s.11(b). See CARE ORDER; CHILD ABDUCTION; CHILD IN CARE; GUARDIAN; MOOT; NATURAL PARENTS.

**child, crime and.** A court is empowered to require a parent or guardian to pay a fine, damages or costs imposed on or awarded against a child or young person: Childrens Act 1908 s.99. The parent or guardian can be required to attend the court before which the case is heard (ibid s.98). See also Defence Act 1954 s.107(3) and (4). See also COMPENSATION ORDER; DEPRAVED; DOLI INCAPAX; REFORMATORY SCHOOLS; YOUNG PERSON.

**child, employment of.** For the purposes of employment, a child is a person who is under the school leaving age (qv), currently 15 years. It is an offence for an employer to employ a child to do work, except that an employer may employ a child over the age of 14 years to do light non-industrial work provided (a) that it is not harmful to health or normal development and does not interfere with schooling, (b) that it does not exceed specified hours and is not in the period 8pm to 8am, (c) that a birth certificate or satisfactory evidence of age has been produced and (d) that written permission from the parent or guardian has been obtained by the employer. See Protection of Young Persons (Employment) Act 1977; Intoxicating Liquor Act 1988 s.38. See YOUNG PERSON.

**child, evidence of.** In civil cases, a child will not be permitted to give evidence unless he understands the nature of an oath (qv); the child's understanding is the test, not his age, and this will be determined by the judge. It has been held that a child's unsworn evidence in a civil case cannot be accepted even if both parties to the action agreed to such a course: Mapp v Gilhooley (1991 SC) ILRM 695.

In criminal proceedings, the unsworn evidence of a child under 14 years of age may be received in evidence if the court is satisfied that he is capable of giving an intelligible account of events which are relevant to the proceedings: Criminal Evidence Act 1992 s.27. The Childrens Act 1908 s.30 required that the unsworn evidence of a child of tender years be corroborated; this requirement has been abolished (ibid 1992 Act s.28(1)). Also there is no longer a requirement for a judge to warn a jury on the danger of convicting an accused on the uncorroborated evidence of a child (ibid s.28(2)(a)). A judge may in his discretion give such a warning (ibid s.28(2)(b)). Unsworn evidence of a child may corroborate evidence (sworn or unsworn) given by any person (ibid s.28(3)). See Attorney General v Sullivan (1930) IR 552. [Text: Spenser & Flin UK]. See OATH.

**child, illegitimate.** A child born to parents who are not validly married to each other. Previously, a child born to a void marriage (qv) was illegitimate: N otherwise K v K [1986] 6 ILRM 75, while children born of a voidable marriage were illegitimate from the granting of an annulment. An illegitimate child had no succession rights on the death of her father intestate: In the Goods of Walker (1985) ILRM 86; an illegitimate child had rights to succeed

to the estate of his mother: Legitimacy Act 1931 s.9. However, recent legislation provides that relationships shall be deduced for the purposes of the Succession Act 1965 irrespective of the marital status of a person's parents: Status of Children Act 1987 s.29. Illegitimate children are now *children whose parents are not married to each other.*

The new provisions will not retrospectively affect any rights under the intestacy of a person who died before commencement of Part V of the 1987 Act. In addition, the rule is now abrogated which rendered void, as contrary to public policy, a provision in a disposition for the benefit of an illegitimate child not in being when the disposition takes effect (ibid s.27(5)).

The 1987 Act has enabled the State to ratify the European Convention on the Status of Children Born out of Wedlock, which came into force for Ireland on 6 January 1989. See LRC 4 of 1982. See AFFILIATION ORDER; CONSTRUCTION OF DISPOSITIONS; PATERNITY, PRESUMPTION OF.

**child, legitimate.** The status of a child arising where his parents were married to each other at the time of his conception or at the time of his birth. There is a presumption that a child born in wedlock is legitimate until the contrary is proven beyond reasonable doubt. Legitimate children are now known as *children whose parents are married to each other:* Status of Children Act 1987. See CHILD, LEGITIMATED.

**child, legitimated.** A child was legitimated upon the subsequent marriage of his parents, provided the father was domiciled in the State at the time of such marriage, and both he and the mother could have been lawfully married to each other at the time of the birth or at some time during the period of ten months preceding the birth: Legitimacy Act 1931 s.1. The child was legitimated from the date of the marriage.

However, under recent legislation, the subsequent marriage of the parents of a child born outside marriage, who remains unadopted, will always render that child legitimate, irrespective of the marital situation of the parents at the time of the birth: Status of Children Act 1987 s.7.

A legitimated child had most of the

succession rights of a legitimate child; however he could only share in a distribution on intestacy where he was legitimated at the date of death of the intestate and he could not take by descent under an entailed interest created before the date of his legitimation. See Succession Act 1965 s.110; also In re P [1945] Ir Jur Rep 17.

Under the Status of Children Act 1987 s.29, provision is made that relationships shall be deduced for the purposes of the Succession Act 1965 irrespective of the marital status of a person's parents. The new provisions will not retrospectively affect any rights under the intestacy of a person who died before commencement of Part V of the 1987 Act. See CONSTRUCTION OF DISPOSITIONS.

**child, liability relating to .** See OCCU-PIERS' LIABILITY TO CHILDREN; NEGLIGENCE.

**child, provision for.** Where the court is of the opinion that a *testator* has failed in his moral duty to make proper provision for a child in accordance with his means, the court may order that suitable provision be made out of the estate, provided it does not diminish a gift by will to the surviving spouse or her *legal right* (qv). See Succession Act 1965 s.117; also FM v TAM (1970) 106 ILTR 82; L v L (1978) IR 288; MH and NMcG v NM and CM (1983) ILRM 519; In b.GM (1972) 106 ILTR 82. There was a relatively high onus of proof on the applicant which required that a positive failure of moral duty be established: C & F v WC & TC (1989 SC) ILRM 815.

Recent legislation has amended s.117 of the 1965 Act to ensure that in any case where a testator has not married the other parent of his child, the child will have a right to apply for proper provision out of the estate, irrespective of whether the will was made before or after commencement of the recent legislation: Status of Children Act 1987 s.31. See also JUDICIAL SEPARATION.

**child, removal from the State.** See CHILD ABDUCTION; PASSPORT.

**child, rights of.** The United Nation's Convention on the Rights of the Child was adopted by the UN General Assembly on 20 Nov 1989 and ratified by Ireland in Sept 1992. The Convention treats the child as a juristic person with a special status needing special care and attention. The rights which are recognised are survival, development and protection rights. See Blake in 9ILT & SJ (1991) 114 and Horgan in 9ILT & SJ (1991) 161.

**child, status of.** The relationship of every person is now determined, unless a contrary intention appears, irrespective of whether his father or mother are or have been married to each other: Status of Children Act 1987 s.3. This now also applies to taxation legislation: Finance Act 1988 s.74. See District Court (Status of Children Act 1987) Rules 1988 (SI No 152 of 1988) and Circuit Court Rules (SI No 152 of 1990).

**child in care.** Where a child is *in the care* of a health board, the board must provide care for him (a) by placing him with a foster parent, or (b) by placing him in residential care, or (c) by placing him with a suitable person with a view to his adoption, or (d) by making other suitable arrangements: Child Care Act 1991 s.36. The board must facilitate reasonable access to the child by his parents; such access may include allowing the child to reside with his parents (ibid s.37). The board may remove a child in its care from the custody of any person with whom he has been placed under s.36 (ibid s.43(1)). The Minister is required to make regulations governing the placement of children with relatives (ibid s.41). See also Report on Child Sexual Abuse (LRC 32 — 1990). See AFTERCARE; CARE ORDER; CHILDREN'S RESIDENTIAL CENTRE; WELFARE OF CHILDREN.

**child stealing.** The offence committed by any person who unlawfully, either by force or fraud, leads or takes away any child under the age of fourteen years or who harbours such a child. It is a felony (qv). See Offences Against the Person Act 1861 s.56.

**childbirth, attendance at.** It is an offence for a person to attend a woman in childbirth unless that person is a midwife, a registered medical practitioner, or a student undergoing professional training, except in a case of sudden or urgent necessity: Nurses Act 1985 s.58. See MIDWIFE.

**children's residential centre.** Any home or other institution for the residential care of children in the care of health boards or other children who are not receiving adequate care and protection: Child Care Act 1991 s.59. Health boards (qv) are required to establish and maintain a register of children's residential centres; it is an offence to carry on such a centre unless it is registered (ibid ss.60-64). Health Boards are also required to make arrangements to ensure the provision of an adequate number of residential places for children in care (ibid s.38). The Minister is required to make regulations for the purpose of ensuring proper standards (ibid s.63) and in relation to the placing of children in residential care (ibid s.40).

When Part VIII of the 1991 Act has come into operation, every institution which was an industrial school certified under the Children's Act 1908 or was a school approved under the Health Act 1953 s.55, will be deemed to be registered as a children's residential centre. See CARE ORDER.

**chinese wall.** A metaphor to describe a set of internal rules and procedures established by an organisation for the purpose of preventing certain types of information in the possession of one part of the organisation from being communicated to other parts of the same organisation. A chinese wall will sometimes be provided eg to prevent insider dealing (qv) or to protect the confidentiality of a tax amnesty. See Companies Act 1990 s.108(7); Waiver of Certain Tax, Interest and Penalties Act 1993 ss.7-8.

**chirographum apud debitorum repertum praesumitur solutum.** [A deed or bond found with the debtor is presumed to be paid].

**chirograph.** Formerly, a deed was written in two parts on the same paper or parchment, with the word *chirographum* (ie autograph) written in capital letters between the two parts; it was then cut through the middle of the letters and a part given to each party. When the cutting was indented, the deed was known as an *indenture* (qv).

**chose.** A thing. A *chose in possession* is a movable chattel in the custody or control of the owner or the right to which can be enforced by taking physical possession eg of one's own goods. A *chose in action* is a right of proceeding in law to procure the payment of a sum of money or to recover pecuniary damages for a wrong inflicted or the non-performance of a contract. A *legal chose in action* is a right of action which could be enforced in a court of law eg debts; an *equitable chose in action* is a right which formerly could only be enforced in a court of chancery eg an interest in a trust. See Patents Act 1992 s.79.

**Christian name.** Includes any forename: Registration of Business Names Act 1963 s.2. See NAME, CHANGE OF.

**Church annulment.** Refers generally to a decree of nullity of marriage granted by an Ecclesiastical Tribunal of the Catholic Church; it cannot be a factor bearing on the decision of the courts whether to grant a nullity decree: N (otherwise K) v K (1986) ILRM 75. See MARRIAGE, NULLITY OF.

**Church holidays.** Days which an employer may substitute for a public holiday (qv) by giving the employee notice of the substitution at least 14 days beforehand. They are Ascension Thursday, Feast of Corpus Christi, and the following except when they fall on a Sunday: January 6th, August 15th, November 1st, December 8th. See Holiday (Employees) Act 1973.

**c.i.f.** [Cost, insurance, freight]. If a seller agrees to sell goods to a buyer at a price *c.i.f. Dublin Docks*, the price includes the price of the goods, the insurance premium and freight payable as far as Dublin Docks. See Michel Freres Societe Anonyme v Kilkenny Wollen Mills Ltd (1959) IR 157.

**cigarettes.** See TOBACCO PRODUCT.

**cinematograph film.** Any sequence of visual images recorded on material of any description (whether translucent or not) so as to be capable, by use of that material (a) of being shown as a moving picture or (b) of being recorded on other material by the use of which it can be shown: Copyright Act 1963 s.18(10). Copyright subsists in a cinematograph film for fifty years from the end of the year in which the film was first *published*, or in the case of a newsreel, fifty years from the end of the year in which the principal events depicted in the film occurred (ibid s.18(2) and (7)).

*Published* means the sale, letting on hire, or offer for sale or hire, of copies of the film to, or by showing by any means to, the public (ibid s.18(10)). A film is to be taken as including the sounds embodied in any sound track associated with the film (ibid s.18(8)). A video cassette has been held to come within the definition of a cinematograph film: DPP v Irwin (1985) HC. A video recording is included in the definition of cinematograph film in the Broadcasting and Wireless Telegraphy Act 1988 s.1. See CENSORSHIP; COPYRIGHT; INFRINGEMENT OF COPYRIGHT; VIDEO.

**Circuit Court.** The court above the District Court (qv) in the hierarchical system of courts. The country is divided into a number of circuits; a Circuit Court judge is assigned to each circuit and travels to several towns in that circuit to hear cases, sitting alone in civil cases and with a jury in criminal cases when the accused is so entitled. There are permanent Circuit Courts in Dublin and Cork to which there are 8 and 2 judges assigned respectively.

On civil matters, the court can award damages of up to £30,000. It can deal with proceedings relating to the execution of trusts where the trust estate (in so far as it relates to land), does not exceed £200 rateable valuation. Failure to give formal proof of rateable valuation does not deprive the Circuit Court of jurisdiction: Harrington v Murphy (1989) IR 207. It can also deal with matters relating to registered land with a similar valuation.

On criminal matters the Circuit Court hears *indictable* (qv) offences sent to it by the District Court. The judge may impose whatever punishment is permitted by statute or common law. An appeal lies from the decision of the Circuit Court to the High Court in civil cases and to the Court of Criminal Appeal in criminal cases.

The Circuit Court also hears appeals from the District Court, both civil and criminal, which appeal consists of a rehearing of the case and the substitution of the court's decision for the District Court's decision, but limited to the jurisdiction in that regard of the lower court.

The jurisdiction of the Circuit Court is conferred on that court and upon its judges collectively, and accordingly the jurisdiction of the court is capable of being transferred from one individual of the several circuit judges to another: The State (Boyle) v Nealon Ors (1986) ILRM 337. See Courts (Supplemental Provisions) Act 1961; Courts Act 1981 and 1991; Jurisdiction of Courts and Enforcement of Judgments (European Communities) Act 1988 s.14; Companies (Amendment) Act 1990 s.3(9). [Text: Lee]. See ENLARGEMENT OF JURISDICTION; FAMILY COURT; FAMILY LAW PROCEEDINGS; REMITTAL OF ACTION; RULES OF COURT.

**circuits.** The division of the State for judicial business. See CIRCUIT COURT.

**circular.** See ADVERTISEMENT.

**circumstantial evidence.** Evidence of a fact relevant to a fact in issue (qv), from which the fact in issue may be inferred. Before an accused person may be found guilty on circumstantial evidence, the court must be satisfied not only that the circumstances are consistent with his guilt but also that they are inconsistent with any other rational conclusion that he is the guilty person. In cases of manslaughter and murder, the fact of death can be proved by circumstantial rather than by direct evidence; death can be inferred from such strong and unequivocal circumstances of presumption as to render it morally certain and leaves no room for reasonable doubt: The People (Attorney General) v Thomas (1954) IR 319. See also R v Exall (1886) 4 F F 922.

**citation.** (1) The calling upon a person who is not a party to an action or proceedings to appear before the court eg a person interested in the estate of a deceased may issue a citation requiring the executor to prove the will where he has failed to do so: RSC O.79 rr 52-57; O.80 rr.56- 57.

(2) The quotation of a decided case in legal argument as an authority supporting the argument.

**citizenship.** The civil status which determines the rights and obligations of a person under the domestic law of the State. Fidelity to the nation and loyalty to the State are fundamental political duties of all citizens: 1937 Constitution, art.9(2). No person may be excluded from Irish citizenship by reason of the sex of that person (ibid art.9(1)(3)). Citizenship can be acquired by birth, by marriage, by grant as a token of honour, and by naturalisation (qv): Irish Nationality and Citizenship Act 1956.

Every person born in Ireland is a citizen by birth, but not if born in Northern Ireland on or after 6th December 1922 unless a *declaration of citizenship* is made. Every person is a citizen if either of his parents was a citizen at the time of his birth; in future however, persons of Irish descent who acquire Irish citizenship will be deemed Irish from the date of registration and not from birth: Irish Nationality and Citizenship Act 1986 s.2. The fact that a person's parents have not married each other is not a bar to Irish citizenship: Status of Children Act 1987 s.5. As a consequence, a person born abroad whose parents have not married each other is an Irish citizen if either of his parents was an Irish citizen at the time of the person's birth.

Formerly every woman, if not already a citizen, acquired Irish citizenship from the date of her marriage to a citizen; a man did not so acquire: Somjee v Minister for Justice (1981) ILRM 324. Now, the acquisition of Irish citizenship by post-nuptial declaration is available to the alien spouse, whether male or female, of a person Irish by birth or descent, at any time after a three year period following marriage (or acquisition of citizenship by the Irish spouse if later) provided the marriage is still subsisting in law and fact: 1986 Act s.3.

Citizens of the State who are part of a family unit are entitled to exercise their right to the company, care and parentage of their parents within the State: Fajujonu v Minister for Justice (1990 SC) ILRM 234.

The President of Ireland may grant citizenship as a token of honour to a person, or his child or grandchild, who in the opinion of the government has rendered signal honour to the nation. The first honorary Irish Citizen was Sir Alfred Chester Beatty in 1957; he bequeathed his famous library in Dublin for the use and enjoyment of the public on his death in 1968 (see Chester Beatty Library Act 1968 and 1986).

Provision is made for the introduction of *European citizenship*: Maastricht Treaty 1992 art.G(C) inserting new art.8 in Rome Treaty 1957. Every person holding the nationality of a member State will be a citizen of the European Union (qv) with rights and duties eg to move and reside freely within the territory of the member States of the Union; to vote and stand as a canditate at local and European Parliament elections in the member State in which he resides; to make complaints to the European Ombudsman; and the right to consular protection outside the Community from the embassy of any member State. See NATURALISATION; PASSPORT; PETITION; TITLE OF NOBILITY.

**citizen's arrest.** Popular expression meaning the power of an individual person to arrest another in certain circumstances. See ARREST WITHOUT WARRANT.

**city code.** See MERGERS.

**city council.** See BOROUGH.

**civic honour.** The honour previously conferred on a person by a city or county borough: Municipal Privileges (Ireland) Act 1876 ss.11-12 and Local Government (Repeal of Enactments) Act 1956 s.1, sch. Now, any local authority may confer a civic honour on a distinguished person, including the admission of the person to the *honorary freedom* of its functional area: Local Government Act 1991 s.48. It is a reserved function (qv) of the authority. See BURGESS; HONOUR; TITLE OF NOBILITY.

**civil.** As opposed to criminal, ecclesiastical, or military. See CIVIL LAW.

**civil arrest.** The arrest of a person by order of the court in connection with a civil matter eg (a) the arrest of a contributory of a company about to quit the State or otherwise to abscond: Companies Act 1963 s.247; In re Ulster Land, Building & Investment Company (1887) 17 LR Ir 591; In re Central Trust Investments Society (1982); In re O'Shea's (Dublin) Ltd (1984 HC); (b) an arrest in relation to bankruptcy: Bankruptcy Act 1988 ss.9 & 23; In re O'M, a bankrupt (1988 HC); (c) the arrest of a debtor about to quit Ireland under the Debtors Act (Ireland) 1872 s.7 and RSC O.69. See Courtney in 8 ILT & SJ (1990) 2OO.

**civil bill.** The legal document whereby civil proceedings are commenced in the Circuit Court (qv); an equity civil bill is required for equitable relief and a testamentary civil bill for probate actions: RCC O.5 r.1; O.34. A Circuit Court judge is empowered to amend a civil bill to an equity civil bill, the latter being a derivative of the former: Kearns v Deery (1993 HC) ILRM 496. See APPEARANCE; PLEADINGS; SUMMONS, SERVICE OF.

**civil custody.** The custody of the Garda Siochana or other lawful civil authority authorised to retain in custody civil prisoners and includes confinement in a public prison: Defence Act 1954 s.2(1).

**civil law.** The body of law dealing with the resolution of disputes between individuals; it provides a remedy, usually a financial one, to the aggrieved party against the wrongdoer by way of compensation rather than as punishment.

**civil power, in aid of.** A reservist may be called out in aid of the civil power, on the direction of the Minister, in the maintenance or restoration of the public peace: Defence Act 1954 s.90

**civil proceedings.** Proceedings in the civil courts which are commenced in the High Court by originating summons or by petition, in the Circuit Court by civil bill and petition, and in the District Court by civil process. See RSC O.1 r.1; RCC O.5 r.1; DCR r.114.

Civil proceedings are generally delayed pending the outcome of criminal proceedings in the same matter, but this is not an immutable rule. See O'Flynn & O'Regan v Mid-Western Health Board (1991 SC) 2 IR 223. See PLEADINGS; SUMMONS, SERVICE OF.

**civil process.** The legal document whereby civil proceedings are commenced in the District Court (qv): DCR r.114. See APPEARANCE; PLEADINGS; SUMMONS, SERVICE OF.

**civil remedy.** The remedy available to an aggrieved person following civil proceedings by way of compensation rather than punishment of the wrongdoer eg damages, specific performance, injunction, judicial review (qqv). [Text: Kerr (2)].

**civil servant.** A servant of the State, other than the holder of political or judicial office, who is employed in a civil capacity and whose remuneration is paid wholly and directly out of monies voted by the Oireachtas. Civil servants who are *established* (ie permanent) hold office at the will and pleasure of the government whereas *unestablished* (ie temporary) officers may have their services terminated by the appropriate authority: Civil Service Regulations Act 1956 ss.5-6. Other conditions of employment are fixed by the Minister (ibid s.17).

It has been held that the power of termination of a civil servant (during, or at the end of, a probationary period) is not one which can be exercised arbitrarily: The State (Daly) v Minister for Agriculture (1988) ILRM 173. Also an extension of a probationary period must be explicit and the appropriate authority must have been satisfied during the period of probation of a failure of the civil servant to fulfil a condition of the probation: Whelan v Minister for Justice (1991 HC) 2 IR 241 — see Barry in 9ILT & SJ (1991) 2 and 9ILT Dig (1991) 73. See also Civil Service Regulations (Amendment) Act 1958. See Flynn v An Post (1987 SC) IR 68; Reidy v Minister for Agriculture (1989 HC) ITLR (4 Sep); O'Reilly v Minister for Industry and Commerce (1993 HC). See INCITEMENT; MARRIAGE BAR; VICARIOUS LIABILITY.

**civil wrong.** A tort (qv).

**civilian.** A person who is not a member of the defence forces.

**claim.** The assertion of a right. See INDORSEMENT OF CLAIM; STATEMENT OF CLAIM.

**clam vi, aut precario.** [By stealth, violence or entreaty]. See PRESCRIPTION.

**class gift.** A gratuitious grant to a number of persons of the same description eg *to X's brothers.* A class gift in a will, speaks from the date of death of the testator. If any member of the class is alive at the testator's death, membership of the class is fixed at that moment. If no member of the class is alive at the testator's death, then prima facia, the gift includes all members born at any future date. If a life interest precedes the class gift, then all those of the class alive when the life interest ceases are entitled to share in the gift. See Succession Act 1965 ss.91 and 98. See LAPSE.

**class rights.** The special rights attaching to different classes of shares in a company. In certain circumstances, class rights are not *ipso facto* deemed to vary in two major kinds of change to the capital structure, in the absence of some provision to the contrary, eg the issue of additional shares ranking *pari passu* with the existing ones, and the issue of new shares carrying preferential rights as regards voting, dividend, return of capital or otherwise: Companies Act 1963 Table A.

For variation of class rights see Companies Amendment Act 1983 s.38. Class rights may not be varied in a capital reduction without the requisite class approval (ibid s.38(3)). Where a proposed variation of class rights obtains the requisite approval of the class affected, dissenting shareholders representing 10 per cent in value of the class may apply to the court to stop the proposal being put into effect: Companies Act 1963 s.78. See In re Holders Investment Trust (1971) 2 All ER 289. See RECONSTRUCTION OF COMPANY; TAKE OUT MERGER.

**clause.** A sub division of a document.

**clausulae inconsuetae semper inducunt suspicionem.** [Unusual clauses always excite suspicion].

**clausum fregit.** [He broke the close].

**Clayton's case.** The rule that in a running account in the absence of special agreement a creditor may treat the earliest credit as being in repayment of the earliest debt: Clayton's Case (Devaynes v Noble (1816) 1 Mer 572). However, see Companies Act 1963 s.288 as amended by Companies Act 1990 s.136 and Smurfit Paribas Bank Ltd v AAB Export Finance Ltd (1991 HC) 2 IR 19.

**clean hands.** A maxim of equity (qv) — *he who comes to equity must come with clean hands.* See Ardent Fisheries v Minister for Tourism and Forestry (1987) ILRM 528.

**clear days.** Complete days. Days prescribed in the Rules of the Superior Courts which are not expressed to be clear days, are to be reckoned exclusively of the first day and inclusively of the last day: RSC O.122 r.10. See TIME, COURT RULES.

**cleared site value.** The value of land as a site cleared of buildings, less such sum as the arbitrator determines to be the cost of clearing and levelling the land, to which the owner of a house is entitled as compensation in relation to a *compul-*

*sory purchase* (qv) effected under the provisions of the Housing Act 1966 and where the acquired property includes the house which, in the opinion of the housing authority (qv), is unfit for human habitation and not capable of being rendered fit for human habitation at reasonable expense (ibid s.84(1)). See also Housing Act 1966 (Acquisition of Land) Regulations 1966 (SI No 278 of 1966). See COMPENSATION AND COMPULSORY PURCHASE.

**clerical error.** A mistake made in a mechanical process such as writing or copying as opposed to the intellectual process of drafting: Maere's Application (1962) RPC 182. See ORDER; SLIP RULE; TYPOGRAPHICAL ERROR.

**client account.** The account required to be kept by a solicitor (qv) in relation to a client. Money in a client account is held by a solicitor in trust for his clients; he is not beneficially entitled to it and he is not entitled to draw a cheque on the account for the purposes of discharging an amount due by him to an other person: Incorporated Law Society v Owens (1990) 8ILT Dig 64. See Solicitors' Accounts Regulations 1984 (SI No 204 of 1984). See also AUCTIONEER; INSURANCE BROKER.

**clinical trials, conduct of.** The conducting of a systematic investigation or series of investigations for the purpose of ascertaining the effects (including kinetic effects) of the administration of one or more substances or preparations on persons where such administration may have a pharmacological or harmful effect: Control of Clinical Trials Acts 1987 s.6(2) and 1990 s.2.

Excluded from clinical trials are the administration of substances or preparations in the ordinary course of medical or dental practice where the principal purpose is to prevent disease in, or to save the life, restore the health, alleviate the condition or relieve the suffering of, the patient (ibid 1990 Act s.2).

A person must not conduct a clinical trial unless (a) he is a registered medical practitioner or a registered dentist, and (b) there is a subsisting permission granted by the Minister in respect of the trial, and (c) an *ethics committee* has given its approval (ibid s.6(1)). These provisions do not apply in specified circumstances to a clinical trial of a substance or preparation which has been granted a *product authorisation* under the Medical Preparations (Licensing, Advertisement and Sale) Regulations 1984 (SI No 210 of 1984) (ibid 1987 Act s.2).

Consent in writing to participation in a clinical trial is required (ibid s.9). Prior to a clinical trial being arranged or conducted, the Minister must be satisfied on the adequacy of security to compensate participants who may suffer injury, loss or damage (ibid 1990 Act s.3). See SI No 321 of 1988. See ETHICS COMMITTEE.

**clog on equity of redemption.** The equitable doctrine which does not permit the equity of redemption (qv) to be fettered or unreasonably restricted by any provision which would make it difficult for the mortgagor (qv) to redeem a mortgage after the date for repayment of the mortgage debt.

**close.** (1) The termination of pleadings, as in *close of pleadings*. (2) Enclosed land. See WAY, RIGHT OF.

**close company.** A company which, for the purposes of corporation tax, is considered as under the control of five or fewer participators or by any number of participators who are directors. A *participator* is one who owns share capital and has voting rights in the company: Corporation Tax Act 1976 Part X; ss.94-104. See Rahinstown Estates v Hughes (1987) ILRM 599.

**close season.** The varying periods of the year during which it is unlawful to hunt game. See OPEN SEASON.

**closed shop.** The term used to describe agreements between employers and trade unions whereby jobs are only to be obtained or retained if the employee is, or becomes and remains, a member of a specified union. They can be *pre-entry* agreements where the individual must be a trade union member before he can be employed, or *post-entry* where the employer is entitled to employ a non-trade unionist provided he agrees to join the union immediately or shortly after employment.

It has been held that the imposition of a closed shop on existing employees, being a restriction on their right to disassociate, is unconstitutional: Educational Co of Ireland Ltd v Fitzpatrick (No 2) (1961) IR 345; Meshell v CIE

(1973) IR 121. The practice of requiring potential employees to join specific trade unions as a pre-condition to obtaining employment may be unconstitutional and contrary to Art 11 of the European Convention of Human Rights (Young, James Wester v UK [1981] IRLR 408; 75 Gazette ILSI 237).

**closing order.** See UNFIT HOUSE.

**closing speeches.** In a trial on indictment, the prosecution has the right to a closing speech, except where the accused is unrepresented and does not call a witness other than a witness of character only: Criminal Justice Act 1984 s.24. The defence has a right to a closing speech in all cases; the closing speech of the defence is made after that for the prosecution.

**club.** A voluntary association of persons combined for purposes other than carrying on business. It is not a partnership. A club sues and is sued in the names of the members of its committee, or the officers, on behalf of themselves and all other members of the club. A club is founded on the contract between the members; in the absence of a contrary provision, members are liable only to the extent of their subscriptions, and payments by members become the property of all the members and cannot be the subject of a resulting trust if the club is wound up, in which case any surplus assets are distributed to the members for the time being per capita. The property of a club is usually vested in trustees who hold it on behalf of the members. A club often has no legal persona apart from that derived from all the members and consequently cannot incur liability from wrongs at the suit of a member of that body: Murphy v Roche (1987 HC) IR 106.

Frequently clubs are registered under the Registration of Clubs (Ireland) Act 1904 to 1988 in order to avail of the provisions to supply their members with excisable liquors without a licence: see In re Parnell GAA Club Ltd (1984) ILRM 246. For the steps to be taken for a club to apply for and hold a Certificate of Registration, see Cassidy in 7ILT & SJ (1989) 112. Registered clubs are restricted on advertising functions to be held by the club: Intoxicating Liquor Act 1988 s.45.

Some clubs are *proprietary clubs* wherein the property of the club is owned by the proprietor who bears the expenses but who also receives the subscriptions of the members; such a club cannot be registered under the 1904 Act. Alternatively, some clubs incorporate themselves as companies usually *limited by guarantee.*

Any proposal to expel a member from a club must comply with the principles of *natural justice;* he must be informed of the complaint against him and be given an opportunity to be heard in his own defence. See Rochford v Storey (1982) HC. See also Courts (No 2) Act 1986 s.9; Intoxicating Liquor Act 1988 ss.42-46. [Text: Woods (3); Palmer UK]. See WILDLIFE DEALING.

**CMR.** [Convention relative au contrat de transport international de merchandises par route]. The Convention on the Contract for the International Carriage of Goods by Road as given effect in Ireland by the International Carriage of Goods by Road Act 1990. The Convention lays down standard conditions of contract for the international carriage of goods. It defines the rights and obligations of the consignor, carrier and the consignee eg the carrier is generally liable for loss, damage or delay to the goods, but the liability is limited unless there has been wilful misconduct or a special value for the goods has been declared. Limits set on liability in the Canals Act 1830, the Railway and Canal Traffic Act 1854 s.7, or the Sale of Goods Acts 1893–1980 do not apply to contracts for the carriage of goods governed by the Convention (ibid 1990 Act s.3(3)). The Statute of Limitations 1957 Part III (which allows for exceptions for fraud, mistake and disability) applies to actions under the CMR. See CMR Contracting Parties Order 1991 (SI No 160 of 1991).

**co.** Abbreviation of *company* (qv).

**co-authors.** See JOINT AUTHORSHIP.

**co-defendants.** See DEFENDANT, JOINT.

**co-operatives.** As a general rule, co-operatives are commercial enterprises which tend to do business principally with their own members with the object of providing a product or service at minimal cost; while a dividend may be payable to members, its maximisation is not necessarily the primary objective.

Co-operatives are usually registered as companies under the Companies Acts 1963-1988 or as societies under the Industrial & Provident Societies Acts 1893-1978. Special legislation exists for building societies and credit unions: Building Societies Act 1989 and Credit Union Act 1966. A disciplinary hearing of a co-operative must observe the requirements of natural justice (qv): Ryan v VIP Taxi Co-operative Society Ltd (1989) ITLR (10 Apr). See In re Belfast Tailors' Co-Partnership (1909) 1 IR 49.

**co-ownership.** The concurrent ownership of two or more persons in the same property. See Patents Act 1992 s.80. See JOINT TENANCY; TENANCY IN COMMON.

**coarse fish.** Any freshwater fish or the spawn or fry thereof other than salmon, trout (including rainbow trout and char) or eels or their spawn or fry: Fisheries (Amendment) (No 2) Act 1987 s.2. See FISHING LICENCE; TROUT.

**code.** A systematic collection in comprehensive form of laws or a branch of law eg the Sale of Goods Act 1893 and the Bills of Exchange Act 1882 were statutes collecting and stating the whole of the law, as it stood at the time they were enacted.

**code of conduct.** Rules for practical guidance in relation to practices to be followed eg under the Insurance Act 1989, the Minister may by order prescribe the practices to be followed by insurance brokers (qv) or insurance agents (qv) in their dealings with their clients or undertakings or with other persons (ibid s.56).

**code of practice.** Rules for practical guidance with respect to the requirements of some statute or with respect to the manner in which business is conducted.

Failure to observe a code does not of itself generally render a person liable to legal proceedings, but it may be admissible in evidence eg see Safety, Health and Welfare at Work Act 1989 ss.2, 30 and 31; Industrial Relations Act 1990 ss.42-43; Environmental Protection Agency Act 1992 ss.76-77. Provision however has been made that any code of practice prepared by bodies representing data controllers (qv) or data processors (qv) will have the force of law where approved by a resolution of each House of the Oireachtas: Data Protection Act 1988 s.13. Also the Central Bank can compel compliance with a code of practice it draws up: Central Bank Act 1989 s.117. Eolas (now Forfas) is empowered to issue codes of recommended practice: Industrial Research & Standards Act 1961; Science and Technology Act 1987; Industrial Development Act 1993 ss.9 and 18. The Labour Court is empowered to investigate a complaint that there has been a breach of a code of practice concerning industrial relations: Industrial Relations Act 1990 s.43. See UNFAIR DISMISSAL; WORKER PARTICIPATION.

**codicil.** An instrument executed by a testator for adding to, altering, explaining or confirming a will previously made by him. A codicil must be executed with the same formalities as a will, as a will is defined as including a codicil: Succession Act 1965 s.3(1). The effect of the codicil is to bring the will down to the date of the codicil and both instruments are read together, with the original dispositions as altered by the codicil. See Earl of Mountcashell v Smyth (1895) 1 IR 346. See RSC O.79 r.85; O.80 r.84. See SUPPLEMENTAL PROBATE, GRANT OF.

**coercion.** See DURESS; MARITAL COERCION.

**cogitationis poenam nemo patitur.** [The thoughts and intents of men are not punishable]. See INTENTION.

**cognates.** Those persons who are related on the mother's side. See AGNATES.

**cognisance, judicial.** Judicial notice (qv) or knowledge.

**cohabitation.** Living together as or as if husband and wife. The guarantees in the 1937 Constitution relating to the family are confined to families based on marriage: The State (Nicolaou) v An Bord Uchtala (1966) IR 567. See also Mulhern v Clery (1930) IR 649. The favourable treatment that cohabiting claimants enjoyed as regards social welfare, over their married counterparts was removed by the Social Welfare (No 2) Act 1989. See CONJUGAL RIGHTS, RESTITUTION OF; DIVORCE A MENSA ET THORO; FAMILY INCOME SUPPLEMENT; SPOUSE.

**cohaeredes sunt quasi unum corpus, propter unitatem juris quod habent.** [Co-heirs are regarded as one person on account of the unity of title which they possess]. See COPARCENARY.

**cohesion.** Term in EC law to describe the process whereby economic and social disparities between the richer and the less well-off regions of the Community are to be reduced progressively: Treaty of Rome 1957. The Maastricht Treaty 1992 reinforces the objective of *economic and social cohesion* in the Rome Treaty and specifies many of the means to be used to achieve it eg the principles of cohesion are included in arts.2 and 3; actions to strengthen cohesion are specified in arts.130a-130e, including the establishment of a *Cohesion Fund* and there is a specific Protocol (15) on cohesion which contains several important commitments on funding.

**cohesion fund.** Provision has been made for the establishment of a new EC *Cohesion Fund* before the end of 1993 which will provide financial contributions towards projects in the environment and *trans-European networks* in the area of transport infrastructure: Treaty of Rome 1957 art.130d inserted by Maastricht Treaty 1992 art.G(D)(38). The Fund will be for the benefit of member States with a GNP per capita of less than 90% of the EC average which have a programme leading to the fulfilment of the conditions of *economic convergence* as set out in art.104c: Protocol on Economic and Social Cohesion.

**coif.** A white silk cap which serjeants-at-law (qv) wore in court.

**coins, coinage.** There is provision for coins of 1p, 2p, 5p, 10p, 20p, 50p and £1: Decimal Currency Acts 1969 to 1990; New Coinage (Twenty Pence) Order 1986 (SI No 52 of 1986); Coinage (Dimensions and Design) (One Pound Coin) Regulations 1990 (SI No 83 of 1990). A perpetual copyright subsists in all coins of the State and in the artistic work defining the design of such coins and belongs to the Minister: Copyright Act 1963 s.57.

As the EC moves towards full economic and monetary union, member States may issue coins subject to approval by the European Central Bank (qv) of the volume of the issue: Treaty of Rome 1957 art.105a(2) as inserted by Maastricht Treaty 1992 art.G(D)(25). The EC Council may adopt measures to harmonise the denominations and technical specification to permit smooth circulation within the Community. See COUNTERFEIT; LEGAL TENDER.

**collateral.** [By the side of]. An additional contract, agreement, or assurance, which is independent of, but subordinate to the main contract, agreement, or assurance affecting the same subject-matter. A collateral security is one given additional to the main security. See McCullough Sales Ltd v Chetham Timber Co Ltd (1983) HC; Namlooze Venootschap De Faam v Dorset Manufacturing Co (1949) IR 203.

**collection.** A collection of money from the public in any public place or places or by house to house visits or both in such place or places and by such visits for the benefit (actual, alleged or implied) of a particular object, whether charitable or not charitable, and whether any badge, emblem or other token is or is not exchanged or offered in exchange for money so collected: Street and House to House Collection Act 1962. A *collection permit* is required; otherwise such a collection by a person will constitute an offence. See also House to House Collection Order 1972 (SI No 75 of 1972). See also PUBLIC APPEAL, MONEY COLLECTED IN.

**collective agreement.** Generally an agreement by or on behalf of an employer, on the one hand, and by or on behalf of an *authorised* trade union (qv), representative of the employees to whom the agreement relates, on the other hand. A collective agreement may be incorporated into a contract of employment; enforceability of such an agreement may depend on whether it was intended to create legal relations. See Allied Irish Banks Ltd v Lupton (1985) ILRM 170; Kenny & Ors v An Post (1988) IR 285.

A rule in a collective agreement which does not comply with the principle of equal treatment is null and void: Pensions Act 1990 s.74. See also Employment Equality Act 1977 s.10. See CUSTOM AND PRACTICE.

**collective responsibility.** The government (qv) is *collectively responsible* to Dail Eireann for the Departments of State administered by the members of the government: 1937 Constitution, art.28(4). This involves an obligation to accept collective responsibility for deci-

sions, and the non-disclosure of dissenting or different views of members of the government prior to the making of decisions: Attorney General v The Sole Member of the Tribunal of Inquiry into the Beef Processing Industry (1993 SC) ILRM 81. See EUROPEAN COMMISSION; RECKLESS TRADING.

**colligenda bona.** See AD COLLIGENDA BONA.

**collision of ship.** Civil jurisdiction in relation to the physical collision of ships (and also where a ship has suffered damage due to evasive action to avoid a collision) has been agreed in a 1952 international convention which is given domestic effect in Ireland by the Jurisdiction of Courts (Maritime Conventions) Act 1989. Jurisdiction may be in the courts:- where the defendant has his place of business or residence; where the defendant's ship has been arrested; where the collision took place if in a port or inland waters; or where the parties agree. The choice is normally at the option of the plaintiff. See ASSESSOR.

**collop.** The unit, under the *common* (qv) of pasture, by which the right to graze animals upon a common grazing was measured; a cow was the equivalent of two collop, a horse was a collop and a half. In the Land Registry (qv) a collop has been registered as appurtenant to the land. [Text: Healy].

**collusion.** An agreement, usually secret, for some deceitful or unlawful purpose. It may amount to the crime or tort of conspiracy (qv). See also PRINCIPAL IN CRIME.

**colore officii.** [By virtue of a person's office]. See Steele v Williams (1853) 8 Exch 625.

**colour.** See HATRED, INCITEMENT TO; RACE.

**colourable.** Term to indicate that which is pretended. See McCartaigh v Daly (1986) ILRM 116.

**colourable device.** The term sometimes referred to in relation to an arrest under the Offences Against the State Act 1939 s.30 where the arresting garda has no bona fide suspicion that the person arrested has committed an offence under that Act, but wishes to detain and question him in respect of another offence. See The People (DPP) v Quilligan (1987) ILRM 606. See SCHEDULED OFFENCE.

**colouring agent.** See E-NUMBER.

**comfort, letter of.** See LETTER OF COM-FORT.

**combined drain.** A drainage pipe, or a system of such pipes, that is not vested or controlled by a sanitary authority and is used to convey trade effluent or other matter (other than storm water) from two or more premises to any waters or to a sewer: LG (Water Pollution) (Amendment) Act 1990 s.2. A local authority is empowered to declare a specified combined drain to be a *sewer*; this enables the authority to treat each discharge into a private drain as a discharge to a sewer and thereby exercise greater control on the effluent (ibid s.22).

**Comhairle na n-Ospideal.** The statutory body with power to regulate the number and type of consultant medical appointments in hospitals taking patients under the Health Acts and to specify the qualifications for such appointments: Health Act 1970 s.41.

**comity.** Courtesy. The comity of nations is the friendly recognition of each other's laws. As regards comity of courts, see Rowan v Rowan (1987) HC.

**commencement.** The time at which an act, regulation, statutory instrument, or section or part thereof, comes into operation. A bill becomes law on and from the day it is signed by the President of Ireland and, unless the contrary intention appears, comes into operation on that day: 1937 Constitution, art.25(4)(1). A *commencement order* is an order made, usually by a Minister under a statutory power, specifying a commencement date, where such an order is required. See Interpretation Act 1937 s.12 sch. See REPEAL.

**commercial credit.** See LETTER OF CREDIT.

**commercial law.** The body of law dealing with contracts, (eg sale of goods and supply of services), intellectual property, bankruptcy, banking, insurance, agency, companies and partnership (qqv). [Text: Byrne R (1); Doolan (5); Forde (5); Sheeran].

**commission.** (1) An order or authority to do an act or exercise a power eg an authority to an agent to enter into a contract. (2) A body charged with a commission eg Civil Service Commission. (3) The remuneration of an agent or an employee.

As regards companies, it is not permissable for a company to apply any of its shares or capital money in payment of any commission to any person, in consideration of the subscription for any shares in the company, except where permitted by its *articles of association* and the commission does not exceed ten per cent of the issued price of the shares: Companies Act 1963 s.59.

As regards auctioneer's commission, the test applied by the court in relation to a dispute over commission is whether the event contracted for by the principal actually happened and whether the agent was the cause of the happening. It has been held that a *sole agent* is not entitled to commission where the exertions of the sole agent had not played any part in effecting a sale and the agency agreement did not contain any express term prohibiting the principal from negotiating a sale during the continuance of the agency: Murphy, Buckley Keogh Ltd v Pye (Ireland) Ltd (1971) IR 57. See also Cusack v Bothwell (1943) 77 ILTR 18; Stokes Quirke Ltd v Clohessy (1957) IR 84; Henehan v Courtney (1967) 101 ILTR 25; Walkin v Murphy (1991 DC) 9ILT & SJ 247; Kehoe & Haythornwaite (1991 CC) 10 ILT & SJ (1992) 50. [Text: Mahon; Murdoch UK].

As regards insurance, the Minister is empowered to reduce the commission payments to insurance intermediaries (qv), where he is of the opinion that these are excessive: Insurance Act 1989 s.37. He is also empowered to prohibit commission payments in the form of benefits-in-kind or loans (ibid s.38). A life assurance policy which is in contravention of these provisions is voidable at the instance of the policyholder within one month of conviction of the insurer and the premium will be refunded together with interest (ibid s.42).

As regards building societies, a commission includes any gift, bonus, fee, payment or other benefit: Building Societies Act 1989 s.2(1). There are prohibitions on the acceptance of commissions eg by a person authorising the making of a loan (ibid s.25). See AUCTIONEER; EUROPEAN COMMISSION; UNDER-SUBSCRIBED; UNDERWRITER; WRONGFUL DISMISSAL.

**commission, evidence to.** The taking

of evidence on oath from a witness whose attendance at court ought for some sufficient reason be dispensed with: RSC O.39.

**commission agent.** An incomplete form of agency by indirect representation eg where a principal appoints a person to deal (especially to buy) on his behalf, on the understanding that when dealing with any third party, the agent will deal in his own name as principal; he is normally remunerated by commission; he is a fiduciary also and consequently may not without disclosure take a commission from the third party. See Montgomerie v UK Mutual SS Assn (1891) 1 QB 370.

**commission de lunatico inquirendo.** An enquiry carried out persuant to the Lunacy Regulations (Ireland) Act 1871. See RSC O.67 r.10-16.

**Commission of EC.** See EUROPEAN COMMISSION.

**commission rogatoire.** See LETTER OF REQUEST.

**commissioner for oaths.** A person appointed to administer oaths and to take affidavits for the purpose of any court or matter: Commissioners for Oaths Act 1889 s.1. Oaths include affirmations and declarations (ibid s.11). Judicial and official notice must be taken of the seal or signature of a commissioner for oaths (ibid s.3(2)). A statutory declaration may be taken and received by a commissioner for oaths: Statutory Declarations Act 1938 s.1(1). See CHIEF JUSTICE.

**Commissioner of Garda Siochana.** See GARDA SIOCHANA; TRAFFIC MANAGEMENT.

**commissioners, town.** See TOWN COMMISSIONERS.

**commissioners of charitable donations and bequests.** The statutory body, appointed by the government, with responsibility for the general administration of charities in the State. They act as trustees of some charitable trusts and hold funds on behalf of others. They are empowered to invest, and authorise charity trustees to invest, in securities outside the ordinary range of trustee securities. Their functions also include the appointment of new trustees and the authorisation of sale of charity property. See Charities Act 1963 and 1973 wherein the Commissioners are referred to as *the Board*. See CHARITIES; CHARITABLE DEVISE OR BEQUEST.

**committal, order of.** An order which directs that a person upon his arrest be lodged in prison until he purges his contempt (qv) and is discharged pursuant to further order of the court: RSC O.44 r.2. See also RCC O.36.

**committal warrant.** An order of committal to imprisonment for the non-payment of a fine or the non-performance of a condition imposed on a person convicted of an offence in a summary jurisdiction; the order may be made by a district court judge within six months from the date fixed for the payment of the fine or the performance of the condition: Petty Sessions (Ireland) Act 1851 s.23 as amended by the Courts (No 2) Act 1991.

**committee.** A person to whom the custody of another person of unsound mind or the estate of that other person is committed by order of the High Court. See RSC O.67 rr.57-69.

**committee of inspection.** See WINDING UP BY TRUSTEE; WINDING UP, VOLUNTARY.

**committee of the regions.** A new consultative body of 189 members which will be asked for its opinion in the areas of education, culture, public health, trans-European networks and economic and social cohesion (qqv); it is appointed by the EC Council on the basis of nominations from the member States; Ireland will appoint 9 members: Treaty of Rome 1957 arts.198a, b, and c inserted by Maastricht Treaty 1992 art.G(E)(67).

**commodatum.** [Loan for use]. See BAILMENT.

**common.** A right of *common* is the right to take some part of any natural product of the land or water belonging to another. It may be created by grant or claimed by prescription (qv). The principal rights of common are: pasture, piscary, estovers and turbary (qqv). See also Wildlife Act 1976 s.55(1).

**common, tenancy in.** See TENANCY IN COMMON.

**common agricultural policy; CAP.** The main instrument through which EC support is channelled to agriculture: Treaty of Rome 1957 arts.38-47. Its main objectives are: to increase agricultural productivity, to ensure a fair standard of living for farmers, to stabilise agricultural markets, to guarantee regular supplies of food, and to ensure reasonable prices for consumers (ibid art.39). The CAP operates through various instruments which vary from commodity to commodity. These include: guaranteed prices with intervention purchasing of commodities in surplus supply; quotas, levies and tariffs on imports to prevent external supplies undercutting EC produced commodities; support for Community exports mainly by way of refunds to allow them compete on world markets and a range of direct supports to producers or processors.

**common assault.** An assault at common law, not amounting to an aggravated assault. See Offences Against the Person Act 1861 ss.42 and 47. See also Criminal Justice Act 1951 s.11, as proposed to be amended by the draft Criminal Justice (Public Order) Bill 1993 s.11. While common assault is triable summarily, it is also triable on indictment (qv) at the option of the prosecution: McGrail v Ruane (1989) 7ILT Dig 81. See ASSAULT.

**common carrier.** See CARRIER, COMMON.

**common commercial policy.** The policy of the EC which is required to be based on uniform principles, particularly in regard to tariff rates, the conclusion of tariff and trade agreements, the achievement of uniformity in measures of liberalisation, export policy and measures to protect trade such as those to be taken in the event of dumping or subsidies: Treaty of Rome 1957 art.113 as replaced by Maastricht Treaty 1992 art.G(D)(28).

**common control.** See MONOPOLY.

**common employment.** The common law rule that a master was not liable to his servant for injuries resulting from the negligence of a fellow servant in the course of their common employment. The doctrine was eroded by successive judicial decisions and eventually by the Law Reform (Personal Injuries) Act 1958. See also Doyle v Flemings Coal Mines Ltd (1955) SC.

**common foreign and security policy; CFSP.** The policy provisions in the Maastricht Treaty 1992 (art.J) which will replace the provisions on European Political Cooperation in the Single European Act 1987. The objectives of the CFSP are to strengthen the common values, interests and independence of the European Union (qv); to strengthen the security of the Union and its member States; to preserve peace and international security; to promote international cooperation; and to develop and consolidate democracy, the rule of law, human rights and fundamental freedoms (art.J.1). Provision is made: for *systematic cooperation* between member States on international issues; for *joint action* on foreign policy and security issues; and for an intergovernmental conference in 1996 to review the CFSP and the framing of a common defence policy. The powers of the European Court of Justice will not apply to the provisions on the CFSP.

**common form.** See WILL, PROOF OF.

**common informer.** A member of the public capable of giving information in respect of the commission of an offence: The State (Cronin) v CJ Western Circuit (1936) 71 ILTR 3. The person need not be an eyewitness of the event: McCormac v Carroll (1910) 45 ILTR 7. It has been held that a common informer has a common law right of access to the courts to lay a complaint and to prosecute for an offence in a court of summary jurisdiction and any restrictions upon such a right would require clear statutory expression: The State (Collins) v Ruane (1984) IR 105; O'Donnell v DPP (1988) HC. A fire authority cannot be a common informer: Dublin Corporation v Cumann Luthchleas Gael Teo (GAA) (1993 SC) — Irish Times 23/6/1993. See DIRECTOR OF PUBLIC PROSECUTIONS; INFORMATION; PROSECUTOR; INDICTABLE OFFENCE.

**common law.** Originally the ancient unwritten law of England, so called because it became common to the whole of England and Wales after the Norman Conquest in 1066. In time it came to mean judge-made law as opposed to statute law. [Text: O'Higgins & McEldowney].

**common law marriage / wife / husband.** (1) Colloquial terms sometimes used to denote the relationship of a man and a woman who live together as if man and wife but without having gone through a legal ceremony of marriage; the terms have no legal significance in the terms as stated. (2) The essential conditions for a valid marriage at common law are: contracting parties, intending there and then to get married, interchanging their mutual consent, one to be husband, the other to be wife, in the presence of a priest in holy orders: Ussher v Ussher (1912) 2 IR 482. The existence of a common law marriage must be determined by the nature of the ceremony and the intention of the parties to that ceremony and not as to their belief as to its effects: Conlan v Mohamed (1987) ILRM 172. See COHABITATION; FAMILY INCOME SUPPLEMENT; MARRIAGE; SPOUSE.

**Common Market.** Formerly, the popular name for the European Economic Community (qv) when its focus was primarily to create a *common market* for goods and services and before its development in the social, economic, monetary and political fields. See HARMONISATION OF LAWS.

**common policies.** The European Community is required to have *common policies* in the following spheres — commercial, agriculture and fisheries, and transport: Treaty of Rome 1957 art.3 as replaced by Maastricht Treaty 1992 art. G(B)(3). In addition the Community is entitled to have *common rules* applying to such areas as transport, competition, taxation and approximation of laws. Member States of the European Union (qv) are required to regard a number of areas as matters of *common interest* eg asylum policy, immigration policy, combatting drug addiction, combatting international fraud, judicial co-operation in civil and criminal matters, customs cooperation, and police cooperation: Maastricht Treaty 1992 art.K.1.

**commorientes.** Persons dying together on the same occasion where it cannot be ascertained by clear evidence who died first. See DEATH, SIMULTANEOUS.

**communicate, right to.** See EXPRESSION, FREEDOM OF; INFLUENCE, IMPROPER; PRISON.

**communications, privileged.** See PRIVILEGE, EVIDENTIAL.

**communis error facit jus.** [Common mistake sometimes makes law].

**Community law.** The body of law arising from membership of the EC. It arises from the treaties of the Community with their annexes and protocols; conventions between member States; legislation; and judicial determinations of the European Court of Justice (qv). It takes precedence over the domestic law of Ireland in the event of conflict. Legislation of the Community consists of: (a) *regulations* — which have a general application and are binding in their entirety and directly applicable in all member States; (b) *directives* — which state an objective which the member State must realise within a stated period; (c) *decisions* — which are binding on those to whom they are addressed. There are also *recommendations* and *opinions* which do not have any legal effect. [Text: Butterworth Ireland (1); Collins & O'Reilly; Curtin & O'Keeffe; McMahon & Murphy; EC Pub (1)]. See EUROPEAN ECONOMIC COMMUNITY; PRELIMINARY RULINGS; SINGLE EUROPEAN ACT.

**Community Patent Agreement.** The Agreement of 1989 which has as its objective the creation of a Community patent system for the European Community (EC) (qv) with a view to ensuring the free movement within the EC of goods protected by patents. It amends and supersedes the original Community Patent Convention of 1975. It constitute a special agreement within the meaning of Part IX of the European Patent Convention (qv) and it is one of the measures identified by the EC Commission as necessary for completion of the internal market.

The Agreement provides for the grant by the European Patent Office of *unitary patents* valid for, and having equivalent effect in, the member States of the EC. These Community patents may be transferred, revoked, allowed to lapse etc, in respect of the whole of the EC. In contrast, a European patent designating a member State has the effect of a national patent in that State and is subject to the national law.

The Agreement creates a centralised litigation procedure for Community patents, involving a common *patent appeal court* to be set up under the Agreement; it will have jurisdiction to determine certain matters concerning Community patents raised on appeal from decisions of national courts in domestic litigation concerning such patents.

The Agreement will enter into force upon ratification by all member States of the EC. By early 1993, only four member States had ratified viz Germany,

France, Portugal and Greece. A perceived constitutional problem in ratifying the Agreement in Ireland led to an amendment to the Constitution in 1992 to permit ratification which was approved by the people: 1937 Constitution art.29(4)(6). See PATENT; EUROPEAN PATENT CONVENTION.

**community service order.** An order under which an offender is obliged to complete between 40 and 240 hours of unpaid work under the supervision of a probation officer; the order may be made by any court, other than the Special Criminal Court, in respect of any offender over 16 years of age who has been convicted of an offence for which the appropriate sentence would otherwise be one of penal servitude (qv) or detention in St Patrick's Institution: Criminal Justice (Community Service) Act 1983.

The court may only make such an order if the offender consents and if it is satisfied, having considered the offender's circumstances, the offender is suitable to perform work under the order. It is an offence to fail to perform the community work under such an order (ibid s.7). See PROBATION AND WELFARE OFFICER; PUNISHMENT.

**Community trade mark.** There is no EC trade mark system yet in operation, although it has been recognised that separate national trade mark registration systems can operate as a barrier to free trade in the Community.

A proposal for a EC Council regulation published a number of years ago would, if adopted, create the possibility to obtain registration of trade marks on a Community-wide basis. However, the Regulation which would establish a *Community trade mark office* was still being debated in 1993. Consequently, businesses wishing to protect trade marks in each EC member State by registration, must seek separate national registrations.

An EC Council Directive approximating the national laws of the member States relating to trade marks was adopted in December 1988 and entered into force with effect from 1st January 1993 (Directive 89/104/EEC). It is intended that the Directive will be given effect in Ireland by a new trade marks Act, which will also up-date the law generally on the registration of marks. See Consten and Grundig v Commission (1966) CMLR 418; Toltee v Dorcets (1985) FSR 533. See Doyle — "Unifying Europe – The EC Trademark Harmonisation Directive and Irish Law" in 11 ILT & SJ (1993) 76. See PARIS CONVENTION; TRADE MARK.

**commutation.** The conversion of the right to receive a variable or periodic payment into the right to receive a fixed or gross payment eg the commutation of a pension.

**commute.** To substitute one punishment for another. For restriction on power to commute punishment for treason (qv) and aggravated murder (qv), see Criminal Justice Act 1990 s.5. See CAPITAL PUNISHMENT; PARDON.

**companies office.** See REGISTRAR OF COMPANIES.

**company.** An association of persons formed for the purpose of some business or undertaking, carried on in the name of the association, each member having the right to assign his shares to any other person, subject to the regulations of the company. Companies are either incorporated or unincorporated. An *unincorporated* company has no existence separate from its members who are individually liable for its debts without limit eg a partnership. An *incorporated* company is a legal entity distinct from its members. Companies are incorporated (1) by charter (2) by statute and (3) by registration.

Companies are limited or unlimited, depending on whether the liabilities of their shareholders is limited or not. A *limited* company may be either a *private* company or a *public* company. A private limited company must include *limited* or *teoranta* in its name. A public limited company must include *public limited company* or *cuideachta phoibli theoranta* in its name. The transferability of the shares of a private limited company is restricted but is not restricted in the case of a public limited company. A private company must have at least two members whereas the minimum number in a public company is seven.

The statute law relating to companies is mainly contained in the Companies Act 1963 and the Companies Acts 1977, 1982, 1983, 1986 and 1990 (two Acts);

Stock Transfer Act 1963; Registration of Business Names Act 1963; Mergers, Take-Overs and Monopolies Control Act 1978; Competition Act 1991. [Text: Ford (1); Keane (1); MacCann; McGahon; Phelan; McCormack; Ussher; Dine (UK); Palmer (UK)]. See COMPANY, LIMITED; COMPANY, UNLIMITED; COMPANY, REGISTERED; COMPANY, PUBLIC LIMITED; EUROPEAN ECONOMIC INTEREST GROUPING; NAME OF COMPANY; ONE MAN COMPANY; REGISTERED OFFICE.

**company, chartered.** A corporation established by *charter* with a legal identity separate from its members; originally granted by the Crown in exercise of the royal prerogative. In earlier times, trading companies were created by royal charter (see In re Commercial Buildings Co of Dublin [1938] IR 477) but later charters were mainly granted to non-trading corporations eg Incorporated Law Society of Ireland. Charters may now be granted by the State: Adaption of Charters Act 1926; Executive Powers (Consequential Provisions) Act 1937.

**company, division of.** See DIVISION OF COMPANY.

**company, European.** See EUROPEAN COMPANY.

**company, inspection of.** See INVESTIGATION OF COMPANY.

**company, limited.** An incorporated company with limited liability. The liability of members of such a company may be limited to the amount, if any, unpaid on the shares respectively held by them, in which case it is known as a *company limited by shares*. Alternatively, liability may be limited to the amount which the members respectively undertake to contribute to the assets of the company in the event that the company is wound up, in which case it is known as a *company limited by guarantee*. In practice, companies limited by guarantee are generally non-profit type companies.

Limited companies may be registered as private or public; however a *company limited by guarantee having a share capital* which is a hybrid type company, cannot be formed as or become a public limited company (plc).

Limitation of liability may be lost where the number of members falls below the minimum amount and the company continues to carry on business for more than 6 months at the reduced membership. It can also be lost in the event of *fraudulent trading*. See Companies Act 1963 ss.5(2)(a), 5(2)(b), 26(2), 207(1)(d), 207(1)(e) and 207(3); Companies Amendment Act 1983 ss.7 and 53(7)(a). See COMPANY, PRIVATE; COMPANY, PUBLIC; COMPANY, PUBLIC LIMITED; FRAUDULENT TRADING; PERSONAL LIABILITY.

**company, merger of.** See MERGER OF COMPANY.

**company, migration of.** See MIGRATION OF COMPANY.

**company, private.** An incorporated company which has been registered as a private company; such registration is permitted provided certain criteria are met. The company must have a minimum of two members and its *articles of association* (qv) must require that (1) its membership will not exceed 50, apart from worker shareholders, (2) the transferability of its shares is restricted and (3) the public are not to be invited to subscribe for shares or debentures in the company. A private company becomes a public company when any of these three requirements is removed from the articles of association. When a private company contravenes any of the three requirements eg by offering its shares or debentures to the public, it loses the legal privilege of private status and a criminal offence will have been committed.

Formerly, the principal advantage of a private company was that it was not required to disclose its financial and trading position to the public via the registry of companies and many EC directives did not apply to it. This has changed since the enactment of the Companies Amendment Act 1986, which implements the Fourth EC Directive on Company Law, and which specifies new disclosure requirements for all companies. However there are important reliefs for a private *small company* (qv) and a private *medium sized company* (qv), which are not required to prepare and publish a full set of accounts.

A person with a financial interest in a private company can obtain a court order (a *disclosure order*) compelling disclosure of interest in shares and debentures in the company in certain circumstances: Companies Act 1990 ss.97-104.

See Companies Act 1963 s.5(1), 33,

34(1), 34(2), 35; Companies Amendment Act 1983 s.21 and First Schedule para 6; Companies Amendment Act 1986 ss.8-11. See DISCLOSURE ORDER; SHARES, VALUE OF.

**company, public.** A company which is not a private company: Companies Amendment Act 1983 s.2(1). Since 1983, it has been possible to create a new type of public company called *a public limited company* (qv) or plc. An old public company with limited liability had to become a plc or else re-register under some other form (ibid s.13). See COMPANY, PRIVATE; ASSOCIATION, ARTICLES OF.

**company, public limited.** [plc]. A public company limited by shares with a minimum of seven members, which complies with specific requirements of the Companies Acts. To become and remain a plc, the company must have a minimum authorised share capital of at least £30,000; at least one-quarter of the nominal amount must have been paid up on its issued share capital, together with any premium on its shares; it must not have allocated any shares it offered for subscription when the offer was *under-subscribed*; it must not have allocated shares for service contracts, or for contracts that can be performed more than five years from the allotment date; an independent valuation must have been made of non-cash consideration transferred in order to acquire shares in it, and of major transactions between it and its first members during its first two years' commercial existence; shares taken by its subscribers must have been paid for in cash; any lien or other charge on its own shares is void; and it may not pay a dividend if it is insolvent in that its net assets are less than its called up share capital and its undistributed reserves: Companies Amendment Act 1983 ss.5(2), 17(1), 19(1), 22, 26(2), 28-35, 44 and 46.

A *company limited by guarantee and having a share capital* cannot be formed as or become a plc (ibid s.7). A building society may convert itself into a public limited company: Building Societies Act 1989 s.101. See VALUATION REPORT.

**company, registered.** A company registered in the registry of companies: Companies Act 1963 s.18. It may be registered with either *limited* or *unlimited*

liability, and it may be registered as a *private* or as a *public limited company*. A company, association or partnership must be registered as a company if it consists of more than 20 persons formed for the purpose of carrying on any business that has as its object the acquisition of gain; in the case of a bank it must be registered if it consists of more than 10 persons (ibid ss.372 and 376). Partnerships of solicitors and accountants are excluded from these requirements: Companies Amendment Act 1982 s.13.

A registered company has perpetual succession and has legal rights and duties separate from its owners' own entitlements and duties; in law the company and its owners are separate and distinct entities. See Salomon v Salomon Co (1897) AC 22; Roundabout Ltd v Beirne (1959) IR 423; Irish Permanent Building Society v Registrar of Building Societies (1981) ILRM 242. See REGISTRAR OF COMPANIES.

**company, sham.** See LIFTING THE CORPORATE VEIL.

**company, statutory.** A statutory corporation, colloquilly known as a *state sponsored* or *semi-state* body; a company established by special legislation. Many of the state sponsored organisations are statutory companies eg the ESB by the Electricity (Supply) Act 1927. In the last century, special general enactments established public utilities eg Companies Clauses Acts.

Statutory companies are restricted to the statutory purposes of their establishment and cannot apply funds to purposes not authorised by their constituting statute. They are subject to the *ultra vires* (qv) doctrine. They may have extensive powers including, in many cases, the power to acquire land compulsorily eg ibid 1927 Act s.45. See Linnane in 8ILT & SJ (1990) 144. See EQUALITY BEFORE THE LAW; PRIVATISATION.

**company, unlimited.** An incorporated association, the members of which wish to engage in business in common but for one reason or another, do not wish their liability to be limited. Because of the numerical limit on the size of partnerships (other than solicitors or accountants), an unlimited company is registered where there are more than 20 such members, or more than 10 in the case of bankers.

The advantages of an unlimited company are that it is exempted from many of the Companies Acts disclosure requirements, it is relatively easy to return contributed capital to its members, and it enjoys certain fiscal and tax advantages. Unlike a partnership, unpaid creditors of an unlimited company have no direct claim against the members and must secure the winding up of the company, and the liquidator will then attempt to recover outstanding amounts from the members with unlimited liability. See Companies Act 1963 ss.372 and 376; Companies Amendment Act 1982 s.13; Finance Act 1973 ss.67- 68; Corporation Tax Act 1976. See PARTNERSHIP; COMPANY, REGISTERED.

**company secretary.** See SECRETARY.

**compellable witness.** See SUB- POENA; WITNESS, COMPETENCE OF.

**compensation.** A payment to make amends for loss or injury to person or property, or to compensate for some deprivation. See MOTORWAY; PATENT; WAY-LEAVE.

**compensation and compulsory purchase.** The compensation to which the owner in land is entitled where his land is compulsorily acquired; he is entitled to get for his land precisely what it is worth to him in money terms immediately before the acquisition and in deciding how much it is worth, both its advantages and disadvantages have to be taken into account: In re Lucas and Chesterfield Gas and Water Board (1909) I KB 16; Acquisition of Land (Assessment of Compensation) Act 1919 as amended by the LG(P&D) Act 1963 s.69(1). These Acts set out rules for determining compensation; these rules do not affect the assessment of compensation for *disturbance* or for *severances and injurious affection* (qv).

Interest on a compulsory purchase award is payable at the *local loans fund rate* where there is entry on the land following service of a notice of entry: Housing of the Working Classes Act 1890, second schedule, art.24 and Murphy v Dublin Corporation (1972) IR 215. Where there is no entry before compensation is agreed or assessed, the local authority is obliged to pay interest on the award at the rate appropriate to

an ordinary contract for sale of land from the time a good title is shown: In re Piggot and Great Western Railway (1881) 18 Ch D 146. Compensation is statutorily provided for when the ESB exercises its power to acquire land compulsorily: Electricity Supply (Amdt) Act 1985. See also Housing (Miscellaneous Provisions) Act 1992 s.35; Roads Act 1993 s.52. [Text: McDermott & Woulfe]. See ARBITRATION; CLEARED SITE VALUE; COMPULSORY PURCHASE ORDER; NOTICE TO TREAT.

**compensation and planning permission.** A person who is refused planning permission (qv) to develop land or is granted permission subject to conditions, has a right to be paid by the planning authority by way of compensation, the amount of the reduction in value of his interest in the land *at the time of the decision* and in the case of the occupier of the land, the damage (if any) to his trade, business or profession carried out on the land: LG(P&D) Act 1990 s.11.

However, there are significant restrictions on the right to compensation eg compensation is not payable in respect of (a) a refusal of permission for any development described in the *Second Schedule* eg demolition of a habitable house; (b) a refusal of permission where the reason for the refusal is a reason set out in the *Third Schedule* eg premature development; (c) a condition imposed on a permission as set out in the *Fourth Schedule* eg requiring a contribution towards the expenditure of the local authority; (d) a refusal of permission or conditions imposed for retention of structures to which the LG (P&D) Act 1963 s.28 applies: (e) land where it is a duty of the local authority to acquire under the 1963 Act s.29 (ibid 1990 Act s.12). Compensation is also not payable where the refusal of permission, or a condition imposed, relates to specified matters concerning motorways, busways and protected roads: Roads Act 1993 s.46(3). See also 1993 Act s.52(6).

A local authority can avoid paying compensation by serving a notice on the claimant stating that, in their opinion, the land is capable of other development for which planning permission ought to be granted (ibid 1990 Act s.13).

Compensation may also be payable

where by notice a planning permission is revoked or modified; where by notice there is removal or alteration of a structure; where by notice there is discontinuance of use of land, removal or alteration of a hedge; or in relation to a tree preservation order, or refusal to grant permission for the erection of a new structure substantially replacing a structure demolished or destroyed by fire (ibid ss.15, and 18-21).

Compensation claims must be made within 6 months (ibid s.4) and are determined, in the absence of agreement, by arbitration under the Acquisition of Land (Assessment of Compensation) Act 1919 subject to the proviso that the arbitrator may make a nil award and the *Rules for Determination of the Amount of Compensation* — (ibid 1990 Act s.5 and *First Schedule*).See ARBITRATION; PARKS, PUBLIC; PURCHASE NOTICE; SPECIAL AMENITY ORDER.

**compensation for criminal injuries.** See COMPENSATION ORDER; CRIMINAL INJURIES COMPENSATION TRIBUNAL.

**compensation for disturbance.** See DISTURBANCE, COMPENSATION FOR.

**compensation for improvements.** See IMPROVEMENTS, COMPENSATION FOR.

**compensation fund.** The fund maintained by the Incorporated Law Society (qv) out of which the Society shall make a grant to any person who has sustained loss in consequence of dishonesty on the part of any solicitor or any clerk or servant of a solicitor in connection with that solicitor's practice *as a solicitor* or in connection with any trust of which that solicitor is a trustee: Solicitors (Amendment) Act 1960 s.21 and third schedule. Compensation from the fund is not confined to clients of the dishonest solicitor: Trustee Savings Bank v Incorporated Law Society (1989 SC) ILRM 665.

**compensation order.** An order which a court may make on conviction of any person of an offence, requiring him to pay *compensation* in respect of any *personal injury* or *loss* resulting from the offence to any person who suffered such injury or loss (the *injured party*): Criminal Justice Act 1993 s.6. The compensation order may be in addition to any other sentence or fine which the court may impose but the amount of the compensation (a) must not exceed the amount of damages which, in the opinion of the court, the injured party would be entitled to recover in a civil action and (b) must have regard to the means, including financial commitments, of the convicted person (or his parent or guardian where applicable).

There are restrictions in respect of injury or loss that results from the use of a mechanically propelled vehicle (ibid s.6(4)). Where death has resulted from the offence, *loss* means any matter for which damages could be awarded in respect of the death, and *injured party* includes a dependant of the deceased (ibid s.6(12)(a)). Also provision has been made for payment to a district court clerk for transmission to the injured party and for payment by way of attachment of earnings (ibid s.7). See DAMAGE TO PROPERTY.

**compensatory damages.** Damages (qv) awarded as compensation for and measured by the material loss suffered by a plaintiff. *Aggravated damages* may be awarded when the motives and conduct of the defendant aggravate the injury to the plaintiff. *Exemplary damages* may be awarded to reflect the proper indignation of the public and to reflect disapproval. See McIntyre v Lewis & Dolan (1991 SC) 1 IR 121. See DAMAGES.

**competence of witnesses.** See WITNESS, COMPETENCE OF.

**competition, common detriment.** The 1937 Constitution provides that the operation of free competition will not be allowed so to develop as to result in the concentration of the ownership or control of essential commodities in a few individuals to the common detriment (art.45(2)(iii)). See MONOPOLY.

**competition, distortion of.** All agreements between undertakings, decisions by associations of undertakings and concerted practices which have as their object or effect the prevention, restriction or distortion of competition in trade in any goods or services in the State or in any part of the State are prohibited and void: Competition Act 1991 s.4(1). Included are agreements which:- fix purchase or selling prices; limit or control markets or production; share markets; apply dissimilar terms to similar contracts.

The Competition Authority (qv) may grant a certificate which states that in its opinion an agreement, decision or concerted practice does not offend s.4(1) (ibid s.4(4)). The Authority has expressed its view that the prohibition in s.4(1) only applies to a current or continuing contractual commitment or one entered into subsequent to the coming into force of the 1991 Act: Iris Oifigiuil 14 May 1993 p.367. The Authority may also grant a licence in respect of an agreement, decision or concerted action (ibid ss.4(2) and 8); in effect this gives an exemption. There is no appeal against a refusal to grant a licence (ibid s.9). A person who is aggrieved in consequence of any prohibited agreement, decision or concerted practice has a right of action for relief against any undertaking which has been a party to such (ibid s.6). See SI No 76 of 1992.

The Competition Authority has refused to grant a certificate or licence in respect of an agreement which contained a restriction which exceeded what was required for legitimate commercial interest and which applied for a period of 18 months after termination of employment: Notification Apex / Murtagh – Iris Oifigiuil 18/6/1993.

The Competition Authority has decided that mergers and acquisitions between competing firms will offend against the prohibition on restrictive agreements contained in the 1991 Act s.4(1) where they would, or would be likely to, result in a diminution of competition in the market concerned: Woodchester Bank Ltd – UDT Bank Ltd as reported by Cagney in 11 ILT & SJ (1993) 23.

The Treaty of Rome 1957 art.85 prohibits as incompatible with the Common Market all agreements between undertakings and all concerted practices which may affect trade between member states and which have as their object or effect the prevention, restriction or distortion of competition within the Common Market. Any agreement or decision prohibited by this Article is void. Any abuse by one or more undertakings of a *dominant* position within the Common Market or in a substantial part of it, is prohibited as incompatible with the Common Market in so far as it effects trade between member states (ibid art.86). It is not sufficient however to prove that the undertaking is in a dominant position, the practice complained of must also constitute an abuse of that position: Masterfoods Ltd v H B Ice Cream Ltd (1993 HC) ILRM 145.

For procedures on the application of EC rules on competition relating to restrictive practices between undertakings which affect trade between member States and abuses of dominant positions with respect to arts.85-86 of the Treaty of Rome, see EC (Rules on Competition) Regulations 1993 (SI No 124 of 1993).

Provision has been made for open competition in public works and public supply contracts in the EC: SI Nos 36-38 of 1992. See also Meade in ILSI Gazette (Jan/Feb 1992) 7. [Text: Brown; Competition Authority; ICEL; Power; Jones (UK)]. See BELOW COST SELLING; DOMINANT POSITION, ABUSE OF; HELLO MONEY; MERGER OF COMPANY, EC REGULATIONS; RESTRAINT OF TRADE, CONTRACT IN; SOLUS AGREEMENT.

**Competition Authority.** The body appointed by the Minister to exercise the functions assigned to it by the Competition Act 1991 s.10 and Schedule. These include: – granting licences; carrying out studies and analyses as requested by the Minister; carrying out an investigation into a possible abuse of a dominant position if requested by the Minister; reporting on merger or takeover proposals referred to it by the Minister; submitting an annual report on its activities. Officers of the Authority have wide powers of entering and inspecting premises or vehicles, and of requiring production of books and records (ibid s.21).

**competition law.** The body of law dealing with such matters as monopolies, mergers, restraint of trade, trade regulation, and distortion of competition. [Text: Brown; Whish UK].

**competitive tender.** See CONSUMER, DEALING AS.

**compilation.** A collection into serviceable form of, for example, facts, statistics, tables, and quotations. *Copyright* can exist in compilations; the copyright of a work of compilation is infringed where another person, relying on the efforts and the compilation of the copyright owner, reproduces all or part of such a work in any material form without any or only minimal input of his own: Allied Discount Card Ltd v Bord Failte Eireann (1990) ITLR (6 Aug). See LITERARY WORK.

**complainant.** The person who makes a complaint: includes the prosecutor or party at whose instance any proceeding is taken, whether he be an informant, complainant, prosecutor or otherwise: DCR r.3. See COMMON INFORMER.

**complaint.** (1) The issue of a summons (qv) must be grounded on the making of a complaint to either a district court judge, a peace commissioner (qv) or a district court clerk: DCR rr.29 and 30. There is no form prescribed for making a complaint: Irish Insurance Commissioners v Trench (1913) 47 ILTR 115. In general a complaint must be made within six months from the time when the cause of complaint has arisen: Petty Sessions (Ireland) Act 1851 s.10; Minister for Agriculture v Norgro Limited (1980) IR 155; The State (Byrne) v Plunkett (1985) HC. See also DPP v District Justice Roche and Paul Kelly & DPP v Arthur Nolan (1988) SC. See Courts (No 3) Act 1986. See SUMMONS.

(2) A statement made to a third party by a female against whom a sexual offence is alleged to have been committed. To be admissible, the complaint must have been made at the first opportunity which reasonably offers itself and it must be voluntary and spontaneous, and must not be elicited by leading, intimidating or inducing questions. A complaint is not admissible to prove the truth of the matters stated but after proof of such facts to confirm the testimony of the prosecutrix and to disprove consent where consent is in issue. See R v Lillyman (1896) 2 QB 167; R v Osborne (1905) 1 KB 551; People (DPP) v Brophy (1992 CCA) ILRM 709; The People (DPP) v G (1993 CCA) 11 ILT Dig 186.

**complete specification.** Formerly, the full description of an invention which was required to be filed before action towards granting a patent could be taken: Patents Act 1964 ss.8-11. An application for a patent could be accompanied by a *provisional specification* initially, the advantage being that the applicant could, at minimal cost, protect his priority while he determined whether there was a prospect of using the invention profitable. Provisional patent protection has been abolished and replaced by a system of claiming priority from earlier applications. Also a less costly *short-term* patent has been introduced. See RSC O.94 rr.15-22. See PATENT, APPLICATION FOR; SHORT-TERM PATENT.

**completion.** Final stages in a contract for the sale of land which is effected by the delivery up by the vendor of a good title and of the actual possession or enjoyment thereof to the purchaser and by the purchaser in accepting such title, and paying the agreed purchase price. See Report on Conveyancing Law — Service of Completion Notices (LRC 40 — 1991).

**compos mentis.** [Of sound mind].

**composition.** A sum of money accepted by creditors in satisfaction of debts. A debtor may propose to his creditors a composition in satisfaction of his liabilities as an alternative to *bankruptcy*. A debtor following adjudication as a bankrupt, may with the consent of the majority of creditors and despite opposition from the minority, offer and carry a composition after bankruptcy.

The court has now got full control over a composition ie it must approve of it before it is binding, which it will do where three fifths in number and value of creditors accept the offer of composition; any creditor whose debt is less than £100 will not be entitled to vote: Bankruptcy Act 1988 s.39. However, an instalment in the payment of a composition may not be secured by a bill, note or other security signed by or enforceable against the bankrupt alone (ibid s.40(2)). Also, the court has a discretion to refuse an offer of composition if the final offer is not payable within two years (ibid s.40(3)).

The court is empowered to discharge the bankruptcy *adjudication order* on the application of the bankrupt and on the report of the Official Assignee (qv) after lodgment with him of cash or specified securities to satisfy the composition (ibid s.41). See BANKRUPTCY; BANKRUPTCY, DISCHARGE OF; CORRUPT AGREEMENT WITH CREDITOR.

**compound.** To settle or adjust by

agreement eg to agree to accept a composition (qv).

**compound interest.** Interest calculated on both the principal and its accrued interest.

(1) The law does not permit compound interest except on commercial or mercantile accounts which are still running. The relationship between banker and customer is merchantile in nature so as to permit charging of compound interest even without express agreement, it being taken that the customer acquiesces in the compounding. Demand for repayment brings the banker/customer relationship to an end and the automatic right to charge compound interest ceases as the relationship is now of creditor and debtor.

The practice in the Master's (High) Court is to allow compounding of interest only to issue of summons and simple interest thereafter. See Yourrell v Hibernian Bank (1918) AC 372; Allied Irish Bank v The George Ltd (1975) HC; National Bank of Greece v Pinios Shipping Co (1989) 1 All ER 213 & (1990) 1 All ER 78. See Doyle in 7ILT & SJ (1989) 215; 8ILT & SJ (1990) 94; and 10 ILT & SJ (1992) 66. However, in a particular case, the court held that a bank had no implied right to charge compound interest or interest at a specially high default rate: Trustee Savings Bank v Maughan (1991 HC) in 10 ILT & SJ (1992) 66 and 265. It is likely that the law now leans against a presumption of compounding interest unless by agreement, express or implied, whether by custom or otherwise.

(2) As regard building societies, for compound interest to be chargeable, provision for such interest must be provided for in the mortgage deed: Eastern Counties Building Society v Russell (1947) 1 All ER 500. It is now general practice for building societies to carry forward annually, the total outstanding indebtedness of the borrower in one sum (which may include arrears in accrued interest) and to charge the borrower with interest on that one sum for the ensuing account period, which arrangement may include an element of compound interest.

(3) A contract for the loan of money by a moneylender (qv) is illegal in so far as it provides directly or indirectly for the payment of compound interest: Moneylenders Act 1933 s.12.

**compound settlement.** A settlement constituted by more than one document eg deeds or wills over a period of time. See SETTLEMENT.

**compounding a felony.** A common law misdemeanour, committed by a person who bargains for value to abstain from prosecuting an offender.

**compromise.** A settlement (qv); an agreement between parties to a dispute to settle it out of court. In general, a compromise must satisfy these conditions: (a) the initial claim must have been reasonable and not vexatious and frivolous; (b) the plaintiff must have had an honest belief in the chances of its success; (c) the party contending that the compromise is valid must not have withheld or suppressed facts that would have shown the claim in a truer light.

It has been held that a defendant was not bound by a settlement where counsel were not *ad idem* because of mutual mistake regarding a compromise: Mespil Ltd v Capaldi (1986) ILRM 373. A plaintiff can be estopped from asserting in proceedings that which he has abandoned in a compromise to previous proceedings: Hennerty v Bank of Ireland (1989) 7 ILT Dig 24. A dependant is not entitled to maintain an action where her deceased husband had compromised the action prior to his death: Civil Liability Act 1961 ss.7, 48 & 49; Mahon v Burke (1991 HC) ILRM 59. A compromised appeal against assessment to tax may properly be the subject of a subsequent additional assessment: Hammond Lane Metal Co Ltd v O'Culachain (1990 HC) ILRM 249. See also Leonard v Leonard (1812) 2 Ball B 171; O'Donnell v O'Sullivan (1913) ILTR 253; O'Neill v Ryan, Ryan O'Brien (1991 HC) ITLR (2 Sep). See RSC O.22 r.10; O.75 r.4(k). See LODGMENT IN COURT; RECONSTRUCTION OF COMPANY; SETTLEMENT; SETTLEMENT, EC.

**Comptroller and Auditor General.** The office holder, appointed by the President of Ireland on the nomination of the Dail, to control on behalf of the State all disbursements and to audit all accounts of moneys administered by or under the authority of the Oireachtas: 1937 Constitution art.33.

In 1993, the nature of the audit process carried out by the C & A G was extended to cover, at his discretion, statutory examinations of economy, efficiency in the use of resources and management effectiveness; the range of bodies covered by his audit and examination processes was also extended to include Vocational Education Committees, third level educational bodies and health boards: Comptroller and Auditor General (Amdt) Act 1993. In addition, he was empowered at his discretion to carry out inspections of the accounts of harbour authorities, regional tourism organisations, and bodies which receive the bulk of their receipts from public funds, to check that public moneys have been spent for the purposes for which they were provided (ibid s.8). The C & A G must not question or express an opinion on the merits of policy or of policy objectives in any of his reports (ibid s.11(5)).

**compulsory licence.** See LICENCES OF RIGHT.

**compulsory purchase of shares.** See SHARES, COMPULSORY PURCHASE OF.

**compulsory purchase order.** An order by which a local authority may compulsorily acquire land for the purposes of any of their statutory powers and duties, in whatever capacity such powers and duties are conferred on them: Public Health (Ireland) Act 1878 s.10; Local Government (No 2) Act 1960 s.10 as substituted by the Housing Act 1966 s.86; 1960 Act s.11. Local authorities are entitled to use the procedure under the Housing Act 1966 under which an order when made, must be submitted to the Minister for confirmation. If an objection is received by the Minister he must cause a *public local inquiry* to be held and he must consider the objection and the report of the inquiry before he annuls the order by an *annulment order* or comfirms it, with or without modification, by a *confirmation order*.

A compulsory purchase order becomes operative on final determination of the proceedings if it is challenged, or if no challenge is made, within a period of three weeks; following which, the local authority is entitled to serve a *notice to treat* (qv) on the persons interested in the land. The relevant date for assessing the value of the land is the date of the first notice to treat: 1966 Act s.84(1); Murphy v Dublin Corporation (1972) IR 215. Fourteen days *notice of entry* by the local authority on the land may be given after service of the notice to treat: 1966 Act s.80.

Certain other bodies are given power by statute to acquire land compulsorily eg the Custom House Docks Development Authority under the Urban Renewal (Amendment) Act 1987; health boards (qv) for their own use and for voluntary bodies by virtue of the Health Act 1947 Part Vlll and Health Act 1970 s.40. Failure of such bodies to exercise this power within a reasonable time from the date of giving notice may result in their losing the right to enforce the notice: Van Nierop v Commissioners for Public Works (1990) 2 IR 189. [Text: McDermott & Woulfe]. See COMPENSATION AND COMPULSORY PURCHASE; OPEN SPACE; MOTORWAY; URBAN RENEWAL.

**compulsory winding up.** See WINDING UP, COMPULSORY.

**computer.** The unauthorised operation of a computer with intent to access *data*, whether or not any data accessed are modified, is an offence: Criminal Damage Act 1991 s.5. Any modification of data after access has been obtained constitutes *damage* to the data and is also an offence (ibid s.2). To *damage* in relation to data is to add to, alter, corrupt, erase or move to another storage medium or to do any act that contributes towards causing this (ibid s.1(b)). *Data* means information in a form in which it can be accessed by means of a computer and includes a program.

As regards the law of evidence, computer printouts may be admissible if they constitute "real evidence" ie if tendered to show what is recorded without human intervention eg printout of a machine monitoring guests' phone calls in an hotel. But they may infringe the hearsay (qv) rule. Foundation testimony may be required to authenticate that the computer and its progamme was operating properly eg a copy record of a register kept in computer by the Environmental Protection Agency may be given in evidence and is prima facie evidence of any fact therein stated, provided that the court is satisfied of the the reliability of the system used to make the copy record and the original entry on which it was based: Environmental Protection Agency Act 1992 s.112(4).

In criminal proceedings, information contained in a document is prima facie admissible in evidence of any fact contained in it, where the information has been compiled in the ordinary course of business on computer; information in the computer printout however must have been reproduced in the course of the normal operation of the reproduction system concerned: Criminal Evidence Act 1992 s.5. See DOCUMENTARY EVIDENCE.

Statutory provision is made for the admissibility of certain computer records eg bankers' books and records: Central Bank Act 1989 s.131(a); social welfare records: Social Welfare Act 1989 s.20. The books and records of a company may be kept on computer: Companies Acts 1977 s.4 and 1990 s.202(1) and (7). Also the Minister is empowered to make regulations to enable the title to shares in companies to be transferred without a written instrument (ibid 1990 Act s.239). A cheque can be presented electronically eg by computer or fax: Central Bank Act 1989 ss.132 and 133. Schedules and maps of public roads can be kept on computer: Roads Act 1993 s.10(5)(d).

Where an officer of the Revenue Commissioners has power to inspect records and those records are kept on computer, the officer is entitled to access to the data equipment and any associated software and to be afforded reasonable assistance: Finance Act 1992 s.237. See also Building Societies Act 1989 s.117(2); Finance Act 1986 s.113 as amended by Finance Act 1993 s.99. See Dwyer in 9ILT & SJ (1991) 192. See LRC No 9 of 1980 and LRC No 25 of 1988. See BANKERS' BOOKS; CHEQUE, PRESENTATION BY NOTIFICATION; CRIMINAL DAMAGE TO PROPERTY; DATA PROTECTION; FAX; HACKING; MEDICAL PRACTITIONER; PATENTABLE INVENTION; TRADING HOUSE, SPECIAL; WORKSTATION.

**computer programme.** Legal protection is given to computer programmes by the EC (Legal Protection of Computer Programs) Regulations 1993 (SI No 26 of 1993). See CRIMINAL DAMAGE TO PROPERTY; PATENTABLE INVENTION; TRADING HOUSE, SPECIAL.

**conacre.** A licence to enter land and to till the land, sow crops and reap the harvest, generally for an eleven month period. Such a licence does not create the relationship of landlord and tenant. The Land Act 1984 was introduced to facilitate the leasing of agricultural land without creating rights in the lessee eg of automatic renewal or compensation for disturbance, the lessor and lessee being treated as of equal status.

**concealed danger.** The source of danger concerning which an occupier may have a duty of care to warn a licensee. See Shelton v Crean (1987) HC. See OCCUPIER'S LIABILITY TO LICENSEES.

**concealment.** Suppression of, or neglect to communicate, a material fact. If it is fraudulent, it may provide grounds for rescission of a contract. Even if not fraudulent, concealment may be fatal to a contract *uberimae fidei* eg a contract of insurance. See UBERRIMAE FIDEI; MISREPRESENTATION.

**concealment of birth.** The offence committed by the secret disposition by any person, of the dead body of a child, whether such child dies before, at, or after, birth, in an endeavour to conceal the birth of the child: Offences Against the Person Act 1861 s.60.

**concentrations, control of.** See MERGER OF COMPANY, EC REGULATIONS.

**concert party.** As regards a public limited company (plc), a group of persons acting together so as to avoid the object of legislation on disclosure of shareholding of the notifiable percentage (5%), the interest of none of them reaching that percentage, but that of all of them together amounting to a substantial or even controlling interest: Companies Act 1990 ss.73-75.

All the persons involved in a concert party are attributed with the interests of all the others in the shares of the target company as regards the obligation to notify that company of the amount of shares they are able to control acting in concert (ibid s.74). See also MONOPOLY.

**conciliation.** The bringing together of employers and employees in an endeavour to settle disputes. See INDUSTRIAL RELATIONS OFFICER; LABOUR RELATIONS COMMISSION.

**conciliation and arbitration schemes.** The schemes for dealing with claims relating to pay and conditions of employment in parts of the public service eg civil service, local authorities. They are non-statutory and have been described as merely contracts. See Inspector of Taxes Association v Minister for the Public Service (1983 HC) & (1986) ILRM 296.

**concurrent ownership.** The co-ownership of two or more persons in the same property. See JOINT TENANCY; TENANCY IN COMMON.

**concurrent sentences.** When an accused is convicted of several offences at the same trial, the court, in general, is empowered to impose separate sentences to be served concurrently ie together and at the same time. Contrast with CONSECUTIVE SENTENCES. See BAIL, OFFENCES COMMITTED ON.

**concurrent wrongdoers.** Persons who are responsible to an injured party for the *same damage*: Civil Liability Act 1961 s.11. This may arise as a result of vicarious liability (qv), breach of joint duty, conspiracy, concerted action to a common end or independent acts causing the same damage. The wrong may be a tort, breach of contract or breach of trust.

Each concurrent wrongdoer is liable for the whole of the damage done to the injured party (ibid s.12); the constitutionality of this section may be challenged: Gaspari v Iarnrod Eireann & Diskin (1993 HC) — Irish Times 27/2/ 1993. Satisfaction by any concurrent wrongdoer will discharge the other (ibid s.16) as will a release which indicates such intention (ibid s.17); however, settlement of a personal injuries action with one co-defendant does not constitute "satisfaction" as against all the defendants: Murphy & Murphy (infants) v Donohue Ltd & Ors (1992 SC) ILRM 378. Judgment against a wrongdoer is not a bar to an action against another concurrent wrongdoer (ibid s.18).

A third party notice to join an alleged concurrent wrongdoer cannot be issued after conclusion of the trial of the action: Kelly v St Laurence's Hospital (1989 SC) ITLR (20 Nov). Independently of a third party notice, a concurrent wrongdoer may sue any other for a *contribution* to the extent of that wrongdoer's responsibility for the injury (ibid s.21). Where persons cause independent

items of damage, they are not concurrent wrongdoers. See also Liability for Defective Products Act 1991 s.8. See Crowley v Allied Irish Banks (1988) ILRM 225; Cowan v Faghaile, Cumann Lutchleas Gael Teo, McInerney (1991 HC) 1 IR 389. See NEXT FRIEND .

**condemnation of will.** Refusal to grant probate of a purported will where the statutory provisions are not complied with. See RSC o.79 r.7; O.80 r.9. See Glynn v Glynn (1987) ILRM 589.

**condition.** An assurance or guarantee. A provision which makes the existence of a right dependent on the happening of an event; the right is then *conditional* as opposed to an *absolute* right. An *express* condition is one set out as a term in a contract or a deed. An *implied* condition is one derived from law on the presumed intention of the parties. A *condition precedent* is one which delays the vesting of a right until the occurrence of a particular event; a *condition subsequent* is one which provides for the defeat of an interest on the occurrence or non-occurrence of a particular event. A *condition concurrent* is one under which performance by one party is rendered dependent on performance by the other at the same time.

A condition in a contract of sale of goods is a stipulation which goes to the root of the contract, the breach of which gives rise to a right to treat the contract as repudiated. A stipulation may be a condition, though called a warranty in such a contract; and a condition may in certain instances be treated as a warranty eg where the contract is not *severable* and the buyer has accepted part of the goods. See Sale of Goods Act 1893 s.11; SGSS Act 1980 s.10.

Where a buyer *deals as a consumer* and there is a breach of a condition by the seller, which the buyer would be compelled to treat as a breach of warranty, the buyer is entitled to reject the goods and repudiate the contract, or, to have the defect constituting the breach remedied elsewhere and to maintain an action against the seller for the cost thereby incurred by him; provided that the buyer, promptly, upon discovering the breach, makes a request to the seller that he either remedy the breach or replace any goods which are not in comformity with the condition, and the seller refuses to comply with the request or fails to do so within a reasonable time. See Sale of Goods Act 1893 s.53; SGSS Act 1980 s.21.

In a contract of sale of goods, there is an implied condition that the seller has a right to sell the goods or, in the case of an *agreement to sell,* that he will have a right to sell the goods at the time the property is to pass (ibid 1893 Act s.12; ibid 1980 Act s.10).

There are similar provisions concerning implied conditions in hire-purchase agreements (ibid 1980 Act s.26).

Contrast with WARRANTY. See CONSUMER, DEALING AS; DESCRIPTION, SALE BY; FAIR AND REASONABLE TERMS; IMPLIED TERM; QUALITY OF GOODS.

**conditions of employment.** See CON-TRACT OF EMPLOYMENT.

**conditions of sale.** (1) The terms under which a purchaser is to take property sold by auction. The usual terms state: the number of years title to be shown; the title which is to be a good *root of title* (qv); the time within which *requisitions on title* are to be made; the rescission by the vendor on onerous conditions being made; the deposit and conditions for forfeiture; the compensation for misdescription; the payment of the purchase money and the interest thereon. It is usual to adopt the standard form of conditions issued by the Incorporated Law Society (qv). See Report on Conveyancing Law — Passing of Risk from Vendor to Purchaser (LRC 40 of 1991). See AUCTION SALES; SALE OF LAND.

(2) The court has power to determine the conditions upon which property is to be sold. See RSC O.51 r.4 (pursuant to a judgment or order); O.76 r.123 (bankruptcy); O.74 r.124 (company); and O.67 r.81 (e,f) (wards of court).

**condominium.** Joint sovereignty over territory eg (a) the territory of Andorra administered by Spain and France; (b) arises where title over a block of apartments is vested in a company and each apartment owner possesses a transferable share in the company which represents his interest. See FLAT.

**condom.** Colloquial term to describe a contraceptive sheath (qv).

**condonation.** The voluntary forgiveness and re-instatement of the erring party to a marriage by the wronged spouse with knowledge of the offence of the former. It was a complete defence to a charge of cruelty or adultery (qv) by a petitioner for a *divorce a mensa et thoro* (qv). Condonation could be express or implied, eg the latter in the case of the continuance or resumption of sexual intercourse. See O'Reardon v O'Reardon (1975) HC. However, condonation on the part of an applicant is no longer a bar to the grant of a decree of *judicial separation*: Judicial Separation and Family Reform Act 1989 s.44. However see s.4 which seems to retain it in a modified form. See CONNIVANCE.

**conduct, previous.** See PREVIOUS CON-DUCT.

**conference.** A meeting between counsel and solicitor and sometimes the client, to discuss a case. See also CONSULTATION.

**confession.** An admission of guilt made to another by a person charged with a crime. A confession may be in writing, signed or acknowledged by the accused, or it may be verbal or by conduct. A confession is admissible as evidence of the facts stated therein, but only if the prosecution establish that it was *voluntarily* made; a confession induced by any promise or threat in relation to the charge, made by or with the sanction of any *person in authority*, or in breach of the accused's constitutional rights, is deemed not to be voluntary.

An appeal to the accused on moral or religious grounds is not an inducement which will render a confession inadmissible. A *person in authority* is someone engaged in the arrest, detention, examination or prosecution of the accused; one who is in a position to press for punishment or to plead for leniency. An incriminating statement made by an accused when his detention is unlawful, is not admissible in evidence: The People (DPP) v Coffey (1987) ILRM 727. See The People (Attorney General) v Galvin (1964) IR 325; The People (Attorney General) v O'Brien (1965) IR 142; The People (DPP) v Byrne (1987 SC) IR 363; The People (DPP) v Hoey (1988 SC) ILRM 666. See INCRIMINATE; JUDGES' RULES; SOLICITOR, ACCESS TO.

**confidence, breach of.** Disclosure of confidential information may amount to a breach of contract where so provided in such a contract. In the absence of contract, the donee of confidential information may be under a duty, in equity, not to use that information to the donor's detriment. There is no absolute confidentiality where the parties concerned are a government and a private individual: The AG for England and Wales v Brandon Books (1987) ILRM 135. However, discussions at meetings of the government are absolutely confidential as a constitutional right: AG v The Sole Member of the Beef Processing Tribunal (1993 SC) ILRM 81. Disclosure of confidential information obtained by way of discovery (qv) can amount to contempt of court eg the use of the discovered material for any purpose extraneous to the proceedings: Ambiorix Ltd v Minister for the Environment (1992 SC) ILRM 209. See also Prince Albert v Strange (1841) 1 Mac G 25; Seager v Copydex Ltd (1967) 2 All ER 415; Aksjeselskapet Jutul v Waterford Ironfounders Ltd (1977) HC; House of Spring Gardens v Point Blank (1984) IR 611; Kennedy & Arnold v Ireland (1988) ILRM 472. [Text: Clarke (UK); Gurry (UK)]. See BANKER AND CONFIDENTIALITY; EMPLOYEE; EMPLOYER, DUTY OF; JURY; OFFICIAL SECRET; SPRING BOARD; TRADE SECRETS; UTTERANCE.

**confidential communications.** Communications which are privileged from disclosure or discovery eg professional communications between counsel or solicitor and client, between parishioner and parish priest, matrimonial communications, and discussions at meetings of the government. See PRIVILEGE, EVIDENTIAL; UTTERANCE.

**confidential information.** Attempts by an employee to access confidential computer data has been held to justify the dismissal of the employee: Mullins v Digital Equipment International BV (1990) ELR 139.

**confirmation order.** See COMPULSORY PURCHASE ORDER.

**confiscate.** To deprive of property by seizure. The government announced in 1993 its intention to introduce legislation to provide for the seizure and confiscation of the proceeds of crime and to enable ratification of the UN Drugs Convention 1988. See Report on Confiscation of the Proceeds of Crime (LRC 35 of 1991).

**conflict of interest.** A company director has a duty to avoid placing himself in a position where his personal interest conflict with those of his principal, the company. Substantial property transactions between a company and its directors must be approved at a general meeting of the company: Companies Act 1990 s.29. The non-cash asset must exceed in value either £50,000 or 10 per cent of the company's assets, with a minimum threshold of £1,000. See MacCann in 9ILT & SJ (1991) 81. See also Building Societies Act 1989 s.56. See DIRECTOR, ARM LENGTH; GOVERNMENT.

**conflict of laws.** An alternative name for private international law (qv). [Text: Binchy (1)].

**conformity, certificate of.** See BANKRUPTCY, PETITION FOR.

**confusion of goods.** See INTERMIXTURE OF CHATTELS.

**congested district.** A district within which it was estimated that the population could not be adequately supported on the arable land which was available: Purchase of Land (Ireland) Act 1891 s.36. The Congested District Boards set up by this Act had the power to purchase estates and sell them to tenants under the land purchase schemes. Certain counties were designated as congested. See LAND COMMISSION.

**conjugal rights.** The right of a married person to the society and cohabitation of his or her spouse. It is not an unqualified right eg it is placed in suspense if and when one or both of the spouses is imprisoned and thereby deprived of personal liberty in accordance with law: Noel & Marie Murray v Ireland & the AG (1991 SC) ILRM 465. See BEGET; CONSORTIUM.

**conjugal rights, restitution of.** Formerly a decree which a party to a marriage could obtain to compel the other party to resume cohabitation. To obtain the decree the petitioner had to prove that the respondent had refused to comply with a written demand to resume cohabitation; it was a good defence to prove that the petitioner had committed a matrimonial offence sufficient to ground an action for a *divorce a mensa et thoro*. It was a rarely sought remedy and the Law Reform Commission had recommended its abolition: LRC

Report No 6 of 1983. Actions for restitution of conjugal rights were abolished as from 22 November 1988: Family Law Act 1988. See Molloy v Molloy (1871) IR 5 Eq 367; Bell v Bell (1922) IR 103; Hood v Hood (1959) IR 225; RSC O.70 r.4.

**connected person.** The spouse, parent, brother, sister or child of a director of a company; a partner of the director; a trustee of a trust the principal beneficiaries of which are the director, his spouse, or any of his children or any body corporate which he controls: Companies Act 1990 s.26. There are restrictions on loans by a company to *connected persons*. See also Building Societies Act 1989 s.52. See LOAN TO DIRECTOR; FRAUDULENT PREFERENCE.

**connemara voting.** Popularly understood to mean "public voting" whereby a person declares his voting preference before a returning officer. It was originally introduced to facilitate voting by illiterate persons. See DISABLED VOTER; VOTERS, SPECIAL.

**connivance.** The intentional active or passive acquiescence by the petitioner for a decree of *divorce a mensa et thoro* (qv) in the adultery of the respondent. When connivance was proved it could act as a complete bar to the petitioner alleging adultery (qv) as a ground for such a decree. See Harris v Harris (1829) 162 ER 894. Now, where an application for a decree of *judicial separation* is made on the ground of adultery and the respondent proves that the adultery was committed with the connivance of the applicant, the court may refuse the application: Judicial Separation and Family Law Reform Act 1989 s.44(2). See CONDONATION.

**consanguinity.** [Of the same blood] Relationship by descent. The relationship may be *lineally* eg as between father and son; or *collaterally* eg as between cousins where descent is from a common ancestor. See AFFINITY; MARRIAGE.

**consecutive sentences.** The sentences which a court generally is empowered to impose on an accused, who has been found guilty of several offences at the same trial, which sentences are to follow one another in time of service. The District Court is not prohibited by statute from imposing consecutive periods of *detention* exceeding 12 months: The State (Clinch) v Connellan (1986) ILRM 455. See BAIL, OFFENCES COMMITTED WHILE ON; INDICTABLE OFFENCE.

**consensus ad idem.** [Agreement as to the same thing]. The common consent necessary for a binding contract. See Mespil Ltd v Capaldi (1986) ILRM 373; Minister for Education v North Star Ltd (1987) HC; Boyle & Boyle v Lee & Goyns (1992 SC) ILRM 65. See AD IDEM.

**consensus facit legem.** [Consent makes law]. Parties to a contract are legally bound to do what they agree to do. See SPECIFIC PERFORMANCE.

**consensus non concubitus facit matrimonium.** [Consent and not cohabitation constitutes a valid marriage]. See MARRIAGE; COMMON LAW MARRIAGE.

**consensus tollit errorem.** [Consent takes away error]. See ACQUIESCENCE.

**consent.** Acquiescence or compliance with or deliberate approval of or agreement to a course of action. Consent is inoperative if obtained by coercion, fraud or undue influence (qqv). Consent is a good defence to charges of offences against the person, except in the case of: – homicide, an assault which is a breach of the peace or is carelessly dangerous, or certain indecent offences created by the Criminal Law Amendment Act 1935. Failure or omission by a person to offer resistance to a criminal act done to that person does not of itself constitute consent to the act: Criminal Law (Rape) (Amdt) Act 1990 s.9. Inability to give a true consent to marriage is a ground for nullity: DB v O'R (1991 SC) ILRM 160. See ADOPTION, CONSENT TO.

**consent, age of.** Usually refers to the age, currently 17, at which a person is legally competent to consent to sexual intercourse. See SEXUAL OFFENCES; RAPE.

**conservation order.** The order which a planning authority (qv) is empowered to make to preserve from extinction or otherwise any flora or fauna in an area to which a special amenity area (qv) order relates; the conservation order may prohibit the taking, killing or destroying of such flora or fauna: LG(P&D) Act 1963 s.46(1) as inserted by the LG(P&D) Act 1976 s.40(b). See also SI No 65 of 1977, art.64.

**consideration.** Some valuable benefit

received by a party who gives a promise (*promisor*) or performs an act, or some detriment suffered by a party who receives a promise (*promisee*). *Some right, interest, profit or benefit accruing to one party, or some forbearance, detriment, loss, or responsibility given, suffered or undertaken by the other*: Currie v Misa (1875) 10 Ex 153. Consideration is necessary to the validity of every *simple contract* (qv), including those in writing. Consideration must be *real*; it need not be adequate to the promise, but it must have some ascertainable value. Consideration must be *legal*. Consideration must move from the promisee. A person may be a party to a contract but a stranger to the consideration.

Consideration may be *executed* or *executory* but not *past*. Consideration is *executed* when the act constituting the consideration is performed; consideration is *executory* when it is in the form of a promise to be performed at a future date. A *past* consideration is one which is wholly executed and finished before the promise is made. For consideration to support a bill of exchange, see HOLDER FOR VALUE. See CONTRACT; EQUAL PAY; STRANGER TO CONSIDERATION; UNCONSCIONABLE BARGAIN; VALUABLE CONSIDERATION.

**consignment.** Goods delivered by a carrier (qv) to a consignee at the instance of the consignor. The consignor has a duty to pre-pay a reasonable charge for the carriage of the goods and impliedly warrants that the goods rendered for carriage are fit to be carried in the ordinary way and that they are not dangerous. See Farrant v Barnes (1862) ii CB (ns) 553.

**consignment note.** See TOXIC AND DANGEROUS WASTE.

**consignor.** See CONSIGNMENT.

**Consolidation Act.** An Act of the Oireachtas which repeals or re-enacts or collects in a single statute previous enactments and amendments relating to a particular topic eg the Social Welfare (Consolidation) Act 1981. Such an Act is subject to a rebuttable presumption that no change in the pre-existing law was intended: Harvey v Minister for Social Welfare (1989) ITLR (7 Aug).

The Attorney General certifies that a Bill is a consolidating Bill. Substantial amendments of the statute law are not permissible; the only permissible amendments are those designed to remove ambiguities or inconsistencies, substitute modern for archaic language and to achieve uniformity of expression: Explanatory Memorandum to Social Welfare (Consolidation) Bill 1993. See CODE.

**consolidated accounts.** See HOLDING COMPANY.

**consolidation of actions.** Causes or matters pending in the court may be ordered to be tried together on the application of any party and whether or not all the parties consent to the order: RSC O.49 r.6. The court has an inherent jurisdiction to order that proceeding be heard together, taking account of the possibility of substantial saving of expense or inconvenience even though otherwise it would not be appropriate to have the proceedings consolidated: O'Neill v Ryan, Ryanair Ltd & Ors (1990 HC) ILRM 140. The tests applied are:- (a) is there a common question of law or fact of sufficient importance; (b) is there a substantial saving of expense or inconvenience; (c) is there a likelihood of confusion or miscarriage of justice: Duffy v Newsgroup Newspapers Ltd (1992 SC) ILRM 835. Defamation actions will not be consolidated where there is a likelihood of confusion (ibid Duffy case). See DEFENDANTS, JOINT.

**consolidation of mortgages.** The equitable doctrine that a mortgagee (qv) who holds two or more mortgages made by the same mortgagor (qv) on different properties, can consolidate them into one and refuse to be redeemed as to one without payment of what is due to him on all. The time for repayment on the mortgages being consolidated must have passed and at least one of the mortgage deeds must contain a clause permitting consolidation: Conveyancing Act 1881 s.17.

**consortium.** (1) A business combination. (2) The right of one spouse to the companionship and affection of the other. *The sum total of the benefits which a wife may be expected to confer on her husband by their living together — help, comfort, companionship, services and all the amenities of family and marriage*: O'Haran v Divine (1966) 100 ILTR 53. Damages may be recovered for the total loss of a wife's society or consortium as a result of the negligence of another but not for an impairment of consortium: Spaight v Dundon (1961) IR 201. There is now an analogous right in a wife to sue for the loss of her husband's society or companionship: McKinley v Minister for Justice (1990 HC) ITLR (7 May) and (1993 SC) 11 ILT Dig 115. Damages for loss of consortium are to be related to the damages recoverable for the death of a spouse (ibid McKinley case). See Civil Liability Act 1961 s.35; LRC 1 of 1981. See CONJUGAL RIGHTS; PER QUOD SERVITIUM AMISIT.

**conspiracy, crime of.** The crime of conspiracy involves the agreement of two or more persons to effect an *unlawful purpose*; it is a misdemeanour (qv). An unlawful purpose includes an agreement to commit a crime, or a tort which is malicious or fraudulent, or other acts which are extremely injurious to the public while not being a breach of law. It has been held that conspiracy to commit an offence should not be charged where the substantive offence can be laid: The People (Attorney General) v Singer (1975) IR 408; The People (Attorney General) v Keane (1975) 109 ILTR 1.

The combination of a conspiracy charge with the substantive offence might be regarded as leading to the possibility of unfair procedures: Walsh J in Ellis v O'Dea & Shields (1990 SC) ITLR (8 Jan). It is a fundamental principle of Irish *common law* (qv) that a person joining in a conspiracy or a joint venture outside the State, in furtherance of which an overt criminal act is committed within the State, will be amenable to the jurisdiction of the Irish courts even where he has not committed an overt act within the State: Ellis v O'Dea and Governor of Portlaoise Prison (1991 SC) ITLR (14 Jan).

See also The State (McCaud) v Governor of Mountjoy Prison (1986) ILRM 129; McDonald v McMahon (1990) 8 ILT Dig 60. See also Industrial Relations Act 1990 s.10.

**conspiracy, tort of.** The tort (qv) of conspiracy involves the combination of two or more persons with intent to injure another in his trade or business, without lawful justification, thereby causing damage or to perform an unlawful act thereby causing damage. Persons are given immunity from actions in conspiracy in respect of acts done in combination, in contemplation or furtherance of a *trade dispute*, which would not be actionable if done by one person alone: Industrial Relations Act 1990 s.10. See Crofter Hand Woven Harris Tweed Co v Veitch (1842) AC 435; Connolly v Loughney 87 ILTR 49; Taylor v Smyth (1990) ILRM 377.

**conspiracy and companies.** A company can in appropriate circumstances commit the crime and tort of conspiracy. See Taylor v Smyth (1990 SC) 8ILT & SJ 298; Belmont Finance Corporation Ltd v Williams Furnituire Ltd (1979) 1 All ER 118; and MacCann in 8ILT & SJ (1990) 197.

**conspirator.** A person who commits the offence of conspiracy (qv). Everything said, done or written by one conspirator is relevant against each of them, provided it was in the execution of their common purpose: R v Blake (1844) 6 QB 126.

**constat.** [It appears]. It follows; it is clear beyond argument.

**constituency.** A geographic area for parliamentary and local government elections. The number of constituencies for the Dail Eireann elections is as determined by law: 1937 Constitution art.16(2). However, no law may be enacted whereby the number of Dail members to be returned by any constituency, may be less than three. Also the Oireachtas is required to revise the constituencies in every twelve years, with due regard to changes in distribution of the population. When a census return discloses major changes in the distribution of the population, there is a constitutional obligation on the Oireachtas to revise the constituencies: O'Malley v An Taoiseach (1990) ILRM 460. The recommendation on this revision is usually made by a non-statutory electoral commission, headed by a Superior Court judge, whose recommendations are usually accepted and enacted into legislation. See Electoral (Amendment) Act 1990; Electoral Act 1992 ss.19 and 29.

The Minister is required to submit proposals for the review of the European Parliament constituencies by 1st December 1993 and at least once every ten years thereafter: European Assembly

    

Elections Act 1977 s.12(2) as amended by Electoral Act 1992 s.172(a). A presidential election is normally conducted by reference to Dail constituencies, but, under proposed draft legislation, the Minister will be able to order it to be conducted by reference to counties and county boroughs eg to facilitate the holding of local government elections and a presidential election at the same time: Presidential Elections Bill 1993 s.12. See DAIL EIREANN; RESIDENCE.

**constitution, bill to amend.** A bill to amend the Constitution must be initiated in Dail Eireann and must be submitted by referendum (qv) to the decision of the people, having been passed or deemed to have been passed by the two Houses of the Oireachtas (qv): 1937 Constitution, art.46.

**Constitution of Ireland.** The written Constitution which was adopted by the people in a referendum and came into effect on 29th December 1937. It continued in force the laws in Saorstat Eireann prior to its adoption, except in so far as they were inconsistent with the Constitution. Notice must be served on the Attorney General (qv), if the court so directs, where in any proceedings a question as to the interpretation of the Constitution arises: RSC O.60 rr.1-2.

The Constitution may be amended by a majority of votes in a referendum (qv). It has been amended a number of times eg to reduce the voting age, to remove the special position of some churches, to alter the Seanad representation from universities, to remove doubts as to certain adoptions, to protect the life of the unborn, to extend the Dail franchise to non-citizens, to provide for the State to join the European Economic Community, to ratify the Single European Act (qv) and the Maastricht Treaty. Constitutional amendments were rejected which sought to provide for the removal of the prohibition on divorce (qv), the removal of proportional representation (qv) as the election system, and to amend the provision dealing with the life of the unborn. [Text: Casey; Doolan (3); Curtin & O'Keeffe; Finlay (1); Forde (2); Kelly; Mackey N; Morgan; O'Reilly & Redmond]. See LANGUAGE; LEGISLATION, CONSTITUTIONALITY OF; SUPREME COURT.

**constitutional right, interference with.** See ABANDONMENT; EVIDENCE AND CONSTITUTIONAL RIGHTS; PRIVATE PROSECUTION; SOLICITOR, ACCESS TO; UNLAWFUL INTERFERENCE WITH CONSTITUTIONAL RIGHT.

**constitutionality of legislation.** See LEGISLATION, CONSTITUTIONALITY OF; RESOLUTION.

**construction, rules of.** Rules laid down by statute or by the courts for the interpretation of documents or of legislation. Every power conferred by an Act of the Oireachtas (qv) to make any regulations, rules or bye-laws is to be construed as including the power to revoke or amend any regulation, rule or bye-law made under such power: Interpretation Act 1937 s.15(3). It would appear that this rule of construction does not apply to *resolutions* unless specifically provided for in particular legislation relating to such resolutions. See SECTION 4 RESOLUTION; CONTRA PROFERENTEM; CONTRACT, INTERPRETATION OF; EJUSDEM GENERIS; LEGISLATION, INTERPRETATION OF; PUNCTUATION; TRANSPOSING OF WORDS.

**construction of dispositions.** Words denoting *family relationships* when used in wills, deeds and other instruments, are in future to be interpreted in respect of dispositions after the commencement of Part V of the Status of Children Act 1987, without regard to whether the parents of any person involved are or were married to each other (ibid s.27). If a disposition is expressed to be *to the children of X*, then X's legitimate, legitimated and illegitimate children are entitled to benefit. However, if the disposition is *to the legitimate children of X*, legitimated children will be entitled to benefit as if born legitimate (ibid s.27(2)). See ARMCHAIR PRINCIPLE; CONSTRUCTION SUIT.

**construction law.** Law dealing with building contracts eg variations, liquidated damages, prolongation and disruption claims. [Text: Kilty; Lyden & MacGrath; Powell-Smith UK]. See ENGINEERING LAW

**construction suit.** A procedure to discover the meaning of a deed, will or other written instrument where the sense or intention is not clear. It is instituted by special summons in the High Court or by equity civil bill in the Circuit Court. The court will determine any question of construction arising under the instrument and will give a declaration of the rights of the person interested. The courts will construe a will to give effect to the intention of the testator but will not make a will for the testator: Curtin v O'Mahony & AG (1992 SC) ILRM 7. See also In re Prescott, deceased (1990) 2 IR 342. See RSC O.83; O.125 r.1; O.4 r.2 (app B, part ll); RCC O.34.

**constructive.** Inferred; not directly expressed.

**constructive desertion.** See DESERTION.

**constructive dismissal.** A dismissal which is inferred where it is reasonable for the employee to terminate the contract of employment because of the employer's conduct: Unfair Dismissals Act 1977 s.1. The resignation of a manager whose position has been undermined may amount to a constructive dismissal: O'Beirne v Carmine Contractors (1990) ELR 232. A constructive dismissal may arise where an employee leaves because of the failure of the employer (a) to relieve a bad atmosphere in the workplace: Smith v Tobin (1992 EAT) ELR 253 or (b) to comply with a requirement of the Health & Safety Authority: Burke & Ors v Victor Collins Enterprises Ltd (1993 EAT) ELR 37.

There is no entitlement to notice in the case of a constructive dismissal: Halal Meat Packers Ltd v Employment Appeals Tribunal (1990) ELR 49; Holmes v O'Driscoll (1991 EAT) ELR 80. See McKeon v Murphy Plastics (Dublin) Ltd UD 142/1980; White v Aluset Ltd UD 259/88 — (1989) ILT & SJ 207; O'Connor v Garvey (1990) ELR 228; Lee v Transirish Lines Ltd (1992 EAT) ELR 150. See UNFAIR DISMISSAL.

**constructive notice.** See NOTICE.

**constructive total loss.** In marine insurance where the subject matter insured is reasonably abandoned on account of its actual total loss appearing to be unavoidable, or because it could not be preserved from actual total loss without an expenditure which would exceed its value when the expenditure has been incurred: Marine Insurance Act 1906 s.60. Where there has been a constructive total loss, the assured may either treat the loss as a partial loss, or abandon the subject-matter insured to the insurer and treat the loss as if it

were an actual total loss (ibid s.61). See Assicurazioni Generali v Bessie Morris SS Co (1892) 1 QB 571. See ABANDONMENT.

**constructive trust.** A trust imposed by equity (qv) in the interest of justice, without any reference to the presumed or express intention of the parties, eg a trustee who makes a profit from his position, holds the profit as constructive trustee for the benefit of the beneficiaries. See Keech v Sandford (1726) Sel Cas Ch 261. See GRAFT, DOCTRINE OF; TRUST.

**construe.** To discover and apply the meaning of a written instrument. See CONSTRUCTION, RULES OF; CONTEMPORANEA EXPOSITO.

**construed as one.** Term frequently found in the collective citation of an Act with previous Acts eg the Merchant Shipping Act 1992 s.1(3) requires that the Act "be *construed as one* with the Merchant Shipping Acts 1894 to 1983, and may be cited together therewith as the Merchant Shipping Acts 1894 to 1992". This means that each and every part of each of the Acts has to be construed as if it had been contained in one Act, unless there is some manifest discrepancy, making it necessary to hold that the later Act has to some extent modified something found in the earlier Act: Canada Southern Railway Co v International Bridge Co (1883) 8 App Cas 727.

**consuetudo est altera lex.** [A custom has the force of law]. See CUSTOM AND PRACTICE.

**consuetudo est optimus interpres legum.** [Custom is the best interpreter of the laws].

**consuetudo et communis assuetudo vincit legem non scriptam, si sit specialis; et interpretatur legem scriptam, si lex sit generalis.** [Custom and common usage overcome the unwritten law, if it be special; and interpret the written law, if it be general]. See CUSTOM AND PRACTICE.

**consul.** An agent appointed to protect the interests of the state or its nationals in another country and to further the development of commercial, economic, cultural, scientific and friendly relations between the two states. The duties and privileges of consular officers are set out in the second schedule of the Diplomatic

Relations and Immunities Act 1967. Consuls are divided into four classes: consuls-general, consuls, vice-consuls, and consular agents. The severance of diplomatic relations does not ipso facto involve the severance of consular relations.

Consular officers and employees are not amenable to the jurisdiction of the judicial or administrative authorities of the receiving state in respect of acts performed in the exercise of consular functions, except in respect of a civil action (a) by a third party for damages arising from an accident caused by a vehicle, vessel or aircraft or (b) arising from a contract not on behalf of the sending state (ibid art.43). Privileges and immunities may be waived by the sending state and must be communicated in writing (ibid art.45).

There is provision for the examination of witnesses before Irish consuls in a foreign country and also for the taking of affidavits: RSC O.39 r.5(3); O.40 r.7. See DIPLOMATIC PRIVILEGE.

**consular officer.** A person in the civil service of Ireland who is a consul-general, a consul, or a vice-consul: Interpretation Act 1937, schedule, para 6.

**consultation.** A meeting between counsel and solicitor and sometimes the client, to discuss a case.

**consultative case stated.** See CASE STATED.

**consultative jurisdiction.** See JURISDICTION.

**Consumer Affairs, Director of.** An officer appointed by the Minister who is independent in the performance of his functions which include: keeping under general review practices in relation to advertising; carrying out examinations requested by the Minister or which he the Director considers should be carried out; requesting persons to discontinue or refrain from practices that are or likely to be misleading to the public in a material matter; instituting proceedings in the High Court to prevent such practices; encouraging and promoting the establishment and adoption of codes of standards. Additional functions were given to the Director in 1980 and 1988. The Director is required to make an annual report to the Minister. Authorised

officers have extensive powers to enter premises and inspect books, documents and records for the purpose of obtaining information to enable the Minister, the Director or a local authority to exercise their statutory functions. See Consumer Information Act 1978 ss.9 and 16; SGSS Act 1980 s.55. Restrictive Practices (Amendment) Act 1987 s.32. See RSC O.104.

The functions formerly vested in the Examiner of Restrictive Practices were vested in 1987 in the Director whose title was changed to Director of Consumer Affairs and Fair Trade: Restrictive Practices (Amendment) Act 1987 s.6(1); SI No 2 of 1988; since repealed by the Competition Act 1991 s.22. The Director has been given power to prosecute in respect of a wider range of offences (ibid 1987 Act s.35). The Director is generally not required to permit inspection of documents which have come into his possession as part of a complaint made to him by a member of the public: Director of Consumer Affairs and Fair Trade v Sugar Distributors Ltd (1991 HC) ILRM 395. See ADVERTISING MISLEADING; MONOPOLY; BANKER CUSTOMER RELATIONSHIP.

**consumer contract.** A contract concluded by a person for a purpose which can be regarded as outside his trade or profession, which is a contract for the sale of goods on instalment credit terms, or a contract for a loan payable by instalments, or for any other form of credit, made to finance the sale of goods, or any other contract for the supply of goods or a contract or the supply of services and which meet particular requirements: Jurisdiction of Courts and Enforcement of Judgments (European Communities) Act 1988, first schedule, arts.13-15.

A consumer may bring proceedings against the other party to such a contract in the courts of the *contracting states* of the EC in which that party is domiciled or in the courts of the contracting state in which the consumer is domiciled (ibid art.14). See SMALL CLAIMS; SUMMONS, SERVICE OUT OF JURISDICTION.

**consumer, dealing as.** A party to a contract is said to *deal as a consumer* in relation to another party if (a) he neither makes the contract in the course of a business nor holds himself out as doing so, and (b) the other party does make the contract in the course of a business, and (c) the goods or services supplied under or in pursuance of the contract are of a type ordinarily supplied for private use or consumption: SGSS Act 1980 s.3. A buyer dealing as a consumer is given the protection of certain implied conditions which cannot be excluded.

A buyer is not regarded as dealing as consumer on a sale by competitive tender, or a sale by auction of goods of a type or by or on behalf of a person of a class, defined by the Minister. It is for those claiming that a party does not deal as consumer to show that he does not (ibid s.3(3)). See Rasbora Ltd v JCL Marine Ltd (1977) 1 Lloyd's Reports 645; O'Callaghan v Hamilton Leasing (Ireland) Ltd (1984) ILRM 146; Cunningham v Woodchester Investment Ltd (1984) HC. See QUALITY OF GOODS; EXCLUSION CLAUSES, RESTRICTION OF.

**consumer law.** The general area of law dealing with the sale of goods and supply of services, hire purchase, consumer information and protection. [Text: Grogan, King & Donelan; Linehan].

**consumer price index number.** The All Items Consumer Price Number Index compiled by the Central Statistics Office: Broadcasting Authority (Amdt) Act 1993 s.1(1). The consumer price index in a CSO publication or in a document signed by the director general of the CSO must be accepted as prima facie evidence of that statistic in any legal proceedings: Statistics Act 1993 s.45. See INTEREST AND SOCIAL WELFARE.

**consumer protection.** The EC is required to contribute to a high level of consumer protection through: (a) measures adopted pursuant to Article 100a in the context of the completion of the internal market (ie by adopting measures which have as their objective the establishment and functioning of the internal market); (b) specific action which supports and supplements the policy pursued by the member States to protect the health, safety and economic interests of consumers and to provide adequate information to consumers: Treaty of Rome 1957 art.129A as replaced by Maastricht Treaty 1992 art.G(D)(38).

**consummated.** Completed eg a marriage

is consummated when completed by ordinary and complete sexual intercourse. If either party is impotent (qv) or refuses to consummate the marriage, such marriage is voidable by *decree of nullity.* See R (otherwise W) v W (1980) HC; AMN v JPC (1988) ILRM 170. See MARRIAGE, NULLITY OF; VIRGO INTACTO.

**contemporanea exposito est optima et fortissima in lege.** [The best way to construe a document is to read it as it would have read when made]. Contemporaneous interpretation. See ARMCHAIR PRINCIPLE; CONSTRUCTION, RULES OF; LEGISLATION, INTERPRETATION OF.

**contempt of court.** A failure to comply with an order of the court or an act of resistance to the court or its judges; also conduct liable to prejudice the fair trial of an accused person. *Criminal* contempt is punitive, to punish for the offence; *civil* contempt is coercive, to compel compliance. A contempt committed in the face of the court can be punished immediately: In re Kevin O'Kelly (1974) 108 ILTR 97. In the District Court, contempt must be committed in the face of the court for sanctions to apply: Petty Sessions (Ireland) Act 1851 s.9. A newspaper article concerning an accused, found guilty of an offence but not yet sentenced, may amount to contempt: Kelly v Irish Times Ltd (1993 CC) — Irish Times 25/5/1993.

It is an offence for a person to be in contempt of a courts-martial, even where the person is not subject to military law: Defence (Amendment) Act 1987 s.12; In re Haughey (1971) IR 217.

There are separate rules governing how contempt of court prisoners are treated in prison eg the general rules relating to remission of sentence do not apply to them: Rules for the Government of Prisons 1947 r.270.

See also Keegan v de Burca (1973) IR 223; The State (DPP) v Walsh (1981) IR 294; Weeland v Radio Telefis Eireann (1987) IR 662; Desmond & Dedeir v Glackin & Minister for Industry & Commerce (1992 HC) ILRM 489; Bar Council v Sun Newspapers (1993 HC). See also Offences Against the State (Amendment) Act 1972 s.4; Companies Act 1990 s.10(5) — except the words "punish in like manner as if he had been guilty of contempt of court" which words have been found to be unconstitutional (ibid Desmond case). See Consultation Paper on Contempt of Court (Law Reform Commission 1991). See EUROPEAN COURT OF HUMAN RIGHTS; SCANDALISING THE COURT; SUB JUDICE; SUBPOENA.

**continental shelf.** The sea bed and subsoil outside the seaward limits of the territorial waters; any rights of the State outside territorial waters over the sea bed and subsoil for the purpose of exploring such sea bed and subsoil and exploiting their natural resources are vested in and exercisable by the Minister: Continental Shelf Act 1968 s.2. The government may by order designate any area as an area within which these rights are exercisable (ibid s.2(3)) and any offence taking place on an installation in a designated area or within 500 metres of such installation will be deemed to have taken place in the State (ibid s.3). An agreement between Ireland and the UK concerning the continental shelf between the two countries came into force on 11 January 1990 (Iris Oifigiuil 10 Apr 1990). See PETROLEUM, EXPLORATION FOR; MARITIME JURISDICTION.

**contingency fee.** A fee for a legal service which depends on the result of litigation. A barrister may not accept instructions from a solicitor on condition that payment will be subsequently fixed as a percentage or other proportion of the amount awarded: Code of Conduct for the Bar of Ireland – Rule 11.1 (e). Solicitors have been warned by the Law Society that "a system of percentage charges per se would be champertous and unenforceable even though agreed with the client": Guide to Professional Conduct of Solicitors in Ireland – Appendix E. However, see CHAMPERTY; NO FOAL NO FEE.

**contingent.** Something which awaits or depends on the happening of an event. See LIABILITY.

**contingent remainder.** A remainder (qv) where the grantee is unascertained or where the title depends on the occurrence of a specified event eg *to A (a bachelor) for life, remainder to his first child to reach 21 years.* A contingent remainder is saved if it is one which can be treated as a legal remainder and if it does not offend against the rule against perpetuities: Contingent Remainders Act

1877. Contingent remainders are alienable *inter vivos* by deed: Real Property Act 1845 s.6; and are devisable by will: Succession Act 1965 s.76. See PERPETUITIES, RULE AGAINST.

**continuance, presumption of.** See PRESUMPTION OF CONTINUANCE.

**continuity of employment.** See REDUNDANCY; UNFAIR DISMISSAL.

**contra.** [Against; opposite].

**contra bonos mores.** [Against good morals]. See also EXPRESSION, FREEDOM OF.

**contra proferentem.** The doctrine that the construction least favourable to the person putting forward an instrument should be adopted against him, provided that this works no wrong. This doctrine has been used in contracts of insurance to lighten the effects of a non-disclosure of material facts; ambiguous expressions will be held against those using them: In re Sweeney Kennedy Arbitration (1950) IR 85. See also Brady v Irish National Insurance (1986) ILRM 669; Capemel Ltd v Lister (1989) IR 319 and 323.

**contraceptive.** Any appliance, or instrument, excluding contraceptive sheaths (ie condoms), prepared or intended to prevent pregnancy resulting from sexual intercourse between human beings: Health (Family Planning) Act 1979 s.1 as amended by Health (Family Planning) (Amdt) Act 1993 s.2. Only certain persons are authorised to sell contraceptives eg chemists, medical doctors, health board employees, and only in respect of a prescription or authorisation of a registered medical practitioner; in addition the person to whom the contraceptive is sold must be over 17 years of age or married: Health (Family Planning) (Amdt) Act 1992 s.4 as amended by 1993 Act s.5. The former licensing requirement for importers and manufacturers of contraceptives has been repealed (ibid 1993 Act s.18). See McGee v Attorney General (1974) IR 284; Director of Public Prosecutions v McCutcheon (1986) ILRM 433. See CONTRACEPTIVE SHEATH; FAMILY PLANNING SERVICE; MARITAL PRIVACY; MEDICAL PREPARATIONS.

**contraceptive sheath.** Includes a contraceptive sheath designed and intended for use by a male person and a contraceptive sheath designed and intended for use by a female person: Health (Family Planning) (Amdt) Act 1993 s.1. The only control over contraceptive sheaths are the power of the Minister to prescribe standards for them (ibid s.4) and to prohibit their sale by vending machines at a place of a class specified in regulations (ibid s.3).

**contract.** A legally binding agreement. A *speciality contract* (qv) is one which is in writing and is sealed and delivered; it is also known as a *deed* or a *contract under seal.* A *simple contract* (qv) is one which is not under seal; all simple contracts require *consideration* (qv) to support them. An *implied contract* arises from the assumed intention of the parties. A *quasi-contract* arises by operation of law, irrespective of the intention of the parties. A *contract of record* arises from obligations imposed by a court of record eg a recognisance.

In general, for a contract to be valid and legally enforceable, there must be (1) an offer and unqualified acceptance; (2) an intention to create legal relations; (3) consensus ad idem; (4) legality of purpose; (5) contractual capacity of the parties; (6) possibility of performance; (7) sufficient certainty of terms; (8) valuable consideration. In some cases, a contract or evidence of it must be in a prescribed form ie in writing or by deed. A contract by deed does not require consideration to support it.

A contract may be enforceable by way of judicial review (qv), in which case the court will make the appropriate order unless it would be unfair to do so: Browne v Dundalk UDC (1993 HC) ILRM 328.

A person domiciled in a *contracting* state of the EC may, in another contracting state, be sued in matters relating to a contract, in the courts for the the place of performance of the obligation in question: Jurisdiction of Courts and Enforcement of Judgments (European Communities) Act 1988, first schedule, art.5. As regards contracts and EFTA countries, see Jurisdiction of Courts and Enforcement of Judgments Act 1993, sixth schedule, art.5. Regulation of the *choice of law* in contract is provided by the Contractual Obligations (Applicable Law) Act 1991. The basic rule is that the parties to a contract are free to select the applicable law to govern the contract; there are rules to determine the applicable law in the absence of an express or implied choice. [Text: Clark (1); Doolan (4); Cheshire, Fifoot & Furmston UK; Chitty UK]. See POST, CONTRACTS BY; PROPER LAW OF A CONTRACT; STATUTE OF FRAUDS; SUBJECT TO CONTRACT; SUMMONS, SERVICE OUT OF JURISDICTION.

**contract, assignment of.** See ASSIGN-MENT OF CONTRACT.

**contract, breach of.** See BREACH OF CONTRACT.

**contract, discharge of.** See DISCHARGE OF CONTRACT.

**contract, interpretation of.** It is an important principle for the interpretation of all contracts that it is not legitimate to use as an aid in the construction of a contract, anything said or done by the parties after the contract was made: In re Wogan's (Drogheda) Ltd (1993 SC) 11 ILT Dig 67. See CONSTRUCTION, RULES OF.

**contract, naked.** See NUDUM PACTUM.

**contract, printed.** See TYPE, SIZE OF.

**contract, privity of.** See PRIVITY OF CONTRACT.

**contract, standard form of.** See CON-TRACT OF ADHESION; STANDARD FORM OF CONTRACT.

**contract, subject to.** See SUBJECT TO CONTRACT.

**contract, time of essence of.** See TIME OF ESSENCE OF A CONTRACT.

**contract, triparite.** See TRIPARTITE CON-TRACT.

**contract, unconstitutional.** See UNCON-STITUTIONAL CONTRACT.

**contract for services.** A contract with an independent contractor. See An Foras Aiseanna Saothair v Minister for Social Welfare & Ryan (1991 HC No 653 Sp). See INDEPENDENT CONTRACTOR.

**contract for the sale of land.** See CONDITIONS OF SALE; STATUTE OF FRAUDS.

**contract of adhesion.** A standardised form of contract which the customer must accept or reject, but which the supplier may vary unilaterally as it may think fit. Where it involves a monoply supplier of a vital public utility, its terms may have to be construed not simply as contractual elements but as component pieces of delegated legislation: McCord v ESB (1980) ILRM 153.

**contract of employment.** A contract of service or of apprenticeship whether it is express or implied and (if it is express) whether it is oral or in writing: Unfair Dismissals Act 1977. A contract of employment may be created by deed, be in writing or be verbal.

In certain employments, the employer is required to give to each employee a written statement setting out the conditions under which he is employed: Minimum Notice and Terms of Employment Act 1973 s.9; and to keep a copy of it for two years: Social Welfare Act 1981 s.294G as inserted by Social Welfare Act 1993 s.27. It is inadequate that revised conditions of service be displayed only on a notice board; they should be sent directly to the personnel concerned: Hayes v Longford Co Council (1990 EAT) ELR 93. The imposition of revised conditions of employment may amount to the *constructive dismissal* of an employee: Pender & Ors v Trinity Sports & Leisure Club (1990) ELR 106.

A contract of employment in restraint of trade (qv) is generally void. While an individual contract of employment may include an arbitration clause, the staying by a court of legal proceedings in contravention of the clause generally does not apply: Arbitration Act 1980 s.5. However legal proceedings may be stayed in the case of an arbitration clause in a contract for services: Williams v Artane Service Station Ltd (1991 HC) ELR 126. An employer cannot generally deprive an employee of the protection given by Irish law by choosing another law to apply to the contract of employment: Contractual Obligations (Applicable Law) Act 1991, first schedule, art.6. See COMPETITION, DISTORTION OF; EMPLOYEE; SPECIFIC PERFORMANCE.

**contract of guarantee.** Generally, a contract whereby the guarantor, in consideration of the creditor making a loan to the principal debtor, agrees that in the event of the default of the principal debtor, payment shall be made by the guarantor within a certain time of all monies due: International Commercial Bank plc v Insurance Corporation of Ireland (1990 HC) ITLR (3 Dec). See also Hong Kong and Shanghai Banking Corp v Icarom plc (1993 SC) 11 ILT Dig 142.

As regards any hire-purchase agreement or credit-sale agreement, a contract of guarantee is a contract made at the request express or implied of the hirer or buyer, to guarantee the performance of the hirer's or buyer's obligations: Hire-Purchase Act 1946 s.1. See CREDIT GUARANTEE; GUARANTEE; LETTER OF CREDIT; TYPE, SIZE OF.

**contract of record.** Judgments and recognisances of courts of record. A judgment imposes an obligation to pay the sum awarded; a recognisance imposes an obligation or bond on an offender eg to be of good behaviour subject to a money penalty if the obligation is broken.

**contract of sale.** See SALE.

**contract of service.** A contract of employment. Contrast with a CONTRACT FOR SERVICES. See EMPLOYEE.

**contracts, doorstep.** See DOORSTEP CONTRACTS.

**contracts, evidenced in writing.** See SIMPLE CONTRACTS; STATUTE OF FRAUDS.

**contracts, illegal.** See ILLEGAL CONTRACTS.

**contracts, quasi-.** See QUASI- CONTRACTS.

**contracts, required to be in writing.** See DEED; SALE OF GOODS; SIMPLE CONTRACTS; STATUTE OF FRAUDS.

**contracts, void.** See VOID CONTRACTS.

**contracts for differences.** An agreement between two persons who agree that they will ascertain the difference in price of certain shares on one day and their price at a later date, with no intention that the shares will be purchased, and with payment being made from one to the other based on the difference. Such an agreement is void as a wager. See also Byers v Beattie (1867) IR ICL 209 (Exch).

**contractual obligations.** See CONTRACT.

**contravention.** Includes failure to comply: Building Societies Act 1989 s.2(1).

**contribution.** (1) Payment made by or imposed on some person. (2) Payment of a proportionate share of a liability which has been borne by one, or some only, of a number of persons liable eg where there are a number of insurance policies in respect of a particular risk and one insurer pays out on that risk, he may bring an action against the other insurers for a rateable contribution. Also an employee who has been unfairly dismissed may have an award of compensation abated to have regard to the contribution he made to his dismissal eg see Pritchard v Oracle (1992 EAT) ELR

24. See CONTRIBUTORY NEGLIGENCE.

**contributory.** Every person liable to contribute to the assets of a company in the event of the company being wound up. The present and past members are liable to contribute to the assets to an amount sufficient for the payment of its debts and liabilities and the costs of the winding up, and for an adjustment of the rights of the contributories between them: Companies Act 1963 s.207.

The list of contributories is made out by the *liquidator* in two parts, *A* contributories consisting of present members who are primarily liable and *B* contributories consisting of past members within the year preceding the winding up. *B* contributories are liable to contribute only after the *A* contributories are exhausted, and are not liable for debts contracted since they ceased to be members.

In the case of a company *limited by guarantee,* a contributory's liability is limited to the amount he undertook to contribute in the event of a winding up. In a company *limited by shares,* a contributory's liability is limited to the amount, if any, unpaid on his shares. See RSC O.74 rr 50-83, 86-89. See SHARES; PERSONAL LIABILITY; WINDING UP.

**contributory negligence.** Negligence or want of care on the part of the plaintiff to an action or of one for whose acts he is responsible: Civil Liability Act 1961 s.34. Where there is contributory negligence on the part of the plaintiff, his damages are reduced by such amount as the court thinks just and equitable having regard to the degrees of fault of the parties (ibid s.34); if it is not possible to establish different degrees of fault, the liability is apportioned equally. The onus on establishing contributory negligence is on the defendant: Clancy v Commissioners of Public Works (1991 SC) ILRM 567. See O'Leary v O'Connell (1968) IR 149; Sinnott v Quinnsworth Ltd (1984) ILRM 523; Conley v Stram (1988) HC.

The negligence of the plaintiff in an action for breach of contract may be pleaded and result in a reduction of damages for such breach; this arises because a *wrong* is defined in the Civil Liability Act 1961 s.2, as including *a tort, breach of contract or breach of trust.*

See Lyons v Thomas (1985) HC. See also Health (Amendment) Act 1986 s.2(2)(a). See PLEADINGS; SAFETY BELT.

**control, common.** See MONOPOLY.

**control of monopoly.** See MONOPOLY, CONTROL OF.

**controlled drugs.** Any substance, product or preparation specified or declared to be a controlled drug; possession of a controlled drug may be an offence: Misuse of Drugs Act 1977 ss.2-3, schedule. [Text: Charleton]. See DRUGS, MISUSE OF.

**controlled dwelling.** A house which is subject to statutory rent control, let as a separate dwelling, or a part so let, of any house, whether or not the tenant shares with any other persons any portion thereof or any accommodation, amenity or facility in connection therewith: Housing (Private Rented Dwellings) Act 1982.

For such a dwelling to be subject to control, there must be a letting of not greater than year to year. There is no control where the rateable valuation exceeds certain limits; where the dwelling is erected on or after 7th May 1941 or let by local authorities or furnished; or is subject to a service letting, or where let bona fide for *temporary convenience* or to meet a temporary necessity; or in certain cases where it is a separate and self-contained flat. See also Housing (Private Rented Dwellings) Act 1983.

The amount of the landlord's income is only a relevant factor in determining the tenant's rent if the landlord seeks to make it so: Quirke v Folio Homes (1988 SC) ILRM 496. See Foley v Johnson (1988 HC) IR 7. See RSC O.112. See Housing (Rent Tribunal) Regulations 1983 and 1988 (SIs 222 of 1983 and 140 of 1988). For discussion on whether the State is bound by the 1983 Act, see de Blacam in 7ILT & SJ (1989) 33. See also Housing (Miscellaneous Provisions) Act 1992 ss.17, 18, 20. See also 7ILT & SJ (1989) 209. [Text: de Blacam (1)]. See RENT CONTROL.

**Controller of Patents.** The office, being a corporate sole with perpetual succession and an official seal, known as the Controller of Patents, Designs and Trade Marks: Patents Act 1992 ss.6 and 97. The Controller, who is appointed by the government, may sue and be sued in that name, and has a wide range of functions, powers and authority under the 1992 Act in respect of patents (qv), under the Trade Marks Act 1963 in respect of trade marks (qv), under the Industrial and Commercial Property (Protection) Act 1927 in respect of designs (qv), and under the Copyright Act 1963 in respect of licences of copyright (qv).

Under the Patents Act 1964 (since repealed) the Controller did not have the authority and power to direct his Examiners to dispense with statutory investigations in the course of examination of certain patent applications for registration: The State (Rajan) v Minister for Industry Commerce (1988) ILRM 231. It has also been held that the Controller is required, having been requested so to do, to give in writing his reasons for dismissing an application for removal of a trade mark: Anheuser Busch v Controller of Trade Marks (1988) ILRM 247. The Controller is required to prepare an annual report: Patents Act 1992 s.103. See IMMUNITY; PATENTS OFFICE JOURNAL.

**Controller of Trade Marks.** See CONTROLLER OF PATENTS.

**convenience, balance of.** See BALANCE OF CONVENIENCE.

**convention.** (1) A treaty between states. (2) Agreed usuage and practice.

**convention application.** An application for a patent from an applicant in a country, which is a member of the Paris Convention (qv), to another convention country for protection in that other country. See Patents Act 1992 s.25. See PATENT.

**convergence criteria.** The conditions which are required to be met by member States of the EC in order to achieve *economic and monetary union* (qv). The criteria are: achievement of a high degree of price stability, absence of excessive budget deficit, observance of exchange rate mechanism of the European Monetary System, and durability of convergence as reflected in long-term interest rates: Treaty of Rome 1957 art.109j(1) as replaced by Maastricht Treaty 1992 art.G(D)(25) and Protocol on Convergence Criteria. See also COHESION FUND; EUROPEAN COMMUNITY.

**conversion.** A building society may convert itself into a public limited company by approving a *conversion scheme*: Building Societies Act 1989 s.101. See also TRUSTEE SAVINGS BANK.

**conversion, fraudulent.** See FRAUDULENT CONVERSION.

**conversion grant.** See LEASE FOR LIVES RENEWABLE FOREVER.

**conversion in equity.** In equity, conversion is the notional change of realty into personalty, or personalty into money, which arises as soon as the duty to convert arises.

Conversion may arise: (a) under a trust eg where a testator or settlor directs trustees to convert realty into personalty or vice versa, the property will be treated as having been converted from the time the instrument containing the direction came into operation; (b) under the Partnership Act 1890 where freehold land has become partnership land, it is treated as between the partners as personalty (ibid s.22); (c) under a sale by court order, conversion takes place from the date of the order, provided the order is final and conclusive; (d) under a specifically enforceable contract for sale of realty, the vendor's interest is converted to personalty and the purchaser's into realty as from the date of the contract.

In the event of total failure of the objects for which the conversion was directed in a deed or will, no conversion takes place. There are other rules for partial failure. [Text: Keane (2)]. See RECONVERSION; FRAUDULENT CONVERSION.

**conversion in tort.** A tort (qv) committed by a person who deals with chattels not belonging to him in a manner inconsistent with the rights of the owner. There must be *dealing* with the goods and there must be the *intention* to deny the right of ownership on the part of the wrongdoer. As to goods the subject of a hire-purchase agreement, see the Hire-Purchase Act 1946 ss.11 and 18. See British Wagon Co Ltd v Shortt (1961) IR 164; Morgan v Maurer Son (1964) Ir Jur Rep 31.

**convertible security.** See DEBENTURE.

**conveyance.** The transfer of the ownership of property; the instrument effecting the transfer. The deed of conveyance will contain the date, names of the parties, narrative recitals or introductory recitals, testatum, operative clause, parcels, habendum, and testimonium (qqv). Conveyancing for any fee, gain or reward is primarily restricted to solicitors (qv): Solicitors Act 1954 s.58. The Law Reform Commission has proposed changes in the law to simplify conveyancing, including reducing the period of title which has to be investigated from 40 to 20 years: Ninth Report of LRC (1986/87). See also Report on Land Law and Conveyancing Law — General Proposals (LRC 30 of 1989); Restrictive Practices Commission Report "Solicitors — Conveyancing & Advertising" (1982). [Text: Laffoy & Wheeler; Linehan; Wylie (2)]. See MARKETABLE TITLE; OVERREACHING CONVEYANCING; VOLUNTARY CONVEYANCE.

**conveyancing services.** The Minister is empowered to make regulations authorising building societies to provide conveyancing services: Building Societies Act 1989 s.31(1). *Conveyancing services* are the preparation of transfers, conveyances, contracts, leases or other assurances in connection with the disposition or acquisition of estates or interests in land (ibid s.31(13)).

**convict.** A person sentenced to death or penal servitude (qv) for treason (qv) or a felony (qv): Forfeiture Act 1870 s.6. A convict is incapable of making any contract, express or implied (ibid s.8; O'Connor v Coleman (1947) 81 ILTR 42). See also Statute of Limitations 1957 s.48(1)(c).

**conviction.** The finding of a person guilty of an offence after trial. Dismissal of an employee convicted of a serious offence unconnected with his work, may be an *unfair* dismissal: Brady v An Post (1992 EAT) ELR 227. A conviction, quashed on certiorari (qv) on the ground that the sentence pronounced is in excess of the jurisdiction of the court, is null and void ab initio and consequently the accused may be put on trial again for the same charge: State (Tynan) v Keane (1968) IR 348 cited in Sheehan v District Judge O'Reilly (1993 SC) ITLR (15 Mar). See SUMMARY OFFENCE; SUMMARY PROCEEDINGS; PROVISIONAL CONVICTION.

**conviction, evidence of.** Evidence of previous conviction of a crime is admissible in civil cases where the fact that a party has been convicted is in issue eg malicious prosecution (qv). Such evidence is also admissible in both civil and criminal cases, where a witness denies his conviction when cross-examined as to credit: Criminal Procedures Act 1865. In criminal cases, evidence of a previous conviction is admissible: (a) on any charge to which a previous conviction is essential to the charge eg being a habitual criminal: Prevention of Crime Act 1908; (b) formerly, evidence of conviction of fraud or dishonesty in the previous five years, to show guilty knowledge on the former charge of receiving stolen goods: Larceny Act 1916; (c) after conviction to assist the judge in imposing a proper sentence; (d) in circumstances where evidence of the bad character of the accused is admissible. See The People (Attorney General) v Kirwan (1943) IR 279. See CHARACTER, EVIDENCE OF.

**conviction, proof of.** A previous conviction may be proved against any person by production of a certificate of conviction: Prevention of Crimes Act 1871 s.18; or in the case of proof for the purpose of discrediting a witness by a certificate: Criminal Procedure Act 1865 s.6; or to assist the judge in imposing a proper sentence by oral recitation by a garda witness of previous convictions from a list already acknowledged by the accused as correct.

**convictions, freedom to express.** See EXPRESSION, FREEDOM OF.

**cooling-off period.** Popularly understood to mean the period during which a buyer or a hirer of goods may withdraw from a contract or hire-purchase agreement. The Minister may provide by order that there shall be a specified period within which the customer shall be entitled to withdraw his acceptance of such a contract: SGSS Act 1980 s.50. See CODE OF PRACTICE; DOORSTEP CONTRACTS.

**coparcenary.** The ownership in land which formerly arose on an *intestacy* where no sons survived the deceased and the nearest relatives were females, those relatives collectively constituted the heir and took the realty as coparcerers. It was a hybrid form of *co-ownership;* there was no right of survivorship and the interests of each coparcener passed under her will or on an intestacy; each coparcener held an undivided share in the property and union in a sole tenant destroyed the coparcenary. Effectively abolished by the Succession Act 1965 ss.10(1) and 11(1) except in relation to the descent to an unbarred entail. See Re Matson (1897) Ch 509. See BARRING THE ENTAIL; JOINT TENANCY.

**copy.** See DOCUMENTARY EVIDENCE; OFFICE COPY.

**copyright.** Copyright in an *original* literary, musical, dramatic or artistic work is the exclusive right to do, or to authorise other persons to do, certain acts in relation to that work: Copyright Act 1963 ss.7-9. Such acts include eg reproducing the work in any material form, publishing it, performing it in public, broadcasting it, or making an *adaptation* (qv) of it (ibid s.8(6) and 9(8)). The term of copyright continues generally for the lifetime of the author of the work and a period of fifty years from the end of the year in which he died (ibid ss.8(4) and 9(5)) and in certain cases from the end of the year in which it was first *published* eg engravings and photographs (ibid s.9(6) and (7)). Infringement of copyright is actionable at the suit of the owner and the remedies are generally an injunction, an order for account and damages (ibid s.22).

An assignment of copyright is not valid unless it is in writing and signed by or on behalf of the assignor (ibid s.47(3)). Licences may be granted in respect of copyright by the owner and are binding on every successor in title of his interest, except a purchaser in good faith for valuable consideration and without notice (ibid s.47(4)). The Controller of Patents, Designs and Trade Marks has jurisdiction to determine disputes arising between licensing bodies and persons requiring licences (ibid ss.29-42). A licence scheme is in the nature of a standing invitation to treat: Phonographic Performance (Irl) Ltd v Controller of Industrial and Commercial Property (1993 HC) 11 ILT Dig 162. See also Phonographic Performance (Ire) Ltd v Chariot Inns Ltd (1993 HC) 11 ILT Dig 162.

International protection of copyright is obtained via the Berne Copyright Union (qv) and the Universal Copyright Convention (qv). See Copyright (Proceedings before the Controller) Rules 1964 (Amdt) Rules 1992 (SI No 149 of 1992) and 1993 (SI No 218 of 1993). [Text: Copinger UK; Laddie UK]. See Allibert SA v O'Connor (1982) ILRM 40. See BREHON LAWS; DESIGN; INFRINGEMENT OF COPYRIGHT; IRISH COPYRIGHT LICENSING AGENCY; JOINT AUTHORSHIP; LITERARY WORK; ORIGINAL; PUBLICATION; THIRD PARTY INFORMATION VIDEO.

**copyright, infringement of.** See INFRINGEMENT OF COPYRIGHT.

**copyright, international.** See BERNE COPYRIGHT UNION; UNIVERSAL COPYRIGHT CONVENTION.

**copyright, ownership of.** Generally the author of an original literary, dramatic or musical or artistic work is entitled to the copyright subsisting in that work: Copyright Act 1963 s.10(1). Where such a work is made by the author in the course of employment under a *contract of service* (qv) or apprenticeship (qv), it will be a matter for interpretation of the contract as to who owns the copyright. However, in respect of literary, dramatic or artistic works where the employer is the owner of a newspaper, magazine or similar periodical, the copyright subsists in that owner unless a contrary intention appears by agreement (ibid s.10(2) and (4)).

Where a person commissions the taking of a photograph, or the printing or drawing of a portrait, or the making of an engraving and pays, or agrees to pay, for it in money or money's worth and the work is made in persuance of that commission, that person and not the author is entitled to the copyright (ibid s.10(3)). See PHOTOGRAPH.

**copyright, perpetual.** See PERPETUAL COPYRIGHT.

**copyright royalty.** See ROYALTY.

**coram judice.** [In the presence of the judge].

**cor; coram.** [In the presence of].

**coram non judice.** [Before a person who is not a judge].

**coroner.** An office holder, appointed by the local authority in whose area the coroner's district is situated, with the general duty to hold inquests (qv) or to cause a post-mortem examination to be made in lieu of an inquest in respect of certain deaths in his district: Coroners Act 1962 ss.8, 17-19. A coroner has jurisdiction to enquire into the finding of treasure trove (qv) (ibid s.49). See also Dangerous Substances Act 1972 s.28. See EXHUMATION; INQUEST.

**corporal punishment.** Physical force against a person which may be permitted by law (eg whipping) or may amount to a crime (eg assault and battery) or a tort (eg trespass to the person). Parents have a broad discretion as to how they maintain discipline among their children; physical force or confinement is permissible, provided it is not excessive. Schoolteachers also had such a discretion previously (McCann v Mannion 66 ILTR 161); however, corporal punishment in schools has been forbidden by the Minister since 1982; a teacher who uses corporal punishment is "regarded as guilty of conduct unbefitting a teacher and will be subject to severe disciplinary action" (Department of Education Circular 9/82 dated January 1982).

"Teachers have most unwisely been deprived of the power of inflicting reasonable corporal punishment which could deal with disobedience": Carrol J in Walsh v St Joseph's National School (1990 CC) — reported in Irish Times 11 Oct 1990. See DISCIPLINE IN SCHOOL; WHIPPING.

**corporate trades, investment in.** The relief from income tax in respect of the investment by individuals in corporate trades, known generally as the *business development scheme; BES* (qv) or the *business expansion scheme.*

**corporate veil.** See LIFTING THE CORPORATE VEIL.

**corporation.** A body of persons having in law an existence and rights and duties distinct from those of the individual persons who from time to time form it. A corporation *sole* consists of only one member at a time in succession eg a bishop. A corporation *aggregate* consists of a number of persons eg an incorporated company and a municipal corporation. A partnership has no legal personality of its own and consequently a partnership firm is not a corporation. See CORPORATION AGGREGATE; CORPORATION SOLE.

**corporation aggregate.** A corporation consisting of more than one member eg a company registered under the Companies Acts. A corporation aggregate must have at least two members, although one may be the nominee of the other. See COMPANY; CORPORATION SOLE.

**corporation sole.** A corporation consist-

ing of a single person whose corporate status arises from an office or function. The object of a corporation sole is to make it possible to distinguish the holder of the office or function in his official and in his private capacity eg a bishop, a minister of State. The property of a corporation sole is treated for the purposes of the Act as belonging to the corporation notwithstanding a vacancy in it: Criminal Damage Act 1991 s.1(5).

**corporation tax.** A tax charged on the profits of companies: Corporation Tax Act 1976 as amended by annual Finance Acts. Corporation tax in respect of interest earned by monies kept on deposit by the liquidator of a company, is a liability properly incurred: Companies Act 1963 s.281; Burns v Hearne (1987) ILRM 508. [Text: Moore & Brennan; Williams]. See MANUFACTURED; PROFIT & LOSS; TRADING HOUSE, SPECIAL.

**corporeal property.** Property which is visible or tangible eg land and goods. See OWNERSHIP.

**corpus delicti.** The body of an offence; the facts which constitute an offence. The prosecution must first prove that the offence has been committed by someone; in murder cases this is usually proved by production of a dead body, though this is not necessary: Attorney General v Edwards (1935) IR 500.

**correction.** See SLIP RULE.

**corresponding offence.** The offence specified in an extradition warrant must *correspond* with an offence under Irish law which is an indictable offence or is punishable on summary conviction by imprisonment for a period of at least 6 months: Extradition Act 1965 s.47. The judge must satisfy himself before ordering the extradition of the accused whether there is a sufficient statement of the ingredients of the alleged offence to enable him to determine whether the acts alleged would constitute an offence under Irish law: The State (Furlong) v Kelly (1971) IR 132.

It is preferable that a judge of the District Court, making an order for extradition, should specify the nature of the offences which he considered to be *corresponding*, but failure to do so is not fatal once correspondence was in fact established in the High Court: Sey v Johnston (1989) IR 516.

**corroboration.** Independent evidence which tends to show that the principal evidence is true; independent evidence of material circumstances tending to implicate the accused in the commission of the crime with which he is charged: Attorney General v Williams (1940) IR 195; People (AG) v Trayers (1956) IR 110.

The general rule of law is that a court can act on the testimony of one witness. However, corroboration of another witness is required by law for: perjury; treason: Treason Act 1939; affiliation orders: Illegitimate Childrens Act 1930 (now repealed); offence of procuring defilement of a girl by threats or fraud or administering drugs: Criminal Law (Amendment) Act 1885.

Corroboration is required as a rule of practice to support the evidence of an *accomplice* (qv) and formerly of the injured party in a sexual assault; the jury could convict on the uncorroborated evidence of one witness in these cases, but the judge had to warn the jury of the danger of acting on such evidence. A warning is no longer a requirement in relation to offences of a sexual nature but the judge retains a discretion, having regard to all the evidence given, to decide whether the jury should be given a warning; no particular form of words is required: Criminal Law (Rape) (Amendment) Act 1990 s.7; DPP v Riordan (1992 CCA) ITLR (30 Nov). See The People v Cradden (1955) IR 130; DPP v Reid (1991 CCA) as reported by Whelan in 9ILT & SJ (1991) 109 and 266. See CHILD, EVIDENCE OF.

**corrupt agreement with creditor.** A creditor commits an offence who accepts property from a bankrupt (qv) or an arranging debtor (qv) or any other person as an inducement for forbearing to oppose or for accepting a proposal or an offer of composition (qv). The person offering the inducement also commit an offence and the claim of the creditor will be void and irrecoverable: Bankruptcy Act 1988 s.125.

**corruption.** An inducement by means of an improper consideration to violate some duty. See Prevention of Corruption Act 1916. See BRIBERY AND CORRUPTION; ILLEGAL CONTRACTS; INFLUENCE, IMPROPER; PERFORMANCE, INDECENT OR PROFANE.

**costs and criminal proceedings.** The court has jurisdiction to award costs to an accused person who is acquitted of a criminal charge, but as legal aid will have been granted in most of such cases, the issue does not normally arise: The People v Bell (1969) IR 24. The Court of Criminal Appeal no longer has jurisdiction to award costs in respect of proceedings for which a legal aid certificate has been granted: Criminal Justice (Legal Aid) Act 1962 s.8. Where that court reverses a conviction and orders the appellant to be re-tried for the same offence, it may order the costs of the re-trial (in the absence of a legal aid certificate) to be paid by the State unless the court is of the opinion that the cause of the new trial has been caused or contributed to by the defence: Court of Justice Act 1928 s.5 and 1962 Act s.8; The People v Moran (1974) Frewen 380.

Where an offender is released on probation (qv), the court may order the offender to pay the costs of the proceedings: Probation of Offenders Act 1907 s.1(3). Also a person convicted of an offence under the Environmental Protection Agency Act 1992 will be ordered to pay to the Agency its costs in relation to the investigation, detection and prosecution of the offence unless the court is satisfied that there are special and substantial reasons for not so doing (ibid s.12).

**costs in civil proceedings.** The court has a discretion in awarding costs in civil proceedings; however, the general practice is that the costs follow the event, ie the successful litigant is generally entitled to his costs: RSC O.99 r.1(4). It would require very substantial reasons of an unusual kind before the Court would depart from that principle: SPUC v Coogan & Ors (1990) 8ILT Dig 156. A plaintiff who failed to prove an actionable defamation none the less had costs awarded in his favour, where the newspaper defendant acknowledged a serious misstatement in the newspaper article only at the appeal hearing: Harkin v Irish Times (1993 HC) — Irish Times 2/4/1993.

There are three requirements to enable costs to be recovered by a party to litigation: (a) an order for costs had to be made in his favour; (b) the matters claimed as costs must have been properly incurred in the course of litigation; and (c) he must be under a legal liability to pay costs in the action: AG v Sligo Co Council (1989) ILRM 785. There is no longer a justification for allowing a wife her costs against her husband in matrimonial proceedings: F v L (1990 HC) ILRM 886.

Costs may be payable on (a) a *party and party* basis, ie all cost which were necessary and proper for the attainment of justice or for enforcing or defending the rights of the party whose costs are being *taxed* and on (b) a *solicitor and client* basis, ie the costs normally associated between a solicitor and his own client.

There are limitations on the amount of costs which may be recovered by a plaintiff in particular circumstances. If a plaintiff is awarded damages which could have been awarded in a lower court, the plaintiff will be entitled to the costs appropriate to the lower court: Courts Act 1991 s.14 inserting a new s.17 to the Courts Act 1981. In the High Court (a) if an award is made between £25,000 and £30,000 the plaintiff will be entitled to Circuit Court costs except where the trial judge grants a special certificate; (b) if the award is between £15,000 and £25,000 the plaintiff will be entitled to Circuit Court costs; (c) if the award is between £5,000 and £15,000 the plaintiff will be entitled to the lesser of Circuit Court costs or costs equivalent to the damages awarded. The judge has a discretion to order the plaintiff to pay the additional costs incurred by the defendant in defending in a higher court than was necessary (ibid 1981 Act s.17(5)).

For provisions on costs in the Circuit and District Courts, see respectively RCC O.58 and DCR r.147 as substituted by District Court Rules (No 2) 1955 r.6. For interest on costs, see Lambert v Lambert (1987) ILRM 390. For costs in winding up of a company, see MacCann in 8ILT & SJ (1990) 245. See also O'Neill v Adidas Sportschuhfabriken (1992 SC) ITLR (17 Aug); In re Hibernian Transport Companies Ltd (in liquidation) (1992 SC) ITLR (20 Apr). See LODGMENT IN COURT; REPETITIVE LEGAL WORK; SECURITY FOR COSTS; TAXATION OF COSTS.

**cottier.** A letting by agreement or memorandum in writing of a dwelling-house or cottage without land or with any portion of land not exceeding half an acre, at a rent not exceeding £5 per year for one month or from month to month or for any lesser period and under which the landlord is bound to keep and maintain the dwelling-house or cottage in tenantable condition and repair: Deasy's Act 1860 s.81; Cottier Tenant (Ireland) Act 1856. Such tenancies have now become obsolete. See also Deasy's Act s.84. See Murphy v Kenny (1930) 64 ILTR 179.

**couchant.** Cattle lying down.

**council.** See COUNTY COUNCIL; URBAN DISTRICT COUNCIL; BOROUGH.

**Council of Ministers.** The main decision making institution of the European Community (qv), represented by one member from each member State, presided over by a President which office rotates every six months. See Treaty of Rome 1957 art.145-154 as amended by Maastricht Treaty 1992 art.G(E)(43)-(47). The members must be at Ministerial level and be authorised to commit their government. See COMMUNITY LAW; SINGLE EUROPEAN ACT.

**Council of State.** The advisory body established by the 1937 Constitution to aid and counsel the President of Ireland (qv) on all matters relating to the exercise and performance by her of her powers and functions (ibid art.31). Its ex-officio members are: the Taoiseach, the Tanaiste, the Chief Justice, the Chairman of Dail Eireann, the Chairman of Seanad Eireann, and the Attorney General. In addition, the President may appoint not more than seven persons to be members; also every *former* President, Taoiseach and Chief Justice, able and willing to act is a member.

**councillor.** An elected or co-opted member of a local government body; there is no residence or property ownership requirement to be eligible: Electoral Act 1963 repealing both the Local Government (Ireland) Act 1898 s.2(5) and Local Government Act 1925 s.57. Persons are disqualified from being councillors in a variety of circumstances eg being under eighteen years; failing to pay rates; being

COUNTY COUNCIL

convicted within five years before election of any crime and sentenced to imprisonment without the option of a fine and not having received a free pardon; being absent from council meetings; failing to pay a sum surcharged (qv) on him by the auditor; making false claims for expenses: Local Government (Ireland) Act 1898 s.94(3); Local Government (Application of Enactments) Order 1898 as amended by the Local Elections (Petitions and Disqualifications) Act 1974 s.24; Local Government Act 1925 s.62; Local Government Act 1941 s.57.

**councillor, disclosure of interest.** Councillors must not influence or seek to influence any planning decision (qv) in which they have a pecuniary or beneficial interest, and are required to disclose any estate or interest which they have in lands situated in the area of their planning authority, any business of dealing in or developing land in which they are engaged or employed, and any profession, business or occupation in which they are engaged which relates to dealing in or developing land: LG(P&D) Act 1976 s.32 and 33(3). It is an offence for a councillor not to give such particulars or to give particulars which are false or, to the knowledge of the member, misleading in a material respect.

There is also a prohibition on persons voting as members of a housing authority, or of certain committees, on resolutions or questions relating to any house or any land in which they are beneficially interested: Housing Act 1966 s.115. See LOCAL ELECTION.

**counsel.** See BARRISTER; SENIOR COUNSEL.

**count.** Sections in an *indictment*, each containing and charging a different offence. See INDICTMENT; RECOUNT.

**counterclaim.** A claim by a defendant for relief or remedy against a plaintiff and maintained in the same action. Where a defendant seeks to rely upon any grounds as supporting a counterclaim, he must in his defence, state specifically that he does so by counterclaim; if such counterclaim raises questions as between himself and the plaintiff along with any other person, he is required to add a title setting forth the names of the defendants to such cross-action: RSC O.21 rr.9-16. For provisions dealing with counterclaims in the Circuit

and District Courts, see respectively RCC O.12 r.7; DCR r.144 amended by DCR 1992 (Set-off or Counterclaim) (SI No 317 of 1992). See also Murphy v Hennessy (1985) ILRM 100. See DEFENCE; PLEADINGS.

**counterfeit.** To make an imitation. The making of false or counterfeit coins is a felony: Coinage Act 1861; Currency Act 1927 s.11. The making or issuing of any piece of metal or mixed metal of any value whatsoever as a coin or token for money or purporting that the holder thereof is entitled to demand any value denoted thereon, is an indictable offence (qv): Decimal Currency Act 1969 s.14. The possession of any false or counterfeit coins is a misdemeanour, as is the uttering of such coins: 1861 Act. For counterfeiting currency notes or postal stamps, see Central Bank Act 1942 s.56; Post Office Act 1908 s.65. Where the intent is to deceive or defraud, the offence is that of forgery. See CURRENCY, FOREIGN; FORGERY.

**counterpart.** A lease is generally prepared in two identical forms, one called a lease and the other a counterpart, the lease being signed by the lessor and the counterpart by the lessee and then exchanged and signed. The contents of a lease may be proved by its counterpart: Deasy's Act 1860 s.23. See Jagoe v Harrington (1882) 10 LR Ir 335.

**counter-offer.** See OFFER.

**county borough.** See BOROUGH.

**county council.** The body, consisting of a chairman and councillors (qv), established in every administrative county with responsibility for the management of the administrative and financial business of the county: Local Government (Ireland) Act 1898 s.1. A council is a body corporate having perpetual succession and a common seal: Local Government (Application of Enactments) Order 1898, schedule, art.13(1). County Councils are *housing authorities* under the Housing Acts 1966-1979; *planning authorities* under the LG(P&D) Acts 1963 and 1976; *fire authorities* under the Fire Services Act 1981. They are also *sanitary authorities* in respect of sewers, water supply, dangerous buildings, abatement of nuisances, refuse collection and street cleaning, baths, wash-houses, bathing places, sanitary conveniences, offensive trades, burial grounds, temporary dwellings, building bye-laws, street lighting, markets and slaughterhouses (qqv).

Many important functions relating to health matters, formerly the responsibility of county councils, were transferred to the health boards under the Health Act 1970. See LOCAL AUTHORITY; LOCAL GOVERNMENT, ELECTION OF; GRAND JURY; BOARDS OF GUARDIANS; BOROUGH; HEALTH BOARD.

**county manager.** The office holder for a county, with responsibility to manage every *elective body*, whose functional area is wholly within the county, such body being the corporation of a borough, an urban district council, the commissioners of a town: County Management Act 1940 ss.1 and 3. The manager holds office until he dies, resigns or is removed from office; he can only be removed from office by the council with the sanction of the Minister (ibid s.5-6; Local Government Act 1941 s.23(1)). However, for appointments since 1991, the manager ceases to hold office after 7 years or on attaining 60 years of age: Local Government Act 1991 s.47 and SI No 128 of 1991.

The functions of a council which are exercisable only by the council are called *reserved functions* (qv), and must be done by way of a resolution of the council; all other functions are called *executive functions* and are exercisable only by the manager: 1940 Act s.17. An executive function is done by the manager by the signing of an order in writing, containing a statement of the time at which it was so signed; the manager must keep a register of all orders made by him (ibid s.19). See SECTION 4 RESOLUTION.

**county registrar.** An officer of the court attached to the Circuit Court office in each county: Court Officers Act 1926 s.35. He sits as registrar to the Circuit Court judge assigned to the county. Apart from controlling and managing the Circuit Court office, he is responsible, outside the Counties Dublin and Cork, as sheriff, for executing all orders of the court lodged with him for execution and for elections and referenda; these specific functions are the responsibility of independent sheriffs in Counties Dublin and Cork. A solicitor of not less than eight years standing may be appointed county

registrar. Provision is made for the poundage fees of a county registrar or sheriff in relation to the execution of an order of the court: Finance Act 1988 s.71. See DISTRICT PROBATE; RETURNING OFFICER; SIDE-BAR ORDERS; SUBPOENA; TAXATION OF COSTS.

**county road.** See PUBLIC ROAD.

**course of trade.** The term which is of significance in relation to trade marks, their registration and any infringement thereof. It has been held that the word *Pass* in relation to a banker's card is not a trade mark as defined, meaning a mark used or proposed to be used in relation to goods for the purpose of indicating , or so as to indicate, a connection *in the course of trade* between the goods and some person having the right to use the mark: Bank of Ireland v Controller of Trade Marks (1987) HC. See also Gallagher (Dublin) Ltd v Health Education Bureau (1982) ILRM 240; ITT World Directories Inc v Controller of Patents, Designs and Trade Marks (1985) ILRM 30; Eurocard International v Controller of Trade Marks (1987) HC.

The term "course of trade" is also important as regards income tax. See Browne v Bank of Ireland Finance Ltd (1991 SC) 9ILT Dig 268. See TRADE MARK.

**court.** A place where justice is administered; the judge or judges who sit in court. Justice is required to be administered in courts established by law by judges appointed in the manner provided by the Constitution: 1937 Constitution, art.34. The *superior* courts are the High Court and the Supreme Court as required by the Constitution; other courts, known as *inferior* courts, of a limited and local nature, are established by statute eg District Court and Circuit Court: Courts (Establishment and Constitution) Act 1961. These *ordinary* courts also include the Central Criminal Court and the Court of Criminal Appeal. There are also *special* courts (qv) which may be established under the Constitution. [Text: Delaney H].

**Court of Criminal Appeal.** The court which hears appeals from the judgments of the Central Criminal Court, the Circuit Criminal Court and the Special Criminal Court: Courts (Establishment and Constitution) Act 1961. The court consists of one Supreme Court judge and two judges of the High Court. The appeal is not a rehearing of the case but is based on a transcript (qv) of the evidence and is usually confined to points of law or that the verdict was against the weight of the evidence. The Court, however, cannot substitute its own subjective view of evidence for the verdict of a jury: DPP v Egan (1990 SC) ITLR (8 Oct). The court may consider grounds of appeal which are contradictory to the trial submission: DPP v Hardy (1992 SC) ITLR (16 Nov). The decision of the court is by a majority and only one judgement is given.

When hearing an appeal from the Special Criminal Court, the Court of Criminal Appeal will consider whether any inference of fact drawn by that court could properly be supported by the evidence: People v Madden (1977) IR 336 cited in People (DPP) v Farrell (1993 CCA) ITLR (5 Apr). When hearing appeals from courts martial, the court is known as the *Courts Martial Appeal Court*. The role of the Court of Criminal Appeal has been affected by the decision that the Supreme Court may hear an appeal directly to it from the Central Criminal Court: The People (AG) v Conmey (1975) IR 341.

The Court of Criminal Appeal has recently been given a new role of reviewing the sentence imposed by a court which appears to the DPP to be unduly lenient: Criminal Justice Act 1993 s.2. It is proposed to give it a new role also in relation to alleged miscarriages of justice. See BOOK OF EVIDENCE; MISCARRIAGE; REVIEW OF SENTENCE.

**court of first instance.** See FIRST INSTANCE, COURT OF.

**court of last resort.** A court from which there is no appeal.

**court of record.** A court which has the records of its acts and judicial proceedings maintained and preserved and which has power to fine and imprison for contempt (qv) of its authority. The Supreme, High and Circuit Courts are courts of record as is the District Court: Courts (Supplemental Provisions) Act 1961 ss.7, 8 and 21; Courts Act 1971 s.13 respectively.

**court protection of company.** A new legal mechanism for the rescue or reconstruction of ailing but potentially viable companies: Companies (Amendment) Act 1990. The central feature of the provision is the appointment by the court of an *examiner* and the placing of the company concerned under the protection of the court for three or four months. While the company is so protected, it may not be wound up, a receiver may not be appointed, and debts or securities may not be executed against it.

If the examiner considers that the company, or part of it, can be saved and that this would be more advantageous than a winding up, the examiner is required to prepare a draft *rescue plan*. This must be put to appropriate meetings of members and creditors and, if agreed, will be put to the court for confirmation. If the court confirms the plan, it becomes binding on those concerned and the examiner's appointment will be terminated. Where the plan is rejected by the court because it contains defects which are not remediable, the examiner's costs and expenses will be refused: In re Wogan (Drogheda) (1993 HC) — Irish Times 10/2/1993.

An examiner may be appointed by the court where the company is or is likely to be unable to pay its debts, and no order has been made for its winding up (ibid s.2 as amended by the Companies Act 1990 s.181(1)(a)). The petitioner does not have to establish as a matter of probability that the company is capable of surviving as a going concern: In re Atlantic Magnetics Ltd (1992 SC) ITLR (16 Mar). See also In re Jetmara Teo (1992 HC) 10 ILT Dig 197.

The appointment of the examiner does not automatically suspend the directors' management powers, although he can apply to the court to have all or any of the directors' functions or powers exercised or performed only by him (ibid 1990 (Amdt) Act s.9). A duty is imposed on the examiner, on appointment and after his investigation, to disclose to the court if misleading information in relation to assets or liabilities had led to his appointment: In re Wogans (Drogheda) Ltd (1992 HC).

For amendments to the 1990 (Amdt) Act, see Companies Act 1990 ss.180-181. See also Companies (Forms) Order

1990 (SI No 224 of 1990). See Rules of Superior Courts (No 3) 1991 (SI No 147 of 1991) for rules governing the procedures to be followed. [Text: Forde (9)]. See DISQUALIFICATION ORDER; OPPRESSION OF SHAREHOLDER.

**court sittings.** See SITTINGS, COURT.

**courts martial.** A military tribunal for the trial of a member of the defence forces on active service. The choice by an accused of an alternative representative does not breach court-martial rules: Private William Murphy (appellant) (1993) ITLR (1 Mar) and 11 ILT Dig (1993) 187. See 1937 Constitution, art.38(4); Courts-Martial Appeals Act 1983; Courts-Martial (Legal Aid) Regulations 1987 (SI No 46 of 1987). [Reports: Frewen]. See CONTEMPT OF COURT.

**courts martial appeal court.** See COURT OF CRIMINAL APPEAL.

**covenant.** (1) An international agreement providing for binding legal obligations. See HUMAN RIGHTS COVENANTS.

(2) A clause, usually in a deed, which binds a party to do some act or to refrain from doing some act. No technical words are necessary to constitute a covenant: Lant v Norris (1757) 1 Burr 287.

*Usual* covenants in a lease refer to the covenant of the landlord that the tenant will have quiet enjoyment; and refer to the covenants of the tenant to pay the rent and rates; to keep the premises in repair and to deliver them up at the end of the tenancy in good repair; to permit the landlord to enter and inspect the premises from time to time.

*Restrictive* covenants in certain leases, absolutely prohibiting a change in use or improvements, are to be construed as prohibiting same without the licence or consent of the lessor, which shall not be unreasonably withheld: Landlord and Tenant (Amendment) Act 1980 ss.64-69. There may be a refusal of consent based on valid estate management grounds: OHS Ltd v Green Property Co Ltd (1986) ILRM 451. A restrictive covenant (eg not to build a structure in excess of a certain height) is enforceable by a tenant against the assignee of the landlord: Tulk v Moxhay (1848) 2 Ph 774; Whelan v Cork Corporation (1991 HC) ILRM 19. For discussion on how restrictive covenants might be dis-

charged, see Lyall in 9ILT & SJ (1991) 156.

A covenant is said to *run with the land* when the advantage or liability of it passes to the assignee of the land. Covenants may be registered as burdens affecting registered land: Registration of Title Act 1964 s.69. See also Deasy's Act 1860 ss.41-42. See Hampshire v Wickens (1878) 7 Ch D 555; White v Carlisle Trust Ltd (1977) HC; Green Property Co Ltd v Shalame Modes Ltd (1978) HC; Belmont Securities Ltd v Crean (1989) 7 ILT Dig 22. See GROUND RENT; PRIVITY OF CONTRACT.

**covenant, deed of.** A person may covenant to make annual payments to a beneficiary for a minimum period whereby his own total income for tax purposes is reduced and the beneficiary's income is thereby increased: Income Tax Act 1967 s.439. The minimum period is three years where the beneficiary is a university, college or school in the State or a body having consultative status with the United Nations (qv) or the Council of Europe (qv). The period in the case of an individual recipient must exceed six years and must not be a minor child of the convenantor.

A covenant to a student son or daughter of a covenantor over 18 years of age could have tax advantages; the covenant, to comply with the requirements of the legislation, could provide for annual payments *for the period of seven years, or for the period of our joint lives, or until he/she ceases to be receiving full-time education at any university, college, school or other educational establishment (whichever is the shortest period)*: Specimen Form of Covenant, issued by the Revenue Commissioners. [Text: Judge].

**covenant to insure.** A lease will often have a covenant requiring the lessee to reimburse the lessor in respect of the cost of insuring the demised premises. There is a heavy onus of proof on a lessee who challenges the lessor's insurance charges; it is not sufficient for the lessee to show that a quotation for a smaller figure could be obtained elsewhere: Sepes Establishment v KSK Enterprises Ltd (1993 HC) ILRM 46.

**cover note.** A document issued by an insurer to the insured covering risks until issue of a policy of insurance. It is a separate contract distinct from the policy and is operative for a specific period. In marine insurance, the contract is deemed to be concluded when the proposal of the assured is accepted by the insurer, whether the policy is issued or not; for the purposes of showing when the proposal was accepted, reference may be made to the slip or covering note or other customary memorandum of the contract: Marine Insurance Act 1906 s.21. See Mackie v European Assurance Society (1869) 21 LT 102.

**covert take-over.** An EC directive, aimed at identifying any person launching a covert take-over bid for a company, requires obligatory disclosure by a person who acquires or sells large number of shares in a company: Council Directive 88/627/EEC. This directive is given effect in the State by the Companies Act 1990 which requires any person who acquires or disposes of shares of a public limited company, which is officially listed on the Irish Stock Exchange, to notify the Exchange when following such acquisition or disposal his shareholding exceeds or falls below the 10%, 25%, 50% or 75% disclosure thresholds (ibid ss.89-96). The Exchange must publish this information unless it considers that this would be contrary to the public interest or seriously detrimental to the company or companies concerned. See SHARES, DISCLOSURE OF.

**coverture.** The condition of being a married woman.

**cpt.** See PUBLIC LIMITED COMPANY.

**crash helmet.** The driver of a motorcycle and a passenger carried on a motorcycle must each wear a crash helmet while the motor cycle is used in a public place: SI No 360 of 1978.

**creche.** See PRE-SCHOOL SERVICE.

**credibility.** Worthy of belief. It has been held that it would be an injustice if the Supreme Court, on appeal, were to reject the determination of a court of trial as to the *credibility* of witnesses who gave evidence before it except in cases of manifest perversity: People v Mulligan 2 Frewen 16 cited in DPP v Egan (1990 SC) ILRM 780. See also dictum (qv) in Northern Bank Finance Corporation Ltd v Charlton (1979) IR 172 at 181. See DPP v McDonagh and Cawley (1991 CCA) 9 ILT Dig 171. See DOCUMENTARY EVIDENCE; PREVIOUS STATEMENT, INCONSISTENT.

**credit.** The time which a creditor allows his debtor to pay a debt; the total amount he permits the debtor to borrow or to owe. Cross-examination *as to credit* means asking questions of a witness with the objective of testing his credibility. See CONVICTION, EVIDENCE OF; EXAMINATION.

**credit guarantee insurance.** In a particular case it was held that a credit guarantee insurance agreement was a *contract of guarantee* and not a contract of insurance: International Commercial Bank plc v Insurance Corp of Ireland (1990 HC) ITLR (3 Dec). In that case, the indemnifier agreed in the event of default of the principal debtor repaying a loan from the creditor, the indemnifier would pay all monies due, the principal debtor having paid the indemnifier a premium for such indemnity. See CONTRACT OF GUARANTEE.

**credit, letter of.** See LETTER OF CREDIT.

**credit by fraud, obtaining.** The misdemeanour (qv) committed by a person who, in incurring any debt or liability, has obtained credit under false pretences, or by means of any other fraud: Debtors (Ireland) Act 1872 s.13(1). It is an offence for a bankrupt (qv) or arranging debtor (qv), to obtain credit without disclosing the fact that he is a bankrupt or arranging debtor: Bankruptcy Act 1988 s.129.

**credit card.** A credit instrument issued to an individual by a bank (qv) or other body by means of which cash, goods or services may be obtained by the individual on credit on production of the instrument, the issuer undertaking to pay the supplier of the cash, goods or services in return for payment to him (the issuer) by the individual. A credit card is also a card issued by a bank to an individual having an address in the State whereby the amounts in respect of the goods, services and cash supplied may be charged to the account of the individual: Finance (No 2) Act 1981 s.17(1)(a). See Diners Club Ltd v Revenue Commissioners (1988 HC) IR 158; Eurocard International v Controller of Trade Marks (1987) HC.

**credit institution.** (1) An undertaking, other than a credit union or friendly society, whose business it is to receive deposits or other repayable funds from the public and to grant credit on its own account: EC (Licensing and Supervision of Credit Institutions) Regulations 1992. These regulations, inplementing Council Directive 89/646/EEC, lay down common Community-wide provisions for the licensing and supervision of credit institutions and the provision of banking services in the EC.

(2) A holder of a licence under the Central Bank Act 1971, a building society, a trustee savings bank, any other deposit-taking institution supervised by the Central Bank or a credit institution authorised in a member State of the Community: EC (Consolidated Supervision of Credit Institutions) Regulations 1992 (SI No 396 of 1992). These regulations, implementing Council Directive 92/30/EEC, require the Central Bank to supervise credit institutions and their subsidiary and associated companies on a consolidated basis ie taking account of the entire group activity and relationships rather than on a single company basis. See OMBUDSMAN FOR THE CREDIT INSTITUTIONS.

**credit-sale agreement.** An agreement for the sale of goods under which the price is payable by five or more instalments: Hire-Purchase Act 1946 s.1. Unlike a hire-purchase agreement, ownership passes in a credit-sales agreement immediately and is not dependent on payment of the purchase price. In hire-purchase, the hirer may terminate the agreement before it has run its course; he may not do so in a credit-sales agreement.

A credit-sales agreement must comply with certain statutory requirements eg there must be a note or memorandum of the agreement; it must contain the *total purchase price*, the *cash price* of the goods, the amount of each instalment and date payable; a copy of the note or memorandum must be delivered or sent to the buyer within 14 days of the making of the agreement (ibid s.4; Hire-Purchase Amendment Act 1960 s.22). The Minister may by order, provide that there be a specified period within which the hirer is entitled to withdraw his acceptance: SGSS Act 1980 s.50.

An agreement not coming within the definition of a credit-sale or hire-

purchase agreement may still be subject to the Factors Act 1889. See Leavy v Butler (1893) 2 QB 318; Helby v Matthews (1895) AC 471. See Courts Act 1991 s.6(2). See RSC O.4 r.13; O.13 rr.3, 15; O.27 rr.2, 16. See ANNUAL PERCENTAGE CHARGE; PRICE CONTROL.

**credit union.** A co-operative society consisting of persons with a common bond which has as its objects (a) the promotion of thrift among its members by the accumulation of their savings, (b) the creation of sources of credit for the benefit of its members at a fair and reasonable rate of interest and (c) the use and control of members' savings for their mutual benefit: Credit Union Act 1966 s.2(1)(a). The common bond includes those of association, employment, residence, and membership. A credit union may be registered under the Industrial & Provident Societies Act 1893. Regulatory power is vested in the Registrar of Friendly Societies. See also Industrial Provident Societies Act 1978 ss.20-27. See Prison Credit Union v Registrar of Friendly Societies (1987) ILRM 367.

**creditor.** A person to whom a debt is owing. A *secured creditor* is one who holds a mortgage (qv), or charge (qv), or lien (qv) on the debtor's property eg Bankruptcy Act 1988 s.3. An *unsecured creditor* is one who does not so hold. A *judgment creditor* is a person in whose favour a judgment for a sum of money has been entered against the debtor. A *maintenance creditor* is the applicant spouse for a maintenance order.

A secured creditor of a bankrupt debtor has a right to realise his security outside of the bankruptcy: Bankruptcy Act 1988 s.136(2). See also 1988 Act, first schedule, para 24. Company directors have a duty to consider the interests of creditors of the company. See McCann in 9ILT & SJ (1991) 30. However, any conveyance or assignment by a company of all its property to trustees for the benefit of its creditors is void: Companies Act 1963 s.286(2) as amended by the Companies Act 1990 s.135. See BANKRUPTCY; CORRUPT AGREEMENT WITH CREDITOR; MAINTENANCE ORDER; WINDING UP.

**creditor, statutory notice to.** The statutory notice given by a personal representative (qv) to creditors with claims against the estate of a deceased, usually in practice by advertising twice at intervals of one week in a newspaper, with a time limit for receipt of claims expiring four weeks after the last insertion. Such notice gives statutory protection to the personal representative but does not prevent a creditor following the assets into the hands of any person who has received them. See Succession Act 1965 s.49.

**creditors' assignee.** See BANKRUPTCY, ADJUDICATION OF.

**creditors' meeting.** A meeting in relation to a company whereby a *voluntary winding up* of the company may be achieved: Companies Act 1963 ss.266-267. The court is not empowered to extend the time for holding a creditors' meeting: Walsh v Registrar of Companies (1987) HC. See also ARRANGING DEBTOR; COMPOSITION; WINDING UP BY TRUSTEE; WINDING UP, VOLUNTARY.

**creditors' winding up.** See WINDING UP, VOLUNTARY.

**cremation.** The burning of a dead body in a crematorium. See BURIAL GROUNDS.

**crime.** An unlawful act or default which is an offence against the public and renders the person guilty of the act or default liable to legal punishment. Whether there is a crime against the community can only arise if an offence is clearly established: McLoughlin v Tuite (1986) ILRM 304. Crimes are either *minor* (summary) or *indictable* (qv) depending on whether the offence entitles the accused to a trial with a jury or not; minor offences are tried by courts of summary jurisdiction: 1937 Constitution, art. 38.2.

The common law divided crimes into *treason*, *felonies* and *misdemeanours* (qqv). Formerly a felon was liable to lose his life and forfeit his property; the distinction between felonies and misdemeanours is now less than formerly. [Text: Carroll; O'Higgins; O'Siochain; Ryan & Magee; Archibald UK]. See DEFENCE; INJUNCTION, CRIMINAL.

**crimen laesae majestatis.** [The crime of injured majesty]. For example, treason (qv).

**criminal.** (1) A person found guilty of an indictable offence.(2) Pertaining to a crime. See INDICTABLE OFFENCE.

**criminal conversation.** The common law remedy by which a man had a right of action for damages against a person who had sexual intercourse with his wife; the consent of the wife to the act of intercourse did not affect the issue. Abolished by the Family Law Act 1981 s.1. See LRC 1 of 1981.

**criminal damage to property.** The offences committed by a person who (a) without lawful excuse damages the property of another intending to damage it or being reckless as to whether it would be damaged; (b) without lawful excuse damages any property intending to endanger the life of another or being reckless in that regard; (c) damages any property with intent to defraud: Criminal Damage Act 1991 s.2. A person is *reckless* if he has foreseen that the particular kind of damage that in fact was done might be done and yet has gone on to take the risk of it (ibid s.2(6)). An offence committed under section 2 by damaging property by fire must be charged as arson (qv).

It is also an offence to threaten damage to property and to have possession of any thing with intent to damage property (ibid ss.3-4). *Property* means (a) property of a tangible nature, whether real or personal, including money and animals that are capable of being stolen, and (b) data ie information in a form in which it can be accessed by means of a computer and includes a program (ibid s.1(1)). To *damage* includes to destroy, deface, dismantle or, whether temporarily or otherwise, render inoperable or unfit for use or prevent or impair the operation of property (ibid s.1(1)). See SI No 226 of 1992. See COMPUTER; DAMAGE TO PROPERTY; MALICIOUS INJURIES SCHEME.

**criminal information.** A written complaint made *ex officio* by the Attorney General and filed in the High Court; it is limited to misdemeanours (qv) of a public nature eg libel on judges, and is tried on the civil side of the court. No criminal information has been filed in recent years; the modern practice is to proceed by way of indictment (qv).

**criminal injuries.** See MALICIOUS INJURIES SCHEME.

**Criminal Injuries Compensation Tribunal.** A tribunal established in 1974 to deal, on an *ex gratia* basis, with applications for compensation from persons injured (or from their dependants in fatal cases) in the course of crimes of violence or in the course of assisting the prevention of crime or the saving of human life. The injury must be serious enough to justify an award of at least £50. The scheme was revised as from 1st April 1986, from which date claims for pain and suffering are excluded; only *special damages* are now claimable.

According to the scheme, the decision of the tribunal is final; however in recent cases the decisions of the tribunal have been the subject of review by the courts: O'Toole v CICT (1988) HC; State (Creedon) v CICT (1989) ILRM 104; Hill v CICT (1990 HC) ILRM 36. See GARDA COMPENSATION.

**criminal jurisdiction, place.** Generally the jurisdiction of our courts extends only to criminal activity in the State, its land, islands and waters. The main exceptions are (a) certain specified offences which are committed in Northern Ireland: Criminal Law (Jurisdiction) Act 1976; (b) larceny committed in any part of the United Kingdom: Larceny Act 1916; (c) certain offences committed by Irish seamen abroad: Merchant Shipping Act 1894; The People (Attorney General) v Thomas (1954) IR 168; (d) treason committed by an Irish citizen: Treason Act 1939; (e) murder, manslaughter, and bigamy: Offences Against the Person Act 1861; (f) forgery: Forgery Act 1913. See JURISDICTION.

**criminal jurisdiction, time.** There is generally no time limit for commencing proceedings for indictable (qv) offences, although some statutes prescribe a time limit. For summary offences (qv), unless a time limit is specified in the statute governing the offence, an information (qv) must be laid or a complaint (qv) must be made within six months from the time when the matter of such information or complaint arose: Petty Sessions (Ireland) Act 1851.

**criminal law.** The body of law which defines the variety of actions (or omissions) which are forbidden by the State and which provides punishment as a sanction. [Text: Carroll; Charlton (1-3); O'Siochain; Ryan & Magee; Reports: Frewen; Casey; Irish Criminal Law Journal].

**criminal libel.** See LIBEL.

**criminal lunatic.** Generally understood to be a person who has been found to be insane in any of the following circumstances: (a) while on remand or awaiting trial; (b) while undergoing sentence; (c) while awaiting the pleasure of the government, having been found to be insane on arraignment; (d) while awaiting the pleasure of the government, having been found *guilty but insane* (ie guilty of the act charged against him but insane at the time; it is a verdict of acquittal on the charge). Criminal lunatics are confined in the Central Mental Hospital Dundrum or in a district mental hospital. See SPECIAL VERDICT.

**criminating questions.** See INCRIMINATE.

**crossing of cheque.** See CHEQUE.

**cross-action.** An action by a defendant against the plaintiff in respect of the same subject matter. See COUNTERCLAIM.

**cross-appeals.** Appeals by both plaintiff and defendant against judgment in a case eg see Clancy v Commissioners of Public Works (1991 SC) ILRM 567.

**cross border shopping.** See DUTY FREE.

**cross-examination.** See EXAMINATION.

**crowd control.** Under proposed draft legislation, the gardai will be given power to erect barriers on any road, street, lane or alley not more than one mile from where an event, which is likely to attract a large assembly of persons, is taking place: Criminal Justice (Public Order) Bill 1993 s.23. Power will be given to direct persons and, where possession of a ticket is required for entry to the event, to prohibit persons who have no ticket from passing the barrier. The gardai will also have power to search a person going to an event, and to seize intoxicating liquour or any article which could be used to cause injury (ibid s.24).

**cruelty.** Conduct which causes danger to life or health, physical or mental, of the other party; it is a ground for a *judicial separation* (qv). See DIVORCE A MENSA ET THORO.

**cruelty to animals.** It is an offence cruely to beat, kick, ill-treat, over-ride, over-drive, over-load, torture, infuriate, or terrify any animal, or to abandon it in circumstances likely to cause it unnecessary suffering: Protection of Animals Act 1911 s.1 and 1965 s.4; Control of Dogs Act 1986 s.20. A person convicted of the offence of cruelty to a dog may be disqualified from keeping a dog (ibid 1986 Act s.18). See ANIMALS.

**cruelty to children.** The misdemeanour (qv) which may be committed by a person over 17 years of age who has the custody charge or care of any child or young person who wilfully assaults, ill-treats, neglects, abandons or exposes such child or young person to unnecessary suffering or injury to health: Children Act 1908 s.12; Children (Amendment) Act 1957 s.4. See CARE ORDER.

**crystallisation.** See FLOATING CHARGE.

**cuideachta phoibli theoranta; cpt.** [Public limited company (qv)].

**cujus est dare ejus est disponere.** [He who gives anything can also direct how the gift is to be used]. See PRECATORY TRUST.

**cujus est instituere ejus est abrogare.** [He who institutes may also abrogate].

**cujus est solum ejus est usque ad coelum et ad inferos.** [Whose is the soil, his is even to the heaven and the depths of the earth]. However, there can be separate ownership of the airspace above the surface of land just as there can be such ownership of the subterranean area below the surface: Humphreys v Brogden (1850) 12 QB 739. See AIRSPACE, INTERFERENCE WITH; FLAT; PLANNING PERMISSION; PRIVATE PROPERTY; WAYLEAVE.

**culpable.** Blameworthy; being responsible for a breach of legal duty.

**culture.** The EC is required to contribute to the flowering of the cultures of the member States, while respecting their national and regional diversity and at the same time bringing the common cultural heritage to the fore: Treaty of Rome 1957 art.128 as replaced by Maastricht Treaty 1992 art.G(D)(37). See also ibid 1957 Treaty art.92(d) as inserted by 1992 Treaty art.G(D)(18). See ARTIST, TAX EXEMPTION OF; COMMITTEE OF THE REGIONS; EDUCATION.

**cum.** [With].

**cum div.** [With dividend]. Stock exchange quotation relating to stocks and shares, indicating that the price includes dividends accrued to date. See BOND WASHING; EX DIV.

**cum testamento annexo.** [With the will annexed]. See LETTERS OF ADMINISTRATION; PROBATE.

**cur adv vult.** [Curia advisari vult (qv)].

**curia advisari vult.** [The court wishes to be advised]. Indicates in a law report (qv) that the judgment of the court was not delivered immediately, but given later after further deliberation.

**currency, decimal.** See COINS; POUND.

**currency, foreign.** A plaintiff may sue for amounts expressed in a foreign currency when the proper law of the contract is that of the foreign country or when a term of the contract so provides. Judgment may be given in the foreign currency or the Irish currency equivalent thereto at the time when the order is made or, in summary judgment proceedings, when judgment is entered in the office: Damen v O'Shea (1977) HC.

In relation to the enforcement of *maintenance orders* of other contracting EC states where the amount stated therein is in a currency other than that of the State, payment must be made on the basis of the exchange rate prevailing, on the date of making of an *enforcement order*, between that currency and the currency of the State: Jurisdiction of Courts and Enforcement of Judgments (European Communities) Act 1988 s.9.

Foreign currency notes are bank notes within the meaning of the Forgery Act 1916: Central Bank Act 1942 s.53. A building society may make loans or raise funds in foreign currency: Building Societies Act 1989 ss.18, 22(1), 23. See also Northern Bank v Edwards (1986) ILRM 167. See POUND.

**current account.** A running account kept between parties with debits and credits eg a current banking account. See also Building Societies Act 1989 s.29(2)(f). See OVERDRAFT.

**current cost accounting convention; CCA.** The convention by which accounts are prepared having regard to replacement costs rather than historic or actual costs. It has been held that, in the light of the judicial meaning consistently given to profits, the CCA method was not an appropriate method for calculating profit for tax purposes: Carroll Industries plc v O'Culachain (1989 HC) ILRM 552.

**curtesy.** The life estate which a husband who survived his wife had in her heritable freeholds ie fee simple and fee tail, provided that his wife died intestate and a child of the marriage was born alive capable of inheriting the freehold. Abolished for registered land by the Registration of Title Act 1964 and abolished entirely by the Succession Act 1965 s.11. See DOWER.

**curtilage.** A courtyard, garden, yard, field, or piece of ground lying near and belonging to a dwellinghouse. See DRUN-KEN DRIVING.

**custody.** (1) Confinement or imprisonment of a person. (2) Control and possession of some person or thing. See DETENTION; ESCAPE; PUNISHMENT.

**custody of children.** See CHILD ABDUC-TION; CHILD, CUSTODY OF.

**custom and practice (or usage).** A rule of conduct established by long usage, which if valid, has the force of law. A valid custom must have been exercised from time immemorial (qv); it must be certain, reasonable, and not be contrary to statute law. Custom may be proved by the direct evidence of witnesses of their personal knowledge of its existence; by evidence of a similar custom in an analogous trade or in another locality; by the declaration of a person, now deceased, of competent knowledge. See Mills v Mayor of Colchester (1867) LR 2 CP 567.

Customs and practices may be implied as terms of an employment contract where they are so universal that "no workman would be supposed to have entered into the service without looking to it as part of the contract": Devonald v Rosser & Sons (1906) 2KB 728. The immunity given to authorised trade unions and their members as regard acts done in furtherance of a trade dispute, is only available where agreed procedures availed of by custom and practice, or in a collective agreement, have been resorted to and exhausted: Industrial Relations Act 1990 s.9.

**custom house docks development authority.** See URBAN RENEWAL.

**customary authority.** The implied authority which an *agent* has, who carries on a particular trade, profession or calling, to perform such acts as are usual in that trade, profession or calling eg a stockbroker on the Stock Exchange (qv).

**customs duties.** Taxes on imports and exports. The government is empowered to impose, vary or terminate customs duties by order: Imposition of Duties Act 1957, provided the order is confirmed by the Oireachtas. Customs officers are given wide powers of detention of goods reasonably suspected of being imported without payment of duty, including detention of the means of conveyance of the goods (eg ship, car), and of forfeiture of goods where they were imported without payment of duty: Customs Consolidation Act 1876 s.177 and Customs & Excise (Miscellaneous Provisions) Act 1988 ss.7-8. See also Mc Daid v Sheehy (1991 SC) ILRM 250.

**cycleway.** A public road (qv) or proposed public road reserved for the exclusive use of pedal cyclists or pedal cyclists and pedestrians: Roads Act 1993 s.68. A road authority may construct (or otherwise provide) and maintain a cycleway (ibid s.68(2)(a)).

**cy-pres.** [As near]. The doctrine by which a trust, which discloses a general charitable intention, will not be permitted to fail because the particular mode of application specified by the testator cannot be carried out; the law will substitute another mode *cy-pres*, that is, as near as possible to the mode specified by the testator.

Failure of purposes justifying recourse to cy-pres include where: the purposes are fulfilled; or the purposes cannot be carried out in the spirit of the gift; or the gift is too large; or the purposes are adequately provided for by other means; or the purposes are no longer charitable; or the purposes are not providing a suitable and effective application of the gift: Charities Act 1961 s.47; Royal Kilmainham Hospital (1966) IR 451. The cy-pres doctrine may also apply where a conjuncture of funds would result in the gift being more effectively used (ibid s.47).

Where the purposes fail or where difficulty arises in applying the charity property so that it is available to return to the donor, there are provisions by which it will be applied cy-pres to charitable purposes where the donor cannot be found or in other particular circumstances (ibid s.48). See also Governors of Erasmus Smith School v AG (1932) 66 ILTR 57. See CHARITIES; PUBLIC APPEAL, MONEY COLLECTED IN; SIGN MANUAL.

# D

**Dail Eireann.** The house of representatives of the national parliament (the Oireachtas): 1937 Constitution, art.15. The sole and exclusive power of making laws for the State (otherwise than by the EC) is vested in the Oireachtas. The number of members of the Dail is fixed from time to time by law but must not be fixed at less than one member for each thirty thousand of the population, or at not more than one member for each twenty thousand of the population. There must be as far as practicable uniformity of representation (ibid art.16(2)(3) and O'Donovan v AG (1961) IR 114). The Dail currently consists of 166 members: Electoral (Amendment) Act 1990 s.2. The same Dail must not continue for more than seven years, although a shorter period may be fixed by law (ibid Constitution art.16(5)); a five year period has been fixed: Electoral Act 1992 s.33. A member of the Dail is generally known by the title *TD*. See CONSTITUENCY; COMMUNITY LAW; FRANCHISE; TD; UTTERANCE.

**Dail election.** An election of a member or members to serve in the Dail and includes a bye-election as well as a general election: Electoral Act 1992 s.2(1). A person is entitled to be registered as a Dail elector if he has reached the age of 18, is a citizen of Ireland, and is ordinarily resident in the constituency (ibid s.8(1)). In addition, (a) a British citizen and (b) a national of an EC member State which permits Irish citizens to vote in their national parliaments, are entitled to be registered as Dail electors (ibid s.8(2)). Election is by proportional representation (qv) with each elector having one transferable vote (ibid s.37).

**damage.** Loss or harm, physical or economic, resulting from a wrongful act or default and generally leading to an award of a measure of compensation. Generally a wrong to be actionable must result in damage, except that some wrongs (eg libel, trespass) are actionable

*per se.*

**damage-feasant.** [Doing damage]. See DISTRESS DAMAGE FEASANT.

**damage, malicious.** See MALICIOUS DAMAGE.

**damage, remoteness of.** See REMOTENESS OF DAMAGE.

**damage to property.** Compensation for loss due to damage to property may be recovered by the party suffering the loss (the *injured party*) by way of a *compensation order* (qv) made against a convicted person. Where the commission of the offence by the convicted person involved the taking of property out of the possession of the injured party and the property has been recovered, any loss occuring to the injured party by reason of the property being damaged while out of his possession is treated as having resulted from the offence, irrespective of how the damage was caused or who caused it: Criminal Justice Act 1993 s.6(3). This applies to loss resulting from the use of a mechanically propelled vehicle (ibid s.6(4)(b)). See also CRIMINAL DAMAGE TO PROPERTY; MALICIOUS INJURIES SCHEME.

**damages.** The compensation in money for loss suffered by a person owing to the tort, breach of contract, or breach of statutory duty of another person. The test by which the amount of damages is ascertained is known as the *measure of damages* (qv). The general principle is that the injured or aggrieved person should be put as nearly as possible in the same position, so far as money can do it, as if he had not suffered injury or loss: Robinson v Harman (1848) 1 Exch 850.

Damages may be *general* or *special* (qqv). Damages can be classified as (a) *nominal* — where there has been no loss, and the damages recognise that the plaintiff has had a legal right infringed; (b) *contemptuous* — where the amount awarded is derisory: Dering v Uris (1964) 2 QB 669; (c) *vindictive, punitive* or *exemplary* — where awarded to punish the defendant: Garvey v Ireland (1979) 113 ILTR 61; McIntyre v Lewis & Dolan (1991 SC) 1 IR 121; (d) *speculative* — calculated having regard to events which may happen in the future: Hickey & Co Ltd v Roches Stores (Dublin) Ltd (No 2) (1980) ILRM 107; (e) *liquidated*

— where fixed or ascertained by the parties in the contract; (f) *unliquidated* — dependant on the circumstances of the case to be determined by the court.

An appellate court may overturn an award of damages where no reasonable proportion exists between what was awarded and what the appellate court would have awarded: McGrath v Bourne (1876) IR 10 CL 160; Foley v Thermocement Products Ltd (1954) 90 ILTR 92; McKevitt v Ireland (1987) ILRM 542.

Certain payments under the Social Welfare Acts are to be taken into account in assessing damages for personal injuries arising out of a mechanically propelled vehicle being used in respect of which liability is required to be covered by an approved policy of insurance: Social Welfare Act 1984 s.12.

It is unusual for damages to be assessed in the first instance by the Supreme Court; however that court can assess and award damages where finality is desireable and where the cost of referring a case back to the High Court is out of all proportion to the amount of damages likely to be awarded: Bakht v The Medical Council (1990 SC) ILRM 840. [Text: White; Ogus UK; McGregor UK]. See QUANTUM; DISABILITY PENSION; REMOTENESS OF DAMAGE; STAY OF EXECUTION.

**damages, aggravation of.** See AGGRAVATION OF DAMAGES.

**damages, exemplary.** See EXEMPLARY DAMAGES.

**damages, general.** See GENERAL DAMAGES.

**damages, measure of.** See MEASURE OF DAMAGES.

**damages, mitigation of.** See MITIGATION OF DAMAGES.

**damages, special.** See SPECIAL DAMAGES.

**damnum absque injuria.** [Loss without wrong]. See DAMNUM SINE INJURIA.

**damnum sine injuria.** [Damage without wrong]. The phrase used to indicate that damage may be caused without any infringement of a legal right of another eg by a person exercising rights over his own property: Mayor of Bradford v Pickles (1895) AC 587. See INJURIA SINE DAMNUM.

**dangerous building, potentially.** See FIRE SAFETY NOTICE.

**dangerous building notice.** See DANGEROUS STRUCTURE.

**dangerous conditions and practices.** See PROHIBITION NOTICE, WORK.

**dangerous dogs.** Although not described as "dangerous", restrictions have been placed on certain dogs: Control of Dogs (Restriction of Certain Dogs) Regulations 1991 (SI No 123 of 1991 as amended by SI No 146 of 1991). The restrictions include the requirement that certain breeds be securely muzzled in a public place and be on a strong chain or leash held by a person over 16 years of age. The breeds specified include bulldogs, rottweilers, and certain bull terriers. The courts have power to order the destruction of "dangerous" dogs: Control of Dogs Act 1986 s.22. See DOGS.

**dangerous driving.** The offence committed by a person who drives a vehicle in a public place in a manner (including speed) which, having regard to all the circumstances of the case (including the condition of the vehicle, the nature, condition and use of the place and the amount of traffic which then actually is or might reasonably be expected then to be therein) is *dangerous to the public*: Road Traffic Act 1961 s.53(1) as amended by the Road Traffic Act 1968 s.51(a).

The prosecution does not have to prove intent; whether a person has driven in a manner *dangerous to the public* is a question of fact to be decided by the court in each particular case. There are higher penalties where dangerous driving is prosecuted on indictment (qv) where the contravention causes death or serious bodily harm to another person (ibid 1961 Act s.53(2)(a)). See The People (Attorney General) v Gallagher (1972) IR 365; Attorney General v Dunleavy (1947) ILTR 71. See CARELESS DRIVING; FURIOUS DRIVING.

**dangerous place.** An excavation, quarry, pit, well, reservoir, pond, stream, dam, bank, dump, shaft or land that, in the opinion of the sanitary authority (qv) in whose sanitary district it is situate, is or is likely to be dangerous to any person: Local Government (Sanitary Services) Act 1964 s.1. A sanitary authority is empowered to carry out such works as will, in the opinion of the authority, prevent the place from being a dangerous place (ibid s.2). There is provision for *notice* to be given by the authority and for an appeal to the District Court to annul the notice (ibid s.5).

**dangerous occurrence.** A specified occurrence which occurs at any place of work eg the collapse or failure of a crane, the escape of a substance which might be liable to cause serious injury, an unintentional ignition of explosives, an incident during the conveying of a dangerous substance by road: Safety Health and Welfare at Work (General Application) Regulations 1993 (SI No 44 of 1993) reg.58. There is a requirement to send a written report to the Health & Safety Authority of a dangerous occurrence (ibid reg.59 (1)(ii)) and to keep records (ibid reg.60).

**dangerous premises.** The liability to compensate persons injured on premises due to their dangerous state is generally upon the occupier and not the owner. If the owner has a duty to repair, liability may fall on him. An independent contractor may be liable: Haseldine v Daw (1941) 2 KB 243. See OCCUPIER'S LIABILITY.

**dangerous structure.** Any building, wall or other structure of any kind, or any part of, or anything attached to, a building, wall or other structure of any kind, that, in the opinion of the sanitary authority (qv) in whose sanitary district it is situate, is or is likely to be dangerous to any person or property: Local Government (Sanitary Services) Act 1964 s.1. A sanitary authority may give notice (generally referred to as a *dangerous building notice*) requiring the carrying out of such works, including demolition, as will prevent the building from being a dangerous structure and to terminate or modify any use of the structure. The sanitary authority may carry out the works necessary itself. It may also obtain an order of the District Court requiring compliance with the notice (ibid s.3(5-6)). See The State (McGuinness) v Maguire (1967) IR 348.

Also the owner or occupier of any structure must take all reasonable steps to ensure that it is not a hazard or potential hazard to persons using a public road: Roads Act 1993 s.70(1). The road authority may serve a notice on the owner or occupier of a hazardous structure to remove, modify or carry out specified works to the structure (ibid s.70(1)(b)). An appeal lies to the District Court (ibid s.70(3)(a)). See SUPPORT, RIGHT TO.

**dangerous substance.** A substance which the Minister by order declares to be such on the ground that in his opinion it constitutes a potential source of danger to person or property: Dangerous Substances Act 1972 s.24. A person engaged in the storage, labelling, packing or conveyance of any dangerous substance must take all practical steps to prevent risk of injury to person or property (ibid s.25). The Minister may make regulations for the protection of persons against risk of injury caused by any dangerous substance (ibid s.26). Certain other sections of the 1972 Act are repealed when particular sections of the Safety, Health and Welfare at Work Act 1989 come into force.

**dangerous things.** See PRODUCT LIABILITY; RYLANDS & FLETCHER, RULE IN.

**dangerous tree.** See TREE.

**dangerous waste.** See TOXIC AND DANGEROUS WASTE.

**data.** Information in a form in which it can be processed ie in a form in which logical or arithmetical operations can be performed automatically on it: Data Protection Act 1988 s.1(1). See also CRIMINAL DAMAGE TO PROPERTY.

**data, inaccurate.** See INACCURATE DATA.

**data, personal.** See PERSONAL DATA.

**data controller.** A person who, either alone or with others, controls the contents and use of *personal data* (qv): Data Protection Act 1988 s.1(1). A data controller has an obligation in relation to the collection, accuracy, adequacy, relevance, storage and security of personal data kept by him. He must ensure that the data is not used or disclosed in a manner incompatible with the specified and lawful purposes for which they are kept (ibid s.2).

A data controller also has to comply with an *enforcement notice* (qv) issued by the Data Protection Commissioner (ibid s.10). Certain data controllers are required to be registered eg (a) data controllers who keep personal data relating to racial origin, political opinions, religious or other beliefs, physical or mental health or sexual life, or criminal convictions; (b) data controllers being financial institutions, credit reference agencies, debt collecting agencies, or direct marketing agencies; (c) data controllers being public authorities and other bodies and persons as specified; (d) certain data processors; and (e) other data controllers as prescribed (ibid s.16(1)). See Data Protection Act 1988 (Section 5(1)(d)) (Specification) Regulations 1993 (SI No 95 of 1993). See PERSONAL DATA.

**data processing equipment.** See TRADING HOUSE, SPECIAL.

**data processor.** A person who processes personal data on behalf of a data controller (qv) but does not include an employee of a data controller who processes such data in the course of his employment: Data Protection Act 1988 s.1(1). He is required to ensure that appropriate security measures are taken to protect the data (ibid s.2(2)).

**data protection.** The statutory protection provided to protect the privacy of individuals with regard to automated personal data; it entitles individuals to establish the existence of automated *personal data* kept in relation to them, to have access to the data (with some exceptions); and to have inaccurate data rectified or erased: Data Protection Act 1988 ss.3-6.

Various obligations are imposed on persons who keep automated personal data eg that the data must be accurate, be kept for lawful purposes, not be disclosed in any manner incompatible with those purposes and be protected by adequate security measures (ibid s.2). Persons keeping such data, ie data controllers (qv) and data processors (qv), owe a *duty of care* to the data subjects (qv) concerned to the extent that the law of torts (qv) does not already provide (ibid s.7).

The legislation provides for the appointment of a Data Protection Commissioner (qv). Certain categories of persons and bodies who keep personal data are required to register with the Commissioner eg those who keep particularly sensitive data (political opinions, health, criminal convictions etc), the public sector and financial institutions (ibid s.16 and third schedule; SI Nos 350 and 351 of 1988).

The legislation does not apply to (a) personal data kept for State security purposes or kept by an individual only for recreational purposes; (b) personal data kept on manual files; or (c) non-personal data eg data concerning companies and partnerships (ibid s.1(4)). Various regulations (a) prohibit the supply of data to a person where it could cause serious harm to his health, (b) restrict access to data which would prejudice the performance of certain functions eg by the Central Bank, and (c) continue in force certain existing statutory restrictions to data eg information obtained by the Ombudsman: (SIs Nos 81, 82, 83 and 84 of 1989). See also SI No 95 of 1993. [Text: Clark (2)]. See CRIMINAL DAMAGE TO PROPERTY; PERSONAL DATA.

**Data Protection Commmissioner.** A body corporate appointed by the government; the Commissioner is independent in the exercise of his function and is empowered to enforce compliance with the statutory provisions dealing with the protection of personal data (qv), either on his own initiative or following complaints from data subjects (qv): Data Protection Act 1988 ss.9-15 and second schedule.

The Commissioner's functions include the maintenance of a register of data controllers (qv) and data processors (qv), the encouragement of preparation and dissemination of codes of practice, the issuing of enforcement notices (qv); prohibition notices (qv) and information notices (qv), and he is also the *designated officer* for the purpose of the *mutual assistance* provisions of the Data Protection Convention (qv).

The Commissioner is entitled to obtain data on a data subject from the Revenue Commissioners to enable him to determine whether he should serve an enforcement notice on the Revenue Commissioners to make the data available to the data subject: Data Protection Commissioner v Revenue Commissioners (1992 CC) — Irish Times 8/12/1992. See DATA PROTECTION.

**Data Protection Convention.** The Convention of the Council of Europe done at Strasbourg on the 28th day of January 1981, which has as its purpose to secure in the territory of each party to the Convention, for every individual, whatever his nationality or residence, respect for his rights and fundamental freedoms, and particularly his right to privacy, with regard to automatic processing of personal data relating to him (*data protection*): art.1. The Convention has been given effect within this State by the Data Protection Act 1988 and is printed in full in the first schedule to the Act.

**data subject.** A person who is the subject of *personal data* (qv): Data Protection Act 1988 s.1(1).

**day.** See CLEAR DAY; TIME.

**day nursery.** See PRE-SCHOOL SERVICE.

**days of grace.** Days allowed for making a payment or doing some other act after the time limited for same has expired. Formerly, three days of grace were added to the period in which a *bill of exchange* had to be paid, unless the bill provided to the contrary eg where it was payable on demand or was a fixed dated bill: Bills of Exchange Act 1882 s.14. As a *cheque* is a bill payable on demand, the drawer thereof was not entitled to any days of grace (ibid ss.14 and 73; M'Lean v Clydesdale Banking Co (1883) 9 App Cas 95). Days of grace as regards bills of exchange have been abolished: Central Bank Act 1989 s.132. See BANK HOLIDAY; BILL OF EXCHANGE.

**de bene esse.** [Of well being]. Anticipating a future occasion. See PERPETUATING TESTIMONY.

**de bonis asportasis.** [Of goods carried away].

**de bonis non.** [Of goods not administered]. An administrator appointed to succeed a deceased administrator or executor to complete the administration of an estate. See In b. Stuart (1944) Ir Jur Rep 62. See Succession Act 1965 s.19.

**de bonis propriis.** [From one's own goods].

**de die in diem.** [From day to day].

**de facto.** [In fact].

**de jure.** [By right].

**de minimis non curat lex.** [The law does not concern itself with trifles]. See Molloy & Walsh v Dublin Co Council (1989 HC) ILRM 633. See PLANNING PERMISSION, DECISION ON.

**de non apparentibus, et non existentibus, eadem est ratio.** [Of things which do not appear and things which do not exist, the rule in legal proceedings is the same].

**de novo.** [Anew]. There is a hearing of a case *de novo* when an appeal is made to the Circuit Court to challenge an order of the District Court on the merits. All questions of law and fact are open to review and either party may call fresh evidence.

**de sont tort.** [Of his own wrong]. See EXECUTOR DE SON TORT.

**dealer, general.** See GENERAL DEALER.

**dealing as consumer.** See CONSUMER, DEALING AS.

**dealing in securities.** Acquiring, disposing of, subscribing for or underwriting securities, or making or offering to make, an agreement to do any of the foregoing: Companies Act 1990 s.107. See EXCHEQUER BILLS; INSIDER DEALING.

**Deasy's Act.** [Landlord and Tenant (Ireland) Act 1860]. The consolidating Act, which introduced the notion that the relationship of landlord and tenant is one of contract; so called after Serjeant Deasy, then Attorney General for Ireland, who piloted the Act through parliament. It continues as the foundation of the law of landlord and tenant in Ireland. [Text: Deale; Wylie (1)].

**death, effect of.** On the death of any person, all causes of action vesting in him or subsisting against him survive for the benefit of his estate or against it, as the case may be: Civil Liability Act 1961 ss.7-8. However, no action against the estate of a deceased person may be maintained unless (a) the proceedings against the deceased person were commenced within the relevant *limitation* period and were pending at the date of death, or (b) the proceedings were commenced within the relevant limitation period, or within the period of two years after the death, whichever period expires first (ibid s.9(2)). See McCullough v Ireland (1990) 8ILT Dig 83.

An action in respect of personal injuries to a person now deceased, may be brought for the benefit of his estate within three years from the date of his death, or the date of his personal representative's knowledge of the cause of action, whichever is the later: Statute of Limitations (Amdt) Act 1991 s.4. In the case of criminal libel involving a deceased person, the mere vilifying of the deceased is not enough; there must a vilifying with a view to injuring his posterity: R v Ensor (1887) 3 TLR 366 cited in Hilliard v Penfield Enterprises Ltd (1990) 1 IR 138.

The authority of an agent is terminated by his or his principal's death. As regards contracts, an offer lapses on the death of the offeror or offeree before acceptance. Death may also terminate a contractual obligation through the doctrine of frustration (qv). If a bankrupt should die after his adjudication as a bankrupt, the court may proceed in the bankruptcy as if the bankrupt were living: Bankruptcy Act 1988 s.42. A *death grant* may be payable on the death of prescribed persons: Social Welfare (Consolidation) Act 1981 ss.107-109.

A building society is empowered to pay to such person who appears to the society to be entitled to receive it, the funds of a deceased shareholder, up to such amount as is fixed from time to time by the Central Bank: Building Societies Act 1989 s.19. See Moynihan v Greensmith (1977) IR 55. See CAUSE OF ACTION; COMPENSATION ORDER; COMPROMISE; CORONER; FATAL INJURIES; LIMITATION OF ACTIONS.

**death penalty.** The sentence that a person shall suffer death for an offence. The death penalty was retained until 1990 but only for capital murder (qv) and treason (qv) and certain offences by a person subject to military law under the Defence Act 1954 ss. 124, 125, 127 or 128. See Criminal Justice Act 1964 s.1. The death penalty was abolished in 1990 — *no person shall suffer death for an offence*: Criminal Justice Act 1990 s.1. See HANGING; PARDON.

**death, presumption of.** The presumption in law that a person is dead arises when it is proved (a) that the person has not been heard of for seven years by persons who would be likely to have heard of him, and (b) that all appropriate enquiries have been made. There is no presumption as to the time the person died or the age at which he died; the burden of proving his death at a particular time rests on the person who asserts it. See McMahon v McElroy (1869) Ir R 5 Eq 1; In re Lavelle (1940) Ir Jur Rep 8; In re Doherty (1961) IR 219. See DEATH, SIMULTANEOUS.

**death, proof of.** The establishment of death in evidence by: production of a death certificate and proof of identity; or identification of the corpse; or identification of the person at the time of death; or presumption of death. See BRAIN DEATH; DEATH, PRESUMPTION OF.

**death, registration of.** The registration of death, the duty of which rests on the local registrar who must be informed of such death by the nearest relative of the deceased present at his death or in attendance during his last illness or the occupier of the house or hospital where the death took place: Births and Deaths Registration (Ireland) Acts 1863 and 1880. The cause of death is usually certified by the medical practitioner who attended the deceased in his last illness; where a post mortem is held, the coroner's certificate as to the cause of death is sent to the registrar. See Vital Statistics and Birth Deaths and Marriages Registration Act 1952; Vital Statistics Regulations 1954 (SI No 280 of 1954). See FOETAL DEATH.

**death, simultaneous.** The presumption in law which deems that two or more persons died simultaneously, where they died in circumstances which render it uncertain which of them survived the other; the presumption is only for the purposes of distribution of the estate of any of them: Succession Act 1965 s.5. See In the goods of Murphy (1973) ILT & SJ 267.

**debenture.** An instrument, often but not necessarily under seal, issued by a company or public body as evidence of a debt or as security for a loan of a fixed sum of money upon which interest is payable. It is usually called a *debenture* on the face of it and it contains a promise to pay the amount mentioned on it. *Debenture* includes debenture stock, bonds and any other security of a company whether constituting a charge on the assets of the company or not: Companies Act 1963 s.2(1). Debentures do not form part of the capital of a company; debenture holders are creditors of the company not shareholders.

A debenture usually gives a charge over the company's assets or some form of security. Power to issue debentures is usually stated in express terms in the memorandum of association. A *convertible* debenture is one that the holder can at some stage convert into shares in the company. Debentures can be made redeemable on the remotest of contingencies, or even be irredeemable or perpetual (ibid s.94).

A company may issue *debenture stock* which is transferrable, registered, and changes hands in much the same way as shares. When a company issues such stock in a series ranking *pari passu,* a register must be kept which is open to inspection by any person (ibid s.91 and 92; Listing Agreement s.9 chs 3 and 4). When debenture stock is issued to a large number of persons, it is usual to appoint a trustee to act on the stockholders' behalf, with the function of ensuring that the loan agreement is adhered to and to protect the lenders and their successors' interests.

A debenture holder who has neglected to cash cheques for interest before the winding up of a company, does not lose his right to be paid arrears of interest: In re Defries & Sons (1909) 2 Ch 423.

The Minister is empowered to obtain information on the ownership of shares and debentures of a company and to impose restrictions on them: Companies Act 1990 ss.15-16 eg restrictions imposed by the Minister on debentures issued by Siuicre Eireann cpt to Talmino Ltd (Iris Oifigiuil — 25 October 1991). See also Companies Act 1963 s.93 and 200; Listing Agreement s.9 ch 2. See Platt v Casey's Drogheda Brewery Co (1912) 1 IR 279; Daly v Allied Irish Banks (1987) HC; In re Tullow Engineering (Holdings) Ltd (in receivership) (1990) 1 IR 452. See SHARES; FLOATING CHARGE; INTEREST; MAREVA INJUNCTION; OPTION; RECEIVER, COMPANY.

**debitor non praesumitur donare.** [A debtor is not presumed to give].

**debitum in praesenti, solvendum in futuro.** [Owed at the present time, payable in the future].

**debt.** A sum of money which one person is bound to pay to another. Debts are: (a) *simple* contract debts; (b) *specialty* debts, created by a document under seal; (c) debts of *record* eg recognisances and judgment debts; (d) *secured* debts, for which security has been given; (e) *preferential* debts. A contract by way of guarantee to pay for the debts of another must be evidenced in writing: Statute of Frauds (Ireland) 1695 s.2.

As regards debts provable and proof of debts in bankruptcy, see Bankruptcy Act 1988 ss.75, 76, 79. As regards infants and debts, see ACCOUNT STATED; RATIFICATION. See also BOOK DEBTS; CLAYTON'S CASE; PREFERENTIAL PAYMENTS.

**debtor.** One who owes a debt. A *judgment debtor* is a person against whom a judgment for a sum of money has been made. A *maintenance debtor* is a spouse ordered to pay maintenance. See BANKRUPTCY; EXAMINATION ORDER; FRAUDULENT DEBTOR; MAINTENANCE ORDER.

**debtor, imprisonment of.** A debtor may be imprisoned for failure to obey a court order directing him to pay a debt either in one payment or by instalments: Enforcement of Court Orders Act 1940 s.6. If a bankrupt is in prison by virtue of that section in respect of a debt incurred before he was adjudicated a bankrupt, the court may order his release: Bankruptcy Act 1988 s.26. The traditional protection from imprisonment for debt for non-commissioned personnel of the defence forces is now restricted to personnel on active service: Defence (Amendment) Act 1987 s.10. There are separate rules governing how debtor prisoners are treated in prison eg remission of sentence does not apply to them: Rules for the Government of Prisons 1947 r.270. See also 1988 Act s.87(6).

**debtor's summons.** Formerly, a summons served by a creditor on a debtor in bankruptcy proceedings, requiring payment of the debt of not less than £20. Failure to comply with the summons was deemed to constitute an *act of bankruptcy.* A debtor's summons has being replaced by a *bankruptcy summons* (qv) and the minimum amount of debt has been increased to £1500: Bankruptcy Act 1988 ss.3 and 8. See also s.7(2). See O'Maoileoin v Official Assignee (1989) IR 647. See BANKRUPTCY, ACT OF.

**decedent.** A deceased person.

**deceit.** A tort (qv) arising from a false statement of fact made by a person, knowingly or recklessly, with the intent that it be acted on by another, who as a result suffers damage. Also known as *fraud* (qv). It has been held that while the standard of proof in fraud is that of the balance of probability, where such proof is largely a matter of inference, such inference must not be drawn lightly: Banco Ambrosiano v Ansbacher Co (1987) ILRM 669.

To establish a cause of action in deceit for damages in relation to the acquisition of securities in a company, it is necessary to show that the defendant made, or authorised the making of, a false statement of fact so as to induce the plaintiff to acquire the securities in question, and that the inducement worked. As regards agency, a principal is not liable for the deceit of his agent: United Dominions Trust (Ireland) Ltd v Shannon Caravans Ltd (1976) IR 225. See Derry v Peak (1889) 14 App Cas 337; Jury v Stoker (1882) 9 LR Ir 385; Lombard Bank Ltd v P McElligot Sons Ltd (1965) 99 ILTR 9; Northern Bank Finance Corp v Charlton (1979) IR 149. See INJURIOUS FALSEHOOD; MISREPRESENTATION; PLEADINGS.

**deceptive acronym.** An acronym which is identical with the acronym of another will be refused registration as a trade mark eg *ANCO* was refused registration as it would indicate, contrary to the facts, a connection between goods thus marked with those produced in connection with the activities of An Chomhairle Oiliuna (AnCO). See also The Anderson Company Application (1972) Supp OJ No 1159 p.1.

**deciding officer.** A person appointed to determine a variety of claims and disputes arising under social welfare law eg under the Redundancy Payments Act 1967 (ibid ss.37-38). A deciding officer is entitled to take into account an applicant's personal circumstances: Corcoran v Minister for Social Welfare (1992 HC) 10 ILT Dig 268.

**decision of EC.** See COMMUNITY LAW.

**declaration, statutory.** See STATUTORY DECLARATION.

**declaration by deceased.** Declarations by a deceased person are admissible in evidence, as an exception to the *hearsay* rule, as follows: (a) a declaration which was opposed to his pecuniary or proprietary interest, in a matter that he had peculiar means of knowledge and no interest to misrepresent the declaration; (b) a declaration made in the course of duty, made contemporaneously with the facts stated, and with no interest to misrepresent the facts; (c) a declaration made as to public or general rights, made *ante litem motam* by some person having competent means of knowledge; (d) a declaration as to pedigree, where pedigree is in issue, made ante litem motam by a person related by blood or marriage; (e) a declaration by a testator as to his will, where the will has been lost, or where the question is whether a will is genuine or was improperly obtained, or where the question is whether which of several documents constitute the will; (f) dying declarations. See ANTE LITEM MOTAM; DYING DECLARATIONS; PEDIGREE.

**declaration of intention.** A declaration by a person that he intends that an offer will be made or invited in the future. It does not mean that an offer is made now and consequently it gives no right of action to another who suffers loss because he does not carry out his intention. See Harris v Nickerson (1873) LR 8 QB 286. See OFFER.

**declaration of interest.** See ARMS LENGTH; CONFLICT OF INTEREST.

**declaration of solvency.** See WINDING UP.

**declaration statute.** A statute which declares or formally states the existing law in order to remove any doubts.

**declaratory judgment.** A declaration by the High Court of the rights of a person eg having regard to the determination of any question of construction of any deed or will or other written instrument; the proceedings are commenced by special summons: RSC O.3 r.7. The court may make binding declarations of right, whether any consequential relief is or could be claimed or not: RSC O.19 r.29.

A plaintiff may be entitled to declaratory relief only and not to damages: Greene v Minister for Agriculture (1990) 2 IR 17. It has been held that Order 84 RSC (ie regarding judicial review) is not to be construed as providing an exclusive procedure for persons seeking declaratory relief in matters of public law: O'Donnell v Corp of Dun Laoghaire (1991 HC) ILRM 301. The jurisdiction of the courts to grant declaratory relief was conferred by the Chancery (Ireland) Act 1867 s.155.

As regards patents, the proprietor or exclusive licensee may be entitled to a declaration from the court (a) that his patent is valid and has been infringed;

(b) that threats of infringement proceedings are unjustified; (c) that the use by a person of a process or product would not constitute an infringement: Patents Act 1992 ss.47, 53 and 54. See INFRINGEMENT OF PATENT; JUDICIAL REVIEW; PARENTAGE, DECLARATION OF.

**decree.** An order of the court embodying its judgment: RCC p.7. The term is generally used to indicate an order (decree) of nullity of marriage and to indicate an order of the District Court. In District Court proceedings, cross-decrees between the same parties may be set-off against each other: DCR r.145. Also a decree of the District Court may now be registered as a judgment mortgage (qv) and may also be registered in the Central Office (qv): Courts Act 1981 s.24-25. See JUDGMENT; MARRIAGE, NULLITY OF.

**decree absolute.** A final and conclusive decree.

**decree nisi.** A conditional decree. See NISI.

**dedication.** Formerly, the creation of a public road by dedication and acceptance. See PUBLIC ROAD.

**deed.** An instrument which is in writing, sealed and delivered, to prove and testify the agreement of the parties whose deed it is, as to its contents. It is usually signed. The seal is usually fixed to the deed before execution. The deed is sealed by placing a finger on the seal with the intention of sealing it; delivery is effected by handing the deed to the other party or by words indicating an intention to deliver it. A deed takes effect from the date of delivery. It is known as an *escrow* (qv) when it is delivered subject to a condition.

Certain contracts must be made under seal eg contracts made without consideration; authorisation of an agent to execute a deed; the transfer of a ship; contracts made by corporations (with exceptions). A right of action on a contract made under seal is statute barred after 12 years, while it is 6 years for a similar right under a simple contract. [Text: Madden]. See ESCROW; NON EST FACTUM; ORAL AGREEMENT, MODIFICATION OF CONTRACT BY.

**deed of conveyance.** The deed to effect the transfer of property. It often includes: recitals; testatum; parcels; operative words; habendum; tenendum; reddendum; conditions; powers; covenants; testimonium (qqv).

**deed of retirement.** See TRUSTEE, RETIREMENT OF.

**Deed of Settlement company.** Formerly an unincorporated company established by promoters who attempted, by using devices of contract and trust, to endow the company with many of the privileges and advantages normally reserved to corporations, which in those days could only be obtained by royal charter or special act of parliament. It is virtually extinct today.

**deed poll.** A deed which is *polled* or smooth ie not indented; a unilateral deed eg a declaration by a party of his intention to change his name. See INDENTURE; NAME, CHANGE OF.

**deeds, registration of.** The system which provides for the registration of deeds, conveyances and wills at the Registry of Deeds situated in Dublin: Registration of Deeds (Ireland) Act 1707. The document registered continues to be the evidence of title, unlike the system of registration of title. Registration is voluntary and a wide variety of documents dealing with interest in land may be registered. Failure to register may mean a *loss of priority* against other interests charged against the land.

A search in the Registry of Deeds will inform a purchaser of certain transactions affecting the title of the *unregistered* land, with the assurance that all transactions which were capable of being registered but which were not registered, will be treated as fraudulent and void, unless actual notice of them was brought to the attention of the purchaser. See Fullerton v Provincial Bank of Ireland (1903) IR 483. [Text: Ellis & Eustace]. See LAND REGISTRATION; MEMORIAL; OFFICIAL SEARCH.

**deemed.** To be treated as; supposed; eg the law deems the dismissal of an employee to be an unfair dismissal (qv) unless there are substantial grounds justifying the dismissal: Unfair Dismissal Act 1977 s.6.

**deer.** See WILD ANIMALS, PROTECTED.

**defamation.** The tort (qv) consisting of the publication of a *defamatory* statement concerning another without just cause or excuse, whereby he suffers injury to his reputation. A *defamatory statement* is a false statement which exposes the person to hatred, ridicule or contempt, or which causes him to be shunned or avoided, or which tends to injure him in his office, calling or business. The test is whether the words tend to lower the person in the estimation of right-thinking members of society. Defamation may be a *libel* (qv) or a *slander* (qv).

To establish an action for defamation, the plaintiff must prove (a) that the words complained of are defamatory; (b) that they refer to the plaintiff; (c) that they were *published* by the defendant; and (d) in the case of slander, *special damage* (ie some definite material loss) was suffered by the plaintiff or that the slander comes within a category which is actionable without proof of special damage. *Publication* means making known the defamatory matter to some person other than the person of whom it is made: see Berry v Irish Times Ltd (1973) IR 368.

The words complained of must be defamatory in their ordinary meaning or by *innuendo* (qv). It is for the judge to say whether the words are capable of bearing a defamatory meaning and for the jury (or the judge where there is no jury) to decide if the words in the circumstances of the case in fact bear that meaning. See Barrett v Independent Newspapers (1986) IR 13.

The defences to a defamation action are: (a) consent by the plaintiff; (b) privilege, absolute or qualified; (c) fair comment; (d) apology; (e) offer of amends; (f) fair and accurate report; (g) justification (qqv). The Law Reform Commission has made recommendations for major changes in the law of defamation: LRC 38 of 1991 and also see O'Dell in 9ILT & SJ (1991) 181. See Defamation Act 1961. [Text: McDonald (1); Duncan & Neill UK; Gatley UK]. See INJURIOUS FALSEHOOD; LODGMENT IN COURT; MALICE; MITIGATION OF DAMAGES; NAME, RIGHT TO GOOD; OFFENSIVE WORDS; PUBLICATION.

**default.** To fail to do something required by law eg non-payment of a sum by the due date; failure to deliver a defence to an action within the prescribed time. See eg JUDGMENT IN DEFAULT OF DEFENCE; PLEADINGS.

**default permission.** Generally understood to mean the grant of planning permission (qv) which is deemed to have been given where the planning authority fails to give its decision within the appropriate period. See Calor Teo v Sligo Co Council (1991 HC) 2 IR 267. See PLANNING PERMISSION, DECISION ON.

**defeasible.** Capable of being annulled.

**defect.** An irregularity or fault. A *patent* defect is one which ought to be discovered by ordinary vigilence; a *latent* defect is one which could not be discovered by reasonable examination. See Ashburner v Sewell (1891) 3 Ch 405.

**defective building.** See BUILDER, DUTY OF.

**defective goods/products.** See MERCHANTABLE QUALITY; PRODUCT LIABILITY.

**defective motor vehicle.** See MOTOR VEHICLE, SALE OF.

**defectum sanguinis.** [Failure of issue]. See ESCHEAT.

**defence.** (1) The opposition or denial by a defendant of the prosecutor's case. (2) A written statement in reply to a *statement of claim* (qv) in a High Court action which must be served within 28 days of delivery of the statement of claim or from the time limited for appearance, whichever be later: RSC O.21 r.1. Facts not denied specifically or by necessary implication are taken to be admitted; a mere denial of a debt or liquidated demand in money is inadmissible; in some other actions it is necessary to deny some matter of fact (ibid rr.3-8). In default of defence, the plaintiff may be permitted to *enter judgment*.

In the Circuit Court, a defence is required to be given or sent by post to the plaintiff within ten days of entering an appearance: RCC O.12 rr.4-5. In the District Court, *notice of intention to defend* a civil process must be given four clear days before the day fixed for the hearing: DCR r.153. See COUNTER CLAIM; DEFEND, RIGHT TO; JUDGMENT IN DEFAULT OF DEFENCE.

**defence, self.** See SELF DEFENCE.

**defence forces.** The right to raise and maintain military or armed forces is vested exclusively in the Oireachtas (qv): 1937 Constitution, art.15(6). The President of Ireland is the supreme commander of the defence forces and all officers hold their commission from her (ibid art.13(5)(2)). Everyday control of the defence forces rests with the Minister: Defence Act 1954. There is no immunity at common law from suit by, or the negation of any duty of care to, a serving soldier, in respect of operations consisting of armed conflict or hostilities; superior officers owe a duty of care to serving soldiers: Ryan v Ireland (1989) 7ILT & SJ 118 & 204 and (1990) ITLR (3 Apr).

Certain members of the defence forces are liable for service with an International United Nations Force; such a force, being a force established by the Security Council or the General Assembly of the UN, is no longer required to be of a police character only and may be engaged in peace *enforcement* as well as peace *keeping:* Defence (Amendment) (No 2) Act 1960 as amended and extended by Defence (Amdt) Act 1993. See Kimber in ISLR (1993) 48 on "UN Enforcing the Peace".

Representative bodies may be established in the defence forces to deal with such non-operational matters as remuneration; such bodies must not be constituted as trade unions: Defence (Amdt) Act 1990. There is provision for deductions from pay of members of the defence forces who have children in care: Child Care Act 1991 s.78. See PEACE OFFICER; MILITARY LAW; RETIREMENT, EARLY; UNITED NATIONS.

**defence policy.** See COMMON FOREIGN AND SECURITY POLICY.

**defences, criminal.** The defences which may be relevant to answer a criminal charge include: insanity, infancy, consent, obedience to orders, self-defence, duress, mistake, drunkeness, immunity, and absence of mens rea (qqv).

**defend, right to.** The right to defend an action has been recognised as part of the constitutional right of access to the courts: Calor Teoranta v Colgan (1990 SC); see Doyle in 8ILT & SJ (1990) 255.

**defendant.** The person against whom an action, information or other civil proceeding is brought; also a person charged with an offence. Where a defendant has been *added* to proceedings, the proceedings are deemed against the added defendant to have begun on the making of the order adding the defendant, thereby treating the added defendant in a like manner as the original defendant

as regards the Statute of Limitations: RSC O.15 r.13. See McMeel v Minister for Health (1986) HC; Fincorig SAS v Ansbacher Co (1987) HC.

The person against whom a petition (qv) is presented is known as a respondent (qv). See also RSC O.15 r.4; RCC O.6 r.2; DCR r.134. See O'BYRNE LETTER.

**defendants, joint.** Co-defendants; persons charged jointly with the same offence. Several persons may be joined in the same indictment (qv); one or more counts may charge several persons with the same crime eg where they are concerned, albeit in different capacities, in say robbing a bank.

In general two or more persons who are charged with the same offence, are tried together. They are not entitled, as of right, to separate trials; it is a matter of discretion for the judge: The People (Attorney General) v Carney & Mulcahy (1955) IR 324. The judge will order separate trials where an accused would be prejudiced by being tried with another eg where one accused has made a statement implicating the other, or where the prosecution or the defence wishes to call a witness who could not be called if the accused were tried with others.

A joint defendant is a competent (qv) but not compellable witness for the prosecution against the other co-defendant: Attorney General (Ryan) v Egan (1948) IR 433. However, once a co-defendant offers himself as a witness on his own behalf, he is bound by the terms of his oath to tell the truth and he may be cross-examined by his co-accused, and his evidence is admissible against his co-accused: Attorney General v Joyce & Walsh (1929) IR 526. See Criminal Evidence Act 1992 s.24.

Where persons are charged on separate summones or charge sheets with similar offences arising out of the same set of facts, in the absence of their consent to being tried together, they are entitled to separate trials: Aldas & Anor v Watson (1973) RTR 466. See also The People v Murtagh (1966) IR 361.

As regards certain civil matters involving defendants in different EC states, a connection must exist between the different actions brought by a plaintiff against the defendants which is such as makes it expedient to have the actions tried together to avoid the risk of irreconcilable judgments arising from separate proceedings: Kalfelis v Banque Schroder (1988) European Court — (1989) 7ILT & SJ 2. See CONSOLIDATION OF ACTIONS; JOINDER OF DEFENDANTS.

**defensive trade mark.** A trade mark (qv), the registration of which is permitted in the absence of any use or intention to use the mark in connection with *other goods*, where the trade mark consists of an invented word or words and has become so well known as respects any goods of which it is already registered and in relation to which it has been used, and the use thereof in relation to the other goods would likely be taken as indicating a connection in the course of trade (qv) between the goods and the other goods: Trade Marks Act 1963 s.35.

**deferred shares.** See FOUNDERS SHARES.

**definition order.** An order which the Minister may make to assign meanings to words or expressions used as, or as part of, a trade description applied to goods, services, living accommodation or facilities, of that description. See Consumer Information Act 1978 s.12.

**deforcement.** The wrongful holding of the land of another.

**defraud.** See FRAUD; ILLEGAL CONTRACTS.

**degree.** A step in the line of descent (qv) or consanguinity (qv). See MARRIAGE.

**dehors.** [Without]. Irrelevant; outside the scope of.

**del credere agent.** [Of belief]. An agent for the sale of goods, who in consideration of a higher rate of commission than is usual, guarantees that his principal will receive due payment for the price of all goods sold by him. The contract of agency is not required to be evidenced in writing under the Statute of Frauds, as the guarantee given is only incidental to the larger contract of agency. See Hamburg India Rubber Comb Co v Martin (1902) 1 KB 778.

**delay.** Negligent or unreasonable delay will defeat an action to enforce ones rights; equity aids the vigilent and not the indolent. The test which applies in all cases involving delay in criminal proceedings is whether or not it is shown that the delay is prejudicial to the fair trial of the accused: Maguire v DPP and Kirby (1988) ILRM 166; O'Connor v DPP (1987) ILRM 723; O'Flynn &

Hannigan v Clifford (1989) 7ILT Dig 124 & (1990) 8ILT Dig 160; Fitzpatrick v Sheilds (1989 HC) ILRM 243; DPP v Ryan (1989 CCA) ITLR (3 Apr).

As regards delay in civil cases, where the delay has been both *inordinate and inexcusable*, the court will decide whether the balance of justice is in favour of, or against, the proceeding of the case; where the delay is not both inordinate and inexcusable, it would appear that there are no real grounds for dismissing the proceedings; also while a party acting through a solicitor is to an extent vicariously liable for the activity or inactivity of the solicitor, the court must consider the litigants' personal blameworthiness for the delay: O'Domhnaill v Merrick (1984) IR 151 cited in Guerin v Guerin & McGrath (1993 HC) ILRM 243.

In relation to whether an accused is entitled to have extradition (qv) refused on the ground of excessive delay, see Harte v Fanning (1988) ILRM 70. Delay in a county registrar or sheriff in executing certificates issued by the Collector General persuant to s.485 of the Income Tax Act 1967 does not invalidate the certificates: Weekes v Revenue Commissioners (1989 HC) ILRM 165. Summonses should be issued within a reasonable time of being applied for: DPP v Byrne (1993 HC) ILRM 475. See also Sweeney v Horan's (Tralee) (1987) ILRM 240; The State (Brennan) v Connellan (1986) HC; DPP v Carlton (1991 HC) ITLR (4 Nov); DPP v Cahalane (1993 HC) – Irish Times 14/8/1993. See LACHES; LIMITATION OF ACTIONS; STRIKE OUT.

**delegated legislation.** Subordinate legislation; rules or law as laid down by some person or body under authority delegated by legislation. Examples are: (a) *orders* permitted to be made by the government under legislation eg the government may by order activate part of the Offences Against the State Act 1939 which established the Special Criminal Court; (b) *statutory instruments* which designated Ministers are permitted to make under various statutes eg the Minister for the Environment may make instruments dealing with a wide range of matters in the area of planning and development under the LG(P&D) Act

1963; (c) *bye-laws* which local authorities and other bodies are empowered to make eg the Garda Commissioner is empowered to make bye-laws in relation to stands and stopping places for buses and taxis and for the general control of traffic and pedestrians under the Road Traffic Act 1961; (d) *autonomous* regulations eg the power given to the Incorporated Law Society by the Solicitors Act 1954 to make regulations governing the conduct of its members.

Delegated legislation must in its method of enactment apply basic fairness of procedures; it must be reasonable, ie it must not be arbitrary, unjust or partial; and it must not be ultra vires (qv). See Cassidy v Minister for Industry Commerce (1978) IR 297; Burke v Minister for Labour (1979) IR 354; Cityview Press v An Chomhairle Oiliuna (1980) IR 381; Cooke v Walsh (1984) ILRM 208.

**delegatus non potest delegare.** [A delegate cannot delegate]. A person to whom powers have been delegated cannot delegate them to another. An agent cannot delegate his authority without the express or implied authority of the principal. However authority to delegate may be implied: (a) where justified by usage of a particular trade; (b) where unforeseen emergencies arise which render it necessary for the agent to delegate; or (c) where the act done is purely ministerial and does not involve confidence or discretion. For delegation by company directors, see MacCann in 9ILT & SJ (1991) 60. See De Bussche v Alt (1878) 8 Ch D 286. See AGENT OF NECESSITY; TRUSTEE, DUTY OF.

**delict.** A wrongful act. See TORT.

**deliverable state.** See GOODS, DELIVERABLE STATE.

**delivery of deed.** See DEED.

**delivery of goods.** The voluntary transfer of possession of goods from one person to another: Sale of Goods Act 1893 s.62. Delivery may take place by physical transfer of the goods; by physical transfer of a document of title eg a bill of lading; by physical transfer of the means of control eg a key to a warehouse with the goods therein; by attornment (qv); or by the seller becoming a bailee for the buyer. Whether it is for the buyer to take possession of the goods or for the seller to send them to the buyer is a question depending in each case on the contract, express or implied, between the parties (ibid s.29). Delivery of goods to a carrier is deemed prima facie to be a delivery to the buyer (ibid s.32). See Board of Ordnance v Lewis (1855) 7 Ir Jur (os) 17; Bonner v Whelan (1905) 39 ILTR 24. See CARRIER, DELIVERY OF GOODS TO; INSTALMENT DELIVERIES; WRONG QUANTITY.

**delusion.** Self-deception relating to some matter. In relation to delusions and wills, see SOUND DISPOSING MIND. In relation to insane delusions, see McNAGHTEN RULES.

**demanding with menaces.** See EXTORTION BY MENACES.

**demesne.** [Own]. The part of the manor occupied by the lord.

**demise.** (1) The grant of a tenancy or lease; to let or lease land. Land which is let or leased is often referred to as *demised premises*. (2) A person's death.

**democracy.** See ELECTION; WORKER PARTICIPATION.

**demolition.** See DANGEROUS STRUCTURE; UNFIT HOUSE; HABITABLE HOUSE.

**demonstrative legacy.** A gift of personal property by will which is general in nature but which is directed to be paid out of a specific fund or part of the testator's property eg £*1000 to X to be paid out of my Irish Permanent Building Society shares*: McCoy v Jacob (1919) IR 134.

**demurrage.** An agreed sum fixed by a charterparty (qv) payable to the shipowner for the detention of a ship beyond the number of days allowed for loading and unloading. [Text: Tiberg (UK)].

**dentistry, practice of.** The performance of any operation and the giving of any treatment, advice, opinion or attendance which is usually performed or given by a dentist and includes the performance of any operation or the giving of any treatment, advice or attendance on or to any person preparatory to, for the purpose of, or in connection with, the fitting, insertion or fixing of artificial teeth: Dentists Act 1985 s.2. A person who is not a *registered dentist* is prohibited from using the title of dentist, dental surgeon or dental practitioner or from practising dentistry (ibid ss.50-51). See also Hennan & Co Ltd v Duckworth

(1904) 90 LT 546.

**dependant.** See FATAL INJURIES; CHILD, PROVISION FOR.

**dependant in fatal injury cases.** See FATAL INJURIES.

**dependent child.** For the purposes of a claim for a *maintenance order* (qv), a child under the age of sixteen years who is the natural child of the spouses, or an adopted child, or a child in whom the spouses stand in loco parentis (qv), or a child of one spouse who is known by the other spouse not to be his child but who is treated as a member of the family and includes a child whose parents are not married to each other: Family Law (Maintenance of Spouses and Children) Act 1976 s.3(1), as amended by the Status of Children Act 1987 s.16.

A child over the age of sixteen is dependent if receiving full time education and is under the age of twenty-one years, or if suffering from some mental or physical handicap which prevents the child from maintaining himself fully. Any income of the dependent children will be taken into consideration by the court in determining whether a maintenance order should be made and how much should be awarded. See DISABLED PERSON AND SEPARATION; JUDICIAL SEPARATION; MAINTENANCE ORDERS; SEPARATION AGREEMENT; SUCCESSION, LAW OF.

**dependent relative revocation.** A conditional revocation of a will where revocation is relative to another will and intended to be dependent on the validity of that will; the revocation is ineffective unless the other will takes effect. See Brady "A case of dependent relative revocation" (1981) 75 ILSI Gazette 5.

**deponent.** A person who makes an affidavit (qv) or deposition (qv).

**deportation.** Expulsion from the State. Deportation of an *alien* does not constitute an infringement of any of the constitutional provisions for the protection of marriage and the family: Osheku v Ireland (1987) ILRM 330. See ALIEN.

**depose.** To make a deposition or statement on oath (qv).

**deposit.** (1) In a contract for the sale of land, a part-payment of the purchase price; it is a usual condition of such sale that where the purchaser makes default, the vendor may forfeit the deposit and resell the land, and recover any deficiency

and expenses on resale from the purchaser, being allowed this amount or the deposit, whichever is the greater. In auction sales, the conditions usually require the deposit to be paid to the auctioneer, who holds as stakeholder (qv). In the absence of agreement to the contrary, a deposit paid to the vendor's solicitor is treated as paid to him as the vendor's agent rather than as a stakeholder. See Leemac Overseas Investments Ltd v Harvey (1973) IR 160; Desmond and Boyle v Brophy (1986) ILRM 547.

(2) In a contract for the sale of goods, a deposit is a guarantee that the purchaser means business: Soper v Arnold (1889) 61 LT 702.

(3) As regards financial institutions, a deposit is generally understood to be a sum of money paid on terms whereby it will be returned with or without interest. "There is no definition in Irish law as to what is or is not a deposit": In re Irish Commercial Society Group Ltd (in receivership and in liquidation) (1987) p.828. A building society is empowered to accept deposits: Building Societies Act 1989 s.18(1). Small deposits of a deceased depositor in savings banks and building societies may be paid to the beneficiaries without the necessity for probate (qv) or letters of administration (qv): Building Societies Act 1989 s.19 and Trustee Savings Bank 1989 s.60. See also HIRE-PURCHASE PRICE; INDUSTRIAL & PROVIDENT SOCIETY; INVESTMENT TRUST COMPANY.

**deposit interest retention tax; DIRT.** The taxation at source of interest paid or credited on *relevant deposits* with banks, building societies and certain other bodies: Finance Act 1986 ss.31-40. A relevant deposit is any deposit other than an *exempted deposit*; an exempted deposit includes eg a deposit in respect of which no person ordinarily resident in the State is beneficially entitled to any interest (ibid s.31(1)). Apart from companies chargeable to corporation tax, only three classes of persons may claim repayment of retention tax: incapacitated persons, persons aged 65 or over, and charities (ibid s.39). Taxation is now at the standard rate: Finance Act 1992 s.22; and for all taxpayers this deduction is regarded as the individual's full liability to income tax in respect of the interest: Finance Act 1993 s.15. See SPECIAL SAVINGS ACCOUNT.

**deposit of goods.** See BAILMENT.

**deposit of title deeds.** The delivery of title deeds to lands which creates an *equitable mortgage* (qv) thereon. The title deeds may be deposited to secure a debt antecedently due, or a sum then advanced or future advances; the depositee acquires a right to hold the deeds until the debt is paid and also acquires an equitable interest in the lands. Where the title deeds are accompanied by a memorandum of deposit signed by the mortgagor (qv), the mortgagee (qv) can protect his interest by registering the memorandum in the Registry of Deeds (qv). The mortgagee's remedy to obtain repayment of debt and interest is by way of mortgage suit (qv). See CHARGE, REGISTERED; FAMILY HOME; LAND CERTIFICATE; TITLE DEEDS.

**deposition.** A statement on oath of a witness in a judicial proceeding eg the statement of witnesses in criminal matters before the committing justice: RSC O.86 r.15. Generally a deposition may not be given in evidence at a trial without the consent of the party against whom it may be offered, unless the deponent is dead, or beyond the jurisdiction of the court, or unable from sickness or other infirmity to attend the trial: RSC O.39 r.17. If the deponent refuses to sign the deposition, it must be signed by the examiner: RSC O.39 r.11, 15. An accused before the Central Criminal Court is entitled to have supplied to him the depositions relating to the offences with which he is charged: RSC O.85 r.5. See Bankruptcy Act 1988 s.140.

In criminal proceedings, a deposition may be taken in the presence of a district judge and the accused: Criminal Procedure Act 1967 s.14. Where this is not possible or practicable, a document will be admissible which contains information compiled in the presence of a district judge from a non-resident victim of an offence where the victim has died or where it is not reasonably practicable to secure the victim's attendance at the trial: Criminal Evidence Act 1992 s.5(4). See DOCUMENTARY EVIDENCE; FRESH EVIDENCE; PERPETUATING TESTIMONY; SHIPS PROTEST.

**depositum.** [Deposit]. See BAILMENT.

**deprave.** To corrupt. See PERFORMANCE, INDECENT OR PROFANE.

**depraved.** A judge of the District Court is empowered to certify that a young person is so *depraved* a character that he serve his sentence in a prison rather than in an institution for young offenders: "depraved" is not defined: Childrens Act 1908 s.102 and G & McD v Governor of Mountjoy Prison (1991 HC) 9ILT Dig 266. See DICTIONARY.

**depreciation.** Depreciation in the value of property in the vicinity is a valid reason for refusing planning permission: Maher v An Bord Pleanala (1993 HC) ILRM 359. See ASSET VALUATION; PROVISION; RESERVE.

**derelict site.** Any land which detracts, or is likely to detract, to a material degree from the amenity, character or appearance of land in the neighbourhood of the land in question because of: (a) the existence on the land of structures which are in a ruinous, derelict or dangerous condition, or (b) the neglected, unsightly or objectionable condition of the land or any structures, or (c) the presence, deposit or collection on the land of any litter, rubbish, debris or waste: Derelict Sites Act 1990 s.3.

There is a general duty on owners and occupiers of land to prevent land from becoming or continuing to be a derelict site (ibid s.9). There is also a duty on a local authority to prevent land in its functional area becoming or continuing to be a derelict site (ibid s.10) and a duty to establish and maintain a *derelict site register* (ibid s.8). An annual *derelict site levy* in respect of urban land on the register, is payable by the owner; the levy is fixed at 3% of the market value in the first year and a maximum of 10% is stipulated and is a charge (qv) on the land (ibid ss.21-26).

A local authority may acquire by agreement or compulsorily any derelict site situate in their functional area (ibid s.14). They may also require the owner by notice to carry out such works as are necessary to prevent the land from continuing to be a derelict site (ibid s.11). They may also enter on the site themselves, carry out the works and recover the expenses of so doing from the owner (ibid s.11). See Derelict Sites

(Urban Areas) Regulations 1991 (SI No 362 of 1991). See VESTING ORDER.

**dereliction.** The act of abandoning.

**derivative action.** A company's action, the right to which is derived from the company, brought by a *minority shareholder* or shareholders. It is an exception to the rule that the proper plaintiff in respect of a wrong alleged to be done to a company is, prima facie, the company. It arises where the company is controlled by the defendant and the only way in which the wrong can be remedied is to allow any member to bring suit on the company's behalf. See Prudential Assurance Co v Newman Industries Ltd (1981) 1 Ch 229.

The Central Bank may bring proceedings in the name of a building society in respect of any fraud (qv), misfeasance (qv) or other misconduct in connection with the management of its affairs: Building Societies Act 1989 s.47(6). See also MacCann in 8 ILT & SJ (1990) 71. See FOSS V HARBOTTLE, RULE IN.

**derogate.** To destroy, prejudice or evade a right or obligation. No man may derogate from his own grant: Wheeldon v Burrows (1879) 12 Ch 31.

**descendant.** A person descended from an ancestor (qv).

**descent.** The devolution of an interest in land upon the death intestate of the owner to a person or persons by virtue of consanguinity with the deceased. Under the Canons of Descent, applicable to deaths prior to 1st January 1967, *realty* (except freehold registered land — Part 1V of Registration of Title Act 1891) went to the heir-at-law traced as follows: (a) inheritance descended lineally to issue of the last purchaser; (b) males took before females; (c) elder males took before a younger male in the same degree but females took equally as coparceners (qv); (d) lineal descendants represented their ancestor eg eldest son's son took before the younger son of the purchaser; (e) nearest lineal ancestor took on failure of lineal descendants; (f) relatives of the half-blood were admitted by the Inheritance Act 1833; (g) where there was a total failure of heirs of the last purchaser, the descent was traced to the last person entitled as if he had been the purchaser; (h) escheat (qv) then occurred but if the widow of the last person entitled survived, she took instead under the Intestate's Estates Act 1954.

Cannons of Descent were abolished by the Succession Act 1965 s.11 except in so far as they apply to the descent of an *estate tail*; new rules for intestate succession were introduced under which realty and personalty devolve in the same way. See INTESTATE SUCCESSION.

**description, sale by.** Where there is a sale of goods by *description*, there is an implied condition (qv) that the goods will correspond with the description. A sale of goods is not prevented from being a sale by description by reason only that, being exposed for sale, they are selected by the buyer. A reference to goods on a label or other descriptive matter accompanying goods exposed for sale may constitute or form part of a description. See Sale of Goods Act 1893 s.13; SGSS Act 1980 s.10. Similar provisions apply as regards goods let by description under a hire-purchase agreement (ibid 1980 Act s.27). See Arcos Ltd v Ronaasen (1933) AC 470; Goff v Walsh (1940) Ir Jur Rep 49; Egan v McSweeney (1956) 90 ILTR 40; Reardon-Smith v Hansen-Tangen (1976) 1 WLR 989; T O'Regan & Sons Ltd v Micro-Bio (Ireland) Ltd (1980) HC. See SELF-SERVICE; TRADE MARK.

**deserter.** A person, subject to military law, who deserts or attempts to desert the defence forces is guilty of an offence against military law; *desertion* includes being absent without due authority having been warned for hazardous duty or important service, with the intention of avoiding that duty or service: Defence Act 1954 ss.2(1) and 135.

**desertion.** (1) Cessation of cohabitation (qv) which may be a ground for refusing a *maintenance order* (qv) to an applicant spouse who has deserted: Family Law (Maintenance of Spouses and Children) Act 1976 s.5(2). *Desertion* requires actual separation and an intention to desert. The definition of "desertion" clearly and unambiguously envisages constructive desertion: K v K (1992 SC) ITLR (4 May). The spouse who physically leaves the matrimonial home is not necessarily the deserter; the spouse who intends to bring the cohabitation to an end and whose conduct causes its termination, commits the act of desertion. See RK v MK (1978) HC. Constructive desertion is normally a bar to a claim for maintenance (ibid 1976 Act s.5(2)) unless it would be repugnant to justice not to make a maintenance order (Judicial Separation & Family Law Act 1989 s.38).

Desertion is a ground for a decree of *judicial separation* in marriage; desertion in this case includes conduct by one spouse that results in the other spouse, with just cause, leaving and living apart from the other spouse (ibid 1989 Act s.2(3)(b)). The court will not normally make an order for the support of a spouse who has deserted (ibid s.20(3)).

Compulsory deductions from the pay of a member of the Defence Forces may be made where he has deserted his wife and left her in destitute circumstances: Defence Act 1954 s.99; Status of Children Act 1987 s.24(2). See ATTACH-MENT; JUDICIAL SEPARATION; UNWORTHINESS TO SUCCEED.

(2) As regards the desertion of children, see ADOPTION; CRUELTY TO CHILDREN; FOSTER PARENTS.

**design.** The features of shape, configuration, pattern, or ornament applied to any *article* by any industrial process or means, whether manual, mechanical, or chemical, separate or combined, which in the finished article appeal to and are judged solely by the eye, but does not include any mode or principle of construction, or anything which is in substance a mere mechanical device: Industrial & Commercial Property (Protection) Act 1927 s.3. *Article* in this context means any article of manufacture and any substance artificial or natural or partly artificial and partly natural.

There is provision for the registration of designs on the application of the *proprietor of any new or original design* (qv). A design when registered is registered as from the date of registration (ibid s.64). Registration confers on the registered proprietor a *copyright* in the design for five years from the date of registration, which period may be extended for two further periods each of five years on application and payment of the prescribed fee (ibid s.70; Copyright Act 1963 s.59). *Copyright* in this context means the exclusive right to apply the design to any article in any class in which the design is registered (ibid 1927

Act s.3). This copyright is without prejudice to the copyright conferred in certain artistic works (ibid s.70). However, copyright in functional designs which are commercially produced has been abolished: Copyright (Amdt) Act 1987 s.1. See also Allibert SA v O'Connor (1981) FSR 613 and (1982) ILRM 40.

A register of designs must be kept at the Patents Office by the Controller of Patents; there are restrictions on its inspection by the public (ibid 1927 Act ss.69 and 73). See also Industrial & Commercial Property (Protection) (Amendment) Act 1957 s.5 and Copyright Act 1963 s.59.

**design, proprietor of new or original.** See PROPRIETOR OF NEW OR ORIGINAL DESIGN.

**designated.** When considered in its Latin etymological sense relates to a sign or a mark of approval; the formal introduction to an accused renders a doctor a *designated* registered medical practitioner under the Road Traffic Acts: DPP v Hyland (1991 HC) ITLR (28 Jan). See BLOOD SPECIMEN; URINE SPECIMEN.

**destructive insect.** See INSECT.

**detain.** See DETENTION.

**detection devices.** See METAL DETECTORS.

**detention.** (1) A sentence of detention eg in St Patrick's Institution, which is distinct from a sentence of imprisonment: The State (Clinch) v Connellan (1986) ILRM 460; The State (White) v Martin (1976) 111 ILTR 21.

(2) A chief medical officer, with the agreement of a second medical practitioner, may order the detention of a person who is a probable source of certain infections in a hospital or other place: Health Act 1947 s.38 as amended by Health Act 1953 s.35; Infectious Diseases Regulations 1981 art.8 (SI No 390 of 1981).

(3) The Garda Siochana are empowered to detain a person following arrest on reasonable suspicion of having committed an *indictable offence* (qv) attracting a penalty of five years or more imprisonment: Criminal Jurisdiction Act 1984 s.4-10. Detention is for a maximum of six hours, which is renewable up to a maximum of twelve hours; time spent overnight is not normally reckonable, and the maximum time a person may be in custody before release is twenty hours. The gardai have a duty to arrange access

to a solicitor (qv) and to notify a parent or guardian (qv) in the case of a juvenile. For application for the re-arrest of a person previously detained under s.4 of the 1984 Act, see District Court Rules 1988 (SI No 158 of 1988).

It has been held that it would be an unwarranted and unlawful usurpation of the constitutional role of the High Court for any inferior court to embark on an enquiry under Article 40 of the 1937 Constitution with a view to holding that a person is being unlawfully detained: Keating v Governor of Mountjoy Prison (1990 SC) ILRM 850. See BODILY SAMPLE; HABEAS CORPUS; IDENTIFICATION PARADE; IN-TERNMENT; RECEPTION ORDER; MENTAL TREATMENT; PREVENTATIVE DETENTION; REF-ORMATORY SCHOOLS; SOLICITOR, ACCESS TO; SPECIAL VERDICT; UNFIT TO PLEAD.

**detention of ship.** The *arrest* of ships within the jurisdiction of the State in respect of *maritime claims* is authorised by the Jurisdiction of Courts (Maritime Conventions) Act 1989 which gives effect to the International Convention on the Arrest of Sea-going Ships 1952. Maritime claims include claims arising out of salvage, loss of life or personal injury in connection with the operation of the ship, agreements relating to carriage of goods or use or hire of the ship by charterparty or otherwise, the mortgage (qv) or hypothecation (qv) of the ship (ibid 1952 Convention, art.1). Arrest means the detention of a ship by judicial process but not seizure in execution or satisfaction of a judgment. The High Court has jurisdiction in these admiralty proceedings (ibid 1989 Act s.5).

**deterioration, medical.** The Supreme Court will not consider facts concerning an alleged medical deterioration of a plaintiff subsequent to the trial of an action in the High Court. "To allow the plaintiff to appeal by reference to facts which had come to light after the hearing of the claim in the High Court would undermine the finality of legal proceed-ings....": Dalton v Minister for Finance (1989) ILT Dig 230.

**determinable fee.** See FEE SIMPLE.

**determine.** To come to an end or to bring to an end.

**detinue.** A tort (qv) which consists of the withholding of goods from the person who is immediately entitled to their possession. An *action in detinue* is one by which a person claims the specific return of goods wrongfully detained or their value and damages for detention. Detinue is proven by evidence that a demand for the return of the goods was made by the plaintiff and yet the defendant failed to deliver them up. As to goods the subject of a hire-purchase agreement, see the Hire-Purchase Act 1946 ss.11 and 18. See Poole v Burns (1944) Ir Jur Rep 20; Treasure Island v Zebedee Enterprises (1987) HC; Mc-Crystal Oil Co Ltd v Revenue Commis-sioners (1993 HC) ILRM 69. See Courts Act 1991 s.7. See BAILMENT.

**Deus solus haeredem facere potest non homo.** [God alone, and not man, can make an heir]. See SUCCESSION.

**devastavit.** [He has wasted]. The wasting or converting to his own use by a personal representative (qv) of any part of the estate of a deceased. Devastavit may be by *misfeasance* eg by the personal representative using the estate for his own benefit; or by *non-feasance* eg by the personal representative neglecting to invest funds in his hands for the benefit of the estate. The personal representative is liable for such waste and his own estate is similarly liable in the event that he dies: Succession Act 1965 s.24. This provision also applies to an *executor de son tort* (qv): Ennis v Rochford (1884) 14 LR Ir 285. See WASTE.

**development.** The carrying out of any works on, in or under land or the making of any material change in the use of any structures or other land: LG (P&D) Act 1963 s.3(1); Environmental Protection Agency Act 1992 s.3(1). See Flanagan v Galway City and County Manager (1990) 2 IR 66; Hoburn Homes Ltd v An Bord Pleanala (1993 HC) ILRM 368. See PLANNING PERMISSION; EXEMPTED DEVELOP-MENT.

**development costs.** See ASSET VALUATION.

**development plan.** The plan, which consists of a written statement and a plan indicating the development *objec-tives*, which each planning authority (qv) is obliged to make and which must be reviewed at least once in every five years after the date of making the plan: LG(P&D) Act 1963 ss.19 and 20(1) as amended by the LG(P&D) Act 1976 s.43(1)(f).

In the case of *urban areas*, the mandatory objectives include: (a) indicating uses for particular areas for particular purposes, such as residential, commercial, agricultural (commonly known as *zoning*), (b) securing the greater convenience and safety of road users and pedestrians by the provision of parking places or road improvements; (c) the development and renewal of obsolete areas; (d) the preservation, improvement and extension of amenities. In the case of *rural areas* the objectives must include (c) and (d) above, in addition to the provision of new water supplies and sewage services and the extension of existing such services.

The *draft plan* or *draft variation* must be kept on public exhibition for three months, certain persons and bodies must be notified, and objections or representations must be taken into consideration before the plan or variation to the plan is made. The planning authority having gone through this process is empowered to make an amendment to the plan, unless the proposed amendment would be a *material alteration* of the draft in which event they must go through the statutory process of notification and exhibition again: 1963 Act s.21(A) as inserted by the 1976 Act s.37.

The making of the plan or any variation of it, is a *reserved function* (qv). The reduction or prevention of noise may now be included as an objective in a development plan: Environmental Protection Agency Act 1992 s.106(3). See also LG (P&D) Regulations 1977 (SI No 65 of 1977). See An Taisce v Dublin Corporation (1973) HC; O'Leary v Dublin Co Council (1988 HC) IR 150; Sharpe v Dublin City & County Manager (1989 SC) ILRM 565; AG v Sligo Co Council (1989 SC) ILRM 768; Hoburn Homes Ltd v An Bord Pleanala (1993 HC) ILRM 368. See PLANNING PERMISSION.

**deviation.** In marine insurance, where a ship, without lawful excuse, deviates from the voyage contemplated by the policy, the insurer is discharged from liability as from the time of the deviation, and it is immaterial that the ship may have regained her route before any loss occurs: Marine Insurance Act 1906 s.46.

**devil.** See BARRISTER.

**devise.** A gift of real property by will, either specific or residuary; to make such a gift. The recipient is the *devisee*. An *executory* devise is one limited to take effect in the future on fulfilment of a condition eg marriage. See LAPSE.

**devolution.** The passing of property or rights from one person to another eg on death.

**diagnosis, incorrect.** An incorrect diagnosis has been held not to be in itself evidence of bad faith or want of reasonable care: Murphy v Greene (1991 SC) ILRM 404. A doctor however was found to be in breach of duty in failing to take account of information in a general practitioner's referral letter and in failing to consult the log book notes concerning the plaintiff's previous tendencies: Armstrong v Eastern Health Board (1991 HC) 9ILT Dig 199 & 227.

**dictionary, use of.** A dictionary may be used by the court to ascertain the meaning of words to which no particular legal interpretation attaches. See R v Peters (1866) 16 QBD 636; McCann v O'Culachain (1986) ILRM 229; G & McD v Governor of Mountjoy Prison (1991 HC) 9ILT Dig 266; DPP v Cafolla (1992 SC) ITLR (22 Jun); Trustees of Kinsale Yacht Club v Commissioner of Valuations (1993 HC) ILRM 393; Hoburn Homes Ltd v An Bord Pleanala (1993 HC) ILRM 368; Madden v Minister for the Marine (1993 HC) ILRM 446. [Text: Stroud UK].

**dictum.** See OBITER DICTUM.

**dictum meum pactum.** [My word is my bond]. See ORAL AGREEMENT.

**die without issue.** The phrase which in a devise or bequest of real or personal property, is to be construed to mean a want or failure of issue during the lifetime of the person or at the time of his death, and not an indefinite failure of issue, unless a contrary intention appears: Succession Act 1965 s.96. See In re Mooney (1925) 29 ILTR 57. See ISSUE.

**differences, contract for.** See CONTRACTS FOR DIFFERENCES.

**digest.** A summary of the main points of cases, arranged by branch of law in an alphabetical order eg The Irish Digest, the Irish Law Times Digest (ILT Dig). See APPENDIX I — LAW REPORTS.

**diminished responsibility.** The defence

allowed in England to a charge of murder (qv) which if proved reduces the offence to manslaughter (qv). It has been held that such a defence cannot exist in this State side by side with a defence of insanity: The People (DPP) v O'Mahony (1986) ILRM 244. [Text: McAuley].

**diplomatic privilege.** The exemption of a diplomatic agent of a foreign state from the ordinary law of the state to which he is accredited. A diplomatic agent enjoys immunity from the criminal jurisdiction of the receiving state. He also enjoys *immunity* from its civil and administrative jurisdiction except in cases, not involving his mission, of a real action to private immovable property or an action relating to succession or relating to any professional or commercial activity by the agent.

A diplomatic agent is not obliged to give evidence as a witness and his person and his private and official residence is inviolable. He is not liable to any form of arrest or detention. Members of his family, if they are not nationals of the receiving state, enjoy the privileges and immunities of the agent.

The immunity from jurisdiction may be waived by the sending state but it must be express; the initiation of proceedings by a diplomatic agent precludes him from invoking immunity in respect of any counter claim. See Diplomatic Relations and Immunities Acts 1967 and 1976. See McMahon v McDonald (1988) HC & SC. See IMMUNITY; PERSONA NON GRATA; CONSUL; AMBASSADOR.

**direct applicability.** The term used to describe EC law which enters into force in each Member State without any national act of reception or incorporation. A provision of the EC Treaty is *directly applicable* in the domestic law of a Member State if it is (a) clear and precise, (b) unconditional, and (c) of such a kind that it requires no further action on the part of the Community institutions or the Member States or, if the measure requires execution, that it leaves no discretion to the Member State in the execution of the measure: Van Gend en Loos v Netherlandse Belastingsadministratie (1963) ECR 1; (1963) LMLR 105. See DIRECTIVE, EC; REGULATION, EC.

**direct effect.** See DIRECTIVE, EC.

**direct evidence.** See EVIDENCE.

**direct examination.** Examination-in-chief. See EXAMINATION.

**direct mailing list.** The mailing or marketing list, from which a data subject (qv) will be entitled to have his name removed, by requesting the data controller (qv) in writing to cease using the data for that purpose: Data Protection Act 1988 s.2(7). See DATA PROTECTION.

**direct marketing list.** See DIRECT MAILING LIST.

**direction.** An instruction from the court eg an instruction given by a judge to a jury on a relevant point of law to be applied to the facts they are considering.

In a criminal trial, a direction may be given by the judge to the jury to find the accused not guilty at the close of the prosecution case. When an application for a direction is made, it is the function of the judge to consider whether there is evidence which a jury might reasonably accept as establishing the guilt of the accused; it is not his function to make any finding on the alleged facts: DPP v Gilligan (1992 CCA) ITLR (30 Mar). A judge must not direct a jury to enter a verdict of guilty in a case where he felt that to be the only proper verdict: DPP v Davis (1993 SC) ILRM 407.

In civil proceedings, a direction may be sought by a defendant at the end of the plaintiff's case for a non-suit ie a dismissal of the plaintiff's action. Where the trial is *before a jury*, a direction will be given to the jury to dismiss the action where the judge, assuming that all matters in controversy will be resolved according to the evidence in favour of the plaintiff, nevertheless holds that even in those circumstances there is not sufficient evidence to support the plaintiff's case.

Where the judge is sitting *without a jury*, he should enquire if the defendant intends, if refused the direction, to go into evidence. If the defendant intends to present evidence, the judge must decide whether the plaintiff has made out a *prima facie* case; if the judge decides in the affirmative, a direction to dismiss the action will be denied. However, if the defendant does not intend to present evidence on liability, the judge must decide if the plaintiff has established as a matter of *probability* the facts necessary to support a verdict in his favour; if the plaintiff has, then the judge will give judgment for the plaintiff; if the plaintiff has not, then the judge will dismiss the action: O'Toole v Heavey (1993 SC) ILRM 343 expanding and clarifying Hetherington v Ultra Tyre Service Ltd (1991 SC) ITLR (22 Jul) and (1993) ILRM 353.

Also where more than one defendant is sued, the judge should decide on an application for a non-suit by a defendant only where he is completely satisfied that another defendant could not escape liability by affixing blame in evidence on the defendant applying for the direction to be dismissed from the action (ibid O'Toole case). See MISDIRECTION; SUMMING UP; SUPREME COURT.

**directions, summons for.** The receiver of a company may apply by special summons to the court for directions in relation to any particular matter arising in connection with the performance of his function: Companies Act 1963 s.316. See In re Tullow Engineering (Holdings) Ltd (in receivership) (1988) HC. See RECEIVER, COMPANY.

**directive, EC.** Legislation of the EC which states an objective which each member state must realise within a prescribed period. "A directive shall be binding, as to the result to be achieved, but shall leave to the national authorities the choice of form and methods": Treaty of Rome 1957 art.189(3).

The principles contained in an EC Directive do not normally have the direct force of law in the member States and will usually require a legislative process to be legally binding, although in some instance the directive can have direct effect between the member state and its citizens, by which the member state will be *estopped* from denying the effect of the directive and will be bound by the law not as it is but as it should be: Browne v An Bord Pleanala (1989 HC) ILRM 865.

Where the provisions of a directive appear, as far as their subject matter is concerned, to be unconditional and precise, individuals may rely on those provisions in the absence of implementing measures adopted within the prescribed period as against a national provision incompatible with the directive: McDermott & Cotter v Minister for Social Welfare (1987) ILRM 324. See also Greene v Minister for Agriculture (1989 HC) ILRM 364; Carberry v Minister for Social Welfare (1989) ITLR (5 Jun).

EC directives have been implemented in Ireland by new legislation (ie Acts of the Oireachtas) and by delegated legislation (ie by ministerial decisions in the form of regulations / statutory instruments). See REGULATION.

**director, managing.** See MANAGING DIRECTOR.

**Director of Consumer Affairs.** See CONSUMER AFFAIRS, DIRECTOR OF.

**Director of Public Prosecutions; DPP.** The independent office established by statute by which all serious crimes are prosecuted in the name of the People: Prosecution of Offences Act 1974. The holder of the office is a civil servant and is independent in the exercise of his function. The function of the DPP in deciding whether or not to prosecute an individual for the alleged commission of a criminal offence is an executive one, and it is not reviewable by the courts, as this would interfere with his independence: The State (McCormack) v Curran (1987) ILRM 225.

He performs all functions formerly capable of being prosecuted by the Attorney General in relation to criminal matters. He is not confined in his nomination or appointment of a solicitor to conduct a charge on an indictable offence (qv) to solicitors employed in the public service: Flynn v DPP (1986) ILRM 290. See 1937 Constitution, art.30(3). See RSC O.97. See COMMON INFORMER; INDICTMENT; LOCUS STANDI; PROSECUTOR; SPECIAL COURTS.

**directors.** The persons with powers and duties to manage the business of a company: Companies Act 1963, Table A, arts 80-90. They are agents of the company, trustees of its money and property, and they occupy a fiduciary position. Their powers and duties are governed by the *articles of association* of the company. Every company must have at least two directors (ibid s.174). A body corporate may not be a director nor may an undischarged bankrupt nor any person convicted on indictment of either an offence in connection with their involvement with a company or any offence involving fraud or dishonesty (ibid ss.176, 183 and first schedule para.91, and Companies Act 1990 ss.149-169).

A person (eg a *shadow* or *de facto* director) is deemed to be a director if the directors are accustomed to act on his directions or instructions (ibid 1990 Act s.27). A director is an officer of the company; whether or not a director is an employee of the company depends on the facts (eg see Stakelum v Canning [1976] IR 314).

Service contracts of directors lasting for more than five years must be approved at a general meeting of the company (ibid 1990 Act s.28). The names of directors must be shown on all business letters of the company and their nationality if not Irish (ibid 1963 Act s.196) and a register of the directors, including other directorships held, must be kept at the registered office of the company (ibid 1963 Act s.195 as inserted by 1990 Act s.51).

Shareholders may by ordinary resolution remove a director from the board before his period of office expires (ibid 1963 Act s.182). The office of director is normally deemed vacated if the director is adjudged bankrupt, makes an arrangement or composition with his creditors generally, becomes of unsound mind, or is absent for more than 6 months from board meetings without the board's consent (ibid Table A, art 91). See Glover v BLN Ltd (1973) IR 388; Carvill v Irish Industrial Bank Ltd (1968) IR 325; Healy v Healy Homes Ltd (1973) IR 309; In re City Equitable Fire Insurance Co (1925) Ch 407.

Where a company is *insolvent* in its winding up, the court must declare that any person who was a director at the commencement of the winding up or within the previous 12 months, must not be appointed as a director or secretary or take part in the promotion or formation of any company for 5 years, unless that company has a share capital of £100,000 if it is a public limited company (plc), or £20,000 if it is a private company, fully paid up in cash in each case (ibid 1990 Act s.150).

There are some exceptions eg that the person acted honestly and responsibly in relation to the conduct of the affairs of the company (ibid s.150(2)). Similar provisions apply where a company is in *receivership* (ibid s.154). In addition, the provisions concerning the disqualification of directors and other officers is widened (ibid s.160).

Directors have a duty to have regard to the interests of the company's employees (ibid 1990 Act s.52(1)). For duty of directors to their company, shareholders, creditors and employees, see MacCann in 9ILT & SJ (1991) 3, 30, 56, 80. For article on directors' remuneration and loans, see MacCann in 9 ILT & SJ (1991) 250 and 276. See also Building Societies Act 1989 ss.48-49. [Text: Doyle; McCann (2)]. See DISQUALIFICA-TION ORDER, COMPANY; FIDUCIARY; LOAN TO DIRECTOR; PROSPECTUS; REMUNERATION OF DIRECTORS; RESTRICTION ORDER; WORKER PAR-TICIPATION.

**directors' report.** The report that directors are required to make on the state of the company's affairs, the dividend they recommend and the amount they propose to carry to reserves; the report, which must be attached to the balance sheet laid before the annual general meeting, must be signed by two directors: Companies Act 1963 s.158.

In addition, the report must give a fair view of the development of the company's business, an indication of any important events which have occurred, of likely future developments in broad terms and of research and development undertaken by the company: Companies (Amendment) Act 1986 s.13. The report must also include particulars of the acquisition by the company of its own shares, or of the acquisition by other persons with financial assistance given by the company, and also of the forfeiture (qv) and surrender of shares and of shares being made subject to a lien (qv) or a charge (ibid s.14).

**directory entries.** A person is not liable for any payment by way of charge for inclusion in a directory of an entry relating to that person or his trade or business if the entry is unsolicited. It is an offence to make a demand for payment therefor. See SGSS Act 1980 s.48. In relation to *invoices* see s.49.

**DIRT.** Deposit interest retention tax (qv).

**disability pension.** The Minister cannot, without considering all relevant factors, abate the disability pension of a person who has received damages: Breen v Minister for Defence (1990 SC) ITLR (5 Nov).

**disability, person under.** A person who lacks legal capacity eg a minor (qv) or a person of unsound mind (qv). Where a person is under a disability, time does not run as regards the Statute of Limitations, until the person ceases to be under a disability: Statute of Limitations (Amdt) Act 1991 s.5; Rohan v Bord na Mona (1990) 2 IR 425. See LIMITATION OF ACTIONS.

**disabled and education.** See DEPENDENT CHILD; EDUCATION.

**disabled and housing.** See BUILDING REGULATIONS; HOUSING.

**disabled driver.** There is provision for repayment of excise duty, value-added tax and remission of road tax in respect of a motor vehicle (and hydrocarbon oil) used by a severely and permanently disabled person where he could not drive the vehicle unless it was specially constructed or adapted to take account of the disablement: Finance Acts 1989 s.92 and 1991 s.124. There are also tax concessions for a disabled person as a passenger. See Wiley v Revenue Commissioners (1993 SC) ILRM 482. See SAFETY BELT.

**disabled person and employment.** Places of work must be arranged to take account of employees with disabilities: SI No 44 of 1993, reg.17, third schedule para 13 and fourth schedule para 10. This applies to places of work used for the first time after 1992, to places of work which undergo modifications after 1992, or to other places whenever required by the features of the workplace. See REHABILITATION.

**disabled person and separation.** The physical or mental disability of a spouse or any dependent child of the family is a consideration which the court must have regard for in providing for that spouse and/or child arising from the granting by the court of a decree of judicial separation (qv): Judicial Separation and Family Law Reform Act 1989 s.20(2)(e) and 20(4)(c).

**disabled person and severance.** A severance payment made to an employee on account of his disability is exempt from income tax: Income Tax Act 1967 s.115 and Cahill (Inspector of Taxes) v Harding (1991 HC) 9 ILT Dig 147.

**disabled person and tax.** See DISABLED DRIVER; INCOME TAX.

**disabled vehicle.** A vehicle which stands so substantially disabled (either through accident, break down or the removal of the engine or other such vital part) as to be no longer capable of being propelled mechanically; it is regarded as not being a *mechanically propelled vehicle* (qv): Road Traffic Act 1961 s.3(2).

**disabled voter.** A disabled person is entitled to vote from his home in elections if he is qualified as a *special voter* (qv). A disabled person who does not so qualify, may be authorised to vote at another polling station where it would be more convenient for the elector because of his disability. See Electoral (Amdt) (No 2) Act 1986; Electoral Act 1992 s.100.

A blind or otherwise physically handicapped person may have his ballot paper marked for him by either a companion or the presiding officer; an illiterate person may also have his ballot paper marked for him by the presiding officer: ibid 1992 Act s.103; Referendum Act 1942 first sch r.18 as amended by Electoral Act 1963 s.75. See also Referendum (Amdt) (No 2) Act 1992. See VOTERS, SPECIAL.

**disabling statute.** Legislation which restricts a pre-existing right. See ENABLING ACT.

**disbar.** To expel a barrister from the Honorable Society of King's Inns. A barrister may apply to have himself disbarred eg in order to become a solicitor. See BARRISTER; KING'S INNS, HONORABLE SOCIETY OF.

**discharge.** To release from an obligation; to release a person from prison.

**discharge from bankruptcy.** See BANKRUPTCY, DISCHARGE FROM.

**discharge of bill.** Release from the obligations of a *bill of exchange* which occurs when all the rights and obligations attached to it are released, in one of the following ways: by payment in due course; by remuneration; by cancellation; by material alteration; by delivery up. See Bills of Exchange Act 1882 ss.59 and 61-64. See PAYMENT IN DUE COURSE.

**discharge of contract.** The release from the obligations of a contract which may arise by performance, agreement, release, rescission, accord and satisfaction, breach, impossibility of performance, frustration, merger, judgment of a court, or bankruptcy (qqv).

**disciplinary proceedings.** Disciplinary hearings must observe the requirements of natural justice: Ryan v VIP Taxi Co-Operative (1989) ITLR (10 Apr). Where the High Court is reviewing disciplinary proceedings in which the issues on review are direct issues of fact, it must itself decide those contested issues of fact; it may mot merely endorse the findings of fact of the disciplinary body: Kerrigan v An Bord Altranais (1990 SC) ITLR (30 Jul). An employee is entitled to know the nature and extent of any proposed disciplinary action against him: Deegan & Ors v Dunnes Stores (1992 EAT) ELR 184. See ADMINISTRATIVE TRIBUNAL; GARDA, DISCIPLINE OF; PROFESSIONAL DISCIPLINARY BODIES.

**discipline in school.** Teachers in schools are required to have a lively regard for the improvement and general welfare of their pupils, to treat them with kindness combined with firmness and to aim at governing them through their affections and reason and not by harshness and severity; ridicule, sarcasm or remarks likely to undermine a pupil's self-confidence are prohibited: Department of Education Circular 9/82 of January 1982. The enforcement of discipline in a national school has been held to be a matter for the teachers and the board of management; "it is not a matter for the courts, whose function, at most, is to ensure that the disciplinary complaint was dealt with fairly": Murtagh & Murtagh v Board of Management of St Emer's National School (1991 SC) ILRM 549. See CORPORAL PUNISHMENT.

**disclaimer.** A renunciation. See ONEROUS PROPERTY.

**disclaimer clause.** See EXCLUSION CLAUSE.

**disclosure in criminal proceedings.** In the UK, it has been held that there is a common law duty on the prosecution to disclose relevant evidence, which duty exists irrespective of any request by the defence and which continues throughout the trial: Judith Ward (1992) 142 NLJ 859. See BOOK OF EVIDENCE.

**disclosure of interest.** See ARMS LENGTH, AT; CONFLICT OF INTEREST; COUNCILLOR, DISCLOSURE OF INTEREST.

**disclosure of invention.** An essential element in an application for a patent; a failure to *disclose* the invention is also a ground for the revocation of a patent which has been granted: Patents Act 1992 ss.19 and 57-58. See PATENT, APPLICATION FOR.

**disclosure order.** The order which a court may make to oblige any person whom the court believes to have relevant information about share or debenture ownership in a private company, to give such information to the court: Companies Act 1990 ss.97-104. A person with a defined *financial interest* in a company may apply to the court for such an order. The court will only make a *disclosure order* if it deems it just and equitable to do so and if it is of the opinion that the financial interest of the applicant is or will be prejudiced by the non-disclosure. See SHARES.

**discontinuance.** The voluntary putting to an end of an action by a plaintiff. The plaintiff may at any time before the receipt of the defendant's defence, or after receipt thereof before taking any other proceeding in the action, discontinue his action by producing to the proper officer a consent signed by all the parties: RSC O.26. There are no particular rules for discontinuing an action in the District Court. For Circuit Court provisions, see RCC O.18.

**discount, issue of shares at a.** The allotment of shares in a registered company at less than their *par* value. Such allotment is not permitted otherwise than for brokerage and commissions authorised by the Companies Act 1963 s.59: Companies Amendment Act 1983 s.27.

**discoverability test.** The concept that a *cause of action* in respect of a wrong, accrues on the date of discovery of damage caused by the wrong, rather that on the date of occurrence of the damage. This concept had not been incorporated into Irish law until 1991. The Law Reform Commission had recommended a discoverability test in respect of personal injuries: LRC 21-1987. See Statute of Limitations (Amdt) Act 1991. See CAUSE OF ACTION.

**discovert.** A woman who is unmarried or a widow.

**discovery of documents.** The process whereby the parties to an action disclose to each other on affidavit all documents in their possession or power, relating to matters in issue in the action. In High Court actions, discovery or inspection of documents is obtained by application to the Master by *notice of motion* (qv); discovery will not normally be ordered against a defendant before the plaintiff has issued his statement of claim or against a plaintiff before the defence is delivered unless in an exceptional case where it is considered necessary. See RSC O.31 r.12.

Discovery is also available as a substantive remedy against a defendant where that person has become inadvertently involved in a tortious activity and is in possession of information which will assist the plaintiff obtain justice; however this jurisdiction of the court must be used sparingly and only to seek the identity of the wrongdoer rather than factual information concerning the commission of the wrong: Megaleasing UK Ltd v Barrett (No 2) (1993 SC) ILRM 497.

Discovery is not allowed for the purpose of *fishing* out a case and can be resisted on a number of grounds eg that the documents are protected by privilege (qv): eg Incorporated Law Society v Minister for Justice (1987) ILRM 42; PMPS Ltd v PMPA Insurance plc (1989 HC) ITLR (11 Dec); or that the documents do not pass the relevancy test (qv).

An order for discovery is complied with by an *affidavit of discovery*. Failure to comply with an order for discovery may lead to the action being dismissed or the defence being struck out: RSC O.31 r.21. Where privilege (qv) is claimed, the deponent in the affidavit of discovery, should list and briefly describe each document over which privilege is claimed, specifying in respect of each such document the precise basis or ground of privilege relied on: Bula Ltd v Tara Mines Ltd (1990 SC) ITLR (20 Aug); Bula Ltd v Crowley (1990 SC) ILRM 756.

Discovery is also permitted to be made against a *third party* (a stranger) not involved in the proceedings, in respect of relevant documents; the party seeking such order must indemnify the third party in respect of any costs reasonably incurred (ibid RSC O.31 r.29). This rule does not give the court power to make an order which would permit a party to search the files of a stranger to the action for the purpose of finding relevant documents; the party seeking the order must also serve notice of his motion on all parties to the action: Holloway v Belenos Publications (1987) ILRM 791; (1987) IR 405. Also the court must be satisfied that the third party is likely to have the documents in its possession, that they are relevant to the issues in the case, and that discovery is not unduly oppressive: Allied Irish Banks plc v Ernst & Whinney (1993 SC) 11 ILT Dig 116. See also Silver Hill Duckling v Minister for Agriculture (1987) ILRM 516; Fitzpatrick v Independent Newspapers Ltd (1988 HC) IR 132. See also RSC O.63 r.1(6).

In civil proceedings, documents may be discovered which were brought into being in the course of investigations by the gardai of the incident which gave rise to the civil proceedings: Walsh v Peters (1993 CC) 11 ILT & S.J 182 applying DPP v Holly (1984) ILRM 149.

In Northern Ireland, it has been held that there is a distinction made between discovery in judicial review (qv) and in plenary actions: In re Glor na nGael (1991 HC of J) ITLR (19 Aug).

For Circuit Court provisions on discovery and inspection, see RCC O.29. In the District Court, notice may be given to a party *to produce* documents, although there is no specific provision in the rules of this court dealing with discovery. See CONSUMER AFFAIRS, DIRECTOR OF; LEGISLATION, MOTIVATION FOR; NOTICE TO PRODUCE; PUBLIC POLICY; RELEVANCY TEST; STAY OF EXECTION.

**discretion to prosecute.** It is for the Director of Public Prosecution (qv) to decide whether or not to prosecute an individual for an alleged indictable offence (qv). Such a decision is not reviewable by the courts: The State (McCormack) v Curran (1987) ILRM 225.

**discretionary trust.** A trust where

property is vested in trustees who have a discretion as to which members of a specified class, such as the children of the settlor or testator, they will pay the income of the trust property or transfer the capital to and in what proportions. It is a trust whereby a beneficiary has no right to any part of the income of the trust property and where the trustees have discretionary power to pay him such income as they deem fit, eg a conveyance to trustees of land to apply the rents and profits *for the benefit of X in the absolute discretion of the trustees.*

Provision has been made by the courts for an adult child, who was seriously mentally ill, by means of a discretionary trust of which all the testator's children would be benificiaries: In re FF, HL v Bank of Ireland (1978) HC. See also MPD v MD (1981) ILRM 179; L v L (1984) ILRM 607. See TRUST.

**discrimination.** The Constitution provides that all citizens shall, as human persons, be held equal before the law: 1937 Constitution, art.40(1). Statute law provides that it is unlawful to discriminate on grounds of sex or marital status in recruitment for employment, in training or in work experience, in opportunities for promotion or in conditions of employment: Employment Equality Act 1977 s.2.

Discrimination is taken to occur (a) where by reason of his sex or marital status a person is treated less favourably than a person of the other sex or (b) where by reason of his sex or marital status a person is obliged to comply with a requirement which is not an essential requirement for membership of certain specified bodies or for employment or (c) where a person is penalised for having in good faith taken action to protect his employment rights (ibid s.3). It is also an offence to publish or display an advertisement which relates to employment which is discriminatory.

A person proposing to refer a dispute concerning discrimination to the Labour Court is entitled to seek from his employer a written explanation for the act believed by the employee to constitute the discrimination (ibid s.28).

The Act does not apply to employment in the Defence Forces, the Garda Siochana, the prison service, a private residence or employment by a close relative or where the sex of the person is an occupational qualification for the job eg female model. See Murphy v Attorney General (1980) SC; The State (Aer Lingus) v The Labour Court (1987) ILRM 373 & (1990) 8 ILT Dig 238; Aer Lingus Teo v Labour Court (1990) ELR 113; Vavasour v EEA (1991 LC) ELR 199; North Western Health Board v Martyn (1988 SC) ILRM 519; Cadwell v Labour Court (1989) IR 280; Natham v Bailey Gibson Ltd (1992 HC) reported by Flynn in 11 ILT & SJ (1993) 96. See also UN Convention on the Elimination of all Forms of Discrimination Against Women 1979 acceded to by Ireland in 1985 with some reservations: see Mullally in 10 ILT & SJ (1992) 6. See also Pensions Act 1990 ss.65-81. [Text: Curtin]. See ADVERTISEMENT; EQUAL PAY; EQUALITY BEFORE THE LAW; INDIRECT DISCRIMINATION; INTERVIEW, EMPLOYMENT; LABOUR COURT; MENSTRUATION; NON-DISCRIMINATION NOTICE; OMBUDSMAN; PENSION SCHEMES; RELIGIOUS FREEDOM; SEXUAL HARASSMENT; VICTIMISATION; WORK, RIGHT TO; WORKERS, FREEDOM OF MOVEMENT OF.

**disentailing deed.** See FEE TAIL.

**disfigurement.** A ground for damages in respect of injuries where suffered as a result of the negligence of another. A plaintiff is entitled to damages for the embarrassment she would suffer in the future as a woman with a major disfigurement and her inability to wear without major embarrassment various quite ordinary types of clothing: Rooney v Connolly (1987) ILRM 768. See FACIAL INJURIES.

**disfranchise.** To deprive of a right. See FRANCHISE; FELONY.

**disherison.** Disinheriting. See DISINHERITING DISPOSITION.

**dishonesty.** The Law Reform Commission has recommended that a range of larceny (qv) offences be replaced by one offence of dishonest appropriation or theft. See The Law Relating to Dishonesty (LRC 43 of 1992). See DISQUALIFICATION ORDER, COMPANY.

**dishonour of bill.** A *bill of exchange* is dishonoured if the drawee refuses to accept it or having accepted it fails to pay it: Bills of Exchange Act 1882 s.47. *Dishonour* gives the holder an immediate right of recourse against the drawer and endorsers of the bill; but notice of such dishonour must be given to those whom the holder wishes to hold liable. Where a *foreign bill* is dishonoured, formal notice of dishonour must be given by the process of *noting and protesting* (qv). See Walex & Co v Seafield Gentex Ltd (1978) IR 167; Spicer-Cowan Ireland Ltd v Play Print Ltd (1980) HC. See CHEQUE, COUNTERMAND OF; CHEQUE, DISHONOUR OF.

**disinheriting disposition.** A voluntary disposition by a deceased within three years before his death of his property for the purpose of defeating the share of his spouse, as a legal right (qv) or on intestacy, or of leaving his children insufficiently provided for. It includes a *donatio mortis causa* (qv). The court may order that such a disposition be deemed to be a gift made by will and to form part of the estate of the deceased. See Succession Act 1965 s.121; also MPD v MD (1981) ILRM 179.

**dismissal, constructive.** See CONSTRUCTIVE DISMISSAL.

**dismissal for want of prosecution.** The dismissal of an action, which the defendant may apply to the court for, where there has been no proceedings for two years; or where the plaintiff in a *plenary* summons has failed to deliver a statement of claim (qv) within the specified time; or where the plaintiff fails to comply with any order to answer interrogatories or for discovery or inspection of documents; or where the plaintiff fails to serve notice of trial after the close of pleadings; or where there is no attendance of the plaintiff at the trial. The balance of justice will be considered by the court in making a decision to dismiss for want of prosecution: Sweeney v Horan's (Tralee) Ltd (1987) ILRM 240. See also Toal v Duignan (1991) ILRM 135,140; Celtic Ceramics Ltd v IDA (1993 HC) ILRM 248 and (1993 SC). See RSC O.31 r.21; O.36 rr.12, 13, 32; O.122 r.11.

In Circuit Court proceedings, the defendant may apply for a similar order (a) if the plaintiff does not serve notice of trial within six weeks after service and entry of the defence or (b) if there is no appearance at the trial by the plaintiff. See RCC O.30 rr.5 and 13. A dismissal for want of prosecution is not a bar to a future action on the same cause of action. See DELAY; LIMITATION OF ACTIONS.

**dismissal of action.** The dismissal of proceedings to which a defendant may be entitled to eg where the *statement of claim* (qv) discloses no cause of action, or the proceedings constitute an *abuse* of the process of the court. The High Court has an inherent jurisdiction to dismiss an action on the basis that, on the admitted facts, it could not succeed: Barry v Buckley (1981) IR 306. However, the court should be slow to dismiss such an action and should not do so where the statement of claim admits of an amendment which might save the action: Sun Fat Chan v Osseus Ltd (1991 SC) ITLR (9 Dec). See Supreme Court of Judicature (Ireland) Act 1877 s.27(5). See also ABUSE OF PROCESS; DIRECTION; DISMISSAL FOR WANT OF PROSECUTION.

**dismissal of employee.** See INCOMPETENCE; NOTICE, EMPLOYMENT; REASONABLENESS; SUMMARY DISMISSAL; TERMINATION OF EMPLOYMENT; UNFAIR DISMISSAL; WRONGFUL DISMISSAL.

**dismissal, summary.** See SUMMARY DISMISSAL.

**dismissal, unfair.** See UNFAIR DISMISSAL.

**dismissal, wrongful.** See WRONGFUL DISMISSAL.

**dismissal of garda.** See GARDA, DISMISSAL OF.

**disorderly conduct.** Under draft legislation, it is proposed to be an offence for any person in a public place to engage in any shouting, singing or boisterous conduct between midnight and 7am, or at any other time after being requested by a garda to desist, in circumstances likely to give reasonable cause for annoyance to others: Criminal Justice (Public Order) Bill 1993 s.5. It will also be an offence for a person to act in a disorderly manner at a public meeting (ibid s.8), or to distribute or display material in a public place which is threatening, abusive, insulting or obscene (ibid s.7), or to use or engage in any threatening, abusive or insulting words or behaviour in a public place (ibid s.6). A garda will be empowered to give a direction to a person to leave immediately the vicinity of the place concerned (ibid s.9). See VIOLENT DISORDER.

**disorderly house.** Any house, room,

168

garden or place kept or used for any of the purposes of public music, singing or other public entertainment of a like kind, without a licence: Public Health Acts Amendment Acts 1890 s.51(5).

**disparagement of property.** See SLANDER OF TITLE.

**display screen equipment.** Any alphanumeric or graphic display screen, regardless of the display process involved: Safety Health & Safety at Work (General Application) Regulations 1993 (SI No 44 of 1993) reg.29. See WORKSTATION.

**disponer.** In relation to a disposition (qv), *disponer* means the person who directly or indirectly provided the property comprised in the disposition: Capital Acquisitions Tax Act 1976 s.2.

**disposal.** In relation to waste, includes the collection, sorting, carriage, treatment, storage and tipping above or under ground, and the transformation operations necessary for its recovery, reuse or recycling: Environmental Protection Agency Act 1992 s.3(1). See EMISSION; WASTE OPERATION; WASTE OIL, DISPOSAL OF.

**disposal of goods.** As to reservation of the right of disposal of goods by the seller, see Sale of Goods Act 1893 s.19.

**disposition.** The passing of property, whether by act of parties or act of law. For capital acquisition tax purposes, includes a will, an intestacy, a donatio mortis causa (qv) or gift made within two years of the disponer's death: Capital Acquisitions Tax Act 1976 s.2. A *testamentary disposition* is a will or other testamentary instrument or act: Succession Act 1965 s.101. See CONSTRUCTION OF DISPOSITION; ISSUE.

**dispute.** A conflict of claims or rights. See ALTERNATIVE DISPUTES RESOLUTION.

**dispute, trade.** See TRADE DISPUTE.

**disqualification.** A deprivation of a right, power or privilege. Disqualification from holding a driving licence is mandatory in the case of certain offences: Road Traffic Act 1961 ss.26-27. Conviction of certain offences may disqualify a person from serving on a jury: Juries Act 1976 s.8. Conviction of a felony (qv) or treason (qv) can result in disqualification from certain public offices. Conviction of offences can also lead to disqualification from being a director of a company or of a building society or from pursuing a particular profession eg Companies Act

1990 ss.149-169; Unit Trust Act 1972 s.16; Auctioneers & House Agents Act 1947 s.18; Solicitors Act 1954 s.34; Health (Nursing Homes) Act 1990 s.6(4); Electoral Act 1992 s.41(j). See SCHEDULED OFFENCE.

**disqualification order, company.** An order that a person shall not be appointed or act as an auditor, director or other officer, receiver, liquidator or examiner or be in any way, directly or indirectly, concerned or take part in the promotion, formation or management of any company: Companies Act 1990 s.159. The order will be made by the court where it is satisfied that the person has been guilty of any fraud or breach of duty in relation to a company or has been made personally liable for the company's debts or his conduct is such as to make him unfit to be concerned in the management of the company or where the person has been persistently in default in relation to certain reporting requirements of the Companies Acts (ibid s.160(2)).

A person is deemed to be subject to a disqualification order for 5 years where he is convicted on indictment of any indictable offence in relation to the company, or involving fraud or dishonesty (ibid s.160(1)). A person who is subject to a disqualification order may apply to the court for relief (ibid s.160(8)). See also ibid s.144. There are penalties and civil consequences for breaching a disqualification order or for acting under the direction of a disqualified person (ibid ss.161, 163-165) See also Building Societies Act 1989 s.64.

**disqualification order, driving.** An order disqualifying a person from driving a motor vehicle which is either a *consequential* disqualification or an *ancilliary* disqualification and which normally comes into operation on the fifteenth day after it is made and an application for removal of which may be made three or two months respectively from the date of the beginning of the period of disqualification: Road Traffic Act 1961 s.29 as amended by the Road Traffic Act 1968 s.19.

Disqualification is not a primary punishment but an adjudication on the person's fitness to drive: Conroy v AG (1965) IR 411; consequently, in an application for removal of a disqualification, the court will consider the applicant's fitness to drive, the nature of the offence and his conduct since the original conviction: DPP v O'Byrne (1989) ITLR (19 Jun).

Under draft legislation, it is proposed that a person found guilty of certain specified drink driving and other road traffic offences will be automatically disqualified from holding a driving licence for a minimum period and also until a certificate of competency (driving test) or a certificate of fitness is obtained (ibid 1961 Act s.26 to be replaced by Road Traffic Bill 1993 s.26). It is also proposed to increase the minimum period which must pass before an application may be made to the court to review a disqualification order (ibid 1961 Act s.29 to be replaced by 1993 Bill s.27).

**disregard clause.** Generally understood to mean a clause in a lease (qv) whereby the review of rent provided for in the lease must not take into consideration any future rent reviews, notwithstanding that provision may have been made for such reviews to be carried out on a regular basis. See RENT REVIEW CLAUSE.

**diss; dissentiente.** Delivering a dissenting judgment. See NEM DIS.

**dissection.** Dissection of the human corpse was originally a punishment for the crime of murder: Geo.3, c.17 (1791). It was abolished as a punishment by the Anatomy Act 1832 (2 & 3 Will.4, c.75). Bodies can be handed over for dissection unless the deceased or a surviving spouse objects: 1832 Act & 1871 Act (34 & 35 Vict, c.16). There is provision for the appointment of an Inspector of Anatomy to whom anatomists are accountable for bodies in their possession. See SI No 256 of 1949, sch, pt 1. See also Doherty in ISLR Vol 2 (1992) 84.

**disseisin.** The wrongful putting out of a person seised of a freehold. See SEISIN.

**dissolution.** Breaking up; bringing to an end; eg dissolution of a partnership under the Partnership Act 1890 ss.32-35 or of a company under the Companies Act 1963. The dissolution of Dail Eireann is performed by the President of Ireland on the advice of the Taoiseach: 1937 Constitution art.13(2). A general election for the Dail must be held within thirty days of the dissolution (ibid art.16(3)(2)). The clerk of the Dail is required

immediately on dissolution to issue a writ to each returning officer (qv) directing him to cause an election to be held of the full number of members of the Dail: Electoral Act 1992 s.39(1) and fourth schedule.

The Seanad is not dissolved with the dissolution of the Dail; members of the Seanad hold office until the day before the polling day for the panels for the new Seanad (ibid Constitution art.18(9)). It has been held that the Courts have no jurisdiction to place any impediment between the President and the Taoiseach in relation to the dissolution of the Dail: O'Malley v An Taoiseach (1990 HC) ILRM 460. See FINANCIAL RESOLUTIONS; PRESIDENT OF IRELAND; PRESIDENTIAL COMMISSION; SEANAD EIREANN; WINDING UP.

**distinctive mark.** For the purposes of registration of a mark in Part A (qv) of the register of trade marks, a mark is *distinctive* if it is *adapted* to distinguish the goods with which the proprietor of the trade mark is or may be connected in the *course of trade*, from goods in the case of which no such connection subsists: Trade Marks Act 1963 s.17(2). Registration of *Dunlop Weather coat*, *Mothercare, Bond Street* as marks were refused on the ground that the words were not adapted to distinguish the goods to which they referred from the goods of others.

Marks which are refused registration in Part A may be registered in Part B (qv) if they meet the lesser requirement of being *capable* of distinguishing the applicant's goods from the goods of others (ibid s.25(3)). See British Colloids v Controller of Industrial Property (1943) IR 56; Ideal Weatherproofs Ltd v Irish Dunlop Ltd (1938) IR 295; In re Mothercare Ltd (1968) IR 359; Philip Morris Inc (1970) IR 82; Waterford Glass Ltd v Controller of Patents, Designs and Trade Marks (1984) ILRM 565. See TRADE MARK.

**distinguishing a case.** Where a court does not follow a previous decision and does not overrule it, (because it considers that there are important differences between that the decision and the case on which it was based and the case it is now considering), the previous case is said to be *distinguished*. See PRECEDENT.

**distortion of competition.** See COMPE-

TITION, DISTORTION OF.

**distrain.** To seize goods by way of distress (qv).

**distress.** (1) A ground for damages in fatal injury cases.

(2) The act of taking movable property out of the possession of a wrongdoer, to compel the performance of an obligation, or to procure satisfaction for a wrong committed. As to goods the subject of a hire-purchase agreement, see the Law of Distress Amendment Act 1908 s.4 and the Hire-Purchase Act 1946 s.17. Distress may not be levied on the goods of a bankrupt (qv) or an arranging debtor (qv) after the date of adjudication or order for protection: Bankruptcy Act 1988 s.139. Distress is a form of legal *self-help* eg distress for rent due. However, a landlord is now prohibited from using distress as a means of enforcing payment of rent due on a premises let solely as a dwelling: Housing (Miscellaneous Provisions) Act 1992 s.19. Distress also refers to the goods seized. Generally the law does not look favourably on distress. For *distress warrants* for revenue offences, see Murphy v D J Wallace (1990 HC) ITLR (24 Dec). See MENTAL DISTRESS; FATAL INJURIES.

**distress damage feasant.** The seizure and detention of animals or other chattels which are unlawfully on a person's land by the occupier thereof and which have caused damage thereto, in order to compel the owner to make reasonable compensation for the damage done. The right of distress damage feasant is no longer available for animals as the Summary Jurisdiction (Ireland) Act 1851 provided that animals are to be returned to their owner where known, or taken to a local pound where unknown, and compensation in the former case claimed on a scale specified in the Act. Pounds are regulated by the Pounds Act 1935. See also Animals Act 1985 ss.5 and 7. See Pounds (Amendment) Regulations 1990 (SI No 4 of 1990).

**distribution.** The division of the personal property of an *intestate* among his next-of-kin, the rules for which were laid down in the Statute of Distribution 1695, now replaced by the Succession Act 1965. See INTESTATE SUCCESSION.

**distribution, company.** See DIVIDEND.

**District Court.** The lowest court in the hierarchical system of courts, with *original* jurisdiction in civil matters and jurisdiction to hear *summary* offences (qv) and, in certain instances, *indictable* offences (qv). The country is divided into over 200 District Court areas. Cases are heard by a judge sitting alone without a jury. On civil matters, the court can award damages of up to £5,000; it has jurisdiction over a wide range of matters but has no jurisdiction in actions in tort for defamation, slander of title, malicious prosecution or false imprisonment. Where the parties consent in civil matters the District Court has unlimited jurisdiction: Courts Act 1991 s.4(c).

An appeal from the District Court lies to the Circuit Court (qv). See District Court Rules. See Jurisdiction of Courts and Enforcement of Judgments (European Communities) Act 1988 s.14 and District Court Rules 1988 (SI No 173 of 1988). [Text: Woods]. See CIVIL PROCESS; REMITTAL OF ACTION; SMALL CLAIMS PROCEDURE.

**District Court, preliminary examination.** In criminal matters, where a defendant is entitled to elect for trial by jury, the District Court conducts a *preliminary examination* to determine if there is sufficient evidence to return the defendant for trial by jury to a higher court. If the judge is not satisfied he *discharges* the defendant. A defective preliminary examination in the District Court invalidates the entire criminal proceedings against an accused: Glavin v Governor of Mountjoy Prison (1991 SC) ITLR (25 Mar).

There is a prohibition on publication of information about a preliminary examination other than a statement of the fact that such examination has been held, the name of the person, the charge and the decision thereon: Criminal Procedure Act 1967 s.17.

In cases involving physical or sexual abuse, evidence may be given at the preliminary examination by means of a video recording of the statements of the alleged victim (under 14 years of age or where mentally handicapped) during an interview with a garda or other competent person: Criminal Evidence Act 1992 s.15. Notice must be given to the accused and the alleged victim must be available for cross-examination. Such a video recording, together with a video recording of evidence given through a live television link at the preliminary examination, is admissible at the trial of the accused, so that young witnesses or witnesses with a mental handicap may not be required to give evidence again (ibid s.16).

It has been held that the statutory power of the Director of Public Prosecutions to return a person for jury trial after his discharge by the District Court is unconstitutional: Costello v Director of Public Prosecutions (1984) ILRM 413. See Criminal Procedure Act 1967 Part II as amended by Courts (No 2) Act 1986 s.8. See also Criminal Justice Act 1993 s.11. See INDICTMENT; LEGAL AID; PUBLICATION, RIGHT OF; TELEVISION LINK; VIDEO RECORDING.

**District Justice.** The former name of a judge of the district court, now called a "judge": Courts Act 1991 s.21 amending the Courts (Establishment and Constitution) Act 1961. See CHIEF JUSTICE; JUDGES.

**district probate registry.** A registry with authority to issue *grants of representation* in the name of the High Court, where the deceased had a fixed place of abode within the district where the application for the grant is made. There are currently 14 such registries controlled by County Registrars. See Succession Act 1965 ss.36 129. See RSC O.80. See PROBATE.

**distringas notice.** The name formerly given to the notice which a person, who claims to be interested in any stock (which includes shares, securities or dividends) of a company, may give to that company, whereupon it is not lawful for the company to permit the stock specified in the notice to be transferred or to pay the dividends, as long as the notice remains operative. The notice is now governed by RSC O.46 rr.5-13 which provides that the person must serve on the company an attested copy of an affidavit, which has been filed in the Central Office (qv), and a duplicate notice in a prescribed form. See STOP ORDER.

**disturbance.** Interference with the existence or exercise of a right eg by trespass or nuisance. See Fitzgerald v Forbank (1897) 2 Ch 96.

**disturbance, compensation for.** The compensation payable to a business tenant (qv) with a business equity of renewal, who is not entitled to a new tenancy in certain specified circumstances eg where the landlord is to pull down and rebuild or reconstruct the property or where the landlord requires vacant possession to carry out a scheme of development for which he has planning permission: Landlord and Tenant (Amendment) Act 1980. The amount of compensation will usually be the pecuniary loss, damage or expense which the tenant sustains or incurs or will sustain or incur by reason of his quitting the tenement (ibid s.58).

**divest.** To take away an estate or interest which had already vested.

**dividend.** (1) The amount payable upon each pound of a bankrupt's liabilities or of a company's liabilities to creditors in a winding up of the company. See RSC O.74 rr.112-116.

(2) Also in a company, the payment made out of profits to its shareholders. Also called a *distribution*. The directors' report to the annual general meeting must state the amount, if any, which the board recommends should be paid in dividends and how much is to be retained in the reserves: Companies Act 1963 s.158. The shareholders decide the dividend at the agm but it must not exceed the amount recommended by the directors (ibid Table A, art 116). Special classes of shareholder, such as those owning preference shares, may be entitled to be paid in priority to other classes, such as *ordinary* or *deferred* shareholders.

In all *registered* companies, distributions may only be made from the company's accumulated realised profits, so far as not previously utilised by distribution or capitalisation, less its accumulated realised losses, so far as not previously written-off in a reduction or reorganisation of capital ie current profits and any profits carried forward, less current losses and any losses carried forward: Companies Amendment Act 1983 s.45.

In a *public limited company* (plc), there is an additional safeguard requiring a balance sheet surplus, as distributions may only be made when the amount of the company's net assets is not less than the aggregate of its called-up share capital and its undistributable reserves ie the value of the company's assets less its liabilities must exceed its called-up share capital together with any undistributable reserves (ibid s.46). See DISTRINGAS NOTICE.

**divisible contract.** A contract which is made up of a series of separate obligations eg where the contract provides that payment is to be made during the process of the contract. An *entire* or *indivisible* contract is one where neither party may demand performance until he is ready to fulfil, or has fulfilled, his obligation. See Verolme Cork Dockyards Ltd v Shannon Atlantic Fisheries Ltd (1978) HC.

**division of company.** The dissolution of a company by the acquisition of its assets and liabilities by more than one other company; such division may be a division by acquisition or by formation of new companies. A *division by acquisition* is an operation whereby two or more companies (the acquiring companies) of which one or more but not all may be a new company, acquire between them all the assets and liabilities of another company in exchange for the issue to the shareholders of that company of shares in one or more of the acquiring companies with or without any cash payment and with a view to the dissolution of the company being acquired.

A *division by formation of new companies* means a similar operation whereby the acquiring companies have been formed for the purposes of such acquisitions. Regulations now govern such divisions of companies since 1987 in respect of plcs and some specified unregistered companies: European Communities (Mergers and Divisions of Companies) Regulations 1987. See also MERGER, COMPANY.

**divisional court.** See HIGH COURT.

**divorce.** The termination of a valid marriage (qv) otherwise than by death or annulment. No law can be enacted providing for the grant of a dissolution of marriage: 1937 Constitution, art.41(3)(2). A referendum (qv) in 1986 to remove this constitutional prohibition on divorce was defeated. The prohibition however does not prevent the courts from granting a *decree of nullity* which is a declaration that no valid marriage ever existed, or from granting a *judicial separation* (qv), or from upholding *separation agreements* (qv), or from recognising foreign divorces. However, only in the case of a decree of nullity or a recognised foreign divorce may the parties remarry. The government has proposed that, following the enactment of legislative proposals in the area of family law, there should be a further divorce referendum: 1992 White Paper on Marital Breakdown. The referendum is planned for 1994. [Text: Brown; Shatter]. See BIGAMY; DIVORCE A MENSA ET THORO; JUDICIAL SEPARATION; MARRIAGE, NULLITY OF.

**divorce, foreign, recognition of.** A foreign divorce is recognised in the State if the parties were *domiciled* (qv) in the place where the divorce was granted: Bank of Ireland v Caffin (1971) IR 123. Formerly, a married woman's domicile was deemed to be that of her husband, but now she is entitled to an independent domicile: Domicile and Recognition of Foreign Divorces Act 1986 ss.1-3. The former presumption was held to be unconstitutional: CM v TM (1991) ILRM 268; W v W (1993 SC) ILRM 294. A foreign decree of divorce is recognised in the State if either spouse is domiciled within the jurisdiction of the foreign court which grants the divorce decree, at the date of the institution of the divorce proceedings (ibid 1986 Act s.5).

Ancillary foreign matrimonial orders which are severable from the foreign divorce (eg maintenance orders) will be enforced in the State but not otherwise: contrast Mayo-Perrott v Mayo-Perrott (1958) IR 336 and Mahon v Mahon (1978) HC. On the granting of a foreign divorce absolute to a husband, it has been held that his wife has no right to claim maintenance (qv) for herself or her children under the Family Law (Maintenance of Spouses and Children) Act 1976, but can claim for maintenance for her children under the Guardianship of Infants Act 1964: CM v TM (1978) HC applying T v T (1983) IR 29; LB v HB (1980) ILRM 257. See Kaczorowska in 11 ILT & SJ (1993) 39. See LRC 10 and 20 of 1985. See also 1937 Constitution, art.41(3)(3).

**divorce a mensa et thoro.** [Judicial separation from table and board]. Formerly, a judicial separation which did not dissolve a marriage (qv) but relieved the parties thereto of the obligation to cohabit with each other. Such a judicial separation was granted on the ground of *adultery* (qv) or of unnatural practices or of the *legal cruelty* of the other party. Legal cruelty was conduct which caused danger to the life or health, physical or mental, of the other party. See McA v McA (1981) ILRM 361.

The decree of divorce a mensa et thoro has been abolished; it has been replaced by a decree of *judicial separation*: Judicial Separation and Family Law Reform Act 1989. See LRC 8 of 1983. See ALIMONY; CONDONATION; CONNIVANCE; DIVORCE; JUDICIAL SEPARATION; MARRIAGE, NULLITY OF; RECRIMINATION; SEPARATION AGREEMENT; UNWORTHINESS TO SUCCEED.

**divorce a vinculo matrimonii.** [Divorce from the bond of matrimony]. See DIVORCE.

**DNA.** [Deoxyribo nucleic acid]. The basic genetic material, made up of long chains of amino acids, found in all animal cells, the precise configuration and formation of which controls the development and functioning of most living things. A genetic profile of a person is obtainable by the examination of his skin, hair or bodily fluids. For example of the use of DNA in a paternity suit, see JPD v MG (1991) ILRM 212. See also R v Cramer (1988) 10 Cr App 485; DPP v Barr (No 2) (1993 CCA) 11 ILT Dig 185. See Fennell in 8ILT & SJ (1990) 227. See BODILY SAMPLE; GENETIC FINGERPRINTING.

**doctrines of equity.** See EQUITY, DOCTRINES OF.

**document.** Something upon which there is writing, printing or inscriptions and which gives information.

**document of title.** A document which enables the possessor to deal with the property described in it as if he were the owner eg a bill of lading: Factors Act 1889 s.1(4).

**document, unstamped.** See UNSTAMPED DOCUMENT.

**documentary evidence.** In an exception to the hearsay rule, information contained in a document is prima facie admissible in criminal proceedings as evidence of any facts contained in it; the information must have been compiled, whether on computer or otherwise, in the course of a *business* and must have been supplied, either directly or indirectly, by someone who had, or may reasonably be supposed to have had, personal knowledge of the matters dealt with in the document recording the information: Criminal Evidence Act 1992 s.5. "Business" is very widely defined eg trade, profession, or other occupation, performance of functions by persons or bodies paid or financed out of public funds and by EC and international institutions (ibid s.4).

A certificate is required stating that the conditions for admissibility have been fulfilled (ibid s.6); advance notice must be given to the other party (ibid s.7); evidence may be given as to the credibility of the supplier of the information (ibid s.9); and the court may exclude the evidence or, if included, estimate the weight to be given to it (ibid s.8).

Certain documents are inadmissible such as those covered by legal professional privilege or containing information supplied by a person who is not compellable to give evidence (ibid s.5(3)). All documents which are admissible (not just under s.5) may be given in evidence by producing an authenticated copy; this includes films, sound recordings, video recordings, and a fax copy (ibid s.30). See MEDICAL PRACTITIONER.

**documents, construction of.** Rules are laid down by statute and by the courts for the interpretation of documents eg planning documents are to be construed in their ordinary meaning as it would be understood by a member of the public, unless such documents read as a whole indicate some other meaning: In re JS Investments (1987) ILRM 659. See CONSTRUCTION, RULES OF; CONSTRUCTION SUIT; CONTRA PROFERENTUM; PUNCTUATION; TRANSPOSING OF WORDS.

**documents, discovery of.** See DISCOVERY OF DOCUMENTS.

**documents, joinder of.** See JOINDER OF DOCUMENTS.

**documents, presumptions as to.** Where a document, which is at least 30 years old, is produced from proper custody, there is a presumption in law that the signature and handwriting thereon is genuine; attestation (qv) or execution need not be proved. Where a deed has been proved to have been signed and attested, it is presumed to have been sealed and delivered, even though no impression of seal appears thereon. An alteration in a deed is presumed to have been made prior to execution, and in a will is presumed to have been made after execution. There is no presumption about documents not under seal, except the presumption of legality ie that they were made so as not to commit an offence.

**dogs.** Under the Control of Dogs Act 1986 responsibility for the control of dogs is delegated to the local authorities; they are required to employ dog wardens and erect dog shelters. Dogs are required to be kept under effectual control and dog wardens are empowered to seize stray dogs.

It is unlawful for a person to keep a dog without a licence (ibid s.2). There is provision for dealing with dangerous dogs (ibid s.22). It is a good defence to an action for shooting a dog if the defendant proves that the dog was worrying, or was about to worry livestock (ibid s.23). There is provision for the District Court to deal with the nuisance of excessive barking of a dog (ibid s.25).

There is also *strict liability* (qv) in damages for any damage caused by a dog and it is no longer necessary to show a previous *mischevious propensity* in the dog (ibid s.21(1)). Apart from this statutory remedy, the owner or keeper of a dog may be liable in negligence (qv) – see Kavanagh v Stokes (1942) IR 596; or in trespass (eg if he commanded the dog to attack). See SI Nos 30 and 59 of 1987 and 255 of 1988.

The 1986 Act was amended in 1992 to provide additional powers to deal more effectively with dangerous dogs, to increase licence fees, and to amend the earlier Act where it had been found to be deficient: Control of Dogs (Amdt) Act 1992. See ANIMALS; BEWARE OF DOG SIGN; DANGEROUS DOGS; GUARD DOG; SCIENTER; STRAY DOG.

**dole.** A share; the popular name given to unemployment benefit and assistance. See SOCIAL WELFARE LAW.

**doli capax.** [Capable of crime]. See DOLI INCAPAX.

**doli incapax.** [Incapable of crime]. There is an irrebuttable presumption that a child under the age of 7 years is incapable of committing a crime. A minor between the age of 7 and 14 years is presumed to be doli incapax, but the presumption is rebuttable by evidence of *mischievous discretion* ie knowledge that what was done was morally wrong. Formerly, a boy under 14 years of age was irrebuttably presumed incapable of rape or of an attempt thereat. Now the rule of law which treated a male person by reason of his age as being physically incapable of committing an offence of a sexual nature is abolished: Criminal Law (Rape) (Amendment) Act 1990 s.6. A minor on reaching his fourteenth birthday becomes fully responsible for his criminal behaviour. See Cashman v Cork County Council (1950) Ir Jur Rep 7; Goodbody v Waterford Corporation (1953) Ir Jur Rep 39; Monagle v Donegal Co Co (1961) Ir Jur Rep 47.

**domain.** The territory over which authority is exercised.

**domestic agreements.** Agreements made in the course of family life and which are not intended to create legal relations. See Balfour v Balfour (1919) 2 KB 571. See LEGAL RELATIONS, INTENTION TO CREATE.

**domestic animals.** See ANIMALS.

**domestic refuse.** See HOUSEHOLD REFUSE.

**domicile.** The place in which a person has a fixed and permanent home, and to which, whenever he is absent, he has the intention of returning. It depends on the physical fact of residence in addition to the intention of remaining. The domicile of a married woman was deemed to be that of her husband notwithstanding that she was permanently resident abroad: see Gaffney v Gaffney (1975) IR 133; this common law rule was held to be unconstitutional: CM v TM (1991) ILRM 268; W v W (1993 SC) ILRM 294. A married woman's domicile is now determined by the same factors as applied in the case of any person capable of having an independent domicile: Domicile and Recognition of Foreign Divorces Act 1986. See W v S (1987) HC; In re Fleming, deceased (1987) ILRM 638; Rowan v Rowan (1988) ILRM 65.

The domicile of a minor at common law was that of his father; but where the child was born after the father's death or where the parents were not married to each other, the domicile was that of the mother. The common law rules were amended by the 1986 Act to provide that the domicile of the minor is that of the mother where the mother and father are living apart and the minor has a home with the mother and not with the father (ibid 1986 Act s.3(1)).

An individual is domiciled in the state, or in a state other than a *contracting* state if, but only if, he is ordinarily resident in the state or in that other state: Jurisdiction of Courts and Enforcement of Foreign Judgments (European Communities) Act 1988 (first schedule, part 1) as amended and extended to EFTA countries by Jurisdiction of Courts and Enforcement of Foreign Judgments Act 1993. See LRC 7 of 1983. See DIVORCE, FOREIGN, RECOGNITION OF; SEAT OF CORPORATION; WILL, INTERNATIONAL.

**dominant position, abuse of.** Any *abuse* by one or more undertakings of a dominant position in trade for any goods or services in the State or in a substantial part of the State is prohibited: Competition Act 1991 s.5. "Abuse" may consist in:- imposing unfair purchase or selling prices; imposing unfair trading conditions; limiting production, markets or technical development; applying dissimilar conditions to equivalent transactions with other trading parties (ibid s.5(2)). Any person who is aggrieved in consequence of any prohibited abuse has a right of action for relief against any undertaking which has been a party to the abuse (ibid s.6). Relief is by way of an injunction, a declaration, and damages including exemplary damages (qv). An action in respect of a prohibited abuse may be brought in the Circuit Court (ibid s.6(2)(b)).

*Dominance* in EC law is a position of strength enjoyed by an undertaking which enables it to prevent effective competition being maintained on the relevant market by affording it the power to behave to an appreciable extent independently of its competitors, its customers and ultimately of the consumers: Hoffman – La Roche v EC Commission (1979) ECR 461 Case 85/76 cited in Master Foods Ltd t/a Mars Ireland v HB Ice Cream (1993 HC)

ILRM 145. See ABUSE OF MONOPOLY RIGHT; COMPETITION, DISTORTION OF.

**dominant tenement.** See EASEMENT.

**dominium.** Ownership.

**domitae naturae.** [Of tame disposition]. See ANIMALS.

**domus sua cuique est tutissimum refugium.** [To every person his house is his surest refuge]. See Seymayne's Case (1604) 5 Co Rep 91. See INVIOLABILITY OF DWELLING.

**dona clandestina sunt semper suspiciosa.** [Clandestine gifts are always to be regarded with suspicion].

**donatio mortis causa.** A gift of personal property in anticipation of death. To be a valid gift it must be made in contemplation of the donor's death, be intended to take effect from his existing illness (unless the donor indicates otherwise) and be completed by delivery at the time to the donee. See In re Beaumont (1902) 1 Ch 889. See also Judicial Separation and Family Law Reform Act 1989 ss.10 and 29. See proposed draft legislation, Matrimonial Home Bill 1993 s.2(1). See DISINHERITING DISPOSITION.

**donee.** A gratuitious recipient; a person who takes a gift (qv); a person who is given a power of appointment (qv).

**donor.** A giver; a person who makes a gift (qv); a person who makes a power of appointment (qv).

**doom; dome.** A judgment (qv).

**doorstep contracts.** Contracts between a consumer and trader when negotiations have been initiated away from business premises. An EC Directive has been adopted on doorstep contracts: Council Directive 85/577/EEC and implemented in the State by the European Communities (Cancellation of Contracts Negotiated Away from Business Premises) Regulations 1989, SI No 224 of 1989. See also Dunn in 7ILT & SJ (1989) 309. See also SGSS Act 1980 s.50. See COOLING OFF PERIOD.

**dormant partner.** A sleeping partner. See LIMITED PARTNERSHIP.

**dosage.** The court will not decide the appropriate level of dosage for a patient plaintiff where his doctor had acted bona fide and in the best interest of the patient and where the dosage was within an appropriate range advised in accordance with a practice approved by a reputable body of medical opinion: Hughes v Staunton (1991 HC) 9ILT Dig 52. See MEDICAL NEGLIGENCE.

**double employment.** Where an employee works for two or more employers on the same day. It is an offence for an employer to permit an employee to work for him on a day on which the employee has worked for another employer, where the aggregate hours worked for both employers exceeds the lawful maximum that the employee could work for the one employer. A young person can commit an offence in such a circumstance, as can a parent or guardian who aids or abets an employer. See Protection of Young Persons (Employment) Act 1977 s.16. See WORKING HOURS; CHILD, EMPLOYMENT OF; YOUNG PERSON.

**double insurance.** Insurance by the insured, with more than one insurer, of the one risk on the same interest in the same subject-matter. Provisions for dealing with double marine insurance is provided for by s.32 of the Marine Insurance Act 1906 s.32. See Zurich Insurance v Shield Insurance (1987) SC.

**double jeopardy.** The common law rule that a person should not face repeated prosecution for the same offence. However, it has been held that an appeal lies to the Supreme Court from an acquittal by direction of the trial judge in the Central Criminal Court: The People (Director of Public Prosecutions) v O'Shea (1982) IR 384. See AUTREFOIS ACQUIT.

**double portions, rule against.** The rule that where a father (or other person *in loco parentis*) makes provision for his child by will, and subsequently provides a portion (qv) inter vivos for the child, the portion is presumed to take the place of the legacy in whole or in part. Equity leans against double portions. See Succession Act 1965 s.63(9). See ADEMPTION; HOTCHPOT.

**double probate, grant of.** A grant of representation to another executor, whose rights had been reserved by the first executor, who is still alive and who has already extracted a grant of probate.

**double taxation agreement.** A tax treaty or convention; a bilateral agreement between the State and another state containing rules aimed at avoiding the taxation twice of income flowing from sources in one of the countries to residents of the other and vice versa, thereby facilitating the movement of capital, labour and commercial activity between the two states. The agreement may also provide for the relief or prevention of double taxation of capital gains or of capital. The government is empowered to make such agreements: Income Tax Act 1967 s.361 and Finance Act 1983 s.47.

The countries with which the State has double taxation agreements in force (August 1993) are: Australia, Austria, Belgium, Canada, Cyprus, Denmark, Finland, France, Germany, Italy, Japan, Korea, Luxembourg, The Netherlands, New Zealand, Norway, Pakistan, Sweden, Switzerland, United Kingdom, United States, Zambia. Proposed double taxation agreements are at various stages of negotiation with Hungary, Poland, Russia, and nearly concluded with Spain and Portugal.

There is an agreement to provide for the avoidance of double taxation of air transport undertakings and their employees between the State and the former USSR (SI No 349 of 1987). Also sea and air transport agreements have been agreed with Spain and South Africa (SIs No 26 of 1977 and No 210 of 1959 respectively).

It would appear that where there is conflict between a Double Taxation Agreement and domestic legislation, the former would prevail: Murphy v Asahi Synthetic Fibres (1986) ILRM 24.

**doubt, beyond reasonable.** See BEYOND REASONABLE DOUBT.

**dower.** The right which a widow had to a life estate in one third of her deceased husband's heritable freeholds, ie fee simple and fee tail, provided her husband died intestate, birth of heritable issue was possible, and the husband had not defeated the widow's right to dower under the Dower Act 1833. Abolished for registered land by the Registration of Title Act 1964 and abolished entirely by the Succession Act 1965 s.11. See CURTESY.

**DPP.** Director of Public Prosecutions (qv).

**draft.** (1) An order for the payment of a sum of money. (2) A rough copy of a document. See BANKERS' DRAFT.

**drain.** A road authority may construct and maintain drains in, on, under, through or to any land for the purpose of draining water from, or preventing water flowing onto, a public road (qv): Roads Act 1993 s.76(1)(a). See COMBINED DRAIN; SEWERS; TRADE EFFLUENT.

**dramatic work.** For the purpose of copyright protection, a dramatic work includes a choreographic work or entertainment in dumb show if reduced in writing in the form in which the work or entertainment is to be presented, but does not include a cinematograph film as distinct from a scenario or script for a cinematograph film: Copyright Act 1963 s.2(1). It is an offence to make a dramatic work with the intent that it may comprise or be included in an illegal broadcast: Broadcasting and Wireless Telegraphy Act 1988 s.5(2)(b). See ARTIST, TAX EXEMPTION OF.

**drawback.** The refund of duty made on the exportation of goods for which customs duties have been paid on importation. It is an offence to claim drawback unlawfully: Customs Consolidation Act 1876 s.108 as amended by the Finance Acts 1963 s.34(4) and 1976 s.44.

**drawee.** The person to whom a bill of exchange (qv) is addressed eg a bank.

**drawer.** The person who signs a bill of exchange (qv) as the maker thereof.

**drawing of cheque.** See CHEQUE, DRAWING OF.

**dress in court.** The costume which judges and counsel are ordinarily required to wear in the superior courts during sittings: RSC O.119. For judges, it is a black coat and vest of uniform make and material of the kind worn by senior counsel (qv), a black Irish poplin gown of uniform make and material, white bands, and a wig of the kind known as the small or bobbed wig. Counsel may not be heard in any case during *sittings* unless wearing the prescribed costume. However, in family law proceedings in the Circuit and High Courts, judges, barristers and solicitors are prohibited from appearing with wig and gown: Judicial Separation and Family Law Reform Act 1989 ss.33 and 45. See FAMILY COURT; TELEVISION LINK.

**drinking up time.** Colloquial expression describing the time permitted after closing time in a licensed premises for the consumption of intoxicating liquor supplied during permitted hours; it was increased from 10 to 30 minutes: Intoxicating Liquor Act 1988 s.27.

**drinking water.** A sanitary authority has a duty to monitor the quality of water intended for human consumption: EC (Quality of Water Intended for Human Consumption) Regulations 1988 (SI No 82 of 1988) which give effect to Council Directive 80/778/EEC. The Environmental Protection Agency may require a sanitary authority to submit to it information on such monitoring; the Agency is required however to carry out its own monitoring and to prepare a public annual report on such monitoring: Environmental Protection Agency Act 1992 s.58. See SEWAGE EFFLUENT.

**driver, uninsured.** See MOTOR INSURER'S BUREAU OF IRELAND; UNTRACED DRIVER.

**driving, careless.** See CARELESS DRIVING

**driving, furious.** See FURIOUS DRIVING.

**driving, dangerous.** See DANGEROUS DRIVING.

**driving licence.** It is an offence for a person to drive a *mechanically propelled vehicle* (qv) in a public place unless he holds a driving licence for the time being having effect and licensing him to drive the vehicle: Road Traffic Act 1961 s.38. See Road Traffic (Licensing of Drivers) Regulations 1964 (SI No 29 of 1964). See Joyce v Esmonde (1987) ILRM 316.

Under draft legislation, it is proposed that a person will commit an offence if he refuses or fails to produce a driving licence there and then when so requested by a garda (ibid s.40 to be amended by Road Traffic Bill 1993 s.25). The option for a garda to require production of the licence within ten days will be retained. See DISQUALIFICATION.

**driving of vehicle.** The general regulation of traffic on roads and the driving of vehicles is governed by the Road Traffic Bye-Laws 1964 (SI No 294 of 1964) which were made under the Road Traffic Act 1961 s.88 and now deemed to be regulations made under the Road Traffic Act 1968 s.60(4). See DANGEROUS DRIVING; DISQUALIFICATION ORDER, DRIVING; DRUNKEN DRIVING; FURIOUS DRIVING.

**driving without reasonable consideration.** The offence committed by a person who drives a vehicle in a public place without reasonable consideration for other persons using the place: Road Traffic Act 1961 s.51A as inserted by the Road Traffic Act 1968 s.49.

**drugs, misuse of.** To prevent the misuse of drugs, various statutory provisions have been made including: powers of search of persons, vehicles, vessels and aircraft; powers of inspection and arrest; procedures for investigation and dealing with irresponsible prescribing of drugs by practitioners; provisions governing the production and supply of drugs; and prohibition on printing of publications which encourage drug abuse: Misuse of Drugs Act 1977 and 1984.

Additional powers have been given to officers of customs and excise to deal with drug smuggling, including powers to detain and search, without warrant, persons and vehicles: Customs and Excise (Miscellaneous Provisions) Act 1988. [Text: Charlton (1)]. See CLINICAL TRIALS; MEDICAL PREPARATIONS; POLICE COOPERA-TION; PUBLIC HEALTH.

**drunken driving.** There are three separate offences of drunken driving: Road Traffic Act 1961 s.49 as inserted by the Road Traffic (Amendment) Act 1978 s.10. It is an offence for a person to drive or attempt to drive a mechanically propelled vehicle in a public place (a) while under the influence of an *intoxicant* to such an extent as to be incapable of having proper control of the vehicle or (b) while there is in his body a quantity of *alcohol* such that, within three hours after so driving or attempting to drive, (i) the concentration of alcohol in his blood exceeds a concentration of 100 milligrammes of alcohol per 100 millilitres of blood, or (ii) the concentration of alcohol in his urine exceeds a concentration of 135 milligrammes of alcohol per 100 millilitres of urine. Failure to prove compliance with the 3 hour requirement will lead to an acquittal: DPP v Doyle (1992 HC).

The description of *drunk driving* may be applied equally to the offences under s.49(2) and (3) of the 1961 Act as amended; the use of the phrase "drunk driving" is sufficient communication by a garda of the reason for an arrest; a technical explanation is not required: DPP (Cloughley) v Mooney (1993 HC) ILRM 214.

An *intoxicant* includes alcohol and drugs and any combination of them. The alcohol level may be proved by the production of a certificate of analysis from the Medical Bureau of Road Safety. It is also an offence to be drunk *in charge* of a mechanically propelled vehicle: 1978 Act s.50.

The decision to prosecute for drunken driving where there is a fatality has, since 1991, been taken by the Director of Public Prosecutions rather than by the gardai. A garda is empowered to arrest a person without a warrant who, in the garda's opinion, was committing or had committed an offence of drink or drug-related driving (ibid s.49(6)). The garda must inform the accused at the time of the arrest that he has formed such opinion: DPP v Lynch (1991 HC) 1 IR 43. An arrest on a person's driveway amounts to trespass and is not a valid arrest; the driveway in the immediate vicinity of the dwellinghouse and forming part of its curtilage attracts the protection of the 1937 Constitution art.40(5): DPP v McCreesh (1991 SC) ITLR (19 Aug). See also DPP (Crowley) v Connors (1991 HC) 9ILT Dig 73; DPP v O'Suilleabhain (1993 HC) ILRM 14. See SI No 218 of 1987. [Text: de Blacam (2)].

Under draft legislation, it is proposed that (a) the maximum permissible levels of alcohol are to be reduced to 80 milligrammes per 100 millilitres of blood and, to 107 milligrammes per 100 millilitres of urine; (b) a new maximum permissible alcohol level of 35 microgrammes of alcohol per 100 millilitres of breath is to be introduced; (c) the gardai are to be given power to enter on private property to secure an arrest; (d) a garda or designated doctor will be empowered to enter a hospital to take a blood or urine sample from a driver suspected of being involved in a traffic accident; (e) new powers will be given to detain an intoxicated driver who could be a threat to himself or other persons, and (f) the court will be empowered to order a person found guilty to pay a contribution to the costs incurred in detection and prosecution of the offence: Road Traffic Bill 1993, Part III, ss.9-24. The Bill was being debated at the time of writing, with questions being raised as to the constitutionality of (c) and (d). See

BREATH ANALYSIS; BLOOD SPECIMEN; HIP FLASK DEFENCE; INCAPABLE; ROAD TRAFFIC CHECK; STOP, OBLIGATION TO; URINE SPECIMEN; .

**drunken person.** Where a contract is made by a person who is so drunk at the time as not to understand what he is doing, such contract is *voidable* (qv) at the option of the drunken person, provided the other party knew of his condition. The burden of proof is on the person suffering the incapacity to prove the knowledge of the other party. A contract made by a drunken person can be *ratified* when he is sober. A drunken person is liable for *necessaries* (qv) supplied to him: Sale of Goods Act 1893 s.2. See CAPACITY TO CONTRACT; INTOXI-CATED.

**drunkenness.** Intoxication. Drunkenness may be a constituent part of an offence eg driving a motor vehicle while under the influence of alcoholic drink. Drunkenness generally is not a defence to a crime; merely to establish that a person's mind was so affected by drink that he more readily gave way to some violent passion, forms no excuse. However if actual *insanity* (qv) in fact supervenes, even as a result of alcoholic excess, it furnishes as complete an answer to a criminal charge as insanity induced by any other cause. Drunkenness which *renders the accused incapable of forming the specific intent essential to constitute the crime should be taken into consideration, with the other facts proved, in order to determine whether or not he had this intent*: DPP v Beard (1920) AC 479. See also R v Gamlen (1858) 1 F F 90; AG for Northern Ireland v Gallagher (1963) AC 359; The People (Attorney General) v Regan (1975) IR 367.

The behaviour of an employee while drunk on duty can be sufficiently serious to warrant dismissal: Quinn v B & I Line (1990) ELR 175. See ALCOHOL, CONSUMPTION OF; INTOXICATED; MENS REA; McNAGHTEN RULES.

**dry rent.** See RENT SECK.

**dual carriageway.** A road the roadway of which is divided centrally so as to provide two separate carriageways, on each of which traffic is required by road regulation to proceed in one direction only: Road Traffic (Signs) Regulations 1962 art.2.

**dubitante.** [Doubting].

**Dublin agent.** A solicitor in the City of Dublin near the Four Courts who acts for another solicitor situated elsewhere. Formerly, a solicitor wishing to undertake work in the Dublin High Court was required to have a registered office within a radius of 2 miles from the Four Courts eg for the service of documents. This led to the practice of solicitors outside Dublin having a Dublin agent. Although no longer a requirement, the practice continues for convenience and efficiency. See LAW AGENT.

**duces tecum.** [Bring with you]. See SUBPOENA.

**duck.** See GAME.

**due.** Owed eg a debt.

**due course of law.** No person shall be tried on any criminal charge save in *due course of law*: 1937 Constitution art. 38(1). The phrase "due course of law" requires a fair and just balance between the exercise of individual freedoms and the requirements of an ordered society: O'Higgins CJ in In re Criminal Law (Jurisdiction) Bill 1975 (1977) IR 129 cited in O'Callaghan v AG & DPP (1993 HC) ILRM 267.

**due process of law.** The term used to describe the regular application of the law through the courts. See Gill v Connellan (1988 HC) ILRM 448.

**dum bene se gesserit.** [During good conduct].

**dum casta clause.** A clause which is sometimes included in a *separation agreement* (qv) whereby a spouse's obligation to maintain the other terminates upon the other committing adultery or ceasing to lead a chaste life. In the absence of such a term the courts will not imply such a term: Lewis v Lewis (1940) IR 42; Ormsby v Ormsby (1945) 79 ILTR 97.

**dum casta vixerit.** [While she lives chastely].

**dum fuit infra aetatem.** [While he was within age].

**dum sola.** [While single or unmarried].

**dump.** Popularly understood to mean a landfill site for the disposal of waste; a *permit* is required for such a site if operated by a person other than a *public waste collector* (qv). Dumping near aerodromes may be restricted: Air Navigation and Transport Act 1988 s.23. See LANDFILL SITE; WASTE OPERATION.

**dumping.** The selling of products in a national market at a price below the price commanded by the same products in their country of origin; it can also include price discrimination as between national markets. Dumping is regulated by EC Regulation 3017/79 amended by Regulation 2176/84; penalties are determined by the *dumping margin*, which is the amount by which the *normal value* of the product exceeds the *export price*. See NTN Toyo Bearing Co v Council (1989) 2 CMLR 76. See also Friel in 8ILT & SJ (1990) 96. See COMMON COMMERCIAL POLICY.

**dumping at sea.** It is an offence deliberately to dump any substance or material at sea, or to load such material onto a vessel, aircraft or marine structure in the State for dumping, except in accordance with a *permit* issued by the Minister: Dumping at Sea Act 1981 s.2. Forty-three signatory countries of the London Dumping Convention 1990, including Ireland, have agreed to phase out the dumpimg at sea of industrial wastes by 1995 (Irish Times 3/11/90). See OIL POLLUTION; SEA POLLUTION; WASTE OPERATION.

**durable.** See MERCHANTABLE QUALITY.

**durante absentia.** [During absence]. Special administration *durante absentia* may be granted during the absence abroad of a personal representative. See Succession Act 1965 s.31; also In the Goods of Cassidy (1832) 4 Hag 360.

**durante bene placito.** [During the pleasure of the Crown].

**durante minore aetate.** [During minority]. The High Court has power to appoint an administrator *durante minore aetate* where a minor is the sole executor. See Succession Act 1965 s.32; also In re Thompson and McWilliams Contract (1896) 1 IR 356. See CESSATE GRANT.

**durante viduitate.** [During widowhood].

**durante vita.** [During life].

**duress.** Actual or threatened physical violence or unlawful imprisonment or threat of criminal proceedings. An act done under duress is generally not valid. A contract entered into under duress is voidable at the option of the party coerced. The person threatened need not be the actual contracting party, but may be the husband or wife or near relative of that party: Kaufman v Gerson (1904) 1 KB 591.

A threat of imprisonment and dishonour has been held to be sufficient to render void a contract of marriage for duress, as has extreme pressure from parents which drove the parties unwillingly into a union which neither party desired: Griffith v Griffith (1944) IR 35; M K (McC) v McC (1982) ILRM 277. See also Smelter Corporation of Ireland v O'Driscoll (1977) IR 305. See INEQUALITY OF POSITION; MARRIAGE, NULLITY OF; UNDUE INFLUENCE.

**duress in crime.** Duress *per minas* may be a good defence to some crimes. Threats of immediate death or serious personal violence which is so great as to overbear the ordinary power of human resistance will be accepted as a justification for acts which would otherwise be criminal, but not for murder, no matter how great the duress: Attorney General v Whelan (1934) IR 526. The defendant to succeed in this defence must show clearly that the overpowering of the will was operative at the time the crime was actually committed. If there was reasonable opportunity for the will to reassert itself, no justification can be found in antecedent threats.

It has been held in Northern Ireland that it is open to a person accused of murder as a principal (qv) *in the second degree* to plead duress: Lynch v DPP for Northern Ireland (1975) AC 653.

**duress of goods.** Doctrine whereby a transaction is voidable where a person in legal possesion of goods (eg pawner) demands more than is justifiably due because of his stronger bargaining position; any excess paid is recoverable: Lloyds Bank v Bundy (1975) QB 326. See INEQUALITY OF POSITION.

**dutch auction.** See AUCTION SALES.

**duty.** (1) An act which is required as a result of a legal obligation; the correlative of a right. Every *duty* imposed by an Act of the Oireachtas or by an instrument made wholly or partly under any such Act shall, unless the contrary intention in such Act or instrument, be performed from time to time as occasion requires: Interpretation Act 1937 s.16(1). Contrast with POWER.

(2) A tax levied. See DUTY OF CARE; DRAWBACK.

**duty-free.** Generally understood to mean

the freedom from liability to pay a tax on goods imported from another state. There is a personal limit on the importation of certain goods. Duty-free shops (eg at airports and on ferries) in the EC are being permitted to continue until 30th June 1999. See EC Council Directive 92/12/EEC of 25th February 1992. For cross border shopping and tax free allowances, see Travers in 10 ILT & SJ (1992) 224 and 254.

**duty of care.** *You must take reasonable care to avoid acts or omissions which you can reasonably foresee would be likely to injure your neighbour. The answer seems to be — persons who are so closely and directly affected by my act that I ought reasonably to have them in contemplation as being affected when I am directing my mind to the acts or omission which are called in question*: Donoghue v Stevenson (1932) AC 562. It has been held that the person whose negligence has caused injuries to another, does not owe a duty of care to that other's children not to deprive them of the non-pecuniary benefits derived from the parent-child relationship: Hosford v John Murphy & Sons (1988) ILRM 300. See also Ward v McMaster (1989 SC) ILRM 400; McEleney v McCarron (1992 SC). See DEFENCE FORCES; MEDICAL NEGLIGENCE; NEGLIGENCE; NEIGHBOUR PRINCIPLE; ROAD USER'S DUTY; SCHOOL AUTHORITY'S DUTY.

**dwelling, inviolability of.** See INVIOLABILITY OF DWELLING.

**dying declaration.** A statement made by a person, since deceased, as to the cause of death, made in the settled hopeless expectation of imminent death. Such a declaration is admissible in trials for murder and manslaughter of the deceased, as an exception to the hearsay rule. The declarant victim must have realised that he was in actual danger of death and had given up all hope of recovery. See R v Woodcock (1789) 1 Leach 500; Q v Jenkins (1869) 20 LT 178.

# E

**e converso.** [Conversely].

**E & OE.** [Errors and omissions excepted].

Often noted on commercial documents with the intention of protecting the maker thereof from mistakes.

**earnest.** A nominal sum given to bind a bargain.

**easement.** A right enjoyed by the owner of land over the lands of another eg a right of way, right to water, right to light, right of support. An easement cannot exist *in gross* ie independently of property, otherwise it may amount to a mere licence; it is a right which is annexed to property, in alieno solo (qv), rather than to an individual. The *dominant* tenement is the land owned by the possessor of the easement, and the *servient* tenement is the land over which the right is enjoyed.

An easement may be created by statute; by deed; by an implied grant; by presumed grant under the doctrine of the *lost modern grant* (qv), by *prescription* (qv) including by the Prescription Act 1832 (applied to Ireland in 1859).

An easement may be lost by abandonment, or by release expressly or by implication by the non-user of the easement over a long period of time. See Gaw v CIE (1953) IR 232; Carroll v Sheridan (1984) ILRM 451.

**Easter.** A sitting of the court. See SITTINGS OF COURT.

**eat inde sine die.** [Let him go without a day].

**EC.** European Economic Community (qv).

**eco-labelling scheme.** See LABELLING.

**economic and monetary union; EMU.** The Maastricht Treaty 1992 provides the legal base and sets out a procedure for moving to full *economic and monetary union* in the EC by 1999 at the latest and, subsequently, replacing the national currencies with a single currency. There is a three stage process; the *first* stage which began in July 1990 completes the Single Market; the *second* stage will begin on 1 January 1994 during which the process of policy coordination will be intensified with the assistance of the European Monetary Institute which will be a forerunner of the European Central Bank; the *third* stage will begin on 1 January 1999 at the latest, or at an earlier date if all the relevant conditions have been met, at which stage the *ECU* will become the single currency of the member States participating in the

Union. At that stage also the European System of Central Banks, consisting of the European Central Bank (ECB) and the central banks of the member States will come fully into operation. See Maastricht Treaty art.G(D)(25) replacing arts.102-109 in Treaty of Rome 1957. See BUDGETRY RULES; CONVERGENCE CRITERIA.

**economic and social cohesion.** See COHESION; COMMITTEE OF THE REGIONS.

**economic and social committee.** The 189 member EC advisory committee to the Commission and the Council, representative of employers, workers and other economic interests, which is consulted on a broad range of economic and social aspects of EC policy: Treaty of Rome 1957 arts.194-198 as amended by Maastricht Treaty 1992 art.G(E)64-66. Ireland has 9 members on this committee.

**economic duress.** Concept by which consent (eg in a contract) is treated in law as revocable where the apparent consent is induced by illegitimate pressure (eg threatened breach of contract unless the contract is renegotiated). See Universal Tankerships v International Transport Workers Federation (1983) 1 AC 366; Atlas Express Ltd v Kafco (1989)1 All ER 641. See also Smelter Corp of Ireland v O'Driscoll (1977) IR 305 where "fundamental unfairness" negatived valid consent.

**economic relations.** See UNLAWFUL INTERFERENCE IN ECONOMIC RELATIONS.

**economic loss.** It has been held that it is foreseeable that there will be economic loss and possible loss of profits if property in a warehouse is damaged: Egan v Sisk (1986) ILRM 283.

**ecu.** European currency unit. The Minister is empowered to issue coins denominated in ECUs but they are not legal tender for the payment of any amount; they are intended to be commemorative coins eg to mark the Irish Presidency of the EC: Decimal Currency Act 1990 s.2. See ECONOMIC AND MONETARY UNION; EXCHANGE RATE POLICY.

**education.** Education essentially is the teaching and training of a child to make the best possible use of his inherent and potential capacities, physical, mental and moral: Ryan v Attorney General (1965) IR 294. The State acknowledges that the primary and natural educator of the child is the family and guarantees to respect the inalienable right and duty of parents to provide, according to their means, for the religious and moral, intellectual, physical and social education of their children: 1937 Constitution, art.42(1). Parents are free to provide this education in their homes or in private schools or in schools recognised or established by the State (ibid art.42(2)).

The State shall, however, as guardian of the common good, require in view of actual conditions that children receive a *certain minimum* education, moral, intellectual and social (ibid art.42(3)(2)). The State has the power to define the minimum standard: In re School Attendance Bill 1942 (1943) IR 334. The duty of the State is to provide *for* free primary education and does not have a duty to provide it: 1937 Constitution, art.42(4); Crowley v Ireland (1980) IR 102. Damages may be awarded for unlawful interference with the constitutional right to free primary education pursuant to the 1937 Constitution, art.42(4): Hayes v Ireland & INTO (1987) ILRM 651; Conway v Ireland & INTO (1991 SC) ILRM 497.

Damages may also be awarded if the State fails to provide for the special primary education needs of a severely and profoundly handicapped child: O'Donoghue v Minister for Health & Minister for Education (1993 HC) – Irish Times 28/5/1993 – under appeal.

A comprehensive Education Act has been promised by government (November 1990). Currently primary education derives its legal status from the Stanley Letter of 1831, and from Royal Charters in 1845 & 1861. Secondary education is governed by the Intermediate Education (Ireland) Act 1878 & 1924. The system of technical education was coordinated by the Vocational Education Act 1930, while higher education relies on royal charters, university legislation (eg University of Limerick Act 1989) and the Higher Education Authority Act 1971, and the National Council for Educational Awards Act 1979. The Dublin Institute of Technology has been established on a statutory basis and given greater independence and authority, as have the 11 Regional Technical Colleges: Dublin Institute of Technology Act 1992; Regional Technical Colleges Act 1992.

Many important decisions relating to educational policy have no foundation in the State's laws; they have no statutory force and the sanction which ensures compliance with them is not a legal one but the undeclared understanding that the Department of Education will withhold financial assistance in the event of non-compliance: Costello J in Callaghan v Co Meath Vocational Education Committee (1990 HC) (Irish Times 21/11/1990). See also Local Authorities (Higher Education Grants) Acts 1968, 1978 and 1992.

The EC is required to contribute to the development of quality education by encouraging cooperation between member States and, if necessary, supporting and supplementing their action, while fully respecting the responsibility of the member States for the content of teaching and the organization of education systems and their cultural and linguistic diversity: Treaty of Rome 1957 art.126 as replaced by Maastricht Treaty 1992 art.G(D)(36). See COMMITTEE OF THE REGIONS; COMPTROLLER AND AUDITOR GENERAL; CORPORAL PUNISHMENT; EXAMINATION RESULTS; EXEMPLARY DAMAGES; SCHOOL AUTHORITY'S DUTY; SUSPEND.

**education, advancement of.** See CHARITIES.

**education awards.** Awards of certificates, diplomas, degrees and post-graduate degrees awarded by educational bodies relying on powers they possess themselves (eg universities) or relying on powers of other bodies (eg National Council for Educational Awards). The National Council for Vocational Awards was established in 1991 on a non-statutory basis. An Foras Aiseanna Saothair (FAS) has authority to award certificates of the attainment of standards recommended by FAS: Industrial Training Act 1967 s.9(2)(d); Labour Services Act 1987.

The Dublin Institute of Technology has power to confer diplomas, certificates or other educational awards; it may also confer degrees, postgraduate degrees and honorary awards by order of the Minister: Dublin Institute of Technology Act 1992 ss.5(1)(b) and 5(2). It may, as may also the Regional Technical Colleges, enter into arrangements with the NCEA or

with a university for the purpose of having awards given (ibid s.5(1)(c) and Regional Technical Colleges Act 1992 s.5(b)).

The Minister is empowered to prescribe that educational achievements secured by a student in an examination centre outside the State may satisfy educational standards for grant purposes, in lieu of the Leaving Certificate: Local Authorities (Higher Education Grants) Act 1992 s.4.

The government has proposed to establish a National Education and Training Certification Board on a statutory basis: Programme for Partnership Government — January 1993.

**EEA Agreement.** The Agreement on the *European Economic Area*: European Communities (Amendment) Act 1993 s.1(1). This is an agreement between the EEC and EFTA and will extend the EEC Treaty concerning the internal market to EFTA contracting states. Ratification of the Agreement by the State is effected by the 1993 Act ss.3 and 4. See EFTA; REGULATION.

**EEC.** [European Economic Community (qv)].

**EEIG.** [European Economic Interest Grouping (qv)].

**effects.** A person's property. See Mitchell v Mitchell (1820) 5 Madd 69.

**effluent.** See SEWAGE EFFLUENT; TRADE EFFLUENT.

**EFTA.** The trade association established in 1960 to eliminate trade tariffs on industrial products between certain countries. Originally comprised of Austria, Denmark, Norway, Portugal, Sweden, Switzerland, and the UK. The UK, Denmark and Portugal left EFTA on joining the EC. EFTA now comprises of Austria, Finland, Iceland, Norway, Sweden and Switzerland. See EEA AGREEMENT; EXECUTION OF JUDGMENTS; FOREIGN JUDGMENTS, ENFORCEMENT OF; JURISDICTION.

**eg.** See EXEMPLI GRATIA.

**egm.** See EXTRAORDINARY GENERAL MEETING.

**ei incumbit probatio qui dicet, non qui negat.** [The burden of proof is on him who alleges, and not on him who denies]. See BURDEN OF PROOF.

**ei qui affirmat, non ei qui nagat, incumbit probatio.** [The burden of proof lies on him who affirms a fact, not on him who denies it]. See BURDEN OF

PROOF.

**Eire.** The name of the State in the Irish language: 1937 Constitution, art.4. The name of the State in the English language is *Ireland*. See STATE.

**ejectment.** The recovery of possession of land. In the Circuit Court, ejectment is usually obtained by *ejectment civil bill* on the title or for overholding, where the rateable valuation of the land does not exceed £200. Ejectment can be obtained for non-payment of rent but this is not usually sought as the defendant in any such proceedings may, at any time before the decree for possession is executed, pay all rents and arrears and costs due and as a consequence the proceedings will be stayed: RCC O.22 r.15; O.35. Similar provisions for ejectment apply in the District Court which has jurisdiction where the rent does not exceed £2500 per annum: DCR r.176. See Deasy's Act 1860 ss.52 and 72; Courts Act 1981 ss.2(1) and 6(a)(ii). An action by a personal representative to recover land in succession to the owner is not statute barred (qv) for 12 years: Gleeson v Feehan & O'Meara (1991 SC) ILRM 783.

**ejusdem generis.** [Of the same kind or nature]. The maxim that where particular words are followed by general words, the general words are limited to the same kind or genus, as the particular words eg *offensive trades* are particularly defined in the Public Health (Ireland) Act 1878 s.128 and all involve the collection of large quantities of animal matter; such trades are also generally defined as consisting of *any other noxious or offensive trade, business or manufacture*; a trade to come within the general category would have to have the features of the particular definition. See In re Miller (1889) 61 LT 365. See also Cronin v Lunham Brothers Ltd (1986) ILRM 415; C W Shipping Ltd v Limerick Harbour Commissioners (1989 HC) ILRM 416. See LEGISLATION, INTERPRETATION OF.

**election.** Choice.

(1) The equitable doctrine of election by which a person who takes a benefit under an instrument must accept or reject the instrument as a whole eg if there is in the will of X *a gift of A's property to B and a gift to A*, A can only take the gift by giving his own property or its value to B. Alternatively he can *elect* to keep his own property and reject the gift. See In re Sullivan (1917) IR 38.

(2) In a will where there is a devise or bequest to a spouse, the spouse may *elect* to take either that gift or the share to which she is entitled as a legal right (qv). In default of election the spouse is entitled under the will only. See Succession Act 1965 s.115; also Reilly v McEntee (1984) ILRM 572.

(3) The system by which the choice of the people is determined in contests for vacancies in parliament and in local government. It has been held that the system by which candidates names are placed in an alphabetical order on the ballot paper, constitutes a reasonable regulation of elections to Dail Eireann: O'Reilly v Minister for the Environment (1987) ILRM 290. Elections for the Dail and European Parliament, Presidential elections, referenda, local elections and elections to Udaras na Gaeltachta can all be held on the same day: Electoral Act 1992 s.165. The conduct of elections and referenda is the responsibility of the county registrars (qv) outside the Counties of Dublin and Cork; in these latter counties it is the responsibility of the sheriff. See Electoral Regulations 1992 (SI No 407 of 1992). See RSC O.97. See CONSTITUENCY; DAIL ELECTION; ISLAND, POLLING ON; PRESIDENT OF IRELAND; FRANCHISE; EUROPEAN ELECTION; LOCAL ELECTION; PROPORTIONAL REPRESENTATION; RECOUNT; SIGN; SPOILT VOTE.

**election agent.** A candidate may appoint one election agent to assist him generally in relation to a Dail election: Electoral Act 1992 s.59. The candidate or his election agent may appoint agents to be present on the candidate's behalf in polling stations and at the counting of votes (ibid s.60); they may also appoint *personation agents* (qv). As regards presidential elections, see draft Presidential Elections Bill 1993 ss.33-35.

**election documents.** Every notice, bill, poster or similar document having reference to an election, except those published by the returning officer, must bear on its face the name and address of the printer and of the publisher thereof: Electoral Act 1992 s.140 and ss.166-170.

**election of local government.** See LOCAL ELECTION.

**election petition, local.** The procedure by which the validity of a local election may be questioned; the petition must be presented to the Circuit Court: Local Elections (Petitions and Disqualifications) Act 1974. The petition may be presented by any person who has reached the age of eighteen years, or by the Director of Public Prosecutions (qv) where it appears to him that a local election may have been affected by the commission of electoral offences (ibid ss.2 and 4). See also Cowan v Attorney General (1961) IR 411.

**election petition, parliamentary.** A petition to the High Court questioning a Dail election: Electoral Act 1992 s.132 and third schedule. The petition may be presented by a person registered as a Dail elector. The Dail election may be questioned on the grounds of want of elegibility, the commission of an electoral offence, obstruction of or interference with or other hindrance to the conduct of the election or mistake or other irregularity which is likely to have affected the result of the election (ibid s.132(5)). The court must either (a) dismiss the petition, (b) declare the correct result, or (c) declare that the election or a specified part is void in which event a fresh election must take place. It is an offence to withdraw a petition corruptly (ibid s.155). As regards petitions in European elections, see European Assembly Elections Act 1977. See RSC O.97.

**election petition, presidential.** Under draft legislation, it is proposed that a person will be able to question the result of a presidential election by way of petition to the High Court: Presidential Elections Bill 1993 ss.57-58. Leave of the Court to present a petition may be sought by the DPP or a candidate or his agent (ibid s.57(6)). The procedures are proposed to be similar to those applying to Dail election petitions (ibid s.58).

**electoral offences.** A variety of offences including personation, bribery, undue influence, interfering with ballot boxes, disorderly conduct at election meetings, breach of secrecy, voting when not entitled to be registered, handling of ballot paper by candidate, canvassing in the vicinity of a polling station: Electoral Act 1992 ss.133-160. See also 1992 Act ss.166-170; draft Presidential Elections Bill 1993 s.59.

**electricity.** Regulations have been made which apply to the generation, transformation, conversion, switching, controlling, regulating, rectification, storage, transmission, distribution; provision, measurement or use of electrical energy in every place of work: Safety Health and Welfare at Work (General Application) Regulations 1993, reg.33 (SI No 44 of 1993). There are separate requirements for mines and quarries: Mines and Quarries Act 1965.

**electricity supply.** It is an offence unlawfully and maliciously to cut or injure any electric line or work with intent to cut off or diminish any supply of electricity: Electricity (Supply) Act 1927 s.111. The relay of cable television and radio signals to domestic householders, transmitted by means of electric current, does not constitute the supply of electricity: Brosnan v Cork Communications (1992 HC) 10 ILT Dig 268. See LIABILITY, STATUTORY EXEMPTION FROM.

**electronic.** See COMPUTERS; FAX.

**elegit.** [He has chosen].

**e-mark.** A mark prescribed in accordance with the Packaged Goods (Quality Control) Act 1980. See PACKAGE.

**embarrassment.** A possible ground for damages arising from injuries caused by the negligence of another. See DISFIGURE-MENT.

**embassy, employee of.** See AMBASSADOR; IMMUNITY.

**embezzlement.** The felony (qv) committed by a clerk or servant, who *fraudulently* appropriates to his own use property delivered to or taken into possession by him on account of his master or employer: Larceny Act 1916 s.17. Property includes chattels, money, or valuable securities. Fraudulent appropriation may be shown eg by the accused having absconded with money or by his wilful omission to pay it over to his employer. See The People (Attorney General) v Warren (1945) IR 24. See FALSE ACCOUNTING; FRAUDULENT CONVERSION.

**emblements.** The profits from sown land; the crops or products as are the result of agricultural labour. The personal representative (qv) of a tenant for life is entitled to take the year's crops when the tenancy determines between seed sowing and harvest time. The right to emblements is lost where a tenancy is ended by the tenant's own act. See GOODS.

**embracery.** The common law misdemeanour of any improper endeavour or attempt corruptly to influence or instruct a jury by money, promises, threats, or by other persuasions or fraudulent devices, other than the strength of evidence and the arguments of counsel in open court.

**embryo implantation.** A child born as a result of the test tube fertilisation of a wife's ova by her husband's semen and borne by the wife following embryo implantation, is legitimate (or now, a child whose parents are married to each other: Status of Children Act 1987). If a third party's semen is used, the child is illegitimate (or now, a child whose parents are not married to each other), although if the wife is living with her husband at the time there may be a presumption that the child is a marital child unless rebutted in court proceedings. See ARTIFICIAL INSEMINATION.

**emergency.** The Minister is empowered, in the interest of the State or of the public, during any emergency, to give directions as to the use, or possession of any aircraft or aerodrome, or any facilities at an aerodrome; failure to comply with a direction is an offence: Air Navigation and Transport Act 1988 s.22. A local authority manager is empowered to deal with an emergency situation without having to inform the elected members: City and County Management (Amendment) Act 1955 s.2 and Housing Act 1988 s.27. See NATIONAL EMERGENCY.

**emission.** An emission into the atmosphere of a pollutant within the meaning of the Air Pollution Act 1987; a discharge of polluting matter, sewage effluent or trade effluent within the meaning of the LG (Water Pollution) Act 1977, to waters or sewers within the meaning of that Act; the disposal of waste; or noise: Environmental Protection Agency Act 1992 s.3(1). See AIR POLLUTION; ASBESTOS.

**emolument.** (1) Some profit or advantage: R v Postmaster General (1878) 3 QBD 428; remuneration. (2) Anything assessable to income tax under Schedule E:

Income Tax Act 1967 s.124. It includes all payments of salaries, fees, wages, and perquisites, whether taxable directly under the main Schedule E charging section (ibid s.110) or by virtue of any other provision in the Income Tax Acts which requires the particular payment to be taxed under Schedule E. The payment of emoluments are subject to the PAYE system of taxation unless the payments are excluded by virtue of s.125 of the 1967 Act as amended by the Finance Act 1985 s.6. (3) The amount of the remuneration and other payments to company directors must be disclosed in the annual accounts: Companies Act 1963 ss.191-193. See PAY AS YOU EARN.

**emotional immaturity.** The incapacity to enter into and to sustain a normal, functional lifelong marital relationship by reason of a lack of *emotional maturity* and of psychological weakness and disturbance, affecting both parties to a marriage is a ground for nullity in Irish law: PC v JC (1989 HC) ITLR (2 Oct). See MARRIAGE, NULLITY OF.

**employee.** (1) A person who is under a *contract of service* to another person, called the employer, under which the employer has the right to direct the employee not only as to what is to be done but as to how it is to be done: Roche v Patrick Kelly & Co Ltd (1969) IR 100. (2) Any person in receipt of emoluments (qv): Income Tax Act 1967 s.124. The parties cannot alter the truth of the employer/ employee relationship by putting a different label on it: Lamb Bros Dublin Ltd v Davidson (1979) HC; Massey v Crown Life Insurance Co (1978) 2 All ER 576. The fact that a person is not paying income tax under the PAYE system is not, of itself, a bar to his being an employee: McCurdy v Bayer Diagnostics Manufacturing Ltd (1993 EAT) ELR 83. An employee generally has access to employment protection legislation.

There is a duty on an employee to do his work with reasonable care and skill; he must be honest and diligent, he must generally obey instructions provided they are reasonable and lawful and he must not wilfully disrupt the employer's business or other activities. He must not disclose confidential information or trade secrets: Faccenda Chicken Ltd v Fowler

(1984) IRLR 61. He also has a duty to take care for his own safety and health and that of any other persons who might be affected by his acts or omissions at work: Safety in Industry Act 1980 s.8(1)(a). See also Minister for Labour v PMPA Insurance (1986) HC; Cervi v Atlas Staff Bureau UD 616/85 EAT 26/11/87; Bank of Ireland v Kavanagh (1987) HC. See EQUAL PAY; UNFAIR DIS-MISSAL; OFFICE HOLDER; EMPLOYER, DUTY OF; INDEPENDENT CONTRACTOR; PROTECTIVE EQUIPMENT; WORKERS, FREEDOM OF MOVE-MENT OF.

**employees and inventions.** See INVEN-TOR.

**employees' share scheme.** A scheme designed to encourage or facilitate a company's employees to acquire its shares or debentures. The holders of such shares must be offered a propor-tionate amount of any further equity which is issued. See Companies Amend-ment Act 1983 ss.2(1) and 23(1)(a). There is provision for income tax relief for an employee who buys new ordinary shares in his employing company; the overall limit has been increased to £3,000: Finance Act 1986 s.12 as amended by Finance Act 1993 s.26. See also PRE-EMPTION.

**employer.** (1) The master of a servant. (2) The person by whom an employee is or was employed. (3) A person for whom one or more workers work or have worked or normally work or seek to work having previously worked for that person: Industrial Relations Act 1990 s.8. (4) Any person paying emoluments (qv) Income Tax Act 1967 s.124.

It has been held that a skipper is not the employer of crew on a trawler for the purposes of income tax regulations: DPP v McLoughlin (1986) ILRM 493. See also Minister for Social Welfare v Griffith (1992 HC) ELR 44. See EMPLOY-MENT AGENCY; EMPLOYMENT LAW; EMPLOYER, DUTY OF; EMPLOYEE.

**employer, duty of.** An employer has a duty to provide a safe place of work, proper equipment and processes, and a safe system of work: Burke v John Paul & Co Ltd (1967) IR 277; O'Hanlon v ESB (1969) IR 75; Kielthy v Ascon Ltd (1970) IR 122. He must provide adequate training and instruction and he must not require the employee to do anything

unreasonable or illegal. He must pay wages or other remuneration but he is generally not required to provide any actual work, except where the employee requires work to develop and maintain special skills relevant to the job (see Nethermere [St Neots] Ltd v Taverna [1984] IRLR 240).

An employer is vicariously liable for the torts of his employee if they are committed within the scope of his employment: Kiely v McCrea Sons Ltd (1940) Ir Jur Rep 1; Byrne v Maguire 60 ILTR 11. An employer may be under a duty not to disclose confidential information concerning its employees: Dagleish v Lothian & Borders Police Board (1991) IRLR 422 as reported by Barry in 10ILT & SJ (1992) 30. Directors of a company must have regard to the interests of the company's employees generally, as well as to the shareholders (members): Companies Act 1990 s.52. See EMPLOYEE; FIRST AID; HEALTH SURVEIL-LANCE; PROTECTIVE EQUIPMENT; SAFETY AT WORK; RESTRAINT OF TRADE.

**employment, contract of.** See CONTRACT OF EMPLOYMENT; TERMS OF EMPLOYMENT.

**employment, minimum age for.** The minimum age for employment is 14 years although employment under the school leaving age, currently 15, is generally prohibited. See Protection of Young Persons (Employment) Act 1977. See CHILD, EMPLOYMENT OF; YOUNG PERSON.

**employment notice.** See NOTICE, EMPLOY-MENT.

**employment agency.** A business in-volved in seeking, whether for reward or otherwise, on behalf of others, persons who will give or accept employment. A licence is required. See Employment Agency Act 1971; Employment Agency Regulations 1993 (SI No 49 of 1993).

For the purposes of unfair dismissal legislation, the person hiring an individ-ual from an employment agency is deemed to be the employer of that individual, irrespective of whether or not the person pays his wages or salary: Unfair Dismissals (Amdt) Act 1993 s.13. Any redress for unfair dismissal will be awarded against the person who hired the individual from the agency (ibid s.13(c)).

**employment agreement.** An agreement relating to the remuneration or the conditions of employment which is registered pursuant to the Industrial Relations Act 1946 ss.25-33. An agreement so registered applies to all workers of the class to which the agreement relates; their employers are bound to grant such workers rates of pay and conditions of employment not less favourable than those fixed by the agreement whether or not they are a party to the agreement. For registration to be valid, fair procedures must be followed and the statutory prerequisites must be complied with: National Union of Security Employers v The Labour Court & Ors (1992 HC) as reported by Barry in 11 ILT & SJ (1993) 50. See also Industrial Relations Act 1990 ss.51-55. See JOINT LABOUR COMMITTEE.

**Employment Appeals Tribunal.** The tribunal which hears appeals, claims and disputes in relation to a wide range of employment legislation eg redundancy, maternity protection, and unfair dismissal. Established by the Redundancy Payments Act 1967 s.39 as the Redundancy Appeals Tribunal, it was renamed by the Unfair Dismissals Act 1977 s.18 and its procedures are governed by the various Acts under which it has jurisdiction, as well as by SI No 24 of 1968 (redundancy) and SI No 286 of 1977 (unfair dismissal).

The tribunal has a chairman who must be a practising barrister or solicitor of at least seven years standing and seven vice-chairmen. It sits in divisions, each division consisting of a chairman (or vice-chairman) and one member each from the nominees of both sides of industry. An appeal from the tribunal lies either to the High Court or to the Circuit Court depending on the matter in dispute. In unfair dismissal an appeal lies to the Circuit Court within 6 weeks from the date on which the tribunal determination is communicated to the parties: Unfair Dismissals (Amdt) Act 1993 s.11(1). Also an appeal lies from the Circuit Court to the High Court: McCabe v Lisney & Son (1981) ILRM 289; an appeal to the Circuit Court is within the time limit if the jurisdiction of the court is invoked within the limitation period: Norris v Power Security Ltd (1990 HC) ELR 181.

An appeal on a point of law should state the decision being appealed against, the question of law which is suggested to be in error, and the grounds of appeal; this summons should be supported by an affidavit which exhibits the determination of the tribunal, including any findings of fact or recital of evidence made by it: Bates v Model Bakery Ltd (1992 SC) ELR 193.

It would appear that relief by way of judicial review (certiori) of the tribunal's decision will be refused where appeal to Circuit and High Court has not been pursued: Memorex v Employment Appeals Tribunal (1989) 7ILT & SJ 154 & 204. The tribunal can only exercise its discretion to exclude a party in exceptional circumstances eg failure to furnish Notice of Appearance within the prescribed time would not be an exceptional circumstance: Halal Meat Packers (Ballyhaunis) Ltd v EAT (1990 SC) ELR 49.

The tribunal does not award costs against any party unless a party has acted frivolously or vexatiously (regulation 19(2) of SI No 24 of 1968): Sherry v Panther Security Ltd (1991 EAT) ELR 239. There are recent provisions for the enforcement by the Circuit Court of determinations made by the tribunal or of orders made by the Court, including interest on any financial compensation awarded, compensation for any delay in implementing re-instatement or re-engagement; the Court may also change an award from re-engagement or re-instatement to financial compensation (ibid 1993 Act s.11). See also IBM Ireland Ltd v Employment Appeals Tribunal (1983) ILRM 50; The State (IPU) v Employment Appeals Tribunal (1987) ILRM 36. See RSC O.105. See APPEARANCE, ENTRY OF; RIGHTS COMMISSIONER.

**Employment Equality Agency.** A body corporate with perpetual succession with the following general functions: (a) to work towards the elimination of discrimination in relation to employment; (b) to promote equality of opportunity between men and women in relation to employment; (c) to keep under review the working of equality and anti-discrimination legislation: Employment Equality Act 1977 ss.34-35. The Agency has power to conduct investigations (ibid ss.39-42) and it may also issue *non-*

*discrimination notices* (qv).

**employment interview.** See INTERVIEW, EMPLOYMENT.

**employment law.** The body of law dealing with the relationship between employer (master) and employee (servant) and organisations representing them. Also known as labour law. Originally the relationship between master and servant was based on contract as between two equal parties; and also trade unions were illegal in so far as their operations were in restraint of trade. Significant changes have taken place in the last century, with trade unions being given statutory recognition in 1871 and immunity from many liabilities in 1906; the Constitution in 1937 recognised the right to work and the right to form associations, and a whole range of employee protection legislation was introduced in the 1960's and 1970's eg equal pay, anti-discrimination, unfair dismissal, maternity protection, holidays, minimum notice and redundancy. [Text: Curtin; FIE (IBEC): Forde (8); von Prondznski; Redmond; Kerr & Whyte]. See COMMON EMPLOYMENT; EMPLOYEE; TRADE UNION.

**employment regulation order.** See JOINT LABOUR COMMITTEE.

**ems.** European monetary system. See Northern Bank v Edwards (1986) ILRM 167.

**emu.** Economic and monetary union (qv).

**E-number.** Generally understood to mean the serial number applying to a particular *colouring agent* in food. A person may not import, distribute, sell or expose for sale any colouring agent other than a permitted colouring agent, for use in the manufacture or preparation of food, or may not import, distribute, sell or expose for sale specified foods which have in or on them any colouring agent other than a permitted agent: SI No 149 of 1973; SI No 140 of 1978; SI No 336 of 1981.

**en autre droit.** [In the right of another].

**en ventre sa mere.** [In the womb of his mother]. An unborn child. Descendents and relatives of a deceased person begotten before his death but born alive thereafter are regarded for the purposes of succession as having been born in the lifetime of the deceased and as having survived him: Succession Act 1965 s.3(2). See also Status of Children Act 1987

s.27(5). See CHILD, ILLEGITIMATE; CLASS GIFT; ISSUE; GESTATION PERIOD.

**enabling Act.** A statute legalising that which was illegal or incompetent; a statute giving obligatory or discretionary powers. For example, see Turf Development Act 1990 which enables Bord na Mona to establish and acquire companies. See also NONFEASANCE.

**enactment.** Legislation (qv). See ACT; BILL.

**enceinte.** [Pregnant]. See PREGNANCY.

**encroachment.** Unauthorised extension of the boundaries of land; unauthorised entrance upon another's rights or possessions. An encroachment by a tenant on another person's land generally enures for the landlord's benefit, unless the conduct of the landlord or the tenant indicates a contrary intention: Meares v Collis (1927) IR 397. See LONG POSSESSION, TITLE BY; TRESPASS.

**encumbrance.** A charge or liability which burdens property eg a mortgage, lease, easement, restrictive covenant (qqv). An *encumbrancer* is a person who has the right to enforce an encumbrance.

**endorsement.** A signature, usually on the reverse side of a document, generally operating as a transfer of rights arising from the document. Endorsement is a mode of transferring bills of exchange and bills of lading. An *endorsement in blank* is an endorsement by the endorser of his own signature without specifying the name of the transferee, under which the bill becomes payable to the bearer. A *special endorsement* is one which specifies the name of the person to whom or to whose order the bill is to be made payable. A *conditional endorsement* is one which is subject to the fulfilment of a specific condition. A *restrictive endorsement* prohibits further transferability (eg *pay John Murphy only — signed* ..... ).

An endorser of a bill agrees to compensate the holder or any endorser subsequent to his own endorsement who is compelled to pay it if the bill is dishonoured when duly presented for payment. See Bills of Exchange Act 1882 ss.32-35. See BILL OF EXCHANGE; CHEQUE.

**endorsement of claim.** See INDORSEMENT OF CLAIM.

**endowment.** (1) Provision for a charity. (2) Formerly, giving a woman a right to dower (qv). See CHARITIES.

**endowment mortgage.** A mortgage wherein the principal sum advanced by the mortgagee (lender) is intended to be repaid by means of a *life-endowment insurance policy* effected by the mortgagor (borrower). The endowment policy from an insurance company will typically provide for the payment of the principal sum at a specified date or on the mortgagor's death, whichever is earlier. If the policy is a *with profits* one, it will provide for the mortgagor to participate in the profitability of the insurance company. The mortgagor pays a regular premium to the insurance company, and interest to the mortgagee on the principal sum advanced. The mortgage deed usually provides that the monthly repayments of the principal sum advanced by the mortgagee are suspended, so long as the endowment policy is kept up and the mortgagor continues to pay interest on that principal sum. An endowment mortgage may also be a *unit-linked* mortgage wherein the premiums are invested in unit trusts whose value may fluctuate. See MORTGAGE.

**enemy.** Includes armed mutineers, armed rebels, armed rioters and pirates: Defence Act 1954 s.2(1). For *enemy aliens,* see Prisoners of War and Enemy Aliens Act 1956 s.1(3).

**enemy of state.** See ILLEGAL CONTRACTS.

**enforcement notice.** The notice which a planning authority (qv) has power to serve where any development of land has been carried out without permission or any condition subject to which the permission was granted has not been complied with: LG(P&D) Act 1963 ss.31-37 as amended by LG (P&D) Act 1992 s.19(1) and (2). Every enforcement notice must be served on both the owner and the occupier of the land and generally must be served (a) within five years of the development having been carried out, or (b) within five years of the date for compliance with a condition, or (c) within five years of grant of permission to retain a structure, or (d) within five years of the expiration of the "appropriate period" where development has commenced but is not in conformity with the permission authorising it. An enforcement notice may require the removal or alteration of any structures, the discontinuance of any use of land or the

carrying out on land of any works. Planning authorities are empowered to enter the land and take the necessary steps to secure compliance with an enforcement notice.

An enforcement notice may also be served by a *building control authority* to ensure compliance with building regulations (qv): Building Control Act 1990 s.8. See Dublin Co Council v Hill (1992 SC) ILRM 397. See WARNING NOTICE.

**enforcement notice, data.** The notice in writing, served on a data controller (qv) or data processor (qv) by which the Data Protection Commissioner (qv) may require such person to take such steps as are specified in the notice within such time as may be so specified, to comply with the data protection legislation: Data Protection Act 1988 s.10(2). This will arise where the Commissioner is of opinion that the person has contravened or is contravening the statutory provisions, other than a provision the contravention of which is an offence. An enforcement notice may be appealed to the Circuit Court. See DATA PROTECTION.

**enforcement of judgment.** See EXECUTION OF JUDGMENT; FOREIGN JUDGMENTS, ENFORCEMENT OF.

**enfranchise.** Conferring the right to vote. See FRANCHISE.

**engaged couple.** Two persons who have agreed to marry each other. In the absence of evidence to the contrary, it is presumed that a gift of property given by another person, is given to them as *joint owners* and subject to a condition that it be returned to the donor if the marriage does not take place: Family Law Act 1981 s.3. A gift of property, including an engagement ring, is presumed to be given subject to a condition that it will be returned if the marriage does not take place, or given unconditionally if on account of the death of the donor, the marriage does not take place (ibid s.4). The rights of spouses in relation to property apply where an agreement to marry is terminated (ibid s.5). See also Married Women Status Act 1957 s.12; Courts Act 1991 s.13. See draft legislation Matrimonial Home Bill 1993 ss.19 and 20. See BREACH OF PROMISE; MATRIMONIAL PROPERTY.

**engineer, professional negligence.** It has been held that an engineer who certifies that a house has been erected above the flood level for the area is guilty of negligence if he does not satisfy himself in an appropriate professional manner that the crucial measurements have been observed: Moran v Duleek Developments Ltd & Hanley (1991 HC) ITLR (14 Oct).

**engineering law.** Generally understood to refer to the body of law dealing with the forms of construction contracts used for engineering works, including matters such as tender and agreement; liability and insurance; sub-contracting; the bond; delay, disruption and acceleration claims; price fluctuation; disputes, arbitration and litigation. [Text: Keane D; Lyden & MacGrath; Abrahamson UK]. See BOND, ENGINEERING CONTRACT; RIAI CONTRACT.

**engraving.** See ARTISTIC WORK.

**engross.** To prepare the text of a document.

**engrossment.** A deed prior to execution. An engrossment of a will must be written in a legible hand or printed or typewritten or, in suitable cases, photocopied and certified as a true copy of the original will. See RSC O.79 r.69.

**enjoyment.** The exercise of a right.

**enlarge.** To free; to extend a limit; to extend a period of time.

**enlargement.** Increasing an estate eg the enlargement of a base fee (qv) into a fee simple (qv).

**enlargement of EC.** Any European State may apply to become a member of the European Union: Maastricht Treaty 1992 art.O. If agreement is reached between the applicant and the existing member States, that agreement must be ratified by all the member States. By 1992, applications to join had been submitted by Austria, Cyprus, Finland, Malta, Sweden and Turkey, and the issue was being debated in Norway and Switzerland. It is expected that Austria, Finland and Sweden will become members by 1995. Agreements which the EC has negotiated with countries of Eastern Europe (eg Poland, Czechoslovakia and Hungary) contain a clear aspiration to eventual membership of the EC by these countries.

**enlargement of jurisdiction.** The parties to proceedings before the Circuit Court may consent to the court having jurisdiction in the action or matter without any limit: RCC O.5 r.9.

**enquiry.** See INQUIRY.

**enrolment.** The registration or recording on an official record of an act or document.

**ens legis.** A legal being or entity.

**entail.** See FEE TAIL.

**enter.** (1) To go onto land so as to assert some right. (2) To record in an account. See also BURGLARY.

**enticement of spouse.** Formerly an actionable tort whereby a spouse was wrongfully enticed away from another. Abolished by the Family Law Act 1981 s.1. See LRC 1 of 1981.

**entrapment.** The enticing of a person into committing a crime in order to prosecute him. See AGENT PROVOCATEUR.

**entry.** An authorised entry by a local authority pursuant to the LG (P&D) Act 1963 s.83 may give rise to compensation to a person who suffered damage thereby: LG (P&D) Act 1990 s.23. See FORCIBLE ENTRY AND OCCUPATION.

**entry, right of.** The right of a local authority to enter upon and take possession of land (eg following a notice of entry served pursuant to the Housing Act 1966 s.80) which the authority can enforce by issuing a warrant to the sheriff (qv) to deliver possession of the land to the person appointed in the warrant to receive possession: Land Clauses Act 1845 s.91. See also MORTGAGEE, RIGHTS OF.

**entry of appearance.** See APPEARANCE, ENTRY OF.

**entry of judgment.** See JUDGMENT; SUMMARY SUMMONS.

**enure.** To take effect; to operate.

**environment assessment directive.** The directive of the European Economic Community, done at Luxembourg on 27 June 1985, which requires developers to produce *environment impact assessments* of a wide range of projects. The assessment is required to identify the direct and indirect effects of a *project* on human beings, fauna, and flora; soil, water, air, climate and landscape; the interaction between these factors; material assets and the cultural heritage (ibid art.3). A *project* means the execution of construction works or of other installation or schemes, or other interventions in the natural surroundings and landscape including those involving the extraction of mineral resources (ibid art.2).

Subject to certain exemption provisions, an environment impact assessment is mandatory for projects of the class listed in Annex 1 (ibid art.4); these projects include crude oil refineries, power stations, integrated chemical installations and waste disposal installations. Member states were required to implement the directive by 3rd July 1988; it was implemented by the European Communities (Environmental Assessment) Regulations 1989 (SI No 349 of 1989) as amended by LG (P&D) Act 1992 ss.22(2) and 3. The earlier Department Circular of 1st July 1988 to local authorities was held not to have had the force of law: Browne v An Bord Pleanala (1989 HC) ILRM 865. See Roads Act 1993 ss.50-51.

The Environmental Protection Agency may, and must if requested by the Minister, prepare guidelines on the information to be contained in the environment impact statements in respect of developments subject to the 1988 and 1989 Regulations: Environmental Protection Agency Act 1992 s.72. The Agency has a right to comment on all environment impact statements and must be consulted before a decision is made to exempt a project from a statutory requirement to prepare such a statement. [Text: Duggan; O'Sullivan & Shepherd]. See BUSWAY; PROTECTED ROAD; MOTORWAY.

**environmental audit.** In relation to any process, development or operation, means a systematic, documented and objective periodic assessment of the organisation structure, management systems, processes and equipment pertaining to, or incidental to, that process, development or operation, for the purposes of environmental protection: Environmental Protection Agency Act 1992 s.74(1). The Agency may promote the carrying out of environmental audits and publish guidelines (ibid s.74(2)).

**environmental law.** The law of planetary housekeeping, concerned with protecting the planet and its people from activities that upset the earth and its life-sustaining capacities: Rodgers "Environmental Law" USA 1977. Environmental law in Ireland is primarily concerned with pollution of the air and water, noise

pollution, waste disposal and resource recovery, pesticides and toxic substances.

EC policy on the environment is required to contribute to pursuit of the following objectives: (a) preserving, protecting and improving the quality of the environment; (b) protecting human health; (c) prudent and rational utilisation of natural resources; and (d) promoting measures at international level to deal with regional or worldwide environmental problems: Treaty of Rome 1957 art.130r as replaced by Maastricht Treaty 1992 art.G(D)(38).

Persons, natural and legal, are entitled to access to information on the environment from public authorities: EC Council Directive 90/313/EEC; Environmental Protection Agency Act 1992 s.110. See also O'Leary in ILSI Gazette (Jan/Feb 1993) 23. [Text: Duggan; Matheson Ormsby Prentice; Scannell].

**environmental medium** . Includes the atmosphere, land, soil and waters: Environmental Protection Agency Act 1992 s.4(3).

**environmental pollution.** Air pollution (qv); the condition of waters after entry of polluting matter; the disposal of waste in a manner which would endanger human health or harm the environment; noise which is a nuisance, or would endanger human health or damage property or harm the environment: Environmental Protection Agency Act 1992 s.4(2). See INTEGRATED POLLUTION CONTROL.

**environmental protection.** Includes (a) the prevention, limitation, abatement or reduction of environmental pollution (qv), and (b) the preservation of the quality of the environment: Environmental Protection Agency Act 1992 s.4(1).

**Environmental Protection Agency.** A body corporate, consisting of a director general and four other directors, with perpetual succession: Environmental Protection Agency Act 1992 ss.19-20. The functions of the Agency include — (a) the licensing, regulation and control of activities for the purposes of environmental protection, (b) the monitoring of the quality of the environment, (c) the provision of support and advisory services, (d) the promotion and co-ordination of environmental research, (e) liaison with the European Environment Agency provided for by Council Regulation 1210/90/EEC (ibid s.52). The Agency may be assigned additional functions and powers and may have certain functions of public authorities transferred to it (ibid ss.53-54; 100-101).

The agency is empowered to delegate functions to any person and to public authorities (ibid ss.25(6) and 45). It is also required to establish regional environmental units (ibid s.43), to make an annual report (ibid s.51) and a report every 5 years on the quality and condition of the environment in the State (ibid s.70). It has power to supervise the performance of statutory functions of local authorities in relation to environmental protection and to give them directions (ibid ss.63 and 68).

The Agency has a major function in relation to *integrated pollution control* (qv) by the issue of licences (ibid ss.82-99). It also may arrange for an inquiry to be held into any incident of environmental pollution and may be directed by the Minister to hold such an inquiry (ibid s.105). See BEST AVAILABLE TECHNOLOGY; COSTS AND CRIMINAL PROCEEDINGS; DRINKING WATER; ENVIRONMENT ASSESSMENT DIRECTIVE; INFLUENCE, IMPROPER; INTEGRATED POLLUTION CONTROL; LABELLING; NOISE; SEWAGE EFFLUENT.

**eo instanti.** [At that instant].

**eo nomine.** [In that name].

**eodem modo quo oritur, eodem modo dissolvitur.** [What has been effected by agreement can be undone by agreement].

**eodem modo quo quid constituitur, eodem modo destruitor.** [A thing is made and is destroyed by one and the same means].

**equal pay.** A woman is entitled to the same rate of remuneration as a man who is employed in the same place by the same employer if both are employed in *like work* (qv). A man is similarly entitled in relation to his remuneration relative to that of a woman. Remuneration includes any consideration, whether in cash or in kind, which an employee receives directly or indirectly from the employer in respect of employment.

It is an offence for an employer to dismiss a person solely or mainly because of making a claim for equal pay and that person may be re-instated to her former position or re-engaged in a different position and obtain compensation to a maximum of 104 weeks' remuneration: Employment Equality Act 1977 ss.30-31.

Equality Officers (qv) of the Labour Relations Commission investigate disputes about equal pay entitlements and issue recommendations; they are empowered to enter premises, to examine records and to seek information. See PMPA Insurance Co Ltd v Keenan (1983) SC; Dept of Public Service v Robinson EP 36/78; The State (Polymark) v ITGWU (1987) ILRM 357. See Anti-Discrimination (Pay) Act 1974; Employment Equality Act 1977. See DISCRIMINATION; LIKE WORK; LABOUR COURT; SOCIAL POLICY.

**equality before the law.** All citizens are required to be held equal before the law: 1937 Constitution, art.40(1). However, the State may in its laws have due regard to differences of capacity, physical and moral, and of social function. See Landers v Attorney General (1975) 109 ILTR 1; de Burca v Attorney General (1976) IR 38.

The first statute to provide for equality in representation as regards men and women on the board of a state-sponsored organisation is the Broadcasting Authority (Amdt) Act 1993 s.7 which provides, inter alia, that where the number of members of the RTE Authority is 7, not less than 3 of them must be men and not less than 3 of them must be women. See DISCRIMINATION; MARITAL COERCION.

**equality clause.** A clause which is deemed to be included as a term in a contract of employment to provide for not less favourable terms for an employee, where the work done by that person is not materially different from that being done by a person of the other sex in the same employment: Employment Equality Act 1977 s.4. See DISCRIMINATION; EQUAL PAY; LIKE WORK.

**equality officer.** Persons appointed by the Labour Relations Commission (qv) and known as equality officers; they are independent in the performance of their function: Industrial Relations Act 1990 s.37. See EQUAL PAY; DISCRIMINATION; LABOUR COURT.

**equitable charge.** See EQUITABLE MORTGAGE.

**equitable doctrines.** The doctrines of

election, performance, satisfaction, conversion and reconversion (qqv).

**equitable estoppel.** A person, who by his words or conduct, wilfully causes another to believe in the existence of a certain state of things, and induces him to act on that belief to his detriment, is estopped from denying that state of things in any subsequent litigation between the parties: Pickard v Sears (1837) 6 A E 469; Doran v Thompson (1978) IR 223. Equitable estoppel may be classified as *promissory* and *propietory*.

*Promissory* estoppel or quasi-estoppel, arises where one party says to another that their existing legal relations are modified in some way, with the intent and result that the other acts on the supposed change of relationship; he is not then permitted, except on reasonable notice to the other party, to revert to their previous relationship: Central London Property Trust Ltd v High Trees House Ltd (1947) KB 130. It has been held that it would be inequitable to allow a party to compensation proceedings to dispute the assumptions on which they were based: Conroy v Commissioner of Garda Siochana (1989 HC) IR 140.

*Proprietory* estoppel arises where the owner of land has encouraged, or acquiesced in, the infringement of his title to the land by another in circumstances which, in the view of the law, renders it inequitable for the owner to assert his legal title to the land in an unqualified manner: Willmot v Barber (1880) 15 Ch D 96; McMahon v Kerry County Council (1981) ILRM 419; Smith v Ireland (1983) ILRM 300; Haughan v Rutledge (1988 HC) IR 295. See EXPECTATION, LEGITIMATE; ISSUE ESTOPPEL.

**equitable execution.** The procedure by which the rights of a *judgment creditor* may be enforced by the appointment of a *receiver*. In general a receiver by way of equitable execution will not be appointed over payments to be made in the future: Ahern v O'Brien (1991) 1 IR 421. For exception, see GROUND RENT. See also ATTACHMENT; JUDGMENT MORTGAGE; RECEIVER, COMPANY; RECEIVER OF MORTGAGED PROPERTY.

**equitable lien.** A lien (qv) which exists independently of possession and which is binding on all who acquire the property with notice of the lien eg a vendor's lien for unpaid purchase money; a purchaser's lien for prematurely paid purchase money. See PURCHASER'S EQUITY.

**equitable mortgage.** The mortgage which arises in equity (qv) by: (a) the agreement to execute a legal mortgage; or (b) the formal mortgage of the *equity of redemption*; or (c) the deposit of title deeds, with or without a memorandum of deposit. A legal mortgage takes priority over an equitable one, even if created after the equitable one, under the equitable maxim *where the equities are equal, the law prevails*. See DEPOSIT OF TITLE DEEDS; EQUITY OF REDEMPTION; MORTGAGE.

**equitable mortgage of shares.** See SHARES, EQUITABLE MORTGAGE OF.

**equitable remedies.** The discretionary remedies that evolved from equity (qv) eg rescission, specific performance, injunction, appointment of receiver (qqv).

**equitable waste.** See WASTE.

**equities.** See ORDINARY SHARES.

**equity.** (1) Fairness, impartiality, natural justice. (2) The doctrines and procedures which developed alongside the common law (qv) and statute law, administered originally by the Court of Chancery to remedy some of the defects of the common law, and which became fused together by the amalgamation of the courts by the Judicature (Ireland) Act 1877. This Act provided that where there is any conflict between the rules of law and equity, equity is to prevail. (3) The issued share capital of a company. [Text: Keane (2); Kiely; Wylie (3); Snell UK]. See CAPITAL.

**equity, maxims of.** Principles which state the fundamental principles of equity eg equity acts *in personam*; equity follows the law; equity will not suffer a wrong to go without a remedy; equity acts on the conscience; equity looks on the intent rather than on the form; where the equities are equal the law prevails; where the equities are equal, the first in time prevails; he who seeks equity must do equity; he who comes to equity must come with clean hands; equity aids the vigilant and not the indolent; delay defeats equity; equity regards the balance of convenience; equity regards as done that which ought to be done; equity imputes an intention to fulfil an obligation; equality is equity; equity will not assist a volunteer; equity never lacks a trustee.

**equity civil bill.** See CIVIL BILL.

**equity of redemption.** The sum total of the mortgagor's rights in equity; it is an equitable estate which can be assigned, devised or mortgaged again. It exists from the moment the mortgage is made. It includes the equitable right to redeem the mortgage when the legal right has been lost by failure to pay the mortgage debt by the due date. There must be no *clogs* (qv) on the equity of redemption. A formal mortgage of the equity of redemption creates an equitable mortgage.

The equity of redemption is lost by: (a) sale by a court in lieu of foreclosure; (b) sale out of court by a mortgagee under an express power of sale given in the mortgage deed or by statutory power of sale given by the Conveyancing Act 1881 s.19; (c) lapse of time under the Statute of Limitations 1957. See FORE-CLOSURE; MORTGAGE; PUISNE MORTGAGE; REDEMPTION.

**equity securities.** See PRE-EMPTION.

**equivocation.** An ambiguity in a document. Where the language of a document, though intended to apply to one person or thing only, applies equally to two or more, and it is impossible to gather from the context which was intended, the document may be interpreted by oral evidence as to the surrounding circumstances of the writer as well as to his direct declaration of intention. Extrinsic evidence is admissible to assist in the construction of a will: Succession Act 1965 s.90. See Richardson v Watson (1833) 4 B Ad 787. See AMBIGUITY.

**erasure.** Erasures or obliterations in a will do not prevail unless proved to have existed in the will prior to its execution, or unless the alterations are duly executed and attested, or unless rendered valid by re-execution or by a codicil: RSC O.79 r.12. See ALTERATION; WILL, REVOCATION OF.

**error.** See PLEADINGS, AMENDMENT OF; SLIP RULE.

**escape.** It is an indictable offence (qv) to aid an escape or attempt to escape from lawful custody: Criminal Law Act 1976 s.6. It is an offence for a person, while under lawful arrest or in lawful custody,

to regain his liberty either by himself or by the voluntary act of his custodian. Prison breaking (qv) is also an offence. See also Convict Prisons (Ireland) Act 1854; Offences Against the State Act 1939 s.32(2); Firearms Act 1964 s.27.

**escape clause.** See EXCLUSION CLAUSE.

**escape of dangerous things.** See RYLANDS FLETCHER, RULE IN.

**escheat.** The *reversion* of land to the lord of the fee or the State on failure of heirs of the owner. It derived from the feudal rule that where an estate in fee simple came to an end, the land reverted to the lord by whose ancestors or predecessors the estate was originally created. Abolished by the Succession Act 1965 s.11. In default of next-of kin, the State takes the estate as ultimate intestate successor (ibid s.73).

**escrow.** A deed delivered to a person who is not a party to it, to be held by that party until certain conditions are performed eg the payment of money, after which it is delivered and takes effect as a deed. See DEED.

**essence of a contract.** The essential conditions of a contract without which agreement would not have been entered into. See CONDITION; TIME OF ESSENCE OF CONTRACT.

**estate.** An interest in land. An estate may be of *freehold* or less than freehold. Freehold estates are those of fee simple, fee tail and a life estate; less than freehold estates are leases and tenancies (qqv).

**estate agent.** See AUCTIONEER; HOUSE AGENT.

**estate duty.** A tax imposed on property which passed on death. Now replaced for deaths on or after 1st April 1975 by a new capital acquisitions tax called *inheritance tax* and, in addition, from 18th June 1993 by a *probate tax* (qv). See Capital Acquisitions Tax Act 1976; Finance Act 1993 ss.109-119. See INHERITANCE TAX; PROBATE TAX.

**estate management.** The refusal of consent by a landlord to an assignment of a lease may be upheld where it is based on valid estate management grounds and is not unreasonable: OHS Ltd v Green Property Co Ltd (1986) ILRM 451. See BUSINESS TENANT; COVENANT.

**estate tail.** See FEE TAIL.

**estimates.** The annual statement of the government's proposals for public expenditure in the ensuing year. See BUDGET.

**estimates meeting.** The statutory meeting, which a local authority (qv) is required to hold, to consider an estimate of expenses and rate in the pound to be levied for the several purposes in the estimate: City and County Management (Amendment) Act 1955 s.10. See Ahern v Kerry County Council (1988) ILRM 392. See RATES.

**estoppel.** A rule of evidence which precludes a person from asserting or denying a fact, which he has by words or conduct led others to believe in. If a person by a representation induces another to change his position on the faith of the representation, he cannot afterwards deny the truth of his representation. Estoppel must be pleaded to be taken advantage of; it provides a shield not a sword and consequently it cannot create a cause of action.

Estoppel can arise under four headings: (1) estoppel by *record:* a party cannot deny the facts upon which a judgment against him was based; the matter is *res judicata*; (2) estoppel by *deed:* a party to a deed cannot deny the facts recited in the deed unless the deed is tainted by illegality or fraud; (3) estoppel by *conduct* (or in pais) eg a tenant who has accepted a lease cannot dispute the lessor's title; (4) *equitable* estoppel (qv). See Boyce v McBride (1987) ILRM 95; Kenny v Kelly (1988) IR 457; Friends Provident v Doherty (1992) ILRM 372. See EXPECTATION, LEGITIMATE; ISSUE ESTOPPEL; RES JUDICATA.

**estovers, common of.** The right to cut wood, gorse or furze on the lands of another. See PROFIT A PRENDRE.

**estreat.** [Extract]. A true copy of a court record, relating to recognisances (qv) and fines (qv). The estreat of a recognisance involves enforcing the record of a recognisance which had become forfeited. See Criminal Procedure Act 1967 s.32. See also Tynan v Attorney General 96 ILTR 144: AG v Sheehy (1990 SC) 8 ILT Dig 239.

**et al; et aliae; et alia.** [And others].

**et al; et alibi.** [And elsewhere]. See ALIBI.

**et seq; et sequentes.** [And those which follow].

**etching.** See ARTISTIC WORK.

**ethics committee.** As regards the conducting of a *clinical trial* (qv), the committee, approved by the Minister, which is required to consider the justification for conducting the proposed trial and the circumstances under which it is proposed to be conducted; it must not consider the proposed trial to be justified unless it is satisfied that the risks to be incurred by the participants would be commensurate with the objectives of the trial: Control of Clinical Trials Act 1987 s.8. The committee is required to consider specified matters, including details of any proposed inducements or rewards, whether monetary or otherwise to be made for becoming a participant (ibid s.8(4)).

**ethics in government.** The government has stated, in 1993, its intention to introduce legislation to give effect to commitments on ethics in government in the Programme for Partnership Government 1993-1997.

**Euro-Jus.** A network of legal experts on Community law, one in each member state of the European Community, whose function is to answer practical questions on Community law, addressed to them by individuals, on matters which affect their everyday life eg right to work and to social security in another member state. The service is provided free of charge to the individual. The Irish Euro-Jus is located at the EC Office in Ireland, Jean Monnet Centre, 39 Molesworth Street, Dublin 2. Telephone: (01) 6712244.

**European Bank for Reconstruction and Development .** The bank established with the object of fostering and promoting the transition of the former command economies of Central and Eastern Europe towards a market-based economic system. See European Bank for Reconstruction and Development Act 1991. See SI No 65 of 1991 for privileges and immunities in Irish law.

**European Central Bank.** Provision has been made for the establishment of a European Central Bank (ECB) and a European System of Central Banks (ESCB): Treaty of Rome 1957 art.4a as inserted by Maastricht Treaty 1992 art.G(B)(7). The ESCB will be composed of the national central banks of the member States and the ECB. See CENTRAL BANK; LEGAL TENDER; MONETARY POLICY.

**European citizenship.** See CITIZENSHIP.

**European Commission.** The civil service of the European Community (qv). It consists of 17 members (a President and Commissioners), each of whom is assigned a particular portfolio and are collectively responsible. Each member State must have a national on the Commission but not more than two. A Commissioner represents the Commission and not his own State. Following the Maastricht Treaty (qv) the Commission retains, with a few exceptions, the sole right to initiate legislation; the term of office of the Commission however will be 5 years (from 1995) to run more closely with the term of the European Parliament which in future must approve the appointment of the Commission: Treaty of Rome 1957 art.158 as inserted by Maastricht Treaty 1992 art.G(E)(48). See also Treaty of Rome 1957 arts.155-163. See SINGLE EUROPEAN ACT.

**European Community; EC.** The Community, established by the Treaty signed at Rome on the 25th day of March 1957. The fourth amendment to the Constitution in 1972 provided for the State to join the Community. By the amendment, no provision of the Constitution invalidates laws enacted, acts done or measures adopted by the State *necessitated by the obligations of membership* or prevents laws enacted, acts done or measures adopted by the Community, or institutions thereof, from having the force of law in the State: 1937 Constitution art.29(4)(3). The Constitution was further amended in 1987 and 1992 by the 10th and 11th referenda to enable the State to ratify the Single European Act (qv) and the Maastricht Treaty (qv) respectively, the two main revisions of the Treaty of Rome (ibid Constitution art.29(4)(3)-(5)).

The Treaty became binding in the State from 1st January 1973 and provision was made for all existing and future acts adopted by the institutions of the Community to be binding on the State and to be part of the domestic law thereof under the conditions laid down in the Treaty: European Communities Acts 1972 s.2 and 1992. A Minister of State may make regulations for enabling

s.2 to have full effect (ibid 1972 Act s.3).

The European Community has a legal personality, and in each of the member States must enjoy the most extensive legal capacity accorded to legal persons under their laws: Treaty of Rome 1957 arts.210-211.

The European Community has as its task, by establishing a common market and an economic and monetary union and by implementing common policies or activities, to promote throughout the community a harmonious and balanced development of economic activities, sustainable and non-inflationary growth respecting the environment, a high degree of convergence of economic performance, a high level of employment and of social protection, the raising of the standard of living and quality of life, and economic and social cohesion and solidarity among member States: Treaty of Rome 1957 art.2 as replaced by Maastricht Treaty 1992 art.G(B)(2).

The tasks entrusted to the Community are carried out by the following institutions: European Parliament, Council, Commission, Court of Justice, Court of Auditors: Treaty of Rome 1957 art.4 as replaced by Maastricht Treaty 1992 art G(B)(6). The Council and Commmission are assisted by an Economic and Social Committee and a Committee of the Regions acting in an advisory capacity. See Greene v Minister for Agriculture (1989 HC) ITLR (12 Jun). [Text: EC Pub (1)]. See COMMUNITY LAW; COUNCIL OF MINISTERS; ENLARGEMENT OF EC; EUROPEAN COMMISSION; EUROPEAN UNION; INTERNAL MARKET.

**European Company.** A company created under EC law and known as a SE (*Societas Europaea*), as proposed in 1988. See Quinn in 8ILT & SJ (1990) 231.

**European Convention on Human Rights.** A convention of the Council of Europe which has been ratified by Ireland in 1953 but has not been incorporated into the domestic law; consequently the courts of the State for the most part refuse to entertain arguments based directly on it. Under the convention was created the Commission on Human Rights and the Court of Human Rights. The convention seeks to protect: the right to life, right to liberty and fair trial; freedom from torture and slavery; freedom of thought and religion. The Commission operates in a conciliatory manner, receiving petitions alleging non-compliance with the convention and initiating investigations.

The European Union (qv) is required to respect human rights, as guaranteed by the Convention, and as they result from the constitutional traditions common to the member States, as general principles of Community law: Maastricht Treaty 1992 art.F.2.See In re O'Laighleis (1960) IR 93; Norris v Attorney General (1982 HC) and (1984 SC) IR 36. See EUROPEAN COURT OF HUMAN RIGHTS.

**European Convention onTorture.** See TORTURE.

**European Council.** See COUNCIL OF MINISTERS.

**European Court of Human Rights.** The judicial body of the Council of Europe which hears cases involving basic rights and freedoms. Member states are not obliged to accept its jurisdiction and its decisions do not bind our courts: Re O'Laighleis (1960) IR 93. However, a judgment of the Court may have a persuasive effect in Ireland in relation to contempt of court: Desmond & Dedeir v Glackin & Minister for Industry & Commerce (1992 HC) ITLR (17 Feb).

The Court has held (a) that internment without trial in Ireland did not breach the Convention on Human Rights as the government had derogated from the terms of the Convention in times of national emergency: Lawless v Ireland (1961) 1 EHRR 15; (b) that inhuman and degrading treatment had been inflicted on certain persons who had been in custody in Northern Ireland: Ireland v United Kingdom (1978) 2 EHRR 25; (c) that the non-availability of state-funded legal aid in matrimonial matters was a breach of the Convention: Airey v Ireland (1979) 2 EHRR 305; (d) that the Convention on Human Rights had been violated as the applicants had not been brought promptly before a judge or other judicial officer following their arrest: Brogan & Ors v United Kingdom: 7ILT & SJ (1989) 16; (e) that a company and an individual had their right to peaceful enjoyment of their possessions interfered with: Healy Holdings Ltd & Healy v Ireland (Irish Times 30/11/1991). [Text: Berger]. See BUGGERY; EUROPEAN CONVEN-

TION OF HUMAN RIGHTS; LEGAL AID.

**European Court of Justice.** The institution of the EC, consisting of 13 judges, which adjudicates on issues between an individual and his government, between member States of the Community, or between institutions of the Community: Treaty of Rome 1957 arts.164-188 as amended by Maastricht Treaty 1992 art.G(E)(49)-(58). Each member State is entitled to nominate a national to the court. Courts of the member States may *refer* matters relating to the Treaty of Rome (qv) to the European Court for determination.

The issue as to what stage a *reference* should be made to the Court of Justice is a matter exclusively for the national courts to determine; the Supreme Court has jurisdiction to grant an interlocutory injunction notwithstanding a reference of separate issues to the Court of Justice: SPUC v Grogan (1990) 8ILT Dig 156 and Treaty of Rome art. 177. A ruling of the European Court may be relied upon retrospectively where that Court, on a question of interpretation of Community law, does not within the same judgment, limit its retrospective effect: Carberry v Minister for Social Welfare (1989) ITLR (5 Jun).

Penalties are introduced to be paid by a member State which is found by the Court of Justice to have failed to fulfil an obligation under the Treaty (ibid art.171 inserted by Maastricht Treaty 1992 art.G(E)(51)). The Court has no jurisdiction over the two non-Community pillars of the European Union (qv) (ie the common foreign and security policy, and judicial and home affairs) or over the common Union provisions in arts.A-F (ibid art.L). See also Portion Foods Ltd v Minister for Agriculture (1981) ILRM 161. See EUROPEAN COMMUNITY; FIRST INSTANCE, COURT OF; PERJURY; PRELIMINARY RULINGS.

**European Economic Area.** See EEA AGREEMENT.

**European Economic Community; EEC; EC.** Term in the Treaty of Rome 1957; it is replaced by the term *European Community*: Maastricht Treaty 1992 art.G.A(1).

**European Economic Interest Grouping (EEIG).** A form of international association which enables its members

to combine part of their activities while retaining their economic and legal independence: EEC Regulation No 2137/85 — OJ 1985 L119 p.1 and SI No 191 of 1989. See Linnane in 7ILT & SJ (1989) 213, 9ILT & SJ (1991) 36, 10 ILT & SJ (1992) 163; Power in 8 ILT & SJ (1990) 19. See also Finance Act 1990 s.29.

**European election.** An election in the State of members to the European Parliament; *European elector* means a person entitled to vote at such election: Electoral Act 1992 s.2(1). A person is entitled to be registered as a European elector in a constituency if he has reached the age of 18 years, is ordinarily resident in that constituency and is either (a) a citizen of Ireland or (b) a national of another EC Member State (ibid s.9). See European Assembly Elections Act 1977 as amended by Electoral Act 1992 ss.171-172.

**European Investment Bank.** The non-profit making bank, comprising the member States of the EC, which has the task of granting loans and giving guarantees which facilitate the financing of a range of projects eg projects for developing less developed regions; projects for modernizing or converting undertakings; projects of common interest to several member States: Treaty of Rome 1957 art.198d-e as inserted by Maastricht Treaty 1992 art.G(E)(68).

The governors of the bank are empowered to establish a European Investment Fund; ratification by the State of the agreement to so empower the governors has been effected by adding the agreement to the list of Treaties governing the EC as they appear in s.1(1) of the European Communities Act 1972: European Communities (Amendment) Act 1993 s.2.

**European law.** See COMMUNITY LAW.

**European ombudsman.** See OMBUDSMAN, EUROPEAN.

**European Parliament.** The institution of the European Economic Community (qv) which generally is elected directly by the peoples of the member States, presided over by a President which office rotates every six months: Treaty of Rome 1957. It has a right to be consulted on all politically important measures; it also has advisory and supervisory powers.

The Council of Ministers (qv) is not obliged to take account of the opinions or amendments put forward by the Parliament. However, the Parliament may, by Motion of Censure, force the resignation of the Commission (ibid art.144).

The role of the parliament has been strengthened by the Maastricht Treaty 1992 eg (a) the parliament has the right to reject legislation in a number of areas; (b) parliament approval is required in a number of areas including the appointment of the Commission; and (c) the parliament has extended rights of involvement in the detailed operation of the Community eg a right of enquiry, a right to receive petitions, a right to call on the Commission to initiate legislation, and the right to appoint the European Ombudsman.

Election in Ireland to the European Parliament is by proportional representation with a form of democratic endorsement for substitutes for the elected member who retires, dies or otherwise relinquishes his seat. See European Assembly Elections Acts 1977 and 1984 as amended by Electoral Act 1992. See CITIZENSHIP; COMMUNITY LAW; CONSTITUENCY; SINGLE EUROPEAN ACT; MAASTRICHT TREATY.

**European patent.** A patent granted under the European Patent Convention (qv): Patents Act 1992 s.2(1). See also COMMUNITY PATENT AGREEMENT.

**European Patent Convention; EPC.** The Convention of 1973 which established a European patent organisation with its own European Patent Office situated in Munich for the granting of *European patents* under the system of law as set out in the Convention. The Convention is expressed to be a special agreement within the Paris Convention (qv). Ireland ratified the Convention on 1st May 1992.

An application under the EPC must designate in which of the contracting States patent protection is desired, and if the application is accepted, a European patent is granted for each of the designated States, which patent must be treated in the State as having the same effect of and subject to the same conditions as are national patents granted by that State (ibid EPC art.2). This is given effect in Ireland by the Patents Act 1992 s.119.

If the language of the specification of the European patent is not English, a translation in English must be filed with the Irish Patents Office for the patent to have effect in Ireland (ibid s.119(6)-(7)). There is provision for the conversion of an application for a European patent into an application for an Irish patent (ibid s.120) and for the High Court to determine questions as to the right to a European patent (ibid s.121). See also ibid ss.122-132. See also EPC Protocol on Recognition. See COMMUNITY PATENT AGREEMENT.

**European Police Office; EUROPOL.** The member States of the EC have agreed to the objective underlying a German proposal to establish a European Police Office for the exchange of information on serious international crime; the member States envisage the adoption of practical measures in many areas eg support of national criminal investigation and security authorities; creation of data bases; drawing up of Europe-wide prevention strategies; with a view to deciding during 1994 at the latest whether the scope for such cooperation should be extended: Maastricht Treaty 1992 — Declaration on Police Cooperation. See COMMON POLICIES; POLICE COOPERATION.

**European Union.** The Union, founded on the European Communities (qv), established by the member States of the EC by the Maastricht Treaty 1992 art.A. The Union includes the European Community together with-separate provisions on common foreign and security policy and on judicial cooperation. The task of the Union is to organise, in a manner demonstrating consistency and solidarity, relations between the member States and between their peoples. The Union has a number of objectives eg (a) to promote economic and social progress, (b) to assert its identity on the international scene, (c) to strengthen the protection of the rights and interests of the nationals of its member States, (d) to develop close cooperation on justice and home affairs (ibid art.B).

The principle of *subsidiarity* must be respected, as must national identities of its member States and fundamental rights (ibid arts.A and F). Ireland may become

a member of the Union: 1937 Constitution art.29(4)(4). No provision of the Constitution invalidates laws enacted, acts done or measures adopted by the State which are necessitated by the obligations of membership of the Union (ibid art.29(4)(5)). See COMMON POLICIES; MAASTRICHT TREATY.

**euthanasia.** The term used to describe the painless killing of a person; it is unlawful. See MURDER; SUICIDE.

**eviction.** Dispossession; recovery of land by due process of law. See EJECTMENT.

**evidence.** The testimony of witnesses and the production of documents and things which may be used for the purposes of proof in legal proceedings. The law of evidence comprises the rules which govern the presentation of facts and proof in proceedings before a court. Evidence may be direct or circumstantial. *Direct* evidence is evidence of a fact in issue (qv); it may be the statement of someone who observed with his senses. *Circumstantial* evidence is evidence of a fact relevant to the *fact in issue;* it is evidence from which the fact in issue may be inferred. [Text: Cole; Fennell; Cross UK; Phipson UK].

**evidence, adducing.** See BURDEN OF PROOF.

**evidence, book of.** See BOOK OF EVIDENCE.

**evidence, circumstantial.** See CIRCUMSTANTIAL EVIDENCE.

**evidence, extrinsic.** Evidence of statements or circumstances or facts not referred to in a document which may explain or vary its meaning. Such evidence is generally inadmissible except to show the intention of a testator and to assist in the construction of or to explain any contradiction in a will. See Succession Act 1965 s.90; also Rowe v Law (1978) IR 55; Clinton, deceased: O'Sullivan v Dunne (1988) ILRM 80. See AMBIGUITY.

**evidence, false.** See PERJURY; PERVERTING THE COURSE OF JUSTICE.

**evidence, fresh.** See FRESH EVIDENCE.

**evidence, hearsay.** See HEARSAY.

**evidence, new.** See FRESH EVIDENCE.

**evidence, preservation of.** Evidence relevant to guilt or innocence must so far as is necessary and practicable be kept until the conclusion of a trial; also articles which may give rise to the reasonable possibility of securing relevant evidence must be preserved also: Murphy

v DPP (1989) ILRM 71; 7ILT & SJ (1989) 158.

**evidence, primary.** Primary evidence is the best evidence available eg primary evidence of a document is the document itself or a duplicate of the original. See BEST EVIDENCE; DOCUMENTARY EVIDENCE; EVIDENCE, SECONDARY.

**evidence, secondary.** Evidence which suggests the existence of better evidence and which may be rejected if that better evidence is available eg a copy of a document, or, oral evidence of the contents of a lost will. See DOCUMENTARY EVIDENCE; OFFICE COPY.

**evidence and constitutional rights.** The courts will rule as inadmissible, evidence obtained in violation of constitutional rights unless the act constituting the breach was committed unintentionally or accidently or there are extraordinary excusing circumstances justifying its admissibility: People (DPP) v Kenny (1990 SC) ILRM 569.

**evidence in previous proceedings.** As an exception to the hearsay (qv) rule, the evidence of a witness in previous proceedings is admissible where the witness is dead, or unable to travel, or is otherwise unprocurable, provided that: (a) the person against whom the evidence is tendered had on the former occasion an opportunity of examining the witness; (b) the question in issue is substantially the same; (c) the proceedings are between the same parties. See DEPOSITION; DISTRICT COURT, PRELIMINARY EXAMINATION; HOSTILE WITNESS; PREVIOUS STATEMENT, INCONSISTENT.

**evidence in rebuttal.** See REBUTTAL, EVIDENCE IN.

**evidence obtained illegally.** Evidence obtained illegally is not necessarily inadmissible. It has been held that it is admissible if it is relevant, the illegality being merely ignored although not condoned; however, the trial judge has a discretion to exclude it, if it appears to him that public policy, based on a balancing of public interests, requires such exclusion. See The People (Attorney General) and O'Brien v McGrath (1964) 99 ILTR 59; The People v O'Brien and O'Brien (1965) IR 142; The People v Madden (1977) 111 ILTR 117; DPP v McMahon (1987) ILRM 87. See CONFESSION; EVIDENCE AND CONSTITUTIONAL RIGHTS.

**evidence of character.** See CHARACTER, EVIDENCE OF.

**evidence of conviction.** See CONVICTION, EVIDENCE OF.

**evidence tending to bastardise children.** The rule of law, known as the *rule in Russell v Russell,* under which neither spouse could give evidence which would tend towards rendering a child of their marriage illegitimate, ceased to have legal effect in the State after the enactment of the 1937 Constitution: S v S (1983) IR 68. Statutory recognition of this is given by the Status of Children Act 1987 s.47 which provides that the evidence of a husband or wife is admissible in any proceedings to prove that marital intercourse did or did not take place between them during any period.

**ex abundanti cautela.** [From excess of caution].

**ex aequo et bono.** [In justice and good faith].

**ex cathedra.** [From the chair]. With official authority.

**ex contractu.** [Arising out of contract].

**ex curia.** [Out of Court].

**ex debito justitiae.** [Arising as a matter of right]. A remedy which the applicant obtains as of right, in contrast with a discretionary right eg in the case of an order of habeas corpus (qv). A petitioning creditor who is unable to have his debt paid by a company is entitled to a winding up order *ex debito justitiae*: Bowes v Hope Life Insurance and Guarantee Co (1865) 11 HLC 389. See also In re Downs & Co (1943) IR 420; Devereaux v Kotsonouris (1992 HC) ILRM 140.

**ex delicto.** [Arising out of wrongs]. See TORT.

**ex diuturnitae temporis omnia praesumuntur esse rite et solemnitur acta.** [From lapse of time, all things are presumed to have been done rightly and regularly]. See ANCIENT DOCUMENT.

**ex div.** Ex dividend; indicates that the price of stocks and shares does not include dividends or interest to date. See BOND WASHING; CUM DIV.

**ex dolo malo non oritur actio.** [No right of action can have its origin in fraud].

**ex gratia.** [As a favour]. Not arising pursuant to a legal liability. See CRIMINAL

INJURIES COMPENSATION TRIBUNAL; UN-
TRACED DRIVER.

**ex informata conscientia.** [From an
informed conscience]. A district court
judge cannot have regard to such matters
*ex informata conscientia* in dismissing a
charge under the Probation of Offenders
Act 1907 where there is no such evidence
before the court. He must have (in the
nature of the offence or the facts
established in evidence before him), the
materials entitling him to apply the Act:
McClellan v Brady (1918) 2 IR 63. See
JUDICIAL NOTICE; LEGISLATION, INTERPRETA-
TION OF.

**ex maleficio non oritur contractus.** [A
contract cannot arise out of an illegal
act]. See ILLEGAL CONTRACTS.

**ex mero motu.** [Of one's own free will].

**ex nudo pacto non oritur actio.** [No
action arises from a nude contract]. See
NUDUM PACTUM.

**ex officio.** [By virtue of office].

**ex-parte.** [On behalf of]. An application
made in a judicial proceedings made by
a party to the proceedings in the absence
of and without notice to the other party
or parties or by a person who has an
interest but is not a party thereto. See
RSC O.40 r.20; RCC form 26. For
contrasting examples, see JUDICIAL REVIEW;
LABOUR INJUNCTION; INJUNCTION.

**ex post facto.** [By a subsequent act].
Retrospectively. See RETROSPECTIVE LEG-
ISLATION; ULTRA VIRES.

**ex proprio motu.** [Of his own accord].
Refers to an action taken by the court
on its own initiative.

**ex relatione; ex rel.** [From a narrative
or information].

**ex tempore judgment.** See EXTEMPORE
JUDGMENT.

**ex turpi causa non oritur actio.** [An
action does not arise from a base cause].
An illegal contract is unenforceable as it
is void. See Scott v Doering (1892) 2
QB 724; Brady v Flood (1841) 6 Circuit
Cases 309. See ILLEGAL CONTRACTS.

**exacta diligentia.** [Utmost diligence].
See BREACH OF TRUST.

**examination.** Interrogation of a person
on oath. *Examination-in-chief* (or direct
examination) is the examination of a
witness by the party who has called him.
*Cross-examination* is the examination of
that witness by the opposite party with
a view to diminishing the effect of his

evidence. *Re-examination* is the further
examination of the witness by the party
who called him, with a view to explaining
or contradicting any false impression
created by the cross-examination; re-
examination must be confined to matters
arising out of the cross-examination.
*Leading questions* (qv) must not be asked
in the examination-in-chief or re-examination; they may be asked in cross-
examination. A judge may disallow any
question put in cross-examination which
may appear to him to be vexatious and
not relevant: RSC O.36 r.37. In the
district court, it is part of a judge's
function to decide what sort of examination-in-chief and cross-examination
may be pursued; if his error in refusing
cross-examination is so gross, it may
oust his jurisdiction: O'Broin v D J
Ruane (1989 HC) ILRM 732. As a
general rule, the prosecution are not
bound to inform the defence of matters
which they may put in cross-examination
to witnesses for the defence: People
(DPP) v James Ryan (1993 CCA) ITLR
(19 Apr). See also Arbitration Act 1954
s.22(1)(d). See also CONVICTION, EVIDENCE
OF; DISTRICT COURT; HOSTILE WITNESS.

**examination of goods.** Where goods are
delivered to a buyer which he has not
previously examined, he is not deemed
to have accepted them unless and until
he has had a reasonable opportunity of
examining them for the purpose of
ascertaining whether they are in conformity with the contract: Sale of Goods Act
1893 s.34; SGSS Act 1980 s.20. See
White Sewing Machine v Fitzgerald
(1895) 29 ILTR 37; Marry v Merville
Dairy Ltd (1954) 88 ILTR 129.

**examination order, district court.** The
order which a judge of the district court
may make to compel a debtor to attend
before him on a specified date to be
examined as to his means and to compel
lodgement of a statement in writing
setting forth his assets and liabilities, his
income earned and unearned, and the
means by which it is earned or the
source from which it is derived and the
persons for whose support he is legally
or morally liable: Enforcement of Court
Orders Act 1926 s.15 as amended by the
Courts (No 2) Act 1986 ss.1 and 3.

Following examination, the judge may
make an *instalment order* requiring the

debt to be repaid by instalments, in default of which the debtor may be imprisoned by order.

**examination re bankrupt.** The court may summons a bankrupt or any person who is known or suspected to have property of the bankrupt; a person is not entitled to refuse to answer on the grounds that his answer might incriminate him but his answers will not be admissible in evidence against him in other proceedings: Bankruptcy Act 1988 s.21. See also Re Wilson ex p. Nicholson (1880) 14 Ch D 243.

**examination re company.** As regards a company which is compulsorily or voluntarily being wound up, the court has extensive power to examine persons on oath and they may not refuse to answer any question on the grounds that they may be incriminating themselves; however, any answers given will not be admissible in evidence in any other proceedings, except in regard to perjury in respect of the answers. The court has power to order a person being examined to pay his debt owed to the company or to return to the liquidator any money, property or books and papers of the company on such terms as the court directs. See Companies Act 1963 ss.245 and 245A as amended or inserted by the Companies Act 1990 ss.126-127; RSC O.74 r.125; O.39 r.4. See Re Aluminium Fabricators Ltd (1983 HC). See COURT PROTECTION OF COMPANY; INVESTIGATION OF COMPANY.

**examination results.** Special provisions have been made concerning the right of individuals to personal data (qv) regarding examination results; examination authorities are required to comply with a request for a copy of any such personal data within 60 days from the date of the request or from the date of first publication of the results whichever is the later: Data Protection Act 1988 s.4(6).

**examiner of company.** See COURT PROTECTION OF COMPANY.

**Examiner of Restrictive Practices.** Formerly, the person appointed by the Minister with many functions relating to the supply or distribution of goods or of the provision of a service: Restrictive Practices Acts 1972 and 1987, now repealed. See Competition Act 1991 ss.2(2) and 22. See COMPETITION AUTHORITY.

**excardination.** See INCARDINATION.

**exception.** (1) In proceedings, an objection to an answer. (2) In a deed, a *saving clause* to prevent the passing of something which otherwise would pass.

**excess clause.** A clause in an insurance policy whereby the insured is to bear the first specified amount of any loss. See INSURANCE.

**exchange.** (1) Reciprocal transfer of ownership or possession. (2) A place for the purchase and sale of, for example, stocks and shares. (3) A transfer of settled land for other land. See SETTLEMENT; STOCK EXCHANGE.

**exchange, bill of.** See BILL OF EXCHANGE.

**exchange control.** The restricting of certain outward movement of funds from the State and ensuring that funds accruing to Irish residents from external sources are not withheld from the country's external reserves: Exchange Control Acts 1954 to 1990. Breach of an exchange control regulation constituted an offence; however, as regards civil proceedings, the courts would enforce a contract even if the consequences of so doing would involve a breach of exchange control regulations: Fibretex v Belier Ltd (1954) 89 ILTR 141; Shelley v Pollock (1980) QB 348. There was nothing illegal or improper in an inspector, validly appointed to investigate a company pursuant to the Companies Act 1990, obtaining through the Minister information from the Central Bank concerning exchange control transactions: Desmond & Dedeir Ltd v Glackin & Minister for Industry and Commerce (1992 SC) ITLR (7 Dec).

Full liberalisation of capital investment within the EC is the objective of the Treaty of Rome 1957 art.8A (as inserted by the Single European Act 1986 art.13). In accordance with this objective, exchange controls with all countries were abolished as from 1st January 1993 as the 1990 Act lapsed on 31st December 1992. However, the Minister may by regulation impose restrictions on *financial transfers* involving specified States: Financial Transfers Act 1992. Financial transfers, without prejudice to the generality of the expression, includes all transfers which could be movement of capital or payments within the meaning of the treaties governing the EC if made between member States of the Community (ibid s.3). Restrictions were imposed in 1992 on financial transfers involving Iraq and the Federal Republic of Yugoslavia as part of UN agreed sanctions: SI Nos 414 and 415 of 1992. See also Luisi and Carbone v Ministero de Tesero (1984) ECR 377. See CAPITAL LIBERALISATION.

**exchange rate.** See RATE OF EXCHANGE.

**exchange rate policy.** The Council of Ministers are empowered to conclude formal agreements on the exchange rate system for the *ECU* in relation to non-Community currencies: Treaty of Rome 1957 art.109 inserted by Maastricht Treaty 1992 art.G(D)(25).

**exchequer bills.** Bills of credit issued by government under the authority of parliament; they are for various sums and bear interest according to the usual rate at the time. The Minister is empowered to create and issue securities bearing interest at such rate and subject to such conditions as to repayment, redemption or any other matter as he thinks fit: Finance Act 1970 s.54 as amended by Finance (No 2) Act 1970 s.6. The National Treasury Management Agency offers for sale: (a) *exchequer bills* which are sold by tender every week and have a maturity of 91 or 182 days, and (b) *exchequer notes* which are sold directly daily and have a range of maturity dates, not less than 7 and not more than 120 days. See also National Treasury Management Agency Act 1990.

**excise duty.** A duty chargeable on certain goods eg intoxicating liquors and tobacco. The government is empowered to impose, vary or terminate excise duties by order, provided the order is validated by confirmation by the Oireachtas (qv): Imposition of Duties Act 1957; McDaid v Judge Sheehy (1989 HC) ILRM 342 & (1991 SC) ILRM 250. The Director of Public Prosecutions has a year to apply for a summons in certain excise matters: DPP v Howard (1990 HC) ITLR (26 Feb).

As regards the EC, the general principle is that excise duty becomes payable at the time of production of the product within in or its entry into the Community in the relevant member State: Council Directive 92/12/EEC of 25th February 1992. It is in the member State of consumption where excise duty is to be paid, except products acquired by private individuals for their own use and transported by them, in which case duty is charged in the member State where they are acquired. See Control of Excisable Products Regulations 1992 (SI No 430 of 1992). See Travers in 10 ILT & SJ (1992) 254. See BET.

**exclusion clause.** A clause in a contract which excludes or modifies an obligation, whether primary, general secondary or anticipatory secondary, that would otherwise arise under the contract by implication of law: Photo Productions Ltd v Securicor Transport Ltd (1980) AC 827. It has been held that an exclusion clause in a loan application form which stated "no responsibility can be accepted by the Society for the condition of the property", absolved the Society from any liability in respect of the condition of the property and the clause was binding: O'Connor v First National Building Society (1991 HC) ILRM 208. See EXCLUSION CLAUSES, RESTRICTION OF.

**exclusion clauses, restriction of.** Any term which exempts a seller from certain implied conditions in a contract for the sale of goods is void where the buyer *deals as a consumer* (qv) and, in any other case, is not enforceable unless it is shown that it is *fair and reasonable*: Sale of Goods Act 1893 s.55; SGSS Act 1980 s.22. Similar provisions apply also in relation to a term of a hire-purchase agreement (ibid 1980 Act s.31). A condition or warranty is not negatived except by clear words (ibid 1893 Act s.55(2)) and an exclusion clause may also be ineffective under the doctrine of fundamental breach eg where the performance is totally different from that which the contract contemplated or there is some other breach going to the root of the contract (ibid s.55(5)).

A producer of a *defective product* cannot limit or exclude his liability, contractually, by notice or by any other provision: Liability for Defective Products Act 1991 s.10. See Clayton Love v B & I Steamship Co Ltd (1970) 104 ILTR 157; Tokn Grass Products Ltd v Sexton Co Ltd (1983) HC. See CONSUMER,

DEALING AS; FAIR AND REASONABLE TERMS.

**exclusion order.** An order excluding a spouse from occupation of the family home (qv) which may be made following the grant of a decree of judicial separation: Judicial Separation & Family Law Reform Act 1989 s.16(a). Contrast with a *barring order* (qv), the breach of which may lead to a criminal sanction whereas breach of s.16(a) does not.

**exclusionary rule.** The rule whereby otherwise admissible evidence is excluded because of the constitutional imperative of protecting the personal rights of the citizen as far as possible eg evidence obtained pursuant to an invalid search warrant. See DPP v Kenny (1990) ILRM 569. See O'Gorman in 9ILT & SJ (1991) 142. See EVIDENCE AND CONSTITUTIONAL RIGHTS.

**exclusive.** In a particular case, the Supreme Court refused to require that machinery be used *exclusively* in a designated area to qualify for an investment allowance, where the legislation did not include this restriction: McNally v O'Maoldomhnaigh (1990 SC) ITLR (22 Oct).

**exclusive dealing.** A term in a contract which restricts a party to dealing only with the other party; it may constitute a restraint of trade (qv) and thereby render it void: McEllistrem v Ballymacelligott Cooperative Agricultural and Dairy Society (1919) AC 548. See SOLUS AGREEMENT.

**exclusive jurisdiction.** As regards the EC, the courts of the State have exclusive jurisdiction regardless of domicile of the parties in certain specified proceedings eg proceedings which have as their object rights *in rem* in, or tenancies of, immovable property situated in the State; proceedings which have as their object the constitution, nullity or dissolution of a company which has its *seat* in the State; certain specified proceedings regarding validity of public registers, the registration or validity of patents, trade marks or designs, and the enforcement of judgments: Jurisdiction of Courts and Enforcement of Judgments (European Communities) Act 1988, first schedule, art.16. As regards EFTA countries, see Jurisdiction of Courts and Enforcement of Judgments Act 1993, sixth schedule, art.16. See SEAT OF CORPORATION.

**exclusive licence.** In respect of patents of invention, means a licence from a proprietor of or applicant for a patent which confers on the licensee and persons authorised by him, to the exclusion of all other persons (including the proprietor or applicant for the patent), any right in respect of the invention: Patents Act 1992 s.2(1). The holder of an exclusive licence has the like right as the proprietor of the patent to take proceedings in respect of any infringement of the patent (ibid s.51). Contrast with *sole* licence which does not exclude the proprietor himself; a sole licensee cannot sue for infringement. An exclusive licence may be partially written and partially oral: Morton-Norwich v United Chemicals (1981) FSR 337. See INFRINGEMENT OF PATENT; LICENCES OF RIGHT.

**exeat.** [Let him go]. Permission to leave.

**executed.** That which is done or completed. Contrast with EXECUTORY. See DEATH PENALTY.

**execution.** (1) The act of completing or carrying into effect, particularly of a judgment.

(2) The execution of deeds is accomplished by the signing sealing and delivery of them by the parties as their own acts and deeds in the presence of witnesses. (3) Formerly, the carrying out of a court's sentence of death. See DEATH PENALTY; DEED; STAY OF EXECUTION; WILL.

**execution debtor.** A person against whom judgment has been given for a sum of money, whose property is taken in execution. See FIERI FACIAS.

**execution of judgment.** The act of completing or carrying into effect the judgment of a court, which is usually done by fieri facias, by attachment, by order of garnishee, by appointment of a receiver by way of equitable execution, by a stop order, by a charging order, by examination order and instalment order, or by judgment mortgage (qqv). Execution of a judgment may issue at any time within six years from judgment: RSC O.42 r.23. Application to the court for liberty to issue execution is necessary (a) where six years has elapsed; or (b) where a change has taken place in the parties by death or otherwise; or (c) where judgment is upon assets *in futuro* (ibid r.24).

An action on a judgment is statute

barred after 12 years from the date on which the judgment became enforceable: Statute of Limitations 1957 s.11. For execution of judgments in the Circuit and District Courts, see RCC O.33 and DCR r.140 respectively. See also Enforcement of Court Orders Acts 1926 and 1940; Courts of Justice Act 1936 s.61; Bankruptcy Act 1988 s.50. See Minister for Social Welfare v Riordan (1966) IR 556.

There is reciprocal recognition and enforcement of judgments in civil and commercial matters between EC States and, since 1993, between EC States and EFTA countries (ie Austria, Finland, Iceland, Norway, Sweden, and Switzerland) and vice versa: Jurisdiction of Courts and Enforcement of Judgments Acts 1988 and 1993. See JUDGMENT; FOREIGN JUDGMENTS, ENFORCEMENT OF; RECEIVER OF MORTGAGED PROPERTY; STAY OF EXECUTION.

**execution order.** An order which includes an order of fieri facias, of sequestration, or of attachment (qqv): RSC O.42 r.8. An execution order in respect of High Court matters may not issue without the filing of a *praecipe* for that purpose (ibid r.11); if unexecuted, such an order remains in force for one year from the date of issue but it may be renewed (ibid r.20). For Circuit Court orders see RCC O.33. See DECREE.

**executive.** See SEPARATION OF POWERS.

**executive functions.** As regards a local authority, all the functions of the council, except those reserved to and exercisable only by the council, which are exercisable only by the manager: County Management Act 1940 s.17. See COUNTY MANAGER; HEALTH BOARD; RESERVED FUNCTIONS; SECTION 4 RESOLUTION.

**executor.** An *executor* is the person to whom the execution of a will, ie the duty of carrying its provisions into effect, is confided by the testator. The duties of an executor are: to bury the deceased; to prove the will; to collect the estate and, as necessary, to convert it into money; to pay the debts in their proper order; to pay the legacies and to distribute the residue among the persons entitled. The executor may bring actions against persons who are indebted to the testator or are in possession of property belonging to the estate. When several executors are appointed and only some of them prove the will, they are called the *proving* or *acting executors*.

It is the duty of an executor to notify a spouse in writing of the right of election between the spouse's *legal right* (qv) and any rights under the will: Succession Act 1965 s.115. Executorship is a *financial service* which a building society may be empowered to provide: Building Societies Act 1989 s.29(2)(n). See ADMINISTRATOR; MURDER; PERSONAL REPRESENTATIVE; PROBATE; PROBATE TAX; STATUTE OF FRAUDS.

**executor according to the tenor.** A person named in a will, wherein no executor is named, whose duties are described in terms sufficient to constitute him executor; a grant of probate may be given to such a person: RSC O.79 r.5(8)(c). See TENOR.

**executor de son tort.** A person who in defraud of creditors or without full valuable consideration, obtains, receives or holds any part of a deceased's estate or effects the release of any debt or liability due to the estate; he is chargeable as executor in his own wrong (de son tort). See Succession Act 1965 s.23; In b. Leeson (1937) 71 ILTR 82.

**executorship by representation.** Doctrine under which an executor of a sole or last surviving executor of a testator became the executor of that testator without the need for a new grant. Abolished by the Succession Act 1965 s.19.

**executory.** That which remains to be done. See TRUST.

**executory interest.** A future interest in land which is not a reversion (qv) or a remainder (qv). Legal executory interests can arise under the Statute of Uses 1634 and under the Statute of Wills 1540, namely springing and shifting uses and devises.

**executor's year.** The period allowed for the personal representative of a deceased to distribute the estate. An action for failure to distribute within this year is not permissible without leave of the court. This does not affect the right of creditors to bring proceedings. See Succession Act 1965 s.62.

**executrix.** The feminine form of executor (qv).

**exemplary damages.** Damages awarded

by way of punishment of the defendant for a breach of contract or statutory or constitutional right or duty or a tort. *Punitive* and *exemplary* damages are recognised as constituting the same element in that awarding damages for the purposes of making an example of a defendant to some extent punishes the person and vice versa: Conway v INTO (1991 SC) ILRM 497.

One of the ways in which the rights of citizens is vindicated, when subjected to oppressive conduct by employees of the State, is by an award of exemplary damages; exemplary damages do not have to be pleaded under the rules of court, but it is desireable that defendants be put on notice of an intention to claim such damages: McIntyre v Lewis & Dolan (1991 SC) ITLR (22 Apr). See Kinlan v Ulster Bank (1928) IR 171; Rookes v Barnard (1964) AC 1129 as applied by Garvey v Ireland (1979) 113 ILTR 61; Kennedy v Ireland (1987) HC. See also Competition Act 1991 s.6(3)(b).See UNLAWFUL INTERFERENCE WITH CONSTITUTIONAL RIGHTS.

**exempli gratia.** [For example]. Usually abbreviated to eg.

**exempted developments.** Developments for which planning permission (qv) is not required: LG(P&D) Act 1963 s.4. These include: (a) development consisting of the use of any land for the purpose of agriculture or forestry; (b) development by a planning authority within its functional area; (c) development consisting of the carrying out of works for the maintenance, improvement or other alteration of a structure which affects only the interior of the structure (with exceptions) or which do not materially affect the external appearance of the structure so as to render its appearance inconsistent with the character of the structure or of neighbouring structures; (d) development consisting of the use of any structure or other land within the curtilage of a dwellinghouse for any purpose incidental to the enjoyment of the dwellinghouse as such (ibid s.4 and LG(P&D) Act 1976 s.43(1)(c)).

The Minister is empowered to make regulations providing for any class of development being an exempted development: 1963 Act s.4(2) and LG(P&D) Regulations 1977, Part III (SI No 65 of 1977). The question as to what constitutes an exempted development is to be decided by An Bord Pleanala: 1976 Act s.14(9)(b). In 1993, the Minister was empowered to establish, by regulations, a procedure of public notice and consultation for developments by local authorities: LG (P&D) Act 1963 s.78 as amended by LG (P&D) Act 1993 s.3. See also SI No 403 of 1983; SI No 1 of 1984; SI No 348 of 1984; SI No 130 of 1985. See SPECIAL AMENITY ORDER.

**exemption clauses.** See EXCLUSION CLAUSES, RESTRICTION OF.

**exequator.** The authorisation from a receiving state to the head of a consular post, admitting him to the exercise of his functions: Diplomatic Relations and Immunities Act 1967, second schedule, art.12.

**exhibit.** A document or thing produced for the inspection of the judge or jury, or to be shown to a witness who is giving evidence, or referred to in an affidavit. In a criminal trial, the accused is entitled to be given a list of the exhibits and an opportunity to inspect the exhibits: Criminal Procedure Act 1967. See The State (Pletzer) v Magee (1986) ILRM 441.

**exhumation.** The disinterring of a buried corpse; it is an unlawful act unless authorised. The Minister may order the exhumation by the Garda Siochana of a body on being requested so to do by a coroner (qv): Coroners Act 1962 s.47(2). Where a coroner is informed by a member of the Garda Siochana not below the rank of inspector that, in his opinion, the death of any person whose body has been buried in the coroner's district may have occurred in a violent or unnatural manner, the coroner may request the Minister to order the exhumation of the body by the Garda Siochana (ibid s.47(1)). Following exhumation, the coroner has like powers and duties as if the body had not been buried (ibid s.47(4)). Also, a local authority has power to exhume the body of a person if the burial appears to threaten public health: Public Health (Ireland) Act 1878.

**exitum.** [The will of the testator is ambulatory down to the very end of his life]. See WILL, REVOCATION OF.

**exoneration.** To relieve from liability; to

clear from an accusation.

**exor.** An executor.

**expectation, legitimate.** The doctrine by which a person may obtain a remedy where he has had a *legitimate expectation* regarding some representations made to him eg an undertaking to be consulted in relation to a change in the law: Pesca Valentia Ltd v Minister for Fisheries & Forestry (1989) 7ILT Dig 324; Wiley v Revenue Commissioners (1989) IR 350 and (1992 SC); Nolan v Minister for the Environment (1989) 7ILT Dig 325. It is an aspect of the equitable concept of *promissory estoppel*: Webb v Ireland (1988) IR 353. It is sometimes decribed as *reasonable expectation*.

The test to be applied is whether in all the circumstances it would be unfair or unjust to allow a party to resile from a position created or adopted by that party which at that time gave rise to a legitimate expectation in the mind of another person that that situation might continue and might be acted on by that other person to their advantage: Cannon v Minister for the Marine (1991 HC) ILRM 261. A prisoner who has been granted regular periods of temporary release may develop a legitimate expectation to a renewal or, if not, to an explanation: Sherlock v Governor of Mountjoy Prison (1991 HC) 1 IR 451. The court will not extend the boundaries of legitimate expectation in a way which would result in the court ordering a statutory body to act ultra vires its powers: Wiley v Revenue Commissioners (1993 SC) ILRM 482. See also Donegal Co Council v Porter (1993 HC) ELR 101 and (1992 EAT) ELR 222. See EQUITABLE ESTOPPEL.

**expectation of life, loss of.** In an action for damages for personal injuries, compensation may be recovered for shortening of life arising therefrom, but the compensation must be moderate: McMorrow v Knott (1959) SC; O'Sullivan v Dwyer (1971) IR 275. Where a cause of action survives for the benefit of a deceased person's estate, damages for loss or diminution of expectation of life are not recoverable: Civil Liability Act 1961 s.7(2). See FATAL INJURIES.

**expert opinion.** The opinion of experts is admissible in evidence whenever the subject is one upon which competency to form an opinion can only be acquired by special study or experience eg in science, art, trade, hand-writing, fingerprints, ballistics, or foreign law. See McFadden v Murdock (1867) IR 1 CL 211; Poynton v Poynton (1903) 37 ILTR 54. See PROFESSIONAL WITNESS; REFRESHING MEMORY; STANDBY FEE.

**explanatory memorandum.** A memorandum which sometimes accompanies a Bill with the purpose of explaining the proposed legislation. It may be examined by the court to discover the purpose of an enactment: McLoughlin & Ors v Minister for the Public Service (1986) ILRM 28.

**exploration for petroleum.** See PETROLEUM, EXPLORATION FOR.

**explosive.** A substance of a kind used to produce a practical effect by explosion or a pyrotechnic effect or anything of which that substance is an integral part; a *licence* is required to import, manufacture, keep, sell or purchase any explosive: Dangerous Substances Act 1972 ss.9-15. The Minister may also regulate the manufacture, storage, marking, packing, conveyance, purchase, sale and keeping of fireworks, safety, signalling and rescue devices and other prescribed articles and substances (ibid s.19). Ammunition is governed by the Firearms Act 1925. Sodium chlorate is an explosive substance within s.9 of the Explosive Substances Act 1883, as are mercury tilt switches: DPP v Hardy (1992 SC) ITLR (16 Nov). See PROPERTIES.

**exposure, indecent.** The deliberate exposure of the person which may amount to the offence of an act of an indecent nature, if committed at or near or in the sight of any place along which the public habitually pass: Criminal Law Amendment Act 1935 s.18. See INDECENCY.

**express.** Directly and distinctly stated, rather than implied eg an express trust.

**express trust.** See TRUST, EXPRESS.

**expressio unius personae vel rei, est exclusio alterius.** [The express mention of one person or thing is the exclusion of another]. A maxim sometimes used in the interpretation of a document or statute but has to be handled with caution. See Wavin Pipes Ltd v Hepworth Iron Co Ltd (1981) HC; Doyle v Hearne (1988) ILRM 318.

**expression, freedom of.** The State

guarantees, subject to public order and morality, liberty for the exercise of the right of citizens to express freely their convictions and opinions: 1937 Constitution, art.40(6)(1)(i). The State however must endeavour that the organs of public opinion, such as the radio, the press, the cinema, while preserving their rightful liberty of expression, including criticism of government policy, are not used to undermine public order or morality or the authority of the State. The publication or utterance of blasphemous, seditious, or indecent matter is stated by the Constitution to be an offence which is punishable in accordance with law. Also the right of freedom of expression may be restricted as necessary to maintain the authority and impartiality of the judiciary: Desmond & Dedeir v Glackin & Minister for Industry (1992 HC) ILRM 489. See The State (Lynch) v Cooney (1983) ILRM 89; The AG for England and Wales v Brandon Books (1987) ILRM 135; Weeland v Radio Telefis Eireann (1987 HC) IR 662. See CENSORSHIP; DEFAMATION; LIBEL; SECTION 31.

**expressum facit cessare tacitum.** [When there is express mention of certain things, then anything not mentioned is excluded]. See EXPRESSIO UNIUS.

**extempore judgment.** The formal decision of a court made immediately at the conclusion of the trial of an action. Where there are no *primary facts* relevant to an issue which have not previously been decided, it is not necessary for the trial judge to set out in an *extempore judgment* the precise findings of primary fact on which he reaches his conclusion: K v K (1992 SC) ITLR (4 May). Contrast with RESERVED JUDGMENT. See JUDGMENT.

**extension of time.** See TIME, COURT RULES.

**extinguishment.** The ceasing of a right or obligation eg an easement (qv) is extinguished when the *dominant* and *servient* tenements are united in the same person. See also CONSOLIDATION; MERGER.

**extortion by menaces.** The offence, popularly known as *blackmail*, committed by a person who (a) utters, knowing the contents, a letter or writing demanding with *menaces*, and without reasonable or probable cause, any property or (b) accuses any person, living or dead, of a crime with intent to gain property:

Larceny Act 1916 s.29. To constitute a *menace*, a threat need not be one of injury to person or property; it is sufficient that the threat should produce in an ordinary man such a degree of fear as would unsettle his mind. If the demand is reasonable there will be no offence. It is also an offence to demand with menaces or by force anything capable of being stolen with the intent to steal it (ibid s.30). See also Criminal Damage Act 1991 s.3.

Under draft legislation to deal with the problem of racketeering, it is proposed that it will be an offence for any person, who, with a view to gain for himself or another or with intent to cause loss to another, makes any unwarranted demand with menaces: Criminal Justice (Public Order) Bill 1993 s.18. See POSSESSION, CRIME.

**extradition.** The formal surrender, based upon reciprocating arrangements by one nation with another, of an individual, accused or convicted of an offence, who is within the jurisdiction of the requested country when the requesting country, being competent to try and punish him, demands his surrender: Wyatt v McLoughlin (1974) IR 378. The formal arrangements by which this may be secured and the principles of reciprocity enshrined are either by way of treaties or by reciprocal legislation. The term *extradition* is often used to embrace the term *rendition* (qv) which is the backing of warrants as between states.

Extradition cannot be granted for an offence which is a *political offence* or an offence connected with a *political offence*: Extradition Act 1965 s.11. The High Court may release a person where the offence to which the extradition warrant relates is a revenue offence (qv) or does not *correspond* with any offence under the law of the State which is an indictable offence (qv) or punishable on summary conviction by imprisonment for at least six months (ibid s.50(2)). Also, a warrant for the arrest of a person ... must not be endorsed for execution .. if the Attorney General (qv) so directs; such a direction not to endorse must be given unless the Attorney General having considered such information as he deems appropriate, is of opinion that (a) there is a clear intention to prosecute the person and (b) such intention is founded on the existence of sufficient evidence: Extradition (Amendment) Act 1987. These functions of the AG are procedural and not judicial in nature: Wheeler v Culligan (1989) IR 344.

Extradition must be refused where the court is satisfied that there is a real danger that the person whose extradition is sought will suffer ill-treatment in breach of his constitutional rights if delivered out of the jurisdiction: Finucane v McMahon (1990 SC) ILRM 505. Also the court cannot properly undertake an investigation into the validity of a conviction recorded in a requesting state: Clarke v Mc Mahon (1990 SC) ILRM 648. Both of these cases involved extradition to Northern Ireland.

See also Criminal Procedure Act 1967 ss.35-38; Criminal Law (Jurisdiction) Act 1976 s.20; Air Navigation and Transport Acts 1973 and 1975; SI No 275 of 1971; Extradition Act 1965 (Part 11)(No 19) Order 1984; Washington Treaty on Extradition (SI No 33 of 1987). See also SI Nos 115 of 1989 and 131 of 1990. See also McMahon v McDonald (1988 HC) 6 ILT 263. See RSC O.98. [Text: Forde (3)]. See CORRESPONDING OFFENCE; POLITICAL OFFENCE; RENDITION.

**extraordinary general meeting; egm.** As regards companies, a meeting other than an annual general meeting: Companies Act 1963, Table A, art 49. Where members of a company representing at least one tenth of the paid up capital with voting rights request the board to call an extraordinary general meeting and it does not do so for 21 days, the meeting may be convened by at least half of those requisitionists (ibid s.132). An extraordinary general meeting of every registered company must be convened whenever a director knows that the net assets of the company are half or less of the company's called-up share capital, for the purpose of considering the measures to be taken to deal with the situation: Companies Amendment Act 1983 s.40. See ANNUAL GENERAL MEETING; RESOLUTION; VOTING AT MEETINGS.

**extra-territorial jurisdiction.** See JURISDICTION.

**extra-territoriality.** The legal fiction by which certain persons and things are deemed for the purpose of jurisdiction and control to be outside the territory of the state in which they really are and within that of another state eg ambassadors and other diplomatic agents while in the country to which they are accredited.

**extrinsic evidence.** See EVIDENCE, EXTRINSIC.

# F

**facial injuries.** The courts regard facial injuries as more important for women than for men when considering compensation for such injuries. See Foley v Thermocement Products Ltd (1954) 90 ILTR 92; Ronayne v Ronayne (1970) SC. See DISFIGUREMENT.

**facsimile.** See FAX.

**fact.** That which is in actual existence; an event or circumstance which is in issue between parties to a dispute before a court. In general, questions of fact are decided by a jury in jury trials and questions of law by the judge. Findings of facts, for the purposes of an appellate review thereof, are either *primary* or *secondary*; the Supreme Court is entitled to reject a trial judge's finding of a secondary fact: JM and GM v An Bord Uchtala (1988) ILRM 203; Hanrahan v Merck Sharpe & Dohme (Ire) Ltd (1988 SC) ILRM 629. The state of a person's mind at a relevant time is necessarily a matter of inference or opinion ie a secondary fact rather than a primary fact, and it is open to the Supreme Court to decide whether the inference drawn by the trial judge was correct. See Metropolitan Railway v Jackson (1887) 7 App Cas 193; Coleman v Clarke (1991 SC) ILRM 841. See INFERENCE; MOOT; PRIMARY FACTS; SECONDARY FACTS.

**fact in issue.** In civil cases, that which is alleged by one party and denied by the other in the pleadings (qv). In criminal cases, it is the constituents of the offence alleged by the prosecution and the facts alleged by the defence and denied by the prosecution eg an alibi (qv). See RELEVANT.

**factor.** A merchantile agent; a person who, in the customary course of his business has possession of goods of his principal, or the documents of title to such goods, with authority to sell, pledge, or raise money on the security of same: Factors Act 1889 s.1(1). The principal is bound by such sale or pledge even though he has forbidden it, unless there is notice of such prohibition (ibid s.2). As regards the rights of an owner of goods in the case of the bankruptcy of a merchantile agent to whom they have been entrusted, see 1889 Act s.12(2) and Bankruptcy Act 1988 s.77. See CREDIT-SALE AGREEMENT; AGENT.

**factory.** A premises or workplace in which persons are employed in manual labour in any process for or incidental to (a) the making of any article or part of an article or (b) the altering repairing ornamenting finishing cleaning or washing, or breaking up or demolition, of any article or (c) the adapting for sale of any article. It also includes a wide range of specifically defined premises eg a laundry, fish net making or mending, printing works, docks, wharfs, quays, warehouses, electrical stations and certain institutions and training establishments. See Factories Act 1955 s.3; Safety in Industry Act 1980 s.3. Certain other sections of the 1955 Act are repealed when particular sections of the Safety, Health and Welfare at Work Act 1989 come into force. See AIR POLLUTION; DANGEROUS CONDITIONS AND PRACTICES; SAFE SYSTEM OF WORK.

**factum.** An act or deed.

**factum probanda.** Facts which have to be proved.

**factum probantia.** Facts which are given in evidence to prove those other facts which are in issue.

**fair and accurate report.** A fair and accurate report, published in any newspaper, or broadcast of court proceedings is *privileged* if published or broadcast contemporaneously; the privilege does not cover blasphemous or obscene matter: Defamation Act 1961 s.18. Privilege extends to reporting of litigation only where a judge becomes involved in some substantive way, not to the preliminary administrative or office stage of litigation: Stringer & Murray v Irish Times Ltd (1993 HC) — Irish Times 4/4/1993.

*Qualified* privilege is given to newspapers and broadcasts in respect of fair and accurate reports, without obligation to publish explanation or contradiction, concerning public proceedings of foreign legislatures, or of international conferences to which the government sends a representative, or proceedings before foreign courts, or an extract from a register open to public inspection or a court notice (ibid 1961 Act s.24(1); *malice* will destroy the privilege.

Qualified privilege is also given, but subject to the obligation to publish a reasonable explanation, in respect of fair and accurate reports concerning: (a) findings of associations for science or learning, or for professional interests or for sport; (b) a public meeting, being a meeting bona fide and lawfully held for discussion on any matter of public concern, whether admission is general or restricted; (c) meetings of a local authority, commission of inquiry or statutory board; (d) general meeting of any company (other than a private company); or (e) a government notice or garda notice (ibid s.24(2)). See Nevin v Roddy Carthy (1935) IR 392. See MALICE; PRIVILEGE.

**fair and reasonable terms.** In determining whether a term in a contract for the sale of goods or supply of services is *fair and reasonable* regard will be had to the following: (a) the strength of the bargaining position of the parties to each other, (b) whether the customer received an inducement to agree to the term, (c) whether the customer knew or ought reasonably to have known of the existence and extent of the term, (d) whether compliance with a condition imposed would be practicable, (e) whether the goods were manufactured, processed or adapted to the special order of the customer: SGSS Act 1980, schedule. See EXCLUSION CLAUSES, RESTRICTION OF.

**fair comment.** The defence which may be pleaded in an action for *defamation* (qv). To succeed it must be proved that the comment is based on true facts, the comment must be on some matter of general public interest, and the comment must be fairly and honestly made: Lefroy v Burnside (1879) 4 LR Ir 556; McQuire v Western Morning News (1903) 2 KB 100. *Malice* will destroy the defence of fair comment. See MALICE; ROLLED-UP PLEA.

**fair dismissal.** The dismissal of an

employee where there are substantial grounds justifying the dismissal; the onus of proof is on the employer: Unfair Dismissal Act 1977 s.6. See UNFAIR DISMISSAL.

**fair practice rules.** Rules which in the opinion of the Fair Trade Commission, represented fair practice conditions with regard to the supply and distribution of goods or the provision of services: Restrictive Practices Act 1972 s.4, since repealed. See Competition Act 1991 ss.2(2) and 22. See COMPETITION, DISTORTION OF; DOMINANT POSITION, ABUSE OF.

**fair procedures.** The rules and procedures which must be followed by all persons and bodies making decisions affecting the individual and which must be fair and seen to be fair. The courts will protect the right of its citizens to fair procedures. The Court will intervene where a procedure is unfair and oppressive, eg see McGrath v Garda Commissioner (1990) ILRM 817. The rules of fair procedure do not necessarily apply to decisions made by a religious superior about a member of her community: Sister O'Dea v O'Briain (1992 HC) ILRM 364. The absence of an appeal against the test findings of a veterinary surgeon in the TB eradication scheme did not amount to an unfair procedure: Carroll v Minister for Agriculture (1991 HC) 1 IR 230. See also Ryan v VIP Taxi Co-operative (1989) ITLR (10 Apr). See NATURAL JUSTICE; VOW.

**Fair Trade Commission.** Formerly, the Commission which had a number of functions relating to the supply and distribution of goods or the provision of service: Restrictive Practices Acts 1972 and 1987, now repealed. See Competition Act 1991 ss.2(2) and 22. See COMPETITION AUTHORITY.

**fair trial.** Every accused is entitled to a fair trial. See PUBLICITY; SUB JUDICE.

**fait.** [A deed].

**falsa demonstrationon nocet cum de corpore constat.** [A false description does vitiate a document when the thing is described with certainty]. The maxim was held not to be applicable to the use by the plaintiffs of the phrase "Cost of Living Index" (which did not then exist) as they had chosen the phrase and it was not open to them now to substitute an alternative phrase: Bank of Ireland v Fitzmaurice (1989 HC) ILRM 452. See also Pratt v Mathew (1856) 22 Beav 328; Boyle v Mulholland (1860) 10 ICLR 150.

**false accounting.** The misdemeanour (qv) committed by a clerk or servant who wilfully, and with intent to defraud, alters, or makes a false entry in, or omits material particular from, any account of his master: Falsification of Accounts Act 1875. See DPP v Ryan (1989 CCA) ITLR (3 Apr). See ACCOUNTS; EMBEZZLEMENT.

**false alarm.** It is an offence to give knowingly, or to cause to be given, a false alarm which interferes with the operation of any aircraft, aerodrome or air navigation installation: Air Navigation and Transport Act 1988 s.43.

**false evidence.** See PERJURY; PERVERTING THE COURSE OF JUSTICE.

**false imprisonment.** The offence comprising the total and unlawful restraint of the personal liberty of another whether by constraining or compelling him to go to a particular place, confining him in a prison or police station, or private place, or detaining him against his will in a public place. See Criminal Law Act 1976 s.11. For the tort of false imprisonment, see TRESPASS TO THE PERSON. See KIDNAPPING.

**false pretences.** The misdemeanour (qv) committed by a person who by a false *statement* of fact, knowing it to be false, obtains from another any chattel, money or valuable security, with the *intention* to cheat or defraud that other: Larceny Act 1916 s.32. The statement must relate to some fact, past or present, although a statement about the future may imply a representation about the present eg drawing (qv) a cheque. There must be an intention to defraud; where money is obtained by false pretences there is a prima facie case of intent to defraud: The People (Attorney General) v Thompson (1960) CCA Frewen 201. It is also a misdemeanour to obtain from any person by any false pretence anything capable of being stolen with intent to defraud: Criminal Justice Act 1951 s.10. See also The People (Attorney General) v Finkel (1951) CCA. See OBTAINING CREDIT BY FRAUD; POSSESSION, CRIME.

**false trade description.** A trade description (qv) which is false in a material respect as regards the *goods* to which it is applied, and includes every alteration of a trade description, whether by way of addition, effacement, or otherwise, where that alteration makes the description false in a material respect, and the fact that a trade description is a trade mark, or part of a trade mark, shall not prevent such trade description being a false trade description: Merchandise Marks Act 1887 s.3(1).

*Goods* include vehicles, ships and aircraft, land, things attached to land and growing crops: Consumer Information Act 1978 s.2(1). *False in a material respect* is to be construed as false to a material degree and is to include being misleading to a material degree (ibid s.2(2)). The definition of false trade description is further extended by including anything which is not a trade description but is likely to be taken for an indication of any of the matters specified in the 1887 Act (ibid s.2(2)).

Every person is guilty of an offence who in the course of any trade, business or profession, *applies* any false trade description to goods, or sells or exposes for sale, or has in his possession for sale, any goods or things to which any false trade description is applied (ibid 1887 Act s.2; ibid 1978 Act s.4(1)-(2)). A wide definition is given to *applies* including an oral statement (ibid 1978 Act s.4(3)). See Lemy v Watson (1915) 32 RPC 508; R v Hammertons Cars Ltd (1976) 1 WLR 1243; Donnelly v Rowlands (1970) 1 WLR 1600; O'Neill & Co v Adidas (1992 SC) ITLR (17 Aug); Director of Consumer Affairs & Fair Trade v Barden (1991 HC). See also Hallmarking Act 1981 ss.5-6. See UNLAWFUL INTERFERENCE IN ECONOMIC RELATIONS.

**falsification.** It is an offence for an officer of a company to destroy, mutilate or falsify any document affecting or relating to the property or affairs of the company: Companies Act 1990 s.243. See also Building Societies Act 1989 s.120(3).

**family.** The natural primary and fundamental unit group of society, and a moral institution possessing inalienable and imprescriptible rights, antecedent and superior to all positive law, and recognised by the State as such: 1937 Constitution, art.41(1)(1). The State is required to guarantee to protect the family in its constitution and authority, as the necessary basis of social order and as indispensable to the welfare of the Nation and the State (ibid art.41(1)(2)).

The family is based on the institution of marriage: The State (Nicolaou) v An Bord Uchtala (1966) IR 567. Family rights include such matters as succession, maintenance, family home, adoption, guardianship, education, and marital privacy (qqv). See also In re J an infant (1966) IR 295. For constitutional protection for the married family, see Whyte in 7ILT & SJ(1989) 115. See ALIEN; EDUCATION; MARRIAGE.

**Family Court.** The Circuit Court is known as the Circuit Family Court when dealing with *family law proceedings* (qv): Judicial Separation and Family Law Reform Act 1989 s.31. Its proceedings must be as informal as practicable and consistent with the administration of justice; no wigs and gowns are allowed (ibid s.33). It must sit in a different place or time from ordinary sittings of the Circuit Court (ibid s.32). In judicial separation applications involving land with a rateable valuation exceeding £200, the matter must be transferred to the High Court if the respondent so requires (ibid s.31(3)). See Circuit Court Rules (No 1 of 1991) (SI No 159 of 1991). See FAMILY LAW PROCEEDINGS.

**family home.** A dwelling in which a married couple ordinarily reside; it includes a dwelling in which a spouse whose protection is in issue ordinarily resides, or if that spouse has left the other spouse, ordinarily resided before so leaving: Family Home Protection Act 1976; Judicial Separation and Family Law Reform Act 1989 s.10. It includes any building, or any structure vehicle or vessel (whether mobile or not), or part thereof, and includes a garden.

If a spouse conveys any *interest* in the family home to a person other than the other spouse, such conveyance is void unless the prior consent in writing of that other spouse has been obtained (ibid s.3(1)). If both spouses join in the sale of the family home, one spouse cannot subsequently object to the sale on the ground that a consent in writing of that spouse had not been obtained: Nestor v Murphy (1979) IR 326. A consent by a spouse to the property being security to a loan should be contemporaneous with the making of the loan: Standard Life Assurance Co Ltd v Satchwell (1990 HC).

If a spouse omits or refuses to consent to a disposal of the family home, the court may order the dispensing of such consent eg where the non-owning spouse has deserted the other spouse (ibid s.4; R v R (1978) HC). Also, the court may make such order as is just and equitable, where it appears to the court on the application of a spouse, that the other spouse is engaging in such conduct as may lead to the loss of any interest in the family home, or may render it unsuitable for habitation as a family home with the intention of depriving the applicant spouse or a dependent child of his residence in the family home: ibid s.5(1) and S v S (1983) ILRM 387.

The provisions of the 1976 Act apply only where one spouse has any estate, right, title or other interest, legal or equitable in the family home (ibid s.1(1)). It has been held that a house, owned by a company in which the husband was the major shareholder, was a family home: LB v HB (1980) HC; C v C (1983) HC.

Also, a spouse's prior consent is not required to render a *judgment mortgage* (qv) effective against a family home: Containercare (Ireland) Ltd. v Wycherley (1982) IR 143; Murray v Diamond (1982) 2 ILRM 113. However, conduct of a wife which resulted in the registration of a judgment mortgage has been held to entitle the husband to an order under s.5(1) of the 1976 Act; the order made was to transfer the wife's interest to trustees to protect the family home for the husband and children: O'N v O'N (1989 HC) ITLR (4 Dec), also reported by Woulfe in 8ILT & SJ (1990) 165.

Also, the deposit of title deeds of a family home in 1975 did not provide a lender with security for the repayment of advances made after the passing of the 1976 Act: Bank of Ireland v Purcell (1988 HC) ILRM 480; (1990 SC) ILRM 106.

Following the granting of a decree of *judicial separation* (qv), the court may make a number of orders relating to the family home, including an order for its sale, an order conferring on one spouse

the right to occupy the family home to the exclusion of the other spouse; the court must take into consideration that proper and secure accommodation be provided for a dependent spouse and any dependent children (ibid 1989 Act ss.16(a) and (b), and 19). See MK v PK in 9ILT & SJ (1991) 176.

Any disposition of the property of a bankrupt (qv), an arranging debtor (qv), or a person dying insolvent, which comprises a family home without the prior sanction of the court, is void: Bankruptcy Act 1988 s.61(4) and 61(5). See also Friends Provident v Doherty (1992 HC) ILRM 372. See Mee in 10 ILT & SJ (1992) 213. See also Family Law Act 1981 s.10; Criminal Damage Act 1991 s.1(3). [Text: Sanfey & Holohan; Shatter; Wylie (1)]. See MATRIMONIAL HOME; MATRIMONIAL PROPERTY; MORTGAGEE, RIGHTS OF.

**family income supplement.** A statutory scheme designed to provide financial assistance to families where one or more of the couple are in full time employment but net family income falls below the level prescribed in the legislation. *Couple* was extended in 1991 to include a man and a woman who are not married to each other but are cohabiting as man and wife. See Social Welfare Acts 1984 s.13; 1988 s.5; 1991 s.47; 1992 ss.6, 39 and 50; 1993 s.7.

**family law.** The body of laws dealing with marriage, divorce, separation, guardianship, adoption, maintenance of spouse and children, custody of and access to children, and matrimonial property including the family home (qqv). [Text: Shatter]

**family law proceedings.** Proceedings before a court of competent jurisdiction (eg the Circuit Family Court or High Court) under the following enactments: Judicial Separation and Family Reform Act 1989; Adoption Acts 1952-1988; Family Home Protection Act 1976; Family Law (Maintenance of Spouses and Children) Act 1976; Family Law (Protection of Spouses and Children) Act 1981; Family Law Act 1981; Guardianship of Infants Act 1964; Legitimacy Declaration Act (Ireland) 1868; Married Women Status Act 1957; Status of Children Act 1987: ibid 1989 Act s.30. Also included are proceedings between spouses under the Partition Acts 1868 and 1876 where the fact that they are married to each other is of relevance to the proceedings.

**family planning service.** A service for the provision of information, instruction, advice, or consultation in relation to one or more of the following: family planning, contraception, contraceptives (qv); it does not include the provision or supply of contraceptives: Health (Family Planning) Act 1979 s.1.

The Minister is required to secure the orderly organisation of comprehensive family planning services; he may make regulations for the making available of a comprehensive family planning service by a health board or by other persons: Health (Family Planning) (Amdt) Act 1992 s.8. The former requirement regarding a *natural* family planning service has been repealed. See Health (Family Planning) Regulations 1992 (SI No 312 of 1992).

**famosus libellus.** [A scandalous libel]. See LIBEL.

**fatal injuries.** At common law there was no right to dependants to sue in respect of a death from fatal injuries. Under the Civil Liabilities Act 1961, the *dependants* of a deceased may recover damages; *dependants* include any members of the deceased's family who suffers injury or mental distress ie wife, husband, father, mother, grandfather, grandmother, stepfather, stepmother, son, daughter, grandson, granddaughter, stepson, stepdaughter, brother, sister, halfbrother, half-sister: Civil Liability Act 1961 ss.47-51 and Courts Act 1981.

The damages which may be awarded are under three headings: (a) loss of pecuniary benefits which could have been reasonably expected but for the wrongful act of the defendant; (b) reasonable compensation for mental distress as determined by the judge, subject to a maximum award of £7,500; (c) funeral and other expenses actually incurred by reason of the wrongful act (ibid 1961 Act s.49; 1981 Act s.28(1)). The basis of assessment of damages for fatal injuries is the balancing of losses and benefits accruing to dependants; this can include the effect of remarriage of a widow the likelyhood of which is to be calculated at the time of death: Fitzsimons v Bord

Telecom & ESB (1991) ILRM 277.

An action must be brought within 3 years of the date of death or the date of knowledge of the person for whose benefit the action is brought, whichever is the later: Statute of Limitations (Amendment) Act 1991 s.6. See Wates v Cruickshank (1967) IR 378; O'Sullivan v CIE (1978) IR 407. See DAMAGES; MENTAL DISTRESS.

**father.** See PARENTAGE, DECLARATION OF; PATERNITY, PRESUMPTION OF.

**fauces terrae.** A narrow inlet of the sea; a gulf.

**fault liability.** See STRICT LIABILITY.

**fax.** Transmission of documents by fax has been held in the District Court to be good service of the documents: ICDS Recruitment Consultants Ltd v Gillespie (1992 DC) as reported in ILS Gazette (Jan/Feb 1993) 10. Where a document is admissible in criminal proceedings, it may be given in evidence by producing an authenticated copy of it, including a fax copy: Criminal Evidence Act 1992 s.30. Under draft legislation it is proposed that the results of the counting of votes in a presidential election may be transmitted to the presidential returning officer by fax or otherwise: Presidential Elections Bill 1993 s.53. See also Statistics Act 1993 s.28(2); Stock Transfer Forms Regulations 1991 (SI No 77 of 1991); Hastie v Jenkerson and McMahon (1990) 1 WLR 1575. See also COMPUTERS; DOCUMENTARY EVIDENCE.

**feadhmannaigh shiochana.** [Peace Commissioners (qv)].

**fee.** (1) The term used in land law to denote that an estate is capable of being inherited. A fee was originally a feudal benefice of land granted to a man and his heirs in return for services to be rendered to the grantor. (2) A financial charge made for a privilege eg a certificate or licence. The Public Offices Fees Act 1879 provides for the collection of fees payable in any public office by means of stamps. Its provisions are often excluded eg Merchant Shipping Act 1992 s.31(4).

Where a fee is paid by cheque, it is received when it is delivered provided it is subsequently honoured in the normal way; acceptance of a blank cheque for a fee implies an agreement to act on an inferred authority to fill in the amount of the prescribed fee: Maher v An Bord

Pleanala (1993 HC) ILRM 359.

**fee farm grant.** A *fee simple* estate with a rent reserved to the grantor. Since the Renewable Leasehold Conversion Act 1849, a *lease for lives renewable forever* (qv) operates as a fee farm grant if the lessor is capable of making such a grant. A fee farm grant creates the relationship of landlord and tenant between the parties: Deasy's Act 1860. A fee farm rent, whether rent seck (qv) or rent charge (qv) may be recovered by various remedies: Conveyancing Act 1881 s.44. See FEE SIMPLE.

**fee simple.** An estate of freehold being the most extensive that a person can have. A fee simple estate may be: (a) a *fee simple absolute*, which is an estate which continues forever; (b) a *determinable fee*, which is a fee simple which will automatically determine on the occurrence of some specified event which may never occur; (c) a *fee simple upon condition*, which may be upon a condition precedent or a condition subsequent; (d) a *base fee*, which is a particular kind of determinable fee; and (e) a *fee farm grant* which is a fee simple with a rent reserved to the grantor.

To convey a fee simple estate it is essential to use the correct words of limitation: *to A and his heirs* or *to A in fee simple*; or *to A and successors* in the case of a grant to a corporation sole. No words of limitation are required in a devise by will or a grant to a corporation aggregate (eg a limited company). For determination of the purchase price of the fee simple, see Landlord Tenant (Amendment) Act 1984 s.7. See also Conveyancing Act 1881 s.51. See BASE FEE; SHELLEY'S CASE, RULE IN; GROUND RENT.

**fee tail.** An entail; an estate tail; a freehold estate which continues for as long as the original tenant and any of his descendants survive. It is created by the words of limitation *heir* followed by some words of procreation eg *To A and the heirs of his body*, or *to A in tail* since the Conveyancing Act 1881. An estate tail may be created by will only by the same words of limitation as those required in a deed: Succession Act 1965 s.95.

The owner of the estate tail is known as the *tenant-in-tail*. A *tail male* or a *tail female* are entails where the property descended to males or females exclusively. In order to *bar* the entail and create a fee simple (qv) estate, it is necessary for the tenant-in-tail to execute a *disentailing deed* which must be enrolled in the Central Office (qv) within six months of execution: Fines and Recoveries Act 1833. An entail cannot be barred by will. See In re Fallon (1956) IR 268; Bank of Ireland v Domville (1956) IR 37.

Canons of descent (qv) have been abolished except in so far as they apply to the descent of an estate tail: Succession Act 1965 s.11. See BARRING THE ENTAIL; PROTECTOR OF THE SETTLEMENT.

**felo de se.** [Felon of himself]. Formerly, a person who committed suicide (qv).

**felon.** A person who commits a felony (qv).

**felony.** A crime which at common law carried the penalty of death and forfeiture of the land and goods of the offender. All other crimes were *misdemeanours*. Many crimes were made felonies by statute. Forfeiture was abolished by the Forfeiture Act 1870. The distinction between felonies and misdemeanours are now less than formerly, although felonies generally carry heavier penalties; also a person may be arrested without penalty when suspected of commiting a felony, whereas an arrest warrant is required for a misdemeanour unless the offender is caught actually committing the misdemeanour. Additionally, only in felonies is the distinction drawn between principals (qv) and accessories (qv). See also COMPOUNDING A FELONY; MISPRISION OF FELONY; TRANSPORTATION.

**feme covert.** A married woman.

**feme sole.** An unmarried woman.

**feodum.** A fee (qv).

**feoffee to uses.** See USE.

**ferae naturae.** [Of a wild nature]. See ANIMALS.

**feudal system.** The system under which the king was lord of all land; he granted land to his lords in return for military and other services. The lords in turn granted land to others, the process being known as *subinfeudation*. The unit of land in the system was the *manor*, each of which had a lord; he exercised jurisdiction over the servile tenants of the manor and all owed allegiance to the king.

**fi fa.** See FIERI FACIAS.

**fiat.** [Let it be done]. A decree, an order, a warrant.

**fiat justitia, ruat coelum.** [Let justice be done, though the heavens fall]. However, see FINALITY IN LITIGATION.

**fictio legis non operatur damnum vel injuriam.** [A legal fiction does not work loss or injustice]. See FINE.

**fiduciary.** A person who has been entrusted with powers for the benefit of others but who in the exercise of those powers is not subject to the direct and immediate control of those others eg company directors, trustees, liquidators, executors and court appointed receivers (qqv). The general rule is that a person in a fiduciary position is not entitled to make a profit and he is not allowed to put himself in a position where his interest and his duty conflict.

Any provisions in a company's regulations are proscribed which exempt or indemnify an officer of the company in respect of any liability which attaches to him in respect of his negligence, default, breach of duty or breach of trust: Companies Act 1963 s.200 as amended by Companies Amendment Act 1983, first schedule para 16. The court may excuse an officer from such liability if he acted reasonably and honestly (ibid s.391). See Jackson v Munster Bank (1885) 15 LR Ir 356; Cockburn v Newbridge Sanitory Steam Laundry Co (1915) 1 IR 249; Nash v Lancegaye Safety Glass (Ireland) Ltd (1958) 92 ILTR 1; Clark v Workman (1920) 1 IR 107; Irish Microforms v Browne (1987) HC. See also Building Societies Act 1989 s.114(1). For fiduciary duties of company directors, see MacCann in 9 ILT & SJ (1991) 30 & 104. See DIRECTOR; RETENTION OF TITLE CLAUSE.

**fieri facias; fi fa.** [Cause to be made]. An order of *execution* directing the sheriff (qv) to whom it is addressed to levy from the goods and chattels of the debtor a sum equal to the amount of the judgment debt, interest, and costs of execution. The sheriff seizes the goods and sells them by auction. See Incorporated Law Society v Owens (1990) 8 ILT Dig 64. See RSC O.42-43. See VENDITIONI EXPONAS.

**fieri feci.** [I have caused to be made]. The return of a sheriff (qv) to an order of *fieri facias*. An order binds the property in the goods of the execution debtor as from the delivery of the order to the sheriff: Sale of Goods Act 1893 s.26. See RSC O.42 r 35.

**filius nullius.** [Son of nobody]. An illegitimate child; a bastard; now referred to as *a child whose parents are not married to each other*: Status of Children Act 1987. See CHILD, ILLEGITIMATE.

**film.** See CINEMATOGRAPH FILM; DOCUMENTARY EVIDENCE.

**final certificate.** Often refers to the certificate of an architect pursuant to a standard building contract, which provides that the certificate is conclusive evidence that the works have been properly carried out and completed in accordance with the contract. See Elliot & Co v Minister for Education (1987) ILRM 710. See RIAI CONTRACT.

**final judgment.** Judgment awarded when an action is ended.

**finality in litigation.** It is of the essence of litigation that, subject to a proper right of appeal, the judgment of a court should be a final one: Dalton v Minister for Finance (1989 SC) ILRM 519. Decisions of the Supreme Court are final and conclusive; however a decision can be set aside for fraud, pleaded with particularity and established on the balance of probability: 1937 Constitution art 34(4)(6); Bruno Tassan Din v Banco Ambrosiano SPA (1991 HC) 1 IR 569. Even if a decision of the Supreme Court on a matter of law is established to have been wrong by a subsequent decision of the Supreme Court, such a correction is not a valid ground for upsetting the original judgment: AG v Ryans Car Hire Ltd (1965) IR 642 and ibid Bruno Tassan Din case. See FRESH EVIDENCE; GENERAL DAMAGES; FOREIGN LAW; SET ASIDE.

**finance house, liability of.** A finance house is deemed to be a party to the sale of goods to a buyer *dealing as consumer*, and the finance house and the seller of the goods are *jointly and severally* answerable to the buyer for any breach of contract and for any misrepresentation made by the seller with respect to the goods, where the buyer has entered into an agreement with the finance house for the repayment to the finance house of money paid by the finance house to the seller in respect of the price of goods.

See SGSS Act 1980 s.14. See CONSUMER, DEALING AS.

**financial institution.** See BANKER AND CONFIDENTIALITY.

**financial resolutions.** Resolutions of Dail Eireann, sitting as a committee of the whole House, to give temporary effect to certain tax measures announced in the government's budget statement: Provisional Collection of Taxes Act 1927. The resolutions may increase, reduce, vary or abolish a specified permanent tax, or renew a specified temporary tax, which was in force immediately before the end of the previous financial year, or may create a new tax. The maximum period for which a Dail financial resolution can have a statutory force is four months unless enacted into law (ibid s.4) (eg by the subsequent Finance Act). However any period of dissolution of the Dail after the resolution is passed is disregarded: Finance Act 1992 s.250.

**financial transfer.** See EXCHANGE CONTROL.

**finding.** (1) The conclusions of an enquiry of fact. (2) The finder of goods has a better title to them against everyone except the true owner. If the finder is under a duty to hand over found property to another, and if the true owner is not found, the goods belong to that other. See Quin v Coleman (1898) 32 ILTR 79; Crinion v Minster for Justice (1959) Ir Jur Rep 433. See TREASURE TROVE.

**finding, bailment by.** The custody of a lost chattel, found in a public place, which gives to the finder all the rights which belong to a bailee by virtue of his possession. The finder has the obligations of a depository to the true owner, including the obligation to return the chattel to him on demand. The finder does no wrong to the true owner, unless he takes it, meaning to appropriate it to himself, knowing or having reasonable grounds for believing that the owner can be found, in which case the taking would be a *trespass* and the finder would be guilty of *larceny* (qv). See Bridges v Hawkesworth (1851) 21 LJ QB 15; Webb & Webb v Ireland & The AG (1988 SC) IR 353.

**finding, larceny by.** See LARCENY BY FINDING.

**finding is keeping.** Popular misconception that the finder of property acquires a title as against all others, including the rightful owner. See LARCENY BY FINDING.

**fine.** (1) A monetary penalty payable on conviction. (2) A lump sum payment for the grant of a lease (qv).

(3) A fictitious collusive action which resulted in an agreement to convey land being entered in the court records as a compromise to an action. It was used to *bar an entail*. It was abolished by the Fines and Recoveries Act 1833 which substituted a simple disentailing assurance. See also Report on the Indexation of Fines (LRC 37 of 1991). See BARRING THE ENTAIL.

**fine, on-the-spot.** See ON-THE-SPOT FINE.

**fineness, standard of.** The standard of fineness, known as the *Irish Standard of Fineness*, which the Minister may by regulation prescribe for articles of precious metal and for solders of such articles: Hallmarking Act 1981 s.7.

**fingerprints.** The clear prints of the external filaments of the skin surface which are obtained by pressing the fingers and thumbs of both hands on paper or cardboard, having first pressed them upon an inked plate: Regulations as to the Measuring and Photographing of Prisoners 1955 (SI No 114 of 1955); Penal Servitude Act 1891. These regulations permit the photographing, measuring and fingerprinting, which includes the taking of palm prints, of a convicted person at any time during his imprisonment, and of an untried person if he does not object or with the authority of the Minister if the prisoner objects.

Good practice requires 12 points of comparison in fingerprints as regards an accused, but a lesser amount will be admissible as regards a witness: People (DPP) v James Ryan (1993 CCA) ITLR (19 Apr) and 11 ILT Dig (1993) 185.

There are further powers given to the gardai in relation to fingerprinting of persons detained under the Offences Against the State Act 1939 s.30: Criminal Law Act 1976 s.7(1). Also provision has now been made for fingerprinting of persons who are prosecuted for an indictable offence, or convicted, or who are detained under powers of detention (qv) contained in the Criminal Justice Act 1984 (ibid ss.6 and 28). For application in connection with the preservation of fingerprints, palm prints and photographs pursuant to the 1984 Act s.8(7), see DCR 1988 (SI No 158 of 1988). See GENETIC FINGERPRINTING.

**finis finem litibus imponit.** [A fine puts an end to legal proceedings].

**fire authority.** The council of a county, the corporation of a county borough, the corporation of Dun Laoghaire and any other borough corporation or urban district council which has established and is maintaining a fire brigade at the commencement of this section: Fire Services Act 1981 s.9(1). A duty is imposed on fire authorities: (a) to make provision for the prompt and efficient extinguishing of fires occuring in buildings and other places of all kinds in their functional areas and for the protection and rescue of persons and property from injury by fire; (b) to establish and maintain a fire brigade; (c) to make adequate provision for the reception of and response for the assistance of the fire brigade. See FIRE SAFETY NOTICE.

**fire, liability for.** At common law, a person was liable for damage caused by fire escaping from his premises. However, by statute there is no liability if the fire accidentally occurs on land or in buildings and escapes without negligence: Accidental Fires Act 1943 s.1. An occupier is liable if he or his servant negligently started the fire, or negligently allows it to escape after being started without negligence. The 1943 Act does not apply to any claims for damages under the Hotel Proprietors Act 1963.

A tenant is generally required to give up possession of premises on determination of a lease in good and substantial repair, except in the case of accidents by fire without the tenant's default: Kiernan v O'Connell (1938) 72 ILTR 205. See also Bradley v Donegal Co Council (1990 HC) ITLR (29 Jan). See RYLANDS v FLETCHER, RULE IN.

**fire brigade.** See FIRE AUTHORITY.

**fire safety notice.** The notice which a fire authority may serve on the owner or occupier of any building which appears to the authority to be a *potentially dangerous building* ie a building which would, in the event of a fire occuring therein, constitute a serious danger to life for any one of specified reasons: Fire Services Act 1981 ss.19-20. A *fire safety notice* imposes on the owner or the occupier certain specified requirements eg the provision and maintenance of exit signs. An appeal lies against such a notice (ibid s.21). The fire safety notice provisions are extended to factories and other premises covered in the Safety in Industry Act 1955 & 1980: Safety, Health and Welfare at Work Act 1989 s.55.

**firearm.** A *lethal* (qv) firearm or other lethal weapon of any description from which any shot, bullet, or other missile can be discharged: Firearms and Offensive Weapons Act 1990 s.4. A firearm also includes a crossbow, a stun gun, and an air gun (which expression includes an air rifle and an air pistol and any other weapon incorporating a barrel from which metal or other slugs can be discharged), a defective firearm, and a prohibited weapon (qv) (ibid s.4(1)). Generally it is not lawful for a person to have in his possession, use, or carry any firearm or amunition save in so far as such possession, use, or carriage is authorised by a *firearms certificate*: Firearms Act 1925 s.2. See also Firearms (Proofing) Act 1968; Firearms Act 1964 and 1971; Firearms Regulations 1976.

It is an offence to have possession of a firearm *with intent* to endanger life; pointing a loaded gun at a person establishes the required intent: ibid 1925 Act s.14(a) as amended; People (DPP) v Farrell (1993 CCA) ITLR (5 Apr).

Using or producing a firearm or an imitation firearm for the purpose of, or while, resisting arrest by a member of the Garda Siochana, or in the course of aiding or abetting an escape or rescue from lawful custody is an indictable offence (qv): ibid 1964 Act s.27. The 1990 Act extended the definition of *firearm*, introduced strict controls on silencers and *offensive weapons*. It also introduced a new offence of reckless discharge of a firearm (ibid s.8). See BURGLARY, AGGRAVATED; HUNT; LETHAL; OFFENSIVE WEAPON; WITHHOLDING INFORMATION.

**firearms certificate.** A certificate issued by a superintendent of the garda siochana to a person residing in his district or by the Minister to a person not ordinarily resident in the State: Firearms Act 1925 s.3; Wildlife Act 1976 s.62. A licence to hunt game with firearms in open season, is required, and is effected by way of endorsement on the firearms certificate or otherwise as provided: 1976 Act ss.20 and 29. Revocation of a certificate by a garda superintendent must not be made without the holder being given an opportunity to state his case: *Hourigan v Supt Kelly* (1992 HC) 10 ILT Dig 266.

**fireplace.** See FUEL.

**fireworks.** It is an offence for any person to throw or cast any fireworks in or into, or to ignite any fireworks in, any highway, street, thoroughfare or public place: Dangerous Substances Act 1972 s.61. See EXPLOSIVE

**firm.** Persons who have entered into partnership with one another; the name under which their business is carried on is called the firm name: Partnership Act 1890 s.4. In the event that partners trade under names other than their own, they must comply with the Registration of Business Names Act 1963. An action may be brought by or against a firm in the name of the firm. See RSC O.14. See BUSINESS NAME.

**first aid.** Treatment of an injury which does not need treatment by a registered medical practitioner or registered general nurse, or otherwise treatment for the purpose of preserving life or minimising the consequences of injury or illness until the services of such a practitioner or nurse are obtained: Safety Health & Welfare at Work (General Application) Regulations 1993 (SI No 44 of 1993) reg.54. It is the duty of every employer to provide where required first-aid equipment, suitably marked and easily accessible, and to provide occupational first-aiders as are necessary (ibid reg.56).

**first instance, court of.** A court in which proceedings are initiated. See 1937 Constitution, arts.34(2); 34(3)(1); 34(3)(4). The Single European Act (qv) has provided for the creation of a Court of First Instance to supplement the European Court of Justice (qv): Treaty of Rome 1957 art.168a as replaced by the Maastricht Treaty 1992 art.G(E)(50).

**first refusal.** An option (qv) to purchase any property on the same terms as offered by another party. A right of first refusal must be supported by consideration (qv) to be enforceable. Where the property is land, the right of first refusal does not constitute an interest in that land: *Aga Khan v Firestone* (1992 HC) ILRM 31.

**fishery harbour centre.** A harbour or the land adjoining it, or both, declared by Ministerial order to be a fishery harbour centre: Fishery Harbour Centres Act 1968 ss.1-2 and 1980. Howth and Dunmore East Harbours were declared to be fishery harbour centres in 1989; their ownership and management was transferred from the Commissioners of Public Works to the Minister: SI Nos 336 and 337 of 1989. The seaward limits of Castletownbere harbour have been defined so as to include Berehaven Sound within its limits and consequently facilitate the collection of harbour dues from foreign factory ships anchored in the Sound: Fisheries Harbour Centres (Amdt) Act 1992.

**fishery limits, exclusive.** The exclusive fishery limits of the State comprises all sea areas which lie within the line every point of which is at a distance of twelve nautical miles (qv) from the nearest point of the *base line*: Maritime Jurisdiction Act 1959 s.6 as amended by the Maritime Jurisdiction Act 1964 s.2. See MARITIME JURISDICTION.

**fishery rights.** Interference in public rights of fishery must not take place without notice or without access to the courts where the Oireachtas (qv) so provides: *Madden v Minister for the Marine* (1993 HC) ILRM 436.

**fishery society.** A society where the number of the society's members is not less than 50 and all or a majority of its members are persons who are mainly engaged in, and derive the principal part of their income, from fishing; the Minister may give a certificate that a society is to be treated as a fishery society: Finance Act 1978 s.18(1). The trading profits of such a society from certain transactions are exempt from corporation tax. For *fishing co-operative society* see Industrial & Provident Societies Act 1978 s.4; Fisheries (Amdt) Act 1991; Fisheries Co-operative Societies Order and Rules 1992 (SI Nos 126 and 127 of 1992). See also TROUT.

**fishing interrogatories.** See INTERROGA-TORIES, FISHING.

**fishing licence.** The licence required to

angle for salmon; or which may be required, by way of a share certificate in a Fisheries Co-operative Society, to angle for trout or coarse fish: Fisheries (Amendment) Act 1991. See In re Beara Fisheries and Shipping Ltd (1988) ILRM 221. See TROUT; SALMON ROD LICENCE; COARSE FISH.

**fishing rights.** See RIPARIAN OWNER.

**fishing vessel.** A vessel used for sea-fishing or for angling in the sea or in freshwater other than such a vessel so used otherwise than for profit; it does not include a vessel registered outside the State: Merchant Shipping Act 1992 s.2(1). The Minister is empowered to make regulations for the purpose of ensuring the safety of fishing vessels and their crews. See Merchant Shipping (Musters) (Fishing Vessels) Regulations 1993 (SI No 48 of 1993).

**fitness for purpose.** See QUALITY OF GOODS.

**fixed charge.** A specific charge on specific property of say a company eg on land and buildings of the company, as security for a loan, as contrasted with a *floating charge*. A *fixed charge* invariably involves the vesting of a legal interest in the vendor of the loan at the time of the transaction. See DEBENTURE; FLOATING CHARGE; CHARGE, REGISTRATION OF.

**fixed term contract.** Unfair dismissal legislation does not apply to fixed term contracts of employment where the dismissal consists only of the expiry of the term or cesser of the purpose: Unfair Dismissals Act 1977 s.2(2)(b). However, s.2(2)(b) only applies where the fixed term contract specifically states that the 1977 Act shall not apply to a dismissal consisting of an expiry or cesser: Sheehan v Dublin Tribune Ltd (1992 EAT) ELR 239. Also a recent amendment to s.2(2)(b) provides for the application of the Act to a dismissal where the employee is re-employed within three months of the dismissal and it is found that the entry by the employer into the subsequent contract was wholly or partly for the purpose of avoiding liability under the Act: Unfair Dismissals (Amdt) Act 1993 s.3(b). Also re-employment by the same employer not later than 26 weeks after the dismissal will not operate to break continuity of service (ibid 1993 Act s.3(c)).

A *fixed-term employee* means an employee whose employment is governed by a contract of employment for a fixed term or for a specified purpose: Safety Health and Welfare at Work (General Application) Regulations 1993 (SI No 44 of 1993) reg.2(1). These regulations apply to employers of fixed-term employees, temporary employees, as well as of permanent employees (ibid reg.4(2)).

**fixtures.** (1) Personal chattels annexed to the freehold by a temporary occupier and which are removable by him. A chattel which, judging from the mode in which it is affixed and all the surrounding circumstances, was affixed by the occupier to be enjoyed as a chattel is removable. If it was affixed to constitute an improvement to the house or land, it is not. See Deasy's Act 1860 s.17.

(2) Television aerials are *fixtures* within the meaning of the Value-Added Tax 1972 s.10(8): Maye v The Revenue Commissioners (1986) ILRM 377.

**flag.** The national flag is the tricolour of green, white and orange: 1937 Constitution, art.7.

**flag officer.** An officer holding the commissioned naval rank of commodore: Defence Act 1954 s.2(1).

**flagrante delicto.** [In the commission of the offence].

**flat.** Colloquially, a suite of rooms in a building, usually on one floor of a building which has a number of floors. A leasehold or freehold interest may be created in a flat; there is no reason at common law why the owner of land cannot convey horizontal slices of the air space above it to others, whether by way of lease or freehold interest: Humphries v Broghen (1850) 12 QB 739.

A flat is entitled to vertical support from the lower part of the building and to the benefit of such lateral support as may be of right enjoyed by the building itself: Dalton v Angus (1881) 6 App Cas 740. There is provision for the registration of land which is a *flat or floor, or part of a flat or floor, of a house*: Land Registration Rules 1972 r.30(1)(a).

A housing authority is empowered to sell a flat in like manner as a house, except that it may make a management charge in respect of areas common to two or more such flats; alternatively it may transfer responsibility for such areas to a company or other body: Housing Act 1966 s.90(6) as inserted by Housing (Miscellaneous Provisions) Act 1992 s.26(1). See also s.90(11)(a). See CONDOMINIUM; FLOOR AREA CERTIFICATE; MULTI-STOREY BUILDINGS.

**floatation.** The offer of a large block of shares in a public company either to the public at large or to clients of an issuing house ie a merchant bank or similar financial institution specialising in this business. A company may be *floated*: (a) by a *direct offer* of shares to the public by prospectus; or (b) by *an offer for sale* by which the entire issue is sold to an issuing house which then offers the shares to the public by prospectus; or (c) by an allotment of shares to an issuing house which *places* them with its clients; or (d) by an offer of shares by *tender* with the shares going to the highest bidder. See ALLOTMENT; PROSPECTUS; SHARES.

**floating charge.** An equitable charge or mortgage on the assets for the time being of a going concern. It attaches to the subject charged in the varying conditions it happens to be in from time to time. The charge remains dormant or floats over the assets until the undertaking ceases to be a going concern, or until the person in whose favour the charge is created (the *chargee*) intervenes.

A floating charge becomes a fixed charge, and is said to *crystalise*, when a receiver is appointed, or a winding up commences, or if the chargee intervenes when entitled so to do. An *automatic crystallisation clause* is one stipulating that a floating charge will crystalise on some specific event occurring. Debentures issued by a company are often secured by a floating charge on the property, present and future, of the company.

A floating charge given within twelve months of a company being wound up is invalid if the company was insolvent at the time it created the charge; there is an exception for *cash paid*: Companies Act 1963 s.288 as amended by the Companies Act 1990 s.136. The test of solvency is whether immediately after the floating charge was given, the company was able to pay its debts as they became due: Re Creation Printing Company Ltd (1981) IR 353. The onus

of proof lies on the person who asserts the validity of the floating charge: Crowley v Northern Bank Finance Corp (1981) IR 353. See also Evans v Rival Granite Quarries Ltd (1910) 2 KB 979; In re Bushmills Distillery Co (1896) 1 IR 301; Welch v Bowmaker (Ireland) Ltd (1980) IR 251; In re Keenan Bros Ltd (1984) HC; In re Tullow Engineering (Holdings) Ltd (in receivership) (1990) 1 IR 452.

The 1990 Act amended s.288 to include goods and services sold or supplied to the company as an exception on the same basis as *cash paid*; also it provided that a floating charge is invalid if given to a person *connected* with a company up to two years before the company went into liquidation, unless it could be shown that the company was solvent after the creation of the charge. See FIXED CHARGE.

**floating policy.** A policy of marine insurance (qv) which describes the insurance in general terms, and leaves the name of the ship or ships and other particulars to be defined by subsequent declaration: Marine Insurance Act 1906 s.29.

**floor area certificate.** The certificate required in order to gain exemption from stamp duty on the purchase of new houses and flats: Housing Regulations 1980 art.8 (SI No 296 of 1980). The gross area must be not more than 125 square metres (1,346 sq ft) and must not be less than 35 sq m (377 sq ft) for a house and 30 sq m (323 sq ft) for a flat.

**flora and fauna.** See CONSERVATION ORDER; NATURE RESERVE; RESERVE.

**flotsam.** Goods of a shipwreck which remain floating on the sea. See Larceny Act 1916 s.15. See JETSAM; LAGAN.

**f.o.b.** Free on board. A price for goods which is quoted f.o.b. includes the cost of placing the goods on board ship.

**foetal death.** The death of a human embryo. When a foetal death occurs after the twenty-eighth week of pregnancy, the medical practitioner (or midwife) is required to send statistical information to the local medical officer of health eg date and place of confinement, estimated period of gestation, sex of foetus, putative cause of death: Vital Statistics (Foetal Death) Regulations 1956 (SI No 302 of 1956). The government indicated in 1993 its intention to introduce a statutory register of babies who were stillborn.

**folio.** In relation to taxation of costs, a folio comprises 72 words, every figure comprised in a column or authorised to be used being counted as one word: RSC O.99 r.37(9). See also LAND REGISTRATION.

**food.** It is an offence to expose for sale foodstuffs which are unfit for human consumption: Public Health (Ireland) Act 1878 s.133. It is an offence to mix into foodstuffs any ingredient or material which thus renders the article injurious to health with the intention that the article will be sold: Sale of Food and Drugs Acts 1875–1936. The extent to which chemical substances and drugs may be used in foodstuffs is also controlled or prevented eg control of chemical and antibiotic residues in meat and dairy products (SI No 236 of 1986).

Minimum standards are laid down by the Food Standards Act 1974 and the regulations which may be made thereunder. Potato growers and packers are required to register and to identify themselves on packages sold by them: Potato Growers and Packers Act 1984. See also Hinde v Allmand (1918) 87 LJ KB 893. See also Health Act 1947 s.56 as amended by Health Act 1953 s.38. See ANIMAL REMEDY.

**food, standard of.** Provisions for the establishment and enforcement of standards for food or drink used by human beings are contained in the Food Standards Act 1974. The Minister is empowered to make regulations in relation to food, regarding: name; description; composition and quality; method of manufacture and preparation; additives; contaminants (including pesticide residues); hygiene; time limits for consumption; packaging, labelling and presentation; transportation, storage and distribution; weights and measures (ibid s.2).

**food and medicines, patents for.** Where the Controller of Patents makes an order to grant a *compulsory* licence relating to a patent for food and medicine, he must in settling the terms, endeavour to secure that food and medicine will be available to the public at the lowest prices consistent with the proprietors of patents deriving reasonable remuneration having regard to the nature of the inventions:

Patents Act 1992 s.70(3)(f). See Pfizer Corporation v Minister for Health (1965) 1 AE 450. See LICENCES OF RIGHT.

**food business, suspension of.** Whenever, as respects any food premises or any food stall or food vehicle used in connection with a food business, the Minister is of opinion that there is a grave and immediate danger that food intended for sale for human consumption, is liable to cause serious illness if consumed, he may by order direct that such premises stall or vehicle be not used in connection with a food business: Food Hygiene Regulations 1950 art.34 (SI No 205 of 1950). An appeal lies to the District Court (qv). See also SI No 322 of 1971.

**food unfit for human consumption.** Food which is or is suspected by an *authorised officer* to be diseased, contaminated or otherwise unfit for human consumption; the authorised officer may seize, remove and detain any such article of food intended for sale for human consumption and to destroy it in specified circumstances: Food Hygiene Regulations 1950 art.11 (SI No 205 of 1950). An authorised officer is defined as health officer, a veterinary officer, an officer of the Minister for Agriculture, or a garda authorised by the Minister (ibid art.2). The local chief medical officer may make a *prohibition order* in respect of food which has been or is about to be imported into the State (ibid art.13). See also SI No 322 of 1971.

**footpath.** A road over which there is a public right of way for pedestrians only, not being a footway (qv): Roads Act 1993 s.2(1). See ROAD.

**footway.** The portion of any road which is provided primarily for the use of pedestrians: Road Traffic Act 1961 s.3. That portion of any road associated with a roadway (qv) which is provided primarily for use by pedestrians: Roads Act 1993 s.2(1). See ROAD.

**forbidden degrees.** The prohibited degrees of relationship in relation to marriage; there are 28 such degrees. See PROHIBITED DEGREES.

**force.** Violent action; it is generally unlawful to use force on another. However a person who is attacked is entitled to use *proportionate* force in retaliation to protect himself and his family and anyone attacked in his presence: The People v Keatley (1954) IR 12. See SELF DEFENCE.

**force majeure.** An overpowering event which could not be anticipated or controlled eg an Act of God (qv). Contracts often contain a *force majeure clause.* A force majeure may amount to a frustration (qv) of the contract.

**forcible entry and occupation.** A person who forcibly enters land (which includes houses or other buildings or structures) or a vehicle or who remains in forcible occupation thereof is guilty of an offence, except where the person does not interfere with the use and enjoyment of the land or vehicle by the owner and leaves when requested to do so: Prohibition of Forcible Entry and Occupation Act 1971. *Forcibly* is defined as using or threatening to use force in relation to person and property. The Act also defines *forcible occupation.* It is a good defence to prove that the accused is the owner, or bona fide claimant of the property. Evidence obtained as a result of a forcible entry on foot of an invalid search warrant is not admissible: People (DPP) v Kenny (1990 SC) ILRM 569. See Ross Co Ltd v Swan (1981) ILRM 416. See SIT-IN.

**forebearance.** Refraining from enforcing a right eg for a debt. A forebearance to sue may be adequate consideration (qv) to support a contract. See Fullerton v Bank of Ireland (1903) AC 309.

**foreclosure.** The forfeiture by a mortgagor (qv) of his *equity of redemption* (qv). The mortgagee's right to foreclosure is the right to apply to the court for an order directing the mortgagor to redeem his mortgage within a certain time or in default to be deprived of his right to redeem forever. See MORTGAGE SUIT.

**foreign adoption.** See ADOPTION, FOREIGN.

**foreign bill.** See INLAND BILL.

**foreign company.** A company which is incorporated outside Ireland but which establishes a place of business in the State, is required to provide the Registrar of Companies with particular information eg the address of the company's principal place of business in the State and the name and address of one or more persons resident in the State authorised to accept service on behalf of the company: Companies Act 1963 s.352.

Where a foreign company has no place of business within the State, the court will not make any order which would amount to regulating the internal affairs of a company not amenable to its jurisdiction: Balkanbank v Naser Taher & Ors (1992 HC) ITLR (13 Apr). See also Gill in 7ILT & SJ (1989) 264.

**foreign currency.** See CURRENCY, FOREIGN.

**foreign judgments, enforcement of.** A foreign judgment is generally enforceable in Ireland if it has been rendered by a court of competent jurisdiction, is final and conclusive and is for a fixed sum of money. In relation to judgments of *contracting* states of the EC, the jurisdiction of the court of the state giving judgment may not be reviewed; there is also provision for enforcement of judgments of periodic payments (eg maintenance orders) as well as fixed sums, and of non-money judgments: Jurisdiction of Courts and Enforcement of Judgments (European Communities) Act 1988.

This Act which enabled the State to ratify the 1968 EC Convention in that regard, which Convention deals with civil and commercial matters only; excluded are judgments concerning status, matrimonial property, wills, succession, bankruptcy, arbitration, social security, revenue, customs and administrative matters.

The Master of the High Court is bound to grant protective measures where an *enforcement order* under the 1968 Convention is granted; such protective measures include eg an injunction to prevent the defendant reducing his assets below the judgment sum pending enforcement: Elwyn (Cottons) Ltd v Master of the High Court (1989) ITLR (6 Mar & 22 May). The law of the state in which enforcement is sought governs the entire procedure: Rhatigan v Textiles y Confecciones Europeas SA (1990 SC) ILRM 825. See also Byrne in 9ILT & SJ (1991) 64.

The 1988 Act has been amended to take account of the accession of Spain and Portugal (the 1989 Accession Convention) and also to bring the 1968 EC Convention into line with the Lugano Convention, which governs the enforcement of judgments between EC and EFTA member States: Jurisdiction of Courts and Enforcement of Judgments

Act 1993.

See also Maintenance Orders Act 1974; European Communities (Enforcement of Community Judgment) Regulations 1972 (SI No 331 of 1972); SI No 91 of 1988 and District Court (Jurisdiction of Courts and Enforcement of Judgments European Communities Act 1988) Rules 1988 (SI No 173 of 1988). See Rules of the Superior Courts (No 1) 1989 Order 42A (SI No 14 of 1989) and SI No 155 of 1990 (Circuit Court Rules). [Text: Byrne P]. See MAREVA INJUNCTION; SET ASIDE; SUMMONS, SERVICE OUT OF JURISDICTION.

**foreign law.** The law of a foreign country which must be proved as a matter of *fact* in Irish courts, if a question depending on that law is in dispute: McNamara v Owners of SS Hatteras (1933) IR 675. *Canon* law is foreign law in this context: O'Callaghan v O'Sullivan (1925) 1 IR 90. The opinion of an expert as to the foreign law is admissible and generally required. The decision of an Irish court adjudicating on a question of foreign law is on the basis of the evidence presented to it and its decision thereon is final: Tassan Din v Banco Ambrosiano (1991 HC) 1 IR 569. See also The State (Griffin) v Bell (1962) IR 355. See EXPERT OPINION.

**foreign tribunal, evidence for.** See LETTER OF REQUEST.

**foreign trust.** A trust in respect of which the settlor and the beneficiaries are not resident, ordinarily resident or domiciled in the State; the assets are situated outside the State; the income arises from sources outside the State; and the trustees, other than certain Irish resident trustees, are not resident, ordinarily resident or domiciled in the State: Finance Act 1993 s.49. For tax treatment of foreign trusts which, aside from an approved Irish resident trustee, have no connection with Ireland, see 1993 Act.

**foreman of jury.** The member of a jury (qv) who is chosen to be their chairman and who announces their verdict. See ISSUE PAPER; VERDICT.

**forensic.** Relating to legal matters.

**forensic examination.** Where stolen property becomes the subject matter of criminal proceedings, any forensic examination (whether by the prosecution or by the defence) should take place within a reasonable time, having regard to all the circumstances, so that the property can then be returned as expeditiously as possible to its true owner: Rogers v DPP (1993 HC) 11 ILT Dig 164.

**forensic medicine.** Medical jurisprudence; the application of medical knowledge to the purposes of the law.

**forensic testing.** See BODILY SAMPLE.

**foreseeable damage.** See REMOTENESS OF DAMAGE; RESCUER.

**foreshore.** The bed and shore, below the line of high water of ordinary or medium tides, of the sea and of every tidal river and tidal estuary and of every channel, creek, and bay of the sea or of any such river or estuary: Foreshore Act 1933 s.1. The foreshore belongs to the State: 1937 Constitution, art.10(2). The Minister is empowered to make leases and licences of the foreshore (ibid 1933 Act ss.2-3 as amended by Foreshore (Amdt) Act 1992 s.2). No registration of land which appears to comprise the foreshore may be made without sending prior notice to the Minister: Registration of Title Act 1964 s.125. See Attorney General v McCarthy (1911) 2 IR 260; Madden v Minister for the Marine (1993 HC) ILRM 436. See also Foreshore (Environmental Impact Assessment) Regulations 1990 (SI No 220 of 1990). See BEACH MATERIAL; SEASHORE; SEAWEED.

**foresight.** Looking forward. A person has a duty of care to avoid acts or omissions which he can reasonably foresee. Also in relation to murder, the accused is presumed to have intended the natural and probable consequences of his conduct. See DUTY OF CARE; ECONOMIC LOSS; MURDER; RESCUER.

**forestry.** A commercial company to implement the afforestation programme of the State is provided for in the Forestry Act 1988. The Act also amends the penalties for certain offences, mostly relating to tree felling. See also VESTING ORDER.

**forfeiture.** The deprivation of a person of his property as a penalty for some act or omission. Forfeiture may take place by agreement or by operation of law eg a forfeiture clause in a lease may enable the lessor to determine the lease; the government is empowered to order the forfeiture of the property of an unlawful organisation. Fishing gear and catch may be forfeited pursuant to the Fisheries (Consolidation) Act 1959 but not summarily: Kostan v AG (1978 HC). Forfeiture of the lands and goods of a felon was abolished by the Forfeiture Act 1870.

An offensive weapon may be forfeited by order of the court: Firearms and Offensive Weapons Act 1990 s.13. A covenant for the forfeiture of a lease on the bankruptcy (qv) of the lessee is void as against the Official Assignee (qv): Bankruptcy Act 1988 s.49(1). A vessel may be forfeited on a second conviction on indictment of certain offences under the Merchant Shipping Act 1992 (ibid s.22). The sale or use of a product forfeited under the Customs Acts does not constitute an infringement of a patent: Patents Act 1992 s.116. See FELONY; LEASE, DETERMINATION OF; PRESERVED BENEFIT; SCHEDULED OFFENCE; UNLAWFUL ORGANISATION.

**forfeiture of shares.** In a company, the shares of a member may be forfeited by resolution of the directors if such power is given in the company's *articles of association:* Companies Act 1963, Table A, art 35. However, a power claimed by a company to forfeit its own shares is invalid as an unauthorised return of capital, unless it is for non-payment of calls: Hopkinson v Mortimer, Harley Co (1917) 1 Ch 646. The courts interpret the power to forfeit very strictly. The prescribed detail must be followed scrupulously; *mala fides* or abusive exercise by the directors of their fiduciary power will cause the forfeiture to be struck down. See Ward v Dublin North City Milling Co (1919) 1 IR 5. See SURRENDER OF SHARES; SHARES.

**forged endorsement.** See CHEQUE, LIABILITY ON.

**forgery.** The offence committed by a person who makes a false document in order that it may be used as genuine or who counterfeits certain seals or dies with an unlawful intent: Forgery Act 1913. The offence covers any writing the falsification of which can prejudice any person; the document must not only tell a lie, but must tell a lie about itself. Documents covered by the offence include wills and codicils, deeds and bonds, bank notes and valuable securities, documents of title to lands and goods,

and policies of insurance.

Most forgeries (eg of private documents) require *intent to defraud* ie to deprive by deceit; some forgeries however (eg of public documents) only require an *intent to deceive* ie to induce another to believe something is true which is in fact false and which the person practising the deceit believes to be false. See also Dangerous Substances Act 1972 s.50; Hallmarking Act 1981 s.13; Finance Act 1989 s.69. See also DPP v Harrington (1991 CCA) 9ILT Dig 171. See COUNTERFEIT; UTTER.

**forinsecus.** [Outside].

**forma pauperis.** See IN FORMA PAUPERIS.

**forms, legal.** See PRECEDENT.

**fortuna.** [Treasure trove (qv)].

**fortune telling.** Telling of fortunes for money may amount to the offence of false pretences (qv).

**forum non conveniens.** Common law doctrine whereby the court refuses to exercise its right of jurisdiction because, for the convenience of the parties and in the interest of justice, an action should be brought elsewhere. See now EC Convention on Jurisdiction and Enforcement of Judgments. See Overseas Union Insurance Ltd v New Hamshire Insurance Co Ltd — Court of Justice of EC (Case C-351/89). See Byrne in 10 ILT & SJ (1992) 230 and 11 ILT & SJ (1993) 63. See JURISDICTION.

**Foss v Harbottle, rule in.** The rule in company law that only a company can maintain proceedings in respect of wrongs done to it: Foss v Harbottle (1843) 2 Hare 461. The exceptions to the rule include the right of an individual shareholder to bring proceedings in respect of an act done on behalf of the company which is illegal or ultra vires (qv) the company or where there is *oppression of a shareholder* (qv). It has been held that a 50% shareholder outvoted by the casting vote of a chairman to the detriment of the company is a minority shareholder entitled to sue for the purposes of the rule: Balkanbank v Naser Taher & Ors (1992 HC) ITLR (13 Apr). See Moylan v Irish Whiting Manufacturers Ltd (1980) HC; Duggan v Bourke & Bank of Ireland (1986) HC. See O'Neill v Ryan (1993 SC) ILRM 557 and MacCann in 8 ILT & SJ (1990) 68–74. See DERIVATIVE

ACTION; OPPRESSION OF SHAREHOLDER.

**foster-child.** Prior to commencement of Part VI of the Child Care Act 1991, a child taken into care by a health board (qv) by the *boarding out* of the child to foster parents: Health Act 1953 s.55; Boarding Out of Children Regulations 1983 (SI No 67 of 1983). The child had to be under 16 years of age and either be (a) a legitimate child (now, a child *whose parents are married to each other*) whose parents were dead or who was deserted by his parents or (where one of them was dead) by the surviving parent, or (b) an illegitimate child (now, a child *whose parents are not married to each other*) whose mother was dead or who was deserted by his mother. However, a health board could continue to support such a child beyond 16 years of age until the completion of his education.

On commencement of Part VI of the 1991 Act, a child boarded out by a health board is deemed to have been placed in *foster care* under an arrangement made under section 36 (ibid 1991 Act s.6). A foster child is now a person under the age of 18 years (ibid s.2(1)). See CHILD; FOSTER-PARENTS; WELFARE OF CHILDREN.

**foster-parent.** Prior to commencement of Part VI of the Child Care Act 1991, a *foster parent* was a person into whose foster care a health board (qv) placed a child, where such care was paid for by the board: Health Act 1953 s.55; Boarding Out of Children Regulations 1983 (SI No 67 of 1983). Foster parents had to be properly assessed by the board and their suitability and the suitability of their home determined (ibid reg.7). A foster parent could not be of a different religion to the child unless (a) each of the child's parents or (b) where the child's parents were not married to each other, the mother or (c) the child's guardians, knew the religion of the foster parent and consented (ibid reg.8) In the case of desertion of the child or death of the parents, it sufficed if the foster parent undertook to bring up the child in the religion to which the child belonged.

On commencement of Part VI of the 1991 Act, *foster parent* means a person other than a relative of a child who is taking care of the child on behalf of a health board in accordance with regula-

tions made under s.39 and *foster care* is construed accordingly (ibid 1991 Act s.36(2)). These regulations may fix the conditions under which children may be placed in foster care, prescribe the form of contract to be entered into by a health board with foster parents, and provide for supervision and visiting (ibid s.39(2)). Also where a foster-child is *adopted* by the foster-parent, the health board may continue to contribute to the maintenance of the child as if he continued to be in foster care (ibid s.44(1)). See FOSTER-CHILD.

**founders' shares.** Deferred shares which do not receive a dividend until other shareholders have been paid a dividend. Founders' shares sometimes entitle the holders to the whole or a substantial part of the distributable profits but are now rarely issued. See SHARES.

**foundling.** An abandoned infant whose parents are not known. Such a child may be adopted. See Adoption Act 1988. See ADOPTION.

**Four Courts.** The buildings in Dublin, designed by Gandon, opened in 1796; the *four* courts leading from the round hall were originally Exchequer, Chancery, King's Bench and Common Pleas. The buildings, as extended, now comprise courts from the District to the Supreme Court, the Law Library (qv), consultation rooms of the Incorporated Law Society (qv), the Central Office (qv) and other court offices.

The burning of the Four Courts in 1922 destroyed many legal records which in many cases barred person from making claims to moneys paid into the court to which they may have been entitled; this is one reason for the accumulation of unclaimed assets in the *funds of suitors*. See SUITORS, FUNDS OF.

**four unities.** See JOINT TENANCY.

**fractionem diei non recipit lex.** [The law does not recognise any fraction of a day]. See CLEAR DAYS; GALE DAY.

**franchise.** (1) The right to vote in a parliamentary or local authority election. Every citizen of the State who has reached the age of eighteen years and who is not disqualified by law has the right to vote in an election for members of Dail Eireann: 1937 Constitution (as amended), art.16(1)(2). The Constitution was amended in 1984 to permit the extension of this franchise by statute law to non-citizens; it was extended to British citizens resident in the State by the Electoral (Amendment) Act 1985; similar voting rights may be extended by order to nationals of member States of the EC resident in Ireland, provided reciprocal voting rights are extended to Irish citizens. Only *presidential electors* are entitled to vote in a referendum (qv) or presidential election. The constitutional ban on double voting did not forbid double registration: 1937 Constitution, art.16(4); Quinn v Mayor of City of Waterford (1991 SC) ILRM 433. Now, a person must not be registered as an elector more than once in any registration area nor in more than one such area: Electoral Act 1992 s.11(1). See also CITIZEN; LOCAL GOVERNMENT, ELECTION OF; PERSONATION; PRESIDENT OF IRELAND; PROPORTIONAL REPRESENTATION; VOTERS, SPECIAL.

(2) A liberty or privilege eg to hold fairs and markets. At common law a franchise was a royal privilege which not only authorised something to be done, but gave the owner the right to prevent others from interfering with the right. The 1937 Constitution provides that all royalties and franchises in the State belong to the State subject to all estates and interests therein for the time being lawfully vested in any person or body (ibid art.10(1)). Franchises are burdens (qv) which can affect registered land without registration: Registration of Title Act 1964 s.72(1). See Skibbereen UDC v Quill (1986) ILRM 170.

(3) A right to trade under the name of another. See Dunlea v Nissan (1991 HC) 9ILT Dig 74.

**fraud.** (1) The crime which may involve a false pretence, false accounting, forgery, embezzlement or fraudulent conversion (qqv). As regards a body corporate or public company, a director of which who makes, circulates or publishes, or concurs in making, circulating or publishing any statement or account which he knows to be false in any material particular, with intent to induce any person to become a shareholder or partner therein, is guilty of a misdemeanour: Larceny Act 1861 s.84. See also Debtors (Ireland) Act 1872 s.13.

(2) Fraud is also the tort of *deceit* (qv).

For fraud as a ground for setting aside the judgment of a court, see SET ASIDE. See Superwood Holdings Ltd v Sun Alliance (1991 HC). See Report of the Government Advisory Committee on Fraud ("Maguire Committee") (1992). See also CONSPIRACY, CRIME OF; INJUNCTION, PLANNING; INSURANCE, CONTRACT OF; PLEADINGS; STATUTE OF FRAUDS; VOIDABLE; UBERRIMAE FIDEI.

**fraud, international .** See POLICE COOPERATION.

**fraudulent conversion.** The misdemeanour (qv) committed by a person who *fraudulently converts* to his own use any property with which he has been entrusted to keep in safe custody or to deliver to another or which he has received for, or on account of, any other person: Larceny Act 1916 s.20. In relation to trusts, it is an offence for a person with intent to defraud, to convert or appropriate to any purpose other than that of his trust, any property given to him on an express trust (qv) created in writing (ibid s.20).

Fraud must be present to constitute the offence; the conversion must be done wilfully and knowingly. When money is received by a person under circumstances which impose on him a definite legal obligation to pay it over to another person, it is money *received for, or on account of, any other person*: Attorney General v Lawless (1930) IR 247; The People (Attorney General) v Heald (1954) IR 58. See also The People (Attorney General) v Murphy (1947) IR 236; The People (Attorney General) v Cowan (1957) CCA; The People (Attorney General) v Singer (1975) IR 408. See EMBEZZLEMENT.

**fraudulent debtor.** A wide range of offences which a bankrupt (qv) or an *arranging debtor* (qv) may commit eg concealing or fraudulently removing any part of his property to the value of £500 or upwards: Bankruptcy Act 1988 s.123. It is also an offence for a person, including persons who subsequently become bankrupts or arranging debtors, to do certain acts with intent to defraud their creditors; there is a rebuttable presumption that the act constituting the offence was done with that intent if it occurred within twelve months before *adjudication* of the person as a bankrupt or of the granting of an *order for protection* to the person (ibid s.123(3)).

**fraudulent misrepresentation.** See MIS-REPRESENTATION.

**fraudulent preference.** Any conveyance, mortgage, delivery of goods, payment, execution or other act relating to property, by a company (within 6 months of being wound up) in favour of any creditor, with the view to giving such creditor, or any surety or guarantor for the debt due to such creditor, a preference over other creditors. A fraudulent preference is invalid. However, for a transfer of property to be caught by this prohibition, the company must have been unable to pay its debts as they fell due at the time the preference was made. See Companies Act 1963 s.286 as amended by the Companies Act 1990 s.135.

The 6 month period has been extended to 2 years in the case of transactions in favour of persons *connected* with the company eg directors, shadow directors, close relatives, and related companies. The onus of establishing the legitimacy of the transaction is placed on the connected person. See In re John Daly Co Ltd (1886) 19 LR Ir 83; In re Olderfleet Shipbuilding Co Ltd (1922) 1 IR 26; Eddison v Allied Irish Banks (1987) HC.

It has been held that the giving of security by a third party to a creditor of an insolvent company in circumstances where the payment would constitute a fraudulent preference if made by the insolvent company, cannot amount to a fraudulent preference: Parkes & Sons Ltd v Hong Kong & Shanghai Banking Corporation (1990 HC) ILRM 341. For provisions governing fraudulent preference by a person who is unable to pay his debts as they become due, see Bankruptcy Act 1988 s.57.

**fraudulent trading.** The offence committed by a person who is knowingly a party to the carrying on of the business of a company with intent to defraud creditors of the company or creditors of any other person or for any fraudulent purpose: Companies Act 1963 s.297 as amended by the Companies Act 1990 s.137.

Such a person may also be declared by the court to be personally responsible

without limitation of liability for the debts or other liabilities of the company, on the application of the receiver, examiner, liquidator or any creditor or contributory of the company: 1963 Act s.297A inserted by 1990 Act s.138. See RSC O.74 r 49. See also In re Aluminium Fabricators Ltd (No 2) (1984) ILRM 399; In re Kelly's Carpetdrome Ltd (1983 & 1984) HC; In re Hunting Lodges Ltd (1985 HC) ILRM 75. See RECKLESS TRADING.

**fraus omnia vitiat.** [Fraud (qv) vitiates everything].

**free movement.** The phrase used in the Treaty of Rome 1957 in relation to the movement of persons, services and capital within the EC. See ALIEN; EXCHANGE CONTROL; INTERNAL MARKET; WORKERS, FREEDOM OF MOVEMENT.

**free port.** The land enclosed within the limits defined by an order made by the Minister: Free Ports Act 1986 s.2. The principal benefits of free port status is the deferral of payments of custom duties and value-added tax on imports and simplified customs documentation and procedures. See Ringaskiddy Free Port (Establishment) Order 1988 (SI No 113 of 1988).

**freedom, honorary.** See CIVIC HONOUR.

**freedom of assembly.** See ASSEMBLY, FREEDOM OF.

**freedom of association.** The right of citizens guaranteed by the State under the Constitution to form associations and unions, subject to public order and morality (art 40.6.1). Laws regulating the right must not contain political, religious or class discrimination (art 40.6.2). See TRADE UNION.

**freedom of expression.** See EXPRESSION, FREEDOM OF.

**freehold.** An interest in land being either a fee simple, a fee tail or a life estate (qqv). Interests which are less than freehold are leases and tenancies (qqv).

**freeman.** A person who possesses the *freedom* of a city or borough with its rights and privileges. Honorary freedom can be conferred by a local authority. See CIVIC HONOUR.

**freeze assets.** The colloquial term to describe an order of the court which prevents any dealing in assets to which the order relates eg an order to prevent monies leaving a bank account under powers conferred by the Finance Act 1983 s.18. See ATTACHMENT OF FUNDS; BANKER CUSTOMER RELATIONSHIP; INJUNCTION; STOP ORDER.

**freight.** The consideration (qv) paid to a carrier for the carriage of goods.

**fresh evidence.** New or additional evidence which an appellant (qv) in an appeal may call with the leave of the court. In relation to the Supreme Court, the evidence must have been in existence at the time of the trial; it must have been such that it could not have been obtained with reasonable diligence for use at the trial; it must be credible though it need not be incontrovertible and it must be such that if given it would probably have an important influence on the result of the case: Murphy v Minister for Defence & AG (1991 SC) 2 IR 161.

If leave is given, the evidence will normally be heard by the Court, although it may order that it be taken on deposition (qv). A witness however will not be permitted to give evidence at the appeal which recants his earlier sworn evidence and supports a different case: Smyth & Ors v Tunney & Ors (1992 SC) ITLR (7 Sep).

In certain circumstances the need for finality in litigation would be outweighed by the need to do justice: O'Connor v O'Shea (1989 SC) ITLR (18 Sep). Fresh evidence which was available but was not used will only be admitted in the most exceptional cases; however regard will be had to one of the principal objects of a criminal trial, being to ensure that an innocent person is not convicted: Attorney General v Kelly (1937) IR 315.

Further evidence may be allowed in a case at the judge's discretion after the close of the case for the prosecution and the case for the defence: The People v O'Brien (1969) Frewen 343. However, a judge of the district court acted in excess of jurisdiction in re-opening a case to hear fresh evidence at an adjourned hearing, in the absence of the accused's counsel of choice, the counsel having previously been excused from appearing: Dawson v Hamill (1990) ILRM 257.

The decision of the Supreme Court cannot, in the absence of fraud, be challenged in subsequent proceedings on the basis of new evidence: Tassan Din v Banco Ambrosiano (1991 HC) 1 IR 569. See also DPP v Quirke (1991) CCA. See also RSC O.86 r.24. See DE NOVO; FINALITY IN LITIGATION; SET ASIDE.

**friend, my.** The term used by counsel in a case to refer to counsel on the opposing side.

**friend, next.** See NEXT FRIEND.

**friendly society.** A society established for the purpose of providing by voluntary subscription of its members for the relief or maintenance of its members and their families during sickness or other infirmity or in old age or in widowhood or for the relief or maintenance of their orphan children during minority: Friendly Societies Act 1896 s.8. It also includes a society providing for life and endowment insurance, or established for a social educational or recreational purpose and includes working-men's clubs.

A friendly society may be registered with the Registrar of Friendly Societies; certain privileges apply to registered societies (ibid s.32-37). A friendly society is not a corporation; consequently its property is vested in its trustees (ibid s.49). See also Friendly Societies Acts 1936 and 1977. An arranging debtor (qv) or a bankrupt (qv) who is a treasurer of a friendly society, must pay the full amount of his debt to the society before paying his other creditors a composition (qv) or dividend (ibid 1896 Act; Bankruptcy Act 1988 s.81(10)).

New rules governing the qualification for appointment as auditors to friendly societies have been enacted: Companies Act 1990 s.187. Additionally, insurance activities permitted to be carried on by friendly societies are now limited to mutual, self-help and small scale activities: Insurance Act 1989 s.28. See Friendly Society Regulations 1988 (SI No 74 of 1988). Compare with INDUSTRIAL & PROVIDENT SOCIETY.

**frivolous action.** See ABUSE OF PROCESS.

**fructus industriales.** [Fruits of industry].

**fructus naturales.** [Fruits of nature].

**frusta legis auxilium quaerit qui in legem committit.** [He who offends against the law vainly seeks the help of the law]. He who comes to equity must come with clean hands. See EQUITY, MAXIMS OF.

**frustration of contract.** Impossibility of performance of a contract which excuses the parties from performance. *Frustration is the premature determination of an agreement between parties, lawfully entered into and in course of operation at the time of its premature determination, owing to the occurrence of an intervening event or change or circumstances so fundamental as to be regarded by the law both as striking at the root of the agreement and as entirely beyond what was contemplated by the parties when they entered into the agreement*: Cricklewood Property and Investment Trust v Leightons Investment Trust (1945) AC 221.

Frustration may arise: (a) by statutory interference: Baily v De Crespigny (1869) LR 4 QB 180; (b) the destruction of a specific object necessary for the performance of the contract: Taylor v Caldwell (1863) 2 B S 836; (c) the non-existence of a state of things, the continued existence of which formed the basis of the contract: Herne Bay SS v Hutton (1903) 2 KB 123; (d) personal incapacity in contracts where the personal qualifications of one of the parties are important: Robinson v Davison (1871) LR 6 Ex 269; (e) frustration of the adventure or of the commercial or practical object of the contract: Metropolitan Water Board v Dick Kerr & Co Ltd (1918) AC 119.

On frustration, a contract is automatically discharged from the time of the event and cannot give rise to liabilities subsequent to the time of discharge. However a contract cannot normally be discharged through the doctrine of frustration if a contract term covers the events which are alleged to constitute frustration: Mulligan v Browne (1976) SC. See also Fibrosa Spolka Cheyjna v Fairbairn, Lawson, Combe Barbour Ltd (1943) AC 32; Kearney v Saorstat Continental Shipping (1943) Ir Jur Rep 8; Herman v Owners of SS Vicia (1942) IR 304; Mc Guill v Aer Lingus & United Airlines (1983) HC.

In relation to a lease (qv), in the absence of any express covenants to repair, a tenant may surrender his tenancy if the premises are destroyed or rendered uninhabitable by fire or some other inevitable accident: Landlord and Tenant Law Amendment Act (Ireland) 1860 (Deasy's Act) s.40. See also Irish Leisure Industries Ltd v Gaiety Enterprises Ltd (1975) HC; National Carriers Ltd v Panalpina (Northern) Ltd (1981) AC 675; FRUSTRATION, SELF INDUCED.

**frustration, self-induced.** Frustration of a contract as a result of a person's own conduct or the conduct of other persons for whom he is responsible. Self-induced frustration will not relieve that party from liability under the contract. The party pleading frustration must show that he took all reasonable steps to prevent the contract being frustrated. See Herman v Owners of SS Vicia (1942) IR 304; Byrne v Limerick Steamship Co Ltd (1946) IR 138.

**fuel.** The Minister, for the purpose of preventing or limiting air pollution, is empowered to make regulations in relation to the standard, specification, composition and contents of fuel which is used in mechanically propelled vehicles or which is burnt in fireplaces: Air Pollution Act 1987 s.53.

**fugam fecit.** [He has made flight].

**full age.** See AGE OF MAJORITY.

**functions.** Term often used to describe powers and duties eg functions of the chief executive officer of a health board: Health Act 1970 s.17(4). See also Patents Act 1992 s.2(1); Environmental Protection Agency Act 1992 s.3(1).

**functus officio.** [Having discharged his duty]. Refers to a person who has exercised his authority and brought it to an end in a particular case. When a local government auditor has made a decision in relation to his functions, he is a *functus officio* and cannot alter or vary his decision: R (Bridgeman) v Drury (1894) 2 IR 489. Once an arbitrator makes an award, he is functus officio: McStay v Assicurazioni Generali Spa (1990) 8ILT Dig 105. A judge of the district court having granted a public music or dance licence is funtus officio; he is not entitled to grant, in effect, a reviewable licence: Sheehan v Reilly (1992 HC) 10 ILT Dig 267.

**fundamental breach.** A breach of contract which goes to the root of the contract entitling the innocent party to treat the contract as terminated and to sue for damages. To determine if a breach is fundamental, consideration is given to the seriousness of the breach, the effect of the breach and the likelihood of it recurring. See Dundalk Shipping Centre Ltd v Roof Spray Ltd (1979) HC. See also Robb v James (1881) 15 ILTR 59. See BREACH OF CONTRACT; EXCLUSION CLAUSES, RESTRICTION OF.

**fundamental rights.** Interests recognised and protected by the courts, which are superior to the law, the respect of which is a duty and the disregard of which is a wrong. Certain fundamental rights are *declared* in the constitution eg personal rights and rights relating to the family, education, private property and religion: 1937 Constitution arts. 40-44. It has been held that fundamental rights declared in the Constitution are not created by it; they are an acknowledgement that the individual has an inalienable possession of them: McGee v Attorney General (1974) IR 101.

Not all fundamental rights are declared; there are many *implied* rights which the courts will declare as the occasion arises: Ryan v Attorney General (1965) IR 294. These rights are not absolute rights, as their exercise may be regulated by the Oireachtas (qv) for the common good. Some fundamental rights are declared to attach to *citizens* and some to *persons*.

Examples of fundamental rights are: right to life; right to bodily integrity; equality before the law; inviolability of dwelling; personal liberty; freedom of expression; freedom to communicate; freedom to publish information; freedom of assembly; freedom to form associations and unions; freedom to travel; religious freedom; right to the private ownership of property; rights in relation to the family, marriage and education (qqv). See PERSONAL RIGHTS.

**funds of suitors.** See SUITORS, FUNDS OF.

**funeral expenses.** Priority in payment out of a deceased's estate is given to funeral and testamentary expenses. See Succession Act 1965 ss.45-46; first schedule. See ADMINISTRATION OF ESTATES; INSOLVENT ESTATE.

**furious driving.** The misdemeanour (qv) committed by a person who, having the charge of any carriage or vehicle, do or cause to be done any bodily harm to any person, by wanton or furious driving or racing or other wilful misconduct: Offences Against the Person Act 1861 s.35. See also Defence Act 1954 s.159.

**future goods.** See GOODS.

**future interest.** An interest limited to come into existence at some time in the future. A future interest in land is an interest which confers a right to the enjoyment of the land at a future time eg the right to land after the death of a living person. A future interest may be *vested* or *contingent*. A *vested* future interest is where the persons entitled to the interest are ascertained and the interest in ready to take effect on the determination of all the preceding interests; a *contingent* interest arises where either of these conditions is absent. Future interests can be classified also as reversions, legal remainders, future trusts and legal executory interests (qqv).

**future trust.** A trust limited to come into existence at some time in the future. Future trusts are classified as: (a) equitable remainders, which, at the time of their creation, are capable of complying with rules governing legal remainders and (b) equitable executory interests, which at the outset infringe one or more of these rules eg springing trusts and shifting trusts.

# G

**Gaeltacht.** [Irish speaking district]. An area designated as an area for the preservation and usage of the Irish language as the vernacular language. See Gaeltacht Areas Order 1956; Ministers and Secretaries (Amdt) Act 1956 s.2(2). The Gaeltacht area in Rathcarn in Co Meath was created in 1935 by the migration of 27 families from Connemara, as part of the work of the Land Commission (qv) in the enlargement and rearrangement of small holdings and the relief of congestion.

Payments received by persons who live in Gaeltacht areas who accommodate students of the Irish language (who wish to improve their fluency in the language) are not taken into consideration as regards means tests for social assistance: Social Welfare Act 1990 s.34. See also Social Welfare (Consolidation) Act 1981 s.288.

**gage.** A pledge or pawn. See MORTGAGE.

**gain.** Acquisition; something obtained or acquired; it is not limited to pecuniary gain nor to commercial profit: Re Arthur Association for British and Colonial Ships (1875) LR 10 Ch App 542 as cited in Deane v VHI (1992 SC) ITLR (31 Aug). *For gain* denotes an activity carried on, or a service supplied, which was done for a charge or payment (ibid Deane case). See VOLUNTARY HEALTH INSURANCE.

**gale.** A rent or duty; a periodic payment of rent.

**gale day.** A rent day. Every tenancy from year to year is presumed to have commenced on the last *gale day* of the calendar year on which rent has become due and payable in respect of the premises, unless a contrary intention appears: Deasy's Act 1860 s.6. It has been held that the consistent and regular recognition by parties to a tenancy of a particular day of each month as the gale day, is prima facie evidence of the commencement of the tenancy on that day of some month, and of its being a monthly tenancy: White v Mitchell (1962) IR 348.

**game.** Wild birds, the hunting of which, the Minister may declare open season (qv) by order: Wildlife Act 1976 s.24. They include grouse, cock pheasant, woodcock, partridge, wild duck, mallard and certain species of wild goose and plover.

**gaming.** Playing a game (whether of skill or chance or partly of skill and partly of chance) for stakes hazarded by the players: Gaming and Lotteries Act 1956 s.2. Gaming is unlawful if (a) the chances of all of the players, including the banker, are not equal; or (b) if a portion of the stakes are retained by the banker otherwise than as winnings; or (c) gaming is conducted by way of slot machines (ibid s.4). Gaming is lawful in specific instances at a circus, travelling show, carnival, public house, amusement hall and funfair. The winner of a lawful game can sue for the prize provided it is not a stake (ibid s.36(4)).

Part lll of the 1956 Act dealing with the licensing of amusement halls and funfairs, does not have effect in any area unless there is for the time being in force a resolution by the local authority under s.13 adopting it for its area: The State (Divito) v Arklow (1986) ILRM 123.

It has been held that before a District Court grants a certificate authorising the issue of such a licence to permit gaming, it must be satisfied that the local authority had adopted such a resolution allowing gaming in its area; unless such a resolution is in force, neither the District Court or the Circuit Court has jurisdiction to grant a certificate or the Revenue Commissioners to issue a licence: Camillo v O'Reilly (1988 SC) ILRM 738. See also Cafolla v Ireland (1986) ILRM 177; DPP v Olympic Amusements (1987) ILRM 320; DPP v Cafolla (1992 SC) ITLR (22 Jun).

For provisions on gaming machine licence duty, see Finance Act 1975 s.43 as amended by Finance Act 1993 s.71. The 1993 Act replaces the system of licensing based on the number of machines in a particular premises with a system based on the individual licensing of each machine. See CHEATING; LOTTERY; WAGERING CONTRACT.

**garda as prosecutor.** See PROSECUTOR.

**garda, complaints against.** A system of investigation and adjudication of complaints made by the public about the conduct of members of the Garda Siochana (other than the Commission of the garda) is provided for in the Garda Siochana (Complaints) Act 1986 and the Garda Siochana (Complaints) (Tribunal Procedure) Rules 1988 (SI No 96 of 1988); Appeal Board Procedure Rules 1988 (SI No 192 of 1988).

**garda, discipline of.** Special considerations apply to the power of the State to dispense with the services of members of the armed forces, of the Garda Siochana, and of the prison service, because it is of vital concern to the community as a whole that the members of these services, should be completely trustworthy: The State (Jordan) v Commissioner of Garda Siochana (1987) ILRM 107.

An inquiry under the Garda Siochana (Discipline) Regulations is one which must be conducted judicially in accordance with the procedures laid down, but this does not constitute the exercise of judicial power: Keady v Garda Commissioner (1989) 7ILT Dig 260. It has also been held that to allow a garda disciplinary inquiry to proceed after the accused member had been acquitted of identical criminal charges would be unfair and oppressive: McGrath v Garda Commissioner (1990 SC) ILRM 817, and Regulation 38 of Garda Siochana (Discipline) Regulations 1989 (SI No 94 of 1989). See also Stroker v Doherty (1991 SC) 1 IR 23; Ryan v Commissioner (1992 HC). However, allegations of criminal conduct, which have been the subject of a nolle prosequi (qv) before a court, may be aired before a garda disciplinary inquiry: Keady v Garda Commissioner (1992 SC) ILRM 312. The 1989 Regulations cannot be applied to conduct or events occurring before they were brought into force: Healy v Garda Commissioner (1993 HC) – Irish Times 14/7/1993. See also O'Shea v Garda Commissioner (1993 HC) – Irish Times 26/3/1993. See ACQUITTAL; ADMINISTRATIVE TRIBUNAL.

**garda, identification of.** In relation to road traffic matters, a person is not bound to comply with a request, demand or requirement of a garda unless he is either in uniform or produces, if requested, an official identification or such other evidence of his identity as may be prescribed: Road Traffic Act 1961 s.111.

**garda compensation.** The scheme whereby compensation is paid out of public monies in respect of injury to, or death from injury of, a garda which injury was maliciously inflicted on him in the course of or in relation to the performance by him of his duties as a member of the Garda Siochana: Garda Siochana (Compensation) Act 1941.

An application for compensation is made to the Minister who will authorise the applicant to apply to the High Court, unless the Minister is of opinion that the injuries are of a minor character (ibid s.6). The High Court is empowered to fix the amount of compensation in acordance with the Act: ibid ss.8 and 10 as amended by the Garda Siochana (Compensation) (Amendment) Act 1945 s.2. See McLoughlin & Ors v Minister for the Public Service (1986) ILRM 28; Conroy v Commissioner of Garda Siochana (1988) HC.

**Garda Siochana.** The national police force, the general direction and control of which is vested in the Commissioner of the Garda Siochana, who is appointed by and may be removed by the government: Police Force Amalgamation Act 1925 ss.6 and 8. He is responsible to the Minister for Justice. The Commissioner is authorised to enrol and appoint women to be members of the force by the Garda Siochana Act 1958.

Provision has been made for the admission of persons as *trainees*, who may subsequently be appointed as gardai; such subsequent appointment must be on *probation* (qv) for a period of two years: Garda Siochana (Admissions and Appointments) Regulations 1988 (SI No 164 of 1988). The Commissioner exercising the power to dismiss a trainee must observe the rules of natural justice and fair procedures; his decision is one which comes within the ambit of decisions which are subject to judicial review: Beirne v Garda Commissioner (1993 SC) ILRM 1.

Members of the garda may serve outside the State with the peace-keeping forces of the United Nations: Garda Siochana Act 1989. See Garvey v Ireland (1979) 113 ILTR 61. See also Garda Siochana Act 1924. See COMMON POLICIES; EUROPEAN POLICE OFFICE; PEACE OFFICER; POLICE COOPERATION; PROSECUTOR.

**garnish.** To warn.

**garnishee.** A debtor in whose hands a debt has been attached by a court. Garnishee proceedings enable a judgment creditor (qv) to have assigned to him the benefit of any debt owed by the garnishee to the judgment debtor (qv). A *garnishee order* is an order, served on a garnishee, attaching a debt in his hands. See RSC O.45 rr.1-8; RCC O.37. See Fitzpatrick v Daf Sales & Allied Irish Finance Ltd (1989) ILRM 777. See ATTACHMENT.

**gazumping.** Popularly understood to describe the situation in which a vendor of a house which is sold *subject to contract*, withdraws from the sale or threatens to do so, in expectation of receiving a higher price elsewhere. A Supreme Court judge has expressed the view that he would prefer that the occasional gazumper go unbound rather than that people be involved in needless uncertainty leading often to long drawn out litigation: O'Flaherty J in Boyle & Boyle v Lee & Goyns (1992 SC) ILRM 65. See SUBJECT TO CONTRACT.

**gearing.** The ratio between a company's debt and its equity. A company is said to be highly geared where it has borrowed heavily in relation to its share capital.

**general agent.** See AGENT.

**general average.** See AVERAGE.

**General Council of the Bar of Ireland.** See BAR COUNCIL.

**general damages.** The damages which the law presumes to flow from the defendant's act eg damages for pain and suffering in the case of personal injury. Because of the need for *finality in litigation*, the damages must be assessed once and for all, so the plaintiff is entitled to *prospective damages* to compensate him for future suffering or future loss of earnings. A plaintiff cannot seek a variation of damages based on matters occurring after a trial eg where he has suffered more damages than appeared probable on the evidence given at the trial: Dalton v Minister for Finance (1989) ILRM 519. However, where a dramatic alteration has taken place it may be proper to consider evidence of that alteration: O'Connor v O'Shea (1989 SC) ITLR (18 Sep).

The poverty of the plaintiff is not to be taken into account in assessing damages. Also no account is to be taken of any sum payable by way of insurance or pension or gratuity in consequence of an injury sustained by the plaintiff: Civil Liability (Amendment) Act 1964 s.2. See DAMAGES; FRESH EVIDENCE; SPECIAL DAMAGES.

**general dealer.** Any person buying otherwise than at a public auction held by a licensed auctioneer (qv), or selling old metal, scrap metal, broken metal or partly manufactured metal goods in specified quantities: General Dealers (Ireland) Act 1903 s.12. It is an offence to act as a general dealer without a licence (ibid s.1). See Dunne v Lee (1913) 2 IR 205.

**general election.** A general election for members of Dail Eireann (qv) held in accordance with the 1937 Constitution, art.16(3)(2): Electoral Act 1992 s.2(1).

**general legacy.** See LEGACY.

**general meeting.** See ANNUAL GENERAL MEETING; EXTRAORDINARY GENERAL MEETING.

**general power.** See POWER OF APPOINTMENT.

**generalia specialia derogant.** [Special things derogate from general things].

**generalia specialibus non derogant.** [General things do not derogate from special things]. General statutes do not affect particular statutes unless the contrary intention appears. "Where there are general words in a later Act capable of reasonable and sensible application without extending them to subjects specially dealt with by earlier legislation, you are not to hold that earlier and special legislation indirectly repealed, altered or derogated from merely by force of such particular words, without any indication of a particular intention to do so": Seward v Vera Cruz (1884) 10 App Cas 59 at 68, cited with approval in Hatch v Governor of Wheatfield Prison (1993 SC) ITLR (29 Mar) and 11 ILT Dig 142.

The maxim is often given statutory recognition eg the exemptions from liability conferred by statute are unaffected by the SGSS Act 1980, see ibid s.4(2). See also Welch v Bowmaker (Ireland) Ltd (1980) IR 251. See LEGISLATION, INTERPRETATION OF.

**generalia verba sunt generaliter inteligenda.** [General words are to be understood generally].

**genetic engineering.** See MICROORGANISM.

**genetic fingerprinting.** The production of a genetic profile of a person through the examination of his skin, hair or bodily fluids. It is claimed that the likelyhood of two persons having the same DNA genetic code are less than one in five billion and that DNA fingerprinting will consequently have an important role to play in cases involving murder, rape, assault and in declarations of parentage (qqv). The *blood test* which can be ordered to determine parentage includes genetic fingerprinting carried out with the objective of ascertaining inheritable characteristics: Status of Children Act 1987 s.38 and JPD v MG (1991 SC) 1 IR 47. Genetic fingerprinting can also be utilised in particular instances where the taking of *bodily samples* is permitted. See Fennell in 8ILT & SJ (1990) 227. See BODILY SAMPLES; DNA.

**genetically modified organism.** An *organism* derived from the formation of a combination of genetic material by artificial techniques, or an organism inheriting such combination of genetic material: Environmental Protection Agency Act 1992 s.111(7). *Organism* means any multicellular, unicellular, subcellular or a cellular entity capable of replication or of transferring genetic material whether by natural or artificial processes (ibid s.111(7)). The Minister may make regulations for the control, management, regulation or prohibition of any process or action involving a genetically modified organism (giving full effect to Council Directives 90/219/EEC and 90/220/EEC): (ibid s.111(1)). See BEST AVAILABLE TECHNOLOGY.

**genocide.** The offence committed by a person who commits certain acts with intent to destroy, in whole or in part, a national, ethnical, racial or religious group, by (a) killing members of the group, or (b) causing serious bodily or mental harm to members of the group, or (c) deliberately inflicting on the group, conditions of life calculated to bring about its destruction in whole or in part, or (d) imposing measures intended to prevent births within the group, or (e) forcibly transferring children of the group to another group: Genocide Convention, art.2 (United Nations 9th December 1948); Genocide Act 1973.

**gentleman's agreement.** Popularly understood to mean an agreement, the performance of which rests on the honour of the parties and is not intended to create legal relations between the parties or to be enforceable in a court of law. See LEGAL RELATIONS.

**geographical name as trade mark.** It is possible to register a prominent geographical name as a trade mark in Part B (qv) of the register of trade marks if there is very compelling evidence of *distinctiveness* (qv). See Waterford Glass Ltd v Controller of Trade Marks (1984) ILRM 565. See TRADE MARK, REGISTERED.

**gestation period.** The extension to the perpetuity period which is permitted to take account of children *en ventre sa mere* (qv), where the gestation period actually exists and where the subsequent birth is relevant to the perpetuity period eg a gift *to the first son of A to reach the age of 21* is valid if A is alive at the time of the gift and dies subsequently leaving his wife pregnant with their first child, who is subsequently born a son and attains 21. See PERPETUITIES, RULE AGAINST.

**gift.** A gratuitious grant or transfer of property. The person giving the gift is the *donor* and the recipient is the *donee*. For a valid gift there must be an intention to give and such acts as are necessary to give effect to the intention. A gift in a will is a *devise* (real property) or a *bequest* (personal property). See CLASS GIFTS; DONATIO MORTIS CAUSA; LAPSE; UNSOLICITED GOODS.

**gift tax.** A tax applicable to gifts *inter vivos* introduced by the Capital Acquisitions Tax Act 1976. [Text: Bale & Condon]. See CAPITAL ACQUISITION TAX; SELF ASSESSMENT.

**global maritime distress and safety system; GMDSS.** The radio communications equipment required to be carried on cargo ships of 300 tons or more and on passenger ships registered in the State and on other such ships registered outside the State while they are in a port in the State: Merchant Shipping (Radio) Rules 1992 (SI No 224 of 1992). There is provision for the phased introduction of the GMDSS between 1992 and 1999.

**global valuation.** The valuation (qv) of properties taken as a whole, wherever situated, of a specified *public utility undertaking* or such undertakings of a specified description, which the Minister may by order direct the Commissioner of Valuations to provide for the determination of: Valuation Act 1988 s.4. This provides a special method of establishing the valuation of such undertakings (eg ESB, Bord Gais) and is an exception to the Valuation Act 1852 s.11. See SI No 268 of 1988.

**glue-sniffing.** See SOLVENTS, SALE OF.

**going concern.** The concept concerning a company which implies that the enterprise will continue in operational existence for the foreseeable future; in particular that the profit and loss account and balance sheet assume no intention or necessity to liquidate or curtail significantly the scale of the operation: Standard Accounting Practice as cited In re Clubman Shirts Ltd (1991 HC) ILRM 43. In determining the value of shares of an oppressed minority shareholder of a company which cannot be regarded to be a going concern, the assets of the company should be valued on a break up basis. See ACCOUNTING

PRINCIPLES; SHARES, COMPULSORY PURCHASE OF.

**golden handcuff.** Colloquial expression to describe a restrictive covenant in an employment contract for which the employee may be given a substantial sum of money (hence "golden"), with the objective of preventing him setting up in competition with his employer for a period of time in the event that he should terminate his employment. Such a covenant may be void as being in restraint of trade and a restriction on competition. See RESTRAINT OF TRADE.

**golden handshake.** Popularly understood to mean payments made as compensation for loss of office or as consideration for or in connection with retirement from office: Companies Act 1963 ss.186-189. These payments must not be paid tax-free, except for the first £6000, and the aggregate amount of them in any year must be disclosed in or along with the annual accounts (ibid ss.185 and 191(1)(c) and (4)). See REDUNDANCY.

**golden rule.** The rule of construction for interpreting a statute which is utilised where the literal interpretation of the words would lead to such an absurdity that it is self evident that the legislature could not have meant what is stated. Under the rule the grammatical and ordinary sense of the words may be modified so as to avoid an absurdity, repugnancy or inconsistency. See Grey v Pearson (1857) 6 HLC 61. See LEGISLATION, INTERPRETATION OF.

**golden share.** Popularly understood to refer to a special share arrangement, combined with provisions of a company's memorandum, whereby one shareholder can effectively prevent the takeover of a company eg by limiting the size of shareholding of any one shareholder or consortium of shareholders. It is sometimes utilised in the privatisation of a state owned company where the government wishes to prevent foreign ownership eg in the case of the privatisation of Irish Life Assurance plc.

**golden umbrella.** Popularly understood to mean service contracts made with company directors which are for a long duration and at high remuneration, often with the objective of deterring shareholders from removing them due to the prohibitive damages which might ensue.

Also known as a *golden parachute*. Service contracts of longer than 5 years are prohibited unless approved by the members of the company in meeting by ordinary resolution: Companies Act 1990 s.28. See REMUNERATION OF DIRECTORS.

**Goldsmiths of Dublin, Company of.** The company, established and incorporated by royal charter of Charles I on 22nd December 1637, with power of enforcing prescribed minimum standards of *fineness* for the quality of gold, silver and platinum to be used in manufacture, and the assay and hallmarking of all gold, silver and platinum wares submitted to it. It also has power to make bye-laws, and the powers of search seizure and destruction of sub-standard wares. The company controls the assay office and is described in the charter as the *Wardens and Commonality of Goldsmiths of the city of Dublin*. See Hallmarking Act 1981. See HALLMARKING.

**golf.** A golf course need not be constructed so that greens and tees are not close to one another for safety reasons; such a rule would impose serious limitations on where golf could be played: Potter v Carlisle & Cliftonville Golf Club Ltd (1939) NI 114 (CA). A golf spectator at the 1990 Irish Open, who was struck on the head by a golf ball, had her action dismissed, the judge finding that the defendants did not have a duty to provide against improbable or unlikely happenings: Dalton v Portmarnock Golf Club and PJ Carroll & Co plc (1992 CC).

**good consideration.** Consideration founded on generosity, natural affection or love or relationship. It is not regarded as *valuable consideration* (ie money or money's worth). See CONSIDERATION.

**good faith.** In relation to contracts for the sale of goods, *good faith* means done honestly, whether negligent or not: Sale of Goods Act 1893 s.62(2). See MARKET OVERT; STOPPAGE IN TRANSITU; VOIDABLE TITLE, SALE UNDER.

**good name.** See NAME, RIGHT TO GOOD; TRIBUNALS OF INQUIRY.

**good title.** See MARKETABLE TITLE.

**goods.** The term includes all *chattels personal* other than things in action and money; it also includes emblements, industrial growing crops, and things attached to and forming part of the land which are agreed to be severed before sale or under the contract of sale. *Things in action* include debts, cheques, bills of exchange, shares and patents. *Future goods* means goods to be manufactured or acquired by the seller after the making of the contract of sale. *Specific goods* means goods identified and agreed upon at the time a contract of sale is made. See Sale of Goods Act 1893 ss.5 and 62. See MANUFACTURED GOODS; UNASCERTAINED GOODS; UNSOLICITED GOODS.

**goods, acceptance of.** See ACCEPTANCE OF GOODS.

**goods, character and quality of.** See CHARACTER AND QUALITY OF GOODS.

**goods, deliverable state.** Goods are in a deliverable state when they are in such a state that the buyer would under the contract be bound to take delivery of them: Sale of Goods Act 1893 s.62. See DELIVERY OF GOODS; GOODS, PROPERTY IN.

**goods, examination of.** See EXAMINATION OF GOODS.

**goods, international classification of.** See INTERNATIONAL CLASSIFICATION OF GOODS.

**goods, property in.** In a contract for the sale of goods, unless a different intention appears, the following are rules for ascertaining the intention of the parties as to the time at which the *property* in the goods is to pass to the buyer:

Rule 1 — Where there is an unconditional contract for the sale of specific goods, in a deliverable state, the property in the goods passes to the buyer when the contract is made, and it is immaterial whether the time of payment or the time of delivery, or both, be postponed. See Clarke v Reilly (1962) 96 ILTR 96.

Rule 2 — Where there is a contract for the sale of specific goods and the seller is bound to do something to the goods, for the purpose of putting them into a deliverable state, the property does not pass until such thing be done, and the buyer has notice thereof.

Rule 3 — Where there is a contract for sale of specific goods in a deliverable state, but the seller is bound to weigh, measure, test, or do some other act or thing with reference to the goods for the purpose of ascertaining the price, the property does not pass until such act or thing be done, and the buyer has notice thereof.

Rule 4 — See APPROVAL, SALE ON.

Rule 5 — Where there is a contract for the sale of unascertained or future goods by description, and goods of that description and in a deliverable state are unconditionally appropriated to the contract, either by the seller with the assent of the buyer, or by the buyer with the assent of the seller, the property in the goods thereupon passes to the buyer. Such assent may be express or implied, and may be given either before or after the appropriation is made.

*Property* in goods means the ownership of them rather than the mere physical possession. See In re Interview Ltd (1975) IR 382; Cronin v IMP Midleton Ltd (1986) HC. See Sale of Goods Act 1893 s.18. See APPROPRIATION; RETENTION OF TITLE.

**goods, receiving stolen.** See HANDLING STOLEN PROPERTY; RECEIVING STOLEN GOODS.

**goods, recovery of.** See RECOVERY OF GOODS.

**goods, rejected.** See REJECTED GOODS.

**goods, sale of.** See SALE OF GOODS.

**goods, title to.** See TITLE TO GOODS.

**goods, unlawful possession of.** See UNLAWFUL POSSESSION OF GOODS.

**goodwill.** An intangible asset of a business arising from the advantage the business derives from its past reputation and its connection with its customers. It has been described as the attractive force which brings in custom: Inland Revenue v Muller (1901) AC 224. The sale of a business usually includes the sale of the goodwill, in which circumstance the vendor may be restrained from soliciting his former customers: Trego v Hunt (1896) AC 7. A charge (qv) on goodwill of a company must be registered under s.99 of the Companies Act 1963 (as amended by Companies Act 1990 s.122) to prevent the security being void as against a liquidator or creditor of the company. See ASSET VALUATION.

**goose.** See GAME.

**government.** The body through which the executive power of the State is exercised; it consists of not less than seven and not more than fifteen members appointed by the President of Ireland: 1937 Constitution, art.28. The head of the government is the Taoiseach (qv). The government meets and acts as a *collective authority* and is responsible to Dail Eireann. The contents and details of discussions at meetings of the government are absolutely confidential as a constitutional right and this right cannot be waived by any member of the government: Finlay CJ in AG v The Sole Member of the Beef Tribunal (1993 SC) ILRM 81.

The Taoiseach, the Tanaiste (qv) and the member of the government in charge of the Department of Finance must be members of the Dail. The other members of the government must be members of the Dail or the Seanad (qv) but not more than two may be members of the Seanad.

The Taoiseach may at any time for reasons which to him seem sufficient request a member of the government to resign; should the member concerned fail to comply with the request, his appointment will be terminated by the President if the Taoiseach so advises (ibid art.28(9)(4)). See Treoracha Faoi Nos Imeachta an Rialtais (Government Procedure Instructions) which sets out the rules for day-to-day operations of government, including submission of memoranda, government appointments, and conflicts of interest. See ETHICS IN GOVERNMENT; SEPARATION OF POWERS; OBSTRUCTION OF GOVERNMENT; TREASON; USURPATION OF GOVERNMENT.

**go-slow.** See WORKING TO RULE.

**Governor of Central Bank.** The person appointed as Governor of the Central Bank of Ireland by the President of Ireland on the advice of the Government: Central Bank Act 1942 s.19. His term of office is for seven years; he is ineligible for election as a director of any bank whatsoever; and he is prohibited from holding shares in any bank. See also Central Bank Act 1989 s.14. See CENTRAL BANK.

**grace, days of.** See DAYS OF GRACE.

**graft, doctrine of.** The equitable doctrine whereby in a constructive trust (qv) the profit or accretion (eg obtained by a person in a fiduciary position) is deemed to be *engrafted* upon the original trust property and thereby held upon the same trusts. See Dempsey v Ward (1899) I IR 463. For an example of a statutory provision on grafting, see Land Law (Ireland) Act 1887 s.14(3).

**grandfather clause.** Colloquial expression to describe a provision whereby, in

the introduction of new minimum levels of qualifications, persons are deemed to meet the qualification requirement on the basis of practice, experience and expertise eg Companies Act 1990 s.188 regarding qualifications of company auditors.

**grand jury.** Formerly, the jury with no corporate or continuous existence, appointed by the Lord Lieutenant, with responsibility for making and repairing roads and bridges and the construction and maintenance of court houses and the support of lunatic asylums, county infirmaries, industrial schools and coroners (qv), financed by a local revenue known as a *county cess* or *grand jury cess*: Grand Jury (Ireland) Act 1836. Its expenditure proposals, known as *presentments* had to be submitted to the judge of the assizes for approval; when its work was completed, it was discharged by the judge and ceased to exist for any purpose. Its local government functions were transferred to the county councils (qv): Local Government (Ireland) Act 1898 s.4. See The State (Feeley) v O'Dea (1986) HC.

**grant.** The allocation of rights and powers by an authority to a particular person or persons and for particular purposes eg grant of letters of administration, grant of probate, grant of a patent. A conveyance is a deed of grant. See PATENT, GRANT OF.

**gratis.** [Free]. Without recompense or charge.

**gratis dictum.** [Mere assertion].

**gratuitous agent.** See AGENT, GRATUITOUS.

**gratuitous bailment.** See BAILMENT.

**Great Britain.** Does not include the Channel Islands or the Isle of Man: Interpretation Act 1937, schedule, para 12. See BRITISH CITIZEN.

**greyhounds, control of.** Greyhounds must be led by a chain or leash in any public place and one person must not lead more than four greyhounds: Control of Dogs Act 1986 s.10.

**grievous bodily harm.** See BODILY HARM, GRIEVOUS.

**Griffith's valuation.** The valuation (qv), called after the first Commissioner of Valuation, carried out of the entire country under the Valuation (Ireland) Act 1852, which is still the valuation in force today, except where a re-valuation has been carried out under s.34 of the 1852 Act or s.65 of the Local Government (Ireland) Act 1898. See VALUATION.

**gross.** Entire; exclusive of deductions. See IN GROSS.

**gross indecency.** Acts of a gross nature and purpose between male persons which fall short of buggery (qv) and which are an offence. It is an offence for a male person to commit an act of gross indecency with another male person under the age of 17 years or with a mentally impaired male person of any age: Criminal Law (Sexual Offences) Act 1993 ss.4 and 5(2). An attempt is also an offence, as is soliciting or importuning for the purposes of gross indecency (ibid s.6). See BUGGERY; MENTALLY IMPAIRED; SOLICIT.

**gross negligence.** Colloquial phrase referring to a very high degree of negligence. The gross negligence of an employee may be a ground for dismissal: O'Brien v Heinz Pollmeier (1991) ELR 157. See MANSLAUGHTER.

**ground rent.** A lease may determine by enlargement by *buying out the ground rent*, whereby the lessee can require the ground landlord to transfer the *fee simple* to the lessee. A wide category of lessees are entitled to acquire the fee simple, including persons holding under building (qv) and proprietary (qv) leases, under long leases with low rent, and under certain local authority leases: Landlord and Tenant (Ground Rents) (No 2) Act 1978 ss.9-15 as amended by the Landlord and Tenant (Amendment) Act 1980 ss.70-73. The 1978 Act does not apply to a shared ownership lease (qv): Housing (Miscellaneous Provisions) Act 1992 s.2(3). The creation of new ground rents is prohibited. See also Landlord and Tenant (Ground Rents) Acts 1984 and 1987.

When a lessee enlarges his interest into a fee simple pursuant to the 1978 Act s.8, all covenants subject to which he held the land, including those for the benefit of third parties, cease to have effect: Whelan & Whelan v Cork Corporation (1991 HC) ILRM 19.

The 1984 Act s.7 enacted new provisions regarding the determination of the purchase price by arbitration, particularly to deal with the case of a lease with less than 15 years to run,

following the ruling in Gilsenan v Foundary House Investments Ltd and Rathmines Property Ltd (1980) ILRM 273. The 1987 Act extended indefinitely the period of operation of Part III of the 1978 Act; this provides ground rent tenants of domestic dwellinghouses with a cheap and expeditious method of buying out the ground rent. A receiver by way of equitable execution may be appointed over ground rents in certain circumstances: Ahern v O'Brien (1991) 1 IR 421. See SPORTING LEASE.

**group accounts.** See HOLDING COMPANY.

**grouse.** See GAME.

**guarantee.** A collateral promise to answer for the debt, default or miscarriage of another person. It is a contract by which a person (known as the *surety*) becomes bound to another (the *creditor*) for the fulfilment or performance of a promise or engagement or other duty of a third party (the *principal*). Although guarantees most often relate to a debt, they can pertain to any type of duty or obligation. Contrast with *warranty* which generally bears no obligations to third parties. See Lombard & Ulster Banking v Murray (1987 HC) ILRM 522.

The Minister for Finance is empowered to guarantee the due payment by a *scheduled body* of the principal (and/or interest on the principal) of all monies, including foreign currency, borrowed by such body with the consent of the Minister: State Guarantees Acts 1954 s.2 and 1964 s.2. See also Building Societies Act 1989 ss.29(2)(b), 36(11)(f), 57(1)(d). [Text: Rowlatt UK]. See CONTRACT OF GUARANTEE; DEBT; MEMORANDUM, STATUTE OF FRAUDS; PERFORMANCE BOND; SURETY.

**guarantee, contract of.** See CONTRACT OF GUARANTEE.

**guarantee, sale of goods.** Any document, notice or other written statement, however described, supplied by a manufacturer or other supplier, other than a retailer, in connection with the supply of any goods, and indicating that the manufacturer or other supplier will service, repair or otherwise deal with the goods following purchase: SGSS Act 1980 s.15. A guarantee must comply with a particular format (ibid s.16). The seller of goods who delivers a guarantee to a buyer is liable to the buyer for the observance of its terms (ibid s.17).

Rights under a guarantee may not in any way exclude or limit the rights of the buyer at common law or pursuant to statute and every provision in a guarantee which imposes obligations on the buyer which are additional to his obligation under the contract is void (ibid s.18). A buyer of goods may maintain an action against a manufacturer or importer or other supplier who fails to observe the terms of a guarantee; a buyer in this context includes all persons who acquire title to the goods within the duration of the guarantee. See Tokn Grass Products Ltd v Sexton Co Ltd (1983) HC.

**guarantee company.** See COMPANY, LIMITED.

**guarantor.** A person who binds himself by a guarantee; a person who promises to answer for another; a surety (qv).

**guard dog.** A dog which is being used (a) to protect premises, or (b) to protect goods or property kept on premises, or (c) to protect a person guarding premises or such goods or property: Control of Dogs Act 1986 s.19 substituted by Control of Dogs (Amdt) Act 1992 s.8(1) and (Guard Dogs) Regulations SI No 255 of 1988 and No 329 of 1989. Controls on the use of guard dogs include an identification system consisting of a collar and a skin implanted electronic encoded device, registration by local authorities, and standards for operation of kennels. Notices must be placed on buildings where guard dogs are present.

**guardian.** A person having the right and duty of protecting the person, property or rights of another who has not full legal capacity or otherwise incapable of managing his own affairs eg the parent of a minor (qv). All matters concerning guardianship and custody of children have to be decided on the basis of the welfare of the child and to the constitutional principle that parents have equal rights to, and are joint guardians, of their children: Guardianship of Infants Act 1964 ss.3 and 6. Custody and guardianship are not synonymous; a parent deprived of custody of a child is not deprived of the rights of guardian: B v B (1975) IR 54.

The mother of an illegitimate child (now a child whose parents have not married each other) is its guardian and consequently may abandon the right by placing the child for adoption: 1964 Act, s.6(4); G v An Bord Uchtala (1980) IR 32. The father of a child whose parents have not married each other, can now become guardian of the child jointly with the mother on application to the court; the mother is now the sole guardian of the child unless the father has been appointed guardian jointly with her: Status of Children Act 1987 ss.11-12.

The 1987 Act does not give the natural father a right to be appointed guardian but only a right to apply to be appointed; he has no constitutional right to guardianship; the welfare of the child is the first and paramount consideration: K v W (1990 SC) ILRM 121. See also PQ v CL (1990 CC) 8ILT & SJ (1990) 269.

A parent in whose custody a child is, can apply to the courts for a *maintenance order* (qv) requiring the other parent to provide financial support for the child: 1964 Act s.11(2); Family Law (Maintenance of Spouses and Children) Act 1976 s.5(1). See also Child Care Act 1991 ss.20, 76-77. See also Cosgrove v Ireland (1982) ILRM 48. [Text: Shatter]. See TESTAMENTARY GUARDIAN; UNDUE INFLUENCE; UNSOUND MIND; WARD.

**guardian ad litem.** See AD LITEM.

**guardians, boards of.** See BOARDS OF GUARDIANS.

**guilty.** (1) The finding after trial that the accused committed the offence with which he is charged. (2) A plea by an accused that he committed the offence. See ALTERNATIVE VERDICT; SPECIAL VERDICT..

**guilty but insane.** See SPECIAL VERDICT.

**guilty mind.** See MENS REA.

# H

**habeas corpus.** [That you have the body]. An order of the High Court to compel a person in whose custody another person is detained to produce the body of that other person before the court and to certify in writing the grounds of his detention; the court having given the person in whose custody he is detained an opportunity of justifying the detention, will order the release of the person from detention unless satisfied that he is being detained in accordance with law: 1937 Constitution, art.40(4)(2).

It is open to any person, citizen or non-citizen, to make an application for habeas corpus: The State (Kugan) v O'Rourke (1985) IR 658. Applications which clearly raise an issue as to the legality of the detention of a person must be treated as applications under art.40 no matter how they are described eg as judicial review or otherwise: Sheehan v District Judge O'Reilly (1993 SC) ILRM 427. The Supreme Court has confirmed that it has no power to put a *stay* on an order for release made by the High Court: The State (Trimbole) v Governor of Mountjoy Prison (1985) IR 550. [Text: Collins & O'Reilly]. See RSC O.84 rr.2-13. See ATTORNEY GENERAL'S SCHEME; DETENTION.

**habendum.** [To have]. The clause in a conveyance which defines the estate to be taken by the purchaser eg *To have and to hold in fee simple.*

**habitable house.** A building or part of a building which is used as a dwelling; or which is not used as a dwelling but which, when last used, was used as a dwelling: Housing Act 1969 s.1. The demolition of a habitable house was prohibited, as was the use otherwise than for human habitation, save under and in accordance with permission from the housing authority, which could either grant the permission, subject to or without conditions, or could refuse permission (ibid s.4). Two separate permissions had to be obtained for *change of use* of a habitable house; planning permission (qv) had to be obtained but only after permission had already been obtained under the 1969 Act (ibid s.10).

If the housing authority was of the opinion that a person had, for the purpose of avoiding the provisions of the Act, caused or permitted a house to deteriorate to such an extent that it ceased to be a habitable house, they could, if they thought fit, serve on the owner of the house a *reinstatement notice*, requiring him to execute such works as might be necessary to make the house fit for human habitation (ibid s.5).

The Act, which was intended to be temporary in nature, expired on 31st December 1984 (ibid s.13), and now stands repealed: Housing Act 1988 s.30. See State (MacGauran) v Dublin Corporation (1979) HC; Dublin County Council v Baily Holdings Ltd (1978) SC; Creedon v Dublin Corporation (1978) HC. See HOUSING.

**habitual criminal.** A person can be pronounced a habitual criminal where the court has sentenced that person to penal servitude (qv) for having committed a felony, the person having had at least three previous serious convictions since the age of sixteen. See Prevention of Crime Act 1908 s.10. See PREVENTATIVE DETENTION.

**hacking.** Generally understood to mean the unauthorised access to or acquisition of information automatically processed on computers. It is an offence for a person who obtains personal data without the prior authority of the data controller (qv) or data processor (qv) by whom the data are kept, and *discloses* the data to another person: Data Protection Act 1988 s.22. See COMPUTERS; DATA PROTECTION.

**half-blood.** See BLOOD.

**hallmarking.** The marking of articles of the precious metals of gold, silver and platinum by a sponsor's mark (qv), indicating the distinctive mark of the sponsor, or assay mark, indicating standard of fineness and place where assay took place. An *approved* hallmark is: (a) a mark lawfully struck by the assay master; or (b) a mark struck in an assay office of the United Kingdom before the 21st day of February 1927; or (c) a mark, to be known as an *international hallmark* which is prescribed by regulations: Hallmarking Act 1981 ss.2-4. Permissible descriptions of unhallmarked articles are specified (ibid s.6). See SI Nos 327 and 328 of 1983. See GOLDSMITHS OF DUBLIN, COMPANY OF.

**halting site.** See TRAVELLER.

**handling stolen property.** The offence committed by a person who handles *stolen* property knowing or believing it to be stolen property: Larceny Act 1916 s.33 as inserted by Larceny Act 1990 s.3. A person commits the offence if, *knowing or believing* it to be stolen property, he *dishonestly* (a) receives it, or (b) retains, removes, disposes or realises it by or for the benefit of another person, or (c) arranges to do any of these things. The property must have been *stolen*, ie stolen, embezzled, fraudulently converted, obtained by false pretences, or through blackmail or extortion (ibid 1990 Act s.7).

*Stolen property* includes property into which the original stolen property has been converted or exchanged, and *property* includes any description of real and personal property, money, debts, and legacies, and all deeds and instruments relating to or evidencing the title or right to any property (ibid ss.7(5) and 12(4)).

The mens rea (qv) for the crime consist of "knowing or believing" and "dishonestly" - see Hanlon v Fleming (1981) IR 489 and R v Feely (1973) QB 530. It is permissible to direct a jury that they may infer knowledge or belief from the accused's conduct (ibid s.33(2)(b)) and The People v Oglesby (1966) IR 163. See RECEIVING STOLEN PROPERTY; UNLAWFUL POSSESSION OF GOODS.

**hanging.** The ordinary way in which the death penalty (qv) was carried out: The People v Pringle (1981) CCA. The sentence was required to be carried out within the walls of the prison in which the prisoner was confined up to the time of execution: Capital Punishment Amendment Act 1868 s.2. *If at the first attempt the criminal is not thoroughly hanged, and is afterwards revived, he shall be hanged again, for the former hanging was not an execution of the sentence which implies a completion of the punishment*: 2 Hale 412. The last hanging in Ireland took place in 1954. Prior to the abolition of the death penalty in 1990, the practice has been to commute the death sentence to imprisonment for 40 years. See DEATH PENALTY.

**harbour authorities.** Statutory bodies established to operate and maintain specified harbours, the members of which are elected and are representative of users of the harbours, local authorities, commercial and labour interests, with some members being nominated by the Minister: Harbours Acts 1946 to 1976. Rosslare Harbour is managed by Coras Iompair Eireann; fishing harbours not specified by the Harbour Acts are the responsibility of the Minister. Responsibility for Dun Laoghaire Harbour was transferred to the Minister in April 1990:

Dun Laoghaire Harbour Act 1990. Pilotage is the responsibility of harbour authorities: Pilotage Act 1913; SR & O No 311 of 1940.

The primary duty of care for cargo stored on an unenclosed quay, where damage is foreseeable, rests with the owner and not the harbour authority: John C Doherty Timber Co Ltd v Drogheda Harbour Commissioners (1993 HC) ILRM 401. See C W Shipping Ltd v Limerick Harbour Commissioners (1989 HC) ILRM 416. See also Oil Pollution of the Sea (Civil Liability and Compensation) Act 1988 s.3(1). See also State Harbours Act 1924. See COMPTROLLER AND AUDITOR GENERAL; FISHERY HARBOUR CENTRE.

**harbouring of spouse.** Formerly an actionable tort (qv) whereby a person harboured another man's wife after notice that she had left that other without his consent. Abolished by the Family Law Act 1981 s.1.

**hard labour.** See PUNISHMENT.

**hare.** See WILD ANIMALS, PROTECTED.

**harmonisation of laws.** The approximation of the laws of the member States of the EC to the extent required for the functioning of the common market: Treaty of Rome 1957 art.3(h). The Council has powers to issue directives for the approximation of national measures which have as their object the establishment and functioning of the common market (ibid art.100a). Harmonisation of national technical standards is also required. See Cassis de Dijon Case 120/78 (1979) ECR 649. See Travers in 11 ILT & SJ (1993) 4. See EUROPEAN ECONOMIC COMMUNITY.

**hatred, incitement to.** It is an offence to incite hatred of persons in the State or elsewhere on account of their race, colour, nationality, religion, ethnic or national origins, membership of the travelling community or sexual orientation: Prohibition of Incitement to Hatred Act 1989. See also VIDEO RECORDING.

**hawker.** A travelling seller of goods: Hawkers Act 1888 s.1 since repealed by Finance Act 1989 s.49.

**hazardous waste.** See TOXIC AND DANGEROUS WASTE; TRANSFRONTIER SHIPMENT.

**head lease.** The lease from which lesser interests (ie sub-leases) have been created. See LEASE.

**headings.** Words prefixed to sections of a statute, and regarded as a preamble. See MARGINAL NOTES.

**headnote.** A summary of the points decided in a case, which is found at the commencement or head of a law report.

**health and EC.** See PUBLIC HEALTH.

**health and safety.** See SAFETY AT WORK.

**health board.** A body corporate with perpetual succession, established by the Minister, to perform functions conferred on it and other functions in its functional area which, before its establishment, were performed by a local authority (other than as a sanitary authority) in relation to the operation of services provided under various specified enactments: Health Act 1970 ss.4(1) and 6. The Minister is empowered to establish the number of health boards as appear to him to be appropriate and to define the functional area of each board so established (ibid s.4(1)). Membership of a health board consists of persons (a) appointed by relevant local authorities, (b) appointed by election by registered medical practitioners and ancillary professions and (c) appointed by the Minister (ibid s.4(2)). Board members may be removed by the Minister by order in specified circumstances (ibid s.12(1)).

Each health board must have appointed a chief executive officer (ibid s.13(1)) who holds his office on such terms and conditions and performs such duties as the Minister from time to time determines (ibid s.13(4)) and who may be suspended by the board by resolution where not less than two-thirds of the board voted, or by the Minister, and may be removed by the Minister following a local inquiry (ibid s.21).

The board must not take any decision or give any direction to the chief executive officer in relation to any matter which is a *function* of that officer (ibid s.17(3)). *Functions* of a chief executive officer include: (a) any function specified to be a function of the officer, or as may be prescribed; (b) any function with respect to a decision as to whether or not any particular person is eligible to avail of a service, grant, or allowance; (c) any function with respect to a decision as to the making or recovery of a charge, or the amount of any charge for a service

for a particular person; (d) any function with respect to the control, supervision, service, remuneration, privileges or superannuation of officers and servants of the board (ibid s.17(4); Murphy v Minister for Health (1987) HC). See also O'Flynn & O'Regan v Mid-Western Health Board & Ors (1991 SC) 2 IR 223. Additional functions have been assigned to chief executive officers in the area of child care: Child Care Act 1991 s.72.

A health board must not incur expenditure within any period in excess of such sum as may be specified by the Minister in respect of that period (ibid 1970 Act s.31). [Text: Hensey]. See COMPTROLLER AND AUDITOR GENERAL; HEALTH SERVICES; AUDITOR, LOCAL GOVERNMENT; NATURAL JUSTICE; PATIENT CHARGES.

**health insurance.** See PERMANENT HEALTH INSURANCE; VOLUNTARY HEALTH.

**health mark.** See ABATTOIR.

**health services.** Persons who are entitled to *full eligibility* for health services are those adults who are ordinarily resident in the State and who are unable without undue hardship to arrange general practitioner medical and surgical services for themselves and their dependants; and also the spouses of such adults: Health Act 1970 s.45 as amended by the Health (Amendment) Act 1991 s.2. A person ordinarily resident in the State who is without full eligibility, has *limited eligibility* ie entitled to public consultant care in public hospitals free of charge (ibid 1990 Act s.3). Persons lose their eligibility if and when they opt for private treatment (ibid s.5).

These provisions are without prejudice to the operation of the EC Regulations in relation to the provision of health services to residents of other EC states who are temporarily resident in Ireland (ibid ss.6 and 9). See also Health Services Regulations 1991 (In-Patient — SI No 135 of 1991; Out-Patient — SI No 136 of 1991).

**health surveillance.** The periodic review, for the purpose of protecting health and preventing occupationally related disease, of the health of employees, so that any adverse variations in their health which may be related to working conditions are identified as early as possible: Health Safety and Welfare at

Work (General Application) Regulations 1993 (SI No 44 of 1993) reg.15(3). It is the duty of every employer to ensure that health surveillance is made available for every employee. See MATERNITY LEAVE.

**hearing.** (1) The trial of a cause or action. (2) Proceedings before a court, arbitrator or tribunal.

**hearsay.** Evidence of a fact not perceived by a witness with his own senses, but asserted by him to have been stated by another person; *what someone else has been heard to say*. It is hearsay evidence if it is offered to prove the truth of the facts stated therein and generally will not be admissible; however hearsay evidence is admissible if its purpose is to show that the statement was made (eg to explain the mental state or conduct of the witness) rather than to prove the truth of the facts therein.

Exceptions to the general rule are: informal admissions; confessions; declarations of deceased persons; evidence in former proceedings; statements in public documents (qqv). Hearsay evidence cannot establish the truth of the answer given: Mullen v Quinnsworth Ltd (1991 SC) ILRM 439. However, hearsay evidence (eg medical records) is admissible on consent of the parties: Hughes v Staunton (1991 HC) 9ILT Dig 52. See Cullen v Clarke (1963) IR 368. For exceptions in criminal proceedings regarding documents, see DOCUMENTARY EVIDENCE. The Law Reform Commission has recommended that generally hearsay evidence should be allowed in civil cases: LRC 25 of 1988. See DYING DECLARATIONS; EVIDENCE IN PREVIOUS PROCEEDINGS.

**hedge.** (1) To reduce by contract the risk of loss arising from changes in interest rates, currency exchange rates or other similar factors affecting ones business. See Building Societies Act 1989 s.34. See SWAP TRANSACTION.

(2) A hedge may be required by notice to be removed or altered: LG (P&D) Act 1963 s.44. Compensation may be payable: LG (P&D) Act 1990 s.20. See also Roads Act 1993 s.70. See TREE.

**heir.** A person who succeeds to property by descent (qv); now *heirs* for the purpose of devolution mean the persons entitled to succeed on intestacy under Part VI of the Succession Act 1965. When the word *heirs* is used in any enactment or deed passed or executed after the lst January 1967 as a *word of purchase* (qv), it is to be construed to mean those entitled under the Succession Act 1965 (Part VI), and when used as a *word of limitation* (qv) to have the same effect as if the Act had not been passed: Succession Act 1965 s.15. See In re McIntyre, Crawford v Ruttledge (1970) HC.

**heir apparent.** A person who, if he survived his ancestor, would be his heir. He was not the heir until after death as nobody could be the heir of a living person — *nemo est heres viventis*.

**heirloom.** (1) *Such goods and personal chattels as shall go by special custom to the heir along with the inheritance*: Blackstone (Commentaries, Book ll p.427). (2) Personal chattels (qv) settled so as to devolve with the land, such as family pictures, tapestries, antiques and furniture: Settled Land Act 1882 s.37. See Gormanstown v Gormanstown (1923) 1 IR 137.

**hello money.** Popularly understood to mean money paid by a supplier of grocery goods to a wholesaler or retailer in consideration of (a) the carrying out by that person of advertising of such goods or (b) the making available of selling space on the opening of a new retail outlet or the extension of an existing outlet, or after the change of ownership of an existing outlet.

The payment of such money or the making of an allowance or the giving of a reduction of or discount on the price of grocery goods or the giving of any other benefit is prohibited, as is the receipt of such benefit: Restrictive Practices (Groceries) Order 1987 (SI No 142 of 1987); Restrictive Practices (Confirmation of Order) Act 1987.

**hereditament.** Real property which on the death intestate of the owner devolved on an heir. *Corporeal* hereditaments are visible and tangible property eg land and structures thereon. *Incorporeal* hereditaments are intangible property eg easements (qv) and profits a prendre (qv).

**High Court.** The court above the Circuit Court (qv) in the hierarchical system of courts, which is invested with full *original* jurisdiction in and power to determine all matters and questions whether of law or fact, civil or criminal: 1937 Constitution art.34(3)(1). It sits in Dublin and at other locations in the State as required.

In civil matters the High Court can award unlimited damages; in criminal matters it is known as the *Central Criminal Court* and hears only very serious crimes such as treason, murder, attempted murder, conspiracy to murder, or rape (qqv). The judge sits alone except (a) in criminal cases and in certain civil actions eg defamation, false imprisonment or intentional trespass to the person, when he sits with a jury and (b) in cases of importance at the direction of the President of the High Court, when three judges sit as a *divisional court*, and may give separate judgments, although the decision of the court is the majority.

The High Court exercises considerable supervisory jurisdiction over inferior courts, administrative bodies and individuals by way of *judicial review* (qv). An appeal from the High Court lies to the Supreme Court (qv). See Rules of the Superior Courts 1986 as amended. See JURY, ABOLITION OF; REMITTAL OF ACTION; STATE SIDE ORDERS.

**highway.** Prima facie the space between the fences and not merely the metalled part of the road and includes the footpath: McKee v McGrath (1892) 30 LRI 41; Collen v Ellis (1893) 32 LRI 491; Attorney General v Mayo County Council (1902) 1 IR 13. See PUBLIC ROAD; ROAD.

**hijacking.** A person is guilty of an offence who unlawfully by force or threat or by other form of intimidation, seizes or exercises control of or otherwise interferes with the control of, or compels or induces some other person to use for an unlawful purpose, any vehicle (whether mechanically propelled or not) or any ship or hovercraft: Criminal Law (Jurisdiction) Act 1976 s.10(1). See AIR LAW.

**Hilary.** A sitting of the court. See SITTINGS OF COURT.

**hip flask defence.** Refers to where a person takes or attempts to take any action, including the consumption of alcohol, with the intention of frustrating a prosecution for drunken driving (qv) or for being drunk in charge of a mechanically propelled vehicle; it is an offence: Road Traffic (Amendment) Act 1978 s.18 (3).

Under draft legislation, it is proposed that, in addition, the court will be required to disregard any evidence of having consumed alcohol between the time of the alleged offence and the giving of a specimen: Road Traffic Bill 1993 s.20.

**hire.** Payment for the temporary use of something. Where goods are let, otherwise than under a hire-purchase agreement, to a person *dealing as consumer* (qv), all the conditions and warranties implied in hire-purchase agreements apply to such an agreement, except the implied terms as to title; however, there is an implied warranty that the goods are free from an undisclosed charge or encumbrance and that the hirer will enjoy quiet possession. See SGSS Act 1980 s.38.

**hire-purchase agreement.** An agreement for the bailment of goods under which the bailee may buy the goods or under which the property in the goods will or may pass to the bailee: Hire-Purchase Act 1946 s.1. In practice, the buyer selects goods which the seller sells to a finance house, which then enters into a hire-purchase agreement with the buyer. There is no contract between the seller and the hirer although the hirer may have a cause of action against the seller for breach of an express warranty or condition. The hirer (bailee) has an option to buy the goods on fulfilment of certain conditions, or he may return the goods to the owner on payment of the sum stated in the agreement.

A hire-purchase agreement must meet particular statutory requirements eg there must be a note or memorandum in writing of the agreement; it must contain the *hire-purchase price* (qv), the *cash price* of the goods; the amount of each instalment and date payable; and a statutory notice on the rights of the hirer to terminate the agreement and on the restrictions on the owner's right to recover the goods; a copy of the note or memorandum must be delivered or sent to the hirer within 14 days of the making of the agreement (ibid s.3; Hire-Purchase (Amendment) Act 1960 s.21). Certain provisions in agreements are void (1946 Act s.6; 1960 Act s.16(1). The Minister may by order provide that there be a specified period within which the hirer is entitled to withdraw his acceptance:

SGSS Act 1980 s.50.

In a hire-purchase agreement there is an implied condition (qv) on the part of the owner that he will have the right to sell the goods at the time the property is to pass and an implied warranty that the goods are free from any charge or encumbrance not disclosed to the hirer and that the hirer will enjoy quiet possession (ibid 1980 Act s.26). Parties to an agreement are entitled to arrange the relationship between themselves such as not to constitute in law a hiring: O'Grady (Inspector of Taxes) v Laragan Quarries Ltd (1991 HC) 1 IR 237. Leasing of aircraft or spare parts of aircraft are excluded from the scope of the hire-purchase Acts: Air Navigation and Transport Act 1988 s.48.

See United Dominions Trust (Commercial) Ltd v Nestor (1962) IR 140; British Wagon Credit Company Ltd v John Henebry 97 ILTR 123; McMullan Brothers Ltd v James J Ryan (1958) IR 94; Mercantile Credit Company of Ireland v Cahill 98 ILTR 79; Henry Ford & Son Finance v Forde (1986) HC. See also Building Societies Act 1989 s.29(2)(j); Courts Act 1991 s.6. Contrast with CREDIT-SALE AGREEMENT. See HIRER, HIRE-PURCHASE; PRICE CONTROL; RECOVERY OF GOODS; SMALL CLAIMS.

**hire-purchase price.** The total sum payable by the hirer under a hire-purchase agreement in order to complete the purchase of the goods to which the agreement relates, exclusive of any sum payable as a *penalty* or as compensation for a breach of the agreement: Hire-Purchase Act 1946 s.1. It includes any sum payable by the hirer by way of deposit or other initial payment (eg by a trade-in of goods): Hire-Purchase (Amendment) Act 1960 s.20. As regards *penalty* see Lamdon Trust Ltd v Hurrell (1955) 1 WLR 391. An inaccuracy in the hire-purchase price known to the hirer but not to the owner will not invalidate the agreement: AIF Ltd v Hunt & Hunt (1992 HC) 10 ILT Dig 199. See PENALTY.

**hirer, hire-purchase.** A person who takes or has taken goods from an owner under a hire-purchase agreement and includes a person to whom the hirer's rights or liabilities under the agreement have passed by assignment or by operation of law: Hire-Purchase Act 1946 s.1. A hirer is entitled to determine such agreement by notice in writing and by paying the amount, if any, by which one-half of the *hire-purchase price* (qv) exceeds the total sums paid and due immediately before termination, without prejudice to any liability which has accrued before the termination and to any damage for failure to take reasonable care of the goods (ibid s.5). However, a hirer of plant or machinery (other than mechanically propelled vehicles) intended for use in an industrial process, the *cash price* of which exceeds £200, is not so entitled.

Certain statements purporting to restrict the rights of hirers are prohibited: SGSS Act 1980 s.30. A clause providing for the termination of a hire-purchase agreement on the bankruptcy (qv) of the hirer is void as against the Official Assignee (qv): Bankruptcy Act 1988 s.49. See Lamdon Trust Ltd v Hurrell (1955) 1 WLR 391; Halpin v Rothwell & United Dominions Trust (Ireland) Ltd (1984) ILRM 613.

**hirer-dealer.** A hirer of goods of any class or description who is a dealer in goods of that class or description; a sale by such a person of goods of which he is the hirer when ostensibly acting in the ordinary course of his business as such dealer, shall be as valid as if he were expressly authorised by the owner: Hire-Purchase Act 1960 s.28.

**historic building.** Tax relief is available in respect of the cost of maintenance and restoration of buildings, and their gardens, which are of significant scientific, historical, architectural interest and to which reasonable access is afforded to the public: Finance Act 1982 s.19. The relief has been extended to the cost of maintenance or restoration of gardens that are not attached to such buildings but which are of significant horticultural, scientific, architectural or aesthetic interest: Finance Act 1993 s.29.

**historic cost accounting.** See CURRENT COST ACCOUNTING.

**historic monument.** Includes a prehistoric monument, and any monument associated with the commercial, cultural, economic, industrial, military, religious or social history of the place where it is situated or of the country and includes all monuments in existence before 1700 AD or such later date as the Minister may appoint by regulations: National Monuments (Amendment) Act 1987 s.1(1). All *national monuments* (qv) are historic monuments but historic monuments, being more broadly defined, are not necessarily national monuments. There is provision for the establishment of a national body, the Historic Monuments Council (ibid s.4).

**historic wreck.** See WRECK.

**hit and run.** See MOTOR INSURER' BUREAU OF IRELAND; UNTRACED DRIVER.

**hoax call.** Popular expression which, if it involves (a) the reporting of a bogus crime to the garda whereby the gardai waste time in investigation, will amount to a *public mischief* (qv) or (b) the sending of a message by telephone which is known to be false for the purpose of causing annoyance, inconvenience or needless anxiety to any other person, may be an offence: Post Office (Amendment) Act 1951 s.13.

**holder for value.** A person who takes a bill of exchange (qv) and who has given, or is deemed to have given, valuable consideration for the bill. Valuable consideration for a bill may be constituted by any consideration sufficient to support a simple contact or any antecedent debt or liability. A holder for value obtains no better title to the bill than the transferor had. See Bills of Exchange Act 1882 s.27.

**holder in due course.** A person who takes a bill of exchange (qv), complete and regular on the face of it, before it is overdue and without notice of dishonour (qv), in good faith and for value, without notice of any defect of title of the transferor; such a person holds the bill free from any defect of title of prior parties: Bills of Exchange Act 1882 s.29.

**holding company.** A company which has a subsidiary eg where the holding company is a member of the subsidiary and controls the composition of its board of directors, or holds more than half in nominal value of its equity share capital or of its shares carrying voting rights; a holding company/subsidiary relationship arises also where one company is a subsidiary of another's subsidiary: Companies Act 1963 s.155. Group or consolidated accounts must be laid before the

annual general meeting of the holding company (ibid ss.150-154).

Particulars regarding a company's holding in subsidiary and associated companies must be disclosed in the notes to the company's accounts eg name, registered office, details of share capital and reserves, details of profit and loss of the latest financial accounts: Companies Amendment Act 1986 s.16.

A subsidiary may, subject to certain conditions, acquire and hold shares in its holding company: Companies Act 1990 ss.224-225. A subsidiary to a building society has the same meaning as it has in the Companies Acts: Building Societies Act 1989 s.2(1).

Where a holding company enters into a transaction not for its own benefit but instead to facilitate one of its subsidiary companies in the group or the group as a whole, then the transaction may be ultra vires. See Charterbridge Corp v Lloyds Bank (1970) 1 Ch 74; Power Supermarkets Ltd v Crumlin Investments Ltd (1981) HC. See also Companies Act 1990 ss.41(1) and 43(2). See RELATED COMPANY.

**holding over.** Where a tenant continues in possession of land on termination of his tenancy. See MESNE RATES.

**holidays.** See ANNUAL LEAVE; PUBLIC HOLIDAYS.

**holograph.** A deed or will written entirely in the grantor's or testator's own hand.

**holy hour.** Popularly understood to mean the time between 2.30 pm to 3.30 pm when public houses in the county boroughs of Dublin and Cork were required to be closed during week days; this is no longer a requirement: Intoxicating Liquor Act 1988 s.25.

**home.** See FAMILY HOME; INVIOLABILITY OF DWELLING; MOTHER; NURSING HOME.

**home birth.** See MIDWIFE.

**home brew.** Colloquial expression meaning beer brewed by a private brewer. See BREWER, PRIVATE.

**home nursing service.** A service to give eligible persons advice and assistance on matters relating to their health and to assist them if they are sick: Health Act 1970 s.60. Public health nurses provide the service; in 1985 there were some 1400 such nurses.

**homeless person.** A person must be regarded by a housing authority as being *homeless* if (a) there is no accommodation available which, in the opinion of the authority, he, together with any other person who normally resides with him or who might reasonably be expected to reside with him, can reasonably occupy or remain in occupation of; or (b) he is living in a hospital, county home, night shelter or other such institution, and is so living because he has no accommodation; and he is, in the opinion of the authority, unable to provide accommodation from his own resources: Housing Act 1988 s.2. A housing authority is required specifically to have regard for the needs of homeless persons in making an annual assessment of housing needs (ibid s.9) and is given additional powers to meet those needs (ibid s.10). A health board is required to make available suitable accommodation for a child in its area who is homeless: Child Care Act 1991 s.5. See HOUSING.

**homicide.** The killing of a human being, the death taking place within a year and a day of the assault on the person. Homicides are either *justifiable, excusable* or *felonious. Justifiable* homicides are killings without blame in the execution of a legal duty or in the furtherance of a legal purpose eg formerly, the putting to death of a person pursuant to a legal judicial sentence; or the killing of a doer of a felony of violence if he cannot otherwise be prevented from escaping. *Excusable* homicides are killings which the law excuses eg by misadventure, in self-defence, or by chance-medley (qqv). *Felonious* homicides are killings resulting from murder, manslaughter, infanticide and formerly, suicide (qqv).

**homosexual conduct.** Sexual activity with a member of one's own sex. It may amount to the offence of buggery (qv). A homosexual relationship by a man prior to his marriage may not be sufficient reason to annul the marriage; however, if a person at the time of marriage is, by reason of homosexuality, incapable of entering into and sustaining the relationship which should exist between married couples if a lifelong union is to be possible, this would entitle the other party to a decree of nullity of that marriage: MF McD (otherwise M O'R) v W O'R (1986) ILRM 336. Inherent and unalterable homosexuality may be a ground for marriage annulment, at least in a case where the petitioner had no knowledge of the existence of the homosexuality of the respondent at the time of the marriage ceremony: UF v JC (1991 SC) 2 IR 330. See also F v F (1990) 1 IR 348. See Woulfe in 8 ILT & SJ (1990) 242. See BUGGERY; GROSS INDECENCY; HATRED, INCITEMENT TO; MARRIAGE, NULLITY OF; VIDEO RECORDING.

**hon.** The Honourable. The title of District, Circuit and Superior Court judges. See MODE OF ADDRESS.

**honorary freedom.** See CIVIC HONOUR.

**honorarium.** A voluntary, or honorary, payment or reward eg a barrister's fee. A Trustee Savings Bank may pay its trustees *honoraria* as approved by the Central Bank: Trustee Savings Bank Act 1989 s.20. See BARRISTER; BRIEF.

**honour.** A title of honour may not be accepted by a citizen except with the prior approval of the government; 1937 Constitution, art.40(2)(2). The President of Ireland may grant citizenships as a token of honour to a person. Also the Minister is empowered to award "The Distinguished Service Medal" to members of the defence forces: Defence Force Regulations (A19 Part V). See CITIZENSHIP; CIVIC HONOUR; TITLE OF NOBILITY.

**horse breeding.** The previous requirement that stallions be licensed has been abolished: Horse Breeding Act 1990 repealing the 1934 Act.

**horseplay.** Rough or boisterous play. Dismissal of an employee for engaging in *horseplay* in a factory may be unfair where the horseplay has been an ongoing problem and not brought under control by management: Dunphy v Largo Food Exports Ltd (1992 EAT) ELR 179.

**horticulture.** The branch of agriculture that deals with the cultivation of plants used for food or for the production of food or ornament: Bord Glas Act 1990 s.1(1). The Horticultural Development Board has the general functions of developing and promoting the production, marketing and consumption of horticultural products (ibid s.4).

**hostile witness.** A witness whose mind discloses a bias hostile to the party examining him and who may, with the leave of the court, be cross-examined by the party who called him. Where a witness gives evidence which is inconsistent with a previous statement of his, he may be cross-examined with the leave of the judge: Criminal Procedure Act 1865; The People (Attorney General) v Hannigan (1941) IR 252. It has been held that the trial judge should explain to the jury that in such a case, the written statement is only evidence against the credibility of the witness and not evidence of the truth of the matters contained in it: People v Taylor (1974) IR 97.

**hotchpot.** [Hocher: to share together]. A blending of properties for the purpose of securing an equal division. Where a fund is appointed to be divided amongst a class and one of the class has already received a special share, that person may be required to add his special share to the fund, for the purpose of computing the share of each beneficiary, before it is distributed and he is then said to bring his special share into hotchpot. See Succession Act 1965 s.63. See ADVANCEMENT.

**hotel.** An establishment which provides sleeping accommodation, food and drink for reward for all comers without special contract and includes every establishment registered as a hotel with Bord Failte Eireann: Hotel Proprietors Act 1963 s.1. An hotel proprietor has a duty to receive all comers, unless he has reasonable grounds for refusal, and to take reasonable care for the safety of his guests (ibid ss.3-4). See Duggan v Armstrong & Tighe (1993 SC) ILRM 222.

In repect of guests who engage sleeping accommodation, the hotel proprietor is liable for damage to, or loss of, property received from guests (ibid ss.5-6). He can limit his liability to £100 for any one guest by displaying a notice in a specified form, but this limitation does not apply to a motor vehicle, to property which was deposited for safe custody, or property damaged or lost through the default of the proprietor or his servant (ibid s.7). The proprietor has a lien (qv) on property brought by a guest in respect of a debt due for sleeping accommodation, food or drink (ibid s.8).

Provisions for the health, safety and welfare of persons employed in hotels are contained in the Shops (Conditions of Employment) Acts 1938 and 1942 and the Safety, Health and Welfare at Work Act 1989. See also Courts Act 1991 s.9. [Text: Dempsey; McDonald]. See FIRE, LIABILITY FOR; WILDLIFE DEALING.

**hours of work.** See WORKING HOURS.

**house.** Includes any building or part of a building used or suitable for use as a dwelling and any outoffice, yard, garden or other land appurtenant thereto or usually enjoyed therewith and *housing* shall be construed accordingly: Housing (Miscellaneous Provisions) Act 1992 s.1(1).

**house, disorderly.** See DISORDERLY HOUSE.

**house agent.** A person who, as agent for another person and for or in expectation of reward, purchases, sells, lets or offers for sale or letting, or invites offers to purchase or take a letting of, or negotiates for the purchase, sale or letting of a house otherwise than by auction or attempts to effect such purchase, sale or letting: Auctioneers and House Agents Act 1947 s.2. A person may not carry on or hold himself out or represent himself as carrying on the business of house agent except under and in accordance with a *licence* (ibid s.7).

Any agreement in a contract relating to the sale, lease, or letting of property which makes the purchaser, lessee or tenant liable to pay the fees or expense of an auctioneer or house agent is void: Auctioneers and House Agents Act 1973 s.2. See Law v Roberts Co (1964) IR 292. [Text: Mahon]. See AUCTIONEER; TAX CLEARANCE CERTIFICATE.

**house to house collection.** See COLLECTION.

**household chattels.** Furniture, bedding, linen, china, earthenware, glass, books and other chattels of ordinary household use or ornament and also consumable stores, garden effects and domestic animals but does not include any chattels used by either spouse for business or professional purposes or money or security for money: Judicial Separation and Family Law Reform Act 1989 s.10. The court may make an order for the protection of household chattels (ibid s.11(d)). See also Family Home Protection Act 1976 s.10 as amended by the Courts Act 1991 s.8. See MATRIMONIAL HOME.

**household refuse.** Sanitary authorities (qv) are empowered and may be required by the Minister to undertake, or to contract for, the removal of *household refuse*: Public Health Act 1878 s.52. In the absence of a ministerial order imposing an obligation on a sanitary authority, such an authority is under no statutory duty to provide a refuse collection service: Bradley & Dunne v Meath Co Council (1991 HC) ILRM 179.

In considering whether refuse is *household refuse* or *trade refuse*, regard must be had to its physical nature and not to the process or circumstances by which it was accumulated. The ordinary refuse of an hotel and of a restaurant has been held to be household refuse: Westminster Corporation v Gordon Hotels Ltd (1906) 2 KB 39; J Lyons & Co Ltd v London Corporation (1909) 2 KB 588. It has also been held that a person was not liable to pay a County Council in respect of a refuse service which he did not utilise: Louth County Council v Matthews (1989) ITLR (31 Jul). See LITTER; TRADE REFUSE.

**Houses of the Oireachtas.** See OIREACHTAS.

**housing.** Housing authorities have an express statutory duty imposed on them to assess the adequacy of the supply and condition of housing in their areas and to draw up programmes, known as *building programmes* to meet the needs of the area: Housing Act 1966 ss.53-55. They are required to adopt a written statement of policy for the effective carrying out of their function as regards the management and control of their housing stock: Housing (Miscellaneous Provisions) Act 1992 s.9. They are empowered to provide dwellings and works, services and building sites and amenities (ibid 1966 Act s.56-57). Housing authorities are also empowered to take account of the needs of persons resident outside their functional area and to build and let houses to such persons: Housing Act 1984; this Act was necessitated by the decision in McNamee v Buncrana UDC (1984) ILRM 77.

The letting of a house by a housing authority includes an implied term that the house is fit for human habitation: 1966 Act s.66; Burke v Dublin Corporation (1991 SC) 1 IR 341.

A housing authority had a duty to ensure by a proper valuation that a house, offered as a security for a loan, was a good security for that loan and it owed a duty of care in that regard to the person seeking the loan: 1966 Act s.39; Ward v McMaster (1986 HC & SC) ILRM 43 and 400. However, now the granting of assistance by a housing authority eg by way of grant, loan or subsidy does not imply any warranty as to the condition of the house or its fitness for habitation (ibid 1992 Act s.22).

Legislation in 1988 (a) sought to ensure that the housing needs of categories of persons such as the homeless, the aged, the disabled and travellers obtain due priority and (b) provided a simplified procedure for discharging mortgages in certain cases: Housing Act 1988. A housing authority is required to draw up a scheme of priorities for letting housing accommodation (ibid s.11). The court will not interfere with a decision of the authority in relation to the granting of accommodation pursuant to such a scheme unless the decision flew in the face of reason or was defective on grounds of failure to observe the rules of natural justice or was illegal or ultra vires: Carton v Dublin Corporation (1993 HC) ILRM 467.

Legislation in 1992 — (a) provided a statutory basis for shared ownership, (b) permitted housing authorities to carry out improvements to privately owned houses, (c) provided for a rental subsidy scheme in respect of houses of approved bodies, (d) required measures to counteract social segregation, (e) provided for increased participation by tenants in the maintenance and management of their housing, and (f) added safeguards for tenants in the private rented sector through the use of rent books, minimum notice to quit, minimum physical standards, and abolition of distress for rent: Housing (Miscellaneous Provisions) Act 1992. See also O'Reilly v Limerick Corporation (1988 HC) ILRM 181. See Housing (Misc Provs) (Amdt) Regulations 1993 (SI No 157 of 1993). See Building Societies Act 1989 s.38(3). See FLOOR AREA CERTIFICATE; HABITABLE HOUSE; HOMELESS; OVERCROWDED HOUSE; PLANNING AUTHORITY; UNFIT HOUSE; TENANT PURCHASE SCHEME.

**housing authority.** A county borough, the corporation of such county borough; a country health district, the council of the county in which such county health district is situate; a borough (with exceptions); an urban district (with exceptions); a town having commissioners (with exceptions): Housing (Miscellaneous Provisions) Act 1992 s.23. See SEGREGATION.

**housing body, approved.** A body approved of by the Minister for the purposes of s.5 of the Housing Act 1988, or a society registered under the Industrial and Provident Societies Acts 1893 to 1978, or under the Friendly Societies Acts 1896 to 1977, or a voluntary group: Building Societies Act 1989 s.28(5); Housing (Miscellaneous Provisions) Act 1992 s.6(10). A building society may, subject to the *adoption* of the power and the approval of the Central Bank, support *approved housing bodies* by means of loans, grants, guarantees and the provision of services and property (ibid 1989 Act s.28(1)(b)). See also 1989 Act second schedule, part I, para 3.

A housing authority is empowered to provide assistance to another housing authority or to an approved voluntary housing body in respect of the provision or management by them of housing; assistance may take the form of a loan, grant, subsidy, periodic contribution, guarantee or assistance in kind (ibid 1992 Act s.6). See ADOPTABLE POWERS.

**housing loan.** (1) A loan on the security of a mortgage (qv) of a freehold or leasehold estate or interest in a *house* (qv) for the purpose of enabling a member of a building society to provide or improve the house or to purchase the said estate or interest: Building Societies Act 1989 s.22. A society is empowered to make *housing loans* to members, including, with the approval of the Central Bank, housing loans in a foreign currency.

(2) A loan for (a) the acquisition of estates or interests in or the construction of houses; (b) the carrying out of improvement works to houses; (c) the acquisition of buildings or other land for the purpose of providing housing; (d) the conversion of a building; (e) the provision of hostel accommodation; (f) the payment of a deposit for the purchase of property: Housing (Miscellaneous Provisions) Act 1992 s.11. Housing loans may be made by a housing authority (ibid s.11(4)). Where the terms of the loan have been breached, the housing authority may recover possession by order of the District Court pursuant to the Landlord and Tenant Amendment Act, Ireland, 1860 ss.84-89 (ibid s.11(5)). See ABANDONED HOUSE.

**hue and cry.** An ancient common law procedure for pursuit of a felon with horn and voice.

**human habitation, fit for.** See UNFIT HOUSE.

**human rights.** The Irish Centre for the Study of Human Rights is located in the Law Faculty of University College, Galway. See also O'Flaherty in 9ILT & SJ (1991) 285. [Text: O'Reilly]. See NATURAL RIGHTS.

**human rights, covenants on.** The covenants of the United Nations called the International Covenant on Civil and Political Rights (ICCPR) and the International Covenant on Economic and Social Rights (ICESR) which were unanimously adopted by the UN General Assembly on 16 December 1966. Ireland signed the covenants on 1 October 1973 and announced its intention to ratify the conventions in December 1987. The Covenants are legally binding *in se* and are supported by an integrated enforcement machinery; they are formal international agreements which restate the provisions of the Universal Declaration on Human Rights (qv) as binding legal obligations. See Power & Gill in 7ILT & SJ (1989) 36 and 69; O'Flaherty in 10ILT & SJ (1992) 109 and 128.

**human rights, European Convention of.** See EUROPEAN CONVENTION OF HUMAN RIGHTS.

**human rights, European Court of.** See EUROPEAN COURT OF HUMAN RIGHTS.

**hung jury.** A jury (qv) unable to agree on any verdict. See VERDICT.

**hunt.** In relation to any wild bird or wild animal, whether it be of a protected species or not, means to stalk, pursue, chase, drive, flush, capture, course, attract, follow, search for, lie in wait for, take, trap or shoot by any means whether with or without dogs, and includes killing in the course of hunting: Wildlife Act 1976 s.44(1). It does not include bird watching, wildlife photography, sketching or painting (ibid s.2). A *licence* is required to hunt game (qv) with firearms and only permitted in open season (qv) (ibid ss.20 and 29).

**husband and wife.** At common law a husband and wife were the one person and the wife had limited contractual and property rights; also she was deemed to have the domicile of her husband. A wife is now capable of having an independent domicile, her contractual capacity is unchanged on marriage, the family home cannot be sold without her consent and she cannot be disinherited by her husband. See DOMICILE; FAMILY HOME; MARRIED WOMAN; MATRIMONIAL HOME; LEGAL RIGHT OF SPOUSE.

**hydrometric data.** Information on the levels, volumes and flows of water in rivers, lakes and groundwaters in the State: Environmental Protection Agency Act 1992 s.64(1). The Agency is required to prepare a national programme for the collection, analysis and publication of this information.

**hypothecation.** The pledging by bottomry bond of a ship or her freight or cargo for the payment of money borrowed by the master. See BOTTOMRY; DETENTION OF SHIP.

**hypothetical arguments.** A plaintiff has no locus standi (qv) to advance hypothetical arguments and is limited to showing how he himself is affected: Madigan v Attorney General Ors (1986) ILRM 136. A court cannot take into account assumptions or hypotheses outside the facts or circumstances of the action before the court: MhicMhathuna v Ireland (1990) 8ILT Dig 59. Also a court must determine the actual and not any hypothetical facts surrounding an alleged offence: Carron v McMahon (1990 SC) ILRM 802. See however MOOT.

# I

**ibid, ib, ibidem.** [In the same place]. From the same source.

**id certain est quod certum reddi potest.** [That is certain which can be made certain].

**id est.** [That is]. Usually abbreviated to ie.

**idem.** [The same].

**identification.** As to whether a person has been sufficiently identified as the person named in a warrant, the High Court has authority to reach a different conclusion from that in the District Court as regards uncontested evidence; a person who answers the description in a warrant of name, address and former address, it can be concluded that the person is the person named in the warrant: Crowley v McVeigh (1990) ILRM 220.

**identification, visual.** See VISUAL IDENTIFICATION; PHOTOGRAPHS, USE OF IN IDENTIFICATION.

**identification parade.** A formal procedure whereby persons, including an arrested suspect, are viewed by a witness for the purpose of identification. An accused has a right not to participate in a formal identification parade: The People v Martin (1956) IR 22. In a particular case, it was held that the accused should have been given the option of submitting to an identification parade; the holding of an identity parade had not outlived its usefulness: DPP v O'Reilly (1990) ITLR (9 Jul). Also, an identity parade which consisted of six instead of the recommended eight persons and at which the defendant's solicitor was not present was ruled to have breached fair procedures: DPP v Bates (1992 CCC).

The conducting officer, who should be a garda unconnected with the offence under investigation, must record the proceedings meticulously, and should say to each witness: *This is an identification parade. I want you to look very carefully at this line of men (or women) and see if you can recognise the person (who etc). Do not say anything until I ask you a question.*

When a witness indicates that he has made an identification, he should normally be asked to touch the person whom he purports to identify on the shoulder; however where the witness is a child or an old person or is frightened, it will suffice to point at and describe the person identified. Where a witness gives evidence by means of a live television link in cases of physical or sexual abuse, evidence by a person other than the witness that the witness identified the accused at an identification parade is admissible as evidence that the accused was so identified: Criminal Evidence Act 1992 s.18(b)(ii).

The result of an identification is not conclusive and a warning is required in relation to the dangers of visual identification (ibid O'Reilly case). The gardai are entitled to extend a period of detention (qv) of person under the Criminal Justice Act 1984 s.4 for the purposes of facilitating an identity parade: DPP v O'Toole & Hickey (1990 CCA) 8ILT Dig 298. See also The People v Hughes 92 ILTR 179. [Text: Ryan & Magee]. See TELEVISION LINK; VISUAL IDENTIFICATION.

**identity card scheme.** Provision has been made for the introduction of a voluntary identity card scheme for young persons aged 18 years and over, in an effort to curb under-age drinking of alcohol: Intoxicating Liquor Act 1988 ss.40-41.

**identity of parties.** See PUBLIC JUSTICE.

**ignorantia eorum quae qui scire tenetur non excusat.** [Ignorance of those things which everyone is bound to know does not constitute an excuse].

**ignorantia facti excusat; ignorantia juris neminen excusat.** [Ignorance of the fact excuses; ignorance of the law does not excuse]. See IGNORANTIA JURIS.

**ignorantia juris neminen excusat.** [Ignorance of the law does not excuse]. Every person is presumed to know the law. See O'Loghlen v O'Callaghan (1874) IR 8 CL 116. See MISTAKE.

**illegal.** Unlawful; contrary to law; in violation of a law or a rule which has the force of law.

**illegal contracts.** Contracts which are forbidden by statute or are contrary to common law or to the Constitution; such contracts are void and collateral contracts are also vitiated. Contracts which are illegal at common law include (1) a contract to commit a criminal offence or a civil wrong: Fibretex (Societe Personnes Responsabilite Limite) v Beleir Ltd (1958) 89 ILTR 141; (2) a contract prejudicial to the administration of justice: Nolan v Shiels (1926) 60 ILTR 143; (3) a contract which serves to corrupt public officials: Lord Mayor of

Dublin v Hayes (1876) 10 IRCL 226; (4) a contract tending to encourage immorality: Pearce v Brooks (1867) 11 WR 834; Seidler v Schallhofer (1982) 2 NSWSR 80; (5) a contract to trade with the enemies of the State: Ross v Shaw (1917) 2 IR 367; (6) a contract that is illegal according to the law where it is to be performed: Stanhope v Hospital Trust Ltd (1936) Ir Jur Rep 25: (7) a contract which serves to defraud the Revenue: Lewis v Squash Ireland Ltd (1983) ILRM 363; Winters v Vital Security Ltd UD 852/1987; McCarthy v Alan Hair Studios Ltd (1990) ELR 148; O'Dowd v Crowley (1991 EAT) ELR 97; Tracey v Cheadle Investments (1991 EAT) ELR 130; Aspel v Fame Clothing Co Ltd (1993 EAT) ELR 42.

A contract which is illegal on its face is illegal at its inception and unenforceable: Murphy Co Ltd v Crean (1915) 1 IR 111; Macklin & McDonald v Greacen & Co (1983) IR 61. Where a contract is lawful on its face but one party intends to perform it unlawfully, it will be enforceable: Whitecross Potatoes v Coyle (1978) HC. See TRADE; UNFAIR DISMISSAL; VOID CONTRACTS.

**illegal earnings.** See TRADE.

**illegal means, evidence obtained by.** See EVIDENCE OBTAINED ILLEGALLY.

**illegitimacy, presumption of.** The presumption of illegitimacy arising out of a *divorce a mensa et thoro* (qv) has been abolished and replaced by a presumption of non-paternity. See PATERNITY, PRESUMPTION OF.

**illegitimate.** See CHILD, ILLEGITIMATE; PATERNITY, PRESUMPTION OF.

**ill-health.** See SICKNESS.

**illicit distillation.** See POITIN.

**illiterate person.** See CONNEMARA VOTING; SIGNATURE.

**illness.** See SICKNESS.

**illusory appointment.** See POWER OF APPOINTMENT.

**illusory trust.** A trust whereby a debtor vests property in trustees on trust to pay his debts; it is *illusory* because the creditors do not always have the right to compel the trustee to carry out the trust. Such a trust may be irrevocable in certain circumstances: Simmonds v Pallas (1846) I Eq R. An assignment to a trustee for the benefit of creditors generally is an *act of bankruptcy* and is void unless registered within 7 days of execution: Deed of Arrangements Act 1887; Bankruptcy Act 1988 ss.7(1)(a) and 57.

**imitation.** It is an offence for a person to issue any document not *issued under lawful authority* which by its form, contents, or appearance is calculated or is reasonably likely to lead the person receiving it to believe that it is issued under lawful authority: Courts of Justice Act 1936 s.81. *Issued by lawful authority* means issued by, from, or by order of any court of justice or any judge or justice of any such court or by or from any officer of or office attached to any such court. See COPYRIGHT; FIREARM; FORGERY.

**imitation firearm.** See FIREARMS.

**immemorial.** See TIME IMMEMORIAL.

**immigration.** Member States of the European Union (qv) are required to regard immigration policy and policy regarding nationals of third countries as a matter of *common concern* eg conditions of entry and movement by nationals of third countries on the territory of member States; conditions of residence, family reunion and access to employment: Maastricht Treaty 1992 art.K.1. See ALIEN; EMIGRANT; PASSPORT; PREINSPECTION; VISA.

**immoral contracts.** Agrements which tend to encourage immorality are generally void. See ILLEGAL CONTRACTS.

**immunisation schemes.** Health board prophylactic campaigns have concentrated on diphtheria, poliomyelitis, whooping cough, rubella (german measles) and measles. See Health Act 1947 s.29; Infectious Diseases Regulations 1981 and 1985 (SI No 390 of 1981; No 268 of 1985). See VACCINE, CARE INVOLVING.

**immunity.** The condition of being exempt from some liability to which others are subject eg (1) immunity of a judge when performing his judicial functions: Macauley & Co Ltd v Wyse-Power [1943] 77 ILTR 61; (2) immunity of a trade union from tortious liability: Industrial Relations Act 1990 ss.9-13; (3) immunity of foreign diplomats: Diplomatic Relations and Immunities Acts 1967 and 1976; Saorstat & Continental Steamship Co v de las Morenas (1945) IR 291; McMahon v McDonald (1988) SC; (4) immunity of the President

of Ireland for the exercise and performance of the powers and functions of her office: 1937 Constitution art.13(8); (5) immunity of members of the Houses of the Oireachtas in respect of any utterances in either House: 1937 Constitution art.15(13); AG v The Sole Member of the Tribunal of Inquiry into the Beef Processing Industry (1992 SC) ITLR (23 Nov); (6) immunity of Minister and the Controller of Patents as regards their official acts in respect of patent validity or searches: Patents Act 1992 s.118; (7) immunity of the Environmental Protection Agency and the National Roads Authority in respect of action for damages alleged to have been caused by their failure to perform or comply with any functions conferred on them: Environmental Protection Agency Act 1992 s.15; Roads Act 1993 s.19(4).

It has been held that while the doctrine of absolute sovereign immunity no longer exists, immunity will be accorded to an activity which touches the actual business of the foreign government; consequently, persons employed by embassies who are involved in the employing government's business organisation and interest, do not have access to the Employment Appeals Tribunal: Government of Canada v EAT (1992 SC) ELR 29 and 10 ILT Dig (1992 SC) 295. See also McMahon v Ireland and Registrar of Friendly Societies (1988 HC) ILRM 610. See DEFENCE FORCES; DIPLOMATIC PRIVILEGE; IMPEACHMENT; OIREACHTAS; PRIVILEGE; TRADE UNION; UNLAWFUL INTERFERENCE WITH CONSTITUTIONAL RIGHTS; UTTERANCE.

**impeachment.** The solemn charge which may be preferred by either of the Houses of the Oireachtas against the President of Ireland, for stated misbehaviour: 1937 Constitution, art.12(10). See PRESIDENT OF IRELAND.

**impeachment of waste.** Liability of a person for waste (qv).

**imperitia culpae adnumeratur.** [Inexperience is counted a fault].

**impersonation.** False personation. See PERSONATION.

**implead.** To prosecute or to take proceedings against another.

**implied conditions.** See IMPLIED TERM.

**implied term.** A term in a contract which has not been expressly stated but which must be implied to give effect to the law or to the presumed intention of the parties. See The Moorcock (1889) 14 PD 64.

A term may be a condition (qv) or a warranty (qv). In contracts for the sale of goods, certain conditions and warranties are implied by statute eg an implied condition that goods are of *merchantable quality* and implied conditions in relation to *description* and *samples* and to the sale of motor vehicles. Terms are also implied in contracts for the supply of services where the supplier is acting in the course of a business. A term will not be implied (a) where it is not necessary to give efficacy to the terms of a contract: Grehan v North Eastern Health Board (1989) IR 422; or (b) where it would have the effect of defeating the contract: Aga Khan v Firestone (1992 HC) ILRM 31. See BUSINESS EFFICACY TEST; OFFICIOUS BYSTANDER TEST; SERVICE, SUPPLY OF; SPARE PARTS; TITLE OF GOODS.

**implied trust.** See TRUST, IMPLIED.

**importune.** See PROSTITUTE; SOLICIT.

**impossibility of performance.** As regards contractual obligations, impossibility of performance does not as a general rule, excuse performance: Paradine v Jane (1647) Aleyn 26. However, in certain cases, impossibility will excuse the parties from performance under the doctrine of *frustration*. See FRUSTRATION OF CONTRACT.

**impossibilium nulla obligato est.** [Impossibility is an excuse for the non performance of an obligation]. See FRUSTRATION OF CONTRACT.

**impotence.** The inability to perform the act of sexual intercourse. Impotence, caused by the wrongful act of another, can lead to damages for *loss of consortium* (qv). Impotence is a ground for annulment of a marriage. The impotence however must have existed at the time of the marriage and must be incurable; impotence accruing after marriage is not a ground for nullity. Qualified impotence, ie inability to have sexual intercourse with the partner of the purported marriage but not with another, may be a ground for nullity: S v S (1976) SC; R (otherwise W) v W (1980) HC. See MARRIAGE, NULLITY OF.

**impound.** To seize. A grant of representation is said to be *impounded* where the sole executor or administrator becomes insane. Under draft legislation, it is proposed that the gardai will be given power, by regulation, to detain a mechanically propelled vehicle for motor tax or motor insurance offences or where the driver is too young to hold a driving licence: Road Traffic Bill 1993 s.39.

**imprescriptible.** That which cannot be rightfully taken away, lost or revoked; inviolable. See CARE ORDER.

**imprimatur.** [Let it be printed]. A licence to publish or print a book.

**imprisonment.** The restraint of a person's liberty by another. See BEGET; FALSE IMPRISONMENT; HABEAS CORPUS; PUNISHMENT.

**improvement notice, lease.** The notice which a business tenant (qv) serves on his landlord when he proposes to carry out improvements to the *tenement* (qv). The landlord may within a month serve the tenant with an *improvement consent*, or an *improvement undertaking* where he undertakes to carry out the work himself, or an *improvement objection*. A landlord has only limited grounds upon which he may object to an improvement. A landlord who carries out the improvement himself is entitled to increase the rent; a tenant who carries out improvements may be entitled to compensation when he quits the tenement. See Landlord and Tenant (Amendment) Act 1980. See IMPROVEMENTS, COMPENSATION FOR.

**improvement notice, work.** A notice, signed by an inspector, stating his opinion that a person has contravened or is contravening a statutory provision regarding safety, health or welfare at work and directing that the alleged contravention be remedied by a specified date: Safety, Health and Welfare at Work Act 1989 s.36. The notice may include directions as to the remedial measures required. An improvement notice may also be founded on a failure by a person to submit or implement an *improvement plan* (qv). An appeal lies to the District Court. Contravention of an improvement notice is an offence (ibid s.48(5)).

**improvement plan.** A plan regarding an activity at work, which is required to be submitted to an inspector, specifying remedial action which it is proposed will be taken to rectify matters regarding that activity; the plan may be requested by the inspector when he is of the opinion that the activity involves, or is likely to involve, risk to the safety or health of persons: Safety, Health and Welfare at Work Act 1989 s.35. Failure to submit an improvement plan is an offence (ibid s.48(4)). Implementation of an improvement plan is enforceable by the issue of an *improvement notice* (qv).

**improvements, compensation for.** A business tenant (qv) who quits his *tenement* (qv) is entitled to compensation by the landlord for every improvement made which adds to the letting value of the tenement on the termination date, and which is suitable to the character of the tenement: Landlord and Tenant (Amendment) Act 1980 Part IV. A business tenant who quits by surrender or because of non-payment of rent is not so entitled.

The amount of compensation may be agreed upon by the landlord and tenant or in the absence of agreement, it will be an amount determined by the court, as the *capitalised value* of such addition to the letting value of the tenement at the termination as the court determines to be attributable to the improvement (ibid s.47(1)). The maximum capitalised value which the court may determine is 15 times the annual amount of addition to the letting value. See IMPROVEMENT NOTICE, LEASE.

**in aequali jure melior est conditio possidentis.** [Where the rights of the parties are equal, the claim of the actual possessor is strongest]. See Bailey v Barnes (1894) 1 Ch 25.

**in alieno solo.** On another's land. See EASEMENT.

**in ambiguis orationibus maxime sententia est ejus qui eas protelisset.** [In dealing with ambiguous words the intention of him who used them should especially be regarded].

**in articulo mortis.** [At the point of death].

**in autre droit.** [In the right of another]. An executor holds property in the right of his testator.

**in bonis, in b.** [In the goods of].

**in camera.** The hearing of a case in private eg in court but with the public excluded or in a judge's private room. Justice is required to be administered in public, save in such special and limited

cases as may be prescribed by law: 1937 Constitution, art.34(1).

The law prescribes that justice may be administered otherwise than in public in the case of eg (a) urgent applications for relief by way of habeas corpus, bail, prohibition or injunction; (b) matrimonial cases; (c) lunacy and cases involving minors; (d) cases involving the disclosure of a secret manufacturing process: Courts (Supplemental Provisions) Act 1961 s.45; (e) proceedings under the Data Protection Act 1988 s.28; (f) cases involving rape offences: Criminal Law (Rape) (Amdt) Act 1990 s.11; (g) proceedings for the appointment of an examiner to a company: Companies (Amendment) Act 1990 s.31.

Before ordering that proceedings be heard *in camera*, the Court has to be satisfied that a public hearing of all or part of the proceedings would fall short of the doing of justice, it being as fundamental principle of the administration of justice in a democratic state that justice be administered in public: In re R (1989) IR 126. See In re Kennedy & McCann (1976) IR 382; Companies Act 1963 s.205(7); Criminal Procedure Act 1967 s.16. See OPPRESSION OF SHAREHOLDER; PUBLIC JUSTICE.

**in casu extremae necessitatis omnia sunt communia.** [In cases of extreme necessity, everything is in common].

**in commendam.** [In trust].

**in consimili casu, consimile debet esse remedium.** [In similar cases the remedy should be similar].

**in contemplation of death.** See DONATIO MORTIS CAUSA.

**in contractis tacite insunt quae sunt moris et consuetudinis.** [The clauses which are in accordance with custom and usage are an implied part of every contract].

**in conventionibus contrahentium voluntas potius quam verba spectari placuit.** [In construing agreements the intention of the parties, rather than the words actually used, should be considered].

**in curia.** [In open court].

**in custodia legis.** [In the custody of the law].

**in esse.** [In being]. Actually existing.

**in extenso.** [At full length]. The reporting of a case in full rather than a summary.

**in extremis.** [In last extremity]. Final illness.

**in facie curiae.** [In the face of the court]. See CONTEMPT OF COURT.

**in forma pauperis.** [In the character of a pauper]. See Salomon v Salomon & Co (1897) AC 22. See LEGAL AID.

**in futuro.** [In the future].

**in gremio legis.** [In the bosom of the law].

**in gross.** A right which is not appendant, appurtenant, or otherwise annexed to land. See EASEMENT.

**in invitum.** [Against a reluctant person].

**in jure non remota causa, sed proxima spectatur.** [In law the promimate, and not the remote, cause is to be regarded].

**in lieu.** [In place of].

**in limine.** [On the threshold]. Preliminary. See Comhlucht Paipear Riomhaireachta Teo v Udaras na Gaeltachta (1990 SC) ITLR (19 Feb). See POSTLIMINIUM.

**in loco parentis.** [In the place of a parent]. A person who is not the parent of a particular child but takes on himself parental offices and duties in relation to the child. See SATISFACTION; SUPERVISION ORDER; TRESPASS; TRESPASS TO PERSON; WELFARE OF CHILDREN.

**in media res.** [In the midst of the matter].

**in misericordia.** [At mercy].

**in nomine.** [In the name of].

**in pais.** [In the country]. As contrasted with *in the court*. Refers to that which happens without legal proceedings eg estoppel in pais or estoppel by conduct eg a tenant, having accepted a lease, cannot dispute his lessor's title.

**in pari causa potior est conditio possidentis.** [Everyone may keep what he has got, unless and until someone else can prove a better title].

**in pari delicto, potior est conditio possidentis.** [Where both parties are equally to blame, the condition of the possessor is the best]. See Daly v Daly (1870) IR 5 CL 108.

**in pari materia.** [In an analogous case]. See LEGISLATION, INTERPRETATION OF.

**in-patient services.** Institutional services provided for persons while maintained in a hospital, convalescent home or home for persons suffering from physical or mental disability or in accommodation ancillary thereto: Health Act 1970 s.51.

See also Health (Amendment) Act 1986. See SI No 50 of 1993. See OUT-PATIENT SERVICES.

**in perpetuum.** [For ever].

**in personam.** [Against a person]. An expression to indicate an action against a specific person, as distinct from *in rem* (qv). Equity acted in personam eg by imprisoning a person for disobeying a judgment.

**in pleno.** [In full].

**in posse.** [Potentially existing]. Contrast with actually existing, see IN ESSE.

**in praesenti.** [At the present time].

**in propria persona.** [In his own proper person].

**in re.** [In the matter of].

**in rem.** [Against a thing]. An expression to indicate an action *against the world*, as distinct from an action against a specific person eg an action to assert a right to property. A judgment *in rem* is a judgment of a court of competent jurisdiction determining the status of a person or thing. See Bruno Tassan Din v Banco Ambrosiano SPA (1991 HC) 1 IR 569; Lazarus-Barlow v Regan Estates (1949) 2KB 465. See IN PERSONAM.

**in situ.** [In its original or natural position].

**in specie.** In its own form and essence, and not in its equivalent. See MUTUUM.

**in statu quo.** [In the former position].

**in terrorum.** [By way of terror] eg a penalty in a contract. See PENALTY.

**in totidem verbis.** [In so many words].

**in toto.** [Entirely; wholly].

**in transitu.** [In course of transit]. See STOPPAGE IN TRANSITU.

**inaccurate data.** Personal data (qv) which are incorrect or misleading as to any matter of fact, as distinct from opinion: Data Protection Act 1988 s.1(2). See DATA PROTECTION.

**inalienability.** Not transferable. The general rule of law is that land must not be rendered inalienable; however, no gift for charitable purposes is void merely because it renders land inalienable in *perpetuity*. A condition in a testator's will which prohibited the sale of land to members of a particular family, was held to be void as contrary to public policy: In re Dunne (1988) IR 155. However, a devise in a will which was conditional on the plaintiff being the beneficial owner of land, which the testator had transferred to the plaintiff during his lifetime, was not void; it did not render the land inalienable: Fitzsimons v Fitzsimons (1993 HC) ILRM 478. Social welfare benefits or assistance or children's allowances are inalienable, as are documents upon which they are payable: Social Welfare (Consolidation) Act 1981 ss.290-294, 304. See also Landlord and Tenant (Amendment) Act 1980 s.66. See CHARITIES; MORTMAIN.

**incapable.** As regards the opinion of a garda that a person is *incapable* of driving a motor vehicle, *incapable* connotes that a person is no longer capable of having proper control, whereas "unfit" connotes that he is not suitable or not qualified to drive: DPP v Fanagan (1991 HC); Road Traffic Act 1978 s.49.

**incapacity.** Lack of legal power or competence eg due to being a minor (qv) or being of unsound mind (qv). The incapacity of an employee may be a ground for dismissal eg see Gurr v Office of Public Works (1990) ELR 42; Caulfield v Waterford Foundry Ltd (1991 EAT) ELR 137. See CAPACITY TO CONTRACT; INCOME TAX; INCOMPETENCE; SICKNESS; UNFAIR DISMISSAL.

**incardination.** The act by which a bishop permanently attaches a cleric to his diocese in the Roman Catholic Church. *Excardination* means the act by which a bishop permanently allows one of his own clergy to leave the diocese in order to belong to another. See Buckley v Cahal Daly (1991 NI HC) ITLR (7 Jan).

**incest.** The offence committed by a male person who has sexual intercourse with a female who is, to his knowledge, his mother, sister, daughter or granddaughter; or by a female over the age of sixteen years who permits her father, brother, grandfather or son to have sexual intercourse with her, knowing him to be so related: Punishment of Incest Act 1908. Since 1988, a spouse is a competent and compellable witness against the other spouse charged with the offence of incest: DPP v JT (1988) CCA (see O'Connor in 7 ILT & SJ (1989) 95 and Charlton in 8 ILT & SJ (1990) 140). For statutory provision, see Criminal Evidence Act 1992 ss.20-26. A male convicted of incest is now liable to imprisonment for a term not exceeding 20 years: ibid 1908 Act s.1 as amended

by 1992 Act s.12. See PARENT; WITNESS, COMPETENCE OF.

**inchoate.** Begun, or in an early stage, but not complete. See INCHOATE BILL.

**inchoate bill.** A bill of exchange (qv) which arises when a person signs a blank stamped paper with the intention that it may be converted into a bill; this operates as an authority to fill it up as a complete bill for any amount the stamp will cover, using the signature already on it: Bills of Exchange Act 1882 s.20. Also, where a bill is wanting in any material particular, the holder of it has authority to fill up the omission in any way he thinks fit (ibid s.20). A promissory note (qv) is inchoate and incomplete until delivery to the payee or bearer (ibid s.84).

**inchoate crime.** An offence which is committed even though the substantive crime with which it is connected is not committed eg incitement, conspiracy, attempt (qqv).

**incineration.** A licence is required for an activity involving the incineration of hazardous waste, hospital waste, other waste in plants with a capacity exceeding 1 tonne per hour, or the use of heat for the manufacture of fuel from waste: Environmental Protection Agency Act 1992, first schedule, para 11.

**incitement.** The offence of soliciting some other person to commit a crime. If the crime solicited is actually committed, the inciter will be liable as an *accessory* (qv) *before the fact* if the crime solicited is a felony, and liable as a *principal* offender if it is a misdemeanour. It is an offence to incite or encourage any civil servant to refuse, neglect, or omit to perform his duties: Offences Against the State Act 1939 s.9. See The People (Attorney General) v Capaldi (1949) CCA. See HATRED, INCITEMENT TO.

**include.** The word *include* has been held to be a word of extension when used in a statutory definition: Attorney General (McGrath) v Healy (1972) IR 393. A word in a statute will have its ordinary meaning in addition to that included by the extension where the extension *include* is given in its definition.

**inclusio unius est exclusio alterius.** [The inclusion of one is the exclusion of the other].

**income tax.** The tax on income or profits

comprising income tax, corporation tax and capital gains tax. Individuals are liable in principle to pay income tax on their income and capital gains tax on chargeable gains realised on the disposal of assets; companies and other bodies of persons with corporate status do not in general pay income tax or capital gains tax, but are chargeable to a separate corporation tax levied on their income and chargeable gains.

Income tax was originally designed as a temporary tax which had to be renewed every year: Bowles v Attorney General (1912) 1 Ch 123. It was finally made a permanent tax in 1972: Finance Act 1972.

Income tax is levied on income from sources classified as follows: A — arising from the ownership of land prior to 6th April 1969; B — arising from the occupation of land prior to 6th April 1969; C — collection of tax at source from interest, annuities, dividends or shares of annuities payable in the State out of any public revenue; D — arising from trade (case 1), profession (case II) etc; E — income from other offices and employments; F — company distributions and dividends etc.

There is an exemption from income tax on the income from the proceeds of a court action for compensation for personal injuries where the recipient is *permanently and totally incapacitated* by reason of mental or physical infirmity from maintaining himself: Finance Act 1990 s.5.

Income tax is managed by the Revenue Commissioners; there is provision for appeal. The income tax year runs from April 6 to April 5. A system of *self assessment* for the self employed has been introduced: Finance Act 1988 ss.9-21. See also Income Tax Act 1967, Corporation Tax Act 1976 and Capital Gains Tax 1975 all as amended, and annual Finance Acts.

The State must not by its taxation legislation breach its pledge to guard with special care the institution of marriage and protect it from attack: Murphy v Attorney General (1982) IR 241. It has been held that the recovery of a penalty imposed by the Income Tax Act 1967 s.128 is not a criminal matter within the meaning of the Prosecution

of Offences Act 1974 s.3 and that the Director of Public Prosecutions (qv) has no locus standi (qv) in relation thereto: Downes v DPP (1987) ILRM 665.

It has also been held that publication of an *enforcement notice* in respect of PAYE can constitute a libel (qv): Kennedy v Hearne & Ors (1988) ILRM 52. The provisions under the 1967 Act for the assessment and collection of income tax in default of the making of a return by a taxpayer are not unconstitutional: Deighan v Hearne & Ors (1990 SC) 1 IR 499. Certain penalties under the income tax code are not criminal in character and may be recovered in civil proceedings: McLoughlin v Tuite (1989 SC) IR 82. [Text: Judge; McAteer & Reddin; O'Reilly & Carroll]. See FINANCIAL RESOLUTIONS; QUALIFYING PATENT.

**incompetence.** A ground for dismissal of an employee: Unfair Dismissal Act 1977; O'Neill v Bus Eireann (1990 CC) ELR 135. The test to be used has two elements: (a) the employer's honest belief of incompetence, and (b) reasonable grounds for that belief: McDonnell v Spar Supermarket (1992 EAT) ELR 214.

**inconsistent previous statement.** See PREVIOUS STATEMENT, INCONSISTENT.

**inconvenience.** A court will not award damages for *inconvenience* caused by a local authority which acts bona fide in the ultra vires exercise of its statutory powers (eg disconnecting a water supply): O'Donnell v Dun Laoghaire Corporation (No 2) (1991 HC) 9ILT Dig 199 & 227.

**Incorporated Law Society of Ireland.** The representative body of the solicitors' profession; it operates under a charter. It exercises statutory functions under the Solicitors Acts 1954-1960 in connection with legal education, discipline, and other matters connected with the profession. The Society has no power to impose a limiting quota upon candidates seeking admission and to hold a competitive examination for entry to its law school: McGabhann v ILSI (1989) ITLR (20 Feb). Requirements have been specified for the admission of qualified lawyers from member States of the European Community to the roll of solicitors of the Incorporated Law Society: The Solicitors Acts 1954 and 1960 (European Communities) Regulations 1991 (SI No 85 of 1991). See In re O'Farrell (1960) IR 239. See SOLICITOR.

**incorporation.** Merging together to form a whole; conferring legal personality on an association of persons eg registration of a company: Companies Act 1963 s.18; or incorporation of a building society: Building Societies Act 1989 s.10. See COMPANY; ASSOCIATION, MEMORANDUM OF; BUILDING SOCIETY.

**incorporeal hereditaments.** Intangible property eg easements (qv) and profits a prendre (qv). See OWNERSHIP.

**incriminate.** To involve oneself or another in the possibility of being prosecuted for a criminal offence. Generally a witness, on grounds of *privilege,* need not answer any question which exposes himself to any criminal charge, perjury (qv) or forfeiture (qv). The witness must say on oath that he honestly believes that the answer may tend to incriminate him.

The privilege does not arise if there are no reasonable grounds for his fears, the time for prosecution has passed, he has been prosecuted previously or has been pardoned, or a statute provides for full disclosure. An accused person giving evidence under the Criminal Justice (Evidence) Act 1924 may be asked questions in cross-examination notwithstanding that they would tend to criminate him as to the offence charged. See R v Boyes (1861) 1 B S 311; In re Reynolds (1882) 20 Ch D 294; The State (Magee) v O'Rourke (1971) IR 205. See also Companies Act 1963 s.245(6) as amended by Companies Act 1990 s.126.

There is no rule of law requiring a judge to instruct a jury that, where the only evidence consists of an incriminating statement by an accused, there was a danger of convicting without corroborative evidence; any such warning could involve the implication that the gardai involved in obtaining such a statement were to be treated in the same way as accomplices: People (DPP) v Quilligan & O'Reilly (No 3) (1993 SC) 11 ILT Dig 88. As regards spouses, see WITNESS, COMPETENCE OF. See BANKRUPT, DUTIES OF; EXAMINATION RE COMPANY; SILENCE, RIGHT TO; TRIBUNALS OF INQUIRY.

**indecency.** Any act which offends modesty, causes scandal or injures the morals of the community. A person commits an offence who at, or near, or in sight of any place along which the public habitually pass, commits any indecent act: Criminal Law Amendment Act 1935 s.18 as amended by Criminal Law (Rape) (Amdt) Act 1990 s.18. The publication or utterance of indecent matter is an offence and is required to be punishable by law: 1937 Constitution, art.40(6)(1)(1). Any public sale, or exposure for sale, or exposure to public view of any indecent book, or print is an offence: Censorship of Publications Act 1946; Town Improvements (Ireland) Act 1854 s.72. See CENSORSHIP OF BOOKS; EXPOSURE, INDECENT; PERFORMANCE, INDECENT OR PROFANE.

**indecency, gross.** See GROSS INDECENCY.

**indecent assault.** See ASSAULT, INDECENT.

**indecent exposure.** See EXPOSURE, INDECENT.

**indemnify.** To make good a loss which one person has suffered in consequence of the act or default of another. Normally an employer will be held to have indemnified an employee against all liabilities and expenses incurred by the employee in the proper performance of his employment.

Any provisions in a company's regulations are void if they exempt or indemnify an officer of the company in respect of any liability which attaches to him in respect of his negligence, default, breach of duty or breach of trust: Companies Act 1963 ss.200 and 391. Similar provisions apply to officers of building societies: Building Societies Act 1989 ss.114-115.

A contract of insurance usually indemnifies the insured, in consideration of a premium, against loss he has suffered. See Rohan Construction v Insurance Corporation of Ireland (1986) ILRM 419 and (1988 SC) ILRM 373. See also Hong Kong and Shanghai Banking Corp v Icarom plc (1993 SC) 11 ILT Dig 142.

There may be circumstances which would require the executive to indemnify the judiciary in relation to costs which are properly awarded against them: McIlwraith v Fawsett (1989) 7ILT Dig 326. See Roads Act 1993 s.33. See also CONTRACT OF GUARANTEE; INNOCENT MISREPRESENTATION; INSURANCE; PROFESSIONAL INDEMNITY POLICY; VICARIOUS LIABILITY.

**indenture.** Originally a document written in duplicate on the same parchment or paper and divided in two by cutting through it in a wavy line; the genuineness of the indenture was proved by fitting the two parts (known as *counterparts*) together.

**independent contractor.** A person who contracts to perform a particular task for another and is not under the other person's control as to the manner in which the task is performed. An employer is not normally liable for the torts of an independent contractor, unless the employer has been negligent himself eg in supervising the work. The distinction between an employee (qv) and an independent contractor is important in relation to taxation, social welfare and employment protection legislation. See Walshe v Baileboro Co-operative (1939) 73 ILTR 232; Lynch v Palgrave Murphy (1964) IR 150; Ryan v Shamrock Marine (1992 EAT) ELR 19; Connolly v Dundalk UDC (1993 SC) 11 ILT Dig 144. See VICARIOUS LIABILITY.

**independent radio.** See RADIO AND TELE-VISION COMMISSION.

**independent television programme.** A programme made by a person who (a) has control of the participants, the persons involved in making the programme, and the equipment and facilities used in making the programme, and (b) is neither a subsidiary nor a holding company of a broadcaster: Broadcasting Authority (Amdt) Act 1993 s.5. The RTE Authority is required to keep a special account (termed the "independent television programme account") into which specified amounts of monies are to be made available by RTE for programmes to be commissioned from the independent sector (ibid s.4).

**indicia.** Signs; marks; criteria. In relation to whether a tenancy exists, the courts will look at the document relied upon as a whole and see if the *indicia* exist to constitute a tenancy or other relationship: Gatien Motor Company v Continental Oil Co of Ireland Ltd (1979) IR 406. See also McLoughlin v Tuite (1986) ILRM 304.

**indictable offence.** An offence which the accused is entitled as of right to a trial by jury. If the accused elects for jury trial, the District Court will conduct a *preliminary investigation* to satisfy itself that there is sufficient evidence *to return the accused for trial* to a higher court. Certain cases of indictable offences can be heard by the District Court if the accused consents (and the Director of Public Prosecutions also consents in particular cases), in which event the maximum punishment is twelve months imprisonment and/or a fine. However, a District Court is empowered to impose consecutive sentences up to a maximum of two years imprisonment: Criminal Justice Act 1984 s.12.

Provision has been made for the transfer of the trial of a person charged with an indictable offence from the Circuit Court before which the person is triable to the Dublin Circuit Court: Courts Act 1981 s.31; The State (Boyle) v Nealon (1987) ILRM 535. As regards the prosecution of an indictable offence by a private citizen, he can only go as far as securing a return for trial, after which the DPP, if he so chooses, must prosecute: State (Ennis) v Farrell (1966) IR 107. See also Gilligan v DPP (1987) HC; The State (Daly) v Ruane (1988) ILRM 117. See COMMON INFORMER; DISTRICT COURT, PRELIM-INARY EXAMINATION; INDICTMENT; MINOR OFFENCE; SUMMARY OFFENCE.

**indictment.** A written accusation of a crime made against one or more persons and preferred to a jury; formerly it was made by *The People at the suit of the Attorney General*: 1937 Constitution, art.30(3). An indictment is now brought in the name of *The People at the suit of the Director of Public Prosecutions*: Prosecution of Offences Act 1974. For the rules governing the form of an indictment, see Criminal Justice (Administration) Act 1924; Indictment Rules 1924. For prosecution of a company on indictment, see the Companies Act 1963 s.382.

It has been held that the inclusion of different additional charges in an indictment at the behest of the DPP following the return by a district court judge of an accused for trial, pursuant to the Criminal Procedure Act 1967 s.18 is not unconstitutional: O'Shea v DPP (1989) ILRM 309; Walsh v DPP (1989) 7 ILT Dig 123. A judge is entitled to add a new count to an indictment if satisfied that evidential material put before him justified him in so doing: O'Brien v Patwell (1993 HC) 11 ILT Dig 164. It is not necessary for counsel (qv) to sign an indictment (ibid Walsh case). See INDICTABLE OFFENCE.

**indirect discrimination.** *Direct* discrimination exists where by reason of his sex a person is treated less favourably than a person of the other sex: Employment Equality Act 1977 s.2(a). *Indirect* discrimination is where *because of his sex* or marital status a person is obliged to comply with a requirement related to employment which is not an essential requirement for such employment and in respect of which the proportion of persons of the other sex, or marital status, able to comply is substantially higher (ibid s.2(c)). The words "because of his sex" connote a causal link between the sex of a person and the requirement or condition imposed on the person; discrimination does not occur merely because historical factors, other than sex, have limited the eligible candidates to a pool which contains a larger number of the members of one sex than the other: Nathan v Bailey Gibson Ltd & Irish Print Union (1993 HC) ELR 106. To determine whether discrimination has occurred, the following questions need to be addressed: (a) what is the requirement with which the claimant is obliged to comply; (b) is the requirement such that either a higher proportion of males than of females (or single females than married females) can comply with it; (c) if the answer is yes, is that fact a result of an attribute of their sex or marital status; (d) is the requirement essential for such employment: Vavasour v Northside Centre for the Unemployed Ltd & FAS (1993 HC) ELR 112. See Bolger in ISLR (1993) 1; Cousins in 11 ILT & SJ (1993) 147. See DISCRIMINATION.

**indirect evidence.** Hearsay or circumstantial evidence. See EVIDENCE.

**indivisible contract.** See DIVISIBLE CONTRACT.

**indorsement.** See ENDORSEMENT.

**indorsement of claim.** An indorsement of the relief claimed and the grounds thereof expressed in general terms; in High Court proceedings it is called a *general indorsement of claim* on a plenary summons, and a *special indorsement of claim* on a summary or special summons: RSC O.4. For indorsement of claim on a civil bill in the Circuit Court, see RCC O.9.

**inducement.** Persuasion by promise or threat to a course of action. An improper inducement will render a confession (qv) inadmissible. See The People (DPP) v Hoey (1988 SC) ILRM 666. See ANTECEDENT NEGOTIATIONS; CORRUPT AGREEMENT WITH CREDITOR; FAIR AND REASONABLE TERMS; DURESS; UNDUE INFLUENCE.

**inducing breach of contract.** The tort (qv) at common law whereby a person knowingly and without lawful justification induces another to break a subsisting contract with a third person whereby that third person suffers damage: Lumley v Gye (1853) 2 E B 216. See also Cooper v Millea (1938) IR 749; Hynes v Conlon (1939) Ir Jur Rep; B & I Steampacket Co Ltd v Branigan (1958) IR 128; Flogas Ltd v Ergas Ltd (1985) ILRM 221.

**industrial action.** Any action which affects, or is likely to affect, the terms or conditions, whether express or implied, of a contract and which is taken by any number or body of workers acting in combination or under a common understanding as a means of compelling their employer, or to aid other workers in compelling their employer, to accept or not to accept terms or conditions of or affecting employment: Industrial Relations Act 1990 s.8. See LABOUR INJUNCTION; STRIKE.

**industrial and provident society.** A society for carrying on any industry business or trade specified in or authorised by its rules, whether wholesale or retail and including dealings of any description with land and the business of banking: Industrial & Provident Societies Act 1893 s.4. Registration of such a society renders it a body corporate with perpetual succession and limited liability (ibid s.21). Farmers' and other cooperative societies are often registered as industrial and provident societies; registration is with the Registrar of Friendly Societies. See also Industrial & Provident Societies (Amendment) Acts 1971 and 1978. A society may not accept deposits (ibid 1978 Act s.5(1)).

The members of a society are virtually free to manage the affairs of their society as they see fit; the majority however may not abuse the power to alter the share capital; no shareholder has a legal right to any specific portion of the assets of a society; rules of a society which benefit members who trade with that society over those who prefer not to do so are reasonable and not in restraint of trade: Kerry Co-Operative Creameries Ltd & O'Connell v An Bord Bainne Co-Operative Ltd (1992 SC) 10 ILT Dig 28. The view has been expressed that a shareholding in a society is not intended primarily as an investment but merely as an "entrance fee" (ibid Kerry Co-op case).

New rules governing the qualification for appointment as auditors to industrial and provident societies are contained in the Companies Act 1990 ss.182 and 187. See PMPS Ltd & Moore v Attorney General (1983) IR 339; PMPS Ltd v Moore (No 2) (1989) 7ILT Dig 123; In re Irish Commercial Society Group (1987) HC; McMahon v Ireland (1988) ILRM 610. See also RSC O.109.

**industrial democracy.** See WORKER PARTICIPATION.

**industrial design.** See DESIGN.

**industrial development.** Provision has been made for the development of industry and technology and for the stimulation and encouragement of investment in industrial undertakings from sources whether within or outside the State: Industrial Development Act 1993. This Act provides for the establishment of Forfas, which has the function of advising on the development and co-ordination of policy for Forbairt (development of indigenous industry), IDA (attraction of overseas firms and their development in Ireland) and An Bord Tractala (development of exports). The functions formerly vested in Eolas are vested in Forfas and may be assigned to and exercised by Forbairt or IDA (ibid ss.9 and 18). The Minister is required to prepare every three years a review of national industrial performance and of national industrial policy (ibid s.13). See also Industrial Development Acts 1986 and 1991; Science & Technology Act 1987 and Industrial Research & Standards Act 1961 as amended. See INDUSTRY.

**industrial dispute.** See TRADE DISPUTE.

**industrial plant.** See AIR POLLUTION; VALUATION, INDUSTRIAL PLANT.

**industrial property.** See INTELLECTUAL PROPERTY; PARIS CONVENTION.

**industrial relations law.** The branch of law dealing with, inter alia, industrial action (strikes, lockouts, picketing, "blacking"), collective bargaining, and trade unions (qqv). [Text: Forde (6); Kerr].

**industrial relations officer.** An officer of the Labour Relations Commission (qv) whose main function under the Industrial Relations Act 1990 is to conciliate in industrial disputes (ibid s.33).

**industrial school.** See CHILDRENS' RESIDENTIAL CENTRE; REFORMATORY.

**industry.** The EC and the member States are required to ensure that the conditions necessary for the competitiveness of the Community's industry exist: Treaty of Rome 1957 art.130 as inserted by Maastricht Treaty 1992 art.G(D)(38). Their action is required to be aimed at: (a) speeding up the adjustment of industry to structural change; (b) encouraging an environment favourable to initiative and to the development of undertakings throughout the community, particularly small and medium-sized undertakings; (c) encouraging an environment favourable to cooperation between undertakings; (d) fostering better exploitation of the industrial potential of policies of innovation, research and technological development.

**inequality of position.** The UK doctrine which attempts to fuse into one concept, five areas of law where the normal rules of freedom to contract are waived on the grounds of inequality of the position of the parties viz salvage, duress of goods, coercion, undue influence, and unconscionable bargain (qqv): Lloyds Bank v Bundy (1975) QB 326; National Westminster Bank v Morgan (1985) AC 686. For discussion on whether Irish courts might approve such a doctrine, see Doyle in 8ILT & SJ (1990) 282. See also Vail in 9ILT & SJ (1991) 258.

**inevitable accident.** An unforeseen and unlooked for event which could not be avoided by the exercise of reasonable care and skill. It is a good defence in negligence and in actions for trespass to chattels and to persons. See Stanley v Powell (1891) QB 86. An *Act of God* (qv) is a special form of inevitable accident which can provide a good defence in torts of strict liability (qv).

**infant.** A minor (qv). See Age of Majority Act 1985 s.3.

**infant and crime.** See DOLI INCAPAX.

**infanticide.** The killing of a newly born child. It is a statutory offence with the same punishment as for manslaughter. It arises where a woman by wilful act or omission causes the death of her child under the age of 12 months, at a time when the balance of her mind was disturbed by reason of her not having fully recovered from the effect of giving birth to the child, and where the circumstances are such but for this Act it would be murder: Infanticide Act 1949.

**infectious diseases.** Diseases which the Minister by regulation specifies to be infectious diseases: Health Act 1947 s.29. There is a general duty on persons with an infectious disease to take precautions against infecting others. The infectious diseases for which maintenance allowances from the State are payable are: acute anterior poliomyelitis, diptheria, dysentery, salmonellosis, tuberculosis, typhoid and paratyphoid fevers, typhus and viral haemorrhagic diseases (including lassa fever and marburg disease): Infectious Diseases (Maintenance) Regulations 1988 (SI No 151 of 1988).

A medical practitioner is required to send written notification to the medical officer of health as soon as he becomes aware or suspects that a person on whom he is in professional attendance is suffering from or is the carrier of an infectious disease: SI No 390 of 1981. See also Health Act 1953 ss.34-37; SIs No 136 of 1948; No 170 of 1948; No 268 of 1985; No 213 of 1992. See BURIAL; DETENTION.

**inference.** A conclusion that a court or a jury may properly draw arising from particular evidence eg appropriate inferences may be drawn from the failure or refusal of an arrested person to account to a garda for his presence in a particular place at or about the time an offence was committed, or to account for particular objects or marks: Criminal Justice Act 1984 ss.18-19.

It has been held that where the circumstances of an accident are to be established by inference as well as from direct but limited evidence, the plaintiff must establish facts from which negligence may reasonably be inferred — it is not sufficient that the plaintiff establish merely that negligence could be inferred, but that it ought to be inferred: Clancy v Dublin Corporation (1989) 7ILT Dig 83. See also Clancy v Commissioner for Public Works (1991 SC) ILRM 567.

It has also been held that in criminal proceedings where different inferences can be drawn from certain facts, the court is obliged to draw the inference most favourable to the accused: The People (DPP) v Clare O'Hare (1988) SC. An appellate court has a discretion to reverse inferences of fact drawn by the trial judge from circumstantial (qv) evidence: Best v Wellcome Foundation Ltd (1992 SC) ILRM 609. See DECEIT; FACT; OPINION; SECONDARY FACTS.

**inferior courts.** Courts with a jurisdiction which is limited geographically and as to the value of the matter in dispute, and which are subject to the supervision of the superior courts eg the District Court (qv) and the Circuit Court (qv).

**inflation.** There is no constitutional right that social welfare allowances keep pace with inflation: Mhic Mhathuna v Ireland (1990) 8ILT Dig 59. See CURRENT COST ACCOUNTING CONVENTION; INTEREST AND SOCIAL WELFARE.

**influence, improper.** There is a prohibition on communications with a director, employee, or person connected with the Environmental Protection Agency for the purpose of influencing improperly his consideration of any matter which falls to be considered or decided by the Agency: Environmental Protection Agency Act 1992 s.40. There is a similar prohibition as regards the National Roads Authority: Roads Act 1993 s.39. There is also a prohibition on certain communications to the DPP or Attorney General or to the gardai for the purpose of influencing the making of a decision in relation to (a) the initiation or withdrawal of criminal proceedings or (b) an application for review of a sentence: Prosecution of Offences Act 1974 s.6; Criminal Justice Act 1993 s.2(4).

**influence, undue.** See UNDUE INFLUENCE.

**informal.** Without formality. Certain statutes require proceedings to be informal eg proceedings in the High Court regarding the care of children are required to be as informal as is practicable, consistent with the administration of justice: Child Care Act 1991 s.29(4). See also FAMILY COURT.

**information.** A statement concerning an offence for which a summons or warrant is required. It has been held that the failure to provide or cause to be provided to a person whose extradition (qv) is sought, copies of the sworn *informations* grounding a warrant for his extradition, did not amount to a denial of fair procedures: Ellis v O'Dea & Shiels (1990 SC) ILRM 87. See COMMON INFORMER.

**information, access to.** The public must be given access to information relating to the environment ie any available information in written, visual, aural or data base form on the state of water, atmosphere, soil, fauna, flora, land and natural sites, and on actions or measures affecting or likely to affect these, including administrative measures and environmental management programmes: Council Directive 90/313/EEC: Environmental Protection Agency Act 1992 s.110. This information must be made available by public authorities. Also the public must be given access to information on monitoring which the Agency considers appropriate (ibid s.67).

**information, disclosure of.** Various statutes and rules of court impose a requirement to disclose information eg lodgment by a debtor of a statement setting forth his assets and liabilities on foot of an order therefor. See DISCOVERY OF DOCUMENTS; EXAMINATION RE COMPANY; EXAMINATION ORDER, DISTRICT COURT; SILENCE, RIGHT TO.

**information, withholding.** See WITHHOLDING INFORMATION.

**information notice, data.** The notice in writing, served on a person, by which the Data Protection Commissioner (qv) may require that person to furnish to him such information in relation to matters specified in the notice as is necessary or expedient for the performance by the Commissioner of his functions: Data Protection Act 1988 s.12. An appeal against the requirements in the notice lies to the Circuit Court. See DATA PROTECTION.

**informer.** See COMMON INFORMER.

**infortunium, per.** [Misadventure (qv)].

**infra.** [Below].

**infringement.** Interference with, or the violation of, the right of another. The remedy is an injunction to restrain future infringements, and an action for the recovery of the damage caused or profits made by the past infringements. See INFRINGEMENT OF COPYRIGHT; INFRINGEMENT OF PATENTS; INFRINGEMENT OF TRADE MARK.

**infringement of copyright.** The violation of the right of the owner of a copyright which takes place when a person, without the licence of the owner, does anything in the State, the sole right to do which is conferred on the owner: Copyright Act 1963 s.7(3). Any fair dealing with any work for the purpose of private study, research, criticism, review or newspaper summary is not an infringement of the copyright of that work (ibid ss.12 and 14).

An infringement of copyright is actionable at the suit of the owner of the copyright and the relief is by way of damages, an injunction and an account (ibid s.22). Where infringement is proved or admitted but the defendant was not aware that copyright subsisted at the time of infringement, the plaintiff is not entitled to damages but will be entitled to an account of profits in respect of the infringement (ibid s.22(3)). Additional damages may be awarded where there is a flagrant infringement (ibid s.22(4)).

The owner of the copyright has the same rights in respect of conversion or detention by another person of an *infringing copy* (qv) as if he were the owner of that copy (ibid s.24). Dealing with an infringing copy of a work in which copyright exists is an offence: Copyright (Amendment) Act 1987 s.2. The owner of the copyright can apply to the District Court which if satisfied will authorise a Garda to seize without warrant infringing copies which may be destroyed by order of the court (ibid s.2). Also infringement of copyright in respect of a video recording can lead to forfeiture of a licence to sell or hire such recordings or to disqualification: Video Recordings Act 1989 s.24.

There is no infringement of copyright by reading or reciting in public or in a broadcast of a reasonable extract from a published literary or dramatic work, provided it is sufficiently acknowledged (ibid 1963 Act s.12). See RSC O.94 r.3. See DPP v Irwin (1985) HC; House of Spring Gardens v Point Blank (1985 SC) ILRM 107. See COPYRIGHT; VIDEO.

**infringement of patent.** The violation of the rights of the proprietor of a patent (qv) of invention; he can enforce his rights by civil proceedings: Patents Act 1992 ss.40-41; 47-56. The proprietor may seek (a) an injunction to restrain further infringement; (b) delivery up or destruction of infringing products; (c) damages or an account of the profits derived by the defendant; (d) a declaration that the patent is valid and has been infringed (ibid s.47). As regards a patented process for obtaining a new product, there is a presumption that where the same product is produced, it has been produced by the patented process and the onus of proof of non-infringement passes to the defendant (ibid s.46).

Damages will not be awarded against a defendant who proves that he was not aware that the patent existed, and had no reasonable grounds for supposing it existed; the words *patent* or *patented* on a product without the number of the patent is ineffective to make the defendant aware that a patent had been obtained for the product (ibid s.49(1)). See Lancer Bros v Henley Forklift Co and H M Sideloaders (1974) FSR 14.

A person threatened with an action of infringement may institute proceedings himself for a *declaration* that the threats were unjustifiable and for an injunction and damages, if he has suffered any (ibid s.53). A general warning not directed to any person in particular is not actionable: Speedcranes v Thompson (1978) RPC 221. The validity of a patent may be raised by way of defence in proceedings for infringement (ibid s.61).

Infringement proceedings are taken in the High Court in respect of normal patents (ibid s.47) and in the Circuit Court in respect of *short-term* patents; there are also special provisions governing infringement proceedings in respect of short-term patents (ibid s.66). See RSC O.94 rr.4-14. See DECLARATORY JUDGMENT; PATENT RIGHTS; SECRET PRIOR USE; SHORT-TERM PATENT.

**infringement of trade mark.** As regards a *registered* trade mark, the exclusive right to the use of the trade mark is deemed to be infringed by any person who, not being the proprietor of the trade mark, uses a mark identical with the registered trade mark or so nearly resembling it as to be likely to deceive or cause confusion, in the *course of trade*, in relation to any goods in respect of which it is registered, and in such manner as to render the use of the mark likely to be taken either (a) as being used as a trade mark, or (b) as importing a reference to some person having the same right either as proprietor or as registered user to use the trade mark, or to goods with which such a person as aforesaid is connected in the *course of trade*: Trade Marks Act 1963 s.12(1).

For *course of trade*, see Gallagher (Dublin) Ltd v Health Education Bureau (1982) ILRM 240; Bank of Ireland v Controller of Trade Marks (1987) HC.

It is usual in an action for infringement of a registered trade mark, to combine in one set of pleadings (qv), the common law remedy of passing off (qv) as well — for example see United Biscuits Ltd v Irish Biscuits Ltd (1971) IR 16. See also IBP Industrie Buitoni Perugina Spa v Dowdall O'Mahony Co Ltd (1977) HC; Hennessy Co v Keating (1908) 1 IR 43. See also RSC O.94 rr.4-14 and rr.46-53. See COURSE OF TRADE; PART A; PART B.

**infringing copy.** An article, the making of which constituted an infringement of the copyright in the work, edition, recording, film, broadcast, or in the case of an imported article, would have constituted an infringement if that article had been made in the State: Copyright Act 1963 s.24. It is an offence for a person to make for sale or hire, or to import into the State (otherwise than for his private and domestic use) any article which he knows to be an infringing copy of the work in which the copyright subsists (ibid s.27). See DPP v Irwin (1985) HC. See INFRINGEMENT OF COPYRIGHT.

**ingross.** See ENGROSS.

**inheritance.** An estate in land which descended from a man to his heirs; for capital acquisition tax purposes, the beneficial taking by a successor of a benefit in possession, on a death otherwise than for full consideration. See

Capital Acquisitions Tax Act 1976 ss.10-11.

**inheritance tax.** A capital acquisition tax levied and paid upon the taxable value of every taxable inheritance taken by a successor where the date of inheritance is on or after 1st April 1975; it replaced estate duty: Capital Acquisitions Tax Act 1976 as amended. [Text: Bale & Condon]. See CAPITAL ACQUISITIONS TAX; PROBATE TAX; SELF ASSESSMENT.

**inhibition.** An entry in the register of the Land Registry in respect of registered land in the form of a restriction on registration; the restriction will prevent all registrations except those made in compliance with the inhibition. It imposes on a subsequent applicant for registration the onus of ensuring that the registration he applies for complies with the inhibition. Inhibitions are used to protect interests which are not permitted to be registered as *burdens* (qv). See Registration of Title Act 1964 ss.96-98.

**injunction.** An order of the court directing a party to an action to do, or to refrain from doing, a particular thing. An injunction is enforced by committal for contempt of court in respect of any breach. An injunction is either (a) *prohibitory* (restrictive/preventative) — forbidding continuance of a wrongful act or (b) *mandatory* (compulsive) — directing direct performance of a positive act: Bula Ltd v Tara Mines (1988) ILRM 157; eg payment of wages: Doyle & Ors v An Post (1992 HC) 10 ILT & SJ 150. As regards time, an injunction is either (a) *interim* — restraining the defendant until some specified time; (b) *interlocutory* — a temporary injunction pending trial of the action, only granted where the balance of convenience lies in so granting it and where the recoverable damages would be an inadequate remedy: Campus Oil Ltd v Minister for Industry & Energy (No 2) (1983) IR 88; Westman Holdings Ltd v McCormack & Ors (1991 SC) ILRM 833. The courts are slow to grant mandatory relief on an interlocutory application but will do so in a suitable case: Barrington v Bank of Ireland (1993 HC) ITLR (19 Apr). Difficulty in assessment of damages will not prevent an interlocutory injunction being granted: Curust v Loewe GmbH (1993

SC) ITLR (11 Jan) and 11 ILT Dig 143;

(c) *perpetual* — permanent injunction after hearing of the action.

A *Mareva injunction* (qv) is a particular type of interim injunction granted on an *ex parte* application. A *quia timet* (qv) injunction is one to prevent or restrain some act, merely feared or threatened.

An injunction may be granted to enforce a negative stipulation in a contract, even if it is only inferred from the contract: Metropolitan Electric Supply Co v Ginder (1901) 2 Ch 799. In a contract for personal services, an express negative stipulation (but not an inferred one) may be enforced by an injunction in a suitable case: Lumney v Wagner (1852) 90 RR 125. Termination of employment may be restrained by interlocutory injunction in a case involving alleged oppressive conduct: Irish Press Ltd v Ingersoll Irish Publications (1993 HC) — Irish Times 6/4/1993. See Supreme Court of Judicature Act (Ireland) 1877. See RSC O.50 rr.2 and 12. [Text: Keane (2); Bean UK]. See ANTON PILLER ORDER; BALANCE OF CONVENIENCE; LABOUR INJUNCTION; MAREVA INJUNCTION; QUIA TIMET; STATUTORY POWER, RESTRAINT OF.

**injunction, constitutional right.** Where an injunction is sought to protect a constitutional right, the only matter which could properly be capable of being weighed against the grant of such protection, is another competing constitutional right: SPUC v Grogan (1990 SC) ILRM 350.

**injunction, criminal.** An order which the High Court is empowered to make to prohibit a criminal act; however, it will make such an order only in exceptional cases and will consider the alternative statutory remedy: Attorney General v Paperlink (1984) ILRM 373. The postponement of a trial for a criminal offence, committed by a breach of a licence, is not a bar to the granting of an injunction, but a factor to be considered in weighing the balance of convenience: In re Beara Fisheries and Shipping Ltd (1988) ILRM 221. Where an existing statute renders an activity illegal, the court will not restrain the imposition of preventative measures authorised by the statute: Cooke v Minister for Communications (1989

ITLR (20 Feb). See also Campus Oil v Minister for Industry (No 2) (1983) IR 88.

**injunction, labour.** See LABOUR INJUNCTION.

**injunction, planning.** An order which the High and Circuit Courts have power to make where (a) development of land, being development for which permission is required, has been carried out, or is being carried out without such permission, or (b) an unauthorised use is being made of land: LG(P&D) Act 1976 s.27 inserted by LG(P&D) Act 1992 s.19(4)(g). An application for such an injunction may be made by a planning authority or any other person, whether or not the person has an interest in the land (ibid. 1976 Act s.27(1)).

The order of the court may require any person specified in the order to do or not to do, or cease to do, as the case may be, anything which the court considers necessary to ensure (i) that the development or unauthorised use is not continued, and (ii) in so far as is practicable, that the land is restored to its condition prior to the commencement of the development or unauthorised use (ibid s.27(1)). However, the court is not empowered to enforce, after the construction of buildings authorised by a planning permission (qv), a partial compliance with the terms of the permission: Dublin County Council v Browne (1987) HC.

The procedure under s.27 is not to be used to determine serious allegations of fraud or misapplication of monies by directors of companies: Dublin County Council v O'Riordan (1986) ILRM 104; Corp of Dun Laoghaire v Park Hill Developmemts Ltd (1989) ILRM 235. Also it is not the function of the court to determine what constitutes good planning for the environment of an area; such function is reserved for the relevant planning authority: Furlong v McConnell Ltd & Ors (1990 HC) ILRM 48. See RSC O.103.

The 1992 Act (a) corrected a deficiency in the 1976 Act which prevented the court giving mandatory relief where a development had been carried out without planning permission (eg Dublin County Council v Kirby (1985) ILRM 325); (b) introduced a 5 year limitation in relation to unauthorised use or

development; and (c) extended the jurisdiction of the Circuit Court to include planning injunctions. See Grist in 11 ILT & SJ (1993) 79.

**injuria.** [A legal wrong].

**injuria non excusat injuriam.** [One wrong does not justify another].

**injuria sine damnum.** [A wrong without damage]. The phrase used in the law of torts (qv) to refer to where there is an infringement of a legal right which is actionable without proving any actual damage eg trespass which is actionable *per se*. See DAMNUM SINE INJURIA.

**injurious falsehood.** A tort (qv) consisting of maliciously making a false statement respecting any person or his property with the result that other persons deceived thereby are induced to act in a manner which causes loss to him. It is different from deceit (qv) in that the falsehood in deceit is addressed to the plaintiff who acts on it to his loss, whereas in injurious falsehood, the falsehood is addressed to other persons who act on it and cause loss to the plaintiff.

It is not necessary to prove *special damage*, if the words are calculated to cause pecuniary damage to the plaintiff and are published in permanent form, or if the words are calculated to cause pecuniary damage to his office, profession or calling, trade or business, carried on at the time of publication: Defamation Act 1961 s.20(1). See Ratcliffe v Evans (1892) 2 QB 254; Royal Baking Powder Co v Wright Crossley Co (1901) RPC 95; Irish Toys and Ulilities Ltd v The Irish Times Ltd (1937) IR 298. See DEFAMATION; SLANDER OF GOODS; SLANDER OF TITLE.

**injury.** (1) A violation of a legal right. (2) A disease or impairment of the physical or mental condition of a person. It has been held that the word *injured* is synonymous with *harmed*: Statute of Limitations (Amendment) Act 1991 s.2; Maitland v Swan and Sligo Co Council (1992 HC) ITLR (6 Jul). (3) An actionable wrong. See CAUSE OF ACTION.

**injury, personal.** Includes any disease and any impairment of a person's physical or mental condition: Courts Act 1988 s.1(7). Actions in the High Court for recovery of damages for *personal injuries* are, since 1988, no longer tried with a jury (qv), except in the case of damages for false imprisonment or intentional trespass to the person or both. Claims for damages for personal injuries in the Circuit (qv) and District (qv) Courts are also tried without a jury. [Text: White]. See CAUSE OF ACTION; DEATH, EFFECT OF; JURY, ABOLITION OF; LIMITATION OF ACTIONS.

**inland bill.** A bill of exchange both drawn and payable within Ireland and Britain. A *foreign* bill is any other bill of exchange. See Bills of Exchange Act 1882 s.4. See BILL OF EXCHANGE.

**inland waters.** The internal or inland waters of the State extending to all sea areas which lie on the landward side of the baseline of the *territorial seas*: Maritime Jurisdiction Act 1959 s.5. See MARITIME JURISDICTION.

**inn.** An inn was defined at common law as a house the occupier of which held himself out to the public as willing to receive all travellers provided that they were willing to pay a price adequate to the sort of accommodation given, they came in a proper condition, and the innkeeper had room for them. The term has been replaced by the term *hotel* and the Innkeepers Acts of 1863 and 1878 repealed by the Hotel Proprietors Act 1963. See HOTEL.

**inner bar.** See BAR; SENIOR COUNSEL.

**innocence, presumption of.** See PRE-SUMPTION OF INNOCENCE.

**innocent misrepresentation.** A false statement which is neither negligent or fraudulent, which is of fact, intended to be acted upon, actually misleads and induces a contract. It generally does not entitle the person induced to rescind the contract but does entitle him to an indemnity (qv).

However, since 1980, where a person has entered into a certain type of contract after a misrepresentation has been made to him, and (a) the misrepresentation has become a term of the contract, or (b) the contract has been performed, or both, then, if otherwise he would be entitled to rescind the contract without alleging fraud, he will be so entitled notwithstanding the matters mentioned in (a) and (b): SGSS Act 1980 s.44. This provision applies to contracts of sale of goods, hire-purchase agreements, agreements for letting of goods, and contracts for the supply of service. Provisions in

such agreements excluding liability for misrepresentation are not enforceable unless they are shown to be *fair and reasonable* (qv) (ibid s.46) See Pearson v Dublin Corporation (1907) AC 351.

As regards shares in a company, a person who by a material misrepresentation made innocently and not negligently, induces another to acquire shares, is generally not thereby liable in damages. If, however, the misrepresentation amounts to a warranty, then the party making it may be liable in damages for breach of contract. See Bank of Ireland v Smith (1966) IR 646. See MISREPRESENTATION.

**innuendo.** The claim by the plaintiff in a defamation action that, although the words complained of are not defamatory in themselves, they have a *secondary* meaning which is defamatory. See Campbell v Irish Press Ltd (1955) 90 ILTR 105; Fullam v Associated Newspapers Ltd (1956) Ir Jur Rep 45. See also REFER TO DRAWER.

**inoperative provisions.** Provisions of a statute which no longer have effect eg it has been held that the provisions of s.8(1) of the Petty Sessions (Ireland) Act 1851 are inoperative due to the disappearance of Grand Juries (qv) and county presentments (qv): The State (Feely) v O'Dea (1986) HC.

**inops consilii.** [Without advice]. Eg without legal advice.

**inquest.** An enquiry in relation to the death of a person which a coroner has a duty to hold, upon being informed that the body of a deceased person is lying within his district, if he is of opinion that the death may have occurred in a violent or unnatural manner or suddenly and from unknown causes or in a place or in circumstances which, under provisions in that behalf contained in any other enactment, require that an inquest should be held: Coroners Act 1962 s.17.

Questions of civil or criminal liability must not be considered or investigated at an inquest and accordingly every inquest must be confined to ascertaining the identity of the dead person and how, when, and where the death occurred (ibid s.30; The State (McKeown) v Scully (1986) ILRM 133). An inquest jury is permitted to reach a verdict of murder, manslaughter or infanticide, but this is confined to third party involvement in a death; in all other instances the jury is prohibited from reaching a verdict which involves attaching criminal liability eg formerly suicide: ibid s.40 and Green v McLoughlin (1991 HC) 1 IR 309. The verdict or any rider (qv) to the verdict at an inquest must not contain a censure or exoneration of any person; however, recommendations of a general character designed to prevent further fatalities may be appended to the verdict (ibid s.31).

A coroner must sit with a jury in certain circumstances eg if either before or during the inquest, he becomes of opinion that the deceased person came to his death by murder, infanticide or manslaughter (qqv) (ibid s.40).

A coroner's jury consists of not less than six and not more than twelve persons (ibid s.41). Every citizen of age eighteen and upwards and under the age of sixty-five residing in a coroner's district is qualified and liable to serve on the jury at a coroner's inquest: Juries Act 1976 ss.31-32. A judicial review (qv) has been permitted of the decision of a coroner to hold an inquest in the absence of the next-of-kin: Boyle v Farrelly (1992 HC).

There are special provisions in relation to an inquest into a death arising from a workplace injury or disease: Safety, Health and Welfare at Work Act 1989 s.56. See CORONER.

**inquiry.** The court may, at any stage of a proceedings, direct any necessary inquiries to be made or accounts to be taken: RSC O.33 r.2. See also ENVIRON-MENTAL PROTECTION AGENCY; INVESTIGATION OF COMPANY; TRIBUNALS OF INQUIRY.

**inquisitorial procedure.** The system in force in countries whose legal systems originate in Roman or Civil Law and under which the judge initiates the investigation, summons and examines witnesses and in which the trial is an inquiry by the court. Contrast with ACCUSATORIAL PROCEDURE.

**insane person.** A person of unsound mind. Contracts made by an insane person are valid, but if the other party knew he was contracting with a person, who by reason of the unsoundness of his mind, could not understand the nature of the contract, the contract is *voidable*

(qv) at the option of the insane party. An insane person is liable for *necessaries* (qv) supplied to him: Sale of Goods Act 1893 s.2. See Imperial Loan Co v Stone (1892) 1 QB 559. See CAPACITY TO CONTRACT; UNSOUND MIND.

**insanity.** Unsoundness of mind; mental disease. It is a defence to the charge of a criminal offence; the defence is largely governed by the McNaghten Rules (qv) but these are not the sole rules. It has been accepted that *irresistible impulse* (qv) may be a defence in appropriate cases: Attorney General v O'Brien (1936) IR 263. Mental abnormality does not amount to legal insanity: Attorney General v O'Shea (1931) IR 728. However, insanity as a defence was widened in 1974 to include cases where the defendant is unable to control his actions as a result of illness or disease: Doyle v Wicklow Co Council (1974) IR 55.

Insanity as a defence must be proved on the balance of probability (qv). When the defence succeeds, the accused is found *guilty but insane* and is ordered to be kept in custody until his release is ordered by the Executive: Trial of Lunatics Act 1883; DPP v Gallagher (1991 SC) ILRM 339. The Minister for Justice has established an advisory committee to advise him in relation to applications for release made by persons found guilty but insane. Leave by way of judicial review to challenge a decision of the Minister based on such advice has been granted in a particular case: Gallagher v Minister for Justice — Irish Times 27/7/1993.

In relation to standing for trial, the test is whether the accused has sufficient intellect to comprehend the course of the proceedings of trial, so as to make a proper defence, to challenge a juror and to understand the details of the evidence: The State (Coughlan) v Minister for Justice (1968) ILTR 177. See also The People (DPP) v O'Mahony (1986) ILRM 244.

In 1991 it was held that in an inquest, a coroner must not allow medical evidence as to the deceased's state of mind since it would bring up for the jury the question of criminal liability in respect of a possible suicide: Green v McLoughlin (1991 HC) 1 IR 309. [Text: McAuley]. See MUTE; PSYCHIATRIC DISOR-

DER; SPECIAL VERDICT; SUICIDE; UNFIT TO PLEAD; UNSOUND MIND; WARD OF COURT.

**insect, destructive.** Destructive insects or pests are to be construed as (a) insects fungi or other pests destructive to crops, (b) bacteria or agents causitive of a transmissible crop disease: Destructive Insects and Pests (Consolidation) Act 1958 s.1. The Act empowers the making of orders preventing the import of any insect, fungus, or other pest destructive to agriculture or horticulture crops or to trees and bushes. It also provides for the service on a crop-owner of a *spraying notice*. The offence provisions of the 1958 Act were extended by the Destructive Insects and Pests (Amendment) Act 1991.

**insider dealing.** It is unlawful for a person *connected* with a public limited company to deal in its quoted securities, if he has *inside* information related to it ie information which is not generally available but, if it were, would be likely materially to affect the price of those security: Companies Act 1990 s.108.

A *connected* person is a natural person (a) who is an officer or shareholder of the company or of a related company or (b) who occupies a position that may reasonably be expected to give him access to such information (ibid s.108(11)). Such a person is also precluded from dealing in the securities of any other company if he has *inside information* related to a transaction involving both companies (ibid s.108(2)). A person who receives inside information from a connected person is also precluded from dealing (ibid s.108(3)).

Insider dealing is both a civil wrong and a criminal offence (ibid ss.109-112). The civil wrong creates a liability to compensate any party to the transaction who was not in possession of the information and with liability to account to the company for any profit in the transaction (ibid s.109). A person convicted of insider dealing is prohibited from dealing for 12 months from conviction (ibid s.112). A policing role is given to the Stock Exchange (ibid s.115). See also s.223 regarding the dealings of a company in its own securities.

Insider trading is also prohibited by the Stock Exchange (City Code on Take-Overs, rule 30; Listing Agreement s.5.41-46). Insider dealing (ibid 1990 Act s.108) does not apply to dealings outside the State in securities: SI No 131 of 1992. See also Securities Trust v Associated Properties (1980) HC; Ryan in 7ILT & SJ (1989) 6; MacCann in 9ILT & SJ (1991) 130 & 151. See Insider Dealing Regulations 1991 (SI No 151 of 1991). See also SI No 131 of 1992. [Text: Murphy & Ashe; ICEL].

**insolvency.** As regards the sale of goods, a person is deemed to be insolvent who either has ceased to pay his debts in the ordinary course of business, or cannot pay his debts as they become due, whether he has commited an *act of bankruptcy* (qv) or not: Sale of Goods Act 1893 s.62. See STOPPAGE IN TRANSITU; UNPAID SELLER.

**insolvency, declaration of.** See BANK-RUPTCY, ACT OF.

**insolvency of employer.** An employer is taken to be insolvent if he has been adjudicated bankrupt, or he has died and his estate is insolvent, or being a company a winding up order has been made or a receiver appointed, or he is an employer as specified in regulations: Protection of Employees (Employers' Insolvency) Act 1984 s.1(3). Employees may claim payment of debts from the Redundancy and Employers' Insolvency Fund, where such debts arise from the employment relationship and have not been paid because of the employer's insolvency (ibid s.6). In addition, the Minister may use the Fund to make payments into the assets of an occupational pension scheme to cover contributions not paid on the employer's insolvency (ibid s.7). As regards trade union dues deducted from remuneration of employees, see In re Solus Teoranta (1990 HC) ELR 64.

An order has been made which rectifies an anomoly in the 1984 Act which denied access to the Fund to employees over the age of 66 because their age prevented them from being fully insurable: Protection of Employees (Employers' Insolvency) Act 1984 (Amendment Order) Order 1988 (SI No 48 of 1988).

The moneys in the fund have been transferred to the Social Insurance Fund: Social Welfare Act 1990 ss. 24 and 28. Part-time employees now have the same protection as full-time employees:

Worker Protection (Regular Part-time Employees) Act 1991 s.1. See In re Cavan Rubber Ltd (1992 EAT) 79. [Text: Forde (9)].

**insolvent.** A person who is unable to pay his debts as they become due. See also ADMINISTRATION OF ESTATES; BANKRUPTCY; INSOLVENCY STOPPAGE IN TRANSITU.

**insolvent company.** A company which is unable to pay its debts as they fall due. A company which was thought to have been insolvent at the date of liquidation (qv) but whose assets when realised are sufficient to pay its debts, is not and never was insolvent: In re Lines Bros Ltd (1984) BCLC 215. However, where a company was in fact insolvent at commencement of the winding up, but a surplus subsequently arose from interest earned over a lengthy liquidation, the company could not be deemed to have always been solvent: In the matter of Hibernian Transport Companies Ltd (1990 HC) ILRM 42. [Text: Forde (7); Forde (9)]. See FLOATING CHARGE; FRAUD-ULENT PREFERENCE; WINDING UP, COMPUL-SORY.

**insolvent estate.** Provision has been made for the administration of the estates of persons who die insolvent to be wound up in bankruptcy: Bankruptcy Act 1988 ss.115-122. The petition in the High Court for the administration in bankruptcy may be made by the personal representative (qv) or by a creditor whose debt would have supported a *bankruptcy petition* against the deceased had he been alive (ibid s.115(1)).

A petition may not be presented when proceedings have already begun in the Circuit Court for the administration of the deceased's estate; however that court may, when satisfied that the estate is insolvent, transfer the proceedings to the High Court (ibid s.115(4)). When an order is made by the court for the administration in bankruptcy of the deceased's estate, his property will vest in the Official Assignee (qv) for realisa-tion and distribution (ibid s.118). Priority in payment is given to funeral and testamentary expenses (ibid s.119).

**inspection of company.** See INVESTIGA-TION OF COMPANY.

**inspection of documents.** See DISCOVERY OF DOCUMENTS.

**inspection of property.** The court may order that an applicant be allowed carry out an inspection of a defendant's property (eg re mining activities) in order to ascertain whether a trespass of the applicant's property has taken place: Bula Ltd & Ors v Tara Mines Ors (1988) ILRM 149. See RSC O.50 r.4. See ANTON PILLER ORDER; SOLICITOR, PROFES-SIONAL NEGLIGENCE.

**installation charges.** As to installation charges relating to goods the subject of hire-purchase agreements, see the Hire-Purchase Act 1946 s.19.

**instalment.** A part or portion of the total sum or quantity due, arranged to be taken on account of the total sum or quantity due.

**instalment deliveries.** Unless otherwise agreed, the buyer of goods is not bound to accept delivery thereof by instalments: Sale of Goods Act 1893 s.31. See Wilkinson v McCann Verdon & Co (1901) 35 ILTR 115; Norwell v Black (1931) 65 ILTR 104. See WRONG QUANTITY.

**instalment order.** See EXAMINATION OR-DER, DISTRICT COURT.

**instance, court of first.** See FIRST INSTANCE, COURT OF.

**instruct.** When a solicitor communicates information to counsel in relation to proceedings or authorises him to act, he is said to *instruct* counsel. He is known as the *instructing* solicitor. See BRIEF.

**instruction fee.** The fee charged by a solicitor for instructing counsel in legal proceedings. The Taxing Master is entitled to determine whether an instruc-tion fee sought by a solicitor is the correct fee. The instruction fee cannot be used to compensate the solicitor for the low level of fees allowable for other expenses: Smyth v Tunney (1992 HC) 10 ILT Dig 267. See TAXATION OF COSTS.

**instrument.** A formal legal document in writing which evidences rights and duties eg a deed (qv) or a will (qv). It is also defined as an order, regulation, rule, bye-law, warrant, licence, certificate or other like document: Interpretation Act 1937 s.3.

**insurable interest.** An interest giving an insured person a right to enforce a contract of insurance. An insurance contract is void unless the assured has some *insurable interest* in the life or property which is the subject of the insurance at the time the contract is entered into. The interest exists if the insured is liable to sustain some monetary loss, or if he may be claimed against following a loss to another. In life insurance, no contract of insurance may be made by a person on the life of another unless he has an interest in the life of that other: Life Assurance Act 1774 s.1; Life Assurance Act 1886.

A person has an unlimited interest in his own life. A father may not necessarily have an insurable interest in his son's life: Halford v Kymer (1830) 10 B & C 724; a husband may insure his wife and vice versa: Griffiths v Fleming (1909) 1 KB 805; a trustee may insure in respect of an interest of which he is trustee: Tidswell v Ankerstein (1792) Peake 151; tenants-at-will may insure a premises which they occupy and are required to maintain: Church & General Insurance Co v Connolly (1981) HC.

Statutory provisions prevent insurance being used as a means of gaming and wagering: Gaming and Lotteries Act 1956; Marine Insurance Act 1906 s.4. See also Coen v Employers Liability Assurance Corporation (1962) 104 ILTR 157; P J Carrigan Ltd v Norwich Union Fire Society (1987 HC) IR 619. See INSURANCE, CONTRACT OF.

**insurable value.** The measure of insurable value in marine insurance, in the absence of any express provision in the policy, is provided for by s.16 of the Marine Insurance Act 1906.

**insurance.** A contract whereby a person called the *insurer* agrees in consideration of money paid to him, called the *premium*, by another person called the *assured*, to indemnify the latter against loss resulting to him on the happening of certain events. The event must constitute an *insurable interest* (qv). The *policy* is the document in which is contained the terms of the contract. Insurance is a contract *uberrimae fidei* (of the utmost good faith) and of indemnity only, except in the case of life and accident insurance, when an agreed sum is often payable. For information on the single insurance market of the EC, see Ping-Fat in 11 ILT & SJ (1993) 43. [Text: Hill UK; Ivamy UK; MacGillivray & Parkington UK; Cameron Markby & Hewitt UK]. See INDEMNIFY; INSURANCE BUSINESS; INSUR-

ANCE, CONTRACT OF; INSURANCE OMBUDSMAN; SUBROGATION; ULTRA VIRES.

**insurance, contract of.** Insurance policies fall into two broad categories: *life assurance* which insures against an event which must happen and *liability insurance* which insures against events which may happen. A contract of insurance does not come into effect and the insurer put on risk until the precise time specified in the contract or, if not stated, when the parties intended. Often, this is at the time the first premium is paid: Harney v Century Insurance Co Ltd (1983) HC. Most contracts of insurance provide that disputes between the parties be resolved by arbitration (qv). The High Court has jurisdiction to set aside an arbitration award if there is an error in law on its face: Church & General Insurance Co v Connolly (1981) HC. See also Stanbridge v Healy (1985) ILRM 290. See COVER NOTE; CREDIT GUARANTEE INSURANCE; FRIENDLY SOCIETY; PRIVATE INTERNATIONAL LAW; UBERRIMAE FIDEI.

**insurance, double.** See DOUBLE INSURANCE.

**insurance, over-.** See OVER-INSURANCE.

**insurance, vehicle.** It is an offence for a person to use in a public place a *mechanically propelled vehicle* (qv) unless either a vehicle insurer, or an exempted person would be liable for injury caused by the negligent use of the vehicle by him: Road Traffic Act 1961 s.56 as amended by the Road Traffic Act 1968 (Part IV) and the European Communities (Road Traffic) (Compulsory Insurance) Regulations 1975. A demand for production of a certificate of insurance or a certificate of exemption may be made by a garda: 1961 Act s.69. See Greaney v Scully (1981) ILRM 340; Boyce v McBride (1987) ILRM 95.

Regulations have been made to extend compulsory third party insurance cover to Irish registered vehicles being driven abroad in EC member States or other designated territories on or after 31st December 1995, up to (a) the minimum legal cover required in the EC member State or other designated territory, or (b) the minimum legal cover required in Ireland, whichever is the more beneficial to the injured party: Road Traffic (Compulsory Insurance) (Amendment) Regulations 1992 (SI No 346 of 1992).

See also SI No 347 of 1992. See MOTOR INSURANCE, EC; MOTOR VEHICLE, NEGLIGENT DRIVING OF; MOTOR INSURER'S BUREAU OF IRELAND; UNTRACED DRIVER; VEHICLE INSURER, PROCEEDING AGAINST.

**insurance agent.** Any person who holds an appointment in writing from an insurer enabling him to place insurance business with that insurer, but does not include an *insurance broker* or an employee of an insurer when the employee is acting for that insurer: Insurance Act 1989 s.2(1). Certain conditions are specified for insurance agents eg that an agent must hold appointment from not more than four authorised insurers (ibid s.49). An insurance agent is an *insurance intermediary* (qv) and is governed by the provisions in the 1989 Act concerning such intermediaries.

It has been held that where an insurance agent's authority is confined to submitting proposal forms (and not to completing the forms), the insurer is not bound by any statement or representation by the agent: Connors v London & Provincial Assurance Co (1913) 47 ILTR 148. Under the 1989 legislation, an insurance agent is deemed to be acting as the agent of the insurer when he completes in his own hand or helps the proposer of an insurance policy to complete a proposal (ibid s.51). See INSURANCE BROKER; INSURANCE INTERMEDIARY; INSURANCE OMBUDSMAN; PAYMENT TO AN AGENT; PREMIUM; TIED INSURANCE AGENT.

**insurance and building societies.** Insurance is a *financial service* which a building society may be empowered to provide: Building Societies Act 1989 s.29(2)(g). However, a society must not carry on insurance business otherwise than by a subsidiary or other associated body of the society except where it acts as an insurance intermediary (qv) (ibid s.29(4) as inserted by Housing (Miscellaneous Provisions) Act 1992 s.30).

A building society is prohibited from requiring a member to effect insurance on any security for a loan with an insurer directed by the society or through the agency of the society or of any intermediary directed by the society: Building Societies Act 1986 s.6(1)(c); SI No 27 of 1987; SI No 339 of 1987. Notwithstanding the repeal of the 1986 Act, this provision continues in force (ibid 1989

Act s.6). Any dispute between a member and the society in relation to this matter is to be determined by the Central Bank.

Also continuing in force is the requirement that a society arrange through an insurer or an intermediary nominated by it for the provision of *mortgage protection insurance* in respect of secured loans, the premium to be payable by the member in monthly instalments; there are exceptions eg in respect of loans in excess of £60,000; and in respect of members who by reason of health would not be acceptable to an insurer. The Central Bank is empowered to prescribe, by regulation, rules concerning (a) removing or restricting the right of a society to require a member to effect or keep effected insurance on a housing loan with an insurer directed by the society or of any intermediary directed by the society, and (b) the arranging by a society through an insurer or intermediary nominated by it for the provision of mortgage protection insurance (ibid 1989 Act s.11(2)(b)(iii) and (v)). No such rules had been prescribed by 1993.

**insurance bond.** See INSURANCE COMPANY; INSURANCE BROKER.

**insurance broker.** A person who, acting with freedom of choice (ie being in a position to arrange insurance contracts with at least five insurance undertakings) brings together, with a view to the insurance of risks, persons seeking insurance and insurance undertakings, and carries out work preparatory to the conclusion of contracts of insurance, but does not include an *insurance agent* or an employee of an insurer when the employee is acting for that insurer: Insurance Act 1989 ss.2(1) and 44. Insurance brokers are required to meet certain qualifications eg membership of a recognised body (ibid s.44).

Insurance brokers as *insurance intermediaries* (qv) are governed by the provisions of the 1989 Act regarding such intermediaries. An insurance broker may be negligent in not advising his client to disclose material information to the insurance company: Latham v Hibernian Insurance Co and Sheridan & Co (1992 HC) 10 ILT Dig 266. See Chariot Inns Ltd v Assicurazioni Generali SPA (1981) ILRM 173. Contrast with INSURANCE AGENT. [Text: Ellis]. See INSURANCE INTER-

MEDIARY.

**insurance business.** Insurance business is carried out by insurance companies which are governed by the Insurance Acts 1909 to 1989, and by registered friendly societies which are governed by the Friendly Societies Act 1896-1977, and by subsidiaries or other associated bodies of building societies which are governed by the Building Societies Act 1989. These Acts and regulations made under the European Communities Act 1972, provide the statutory base for supervision by the State in the interest of policy holders. Insurance companies must hold an *authorisation*, maintain a *bond* with the High Court and make annual returns.

The supervising powers of the Minister have been updated and clarified, a system of regulation of insurance brokers and agents has been introduced, and the Minister has been given power to regulate commission payments to insurance intermediaries (qv): Insurance Act 1989. See also European Communities (Non-Life Insurance) Regulations 1976 (SI No 115 of 1976); European Communities (Life Assurance) Regulations 1984 (SI No 57 of 1984). See also RSC O.113. See INSURANCE AGENT; INSURANCE BROKER; COMMISSION.

**insurance compensation fund.** The fund established by the Insurance Act 1964. The right to compensation via the fund, for refunds of premiums or payment of unsatisfied claims to policyholders or claimants of an insurance company being wound up, is restricted to 65% of unsatisfied claims or £650,000 per claim, whichever is the lesser: Insurance Act 1989 s.31.

**insurance intermediary.** An insurance broker or an insurance agent: Insurance Act 1989 s.2(1). Insurance intermediaries are required to keep a separate client bank account (ibid s.48) and to hold a bond in a specified form to a value of not less than £25,000 which, in the event that the intermediary fails to meet his financial obligations, will be available for the benefit of his clients who have thereby suffered loss (ibid s.47).

The Minister may provide by regulation that a person must not act or hold himself out to be an insurance agent or broker unless he effects a policy of *professional indemnity insurance* as the Minister may prescribe (ibid s.45).

Also an insurance intermediary is disqualified from acting as such if adjudged bankrupt (qv); of if convicted of an offence involving fraud (qv) or dishonesty, whether connected with insurance or not; or if he is or was a director in a company involved in insurance which has been wound up (ibid ss.54-55).

Every insurance undertaking is required to keep a register of its appointed insurance intermediaries (ibid s.50). See INSURANCE AGENT; INSURANCE AND BUILDING SOCIETY; INSURANCE BROKER; INSURANCE OMBUDSMAN.

**insurance of unnamed persons.** See UNNAMED PERSONS, INSURANCE OF.

**insurance ombudsman.** An independent and impartial arbitrator of unresolved disputes or claims between a personal policy holder and his insurance company in respect of any insurance taken out in Ireland. The ombudsman can deal with such matters where the amount in dispute is £100,000 or less, or, where the policy concerns permanent health, the basic benefits insured are £10,000 or less per annum.

The Ombudsman cannot deal with (a) any dispute about life assurance which concerns the actuarial standards, tables and principles which the insurance company applies, including the method of calculating surrender values and paid up policy values, and the bonus system and bonus rates applicable; (b) disputes relating to acts or omissions of insurance intermediaries other than those for which the insurance company bears full legal responsibility (eg tied insurance agents); (c) time barred matters; (d) matters more appropriate to a court of law.

The insurance ombudsman is empowered to make a judgment against an insurance company of up to £100,000 which is binding on the company but not on the policy holder. This non-statutory scheme was established in 1992. [Insurance Ombudsman of Ireland, 77 Merrion Square, Dublin 2. Tel: 6620899; Fax 6620890].

**insured.** Includes a person who is indemnified by another (the insurer) against loss resulting to him on the happening of an event.

**insurer.** The person who indemnifies

another (the insured) against loss, in consideration of a premium (qv). An insurer domiciled in a *contracting* state of the EC may be sued in the courts of the state where he is domiciled, or in another contracting state in the courts for the place where the policy-holder is domiciled: Jurisdiction of Courts and Enforcement of Judgments (European Communities) Act 1988, first schedule, arts.8-12a. See VEHICLE INSURER, PROCEEDING AGAINST.

**insurer, administrator of.** See ADMINISTRATOR OF INSURANCE.

**intangible property.** A *chose* in action as compared with corporeal property, such as goods. See CHOSE.

**integrated pollution control.** A single system of licensing to replace separate air and water pollution licensing systems: Environmental Protection Agency Act 1992 Part IV (ss.82-99). A person who carries out an activity listed in the *First Schedule* of the 1992 Act may only do so pursuant to a licence issued by the Agency (ibid s.82). The activities listed include activities relating to minerals, energy, metals, mineral fibres and glass, chemicals, intensive agriculture, food and drink, wood, paper, textiles, leather, fossil fuels, cement, waste, surface coatings, testing of engines, lime, and printed circuit boards.

Procedures for the processing of applications for licences are specified, with provision for notification of the relevant planning authority and for objections, time limits, and possible oral hearing (ibid ss.85-86). There is also provision for review of licences and a register of licences (ibid ss.88-89). A charge may be imposed by the Agency in respect of emissions (ibid s.93).

The Agency must obtain the consent of the relevant sanitary authority in relation to a licence which it proposes to grant which involves a discharge of any trade effluent or other matter (other than domestic sewage or storm water) to a sewer (ibid s.97).

**intellectual property.** Personal property which is given limited protection by the law eg patents, designs, trade marks, copyright, and know-how (qqv). The law attempts to balance the need to reward human ingenuity and inventiveness on the one hand, with the promotion of the public good on the other hand. [Text: ICEL]. See TOPOGRAPHY RIGHT.

**intensive agriculture.** The rearing (a) of poultry in installations where the capacity exceeds 100,000 units (1 broiler = 1 unit; 1 layer, turkey or other fowl = 2 units); (b) of pigs in installations where the capacity exceeds 1,000 units in gley soils or 3,000 units on other soils (1 pig = 1 unit; 1 sow = 10 units): Environmental Protection Agency Act 1992, first schedule. Intensive agriculture is an activity to which Part IV of the 1992 Act applies ie it is subject to *integrated pollution control* (qv).

**intensification of use.** See PLANNING PERMISSION.

**intention.** The general rule of law is that a person is presumed to intend the natural reasonable and probable consequences of his acts, whether in fact he intended them or not. See People (DPP) v Farrell (1993 CCA) ITLR (5 Apr). For ascertaining the intention of parties to a contract for the sale of goods, as to the time at which property in the goods passes to the buyer, see rules in GOODS, PROPERTY IN. See also MALICE; MENS REA; MURDER.

**inter alia.** [Among other things].

**inter alios.** [Among other persons].

**inter arma leges silent.** [Between armies the law is silent]. See WAR CRIMES.

**inter partes.** [Between parties].

**inter se.** [Among themselves].

**inter vivos.** [During life; between living persons].

**interception of aircraft.** There are detailed provisions for the interception (including required landing) of civil aircraft flying without authority or being used for any purpose inconsistent with the 1944 Chicago Convention on International Civil Aviation: Air Navigation (Interception of Aircraft) Order 1990 (SI No 12 of 1990). See Air Navigation and Transport Act 1988 ss.38-39.

**intercourse, sexual.** See SEXUAL INTERCOURSE.

**interesse termini.** [Interest of a term].

**interest.** (1) A right in property.

(2) Rights, titles, advantages, duties and liabilities connected with a thing, whether present or future, ascertained or potential.

(3) Interest on judgment debts under the Debtors (Ireland) Act 1840 s.26 has

been reduced from 11 per cent to 8 per cent as from 23rd January 1989: Courts Act 1981 (Interest on Judgment Debts) Order 1989 (SI No 12 of 1989).

(4) Interest on a dishonoured cheque may be claimed from the time of its presentment for payment: Bills of Exchange Act 1882 s.57(1).

(5) A sum of money payable in respect of the use of another sum of money called the principal. The interest charged by a building society on a mortgage loan provides the cover for the interest paid by the society to its shareholders and depositors.

In a company which is being wound up, interest upon debts of the company which carry interest, ceases to run from the date of commencement of the winding up, unless the assets are sufficient to pay all the debts in full: In re International Contract Company Ltd Hughes Claim (1872) LR 13 Eq 623. See also Daly v Allied Irish Banks (1987) HC; McCairns (PMPA) (In Liquidation) (1992 SC) ILRM 19. See COMPENSATION AND COMPULSORY PURCHASE; INSOLVENT COMPANY; INTEREST ON JUDGMENTS.

**interest, disclosure of.** The duty imposed by law on certain persons to disclose their interest in a matter eg the duty of a director of a company to disclose the nature of his interest in any contract between himself and his company. See ARMS LENGTH, AT; COUNCILLOR, DISCLOSURE OF INTEREST.

**interest and bankruptcy.** Where interest is reserved or agreed for on a debt which is overdue at the date of adjudication of a bankrupt, the creditor is entitled to prove or be admitted as a creditor for such interest up to the date of the adjudication: Bankruptcy Act 1988 s.75(2). See BANKRUPTCY.

**interest and social welfare.** By agreement with the Ombudsman (qv), compensation based on the consumer price index is paid in respect of social welfare payments which are over two years late: Annual Report of Ombudsman 1986 pp.16 and 36.

**interest and tax.** Interest may be awarded on overpaid tax: Navan Carpets v O'Culachain (1988 SC) IR 164. Interest on an overpayment of tax (based on an assessment to tax which is reduced by the High or Supreme Court) is to be calculated by applying the rate applicable under the Courts Act 1981: Texaco (Ireland) Ltd v Murray (1992 SC) ILRM 304. Interest received by a company on advance payments on the sale of goods abroad is not *income from the sale of goods* so exported: Kerrane v Hanlon (Ir) Ltd (1987) HC. See DEPOSIT INTEREST RETENTION TAX.

**interest on awards.** See AWARD.

**interest on judgments.** A court may award interest at 8 per cent from the date of entering up judgment until satisfaction of the judgment: Debtors (Ireland) Act 1840 s.26; Courts Act 1981 s.19(1); SI No 12 of 1989. Judgments on amounts not exceeding £150 do not carry interest (ibid 1981 Act s.23). The rate of interest may be changed by the Minister (ibid 1981 Act s.20(1)). A judge is empowered to award interest between the date the cause of action accrued and the date of judgment (ibid 1981 Act s.22). Only a *judge* can order the payment of such interest and not the Master of the High Court: Mellowhide Products Ltd v Barry Agencies Ltd (1983) ILRM 152.

Interest may also be awarded for the period between a breach of contract and the date of judgment; however the sum must be a *liquidated* or certain amount and the creditor must have served notice in writing of intention to claim interest. Interest on a dishonoured cheque may be claimed from the time of its presentment for payment: Bills of Exchange Act 1882 s.57(1). Interest has been awarded on the recoupment of capital outlay at the average of the overdraft and deposit rates: Dwyer Nolan Developments v Dublin County Council (1986) IR 130.

For interest on judgments obtained in other *contracting* EC states being enforced in this State, see Jurisdiction of Courts and Enforcement of Judgments (European Communities) Act 1988 s.8. In relation to interest on legal costs, see Lambert v Lambert (1987) ILRM 390. See 1840 Act s.53 and 1981 Act s.22. See East Cork Foods v O'Dwyer Steel Co (1978) IR 103; Incorporated Food Products Ltd v Minister for Agriculture (1984) HC. See ACCUMULATION; BREACH OF TRUST; COMPOUND INTEREST; MONEYLENDER; PRE-JUDGMENT INTEREST.

**interest reipublicae ne maleficia re-**

**maneant impunita.** [It is a matter of public concern that wrongdoings are not left unpunished].

**interest reipublicae ne sua re quis male utatur.** [It concerns the state that no one should make a wrongful use of his property].

**interest reipublicae ut sit finis litium.** [It concerns the state that litigation be not protracted]. See FINALITY IN LITIGATION.

**interference.** It is an offence to interfere with the military or police force by violence, with the intent of undermining public order, or the authority of the State: Offences Against the State Act 1939 s.9.

**interference with goods.** See CONVERSION; DETINUE; TRESPASS TO GOODS.

**interim.** In the meantime.

**interim injunction.** See INJUNCTION.

**interim order.** An order of the Court, made in the course of proceedings, pending further directions from the Court.

**interlineation.** See ALTERATION.

**interlocutory.** Not final.

**interlocutory applications.** Applications to the court, made during the course of an action between entry of appearance and close of pleadings for orders, with a view to assisting either party in the prosecution of his case eg orders for discovery of documents, interpleader, and security for costs (qqv). The right of a litigant to seek and obtain an order of inspection is in no way dependent upon the court being satisfied as to the strength of his case: Bula Ltd v Tara Mines (1987) IR 85. For interlocutory applications in the Circuit Court, see RCC O.17. See also INJUNCTION.

**interlocutory injunction.** See INJUNCTION.

**intermediary.** See INSURANCE INTERMEDIARY; THIRD PARTY INFORMATION.

**intermixture of chattels.** The intermingling of chattels so that the several portions are no longer distinguishable. Where by agreement, the chattels of two persons are intermixed, they become *tenants-in-common* in proportion to their respective shares. This also occurs where a bailee intermixes bailed chattels with his own, except that the bailee will be liable for any costs associated with separating the chattels into shares. See TENANCY IN COMMON.

**internal market.** As regards the European Economic Community, means an area without internal frontiers in which the free movement of goods, persons, services and capital is assured in accordance with the provisions of the Treaty of Rome 1957. The Community is required to adopt measures with the aim of progressively establishing the *internal market* over a period which expired on 31st December 1992 (ibid art.8A as inserted by art.13 of the Single European Act). See SINGLE EUROPEAN ACT.

**international agreements.** Every international agreement to which the State becomes a party must be laid before Dail Eireann; the State is not bound by any such agreement involving a *charge on public funds* unless the term of the agreement has been approved by the Dail: 1937 Constitution, art.29(5). This does not apply to agreements or conventions of a technical or administrative character (ibid art.29(5)(3)). See State (Gilliland) v Governor of Mountjoy Prison (1987) ILRM 278. See DOUBLE TAXATION AGREEMENTS.

**international carriage of goods.** See CMR.

**international carriage of passengers.** Regulations on revised common rules for the international carriage of passengers by coach and bus, within member States, have been made, implementing Council Regulation 684/92 and Commission Regulation 1839/92: European Communities (International Carriage of Passengers) Regulations 1992 (SI No 341 of 1992).

**international carriage of perishable foodstuffs.** There is legislative provision for (a) the laying down of technical standards for the thermal efficiency of insulated, refrigerated, mechanically refrigerated or heated equipment used in the international carriage of perishable foodstuffs; (b) the testing of such equipment and its certification; and (c) the requirement that only equipment complying with specified standards will be used in the international carriage of perishable foodstuffs: International Carriage of Perishable Foodstuffs Act 1987. See Consolidated Regulations 1993 (SI No 188 of 1993).

**international classification of goods.**

The classification of goods in the International Classification adopted under the Nice Agreement of 15 June 1957 as revised at Stockholm on 14 July 1967 and at Geneva on 13 May 1977. This classification is used in the registration of trade marks (qv); a trade mark must be registered in respect of particular goods or classes of goods, and any question arising as to the class within which any goods falls is decided by the Controller of Trade Marks: Trade Marks Act 1963.s.11.

**international copyright.** See BERNE COPYRIGHT UNION; UNIVERSAL COPYRIGHT CONVENTION.

**International Court of Justice.** The principal judicial organ of the United Nations: UN Charter, art.92. The court, sometimes called the World Court, is composed of fifteen members sitting at The Hague, no two of whom may be nationals of the same state; they are to be independent and are elected regardless of nationality by the General Assembly and Security Council of the UN. The Court has jurisdiction over all matters specifically provided for in the UN Charter or in treaties and conventions in force, and over all cases which the parties refer to it. Although the court has no power to impose sanctions or to enforce its judgments, it is understood that all of its decisions have been followed, the exception being Corfu Channel Case (United Kingdom v Albania) (1949) ICJ 4. See UNITED NATIONS.

**International Development Association.** An affiliate of the World Bank which provides loans to the world's poorest countries at low or zero rates of interest. See International Development Association Acts 1960 to 1990.

**International Covenants of UN.** See HUMAN RIGHTS COVENANTS.

**international hallmark.** See HALLMARK.

**international haulage.** See CARRIER'S LICENCE.

**international hire-purchase agreement.** See INTERNATIONAL SALE OF GOODS.

**international law.** The body of legal rules applying between states. Ireland accepts the generally recognised principles of international law as its rule of conduct in its relations with other States: 1937 Constitution art.29(3). This refers only to public international law: Heder-

man J in W v W (1993 SC) ILRM 294. The rules which define the rights and duties as between the citizens of different states is known as *private international law* (qv) or *conflict of laws*.

**international road freight licence.** See CARRIER'S LICENCE.

**international sale of goods.** A contract for the international sale of goods is a contract made by parties whose place of business (or, if they have none, habitual residences) are in territories of different states and one of three other conditions are satisfied. Such a contract may negative or vary any right or duty or liability which would otherwise arise by implication of law. See Sale of Goods Act 1893 s.61(6) and SGSS Act 1980 s.24. A similar provision exists for international hire-purchase agreements (ibid s.37).

**internment.** Deprivation of liberty without trial. Internment has been upheld as not infringing the Constitution: Art.26 and the Offences Against the State (Amendment) Bill 1940 (1940) IR 470. Following proclamation by the government that specified powers are necessary to secure the preservation of public peace and order, a Minister may order for arrest and detention of a person, if he is of opinion that that person is engaged in activities prejudicial to the preservation of public peace and order or to the security of the State: Offences Against the State (Amendment) Act 1940.

It would appear now that the courts will look behind the exercise of the administrative power and that any opinion formed by the Minister must be one which is bona fide held and factually sustainable and not unreasonable: The State (Lynch) v Cooney (1983) ILRM 89. Also discovery (qv) may be ordered of documents, relating to the internment of a person, which could be regarded as confidential and sensitive but not as involving national security: Gormley v Ireland (1992 HC) 10 ILT Dig 200. See EUROPEAN COURT OF HUMAN RIGHTS; PREVENTATIVE DETENTION; PRISONER OF WAR.

**interpleader.** A procedure whereby a person (who is sued, or expects to be sued, by rival claimants to property which is in his possession and in which he claims no interest and he knows not to whom he can safely give it up), can compel the claimants to *interplead* ie to take proceedings between themselves to determine who is entitled to it. This is a *stakeholder's interpleader* eg where a bank holds money to which there are opposing claims. Similarly, a *sheriff's interpleader* arises where goods, taken by the sheriff under an order of fi fa (qv), are claimed by a third party. See RSC O.57. For interpleader provisions in the Circuit and District Courts, see respectively RCC O.39; DCR rr.188-189. See also Courts Act 1991 s.5.

**interpretatio chartarum benigne facienda est ut res magis valeat quam pereat.** [The construction of deeds is to be made liberally, that the thing may rather avail than perish].

**interpretation clause.** A clause, eg in a statute or deed, which provides that certain specified words and phrases used therein have certain meanings eg *In this Act, except where the context otherwise requires, "valuable consideration" means consideration in money or money's worth*: Succession Act 1965 s.3(1).

**interpretation of legislation.** See LEGISLATION, INTERPRETATION OF

**interpreters.** See LANGUAGE; OATH, INTERPRETER'S.

**interrogation.** Questioning of suspects. The Minister may provide by regulations for the electronic recording of questioning of persons in police custody: Criminal Justice Act 1984 s.27. See JUDGES' RULES; EXAMINATION; SOLICITOR, ACCESS TO.

**interrogatories.** Written questions, answerable on affidavit, which a party may, with leave, put to the other party to an action. Their purpose is to obtain admissions and to limit the scope of an opponent's case. Answers to interrogatories are binding. See Heaton v Goldney (1910) 1 KB 758. See RSC O.31.

**interrogatories, fishing.** Written questions to elicit answers to support a case which is lacking in substance; a party will not be required to answer such questions. See Pankhurst v Hamilton (1886) 2 TLR 682. See RSC O.31.

**intervener.** A person who voluntarily intervenes in an action with the leave of the court or the Master of the High Court: RSC O.63 r.1(13). It may occur in actions for recovery of land (RSC O.12 r.20), in matrimonial causes (RSC O.70.r.19), in probate actions (RSC O.12 r.14) and in Admiralty actions *in rem* (RSC O.64 r.14).

**intervening act.** See CAUSATION; NOVUS ACTUS INTERVENIENS.

**interview, employment.** Questions asked at an employment interview concerning *marital status* can constitute discrimination contrary to the Employment Equality Act 1977 s.2(a) and 3: Medical Council & Barrington EE9/1988; Trinity College Dublin & McGhee EE1/1988 in 7ILT & SJ (1989) 126.

**intestacy.** Dying intestate ie without making a valid will. Partial intestacy is the leaving of a will which validly disposes of part only of the property of the deceased, so that the rest goes on an intestacy. Equity (qv) leans against an intestacy: In re Estate of Egan (1990) 8ILT Dig 168. See SUCCESSION, LAW OF; INTESTATE SUCCESSION.

**intestate succession.** The residuary estate of an intestate devolves according to the Succession 1965 ss.66 to 73 under rules which apply to both real and personal property:

(1) If there is a surviving spouse and issue, then the spouse takes two-thirds and the issue take one-third.

(2) If there is a surviving spouse and no issue, the spouse takes all.

(3) If there are issue and no spouse, the issue take all; if they are in equal relationship to the deceased, the distribution is in equal shares among them; if they are not, it is *per stirpes* (qv).

(4) If there are no surviving issue or spouse, the parents of the deceased take all in equal shares; if only one parent survives, that parent takes all.

(5) In the event that there are no such survivors, the estate is distributed among brothers and sisters in equal shares. If a brother or sister does not survive the intestate, the children of that brother or sister (where any other brother or sister survive) represent their parent and divide his or her share. If the intestate leaves no surviving brothers or sisters, his estate is distributed in equal shares among the children of his brothers and sisters and not *per stirpes*.

(6) In all other cases, the estate is distributed in equal shares among the next-of-kin.

(7) In default of next-of-kin, the estate passes to the State as ultimate intestate

successor. See LETTERS OF ADMINISTRATION; NEXT-OF-KIN.

**intimidation, tort of.** Arises where harm is inflicted by the use of *unlawful threats* whereby the lawful liberty of others to do as they please is interfered with. It may arise by intimidation of other persons which results in injury to the plaintiff. To constitute the tort there must be a threat, the threat must be to do an unlawful act, and there must be a submission to the threat. See Rookes v Barnard (1964) AC 1129; Whelan v Madigan (1978) HC.

**intoxicated.** Under proposed draft legislation, means under the intoxicating influence of any alcoholic drink, drug, solvent or other substance or a combination of substances: Criminal Justice (Public Order) Bill 1993 s.4. It is proposed to be an offence for a person to be present in any public place while being intoxicated to such an extent as to give rise to a reasonable apprehension that he might endanger himself or any other person in his vicinity (ibid s.4(1)).

**intoxicating liquor.** An application for a declaration that a premises is fit and convenient to receive a transfer of an *intoxicating liquor licence*, can be refused on the grounds that it would have a material adverse effect on the businesses in the neighbourhood: Intoxicating Liquor Act 1960 s.14 and Application of Thank God It's Friday Ltd (1990) ILRM 228. It has been held that a theatre premises is not a suitable premises within the meaning of the Licensing (Ireland) Act 1902 s.3 (as amended) for the grant of a full ordinary seven day publican's licence: In re an Application by Tivoli Cinema Ltd (1992 HC) ILRM 522.

Restaurants may serve beer, spirits and liqueurs with meals, provided the restaurant has a *special licence:* Intoxicating Liquor Act 1988; Special Restaurant Licence (Standards) Regulations 1988 (SI No 147 of 1988).

It is an offence for a person under the age of 18 years to buy alcoholic liquor and for a publican to supply alcohol to such a person; the previous requirement that to constitute an offence the publican had to supply *knowingly,* has been removed (ibid 1988 Act). See Jaggers Restaurant Ltd v Aherne (1988 SC) IR

308. [Text: McDonald; Woods (3)]. See OFF-LICENCE.

**intoxicating liquor licence renewal.** New procedures for the renewal of intoxicating liquor licences and registered club certificates have been in operation since 1988. It is no longer necessary to produce a certificate of the District Court to the Revenue Commissioners, except in specified circumstances eg where a notice of objection has been lodged. Certain licensed hotels now require a certificate from Bord Failte, and club certificates are renewable at the annual licensing District Court and not, as heretofore from the date of issue or date of last renewal. Also a *tax clearance certificate* is now required before a licence will be renewed at the annual licensing: Finance Act 1992 s.242. See Courts (No 2) Act 1986; District Court (Renewal of Intoxicating Liquor Licences) Rules 1988 (SI No 145 of 1988).

**intra vires.** [Within the power of]. See ULTRA VIRES.

**intrinsic.** Essential to, or inherent in, something.

**inure.** Enure; to take effect.

**invasion.** The government is empowered to take whatever steps they consider may be necessary for the protection of the State in the case of an actual invasion: 1937 Constitution, art.28(3)(2).

**invented word.** For the purpose of registration of a trade mark in Part A of the register, a word which is new, which is pronounceable and which has no obvious meaning for an Irishman: In re ACEC (Ireland) Ltd (1964) IR 201. It has been held that the time to be considered as to whether a word is an invented word or not, is the date of the application to register the word and not the date of the hearing: Willys-Overland Motors Inc v Controller of Industrial Property (1947) IR 344. Words such as *cosco, SAF, Jeep,* and *Zing* have been held to be invented words, whereas *Gramaphone* and *cellular* have not been so held. See also In re Hamilton Cosco Inc (1966) IR 266; La Soudure Autogene Francaise v Controller of Patents, Designs and Trade Marks (1982) ILRM 207; Application of Schweppes (Overseas) Ltd (1970) IR 2O9. See DISTINCTIVE MARK; PART A.

**invention.** An invention is not defined in

the Patents Act 1992, although certain matters are excluded (eg an aesthetic creation) and certain requirements are specified for an invention to be patentable eg *new*, involving an *inventive step*, and being susceptible of *industrial application*. Micro-organisms produced by genetic engineering are not excluded from patent protection: National Research Development Corporation's Application (1986) FSR 620, distinguishing Ranks Hovis McDougall Ltd v Controller of Patents (1979) IR 142. See INVENTOR; PATENTABLE INVENTION; MICRO-ORGANISMS; SIMULTANE-OUS INVENTION.

**inventive step.** See PATENTABLE INVENTION.

**inventor.** The actual deviser of an invention: Patents Act 1992 s.2(1). The right to a patent belongs to the inventor or his successor in title; where the inventor is an employee, the right to a patent depends on the law of the State where the employee is employed eg in Ireland in the absence of any express term to the contrary, the employee is presumed to be a trustee for his employer in any invention made in the course of his duty as an employee (ibid s.16). The inventor is entitled to be mentioned as such in any patent granted for the invention (ibid s.17).

**investigation of company.** There are three main investigations which may be made of a company: (a) an investigation of the affairs of a company ordered by the court; (b) an investigation of the true ownership of a company ordered by the Minister, and (c) an examination of company documents without an inspector being appointed: Companies Act 1990 ss.7-24.

(a) The High Court is empowered to appoint inspectors to investigate the affairs of a company on the application of the company, a director, a creditor, or a certain minimum number of members (ibid s.7). In addition, the court may on the application of the Minister appoint inspectors if it is satisfied that there are circumstances suggesting illegality or fraud or of some members being unfairly prejudiced (ibid s.8). The inspectors have wide powers regarding the production of books relating to the company, directors' private bank accounts, and attendance before the inspectors for examination on oath

(ibid ss.9-10). The court having considered the Inspectors' Report, may make such order as it deems fit, including the winding up of a body corporate or the remedying of any disability; the Minister may also present a winding up petition (ibid s.12).

(b) The Minister may appoint inspectors to investigate the membership of any company for the purpose of determining the *true persons* (qv) who are financially interested in the success or failure of the company or able to control or materially to influence the policy of the company (ibid s.14). The inspectors appointed have similar powers to those appointed by the court, except in respect of access to private bank accounts. An inspector can compel production of documents which pre-date the 1990 Act: Chestervale Properties & Hoddle Investments v Glackin & Ors (1992 HC) ILRM 221. An inspector is entitled to "tear the veil of secrecy of ownership from the company" and identify those financially interested in its success or failure, even where the company was registered outside the State: Desmond & Dedeir Ltd v Glackin (1992 SC) ITLR (7 Dec).

An inspector is not required to accept averments (made by a person he wishes to examine on oath) as *prima facie* evidence of their truth: Probets & Freezone Investments Ltd v Glackin (1993 SC) 11 ILT Dig 114. A financial institution must comply with a request for information made by an inspector and does not have to consult with its client; the 1990 Act overrides any question of confidentiality: Glackin v Trustee Savings Bank (1993 HC) 11 ILT Dig 114. See also Lyons v Curran (1993 HC) ILRM 375; Minister for Justice v Siuicre Eireann cpt (1993 HC) 11 ILT Dig 114.

(c) The Minister, without the appointment of inspectors, can compel a wide variety of companies to produce the documents he specifies (ibid ss.19-20). He can also compel disclosure of information as to the persons interested in shares or debentures (ibid s.15). See also Building Societies Act 1989 ss.45-47. See EXAMINATION RE COMPANY.

**investment funds, designated.** Funds in a scheme whereby each participant owns a particular share in a particular company, and in which all subscriptions must be paid up by a specific date, after which no new entrants may join. See Designated Funds Act 1985.

**investment company.** A company limited by shares, the sole object of which is the collective investment of its funds in property with the aim of spreading investment risk and giving members of the company the benefit of the management of its funds: Companies Act 1990 s.253(2). The shareholders may call for the shares to be bought in by the company at any time. A company which falls within the definition of a UCITS is excluded but certain of the UCITS regulations apply to an investment company. To facilitate the operation of these investment companies with variable capital, certain provisions of company law do not apply; however, such companies must be authorised by the Central Bank and are subject to constant supervision by the Bank. See 1990 Act Part XIII ss.252-262. See UNDERTAKINGS FOR COLLECTIVE INVESTMENT IN TRANSFERABLE SECURITIES.

**investment incentive scheme.** A scheme introduced in 1993 to encourage the start-up of new businesses by providing tax relief of £25,000 per year on a retrospective basis against income of any three of the preceding five years to a person who leaves employment (or an unemployed person) to start his own business: Finance Act 1993 s.25. This in practice will allow immediate relief by way of a tax refund on investments up to £75,000. See also BUSINESS DEVELOPMENT SCHEME.

**investment trust company.** A company whose main business consists of the investment of its funds in securities: Central Bank Act 1971 s.2. An investment trust company may not accept or hold deposits: Industrial & Provident Societies (Amendment) Act 1978 s.36. See In re Irish Commercial Society Group (1987) HC.

**investments, trustee.** See TRUSTEE INVESTMENTS.

**inviolability of dwelling.** The *dwelling* of every citizen is inviolable and must not be forcibly entered save in accordance with law: 1937 Constitution, art.40(5). In a case where members of a family live together in the family home, the house as a whole is the *dwelling* of each member of the family; however, if a member of a family occupies a clearly defined portion of the house apart from the other members of the family, then it may well be that the part not so occupied is no longer his dwelling and that the part he separately occupies is his dwelling, as would be the case where a person not a member of the family occupied or was in possession of a clearly defined portion of the house: The People (AG) v O'Brien (1965) IR 142. See also DPP v Gaffney (1988) ILRM 39; McCormack v ICS Building Society (1989 HC); People (DPP) v Kenny (1990 SC) ILRM 569. See also DIPLOMATIC PRIVILEGE; DRUNKEN DRIVING; RECOVERY OF MOTOR VEHICLE.

**invitation to treat.** An offer to receive an offer eg an advertisement to receive tenders. An advertisement or an invitation to make an offer is not an offer which is capable of being turned into a contract by acceptance. A shopkeeper who displays goods in his window with a ticket on them stating a price, does not make an offer for sale, the acceptance of which constitutes a contract; he merely invites the public to make an offer to buy the goods at the price stated. See Fisher v Bell (1961) 1 QB 394; Minister for Industry and Commerce v Pim (1966) IR 154. See COPYRIGHT; OFFER; TENDER.

**invitee.** See OCCUPIER'S LIABILITY TO INVITEES.

**invoices.** See DIRECTORY ENTRIES; UNSOLICITED GOODS.

**involuntary bailment.** Where a person takes possession of a chattel involuntarily (eg a parcel left mistakenly at one's residence), he is the *bailee* of that chattel for the owner. He will be liable to the owner for wilful damage thereto. See Lethbridge v Phillips (1819) 2 Stark 544. See BAILMENT

**IOU.** [I owe you]. A written admission of a debt with an implied undertaking that the debt will be repaid sometime. It is not a negotiable instrument (qv). If it contains a written undertaking to repay at some date it could amount to a promissory note (qv).

**ipse dixit.** [He himself said it].

**ipsissima verba.** [The identical words].

**ipso facto.** [By the mere fact]. By the nature of the case.

**ipso jure.** [By the law itself]. By operation of the law.

**Ireland.** The name of the State in the English language: 1937 Constitution, art.4; Ellis v O'Dea & Shiels (1990 SC) ITLR (8 Jan). An injunction cannot issue against the entity *Ireland*: Pesca Valentia Ltd v Minister for Fisheries (1986) ILRM 68. See STATE.

**Iris Oifigiuil.** The official organ of the government for announcing appointments to public offices and publishing proclamations, statutory instruments, appointment of receivers to companies etc. It is usually published every Tuesday and Friday. Prima facie evidence of any proclamation, order, rule, regulation, byelaw, or other official document may be given in any legal proceedings by production of a copy of the Iris purported to contain such matter: Documentary Evidence Act 1925 ss.3-4. Notices in relation to many matters concerning companies must be published in the Iris within six weeks of the delivery to the Registrar of Companies: SI No 163 of 1973; Companies Amendment Act 1983 s.55. Iris Oifigiuil replaced the Dublin Gazette in 1922: Adaptation of Enactments Act 1922 s.3.

**Irish Aviation Authority.** Under proposed draft legislation, a private limited company, owned by the Minister for Finance, which will have the following functions: (a) the management of Irish airspace, (b) the operation of air navigation services and aeronautical communication services, (c) the regulation of safety aspects of civil aviation, and (d) the implementation of certain international agreements in relation to the safety of civil aviation: Irish Aviation Authority Bill 1993. See AIR LAW.

**Irish Centre for European Law; ICEL.** A charitable company established in May 1988 which has the following objectives: (a) evaluation of the effects of EC law on Irish law; (b) preparing Irish lawyers and other professional advisers to be more competitive in EC law; (c) liaison with EC and Council of Europe institutions; (d) providing a forum for examining practical legal issues between EC and EFTA countries. [ICEL, Trinity College, Dublin 2]. See APPENDIX 3.

**Irish Copyright Licensing Agency.** A recent non-profit making company, limited by guarantee, representative of publishers and authors, incorporated with the objective of acting as a clearing centre between owners and users of copyright material. It will provide users such as schools, universities and libraries with an easy means of obtaining permission to copy and will pass on the fees collected to publishers and authors. See Quinn AP in ILSI Gaz (Apr 1993). See PERFORMING RIGHTS SOCIETY LTD.

**Irish Free State.** See SAORSTAT EIREANN; TREATY, THE.

**Irish language.** See LANGUAGE; TEACHER.

**Irish music rights.** See PERFORMING RIGHTS SOCIETY LTD.

**irrationality, test of.** The test which the court may apply in a judicial review (qv) of the decision of administrative action. Also referred to as the *test of unreasonableness*. The test lies in considering whether the impugned administrative decision (a) is fundamentally at variance with reason and common sense; (b) is indefensible for being in the teeth of plain reason and common sense, and that the court is satisfied (c) that the decision-maker has breached his obligation whereby he must not flagrantly reject or disregard fundamental reason or commonsense in reaching his decision:: The State (Keegan) v Stardust Victims Tribunal (1986) IR 642.

In order for the court to intervene and quash the decision, the applicant must establish that the decision-making authority had before it no relevant material which would support its decision: O'Keefe v An Bord Pleanala & Radio Tara (1992 SC) ILRM 237. A regulation made under an Act may be held to be ultra vires the Act for unreasonableness where it lacks any logical basis: McHugh v AB (1993 SC) 11 ILT Dig 28.

**irrebuttable presumptions.** Inferences which cannot be rebutted as evidence to contradict them is not allowed eg the presumption what a child under the age of seven is incapable of committing a crime. See PRESUMPTION.

**irresistible impulse.** A person is said to act under an *irresistible impulse* to do an act when, from disease of mind, he is incapable of restraining himself from doing it, although he may know at the time of committing it that the act was wrong: Attorney General v O'Brien

(1936) IR 263. It is a defence of insanity which must be proved on the balance of probability. See AUTOMATISM; INSANITY.

**irrevocable.** Incapable of being revoked. See POWER OF ATTORNEY.

**irrevocable letter of credit.** See LETTER OF CREDIT.

**island, polling on.** Provision has been made for taking an election poll on an island on any of the five days before the polling day if the returning officer considers it desireable to do so because of weather or transport problems: Electoral Act 1992 ss.85-86. See also draft Presidential Elections Bill 1993 s.42.

**issue.** (1) In pleadings (qv), a matter which is claimed by one party and denied by the other, is said to be *at issue*.

(2) Offspring. A person's issue consists of his children, grandchildren and other lineal descendants. A gift *to A and his issue* confers a life estate only because of the failure to use the appropriate word *heirs*. The words *die without issue* are to be construed in a will as meaning a want or failure in the lifetime or at the death of the party and not an indefinite failure of issue, unless a contrary intention appears from the will: Succession Act 1965 s.96, re-enacting the Wills Act 1837 s.29.

*Issue* has been held to mean only legitimate issue and consequently illegitimate children had no succession rights on the death of their father: In the Goods of Walker dec'd (1985) ILRM 86. However, legislation in 1987 provided that relationships shall be deduced for the purposes of the Succession Act 1965 irrespective of the marital status of a person's parents: Status of Children Act 1987 s.29. *Issue* however used in a will, does not include adopted children: In re John Stamp (1993 HC) ILRM 383. See CHILD, ILLEGITIMATE; CONSTRUCTION OF DISPOSITIONS.

**issue estoppel.** "Where a clearly identifiable issue has been decided against a party in a criminal trial, by means of a judgment explaining how the decision was reached, such decision may give rise to issue estoppel in subsequent civil proceedings in which that party is involved and in the absence of special circumstances, an effort by a party to challenge by means of civil proceedings a decision made against him by a court

of competent jurisdiction is an abuse of the process of court": Kelly v Ireland (1986) ILRM 318. See also Meath County Council v Daly (1987 HC) IR 391; Breathnach v Ireland (1990) 8ILT Dig 192. See ESTOPPEL; RES JUDICATA.

**issue paper.** A formulation of the charges and indication of the issues to be determined in a trial which is given to the foreman of the jury (qv); a list of questions may be sufficient. See The People v McCormack (1944) Frewen 55.

**issued capital.** See CAPITAL.

# J

**jactitation of marriage.** [Jactitare — to boast]. A procedure by which a person (the respondent) may be prevented by court order from making false assertions of being married to another person (the petitioner). It is not a declaration of nullity and consequently cannot bind third parties. See Duchess of Kingston's case (1776) 168 ER 175. See also Law Reform Commission Report No 6 of 1983.

**jeopardy, in.** In danger of being convicted of a criminal charge. See DOUBLE JEOPARDY.

**jetsam.** Goods of a ship which are cast overboard and sink. See Larceny Act 1916 s.15. See FLOTSAM; LAGAN.

**jet skiis.** Regulations came into operation on 1st April 1993 which enable local authorities, regional fisheries boards, the Commissioners of Public Works and harbour authorities to propose areas as being unsuitable for the operation of jet skiis and fast power boats, in the interest of safety of pleasure craft and their occupants: Merchant Shipping (Jet Skiis and Fast Power Boats) Regulations 1992.

**jettison.** To throw overboard a ship's goods from necessity to lighten the vessel. See Milward v Hibbert (1842) 3 QB 120.

**jobsearch course.** It has been held that decisions to disallow unemployment assistance payments for failure to attend a jobsearch course must be based on the rules in the Social Welfare (Consolidation) Act 1981 and the requirements of natural justice: Thompson v Minister for Social Welfare (1989) IR 618.

**joinder of causes of action.** The uniting in the same action of several causes of action by a plaintiff; a defendant may apply to the court for an order confining the action to such of the causes of action as may be conveniently disposed of together. See RSC O.18. See also RCC O.6 r.1; O.8.

**joinder of defendants.** The adding of a defendant to proceedings. The court is entitled to join as a defendant a party situate outside the jurisdiction where the party could have been named as a co-defendant if the party had been situate within the jurisdiction: RSC O.11 r.1(h); Tromso Sparebank v Byrne & Ors (1990 SC) ITLR (5 Mar). See DEFENDANT; DEFENDANTS, JOINT.

**joinder of documents.** The joining of two or more documents to be read together, so as to satisfy the requirements of the Statute of Frauds (Ireland) 1695. If one of the documents is signed, it must refer to the other document, and the other document must have existed at the time of signature. See McQuaid v Lynam (1965) IR 564; Kelly v Ross & Ross (1980) HC.

**joint account.** A banking account which can be operated either singly or collectively by the parties to the account, as arranged and agreed.

Money is frequently placed in a bank or other account in the joint names of two persons, often the depositor and another person. If it appears that such a deposit is made with the intention of making a testamentary disposition without complying with the statutory provisions, the court will hold that there is a presumption of a *resulting trust* in favour of the depositor's executors: Owens v Greene (1932) IR 225; Lynch v Burke (1990 HC) 1 IR 1. Generally, parties to a joint account are entitled to share the funds in the account equally and not in proportion to their contributions to it: Jones v Maynard (1951) Ch 572. Where a joint account is in the name of a husband and wife and the husband only has contributed to it, the doctrine of *advancement* (qv) may arise. See also Murray v Murray & Anor (1939) IR 317. See DOUBLE PORTIONS; RESULTING TRUST.

**joint and several obligation.** An obligation entered into by two or more persons, jointly and severally, so that each is liable separately, and all liable jointly, and an action may be taken against one or more separately or all jointly. The obligation may arise by agreement of the parties or by operation of law. See ANTECEDENT NEGOTIATIONS; FINANCE HOUSE, LIABILITY OF.

**joint authorship.** A work of joint authorship means a work produced by the collaboration of two or more authors in which the contribution of each author is not separate from the contribution of the other author or authors: Copyright Act 1963 s.16. Joint authors or *co-authors* hold the copyright as *tenants in common* (qv) rather than as joint tenants (qv): Lauri v Renad (1892) 3 Ch 402. In the absence of agreement to the contrary, it has been held that they hold the copyright in equal undivided shares: Redwood Music Ltd v B Feldman & Co Ltd (1979) RPC 1. An author may obtain an injunction to restrain his co-author for infringing their copyright: Cescinsky v George Routledge & Sons Ltd (1916) KB 325. Copyright in works of joint authorship subsists for 50 years from the end of the year in which the sole surviving author died (ibid s.16(3)). See COPYRIGHT.

**joint defendants.** See DEFENDANTS, JOINT.

**Joint Industrial Council.** [JIC]. An association of employers and employees for a particular industry, having as its objective the promotion of harmonious relations. Provided the association fulfils certain conditions, it may be registered as a JIC by the Labour Court. See Industrial Relations Act 1946 ss.59-65.

**Joint Labour Committee.** [JLC]. A committee established by the Labour Court under the Industrial Relations Act 1946 ss.35-41 to determine minimum wages and conditions of employment for all workers covered by it. It consists of an equal number of employer and trade union representatives and of independent persons nominated by the Minister: Industrial Relations Act 1990 s.44 and fifth schedule. The committee formulates proposals for an *employment regulation order* which when agreed by the Labour Court has the effect of automatically amending the contracts of employment of all workers covered by it (ibid s.48). The committee must seriously consider objections put forward by any dissenting members or the resulting order will be invalidated: Burke v Minister for Labour (1979) IR 354. The Labour Relations Commission is required to carry out a periodic review of joint labour committees (ibid 1990 Act s.39). See also Minister for Labour v Costello (1989) ILRM 485. See EMPLOYMENT AGREEMENT.

**joint stock company.** See COMPANY; STOCK.

**joint tenancy.** The ownership of land by two or more persons where there is a *right of survivorship* ie when a joint tenant dies his interest passes to the remaining joint tenants. For this reason it is usual to make trustees joint tenants. The *four unities* of *possession, interest, title* and *time,* must exist or otherwise the ownership will be a tenancy in common (qv).

The joint tenants must have a unity of possession by which they have equal rights to possession of the whole land; they must have the identical share or interest in the land; they must have the same title by taking it from the same instrument; and their interest must have come into existence at the same time, with some exceptions.

Severance of a joint tenancy may be legal or equitable; when severence is legal, the joint tenancy is at an end; when equitable, only the beneficial interest is severed, the legal estate remaining unaffected.

A joint tenancy may be created by grant or devise *to A and B* or *to A and B jointly,* ie without words which indicate that they are to hold separate and distinct shares. A corporation, because its perpetual existence prevented the right of survivorship, originally could not be a joint tenant until the Bodies Corporate (Joint Tenancy) Act 1899. See Maher v Maher (1987) ILRM 582. See MATRIMONIAL HOME; PER MY ET PER TOUT; TENANCY IN COMMON.

**joint tortfeasors.** [Joint wrongdoers]. See CONCURRENT WRONGDOERS.

**joint venture.** A special institutionally fixed form of cooperation between undertakings: EC Commission Notice concerning the assessment of co-operative joint ventures (JV) to Art 85 EEC, OJ (1993) C43/2. A joint venture may infringe competition rules. See Compe-

tition Authority Decision No 24 on Cambridge/Imari (25 June 1993). See Travers in 11 ILT & SJ (1993) 172.

**jointress.** A woman entitled to jointure (qv).

**jointure.** A provision made by a husband for the support of his wife after his death eg an annual income during widowhood. See STRICT SETTLEMENT.

**journalist, communications with.** There is no privilege (qv) attaching to communications with a journalist: O'Brennan v Tully (1935) 69 ILTR 115; In re Kevin O'Kelly (1974) ILTR 97. A tribunal of inquiry is empowered to order a journalist to reveal the source of information on which articles published in his newspaper were based: Kiberd v Tribunal of Inquiry into the Beef Industry (1992 HC) ILRM 574. It has been held that it is improper for a judge presiding at a criminal trial to discuss in any way the trial or any aspect of it with representatives of the media, including vetting in any way the newspaper reports of the trial: DPP v Barr (No 2) (1993 CCA) 11 ILT Dig 185.

**joyriding.** Colloquial expression which may constitute the crime of taking possession of a mechanically propelled vehicle without the consent of the owner and also dangerous driving (qv): Road Traffic Act 1961 ss.53 and 112, Road Traffic Act 1968 s.51.

**judges.** Judges are appointed by the President of Ireland, on the advice of the government, to administer justice in courts: 1937 Constitution, arts.35(1) and 34(1). Judges are independent in the exercise of their judicial functions; they may not be members of the Oireachtas or hold any other office or position of emolument (ibid art.35). They may not be removed from office except for stated misbehaviour and then only upon resolutions passed by both Houses of the Oireachtas. Their remuneration cannot be reduced during their continuance in office. They enjoy immunity (qv) from action when performing their judicial functions: Macauley & Co Ltd v Wyse-Power (1943) 77 ILTR 61.

Barristers and solicitors of 10 years standing may be appointed as district court judges; barristers of 10 years standing may also be appointed as Circuit Court judges, and those of 12 years standing as High Court and Supreme Court judges. The conviction of an accused by a person who was not a judge appointed in accordance with the Constitution cannot be retrospectively validated by legislation: Courts (No 2) Act 1988 and Shelly v Mahon (1990) ITLR (23 Jul). See O'Byrne v Minister for Finance (1959) IR 1; The State (Walshe) v Murphy (1981) IR 275. See also Courts Act 1985 and Courts of Justice (District Courts) Act 1946 s.20. See CHIEF JUSTICE; DRESS IN COURT; JUDICIAL NOTICE; MODE OF ADDRESS.

**judges, temporary.** It has been held that the appointment of judges of the District Court for fixed short periods is not inconsistent with any provision of the 1937 Constitution nor does it in any way interfere with or limit their constitutionally guaranteed independence: Magee v Culligan (1992 SC) ILRM 186. See Courts (Supplemental Provisions) Act 1961 s.48.

**judge's declaration.** The declaration which every judge appointed under the Constitution must make and subscribe: *In the presence of Almighty God I do solemnly and sincerely promise and declare that I will duly and faithfully and to the best of my knowledge and power execute the office of .......... without fear or favour, affection or ill-will towards any man, and that I will uphold the Constitution and the laws. May God direct and sustain me:* 1937 Constitution, art.34(5)(1).

**judge's intervention.** A judge may intervene at a trial to maintain an even balance between the parties, but must not (eg by criticism of a witness) take over the function of counsel. See Donnelly v Timber Factors Ltd (1991 SC) 1 IR 553.

**judges' rules.** Code of guidance for police officers, drawn up by English judges in 1912 relating to questioning and charging a person suspected of having committed a crime. Five more rules were added in 1918. The rules were framed with the object of preventing confessions being improperly elicited from suspects by police officers. They do not have the force of law; a statement obtained from an accused in breach of a provision of the judges' rules is admissible provided it is a voluntary one: McCarrick v Leavy (1964) IR 225. An admission may be admissible — where a previous admission made after caution, was ruled inadmissible due to breach of the Judges' Rules: DPP v Buckley (1990) 1 IR 14. See also The People (Attorney General) v Cummins (1974) 108 ILTR 5. See CAUTION.

**judgment.** The formal decision or sentence pronounced by a court in legal proceedings; also the reasoning of the judge or judges which leads him or them to the decision. A judge may, at or after a trial, direct that judgment be entered for any or either party; no judgment may be entered after a trial without the order of the judge: RSC O.36 r.38. A judgment for the payment of money and/or costs may be registered in the Central Office (qv) within twenty-one days after the entry of the judgment.

District Court decrees may be registered in like manner as a similar judgment of the High Court: Courts Act 1981 s.25. See also Circuit Court (Registration of Judgments) Act 1937 as amended by the Courts Act 1981 s.27.

In civil proceedings in the High Court (qv), judgment *after trial* may be appealed to the Supreme Court within twenty one days from the perfection of the judgment: RSC O.58 r.3. Judgment may also arise *in default of appearance* and *in default of defence* (qqv). See DECREE; DECLARATORY JUDGMENT; DIREC-TION; EXECUTION OF JUDGMENT; FOREIGN JUDGMENTS, ENFORCEMENT OF; OBITER DIC-TUM; ORDER; RATIO DECIDENDI; SUMMARY SUMMONS.

**judgment, liberty to enter.** See SUM-MARY SUMMONS.

**judgment creditor.** One in whose favour a judgment for a sum of money is given against a judgment debtor. In relation to a company which is being wound up, a creditor who has issued execution against the company's property or attached a debt due to it is not entitled to retain the benefit of the process unless it was completed before the winding up commenced or before the creditor received notice of the meeting at which it was proposed to wind it up: Companies Act 1963 ss.291, 292 and 219. See CREDITOR; EXECUTION OF JUDGMENT.

**judgment debtor.** A person against whom a judgment (qv) has been given for a sum of money in favour of a judgment creditor. See EXECUTION OF

JUDGMENT.

**judgment in default of appearance.**
Judgment to which a plaintiff is entitled where the defendant fails to enter an appearance to a summons duly served: RSC O.13. Where the originating summons (whether plenary or summary) is for a liquidated (qv) sum, final judgment may be entered in the Central Office (qv) without an order of the court, except in the case of hire-purchase and moneylending matters when the plaintiff must seek liberty to enter such judgment from the Master (qv) or the court (ibid r.3).

Where the summons is a *plenary* one for an unliquidated sum, the plaintiff must deliver a statement of claim (qv) to the Central Office in lieu of delivery to the defendant and then apply to the court for judgment which, if granted, will be that the plaintiff do recover against the defendant damages (qv) to be assessed by a judge with or without a jury, as the case may be (ibid r.6).

For Circuit Court provisions on judgment in default of appearance, see RCC O.23-24. Where a defendant in the District Court fails to give notice of intention to defend a civil process, the plaintiff may obtain judgment: DCR (1963) r.7.

Pre-judgment interest which is allowed to be claimed by the Courts Act 1981 s.22 cannot be adjudicated upon by the Master or by the Central Office; consequently such a claim must be made to the court: RSC O.13 r.19; Mellowhide Products Ltd v Barry Agencies Ltd (1983) ILRM 152. See APPEARANCE.

**judgment in default of defence.** Judgment to which a plaintiff is entitled where the defendant fails to deliver a defence to a *plenary* summons: RSC O.27. In the case of a claim for a debt or liquidated demand, the plaintiff may have final judgment entered in the Central Office without an order of the court, except in the case of hire-purchase and money lending matters wherein such final judgment may not be entered until after twelve months from the issue of the summons, unless the leave of the court is first obtained by motion on notice on the defendant (ibid rr.2, 15-16).

In claims for unliquidated damages in tort or contract, judgment is obtained by *notice of motion* (qv) to the court, served on the defendant. However, the plaintiff must first serve a 21 days warning letter on the defendant, warning of intention to serve a notice of motion for judgment, and consenting to a further 21 days late delivery of defence; he then allows the defendant deliver his defence even after service of notice of motion for judgment, but not later than 6 days before the return date; in which event if the defence is delivered, the motion is not put in the judge's list and the plaintiff is entitled to a fixed sum of £100 for costs (ibid r.9). However, in continuing default of defence, the court may then order judgment that the plaintiff do recover against the defendant, damages (qv) to be assessed by a judge with or without a jury, as the case may be.

For judgment in default of defence in the Circuit Court, see RCC O.23-24. Where a defendant in the District Court fails to give notice of intention to defend a civil process, the plaintiff may obtain judgment: DCR (1963) r.7.

There is a prohibition on the recognition in an EC State of a default judgment given in another EC State when the document instituting the proceedings was not properly served on the defendant who did not contest the proceedings: Minalmet GmbH v Brandeis Ltd (Case — 123/91 ECJ) reported by Byrne in 11 ILT & SJ (1993) 136. See DEFENCE.

**judgment mortgage.** A mortgage created by the registration as a mortgage, by a judgment creditor against the lands of the judgment debtor, of a judgment of a court for the payment of a sum of money: Judgment Mortgage Acts 1850 and 1858. Judgments which may be registered are such money judgments of the Supreme, High, Circuit and District Courts: Circuit Court (Registration of Judgments) Act 1937; Courts Act 1981 s.24.

A judgment may be registered against all legal and equitable interests of the judgment debtor in freehold and in leasehold property; a judgment mortgage is rarely registered against leaseholds as the judgment mortgagee then becomes liable for rent and convenants therein.

When a judgment is validly registered

as a mortgage, the registration has the effect of a mortgage by deed over the debtor's beneficial interest at the time of registration in the lands set out in the *judgment mortgage affidavit* which is sworn by the judgment creditor: Judgment Mortgage Act 1850 s.7. If the affidavit filed achieves the purpose which the legislature sought to achieve, strict compliance with the statutory provisions will not be required; the mere omission of a requirement of s.6 of the 1850 Act which does not affect the question or the identity of the property or the debtor could not of itself invalidate the charge on the property: Irish Bank of Commerce Ltd v O'Hara (1993 SC) 11 ILT Dig 68 — see Doyle in 7ILT & SJ (1989) 304 and 11 ILT & SJ (1993) 52. However, the affidavit must comply with the relevant Rules of Court and content of affidavits generally: Credit Finance Ltd v Hennessy (1979) as reported by Doyle in 8ILT & SJ (1990) 51.

A judgment mortgage does not obtain priority over a prior unregistered mortgage: Eyre v McDowell (1861) 9 HLC 620, unless the judgment mortgage is carried on the back of a subsequent registered mortgage: Re Scott's Estate (1862) 14 Ir Ch R 57.

The remedy of the judgment mortgagee is to seek a sale by the court by instituting a *mortgage suit* (qv). For *priority* of a judgment mortgage in the event of the judgment debtor becoming bankrupt (qv), see Bankruptcy Act 1988 s.51. [Text: Babington; Madden; Scanlon]. See Registration of Title Act 1964 s.71. See FAMILY HOME; LAW AGENT; SATISFACTION; WIDOW.

**judici officium suum excedenti non paretur.** [Effect is not given to the decision of a judge in excess of his jurisdiction]. See CERTIORARI; JUDICIAL REVIEW;

**judicial authority.** As regards the requirement that an extradition warrant be signed by a judicial authority, it has been held that the term *judicial authority* as used in the Extradition Act 1965, falls to be tested by the law of the place requesting extradition and that there are no grounds for suggesting that a person lacking legal training or security of tenure cannot be a judicial authority: Russell v Fanning (1988) ILRM 333.

For arrangements concerning the endorsement of such warrants, see EXTRADITION.

**judicial notice.** Judicial cognisance. Matters which a judge takes notice or cognisance of, without formal proof, because they are matters of common knowledge and everyday life, or because he is required to take notice of them without proof eg Acts of the Oireachtas. Judicial notice is required to be taken of the EEC Treaties, of the Official Journal and of any decision of, or expression of opinion by, the European Court on any question in respect of which that Court has jurisdiction: European Communities (Judicial Notice and Documentary Evidence) Regulations 1972 (SI No 341 of 1972). See Byrne v Londonderry Tram Co (1902) 2 IR 457; The State (William Taylor) v Circuit Court Judge for Wicklow (1951) IR 311; Waters v Cruickshank (1967) IR 378. See EX INFORMATA CONSCIENTIA; PRELIMINARY RULINGS.

**judicial power.** See SEPARATION OF POWERS.

**judicial review.** A "legal remedy available in situations where a body or tribunal with legal authority to determine rights or impose liabilities, and with a duty to act judicially, has acted in excess of legal authority or contrary to its duty": Murtagh & Murtagh v Board of Management of St Emer's National School (1991 SC) ILRM 549. Judicial review is generally concerned not with the decision of a body or tribunal but with the decision making process: O'Keefe v An Bord Pleanala & Radio Tara (1991 SC) ILRM 237. Judicial review is a review and not an appeal: Garda Representative Association v Ireland, AG and Minister for Justice (1993 SC) ITLR (16 Aug). Excluded from judicial review are decisions made in the realm of private law where the duty being performed by the decision making authority is manifestly a private duty derived solely from contract or solely from consent or agreement of the parties affected: Finlay CJ in Beirne v Commissioner of Garda Siochana (1993 SC) ILRM 1.

An application for judicial review is an application to the High Court for orders of certiorari, prohibition, mandamus or quo warranto (qqv): RSC O.84 r.18. An application for a declaration (qv) or for an injunction (qv) may also be made by an application for judicial review.

Judicial review is now the uniform system for the High Court to exercise its supervisory function over inferior courts, administrative bodies and individuals. An application for judicial review may not be made unless the leave of the court is first obtained, which leave is sought by way of a motion made *ex parte*, grounded upon a supporting statement and verifying affidavit: (ibid r.20).

If leave is granted, the application for judicial review is then made by originating notice of motion unless the court directs that it be made by plenary summons (ibid r.22(1)). The respondent is allowed seven days from service of the notice of motion within which to serve his statement and affidavit (ibid r.22(4)).

Damages may be awarded on an application for judicial review if (a) the applicant has included a claim for such relief in his supporting statement and (b) if the court is satisfied that the applicant would have been awarded damages if the claim had been made in a civil action (ibid r.24(1)).

An application for leave to apply for a judicial review must be made promptly and in any event within three months from the date when grounds for the application first arose, or six months when the relief sought is certiorari (qv) (ibid r.21(1)). However, as regards planning matters, an application for leave to apply for a judicial review must be made, by motion on notice, (not *ex parte*), within two months of the relevant planning decision, and the court must not grant such leave unless it is satisfied that there are substantial grounds for contending that the decision is invalid or ought to be quashed; there are also restrictions on any appeal to the Supreme Court: LG (P&D) Act 1963 s.82(3A) as inserted by LG (P&D) Act 1992 s.19(3).

The court may allow an applicant for judicial review to amend a statement of claim at any time: Molloy v Governor of Limerick Prison (1991 SC) ITLR (2 Dec). See also Solan v DPP (1989) ILRM 491; DPP v McDonnell (1991 HC) 9ILT Dig 128.

In relation to tribunals, it has been held that the proper purpose of the remedy of judicial review of administrative action is to ensure that a decision reached by a tribunal has been open to it upon the evidence before it; it is not the function of the court to substitute its opinion for that of the authority constituted by law to decide such matters: The State (Keegan) v Stardust Victims Tribunal (1987) ILRM 292. Judicial review extends to bodies which exercise functions of a public nature but not a domestic tribunal: Murphy v The Turf Club (1989) IR 171. The factors relevant to whether judicial review extends to a particular body are: the source of power of the body, the nature of its powers, and the effect of the sanctions it can impose — see Taylor in 9ILT & SJ (1991) 14.

For judicial review and employment dismissal cases, see Barry in 9ILT & SJ (1991) 54 and O'Neill v Iarnrod Eireann (1991 SC) ELR 1. See An Post v Brady (1993 HC) ELR 46. See also Delaney in 11 ILT & SJ (1993) 12. For practice and procedure where the State is a party, see [Text: Collins & O'Reilly]. See LRC Working Paper 8 of 1979. See DECLARATORY JUDGMENT; DISCOVERY.

**judicial separation.** The decree granted by the court which relieves the spouses to a marriage of the obligation to cohabit; the marriage however is not dissolved: Judicial Separation and Family Law Reform Act 1989.

A decree may be awarded to an applicant on one or more of a number of grounds eg (a) adultery of the respondent, (b) unreasonable behaviour of respondent; (c) desertion by respondent for at least one year; (d) spouses have lived apart for at least one year and respondent consents to the decree; (e) spouses have lived apart for at least three years; (f) marriage has broken down to such extent that normal marital relationship has not existed for at least one year (ibid s.2(1)).

There are safeguards to ensure the applicant and respondent are aware of the alternatives to separation proceedings and to assist attempts at reconciliation (ibid ss.5-7). Also the court will not grant a decree unless satisfied that proper provision is made for the *welfare* of dependent children of the family; "welfare" comprises the religious and moral, intellectual, physical and social welfare of the children (ibid s.3).

The court is empowered to make ancillary financial, property, custody and other orders, including orders in relation to the *family home* (qv) (ibid Part II). It will generally seek to ensure that provision is made for the spouses and any dependent child of the family as is adequate and reasonable having regard to all the circumstances (ibid s.20). There is also provision for the voidance of transactions intended to prevent or reduce the provision of financial relief of a spouse or child (ibid s.29).

The Circuit Court is established as a Circuit Family Court (ibid s.31). See O'H v O'H (1990 HC) 2 IR 558 reported in 9ILT & SJ (1991) 28; MK v PK (1990 HC) reported by Corrigan in 9ILT & SJ (1991) 176; VS v RS (1991 HC) ITLR (11 Nov). See Circuit Court Rules (No 1) of 1991 — SI No 159 of 1991 and Corrigan in 9ILT & SJ (1991) 204. See also Child Care Act 1991 s.20. [Text: Browne; Duncan & Scully]. See DIVORCE A MENSA ET THORO; SUCCESSION, LAW OF.

**judiciary.** The collective name for judges (qv).

**junior counsel.** See BARRISTER.

**jura eodem modo destituuntur quo constituuntur.** [Laws are abrogated by the same means by which they were made].

**jura publica anteterenda privatis.** [Public rights are to be preferred to private].

**jurat.** A certificate at the end of an affidavit, stating where and when the affidavit was sworn, with the signature and description of the person before whom it was sworn. The jurat must contain a certificate by the person taking the affidavit that he knows the deponent himself, or some person named in the jurat who certifies his knowledge of the deponent: RSC O.40 r.14.

**juratores sunt judices facti.** [Juries are the judges of fact].

**juris et de jure.** [Of law and from law].

**jurisdiction.** (1) The power of a court or a judge to hear and decide an action, petition or other proceeding. (2) The territorial limits within which legal authority may be exercised. (3) The district or limits within which the judgments or orders of a court can be enforced or executed. There are monetary limits set on the jurisdiction of the hierarchy of courts; however, where the parties consent in civil matters the Circuit Court has unlimited jurisdiction (Courts (Supplemental Provisions) Act 1961 s.22(1)(b)), as has the District Court (Courts Act 1991 s.4(c)).

Without prejudice to the right claimed to exercise jurisdiction over the whole of the national territory (qv), the laws of the State have the like area and extent of application as the laws of Saorstat Eireann (qv) and the like extra-territorial effect: 1937 Constitution, art.3. The Criminal Law (Jurisdiction) Act 1976 permits the arrest and trial in the State of persons alleged to have committed certain offences in Northern Ireland.

The jurisdiction of Irish courts has been extended further in civil and commercial matters by the Jurisdiction of Courts and Enforcement of Judgments (European Communities) Acts 1988 and 1993. Persons domiciled in a "contracting state" must be sued in the courts of that state; however (a) in matters relating to a contract they may be sued in the place of performance of the obligation, and (b) in matters relating to tort in the place where the harmful event occurred (ibid 1988 Act, first schedule, arts. 2, 5 and 6; Gannon v B & I and Landliner Travel Merseyside Ltd (1993 SC) 11 ILT Dig 144.

The Irish court has jurisdiction where there is a plausible cause of action against an Irish co-defendant; it is not open to one of a number of defendants from a contracting State to admit liability so as to deprive the plaintiff of the right to pursue a claim in a court in which jurisdiction has been established: Kelly v McCarthy & Ors (1993 HC) ITLR (12 Apr).

A defendant may raise the issue of jurisdiction under the 1988 Act at any time before serving his defence: Campbell International Trading House Ltd v Peter van Aart and Natur Pur gmbh (1992 SC) ILRM 663. The Irish courts do not have jurisdiction as regards a contractural obligation which is to be performed in another EC state: Olympia Productions Ltd v Cameron Mackintosh (1992 HC) ILRM 204. See Ferndale

Films Ltd v Granada Television Ltd (1993 SC) — Irish Times 21/7/1993. It is not sufficient to show that the obligation which it is claimed has been breached *could* have been performed in Ireland: Hanbridge Services Ltd v Aerospace Communications (1993 SC) ITLR (21 Jun). See Contractual Obligations (Applicable Law) Act 1991. The 1993 Act gives force of law to the Lugano Convention on jurisdiction and enforcement of judgments between EC member States and EFTA countries.

The High Court is already empowered to act in aid of the United Kingdom in bankruptcy (qv) matters, and the government may by order extend this aid to other jurisdictions: Bankruptcy Act 1988 s.142; In re Gibson, A Bankrupt in England, Ex Parte Walter (1960) Ir Jur Rep 60. See The State (McCormack) v Curran (1987) ILRM 225. See also Gill in 7ILT & SJ (1989) 2 and 8ILT (1990 179. See also Criminal Damage Act 1991 s.7(1).

For specific jurisdiction of each court, see separate entry under each court. [Text: Byrne P]. See also CRIMINAL JURISDICTION; ENLARGEMENT OF JURISDICTION; EXCLUSIVE JURISDICTION; FOREIGN JUDGMENTS, ENFORCEMENT OF; MARITIME JURISDICTION; SPLITTING OF ACTION; SUMMONS, SERVICE OUT OF JURISDICTION.

**jurisdiction, criminal.** See CRIMINAL JURISDICTION.

**jurisprudence.** The science, philosophy or theory of law. The study of the principles of law.

**juror.** A member of a jury (qv).

**juror, challenge to.** In criminal cases, the prosecution and each accused may challenge without cause shown (called a *peremptory challenge*) up to seven jurors and jurors so challenged are not included in the jury. The prosecution and each accused may challenge for cause shown any number of jurors; the cause must be shown immediately on the challenge being made and the judge will then rule on the challenge; if the challenge is allowed, the juror is not included in the jury. In civil cases, each party may similarly challenge jurors. See Juries Act 1976 ss.20-21.

**juror's oath.** See OATH, FORM OF.

**jury.** A body of persons selected according to law and sworn to give a verdict on some matter according to the evidence. A jury is chosen from panels which are drawn from citizens aged between eighteen and seventy years of age who are registered on the register of electors of Dail Eireann: Juries Act 1976. Certain categories of persons are ineligible, excused or disqualified.

A jury comprises twelve persons; however, if a juror dies or is discharged by the judge (eg due to illness), the jury will remain properly constituted unless the judge directs otherwise or the number of jurors is reduced below ten (ibid s.23). Jurors in criminal matters are provided with meals and other facilities; jurors in civil cases are not.

The deliberations of a jury must always be regarded as completely confidential and must not be published after a trial; it is a well established principle that the deliberations of a jury in a criminal case must not be revealed or inquired into: O'Callaghan v AG (1993 SC) 11 ILT Dig 162. Juries should be warned by the judge not to discuss the case with any person other than another member of the jury: DPP v McKeever (1993 CCA) 11 ILT Dig 186. See RSC O.36 rr.5, 10, 34, 35, 42; O.22 r.7; O.76 r.91. See EMBRACERY; GRAND JURY; HUNG JURY; INQUEST; JUROR, CHALLENGE TO; TRIAL BY JURY; VERDICT; WAGES.

**jury, abolition of.** Juries were abolished for civil actions in the Circuit Court by the Courts Act 1971. Juries were abolished for certain *actions* in the High Court for recovery of damages for *personal injuries* from 1st August 1988: Courts Act 1988 s.1(1). *Personal injuries* include any disease and any impairment of a person's physical or mental condition (ibid s.1(7)).

*Actions* include (a) actions where the personal injuries were caused by negligence, nuisance or breach of duty; (b) actions under the Civil Liability Act 1961 s.48 ie actions brought where death is caused by wrongful act, neglect or default; or (c) actions under the Air Navigation and Transport Act 1936 s.18 (as inserted by the Air Navigation and Transport Act 1965 s.4) ie liability of a carrier in the event of death of a passenger. Such actions do not include actions where the damages claimed consists only of damages for false imprisonment or for intentional trespass to the person or both (ibid s.1(3)).

**jury, trial by.** See TRIAL BY JURY.

**jus.** [A right]. See EURO-JUS.

**jus accrescendi.** [The right of survivorship]. See JOINT TENANCY.

**jus canonicum.** [Canon law].

**jus ex injuria non oritur.** [A right does not arise out of a wrong].

**jus in personam.** [A right against a specific person].

**jus mariti.** [The right of a husband].

**jus publicum privatorem pactis mutari non potest.** [Public law is not to be superceded by private agreements].

**jus quaesitum tertio.** [Rights on account of third parties]. Generally, a contract cannot confer rights on a third party; only a party to a contract can sue on it. However, rights may be conferred on third parties by way of trust. See O'Leary v Irish National Insurance Co Ltd (1958) Ir Jur Rep 1; Cadbury Ireland Ltd v Kerry Co-op Creameries Ltd (1982) ILRM 77; Rooney v Trustees of Textile Operatives Society of Ireland (1913) 47 ILTR 303. See PRIVITY OF CONTRACT.

**jus tertii.** [The right of a third person]. A defendant cannot, unless he has the consent of the true owner, claim as a defence that the plaintiff is not entitled to possession, because a third party is the true owner. See Webb & Webb v Ireland & AG (1988 SC) ILRM 565; O'Beirne v Fox (1990) ELR 151.

**just and equitable.** The phrase sometimes used in statutes conferring power to a judge to make an order where the court is of opinion that it would be *just and equitable* to do so eg in company law, a company may be wound up if the court is of the opinion that it would be just and equitable. See Companies Act 1963 s.213; In re Murph's Restaurant Ltd (1979) HC; In re Vehicle Building (1986) ILRM 239.

**justice.** The impartial resolution of disputes, the upholding of rights, and the punishment of wrongs, by the law. Justice is required to be administered in courts established by law by judges appointed in the manner provided in the Constitution: 1937 Constitution, art.34(1). Certain articles of the Constitution indicate that *justice is placed above the law and acknowledge that natural*

*rights, or human rights, are not created by law but that the Constitution confirms their existence and gives them protection*: McGee v Attorney General (1974) IR 101.

For characteristics of the *administration of justice*, see McDonald v Bord na gCon (1965) IR 217 as cited in Goodman v Mr Justice Hamilton (1992 HC & SC) ILRM 145. Two essential ingredients are that there is a contest between parties and that some form of liability or penalty should be imposed on one of the parties: Keady v Commissioner of Garda Siochana (1992 SC) ILRM 312.

**justice, district.** See DISTRICT JUSTICE.

**justice, natural.** See NATURAL JUSTICE.

**justice, public.** See PUBLIC JUSTICE.

**justice of the peace.** Replaced by Peace Commissioners who have all the powers and authorities which immediately before 6th December 1922 were vested in a Justice of the Peace: Courts of Justice Act 1924 s.88. See PEACE COMMISSIONER.

**justifiable homicide.** See HOMICIDE.

**justification.** A plea in a defamation (qv) action that the statement complained of made by the defendant is substantially true, ie true not only in its allegations of fact but also in any comments made therein. It is a dangerous plea as the onus of proving justification rests on the defendant and if it fails, *exemplary* damages may be awarded. See Defamation Act 1961 s.22. See AGGRAVATION OF DAMAGES.

# K

**kangaroo court.** Colloquial expression to describe a hearing in which the elementary and generally accepted norms of justice have not been observed.

**keeping the peace.** See BINDING TO THE PEACE.

**kerb-crawling.** Colloquial expression to describe soliciting or importuning from or in a motor vehicle for the purposes of prostitution; it is a criminal offence: Criminal Law (Sexual Offences) Act 1993 ss.1(1) and 7. See PROSTITUTE.

**kidnapping.** The offence of stealing and carrying away, or secreting of some person against his will; it is the most aggravated form of false imprisonment. See The People (Attorney General) v Edge (1943) IR 115. See Criminal Law Act 1976 s.11. See CHILD STEALING; FALSE IMPRISONMENT.

**kill.** To cause the death of another. See HOMICIDE; MURDER.

**kin.** Relationship by blood.

**King's Inns, Honorable Society of.** The society, the Benchers of which constitute the governing body of the Bar of Ireland. The Society, founded in 1541, provides a course of education and training which when successfully completed leads to admission of the student by the Benchers to the degree of barrister-at-law and to being called to the Bar by the Chief Justice and thereby to being admitted to practice in the courts. See also King's Inns Library Act 1945 as amended by Copyright Act 1963 s.58. See Kenny in 10 ILT & SJ (1992) 172. [Text: Hogan & Osborough; Kenny]. See BARRISTER; LAW LIBRARY; SUITORS FUNDS OF.

**knackery.** Any premises used for and in connection with the collection, delivery, supply, slaughter, storage, skinning or cutting up of animals or parts of animals which are not intended for human consumption: Abattoirs Act 1988. Knackeries require annual licensing, the objective being to regulate such activities where animal carcases and offals are handled for industrial and other purposes. See ABATTOIR.

**knock for knock.** Phrase used eg to describe an agreement whereby insurance companies pay their own insured on the basis that there will be no action brought by one insured against the other. It also refers to agreements between companies in relation to their employee pension funds, whereby pension liabilities in respect of an employee moving from one company to the other, are borne by the receiving company's fund.

**knowledge.** Awareness of, or acquaintance with, fact or truth. The law can presume knowledge of facts under the *doctrine of notice* where a person would have known if he had made proper enquiries. Everyone is presumed also to know the law. See CAUSE OF ACTION; IGNORANTIA FACTI EXCUSAT; NOTICE.

**know-how.** Industrial information and techniques likely to assist in the manufacture or processing of goods or materials, or in carrying out any agricultural, forestry, fishing, mining, or other extractive operations: Finance Act 1968 s.2. A trader may deduct as a trading expense any expenditure including capital expenditure in acquiring know-how for use in his trade, if it would not otherwise be deductible. However, no deduction is given for capital expenditure where (a) the know-how is acquired as part of the acquisition of the whole or part of a trade from another person or (b) an element of *control* arises as regards the buyer and/or seller within the definition of control in the Income Tax Act 1967 s.299(6). See TRADE SECRET.

# L

**labelling.** A voluntary EC-wide voluntary labelling system is to be introduced for goods which meet strict environmental criteria (called the *eco-labelling* scheme). It will not apply to food, drink or pharmaceuticals, but will apply to a wide range of goods eg batteries, refrigerators, gardening products. See Council Regulation 880/92/EEC.

The Environmental Protection Agency must, if it considers it necessary or desireable to do so, establish or arrange for the establishment of the eco-labelling scheme: Environmental Protection Agency Act 1992 s.78. It will be an offence to use a symbol provided for in such a scheme in respect of a product or service which has not been approved under the scheme (ibid s.78(4)).

**Labour Court.** A tribunal established by the Industrial Relations Act 1946 s.10 with the role of promoting collective bargaining and of resolving industrial conflict; it also adjudicates on disputes under the Anti-Discrimination (Pay) Act 1974 and the Employment Equality Act 1977. A recommendation from an Equality Officer can be appealed by either party to the Labour Court. It is a tripartite tribunal, consisting of a chairman, three deputy chairmen, as well as four members nominated by trade unions and four nominated by employers' organisations; formal legal qualifications are not required.

The Labour Court may not investigate a trade dispute unless the parties to the dispute have requested it to do so and the Labour Relations Commisssion has either (a) waived its functions of conciliation or (b) has given it a report stating that no further efforts on its part will resolve the dispute: Industrial Relations Act 1990 s.26. However, the Labour Court may intervene in exceptional circumstances (ibid s.26(5)) or where there is specific provision for the direct reference of trade disputes to the Court (ibid s.25(3)). Also the Court is required to endeavour to resolve a dispute affecting the public interest, referred to it by the Minister (ibid s.38).

The court is bound by few procedural rules other than the general principles of law and of *natural justice*. It may not use expert evidence without disclosing the substance of that evidence to the parties and allowing them to make submissions on it: State (Cole) v Labour Court 1983 HC.

The court need not first make an initial determination that a complaint is receivable before making the administrative decision to refer the matter to an equality officer (qv) for determination: Aer Lingus Teo v Labour Court (1990 SC) ELR 113. The court cannot refuse to entertain an appeal from the recommendations of an equality officer on the ground that issues raised have already been decided by the court: Aer Rianta cpt v Labour Court (1990 HC) ILRM 193. See also The State (Polymark) v ITGWU (1987) ILRM 357. See RSC O.106. See DISCRIMINATION; EQUAL PAY.

**labour injunction.** An injunction (qv) in a labour dispute, restraining a strike or other industrial action (qv). Where the strike or other industrial action is in accordance with a secret ballot and the trade union has given notice to the employer, the employer cannot seek an injunction unless he gives notice to the trade union and its members (ie no *ex parte* injunction): Industrial Relations Act 1990 s.19. The court cannot grant an injunction where the union establishes a fair case that it was acting in contemplation or furtherance of a *trade dispute* (ibid s.19(2)). If it does not so establish, the court will decide, as it does in other injunction applications, where the balance of convenience lies. See Allied Irish Banks plc v Irish Bank Officials Association (1991 HC); Molloy, Enright & McCarty v IBOA (1992 HC); Draycar Ltd v Whelan (1993 HC) ELR 119; Bus Eireann v SIPTU (1993 HC); Iarnrod Eireann v NBRWU (1993 HC). See Barry in 11 ILT & SJ (1993) 146. See INJUNCTION; TRADE DISPUTE.

**Labour Relations Commission.** The Commission with the general responsibility of promoting the improvement of industrial relations: Industrial Relations Act 1990 ss.24-42. The Commission also provides conciliation and advisory services, prepares and offers guidance on codes of practice; provides an equality officer and rights commissioner service; conducts or commissions research into matters relevant to industrial relations; assists joint labour committees and industrial councils in the exercise of their functions (ibid s.25).

Trade disputes must be referred to the Commission first, except where there is a specific provision for the direct reference of a dispute to the Labour Court (ibid s.25(3)) eg as provided for in the Industrial Relations Act 1969 s.20, or the Labour Court intervenes as it is empowered to do (ibid 1990 Act s.26). The Commission must endeavour to resolve a trade dispute affecting the public interest, referred to it by the Minister (ibid 1990 Act s.38).

**laches.** Negligent or unreasonable delay in asserting or enforcing a right; the equitable doctrine that delay defeats equity, or that equity aids the vigilant and not the indolent. *A court of equity has always refused its aid to stale demands where a party has slept upon his rights and acquiesced for a great length of time. Nothing can call forth this court into activity but conscience, good faith and reasonable diligence*: Smith v Clay (1767) Amb 645. A dismissal from employment which is affected by laches is unfair: Sheehan v M Keating & Son Ltd (1993 EAT) ELR 12. See also In re Sharpe (1892) 1 Ch 154. See LIMITATION OF ACTIONS.

**lading, bill of.** See BILL OF LADING.

**lagan.** Goods which have been cast from a ship in danger but where they are marked with a buoy or other means to facilitate recovery. See FLOTSAM; JETSAM.

**laissez-passer.** [Let pass]. The travel documents issued to officials of the United Nations or of its specialised agencies which are accorded recognition as valid travel documents by the Diplomatic Relations and Immunities Act 1967, second schedule.

**land.** As regards the law of real property or land law, *land* includes things attached to the land, such as buildings and other structures. As regards Acts of the Oireachtas (qv), *land* includes messuages, tenements and hereditaments, houses and buildings of any tenure: Interpretation Act 1937 ss.4 and 12. A general devise of *land* is to be construed as including leasehold land as well as freehold land, unless a contrary intention appears from the will: Succession Act 1965 s.92.

As regards planning permission, *land* includes any structure and any land covered with water, whether inland or coastal: LG(P&D) Act 1963 s.2(1). As regards the Rules of the Superior Courts, *land* includes messuages, tenements, hereditaments, houses and buildings of any tenure: RSC O.125 r.1. In bankruptcy matters, *land* includes any estate or interest in or charge over land: Bankruptcy Act 1988 s.3.

In landlord and tenant matters, *land* includes houses, messuages, and tenements of every tenure, whether corporeal or incorporeal: Deasy's Act 1860 s.1. The words *all lands* are to be taken literally and include land comprising the sea-bed: Trustees of Kinsale Yacht Club v Commissioner of Valuations (1993 HC) ILRM 393. As regards pre 1922 statutes, see Interpretation Act 1889 s.3. See Report on Land Law and Conveyancing Law — General Proposals (LRC 30 of 1989). [Text: Pearse; Wylie (1)].

**land, compulsory acquisition of.** See COMPULSORY PURCHASE ORDER.

**land, planning and control.** See PLANNING PERMISSION.

**land, recovery of.** See EJECTMENT.

**land bond.** An interest bearing bond issued by the Land Commission (qv) to effect the compulsory purchase of land, as part of the scheme commenced in the late nineteenth century for the transfer of land from landlords to tenant farmers: Purchase of Land (Ireland) Act 1891;

Land Act 1923. All remaining land bonds were redeemed in 1989 and the Land Bond Fund dissolved in 1992: Land Bond Act 1992. Payments of annuities by tenant-farmers are now used for the benefit of the Exchequer.

**land certificate.** The certificate of title to which the person registered as owner of *registered* land is entitled: Registration of Title Act 1964 s.28. The land certificate must be produced to the Registrar of the Land Registry for alteration, before any subsequent transaction can be noted on the register (ibid s.105). A lien (qv) is created when a land certificate is deposited to secure an advance of money; the depositee protects his rights by refusing to produce the certificate. See LAND REGISTRATION.

**Land Commission.** The Commission, originally established in 1881, with power (a) to acquire land for distribution among small farmers to relieve congestion and (b) to advance money for the purchase by tenants of landlords' estates: Land Law (Ireland) Act 1881. By 1992, the Commission had overseen the purchase by tenants of approximately 87% of the agricultural land on the whole island (largely achieved prior to independence in 1921) and the structural distribution of about 20% of the agricultural land in the State (largely achieved since 1921).

With the decline in the number of large estates available for acquisition, the rise in land prices and the unacceptability of land bonds (qv) as a means of payment of owners, the Commission ceased to acquire land in 1983. Provision for the Commission to be dissolved was made in 1992; there is provision that the jurisdiction of the Judicial Commissioner and the Appeal Tribunal be vested in the High Court; that any power or duty vested in the Commission or the Lay Commissioners be exercised by the Minister; and that Commission land be vested in the Minister or the Central Fisheries Board: Irish Land Commission (Dissolution) Act 1992. See also Land Law (Commission) Act 1923; Land Act 1933 s.9; Land Act 1950 ss.12 and 14.

**land registration.** There are two mutually exclusive systems of land registration, the *registration of title* and the *registration of deeds*. Under the registration of deeds, the existence of a deed, will or conveyance may be registered; the document remains itself the evidence of title. Under the registration of title, the document ceases to be evidence of title, being replaced by the register which is conclusive evidence of title of the person whose name appears therein.

The registry of title was established by the Registration of Title Act 1891 and continued by the Registration of Title Act 1964. There are three registers, one each for registering the ownership of freehold land, leasehold land, and subsidiary interests (ibid s.8). The register is kept in *folios*, and each folio is in three parts: the first part has a description of the property; the second part describes the owner of the property, including cautions (qv) and inhibitions (qv) restricting the registration of dispositions of the property; the third part contains burdens (qv) and charges (qv), such as mortgages (qv). The register is prepared and maintained in the Land Registry which is situated in Dublin. Each registered holding is marked on the *registry map* by a plan number corresponding to the register.

Registration is compulsory for (a) all freehold and leasehold property acquired by local authorities and state sponsored bodies; (b) freehold property purchased under the various Land Purchase Acts; (c) acquisition on sale of property in areas designated as compulsory registration areas. Currently the counties of Carlow, Laois, and Meath have been so designated. See Land Registration Rules 1972 to 1986 (SI No 230 of 1972 and SI No 310 of 1986). See Courts Act 1991 s.3. [Text: Fitzgerald; McAllister; Wylie (1)]. See DEEDS, REGISTRATION OF; BURDEN; CAUTION; INHIBITION; MEMORIAL; NOTICE; OVERRIDING INTERESTS; QUALIFIED TITLE; QUIT RENT.

**land registry.** The registry which maintains registers in which entries may be made of the ownership of land and of the incumbrances, called *burdens* (qv), affecting ownership. See LAND REGISTRATION.

**landfill site.** Land used for the disposal of waste. The Environmental Protection Agency is required to specify and publish criteria and procedures for the selection, management, operation and termination of the use of landfill sites for the disposal of domestic and other wastes: Environmental Protection Agency Act 1992 s.62(1). The specified criteria and procedures may relate to — eg site selection; design and bringing into operation of sites; impacts on the environment; leachate management, treatment and control; control and recovery of landfill gas; operational guidelines; fire, pest and litter control; appropriate recovery, reuse and recycling facilities; co-disposal of industrial and other wastes; monitoring of leachate, other effluents and emissions; termination of use and subsequent monitoring (ibid s.62(2)).

A landfill site managed or operated by a local authority must comply with the specified criteria and procedures (ibid s.62(5)). Private sites require a permit from the local authority: EC (Waste) Regulations 1979 (SI No 390 of 1979). See LITTER; WASTE OPERATION.

**landlord.** A lessor; the owner or holder of land leased to another called the tenant or lessee. The relationship of landlord and tenant arises *in all cases in which there shall be an agreement by one party to hold land from or under another in consideration of any rent*: Deasy's Act 1860 s.4. A landlord is also defined as the person for the time being entitled to receive (otherwise than as agent for another) the rent paid in respect of premises by the tenant thereof: Landlord and Tenant (Amendment) Act 1980 s.3(1). [Text: Deale; Wylie (4)]. See COVENANT; GROUND RENT; IMPROVEMENT NOTICE; LEASE; RENTED HOUSE, REGISTRATION OF; RENTED HOUSE, STANDARD OF.

**language.** The Irish language as the national language is the first official language; the English language is recognised as a second official language: 1937 Constitution, art.8. In the event of conflict between the text of the Constitution, or of a law enrolled in accordance with the Constitution, in both the official languages, the text in Irish will prevail (ibid arts.25(4)(6) and 25(5)(4)). However, in interpreting the Constitution, where there appears to be a conflict between terms used in the two texts, search must first be made for a common meaning before the Irish language text is permitted to prevail: The State (Guilland) v Governor of Mountjoy Prison (1986) ILRM 381 applying

O'Donovan v Attorney General (1961) IR 114.

A litigant has a constitutional right to conduct his case in the Irish language: R (O'Coileain) v D J Crotty (1927) 61 ILTR 81. He has a similar right in respect of the English language: The State (Buchan) v Coyne (1936) 70 ILTR 185. He has no right to insist on only Irish being spoken in a proceedings: O'Monachain v An Taoiseach (1982) SC.

A person has a constitutional right to Irish language copies of documents required under the Companies Act 1963: O'Murchu v Registrar of Companies (1989) 7ILT Dig 24. There is also a constitutional obligation on the State to make available the Rules of Court (qv) in the Irish language: Delap v An tAire Dli agus Cirt Eire agus An tArd Aighne (1990 HC) ITLR (24 Dec). In Northern Ireland, restrictions on the use of the Irish language by prisoners at the Maze Prison was held not to be unlawful: MacCormaic & Pickering v Governor of HM Prison (1991 HC — NI) ITLR (29 Apr).

There is provision for interpreters in the courts and for the translation of any affidavit, summons, petition or notice from English into Irish and from Irish into English: RSC O.120. The basic records of a company must be kept in an official language of the State: Companies Act 1990 s.202(7). See also RCC O.1 r.5. See also Attorney General v Joyce (1929) IR 526. See Tearmai Dli, Oifig an tSolathair. See also Irish Legal Terms Act 1945; Place Names (Irish Forms) Act 1973.

The Maastricht Treaty 1992 was drawn up in the Danish, Dutch, English, French, German, Greek, Irish, Italian, Portuguese and Spanish languages, the texts in each of these languages being equally authentic: Maastricht Treaty 1992 art.S. The languages of the European Patents Office are English, French and German: see Patents Act 1992 ss.119 and 121. See GAELTACHT; OATH, INTERPRETER'S; TEACHER, LANGUAGE QUALIFICATION; WILL, PROOF OF.

**lapse.** (1) Generally when a person to whom property has been devised or bequeathed dies before the testator, the devise or bequest fails or *lapses* and the property falls into residue; a lapsed share of residue however does not fall into residue, but devolves upon an intestacy. A lapse does not occur if land is given to a person *in tail* who predeceases the testator and who leaves issue living at the testator's death capable of inheriting the entail: Succession Act 1965 s.97.

Also there is no lapse where property is given to issue of the testator and such descendant dies leaving issue living at the testator's death (ibid s.98). Another exception to the doctrine of lapse is where the gift is charitable and the property can be applied *cy-pres* (qv). In the case of a devise to persons as joint tenants (qv), if one dies before the testator the others take his share; whereas if two persons hold as tenants in common (qv), the share of the deceased tenant lapses.

(2) Proceedings lapse in the event of the death of a defendant in criminal proceedings. See DEATH, EFFECT OF.

**lapse of offer.** A lapse of an offer occurs (a) on the death of the offeror or offeree before acceptance; or (b) by non-acceptance within the time prescribed; or (c) by non-acceptance within a reasonable time where no time is prescribed. See Ramsgate Hotel v Montefiore (1866) LR 1 Ex 109 See OFFER.

**larceny.** Stealing. The offence committed by a person who, without the consent of the owner, fraudulently and without a claim of right made in good faith, *takes* and carries away anything capable of being stolen, with intent, at the time of such taking, permanently to deprive the owner thereof: Larceny Act 1916 s.1. The offence is committed also by a person who has lawful possession of the thing, if, being a *bailee* or part owner thereof, he fraudulently converts the same to his own use or the use of any person other than the owner.

There must be a taking, either actual or constructive. An actual taking arises by the seizing of the thing acquisitively and not the mere touching of it or moving it inquisitively. A constructive taking can occur where possession is obtained by a trick (qv); or by intimidation, or under a mistake on the part of the owner with knowledge on the part of the taker; or by finding (qv).

The mens rea (qv) in larceny is the

intention permanently to deprive the owner of the thing stolen. Larceny of shop goods can be committed while the accused is still on the shop premises: DPP v Keating (1989 HC) ILRM 561. Where goods are stolen and the offender is prosecuted to conviction, the property in the goods revests in the person who was the owner notwithstanding any intermediate dealing with them: Sale of Goods Act 1893 s.24. See also Larceny Act 1916 s.45. See The People (Attorney General) v Mill (1955) CCA; The People (DPP) v O'Loughlin (1979) IR 85. [Text: McCutcheon]. See HANDLING STOLEN PROPERTY; REWARD.

**larceny, aggravated.** Larceny (qv) which carries more severe penalties than simple larceny: Larceny Act 1916. Aggravated larceny arises in the case of (a) the particular type of property stolen eg cattle (ibid s.3) or a will (ibid s.6); (b) the manner in which the larceny is committed eg stealing from the person (ibid s.14); (c) the place where it is committed eg a ship (ibid s.15); and (d) the person who commits it eg larceny by a tenant (ibid s.16). See ROBBERY.

**larceny by finding.** The larceny (qv) which occurs where a person finds goods which have been lost and appropriates them to his own use in circumstances where he believes that the owner can be found by taking reasonable steps.

**larceny by trick.** The larceny (qv) which occurs when a person, with the necessary intent, obtains possession of goods, by means of some trick, from the owner who does not intend to part with the entire right to the property but only to the possession. On conviction, the stolen property revests in the true owner.

**last resort, court of.** See COURT OF LAST RESORT.

**last straw.** Colloquial expression meaning the final irritation or problem that stretches a person's endurance or patience beyond the limit. For there to be a "last straw" dismissal of an employee, there must be a blameworthy act by the employee, judged by standards of belief by the employer of misconduct by the employee which is sustained by evidence establishing the facts on the balance of probabilities and ascertained by a full and fair investigation: Donnelly v Arklow Pottery Ltd (1992 EAT) ELR 240.

**lateness.** Lateness in arriving for work may not be a valid ground for dismissal of an employee if it has been tolerated in the past by the employer: O'Connell v Garde (1991 EAT) ELR 105.

**latent ambiguity.** See AMBIGUITY.

**latent defect.** See DEFECT.

**laundering.** Generally understood to mean the processing of money in such a manner that its origin or ownership is concealed or disguised. An EC Directive is proposed which will require financial institutions to challenge cash which is suspected to come from a wide range of illegal activities eg blackmail, terrorism, arms dealing and drug trafficking.

**law.** The written and unwritten body of rules, derived from custom, formal enactment or judicial decision, which are recognised as binding on persons who constitute a community or state, so that they will be imposed upon and enforced among those persons by appropriate sanctions. The law can be classified as municipal (domestic) or international, public or private, criminal or civil. [Text: Byrne & McCutcheon; Doolan (1); O'Higgins; and see Appendix 3]. See RULE OF LAW.

**law, EC.** See COMMUNITY LAW.

**law agent.** A person who is qualified and authorised to conduct the legal business of another; the solicitor employed by a corporate body eg the Law Agent of Dublin Corporation. A judgment mortgage affidavit may be made by the law agent of any corporate body: Judgment Mortgage Amendment Act 1858 s.3.

A full time solicitor employed by a county borough is known as a *law agent* whilst the corresponding post in a county council is known as a *county solicitor*. The first law agent to Dublin Corporation was Edward Scriven who undertook legal work for the Corporation on a commission basis from 1756 until his death in 1794; he prepared a translation of the 17th century Recorder's Book from the original Latin and French. As regards costs and expenses of a law agent allowed in taxation (qv), see Joan O'Reilly v Dublin Corporation (1963 HC). See DUBLIN AGENT.

**law and equity, fusion of.** See EQUITY.

**law and fact.** Law is a conceived principle, a rule of duty; fact is actual, an event which is according to or in contravention of the rule.

**Law Library.** The central and primary place of practice for the Bar of Ireland. Subject to certain exceptions, membership of the Law Library is confined to full time practising barristers. The Library is governed by a committee which is elected by the Bar Council (qv) which is itself elected by members of the Library. Prior to the founding of the Law Library, it was customary for Irish barristers to get many of the books they required on loan from private book sellers who conducted lending libraries. In the early 18th century, one of these book lenders went bankrupt and the Bar decided to set up its own Library. See BARRISTER; LIBRARY.

**law merchant.** The custom of merchants which when proved became part of the common law. It is nothing more or less than the usages of merchants and traders in the different departments of trade, ratified by decisions of courts of law: Goodwin v Robarts (1875) LR 10 Ex 337. See also Sale of Goods Act 1893 s.61(2).

**law of nations.** International law or private international law (qqv).

**Law Reform Commission.** An independent statutory body corporate formally established in 1975. Its function is to keep the national law and the private and public international law of the State under review and to undertake examinations and conduct research with a view to reforming the law and to formulate proposals for law reform. The Commission also examines a particular branch of the law when requested to do so by the Attorney General (qv). There is a president and four commissioners all appointed by the government. See Law Reform Commission Act 1975. For reports of Commission, see APPENDIX 2.

**law report.** A published account of legal proceedings which gives a statement of the facts and the reasons given by the court for its decision. Law reports commenced in the thirteenth century with the Year Books (c.1270-1530) which were written in Anglo-French and Latin. The Incorporated Council of Law Reporting was established in the mid-nineteenth century and produced reports which were written by barristers. The current Irish law reports are contained in the Irish Reports of the Incorporated Council of Law Reporting (IR); the Irish Law Reports Monthly (ILRM); the reports on the Court of Criminal Appeal (Frewen; Casey); the Irish Times Law Reports (ITLR); the Student Law Reporter; Employment Law Reports (ELR); Irish Criminal Law Journal (ICLJ); Irish Journal of European Law (IJEL) and the unreported judgments. See APPENDIX 1: LAW REPORTS; PRECEDENT.

**Law Society.** See INCORPORATED LAW SOCIETY OF IRELAND.

**law terms.** See SITTINGS OF COURT.

**lawful.** Authorised or permitted by the law.

**lawful homicide.** Excusable or justifiable homicide (qv).

**lawsuit.** Contentious litigation.

**lawyer.** A legal practitioner; a barrister (qv) or solicitor (qv).

**lay days.** The days allowed by a charterparty (qv) for loading and unloading a ship.

**laying an information.** See COMMON INFORMER.

**lay-off.** A cessation of employment caused by the employer's inability to provide work but where the employer believes that this is temporary and he gives the employee notice to that effect before the cessation: Redundancy Payments Act 1967 s.11(1). Lay-off may give an entitlement to redundancy payment. An employee who claims and receives redundancy payment in respect of lay-off or short-time is deemed to have voluntarily left his employment: Unfair Dismissals Act 1977 s.20; Scott & Ors v Irish Printed Circuits Ltd (1990) ELR 167; Connolly v McInerney & Sons Ltd (1990) ELR 26. See Industrial Yarns Ltd v Greene (1984) ILRM 15. See SHORT-TIME.

**leading case.** An important case which settles the principles in a particular branch of law and which is cited in court. See PRECEDENT.

**leading question.** A question put to a witness which directly or indirectly suggests the desired answer or one which may be answered simply *yes* or *no*. Leading questions may not be asked of a witness by the party who called him except:- in introductory or undisputed matters; to lead a witness's mind to a particular topic; to identify a person or thing already described; to establish a contradiction to what was said by another witness; where the witness is hostile (qv). See EXAMINATION.

**leap year.** See AGE.

**lease.** A conveyance or grant by a *lessor* to a *lessee* of possession of property, to last for a certain period of time; it must be for a period less than the estate or interest of the lessor as otherwise it is a conveyance or assignment and not a lease. A lease is usually made in consideration of a *fine* (which is a payment from the lessee to the lessor on the creation of the interest) and on the payment of *rent*. The expression *lease* is usually used to denote an interest for a long period of time, whereas *tenancy* is used to denote a relatively short period. A *sub-lease* or *under-lease* is a lease created by a person who himself is a lessee, for a shorter term then he himself holds.

A letting may be *periodic* eg week to week or month to month; it may be expressly created or arise by reference to the payment by the tenant to the landlord of rent. See Davies v Hilliard (1967) 101 ILTR 50. [Text: Deale; Wylie (1)]. See TENANCY, TERMINATION OF; TENANCY AT WILL; TENANCY BY SUFFERANCE; UNAMBIGUOUS.

**lease, creation of.** A lease may be created orally where it is for year certain, from year to year or lesser period: Deasy's Act (qv) 1860; for any other period, writing is required and certain statutes require particular leases to be under seal eg Settled Land Act leases. Also letting, sub-letting or subdividing of agricultural holdings requires the consent of the Land Commission: Land Act 1965 s.12. For the purposes of the Landlord and Tenant (Amendment) Act 1980, a lease is an instrument in writing, whether under or not under seal, containing a contract of tenancy in respect of any land in consideration of a rent or return and includes a *fee farm grant* (qv) (ibid s.3(1)). See LAND COMMISSION.

**lease, determination of.** The ending of a lease or tenancy. It may happen by efflux of time, by surrender, merger, forfeiture or by notice to quit. Where a lease is for a fixed period of time, it automatically expires when the fixed period ends; however certain lessees may

have a statutory right to a new lease eg Landlord and Tenant (Amendment) Act 1980 for business leases (qv).

A lease is *surrendered* when the lessee gives up to the lessor the residue of the term still to run; this may arise by express act of the lessee or by operation of law. *Merger* takes place where the lessee acquires the reversion (qv); the lease is absorbed by the reversion. *Forfeiture* can occur for a breach of a condition in a lease, with or without a forfeiture clause, or a breach of a covenant (qv) with a forfeiture clause (sometimes called a *proviso for re-entry*). Forfeiture is strictly construed against the lessor or landlord: Bennett v Kidd (1926) NI 50.

Where a landlord proposes to forfeit a lease in reliance on a proviso giving a right of re-entry for non-payment of rent or breach of other covenants in the lease, the re-entry may only be effected either by physical possession or by the issue and service of proceedings for recovery of possession of the premises: Bank of Ireland v Lady Lisa Ireland Ltd (1993 HC) ILRM 235.

A yearly, monthly, weekly or other periodic tenancy may be determined by a *notice to quit* but not a lease or tenancy for a fixed period of time unless expressly reserved in the lease. See also Deasy's Act (qv) 1860; Conveyancing Act 1881; Landlord and Tenant Act 1967. See GROUND RENT; TENANCY, TERMINATION OF.

**lease for lives renewable for ever.** A lease granted for the term of lives, usually three, which contained a provision that when any of the lives dropped out, the grantor would grant a renewal of the lease for a new life on the payment of a sum of money called a renewable fine. A *conversion grant* enabled either party to convert the lease into a fee farm grant (qv); also such a lease, if made for the first time since 1849, operates as a fee farm grant if the lessor is capable of making such a grant: Renewable Leasehold Conversion Act 1849.

Surviving *leases for lives renewable for ever* have been converted into *fee simple* estates: Landlord and Tenant (Amendment) Act 1980 s.74.

**leasehold.** The interest created by a lease (qv).

**leasehold, mortgage of.** In order to

prevent the mortgagee (lender) becoming liable to pay the rent and perform the covenants in a lease, it is usual to create a mortgage of a lease, by way of a sub-demise of the residue of the mortgagor's interest in the term, less one day, and by way of a declaration by the mortgagor to hold the nominal reversion of one day as trustee for the mortgagee in order that the mortgagee will be able to sell the whole leasehold interest on exercising his power of sale, should this arise. See REVERSION.

**leave year.** As regards the statutory entitlement to annual leave (qv), the year beginning on 1st April: Holiday (Employees) Act 1973.

**leave to defend.** The permission given to a defendant to a summary summons to defend the proceedings, which permission may be unconditional or subject to such terms as to security, or time and mode of trial, or otherwise as the court may think fit: RSC O.37 r.10. In relation to third parties, see RSC O.16 r.8(1)(c).

**legacy.** A gift of personal property by will; a bequest. The person to whom the property is given is called the *legatee* and the gift or property is called a *bequest*. A *general* legacy is a piece of personal estate which has not been distinguished from personal property of the same kind eg a bequest of a "horse" of which the testator has several. A *specific* legacy is a bequest of a special part of the testator's personal estate eg "my horse which won the Irish Sweep's Derby in 1974." Legacies are also classified as *pecuniary* (qv) and *demonstrative* (qv). See ABATEMENT OF LEGACY; LAPSE.

**legal.** (1) In accordance with the law. (2) In accordance with the common law (qv) as distinct from equity (qv).

**legal aid.** The assistance of a qualified lawyer which a person, accused of a serious charge, is entitled to in the preparation and conduct of his defence, the cost of which is to be borne by the State from public funds: The State (Healy) v Donoghue (1976) IR 325. When the circumstances are such that if, in the event of a conviction, or on a plea of guilty, a sentence of imprisonment is likely, the judge is required to inform an indigent defendant of his right to legal aid under the provisions of the

Criminal Justice (Legal Aid) Act 1962. Legal aid may be available to an accused at the preliminary examination of an offence in the District Court where evidence will be given through a live television link (qv): 1962 Act s.2A as inserted by Criminal Evidence Act 1992 s.15(4). See Cahill v DJ Reilly & DPP (1992 HC) ITLR (13 Jul).

A district court judge should choose a solicitor for a defendant only where he has not nominated one himself, or where any nominated by him are not acceptable to the judge for good and sufficient reasons: The State (Freeman) v DJ Connellan (1987) ILRM 470.

The State was held to have been in breach of the Convention on Human Rights (qv) because of the non-availability of state-funded legal aid in matrimonial matters: Airey v Ireland (1979) 2 EHRR 305. A non-statutory legal aid scheme for civil matters was established in December 1979 under the Legal Aid Board, the purpose of which is to make the services of solicitors and, if necessary, barristers available to persons of modest means at little cost; certain matters are excluded eg land disputes.

To be granted civil legal aid, the applicant must have a reasonable likelyhood of success in relation to the proceedings; however, in cases concerning the welfare of children (eg wardship proceedings brought by a health board), the applicant must be regarded as likely to be successful if the case he wishes to make is likely to be of assistance to the court in making its decision: Stevenson v Legal Aid Board (1993 HC) ITLR (17 May). It has been held that there is no constitutional duty on the State to provide for any form of financial support for civil litigation among citizens; the Board was required however to consider an application for civil legal aid and advice within a reasonable time: Cosgrove v Legal Aid Board (1990 HC) ITLR (19 Nov).

In Northern Ireland it has been held that the fact that a party to a civil action is legally assisted may be a relevant factor to be considered by the judge in deciding whether to dismiss the action due to the failure of the party to attend at court: In the matter of Patricia Murphy (1992 HC NI) ITLR (24 Feb).

See also The State (O'Connor) v Clifford (1987) HC. See Courts-Martial (Legal Aid) Regulations 1987 (SI No 46 of 1987). See European Agreement on the Transmission of Applications for Legal Aid entered into force for Ireland on 15 December 1988. See Cousins in 10ILT & SJ (1992) 41. [Text: Gov Pub (4) & (5)]. See ATTORNEY GENERAL'S SCHEME; EURO-JUS.

**legal costs accountant.** An accountant often engaged by a solicitor to draw, prepare and submit a bill of costs in legal proceedings. It has been held that the cost of using a legal costs accountant is not a cost properly incurred by the official liquidator in a winding up of a company: In re Castle Brand Ltd (in liquidation) (1990 HC) ILRM 97.

**legal costs, investigation of title.** A building society is precluded from requiring a member to pay its costs of legal investigation of title to any property offered as security for a loan: Building Societies Amendment Act 1986 s.6(1)(d); SI No 27 of 1987, first schedule (iv); SI No 339 of 1987 art.6. Notwithstanding the repeal of the 1986 Act, this provision continues in force as if made by the Central Bank: Building Societies Act 1989 s.6. See also ibid s.11(2)(b)(iv)). See COSTS IN CIVIL PROCEEDINGS; SOLICITOR AND CLIENT COSTS.

**legal memory.** See TIME IMMEMORIAL.

**legal mortgage.** See MORTGAGE.

**legal profession.** Barristers (qv) and solicitors (qv). See Fair Trade Commission Report of Study into Restrictive Practices in the Legal Profession (1990).

**legal professional privilege.** See PRIVILEGE, LEGAL PROFESSIONAL.

**legal relations, intention to create.** An essential element in the creation of a valid and legally enforceable contract. In business dealings an intention to create legal relations will be presumed. In social arrangements it will not be so assumed unless the contrary is shown. A condition in a contract expressly excluding legal relations is binding and is not contrary to public policy. See Appleson v Littlewoood Ltd (1939) 1 All ER 464; Balfour v Balfour (1919) 2 KB 571. See GENTLEMAN'S AGREEMENT.

**legal representation.** A person is entitled to be represented in court by a solicitor (qv) or barrister (qv). It has been held

that a judge of the district court was wrong not to allow an adjournment sought by an accused in order that he might secure legal representation: Flynn v DJ Ruane (1989 HC) ILRM 690. An employee may be entitled to have legal representation at a disciplinary hearing, particularly where the charges are serious: Gallagher v Revenue Commissioners (1991 HC) ILRM 632. A person may not be entitled to legal representation where such entitlement is not provided for eg in an appeal hearing under social welfare law: Corcoran v Minister for Social Welfare (1992 HC) ILRM 133. See also LEGAL AID; NATURAL JUSTICE; SOLICITOR, ACCESS TO.

**legal right of spouse.** See SPOUSE, LEGAL RIGHT OF.

**legal separation.** See DIVORCE A MENSA ET THORO; JUDICIAL SEPARATION; SEPARATION AGREEMENT.

**legal tender.** Tender or offer of payment in a form which a creditor is bound to accept. A tender of money in coins is legal tender for 20 times the face value of each denomination of coin tendered: Central Bank Act 1989 s.127. Notes issued by the Central Bank are legal tender in the State for the payment of any amount (ibid s.118). In a tender of money, the exact amount must be tendered without any request for change. A perpetual copyright subsists in legal tender notes and belongs to the Central Bank of Ireland: Copyright Act 1963 s.57.

As the EC moves towards full economic and monetary union, the only banknotes which will have the status of legal tender within the Community will be banknotes issued by the European Central Bank (qv) and the national central banks: Treaty of Rome 1957 art.105a(1) as inserted by Maastricht Treaty 1992 art.G(D)(25). The ECB will have the exclusive right to *authorise* the issue of banknotes within the Community. See COINS; TENDER.

**legal tender note fund.** The fund which was wound up by the Central Bank of Ireland with effect from the close of business on 27 July 1989 pursuant to the Central Bank Act 1989 s.22. The assets of the fund have been transferred to the General Fund of the bank; legal tender notes on issue at any time from

28 July 1989 are a liability on the General Fund (Iris Oifigiuil — 1st August 1989).

**legal year.** The annual period of time constituted by the four sittings of the courts, being Michaelmas, Hilary, Easter and Trinity. See SITTINGS OF COURT.

**legality, presumption of.** See OMNIA PRAESUMUNTUR RITA ESSE ACTA.

**legatee.** A person to whom a legacy is left. See LEGACY.

**leges posteriores priores contrarias abrogant.** [Later laws abrogate prior contrary laws].

**legislation.** (1) The making of laws. (2) The body of enactments or statutes of the legislature. Legislation is either *superior* or *sub-ordinate*. Superior legislation is law as enacted by the legislature ie by the Oireachtas (qv); sub-ordinate legislation is the rules or law as laid down by some person or body under authority delegated by the legislature. See ACT; BILL; DELEGATED LEGISLATION; JURISDICTION.

**legislation, constitutionality of.** The Oireachtas must not enact any law which is in any respect repugnant to the Constitution and any law which is so repugnant is invalid to the extent of the repugnancy: 1937 Constitution art.15(4). The Constitution continued in force the laws in Saorstat Eireann prior to its adoption, except in so far as they were inconsistent with the Constitution (ibid art.50).

A law passed by the Oireachtas is presumed to be constitutional unless and until the contrary is clearly established; all laws in force prior to the coming into operation of the Constitution do not enjoy such a presumption but remain part of the legislative framework until found to be inconsistent with the Constitution. See F v Supt of B Garda Station (1991) 1 IR 189. There is a constitutional prohibition on the enactment of laws applicable in the counties of Northern Ireland (qv) pending the re-integration of the national territory: 1937 Constitution, art.3 and McGimpsey v Ireland (1990 SC) ILRM 440.

The High Court has jurisdiction to decide on the validity of any law having regard to the provisions of the Constitution (ibid art.34(3)). An appeal lies to the Supreme Court. Also that court deals with a referral by the President of Ireland of a Bill under art.26 in which event the Court may deliver only one decision (ibid art.34(4)(5)).

A citizen may only challenge the constitutionality of legislation where his interests have been adversely affected, or they stand in real or imminent danger of being adversely affected by the operation of the legislation: Cahill v Sutton (1980) IR 269. The Supreme Court will not pronounce on the constitutional validity of a statutory provision where such pronouncement can be of no conceivable interest or benefit to the applicant; the court will avoid dealing with a constituitional issue where a case can be decided on some other ground: McDaid v Judge Sheehy (1991 SC) ILRM 250; In re Application of Tivoli Cinema Ltd (1992 HC) ILRM 522,

Notice must be served on the Attorney General in any proceedings wherein any question arises as to the validity of a law, having regard to the provisions of the Constitution: RSC O.60 rr.1-2. See NATIONAL EMERGENCY; RETROSPECTIVE LEGISLATION; SEVERANCE; SUPREME COURT.

**legislation, delegated.** See DELEGATED LEGISLATION.

**legislation, interpretation of.** Statutes are interpreted by the literal rule, the golden rule, the mischief rule, or by the maxims, ejusdem generis, and generalia specialibus non derogant (qqv). The Supreme Court has held that there are three basic rules of interpretation: (a) if the statute is directed to the public at large, a word or expression should be given its ordinary or colloquial meaning; (b) when a word or expression creates a penal or taxation liability, it should be construed strictly; (c) when a word is a simple word which has widespread and unambiguous currency, the judge's own experience of its use should be drawn on to construe it: Inspector of Taxes v Kiernan (1981) IR 117 and (1982) ILRM 13.

In construing a particular statutory provision, no provision of another statute may be used as an aid or a guide unless that other statutory provision is *in pari materia*, that is forming part of the same statutory context: The State (Sheehan) v Ireland (1988 SC) ILRM 437. The long title of an Act is only relevant to the issue of interpretation where the text of a statutory provision is ambiguous or equivocal: The People (DPP) v Quilligan (1987) ILRM 606.

There is a presumption that words in a statute were not used without a meaning and were not tautologous or superfluous; effect must be given, if possible, to all the words used, for the legislature must be deemed not to waste words or to say anything in vain: Egan J in Cork County Council v Whillock (1993 SC) ITLR (8 Feb). Also words or phrases must not be inserted into a statutory provision so as to interpret it: McDonagh v County Borough of Galway (1993 SC) ITLR (23 Aug).

The court cannot rely on the expression of a Minister, given in the Dail, when interpreting an Act: Conaty v Tipperary (NR) Co Council (1989) 7ILT & SJ 222. However, Dail and Seanad debates may be admissible as an aid to understanding what motivated the legislature in framing a statute: Wavin Pipes Ltd v Hepsworth Iron Co Ltd (1982) FSR 32. See also Interpretation Act 1937. See also Cooke v Walsh (1984) ILRM 208; DPP v Go Travel Ltd (1991 SC) ILRM 577; McCann v O'Culachain (1986) ILRM 229; Texaco v Murphy (1992 SC) ILRM 304; Irish Bank of Commerce v O'Hara (1992 SC) ITLR (10 Aug). See Kerr — "Parliamentary History as an Aid to the Interpretation of Statutes" in 11 ILT & SJ (1993) 72. See CONSTRUE AS ONE; EXPLANATORY MEMORANDUM; MARGINAL NOTES; PREAMBLE; REPEAL.

**legislation, motivation for.** The court will not order the discovery of documents to determine the motivation for legislation as it would be meaningless and unjustified by the doctrine of the separation of powers; the validity of legislation must be tested by reference to the document ultimately enacted by the Oireachtas and not on the basis of the motives, intention or purpose of the Minister by whom the legislation is introduced or those of any member of the Oireachtas who supports or opposes it: Blascaoid Mor Teo v Ireland (1992 HC) — Irish Times 28/11/1992.

**legislation, retrospective.** See RETROSPECTIVE LEGISLATION.

**legislative.** See SEPARATION OF POWERS.

**legitimacy, presumption of.** The presumption of legitimacy arising out of marriage has been abolished and replaced by a *presumption of paternity:* Status of Children Act 1987 s.44 and 46. See Russell v Russel (1924) AC 687; AS v RB (1984) ILRM 66. See PATERNITY, PRESUMPTION OF.

**legitimate.** See CHILD, LEGITIMATE.

**legitimate expectation, doctrine of.** See EXPECTATION, LEGITIMATE.

**legitimated.** See CHILD, LEGITIMATED.

**lesbianism.** Female homosexuality. The Defamation Act 1961 s.16 provides that words spoken and published which impute unchastity or adultery to any woman or girl does not require proof of *special* damage to render them actionable. In the UK, it has been held that an imputation of lesbianism is an imputation within the meaning of a similar section in the Slander of Women Act 1891: Kerr v Kennedy (1942) 1 All ER 412. See HATRED, INCITEMENT TO; SLANDER; VIDEO RECORDING.

**lessee.** A person to whom a lease (qv) is granted.

**lessor.** A person who grants a lease (qv).

**lethal.** As regards a *lethal* weapon, means capable of causing death: Moore v Gooderham (1960) 1 WLR 1308. See FIREARM.

**letter of comfort.** In commercial practice, usually a letter from a parent company to the creditor of a subsidiary of the parent in respect of advances made to the subsidiary. Whether it involves an assumption of legal liability for the debts of the subsidiary will depend on the wording of the letter and the intention of the parties. In general, the effect of a letter of comfort is a matter of such uncertainty, they are inadvisable in commercial transactions, a guarantee or indemnity being much more certain. See Kleinworth Benson Ltd v Malaysia Mining Corp (1988) 1 All ER 714; 7ILT & SJ (1989) 235; 8ILT & SJ (1990) 234.

**letter of credit.** An undertaking by a banker acting on the instructions of its customer (eg the buyer of goods) to pay or to meet drafts drawn pursuant to it by the beneficiary of the credit (eg the seller of the goods) in accordance with the terms laid down in the undertaking. The sale of goods worldwide is normally arranged by means of *letters of credit* eg the buyer may instruct his bank to open a credit in favour of the seller, which is a promise by the banker to pay money to the seller in return for, say, shipping documents in respect of the goods.

Letters of credit may be revocable or irrevocable. A *revocable* credit may be amended or cancelled at any time without notice to the beneficiary. An *irrevocable* letter of credit constitutes a definite undertaking of the issuing bank, provided that the terms and conditions of the credit are complied with. See also Building Societies Act 1989 s.29(2)(q). [Text: Paget UK].

**letter of request.** A letter (also known as a *commission rogatoire*) from a foreign court or tribunal that it is desirous of obtaining the testimony of a witness within the jurisdiction of this State; the court in this State is empowered to order the taking of such evidence. See RSC O.39 rr.39-44. See Foreign Tribunals Evidence Act 1856; Extradition Act 1870 s.24; Arbitration Act 1954 s.22(1)(d); Patents Act 1992 s.130.

**letters missive.** See SIGN MANUAL.

**letters of administration.** A *grant of representation* issued from the Probate Office, or from a District Probate Registry (qv), which are part of the High Court, to the effect that administration of a deceased's estate has been granted to the administrator, he having first sworn faithfully to administer same (eg RSC App Q Form 7). The administrator undertakes to exhibit a true inventory of the estate and to render a true account thereof (RSC App Q Form 5).

Persons who have a beneficial interest in the estate of the deceased are entitled to a grant of administration in a specified order of priority depending on whether the deceased died intestate or testate: Succession Act 1965 s.27(3); RSC O.79 r.5. A grant of administration cannot be made to more than three persons unless the probate officer directs otherwise: RSC O.79 r.5(14) and O.80 r.6(13).

A grant of letters of administration intestate is given where the deceased died intestate. A grant of administration with the will annexed, *cum testamento annexo*, is given where the deceased left a will, but some person other than the executor applies for a grant.

A grant may be limited as to duration, limited as to purpose, or limited to a particular part of the estate. See Succession Act 1965 s.27(1); also In re Mathew (dec'd) (1984) 2 All ER 396. See also Status of Children Act 1987 s.30. See ADMINISTRATION OF ESTATES; ADMINISTRATOR; INSOLVENT ESTATE.

**letters of administration, priority for.** Persons having a beneficial interest in the estate of another, who has died wholly intestate and domiciled in Ireland, are entitled to a grant of administration in the following order of priority: (a) the surviving spouse; (b) the surviving spouse jointly with a child of the deceased nominated by the said spouse; (c) the child or children of the deceased; (d) the issue of any child of the deceased who has died during the lifetime of the deceased; (e) the father or mother of the deceased; (f) brothers and sisters of the deceased (whether of the whole or half blood); (g) where any brother or sister survived the deceased, the children of a predeceased brother or sister; (h) nephews and nieces of the deceased (whether of the whole or half blood); (i) grandparents; (j) uncles and aunts (whether of the whole or half blood); (k) great grandparents; (l) other next-of-kin of nearest degree (whether of the whole or half blood) preferring collaterals to direct lineal ancestors; (m) the nominees of the State: RSC O.79 r.5(1).

**letters patent.** Originally, grants by the sovereign of franchises, lands or rights to another, contained in an instrument or charter, which was usually addressed to all subjects in the realm and bore the Great Seal of the Realm. The term *Letters Patent for an Invention* are no longer used; patent grants also are no longer under seal: Patents Act 1992 s.34. See PATENT.

**letting of goods.** See HIRE; HIRER, HIRE-PURCHASE.

**levant and couchant.** [Risen and lain down].

**levy.** To raise money compulsorily eg by means of taxes or distress. Modern examples are the training levies imposed on some employers by the Industrial Training Act 1967 and the employment and training levy imposed on individuals by the Labour Services Act 1987 and the Youth Employment Agency Act 1981.

**lex causae.** [The law governing the matter]. See Mitchelstown Co-operative Agricultural Society v Nestle (1989 SC) ILRM 582.

**lex domicilii.** [The law of the person's domicile].

**lex fori.** [The law of the court in which the case is tried].

**lex loci celebrationis.** [The law of the place where a marriage is celebrated]. A marriage abroad to be recognised by the State must have complied with the law of the place where it was celebrated. Certain marriages solemnised according to religious ceremonies abroad eg in Lourdes, but which did not comply with the local civil formalities, were regularised by the Marriage Act 1972 s.2. See also Conlon v Mohamed (1987) ILRM 172.

**lex loci contractus.** [The law of the place where the contract is made].

**lex loci delicti commissi.** [The law of the place where the wrong was committed].

**lex loci solutionis.** [The law of the place of performance].

**lex non cogit ad impossibilia.** [The law does not compel the impossible].

**lex non requirit verificari quod apparet curiae.** [The law does not require that which is apparent to the court to be verified].

**lex non scripta.** [The unwritten law]. The common law.

**lex posterior derogat priori.** [A later law overrules an earlier one].

**lex rei situs.** [The law of the situation of the thing].

**lex scripta.** [The written law]. Statute law.

**lex situs.** [The law of the place where property is situated]. The general rule is that land and other immovables are governed by the lex situs eg succession to moveable property of an intestate is governed by the law of his domicile and succession to his immovables by the lex situs. See PRIVATE INTERNATIONAL LAW; WILL, INTERNATIONAL.

**lex spectat naturae ordinem.** [The law has regard to the order of nature].

**lex talionis.** [The law of retaliation]. Refers to primative law embodied in the phrase *An eye for an eye, a tooth for a tooth.*

**liability.** Legal obligation or duty; or the amount owed. A person who commits a wrong or breaks a contract or trust is said to be liable or responsible for it. A liability is said to be criminal or civil, depending on whether it is enforced by a criminal or civil court. A *vicarious liability* (qv) is one which falls on one person as a result of his relationship with another eg a master is generally liable for the acts of his servant performed in the course of his employment. A *contingent liability* is a future unascertained obligation. Where the justice of a case so requires it, the Supreme Court can determine the issue of liability instead of referring the matter back to the High Court eg see Phillips v Durgan (1991 SC) ILRM 321. [Text: Kerr (3)]. See LIMITATION OF LIABILITY.

**liability, limited.** See COMPANY, LIMITED; LIMITED PARTNERSHIP; PERSONAL LIABILITY.

**liability, statutory exemption from.** Examples of statutory exemption from liability are in respect of (a) loss arising from the administration of the postal services: Post Office Act 1908 s.13; (b) loss arising from telephone and telegraph services: Telegraph Regulations 1920, Telephone Regulations 1959; (c) exemption from implied terms of carriage contracts: SGSS 1980 s.40(6); (d) terms and conditions of carriage by rail: Transport Act 1958 s.8; (e) power to cut off electricity for non-payment of account: Electricity (Supply) Act 1927 s.99; McCord v ESB (1980) ILRM 153.

**liability, strict.** See STRICT LIABILITY.

**liability, vicarious.** See VICARIOUS LIABILITY.

**liability for products.** See PRODUCT LIABILITY.

**libel.** Defamation in writing or printing or in some other permanent form, such as a statue or film. Broadcasting words by wireless telegraphy is to be treated as publication in a permanent form: Defamation Act 1961 s.15. Libel is actionable *per se*, without proof of actual damages being suffered. See DEFAMATION.

A libel, but not a slander, may also be a crime. *Criminal libel* is a libel which is sufficiently aggravated by its public nature (eg libel on a person in a public position). It has been held that while it is not necessary that a libel should be likely to provoke a breach of the peace in order to constitute a criminal offence, it must be a serious libel so that the public interest requires the institution of criminal proceedings: Hilliard v Penfield Enterprises Ltd and Ors (1990 HC) 1 IR 138. It is a good defence to show the truth of the matter charged and to show that it was for the public benefit that the matters charged were published: Defamation Act 1961 s.6. See RSC O.36 r.36. See Report on the Crime of Libel (LRC 41 of 1991). [Text: McDonald; McHugh; Duncan & O'Neill UK; Gatley UK]. See DEATH, EFFECT OF; DEFAMATION; LODGMENT IN COURT; MITIGATION OF DAMAGES; NAME, RIGHT TO GOOD; OFFER OF AMENDS; PUBLICATION; SLANDER.

**liberty.** (1) Absence of restraint. (2) A necessary condition for freedom. (3) A franchise (qv). [Text: TCD].

**liberty, personal.** See PERSONAL LIBERTY.

**libraries.** Local authorities have power to establish public libraries, museums and schools of science and art: Public Libraries (Ireland) Act 1855 and 1877; LG(P&D) Act 1963 s.77.

In Northern Ireland, it has been held that there is no legal duty to provide a *law library* for the use of personal litigants: In the matter of an application by Jagat Narain (1991 C of A in NI) ITLR (3 Jun). Similarly, in the Republic, it has been held that there is no constitutional duty on the State to provide a law library for personal litigants: MacGairbhit v AG (1991 HC) 2 IR 412. See LAW LIBRARY.

**licence.** An authority to do something which would otherwise be wrongful or illegal. A *bare licence* (qv) can be revoked at any time. A *licence coupled with an interest* is one supported by consideration and can be revoked only in accordance with its terms. Property rights arising in licences created by law are subject to the conditions created by law and to an implied condition that the law may change those conditions; a change in the law which has the effect of reducing property values cannot of itself amount to an infringement of constitutionally protected property rights: Hempenstall v Minister for Environment (1993 HC) ILRM 318. See BARE LICENCE; EXCLUSIVE LICENCE.

**licence, copyright.** See COPYRIGHT.

**licences of right.** A licence to a patent to which any person is entitled, as of right: Patents Act 1992 ss.68(2) and 70(1). The licence may be *voluntary* or *compulsory*. It is *voluntary* where the proprietor of the patent applies to the Controller of Patents for an entry to be made in the register to the effect that licences under the patent are to be made available as of right, in which case renewal fees will be halved and the licence terms will, in default of agreement, be settled by the Controller (ibid s.68).

The licence is *compulsory* where the Controller so orders on application by any person on certain specified grounds for a licence or for an entry in the register that licences be available as of right (ibid s.71). The specified grounds include (a) that the patented invention is not being commercially worked in the State — see s.2(1) and Kamborian's Patent (1961) RPC 403; (b) that the demand in the State for the patented product is not being met on reasonable terms or is being met to a substantial extent by importation; (c) that the commercial working in the State of the patented invention is being prevented or hindered by importation of the patented product; (d) that by reason of the refusal of the proprietor to grant a licence on reasonable terms, or by reason of conditions imposed by the proprietor, the establishment or development of commercial or industrial activities in the State is unfairly prejudiced; (e) that a condition which is null and void has been included in a contract relating to the patented product or process (ibid s.70(2)). A compulsory licence must be non-exclusive and non-transferable (ibid s.70(3)(d)).

The Controller may grant a compulsory licence to the customers of the applicant as well as the applicant (ibid s.71). See Loewe Radio's Application (1929) 46 RPC 479; Hunter v Fox (1965) RPC 416. See PATENT; FOOD AND MEDICINES, PATENTS FOR.

**licensee.** A person who has permission, express or implied, to enter premises for his own purposes, but not for any business of the occupier. See BARE LICENCE; OCCUPIER'S LIABILITY TO LICENSEES.

**lie.** An action is said to *lie* if it can be properly instituted and maintained.

**lien.** The right to hold the property of

another as security for the performance of an obligation. As regards a contract for the sale of goods, an unpaid seller's lien is the right of a seller to retain possession of goods until the payment or tender of the price: Sale of Goods Act 1893 ss.41-43. Any lien or other charge of a public limited company on its own shares is void: Companies Amendment Act 1983 s.44. Exceptions are made for charges that arise from transactions entered into in the ordinary course of business by money lending companies, and charges taken by companies on their own not fully paid shares for any amount not paid on them (ibid s.44(2)). See also Companies Act 1963, Table A, art 11; Companies Act 1990 s.125; Building Societies Act 1989 s.41(6). See RSC O.22 r.10(7); O.45 rr.5-6; O.50 r.9; O.99 r.4. See CARRIER'S LIEN; DEPOSIT OF TITLE DEEDS; FORFEITURE; PRESERVED BENEFIT; SOLICITOR.

**lien, equitable.** See EQUITABLE LIEN.

**lieu, in.** In the place of.

**life, expectation of.** See EXPECTATION OF LIFE, LOSS OF.

**life, right to.** Every individual, as an individual, has certain inherent rights of which the right to life is the most fundamental: Conroy v Attorney General (1965) IR 411. The State is required by its laws to protect as best it may from unjust attack and, in the case of injustice done, to vindicate the life of every citizen: 1937 Constitution, art 40(3)(2). The right to life of the *unborn* has been expressly acknowledged by the Eighth Amendment to the 1937 Constitution, passed by referendum in 1983; the equal right of the mother is also acknowledged in that amendment (ibid art.40(3)(3)). However, the Twelfth Amendment to the Constitution regarding the right to life was rejected by the people in 1992. See also SPUC v Grogan (1990 SC) ILRM 350; (1992 ECJ) ILRM 461. See ABORTION; UNBORN, RIGHT TO LIFE.

**life assurance.** Assurance of a class specified in the European Communities (Life Assurance) Regulations 1984 (SI No 57 of 1984), schedule 1.

From July 1994 EC-based life insurance companies will be permitted to sell their policies anywhere in the EC, subject to supervision of regulations in their base country: EC Third Life Directive. Spain, Portugal and Greece have a longer time period in which to comply with the Directive. See INSURANCE BUSINESS.

**life estate.** A freehold estate for the life of a person which arises by grant. The life estate may be for the life of the tenant eg *to A for life*. It may also be for the life of another, *pur autre vie* eg *to A for the life of B*. B is known as the *cestui que vie* and A the *tenant pur autre vie*; the years remaining in the estate on the death of A may be disposed of by his will or, if he dies intestate, the interest devolves on his personal representatives (qv): Statute of Frauds (Ireland) 1695; Succession Act 1965.

A life tenant is liable for waste (qv). He also has certain rights to emblements (qv) and to fixtures (qv). A life tenancy formerly could be created by operation of law eg curtesy (qv) and dower (qv), but these were abolished by the Succession Act 1965 s.11.

**life imprisonment.** The mandatory sentence of penal servitude for life for non-capital murder: Criminal Justice Act 1964 s.2; The People v Murtagh (1966) IR 361. In practice, a person sentenced to penal servitude for life is released after a period of imprisonment of eight to ten years. However, see TREASON. Longer periods are specified for aggravated murder, which has replaced capital murder. See MURDER, AGGRAVATED; SEXUAL ASSAULT.

**life in being.** See PERPETUITIES, RULE AGAINST.

**life-guards.** See BATHS, PUBLIC.

**lifting the corporate veil.** The phrase used to describe the process whereby the legislature and the court may look behind the corporate curtain and identify a company with its owners, despite being bound by the principle that a company is a separate legal person, distinct from its members. The court will look at the underlying economic reality, especially where the company has been engaged in fraudulent trading or where the company is a mere sham. See Gilford Motor Co v Horne (1933) Ch 935; Powers Supermarkets Ltd v Crumlin Investments Ltd (1981) HC; Dublin County Council v O'Riordan (1986) ILRM 104; Desmond & Dedeir Ltd v Glackin (1992 SC) ITLR (7 Dec). See INVESTIGATION OF COMPANY; PERSONAL LIABILITY.

**lifting weights.** See WEIGHTS, MAXIMUM.

**light, right to.** To constitute an actionable nuisance for obstruction of ancient lights, it is not enough that the light is less than before; there must be a substantial privation of light, enough to render the occupation of a house uncomfortable acording to the ordinary notions of mankind and, in the case of a business premises, to prevent the plaintiff from carrying on his business as beneficially as before: Colls v Home & Colonial Stores (1904) AC 179.

After the actual enjoyment of the access of light to a building has continued for 20 years without interruption, the right is deemed absolute unless enjoyed by written consent: Prescription Act 1832 (in Ireland 1859) s.3. See also O'Connor v Walsh (1907) 42 ILTR 20; Scott v Goulding Properties Ltd (1973) IR 200; Leech v Reilly (1983) HC. See EASEMENT.

**lighting.** See PUBLIC LIGHTING; STREET LIGHTING.

**lighting-up hours.** The period commencing one half-hour after sunset on any day and ending one half-hour before sunrise on the next day: Road Traffic General Bye-Laws 1964 art.2. (SI No 294 of 1964).

**like work.** A man and a woman are regarded as employed on *like work* in relation to entitlement to equal pay (a) where both perform the *same work* under the same or similar conditions or where each is in every respect interchangeable with the other in relation to the work, or (b) where the work performed by one is of a *similar nature* to that performed by the other and any differences between the work performed or the conditions under which it is performed by each, occur only infrequently or are of small importance in relation to the work as a whole, or (c) where the work performed by one is *equal in value* to that performed by the other in terms of the demands it makes in relation to such matters as skill, physical or mental effort, responsibility and working conditions.

A woman can avail of equal pay legislation if doing work of greater value than a male colleague: Murphy v Telecom Eireann (1986) HC, endorsed by opinion of Advocate General of European Court 1987.

See also Dept of Posts & Telegraphs v Kennefick DEP 2/ 1980; Arthur Guinness v Federated Workers' Union of Ireland DEP 11/1983; Comhairle Oiliuna Talmhaiochta v Doyle (1989) IR 33. See Anti-Discrimination (Pay) Act 1974 s.3. See EQUAL PAY.

**limitation, words of.** See WORDS OF LIMITATION.

**limitation of actions.** The provision by which actions to enforce rights are barred if proceedings are not taken within certain periods of time: Statute of Limitations 1957. The time limits prescribed include: (a) simple contract — six years from the date on which the *cause of action* accrued (ibid s.11(1)(a)); (b) quasi-contract — six years (ibid s.11(1)(b)); (c) specialty contract — 12 years (ibid s.11(5)); (d) tort (other than one causing personal injuries or slander) — six years (ibid s.11(2)); (e) personal injury — 3 years from the cause of action or the date of knowledge if later (ibid s.11(2)(b); Statute of Limitations (Amdt) Act 1991); (f) slander — 3 years (ibid 1957 Act s.11(2)(c)); (g) recovery of land — 12 years (ibid s.13(2)); (h) recovery of arrears of conventional rent — six years (ibid s.28); (i) redemption of mortgage — 12 years (ibid s.15); (j) judgment of court of record — 12 years (ibid s.11(6)); (k) salvage claims — 2 years (Civil Liability Act 1961 s.46); (l) contribution from concurrent wrongdoer — same period as the injured person is allowed by law for bringing an action against the contributor, or within the period of two years after the liability of the claimant is ascertained, or the injured person's damages are paid, whichever is the greater (ibid s.31 of Civil Liability Act 1961); (m) damages arising from breach of implied condition arising from defective motor vehicle — 2 years (SGSS Act 1980 s.13(7)); (n) damages in respect of defective products — 3 years (Liability for Defective Products Act 1991 s.7).

There is provision for the extension of the limitation periods in the case of disability, acknowledgement, part payment, fraud, and mistake (ibid 1957 Act ss.47-72; 1991 Act s.5). However, even where an action has been commenced within the time limit fixed by an Act of the Oireachtas, the courts have an inherent jurisdiction to dismiss a claim in the interests of justice where the lapse of time is so great that it would cause injustice to a defendant: Toal v Duignan & Ors (1990 SC) ITLR (26 Nov) — a medical negligence action. See O'Brien v Keogh (1972) IR 144; Campbell v Ward (1981) ILRM 60. [Text: Brady & Kerr]. See CAUSE OF ACTION; PRODUCT LIABILITY, EC; SURGICAL OPERATION; TIME; UNSOUND MIND.

**limitation of liability.** The imposition of a ceiling or limit on liability for damage or loss by contract or by statute. See Dun Laoghaire Corporation v Park Hill Developments Ltd (1989) ILRM 235. See COMPANY, LIMITED; LIMITED PARTNERSHIP; PERSONAL LIABILITY.

**limited administration.** A grant of letters of administration of the estate of a deceased which is limited as to duration, to purpose or to a particular part of the estate. See LETTERS OF ADMINISTRATION.

**limited company.** See COMPANY, LIMITED.

**limited owner.** An owner of an interest in land which is less than a fee simple estate eg a life tenant.

**limited partnership.** A partnership in which there are one or more partners with unlimited liability, known as *general partners*, and other partners known as *limited partners* who contribute to the partnership assets a specified amount in money or money's worth and who enjoy immunity from liability beyond the amount so contributed, provided they take no part in the management of the business: Limited Partnership Act 1907.

A limited partner, also known as a *sleeping partner*, has no power to bind the firm. A limited partnership must be registered with the Registrar of Companies. Bankruptcy provisions apply to limited partnerships in like manner as if they were ordinary partnerships; however when all general partners are adjudicated bankrupt, the assets of the limited partnership vest in the Official Assignee (qv): Bankruptcy Act 1988 s.37. See also 1988 Act s.81(10). See McCartaigh v Daly (1986) ILRM 116. See PARTNERSHIP; PARTNERSHIP AND BANKRUPTCY.

**linea recta semper praefertur transversali.** [The direct line is always preferred to the collateral].

**lineal consanguinity.** See CONSANGUINITY.

**linking services.** There is a prohibition on a building society making it a condition of a housing loan (qv) that the borrower must take other services from the society eg financial, insurance, conveyancing, auctioneering or other services relating to land, whether provided directly by the society itself or through a subsidiary or associated body: Building Societies Act 1989 s.35(1).

**liquid assets.** Assets in readily realisable form or in cash.

**liquidated.** Fixed or ascertained. A company is said to be *liquidated* when it is wound up.

**liquidated damages.** The compensation in money for loss suffered by a person owing to breach of contract by another, which is a fixed and ascertained amount in the contract. In an action where it appears to the court that the amount of damages is substantially a matter of calculation, the court may direct that the amount for which final judgment is to be entered shall be determined by the Master of the High Court: RSC O.36 r.48. See DAMAGES; PENALTY; SUMMONS, HIGH COURT; SUMMARY SUMMONS.

**liquidated demand.** An ascertained demand in money. The recovery of such a demand with or without interest, must be by summary summons where proceeded with in the High Court: RSC O.2 r.1(1). The indorsement of claim on such a summons must state the amount claimed and must state the amount claimed for costs and state that on payment of such amounts within six days after service, further proceedings will be stayed: RSC O.4 r.5.

**liquidation.** See WINDING UP.

**liquidator.** A person appointed to carry out the winding up of a company. The principal duties of the liquidator are to get in and realise the assets of the company, to pay or settle its debts, and to distribute to the members the surplus, if any, that may remain. A liquidator appointed by the court is known as an *official liquidator*. The main difference between a liquidator in a winding up by the court and in a voluntary winding up, is that the former must obtain the consent of the court or of the *committee of inspection* in order to exercise many of his powers: Companies Act 1963 s.231 as amended by the Companies Act 1990 s.124.

It has been held that if a sale by a

liquidator is subject to the court's prior approval, the liquidator must accept the highest offer made, even if that offer was made subsequent to the liquidator having agreed with another party to sell the property subject to the court's consent: Van Hool McArdle Ltd v Rohan Industrial Estates Ltd (1980) IR 237.

Where cause is shown, the court may remove a liquidator in a voluntary winding up and appoint another (ibid 1963 Act s.277(2)). A liquidator must be afforded an opportunity of making his case in respect of his fees: In re Merchant Banking (1987) ILRM 260. The general law of bankruptcy (qv) must be applied by the liquidator to some aspects of winding up of insolvent companies (ibid s.284; In re Irish Attested Sales Ltd (1962) IR 70). See also In re GWI Ltd (1987) HC.

A liquidator is obliged to incorporate, in any returns he is required to make, a report on whether any past or present director or other officer or member of the company is subject to a *disqualification order* (qv) or has been declared personally liable for the debts of the company: Companies Act 1990 ss.144-145.

Persons disqualified for appointment as a liquidator are present or recent officers or servants of the company, its auditors and close relatives of officers (ibid s.146 inserting s.300A in the 1963 Act) or an undischarged bankrupt (ibid 1990 Act s.169 amending s.183 of the 1963 Act). While there are no qualifications specified for liquidators, the Minister is empowered to add to the list of persons who are not qualified for appointment (ibid 1990 Act s.237). See also Building Societies Act 1989 s.109. See RSC O.74 rr.29-48. [Text: Forde (9); Robb]. See WINDING UP; ONEROUS PROPERTY; PROVISIONAL LIQUIDATOR; DISQUALIFICATION ORDER.

**liquor.** See INTOXICATING LIQUOR.

**lis.** An action; a suit; a dispute.

**lis alibi pendens.** [A suit pending elsewhere]. It may be a ground for staying an action. See LIS PENDENS.

**lis moto.** [An existing or pending action]. See ANTE LITEM MOTAM.

**lis pendens.** [Pending action]. The registration of an action against a landowner: Judgment (Ireland) Act 1844

s.10; Byrne v UDT Bank Ltd (1984) ILRM 418. A lis pendens does not bind or affect a purchaser or mortgagee (qv), who has no express notice of it, unless and until a memorandum containing the requisite details concerning the suit is registered in court eg the name and usual or last known abode and title, trade or profession of the person whose estate is intended to be affected by the suit, the court, title of action, and day filed: In re O'Byrne's Estate (1885) 15 LR Ir 373.

A registered lis pendens may be *vacated* on the order of the court, even without the consent of the person who registered it: RSC 0.63 r.1(29); Flynn v Buckley (1980) IR 423; Lis Pendens Act 1867. See also Jurisdiction of Courts and Enforcement of Judgments (European Communities) Act 1988, first schedule, arts.21-23; Jurisdiction of Courts and Enforcement of Judgments Act 1993, sixth schedule, arts.21-23. See PENDENTE LITE.

**list for hearing.** See LODGMENT IN COURT; SET DOWN.

**listing agreement.** See STOCK EXCHANGE.

**lite pendente.** See PENDENTE LITE.

**literal rule.** The rule of construction for interpreting a statute whereby the judge gives to words in the statute their natural and ordinary meaning. Effect is required to be given to a particular provision of legislation unless it would lead to a result so manifestly absurd or unjust that there is good reason to seek an alternative: Rahinstown Estate v Hughes (1987) ILRM 599. See also R v Inhabitants of Ramsgate (1827) 6 B C 712; Inspector of Taxes v Kiernan (1981) IR and (1982) ILRM 13; In re Atlantic Magnetics Ltd (1992 SC) ITLR (16 Mar). See LEGISLATION, INTERPRETATION OF.

**literary work.** For the purposes of copyright protection, literary work includes all original works reduced to *writing* or to some other material form: Copyright Act 1963 ss.3(4) and 8(1). It includes any written table or compilation (ibid s.2(1); Allied Discount Card Ltd v Bord Failte Eireann (1990 HC) ILRM 811. *Writing* includes any form of notation whether by hand or by printing, typewriting or other process (ibid s.2(1)). Literary work includes any written table or compilation: Broadcasting and Wireless Telegraphy Act 1988 s.1. In interpreting the phrase *literary work* the Court must take a broad view; the phrase should be taken to mean any written or printed composition which was an original composition that involved labour, time and skill in its compilation: RTE v Magill TV Guide Ltd (1990 HC) ILRM 534. See COMPILATION; COPYRIGHT; ORIGINAL.

**lithograph.** See ARTISTIC WORK.

**litigation.** Legal action by parties who are known as *litigants*. A solicitor is required to exercise due professional care and skill in the conduct of litigation in respect of a client; if he does not do so, he will be liable in tort as well as in contract: Finlay v Murtagh (1979) IR 249. The duty extends to the drafting of pleadings (qv): McGrath v Kiely (1965) IR 497.

**litis aestimatio.** [Measure of damages].

**litter.** The creation of litter is prohibited and constitutes an offence: Litter Act 1982 s.3. Local authorities are required to take measures for the prevention of litter and for dealing with litter in their areas (ibid s.2). They have enforcement powers in respect of littering, graffiti, flyposting, the abandonment of vehicles and disused articles (ibid ss.11-13). They are required to make provision for the disposal of vehicles and scrap metal (ibid s.9). Occupiers of land are required to keep it free of litter, which is in, or is visible from, a public place (ibid s.4). See WASTE OPERATION.

**livelihood.** A right to trade and earn a livelihood is one of the unspecified personal rights guaranteed by the Constitution art 40.3; it is not an unqualified right: Hand & Ors v Dublin Corporation (1991 SC) ILRM 556. See WORK, RIGHT TO.

**living matter.** It is now possible to patent living matter as an invention. See MICRO-ORGANISMS.

**living memory.** See TIME IMMEMORIAL.

**loan.** A contract whereby one person lends or agrees to lend a sum of money to another, in consideration of a promise express or implied to repay that sum: Chitty. [Text: Burgess]. See LOCAL LOANS FUND.

**loan to director.** Formerly there was no prohibition on the making of a loan by a company to a director; however any such loan had to be disclosed in the accounts of the company: Companies Act 1963 ss.192-193. Recent legislation prohibits, subject to certain limited exceptions, companies from making loans in excess of 10% of the company's assets to a director or a person *connected* to a director: Companies Act 1990 ss.31-37.

The prohibition includes the making of *quasi-loans* to a director or entering into a *credit transaction*, guarantee or security for a director; these are arrangements whereby third parties pay a director's liability in a financial transaction or provide him with goods and services on the understanding that the company will eventually pay the third party.

There are exceptions, eg inter-company loans, director's expenses, and loans entered into by the company in the ordinary course of business (ibid ss.34-37). There are civil remedies and criminal penalties for a breach of the prohibition; also the person who benefitted from the arrangement can be made personally liable without limit for the debts of the company in certain circumstances (ibid ss.38-40). There are disclosure requirements in the annual accounts in respect of loans in excess of £2,500; except in licensed banks where the total amount outstanding and the number of directors only requires disclosure (ibid s.43). See also Building Societies Act 1989 s.57. See DIRECTOR; QUASI-LOAN.

**loc cit; loco citato.** [At the passage quoted]. Reference to a passage in a book.

**local authority.** Each of the following bodies: county councils, county borough corporations, borough corporations, urban district councils, and commissioners of a town. It also includes a committee or joint committee or board or joint board appointed to perform the functions of any of such bodies, or appointed by one or more of such bodies other than a vocational education committee (qv).

The general competence of local authorities has been increased considerably; provision has been made to transfer additional functions to them; and they are required to have regard to certain matters in performing their functions: Local Government Act 1991 ss.5-9.

Certain controls previously exercised by the Minister have been removed eg relating to certain land disposals, delegation of functions by managers, local contributions to local bodies, local authority superannuation, car parks, and certain local authority meetings: Local Government (Removal of Control) Regulations 1993 (SI No 172 of 1993).

Provision has also been made for the establishment of regional authorities for the purpose of promoting the co-ordination in different areas of the State of the provision of public services (ibid 1991 Act s.43). See also Local Government (Ireland) Act 1898; Local Government Act 1941 s.2(2). [Text: Cabot & Haigh; Keane (3)]. See BOUNDARY ALTER-ATION; COUNTY MANAGER; LOCAL GOVERN-MENT; RESERVED FUNCTION.

**local authority, dissolution of.** The termination of the legal existence of a local authority which can be achieved only by a statutory enactment to that effect. However, the Minister may remove from office the members of a local authority for specified reasons and replace them by one or more persons to be commissioner or commissioners to enable the authority to function until the coming into office of members elected at the next election: Local Government Act 1941 s.48.

The specified reasons include: the failure to strike an adequate rate; the refusal to allow audit of accounts; the refusal or neglect to comply with a judgment, order or decree of a court. The removal from office of members and their replacement by commissioners does not effect the continuity of the existence of the local authority (ibid s.55).

**local election.** An election held pursuant to s.81 of the Electoral Act 1963, or a new election within the meaning of Part IV of the Local Government Act 1941: Electoral Act 1992 s.2(1). A *local government elector* means a person entitled to vote at a local election. A person is entitled to be registered as a local government elector in a local electoral area if he has reached the age of 18 years and he was, on the qualifying date, ordinarily resident in that area (ibid s.10). An election must be held every five years. See Local Elections Regulations 1965 (SI No 128 of 1965) amended by 1992 Act s.174. See ELECTION PETITION; VOTERS, SPECIAL.

**local government.** The management of the administrative and financial business of local areas entrusted to the elected bodies of county councils, corporations of county and other boroughs, urban district councils and town commissioners (qqv). A major reform of local government has been provided for by the Local Government Act 1991. [Text: Keane (3); Roche]. See LOCAL AUTHORITY.

**local government, re-organisation of.** Dublin County Council is required to establish and delegate functions to Area Committees for three electoral divisions: Fingal, South Dublin, and Dun Laoghaire-Rathdown, as part of a process by which these areas will eventually achieve county council status: Local Government (Re-organisation) Act 1985 Part III; Local Government Act 1991, Part IV. These new county councils come into effect on 1st January 1994 replacing Dublin County Council and Dun Laoghaire Corporation: Dublin (Preparation of Reorganisation) Regulations 1993 (SI No 52 of 1993).

The 1985 Act also provided for the borough of Galway to become a *county borough* (ibid Part II and SI No 425 of 1985) and for the boundary of County Cork to include Whiddy Island (ibid s.28 and SI No 175 of 1985 implementing recommendation No 45 of the Tribunal of Inquiry into the Disaster of Whiddy Island).

**local loans fund.** A fund established to provide loan capital to local authorities to finance capital expenditure: Local Loans Fund Acts 1935 to 1987. See also Housing (Miscellaneous Provisions) Act 1992 s.15.

**local road.** A public road (qv) other than a national road or a regional road: Roads Act 1993 ss.2(1) and 10(1)(c). See ROAD.

**locatio conductio.** See BAILMENT.

**locatio custodiae.** See BAILMENT.

**locatio operis faciendi.** See BAILMENT.

**lock-out.** An action taken by one or more employers which consists of the exclusion of one or more employees from work or the suspension of work or the collective, simultaneous or otherwise connected termination or suspension of employment of a group of employees: Unfair Dismissals Act 1977 s.5(5). The lock-out of an employee is deemed to be a dismissal and the dismissal is deemed to be an unfair dismissal if after termination of the lock-out (a) the employee is not permitted to resume his employment on terms at least as favourable as those specified in the Act and (b) one or more other employees were so permitted (ibid s.5(1) as amended by Unfair Dismissals (Amdt) Act 1993 s.4).

**loco parentis.** See IN LOCO PARENTIS.

**locum tenens.** [Holding an office]. A person who acts as lawful substitute for another.

**locus in quo.** [The place in which]. The scene of the event. Sometimes a judge will visit the scene: See McAllister v Dunnes Stores (1987) HC.

**locus poenitentiae.** [A place, or opportunity, of repentence]. A planning authority (qv) give themselves a *locus poenitentiae* by serving a notice on an applicant for planning permission, requiring further information or the production of additional evidence in respect of the application. See LG(P&D) Regulations 1977 (SI No 65 of 1977), art.26.

**locus regit actum.** [The place governs the act].

**locus sigilli; L.S.** [The place of the seal].

**locus standi.** [A place of standing]. The right to be heard in court. The question as to whether a person has sufficient interest to maintain proceedings is a mixed question of fact and law: The State (Lynch) v Cooney (1982) IR 337.

A party who has a bona fide concern and interest in an actual or threatened infringement of the Constitution has a locus standi in proceedings to enforce the provisions of the Constitution: SPUC v Coogan & Ors (1989 SC) ITLR (16 Oct). Also, where the plaintiff is an aggrieved person he has, by definition, a locus standi: Chambers v An Bord Pleanala & Sandoz (1992 SC) ILRM 296.

It has been held that the Director of Public Prosecutions (qv) has no locus standi to bring proceedings for recovery of a penalty imposed by the Income Tax Act 1967 s.128: Downes v DPP (1987) ILRM 665; Prosecution of Offences Act 1974 s.3. See also The State (Sheehan) v Ireland (1987) SC; Crotty v An Taoiseach (1987) ILRM 400; Attorney General v Open Door Counselling Ltd and Dublin Wellwoman Centre Ltd (1989 SC) ILRM 19. See also Humphrey

& O'Dowd in 8ILT & SJ (1990) 14; Delaney in 8ILT & SJ (1990) 147.

**lodgment in court.** The payment of money into court which a defendant in an action for debt or damages or in an admiralty action, may make: RSC O.22. The lodgment may be: (a) a lodgment *in satisfaction* of the claim, by which the defendant is taken to admit the claim; or (b) a lodgment *with the defence denying liability*, which remains in court to await the result of the trial if the plaintiff does not accept it; in which event if he succeeds in his claim but is not awarded more than the lodgment, the defendant will be entitled to his costs against the plaintiff from the date of the lodgment; or (c) lodgment *with the defence setting up tender* which lodgment the plaintiff can accept but he is only entitled to his costs if he continues the action and disproves the tender; if he fails to disprove the tender, the defendant is entitled to his costs of the whole action.

A defendant who has made a lodgment is entitled, without court order, to *top up* the lodgment once only by lodging the additional sum in court; the second lodgment date becomes the effective date for determining costs, but only where that lodgment is made at least three months before the date on which the action is first listed for hearing (ibid r.1(2); Donohue v Dillon (1987) HC).

There are special rules governing the lodgment of money in Court in personal and fatal injury cases; the defendant may lodge money in court either at the time of delivery of the defence or within four months from the date of the Notice of Trial, or later, including topping up, by leave of the court (ibid RSC O.22 rr.1(7) and 7(1) inserted by SI No 229 of 1990).

A defendant may be permitted by the court to make a late lodgment but only in special circumstances eg where the defendant discovers, as a result of settlement negotiations, that the plaintiff's injuries were more serious than originally pleaded on his behalf: Brennan v Iarnrod Eireann (1993 HC) ILRM 134.

Lodgment with the defence denying liability is not permitted in actions for libel or slander or where the defence raises a question on the title to land (ibid RSC O.22 r.1(3)). In relation to claims by infants or persons of unsound mind, no settlement or compromise or payment or acceptance of money paid into court, either before or at or after trial, is valid without the approval of the court (ibid r.10 and Civil Liability Act 1961 s.63).

For Circuit and District Court provisions on lodgments, see RCC O.12 rr.8-14; DCR rr.132-133; District Court (Interest on Decrees and Lodgments) Rules 1982 (SI No 140 of 1982). See PAYMENT OUT OF COURT.

**lodgment in court, disclosure of.** In a High Court action, the fact that money has been lodged in court must be stated in the defence; however the fact that money has been lodged or the amount thereof must not be disclosed to a jury in any action tried by judge and jury, (or where the judge sits alone, the amount lodged in court must not be disclosed to him) until all questions of liability and the amount of debt and damages has been decided, except in an action to which a defence of *tender* before action is pleaded or where the plaintiff is a minor (qv) and the direction of the court is sought as to the advisability of accepting or rejecting the lodgment: RSC O.22 r.7.

In personal and fatal injury cases, the pleadings must not disclose the fact that money has been paid into court and this must not be communicated to the judge, except that the judge may enquire, for good or sufficient reasons, whether and in what amount, a payment has been made (ibid RSC O.22 r.1(8) as inserted by SI No 229 of 1990).

In a Circuit Court action, the fact of lodgment need not necessarily be stated in the defence; hoverever, subject to the exceptions stated above, the amount must not be disclosed to the judge prior to judgment. As regards disclosure to a judge in the District Court, it has been held that it is preferable that disclosure should not be made until after the determination of the case: Cosgrove v Molloy (1986) HC.

**loitering.** A garda is empowered to direct a person to leave a street or public place where he has reasonable cause to suspect that the person is loitering in order to solicit or importune another person for the purposes of prostitution: Criminal Law (Sexual Offences) Act 1993 s.8. See also CANVASSING.

**lone parent.** A widow, widower, separated spouse, unmarried person, or a person whose spouse has been committed in custody to a prison or place of detention who has at least one qualified child normally residing with that person: Social Welfare Act 1990 s.12. An allowance is payable to a lone parent.

**long possession, title by.** The title which a person acquires in land by retaining adverse possession of the land for a certain period without acknowledging the true owner's title. An action to recover land from a person in possession must be brought within 12 years (30 years in the case of a State authority) after the right of action accrued or from the last written acknowledgement signed by the person in possession or his agent. Time does not run against the true owner in the case of fraud, until he has discovered the fraud or could with reasonable diligence have discovered it. Time does not run also in the case of a person with a disability.

The right of action to recover land may accrue: (a) on dispossession or discontinuance; (b) on failure to take possession on death or under an assurance. See Statute of Limitations 1957. See Registration of Title Act 1964 s.49. See Maher v Maher (1987) ILRM 582; Durack Manufacturing v Considine (1987) HC. [Text: Wylie (1)]. See CARETAKER; LIMITATION OF ACTIONS.

**long title.** See LEGISLATION, INTERPRETATION OF; PREAMBLE.

**long vacation.** The period beginning on 1st August and ending on 30th September when the Supreme and High Courts are not normally sitting: RSC O.118 r 2. Pleadings are not to be delivered or amended during the long vacation unless directed by the Court or on consent: RSC O. 122 r.4. See TIME, COURT RULES; VACATION.

**lord.** Originally the person from whom a tenant held land.

**lord lieutenant.** Formerly the office created for the purpose of having a representative of the Crown in an area to keep it in military order; prior to the independence of Ireland, the Lord Lieutenant in Dublin was the Chief Governor of Ireland. The government is empowered to exercise the functions formerly exercised by the Lord Lieutenant under the Civil Bill Courts (Ireland) Act 1851. See SI No 174 of 1992. See Adaptation of Enactments Act 1922 s.11.

**lord mayor.** The title given to the chairman of the borough corporation of Dublin by the Municipal Corporations (Ireland) Act 1840 and to the Chairman of the Borough Corporation of Cork (and Belfast) by letters patent. The procedure for electing a lord mayor is governed by the Electoral Act 1963 s.82; Local Elections Regulations 1965 (SI No 128 of 1965). See MAYOR.

**loss.** Unless a policy of insurance provides otherwise, the insurer is liable for any loss proximately caused by a peril insured against. See Marine Insurance Act 1906 s.55. See TOTAL LOSS.

**loss of service.** See PER QUOD SERVITIUM AMISIT.

**lost bill.** A bill of exchange (qv) which is lost before it is overdue. The person who was the holder of the bill prior to its loss, may apply to the drawer for a duplicate which the drawer must provide, but the drawer can demand security from the applicant against the risk of the original bill being found and the drawer being liable on both bills: Bills of Exchange Act 1882 s.69. If the drawer refuses to give such a duplicate, having been requested, he can be compelled to do so.

**lost modern grant.** The doctrine by which a court can presume from long user, that at some time in the past an *easement* (qv) was granted by deed but that the deed has been lost and cannot be produced. See PRESCRIPTION.

**lost years.** See EXPECTATION OF LIFE, LOSS OF.

**lot.** See AUCTION SALES.

**lottery.** Includes all competitions for money or money's worth involving guesses or estimates of future events or of past events the results of which are not yet ascertained or not yet generally known: Gaming and Lotteries Act 1956 s.21. Any kind of skill or dexterity whether bodily or mental in which persons can compete would prevent a scheme from being a lottery, if the result depended partly upon such skill or dexterity: Scott v The Director of Public Prosecutions (1914) 2 KB 868; Attorney General (McGrath) v Healy (1972) IR 393. The law does not require every participant to be a purchaser to constitute a lottery; it is sufficient that there be a substantial number: Flynn v Denieffe & Independent Newspapers plc (1993 SC) ILRM 417.

Generally lotteries are prohibited except where declared not to be unlawful eg private lotteries, lotteries at dances, concerts and carnivals, and lotteries conducted wholly within the State in accordance with a permit or a licence (ibid ss.23-32).

A national lottery was established by the National Lottery Act 1986 which permits the Minister to award a licence to a suitable body to operate the lottery. The surplus funds remaining, after prizes and expenses have been paid, are to be used for sport and other recreation, national culture (including the Irish language), the arts and the health of the community and such other purposes and in such amounts, as the Government may determine from time to time (ibid s.5).

The restriction on advertising and publicity in relation to other lotteries run under authority of a Garda permit or licence has been removed (ibid s.33(1)) and the Minister may by regulation amend the value of prizes in such lotteries (ibid s.33(2)). The maximum prize money now permitted in the case of a lottery under a Garda permit is £3000 and it is £10,000 in the case of a District Court licensed lottery: Lottery Prizes Regulations (SI No 72 of 1987). The National Lottery is prohibited from imposing exclusive agency arrangements on agents who wish to act also for the REHAB and other lotteries: Restrictive Practices (National Lottery) Order 1990 (SI No 130 of 1990). See also Hall v Cox (1899) 1 QB 198; Barrett v Flynn (1916) 2 IR 1; Camillo v O'Reilly (1988 SC) ILRM 738; DPP v Sports Arena & Cafolla (1992 SC); Jacinta Yilmaz v Kemal Yilmaz (1993 HC) — Irish Times 21/1/1993. See GAMING.

**low-tide elevation.** A naturally formed area of land which is surrounded by and above water at low water but submerged at high water: Maritime Jurisdiction Act 1959 s.1. See MARITIME JURISDICTION.

**l.s.** Locus sigilli (qv).

**lucid interval.** A temporary period of rational thought and behaviour between periods of insanity. A will made during such a period may be admitted to probate (qv) if the person had, at the time, a sound disposing mind. See Chambers and Yatman v Queen's Proctor (1840) 2 Curt 415; Banks v Goodfellow (1870) LR 5 QB 549. See SOUND DISPOSING MIND.

**lucri causa.** [For the purpose of gain].

**Lugano Convention.** See FOREIGN JUDGMENTS, ENFORCEMENT OF; JURISDICTION; MAINTENANCE ORDER.

**lump.** The colloquial term to describe the payment of a lump sum to self employed persons on building contracts without deduction of tax at source. For prevention, see SUBCONTRACTORS, PAYMENT OF. See also MAINTENANCE.

**lunatic.** See CRIMINAL LUNATIC; INSANE PERSON; INSANITY.

# M

**Maastricht Treaty.** The Treaty on European Union signed at Maastricht on 7th February 1992 and approved by referendum in Ireland on 18th June 1992. The Treaty amends the Treaty of Rome 1957 and the Single European Act 1987. The main changes are in the areas of economic and monetary union, European citizenship, foreign and security policy, the role of the European Parliament, consumer policy, education, and health. The Maastricht Treaty includes seventeen important Protocols, including the *abortion* protocol (number 17) relating to article 40(3)(3) of the Constitution of Ireland, and the protocol on social policy (number 14) which was agreed by governments of eleven member States but not by the UK. The Treaty also includes a number of Declarations, including one added in Portugal on 1st May 1992 relating to the "abortion" protocol regarding the right to travel and to information. The Treaty enters into force on the first day of the month after the last signatory State has deposited its instrument of ratification. See 1937 Constitution art.29(4)(4). See Government White Paper 1992 "Treaty on European Union" (Pl.8793). See REFER-ENDUM.

**maim.** A bodily harm whereby a person is deprived of the use of any member of his body or of any sense which he can use in fighting, or by loss of which he is generally and permanently weakened. It is an offence to maim another: Offences Against the Person Act 1861 s.18.

**main road.** Formerly, any road which the Minister declared by order to be a main road: Local Government Act 1925 s.1 — repealed by Roads Act 1993 s.4. The words "main road" in the LG (P&D) Act 1963 s.89(10) have been replaced by the words "national road or regional road" (ibid 1993 Act s.6). See PUBLIC ROAD.

**maintenance.** The supply of necessaries (qv). The financial arrangements embodied in a maintenance agreement or order. See MAINTENANCE ORDER.

**maintenance and champerty.** See CHAMPERTY.

**maintenance agreement.** An agreement for the periodic payment of sums of money by one spouse to another usually as part of a separation agreement (qv). Maintenance payments may be ordered by the court to be adjusted downwards as well as upwards: D v D (1990 HC) 2 IR 361. See SEPARATION AGREEMENT.

**maintenance order.** An order of the court which provides for the periodical payment of sums of money by one spouse to the other spouse, where it appears to the court that the spouse has failed to provide such maintenance for the applicant spouse as is proper in the circumstances: Family Law (Maintenance of Spouses and Children) Act 1976 s.5(1). A spouse when applying for a maintenance order, may join a claim in respect of her dependent children (qv).

The applicant spouse is known as the *maintenance creditor* and the spouse ordered to pay maintenance is called the *maintenance debtor*. The court cannot grant a maintenance order where it is proved that the applicant spouse has deserted the other spouse (ibid s.5(2); RK v MK (1978 HC)) unless it would otherwise be repugnant to justice: Judicial Separation & Family Law Reform Act 1989 s.38.

Also where the applicant spouse has committed adultery, the court may refuse to grant a maintenance order unless the other spouse has connived or condoned or by wilful neglect or misconduct, conduced to the adultery: ibid 1976 Act s.5(3); L v L (1979) HC; OC v TC (1981) HC. In considering a maintenance order in favour of a wife, the court must ascertain the income earned or capable of being earned by the wife: RH v NH (1986) ILRM 352.

A maintenance order may be enforced: by seizure of the maintenance debtor's property and effecting its sale; by his imprisonment; by *attachment* of the maintenance debtor's earnings (ibid s.10). Such attachment requires the debtor's employer to deduct the amount of the order from his salary or wages and forward it to the District Court clerk who in turn forwards it to the maintenance creditor.

A maintenance order may be obtained for the support of children whose parents are not married to each other: Status of Children Act 1987 ss.15-25; RB v HR (1990 CC) in 8ILT & SJ (1990) 295.

The court is empowered to make a lump sum order or periodic payments order on granting a decree of judicial separation (qv): Judicial Separation and Family Law Reform Act 1989 s.14. It also may order maintenance pending suit and make retrospective maintenance orders (ibid ss.13 and 21). See also ibid ss.23 and 24.

Also reciprocal enforcement of maintenance orders exists as between the State and the United Kingdom for some years: Maintenance Orders Act 1974; and more recently between the State and other *contracting* states in the EC (1988), and between EC states and EFTA countries (1993): Jurisdiction of Courts and Enforcement of Judgments (European Communities) Acts 1988 (ss.7, 9, and first schedule, art.5) and 1993. See also Sachs v Standard Chartered Bank (1987) ILRM 297; CM v TM (1988) ILRM 262; K v K (1992 SC) ITLR (4 May). See also DCR 1988 (SI Nos 173 and 180 of 1988). [Text: Duncan & Scully]. See AFFILIATION ORDER; DESERTION; DIVORCE; FOREIGN JUDGMENTS, ENFORCEMENT OF; PARENTAGE, DECLARATION OF.

**majority.** See AGE OF MAJORITY.

**majority verdict.** See VERDICT; TRIAL BY JURY.

**mala fides.** [Bad faith]. The court is only entitled to review a scheme (of grant payments to the owners of diseased cattle) where it was satisfied that it was being operated *mala fides*, or at least, where it involved some abuse of power: Rooney v Minister for Agriculture (1992 SC) ITLR (3 Feb). See Foley v DPP (1989 HC) ITLR (25 Sep). See BONA FIDES.

**mala grammatica non vitiat chartam.** [Bad grammar does not vitiate a deed].

**mala in se.** Acts which are wrong in themselves eg murder, as opposed to *mala prohibita*, which are acts which are merely prohibited eg driving a motor vehicle without insurance.

**mala praxis.** Failure of professional duty giving rise to a right of action for damages eg medical negligence.

**maledicta expositio quae corrumpit textum.** [It is a bad exposition which corrupts the text].

**malice.** Malice is a wrong or improper motive, or feeling existing in the mind of the defendant at the time of the publication of a *defamation* (qv) which actuates the publication. A defendant who acts rashly, or stupidly is protected, provided he acts in good faith but not if he uses a privileged occasion for any other purpose other than that for which it was intended. A failure to retract a serious charge may constitute evidence that at the time of the original publication the defendant was actuated by malice. See Coleman v Kearns (1946) Ir Jur Rep 5. See PRIVILEGE.

**malice aforethought.** The element of *mens rea* (qv) in the crime of murder. See MURDER.

**malicious damage.** The offences committed by a person who unlawfully and maliciously causes damage to specified property: Malicious Damage Act 1861. A malicious intention to damage must be present in the mind of the accused; *malicious* means foresight of the consequences, or an intention to do the kind of harm which resulted from the unlawful act, or a recklessness as to whether harm would result or not. See The People (DPP) v Walsh (1988) ILRM 137. See also Electricity (Supply) Act 1927 s.111; Gas Works Clauses Act 1847/71.

The Law Reform Commission recommended major changes to the law on malicious damage: LRC 26 of 1988. The law was changed in 1991: Criminal Damage Act 1991 repealing the Malicious Damage Act 1861 except for sections 35-38 (interference with railways and telegraphs), 40-41 (killing or maiming animals), 47 (exhibiting false signals to shipping), 48 (cutting away buoys), 72 (admiralty offences), 58 (the Act to apply whether or not malice against owner of property): ibid 1991 Act ss.14 and 15. See also Criminal Justice Act 1993 s.13.

The description of *malicious damage* is commonly used to describe damage to property in respect of which compensation is claimed under the *malious injuries scheme* (qv).See CRIMINAL DAMAGE TO PROPERTY; DAMAGE TO PROPERTY.

**malicious falsehood.** Injurious falsehood (qv).

**malicious injuries scheme.** Also referred to as *criminal injuries*. A scheme under which payment of compensation from public funds is made for damage occuring to property in particular instances: Malicious Injuries Act 1981. Restrictions on the scheme were introduced in 1986; compensation is now payable for damage to property (a) caused unlawfully by one or more of a number (exceeding two) of persons riotously assembled together or (b) caused as a result of an act committed maliciously by a person acting on behalf of or in connection with unlawful or certain other organisations: Malicious Injuries (Amendment) Act 1986 s.2. See RSC O.110; District Court (Malicious Injuries) Rules 1987 (SI No 209 of 1987).

The court has power to extend the statutory time limit for malicious injuries claims for good reasons: 1981 Act ss.14 and 23; Cork County Council v Whillock & Murphy (1993 SC) 11 ILT Dig 144. See Dublin Corporation v Murdon Ltd (1988) ILRM 86; Conaty v Tipperary (NR) Co Council (1989) 7ILT & SJ 222; Hutch v Dublin Corporation (1992 SC) ILRM 596. [Text: Kennedy & McWilliam]. See TUMULTUOUSLY.

**malicious prosecution.** A tort (qv) consisting of the institution of unsuccessful criminal proceedings maliciously and without reasonable or probable cause, thereby causing actual damage to the party prosecuted. A plaintiff must prove that the criminal proceedings terminated in his favour, that the defendant instituted and/or participated in the proceedings maliciously, that there was no reasonable or probable cause for such proceedings, and that the plaintiff suffered damage: McIntyre v Lewis & Ors (1991 SC) 1 IR 121. Malicious prosecution also includes malicious civil proceedings involving bankruptcy (qv) or the winding up (qv) of a company. See Brown v Hawkes (1891) 2 QB 718; Berry v British Transport Commission (1962) 1 QB 306.

**malitia supplet aetatem.** [Malice supplements age]. See DOLI INCAPAX.

**mallard.** See GAME.

**man of straw.** A person with little or no means and consequently not worth taking proceedings against for damages.

**manager, local authority.** See COUNTY MANAGER.

**managing director.** The director in a company who is given responsibility for managing the everyday business affairs of the company. A board may appoint a managing director from one of its members and determine his terms of service; he may be entrusted with any of the board's powers: Companies Act 1963. Table A, art 110-112. See also Battle v Irish Art Promotion Centre Ltd (1968) IR 252. See also Building Societies Act 1989 s.49(7).

**mandamus.** [We command]. An order of the High Court to compel a person or body to perform a legally imposed duty; it is an order directed to any person, corporation or inferior court, requiring him or them to do some particular thing, therein specified, which appertains to his or their office and for which the applicant has no other specific means of compelling performance. An order of mandamus will be granted to compel compliance with a statutory duty which is not discretionary irrespective of whether or not the person on whom the duty is placed is a public official or an official body: Minister for Labour v Grace (1993 HC) ELR 50. See The State (Reilly) v D J Clones (1935) IR 908; The State (Turley) v O'Floinn (1968) IR 245. See also Justices Protection (Ireland) Act 1849 s.5. See JUDICIAL REVIEW.

**mandate.** A direction, request or command. A cheque (qv) is a mandate.

**mandatory injunction.** See INJUNCTION.

**mandatum.** [Mandate]. See BAILMENT.

**manslaughter.** A felony (qv) involving an unlawful homicide that is not murder, or infanticide. Manslaughter may be *voluntary* and *involuntary*. A *voluntary* manslaughter is an unlawful homicide where the malice aforethought (qv) of murder may be present but because of provocation (qv), the crime is reduced from murder to manslaughter: The People (DPP) v MacEoin (1978) IR 27.

An *involuntary* manslaughter arises where a person brings about the death of another by acting in some unlawful manner, but without the intention of killing or doing an act likely to kill. It may arise by the person doing an act which is intrinsically unlawful, or doing some lawful act but doing it recklessly, or culpably leaving unperformed some act which he had a legal duty to perform; the fatal negligence involved needs to be of a very high degree and such to involve a high degree of risk of substantial personal injuries to others: The People (Attorney General) v Dunleavy (1948) IR 95. See HOMICIDE; PROVOCATION; UNWORTHINESS TO SUCCEED.

**mansuetae naturae.** [Tame by nature]. See ANIMALS.

**manual handling of loads.** Any transporting or supporting of a load by one or more employees, and includes lifting, putting down, pushing, pulling, carrying or moving a load, which, by reason of its characteristics or of unfavourable ergonomic conditions, involves risk, particularly of back injury, to employees: Safety Health and Welfare at Work (General Application) Regulations 1993 reg.27 (SI No 44 of 1993). Every employer is required to take measures to avoid the need for the manual handling of loads by his employees; however where the need cannot be avoided, he must seek to reduce the risk involved (ibid reg.28 and Eighth Schedule). See WEIGHTS.

**manufactured goods.** It has been held that bananas ripened in the State by a specified artificial process are *goods manufactured* within s.54 of the Corporation Tax Act 1976; Charles McCann Ltd v O'Culachain (1986) IR 196. See Finance Act 1980 s.42 and O'Laochdha

v Johnson (Ire) Ltd (1992 HC) 10 ILT Dig 268. See also Finance Act 1993 s.44 which extends further the definition of *goods* for manufacturing relief purposes eg processing of meat, production of a newspaper.

**manuscript.** In relation to a work, means the original document embodying the work, whether written by hand or not: Copyright Act 1963 s.2(1). See COPYRIGHT.

**mareva injunction.** The *injunction* which the court may grant to restrain a defendant, who is not within the jurisdiction but who has assets within the jurisdiction, from removing these assets from the jurisdiction pending trial of an action for a debt due. So called after Mareva Compania Naviera v International Bulk Carriers (1980) 1 All ER 213.

In deciding whether to grant an interlocutory Mareva injunction, the court will apply the ordinary test as to whether the plaintiff had established that there was a fair question to be tried and where the balance of convenience lay as to the issuing of an injunction, taking account of the risk in the particular case of the Mareva injunction that the refusal to grant relief could involve a real risk that a judgment or award in favour of the plaintiff would remain unsatisfied: Serge Caudron v Air Zaire (1986) ILRM 10.

A mareva injunction can be obtained by way of protective relief associated with an order for enforcement of a foreign judgment pursuant to the Brussels Convention: Elwyn (Cottons) Ltd v Pearle Designs Ltd (1989 HC) ILRM 162. See INJUNCTION.

**marginal notes.** The notes printed at the side of sections of Acts of the Oireachtas which explain the sections. They do not form part of the Act but may be considered to ascertain the *mischief* at which the Act is aimed. See MISCHIEF OF A STATUTE.

**marina.** A floating marina fixed to seabed piles is a development for sport and is not a rateable hereditament: Trustees of Kinsale Yacht Club v Commissioner of Valuations (1993 HC) ILRM 393.

**marine.** Of, in, near, concerned with or belonging to the sea and tidal waters, inhabiting, found or got from the sea or from non-tidal waters: Marine Institute Act 1991 s.1. The Act makes provision for the carrying out of marine research and development and related services.

**marine adventure.** There is a marine adventure where any ship, goods or other moveables are exposed to maritime perils (qv): Marine Insurance Act 1906 s.3. Every lawful marine adventure may be the subject of a contract of insurance (ibid s.3(1)).

**marine incident.** The Minister is empowered to order a formal public inquiry into a marine incident: Merchant Shipping Act 1894 s.466 (eg the inquiry into the sinking of a fishery patrol vessel near Ballycotten in 1990). See also ACCIDENT.

**marine insurance contract.** A contract whereby an insurer, in consideration of a premium (qv) paid to him, agrees to indemnify the insured against marine losses ie losses incident to *marine adventure*: Marine Insurance Act 1906 s.1. A contract of marine insurance is inadmissible in evidence unless it is embodied in a marine policy in accordance with the 1906 Act (ibid s.22). A marine policy is assigned by indorsement thereon or in other customary manner (ibid s.50) See also Finance Act 1959 ss.75 and 80. [Text: Hill UK; Ivamy UK; McGuffie, Fugeman & Gray UK]. See MARINE ADVENTURE.

**marital coercion.** Formerly the rebuttable presumption at common law that a married woman who committed a felony (qv), other than murder, in the presence of her husband, committed it under his coercion and was not guilty of an offence. It has been held that the defence of marital coercion did not survive the enactment of the 1937 Constitution because it offended the guarantee of equality before the law in that a similar defence was not available to a husband: The State (DPP) v Walsh and Conneely (1981) IR 294. See also The People (DPP) v Murray (1977) IR 360. See EQUALITY BEFORE THE LAW.

**marital privacy.** The implied constitutional right of a husband and wife to decide how many children they wish to have, if any: McGee v Attorney General (1974) IR 284. In this case it was held that the prohibition of the importation of artificial contraceptives by the Criminal Law (Amendment) Act 1935 s.17

was an unjustified invasion of the plaintiff's right to privacy in her marital affairs. See WITNESS, COMPETENCE OF.

**marital rape.** At common law a husband could not be guilty of the rape of his wife. "By their mutual matrimonial consent and contract the wife hath given herself.... unto her husband which she cannot retract": Hale CJ (IPC 629) (1736). The marital exemption for rape has been abolished: Criminal Law (Rape) (Amendment) Act 1990 s.5. Criminal proceedings can only be instituted by or with the consent of the Director of Public Prosecutions.

**marital status.** See DISCRIMINATION; INTERVIEW, EMPLOYMENT.

**maritime boundaries.** See Boundary Survey (Ireland) Act 1854. For example under that Act, see Maritime Boundaries (County of Cork) Order 1990.

**maritime jurisdiction.** The *territorial seas* of the State is that portion of the sea which lies between the *baseline* and the *outer limit of the territorial seas*: Maritime Jurisdiction Act 1959 s.2. The territorial seas are stated to be part of the national territory (qv): 1937 Constitution art.2.

The outer limit of the territorial seas is the line every point of which is at a distance of three (now twelve) nautical miles (qv) from the nearest point of the baseline: (ibid 1959 Act s.3). The baseline is low-water mark (a) on the coast of the mainland or of any island, or (b) on any *low tide elevation* situated wholly or partly at a distance not exceeding three (now twelve) nautical miles from the mainland or an island (ibid s.4). The formerly specified three miles is now twelve miles: Maritime Jurisdiction (Amendment) Act 1988 s.2.

Every offence committed within the territorial seas or inland waters (qv) is an offence within the jurisdiction of the State (ibid 1959 Act ss.10-11). Control of fishing in waters in the Foyle area is vested in the Foyle Fisheries Commission by virtue of the Foyle Fisheries Act 1952 (Irish) and the Foyle Fisheries Act (NI) 1952 (UK). Subject to international law, ships of all States have the right of innocent passage through the territorial seas: United Nations Convention on the Law of the Sea 1982 art.18. See also Maritime Jurisdiction (Amendment) Act

1964; Jurisdiction of Courts (Maritime Conventions) Act 1989. See CONTINENTAL SHELF; LOW-TIDE ELEVATION; INLAND WATERS; FISHERY LIMITS, EXCLUSIVE.

**maritime perils.** The perils subsequent on, or incidental to, the navigation of the sea, ie *perils of the sea* (qv), fire, war perils, pirates, rovers, thieves, captures, seisures, restraints, and detainments of princes and peoples, jettisons (qv) and barratry (qv): Marine Insurance Act 1906 s.3. See MARINE INSURANCE CONTRACT.

**mark.** See TRADE MARK.

**mark, distinctive.** See DISTINCTIVE MARK.

**market.** At common law, a market is a franchise (qv) or privilege to establish meetings of persons to buy and sell, derived from a royal grant or from prescription (qv) which implied such a grant. Local authorities are empowered to provide market places in their area: Public Health (Ireland) Act 1878 s.103.

**market, internal.** See INTERNAL MARKET.

**market overt.** [Open market]. An open public and legally constituted market; a market held on days prescribed by charter, statute or custom. Where goods are sold in *market overt,* according to the usage of the market, the buyer acquires a good title to the goods, provided he buys them in good faith and without notice of any defect or want of title on the part of the seller: Sale of Goods Act 1893 s.22. See RESTITUTION OF POSSESSION.

**market right.** A right conferred by franchise (qv) or statute to hold a fair or market, that is to say, a concourse of buyers and sellers to dispose of commodities: Casual Trading Act 1980 s.1. A local authority may acquire any market right in its functional area by agreement or compulsorily and it may extinguish a market right owned by it (ibid ss.8-9). See also Public Health (Ireland) Act 1878. See Skibbereen UDC v Quill (1986) IR 123 and (1986) ILRM 170.

**marketable title.** As regards freehold land, a title which goes back 40 years: Vendor and Purchasers Act 1874 s.1; also known as a *good* title. A contract for the sale of land may stipulate that the title may commence at a more recent date. If the vendor shows the title which he is required to prove, he is said to show a *good* title. The conveyance or document with which the title com-

mences is called the *root of title* (qv). See Maconchy v Clayton (1898) 1 IR 291. See CONVEYANCE; OPEN CONTRACT.

**marking order.** An order which the Minister may make to compel that goods be marked with or accompanied by any information. The Minister may also regulate or prohibit the supply of goods in relation to which the requirements are not complied with. It is an offence to contravene a *marking order.* See Consumer Information Act 1978 s.10.

**marriage.** The voluntary union of one man and one woman to the exclusion of all others: Hyde v Hyde (1868) LR 1 PD 130. The State pledges itself to guard with special care the institution of marriage, in which the family is founded, and to protect it against attack: 1937 Constitution, art.41(3)(1); Murphy v Attorney General (1982) IR 241; Muckley v Ireland (1986) ILRM 364; Greene v Minister for Agriculture (1990 HC) ILRM 364.

A marriage in the State is generally valid if (a) it is solemnised in a church in the presence of two or more witnesses after the *banns* have been notified to the public or (b) it is contracted by civil ceremony before a registrar appointed for that purpose. Marriages abroad must comply with the *lexi loci celebrationis* (qv).

A marriage solemnised between persons, either of whom is under the age of sixteen years is not valid unless the consent of the President of the High Court has been obtained: Marriage Act 1972 s.1(1). Parental consent is required by persons under the age of 21 who wish to marry. The parties to a marriage must not be within the *prohibited degrees* of relationships either by *consanguinity* (qv) or *affinity* (qv); there are twenty-eight prohibited relationships: Marriage Act 1835; Deceased Wife's Sister's Marriage Act 1907; Deceased Brother's Widow's Marriage Act 1921.

An agreement made in consideration of marriage must be evidenced in writing: Statute of Frauds (Ireland) 1695 s.2. An agreement which subverts the sanctity of marriage is void at common law eg marriage broker contracts: Williamson v Gihan (1805) 2 Scholes Lefroy 357.

Full age is conferred on an infant by virtue of marriage: Age of Majority Act

1985 s.2. A contract which provides that one party is to pay a certain sum to support the other in the event of future separation is void as weakening the marriage bond: Marquess of Westmeath v Marquess of Salisbury (1830) 5 Bli (ns). [Text: Duncan & Scully; Shatter]. See COMMON LAW MARRIAGE; CONJUGAL RIGHTS, RESTITUTION OF; CONSORTIUM; JACTITATION OF MARRIAGE; MARRIAGE, NULLITY OF; MARRIAGE REGISTER; PROHIBITED DEGREES.

**marriage, nullity of.** A matrimonial action for the purpose of obtaining a judicial decree that a purported marriage is in fact null and void. A marriage may be *void* or *voidable*. A marriage may be *void* on the grounds of (a) lack of capacity eg where one or both of the parties is within the prohibited degree of relationships, or already married, or under the age of sixteen without consent of the President of the High Court; or (b) non-observance of the appropriate formalities eg lack of parental consent: Ussher v Ussher (1912) 2 IR 445; or (c) lack of consent eg due to duress, parental or otherwise; Griffith v Griffith (1944) IR 35; S v O'S (1978) HC; McK (otherwise M McC) v F McC (1982) ILRM 277; ACL v RL (1982) HC; N (Otherwise K) v K (1986) ILRM 75; W(C) v C (1990) IR 696; DB(D.O'R) v N.O'R (1991 SC) ILRM 160.

A marriage may be *voidable* if either party has not the mental capacity to marry or is impotent (qv) or the marriage is not consummated (qv): RSJ v JSJ (1982) ILRM 263; D v C (1984) ILRM 173; MF McD (Otherwise M O'R) v W O'R (1984) HC; DC v DW (1987) ILRM 58; AMN v JPC (1988) ILRM 170.

A *void* marriage is one which never had legal effect and consequently is void ab initio. Its validity may be challenged by any person with a sufficient interest, even after the death of the parties; a decree of nullity is not necessary though desirable, and children of the marriage are illegitimate (now referred to as *children whose parents are not married to each other*: Status of Children Act 1987).

A *voidable* marriage is one which is valid until it is annulled by a *decree of nullity*; its validity may be challenged only by one of the parties to the marriage during the lifetime of both; and children

of the marriage are legitimate until the marriage is annulled.

Provision has now been made for the father of any child of a void or voidable marriage to be the guardian of that child, if the marriage was a voidable one which was annulled after the child's conception, or in the case of a void marriage, if the father reasonably believed at the appropriate time that it was a valid marriage: Status of Children Act 1987 s.9(3).

It has been held that a valid marriage exists between parties who had entered into the contract of marriage with the intention of divorcing at a later stage: HS v JS (1992 SC) ITLR (29 Jun). See Woulfe in 7ILT & SJ (1989) 130 & 178; 8ILT & SJ (1990) 242. See LRC 9 of 1984, 20 of 1985. [Text: Shatter; Duncan & Scully; Gov Pub (3)]. See CHILD, ILLEGITIMATE; CHURCH ANNULMENT; GUARDIAN; HOMOSEXUAL CONDUCT; PERSONALITY DISORDER; POLYGAMOUS MARRIAGE; PREGNANCY; PSYCHIATRIC DISORDER.

**marriage, presumption of.** The presumption in law that persons are married to each other, when it is proved that they cohabited and were treated as married by those who knew them. Strict proof, by evidence of an apparently valid marriage ceremony, is only required in bigamy (qv) and divorce (qv) proceedings. See Mulhern v Clery (1930) IR 649.

**marriage, registration of.** Two parallel procedures for the registration of marriages exist; one through local registrars for marriages other than those in the Roman Catholic Church: Marriage (Ireland) Act 1844; the other for Catholic marriages which is processed through the registrars for births and deaths: Marriage Law (Ireland) (Amendment) Act 1863. The form of marriage register is the same however. See also Vital Statistics and Births Deaths and Marriages Registration Act 1952.

An error in the marriage register may be corrected in the margin by order of a judge at a sitting of the District Court for the district in which the marriage was solemnised (ibid 1863 Act s.13).

**marriage, solemnisation of.** Provision has been made for the registration of places for the solemnisation of marriages therein, by the Marriage Law (Ireland) Amendment Act 1863 s.12.

**marriage bar.** Generally understood to

refer to the previous requirement on women to retire from employment in the civil service on marriage: Civil Service Regulations Act 1956 s.10. The marriage bar was abolished by the Civil Service (Employment of Married Women) Act 1973 s.3. However, only widows or married women who were not supported by their husbands could apply for reinstatement to the civil service (ibid 1973 Act). These requirements have been held to be discriminatory and contrary to the Employments Equality Act 1977 s.2: Moran v Minister for Finance EE20/1991 & EE21/1991 as reported by Barry in 10ILT & SJ (1992) 2; also (1991) ELR 187 (under appeal). See also Aer Lingus Teo v Labour Court (1990 SC) ILRM 485.

**marriage gratuity.** Term applied to a payment made by an employer to an employee on the occasion of the latter's marriage. It has been held in a particular case and set of circumstances that the refusal to pay a marriage gratuity to a male employee was based on grounds other than sex: Bank of Ireland v Kavanagh (1987) HC. See also Curran v AIB (1992 HC).

**married woman.** Previously married women had limited contractual and property rights. The capacity of a woman to contract is now unchanged upon marriage: Married Women Status Act 1957 s.2(1). See also Social Welfare Act 1952 s.59 as repealed and re-enacted by the Social Welfare (Consolidation) Act 1981 s.121. See MATRIMONIAL PROPERTY; PRIVITY OF CONTRACT.

**marry, breach of promise to.** See BREACH OF PROMISE; ENGAGED COUPLE.

**marshalling.** The equitable doctrine under which if person A has claims against funds X and Y of person B, and person C has a claim only against fund X, A will be required to satisfy himself as far as possible out of fund Y. Marshalling has been given statutory recognition in the administration of estates of deceased persons; if debts are paid out of the permitted order, an adversely affected beneficiary may have recourse to property which should have been used to pay debts before his was resorted to. See Succession Act 1965 s.46(5).

The doctrine of marshalling cannot be relied upon as a defence to proceedings instituted by a creditor against one or more of several co-sureties, where they have separately mortgaged different properties as securities for their separate guarantees: Lombard & Ulster Banking Ltd v Murray & Murray (1987) ILRM 522.

**martial law.** Generally understood to mean the exercise of control and absolute power by military authorities during an emergency when the civil authority cannot function. There is no such power given to the military authorities in the 1937 Constitution. However, the government is empowered to take whatever steps they may consider necessary for the protection of the State in the case of an actual invasion and is given wide powers whenever there exists a *national emergency*. See INVASION; MILITARY TRIBUNALS; NATIONAL EMERGENCY.

**master.** In relation to a vessel (qv), means the person having, for the time being, the command or charge of the vessel: Merchant Shipping Act 1992 s.2(1). See also EMPLOYER; BARRISTER.

**Master of High Court.** An officer attached to the High Court who has a wide jurisdiction in matters which come within that court's jurisdiction, eg orders made on motions of course (qv), orders for discovery (qv) of documents, orders giving liberty to serve third party notices (qv): Courts (Supplemental Provisions) Act 1961, 8th schedule; RSC O.63. An order of *mandamus* may issue against the Master: Elwyn (Cottons) Ltd v Master of the High Court (1989) ITLR (22 May). [Text: Barron & Ford]. See FOREIGN JUDGMENTS, ENFORCEMENT OF; LIQUIDATED DAMAGES.

**material change.** See DEVELOPMENT PLAN; PLANNING PERMISSION.

**material contracts.** In a prospectus offering shares in a company for sale to the public, all material contracts must be disclosed, including the dates, parties and general nature of the contracts. A contract is material if it has been entered into by the company within five years of the prospectus being issued, and is not a contract entered into in the ordinary course of the business carried on or intended to be carried on by the company: Companies Act 1963, third schedule, reg 14. See Jury v Stoker (1882) 9 LR Ir

385. See PROSPECTUS.

**material fact.** A fact which a person has a duty to disclose to an insurer; it is any fact which could affect the renewal of insurance or the premium. See Aro Road & Land Vehicles v Insurance Corporation of Ireland (1986 SC) IR 403. See FACT; PREMIUM; UBERRIMAE FIDEI.

**materials.** See SERVICES, SUPPLY OF.

**maternity leave.** The leave of at least 14 weeks to which female employees are entitled by reason of pregnancy, provided notice is given to the employer at least four weeks before the expected confinement, together with a medical certificate establishing the fact of pregnancy: Maternity Protection of Employees Act 1981. The employee may chose the exact date of leave, but it must cover the four weeks before and the four weeks after the confinement. Maternity leave is now available to regular part-time employees: Worker Protection (Regular Part-time Employees) Act 1991 s.1.

The employee is entitled to return after the birth to her job to the same employer and on the same terms as before, provided she notifies the employer in writing at least four weeks before the date of the return to work. The employer can however provide alternative work provided the terms and conditions of the new contract are not substantially less favourable to the employee than her former contract: Leech v PMPA Insurance Co Ltd P 13/1982.

Failure to comply with giving notice in writing will deny the employee the right to return; however, a contractual obligation may have been established by conduct in respect of previous maternity leave: Scott v Yeates & Sons (1992 EAT) ELR 83. An occupational pension scheme may make special provision in relation to maternity leave: Pensions Act 1990 s.72. A dispute in relation to maternity leave is heard by the Employment Appeals Tribunal (qv). See Orr v Stylus Ltd (1991 EAT) ELR 25.

Under a proposed EC directive (November 1992): (a) paid time off will have to be given to attend ante-natal examinations; (b) before and after the birth, the employee will not be obliged to undertake night work but she may do so if she so wishes; (c) the employer will be required to carry out a health and safety assessment on all pregnant employees; (d) part-time workers will not be required to have a minimum number of hours per week to qualify for maternity leave; (e) any dismissal arising out of pregnancy will be unlawful. See PREGNANCY.

**matricide.** The crime of murder (qv) of one's mother.

**matrimonial communications, privilege of.** See PRIVILEGE, MATRIMONIAL COMMUNICATIONS.

**matrimonial home.** Under proposed draft legislation, the dwelling in which a married couple ordinarily resided, or reside, either immediately before or at any time after the commencement of this section as their sole or principal residence and any easements attached or annexed to such a dwelling and exercisable over any other land: Matrimonial Home Bill 1993 s.2(1). Under the proposed legislation, existing and future matrimonial homes (including mobile homes) and household chattels will vest in both spouses as *joint tenants*; the surviving spouse will acquire the interest of both. The matrimonial home must be a building or part of a building occupied as a separate dwelling (eg a farmhouse, detached or semi-detached house, or flat) and it includes any garden or other land usually occupied with it (but not a farm).

Other features of the proposed provisions are: (a) matrimonial homes already owned by spouses as joint tenants or tenants in common in equal shares are excluded, (b) married couples or a couple contemplating marriage may exclude the provisions, (c) the existing power of the courts to divide up property when granting a decree of judicial separation is unaffected, and (d) the court may exclude the application of the provisions if it is satisfied that it would be unjust not to do so having regard to the circumstances of the spouses. A matrimonial home in which both spouses are living will also be a *"family home"* (qv).

**matrimonial property.** Disputes between husband and wife as to the title to, or possession of, any property, may be resolved by the courts as the courts think proper and just: Married Women's Status Act 1957 s.12. Under proposed draft legislation, new provisions will deal more comprehensively with such matters:

Matrimonial Home Bill 1993 s.19.

When a wife makes payments towards the purchase of a house which is in the sole name of the husband, or the repayment of the mortgage instalments, he becomes a trustee (qv) for her of a share in the house, the size of the share depending on the size of her contribution of which she becomes the beneficial owner: Conway v Conway (1976) IR 254. See also EN v RN and MC (1992 SC) ITLR (27 Jan). An extension of the circumstances in which a wife may claim a beneficial interest in the family home to include a situation where she made no direct or indirect financial contribution, was not upheld: L v L (1992 SC) ILRM 115.

Under draft legislation, it is proposed that existing and future matrimonial homes and household chattels will vest in both spouses as *joint tenants*; a spouse who makes a substantial financial contribution to the improvement of real and personal property (other than household chattels and the matrimonial home) will be entitled to the share agreed between the spouses or as the court may determine: Matrimonial Home Bill 1993 ss.4 and 21. See MATRIMONIAL HOME.

However, on granting a decree of judicial separation (qv), the court has wide powers to make orders affecting matrimonial property, eg an order for the sale of property; a property adjustment order; an order conferring a right to occupy the family home to the exclusion of the other spouse; an order extinguishing succession rights: Judicial Separation and Family Law Reform Act 1989 ss.15-21.

In making a *property adjustment order* (qv), the court must have regard, inter alia, to the contribution made by each spouse to the welfare of the family including any contribution by looking after the home or caring for the family (ibid s.20). See Corrigan in 10 ILT & SJ (1992) 59.

Where an allowance is made by one spouse to another for the purpose of meeting household expenses, the property acquired by it belongs to the spouses as joint owners, in the absence of any agreement to the contrary: Family Law (Maintenance of Spouses and Children) Act 1976 s.21. Where an agreement to marry is terminated, the rights of the previously engaged persons to any property, are governed by the rules applicable to matrimonial property: Family Law Act 1981 s.5; Matrimonial Home Bill 1993 s.20. See Wall v Wall (1986) HC; DMcC v M McC (1986) ILRM 1. See LRC 1 of 1981. See Leahy in ISLR (1993) 65. See FAMILY HOME; HOUSEHOLD CHATTELS.

**mature student.** A person of not less than 23 years of age or such other age as may stand specified from time to time by the Minister; a local authority is empowered to make grants to mature students for the purpose of assisting them to attend approved institutions: Local Authorities (Higher Education Grants) Act 1992 ss.2-3.

**maturity.** The time when a bill of exchange (qv) becomes due.

**maxims of equity.** See EQUITY, MAXIMS OF.

**maximum prices order.** See PRICE CONTROL.

**mayor.** The title given to the chairman of the borough corporations of Limerick and Waterford by the Municipal Corporations (Ireland) Act 1840 s.12 and to the chairman of the borough corporation of Galway by the Local Government (Galway) Act 1937 s.3. The procedure for electing a mayor is governed by the Electoral Act 1963 s.82; Local Elections Regulations 1965 (SI No 128 of 1965). See LORD MAYOR.

**McNaghten Rules.** The rules formulated in 1843 which govern the defence of insanity: McNaghten's Case 10 Cl & Fin 200. The rules are: (a) every man is presumed to be sane and to possess a sufficient degree of reason to be responsible for his crime until the contrary be proved; (b) to establish the defence of insanity, it must be clearly shown that, at the time of committing the act, the accused was labouring under such a disease of mind as not to know the *nature and quality* of his act, or, if he did know this, not to know that what he was doing was wrong; (c) where a criminal act is committed by a man under some *insane delusion* as to the surrounding facts, he will be under the same degree of responsibility as if the facts had been as he imagined them.

The McNaghten rules do not provide

the sole test for determining the issue of insanity; the rules must be read as limited to the effect of insane delusions: Doyle v Wicklow County Council (1974) IR 55. See also The People (DPP) v O'Mahony (1986) ILRM 244. [Text: McAuley]. See INSANITY.

**me judice.** [In my opinion].

**measure, short.** See SHORT WEIGHT.

**measure of damages.** The basis on which monetary compensation for loss is ascertained in the case of an action in tort, breach of contract or breach of statutory duty. In general, in contract, there must be a *restitutio in integrum* (qv); the plaintiff is to be put, as far as money can do it, in the same position as if the contract had been performed: Robinson v Harman (1848) 1 Exch 850. The measure of damages in a breach of contract involving failure to pay a sum of money, is limited to the sum in question and interest: Fletcher v Tayleur (1855) 17 CB 21. Damages are limited to those which are not remote. *Exemplary* damages (qv) may be awarded as may damages for mental distress (qv). See DAMAGES; DETERIORATION; REMOTENESS OF DAMAGES; PENALTY.

**mechanical propelled vehicle.** A vehicle intended or adapted for propulsion by mechanical means, including (a) a bicycle or tricycle with an attachment for propelling it by mechanical power, whether or not the attachment is being used, or (b) a vehicle the means of propulsion of which is electrical or partly electrical and partly mechanical, but not including a tramcar or other vehicle running on permanent rails: Road Traffic Act 1961 s.3(1). It does not include a disabled vehicle (qv). See FUEL.

**mediation.** See ALTERNATIVE DISPUTES RESOLUTION; CONCILIATION; JUDICIAL SEPARATION.

**medical deterioration.** See DETERIORATION, MEDICAL.

**medical jurisprudence.** Forensic medicine (qv).

**medical negligence.** The test of liability in *medical negligence* cases relates to whether the practitioner is guilty of such failure that no practitioner of equal status would have been guilty of the same failure if acting with ordinary care; deviation from an accepted practice will only constitute negligence where such was one which no practitioner of equal status would have followed taking ordinary care; to follow a practice which has inherent defects constitutes negligent behaviour; the trial court is not to choose between alternative courses of treatment which it considers preferable, but to consider whether the course adopted complied with the standard of care; and in developing the principles in this area, the courts must take account, on the one hand, that doctors should not be obliged to carry out their work under frequent threat of unsustainable legal claims and, on the other, that in the view of the complete dependence on doctors, the law must not permit the development of lax or permissive standards: Dunne v National Maternity Hospital (1989 SC) ILRM 735; Hughes v Staunton (1991 HC) 9ILT Dig 52.

The failure by a medical practitioner in general practice to make a house visit to his patient when so requested may constitute professional negligence in a particular case eg where the patient was an ill pregnant mother whose condition had worsened and who failed to keep down prescribed medication: O'Doherty v Whelan (1993 HC) ITLR (16 Apr). See also Walsh v Family Planning Services Ltd (1993 SC) 11 ILT Dig 90; Maitland v Swan & Sligo Co Council (1992 HC) ITLR (6 Jul). See DIAGNOSIS, INCORRECT; DOSAGE; NO FAULT COMPENSATION; RES IPSA LOQUITUR; LIMITATION OF ACTIONS; SURGICAL OPERATION.

**medical practitioner, registered.** A person registered in the General Register of Medical Practitioners established under the Medical Practitioners Act 1978. The Medical Council is obliged under the 1978 Act to make rules specifying the courses of training and examinations required to qualify for registration: Bakht v The Medical Council (1990 SC) ILRM 840. The Council has the responsibility for ensuring that only fully qualified and experienced persons are registered so as to enable them to engage in medical practice in the State.

The register may be kept on computer and also a certificate signed by the Registrar is evidence of the matter stated in the certificate, unless the contrary is shown: 1978 Act ss.26(2), (2A) and s.57 as substituted by Medical Practitioners

(Amdt) Act 1993 s.2 and s.3 respectively.

A consultant physician was awarded damages for breach by the health board of its contractual obligation to supply him with reasonable facilities for the proper discharge of his duties; it was no defence to say that its failure was due to policies imposed by the Minister for Health: Sullivan v Southern Health Board (1993 HC) — Irish Times 30/7/1993. See Treaty of Rome 1957 art.57 as replaced by Maastricht Treaty 1992 art.G(D)(13). See also BLOOD SPECIMEN; BRAIN DEATH; COMHAIRLE NA N-OSPIDEAL; DESIGNATED; PROFESSIONAL NEGLIGENCE; SURGICAL OPERATION; UNDUE INFLUENCE.

**medical preparations.** A substance which is sold under a proprietary designation or any other prophylactic, diagnostic or therapeutic substance, which may be used for the prevention or treatment of any human ailment, infirmity, injury or defect: Health Acts 1947 s.65 and 1953 s.39; Misuse of Drugs Act 1977 s.36. Also included is (a) any drug or preparation intended to prevent pregnancy resulting from sexual intercourse between human beings, and (b) other preparations which may be used for restoring, correcting or modifying physiological functions in human beings: Health (Family Planning) (Amdt) Act 1992 s.7 amending the 1947 Act s.65. Oral contraceptive pills and spermacides are now controlled by the 1947 Act.

Regulations may be made to prohibit the manufacture, preparation, importation, distribution, sale or offering or keeping for sale of medical preparations, either absolutely or subject to specified conditions, including the grant of a licence. Advertising of such preparations may also be controlled. See Medical Preparations Regulations 1974-1993 (SI Nos 39, 40, 68, 69, 70, 71 and 76 of 1993); Medical Preparations (Advertising) Regulations 1993 (SI No 76 of 1993); Pharmacopoeia Act 1931; Therapeutic Substances Act 1932. [Text: EC Pub (2)]. See CLINICAL TRIALS; PRESCRIPTION DRUGS.

**medium-sized company.** A private company which satisfies at least two of the following conditions: (a) the balance sheet total does not exceed £5 million, (b) turnover does not exceed £10 million,

(c) the average number of employees does not exceed 250: Companies Amendment Act 1986 s.8. A medium-sized company may combine some of the items set out in the format specified for the profit and loss account (ibid s.11). See ACCOUNTS.

**meetings.** See ASSEMBLY, RIGHT OF.

**meetings of company.** Meetings of a company attended by its members, comprising (a) the *annual general meeting* held once each year; (b) an *extraordinary general meeting* which may be convened when the directors so wish, and also by requisition of a defined proportion of members: Companies Act 1963 s.132; and (c) a separate *class meeting* of members usually for the purpose of voting on proposals to vary or abrogate the rights attached to the class of shares in question. See ANNUAL GENERAL MEETING; CLASS RIGHTS; EXTRAORDINARY GENERAL MEETING.

**melior est conditio possidentis et rei quam actoris.** [The position of the possessor is the better, and that of the defendant is better than that of the plaintiff]. Possession is prima facie evidence of ownership and may be good against all claims except that of the true owner. The onus of proof in an action generally rests on the claimant or plaintiff.

**membership.** (1) As regards a company, every person who has been allotted one or more shares in a company and has the unconditional right to be included in the company's register of members, is a member of that company. The subscribers of the memorandum and every other person who agrees to become a member of a company, and whose name is entered in its register of members, is a member of the company: Companies Act 1963 s.31.

(2) As regards a building society, every person who holds one or more shares in a building society is a member of that society; however, a society may by its rules, allow a person who does not hold a share to be a member, where that person is an applicant for or a recipient of a *housing loan* (qv). See also Building Societies Act 1989 ss.2(1) and 16(1).

(3) As regards a trade union, see WORK, RIGHT TO. See also OPPRESSION OF SHAREHOLDER.

**memorandum.** A note recording the particulars of any transaction or matter.

**memorandum, sale of goods.** The memorandum required in relation to a contract for the sale of goods of £10 or upwards, in the absence of acceptance and receipt of the goods, or part payment, or something given in earnest to bind the contract: Sale of Goods Act 1893 s.4. In the absence of such memorandum, the contract is unenforceable. The essential requirements of the memorandum are similar to those required in the Statute of Frauds, except that where the price is agreed it must be shown in the memorandum, and where not agreed, a reasonable price will be implied. See MEMORANDUM, STATUTE OF FRAUDS.

**memorandum, Statute of Frauds.** The memorandum required in writing in relation to certain contracts which otherwise are unenforceable: Statute of Frauds (Ireland) 1695. In relation to the memorandum (a) it need not be made at the time of the formation of the contract, provided it is made before action is brought; (b) it must contain the names of the parties or a sufficient description of them; (c) the subject matter must be described so that it can be identified and all material terms of the contract must be stated; (d) the consideration must appear, except in contracts of guarantee where by virtue of the Mercantile Law Amendment Act 1856, consideration must be present but need not appear in the memorandum; (e) it must be signed by the party to be charged or his agent. See Casey v Irish Intercontinental Bank (1979) IR 364; Tradax (Ireland) Ltd v Irish Grain Board Ltd (1983) SC; Morris v Barron (1918) AC 1; Hawkins v Price (1947) Ch 645; Mulhall v Haren (1981) IR 364.

Where a memorandum or note exists which satisfies the Statute, the Court will not imply a term which would have the effect of defeating the contract: Aga Khan v Firestone (1992 HC) ILRM 31. A memorandum which contains any term or expression such as "subject to contract" is not sufficient, even if it can be established by oral evidence that such a term or expression did not form part of the originally concluded oral contract: Boyle & Boyle v Lee & Goyns (1992 SC) ILRM 65. Only in rare and exceptional circumstances, such as arose in Kelly v Parkhall School (1979) IR 349, could the words "subject to contract" be treated as being of no effect: Egan J in Boyle v Lee).

If there is no memorandum, the contract cannot be enforced unless there has been *part performance* of the contract by the plaintiff; equity will then decree *specific performance*. For the acts of part performance regarded as supplanting the memorandum required by the Statute of Frauds, see Hope v Lord Cloncurry (1874) IR 8 Eq 555; Lowry v Reid (1927) NI 142; Kennedy v Kennedy (1984) HC. See PART-PERFORMANCE; STATUTE OF FRAUDS; UNENFORCEABLE.

**memorandum of association.** See ASSOCIATION, MEMORANDUM OF.

**memorial.** An abstract of the material parts of a deed, the enrolment of which is necessary for the registration of a deed in the Registry of Deeds: Registration of Deeds (Ireland) Act 1707 s.7. It must contain: the date of perfection of the deed; the names and addresses of all the parties and witnesses to the deed; and the lands described as in the deed itself. The memorial must be executed by one of the grantors or grantees of the deed, be attested by two witnesses (one of whom was a witness of the grantor's execution of the deed) and be proved by an affidavit made by a witness common to the memorial and the deed (ibid s.6). See also DEEDS, REGISTRATION OF; SIGN MANUAL.

**memory, refreshing.** See REFRESHING MEMORY.

**menaces, extortion by.** See EXTORTION BY MENACES.

**mens rea.** [Guilty mind]. To constitute a criminal offence, the offence must be accompanied by a blameworthy state of mind. What the law considers as blameworthy varies from offence to offence; mens rea must be considered in relation to the crime charged. It may be *intentional* eg in murder where the consequences are foreseen by the accused and desired. It may be *reckless* or be *grossly negligent* where the consequences are foreseen but not necessarily desired eg in manslaughter. It may also be *negligent*, where the consequences are not foreseen but where the law requires foresight eg dangerous driving of a motor vehicle.

An offence at common law requires mens rea. In an offence created by statute, it is a question of construction as to whether it is required; if the statute is silent on mens rea, there is a presumption that it is required: The People (DPP) v Murray (1977) IR 360 adopting Sweet v Parsley (1970) AC 132. See also R v Tolson (1889) 23 QBD 168. See INTENT; MALICE AFORETHOUGHT; STRICT LIABILITY IN CRIMINAL LAW; ACTUS NON FACIT REUM, NISI MENS SIT REA.

**mensa et thoro.** See DIVORCE A MENSA ET THORO.

**menstruation.** Failure to comply with the request for a toilet break by a female employee, who is menstruating, can amount to discrimination: Power Supermarkets t/o Crazy Prices & Purdy EE11/ 1991.

**mental abnormality.** See INSANITY.

**mental disability.** For recommendations on reform of the law relating to liability in tort of mentally disabled persons, see LRC 18 of 1985. See also Report on Sexual Offences against the Mentally Handicapped (LRC 33 of 1990). See MENTAL HANDICAP; SAFETY BELT.

**mental disorder, person suffering from.** Where a member of the Garda Siochana is of opinion that a person is suffering from mental disorder of such a degree that he should, in the interest of his own health and safety or for the protection of other persons or property, be placed forthwith under care and control, he may take the person into custody and remove him to a garda station: Health (Mental Services) Act 1981 s.16. The garda must then apply forthwith to a registered medical practitioner for a recommendation for the reception of that person in a psychiatric centre. The 1981 Act had not been brought into operation by 1993. See PSYCHIATRIC CENTRE; RECEPTION ORDER.

**mental distress.** A ground for damages in fatal injury cases; the judge may award compensation as he considers to be reasonable for the *mental distress* resulting from the death to each dependant: Civil Liabilities Act 1961 s.49. It is subject to a maximum award of £7,500: Courts Act 1981 s.28(1). See Dowling v Jedos Ltd (1977) SC.

Damages for *mental distress* will not automatically be awarded to a plaintiff who can show it arising from breach of contract. It has been held that the *mental distress* suffered by a plaintiff on discovering that the licensed premises he had purchased had a hotel licence and not a public house licence, did not warrant damages (qv) as it was not reasonably foreseeable: Kelly v Crowley (1985) HC. See FATAL INJURIES; WORKSTATION.

**mental handicap.** In all criminal proceedings, a person with a mental handicap may give unsworn evidence if the court is satisfied that he is capable of giving an intelligible account of events which are relevant to those proceedings: Criminal Evidence Act 1992 s.27. This unsworn evidence may corroborate evidence (sworn and unsworn) given by any other person (ibid s.28(3)). A person with mental handicap may also, in criminal proceedings involving physical or sexual abuse, give evidence by means of a live television link. Where the person is the alleged victim, a videorecording of a statement he made to a garda may also be admissible. See DISTRICT COURT, PRELIMINARY EXAMINATION; EDUCATION; MENTALLY IMPAIRED; TELEVISION LINK.

**mental treatment.** Medical treatment for a psychiatric illness. There are three categories of patients in mental hospitals: (a) *voluntary* patients; (b) *temporary* patients, and (c) *persons of unsound mind*. A voluntary patient may be admitted without the recommendation of a medical practitioner (unless the person is under 16 years of age) and may leave on giving three day's notice.

A *reception order* is required in the case of a temporary patient or a person of unsound mind. Where the person is eligible for health board services, it will be an *eligible patient reception order* signed by a medical practitioner and the medical officer of the institution; where the person is a private patient, it will be a *private patient reception order* signed by two medical practitioners who have examined the patient separately.

A person of unsound mind may be detained "until his removal or discharge by proper authority or his death"; whereas, the detention of a temporary patient is limited to 6 months, which may be extended by the chief medical officer of the institution for a maximum of six months at each extension, provided that the total detention period does not exceed two years.

Safeguards to protect persons from wrongful detention include: (a) habeas corpus (qv); (b) patients' right to have a letter forwarded unopened to the Minister, President of High Court, or others; (c) penalties for unlawful detention; (d) any person may apply to the Minister for an order for examination, by two medical practitioners, of a detained patient. See Mental Treatment Act 1945; Health Act 1970; Mental Treatment Regulations 1961; Mental Treatment Acts (Adaptation) Order 1971 (SI No 108 of 1971). See O'Dowd v North Western Health Board (1983) ILRM 186; Murphy v Greene (1991 SC) ILRM 404. Significant changes are contained in the Health (Mental Services) Act 1981 but this Act had not come into force by 1993. See ACCESS TO COURTS; RECEPTION ORDER.

**mentally impaired.** Suffering from a disorder of the mind, whether through mental handicap or mental illness, which is of such a nature or degree as to render a person incapable of living an independent life or guarding against serious exploitation: Criminal Law (Sexual Offences) Act 1993 s.5(5). It is an indictable offence for a person to have sexual intercourse or to commit an act of buggery with a person who is mentally impaired (ibid s.5(1)). An attempt is also an offence, as in an act of *gross indecency* by a male with a mentally impaired male. It is a defence for the accused to be able to show that he did not know and had no reason to suspect that the person was mentally impaired (ibid s.5(3)). See BUGGERY; SOLICIT.

**mercantile agent.** See FACTOR.

**merchandise licence.** A carrier's licence; a national road freight carrier's licence or an international road freight carrier's licence. See CARRIER'S LICENCE.

**merchandise mark.** See TRADE DESCRIPTION; FALSE TRADE DESCRIPTION.

**merchant shipping.** The International Convention for the Safety of Life at Sea, signed in London on 1st November 1974, has been given effect in this State by the Merchant Shipping Act 1981. For safety regulations for commercial ships and ferries, see Merchant Shipping Regulations 1988 (SI Nos 107, 108, 109, 110 of 1988). See also Merchant Shipping Acts 1894-1983. [Text: Power UK]. See PASSENGER BOAT; PASSENGER SHIP.

**merchantable quality.** Goods are of *merchantable quality* if they are fit for the purpose or purposes for which goods of that kind are commonly bought and as durable as it is reasonable to expect having regard to any description applied to them, the price (if relevant) and all the other relevant circumstances: Sale of Goods Act 1893 s.14; SGSS Act 1980 s.10. Where a seller sells goods (or an owner lets goods under a hire-purchase agreement) in the course of a business, there is an implied condition that the goods are of merchantable quality. See Butterly v United Dominions Trust (Commercial) Ltd (1963) IR 56. See CONDITION; QUALITY OF GOODS.

**merger.** The extinguishing of a right, by operation of law, by reason of its coinciding with another and greater right in the same person eg in a contract for the sale of land, the written agreement of sale becomes merged and extinguished in the subsequent conveyance under seal.

If both the benefit of a charge in property and the property subject to the charge vest in the same person, equity will treat the charge as kept alive or merged depending on the circumstances eg where there are mortgages A and B on a property with priority to A, and the owner of the *equity of redemption* (qv) redeems A, he will not be able to keep the redeemed mortgage alive as against B if in fact he created both A and B mortgages. See Lemon v Mark (1899) 1 IR 416.

**merger of company.** The acquisition of one company by another, so that only one company remains. The most common method of merger today is where one company acquires most or all of the shares in another company so that the latter becomes a subsidiary of the former. The offer to acquire the shares may be for cash or for some of the former's own shares or a permutation of both and is usually conditional on a certain proportion being accepted.

A merger can also be accomplished by a company proposed to be, or in the course of being, wound up voluntarily by special resolution authorising the liquidator to transfer the company (the transferor) to the receiving company (the transferee) in return for stocks, shares, debentures or other interests in the transferee company: Companies Act 1963 s.260. This procedure cannot be used where the transferor company is in compulsory liquidation.

Take-overs of companies the shares of which are quoted on the Stock Exchange and of unlisted public companies are governed also by the City Code on Take-Overs Mergers, which is an integral part of the Listing Agreement. Compliance with the Code is supervised by a panel and decisions may be appealed to an appeal committee.

Mergers involving large companies may infringe EC competition law and may be subject to the Mergers, Take-Overs and Monopolies (Control) Act 1978, as amended by the Competition Act 1991 ss.13-18.

The ability of directors to oppose take-over bids may be affected by their fiduciary duty, their power to refuse to register transfers and to issue and allot additional shares. See Kinsella v Alliance & Dublin Consumers Gas Co (1982) HC. See also Hennessy v National Assn (1947) IR 159. [Text: Forde (5); Mason Hayes & Curran; Weinberg & Blank (UK)]. See COMPETITION, DISTORTION OF; COVERT TAKE-OVER; TAKE-OUT MERGERS; SHARES, DISCLOSURE OF; WHITE KNIGHT.

**merger of company, EC regulations.** The regulations which apply to the merger and division of plcs and certain specified unregistered companies since 1st June 1987, implementing the EC Third and Sixth Company Law Directives: European Communities (Mergers and Division of Companies) Regulations 1987 (SI No 137 of 1987). The EC also has control over mergers through its competition policy eg the take-over contest for the shares of Irish Distillers plc in 1988.

The EC Commission now has exclusive jurisdiction, with some rare exceptions, over very large cross-border mergers in the Community. The new merger regulations were adopted in Council Regulation No 4064/89 whereby a merger (concentration) is defined as the merger of two or more previously independent undertakings; or where one or more persons already controlling at least one undertaking or one or more undertakings acquire, by the purchase of securities or assets, direct or indirect control of the whole or parts of one or more undertakings.

Mergers are regulated which have a *community dimension* ie where (a) the aggregate worldwide turnover of all the undertakings concerned is more than 5,000m ECU and (b) the aggregate community wide turnover of each of at least two of the undertakings concerned is more than 250m ECU. The Regulation came into force on 21st September 1990. A proposed concentration is assessed by the EC Commission in consultation with the relevant authority in each member State. A notification from the EC Commission constitutes a notification to the Minister under s.5 of the Merger, Take-overs and Monopolies (Control) Act 1978: Competition Act 1991 s.16. For the procedures on the application of EC rules on competition relating to the control of mergers and take-overs between undertakings with an EC dimension, see EC (Rules on Competition) Regulations 1993 (SI No 124 of 1993). See Keane & Walsh in 8ILT & SJ (1990) 181. [Text: Downes & Ellison UK].See COMPETITION, DISTORTION OF; DIVISION OF COMPANY.

**merger/take-over, domestic statutory provision.** A merger or take-over is to be taken to exist when two or more *enterprises*, at least one of which carries on business in the State, come under *common control* (qv): Mergers, Take-overs and Monopolies (Control) Act 1978 s.1(3)(a). This statutory provision applies to a proposed merger or take-over if, in the most recent financial year, (a) the value of the gross assets of each of two or more of the enterprises is not less than £10 million or (b) the turnover of each is not less than £20 million, excluding VAT or excise duty (ibid s.2(1); SI No 135 of 1993) or (c) where the proposed mergers are of a particular class (ibid 1978 Act s.2(5)).

Enterprises are deemed to come under common control when one obtains the right (a) to appoint or remove a majority of the board of the other, or (b) to 25% of the voting rights of the other after the acquisition (ibid 1978 Act s.1(3)(c) as substituted by Competition Act 1991 s.15(2)). Each of the enterprises is required to notify the Minister of the proposed merger or take-over: 1978 Act s.5 as substituted by 1991 Act s.16.

The Minister may allow the merger to go ahead or he may refer it to the Competition Authority (qv) for investigation (ibid 1978 Act ss.7-8 as amended by 1991 Act s.17). The Minister may, having considered their report, if he thinks that the exigencies of the common good so warrant, by *order* prohibit a proposed merger or take-over either absolutely or except on conditions specified in the order (1978 Act s.9(1) as amended by 1991 Act s.18). For example, see prohibition by Minister on majority shareholding by Independent Newspapers plc in the Tribune Group: SI No 56 of 1992.

Title to any shares or assets in relation to a proposed merger or take-over does not pass, until the Minister has stated in writing that he has decided not to make such an *order* or the *relevant period* has elapsed without the Minister having made an order (ibid 1978 Act s.3). An appeal on a point of law lies to the High Court against such an *order* (ibid s.12). The Minister may on a motion obtain an injunction to enforce compliance with such an *order* (ibid s.13; Restrictive Practices [Amendment] Act 1987 s.26).

An *enterprise* means a person or partnership engaged for profit in the supply or distribution of goods or the provision of services (including an industrial and provident society, friendly society, credit union, building society) and a holding company within the meaning of the Companies Act 1963 s.155 (ibid 1978 Act s.1(1)). See also Restrictive Practices (Amendment) Act 1987 ss.24-25. See also SI No 42 of 1990. See also Linnane in 9 ILT & SJ (1991) 243. See MONOPOLY, CONTROL OF; NEWSPAPER.

**mesne rates.** The damage for trespass arising in an *ejectment action* for non-payment of rent or for overholding to which a plaintiff is entitled: Deasy's Act 1860 s.77. The measure of the mesne rates is the value of the premises during the period of trespass, usually but not invariably, calculated on the rent; there

may also be, if the facts warrant it, damages for deterioration of the premises: Lynham v Butler 67 ILTR 121. See RSC O.41 rr.9-10; RCC O.8 r.2.

**metal detectors.** Detection devices, the use or possession of which, is prohibited in or at a site of a registered monument or other specified monuments or in a registered archaeological area (qv) or a restricted area: National Monuments (Amendment) Act 1987 s.2. It is also an offence to use a detection device or to promote, whether by advertising or otherwise, the sale or use of detection devices, for the purpose of searching for archaeological objects. See ARCHAEOLOGICAL AREA; HISTORIC MONUMENT; NATIONAL MONUMENT; WRECK.

**Michaelmas.** A sitting of the Court. See SITTINGS OF COURT.

**micro-organisms.** Micro-organisms produced by genetic engineering are not excluded from patent protection; it has been held that an application for a patent in respect of an invention entitled *Improvement in or relating to cell lines* should proceed, since the cell lines were articles for use produced from raw materials occurring in nature by giving those materials new forms, qualities and properties, they fell within the definition of an invention in the Patents Act 1964 s.2 as *manufactures*; the fact that the articles consisted of living matter was irrelevant: National Research Development Corporation's Application (1986) FSR 620, distinguishing Rank Hovis McDougall Ltd v Controller of Patents (1979) IR 142 and applying In re Chakrabarty 206 USPQ 193 (1980). See Keane in 10 ILT & SJ (1992) 139.

The Patents Act 1992, which repeals the 1964 Act, provides that rules may prescribe the "disclosure" requirements in respect of an invention which requires for its performance the use of a micro-organism (ibid 1992 Act s.19(2)).

**midnight.** In relation to any particular day, the point of time at which such day ends: Interpretation Act 1937 s.12 sch.

**midwife.** Originally was a woman registered in the roll of midwives in accordance with the Midwives Act 1944. The statutory bar to men becoming midwives was removed by the Employment Equality Act 1977 s.11. A midwife is now a person whose name is registered in the midwives division of the register of nurses: Nurses Act 1985 s.2. It is an offence for a person to use or take the name or title of *midwife* if that person is not registered (ibid s.49). See also 1985 Act s.57.

It has been held that a midwifery service can be provided by the attendance of a medical practitioner at the birth; the health board (qv) does not have to provide a midwife for a *home* delivery: Health Act 1970 s.62; Spruyt v Southern Health Board (1988 HC & SC). See CHILDBIRTH, ATTENDANCE AT; FOETAL DEATH.

**migration of company.** The European Court has held that Articles 52 and 58 of the Treaty of Rome do not confer on companies the right to transfer their central management and control to another member State while retaining their status as companies incorporated under the legislation of the first member State: R v HM Treasury and Inland Revenue Commissioners, ex parte Daily Mail and General Trust plc (1988) STC 787 as described by Gill in 7ILT & SJ (1989) 59.

**mile, nautical.** See NAUTICAL MILE.

**mileometer reading.** A false mileometer reading has been held in the UK to be a false trade description (qv): R v Hammerton Cars Ltd (1976) 1 WLR 1243.

**military convict.** A person under sentence of penal servitude passed by a court-martial: Defence Act 1954 s.2(1).

**military law.** The body of law dealing with the raising, maintenance and command of the defence forces; enlistment, promotion and discharge of personnel; discipline and offences in relation to persons subject to military law; courts-martial, and execution of sentences. The law is primarily contained in the principal statute: Defence Act 1954.

Subsequent legislation has provided for: overseas service with the United Nations (qv) in peace keeping and enforcement: Defence (Amendment) (No 2) Act 1960 as amended and extended by Defence (Amdt) Act 1993; the recruitment of women: Defence (Amendment) Act 1979; appeals from courts martial (qv): Courts-Martial Appeals Act 1983; alteration in punishments in respect of offences against military law and introduction of new forms and penalties in respect of serving

officers, and providing for contempt of a courts-martial: Defence (Amendment) Act 1987. See DEFENCE FORCES.

**military prisoner.** A person under sentence of imprisonment passed by a court-martial: Defence Act 1954 s.2(1).

**military tribunals.** The tribunals which may be established for the trial of offences against military law alleged to have been committed by persons subject to military law and also to deal with a state of war or armed rebellion: 1937 Constitution, art.38(4)(1). See COURTS MARTIAL.

**mine.** Excavations for or in connection with the getting of minerals or mineral products. The Mines and Quarries Act 1965 contains provisions for protecting the lives, health and welfare of workers therein. Women are now permitted to work in all occupations, including manual occupations below ground, in a mine: Employment Equality Act 1977 (Employment of Females on Underground Work in Mines) Order 1989. Certain sections of the 1965 Act are repealed when particular sections of the Safety, Health and Welfare at Work Act 1989 come into force. See Glencar Exploration v Mayo Co Council (1992 HC).

**minimum age for employment.** See EMPLOYMENT, MINIMUM AGE FOR.

**minimum prices.** See BELOW COST SELLING; PRICE CONTROL.

**minimum wages.** See JOINT LABOUR COMMITTEE.

**Minister.** A member of the Government. The President of Ireland (qv) acting on the nomination of the Taoiseach (qv) with the previous approval of Dail Eireann (qv), appoints members of the Government: 1937 Constitution art.13(1)(2). The Taoiseach is empowered to assign Departments of State to members of the Government: Ministers and Secretaries (Amdt) Act 1946 s.4(1). A Minister is disqualified from being a member of a local authority: Local Government Act 1991 s.13. See GOVERNMENT; MINISTERIAL DECISIONS; MINISTERIAL RESPONSIBILITY; SEVERANCE PAY.

**Minister of State.** A member of either House of the Oireachtas, appointed by the government on the nomination of the Taoiseach: Ministers & Secretaries (Amendment) (No 2) Act 1977 s.1. They are not members of the government. Not more than 15 persons may be appointed: Ministers & Secretaries (Amendment) Act 1980 s.2. The government may on the recommendation of the Taoiseach remove a Minister of State. A Minister of State may resign his office by letter addressed to the Taoiseach and the resignation takes effect on and from the day it is accepted by the Taoiseach (ibid s.4). A Minister of State is disqualified from being a member of a local authority: Local Government Act 1991 s.13.

**ministerial announcement.** RTE is required to comply with a direction from the Minister to allocate broadcasting time for any announcements by or on behalf of any Minister of State in connection with the functions of that Minister of State: Broadcasting Act 1960 s.31(2). There is no right of reply to such a broadcast. An application to prevent the Taoiseach from making a broadcast under s.31(2) in favour of the Maastricht Treaty failed, as did the application for a right of reply: McCann v Ireland (1992 HC) — Irish Times 6/12/1992.

**ministerial decisions.** The exercise of a Minister of a statutory power may be subject to *judicial review* and will be upheld if found to be reasonable: The State (Crowley) v Irish Land Commission (1951) IR 250; Egan v Minister for Defence (1989) 7ILT Dig 81. Where a Minister is granted a specific duty to make decisions under a statutory code, and he makes such decisions bona fide having obtained and followed legal advice, he cannot be held to be negligent or to have made negligent misrepresentations, if he is found to have acted ultra vires (qv): Pine Valley v Minister for the Environment (1987) ILRM 747.

A Minister may be required to state the reasons for decisions which he makes in exercise of a statutory power eg where he refuses to grant a sea fishing boat licence to an applicant: International Fishing Vessels Ltd v Minister for the Marine (1989) IR 149. However, his decision made for stated valid reasons is not invalidated by unstated reasons (ibid (1991 SC) 2 IR 379). It has also been held that it is unconstitutional for a Minister to exercise his statutory power in such a way as to negative the expressed intention of the legislature: Harvey v

Minister for Social Welfare (1990 SC) ILRM 185.

A Minister also is required to deal with an application under a statute (to attain a statutory right) within a reasonable time and before any critical "cut-off" time: Twomey v Minister for Transport & Tourism (1993 SC) ITLR (10 May). A Minister must act reasonably: Breen v Minister for Defence (1990 SC) ITLR (5 Nov). The obligation for a Minister to act fairly in exercising his discretion includes ensuring that fair procedures are provided not only for an applicant but also for an objecting party: Madden v Minister for the Marine (1993 HC) ILRM 436. See STATUTORY INSTRUMENT.

**ministerial responsibility.** Ministers as members of the government are *collectively* responsible to Dail Eireann for the Departments of State administered by them: 1937 Constitution, art.28(4). See GOVERNMENT.

**minor.** A person under the age of eighteen years who is not or has not been married: Age of Majority Act 1985 s.2. This interpretation also applies to the terms *infancy, infant* and *minority.* Contracts made during infancy in respect of *necessaries* (qv) and *apprenticeship* (qv) are binding on an infant. When an infant acquires an interest in a subject of a permanent nature, which imposes a continuous liability on him, the contract cannot be enforced against him during infancy eg a lease, a partnership, a shareholding in a company or a marriage settlement.

After the infant attains full age, it will be binding on him unless he avoids it within a reasonable time eg see Davies v Benyon-Harris (1931) 47 TLR 424. All other contracts are unenforceable against the infant. Certain contracts entered into by infants are *absolutely void* eg a contract for repayment of money lent or to be lent; goods supplied or to be supplied (other than necessaries) and accounts stated: Infants Relief Act 1874 s.1. See Coutts v Browne-Lecky (1947) KB 104. See also Family Law Act 1981 s.10; Finance Act 1986 s.112; Law Reform Commission Report on Minors' Contracts LRC 15 of 1985.

A minor is fully liable for his torts (qv) provided he has reached the age of discretion: O'Brien v McNamee (1953)

IR 86. A minor may be made a ward of court. However, parental consent is still required by persons under the age of 21 who wish to marry, and formerly a person could be adopted up to 21 years of age (now, under 18 years: Adoption Act 1988 s.6). See also Building Societies Act 1989 s.16(5). See LRC 17 of 1985. See CHILD, ADOPTED; DOLI INCAPAX; LODGMENT IN COURT; MARRIAGE; PAYMENT OUT OF COURT; NEXT FRIEND; RATIFICATION; WARD OF COURT.

**minor and crime.** See DOLI INCAPAX; YOUNG PERSON

**minor offence.** An offence which may be tried by courts of summary jurisdiction: 1937 Constitution, art.38(2). The Constitution does not define a minor offence. The main criteria for determining whether an offence is a minor one are: the severity of the penalty, the moral quality of the act, how the law stood when the statute was passed, the relationship of the offence to common law offences: Melling v O'Mathghamhna (1962) IR 1; The State (Rollinson) v Kelly (1984) ILRM 625. Secondary penalties authorised under a statute should not be taken into account: Cartmill v Ireland (1987) HC.

It would appear that where the punishment is less than six months imprisonment or the fine is £500 or less, the offence is minor; whereas where the punishment is two years or more or the fine is £100,000 or more, the offence is non-minor. See Conroy v Attorney General (1965) IR 411; The State (Sheerin) v Kennedy (1966) IR 379; Kostan v Ireland (1978) HC; The State (Pheasantry) v Donnelly (1982) ILRM 512; The State (Wilson) v DJ Neylon (1987) ILRM 118. See SUMMARY OFFENCE.

**minority protection.** See OPPRESSION OF SHAREHOLDER.

**minutes.** Notes providing a record of proceedings. A company must keep minutes of all its general meetings: Companies Act 1963 s.145. Such minutes must be signed by the chairman and when so signed are prima facie evidence of what occurred at the meeting. The minutes must also be open to inspection by members of the company: ibid s.146 and Companies (Amendment) Act 1982 s.15. Minutes contemporaneously made of the meeting of members of a board

or of a tribunal are neither a necessary nor the only method of establishing the material that was before that board or tribunal: O'Keeffe v An Bord Pleanala & Radio Tara (1992 SC) ILRM 237.

**misadventure.** The killing of another while doing a lawful act with no intention of causing harm, and with no culpable negligence in the mode of doing it eg death accidentally caused in the course of a lawful game or sport. See R v Young 10 Cox 371; The People (Attorney General) v Dunleavy (1948) IR 95. See HOMICIDE.

**misappropriation.** See DECEIT; FRAUDULENT CONVERSION.

**miscarriage.** A failure of justice. Under draft legislation, a framework is proposed for reviewing alleged miscarriages of justice, broadly implementing the recommendations of the Martin Committee (1990): Criminal Procedure Bill 1993. Under the Bill, a person, who has exhausted the normal appeal procedures, will be permitted to appeal again to the Court of Criminal Appeal for an order quashing a conviction or reviewing a sentence, provided he has a new or newly-discovered fact to support his allegation of a miscarriage of justice. Also, the Minister will be empowered to appoint an ad hoc committee of inquiry, in appropriate cases, with wide powers to examine an alleged miscarriage of justice. See APPEAL; PARDON.

**mischief of a statute.** The wrong which it is intended to redress by an enactment. The mischief is often to be found in the preamble to the Act or from the marginal notes. See MISCHIEF RULE.

**mischief rule.** The rule of construction for interpreting a statute whereby the judge will look at the law which existed prior to the statute, the *mischief of the statute* (qv) which it was intended to remedy and will interpret the statute in a way to suppress the mischief and advance the remedy. See Magdalen College Case (1616) 11 Co Rep 716; Nestor v Murphy (1979) IR 326.

**mischievous propensity.** See SCIENTER; ANIMALS; DOGS.

**misconduct.** A ground for dismissal from employment. See Nugent v CIE (1990) ELR 15; Creed v KMP Co-op Society Ltd (1990 EAP) ELR 140; O'Connor v Brewster (1992 EAT) ELR 10. See

HORSEPLAY; REDUNDANCY; UNFAIR DISMISSAL.

**misdemeanour.** See FELONY.

**misdescription.** As regards property, an error, mistake, or mis-statement in the description of the property. If the misdescription is substantial, the purchaser will be entitled to repudiate the contract; the misdescription will be a good defence to an action for specific performance (qv). However, if the misdescription is one the only effect of which was to induce the purchaser to give a higher price than he otherwise would, and was made innocently, and compensation can be fairly assessed, the court will order specific performance subject to that compensation.

**misdirection.** Failure by a judge to inform the jury adequately as to the evidence or the law or as to the issues requiring a decision or a total failure so to inform. A judge sitting alone can misdirect himself eg by putting the wrong questions to himself to answer. Misdirection is a ground for appeal. See Kelly v Board of Governors of St Laurence's Hospital (1989) 7ILT Dig 23.

**misericordia.** [Mercy].

**misfeasance.** An improper performance of an otherwise lawful act eg where there is an act of positive negligence. A *misfeasor* is a person who is guilty of a misfeasance. Where a local authority performs its duty of repairing the highway but does so in a negligent manner, it is guilty of misfeasance; it may be sued for any resulting damage and cannot escape liability on the grounds that it employed an independent contractor to do the work: Clements v Tyrone County Council (1905) 2 IR 415. Damages for misfeasance will not be granted where the defendants had acted in a bona fide manner and had not acted maliciously: CW Shipping Ltd v Limerick Harbour Commissioners (1989 HC) ILRM 416. See also Kelly v Mayo Co Co (1964) IR 315. See NONFEASANCE; ROAD MAINTENANCE.

**misfeasance suit, company.** A summary procedure by which a company which is being wound up may be compensated for losses arising from various wrongs done to it (including any misfeasance or other breach of duty or trust) by its directors or other officers. The court may, on the application of the liquidator, or of a creditor or contributory, investigate the matter and order restitution and compensation. See Companies Act 1963 s.298 as amended by Companies Act 1990 s.142; RSC O.74 r 49. See In re S M Barker Ltd (1950) IR 123; Jackson v Mortell (1986) HC. See MacCann in 9ILT & SJ (1991) 58. See WINDING UP.

**misjoinder.** Where a person is wrongly joined in proceedings either as plaintiff or defendant. No cause or matter may be defeated by reason of the misjoinder or non-joinder of parties; the court may order that the names of parties improperly joined, be struck out, and to add parties who ought to have been joined: RSC O.15 r.13.

**misleading advertisement.** See ADVERTISING MISLEADING.

**misnomer.** A mis-naming. An amendment to correct the error may be made in a suitable case. See PLEADINGS, AMENDMENT OF.

**misprision of felony.** A common law misdemeanour, committed by a person who knows that a felony (qv) has been committed and can give information which might lead to the felon's arrest, but omits to report it. The offence does not arise by the failure of a legal advisor, a doctor or a clergyman to report the matter, or where the failure is in order to avoid inviting a prosecution against oneself. See Sykes v DPP (1961) 3 All ER 33 at 36. See ACCESSORY.

**misprision of treason.** The offence committed by a person who fails to disclose treason (qv) which is proposed to be, or is being, or has been committed: Treason Act 1939 s.3.

**misrepresentation.** A statement or conduct which conveys a false or wrong impression. A misrepresentation may be *fraudulent, negligent* or *innocent*. As regards contract, a misrepresentation to be *operative*: must be a false representation; it must be one of fact; it must be intended to be acted upon; and it must actually mislead and induce a contract.

A *fraudulent* misrepresentation is one made knowingly or without belief in its truth or recklessly, careless whether it be true or false: Derry v Peek (1889) 14 App Cas 337; Early v Fallon (1976) HC. The person so induced to contract may affirm or rescind the contract and sue for damages in the tort of deceit (qv), although rescission may not be allowed where the parties cannot be restored to their original position: Northern Bank Finance Corp Ltd v Charlton (1979) IR 149; Carbin v Somerville (1933) IR 276.

A *negligent* misrepresentation is one made with no reasonable grounds for believing it to be true. A special duty of care may exist between parties to a contract such as to render *negligent* the failure of one party to ascertain the falsity of a statement, which with reasonable care would have been ascertained: Hedley Byrne & Co Ltd v Heller & Partners Ltd (1964) AC 465; Securities Trust Ltd v Hugh Moore & Alexander Ltd (1964) IR 417; Esso Petroleum Ltd v Mardon (1975) 1 All ER 203; Stafford v Mahoney (1980) HC. The person induced to enter the contract may sue in the tort of negligence (qv).

An *innocent* misrepresentation is one which is not negligent or fraudulent and which may entitle the party misled to rescind the contract if the innocent misrepresentation was of a material fact: Redgrave v Hurd (1881) 20 Ch D 1 ; or to an indemnity to restore the party misled to the position he was in before he entered the contract; or to an abatement (qv). See INNOCENT MISREPRE-SENTATION; NEGLIGENT MIS-STATEMENT; PAT-ENT, REVOCATION OF; PLEADINGS.

**mistake.** Mistake may operate to nullify consent. However, mistake by a party to a contract cannot avoid that contract due to (a) an error of judgement on his part or (b) an underestimation of his own power of performance under the contract or (c) generally an error as to the law and its effects. Mistake may be *mutual* or *common* where the mistake is shared by both parties to the contract, or it may be *unilateral* where it is on one side only.

A *unilateral* mistake generally will not allow a party to a contract to avoid the contract unless there is a mistake as to: (a) the subject matter contracted for: Raffles v Wichelhaus (1864) 2 H & C 906; (b) the identity of the person with whom the contract is made: Cundy v Lindsay (1878) 3 App Cas 459; (c) the promise of one party which mistake is known to the other party: Webster v Cecil (1861) 30 Beav 62; (d) the character

of a written document: see NON EST FACTUM.

A *mutual* mistake as to a fact which goes to the root of a contract will render the contract void ab initio eg mistake as to the fundamental subject matter of the contract or mistake as to the existence of the subject matter eg a life insurance policy taken out in the mistaken belief that the person in question is still alive, is void: Strickland v Turner (1852) 7 Exch 208. See also Bell v Lever Bros (1932) AC 161; Cooper v Phibbs (1867) LR 2 HL 149; Western Potato Co-operative Ltd v Durnan (1985) ILRM 5; Mespil Ltd v Capaldi (1986) ILRM 373; Irish Life Assurance Co v Dublin Land Securities (1986) HC.

Where mistake is *operative* ie operates to render the contract void at common law or voidable in equity, the relief available may be rescission (qv), rectification (qv) or as a defence to specific performance (qv).

Money paid under a mistake of fact is always recoverable as *money had and received* (qv) to the use of the person who has paid it; it now appears that money paid under a mistake of law is also recoverable: Rogers v Louth County Council (1981) ILRM 143; Lord Mayor of Dublin v The Provost of Trinity College Dublin (1984) HC. See COMPRO-MISE; OFFER.

**mistake, sale of goods.** Although parties have reached agreement in the same terms and on the same subject matter, if their agreement is based on a fundamental fact, which turns out to have been mistaken, the courts may treat such a mistake as avoiding the contract which had apparently been made. See Chartered Trust Ireland Ltd v Healy (1985) HC.

**mistake and crime.** Mistake of law is no defence. A mistake of fact may be a good defence to a criminal charge where the mistake of fact, if true, would have justified the act.

**mistake and tort.** Mistake is generally no defence in an action of tort (qv).

**misuse of drugs.** DRUGS, MISUSE OF.

**mitigation of damages.** Diminution of loss. In general there is a duty on a person whose legal rights have been infringed to act reasonably to mitigate his loss. The injured party can recover no more than he would have recovered if he had acted reasonably, because any further damages do not reasonably follow from the defendant's breach. Failure by a plaintiff to mitigate losses he incurred by the defendant's action, may result in a reduction in the costs awarded to the plaintiff eg in a particular case only 19 days costs of a 22 day hearing were awarded to the plaintiff: Deane & Ors v VHI (1993 HC). See also Cullen v Horgan (1925) 2 IR 1; Bord Iascaigh Mhara v Scallan (1973) HC; Malone v Malone (1982) HC.

Where the injured party has received compensation from another source, the common law rule is that this compensation does not reduce damages to the defendant; however statute may require such a deduction. See Social Welfare Act 1984 s.12; Social Welfare Consolidation Act 1981 s.68(1); Civil Liability (Amendment) Act 1964 s.2.

In defamation (qv) actions, the following factors may be taken into account in mitigation of damages: an apology from the defendant: Defamation Act 1961 s.17; receipt by the plaintiff of compensation for the same or similar words already (ibid s.26); provocation by counter-defamations; and the bad reputation of the plaintiff. Where a defendant in such an action intends to give evidence in mitigation of damages, he must furnish particulars thereof to the plaintiff not later than seven days beforehand: RSC O.36 r.36.

**mittimus.** [We send].

**mixed fund.** A fund consisting of the proceeds of sale of both real and personal property.

**mobilia sequuntur personam.** [Movables follow the person]. See FIXTURES.

**mode of address.** Judges of the Superior Courts (qv) must be addressed in Irish or English by their respective titles and names, and may be referred to, in Irish as *An Chuirt* or, in English, as *The Court*: RSC O.119 r.1. It is customary in court to address judges of the Supreme, High and Circuit Courts as *My Lord* or *Your Lordship* or *A Thiarna Bhreithimh* and a judge of the District Court as *Judge* or *A Bhreithimh*.

In writing, it is customary to address judges of the Supreme and High Courts as *The Hon Mr/Mrs/Ms Justice* ...; of the Circuit and District Courts as *His/*

*Her Hon Judge* .... Letters are commenced *Dear Mr/Mrs/Ms Justice* ... (Supreme and High); *Dear Judge* (Circuit and District). An arbitrator is usually addressed as *Arbitrator* or *Mr/Mrs/Ms Arbitrator*. See also RCC O.3 r.2.

**models.** See ARTISTIC WORK.

**modus et conventio vincunt legem.** [Custom and agreement overrule law]. See CUSTOM AND PRACTICE.

**modus legem dat donationi.** [Agreement gives law to the gift].

**modus operandi.** [The way of performing a task].

**molestation.** An act done by a spouse or on his authority, with the intent to annoy the other spouse and in fact be an annoyance to her. A *non-molestation clause* is generally included in a separation agreement (qv) providing that neither spouse will molest, annoy, disturb or interfere with the other. Behaviour in breach of such a clause may be restrained by injunction (qv). See ASSAULT; BARRING ORDER.

**molliter manus imposit.** [He laid hands on him gently]. A defence to a charge of *assault and battery* (qv).

**monetary policy.** The basic task of the European System of Central Banks (ECSB) will be to define and implement the monetary policy of the EC: Treaty of Rome 1957 art.105 replaced by Maastricht Treaty 1992 art.G(D)(25). The primary objective of the ESCB will be to maintain price stability; it will also be required to conduct foreign exchange operations consistent with the exchange rate policy, to hold and manage the official foreign reserves of the member States, and to promote the smooth operation of payments systems. The European Central Bank (qv) will have the exclusive right to authorise the issue of banknotes within the Community (ibid art.105a). There is provision for a Monetary Committee which will be replaced in time by an Economic and Financial Committee (ibid art.109c). See ECONOMIC AND MONETARY UNION.

**monetary unit.** The monetary unit of the State is the Irish pound which is issued in *legal tender* (qv) form: Central Bank Act 1989 s.24(1). The Minister is empowered to vary the general exchange rate for the Irish pound in respect of other monetary units (ibid s.24(2)).

**money.** The medium of exchange and measure and store of value. A *pecunary* legacy includes any direction by a testator for the payment of money: Succession Act 1965 s.3(1). See LEGAL TENDER.

**money bill.** See BILL, MONEY.

**money had and received.** Money which is paid to one person which rightfully belongs to another eg where a person pays money under protest he may recover the sum paid: Gt. Southern and Western Railway Co v Robertson (1878) 2 LR (Ir) 548; or where money is paid under a conditional contract it may be recovered if the condition is not fulfilled: Lowis v Wilson (1949) IR 347; Lord Mayor of Dublin v The Provost of Trinity College Dublin (1984) HC. See MISTAKE; ULTRA VIRES.

**money laundering.** See LAUNDERING.

**money lodged in court.** See LODGMENT IN COURT.

**moneylender.** A person whose business is that of moneylending, or who advertises or announces himself or holds himself out in any way as carrying on the business of moneylending, but not including pawnbrokers, friendly societies, or bodies authorised by law to lend money, bankers, credit unions, or bodies exempted: Moneylenders Acts 1900 s.6 and 1933 s.24(1); Credit Union Act 1966 s.28.

Protection is given to borrowers against excessive rates of interest on loans from moneylenders and where a transaction is *harsh and unconscionable* (ibid 1900 Act s.1). Where interest is in excess of 39% per annum the court is to asssume conclusively that the interest charged is excessive and that the transaction is harsh and unconscionable: Moneylenders Act 1933 s.17.

A moneylender must take out annually a *licence,* granted by the Revenue Commissioners, in respect of every address at which he carries out his business; he must first secure a certificate granted by a District Court judge (ibid 1933 Act ss.5-6). A certificate may be refused on a number of grounds, including lack of satisfactory evidence of good character of the applicant (ibid s.6(8)). The Minister has power to exempt a person from the requirements of the Act. See Thomas v Ashbrook (1913) 2 IR 416. See RSC O.4 r.8; O.13

r.14; O.27 r.15. See COMPOUND INTEREST; DEBTOR'S SUMMONS; SIMPLE CONTRACT; UNCONSCIONABLE BARGAIN.

**monopoly.** Monopoly is now to be construed as a reference to an *abuse of a dominant position*: Mergers, Take-overs and Monopolies Act 1978 ss.11-13; Competition Act 1991 s.14(7). The Minister may request the Competition Authority (qv) to carry out an investigation if he is of the opinion that there is an abuse and he may, if the interests of the common good so warrants, order the prohibition of the continuance of the dominant position or require an adjustment of the dominant position (eg by the sale of assets) (ibid s.14).

The 1937 Constitution provides that the operation of free competition will not be allowed so to develop as to result in the concentration of the ownership or control of essential commodities in a few individuals to the common detriment (Constitution art.45(2)(iii)). [Text: Forde (5); Mason Hayes & Curran]. See ABUSE OF MONOPOLY RIGHT; COMPETITION, DISTORTION OF; CONCERT PARTY.

**month.** The word *month* means a calendar month unless the contrary intention appears: Interpretation Act 1937 s.12 sch. In a contract of sale *month* means prima facie calendar month: Sale of Goods Act 1893 s.10(2). Where time for doing any act or taking any proceedings is limited by months, such time is to be computed by calendar months, unless otherwise expressed: RSC O.122 r 1. See TIME; COURT RULES.

**monuments.** See NATIONAL MONUMENT; HISTORIC MONUMENT.

**moot.** (1) Debate of points of law in a hypothetical case eg to give practice to student lawyers. There is an All Ireland Moot Court competition sponsored by the Bar Council and legal publishers Butterworth Ireland Ltd. Also Irish law students compete in the Irish heats of the American Jessop International Law Moot and in the heats of a European law moot run by the European Law Students Association. See examples in ISLR Vol 2 (1992) 110 and Vol 3 (1993) 147.

(2) The courts should not embark on a *moot issue* where matters of fact have not actually been established in evidence: Brady v Donegal Co Council (1989 SC)

ILRM 282. While the court does not ordinarily give a ruling on a moot, cases concerning the care and custody of children were probably of unique character; and the court would therefore rule on the issues in order to provide guidance to those involved and in particular having regard to the absence of provision for legal assistance for children involved in such proceedings: F v Supt of B.Garda Station (1990) 8ILT Dig 191. See also Murphy v Roche (1987) IR 106; International Fishing Vessels Ltd v Minister for the Marine (1991 SC) 2 IR 379; In re Application of Tivoli Cinema Ltd (1992 HC) ILRM 522. See HYPOTHETICAL ARGUMENTS; OBITER DICTUM.

**morality.** [Text: Daly CB ]. See PUBLIC MORALS.

**moratorium.** An authorised postponement in the performance of an obligation eg on payment of a debt.

**mortgage.** A conveyance of an interest in land or other property as security for a loan. The mortgagor (borrower) normally remains in possession of the land until the debt is repaid. A mortgage may be *legal*, *equitable* or *statutory*. A *legal mortgage* is a transfer of the legal estate or interest in the land or other property; an *equitable mortgage* arises where only an equitable interest is transferred eg by deposit of title deeds (qv); a *statutory mortgage* is one arising by way of judgment mortgage (qv) under the Judgment Mortgage Act 1850.

The mortgagor has a right to redeem his mortgage on repayment of the debt; it is a legal right on the date fixed for redemption and an equitable right thereafter. The mortgagor also has an *equity of redemption*, which is the sum total of the mortgagor's rights in equity, and there must be no *clogs* (qv) on that right.

A mortgage is discharged by redemption (qv), by foreclosure (qv), or by exercise of the mortgagee's right of sale. Mortgages rank in priority according to the date of their registration.

A mortgage on registered land is created by registration of a *charge* as a burden on the land and registration of the *chargeant* as the owner of the charge. The charge operates as a mortgage by deed within the meaning of the Conveyancing Acts: Registration of Title Act 1964 s.62. [Text: Wylie (1); Fisher &

Lightwood UK]. See CHATTEL MORTGAGE; CHARGE ON LAND; CHARGE, REGISTRATION OF; ENDOWMENT MORTGAGE; MERGER; PRIOR MORTGAGE; RECITALS; TRUSTEE INVESTMENT.

**mortgage, equitable.** See EQUITABLE MORTGAGE.

**mortgage, judgment.** See JUDGMENT MORTGAGE.

**mortgage, prior.** See PRIOR MORTGAGE.

**mortgage of goods.** See BILL OF SALE.

**mortgage of leaseholds.** See LEASEHOLDS, MORTGAGE OF.

**mortgage of shares.** See SHARES, EQUITABLE MORTGAGE OF.

**mortgage protection insurance.** See INSURANCE AND BUILDING SOCIETY.

**mortgage suit.** An action in which the plaintiff mortgagee (lender) seeks a sale by the court in lieu of foreclosure (qv). The plaintiff mortgagee usually seeks (a) that his mortgage be declared *well charged* on the lands, (b) an order for payment of the sum due, and (c) an order that in default of payment within the specified time, the lands be sold by the court. A mortgage suit is commenced in the Circuit Court, where the rateable valuation of the land does not exceed £200, or otherwise in the High Court. See RSC O.54 r.3; RCC O.45 r.2. [Text: Scanlon]. See MORTGAGEE, RIGHTS OF.

**mortgagee.** The person to whom property is mortgaged; the lender of the mortgage debt.

**mortgagee, rights of.** A mortgagee (lender) generally has the following rights where the mortgage is by deed: (a) right to possession, but only in suitable cases eg to aid a sale: Ulster Bank Ltd v Conlon (1957) 91 ILTR 193; (b) power of sale out of court where the redemption date has passed and there is either three months default, after notice, in payment of principal or two months arrears of interest or breach of a covenant: Holohan v Friends Provident & Century Life Office (1966) IR 1; (c) power to appoint a receiver, exercisable under the same conditions as a power of sale; the receiver is deemed to be an agent of the mortgagor and consequently the mortgagee is not liable for the defaults of the receiver; (d) power to insure. See Conveyancing Act 1881 s.19.

It has been held that in the case of a default, the mortgagor should be ordered to give up possession as the property, when sold with vacant possession, would realise more: *Irish Permanent Building Society v Ryan* (1950) IR 12. See also *Irish Civil Service (Permanent) Building Society v Ingram's Representative* (1959) IR 181.

However, in the absence of a court order to repossess a *family home*, a building society may be restrained from exercising a right to possession pursuant to a clause in a mortgage deed and be ordered, by way of interlocutory relief, to deliver up possession of the house so repossessed: *McCormack v ICS Building Society* (1989 HC) ITLR (17 Apr).

A mortgagee may obtain an order for sale by the court of the mortgaged property by way of *mortgage suit* (qv). He also has the usual creditors' remedy against a debtor for repayment of the principal and interest due. He is entitled to retain possession of the title deeds until the mortgage is redeemed.

The court has power to adjourn proceedings by a mortgagee for possession or sale of a *family home* (qv) where it appears that the other spouse is desirous and capable of paying the arrears: Family Home Protection Act 1976 s.7. Also, the court can give permission to a mortgagee to bid and purchase at the sale of the property of a bankrupt (qv) or arranging debtor (qv): Bankruptcy Act 1988 s.53.

Where mortgaged property is sold by a building society in exercise of a power of sale, the society must ensure that the property is sold at the best price reasonably obtainable and must notify the mortgagor and any other mortgagee, with particulars of the sale within 21 days thereof: Building Societies Act 1989 s.26(1) and (5). It has been held in the UK that a building society is not bound to retain a property indefinitely until a higher price could be reached: *Reliance Permanent Building Society v Harwood-Stamper* (1944) 2 All ER 75. See RECEIVER OF MORTGAGED PROPERTY; RETENTION OF MORTGAGED PROPERTY.

**mortgages, consolidation of.** See CONSOLIDATION OF MORTGAGES.

**mortgagor.** The person who mortgages his property as security for the mortgage debt; the borrower.

**mortgagor, rights of.** A mortgagor (borrower) has the following rights: (a)

*equity of redemption* which he can assign, devise or mortgage again; (b) possession — he can keep all rents and profits without rendering an account; he is not liable for *waste* (qv) unless it would render the property an inadequate security; he can sue for rent or injury done to the land without joining the mortgagee; (c) leases — a mortgagor in possession may make leases which bind the mortgagor and the mortgagee; however this right is to be exercised by the mortgagee after a receiver has been appointed; Conveyancing Act 1881 s.18; Conveyancing Act 1911 s.3.

A mortgagor may also enforce his right to redeem his mortgage by a *redemption suit*. The mortgagor is entitled to possession of the title deeds on redemption of the mortgage. See EQUITY OF REDEMPTION; HOUSING LOAN; REDEMPTION; WASTE.

**mortmain.** [Dead hand]. Land which is inalienable. Alienation in mortmain was prohibited eg land could not be conveyed originally to a corporation except by statutory authority or by licence. There was a *mortmain* restriction on gifts of land to charities: Charitable Donations and Bequests (Ireland) Act 1844. Mortmain restrictions were repealed by the Mortmain (Repeal of Enactments) Act 1954.

**mortuum vadium.** [Dead pledge; a mortgage (qv)].

**mother.** The State must endeavour to ensure that mothers are not obliged by economic necessity to engage in labour to the neglect of their duties in the home: 1937 Constitution, art.41(2)(2). See *L v L* (1992 SC) ILRM 115.

**motion.** An application to a court or to a judge for an order directing something to be done in the applicant's favour. Generally, a motion may be made only after notice has been given to the parties affected but in certain cases it can be made *ex-parte* (qv). See RSC O.52 r.2; RCC O.51. See MOTION OF COURSE; NOTICE OF MOTION.

**motion of course.** A motion made *ex-parte* which an applicant is entitled to have granted as of right on his own statement and at his own risk.

**motion on notice.** A motion (qv) where notice thereof is given to the other side in legal proceedings. See NOTICE OF

MOTION.

**motive.** That which incites a person to action. Motive is generally irrelevant in the law of torts although in defamation, malice will negative the defence of qualified privilege or fair comment. See MALICE.

**motor insurance EC.** EC insurance undertakings have a right to underwrite motor liability insurance risks in a member State without being established in the State where the risk is situated. This right is given effect in Ireland from 20th November 1992 by the European Communities (Non-Life Insurance) (Amendment) Regulations 1992 (SI No 244 of 1992). Insurers who transact third party motor insurance business in Ireland are required to be members of the Motor Insurers' Bureau of Ireland (qv) (SI No 347 of 1992). See INSURANCE, VEHICLE.

**Motor Insurers' Bureau of Ireland.** A company formed by motor insurers. Formerly, under an agreement between the Bureau and the Minister, dated 30th December 1964, if damages were awarded by a court in respect of the death or personal injury (but not in respect of property) arising out of the use of a mechanically propelled vehicle in a public place in circumstances where the liability was required to be covered by insurance under the Road Traffic Act 1961, and such damages, or any part of them, remained unpaid twenty-eight days after the judgment becomes enforceable, the Bureau would pay the unrecovered amount of such damages to the person in whose favour the judgment had been given. Payment in respect of loss of service of an insured person was specifically excluded.

Where at the time of the accident the vehicle was being used without the consent of the owner, the Bureau would not accept liability for judgments against the owner or the driver of the vehicle in favour of persons travelling in the vehicle. The Bureau would however consider awarding an *ex gratia* payment if satisfied that the passenger was not aware or should not have reasonably known that the vehicle was being used without the owner's consent. It has been held that the onus is on the Bureau to prove that the passenger should have known the driver was uninsured: Kinsella v MIBI

(1993 SC) ITLR (19 July).

A new Agreement between the Minister and the Bureau, covering road accidents occurring on or after 31 December 1988, gives effect to the second EC Directive on Motor Insurance 84/5/EEC of 30/12/1983. The main features of the new Agreement are (a) a victim of an accident involving an uninsured motor vehicle can apply directly to the Bureau for compensation; the securing of a judgment of a court is not a precondition to compensation; redress to the Courts is available, however, where the victim is refused compensation or is not satisfied with the amount offered; (b) compensation is available also as of right for victims of untraced "hit and run" drivers; (c) no compensation will be available for injuries sustained by an uninsured driver in a collision with a motor vehicle driven by another uninsured driver; and (d) compensation for property damage caused by uninsured (including stolen) motor vehicles is available in respect of road accidents occurring on or after 31st December 1992, but not in the case of untraced drivers. For details of Agreements, see Stationery Office (PR 3296 — old; PI 6527 — new). See Ambrose v O'Regan 10 ILT Dig (1992 SC) 200. See also UNTRACED DRIVER.

**motor vehicle, negligent driving of.** Every person using the highway must take reasonable care in doing so, not to cause injury or damage to other users. The duty of care of the driver of a motor vehicle depends on many factors eg time, place, weather, state of light, state of the highway, speed, manner of driving, other traffic, and the state and condition of the driver. A higher standard of care is required when children are known to be present: Brennan v Savage Smyth Co Ltd (1982) ILRM 223. A person in control of a motor vehicle, although not driving it may be held to be negligent: Dockery v O'Brien (1975) 109 ILTR 127. See also Hassett v Skehan (1939) Ir Jur Rep 5.

It has been held that an insurer is not liable in tort or contract to a plaintiff whose claim against a deceased motorist is statute barred: Boyce v McBride (1987) ILRM 95. See PROPER LOOK OUT.

**motor vehicle, recovery of.** See RECOVERY OF MOTOR VEHICLE.

**motor vehicle, sale of.** There is an *implied condition* in a contract for the sale of a motor vehicle, that at the time of delivery of the vehicle, it is free from any defect which would render it a danger to the public, including persons travelling in the vehicle. There is no distinction in this regard between new and second-hand vehicles. The implied condition does not apply in the case of a sale to a dealer eg on a trade-in. See SGSS Act 1980 s.13. See Glorney v O'Brien (1989) 7ILT Dig 104; Sze Ping-Fat in 10 ILT & SJ (1992) 192. See MILEOMETER READING.

**motor vehicle, type approval of.** See TYPE APPROVAL, MOTOR VEHICLES.

**motorist, untraced.** See UNTRACED DRIVER.

**motorway.** A public road (qv) or proposed public road specified to be a motorway in a *motorway scheme* approved by the Minister: Roads Act 1993 ss.2(1), 43, and 49. Pedestrians and pedal cyclists must not use a motorway, and persons must not permit animals to be on a motorway (ibid s.43(4)). There is no right of direct access to a motorway from land adjoining it and no such right may be granted (ibid s.43(2)); this includes a prohibition on the granting of planning permission which would involve direct access (ibid s.46).

However, a road authority must provide such a person with an alternative means of access if the motorway deprives him of his only means of access, and he is entitled to compensation for any reduction in the value of his land which results (ibid s.52(3)-(4)).

A road authority may submit a motorway scheme to the Minister, having first notified the public and affected land owners/occupiers (ibid s.48). The Minister, before approving a scheme, must cause a local public inquiry to be held, must consider any objections, and must consider the report and recommendations of the person conducting the inquiry (ibid s.49).

Approval of the scheme by the Minister has the same effect as if it were a *compulsory purchase order* (qv) made under the Local Government (No 2) Act 1960 s.10 as inserted by the Housing Act 1966 s.86 (ibid 1993 Act s.52).

The road authority is required to prepare an environmental impact statement on the construction of a motorway (ibid s.50). The National Roads Authority is empowered to direct a road authority to make a motorway scheme (ibid s.20(1)(a)).

The normal planning legislation does not apply to an application for permission to erect power lines on lands comprised in a motorway scheme: Nolan v Minister for the Environment and ESB (1991 SC) ILRM 705. See PUBLIC ROAD; SERVICE AREA; SPEED LIMIT.

**movables.** Personal property eg goods, as opposed to real property eg land.

**mugging.** The colloquial term used to describe the crime of robbery (qv) of a pedestrian.

**multinational company.** Generally understood to mean a company which is in effect a cluster of companies registered in different countries and tied together by common ownership and responding to a common management strategy. Every company which is incorporated outside the State which establishes a place of business in the State is required to make up annual accounts and to deliver certain particulars to the Registrar of Companies: Companies Act 1963 ss.351-360.

**multi-storey buildings.** Buildings of five storeys or more, built since 1950 or to be built. Provisions to improve and ensure the safety standards of such buildings are contained in the Local Government (Multi-Storey Buildings) Act 1988. Such buildings must be certified by a chartered engineer with experience related to either structures or gas networks, depending on the kind of appraisal required. See also Building Control Act 1990 s.23. See SI Nos 285 and 286 of 1988; SI No 95 of 1990.

**municipal law.** The domestic or internal law of a country as opposed to international law. It may be classified as *public law* and *private law* (qqv).

**murder.** The unlawful killing with *malice aforethought* of another human being, the death following within a year and a day. The killing need not be by direct violence; abandoning a child so that he dies may suffice. The human being must have had an independent existence; there can be no murder of a child before birth or even during birth. *Malice aforethought* is present where the accused intended to kill, or cause serious injury to, some person, whether it is the person who was actually killed or not: Criminal Justice Act 1964 s.4. The accused person is presumed to have intended the natural and probable consequences of his conduct, but this presumption may be rebutted.

A person convicted of murder is debarred from benefiting under his victim's will: Succession Act 1965 s.120. Also a convicted murderer whose crime accelerated succession will not be permitted to be an executor (qv): In the Goods of Martin Glynn v Kelly & Concannon (1992 SC) ILRM 582. A person convicted of murder must be sentenced to life imprisonment (unless the murder is an aggravated murder): Criminal Justice Act 1990 s.2. See Attorney General v O'Shea (1931) IR 728. See CAPITAL MURDER; CRIMINAL JURIS- DICTION, PLACE; DYING DECLARATION; INSAN- ITY; MANSLAUGHTER; MURDER, AGGRAVATED; PERSUADE TO MURDER; PROVOCATION; SELF- DEFENCE; SPECIAL VERDICT; SUCCEED, UNWOR- THINESS TO; UNBORN, INJURIES TO THE.

**murder, aggravated.** Although not given the description "aggravated" by statute, it is the murder of a member of the Garda Siochana or a prison officer acting in the course of his duty; or murder done in the course or furtherance of specified offences created by the Offences Against the State Act 1939; or murder committed within the State for a political motive of the head of a foreign State or of a member of its government or of its diplomatic officer: Criminal Justice Act 1990 s.3.

It must be proved that the accused knew of the existence of each ingredient of the offence or was reckless as to whether or not that ingredient existed eg in relation to the killing of a garda, by showing that the accused knew the deceased was a garda acting in the course of his duty or was reckless as to whether he was a garda so acting (ibid s.3(2)).

There is a minimum period of imprisonment specified for aggravated murder (40 years) and attempted aggravated murder (20 years); there are also restrictions on the power to commute or remit punishment or to grant temporary release in the case of aggravated murder (ibid ss.4-5). See COMMUTE; RELEASE, TEMPORARY;

REMISSION.

**museum.** The National Museum of Ireland was established by the Science and Art Museums Act 1877. See LIBRARIES.

**musical work.** For the purposes of copyright protection, musical work includes all *original* musical work together with the arranging of existing work or transcription of the work: Copyright Act 1963 s.8(7). See ARTIST, TAX EXEMPTION OF; COPYRIGHT; PERFORMING RIGHTS SOCIETY; ORIGINAL: ROYALTY.

**muster list.** The master of every ship must prepare and maintain a *muster list* which must specify, inter alia — the general emergency alarm signal and the action to be taken by crew and passengers; how the order to abandon ship is to be given; and other emergency signals: Merchant Shipping (Musters and Training) Rules 1990 (SI No 85 of 1990) as amended by Merchant Shipping (Musters and Training) Rules 1993 (SI No 7 of 1993).

**mutatis mutandi.** [The necessary changes being made].

**mute.** Silent. An accused person may stand mute when asked to plead, in which case the judge will decide, after hearing evidence on the matter, if (a) he is standing *mute by malice* (ie deliberately silent) in which case he will be treated as having pleaded not guilty or (b) he is *mute by visitation of God*, in which case he will be treated as insane and unfit to plead, unless he can be made to understand by means of signs with the aid of an interpreter (eg where he is deaf and dumb). See Juries Act 1976 s.28. See PLEA; UNFIT TO PLEAD.

**mutual insurance.** Where two or more persons mutually agree to insure each other against marine losses, there is said to be mutual insurance: Marine Insurance Act 1906 s.85. [Text: Hill UK; Ivamy UK; McGuffie, Fugeman & Gray UK].

**mutual society.** A society which is owned and controlled generally by the persons who consume the product or service which the society provides eg a credit union, a building society. "The term *mutual* (which does not appear in the Building Societies Act 1989 or in previous legislation) is used to indicate an organisation the ownership and ultimate control of which is vested in the members broadly on the basis of equality rather than in proportion to financial interest": Report of Registrar of Building Societies (1981) p.8.

**mutuum.** A quasi-bailment of personal chattels, consisting of a loan thereof to the borrower with the intention that it will be consumed by the borrower and will be returned, not in specie, but by something similar in kind and quantity. It differs from commodatum (loan for use) in that in the latter, possession and not ownership vests in the borrower; in mutuum, the property in the chattel vests in the borrower. See PRO-MUTUUM.

# N

**name, change of.** A change of *surname* is normally effected by formal enrolment of a deed poll (qv); it has the advantage that a record is preserved of the change for future identification. However, a name is not ipso facto changed by such enrolment; the change is effected by reputation and the most the deed does is to assist in the establishment of that reputation. A purely informal change is just as effective as a change effected by a deed poll: In re Talbot (1932) IR 714. It would appear that a *Christian* name may be changed at confirmation.

A company may change its name by special resolution with the consent of the Minister: Companies Act 1963 s.23(1). It has been possible since 1990 to submit a change of name to the Companies Registration Office without obtaining prior approval; however no change of name will have effect until the certificate of change of name has issued. A building society may change its name by special resolution; however the change cannot take effect until the Central Bank is satisfied that the changed name is not undesireable: Building Societies Act 1989 s.14(3).

The change of name of an urban district, townland or town is made by order of the government: Local Government Act 1946 ss.76-77. The change of name of a street or locality is a *reserved function* (qv) of the local authority (ibid

ss.78(2) and 79(1)). See also Williams v Bryant (1839) 5 M & W 447. [Text: Linell (UK)]. See NAME OF COMPANY.

**name, geographic.** See GEOGRAPHICAL NAME AS TRADE MARK.

**name, right to good.** The State is required by its laws to protect as best as it may from unjust attack and, in the case of injustice done, vindicate the *good name* of every citizen: 1937 Constitution, art 40.3(2). See TRIBUNALS OF INQUIRY.

**name of company.** The name under which a company is registered in the Registry of Companies. A name will not be accepted which in the opinion of the Minister is undesireable: Companies Act 1963 s.21. The Minister is empowered to order a change in name which in his opinion is too like the name of a company already registered (ibid s.23(2)). The name of a limited company must include *limited* or *ltd* or the Irish equivalents *teoranta* or *teo* (ibid s.6(1)(a). Where the company is a public limited company, this must be included in its name or the abbreviation *plc* or the Irish equivalents *cuideachta phoible theoranta* or *cpt* : Companies Amendment Act 1983 s.4(1).

The Minister is empowered to dispense with *limited* or *teoranta* in the name of a limited company which has as its objects the promotion of commerce, art, science, religion, charity or other useful object and intends to apply profits or other income to those objects, and the payment of a dividend to its members is prohibited: Companies Act 1963 s.24.

A company which carries on business under a name other than its corporate name is required to register the former name under the Registration of Business Names Act 1963 : Companies Act 1963 s.22. It is an offence to trade under a misleading name: Companies Amendment Act 1983 s.56. An unintentional mis-statement of the correct name of a company applying for planning permission, which did not have the effect of misleading or disadvantaging anyone, could not prevent developers obtaining declarations to which they were otherwise entitled: McDonagh v County Borough of Galway (1993 SC) ITLR (23 Aug). See RSC O.75 r 18. See also Building Societies Act 1989 ss.13-14. See NAME, CHANGE OF; BUSINESS NAME; PASSING OFF; RECEIVER.

**name of State.** See STATE.

**nation.** A body of people recognised as an entity by virtue of their historical, linguistic, or ethnic links and without regard to political or geographic boundaries. The Irish nation affirms its inalienable, indefeasible and sovereign right to chose its own form of government, to determine its relations with other nations and to develop its life, political, economic and cultural, in accordance with its own genius and traditions: 1937 Constitution art.1.

**national archives.** The body established to preserve records and documents previously held in the Public Records Office or the State Papers Office and other public records: National Archives Act 1986 s.2(1). The Act envisages the regular transfer to the National Archives of all over-30 year old records of courts, government departments and other public bodies which are deemed worthy of permanent preservation. The public have a right of access to such records, although certain records of particular sensivity (eg relating to security or affecting individual privacy) or which may be damaged by inspection, may have access limited (ibid ss.10-11). See National Archive Regulations 1988. See Blake in 10ILT & SJ (1992) 43. See CENSUS.

**national debt.** The debt outstanding for the time being of the Exchequer: National Treasury Management Agency Act 1990 s.1. See TREASURY MANAGEMENT, NATIONAL.

**national emergency.** A national emergency exists when each of Houses of the Oireachtas (qv) so resolves *in time of war or armed rebellion*; nothing in the Constitution may be invoked to invalidate any law enacted by the Oireachtas which is expressed to be for the purpose of securing the State in time of war or armed rebellion or to nullify any act done or purporting to be done in time of war or armed rebellion in pursuance of such law: 1937 Constitution art.28(3)(3).

The Houses of the Oireachtas resolved that a *national emergency* arising from the conflict in Europe existed on 2nd September 1939 and continued to 1st September 1976 on which date the Houses of the Oireachtas resolved that a new national emergency arising from the conflict in Northern Ireland existed. See

The State (Walsh) v Lennon (1942) IR 112; Emergency Powers Act 1976.

**national identity.** The European Union (qv) is required to respect the *national identities* of its member States, whose systems of government are founded on the principles of democracy: Maastricht Treaty 1992 art.F.1.

**national lottery.** See LOTTERY.

**national monument.** A monument or the remains of a monument the preservation of which is a matter of national importance by reason of the historical, architectural, traditional, or archaeological interest attaching thereto: National Monuments Act 1930 s.2. The constitutionality of legislation preserving national monuments has been upheld, even where a *preservation order* had the effect of sterilising part of a farmer plaintiff's land without compensation: O'Callaghan v Commissioners of Public Works (1985) ILRM 364. The Commissioners are obliged to take such reasonable steps as are necessary to avoid foreseeable risk to members of the public to whom they permitted access to a national monument: Clancy v Commissioners of Public Works (1991 SC) ILRM 567. It has been held that the proposed use of lands around a national monument as a refuse dump amounted to a breach of the 1930 Act s.14: AG v Sligo Co Council (1989 SC) ITLR (20 Mar). See HISTORIC MONUMENT; METAL DETECTOR.

**national park.** National parks have been created by special legislation eg Phoenix Park Act 1925; Burne Vincent Memorial Park Act 1932; An Blascaod Mor National Historic Park Act 1989. See NATIONAL MONUMENT; NATURE RESERVE.

**national parliament.** The national parliament is called and known as the Oireachtas: 1937 Constitution art.15(1)(1). See OIREACHTAS.

**national road.** A public road (qv) or a proposed public road which is classified as a national road by the Minister: Roads Act 1993 ss.2(1) and 10. See MOTORWAY; WAY, PUBLIC RIGHT OF.

**National Roads Authority.** A body corporate with perpetual succession and with overall responsibility for the planning and supervision of works for the construction and maintenance of national roads: Roads Act 1993 ss.16-42 and third schedule. It is required at least every five years, following public consultation, to prepare a plan for the development of national roads and to review annually implementation of the approved plan (ibid s.18).

It also has the following functions (a) preparing, or arranging for the preparation of road designs, maintenance programmes, and schemes for the provision of road signs (ibid s.19), (b) securing the carrying out of construction or maintenance work on national roads (ibid s.19); (c) allocating and paying grants (ibid s.19(f)), (d) specifying standards and carrying out research (ibid s.19(g-h)); (e) directing road authorities to carry out certain specified functions and carrying out the function itself where the road authority fails or refuses to comply with a direction (ibid s.20); (f) preparing programmes for EC financial assistance (ibid s.21); (g) borrowing in respect of national roads ibid ss.25-27); (h) tolling of national roads (ibid ss.56-66). See MOTORWAY; TOLL ROAD.

**national school.** A public elementary day school for the time being recognised by the Minister as a national school: School Attendance Act 1926. See CORPORAL PUNISHMENT; DISCIPLINE IN SCHOOL; PRE-SCHOOL SERVICE; SCHOOL AUTHORITIES DUTY.

**national territory.** The national territory consists of the whole island of Ireland, its islands and territorial seas: 1937 Constitution, art.2. The restriction imposed by art.3, which prohibits the enactment of laws applicable to the counties of Northern Ireland pending the re-integration of the national territory, in no way derogates from the claim in art.2 of a legal right to the entire national territory: McGimpsey v Ireland & Ors (1990 SC) ILRM 440. See ANGLO-IRISH AGREEMENT; NORTHERN IRELAND; UNITED IRELAND.

**nationalisation.** The bringing of the ownership of a company under the control of the State eg the acquisition of the assets of Dublin Gas by Bord Gais Eireann: Gas (Amendment) Act 1987. See PRIVATISATION.

**nationality.** The legal relationship attaching to membership of a nation. The question whether an individual possesses the nationality of a member State of the EC must be settled solely by reference to the national law of the member State concerned: Maastricht Treaty 1992 — Declaration on Nationality. See CITIZENSHIP; HATRED, INCITEMENT TO; NATURALISATION.

**nations, law of.** International law (qv).

**natural child.** Term sometimes applied to a child whose parents are not married to each other. See NATURAL PARENT.

**natural family planning.** See FAMILY PLANNING SERVICE.

**natural justice.** The rules and procedures to be followed by any person or body with the duty of adjudicating on disputes between, or the rights of, others. The main rules are that a person must not be a judge in his own cause; a person must have notice of what he is accused; and each party must be given an opportunity of adequately stating his case. See Garvey v Ireland (1979) 113 ILTR 61; Gunn v National College of Art and Design (1990 SC) 2 IR 168; Wong v Minister for Justice (1993 HC).

It has been held that it was fallacious to submit that a student, while well educated, did not need representation at a disciplinary hearing: Flanagan v University College Dublin (1989 HC) ILRM 469. It has also been held that the application of the relevent rules of natural justice do not apply to the dismissal of a statutory board officer where the person had not been dismissed for any fault by her in the discharge of her duties: Hickey v Eastern HB (1991 SC) 1 IR 208. See FAIR PROCEDURE; NEMO JUDEX IN SUA CAUSA; AUDI ALTERAM PARTEM.

**natural law.** The law which is based on value judgments which emanate from some absolute source eg God's revealed word. Natural law *is both anterior and superior to positive law or man-made law. There are many personal rights of the citizen which follow from the Christian and democratic nature of the State which are not mentioned in Article 40 (of the 1937 Constitution) at all*: Ryan v Attorney General (1965) IR 294. See O'Hanlon J, Murphy T, Clarke D in 11 ILT & SJ (1993) 8, 81, 129 and 177. See NATURAL RIGHTS.

**natural parents.** The parents of a child as contrasted with adopting parents. A *parent* includes the natural father of an illegitimate child: Adoption Act 1952 s.3. There is a presumption that a child's best interests would best be served in the custody of his natural parents: MC & MC v KC & AC (1986) ILRM 65. See PARENTAGE, DECLARATION OF.

**natural person.** A human being, as contrasted with an artificial person eg a company (qv).

**natural rights.** (1) Rights which come from the natural law (qv). *Natural rights or human rights are not created by law but the Constitution confirms....their existence and gives them protection. The individual has natural and human rights over which the State has no authority*: McGee v Attorney General (1974) IR 284.

(2) The term *natural rights* also refers to rights which exist automatically with land eg the right to support, the right to water flowing in a defined channel. Such rights may also be acquired as easements (qv). [Text: O'Reilly]. See FUNDAMENTAL RIGHTS; RIPARIAN; SUPPORT, RIGHT TO.

**naturalisation.** The process by which a person may have conferred on him *citizenship* of the State by the Minister. The applicant must be of full age; must be of good character; must have had 4 years residence in Ireland of which one year's continuous residence preceded the application; must intend to reside in the State after naturalisation; and must have made a declaration of fidelity to the nation and loyalty to the State: Irish Nationality & Citizenship Act 1956 s.15 as amended by Irish Nationality & Citizenship Act 1986 s.4. The 1986 Act removed the previous requirement of one year's notice of intention to apply for a certificate of naturalisation.

The Minister is empowered to waive the conditions for granting a certificate in a number of instances, including where the applicant is a refugee (qv) or a stateless person (qv) (ibid 1986 Act s.5). The grant or refusal of a certificate of naturalisation is not subject to an order of the courts: Osheku v Ireland (1987) ILRM 330. However, in a particular case, a plaintiff was given a declaration of his entitlement to apply for naturalisation: Wong v Minister for Justice (1993 HC) — Irish Times 10/7/93. See CITIZENSHIP.

**nature reserve.** Land, including inland water, which is by order declared to be a nature reserve: Wildlife Act 1976 s.15. The Minister may make such an order where he is satisfied that the land includes the habitat of a species or community of flora or fauna which is of scientific interest or includes an ecosystem which is of scientific interest and that the habitat or ecosystem is likely to benefit if measures are taken for its protection. For example, see Nature Reserve (Glendalough) Establishment Order 1988 (SI No 68 of 1988). See REFUGE.

**nautical mile.** The length of one minute of an arc of a meridian of longitude: Maritime Jurisdiction Act 1959 s.1.

**navigation, right of.** The right of persons to use a river; it is a *right of way* and may be a private or public right. Work authorised by a *bridge order* may be carried out, notwithstanding any interference it may cause with public or private rights of navigation, except in relation to the river Shannon: Local Government Act 1946 s.52 as amended by the Local Government Act 1955 s.40. Compensation may be payable in respect of interference with a private right of navigation by agreement or in default of agreement under the Acquisition of Land (Assessment of Compensation) Act 1919. See COMPENSATION AND COMPULSORY PURCHASE; SHANNON NAVIGATION; WAY, RIGHT OF.

**ne exeat regno.** [That he shall not leave the kingdom]. An injunction or order that a person not leave the jurisdiction. To obtain the writ a plaintiff must prove:- (a) that there exists an equitable equivalent of an action at law which would prior to the Debtors (Ireland) Act 1872 have entitled the plaintiff to seek the arrest of the defendant; (b) that the plaintiff has a good cause of action against the defendant to the amount of £20 or has suffered damage to that amount; (c) that there is probable cause for believing that the defendant is about to quit Ireland; and (d) that the defendant's absence would materially prejudice the plaintiff in the prosecution of his action. See Courtney in 8ILT & SJ (1990) 222. See also Al Nahkel & Trading Ltd v Lowe (1986) 1 All ER 729; Felton v Callis (1968) 3 All ER 673. See RSC O.40 r.21. See MAREVA INJUNCTION.

**nec vi, nec dam, nec precario.** [Not by violence, stealth or entreaty]. See PRESCRIPTION.

**necessaries.** See ALLOWANCE TO BANKRUPT; CAPACITY TO CONTRACT.

**necessitas inducit privilegium quoad jura privata.** [Necessity gives a privilege as to private rights].

**necessitas non habet legem.** [Necessity knows no law].

**necessitas publica majorest quam privata.** [Public necessity is greater than private]. See NECESSITY.

**necessity.** Circumstances compelling a course of action. (1) In tort (qv), *necessity* may be a good defence where the damage has been caused to prevent a greater evil and the act was reasonable. See Leigh v Gladstone (1909) 26 TLR 139; Cope v Sharpe (1912) I KB 496; Lynch v Fitzgerald (1938) IR 382.

(2) In crime, necessity does not excuse an offence and is not a good defence: R v Dudley and Stephens (1884) 14 QBD 273. See O'Hanlon J in 10 ILT & SJ (1992) 86. See DURESS; OBEDIENCE TO ORDERS.

**necessity, agent of.** See AGENT OF NECESSITY.

**neglect, wilful.** See WILFUL NEGLECT.

**negligence.** A tort (qv) involving the breach of a legal duty of care whereby damage is caused to the party to whom the duty is owed. It is the doing by a person of some act which a reasonable and prudent man would not have done in the circumstances of the case in question, or the omission to do something which would be expected of such a man under such circumstances.

For actionable negligence there must be: (a) a duty of care between the parties; (b) a failure to observe the required duty of care; and (c) reasonably foreseeable damage suffered. The law recognises that many persons owe a duty of care to others eg occupiers, carriers, employers, bailees, highway users, possessors of skills, and producers of goods. The degree of care required is that of reasonable care.

The standard of care is the foresight and caution of the ordinary or average prudent man. But the standard of care is higher where a person puts a dangerous object attractive to children in a place where children may have access to it: Purtill v Athlone UDC (1968) IR 205; Maria Rooney v The Rev Fr Connolly PP (1987) ILRM 768. Persons professing special skills (eg a solicitor) must use such skill as is usual with persons professing such skill.

The burden of proving negligence rests with the plaintiff but where the facts speak for themselves under the doctrine of *res ipsa loquitur* (qv), the plaintiff merely proves the accident.

Where there is *contributory negligence* (qv) on the part of the plaintiff, his damages will be reduced by such amount as the court thinks just and equitable having regard to the degrees of fault of the parties: Civil Liabilities Act 1961 s.34. [Text: McMahon & Binchy; Charlesworth & Percy UK]. See CONCURRENT WRONGDOER; DUTY OF CARE; OCCUPIERS LIABILITY TO CHILDREN; INFERENCE; MEDICAL NEGLIGENCE; MITIGATION OF DAMAGES; PRIMARY FACTS; PROFESSIONAL NEGLIGENCE; SAFETY BELT.

**negligence, presumption of.** See RES IPSA LOQUITUR.

**negligence, professional.** See PROFESSIONAL NEGLIGENCE.

**negligent misrepresentation.** A false statement, made with no reasonable grounds for believing it to be true, which is one of fact, intended to be acted upon, and which actually misleads and induces a contract. A special *duty of care* (qv) has to exist between the parties which would render the misrepresentation a negligent one, entitling the injured party to rescind the contract and to sue for negligence: Hedley Byrne & Co Ltd v Heller & Partners Ltd (1964) AC 465.

Since 1980, a statutory liability in damages is imposed on a party to certain types of contract, who has induced another party to enter into the contract by means of a negligent misrepresentation: SGSS Act 1980 s.45. This provision applies to a contract of sale of goods, a hire-purchase agreement, an agreement for letting of goods, and a contract for the supply of a service. The defendant can avoid liability if he can prove that he had reasonable ground to believe and did believe up to the time the contract was made that the facts represented were true. The court may award damages instead of rescission where it would be equitable to do so (ibid s.45(2)).

**negligent mis-statement.** Where a duty of care exists between two parties, there is a general obligation not to do what foreseeably may damage another: Donoghue v Stevenson (1932) AC 562; and this duty of care applies to economic or financial loss as well as to physical damage caused by another's negligence: Hedley Byrne & Co Ltd v Heller & Partners Ltd (1964) AC 465. As regards the relationship of a company to a shareholder in respect of a negligent mis-statement, see Securities Trust Ltd v Hugh Moore and Alexander (1964) IR 417. See PROSPECTUS; MISREPRESENTATION; NEGLIGENT MISREPRESENTATION.

**negotiable instrument.** An instrument, the transfer of which to the transferee (who takes it in good faith and for value) passes a good title, free from any defects affecting the title of the transferor. Notice is not required to be given to the person liable on the instrument and the transferee may sue in his own name. The most important negotiable instruments are bills of exchange, promissory notes, cheques, share and dividend warrants and debentures payable to bearer (qqv). Negotiability may be conferred by custom or statute and restricted or destroyed by the holder of the instrument. See Bechaunaland Exploration Company v London Trading Bank Ltd (1898) 2 QB 658. See Bills of Exchange Act 1882 ss.31-32. [Text: Richardson UK]. See NEMO DAT QUI NON HABET.

**negotiation licence.** The licence required for any body of persons to carry on negotiations for the fixing of wages or other conditions of employment: Trade Union Act 1941 s.7. The membership requirement for a new union seeking a negotiation licence has been doubled from 500 members to 1000: Industrial Relations Act 1990 s.21(2). See TRADE UNION, AUTHORISED.

**negotiation of a bill.** The transferring of a bill of exchange (qv) from one person to another so that the transferee becomes the holder of the bill: Bills of Exchange Act 1882 s.31(1).

**neighbour principle.** In Northern Ireland, it has been held that where farmer A renders assistance to farmer B, and sustains personal injuries in the course of that work, farmer A is in law the *neighbour* of farmer B and as such owes farmer B the duty to be reasonably careful for his safety in relation to

foreseeable risks of injury: Tanney v Shields (1992 HC – NI) ITLR (19 Oct). See DUTY OF CARE.

**nem con; nemine contradicente.** [No one saying otherwise].

**nem dis; nemine dissentiente.** [No one dissenting]. Term used in a law report (qv) indicating that no judge dissented in the judgment given.

**neminem oportet legibus esse sapientiorem.** [It is not permitted to be wiser than the laws].

**nemo admittendus est inhabili tare seipsum.** [Nobody is to be permitted to incapacitate himself].

**nemo agit in seipsum.** [No one can take proceedings against himself]. See CLUB.

**nemo contra factum suum propriem venire potest.** [No one can go against his own deed]. See NON EST FACTUM.

**nemo dat qui non habet.** [No one gives who possesses not]. A person generally cannot give a better title than he has himself: Sale of Goods Act 1893 s.21. In some instances, however, a buyer acquires a good title, notwithstanding a defect in the seller's title eg transfer of a negotiable instrument; disposition by a mercantile agent; sale under an order of the court; sale under a voidable title; sale in *market overt*; sale by a *hirer-dealer*; and under the doctrine of estoppel (qqv). See HOLDER IN DUE COURSE; NOT NEGOTIABLE.

**nemo debet bis puniri pro uno delicto.** [No one should be punished twice for one fault]. See AUTREFOIT CONVICT.

**nemo est haeres viventis.** [No one is heir of anyone who is alive]. See HEIR APPARENT.

**nemo ex proprio dolo consequitur actionem.** [No one obtains a cause of action by his own fraud]. See EQUITY, MAXIMS OF.

**nemo ex suo delicto meliorem suam conditionem facere potest.** [No one can improve his position by his own wrongdoing]. See EQUITY, MAXIMS OF.

**nemo judex in sua causa.** [No one can be a judge in his own cause]. Also *nemo debet esse judex in propria causa*. One of the principles of *natural justice* (qv). The person or body making a decision must be without bias, and consequently must not have any pecuniary or personal interest in the matter to be decided unless so declared eg a judge having shares in a company which is a party to an action being heard; a foreman of a jury in a fraud case being an investor in the company defrauded: The People (Attorney General) v Singer (1975) IR 408. See AUDI ALTERAM PARTEM.

**nemo plus juris ad alium transferre potest, quam ipse haberet.** [The title of an assignee can be no better than that of his assignor]. See NEMO DAT QUI NON HABET.

**nemo potest esse simul actor et judex.** [No one can be at once suitor and judge]. See NATURAL JUSTICE.

**nemo potest facere per alium, quod per se non potest.** [No one can do through another what he cannot do himself]. See AGENT; AGENT OF NECESSITY.

**nemo potest plus juris ad alium transferre quam ipse habet.** [No one can transfer a greater right to another than he himself has].

**nemo prohibetur pluribus defensionibus uti.** [No one is forbidden to use several defences]. See DEFENCE.

**nemo tenetur ad impossibile.** [No one is required to do what is impossible]. See FRUSTRATION OF CONTRACT; INEVITABLE ACCIDENT.

**nemo tenetur se ipsum accusare.** [No one is bound to incriminate himself]. See INCRIMINATE.

**nervous shock.** A person who suffers nervous shock may receive damages in tort (qv) from the person whose negligence caused the shock. A mother who suffered nervous shock, which changed her personality and lifestyle, as a result of a road accident not involving herself but her husband and two daughters, was awarded £75,000: Kelly v Hennessy (1993 HC) ILRM 530. See Byrne v Southern and Western Ry Co (1882) discussed in Bell v G N Ry Co (1890) 26 LR (Ir) 428; Hogg v Keane (1956) IR 155.

**new evidence.** See FRESH EVIDENCE.

**newspaper.** There is statutory control of any proposed merger or take-over involving at least one enterprise engaged in newspaper production, regardless of turnover or gross assets of either of the enterprises concerned. See Mergers, Take-overs and Monopolies (Control) Act 1978 s.2(5) and Mergers, Take-overs and Monopolies (Newspapers) Order 1979 (SI No 17 of 1979). See also

BUSINESS NAME; MANUFACTURED GOODS; MERGER/TAKE-OVER; TRADING STAMP.

**next friend.** The person through whom a minor (qv) brings an action, generally a close relative. On application by the defendant in an action to join the *next friend* as a third party (qv) in order to claim a contribution against the next friend as a concurrent wrongdoer (qv), the court will balance the disruption to the proceedings which would arise from such joinder, against the convenience of trying all the issues in the one action: Michael Quirke (a minor) *suing by his mother and next friend* Mary Quirke v O'Shea and CRL Oil Ltd (1992 SC) ILRM 286.

On the minor attaining full age, the next friend may apply on affidavit to the Registrar in the Central Office for a certificate that the plaintiff *lately an infant* may proceed in his own name: RSC O.15 rr.6 and 20. As regards the Circuit and District Courts, see RCC O.6 r.5; O.16 r.1; DCR r.8 (as inserted by DCR 1955). See also D'Arcy (a minor) v Roscommon Co Council (1992 SC) 10 ILT Dig 56; Johnston (a minor) v Fitzpatrick (1992 SC) ILRM 269; Hallahan (a minor) v Keane (1992 HC) ILRM 595.

**next-of-kin.** Those who stand nearest in blood relationship to an *intestate*. Degrees of blood relationship of a direct lineal ancestor are counted from the intestate to that ancestor. For any other relative, the degrees are counted from the intestate to the nearest ancestor, common to the intestate and the relative, and down to the relative in question. Where a direct lineal ancestor and any other relative are within the same degree of blood relationship to the intestate, the other relative is preferred to the exclusion of the direct lineal ancestor. Relatives of the *half-blood* share equally with relatives of the *whole blood* in the same degree. See Succession Act 1965 ss.71 and 72. See ANCESTOR; BLOOD RELATIONSHIP; INTESTATE SUCCESSION; RESIDUE.

**nexus.** Connection; bond. See Crowley v Allied Irish Banks (1987 SC) IR 282.

**night.** The period between 9pm in the evening and 6am in the morning of the next succeeding day: Larceny Act 1916 s.46(1). It is an offence to be found by *night* armed with any dangerous or offensive weapon or instrument with intent to commit a burglary (ibid s.28; Criminal Law (Jurisdiction) Act 1976 s.21(3)). Any person may arrest a person found committing an indictable offence (qv) in the night and hand him over to a garda: Prevention of Offences Act 1851 s.11.

**nightwork.** Work between the hours of 8pm and 8am which is prohibited for children under the school leaving age (qv), currently 15, and between 10pm and 6am for young persons (qv) generally, between 8pm and 8am for young industrial workers and between 10pm and 8am for women in industrial work. See Protection of Young Persons (Employment) Act 1977 ss.14-15; Conditions of Employment Acts 1936 ss.3, 38(1)(a) and 46, and 1944 s.2; Nightwork Bakeries Act 1936 and (Amendment) Act 1981. See WORKING HOURS.

**nihil facit error nominiscum de corpore constat.** [A mistake as to the name has no effect when there is no mistake as to who is the person meant]. See MISNOMER.

**nihil; nil.** [Nothing].

**nisi.** An order, rule, declaration, decree or other adjudication of a court is said to be made *nisi* when it is not final or absolute and is not to take effect until the person affected by it fails to show cause against it within a certain time eg a conditional order of garnishee (qv).

**no fault compensation.** Colloquial expression to describe a system by which tortious causes of action are abolished and replaced by a scheme of benefits for accident victims without proof of fault. "Of the many forms of tortious liability, it is difficult to find one more appropriate for *no fault compensation* than that of medical malpractice" McCarthy N, Supreme Court Judge 1987, and in Hegarty v O'Loughran (1990 SC) ITLR (2 Apr). No fault compensation schemes exist in Sweden, Finland and New Zealand but not in Ireland. However, no fault liability has been introduced in 1991 in respect of defective products which cause damage, irrespective of whether the producer was negligent: Liability of Defective Products Act 1991. See Murphy in 7 ILT & SJ (1989) 216. See PRODUCT LIABILITY; STRICT LIABILITY.

**nobility, title of.** See TITLE OF NOBILITY.

**no foal no fee.** Colloquial expression generally understood to mean the provision of a legal service on the basis that no fee will be incurred by the client unless there is a successful outcome. A barrister may accept instructions from a solicitor on the basis that his ordinary fee will be paid in the event of the case being successful and that no fee will be expected if unsuccessful. This most commonly occurs with personal injuries cases but not exclusively so. As regards solicitors, there is concern by the Incorporated Law Society that legal services advertised on a "no foal no fee" basis could be misinterpreted by a client that he will have no liability either to his own solicitor or to the defendant should the plaintiff client be unsuccessful. See CHAMPERTY; CONTINGENCY FEE.

**noise.** The Minister is empowered to make regulations for the prevention or limitation of any noise which may give rise to a nuisance or disamenity, constitute a danger to health, or damage property: Environmental Protection Agency Act 1992 s.106. A local authority or the Environmental Protection Agency may require measures to be taken to prevent or limit noise by serving a notice on the person in charge (ibid s.107).

Where any noise which is so loud, so continuous, so repeated, of such duration or pitch or occurring at such times as to give reasonable cause for annoyance to a person in any premises in the neighbourhood or to a person lawfully using a public place, the District Court may order the prevention or limitation of the noise (ibid s.108). This does not apply to noise caused by aircraft or by a statutory undertaker (qv) or local authority (ibid s.108(4)). Complaint to the District Court may be made by the person affected, the local authority, or by the Agency.

All these provisions are without prejudice to the provisions of the Safety, Health and Welfare at Work Act 1989 (ibid 1992 Act s.109). In addition, the Minister may make regulations requiring road authorities to carry out works or other measures to mitigate the effects of road traffic noise: Roads Act 1993 s.77. See NUISANCE; VIBRATION.

**nolens volens.** [Unwilling or willing].

**nolle prosequi.** [Unwilling to prosecute].

In criminal proceedings, the entry of a *nolle prosequi* by the prosecution before judgment, operates to stay the proceedings; it is not equivalent to an acquittal and is no bar to a new indictment (qv) at a subsequent date for the same offence. See R v Comptroller of Patents (1899) 1 QB 909. See GARDA, DISCIPLINE OF.

**nolo contendere.** [I do not wish to contend].

**nolumus mutari.** [We will not change]. Motto of the Honorable Society of Kings Inns (qv).

**nominal capital.** See CAPITAL.

**nominee.** See REGISTER OF MEMBERS; THIRD PARTY INFORMATION.

**nominis umbra.** [The shadow of a name].

**non aliter a significatione verborum recedi oportet quam cum manifestum est aliud sensisse testatorem.** [There should be no departure from the ordinary meaning of words except in so far as it appears that the testator meant something different]. See CONSTRUCTION, RULES OF; EVIDENCE, EXTRINSIC.

**non cepit modo et forma.** [He did not take it in the manner and the form as alleged]. See REPLEVIN.

**non compos mentis.** [Not sound in mind]. See UNSOUND MIND; MENTAL DISORDER.

**non constat.** [It does not follow].

**non culpabilis.** [Not guilty].

**non debet, cui plus licet, quod minus est non licere.** [It is lawful for a man to do a lesser thing if he is entitled to do a greater thing].

**non est factum.** [It is not his deed]. The plea of a person who has executed a deed in ignorance of its character, that it is not his deed, notwithstanding its execution by him. The person who signs a contract must not have been careless at the time of signing; signing without reading a contract is carelessness. See Bank of Ireland v McManamy (1916) 2 IR 161; Saunders v Anglia Building Society (1971) AC 1004; UDT Ltd v Westen (1976) QB 513.

**non est inventus.** [He has not been found].

**non liquet.** [It is not clear].

**non obstante veredicto.** [Notwithstanding the verdict].

**non omne quod licet honestum est.** [All things that are lawful are not honourable].

**non placet.** [It is not approved].

**non pros; non prosequitor.** [He does not follow up]. See DISMISSAL FOR WANT OF PROSECUTION.

**non sequitor.** [It does not follow].

**non videntur qui errant consentire.** [Those who are mistaken are not deemed to consent]. See MISTAKE.

**nonfeasance.** The neglect or failure to perform an act which one is bound by law to perform. A local authority is not liable for injury to the user of a highway caused by its failure to repair the highway; however, s.60 of the Civil Liability Act 1961 has provided, subject to being brought into operation by order of the government, that *a road authority shall be liable for damage caused as a result of their failure to maintain adequately a public road*. It has been held that s.60(7) is merely enabling and does not impose a duty on the government to bring the section into operation and that the discretion vested in the government was not limited in any way, as to time or otherwise: The State (Sheehan) v Ireland (1988 SC) ILRM 437. The National Roads Authority is not liable for damage caused as a result of any failure to maintain a national road: Roads Act 1993 s.19(5). See Harbinson v Armagh C C (1902) 2 IR 538; Maguire v Liverpool Corporation (1905) 1 KB 767; Kelly v Mayo Co Council (1964) IR 315. See MISFEASANCE.

**non-discrimination notice.** A notice which the Employment Equality Agency (qv) may serve on a person, specifying the act or omission constituting a discrimination (qv) or contravention in relation to the Employment Equality Act 1977 or the Anti-Discrimination (Pay) Act 1974 and requiring the person not to commit the discrimination or contravention and specifying the steps the Agency requires to be taken by the person. An appeal against the notice or any of its requirements may be made to the Labour Court. The Agency is required to keep a register of every notice which has come into operation. See Employment Equality Act 1977.

**non-joinder.** The omission of a person in proceedings either as plaintiff or defendant. No cause or matter may be defeated by reason of the misjoinder (qv) or non-joinder of parties; the court may order that the names of parties improperly joined, be struck out, and to add parties who ought to have been joined: RSC O.15 r.13.

**non-life insurance.** Insurance of a class specified in the European Communities (Non-Life Insurance) Regulations 1976 (SI No 115 of 1976). A person generally may not carry on the business of non-life insurance in the State unless he is the holder of an authorisation granted by the Minister (ibid art.4). There is a requirement to establish and maintain *technical reserves* in respect of underwriting liabilities assumed (ibid arts.14 and 27) and to establish an adequate *solvency margin* (ibid art.16(1) and 28). See INSURANCE.

**non-marital child.** A child whose parents are not married to each other. See Status of Children Act 1987.

**non-minor offence.** See INDICTABLE OFFENCE.

**non-paternity.** See PATERNITY, PRESUMPTION OF.

**non-suit.** (1) Formerly, the abandonment of a case by a plaintiff; now replaced by the procedure of discontinuance (qv).

(2) An application by a defendant for a *non-suit* is an application by a defendant at the end of the plaintiff's case for a *direction* that the evidence adduced by the plaintiff is not sufficient to establish a case against the defendant. See O'Toole v Heavey (1993 SC) ILRM 343. See DIRECTION.

**non-user.** Failure to exercise a right; it may amount to abandonment of the right eg of an easement (qv). See ABANDONMENT.

**Northern Ireland.** The territory comprising the counties of Antrim, Armagh, Down, Fermanagh, Londonderry and Tyrone: Government of Ireland Act 1920 s.1(2). The extent of Northern Ireland is recognised by the Treaty (Confirmation of Amending Agreement) Act 1925. The courts take judicial notice of the existence of Northern Ireland and its courts: The People v McGeough (1978) IR 384; MacB v MacB (1984) HC.

The governments of Ireland and the United Kingdom have affirmed that any change in the status of Northern Ireland would only come about with the consent of a majority of the people of Northern

Ireland: Anglo-Irish Agreement 1985; Crotty v An Taoiseach (1987) ILRM 400.

In relation to a *proposed road development* which is likely to have significant effects on the environment of Northern Ireland, there is a requirement on the road authority to send to the prescribed authority in Northern Ireland a copy of the environment impact statement, and the Minister, before approving the development, is required to consider any views of that prescribed authority: Roads Act 1993 ss.50(3)(c) and 51(5)(b).

A defendant in an action is not entitled to an order for security for costs solely on the grounds that the plaintiff resides in Northern Ireland: RSC O.29 r.2. See also Moyne v Londonderry Port and Harbour Commissioners (1986) IR 299. See Trade Union Act 1975 s.17. See also 1937 Constitution arts.1-3. See ANGLO-IRISH AGREEMENT; CITIZENSHIP; EXTRADITION; FRANCHISE; NATION; NATIONAL EMERGENCY; NATIONAL TERRITORY; ROAD DEVELOPMENT, PROPOSED; SECURITY FOR COSTS; UNITED IRELAND; WHISKEY, IRISH.

**noscitur a sociis.** Known from associates]. The meaning of a word may be determined by reference to its context.

**not guilty.** See ACQUITTAL.

**not negotiable.** The words marked on a cheque which gives the holder no better title than the previous holder: Bills of Exchange Act 1882 s.81. See Great Western Railway Co v London & County Banking Co (1900) 2 QB 464. See CHEQUE; NEMO DAT QUI NON HABET.

**notary public.** A public officer, appointed by the Chief Justice, who certifies the due execution in his presence of a deed, contract, or other writing, or verifies some act or thing done in his presence, which certification or verification he authenticates by his signature and official seal. In certain instances, his signature alone suffices. Unless there are exceptional circumstances, a notary public must be a solicitor: In the matter of Timothy McCarthy (1990 SC) ILRM 84.

The main functions of a notary public include (a) authenticating public and private documents; (b) attesting and verifying signatures to documents in order to satisfy evidential or statutory requirements of foreign governments or of overseas institutions and regulatory authorities; (c) noting and protesting bills of exchange and promissory notes for non-acceptance or non-payment; (d) drawing up ship protests; and (e) giving certificates as to the acts and instruments of persons and their identities.

A statutory declaration (qv) may be taken and received by a notary public: Statutory Declarations Act 1938 s.1(1). See Promissory Notes (Ireland) Act 1864; Courts (Supplemental Provisions) Act 1961 s.10(1)(b). [Text: O'Connor]. See BILL OF EXCHANGE; PROMISSORY NOTE; SHIPS PROTEST; STATUTORY DECLARATION.

**notice.** Knowledge or cognisance. To give *notice* is to bring matters to a person's knowledge or attention. The *doctrine of notice* is often crucial in deciding a contest for priority between competing equitable interests or between equitable and legal interests. Notice can be *actual* where a person is aware by his own knowledge of a previous claim: In re Fuller & Co Ltd (in liquidation) (1982) IR 161; or it can be *constructive*, where the person is not himself aware but could have been, had he made proper enquiries: Northern Bank Ltd v Henry (1981) IR 1; or it may be *imputed*, eg where an agent of the person has either actual or constructive notice of a previous claim: In re Burmester (1858) 9 Ir Ch R 41. See also Conveyancing Act 1882 s.3(1).

In the case of registered land, the register generally governs priorities, except that certain interests and rights may affect registered land without registration: Registration of Title Act 1964 s.31(1); Tench v Molyneux (1914) 48 ILTR 48. In relation to notice and personalty, see Deale v Hall (1823) 3 Russ 1; Molloy v French (1849) 13 Ir Eq R 216. See PRIORITY.

**notice, employment.** The minimum periods of notice to be given by employers and by employees when terminating a contract of employment are specified in the Minimum Notice and Terms of Employment Act 1973 and 1984. The minimum notice which an employer must give varies from one week to eight weeks depending on the length of service of the employee. Minimum notice applies also to regular part-time employees: Worker Protection (Regular Part-Time Employees) Act 1991 s.1.

The minimum notice entitlement may be waived but it must be clear and unambiguous to be effective: Industrial Yarns Ltd v Greene [1984] ILRM 15. While the winding up order of a company is usually notice of discharge of all its employees, the circumstances may justify the continuity of their service and the waiving of the notice: In re Evanhenry Ltd (1986 HC); Dodd & Ors v Local Stores (Trading) Ltd (1992 EAT) ELR 61.

The notice required by the 1976 Act must not be stringently and technically construed; the Act is not concerned with the form of notice but only with the length; the provisions of the Act are complied with once the notice conveys to the employee that he will lose his employment at the end of the period expressed or necessarily implied in the notice, once that period is not less than the statutory minimum: Bolands Ltd (In receivership) v Ward (1988) ILRM 383. See SI No 243 of 1973 and Protection of Employees (Employers' Insolvency) Act 1984 s.13.

Where a contract is for an indefinite period, then reasonable notice must be given provided that it is not less than the statutory minimum. The more important or unique the position, the longer will be the period regarded as reasonable. Even if a post is described as *permanent and pensionable*, it can be determined by reasonable notice. The reasonableness of notice has to be considered in relation to the period which would be reasonable to enable a person to find other employment: Tierney v Irish Meat Packers (1989 HC) 7ILT Dig 5.

As regards the notice which an employee must give to an employer, this will depend on the contract of employment. The remedy for a breach of the notice required in the contract lies in contract law and on the basis of compensation to the employer rather than penalty; deduction of an amount from the wages of an employee for failure to comply with notice, in the absence of an express provision for such deduction, is in contravention of the Payment of Wages Act 1991 s.5: Curust Hardware Ltd v Dalton (1993 EAT) ELR 10. See also McDonnell v Minister for Education

(1940) IR 316; Walsh v Dublin Health Authority (1964) 98 ILTR 82; Scott v Kelly's Express Print (1991 EAT) ELR 160. See CONSTRUCTIVE DISMISSAL; FIXED TERM CONTRACT; SUMMARY DISMISSAL; TRANSFER OF EMPLOYMENT.

**notice of abandonment.** The notice required in marine insurance. See ABANDONMENT.

**notice of dishonour.** The notice which must be given to those whom the holder of a bill of exchange (qv) wishes to hold liable. See DISHONOUR OF BILL.

**notice of motion.** A motion (qv) where notice thereof is given to the other side in legal proceedings. Unless the High Court gives special leave to the contrary, there must be at least two clear days between the service of a notice of motion and the day named in the notice for the hearing of the motion; however, where the notice of motion requires to be served personally out of court, it must be served not less than four clear days before the hearing of the application: RSC O.52 r.6. In the Circuit Court there must be at least four clear days notice: RCC O.51. For notice of motion in the District Court to vary or set aside a decree, see DCR (1963) r.9. See MOTION.

**notice of trial.** The notice which the plaintiff in a High Court action must serve within six weeks of the close of pleadings; otherwise the defendant may do so without court order; twenty one days notice of trial must be given: RSC O.36 rr.12 and 16. The actual setting down for trial must be done within fourteen days after the service of notice of trial, otherwise the notice of trial will no longer be in force (ibid r.18). If the party who has served notice omits to set down the action for trial within seven days, the party to whom the notice has been given may set it down (ibid r.21). In relation to the Circuit Court, see RCC O.30 rr.1-4.

**notice to admit.** A party to an action may serve on the other party a *notice to admit* particular facts or documents. Unreasonable failure to admit matters may render the party in default liable to pay the costs of proving them at the trial. See RSC O.32; RCC O.28.

**notice to proceed.** The notice given by one party in any cause or matter to the other party of his intention to proceed, which is required where there has been no proceedings for one year from the last proceedings; one month's notice must be given: RSC O.122 r.11.

**notice to produce.** The notice given by a party in an action in the District Court to his opponent, requiring production of documents. See DISCOVERY OF DOCUMENTS.

**notice to quit.** A yearly, monthly, weekly or other periodic tenancy may be determined by a *notice to quit* but not a lease or tenancy for a fixed period of time unless expressly reserved in the lease. A minimum period of notice to quit of four weeks has now been provided for: Housing (Miscellaneous Provisions) Act 1992 s.16. See TENANCY, TERMINATION OF. See also EJECTMENT; LEASE, DETERMINATION OF; TENANCY, TERMINATION OF.

**notice to treat.** In relation to the *compulsory purchase* (qv) of land, the notice which a local authority (qv) has power to serve stating that they are willing to *treat* for the purchase of the several interests in the land and requiring each such owner, lessee and occupier to state within a specified period (not being less than one month from the date of service of the notice to treat) the exact nature of the interest in respect of which compensation is claimed by him and details of the compensation claimed and, if the authority so require, distinguishing separate amounts of the compensation in such manner as may be specified in the notice to treat and showing how each such amount is calculated: Housing Act 1966 s.79.

The owner of land who fails to deliver to the acquiring authority a notice in writing of the amount claimed by him as compensation, can be penalised in costs: Acquisition of Land (Assessment of Compensation) Act 1919 s.5(2).

The effect of a notice to treat is to oblige the local authority to take, and the owner to surrender, the land: In re Green Dale Building Company (1977) IR 256. No estate passes to the acquiring local authority by virtue only of the notice to treat: Irish Life Assurance v Dublin Land Securities (1986 HC) IR 332.

**noting a bill.** A brief note or memorandum made by a notary public (qv) as an interim measure, recording that a bill of exchange has been dishonoured, as a first step to a protest (qv). The note must be made at the time of dishonour and is written into the notary's *protest register*. See Bills of Exchange Act 1882 s.51. See NOTING AND PROTESTING.

**noting and protesting.** The process by which formal *notice of dishonour* of a foreign bill of exchange is made: Bills of Exchange Act 1882 s.51. If a foreign bill is not so protested, the drawers and endorsers are discharged (ibid s.51(2)). A notary public (qv) must present the bill for acceptance or payment, must note the reply made on the bill, and issue a formal *certificate of dishonour* called a *protest*.

**notorious facts.** Matters of common knowledge of which judicial notice (qv) may be taken without formal proof.

**nova causa interveniens.** [New intervening cause].

**nova constitutio futuris formam imponere debet, non praeteritis.** [A new law ought to regulate what is to follow, not the past]. See RETROSPECTIVE LEGISLATION.

**novation.** A tripartite contract whereby a contract between two parties is rescinded in consideration of a new contract being entered into between one of the parties and a third party eg where the creditor at the request of the debtor agrees to take another person as his debtor in the place of the original debtor. The effect of novation is to release the original debtor from his obligations under the contract and to impose these obligations on the new debtor. Novation frequently arises in a partnership on a change in membership of the firm, when creditors, expressly or by implication (eg by continuing to trade with the firm), accept the new firm as their debtor.

Novation of a contract may also occur when a party to the contract is adjudicated a bankrupt; the official assignee in bankruptcy becomes entitled to the contractual rights and obligations unless he expressly disclaim's the contract: In re Casey, a Bankrupt (1991 SC) ILRM 385.

**novelty.** One of the requirements for an invention to be patentable: Patents Act 1992 s.9(1). The invention must be *new*; it will be considered new if it does not form part of the *state of the art* (ibid s.11). Under the Patents Act 1964 (since repealed), it was held that the test of novelty should be based on what was published before the priority date (qv) and that publication outside of the State is relevant: Wavin Pipes Ltd v Hepworth Iron Co Ltd (1982) FRS 32.

A *novelty search report* may be requested by an applicant for a patent or, in lieu of making such request, the applicant may submit the grant of a patent obtained in a prescribed foreign State or the result of a search report associated therewith (ibid 1992 Act ss.29-30). See also General Tire & Rubber Co v Firestone Tyre & Rubber Co (1975) 1 WLR 819. See PATENT CO-OPERATION TREATY; PATENTABLE INVENTION; PUBLICATION.

**novus actus interveniens.** [A new act intervening]. A defence in an action in tort (qv) whereby it is claimed that A is not liable for the damage done to B, if the *chain of causation* between A's act or omission is broken by the intervention of a third party, thereby rendering the damage too *remote*. There is a general duty to guard against a novus actus interveniens and consequently the defence will fail if the intervening act is a direct or foreseeable consequence of the defendant's act or is intentionally procured by the defendant. Novus actus interveniens has been pleaded as a defence to a charge of murder: The People (Attorney General) v McGrath (1960) CCA. It is of the essence of novus actus interveniens that the damage complained of should have resulted from the act of another person who is independent of both the plaintiff and the defendant: Coyle v An Post (1993 SC) ILRM 508 at 526. See Cunningham v McGrath Bros (1964) IR 209; Conole v Redbank Oyster Co (1976) IR 191; Crowley v Allied Irish Banks (1988) ILRM 225. See REMOTENESS OF DAMAGE.

**noxious weeds.** Weeds declared by the Minister to be noxious weeds eg thistle, ragworth, dock, common barberry, and the male hop plant: Noxious Weeds Act 1936 s.2. Where noxious weeds are not destroyed in accordance with a statutory notice served on a specified person (eg the owner or occupier of the land), that person commits an offence (ibid s.5).

**nuclear material.** See RADIOACTIVE SUB-

STANCE.

**nudum pactum.** [A nude contract]. An agreement without consideration (qv) and which is consequently unenforceable unless it is under seal.

**nuisance.** A tort (qv) which involves an act or omission which amounts to an unreasonable interference with, disturbance to, or annoyance to another person in the exercise of his rights; if the rights so interfered with belong to the person as a member of the public, the act or omission is a *public nuisance*; if these rights relate to the ownership or occupation of land, or some easement (qv), profit (qv) or some other right enjoyed in connection with land, then the act or omission amounts to a *private nuisance*: Connolly v South of Ireland Asphalt Co (1977) IR 99. See NUISANCE, PRIVATE; NUISANCE, PUBLIC.

**nuisance, private.** The unlawful interference with another's servitude (easement (qv)) or the unauthorised user of a person's own property which causes damage to the property of another or interferes with the enjoyment of the property of another. The interference must be substantial to be actionable: Mullins v Hynes (1972) SC. The remedies are: abatement (qv); damages (which cannot include personal injuries); injunction, including a mandatory or a *quia timet* (qv) injunction to prevent a threatened nuisance: Attorney General (Boswell) v Rathmines & Pembroke Trust Hospital Board (1904) 1 IR 161.

Private nuisances have been held to include interference from: smoke, heat, smell, vibrations, soil erosion, branches of trees, damage to foundations, dust, fumes, sewage, dangerous leaves and blasting operations. See Dewar v City and Suburban Racecourse Co (1889) 1 IR 345; New Imperial Windsor Hotel Co v Johnson (1912) 1 IR 327; Wallace v McCartan (1917) IR 377; Leech v Reilly (1983) HC; McGrane v Louth County Council (1983) HC; Rabette v Mayo County Council (1984) HC; Hanrahan v Merck Sharpe & Dohme (Ire) Ltd (1988 SC) ILRM 629; Fleming, Byrne & Hayden v Rathdown School (1993 HC). See RYLANDS v FLETCHER, RULE IN.

**nuisance, public.** Some unlawful act, or omission to discharge some legal duty that endangers the lives, safety, health or comfort of the public, or by which the public are obstructed in the exercise of some common right. A public nuisance can be committed by either obstruction of a public highway or endangering it: Cunningham v MacGrath Bros (1964) IR 209.

A private person may bring an action for damages or an injunction for public nuisance but only if he has suffered some substantial damage to himself and different in kind from that suffered by the rest of the public: Smith v Wilson (1903) 2 IR 45. Public nuisance is a crime; the Attorney General may institute criminal proceedings or he may sue for an injunction to restrain the nuisance. See SANITARY AUTHORITIES AND NUISANCE.

**nul tiel.** [No such].

**null and void.** Having no force; invalid eg a judgment which has been *set aside* (qv).

**nulla bona.** [No goods]. The return made by a sheriff (qv) to an order of *fieri facias* (which authorised him to seize the goods and chattels of a person) when he has been unable to find any to seize. See BANKRUPTCY, ACT OF; FIERI FACIAS.

**nulla pactione effici potest ut dolus praestetur.** [By no contract may it be arranged that a man be indemnified against responsibility for his own fraud]. See INDEMNITY.

**nulla poena sine lege.** [No punishment except in accordance with the law]. See PUNISHMENT.

**nullity of marriage.** See MARRIAGE, NULLITY OF.

**nullius filius.** A bastard (qv); now a person whose parents are not married to each other. See CHILD, ILLEGITIMATE.

**nullum simile est idem.** [A thing which is similar to another thing is not the same as that other thing].

**nullus videtur dolo facere qui suo jure utitur.** [A malicious or improper motive cannot make wrongful in law an act which would be rightful apart from such motive]. See MOTIVE.

**nunc pro tune.** [Now for then].

**nuncupative will.** A privileged will involving an oral declaration before witnesses, formerly allowed as an exception for soldiers on actual military service and mariners at sea under the Wills Act 1837 s.11, as extended by the Wills

(Soldiers Sailors) Act 1918, even where the testator was under 21 years of age. The exception was not re-enacted by the Succession Act 1965.

**nunquam indebitatus.** [Never indebted].

**nuptias non concubitus sed consensus facit.** [It is consent, not habitation, which makes a marriage]. See COMMON LAW MARRIAGE; MARRIAGE

**nurse.** A woman or a man whose name is entered in the register of nurses established under s.27 of the Nurses Act 1985 (ibid s.2). Statutory provision for the registration, control and education of nurses is contained in the 1985 Act. It is an offence for a person to take or use the title of nurse or midwife (qv) if not registered (ibid s.49). A nurse may have her name erased from the register if convicted of an indictable offence (ibid s.42) or if found guilty of professional misconduct or to be unfit to practise (ibid s.39). See Kerrigan v An Bord Altranais (1990) ITLR (30 Jul); Fennessy v Minister for Health (1991 HC) 2 IR 361. See DISCIPLINARY PROCEEDINGS; HOME NURSING SERVICE.

**nursery.** See PRE-SCHOOL SERVICE.

**nursing home.** An institution for the maintenance of more than two dependent persons: Health (Nursing Homes) Act 1990 s.2. There are certain exclusions eg state institutions, institutions for the care of physically handicapped persons which are grant aided by the State, and premises in which the majority being maintained are members of a religious order or priests. A dependent person is one who requires assistance with the activities of daily living (ibid s.1). A person must not carry on a nursing home unless it is registered (ibid s.3) and must comply with regulations made in relation to standards (ibid s.6).

# O

**oath.** A solemn declaration by which a party calls his God to witness that what he says is true, or that what he promises to do he will do. In general all evidence (qv) must be on oath. An *affirmation* may be made instead of an oath. It is a fundamental principle of the common law that *viva voce* (qv) evidence must be given on oath or affirmation; the purpose being to ensure that such evidence is true by the provision of a moral or religious and legal sanction against deliberate untruth: Mapp v Gilhooley (1991 SC) ILRM 695. See Oaths Act 1888; Interpretation Act 1937 s.12 sch. See Report on Oaths and Affirmations (LRC 34 of 1990). See AFFIRMATION; CHILD, EVIDENCE OF; OATH, FORM OF; PERJURY; UNLAWFUL OATH; UNSWORN STATEMENT.

**oath, interpreter.** An oath in the following or similar form: *I swear by Almighty God that I will well and truly interpret and explain to the court/jury the evidence given in this case/trial/enquiry according to the best of my skill and understanding.*

**oath, jury.** In criminal trials the juror's oath is: *I swear by Almighty God that I will well and truly try the issue whether the accused is (or are) guilty or not guilty of the offence (or the several offences) charged in the indictment preferred against him (or her, or them) and a true verdict give according to the evidence*: Juries Act 1976 ss.18(1) and 19(1).

In relation to the issue as to whether an accused is fit to plead, the oath is: *I swear by Almighty God that I will well and diligently inquire whether (stating the name of the accused person), the prisoner at the bar (qv) be insane or not and a true verdict give according to the best of my understanding* (ibid ss.18(1) and 19(2)).

In civil actions the juror's oath is: *I swear by Almighty God that I will well and truly try all such issues as shall be given to me to try and true verdicts give according to the evidence* (ibid ss.18(1) and 19(3)). See UNFIT TO PLEAD.

**oath, witness.** An oath in the following or similar form: *I swear by Almighty God that the evidence I shall give to this court touching this case/complaint/charge shall be the truth, and nothing but the truth.*

**obedience to orders, defence of.** In some circumstances, obedience to a superior's orders may be relevant in negativing the *mens rea* (qv) required to constitute an offence. As regards military forces, a soldier acting under orders of his superior officer, is justified unless the order be manifestly illegal: Keighley v

Bell (1868) 4 F & F 773. See MARITAL COERCION.

**obiter dictum.** [Saying by the way]. An observation by a judge in a case on a legal question, based on facts which were not present, or not material, in the case, or which arose in such a manner as not to require a decision. The *obiter dictum* is not binding on future cases but may be persuasive. The Supreme Court may treat a decision of the High Court on the question of the constitutionality of legislation as being technically *obiter dicta* when it considers that the latter court should not have engaged in the question: McDaid v Judge Sheehy (1991 SC) ILRM 250. Contrast with RATIO DECIDENDI. See MOOT; PRECEDENT.

**objects clause.** The clause in the *memorandum of association* of a company setting out the objects which a company has been formed to pursue: Companies Act 1963 s.6(1)(c) (as amended by Companies (Amdt) Act 1983, first schedule, para 2). A company may by special resolution alter the provisions of its memorandum by abandoning, restricting or amending any existing object or by adopting a new object; an application to cancel the alteration may be made to the court by a minority of 15 per cent in value of the shareholders or by 15 per cent of the debenture holders (ibid 1963 Act s.10 as amended by 1983 Act, first schedule, para 3). The objects clause cannot be changed with retrospective effect: Northern Bank Finance Corp v Quinn (1979) HC. See also Building Societies Act 1989 ss.9(1) and 10(2)(a). See BELL HOUSES CLAUSE; ULTRA VIRES.

**obligation.** A legal duty arising out of contract (qv) or tort (qv) between two or more persons. See LIABILITY.

**obligee.** A person to whom a bond (qv) is made.

**obligor.** A person who binds himself by a bond (qv).

**obliteration.** See ALTERATION; ERASURE.

**obscene.** See CENSORSHIP OF BOOKS; DISORDERLY CONDUCT; INDECENCY; PERFORMANCE, INDECENT OR PROFANE.

**obscene calls.** A message by telephone which is grossly offensive or of an indecent, obscene or menacing character; the sending of such a message is an offence: Post Office (Amendment) Act 1951 s.13.

**obstruction.** Under draft legislation, it is proposed to increase the fine for willfully preventing or interrupting the free passage of any person or vehicle in any public place: Criminal Justice (Public Order) Bill 1993 s.10.

**obstruction of government.** The offence of preventing or obstructing any arm of government, whether legislative, executive, or judicial, by force of arms or other violent means, or by any form of intimidation: Offences Against the State Act 1939 s.7, as amended by Criminal Law Act 1976 s.2. See also The People (DPP) v Kehoe (1983) IR 136.

**obstruction of the President.** The offence of obstructing the President of Ireland (qv) in the exercise of her duties: Offences Against the State Act 1939 s.8.

**obtaining credit by fraud.** See CREDIT BY FRAUD, OBTAINING.

**O'Byrne letter.** The letter which is normally sent by a plaintiff in an action where there are two or more defendants and he wishes to have evidence to ground a subsequent application to the court, for an order that the unsuccessful defendant pay the costs of the successful defendant.

The format of the letter is typically: *Our client cannot be expected to elect between respective defendants and unless we have an admission of liability by you within 10 days, we will institute proceedings against you and Mr X. In the event that Mr X is not held liable and an order is made dismissing the claim against him with costs, application will be made to the court under the Court of Justice Act 1936 s.78 for an order that, in addition to damages and our client's costs, you should pay to our client such sum as he may have to pay for the costs of Mr X and this letter will be produced at the hearing of the said application.* See Bullock v London Omnibus Co (1907) 1 KB 264; Rice v Toombes (1971) IR 38. See Courts of Justice Act 1936 s.78.

**occasion of qualified privilege.** See PRIVILEGE.

**occasional trading.** Selling goods by retail at a premises or place (not being a public road or other place to which the public have access as of right) of which the person so selling has been in occupation for a continuous period of less than three months ending on the date of such selling: Occasional Trading Act 1979 s.2. It is an offence to engage in occasional trading unless the person has an *occasional trading permit* (ibid s.3). Similar exceptions apply to certain selling transactions as apply in casual trading (qv). See also Casual Trading Act 1980 s.17.

**occupancy.** Formerly, if an estate *pur autre vie* had been granted without any reference to the grantee's heir or successors in the conveyance, the law of occupancy applied ie the first person who entered the land after the grantee's death, succeeded to it eg where A granted land to B for the life of C and B died before C, anyone could enter and occupy the land during C's life. If the person who entered was B's heir, he was known as the *special occupant*; otherwise he was known as a *general occupant*.

The law of occupancy has been abolished; *general occupancy* was abolished by the Statute of Frauds (Ireland) 1695 s.9 and *special occupancy* was abolished by the Succession Act 1965 s.11(1). Now, on the death of a tenant pur autre vie intestate, his land devolves on his personal representatives for distribution with the rest of his estate, real and personal. See LIFE ESTATE; OCCUPANT.

**occupant.** See OCCUPANCY.

**occupation.** (1) The exercise of physical control or possession of land; having actual use of land; taking possession of territory by armed forces. (2) A person's trade, profession or calling. See EMPLOYEE; FORCIBLE ENTRY AND OCCUPATION.

**occupational pension.** See PENSION SCHEME.

**occupier's liability.** The liability of an occupier of unsafe premises to entrants to the premises may depend on whether the entrant is an *invitee*, a *licensee* or a *trespasser*. However, "the law in relation to occupier's liability can no longer be seen as consisting of such watertight compartments": Garvan v Brennan (1989 CC) 7ILT & SJ 319.

It has been held that the test of an occupier's liability is whether what occurred was reasonably foreseeable and in relation to a person who was proximate to the occupier; the court must take account of the entire circumstances, including the nature of the danger involved, the age and knowledge of the person likely to be injured, and the conduct of the person who came onto the premises: Smith v CIE (1991 SC) 9ILT Dig 148. See LRC Consultation Paper on Occupier's Liability (1993).

**occupier's liability to children.** If a premises contains some *allurement*, a child who has trespassed on to the premises will be converted into a *licensee* and the occupier will have a duty of care to protect from concealed dangers. See McNamara v ESB (1975) IR 1; Keane v ESB (1981) IR 44; Maria Rooney v The Rev Fr Connolly PP (1987) ILRM 768. See OCCUPIER'S LIABILITY TO LICENSEES.

**occupier's liability to invitees.** An *invitee* is a person who enters premises with the express or implied invitation of the occupier in a matter in which both have a common interest eg a customer in a shop. The duty of care owed to an invitee is to exercise reasonable care to prevent damages from unusual dangers of which the occupier knows or ought to know.

It has been held that occupiers of supermarket premises owe their customers who are invitees on the premises a duty to take reasonable care, in all the circumstances to see that the premises are reasonably safe, each case necessarily depending on its own particular facts: Mullen v Quinnsworth Ltd (1990 SC) 1 IR 59. Where oil has spilled on a supermarket floor, the onus is on the occupier to prove that reasonable care was taken to ensure that the premises were safe: Mullen v Quinnsworth Ltd (1991 SC) ILRM 439.

The relationship of *invitor and invitee* has been described by a Supreme Court judge as a form of legal fiction which he thought best abandoned: McCarthy J in Clancy v Commissioners of Public Works (1991 SC) ILRM 567. See O'Gorman v Ritz (Clonmel) Ltd (1947) Ir Jur Rep 35; Callaghan v Killarney Race Co (1958) IR 366.

**occupier's liability to licensees.** A *licensee* is a person who enters premises with the express or implied permission of the occupier granted gratuitously in a matter in which the occupier has no interest eg a guest in a private house, worshippers in a church, persons in public paths and forests. The duty of care owed to a licensee is to warn him of any concealed source of danger on the premises, the existence of which is actually known to the occupier and of which the licensee is unaware. See Bohane v Driscoll (1929) IR 428; Boughton v Bray UDC (1964) Ir Jur Rep 57; Maria Rooney v The Rev Fr Connolly PP (1987) ILRM 768.

**occupier's liability to trespassers.** A *trespasser* is a person who enters premises without the express or implied consent of the occupier. The duty of care owed to a trespasser is not to do any act which deliberately, or is recklessly likely, to injure him. An occupier is entitled to protect his premises, but if he creates a danger which he knows a trespasser coming on to the premises will not see, or will see but not realise its danger, he must take reasonable care to prevent injury to the trespasser. See O'Keeffe v Irish Motors Inns Ltd (1978) IR 85. See RECKLESSNESS.

**of course.** See MOTION OF COURSE.

**off record.** A solicitor is said to come *off record* when he obtains an order of the court declaring that he has ceased to be the solicitor acting for a party in any proceedings: RSC 0.7 r.3. An ex-parte application to the court is made by the solicitor; any order made by the court does not affect the rights of the solicitor and the party as between themselves (ibid rr.4-5).

**offence.** Generally, a *crime*.

**offence and sentence.** For comprehensive list of offences, how created, whether felony or misdemeanour, and sentences applicable, see text. [Text: Ryan & Magee, Appendix H].

**offences against property.** The group of crimes including arson, burglary, criminal damage to property, embezzlement, false pretences, forcible entry, forgery, fraudulent conversion, larceny, malicious damage, handling stolen property, and robbery (qqv).

**offences against public order.** The group of crimes including bigamy, blasphemy, contempt of court, indecency, obstruction of government, perjury, riot, sedition, treason, usurpation of the functions of government, and crimes involving official secrets and unlawful organisations (qqv).

**offences against the person.** The group of crimes including adbuction, abortion, assault, bestiality, child stealing, false imprisonment, incest, indecent assault, infanticide, kidnapping, manslaughter, murder, rape, sexual assault, unlawful carnal knowledge (qqv). [Text: Charlton (2)].

**offences against the State.** Offences provided for in the Offences Against the State Acts 1939 to 1985. A garda is empowered to arrest a person in relation to specified offences where he suspects that that person has committed or is about to commit any of those offences: 1939 Act s.30; Trimbole v Governor of Mountjoy Prison (1985) IR 550. Questioning of a person so detained in relation to other crimes does not necessarily affect the legality of the detention: The People (DPP) v Quilligan (1987) ILRM 606. The constitutional guarantee on equality before the law is not breached by detention pursuant to s.30: DPP v Quilligan & O'Reilly (1992 SC) ITLR (2 Nov). See UNLAWFUL ORGANISATION; OBSTRUCTION OF GOVERNMENT; OBSTRUCTION OF PRESIDENT; SECRET SOCIETIES.

**offensive trades.** Blood boiler, bone boiler, fellmonger, soap boiler, tallow melter and tripe boiler, or any other noxious or offensive trade, business or manufacture; it is an offence to carry on an offensive trade in the district of an urban sanitary authority without their approval: Public Health (Ireland) Act 1878 s.128. See EJUSDEM GENERIS.

**offensive weapon.** Includes a firearm that is not loaded and an imitation firearm: Firearms Act 1964 s.25(1). It is an offence to be found at night armed with any dangerous or *offensive weapon* with intent to commit any burglary: Larceny Act 1916 s.28(1); Criminal Law (Jurisdiction) Act 1976 s.21(3).

An *offensive weapon* now includes a wide range of knives and weapons eg flick-knives, knuckledusters, belt buckle knife; it is an offence to manufacture, sell or hire an offensive weapon: Firearms and Offensive Weapons Act 1990 s.12 and SI No 66 of 1991. It is also an offence for a person, without good reason, to have with him in a public place a knife or any article which has a blade or is sharply pointed (ibid s.9).

A *weapon of offence* is any article made or adapted for use for causing injury to or incapacitating a person; it is an offence for a trespasser to have with him a knife or a weapon of offence (ibid s.10). See BURGLARY, AGGRAVATED; FIREARM.

**offensive words.** In a will it is possible for words which are offensive or defamatory and which have no testamentary value to be excluded from probate. See *In the Estate of White* (1914) P 153.

**offer.** A proposal to give or to do something, which when accepted constitutes an agreement. It should be distinguished from an invitation to others to make offers eg as made by an auctioneer or as made in an advertisement inviting tenders. An offer may be *express* or *implied* from conduct. The person making the offer is known as the *offeror* and the person to whom the offer is made is the *offeree*.

The general rules relating to offers are: (1) an offer may be made to a definite person, to the world at large, or to some definite class of persons; (2) an offer may be made by words or by conduct; (3) the terms of an offer must be definite; (4) the offer must be communicated to the offeree before acceptance.

An offer may be withdrawn or revoked at any time before it has been unconditionally accepted, or it may be rejected (eg by a counter-offer), or it may lapse. An offer lapses on the death of the offeror or offeree before acceptance; by non-acceptance within the time prescribed; or where no time has been prescribed, by non-acceptance within a reasonable time.

As regards a *mistaken* offer, the offeror will be bound notwithstanding the mistake between the parties, if the offeree's interpretation of the offer is reasonable when construed objectively: O'Neill v Ryan (1991 HC) ITLR (2 Sep). See LAPSE OF OFFER; REVOCATION OF OFFER.

**offer for sale.** A document offering the shares of a company to the public, issued by a financial intermediary which has bought the shares outright from the company. The offer may be at fixed price or be by way of tender. An offer for sale to the public must comply with prospectus rules. See Companies Act 1963 s.51 and Companies (Amdt) Act 1983 s.21(2). See PROSPECTUS.

**offer of amends.** The offer made by a person in relation to an *unintentional defamation,* consisting of (a) an offer to publish a suitable correction and a sufficient apology and (b) an offer to take reasonable steps to notify persons, to whom the defamatory material has been distributed, that the material is alleged to be defamatory: Defamation Act 1961 s.21. An unintentional defamation is one which the person claims was published by him innocently; the offer must be accompanied by an affidavit specifying the facts relied upon to show that the words were *published innocently* in relation to the party aggrieved.

If an offer of amends is accepted, no further proceedings may follow against the person making the offer. If the offer is rejected, it is a good defence to defamation proceedings. The offer of amends may require the dafamatory words to be republished; such republication is privileged: Willis v Irish Press Ltd (1938) 72 ILTR 238. See PUBLICATION.

**offeree.** See OFFER.

**offeror.** See OFFER.

**office.** A premises, room, suite of rooms or other part of premises in which more than five persons are employed in clerical work: Office Premises Act 1958 s.3. This Act provides for the protection of the health, welfare and safety of person employed in offices. See also Safety, Health and Welfare at Work Act 1989; certain sections of the 1958 Act are repealed when particular sections of the 1989 Act come into force.

**office copy.** Attested copies of all documents filed in the High Court are admissible in evidence in all causes and matters and between all persons or parties to the same extent as the originals would be admissible: RSC O.39 r.3. It has been held in Northern Ireland that an office copy of an instrument deposited in the Supreme Court could not be taken as evidence of the truth of the contents or the genuiness of the execution of the instrument: O'Kane v Mullan (1925) NI 1. See DOCUMENTARY EVIDENCE.

**office holder.** It has been held that the characteristic features of an *office* are that it is created by Act of the national parliament, charter, statutory regulation, articles of association of a company or of a body corporate formed under the authority of a statute, deed of trust, grant or by prescription; and that the holder of it may be removed if the instrument creating the office authorises it: Glover v BLN Ltd (1973) IR 389.

An office holder is entitled to the benefit of the principles of *natural justice* (qv) before being removed from office eg where dismissed for misconduct or failing to perform the duties of the office, but not for redundancy: Hickey v Eastern Health Board (1990 SC) ELR 177. The rights of an employee in regard to dismissal do not depend on whether the person is a servant or an officer, but rather on the reasons for and circumstances surrounding the dismissal (ibid Hickey case). The consent of an office holder may be required, in a particular case, to the abolition of his office: Turley v Laois Co Co (1991 HC) 9ILT Dig 51.

An office might be held for a fixed term of one year from each meeting at which the annual election of officers takes place eg in a trade union: Kenny v Trustees of OP & ATS of I (1991 EAT) ELR 152. Certain office holders are excluded from the protection of the Unfair Dismissals Act 1977. As regards an officer of a local authority, see O'Callaghan v Cork Corporation UD 309/1978. See Garvey v Ireland (1981) IR 75; Henegan v Western Regional Fisheries Board (1986) ILRM 225. See EMPLOYEE; PROBATION IN EMPLOYMENT.

**officer.** In relation to a body corporate, includes a director or secretary: Companies Act 1963 s.2(1). In relation to specific provisions of company law, *officer* may have a wider meaning eg as regards "insider dealing", it includes an employee, auditor, liquidator, receiver, or examiner: Companies Act 1990 s.107. In relation to a building society, an officer means a director, chief executive or secretary of the society: Building Societies Act 1989 s.2(1).

**Official Assignee.** The officer of the High Court in bankruptcy matters: Courts (Supplemental Provisions) Act 1961, eighth schedule, para 3. The bankrupt's property, real and personal, present and future, vested and contingent, vests in the Official Assignee, but not land which the bankrupt holds as a trustee.

The Official Assignee is empowered to perform such duties and functions as are conferred on him by statute or by rules of court; his functions are stated to be to get in and realise the property, to ascertain the debts and to distribute the assets in accordance with the Act: Bankruptcy Act 1988 ss.60-61. He is empowered eg to sell the bankrupt's property by public or private auction; to make any *compromise* (qv) or *arrangement* with creditors or to *compromise* any debts or liabilities; and to mortgage or pledge any property to raise any money (ibid s.61(3)).

He is also entitled to disclaim onerous property (qv), although the previous power which he had to elect not to take leasehold property has been abolished. If he does not expressly disclaim a contract to which the bankrupt was previously a party, the Official Assignee becomes entitled to the contractual rights and obligations under the contract and new terms cannot be implied or inserted by the court: In re Casey, a Bankrupt (1991 SC) ILRM 385. He is not a trustee for the purposes of the Statute of Limitations (ibid s.133). [Text: Holohan & Sanfey]. See ARRANGING DEBTOR; BANKRUPTCY; NOVATION.

**Official Journal of EC.** The publication of the EC dealing with legislation and communications.

**official journal of patents office.** See PATENTS OFFICE JOURNAL.

**official language.** See LANGUAGE.

**official liquidator.** A liquidator appointed by the court. See LIQUIDATOR; WINDING UP.

**official search.** A search made in the Registry of Deeds to discover the existence of all deeds and conveyances affecting unregistered land. It may be a *common* search or a *negative* search, the certificate arising from the latter being signed by the Registrar and Assistant Registrar, who are both liable to a party aggrieved in respect of any fraud, collusion or negligence in the making of such negative search. See DEEDS, REGISTRATION OF.

**official secret.** Information of a military nature or any other matter which prejudices the safety of the State; it is an offence to give or to get or to possess or publish any such information: Official Secrets Act 1963. See also The AG for

England and Wales v Brandon Books (1987) ILRM 135. See also SPYING.

**officious bystander test.** The common law test which may imply a term in a contract. The test is whether the parties at the time they were making their bargain, would have agreed *of course* to a suggested express provision from an officious bystander. See Tradax (Ireland) Ltd v Irish Grain Board Ltd (1983) IR 1.

**off-licence.** A licence for the sale of intoxicating liquor for consumption off the premises. Where licences are offered to be extinguished in substitution for new licences, they must be of the same character eg an on-licence will not substitute for an off-licence even though it might be regarded as "greater" or "more extensive": O'Rourke & Flanagan v Grittar (1990 HC) ILRM 877. See Power Supermarkets v O'Shea (1988) IR 206. See also Beer Retailers Spirit Grocers Retail Licensing (Ireland) Act 1900; Licensing Ireland Act 1902; Intoxicating Liquor Act 1960 s.13. See BAR.

**offshore installation.** Any installation which is or has been maintained, or is intended to be established, for the exploration for or exploitation of minerals and includes any installation providing accommodation for persons who work on or from any such offshore installation so engaged in exploration or exploitation of minerals: Safety, Health and Welfare (Offshore Installations) Act 1987. Previously, workers on offshore installations were protected by the terms of petroleum prospecting licences issued under the provisions of the Petroleum and Other Minerals Development Act 1960. Certain sections of the 1987 Act are repealed when particular sections of the Safety, Health and Welfare at Work Act 1989 come into force.

**oil pollution.** Owners of ships carrying oil in bulk as cargo have *strict liability* (qv) for pollution and damage except where the discharge of oil which caused the damage resulted from an act of war or a natural phenomenon of an exceptional, inevitable or irresistible character, or was due to the act of a third party with intent to do damage, or by the failure of the authorities to maintain navigational aids: Oil Pollution of the Sea (Civil Liability and Compensation) Act 1988 as amended by the Sea Pollution Act 1991 s.37. The 1988 Act gives effect in the State to a number of International Civil Liability Conventions. See SEA POLLUTION.

**Oireachtas.** The national parliament consisting of the President (qv) and two houses, a house of representatives called Dail Eireann (qv) and a senate called Seanad Eireann (qv); the sole and exclusive power of making laws for the State is vested in the Oireachtas: 1937 Constitution, art.15. Members of both houses are privileged from arrest in going to or coming from, and while in the precincts of either House, except in the case of treason, felony or breach of the peace (qqv) (ibid art.15(13)). Certain persons are disqualified from election to either Houses of the Oireachtas eg an undischarged bankrupt: Electoral Act 1992 s.41.

Provision has been made in the Maastricht Treaty 1992, by way of Declaration, of steps to ensure that national parliaments of the EC are better informed eg by ensuring that national parliaments receive Commission proposals for legislation in good time for information or possible examination: Declaration (13) on the Role of National Parliaments in the European Union. See ACT; BILL; COMMUNITY LAW; GOVERNMENT; PRIVILEGE.

**ombudsman.** The office holder, independent in the performance of his functions, appointed by the President of Ireland (qv), with power to investigate administrative actions by public bodies which adversely affect some person: Ombudsman Act 1980 ss.2-3. The ombudsman may investigate any action where it appears to him that the action may have been: taken without proper authority; taken on irrelevant grounds; the result of negligence or carelessness; based on erroneous or incomplete information; improperly discriminatory; based on an undesireable administrative practice; or otherwise contrary to sound or fair administration (ibid s.4(2)(b)).

It must appear to the ombudsman that the action has or may have adversely affected some persons and if the investigation is initiated by way of complaint, rather than by the ombudsman of his own motion, the complainant must have, in the ombudsman's opinion, a sufficient interest in the matter (ibid s.4(2)(a), (3), (9)).

The bodies, against whom the ombudsman may hear a complaint, include local authorities and health boards, most state-sponsored bodies, all departments of State, excluding the government itself (ibid s.4(2) and first schedule; SI No 332 of 1984; SIs 66 and 69 of 1985). See also Finance Act 1981 s.52; Ombudsman (Amendment) Act 1984. [Office of the Ombudsman, 52 St Stephens Green, Dublin 2. Tel: 6785222]. [Text: Hogan & Morgan].

**ombudsman for the credit institutions.** An independent and impartial arbitrator of unresolved complaints between a customer and his bank or building society. The ombudsman is appointed by the Council of the Credit Institutions to whom he is responsible. He is empowered to deal with most complaints (eg unfair treatment, uncorrected mistake, maladministration, negligence, poor service, breach of contract or confidentiality). He cannot deal with complaints which concern (a) a matter where the amount in dispute is more than £25,000, (b) a limited company, (c) the commercial judgement or policy of the bank or building society or its discretion under a will or trust.

He has power to award compensation of up to £25,000 and to give such directions to a bank or building society as will do justice between the parties, which award or direction is binding on the bank or building society but not on the customer who may pursue a legal remedy. This non-statutory scheme was established in 1990. [The Ombudsman for Credit Institutions, 8 Adelaide Court, Adelaide Road, Dublin 2. Tel: 4783755. Fax: 4780157].

**ombudsman, European.** Provision is made for the appointment of an independent ombudsman by the European Parliament to receive complaints from any citizen of the EC or any natural or legal person residing in a member State concerning instances of maladministration in the activities of the Community institutions or bodies, with the exception of the Court of Justice and the Court of First Instance acting in their judicial role: Treaty of Rome 1957 art.138e inserted by Maastricht Treaty 1992

art.G(E)(41).

**ombudsman, insurance.** See INSURANCE OMBUDSMAN.

**omission.** A failure to do something. It may amount to the tort of negligence (qv) where a duty existed to do that something. It may also constitute the *actus reus* (qv) in a crime. See NONFEASANCE.

**omne quod solo inaedificatur solo cedit.** [Everything which is built into the soil is merged therein]. See FIXTURES.

**omne testamentum morte consummatum est.** [Every will is completed by death]. A will is ambulatory until the death of the testator. See AMBULATORY.

**omnes licentiam habent his, quae pro se indulta sunt, renunciare.** [Everyone has liberty to renounce those things which are granted for his benefit].

**omnia praesumuntur legitime facta donec probetur in contrarium.** [All things are presumed to have been legitimately done unless the contrary is proved].

**omnia praesumuntur rite esse acta.** [All acts are presumed to have been done rightly]. This maxim will not be carried to such lengths as to nullify a statutory provision eg the formalities for execution of a will. The maxim cannot be relied on to dispense with formal proof that a doctor is a designated medical practitioner for the purposes of the Road Traffic Act 1978: DPP v O'Donoghue (1992 HC) 10 ILT Dig 74. See Clergy v Barry [1889] 21 LR Ir 152; In re McLean (1950) IR 180; Clarke v Early (1980) IR 223. See BEST EVIDENCE RULE; PRESUMPTION OF REGULARITY.

**omnibus.** A large *public service vehicle* (qv) which is for the time being used on a definite route for the carriage of passengers who are carried at separate fares and are picked up and set down along such routes whether on request or at fixed stopping places: Road Traffic Act 1961 s.3..

**on approval.** See APPROVAL, SALE ON.

**one man company.** A company which has a sole member; it must be a private company, limited by shares or by guarantee: EEC Directive 98/667/EEC (Twelfth Company Law Directive). The purpose of the Directive is to lay down uniform conditions under which single-member companies may be established throughout the European Community. See MacCann in 8ILT & SJ (1990) 166.

**onerous property.** (1) Property of a company being wound up which a liquidator may disclaim with the consent of the court: Companies Act 1963 s.290. It includes land of any tenure burdened by onerous covenants, or unprofitable contracts, property which is unsaleable or not readily saleable. A supplier is entitled to prove as a creditor for the loss sustained by the supplier by reason of the disclaimer: In re Ranks (Ir) Ltd (1988) ILRM 751. See in re Farm Machinery Distributors Ltd (1984) ILRM 273. See RSC O.74 rr.84-85. See also TRANSMISSION OF SHARES.

(2) The Official Assignee (qv) in bankruptcy is empowered to disclaim onerous property of the bankrupt with the leave of the court, eg land with onerous covenants, shares or stocks in companies, unprofitable contracts, property which is unsaleable or not readily saleable: Bankruptcy Act 1988 s.56. See BANKRUPTCY; OFFICIAL ASSIGNEE; REPUDIATION.

**onus of proof.** See BURDEN OF PROOF.

**onus probandi.** [The burden of proof (qv)].

**on-the-spot fine.** A monetary penalty in respect of an alleged offence, which if not paid within a specified period, will lead to a prosecution for the offence eg parking offences. Local authorities are empowered to introduce on-the-spot fines for litter offences: Litter Act 1982 s.5. See also Road Transport Act 1986 s.13; Road Traffic Act 1961 s.103 as amended by the Road Traffic Act 1968 ss.6 and 64; Finance Act 1976 s.74. Dublin Bus introduced on-the-spot fines in 1990 for failing to pay the appropriate fare. See LITTER.

**op cit; opera citato.** [In the work quoted]. The book previously cited.

**open contract.** A contract for the sale of land which is left *open* as to title (qv), in which case the law defines the extent of the vendor's duty as to the length of *title* which he must show. However, it is usual for a contract to be a *closed* one ie where the title to be shown is clearly defined. See MARKETABLE TITLE.

**open court.** See PUBLIC JUSTICE.

**open justice.** See PUBLIC JUSTICE.

**open season.** The period during which it is lawful to hunt game (qv) with firearms, provided the person so hunting has a licence therefor. The duration of the period is specified in an order made by the Minister. See Wildlife Act 1976.

**open space.** Land which is required to be provided or maintained as *open space* as part of a condition to the grant of planning permission (qv) for the development of land; a planning authority (qv) has the power to serve a notice on the owner of such land, requiring him to take such steps, in the nature of levelling or planting the land, as are necessary to make it suitable for open space purposes: LG(P&D) Act 1976 s.25. If the owner fails to comply with such a request, the planning authority may acquire the land compulsorily by means of a *vesting order* (qv). See SI No 226 of 1976.

**opening speech.** See RIGHT TO BEGIN.

**operative mistake.** See MISTAKE.

**operative part.** The part of a deed which carries out the main object as opposed to the recitals (qv). The operative part in a conveyence consists of the testatum, the consideration, the receipt clause, and the operative words.

**operative words.** The words which in a deed, create or transfer an estate. See WORDS OF LIMITATION.

**opinion.** The opinions of witnesses are generally irrelevant and inadmissible; a witness is required to give evidence of facts which he observed, it being left to the court to draw inferences from the facts, to form opinions and to come to conclusions. The exceptions are: opinions of experts; opinion as to the identity of a person; opinion as to handwriting by a person *acquainted* with the handwriting; opinion of a garda as to intoxication: AG v Kenny (1960) 94 ILTR 185; DPP v Donoghue (1987) ILRM 129. See also The People (Attorney General) v McGeogh (1969) CCA. See EXPERT OPINION.

**opinion, freedom to express.** See EXPRESSION, FREEDOM OF.

**opinions, EC.** See COMMUNITY LAW.

**opium poppy.** A plant of the species *papaver somniferum L* or *papaver bracteatum lindl*: Misuse of Drugs Act 1984 s.2. See CANNABIS.

**oppression of shareholder.** Any *member* of a company who complains that the affairs of the company are being conducted or that the powers of the directors are being exercised in a manner oppressive to him or any of the members, or in disregard of his or their interests as members, may apply to the court for intervention: Companies Act 1963 s.205. *Oppression* has been defined as "burdensome, harsh and wrongful"; the court will look at the business realities of the situation as opposed to the narrow legalistic view.

Where the court is of the opinion that there is oppression, it is empowered to make such order as it deems fit with a view to bringing to an end the matters complained of (ibid s.205(3)) or it may order that the company be wound up (ibid s.213(g)). Following an investigation of a company, the Minister may apply to the court for an order against oppression (ibid s.205(2)).

Only those who come within the definition of *member* in s.31 of the 1963 Act may present a petition under s.205(1): O'Tuama v Allied Metropole Hotel Ltd as reported in 7ILT & SJ (1989) 195. In relation to whether such a petition may be held *in camera*, consideration must be given to the obligation under the Constitution art.34(1) to admininster justice in public: ibid s.205(7) and In re R Ltd (1989) ILRM 757.

Complaints concerning the conduct of the affairs of a company which is under the *protection of the court* cannot constitute a basis for the making of an order for relief under s.205: Companies (Amendment) Act 1990 s.5 as amended by Companies Act 1990 s.180(1)(b). See also Scottish Co-op Wholesale Society v Meyer (1959) AC 324; In re Clubman Shirts Ltd (1983) ILRM 323; In re Murph's Restaurants Ltd (No 2) (1979) ILRM 141; In re Greenore Trading Co (1980) HC; In re Williams Group (Tullamore) Ltd (1985) IR 613. A shareholder has no right to being a personal action in respect of the value of his shareholding resulting from damage to the company against the party who caused such damage: O'Neill v Ryan (1993 SC) ILRM 557. See COURT PROTECTION OF COMPANY; FOSS v HARBOTTLE, RULE IN; PETITION FOR WINDING UP; SHARES, COMPULSORY PURCHASE OF; WINDING UP, COMPULSORY.

**oppressive proceedings.** A court has an inherent jurisdiction to *stay* oppressive proceedings which are an abuse of the process of the court eg McGinn v Beegan (1962) IR 364. See ABUSE OF PROCESS; MALICIOUS PROSECUTION.

**optima legum interpres est consuetudo.** [Custom is the best interpreter of the law]. See CUSTOM AND PRACTICE.

**optimus interpres rerum usus.** [The best interpreter of things is usage]. See CUSTOM AND PRACTICE.

**option.** A right of choice. A right conferred by agreement to buy or not any property within a certain time. A right, which may be acquired by contract, to accept or reject a present offer within a given period of time. An *option* is also a right to call for delivery or to make delivery of a specified number of shares or debentures at a specified price and within a specified time (eg *put* and *call*); it is an offence for a director of a company to deal in options to buy or sell listed shares or debentures in the company: Companies Act 1990 s.30. See FIRST REFUSAL; REVOCATION OF OFFER.

**oral agreement.** An agreement which is not reduced to writing or evidenced in writing. Certain oral agreements are unenforceable because they are required to be by deed (qv) or are required to be evidenced in writing under the Statute of Frauds (qv).

**oral agreement, modification of contract by.** A contract in writing may be rescinded or varied by an oral agreement. A contract under seal may be rescinded or varied by a simple contract (qv). However, a contract which is required by the Statute of Frauds to be evidenced in writing, can be rescinded but cannot be varied by an oral agreement: Morris v Barron (1919) AC 1. If a contract, required by statute to be in writing, is varied by oral agreement, the contract can be enforced in its original form, the oral agreement being discarded. See VARIATION.

**oral evidence.** See VIVA VOCE.

**oral smokeless tobacco product.** Any product or substance, made wholly or partly from tobacco, which is intended for use, unlit, by being placed in the mouth and kept there for a period, or by being placed in the mouth and sucked or chewed: Tobacco (Health Promotion and Protection) Act 1988 s.6. Under the

Act, it is offence for any person to import, manufacture, sell or dispose of, or to offer for sale or other disposal, or advertise, an oral smokeless tobacco product. See United States Tobacco (Ireland) Ltd v Minister for Health (1991 HC).

**oral will.** See NUNCUPATIVE WILL.

**order.** (1) A direction or command of the court. A final order of a court which has been perfected can be amended by the court but only in special or unusual circumstances: Belville Holdings Ltd (in Receivership) v Revenue Commissioners (1993 SC) ITLR (3 May). A court can only interfere after the passing and entering of a judgment where there is an accidental slip in the judgment or if the judgment as drawn up does not accurately state what the court actually decided: Ainsworth v Wilding (1895) 1 Ch 673. See also In re Swire (1885) 30 Ch D 239. See SLIP RULE.

(2) The code of procedure of the Superior Courts and the Circuit Court consists of *orders*, subdivided into *rules*. See RSC; RCC.

**order bill.** A bill of exchange payable to order, or which is expressed to be payable to a particular person, or does not contain words prohibiting transfer. An *order* bill is negotiated by an endorsement coupled with delivery, whereas a *bearer* bill is negotiated by delivery alone. See Bills of Exchange Act 1882 s.8(4) and 34. See BEARER BILL; BILL OF EXCHANGE; ENDORSEMENT.

**order for protection.** See ARRANGING DEBTOR.

**order for sale.** See MORTGAGEE, RIGHTS OF.

**orders, obedience to.** See OBEDIENCE TO ORDERS, DEFENCE OF.

**ordinary resolution.** See RESOLUTION.

**ordinary shares.** Shares in a company which do not have any preferential rights attaching to them and which attract dividends after payments are made to the preferential shareholders and debenture-holders. The holders of ordinary shares are regarded as the owners of the equitable interest in the company, as contrasted with the secured lenders, and consequently ordinary shares are often known as *equities* and are traded on the Stock Exchange (qv). See SHARES.

**ordre public.** [Public policy (qv)].

**organisation, unlawful.** See UNLAWFUL ORGANISATION.

**original.** For the purpose of copyright, only *original* literary, dramatic, musical and artistic work is protected. To be *original*, the work must be the result of at least a substantial amount of independent skill, knowledge or creative labour. If the work is partly derived from an earlier work, the later work will be entitled to copyright protection in its own right, although the author may need to obtain a licence from the earlier copyright owner. See COPYRIGHT.

**original jurisdiction.** See JURISDICTION.

**originating summons.** A summons by which civil proceedings in the High Court is instituted. A *plenary* summons is an originating summons for plenary proceedings with pleadings and hearing on oral evidence. A *summary* summons (or a special summons, depending on the claim involved) is an originating summons for summary proceedings without pleadings and to be heard on affidavit with or without oral evidence. See RSC O.1-3. See SUMMONS, HIGH COURT.

**orphan.** A child whose parents are dead: Adoption Act 1952 s.3. An orphan also means a qualified child — (a) both of whose parents are dead, or (b) one of whose parents is dead or unknown, as the case may be, and whose other parent — (i) is unknown, or (ii) has abandoned him, or (iii) has refused or failed to provide for him, where that child is not normally residing with a step-parent or with a person who is married to and living with that step-parent: Social Welfare (Consolidation) Act 1981 s.2(1) as amended by Social Welfare Act 1992 s.15. See FRIENDLY SOCIETY; CHILD AT RISK; WELFARE OF CHILDREN.

**orse.** [Otherwise].

**ostensible authority.** Apparent authority. See Kett v Shannon (1987) ILRM 365.

**oust.** To bar, exclude, eject, dispossess.

**ouster le main.** [Out of hand].

**ouster of jurisdiction.** Removal from the court of its power to hear and determine an action or case. The jurisdiction of the District Court is ousted if, in giving a decision on the case before it, it is called upon to adjudicate on a dispute of title to real property. This rule of law however, does not prevent the District Court trying offences under the Criminal Damage Act 1991 (ibid s.8).

**outgoings.** The necessary expenses and charges which the *receiver* of mortgaged property is required to discharge: Conveyancing Act 1881 s.24(8). See RECEIVER OF MORTGAGED PROPERTY.

**outline permission.** See PLANNING PERMISSION, APPLICATION FOR.

**out-patient services.** Institutional services other than *in-patient services* (qv) provided at, or by persons attached to, a hospital or home and institutional services provided at a laboratory, clinic, health centre or similar premises, but does not include — (a) the giving of any drug, medicine or other preparation except where it is administered direct by the person providing the service or is for psychiatric treatment, or (b) dental, ophthalmic or aural services: Health Act 1970 s.56(1). Charges may be imposed for these services, see Health (Amendment) Acts 1986 and 1987. See also SI Nos 51 and 178 of 1993.

**out-worker.** A person to whom articles or materials are given to be made up, cleaned, washed, altered, ornamented, finished or repaired or adapted for sale in his own house or another premises not under the control or management of the person who gave out the articles or material: Social Welfare (Consolidation) Act 1981, first schedule, para 7. While out-work is an insurable employment, some employment protection legislation does not apply to it eg Holiday (Employees) Act 1973. Whether an outworker is an employee or is on a contract for services is a matter to be determined by the contractual terms. See Minister for Industry v Healy (1941) IR 545.

**overcrowded house.** A house is deemed to be *over-crowded* at any time when the number of persons ordinarily sleeping in the house and the number of rooms therein either (a) are such that any two of those persons, being persons of ten years of age or more of opposite sexes and not being persons living together as husband and wife, must sleep in the same room, or (b) are such that the free air space in any room used as a sleeping apartment for any person is less than four hundred cubic feet (disregarding any height over eight feet): Housing Act 1966 s.63.

It is an offence for the owner of such a house to fail to comply with a notice served on him by the housing authority requiring him to desist from causing or permitting the overcrowding (ibid s.65).

**overdraft.** A loan from a bank to a customer effected by permitting the customer's current account to go into debit. On a current account a cause of action accrues against the debtor in respect of any sum advanced from the date of the advance: Parr's Banking Co v Yates (1898) 2 QB 460. A banker must make a demand before pursuing on an overdrawn current account: Joachimson v Swiss Banking Corporation (1921) 3 KB 112. A cause of action against the guarantor of a current account does not accrue until demand is made: Bank of Ireland v O'Keeffe (1987) IR 47. See also Doyle in 8ILT & SJ (1990) 169. See CHEQUE, DRAWING OF; CLAYTON'S CASE.

**overdue bill.** A bill of exchange (qv) which remains in circulation when the time for its payment has passed or, if it is payable on demand, when it appears to have been in circulation for an unreasonable length of time: Bills of Exchange Act 1882 s.36(3). A person who takes an overdue bill takes it subject to the equities of prior holders (ibid s.36(2)).

**overdue cheque.** See CHEQUE, OVERDUE.

**overreaching conveyance.** A conveyance which enables the owner of an estate to transfer it free from equitable interests or charges to which it is otherwise subject, such interests being shifted from the land to the purchase money eg on the sale of land held on trust, the equitable interest is transferred from the land to the money in the trustee's hands. Overreaching also occurs in settled land when the tenant for life transfers the *fee simple* freed and discharged from all the various estates attaching to the land by or under the settlement. See Connolly v Keating (No 1) (1903) 1 IR 353.

**overriding interests.** The burdens which affect registered land whether they are registered or not eg rights of the public, rights acquired under the Statute of Limitations, rights of persons in actual occupation of the land. See Registration of Title Act 1964 s.72.

**overt.** Open eg as in overt act and market overt (qv).

**overtaking.** A driver of a vehicle must not overtake, or attempt to overtake, if to do so would endanger, or cause inconvenience to, any other person: Road Traffic General Bye-Laws 1964 (SI No 294 of 1964) art.19.

**overtime.** Hours of work in excess of normal hours for which a premium payment is usually paid by agreement. An employee cannot recover for overtime worked in excess of the limit set by legislation: Martin v Galbraith (1942) IR 37. Dismissal for failing to work overtime in excess of the legal limit is an unfair dismissal (qv): Thornton v Coolock Foods Ltd (1990) ELR 40. Requests to work overtime must be reasonable: Holgate v Coolock Foods Ltd (1990 EAT) ELR 91. Notice of a requirement to work overtime given at the normal finishing time is unreasonable: Murray v Mohan (1990) ELR 238. A refusal to work overtime in breach of a contract to do so, is a ground for dismissal: McKenna v Farrell Bros (1991 EAT) ELR 77. See WORKING HOURS; WORKING TIME DIRECTIVE.

**over-insurance.** Where the aggregate of all the insurance contracted for exceeds the total value of the insured's interests which are at risk.

**over-rule.** To set aside eg when a higher court overrules a decision of a lower court.

**ownership.** Right to the exclusive enjoyment of something; it does not necessarily depend on possession. Ownership may be *absolute* where it is without conditions and is complete, or it may be *restricted* where it is subject to some limitation. It may be *corporeal* where it is visible or tangible, or *incorporeal* eg a right to recover a debt, or an easement (qv). It may be *legal* or *equitable* depending on the title eg in a fee simple subject to a trust, the legal fee simple is vested in the trustee, whereas the equitable fee simple resides in the beneficiary. Ownership may also be *vested* where there is a present right to the ownership, or *contingent* where ownership awaits or depends on the happening of an event. Ownership may also be *concurrent* (qv). See GOODS, PROPERTY IN; POSSESSION.

**ozone layer.** There are control measures in the EC to counter depletion of the ozone layer: Council Resolution 594/91. These are equivalent to, or more stringent than, the international measures agreed in the Montreal Protocol on Substances that Deplete the Ozone Layer (June 1990) as amended in December 1991.

# P

**pace.** [By permission or consent of].

**package.** A bag, bottle, box, case, carton, envelope, net, sack or wrapper containing anything which is the subject of trade, manufacture or merchandise: Packaged Goods (Quality Control) Act 1980. There are provisions in this Act imposing duties on packers and importers as regards the quantity of goods included in and the marking of a package, which has been made up otherwise than in the presence of the person purchasing the package, and is a package the contents of which cannot be removed without opening it (ibid Part II). There are also provisions regarding the marking of an *e-mark* (qv) on a package.

**pact.** An agreement; a contract; a treaty between states.

**pacta dant legem contractui.** [Agreements constitute the law of contract].

**pacta sunt servanda.** [Contracts are to be kept].

**pain and suffering, damages for.** Compensation may be awarded for pain and suffering experienced by a person injured as a result of the tort (qv) of another. Compensation may be given for future, as well as past and present pain and suffering, including that which may accompany or result from a medical operation which is reasonably necessary to perform. See Sexton v O'Keeffe (1966) IR 204. See AMENITY, LOSS OF; DISFIGUREMENT; GENERAL DAMAGES; NERVOUS SHOCK.

**painter.** See ARTIST, TAX EXEMPTION OF; HUNT.

**pais.** See IN PAIS.

**palm prints.** See FINGERPRINTS.

**panel.** The list of persons who have been summoned to serve as jurors. See JURY.

**par.** The par value of a company's share is the *nominal* or theoretical specific value of the share contained in its memorandum of association. The authorised or *nominal capital* of a company is the aggregate par value of the shares which its memorandum permits it to issue to subscribers. See PREMIUM; SHARES.

**paramount.** Superior.

**paraphernalia.** The apparel, ornaments and gifts given by a husband to his wife. See MATRIMONIAL PROPERTY.

**parcels.** (1) Parts or plots of land. (2) The part of a conveyance of land, following the operative words (qv), which describes the property and often refers to a plan drawn on the deed.

**parcenary.** Coparcenary (qv).

**pardon.** The excusing of an offence or remission of a punishment. The right of pardon and the power to commute or remit punishment imposed by a court exercising criminal jurisdiction is vested in the President of Ireland: 1937 Constitution, art.13(6). This right or power may, except in capital murder (qv), also be conferred by law on other authorities; the government is given such powers which it may delegate to the Minister: Criminal Justice Act 1951.

It appears that only three Presidential pardons have been granted in the history of the State to remedy miscarriages of justice: Thomas Quinn in December 1940; Walter Brady in February 1943 — both granted by President Douglas Hyde; and Edward (Nicky) Kelly in April 1992 — granted by President Mary Robinson. The effect of the pardon granted to Mr Kelly was "to put him in the same position as he would have been if he had not been convicted of the charges in question": Government Statement. See MISCARRIAGE.

**parens patriae.** [Parent of his country]. Expression used to describe the Attorney General (qv) when he acts on behalf of the community to ensure that the law is enforced eg to prevent an abortion taking place. See AG v X (1992) ILRM 401.

**parent.** Father or mother of another. A birth certificate is admissible in criminal proceedings as evidence of the relationship of the father or mother named therein to the person to whose birth the certificate relates: Criminal Evidence Act 1992 s.5(5). See CORPORAL PUNISHMENT; LONE PARENT.

**parentage, declaration of.** A declaration by the Circuit Family Court that a named person is the parent of the applicant: Status of Children Act 1987 ss.34-36. Applications for such a declaration are confined to persons born in the State and any other person who can show good and proper reason for applying (ibid s.35). In keeping with the policy of the Adoption Acts which secures confidentiality in regard to natural parents, applications will not be accepted from adopted children.

The court will grant the declaration sought where the fact of parentage is proved on the balance of probability. See Legitimacy Declaration Act (Ireland) 1868 for similar declaration which was available to legitimate or legitimated children but not to children whose parents were not or had not been married to each other. See District Court (Status of Children Act 1987) Rules 1988 (SI No 152 of 1988). See BLOOD TEST; BIRTH, REGISTRATION OF; GENETIC FINGERPRINTING; PATERNITY, PRESUMPTION OF.

**parental rights, abandonment of.** See ADOPTION.

**pares.** Equals; peers.

**pari passu.** [With equal step]. Equally; without preference. Shares in a company of a particular class rank *pari passu* for all purposes with shares of the same class: Companies Act 1963 s.80(2). The property of a company in a voluntary winding up is applied in satisfaction of its liabilities *pari passu* (ibid 1963 Act s.275 as amended by Companies Act 1990 s.132). See CLASS RIGHTS; SUBORDINATION.

**Paris Convention.** The International Convention for the Protection of Industrial Property signed in Paris in 1883 and revised on a number of occasions. Ireland formally acceded to the Convention as Saorstat Eireann on 4th December 1925. The Convention provides that, as regards the protection of industrial property, every member country will afford to nationals of other member countries the same protection as it affords to its own nationals and that the filing of an application for a *patent* in one member country gives a *right of priority* to the date of that filing in respect of corresponding applications filed in other member countries within 12 months of that date. The Patents Act 1992 s.25 provides for such *convention applications* (qv).

The Paris Convention also provides for reciprocity of treatment as between proprietors of *trade marks* in the different states which have ratified the Convention. Where a person has applied in a foreign state (which is a party to any international agreement for the mutual protection of trade marks to which the State is a party) for protection of a trade mark, the person is entitled to registration in the State of that trade mark in priority to other applicants and the registration shall have the same date as the date of the application in the foreign state, provided the application is made within 6 months: Trade Marks Act 1967 s.70. See TRADEMARK; PATENT CO-OPERATION TREATY; EUROPEAN PATENT CONVENTION; WORLD INTELLECTUAL PROPERTY ORGANISATION.

**parium judicium.** [Judgment of one's peers]. See JURY.

**park.** In relation to a vehicle, means kept or leave stationary, and cognate words are construed accordingly: Road Traffic Act 1961 s.3. See DPP v Clancy (1986) ILRM 268. See PARKING, DANGEROUS; PARKS, PUBLIC; TRAFFIC REGULATION.

**parking, dangerous.** It is an offence for a person to *park* (qv) a vehicle in a *public place* if, when so parked, the vehicle would be likely to cause danger to other persons using that place: Road Traffic Act 1961 s.55 as amended by the Road Traffic Act 1968 s.52. See PUBLIC PLACE.

**parks, public.** Local authorities are empowered to acquire land compulsorily for the provision of recreation grounds: Local Government (Ireland) Act 1898 s.36. The development plan (qv) of a planning authority may indicate the objective of reserving, as a public park, public garden or public recreation space, land normally used as such: 1963 Act s.19(3), third schedule, part iv, para 2. Conditions may be imposed on a grant of planning permission, without creating a right to compensation, which reserves as a public park, public garden or public recreation space, land normally used as such: LG (P&D) Act 1990 s.12 and Fourth Schedule para 14. See also SI No 65 of 1977, class 26. See NATIONAL PARK.

**parliament.** See EUROPEAN PARLIAMENT; NATIONAL PARLIAMENT.

**parliamentary franchise.** See FRANCHISE.

**parliamentary privilege.** The rights and immunities enjoyed by members of both Houses of the Oireachtas (qv) eg privilege from arrest in going to and from and while in the precincts of either House, freedom of debate, and privilege from defamation for utterances made in either House wherever published. See 1937 Constitution, art.15. See OIREACHTAS; UTTERANCE.

**parol.** Verbal or oral, not in writing or under seal (qv), eg a parol contract. See ORAL AGREEMENT.

**parole.** Release on licence of a prisoner who is serving a sentence. See RELEASE, TEMPORARY; PUNISHMENT.

**part A.** The part of the register kept at the Patents Office which contains registered trade marks, which, if valid, give the registered proprietor the exclusive right to the use of the mark in relation to the goods for which it is registered: Trade Marks Act 1963 s.12(1). The original registration is after the expiration of seven years from the date of that registration, deemed to be valid in all respects unless the registration was obtained by fraud, or the trade mark is likely to deceive or cause confusion, or is contrary to law or morality, or is of a scandalous design (ibid s.21). Contrast with PART B. See also TRADE MARK, REGISTERED.

**part B.** The part of the register kept at the Patents Office which contains registered trade marks, which give the registered proprietor the same rights given by registration in Part A (qv), with the exception that registration in Part B does not become immune from invalidity attack after seven years as it does in Part A: Trade Marks Act 1963 ss.13(1) and 22.

Additionally, the registered proprietor in Part B cannot obtain injunction or other relief from a defendant in an infringement action, if the defendant satisfies the Court that the use of the trade mark complained of is not likely to deceive or cause confusion or to be taken as indicating a connection in the *course of trade* (qv) between the goods and the person having the right as proprietor or as registered user of the trade mark (ibid s.13(2)). See Bismag

Ltd v Ambline (Chemists) Ltd (1940) 57 RPC 209; Winthrop Group v Farbenfabriken Bayer AG (1976) RPC 469; Eurocard International v Controller of Trade Marks (1987) HC; Miller Brewing Co v Controller of Trade Marks (1988) ILRM 259. See TRADE MARK, REGISTERED.

**part-payment.** See SALE.

**part-performance.** The equitable doctrine whereby a defendant will not be permitted to escape from a contract relating to land by pleading the absence of a memorandum in writing as required by the Statute of Frauds (qv), where the plaintiff has partly performed the contract in the expectation that the defendant would perform his part. See MEMORANDUM, STATUTE OF FRAUDS; QUANTUM MERUIT; UNENFORCEABLE.

**part-time worker.** A *regular part-time worker* is an employee who is normally expected to work for at least eight hours a week and who has completed thirteen weeks service: Worker Protection (Regular Part-Time Employees) Act 1991. Regular part-time workers now enjoy the same protection generally as full-time workers ie as regards redundancy, minimum notice, worker participation, unfair dismissal, maternity, employers' insolvency, and holidays legislation. The Minister is empowered to make regulations setting out the details of social welfare entitlements of part-time workers: Social Welfare Act 1991 ss.18-20. See Barry in 9ILT & SJ (1991) 26. See SOCIAL POLICY; UNFAIR DISMISSAL.

**particeps criminis.** [A person who shares in a crime]. An accomplice (qv).

**participation.** See WORKER PARTICIPATION.

**particular average.** See AVERAGE.

**particular estate.** An estate less than the fee simple (qv) ie given for a particular length of time. It is a term used to refer to an estate granted out of a larger estate.

**particulars, land.** The precise physical description of a property to be sold by auction (qv) and a short statement of the nature of the title; these are usually fixed by the auctioneer (qv) following instructions by the vendor's solicitor (qv). See CONDITIONS OF SALE; SALE OF LAND.

**particulars, pleadings.** The details of a claim or a defence in an action which are necessary for a party to know the case he has to meet. A party may by

letter apply to the other party for a full and better statement of the nature of the claim or defence or of *further and better particulars* of any matter stated in any pleadings or notice; the court may order such statement or particulars upon such terms, including costs, as may be just and will take into consideration such letter, but will not normally order such statement or particulars to be given before defence or reply: RSC O.19 r.6.

It has been held that the delivery of a notice for particulars does not prevent a defendant from raising the issue of jurisdiction of the court to hear the action: Campbell International Trading House Ltd v Peter van Aart and Natur Pur gmbh (1992 SC) ILRM 663.

For provisions regarding particulars in Circuit Court proceedings, see RCC O.14. See also "Summary Procedure and the Use of Particulars" - Doyle in 7ILT & SJ (1989) 201. See Cooney v Browne (1986) ILRM 444; Brennan v Kelly (1988) ILRM 306. See PLEADINGS; TRAVERSE.

**partition.** (1) The division of a country into two or more separate nations. See NORTHERN IRELAND.

(2) The division of land owned by persons jointly among the owners in severalty (qv). Co-owners may partition by consent of the other co-owners by deed: Real Property Act 1845. A co-owner may without the consent of his co-owners apply to the court for partition: Partition Acts 1868 and 1876. The court has power to order a sale with division of the proceeds as an alternative to partition (ibid 1868 Act ss.3 and 4 as amended). The Court also has power to order partition of property on granting a decree of judicial separation (qv): Judicial Separation and Family Law Reform Act 1989 ss.16(1) and 30. See FF v CF (1987) ILRM 1. See RSC O.51 r.3; RCC O.6 r.14; O.45.

**partnership.** The relationship existing between two or more persons carrying on business in common with a view of profit: Partnership Act 1890 s.1. *Business* means a series of acts which, if successful, will produce profit or gain; it includes every trade, occupation or profession; *person* means a legal person and includes human and artificial or corporate persons. There are rules in s.2 for determining if a partnership exists.

The essential difference between a partnership and a company is that the former has no legal personality, whereas a company is a body corporate. The property of a partnership firm belongs to the individual members; they are collectively entitled to it; whereas the property of a company belongs to the company. Creditors of a partnership firm are creditors of the members of the firm and on a judgment can levy execution on the property of the partners of the firm; whereas, judgment against a company ordinarily gives no right to levy execution against the members. A partner cannot contract with his firm, whereas a member of a company can contract with the company.

There are two types of partnership: the *ordinary partnership* which is governed by the Partnership Act 1890 and the *limited partnership* formed under the Limited Partnership Act 1907. The ordinary partnership is an important feature in the State, particularly in the field of the professions; however very few limited partnerships are formed. The rights of partners, between themselves, are governed by the partnership agreement or contract or the deed of partnership or partnership articles, if any.

A formal document is not necessary to create a partnership; there may be an implied partnership from the acts of the parties thereto: see Greenham v Gray (1855) 4 ICLR 501. The receipt by a person of a share in the profits of a business is prima facie evidence that he is a partner in the business, but the receipt of a share or payment contingent or varying with the profits does not of itself make someone a partner in a business: O'Kelly v Darragh (1988) ILRM 309.

See Macken v Revenue Commissioners (1962) IR 302; Meagher v Meagher (1961) IR 96; Williams v Harris (1980) SC. See also RSC O.46 rr.3-4. [Text: Keane (1); O'Malley & Courtney; Lindley (UK); Palmer (UK)]. See FIRM; LIMITED PARTNERSHIP.

**partnership, bankruptcy and.** One or more partners may be adjudicated a bankrupt on the presentation of a petition by a creditor whose debt is sufficient ie £1,500: Bankruptcy Act 1988 ss.31 and 8. An adjudication may not be made against the firm, (even though it is permissible to take proceedings or be proceeded against in the name of the firm), but such adjudication will be made against the partner(s) individually with the addition of the firm name (ibid s.36).

The bankrupt partner must deliver to the Official Assignee (qv) a separate *statement of affairs* in respect of the partnership, and the other partners must also deliver such accounts and information as the Official Assignee deems necessary (ibid ss.32-33).

The joint property of partners is applied in the first instance in payment of their joint debts, their separate property being applied to their separate debts. Where there is a surplus of the joint property, it is dealt with as part of the separate properties in proportion to the right and interest of each partner in the joint property. Where there is a surplus of any separate property it is dealt with as part of the joint property so far as necessary to meet any deficiency in the joint property (ibid s.34). See also 1988 Act ss.74, 106, and 138. See ARRANGING DEBTOR; BANKRUPTCY; LIMITED PARTNERSHIP.

**partnership, dissolution of.** Dissolution of a partnership takes place, in general, by agreement, by conduct, or by bankruptcy or death of one of the partners, or by intervening illegality, or by court order on the grounds of insanity, incapacity, misconduct of a partner, or where the court considers it just and equitable: Partnership Act 1890 ss.32-35; RSC O.76 r 43. The court has a discretion not to award costs, arising from a dissolution, out of the partnership assets: Baxter v Horgan (1992 SC) 10 ILT Dig 55.

Where no time limit of a partnership is fixed, it is called a *partnership at will* and may be dissolved by any partner at any time by giving notice (ibid s.26(1)). The High Court is empowered to wind up and settle the affairs of a partnership in which a bankrupt (qv) has an interest: Bankruptcy Act 1988 s.138. See Larkin v Groeger & Eaton 7 ILT Dig (1989) 53.

**partnership, liability in.** In an ordinary partnership, each partner is liable with unlimited liability for the debts of the partnership to the whole extent of his property. As between partners, each partner is bound to contribute to the debts in proportion to his share of the profits unless otherwise agreed. As regards third parties, the act of each partner, within the ordinary scope of the business, binds his co-partners whether they sanctioned it or not: Partnership Act 1890 s.5.

An act or instrument relating to the business of the firm and done or executed in the firms name, or in any other manner showing an intention to bind the firm, by any person so authorised, whether a partner or not, is binding on the firm and on all the partners (ibid s.6). See Allied Pharmaceutical Distributors Ltd v Robert J Kidney (1991) 2 IR 8. See FRAUD; LIMITED PARTNERSHIP.

**partnership, number to form.** The minimum number of persons who can form a partnership is two while the maximum number of a partnership formed for the purpose of carrying on business with the object of acquisition of gain is 20. There are important exceptions in the case of partnerships involving bankers, solicitor and accountants: Companies Act ss.372 and 376; Companies (Amendment) Act 1982 s.13.

**partridge.** See GAME.

**party.** A person who sues or is sued; a person who takes part in a legal transaction eg a party to a contract. A party also includes every person served with notice of or attending any proceedings, although not named on the record: RSC O.125 r.1. Where a bankrupt (qv) is a party to a contract jointly with any other person, that other person may sue or be sued in respect of the contract without joining the bankrupt: Bankruptcy Act 1988 s.35.

**party and party costs.** The costs incurred in contentious legal matters involving two or more parties, which were necessary or proper for the attainment of justice or for enforcing or defending the rights of the party whose costs are being *taxed*; the successful litigant is generally entitled to his costs on this basis. See RSC O.99 r.10. See COSTS IN CIVIL PROCEEDINGS; TAXATION OF COSTS.

**party wall.** The wall between adjoining properties. The general presumption at common law is that adjoining property owners are *tenants-in-common* (qv) of the party wall: Jones v Read (1876) IR 10 CL 315; Miley v Hutchinson (1940) Ir Jur Rep 37. This presumption can be rebutted eg by evidence that the wall was built entirely on one owner's land: Barry v Dowling (1968) HC. An owner is entitled to build a party wall (or banks, trenches, or fences) between adjoining lands and charge half the cost to his neighbour: Boundaries Act (Ireland) 1721. See also Dublin Corporation Act 1890 ss.3-5 and 9-12.

**pass book.** The book in which is recorded the amount invested by a saver in a bank or building society and also subsequent investments and withdrawals. A pass book entry does not on its own, give an investor a legal entitlement to the sum entered: Leen v Irish Permanent Building Society (1976) — Report of Registrar of Friendly Societies (1981) p.12.

**passenger.** A person who is carried in a conveyance for reward. Any person carried on a vessel (qv) other than (a) the owner or (b) a person to whom the vessel is on hire or (c) a person employed or engaged in any capacity on board the vessel or (d) a shipwrecked or distressed person: Merchant Shipping Act 1992 s.2(1). See also Merchant Shipping (Safety Convention) Act 1952 s.43. See PASSENGER BOAT; PASSENGER SHIP; SERVICE, SUPPLY OF.

**passenger boat.** A vessel carrying not more than 12 passengers for reward or on hire excluding a fishing vessel (qv) or a passenger ship (qv) with a certificate: Merchant Shipping Act 1992 s.2(1). A vessel must not be used as a passenger boat unless a licence is in force in respect of it (ibid s.14); the licence will specify the limits (if any) beyond which the vessel shall not ply and the maximum passengers that the vessel is fit to carry (ibid s.15). Where passengers are carried on board a vessel, there is a presumption that the carriage is for reward unless the contrary is proved (ibid s.32(2)). A passenger boat must have painted on it "licensed to carry .. passengers" (ibid s.17(2)). The Minister may make regulations for the purpose of ensuring the safety of passenger boats and their passengers and crew. See PASSENGER; SHIP.

**passenger road service .** A service

provided for separate charges in respect of each passenger; it is an offence to carry on such a service without a licence: Road Transport Act 1932. To constitute an offence the person who received the separate charges from each passenger is required to be the person who owned or otherwise controlled the vehicle: DPP v Go-Travel Ltd (1991 SC) ILRM 577.

**passenger ship.** A vessel carrying more than 12 passengers, excluding a fishing vessel (qv) or a vessel carrying passengers to or from the State; a vessel includes any ship or boat and any other vessel used in navigation: Merchant Shipping Act 1992 s.2(1). A vessel must not be used as a passenger ship unless a certificate is in force in relation to it (ibid s.12) and a policy of insurance is also in force (ibid s.13). There is also a requirement for a survey at least once a year (ibid s.6). The certificate will specify the limits (if any) beyond which the vessel shall not ply and the maximum passengers that the vessel may carry (ibid s.8). See PASSENGER; SHIP.

**passim.** [In various places; here and there]. Term used in relation to a reference appearing throughout a book.

**passing of Act.** The day of the *passing* of every Act is the day on which the Bill for such Act is signed by the President of Ireland: Interpretation Act 1937 s.8(1). See ACT.

**passing off.** A tort committed by a person who, in a manner calculated to deceive, passes off his goods or business as those of another eg by use of a similar name or trade mark (qv) or description or appearance. The remedies for a plaintiff are damages, an account, and an injunction to restrain the defendant for the future. Actual deception or an intention to deceive is not necessary to ground an action in passing off, but proof of such an intention or that a member of the consuming public has been deceived, will help the plaintiff's case. In relation to the name of goods, the test is whether the name used connotes goods manufactured or sold by another or is merely descriptive of the goods.

In relation to packaged goods, the court will consider the general *get up* of the packages; their size and shape; the material used; the combination of colours; the decoration and lettering; the arrangement of labels; the spacing of words; and the overall picture presented from the entire combination. See Polycell Products Ltd v O'Carroll (1959) Ir Jur Rep 34; American Cyanamid v Ethicon Ltd (1975) AC 396; C & A Modes v C & A (Waterford) Ltd (1976) IR 198; Adidas Sportsschuhfabriken Adi Dasler K A v Charles O'Neill & Co Ltd (1980) HC; Three Stripes International v Charles O'Neill & Co Ltd (1988) IR 144; Campus Oil Ltd v Minister for Energy (1983) IR 88; Falcon Travel Ltd v Owners Abroad Group plc (1991 HC) 1 IR 175 and Coughlan in 9ILT & SJ (1991) 138; Muckross Park Hotel v Randles & Dromhall Hotel Co Ltd (1992 HC). [Text: Wadlow UK]. See INFRINGE-MENT OF TRADE MARK; NAME OF COMPANY.

**passport.** A document which contains particulars which enables the holder to be identified and which is intended to allow the holder to pass from one country to another without let or hindrance. Responsibility for issuing passports and visas rests with the Department of Foreign Affairs: Ministers and Secretaries Act 1924 s.1 (xi).

A citizen has a constitutional right to a passport: The State (KM RD) v The Minister for Foreign Affairs (1979) IR 73. A citizen over 18 years of age will be granted a passport who complies with the application requirements eg identity and signature certified by a garda. A child will be included on a parent's passport but only with the consent of the other parent: Cosgrove v Ireland Ors (1982) ILRM 48. A child may be issued with a separate passport but only with the consent of both parents. See also (P)I v Ireland (1989 SC) ILRM 810.

The removal from the State of a child under seven years of age who is an Irish citizen is prohibited (a) without the approval of parents who are married to each other, or (b) without the approval of the mother, guardian or a maternal relation of the child where the child's parents are not married to each other: Adoption Act 1952 s.40. See also Child Care Act 1991 s.18(4). See BANGEMANN WAVE; PREINSPECTION; TRAVEL, RIGHT TO.

**past consideration.** See CONSIDERATION.

**pasturage.** The right to graze animals on the lands of another. See COLLOP; PROFIT A PRENDRE; RUNDALE SYSTEM.

**patent.** An exclusive right conferred pursuant to Part II and Part III of the Patents Act 1992 (ibid s.2(1)). A patent while it is in force confers on its proprietor the right to prevent all third parties from directly or indirectly using the subject matter of the patent (ibid ss.40-41). It is in effect a bargain between the State and the inventor, whereby he is given a monopoly right in his invention for a period of time, in return for the disclosure of his invention.

There are four classes of patent: (1) a *European patent* as granted by the European Patents Office under the European Patent Convention (EPC) which when granted is, in so far as Ireland has been designated, equivalent to an Irish patent; an "international application" under the Patent Cooperation Treaty (qv) which designates Ireland is deemed to be an application for a European Patent (ibid 1992 Act ss.119-132); (2) an *Irish Patent* granted by the Controller of Patents, Designs and Trade Marks and governed by Irish law which while closely modelled on the EPC is fully under the jurisdiction of the Irish Courts and Patents Office (ibid ss.6-62); (3) a *short-term Irish patent* with a different standard of inventive step required; and (4) a proposed *Community Patent* applicable to member States of the EC and subject to a common system of laws (1937 Constitution art.29(4)(6)).

Only certain inventions are patentable. Priority is given on the basis of the date of filing of an application for a patent or on a priority date arising from Ireland's membership of the Paris Convention (qv). The applicant must *disclose* the invention. The Controller of Patents publishes the notice of grant of a patent in the Patents Office Journal.

A patent may be subject to *licences of right* (qv) and there are provisions governing the issue of compulsory licences. A patent once granted can be revoked by the High Court. Renewal fees must be paid annually and there is an annual maintenance fee on pending applications. Infringement (qv) of a patent can be prevented by injunction and an action for damages.

Apart from the changes in the classes of patents, the main changes made by the 1992 legislation are (a) longer patent life (20 years instead of 16 years) and no extensions; (b) abolition of opposition to the grant of a patent, abolition of *patents of addition* and of *provisional* patent protection; (c) minimising of responsibility of Patents Office for examination; and (d) expansion of infringement of patent to include indirect use of an invention. See Patent Rules 1992 (SI No 179 of 1992). See Treaty of Rome 1957 art.85(1). [Text: Murdoch (1); Terrell UK]. See COMMUNITY PATENT AGREEMENT; EUROPEAN PATENT CONVENTION; EXCLUSIVE JURISDICTION; FOOD AND MEDICINE; INFRINGEMENT OF PATENT; PATENTABLE INVENTION; PATENT RIGHTS; PRIORITY DATE; REGISTER OF PATENTS; ROYALTY; SIMULTANEOUS INVENTION.

**patent, application for.** An application for a patent, must contain (a) a request for a grant of a patent; (b) a specification containing a description of the invention; and (c) an abstract: Patents Act 1992 ss.15, 18, 21, 22. The application, not necessarily from the inventor, must also *disclose* the invention in a manner sufficiently clear and complete for it to be carried out by a person skilled in the art (ibid s.19). The *claim* must define the matter for which protection is sought, be clear and concise and be supported by the description (ibid s.20). There are special provisions governing an application for a *short-term* patent (qv).

**patent, infringement of.** See INFRINGEMENT OF PATENT.

**patent, qualifying.** See QUALIFYING PATENT.

**patent, revocation of.** A patent may be revoked on the application of any person on the grounds that (a) the subject-matter of the patent is not patentable; (b) the specification of the patent does not disclosure the invention sufficiently; (c) the matter disclosed in the specification extends beyond that disclosed in the application as filed; (d) the patent protection has been extended by an amendment of the application or the specification; (e) the proprietor of the patent is not entitled to the patent grant: Patents Act 1992 ss.57-58. The Controller of Patents has power to revoke a patent on his own initiative eg lack of novelty apparent after grant, or duplication of patent with European Patent already granted (ibid s.60). A short-term patent (qv) may also be revoked. See Wavin Pipes Ltd v Hepworth Iron Co Ltd (1981) HC.

**patent, surrender of.** The proprietor of a patent may at any time by written notice given to the Controller of Patents offer to surrender his patent: Patents Act 1992 s.39. The patent ceases to have effect from the date when notice of acceptance is published in the Patents Office Journal (ibid s.39(5)). Opposition may be made eg by a licensee. See Patent Rules 1992 r.40 (SI No 179 of 1992).

**patent, term of.** See TERM OF PATENT.

**patent agent.** A person who carries on the business of acting as agent for others for the purpose, inter alia, of applying for patents. Any act which has to be done by or to any person in connection with a patent or any procedure relating to a patent or the obtaining thereof, the act may be done by or to an agent: Patents Act 1992 s.105(1). A person acting for gain must not, either alone or in partnership with any other person, practise, describe himself or hold himself out as a patent agent, unless he is registered as a patent agent in the register of patent agents, or as the case may be, unless he and all his partners are so registered (ibid s.106(2)(a)). There are similar provisions for a company practising as a patent agent.

There are similar prohibitions in relation to European Patents unless the agent is on the list of professional representatives, called European Patent Attorneys, maintained by the European Patents Office (ibid s.125).

As regards priviliged communications, a patent agent is a person registered as a patent agent, a company or partnership lawfully practising as a patent agent in the State or a person or partnership which satisfies the requirements of the European Patent Convention (ibid s.94(3)). See Register of Patent Agent Rules 1992 (SI No 180 of 1992).

**patent ambiguity.** See AMBIGUITY.

**Patent Co-operation Treaty; PCT.** The Treaty of 1970 which has as its object to simplify and render more economical the obtaining of protection for inventions where protection is sought in several countries (ibid art.1(2)). It is not intended to diminish rights under the Paris Convention (qv).

Under the Treaty, where patent protection is sought in a member of the contracting States, a single *international application* may be filed at one of the *receiving offices*, which will usually be the applicant's local national patent office, and the application will have a right of priority from the date of such filing.

A novelty search is carried out by an international search authority whose report is furnished to the national patent office in each country in which protection is sought and a grant of a patent is made under the authority of that national office.

Under Irish law, an international application under the PCT which designates the State is deemed to be an application for a European Patent designating the State; consequently it will only be possible to designate Ireland through a PCT application in the context of a European application: Patents Act 1992 s.127. See EUROPEAN PATENT AGREEMENT.

**patent defect.** See DEFECT.

**patent of addition.** Formerly, the patent which was granted where there had been an improvement in or modification of an invention for which a patent had been granted or applied for: Patents Act 1964 s.28. There is no provision for patents of addition in the Patents Act 1992 which repeals the 1964 Act.

**patent rights.** (1) The right conferred on the proprietor of a patent to prevent all third parties not having his consent from making various direct uses of the invention according as to whether the invention is a product, a process, or the product of a process: Patents Act 1992 s.40. The right is also conferred to prevent indirect use of the invention (ibid s.41). The rights do not extend to acts done for non-commercial purposes, or acts done for experimental purposes, or to prevent the free circulation throughout the EC of patented products put on the market in a member State by the proprietor (ibid ss.42-43). The extent of protection conferred by a patent is determined by the terms of the *claim* filed as part of the application for a patent (ibid s.45).

(2) The right to do or authorise the doing of anything which would, but for that right, be an infringement of a

patent: Income Tax Act 1967 s.284. See INFRINGEMENT OF PATENT.

**patent royalty.** See QUALIFYING PATENT; ROYALTY.

**patentable invention.** An invention to be patentable must be susceptible of *industrial application*, it must be *new* and must involve an *inventive step*: Patents Act 1992 s.9(1). An invention is considered susceptible of *industrial application* if it can be made or used in any kind of industry, including agriculture (ibid s.14). An invention will be considered *new* if it does not form part of the state of art, which comprises everything made available to the public (whether in the State or elsewhere) by means of a written or oral description, by use, or in any other way, before the date of filing of the patent application (ibid s.11). An invention will be considered as involving an *inventive step* if, having regard to the state of art, it is not obvious to a person skilled in the art (ibid s.13). There are special requirements in respect of a short-term patent (qv).

Any of the following are not to be regarded as an invention capable of being patented: (a) a discovery, a scientific theory or a mathematical method; (b) an aesthetic creation; (c) a scheme, rule or method for performing a mental act, playing a game or doing business, or a program for a computer; (d) the presentation of information; (e) a method (other than a product) for treatment of the human or animal body by surgery or therapy and a diagnostic method practised on human or animal body (ibid s.9). Also a patent cannot be granted in respect of a plant or animal variety (other than a microbiological process) or an invention the publication or exploitation of which would be contrary to public order or morality (ibid s.10). See SIMULTANEOUS INVENTION.

**patented.** The words *patent* or *patented* on a product without the number of the patent is ineffective to make a defendant in a patent infringement action aware that a patent has been obtained for the product: Patents Act 1992 s.49(1). A person is guilty of an offence, who falsely represents that an article sold by him is patented; it is sufficient for the offence that the article has on it the words *patent* or *patented* or any words expressing or

implying that the article is patented (ibid s.112). See INFRINGEMENT OF PATENT.

**patents office.** The office established by statute and continued in being for the registration of patents, designs and trade marks: Patents Act 1992 s.6. It is under the control of the Controller of Patents (qv).

**patents office journal.** The Journal in which is published by the Controller of Patents all matters which he is directed by law to publish in the Journal and also such matters and information as appear to him to be useful or important in relation to patents or applications for patents: Patents Act 1992 s.100. The Controller is required to publish a notice of all patent grants, including a specification of the patent containing the description and claims, and drawings if any (ibid s.34); and also entries in the register of licences of right (ibid s.68(5)).

**patents, register of.** The register in which is required to be entered particulars of published patent applications, of patents in force, of assignmments and transmissions of, and of licences under, patents and published applications: Patents Act 1992 s.84.

**pater est quem nuptiae demonstrant.** [He is the father whom marriage indicates]. See PATERNITY, PRESUMPTION OF.

**paternity, presumption of.** Where a married woman, or a woman whose marriage terminated less than ten months beforehand, gives birth to a child, her husband is presumed to be the father of the child (previously, such a child was presumed to be legitimate): Status of Children Act 1987 s.46. However, where the husband and wife are living apart under a decree of *divorce a mensa et thoro* (qv) or a judicial separation (qv) for more than ten months before the birth, the husband will be presumed not to be the child's father (formerly, such a child was presumed to be illegitimate). The person named as father in the births' register kept under the Births and Deaths Registration Acts is presumed to be the father of the child.

These presumptions are rebuttable on the normal standard of proof in civil proceedings ie the balance of probability. Formerly, rebuttal of the presumption of legitimacy required to be proved beyond reasonable doubt. "The truth should prevail over the presumption of legitimacy": JPD v MG (1991 SC) ILRM 217. See BIRTH, REGISTRATION OF; PARENTAGE, DECLARATION OF.

**patient charges.** Statutory provision has been made to permit health boards to impose charges in respect of hospital services provided for persons entitled to recover damages or compensation for injuries sustained in a road traffic accident: Health (Amendment) Act 1986. This statutory provision reverses the effect of Cooke v Walsh (1984) ILRM 208. See ROAD TRAFFIC ACCIDENTS.

**pawn.** To pledge a chattel as security for a debt. The pawner parts with its possession to the pawnee (lender). The pawnee has a power of sale in default of redemption by the pawner. Any person who buys, takes in exchange, or takes in pawn a social welfare document is guilty of an offence: Social Welfare (Consolidation) Act 1981 s.291. See DURESS OF GOODS; PAWNBROKER.

**pawnbroker.** Includes any person who carries on the business of taking goods and chattels in pawn and in particular includes any person who (a) receives or takes from any other person any goods or chattels by way of security for the repayment of any sum of money not exceeding fifty pounds advanced thereon; or (b) purchases, or receives or takes in, goods or chattels and pays or advances or lends thereon any sum of money not exceeding fifty pounds with or under an agreement or understanding expressed or implied or from the nature of the transaction to be reasonably inferred that those goods or chattels may be afterwards redeemed or purchased on any terms: Pawnbrokers Act 1964 s.2.

It is an offence for a person to carry on the business of pawnbroker at any premises unless he holds a licence which is in force in respect of those premises (ibid s.7). The holder of a *pawn-ticket* (qv) is entitled to redeem the pledge (qv) to which it relates (ibid s.22). The pawner (qv) is entitled to the surplus on the sale of a pledge (ibid s.33).

**pawner.** A person delivering an article for pawn to a pawnbroker (qv): Pawnbrokers Act 1964 s.2.

**pawn-ticket.** A receipt in prescribed form which a pawnbroker is required to give to a pawner on taking a pledge (qv) in pawn: Pawnbrokers Act 1964 s.14. A *special contract pawn-ticket* is required where the pawnbroker enters into a special contract in respect of a pledge on which the pawn-broker makes a loan of more than ten pounds (ibid s.15).

**pay as you earn.** The system of collection of income tax from employees; it is deducted at source by employers by reference to tax tables so that the periodical deduction of tax keeps pace with the accruing tax liability of the employee. A person making any payment of any emolument is required to deduct or repay income tax and to account for it to the Revenue Commissioners: Income Tax Act 1967 ss.124-133. See Hearne v J A Kenny & Partners (1989) 7 ILT Dig 24. See also Finance Act 1985 s.6. See EMOLUMENT.

**payee.** The person to whom a cheque (qv) or negotiable instrument (qv) is payable.

**payment.** The passing of money from payer to payee in satisfaction of some debt or obligation. An unindorsed cheque which appears to have been paid by the banker on whom it is drawn is evidence of the receipt by the payee of the sum payable by the cheque: Cheques Act 1959 s.3.

**payment in due course.** Discharge of a bill of exchange (qv) by payment made at or after the maturity of the bill to the holder thereof in good faith and without notice that his title to the bill is defective: Bills of Exchange Act 1882 s.59(1). See DISCHARGE OF A BILL.

**payment into court.** See LODGMENT IN COURT.

**payment of wages.** See WAGES.

**payment out of court.** In the High Court, money lodged in court may be paid out to the plaintiff upon receipt of a notification that the plaintiff accepts the sum lodged in satisfaction, except where the plaintiff is a minor (qv) or a person of unsound mind: RSC O.77 r.32; O.22 r.10. In the Circuit Court, any person entitled to, or claiming to be interested in, any funds in court may file a petition setting forth the substance of the order he seeks to obtain; also where a plaintiff, not under a disability, accepts an amount lodged in court, payment may be made to him by lodging a notice of acceptance: RCC O.48 r.13; O.12 r.12. See LODGMENT IN COURT.

**payment to an agent.** Payment of money to an agent discharges the liability of the payer to the principal, if the agent is authorised to receive the money. Such authorisation exists if (a) the principal has expressly authorised the agent to accept payment or (b) it is the custom of that particular type of agency or (c) the agent had ostensible authority to accept payment. The general rule is that an agent authorised to sell is not authorised to receive payment. See PREMIUM; SECRET PROFIT; COMMISSION; AUCTIONEER.

**pcbs.** See POLYCHLORINATED BIPHENYLS.

**peace, binding to.** See BINDING TO PEACE.

**peace commissioner.** The office created by the District Justices (Temporary Provisions) Act 1923 s.4. The person appointed by the Minister with a number of duties and powers eg signing summonses and warrants, administering oaths and taking declarations, affirmations and informations: Courts of Justice Act 1924 s.88. His former power to remand a person (in custody or in such bail as he deemed fit), who had been brought before him when a District Court judge was not immediately available, has been held to be invalid having regard to the 1937 Constitution art.34.1, because it was a judicial and not an administrative act: O'Mahony v Melia (1990) ILRM 14.

A statutory declaration may be taken and received by a commissioner for oaths: Statutory Declarations Act 1938 s.1(1). See also Ryan v O'Callaghan (1987) HC; Byrne v Gray (1988) IR 31. See JUSTICE OF THE PEACE.

**peace officer.** Under proposed draft legislation, a member of the garda siochana, a prison officer, a member of the defence forces, a sheriff or a traffic warden; it is proposed to be an offence for any person to assault a peace officer acting in the execution of his duty: Criminal Justice (Public Order) Bill 1993 s.20.

**pecunary legacy.** A gift of money by will. It includes an annuity (qv), a general legacy, a demonstrative legacy (qv) so far as it is not discharged out of the designated property, and any other general direction by a testator for

payment of money: Succession Act 1965 s.3(1). See LEGACY.

**pedestrian.** Pedestrians are required to exercise care and to take all reasonable precautions to avoid causing danger or inconvenience to traffic and other pedestrians: Road Traffic General Bye-Laws 1964, Part VI (SI No 294 of 1964). When a vehicle is approaching a zebra crossing (qv) a pedestrian must not step onto that crossing if his action is likely to cause the driver to brake suddenly or to swerve (ibid art.38). See CYCLEWAY; FOOTWAY; MOTORWAY; PROPER LOOK OUT.

**pedigree.** Relationship by blood or marriage between persons. The relationship is proved by such facts as birth, marriage, death or failure of issue and may be proved by declarations made by deceased relatives. See Berkeley Peerage Case (1811) 4 Camp 401. See DECLARATION BY DECEASED.

**penal servitude.** Imprisonment with compulsory labour; it was substituted for transportation (qv) by the Penal Servitude Act 1853. The last statute to prescribe penal servitude as a sentence was the Criminal Justice Act 1964 s.2. In practice there appears to be no distinction in the treatment of prisoners sentenced to penal servitude or imprisonment. See Application of McLoughlin (1970) IR 197. See also SR & O No 203 of 1937. See PUNISHMENT.

**penal statute.** Legislation creating offences or providing for the recovery of penalties in civil proceedings. The Supreme Court has held that a word or expression in legislation which creates a penal or taxation liability, should be construed strictly: Inspector of Taxes v Kiernan (1981) IR 117.

**penal sum.** The amount specified in an *administration bond* to which parties thereto bind themselves. Unless otherwise directed, the sum is double the gross value of the estate of the deceased: RSC App Q Part 11.

**penal warrant.** A warrant (qv) authorising the arrest of a specified person. See Murphy v DJ Wallace (1990 HC) ITLR (24 Dec). See REVENUE OFFENCE.

**penalty.** A punishment; the nominal sum payable on breach of contract or of a term of a contract. In a contract it is usually stipulated *in terrorem* of the other party, to compel performance of the contract by providing for a payment to be made by way of punishment if the contract is not performed.

When a contract provides that, on breach being made, a fixed sum will be payable by the party responsible, it is a question of construction whether this sum is a *penalty* or *liquidated damages*. If it is a penalty, only the actual damages suffered are recoverable; if it is liquidated damages (ie a genuine pre-estimate of damage), the sum fixed may be recovered.

The use of the words *penalty* or *liquidated damages* in a contract is not conclusive; the court will ascertain whether a sum is truly a penalty or liquidated damages. If the sum fixed is extravagant and unconscionable compared with the greatest loss which could conceivably be proved to have followed the breach, it will be held to be a penalty: Dunlop Pneumatic Tyre Co v New Garage Motor Co (1915) AC 79. It will be a penalty also if the breach consists only in paying a sum of money, and the sum stipulated is greater than the sum which ought to be paid: Bradford v Lemon (1929) NI 159.

There is a presumption that a clause is penal when a single lump sum is payable on the occurrence of one or more or all of several events, the events occasioning varying degrees of damages: UDT Ltd v Patterson (1975) NI 142. If the consequences of breach of contract are difficult to estimate in financial terms this, far from being an obstacle to the validity of a clause providing for damages, will point in favour of upholding it, the courts taking the view that it is better for the parties themselves to estimate the damages that will result: Schiesser International (Ireland) v Gallagher (1971) ILTR 22. See also Wall v Rederiaktiebolaget Lugudde (1915) 3 KB 66. See HIRE-PURCHASE PRICE.

**pendens lis.** [A pending action].

**pendente lite.** [While litigation is pending]. After an action has commenced and before it has been disposed of. A *grant pendente lite* is a grant of administration made by a court where any legal proceedings are pending, which touch upon the validity of a will or which seek to recall or revoke a grant already given: Succession Act 1965 s.27(7). See also In re Bevan (1948) 1 All ER 271. See also

RSC O.47. See LIS PENDENS.

**pension scheme, occupational.** Any scheme or arrangement (a) which is comprised in one or more instruments or agreements, and (b) which provides benefits or is capable of providing benefits in relation to employees in any description of employment who reside within the State, and (c) which meets other requirements eg it is approved, or in the process of seeking approval, or is a statutory scheme under the appropriate provisions of the Finance Act 1972: Pensions Act 1990 s.2 as amended by Social Welfare Acts 1992 s.53(b) and 1993 s.42(e). The 1990 Act has been amended by the Social Welfare Acts 1991 ss.60-64; 1992 ss.53-63; and 1993 ss.42-52.

The 1990 Act has four objectives: (1) the establishment of a legal framework and a supervisory system; (2) provision for compulsory preservation of pension entitlements; (3) to ensure that pension expectations in *defined benefit schemes* are backed by adequate assets; (4) progressive implementation of equal treatment of men and women.

The Act provides for the establishment of a Pensions Board to act as the regulatory body and the supervisor of the statutory requirements. It also distinguishes between a *defined contributions scheme* (one which provides benefits the rate or amount of which are determined by the amount of contributions paid by or in respect of a member) and *defined benefit schemes* (which are all others). See Occupational Pension Schemes (Preservation of Benefits) Regulations 1992 (SI No 445 of 1992). See also SI No 216 of 1993 (appointment of trustees); SI No 217 of 1993 (special calculations — preservation of benefits).

In the UK it has been held that there is an implied limitation in pension schemes that the employer will not exercise its rights so as to destroy or seriously damage the relationship of confidence and trust between the company and its employees: Imperial Group Pension Trust Ltd v Imperial Tobacco Ltd (1991) IRLR and Barry in 9ILT & SJ (1991) 150. See also Glen Abbey Pension Trust v County Glen plc (1992 HC).

The principles of equal pay in the EC

Treaty art.119 and Council Directive 75/117/EEC have significant implications for occupational pension schemes eg pension benefits cannot discriminate on grounds of sex directly or indirectly: Barber v GRE Assurance (1990) IRLR 240 & Barry in 8ILT & SJ (1990) 194. However the Protocol to the Maastricht Treaty 1992 (qv), limits retrospection to periods of employment from 17 May 1990 except where legal proceedings had been initiated. See also Social Welfare Act 1992 s.62.

It has been held that the Minister was entitled to abate a "wound pension" previously granted to a member of the defence forces: Breen v Minister for Defence (1990 SC) ILT Dig 299. It has also been held that the children's pension payable to the widow of a garda siochana was the beneficial property of the children and was not to be aggregated with the widow's pension for income tax purposes: O'Coindealbhain v O'Carroll (1989) IR 229. See Buckley in 9 ILT & SJ (1991) 154 for article on Pensions Act 1990. See also Oireachtas (Allowances to Members) and Ministerial and Parliamentary Offices (Amdt) Act 1992. [Text: Forde (8); Inglis-Jones (UK)]. See INSOLVENCY OF EMPLOYER; PREFERENTIAL PAYMENTS; PRESERVED BENEFIT; TRUSTEE, REMOVAL OF.

**peppercorn rent.** See RENT.

**per.** [As stated by].

**per annum.** [By the year]. Annually.

**per autre vie.** See CESTUI QUE VIE; LIFE ESTATE.

**per capita.** [By heads]. Individually. Distribution per capita is where property is divided among those entitled to it in equal shares.

**per cur; per curiam.** [By the court]. Refers to a decision by the court. For example, see N (Otherwise K) v K (1986) ILRM 75; O'Byrne v Gloucester 7 ILT Dig (1989) 56.

**per diem.** [By the day].

**per incuriam.** [Through want of care]. A decision of the court which is mistaken. See Kelly v O'Sullivan (1991 HC) 9ILT Dig 126.

**per infortunium.** [By mischance].

**per mensem.** [By the month].

**per minas.** [By menaces (qv)]. See DURESS IN CRIME.

**per my et per tout.** [By the half and by the whole]. Joint tenants are said to be seised *per my et per tout,* in that they have an equal right to the possession of the whole property and no one is entitled to exclusive possession of any part. See JOINT TENANCY.

**per pro; per procurationem.** [As an agent]. On behalf of another eg where a person signs a document for another.

**per quod.** [Whereby].

**per quod servitium amisit.** [Whereby he lost his service]. An action by an employer for damages for the loss of service of his employee against a third party who had injured the employee. See Bradford Corporation v Webster (1920) 2 KB 135; Cook v Carroll (1945) IR 515.

A similar action is available to a parent against a third party who wrongfully deprives the parent of the legal right which he has to the services of his unmarried minor (qv) who ordinarily lives with him eg by the third party enticing, harbouring or seducing the minor. See Barnes v Fox (1914) 2 IR 276. See LRC Report No 7 of 1979. See CONSORTIUM.

**per se.** [By itself]. Taken alone.

**per stirpes.** [By stock or branches]. Distribution of the property of an intestate is *per stirpes* if it is divided amongst those entitled to it according to the number of stocks of descent ie children representing a deceased parent take in equal shares the share which would have been taken by their deceased parent had he survived, and they may in turn be represented in a similar way by their own issue through all degrees. See Succession Act 1965 s.3. See INTESTATE SUCCESSION.

**per subsequens matrimonium.** [By later marriage]. See LEGITIMATION

**per totam curiam.** [By the whole court].

**peremptory.** An order which allows no excuse for non compliance.

**peremptory challenge.** See JUROR, CHALLENGE TO.

**performance.** (1) The act which, being in accordance with the term or condition of a contract, discharges it eg payment or tender (qv).

(2) The equitable doctrine by which a transfer of property operates in law, whether the donee wishes it or not, as a complete or *pro tanto* discharge of a

previous legal liability of the donor. It derives from the equitable doctrine that *equity imputes an intention to fulfil an obligation.* Equity presumes performance (a) where there is a covenant to purchase and settle lands and a purchase is in fact made: Lechmere v Earl of Carlisle (1733) 3 P Wms 211; (b) where there is a covenant to leave personalty to another and the covenantor dies intestate and property to satisfy the covenant does in fact come to that other: Blandy v Widmore (1716) 1 P Wms 323; In re Shine (1964) IR 32. See IMPOSSIBILITY OF PERFORMANCE; PART-PERFORMANCE.

**performance bond.** A *guarantee* (qv) given by an agency, usually a bank, to secure the beneficiary against, for example, a seller being unable to supply goods under a contract of sale or, more commonly, to secure a beneficiary in an international construction contract against the contractor being unable to complete the project properly. Performance bonds may be (a) *first demand* whereby the issuing agency is required to pay the beneficiary on demand or (b) *conditional* whereby the issuing agency is only required to pay upon evidence eg that a breach of contract has actually occurred. See Hibernia Meats Ltd v Ministre de L'Agriculture (1984) HC. See Gill in 8 ILT & SJ (1990) 41.

**performance, indecent or profane.** It is an offence to show for gain or reward an indecent or profane performance. To constitute an offence, there must be an intention to deprave or corrupt those viewing the performance whose minds were open to such immoral influences: Attorney General v Simpson (1959) 93 ILTR 33. See INDECENCY.

**performers' protection.** A variety of statutory protections are provided for *performances* of literary, dramatic, musical and artistic works, aimed at preventing the unauthorised records, films and broadcasts thereof: Performers' Protection Act 1968. *Performance* means a performance of any actors, singers, musicians, dancers or other persons who act, sing, deliver, declaim, play in or otherwise perform literary, dramatic, musical or artistic works, and includes such performances rendered or intended to be rendered audible or visible by mechanised or electrical means (ibid

s.1(1)). See Mannion in 10 ILT & SJ (1992) 276. See PERFORMING RIGHTS SOCIETY.

**Performing Rights Society Ltd; PRS.** A non-profit making company limited by guarantee and having no share capital formed in the United Kingdom in 1914, which has the objective to protect copyright music from unauthorised exploitation and to grant permission for use on payment of a licence fee. The PRS is open to composers, authors and publishers of music and their heirs, who assign to the PRS the rights which it administers on their behalf.

These rights are the public performing rights, the broadcasting rights and the right to transmit the work to subscribers to a diffusion service, and, in the case of writer members, the film synchronisation rights composed primarily for the purpose of being included in the soundtrack of a particular cinematograph film or films in contemplation when the work was commissioned. The Society grants blanket licences which authorise the licensees to use the PRS rights referred to above. In Ireland, the PRS is now called the Irish Music Rights Organisation Ltd (IMRO).

Analogous societies are the Mechanical Copyright Protection Society Ltd which grants licences to make sound recordings, and the Phonographic Performance (Ireland) Ltd which grants licences for public performances of sound recordings. See Performing Right Yearbooks. See Performing Rights Society Ltd v Marlin Commmunal Aerials (1975) SC. See Tyrrell in ILSI Gazette (Jul/Aug 1992) 235.

**period of time.** See TIME.

**perils of the sea.** In marine insurance, *perils of the sea* refers only to fortuitous accidents or casualties of the seas; it does not include the ordinary action of the winds and waves: Marine Insurance Act 1906, first schedule, art.7. See MARITIME PERILS.

**periodical payments.** See ATTACHMENT; MAINTENANCE ORDER.

**perishable goods.** The court has power to order the sale of perishable goods: RSC O.50 r.3. See INTERNATIONAL CARRIAGE OF PERISHABLE GOODS.

**perished goods.** Where there is a contract for sale of specific goods and the goods without the knowledge of the seller have perished at the time when the contract is made, the contract is void: Sale of Goods Act 1893 s.6. Where there is an agreement to sell specific goods and subsequently the goods, without any fault on the part of the seller or buyer, perish before the risk passes to the buyer, the agreement is thereby avoided (ibid s.7). See SALE OF GOODS.

**perjury.** An offence committed by a person who asserts upon oath (qv), duly administered in a judicial proceeding before a competent court or tribunal at which evidence on oath may be heard, of the truth of some matter of fact, material to the question depending in that proceeding, which assertion the assertor does not believe to be true when he makes it, or on which he knows himself to be ignorant. Perjury by a person before the European Court of Justice arises when he swears anything which he knows to be false or which he does not believe to be true: Courts of Justice of the European Communities (Perjury) Act 1975 s.1. See also Perjury Act 1586; Arbitration Act 1954 s.7. See SUBORNATION OF PERJURY.

**permanent and pensionable.** See NO-TICE, EMPLOYMENT; ACTING CAPACITY.

**permanent health insurance.** The business of effecting and carrying out contracts of insurance, providing specified benefits against risks of persons becoming incapacitated in consequence of sustaining injury as a result of an accident or of an accident of a specified class or of sickness or infirmity and subject to certain provisions regarding period and termination: European Communities (Life Assurance) Regulations 1984 (SI No 57 of 1984), art.8. An authorisation is required to carry on the business of permanent health insurance. Contributions to an approved permanent health insurance scheme are allowable as a tax deduction: Finance Acts 1979 s.8 and 1986 s.7. See INSURANCE OMBUDSMAN; VOLUNTARY HEALTH INSURANCE.

**permanent society.** Originally was a building society which had not by its rules any fixed date or specified result at which it would terminate eg Irish Permanent Building Society: Building Societies Act 1874 s.5, since repealed and only of historical importance now.

Contrast with TERMINATING SOCIETY.

**permissive waste.** See WASTE.

**permit.** An authority; permission; licence.

**perpetua lex est, nullam legem humanam ac positivam perpetuam esse, et clausula quae abrogationem excludit, ab initio non valet.** [It is an everlasting law, that no positive and human law shall be perpetual, and a clause which excludes abrogation is invalid from its commencement].

**perpetual copyright.** The copyright in legal tender notes given to the Central Bank of Ireland and in coins to the Minister: Copyright Act 1963 s.57.

**perpetual fund.** A fund which is established in connection with an undertaking mainly for one or more of a number of purposes eg the provision of superannuation allowances, pensions, periodic allowances to children, or an assurance of capital sums on death: Perpetual Funds (Registration) Act 1933 s.2. Funds registered with the Registrar of Friendly Societies pursuant to this Act are relieved from the operation of the rule of law relating to perpetuities (qv). Total accumulated funds in 1986 amounted to £366m.

**perpetual injunction.** See INJUNCTION.

**perpetuating testimony.** A proceeding to place on record, evidence which is material for establishing a future claim to property: RSC O.39 r.35. The court may allow the deposition (qv) of a witness to be adduced in evidence on such terms as the court directs: RSC O.39 r.34. See also SHIPS PROTEST.

**perpetuities, rule against.** A *limitation* of any interest in land is void if it is capable of vesting outside the perpetuity period, which consists of a life or lives in being at the time of the gift and 21 years thereafter. A *life in being* includes everyone who is alive at the time of the gift and mentioned in it either expressly or by implication. Lives must be human lives and not animals: In re Kelly (1932) IR 255. If there is no reference to lives in being, the period is 21 years.

The rule does not apply to (a) a limitation following an *estate tail* or (b) a gift over from one charity to another. The perpetuity period may be extended for a *gestation period* (qv). The rule against perpetuities does not apply to a shared ownership lease (qv): Housing

(Miscellaneous Provisions) Act 1992 s.2(2). See also Cadell v Palmer (1833) 1 Cl & Fin 372. See CHARITIES; FEE TAIL; PERPETUAL FUND; REMOTENESS; WORDS OF LIMITATION.

**persistent offender.** See HABITUAL CRIMINAL.

**person.** The object of rights and duties ie capable of having rights and being liable to duties. A *natural* person is a human being. An *artificial* person is a collection or succession of natural persons forming a corporation. Under the Interpretation Act 1937, the word *person* is to be construed as importing a body corporate as well as an individual unless a contrary intention appears: ibid ss.11(c) and 11(i). See CORPORATION; STATE; TRUE PERSON.

**person in authority.** See CONFESSION.

**person of unsound mind.** See MENTAL DISORDER; UNSOUND MIND.

**persona non grata.** [Unacceptable person]. A receiving State may at any time and without having to explain its decision, notify a sending State that any member of its diplomatic staff is *persona non grata*, in which case the sending State will either recall the person concerned or terminate his functions with the mission: Diplomatic Relations and Immunities Act 1967, first schedule, art.9.

**personal action.** An action *in personam* (qv) as contrasted with an action *in rem* (qv).

**personal data.** Information in a form in which it can be processed (ie *data*) relating to a living individual who can be identified from the data or from the data in conjunction with other information in the possession of a *data controller* (qv): Data Protection Act 1988 s.1(1).

An individual has a right to establish the existence of personal data and to be given a description of the data and the purposes for which it is kept (ibid s.3). He is also entitled to be supplied, within 40 days, with a copy of any personal data about him on making a request in writing to the data controller and on payment of any fee required (ibid s.4). This right of access to personal data is restricted in certain instances: (a) an *absolute restriction* eg data covered by legal professional privilege (qv); or (b) a *conditional* restriction eg where disclosure

would prejudice the prevention of crime (ibid s.5).

A data subject is entitled to have personal data rectified or erased, as the case may be, if they have been dealt with by a data controller in contravention of the provisions of s.2(1) of the Act eg if inaccurate, or kept for an unlawful purpose (ibid s.6). See DATA PROTECTION.

**personal injuries.** See LRC 21 of 1987. See INJURY, PERSONAL. See also DAMAGES; DISCOVERABILITY TEST; FACIAL INJURIES; INCOME TAX; JURY, ABOLITION OF; LIMITATION OF ACTIONS; MENTAL DISTRESS; NERVOUS SHOCK; PRIMARY FACT; PRODUCT LIABILITY, EC; SURGICAL OPERATION.

**personal liability.** Legal obligation which attaches to a person. A person may become personally liable for the debts of a limited company of which he is a member where eg (a) the number of members is below the minimum required: Companies Act 1963 s.5; (b) where there is a failure to correctly state the company's name: ibid s.114(4); (c) where the memorandum of association so provides: ibid s.197(1); (d) where he is a disqualified or restricted person: Companies Act 1990 s.162; (e) where he acts on the directions of a disqualified or restricted person: ibid 1990 Act ss.164-165; (f) where there is a failure to meet the capital requirements imposed by s.150 of the 1990 Act: ibid s.161(4); (g) where there is a failure to keep proper books of account: ibid 1990 Act ss.204 and 202; (h) where there is an inaccurate statutory declaration of solvency: ibid 1990 Act s.128 inserting new s.256(8) into 1963 Act; (i) where there has been fraudulent or reckless trading (qqv): ibid 1963 Act s.297A as inserted by the 1990 Act s.138. See Guilfoyle v Mark A Synnott (1993 HC) — Irish Times 10/2/1993. See MacCann in 9 ILT & SJ (1991) 206 & 232. See also SURCHARGE. See COMPANY, LIMITED; LIFTING THE CORPORATE VEIL; LIMITATION OF LIABILITY; LOAN TO DIRECTOR.

**personal liberty.** No citizen may be deprived of his personal liberty save in accordance with law: 1937 Constitution, art.40(4)(1). See HABEAS CORPUS; FALSE IMPRISONMENT; TRESPASS TO THE PERSON.

**personal property.** Goods, chattels and leaseholds; personalty. [Text: Bell].

**personal representative.** An executor

or administrator of the estate of a deceased person. The real and personal estate of a deceased person devolve on his death and become vested in his personal representatives, notwithstanding any testamentary disposition. The personal representatives are deemed in law to be his heirs and assigns within the meaning of all trusts and powers. See Succession Act 1965 s.10; Social Welfare Act 1991 s.33. See ADMINISTRATOR; DEVASTAVIT; EJECTMENT; EXECUTOR; INSOLVENT ESTATE; PROBATE TAX.

**personal rights.** Certain *personal rights* are specifically provided for in the Constitution eg right to life, right to information, right to travel, right to a good name, right to equality before the law, right to personal liberty, right to trade and earn a livelihood; right to assembly, to form associations and to freedom of expression: 1937 Constitution, art.40. The State guarantees in its laws to respect, as far as practicable, by its laws to defend and vindicate the *personal rights* of the citizen (qv): ibid art.40(3)(1). See FUNDAMENTAL RIGHTS; CONJUGAL RIGHTS.

**personality disorder.** Gross personality disorder, which renders a person incapable of forming any proper marital relationship, may be a good ground for a nullity decree: W(C) v C (1989) IR 696. See EMOTIONAL IMMATURITY; PSYCHIATRIC DISORDER.

**personalty.** Personal property; includes leaseholds.

**personation.** The offence committed by a person who (a) at an election applies for a ballot paper in the name of some other person or (b) having obtained a ballot paper once at an election, applies at the same election for a ballot paper in his own name: Electoral Act 1992 s.134 and ss.166-170. Compensation may be payable to a person arrested on a charge of personation made by a personation agent (qv) without reasonable or just cause (ibid s.158). See also Local Government Act 1991 s.10 regarding local elections.

**personation agent.** A person appointed in writing by a candidate in a Dail election (or by his election agent) for the purpose of assisting in the detection of personation: Electoral Act 1992 s.60(3). One such person may be appointed as the candidate's agent in each polling station. A personation agent must not leave a polling station without the permission of the presiding officer (ibid s.148). See also draft Presidential Elections Bill 1993 s.34(4).

**persuade to murder.** The misdemeanour committed by a person who persuades, or endeavours to persuade, another to commit a murder (qv): Offences Against the Person Act 1861 s.41.

**persuasive authorities.** Precedents (qv) which are not binding on a court. They include obiter dicta, decisions of inferior courts, and decisions of the U S and Canadian Supreme Courts, and of the English, Australian and New Zealand courts.

**perverse verdict.** A verdict altogether against the evidence. The courts will not interfere with the verdict of a jury in a case where there is evidence to support a verdict, where the trial is conducted in an exemplary manner, with express warnings given to the jury; it is for the jury to assess the evidence and to arrive at a verdict: DPP v O'Brien (1990) 8ILT Dig 157. See VERDICT.

**perverting the course of justice.** Any act tending or intended to pervert the course of justice is a misdemeanour at common law. Manufacturing false evidence is such an offence. R v Vreones (1891) 1 QB 360. See BRIBERY AND CORRUPTION.

**petition.** (1) A written application to the court for relief or remedy which is used in particular cases to commence proceedings eg in matters concerning bankruptcy, matrimonial causes, patents, wards of court and matters relating to professional disciplinary bodies and to the Companies Acts. Unless the court gives leave to the contrary, there must be at least two clear days between the service of a petition and the day for hearing it: RSC O.5 r.17. See also RSC O.5 r.15-17; O.40 r.1. See also RCC O.48 r.1.

(2) A Bill may be the subject of a joint *petition* to the President of Ireland where the majority of Seanad Eireann and not less than one-third of Dail Eireann request the President to decline to sign and promulgate the Bill on the ground that it contains a proposal of such national importance that the will of the

people thereon ought to be ascertained: 1937 Constitution art.27(1). If the President decides that there are such grounds, she will not sign and promulgate the Bill as law unless either the proposal is agreed (a) by the people at a referendum (qv) or (b) by a resolution of the Dail after a dissolution and re-assembly of the Dail (ibid art.27(5)).

(3) Any citizen of the European Union (qv), and any natural or legal person residing or having his registered office in a member State has the right to address, individually or in association with other citizens or persons, a *petition* to the European Parliament on a matter which comes within the Community's field of activity and which affects him directly: Treaty of Rome 1957 art.138d as replaced by Maastricht Treaty 1992 art.G(E)(41). See also ibid art.8d. See ELECTION PETITION; SUMMONS.

**petition for bankruptcy.** See BANKRUPTCY, PETITION FOR.

**petition for winding up.** A petition requesting the court to wind up a company, which is presented by the company itself, or any creditor, any contributory (qv), the Minister, or in the case of oppression (qv) any person entitled by virtue of the Companies Act 1963 s.205. The right to present a petition is a statutory right which cannot be excluded by the *articles of association:* In re Perevil Gold Mines Co Ltd (1898) 1 Ch 122. See also Companies Act 1963 s.215 as amended by Companies (Amdt) Act 1983, first schedule, para 18, and third schedule. See WINDING UP, COMPULSORY; COURT PROTECTION OF COMPANY.

**petroleum.** Includes crude petroleum, oil made from petroleum or from coal, shale, peat or other bituminous substances and other fractions of petroleum: Dangerous Substances Act 1972 s.2(1). *Petroleum spirit* means petroleum which, at normal atmospheric pressure, gives off an inflamable vapour at a temperature of less than 72 degrees Fahrenheit (ibid s.20(1)).

No person may have petroleum spirit in his possession or under his control except in a store licensed by the proper local or harbour authority; this provision does not apply to a quantity not exceeding 3 gallons kept in suitable leakproof containers, securely stopped and containing not more than one gallon each (ibid s.21). See SOLUS AGREEMENT.

**petroleum, exploration for.** It is unlawful for any person to search for petroleum in any area in the State unless he is the licensee under a *petroleum lease;* it is also unlawful for any person to get, raise, take or carry away petroleum unless he is the lessee under a petroleum lease: Petroleum and Other Minerals Developments Act 1960. All *State* petroleum vests in the Minister. See also Continental Shelf Act 1968 s.4.

**pharmaceutical chemist, registered.** A person registered in the Register of Pharmaceutical Chemists for Ireland maintained under the Pharmacy Acts 1875 to 1977. See also Regulations of the Pharmaceutical Society of Ireland 1971 to 1992 (SI No 239 of 1987, 330 of 1991, and Regulation 1992 — Iris Oifigiuil 1st December 1992). See EC (Recognition of Qualifications in Pharmacy) Regulations 1991 (SI No 330 of 1991). See Treaty of Rome 1957 art.57 as replaced by Maastricht Treaty 1992 art.G(D)(13). See FAMILY PLANNING SERVICE; POISON; PRESCRIPTION DRUGS.

**pheasant.** See GAME.

**phoenix company.** The colloquial term to describe a company which is wound up having liabilities in excess of its assets and shortly thereafter re-opens for business under a different name.

In order to curb this abuse of company legislation, the law was changed by widening the provisions dealing with the *disqualification* of directors and by requiring that directors of an insolvent company could only be directors of companies with a minimum share capital, fully paid up in cash: Companies Act 1990. See DIRECTORS; DISQUALIFICATION ORDER.

**photograph.** Any product of photography or any process akin to photography, other than a part of a cinematograph film (qv): Copyright Act 1963 s.2(1). The *author* in relation to a photograph, means the person who, at the time the photograph is taken, is the owner of the material on which it is taken (ibid s.2(1)). Copyright in a photograph continues for a period of fifty years from the end of the year in which the photograph was first published (ibid s.9(7)). See ARTISTIC WORK; COPYRIGHT, OWNERSHIP OF; HUNT.

**photographs, use of in identification.** Where photographs are used for identification of the perpetrator of an offence, a series of at least twelve photographs ought always be presented to a witness for the purpose of such identification, even where the gardai have a particular person in mind as the perpetrator; the witness should be asked whether any of the persons depicted was the perpetrator: *The People v Mills* (1957) IR 106 applying *R v Dwyer* (1925) 2 KB 799. See FINGERPRINTS.

**picketing.** It is lawful to picket in contemplation or furtherance of a trade dispute. It is lawful for one or more persons, acting on their own behalf or on behalf of a trade union in contemplation or furtherance of a trade dispute, to attend at, or where that is not practicable, at the approaches to, a place where their employer works or carries on business, if they so attend merely for the purpose of peacefully obtaining or communicating information, or of peacefully persuading any person to work or abstain from working: Industrial Relations Act 1990 s.11. This protection is confined to *authorised* trade unions holding a negotiation licence and their members and officials (ibid s.9). There is no immunity in respect of picketing of an employer's home: *Dillon v Walsh & Nolan* (1992 DC) — Irish Times 20/12/1992.

The method of picketing and the numbers picketing must be peaceful and be reasonable having regard to all the circumstances: *Brendan Dunne Ltd v Fitzpatrick* (1958) IR 29; *EI Co Ltd v Kennedy* (1968) IR 69. The legal status of *secondary picketing* (qv) was uncertain; the courts tended to regard it as unlawful; contrast *Roundabout Ltd v Beirne* (1959) IR 423 and *Ellis v Wright* (1978) IR 6). It is now lawful in certain circumstances. See SECONDARY PICKETING.

Picketing is not lawful if its purpose is unconstitutional eg if its purpose is to deprive another of their constitutional rights: *Educational Co of Ireland v Fitzpatrick* (1961) IR 323; *Murtagh Properties Ltd v Cleary* (1972) IR 330. Persons engaged in picketing may not indulge in activity which would amount to a criminal offence eg watching and besetting: Conspiracy and Protection of Property Act 1875 s.7; or making use of

threatening abusive and insulting words to provoke a breach of the peace eg Dublin Police Act 1842 s.14(13); draft Criminal Justice (Public Order) Bill 1993 ss.5 and 27. See IMMUNITY; SIT-IN; LABOUR INJUNCTION.

**piller, anton.** See ANTON PILLER ORDER.

**pilotage.** A ship while navigating in a pilotage district in which pilotage is compulsory must be under the pilotage of a licensed pilot for the district or under the pilotage of a master or mate possessing a pilotage certificate; a ship carrying passengers must comply with this requirement even where pilotage is not otherwise compulsory: Pilotage Acts 1913 s.11 and 1962 s.5. See *Turner v Pilotage Committee* (1989) 7ILT Dig 23. See HARBOUR AUTHORITIES.

**pimp.** Colloquial term to describe a person who controls and directs a prostitute and lives in whole or in part on her earnings. See PROSTITUTE.

**pinholes.** Holes or similar marks on a will are deemed to be an indication that there are missing pages or that some other document was attached to the will.

**piracy.** The infringement of copyright. See INFRINGEMENT OF COPYRIGHT.

**piscary.** The right to fish in the waters of another. See PROFIT A PRENDRE.

**place, dangerous.** See DANGEROUS PLACE.

**place of business.** See FOREIGN COMPANY.

**placing.** As regards the shares of a company, the allocation of shares by the company to a financial intermediary (an issuing house) which agrees to purchase and place them with clients. See FLOATATION.

**plagiarism.** See CHEATING.

**plaintiff.** The person who brings a legal action; a plaintiff includes any person seeking relief against any other person by any form of civil proceedings: RSC O.125 r.1. A defendant in an action may be the plaintiff of a counterclaim (qv). See O'BYRNE LETTER.

**planning appeal, proceedings.** A person may seek to change a decision regarding planning permission by (a) appealing the decision of the planning authority to An Bord Pleanala within one month of the decision or (b) seeking a judicial review of the decision of the planning authority or of An Bord Pleanala.

A person is not allowed to question the validity of a decision of a planning authority (qv) on an application for permission or approval or a decision of An Bord Pleanala on any appeal or on any reference otherwise than by way of application to the High Court for judicial review. An application for leave to apply for judicial review must be made, by motion on notice, within two months of the relevant decision. See LG(P&D) Act 1963 s.82(3A) inserted by the LG(P&D) Act 1992 s.19(3). See Inver Resources v Limerick Corporation (1988) ILRM 47; Brady v Donegal Co Council (1987) HC and (1989) 7ILT Dig 21. See Kimber in 11 ILT & SJ (1993) 17. For limitations on judicial review, see JUDICIAL REVIEW. For details on appeal to An Bord Pleanala, see BORD PLEANALA, AN.

**planning authority.** In the case of a county or other borough, the corporation; in the case of a county exclusive of any borough or urban district, the county council (qv); and in the case of an urban district, the urban district council (qv): LG(P&D) Act 1963 s.2(2).

A planning Authority in exercise of its powers under the 1963 Act owes no duty of care at common law towards the occupiers of buildings erected in its functional area to avoid damage due to defective siting and construction: Sunderland v Louth Co Council (1990 SC) ILRM 658.

**planning injunction.** See INJUNCTION, PLANNING.

**planning law.** The body of law dealing with: (a) the permission which is required for every form of development of land, save in the case of *exempted developments* (qv); (b) the statutory duty of local planning authorities (qv) to prepare a *development plan* (qv); (c) the appeal mechanisms which exist where there is an adverse decision of the planning authority; (d) the *compensation* which is payable in respect of a refusal to grant permission or in respect of the conditions imposed; and (e) the enforcement powers of the planning authorities to ensure compliance with the terms of planning permission and to restrain unauthorised development. See LG(P&D) Acts 1963, 1976, 1982, 1983, 1990, 1992 and 1993.

The 1963 Act established the basic framework; the 1976 Act sought to remedy the more serious deficiencies by providing new and more extensive

enforcement machinery and establishing a planning appeal board (An Bord Pleanala); the 1982 Act provided more stringent penalties for breaches; the 1983 Act altered the method of appointing the chairman and members of the planning appeal board; the 1990 Act amended and consolidated the law on planning compensation; the 1992 Act amended the law on planning appeals so that they be dealt with expeditiously; and the 1993 Act regularised the position regarding State authorities (qv) and introduced a procedure of public notice and consultation as regards development by local authorities. [Text: Keane (3); Nowlan; O'Sullivan & Sheppard; Walsh & Keane].

**planning permission.** The permission which is required in respect of any *development* of land other than *exempted* development and development commenced before 1st October 1964; LG(P&D) Act 1963 s.24.

*Development* means the carrying out of any *works* on, in or under land or the making of any *material change* in the *use* of any structures or other land (ibid s.3(1)). *Land* includes any structure and any land covered with water, whether inland or coastal; *work* includes any act or operation of construction, excavation, demolition, extension, alteration, repair or renewal (ibid s.2(1)). *Use*, in relation to land, does not include the use of the land by the carrying out of any works thereon (ibid s.2(1): Viscount Securities Ltd v Dublin County Council 112 ILTR 17); Rehabilitation Institute v Dublin Corporation (1988 HC) 6 ILT 198.

An intensification of an existing use of land can constitute a *material change*: Patterson v Murphy (1978) HC; Stafford & Son v Roadstone Ltd (1980) HC; Monaghan Co Council v Brogan (1987) ILRM 564. The use of the facade of a building to display commercial advertisements unconnected with the present business user, constituted a *material change*: Dublin Corp v Regan Advertising Ltd (1989 SC) IR 61. A *use right* is capable of being abandoned, making its resumption a material change requiring authorisation: Meath Co Council v Daly (1988) ILRM 274. See EXEMPTED DEVELOPMENT; COUNCILLOR, DISCLOSURE OF INTEREST; INJUNCTION, PLANNING; LAND.

**planning permission, appeal.** See PLAN-

NING APPEAL; BORD PLEANALA, AN.

**planning permission, application for.**
The application for permission which
must be made in respect of any
*development* of land. An application may
be for an *outline* permission ie permission
in principle subject to subsequent approval by the planning authority of
detailed plans for the development; or
for *full* permission or approval which
application must contain detailed plans,
drawings and maps: LG(P&D) Regulations 1977 (SI No 65 of 1977).

Notice to the public of intention to
apply for permission must be made (ibid
art.14) and this requirment is strictly
interpreted by the courts: Keleghan &
Ors v Dublin Corporation and Corby
(1977) 111 ILTR 144; Readymix (Eire)
Ltd v Dublin County Council and the
Minister for Local Government (1974)
SC.

An application for planning permission
must be made either by or with the
approval of a person who has a sufficient
legal estate or interest in the property,
which is the subject of the application,
to carry out the proposed development:
Frescati Estates v Walker (1975) IR 177.
See also The State (Alf-a-Bet Promo-
tions) Ltd v Bundoran UDC (1978) 112
ILTR 9.

**planning permission, conditions on.**
The conditions subject to which a
planning authority may grant permission
or approval in respect of any *development*
of land: LG(P&D) Act 1963 ss.26(2) and
LG(P&D) Act 1976 s.39(c). These
include conditions: (a) regulating the
development or use of adjoining or
adjacent land which is under the control
of the applicant; (b) requiring the
carrying out of works (including the
provision of car parks) which the
planning authority consider are required
for the purposes of the development; (c)
requiring the provision of open spaces
and the planting of trees; (d) requiring
the giving of security for satisfactory
completion of the development; (e)
requiring roads, open spaces, car parks
and sewers, in excess of the immediate
needs of the proposed development; (f)
requiring contribution towards expenditure by the local authority which has or
will facilitate the development; (g)
requiring measures for the reduction or

prevention of noise or vibration.

In addition, any conditions imposed:
(a) must fairly and reasonably relate to
the permitted development; (b) must be
relevant to the planning policy; (c) must
not relate to other land which is not
under the applicant's control; (d) must
not be dependent for implementation on
the co-operation of a third party; (e)
may affect the right of the occupier to
use his premises in a particular manner;
and (f) may be void for uncertainty. See
ENFORCEMENT NOTICE.

**planning permission, decision on.** The
decision which a planning authority (qv)
is empowered to make by deciding to
grant the permission or approval, subject
to or without conditions, or to refuse it:
LG(P&D) Act 1963 s.26. In dealing with
any such decision, the planning authority
is restricted to considering the proper
planning and development of the area of
the authority (including the preservation
and improvement of the amenities
thereof), regard being had to the provisions of the development plan, the
provisions of any *special amenity area*
(qv) order relating to the said area and
other specified matters eg provision of
car parks, open spaces, security for
satisfactory completion: 1963 Act s.26(1);
LG(P&D) Act 1976 ss.24 and 39(c); In
re Grange Developments Ltd (1987)
ILRM 245 and 733 and (1989 SC)
ILRM 145.

The decision to grant or refuse permission is an *executive* function of the
manager; however a decision to grant
permission which would contravene materially the development plan or any
*special amenity area* order may be made
by the passing of a resolution where at
least three quarters of the members of
the planning authority have voted in its
favour: 1963 Act s.26(3) as amended by
the 1976 Act s.39(d) and the Local
Government Act 1991 s.45.

A decision to grant planning permission
is deemed to have been given where the
planning authority does not notify the
applicant of its decision within the
*appropriate period*, being the period of
two months beginning on the day of
receipt by the authority of the application: 1963 Act s.26; The State (Murphy)
v Dublin County Council (1970) IR 253;
Dunne Ltd v Dublin County Council

(1974) IR 45. The grant is deemed to have been given if there has been substantial compliance with the regulations by the applicant and any failure came within the *de minimis* rule: Molloy & Walsh v Dublin County Council (1990 HC) ILRM 633.

A planning authority is required to make documents dealing with an application available for inspection by members of the public for one month from the date of their decision on the application: LG (P&D) Act 1992 s.5. The documents include copies of — the planning application, drawings, maps, environmental impact statement, any report on the application, the decision, and notification to the applicant (ibid s.6). See COMPENSATION & PLANNING PERMISSION; DEFAULT PERMISSION; DEPRECIATION; PLANNING APPEAL, PROCEEDINGS; SECTION 4 RESOLUTION.

**planning permission, duration of.** The duration of planning permission is normally five years: LG(P&D) Act 1982 s.2. However, a planning authority has the power to grant permission for a longer period (ibid s.3). There is also provision for an extension of the time limit where *substantial* works were carried out during the relevant period or for a further extension where failure to carry out the works during the extended period was due to circumstances outside the control of the developer (ibid s.4). See The State (Patrick McCoy) v Corporation of Dun Laoghaire (1983) HC.

**planning permission, objection to.** An objector has, under the guarantees of fair procedures inherent in the 1937 Constitution, art.40(3), a right to make his case to a planning authority and, if necessary, to An Bord Pleanala, at the hearing of an appeal from the decision of the planning authority: The State (Haverty) v An Bord Pleanala (1987 HC) IR 485. However, see BORD PLEANALA, AN; PLANNING APPEAL, PROCEEDINGS.

**planning permission, revocation of.** The revocation or modification of a planning permission which a planning authority is empowered to do by notice served on the owner or occupier of the affected land and any other person who in their opinion will be affected by the revocation or modification: LG(P&D) Act 1963 s.30. This power may only be

exercised bona fides (qv) and an appeal lies to An Bord Pleanala. See Listowel UDC v McDonagh (1968) IR 312; The State (Cogley) v Dublin Corporation (1970) IR 244.

**plant varieties.** See VARIETAL NAMES.

**platinum.** See GOLDSMITHS OF DUBLIN, COMPANY OF.

**play-group.** See PRE-SCHOOL SERVICE.

**plc.** [Public limited company]. See COMPANY, PUBLIC LIMITED.

**plea.** In a criminal trial, the accused's response to the indictment (qv), which he may do by pleading guilty or by taking legal objection to the indictment, or by standing mute (qv) or by pleading not guilty. Legal objection to the indictment may be taken by (a) a motion to quash on the ground that the indictment suffers from a defect which cannot be remedied or where the court does not have jurisdiction to try the case or (b) a special *plea in bar* of autrefois acquit (qv) and autrefoit convict (qv). A person who pleads guilty is entitled to withdraw his plea at any time before sentence, by leave of the court: R v Plummer (1912) 2 KB 339.

**plea bargaining.** An informal arrangement by which the defendant to criminal proceedings agrees to plead guilty to one or more charges in return for the prosecution extending some advantage to him eg dropping another charge.

**plea in bar.** See AUTREFOIS ACQUIT; AUTREFOIS CONVICT.

**plead.** To make a plea (qv); to address the court.

**pleadings.** Formal written or printed statements in a civil action, usually drafted by counsel, delivered alternatively by the parties to each other, stating the allegations of fact upon which the parties to the action base their case. Pleadings in the High Court include an originating summons, statement of claim, defence, counterclaim, reply, petition or answer (qqv): RSC O.125 r.1.

In all cases alleging a wrong, within the meaning of the Civil Liabilities Act 1961 and 1964, particulars of such wrong, and personal injuries suffered and any items of special damage, must be set out in the statement of claim or counterclaim and particulars (qv) of any contributory negligence (qv) must be set out in the defence: RSC O.19 r.5(1). In cases alleging misrepresentation, fraud, breach of trust, wilful default or undue influence, particulars with dates and items if necessary, must be set out in the pleadings (ibid rr.5(2) and 6(1)).

It is a well-recognised principle that counsel should not sign pleadings containing an allegation of fraud unless satisfied there are substantial grounds for making such allegation: Administralia Asigurilor de Stat v Insurance Corporation of Ireland (1990) 2 IR 246.

In the Circuit Court, pleadings consist of the indorsement of claim on the civil bill, or equity civil bill, defence, or defence and counterclaim: RCC O.5. In the District Court there are no formal pleadings besides the claim contained in the civil process, notice of intention to defend, set-off or counterclaim, and third party procedure: DCR r.114. [Text: Collins & O'Reilly; Bullen & Leak UK; Odgers UK]. See LITIGATION; LONG VACATION; PARTICULARS, PLEADING; SPECIAL PLEADING; TRAVERSE; UNDUE INFLUENCE IN PLEADINGS.

**pleadings, amendment of.** There are times allowed for the amendment of pleadings without application to the court, or by consent, or by the court; however, the court may grant leave to such amendments as may be necessary for the purpose of determining the real issues in controversy between the parties: RSC O.28 r.1. In the Circuit and District Courts, similar provisions apply: RCC O.57; DCR r.21. See SUMMONS, AMENDMENT OF.

**pleasure craft.** Vessels used otherwise than for profit and used wholly or mainly for sport or recreation but includes mechanically propelled vessels that are on hire pursuant to contracts or other arrangements that do not require the owners of the vessels to provide crews or parts of crew for them: Merchant Shipping Act 1992 s.20(6). The Minister is empowered to make regulations for the purpose of ensuring the safety of pleasure craft and their occupants (ibid s.20)).

**pledge.** An article pawned with a pawnbroker: Pawnbrokers Act 1964 s.2. The transfer of the possession, but not the ownership, of a chattel as security for the payment of a debt or performance of an obligation. On default, the chattel

may be sold. The Official Assignee (qv) has the right to inspect any of a bankrupt's goods which have been pledged or pawned so that he may have a reasonable opportunity of exercising the right of *redemption:* Bankruptcy Act 1988 s.68. See PAWNBROKER.

**plenary.** Full; conclusive; complete.

**plenary summons.** See SUMMONS, HIGH COURT.

**plene administravit.** [He has fully administered].

**plenipotentiary.** A person or persons with full powers.

**plover.** See GAME.

**plural.** The use of a *plural* noun in an Act imports the singular (unless the contrary intention appears): Interpretation Act 1937 s.11(a). This interpretation also applies to nouns in instruments made wholly or partly under an Act.

**pointsman.** A garda in uniform and on traffic control duty: Road Traffic General Bye-Laws 1964 art.2 (SI No 294 of 1964).

**poison.** The felony (qv) committed by a person who unlawfully administers any poison or other destructive or noxious thing so as to endanger life, or to inflict grievous bodily harm: Offences Against the Person Act 1861 s.23. It is a misdemeanour where the intention is to injure, aggrieve or annoy (ibid s.24). There are restrictions on the sale of poisons and regulations on the labelling of containers, the keeping of books and records on sales, and there are special restrictions on the sale of strychnine. See Poisons Act 1961; Pharmacy Acts 1875 to 1977; Poisons Regulations — SI No 188 of 1982; SI No 424 of 1986; SI No 353 of 1991. See ABORTION.

**poitin.** Colloquial term in the Irish language to describe an illicit spirit, the making, possession, selling or delivery of which is an offence: Illicit Distillation Act 1831. See also Spirits (Ireland) Act 1854; Illicit Distillation Act 1857; Revenue (No 2) Act 1861 s.19; Intoxicating Liquor (General) Act 1924; Intoxicating Liquor Act 1960 s.22(1); Customs and Excise (Miscellaneous Provisions) Act 1988 s.14.

**police.** See GARDA SIOCHANA.

**police cooperation.** Member States of the European Union (qv) are required to regard police cooperation as a matter of *common concern*, eg police cooperation for the purpose of preventing and combatting terrorism, unlawful drug trafficking and other serious forms of international crime, and for combatting drug addiction and fraud on an international scale: Maastricht Treaty 1992 art.K.1.

**police property.** See PROPERTY IN POSSESSION OF GARDA.

**policy.** An instrument comprising a contract of insurance and called a life, fire, marine, accident, public liability, aviation, etc policy, according to the nature of the insurance. See INSURANCE, CONTRACT OF; ASSIGNMENT OF CONTRACT; PREMIUM.

**political offence.** Extradition cannot be granted for an offence which is a *political offence* or an offence connected with a *political offence*: Extradition Act 1965 s.11. It has been held that even if the objective of an offence is undoubtedly political, the means used must not be unacceptable in the sense that reasonable, civilised people would not regard them as political acts: McGlinchey v Wren (1982) IR 154. It has also been held in a particular case of murders, that they were so cowardly and callous, that it would be a distortion of language if they were accorded the status of political offences: Shannon v Fanning (1984) IR 569. See also Bourke v Attorney General (1972) IR 36; Quinn v Wren (1985) IR 322; Finucane v McMahon (1990 SC) ILRM 505; Carron v McMahon (1990 SC) ILRM 802.

A number of offences are by statute no longer regarded as political offences and criteria are laid down to be taken into account when evaluating the offences: Extradition (European Convention on Suppression of Terrorism) Act 1987 ss.3(2) and 4(1). It has been held that s.3 of the 1987 Act must be strictly construed: Sloan v Culligan (1992 SC) ILRM 194.

The onus of establishing that offences to which an extradition order relate are political offences is upon the person who seeks asylum in the State: Harte v Fanning (1988) ILRM 75. See also Ellis v O'Dea (1991 SC) ILRM 347; Magee v Culligan (1992 SC) ILRM 186. See EXTRADITION; MURDER, AGGRAVATED.

**political party, register of.** The register of political parties which meet specified criteria, eg that they are genuine political parties and are organised in the State to contest a Dail election or a European election or a local election: Electoral Act 1992 s.25. Registration may be for one or more of such elections and may be for a part or the whole of the State. Registration enables a candidate in an election to add the name of his registered party to his own on the ballot paper (ibid ss.25(13) and 88(2)(b)). See Loftus v Attorney General (1979) IR 221.

**polygamous marriage.** It was held in a particular case that a South African marriage, being potentially polygamous, was not enforceable in Irish law: Conlon v Mohamed (1987) ILRM 172 and 7ILT Dig (1989) 54.

**poll.** Taking a vote on a motion or at an election. At a general meeting of a company, questions are decided by a show of hands but there is a right to demand a poll, unless this right is expressly excluded. The right to demand a poll may be excluded only in respect of electing the chairman of the meeting or in relation to the adjournment of the meeting: Companies Act 1963 s.137. The poll involves the taking of the votes in person (or usually by proxy) by marking a voting paper *for* or *against* the motion or resolution.

A company may create different kinds of voting shares, with one carrying greater voting rights than another, although the Stock Exchange discourages the creation of non-voting shares. In the absence of provisions to the contrary, every member has one vote in respect of each share or each £10 of stock held by him (ibid s.134(e)). See Kinsella v Alliance Dublin Consumers Gas Co (1982) HC. See also Building Societies Act 1989 ss.50(2), 50(13), 73(1) and second schedule, part 11, para 5(q). See PROXY; CHAIRMAN; VOTING AT MEETINGS.

**poll tax.** A tax per person.

**pollutant.** Any substance so specified or any other substance (including a substance which gives rise to odour) or energy which, when emitted into the atmosphere, either by itself or in combination with any other substance, may cause air pollution: Air Pollution Act 1987 s.7(1) as amended by Environmental Protection Agency Act 1992 s.18(2) and third schedule. Specified air pollutants are listed in the 1987 Act, first schedule. See AIR POLLUTION; POLLUTING MATTER.

**pollution control.** See INTEGRATED POLLUTION CONTROL.

**polluting matter.** As regards water pollution, means any poisonous or noxious matter, and any substance (including any explosive, liquid or gas) the entry or discharge of which into any waters is liable to render those or any other waters poisonous or injurious to fish, spawning grounds or the food of any fish, or to injure fish in their value as human food, or to impair the usefulness of the bed and soil of any waters as spawning grounds or their capacity to produce the food of fish or to render such waters harmful or detrimental to public health or to domestic, commercial, industrial, agricultural or recreational uses: Local Government (Water Pollution) Act 1977 s.1. See WATER POLLUTION.

**pollution, civil liability for.** Liability is imposed on the occupier of premises from which effluent originates where that effluent enters waters and causes injury loss or damage to a person or the property of a person: LG (Water Pollution) (Amendment) Act 1990 s.20. Liability is also imposed on the person responsible for the entry if it is a contravention of the Act. This liability is without prejudice to any other cause of action that may lie. Similar provisions apply in respect of air pollution which causes injury, loss or damage to a person or to the property of a person: Air Pollution Act 1987 ss.28A and 28B inserted by Environmental Protection Agency Act 1992 s.18(2) and third schedule, para 4. See AIR POLLUTION; RYLAND V FLETCHER, RULE IN; SEA POLLUTION; WATER POLLUTION.

**polychlorinated biphenyls; pcbs.** The holder of waste polychlorinated biphenyls is required: (a) to notify the Minister of such holding and the manner in which it is proposed to dispose of it; (b) to comply with any direction given by the Minister or by an *authorised person* in relation to such disposal; and (c) to provide evidence, if so required, of the manner in which the *pcb* waste has been disposed of: European Communities (Waste) Regulations (SI No 108 of 1984).

See also Environmental Protection Agency Act 1992 s.54 and second schedule.

**port, free.** See FREE PORT.

**portion.** The provision made for a child by a parent or one *in loco parentis* so as to establish the child for life. See ADVANCEMENT; DOUBLE PORTIONS, RULE AGAINST; SATISFACTION; STRICT SETTLEMENT.

**positive law.** Man-made law as compared with natural law (qv).

**posse comitatus.** [The power of the country]. Formerly, a group of able-bodied men which the sheriff was empowered to call together to assist in keeping the peace.

**possession.** Physical detention with the intention to hold the thing detained as one's own; continuing exercise of a claim to the exclusive use of some material object. Possession is prima facie evidence of ownership and may be good against all claims except that of the true owner. Possession may develop into ownership with the efflux of time eg adverse possession (qv) of land. A seller in market overt (qv), a factor (qv) and the holder of a negotiable instrument (qv) can all give a better title than they themselves have, provided the buyer takes in good faith and for value. See NEMO DAT QUI NON HABET; OWNERSHIP.

**possession and crime.** Possession of certain objects or materials can constitute a criminal offence eg possession of a firearm with intent to endanger life, possession of drugs. It is an offence for a person to be in *possession* of any article with the intention that it be used in a larceny (qv), burglary, damanding with menaces, obtaining by false pretences, or taking a vehicle without the consent of its owner: Larceny Act 1990 s.2. The distinctive character of *possession* is that the accused has control of the article in question and knowledge of its existence: Minister for Posts & Telegraphs v Campbell (1966) IR 69; he does not have to have custody.

**possession, order for.** The order which a court may give to a mortgagee to aid a sale out of court, or a sale by the court in lieu of foreclosure (qv): Ulster Bank Ltd v Conlon (1957) 91 ILTR 193; Irish Permanent Building Society v Ryan (1950) IR 12; Irish Civil Service Building Society v Ingram's Representative (1959)

IR 181.

**possession is nine-tenths of the law.**
Popular paraphrase for the legal concept
that possession is prima facie evidence
of ownership and may be good against
all claims except that of the true owner.
See POSSESSION.

**possession of drugs.** A person who has
possession of a controlled drug may be
guilty of an offence: Misuse of Drugs
Act 1977 s.3.

**possibility.** A future event the happening
of which is uncertain. A possibility in
relation to a future interest in land is
said to be *bare* or *coupled with an interest.*
The possibility of reverter which exists
in the grantor of a determinable fee (qv)
is an example of a bare possibility; it is
not transferable. A contintent remainder
(qv), on the other hand, can give rise to
a possibiliity which can be transferred.

**post.** [After; following].

**post, contracts by.** Generally the rules
governing contracts by post are: (a) an
offer by post may be accepted by post,
unless the offer indicates anything to the
contrary; (b) an offer is only made when
it actually reaches the offeree and not
when it would have reached him in the
ordinary course of post; (c) an acceptance
is complete as soon as the letter of
acceptance is posted, prepaid and properly addressed, whether it reaches the
offeror or not; (d) a revocation is not
complete until it actually reaches the
offeree. See Adams v Lindsell (1818) 1
B Ald 681; Household Fire Insurance
Co v Grant (1879) 27 WR 858; Henthorn
v Fraser (1892) 2 Ch 27. See CONTRACT.
See also FAX; LIABILITY, STATUTORY EXEMP-
TIONS FROM; PRESUMPTION OF REGULARITY.

**post, redirection of.** The existing power
of the High Court to order the redirection
to the Official Assignee (qv) of letters
addressed to a *bankrupt,* has been
extended to telegrams and postal packets:
Bankruptcy Act 1988 s.72. See BANK-
RUPTCY.

**post diem.** [After the day].

**post litem motam.** [After litigation was
in contemplation].

**postal packets.** A number of offences
regarding postal packages (eg the unlawful taking or opening of mailbags or
postal packages, or secreting or destroying by an officer of An Post of a postal
package) are provided for by the Post

Office Act 1908 ss.50-55 as amended by
the Larceny Act 1990 s.10.

There are provisions regarding the
interception of postal packets; they are
similar to those applying to the interception of telecommunications messages ie
requirements for authorisation, complaints procedure, and review by a High
Court judge: Interception of Postal
Packets and Telecommunications Messages (Regulation) Act 1993. See TELE-
PHONE TAPPING.

**postal voter.** A person whose name is
entered in the postal voters list: Electoral
Act 1992 s.2(1). An elector is entitled to
be entered in this list if he is a member
of the garda siochana, is a whole time
member of the defence forces, or is a
person deemed to be ordinarily resident
in the State (ie a member of an Irish
diplomatic mission resident abroad) (ibid
s.14). A postal voter is entitled to vote
by sending his ballot paper by post to
the returning officer for his constituency
(ibid s.38(2)). See also 1992 Act ss.64-
77 and draft Presidential Elections Bill
1993 s.40.

Provision is also made for voting by
post in the election of employees to the
boards of State companies: Worker
Participation (State Enterprises) (Postal
Voting) Regulations 1988 (SI No 171 of
1988). See also Building Societies Act
1989 s.75. See also SEANAD EIREANN.

**posthumous child.** A child born after
the death of the father.

**postliminium.** [Beyond the threshold].
The doctine in international law (qv)
whereby persons, property and territory
tend to revert to their former condition,
following the withdrawal of enemy
control.

**post-date.** To insert a date on a document
subsequent to the date of execution
thereof eg to post-date a cheque. See
CHEQUE, POST-DATED.

**post-mortem.** [After death]. The examination of a body after death to determine
the cause of death. Also referred to as
an *autopsy.* See CORONER.

**potato growers.** A registration scheme is
imposed on all potato growers and
packers by the Registration of Potato
Growers and Potato Packers Act 1984.

**potior est conditio defendentis.** [The
condition of the defendant is better].
The burden of proof is on the plaintiff.

See BURDEN OF PROOF.

**potier est conditio possidentis.** [The condition of the possessor is the better]. The burden of proof is on the claimant to show that he has a superior title to that of the possessor.

**pound.** The *monetary unit* of the State is the Irish pound which is issued in legal tender (qv) form: Central Bank Act 1989 s.24(1). The Minister is empowered to vary the general exchange rate for the Irish Pound in respect of other monetary units (ibid s.24(2)). The one pound coin was introduced by the Coinage (Dimension and Design) (One Pound Coin) Regulations 1990, SI No 83 of 1990: Decimal Currency Act 1990 s.39(c). The £ symbol has no legal significance itself, no more than has the IR£ symbol *which appears to be a banking device*: Northern Bank v Edwards (1986) ILRM 167. However, references in contracts and other instruments to the payment of money are references to Irish pounds unless some other currency is specified: Central Bank Act 1989 s.25. See COINS; LEGAL TENDER.

**poundage.** A fee of a particular amount in each pound; a sheriff is entitled to a *poundage* in respect of that which he takes, or is deemed to have taken, upon an execution against the lands or goods of a defendant. See also Finance Act 1988 s.71. See COUNTY REGISTRAR; SHERIFF. See also RATES.

**pounds.** See DISTRESS DAMAGE FEASANT.

**poverty.** A body, known as the Combat Poverty Agency, has been established to advise on all aspects of economic and social planning in relation to poverty: Combat Poverty Agency Act 1986. See also SECURITY FOR COSTS.

**poverty, relief of.** See CHARITIES.

**power.** The authority conferred on a person by law to determine the legal relations of himself or others. Every *power* conferred by an Act of the Oireachtas or by an instrument made wholly or partly under any such Act, *may*, unless the contrary intention appears in such Act or instrument, be exercised from time to time as occasion requires: Interpretation Act 1937 s.15(1). Contrast with DUTY.

**power boat.** See JET SKIIS.

**power of appointment.** An authority given to a person to dispose of property which is not his. The person giving the authority is called the *donor*, the person to whom it is given, is the *donee* of the power, and the persons in whose favour the donee may make an appointment are called the *objects of the power*.

A power may be *appendant*, *in gross* or *collateral*. It is *appendant* where the donee has an interest in the property and the power is to take effect wholly or in part out of that interest. The power is *in gross*, where the donee is given an interest in the property but the exercise of it will not affect his interest. The power is *collateral* or naked where the donee is not given any interest in the property.

A power of appointment may be classified also as a *general power* which is the power to appoint property to anyone including the donee himself and is almost equivalent to ownership; and a *special power* where the power is to appoint to a special person or among a special class. Several statutes regard a donee of a special power as actual owner: Judgment Mortgage Act 1850; Succession Act 1965 ss.46 and 93. In the absence of a direction to the contrary by the donor, special powers are *exclusive* powers, by which the donee may appoint to any or all of the class: Illusory Appointments Act 1874. See OFFICIAL ASSIGNEE; POWER OF ATTORNEY.

**power of attorney.** A formal instrument under seal by which one person authorises another person to act for him, in relation to certain specified matters. The donor of the power is the *principal* and the donee is the *attorney*. The authorisation must be under seal in order for the attorney to execute a deed on behalf of the principal.

A power of attorney given for value and expressed to be irrevocable, cannot (in favour of a purchaser) be revoked without the agreement of the attorney (donee); a power of attorney, given for value or not, expressed to be irrevocable for a fixed period not exceeding one year is similarly irrevocable: Conveyancing Act 1882 ss.8 and 9.

An instrument creating or revoking a power of attorney may be deposited in or filed at the Central Office (qv); an alphabetical index of the names of donors of such powers of attorney is kept and the index may be searched on payment of the prescribed fee: Conveyancing Act 1881 s.48(1); RSC O.78. Such filing does not afford any protection against a breach of trust or other abuses. See Report on Land Law — Enduring Powers of Attorney (LRC 31 of 1989).

**power of sale.** See MORTGAGEE, RIGHTS OF; SETTLEMENT; TRUSTEE, POWER OF.

**p.p.** See PER PRO.

**practice.** The formal procedures relating to proceedings in a court, governed generally by the Rules of the Superior Courts in respect of the High and Supreme Court (RSC), the Rules of the Circuit Court (RCC) and District Court Rules (DCR). [Text: Collins & O'Reilly; Gannon; Waldron; Woods (1)]. See RULES OF COURT.

**practice directions.** The directions and notes, generally published in the Legal Diary, indicating the views of the judges, the Master of the High Court, and the registrars regarding matters of practice and procedure of the courts. The directions are issued from the Central Office (qv). A court has held that it is not bound by a practice note: Donohoe v Dillon (1988 HC) ILRM 654. Practice notes are also published by the Law Society in its monthly publication "Gazette". For example of practice direction, see SUMMONS, SERVICE OUT OF JURISDICTION.

**practising certificate.** (1) The certificate issued by the Incorporated Law Society of Ireland (qv) certifying that the solicitor (qv) named therein is entitled to practice as a solicitor: Solicitors Act 1954 ss.46-53. (2) The certificate awarded to a person by a body of accountants entitling that person to practise as auditor of a company or as a public auditor: Companies Act 1990 s.182.

**praecipe.** A command. A form used to secure the issue of various orders eg a praecipe delivered to the Central Office of the High Court for the issue of a subpoena (qv).

**praepositus.** [A person put in front]. A person in authority.

**praesumitur pro negante.** [It is presumed for the negative].

**praesumptio.** [Presumption (qv)]

**prank.** In a particular case, a company has been found vicariously liable for the prank of a supervisor which resulted in an employee suffering personal injury:

Kennedy v Taltech Engineering Co Ltd (1990) 8ILT Dig 84.

**preamble.** The introduction to a statute which states the reason for it eg in the Succession Act 1965 — *An Act to reform the law relating to succcession to the property of deceased persons and, in particular, the devolution, administration, testamentary disposition and distribution on intestacy of such property, and to provide for related matters.* It is also referred to as the "long title" of the statute. See Madden v Minister for the Marine (1993 HC) ILRM 436. See LEGISLATION, INTERPRETATION OF; MISCHIEF OF A STATUTE.

**precatory trust.** An express trust created by expressions which prima facie are only recommendatory; a trust which may be created by the use by the donor of *precatory words* accompanying a gift, ie words which express a wish, hope, desire or entreaty, that the donee will dispose of the property in some particular way. The Courts tend to rule against construing precatory words as trusts: In re Adams and Kensington Vestry (1884) 27 Ch D 394. If a gift is given absolutely, the precatory expressions attached to it are regarded as stating the motive that induced the absolute gift, rather than a fetter imposed upon it: O'Donoghue v O'Donoghue (1959) ILTR 56; Chambers v Fahy (1931) IR 17; In re McIntosh (1933) IR 69. See TRUST.

**precedence.** The ceremonial order or priority to be observed by persons on formal occasions. The President of Ireland takes precedence over all other persons in the State: 1937 Constitution art.12(1).

**precedent.** (1) In drafting proceedings or in conveyancing, a *precedent* is a copy of an instrument used as a guide in preparing a similar instrument. [Text: Collins & O'Reilly; Laffoy & Wheeler; Bullen & Leak; Butterworths].

(2) A *precedent* is also a judgment or decision of a court of law which is cited as an authority to justify a decision in a case involving a similar set of facts. A precedent may be *authoritative* where it is binding and must be followed; *persuasive* where it is worthy of consideration but need not be followed (eg based on an orbiter dictum (qv)); *declaratory* where it merely applies an

existing rule of law; and *original* where it creates and applies a new rule of law. A precedent is said to be *applied* when it is followed. It is said to be *distinguished* where a judge holds that there are important differences between the case on which the precedent was based and the case now being considered.

The Supreme Court binds all courts although it is not bound by its own decisions. The High Court binds the Circuit and District Courts; the Court of Criminal Appeal binds the Central Criminal Court, the Special Criminal Court and the Circuit and District Courts on criminal matters. The courts may adopt as *persuasive* precedents, the judgments of the US and Canadian Supreme Courts, and of the House of Lords and Australian and New Zealand courts. "While the Irish High Court should be slow to refuse to follow a principle established since 1883 in England, it was justified in not following it where high legal authority in England had questioned it": Costello J in Tromso Sparebank v Beirne & Ors (1989 HC) ILRM 257. See also Attorney General v Ryan Car Hire Ltd (1965) IR 642; McDonnell v Byrne Engineering Ltd (1978) HC. See STARE DECISIS; RATIO DECIDENDI; OBITER DICTUM.

**precedent, condition.** See CONDITION.

**predecessor.** A person from whom one obtains succession to property ie from a settlor (qv) or testator (qv). A *predecessor in title* is the person through whom one may trace a title in property.

**pre-emption.** The right of purchasing property before or in preference to other persons. As regards companies, there is no general common law principle that requires giving to existing shareholders a pre-emptive claim on new shares. Since 1983 however, pre-emption is now compulsory for every company, subject to some exceptions, and also pre-emption must apply to equity securities for which a Stock Exchange listing is sought: Listing Agreement s.1, ch 2,15; Companies Amendment Act 1983 s.23;

A company proposing to allot any *equity securities* must not allot any of those securities on any terms to any person unless it has made an offer to each person who holds relevant shares to allot to him on the same or more favourable terms a proportion of those securities which is as nearly as practicable equal to the proportion in nominal value held by him of the aggregate of the shares (ibid s.23).

A private company may by its memorandum or articles of association vary the right of pre-emption (ibid 23(10)). The right does not apply to shares that have been allotted for a consideration wholly or partly other than cash (ibid s.23(4)). Waiver of the right is allowed in certain circumstances (ibid s.24).

Only *equity securities* carry the right of pre-emption; these are (a) shares which are not subject to any ceiling on the amounts that may be distributed to their holders by way of dividends and capital, and (b) rights to subscribe for or convert into such shares (ibid s.23(13)). Consequently, they are principally *ordinary* shares and certain *preference* shares. There are special provisions for equity securities of a particular class and for shares held under an *employees' share scheme* (ibid s.23). See SHARES.

**preference shares.** Shares in a company which carry prior or preferential rights over other shares. Usually the preference shareholders must be paid a dividend, or repaid their investment, or both as the case may be, before such payment may be made to the other shareholders.

Preference dividends are presumed to be *cumulative* ie in the absence of a contrary provision, where a preference dividend has not been paid in any year or years, then all arrears of undeclared preference dividends for those years must be paid before any other class of shareholder may get a dividend: Webb v Earle (1875) LR 20 Eq 556. Preference shares are usually *redeemable* at some future date although they may be irredeemable. The *articles of association* usually provide that preference shareholders have no voting rights except in exceptional circumstances.

Usually preference shares are by their terms given priority in respect of payment of capital but are excluded from participating in any surplus which may remain in a winding up. If not specifically provided for, there is doubt as to whether preference shareholders are entitled to participate rateably in a surplus: contrast Cork Electric Supply Co v Concannon

(1932) IR 314 with Scottish Insurance Co v Wilsons Clyde Coal Co (1949) AC 462. See Building Societies Act 1989 s.10. See REDEEMABLE PREFERENCE SHARES.

**preferential creditor.** See PREFERENTIAL PAYMENTS.

**preferential debts.** See PREFERENTIAL PAYMENTS.

**preferential payments.** The payment of debts in priority to others in distributing or realising an estate, as in the administration of a deceased's estate, in the distribution of a bankrupt's estate, or in the winding up of a company.

As regards a company, preferential debts include: (a) one year's rates and taxes, PAYE and social welfare contributions; (b) four months' wages or salary of any clerk, servant, workman or labourer; (c) sums due to employees for sick and holiday pay; (d) payments due for provision of superannuation benefits; (e) compensation and costs in respect of employers' liability for injuries suffered in the course of employment: Companies Act 1963 s.285, Companies Amendment Act 1982 s.10.

There is a limit of £2,500 in each of these categories (ibid s.10(b)). These debts rank equally among themselves and abate in equal proportions if the assets are insufficient to meet them: Companies Act 1963 s.285(7). The liquidator's remuneration, together with all costs, charges and expenses in the winding up, must be paid before all preferred debts. Somewhat similar provisions regarding preferential payments apply to the distribution of the property of a bankrupt (qv): Bankruptcy Act 1988 s.81. See RSC O.74 rr.46 and 128(1).

In order to speed up company liquidations generally, the liquidator is entitled to advertise for preferential creditors and to exclude any creditors who do not come forward within a specified time: Companies Act 1963 s.285(14) as inserted by Companies Act 1990 s.134. See In re Castlemahon Poultry Products (1987 SC) ILRM 222.

As regards preferential payments in bankruptcy, see In an arranging debtor (1921) 2 IR 1. See also In re United Bars (1989) 7ILT Dig 259. See Rules of Superior Courts (No 3) 1989 (SI 79 of 1989) Part XXVII. See also Social Welfare Act 1990 s.45. See CHARGE.

**pregnancy.** The state of being with child; having conceived. The dismissal of an employee by reason of pregnancy, or matters connected therewith, is deemed to be unfair: Unfair Dismissal Act 1977 s.6(2). Dismissal is not unlawful if the employee is unable to do adequately the work for which she was employed: ibid s.6(f)(i)(I) and McCarthy v Sunbeam Ltd (1991 EAT) ELR 38.

For allegation of direct discrimination under s.2(a) of the 1977 Act, see Long v Power Supermarket t/a Quinnsworth EE5/1988 in 7ILT & SJ (1989) 86, where the Equality Officer found as a question of fact that the treatment afforded a pregnant female was the same as that afforded a sick male. See also Maxwell v English Language Institute (1990) ELR (226); O'Leary v Panther Catering (1990) ELR 157; Webb v EMO Air Cargo (UK) Ltd (1993) IRLR 27.

Employers are required to ensure that when places of work undergo modifications extensions or conversions after 1992, or are used for the first time after 1992, pregnant women and nursing mothers must be able to lie down to rest in appropriate conditions: SI No 44 of 1993, reg.17, third schedule, para 11, and fourth schedule, para 8. This requirement also applies to other places of work whenever required by the features of the place of work, the work activity carried on and the circumstances or the hazards prevailing in relation to any such activity (ibid reg.17(2)).

Prior pregnancy can also be a ground for nullity in a subsequent marriage as affecting the true consent required for marriage: contrast WCC v C (1989 HC) IR 696 and DB(O'R) v N'O'R (1988) HC as per Woulfe in 7ILT & SJ (1989) 130. See UNFAIR DISMISSAL. See also ABORTION; MATERNITY LEAVE; SICKNESS; UNBORN, INJURIES TO; UNBORN, RIGHT TO LIFE OF.

**preinspection.** The procedure by which immigration and public health requirements of United States law is completed in Ireland for passengers and crew travelling from Ireland to the US; the procedure is operated by employees of the US Immigration and Naturalisation Service (INS) who are granted certain powers and immunities under Irish law: Air Navigation and Transport (Preinspection) Act 1986. A person refused clearance to enter the USA by the INS is deemed to have arrived in the State of Ireland and to be within the jurisdiction of Irish immigration law and officials (ibid s.7).

**prejudice.** Injury; pre-conceived judgment. See WITHOUT PREJUDICE.

**prejudicial evidence.** Evidence which invites a court to disbelieve a witness on the basis of general bad character, or to believe a witness on the basis of general good character, without being directly probative as to the issue of guilt or innocence of the crime charged. See Newman in ISLR (1993) 96. See CHARACTER, EVIDENCE OF.

**pre-judgment interest.** Interest which a plaintiff in an action may be entitled to between the date his cause of action accrued and the date of judgment: Courts Act 1981 s.22. Such interest may be awarded by the court only and not by the Master of the High Court or by the Central Office (qv): Mellowhide Products Ltd v Barry Agencies Ltd (1983) ILRM 152. See INTEREST ON JUDGMENTS.

**preliminary examination.** See DISTRICT COURT, PRELIMINARY EXAMINATION.

**preliminary issue.** An issue which raises a question of law, which a court considers would be convenient to have decided before any evidence is given or any question or issue of fact is tried, or before any reference is made to an arbitrator; the court may order that such question of law be raised for the opinion of the court either by *special case* or in such other manner as the court deems expedient: RSC O.34 r.2; also RCC O.31 r.1. See SPECIAL CASE.

**preliminary point.** A matter raised usually at the outset in a legal proceedings eg as to the jurisdiction of the court.

**preliminary rulings.** The rulings given by the European Court of Justice concerning: (a) the interpretation of the Treaty of Rome; (b) the validity and interpretation of acts of the institutions of the European Community; (c) the interpretation of the statutes of bodies established by an act of the Council, where those statutes so provide: Treaty of Rome 1957 art.177. The Court may not rule on the interpretation of national laws and regulations or on the conformity of such measures with Community law;

it may only provide the national court with the criteria for interpretation based on Community law which will enable that court to solve the legal problem with which it is faced: Heineken Bronwerijen ECR (1984) 3435.

Every member or tribunal of a member state is entitled to ask the court for a *preliminary ruling,* regardless of the stage reached in the proceedings pending before it and regardless of the nature of the decision which it is called upon to give; an appeal does not lie against a decision to seek a preliminary ruling: Campus Oil Co Ltd v Minister for Industry Energy (1983 SC) IR 82. A preliminary ruling is binding *inter partes;* it may be regarded as authoritative by all national courts where it declares a Council or Commission regulation to be void: Societe des Produits de Mais SA (1985) ECR 719. See also In re Beara Fisheries and Shipping Ltd (1988) ILRM 221; SPUC v Grogan (1989) IR 753; Cotter v McDermott (1991 ECJ) Case 377/89. See EUROPEAN COURT OF JUSTICE.

**preliminary tax.** The tax liability of a self employed person, as assessed by that person, which must be paid within one month of the due date in each tax year, under the "self assessment" provisions introduced by the Finance Act 1988 ss.9-21. Preliminary tax includes income tax, pay related social insurance, health contribution, and the employment and training levy.

If the preliminary tax actually paid is less than 90% of the amount actually due for the year, interest will be charged on the deficiency from the due date. A "Notice of Preliminary Tax" is the Tax Inspector's estimate of the preliminary tax due; however the taxpayer's own estimate of preliminary tax must be paid even if it is higher than that in the Notice or even if no Notice is received by the taxpayer. There is no right of appeal against the tax shown in the Notice and that amount may be pursued for collection by the Revenue Commissioners in the event that the taxpayer fails to pay his own assessment of the preliminary tax.

**premature.** In a particular case involving a Bord Pleanala decision, development which was stated to be *premature* was held to mean action which could be done at a later date but that as yet it was too early to take action: Hoburn Holmes Ltd v An Bord Pleanala (1992 HC) ITLR (20 Jul) and (1993) ILRM 368.

**premises.** [That which went before]. (1) The operative parts of a conveyance (qv) which precede the *habendum* (qv) and come after the *recitals* (qv). (2) Popularly, land and buildings. Includes any messuage, building, vessel, structure or land or any hereditament of any tenure, together with any out-buildings and curtilage: Environmental Protection Agency Act 1992 s.3(1). See also Building Societies Act 1989 s.20.

**premium.** (1) The consideration in a contract of insurance. It is often a periodical payment; an insurer is not bound to accept a *renewal premium* except in the case of a life insurance policy. Policies usually provide that the insurer is not on risk until the premium is paid. There is a duty on the insured to disclose material facts which could affect the renewal or the renewal premium. In marine insurance, where an insurance is effected at a premium to be arranged, and no arrangement is made, a reasonable premium is payable: Marine Insurance Act 1906 s.31. See also ibid ss.52-54.

A premium paid to an insurance intermediary (qv) is treated as having been paid to the insurer when it is paid to the insurance intermediary in respect of a renewal of a policy which has been invited by the insurer, or in respect of an accepted proposal: Insurance Act 1989 s.53.

Additionally, an insurance intermediary must not accept money from a client (a) in respect of a proposal unless it is accompanied by the completed proposal or the proposal has been accepted by the insurer, or (b) in respect of a renewal unless it has been invited by the insurer (ibid s.52).

(2) The amount in excess of the par or nominal value of a share in a company which an applicant for that share is required to pay. It is for the directors to decide whether to issue shares at a premium and the size of any premium: Companies Act 1963, Table A, art 5. The aggregate amount or value of any premium received must be placed in a *share premium account*. It may not be repaid to the shareholders except by the capital reduction mechanism (ibid ss.72-77 as amended). However it may be used to finance the issue to existing members of fully paid up *bonus* shares, or to pay any premium which is due when preference shares or debentures are being redeemed, or to defray the company's preliminary expenses, or the cost of issuing shares or debentures in the company, or to pay commission on such issue (ibid s.62 as amended by the Companies Acts 1983, first schedule, para 11 and Companies Act 1990 s.231(1)). See DISCOUNT, ISSUE OF SHARES AT; INSURANCE, CONTRACT OF; REDUCTION OF CAPITAL; ULTRA VIRES.

**pre-retirement allowance.** A scheme of a pre-retirement allowance for elderly long term unemployed persons who have effectively retired from the labour force has been provided for in the Social Welfare Act 1988 s.28.

**prerogative, royal.** See ROYAL PREROGATIVE.

**prerogative orders.** Orders of certiorari, prohibition, mandamus and quo warranto (qqv). See JUDICIAL REVIEW.

**pre-school service.** Any pre-school, play group, day nursery, creche, day-care or other similar service which caters for pre-school children including those grant-aided by health boards: Child Care Act 1991 s.49. A *pre-school child* is a child who has not attained the age of six years and who is not attending a national school (qv) or a school providing an educational programme similar to a national school (ibid s.49). A person carrying on a pre-school service must give notice to the relevant health board (ibid s.51). There is provision for supervision and inspection by the health board (ibid ss.53-55). Regulations may be made by the Minister (ibid s.50).

A statutory duty is placed on persons carrying on pre-school services to take all reasonable measures to safeguard the health safety and welfare of the children concerned and to comply with the Minister's regulations (ibid s.52). These legal provisions do not apply to a person taking care of not more than 3 pre-school children in that person's home, or care by a relative or spouse of a relative (ibid s.58).

**prescribe.** (1) To lay down with authority;

to set out under a regulation. (2) To claim by prescription (qv).

**prescribed limit of alcohol.** See DRUNKEN DRIVING.

**prescription.** The vesting of a right by reason of the lapse of time eg an easement (qv). Prescription at common law required proof of user since time immemorial (qv), *nec vi, nec dam, nec precario,* ie without force, without secrecy, without permission. The doctrine of the *lost modern grant* (qv) overcame some difficulties in establishing this proof. The Prescription Act 1832, extended to Ireland in 1859, lays down the periods of enjoyment required to establish title to an easement and a profit a prendre (qv). See Scott v Goulding Properties Ltd (1973) IR 200.

**prescription drugs.** Medical preparations which must only be supplied against a prescription issued by a registered medical practitioner or registered dentist. There is a comprehensive system of control on prescriptions eg limit of 6 months for dispensing from date of prescription; labelling requirements eg if for external use must have "for external use only"; pharmacy records; emergency prescribing; prohibition on sale after the expiry date; prohibition on advertisements for prescription-only medical preparations: Medical Preparations (Control of Sale) Regulations (SI No 18 of 1987). See MEDICAL PREPARATIONS.

**present.** To tender or offer eg to present a cheque (qv) for payment.

**presentment.** See GRAND JURY.

**preservative.** Any substance which is capable of inhibiting, retarding or arresting deterioration of food caused by micro-organisms and of concealing the evidence of such deterioration, but does not include some specified substances eg common salt: SI No 337 of 1981. A person may not manufacture, prepare, import, distribute or sell any food which contains any preservative other than a permitted preservative (ibid para.11).

**preserved benefit.** The benefit which a member of an occupational pension scheme is entitled to, whose employment terminates (otherwise than by death) prior to normal retirement age: Pensions Act 1990 ss.28-39 as amended by Social Welfare Acts 1992 s.54 and 1993 s.45.

The qualifying service is 5 years of which 2 years must be since 1 January 1991. A member who is entitled to a preserved benefit is entitled to a transfer payment to another pension scheme or to a life office annuity bond (ibid 1990 Act s.34 as amended by 1992 Act s.55). A preserved benefit cannot be subject to forfeiture or a lien (qv) (ibid 1990 Act s.36). See PENSION SCHEME, OCCUPATIONAL.

**President of Ireland.** The office, established by the 1937 Constitution, and elected by the direct vote of the people, the holder of which takes precedence over all other persons in the State and who may hold office for not more than two terms, each of seven years (ibid arts.12-14). The President, on the nomination of Dail Eireann, appoints the Taoiseach. She also appoints the other members of the government on the nomination of the Taoiseach and with the previous approval of the Dail. The Dail is summoned and dissolved by the President on the advice of the Taoiseach, although she may in her absolute discretion refuse to dissolve the Dail on the advice of a Taoiseach who has ceased to retain the support of a majority in the Dail.

Every Bill passed or deemed to have been passed by both Houses of the Oireachtas requires the signature of the President for its enactment into law. The President may, after consultation with the Council of State (qv) refer a Bill to the Supreme Court for a decision on the question as to whether it is repugnant to the Constitution. The President is also supreme commander of the defence forces and all its officers hold their commissions from her. She is responsible for the accreditation of the diplomatic representatives of the State: Republic of Ireland Act 1948.

Only *presidential electors* ie Irish citizens, 18 years and over, ordinarily resident in the constituency in which they seek to register, are entitled to vote in presidential elections: Electoral Act 1992 s.7. Under draft legislation, it is proposed to amend and consolidate the law relating to presidential elections: Presidential Elections Bill 1993. See also Presidential Establishment Acts 1938, 1973 and 1991.

The Presidents of Ireland have been:

Mary Robinson (1990 to present); Patrick J Hillery (1976-1990); Cearbhall O'Dalaigh (1974-1976); Erskine H Childers (1973-1974); Eamon de Valera (1959-1973); Sean T O'Ceallaigh (1945-1959); Douglas Hyde (1938-1945). See ADDRESS; ELECTION PETITION, PRESIDENTIAL; IMPEACHMENT; OBSTRUCTION OF THE PRESIDENT; PETITION.

**Presidential Commission.** The commission which is empowered to exercise and perform the powers and functions conferred on the President of Ireland, in her absence from the State, or incapacity, or where she has died, resigned, been removed from office or has failed to exercise and perform the powers and functions of her office: 1937 Constitution, art.14. The Commission consists of the Chief Justice, the Chairman of Dail Eireann (An Ceann Comhairle) and the Chairman of Seanad Eireann. The first dissolution (qv) of Dail Eireann ordered by the Presidential Commission (in the absence abroad of the President) took place in 1992 — Iris Oifigiuil 10th November 1992.

**press and privilege.** See FAIR AND ACCURATE REPORT; JOURNALIST, COMMUNICATIONS WITH; PUBLICATION, RIGHT OF.

**presumption.** A conclusion or inference as to the truth of some fact in question, drawn from other facts either proved or admitted to be true. Presumptions may be (a) *presumptions of law* which are *irrebuttable* (praesumptiones juris et de jure) and evidence is not admissible to contradict them eg that a child under seven years cannot commit a crime; (b) presumptions of law which are *rebuttable* (praesumptiones juris) and which are conclusive unless disproved by evidence to the contrary eg the presumption of innocence of an accused; (c) *presumptions of fact* (praesumptiones hominis vel facti) which are inferences which may be drawn from other facts but not compulsorily eg that the possessor of goods recently stolen is either the thief or the receiver (now, handling stolen property (qv)). See Maher v Attorney General (1973) IR 140.

**presumption of constitutionality.** See LEGISLATION, CONSTITUTIONALITY OF; RESOLUTION.

**presumption of continuance.** The presumption of fact that a proven state of affairs can be presumed to have continued in that condition for a reasonable time eg a jury is entitled to draw the inference that if a person was alive on a particular day, he was alive on a subsequent day.

**presumption of death.** See DEATH, PRESUMPTION OF.

**presumption of good faith and value.** The holder of a bill of exchange (qv) is prima facie presumed to be a *holder in due course* (qv): Bills of Exchange Act 1882 s.30(2).

**presumption of innocence.** The presumption in law, which is rebuttable, that an accused is innocent until proven guilty beyond reasonable doubt. See Harvey v Ocean Accident & Guarantee Corporation (1905) 2 IR 1. A trial held otherwise than in accordance with the presumption is not one in due course of law; however a limitation on the presumption of innocence could be constitutionally permissible: O'Leary v AG (1991 HC) ILRM 455. See UNLAWFUL ORGANISATION.

**presumption of legality.** See OMNIA PRAESUMUNTUR RITE ESSE ACTA.

**presumption of legitimacy.** See LEGITIMACY, PRESUMPTION OF.

**presumption of marriage.** See MARRIAGE, PRESUMPTION OF.

**presumption of negligence.** See RES IPSA LOQUITUR.

**presumption of regularity.** Where any judicial or official appointment or act is shown to have been done in a manner substantially regular, there is a presumption in law that the formal requisites for its validity were complied with. See In re McLean (1950) IR 180.

In a particular case concerning whether various assessments and demands had been lawfully posted by the Revenue Commissioners, it was held that the trial judge was entitled to act upon the evidence of the operation of a system and to accept it established as a matter of probability that the various documents had been posted when they were meant to have been: Deighan v Hearne & Ors (1990 SC) 1 IR 499. See OMNIA PRAESUMUNTUR RITE ESSE ACTA.

**presumption of sanity.** The presumption in law that a person is sane until the contrary is proved. See INSANITY; McNAGHTEN RULES; UNFIT TO PLEAD.

**presumption of survivorship.** See

DEATH, SIMULTANEOUS.

**presumptions as to documents.** See DOCUMENTS, PRESUMPTIONS AS TO.

**pretence, false.** See FALSE PRETENCE.

**pre-Union Irish Statute.** An Act passed by a parliament sitting in Ireland at any time before the coming into force of the Union with Ireland Act 1800: Interpretation Act 1937, schedule, para 24.

**preventative detention.** The period of not more than ten, and not less than five years, where a person is convicted as an *habitual criminal:* Prevention of Crime Act 1908. As there are apparently no facilities in the State for providing such detention, in practice the Act cannot be applied: The People (DPP) v Carmody (1988) ILRM 370. Preventative detention, by refusing bail (qv) to a person because of the likelihood of the commission of further offences, has no place in our legal system: The People v O'Callaghan (1966) IR 501. A preventative sentence of a rapist to protect women from him was unknown to the State's judicial system: DPP v Jackson (1993 CCA) — Irish Times 27/4/93. See also DPP v Ryan (1989) 7 ILT Dig 81.

Preventive detention, in terms of civil confinement, is provided for under the Mental Treatments Acts 1945-61, with improved safeguards when the Health (Mental Services) Act 1981 is brought into force. Also the Offences Against the State (Amendment) Act 1940 provides for preventative detention. See O'Malley in 7ILT & SJ (1989) 41. See INTERNMENT; MENTAL TREATMENT; RECEPTION ORDER.

**previous conduct.** Evidence of previous conduct is not admissible generally as it is deemed irrelevant. However, such evidence is admissible: (a) to prove guilty knowledge of a receiver of stolen goods: Larceny Act 1916 s.43 (now, handling stolen property (qv)); (b) to prove facts showing system so as to negative that an act was accidental: Makin v AG for New South Wales (1894) AC 57; (c) to prove the existence of a course of business; (d) to prove a state of mind eg intention, knowledge or malice; (e) to prove the true relationship between the accused person and the prosecutrix in sexual cases, but only when the judge so allows where it would otherwise be unfair to the accused: The People (Attorney General) v Dempsey (1961) IR 288;

Criminal Law (Rape) Act 1981 s.3 as amended by the Criminal Law (Rape) Amdt Act 1990 s.13. See RAPE.

**previous statement, inconsistent.** When a witness gives evidence at a trial which is inconsistent with a previous statement of his, the trial judge should explain to the jury that in such a case, the previous statement is only evidence against the credibility of the witness and not evidence of the matters contained in it: The People v Taylor (1974) IR 97. See HOSTILE WITNESS.

**price.** The money consideration in a contract for the sale of goods: Sale of Goods Act 1893 s.1. The price may be fixed or may be left to be fixed or may be determined by the course of dealing between the parties (ibid s.8). In the absence of the foregoing, the buyer must pay a reasonable price; what is reasonable is a question of fact dependent on the circumstances of each particular case. The time of payment is not deemed to be of the essence of a contract of sale unless a different intention appears from the terms of the contract (ibid s.10(1)). See CAPACITY TO CONTRACT; WARRANTY, BREACH OF.

**price, false or misleading indication of.** It is an offence for a person offering to supply goods of any description or offering to provide any services or living accommodation to give a false or misleading indication of the price or charge for same or of the recommended price (qv) for the goods: Consumer Information Act 1978 s.7.

**price, recommended.** See RECOMMENDED PRICE.

**price, reserve.** See RESERVE PRICE.

**price, retail.** See RETAIL PRICE.

**price control.** Wide statutory power is given to the Minister to make orders regulating the price of goods and services by the Prices Acts 1958, 1965 and 1972. The power extends to the interest charged and other charges made under hire-purchase and credit-sale agreements (ibid 1972 Act s.4). Price control is achieved mainly by *maximum price orders* and *price stabilisation orders*.

These orders must not be arbitrary or unfair or otherwise they may be ultra vires and void: Cassidy v Minister for Industry and Commerce (1978) IR 297. The Minister may also make *retail price display* orders requiring retailers to display in a specified manner the prices charged by them for certain commodities, and there is a prohibition on the sale *below cost* of certain goods.

There is provision for the appointment of *advisory committees* to enquire into and report to the Minister on the pricing and marketing of goods and services; it is an offence for a person to default in attending before such a committee on being duly summoned (ibid 1972 Act s.10). See also Restrictive Practices (Amendment) Act 1987 ss.27-29. See BELOW COST SELLING.

**price discrimination.** Charging different prices for essentially the same product or service. This may amount to an *abuse of a dominant position*. As regards the take-over and merger of companies, the City Code requires that all shareholders of the same class be offered the same price. As far as the law is concerned, generally a shareholder is entitled to sell his shares on the best terms he can get. See DOMINANT POSITION, ABUSE OF; MERGER.

**price list.** See ADVERTISEMENT.

**price variation clause.** In such a clause in a contract, effect must be given to the ordinary meaning of the words in the clause: Marathon Petroleum v Bord Gais Eireann (1986) SC.

**priest and privilege.** See PRIVILEGE, COMMUNICATIONS TO PRIEST.

**prima facie.** [Of first appearance]. On the face of it; a first impression. A *prima facie* case is one in which there is sufficient evidence in support of a party's charge or allegation to call for an answer from his opponent. If a prima facie case has not been made out, the opponent may, without calling any evidence himself, submit that there is no case to answer, whereupon the case may be dismissed. See DIRECTION.

**primary facts.** Basic facts determined by a trial judge; the determination of facts depending on the assessment by the judge of the credibility and quality of the witnesses. The Supreme Court will not normally reverse such findings because it has not had the advantage of seeing and hearing the witnesses as they gave their evidence: JM and GM v An Bord Uchtala (1988) ILRM 203. There are exceptional cases where the evidence is so clearly one way as to require the

intervention of the Supreme Court: Kennedy v Galway VEC (1993 SC) 11 ILT Dig 91. Contrast with SECONDARY FACTS.

Findings of primary facts will not be set aside unless there is no evidence to support them; with regard to inferences drawn from primary facts which are mixed questions of fact and law, these will be set aside only if the conclusions are ones which no reasonable judge could draw: Mara v Hummingbird Ltd (1982) ILRM 421 cited in Browne v Bank of Ireland Finance Ltd (1991 SC) ITLR (18 Mar) and O'Culachain v McMullan Bros Ltd (1991 HC) 1 IR 363. See also S v S (1992 SC) ILRM 732.

While normally bound by the findings by the trial judge of primary fact, the Supreme Court must investigate on appeal whether such findings constitute negligence, this being a matter of law in an action for damages for personal injuries: Moore v Fulleton (1991 SC) ILRM 29.

The Supreme Court has recommended, where judgment is not reserved in any cases tried by a judge, that the judge at the conclusion of the evidence should summarise his findings of primary fact and then invite submissions from both sides: O'Byrne v Gloucester (1989) 7ILT Dig 56. See also FACT; INFERENCE.

**Prime Minister.** Taoiseach (qv).

**primo loco.** [In the first place].

**primogeniture.** [Primo-genitus, first born]. The rule of inheritance according to which the eldest male in the same degree succeeded to the ancestor's land to the exclusion of others. Abolished by the Succession Act 1965 s.11 except as it applies to the descent of an *estate tail* (qv).

**principal.** A person who authorises another, called an *agent*, to act on his behalf. The duty of a principal is to pay the reward or commission to the agent in accordance with the express or implied contract of agency, and to indemnify the agent against losses incurred in execution of the authority.

A principal may revoke his authority at any time except where it has been given under seal or where the authority has been *coupled with an interest*. If a principal has allowed an agent to assume authority, a revocation of authority will only be effective as against third parties, if the third parties are informed of the revocation of authority.

Where a principal represents to a third party that he has authorised an agent to act on his behalf, he may, as against the third party, not be allowed to deny the truth of the representation and be bound by the agent's act whether he in fact authorised it or not; this is known as *apparent* authority: Kilgobbin Mink & Stud Farms Ltd v National Credit Co Ltd (1980) IR 175. See also Kett v Shannon (1987) ILRM 364. See COM-MISSION; SECRET PROFIT; UNDISCLOSED PRINCIPAL.

**principal, undisclosed.** See UNDISCLOSED PRINCIPAL.

**principal in crime.** In a felony (qv), the principal *in the first degree* is the actual offender; the principal *in the second degree* is the person who aids and abets the actual perpetrator of the felony at the time when it is committed. The aider and abetter (qv) is liable for such crimes committed by the principal in the first degree as were done in execution of their common purpose. See The People (Attorney General) v Ryan (1966) Frewen 304; The People (DPP) v Madden (1977) IR 336. See ACCESSORY; DURESS IN CRIME.

**print.** See ARTISTIC WORK.

**printed document.** See TYPE, SIZE OF.

**prior mortgage.** A building society is prohibited from making a *housing loan* (qv) on the security of any freehold or leasehold estate or interest which is subject to a *prior mortgage* unless the prior mortgage is in favour of the society: Building Societies Act 1989 s.22(4). However, the Central Bank may, by regulations, specify charges or descriptions of charges which would not materially affect the security, and a *prior mortgage* will not include any charge so specified (ibid s.22(5)). No such regulations had been made by 1993 and none were planned.

Pending such regulations, a *prior mortgage* does not include charges specified in the Building Societies (Amendment) Act 1983 or in the Land Act 1984 s.4(2), notwithstanding their repeal eg a charge on land to secure payment of the whole or part of a conventional rent, a fee farm rent or a crown rent or to secure payment of a purchase annuity, a land reclamation annuity or any other annual payment to the Land Commission. The 1983 Act was necessitated by the decision in Rafferty v Crowley (1984) ILRM 350.

**priority.** Precedence; the right to enforce a claim in preference to others. As regards *registered land,* the register is conclusive evidence of the title of the owner of the land as appearing on the register and of any right or burden, and such title, in the absence of fraud, is not affected by the owner having notice of any deed relating to the land: Registration of Title Act 1964 s.31. Registered burdens on registered land rank *inter se* according to the order in which they are registered, not according to the order in which they are created (ibid s.75).

As regards *unregistered land,* registered deeds rank inter se according to their date of registration, irrespective of whether the deed passes the legal or equitable estate: Registry of Deeds (Ireland) Act 1707 s.4. As between registered and unregistered deeds, the unregistered deed is deemed fraudulent and void as against the registered one; however a party claiming through a registered deed who has actual *notice* of a prior unregistered deed, cannot rely on the priority given by the 1707 Act (ibid s.5). Registration gives priority but it does not amount to notice.

In the absence of registration, priority as between equitable interests or between legal and equitable interests is determined by the equitable maxims *where the equities are equal, the first in time prevails; where the equities are equal, the law prevails.* See ADMINISTRATION OF ESTATES; DEEDS, REGISTRATION OF; JUDGMENT MORTGAGE; LAND REGISTRATION; NOTICE; OVERRIDING INTEREST; WINDING UP, COMPULSORY.

**priority date.** As regards a patent, the *date of filing* of a patent application; this is the date that the applicant paid the filing fee and filed documents which contain (a) an indication that a patent is sought; (b) information identifying the applicant; and (c) a description of the invention: Patents Act 1992 s.23. The date of filing is also the date which, under the law of the country where the application is made or in accordance with the terms of a treaty or convention to which the country is a party, is to be treated as the date of filing the application or is equivalent to the date of filing of an application in that country (ibid s.2(1)). In the case of a *convention application* (qv), it is generally the date of application for protection in the applicant's convention country under the *right of priority* provision of the Paris Convention (qv). See EUROPEAN PATENT TREATY; SIMULTANEOUS INVENTION.

**prison.** A place of detention for persons committed to custody under the law: Prisons (Ireland) Acts 1926–1972. The prison authorities are required to take all reasonable steps and reasonable care not to expose prisoners to a risk of damage or injury, but not to guarantee that prisoners do not suffer injury during imprisonment: Muldoon v Ireland (1988) ILRM 367. The Safety, Health and Welfare at Work Act 1989 applies to prisons and places of detention unless its application is incompatible with safe custody, good order and security (ibid s.57). Failure to deliver correspondence to a prisoner, which is not found to be objectionable pursuant to the Rules for the Government of Prisons 1947 r.63, can constitute an unjustified breach of a prisoner's right to communicate: Kearney v Minister for Justice (1987) ILRM 52. See also The State (Gallagher) v Governor of Portlaoise Prison (1987) ILRM 45. See PEACE OFFICER.

**prison breaking.** The offence committed by a person who is in lawful custody who uses force to effect his escape (qv). If the prisoner is awaiting trial and the offence with which he is charged is a felony (qv), the prison breaking will also be a felony.

**prison personnel, dismissal of.** See GARDA, DISMISSAL OF.

**prisoner of war.** A person who, in relation to the State and a war in which the State is a participant, is such a *prisoner of war* within the meaning of the Prisoners of War Convention 1949, art.4, para A: Prisoners of War and Enemy Aliens Act 1956 s.1(2). Persons may also be treated as prisoners of war where the State is not a participant in a war. A prisoner of war may be interned. See INTERNMENT.

**privacy.** The right to privacy is not defined by statute or in the Constitution.

*Whilst the personal rights (of the 1937 Constitution, art.40(3)) are not described specifically, it is scarcely to be doubted in our society that the right to privacy is universally recognised and accepted with possibly the rarest of exceptions...*: McGee v Attorney General (1974) IR 284. Protection of privacy is provided by a wide range of torts eg trespass to land, goods and to the person; nuisance; and breach of confidence.

Telephone tapping of a conversation can amount to an infringement of the constitutional right to privacy: Kennedy v Ireland (1988) ILRM 472. An injunction may be obtained to stop the bugging of a telephone: Mangan v McKeown & Kilsaran Concrete Products Ltd (1991 HC). There is also a right to privacy while in police custody, but it is not breached by a medical practitioner giving evidence of his observation of the accused: People (DPP) v Kenny (1991 HC) 9ILT Dig 74. The tort of intentional infliction of mental suffering can afford protection against improper techniques of investigation, intimidatory debt collection and harassment of tenants by landlords. See Janvier v Sweeney (1919) 2 KB 316. See CONFIDENCE, BREACH OF; DATA PROTECTION; HACKING; IN CAMERA; NATIONAL ARCHIVES; TELEPHONE TAPPING; TRANSBORDER DATA FLOWS.

**privacy, marital.** See MARITAL PRIVACY.

**private Act.** A statute concerning a particular person or town or not of general application eg The Limerick Harbour (Bridge) Act 1963, as compared with a public Act, which applies generally within the State. See BILL.

**private bill.** See BILL.

**private brewer.** See BREWER, PRIVATE.

**private carrier.** See CARRIER, PRIVATE.

**private company.** See COMPANY, PRIVATE; SHARE, VALUE OF.

**private international law.** [Conflict of laws]. That part of Irish law which deals with cases involving a *foreign element*. It deals with matters such as (a) what system of law will be applied; (b) whether the Irish courts have jurisdiction over a case; and (c) the recognition and enforcement of judgments of foreign courts. See Jurisdiction of Courts and Enforcement of Judgments (European Communities) Act 1988; Jurisdiction of Courts and Enforcement of Judgments Act 1993.

[Text: Binchy (1)]. See DIVORCE, FOREIGN, RECOGNITION OF; FOREIGN JUDGMENTS, ENFORCEMENT OF; INTERNATIONAL LAW; JURISDICTION; MAINTENANCE ORDER; SUMMONS, SERVICE OUT OF JURISDICTION.

**private law.** The area of domestic law dealing primarily with the relations between individuals within the State, with which the State is not immediately and directly concerned, eg the law of contract and the law of torts. See PUBLIC LAW.

**private member's bill.** A draft legislative proposal which a member of Dail or Seanad Eireann is entitled to initiate, other than a money bill. See BILL, MONEY.

**private nuisance.** See NUISANCE, PRIVATE.

**private property, right to.** The State acknowledges that man, in virtue of his rational being, has the natural right, antecedent to positive law, to the private ownership of external goods; the State accordingly guarantees to pass no law attempting to abolish the right of private ownership or the general right to transfer, bequeath and inherit property: 1937 Constitution, art.43(1). However, the Constitution recognises that the exercise of the rights to private property ought, in civil society, be regulated by the principles of social justice, and consequently provides that the State may delimit by law the exercise of these rights with a view to reconciling their exercise with the exigencies of the common good (ibid art.43(2)).

The right to property is delimited by many statutes eg compulsory purchase of land; planning permission; succession law. Many State agencies have considerable powers to enter, use and acquire land to fulfil their statutory function. Where property is taken by the State, compensation must generally be paid. In some particular cases, social justice may not require the payment of any compensation upon a compulsory acquisition (qv) that can be justified by the State as being required by the exigencies of the common good: Dreker v Irish Land Commission (1984) ILRM 94. See also Blake v Attorney General (1981) ILMR 34; PMPS Ltd v Attorney General (1983) SC; Lawlor v Minister for Agriculture (1988) ILRM 400. See also Electricity Supply Board v Gormley (1985) SC; Electricity Supply Amend-

ment Act 1985. See Minerals Development Act 1979. See COMPULSORY PURCHASE ORDER; DERELICT SITE; FORFEITURE; LICENCE; MOTORWAY; NATIONAL MONUMENT; UNFIT HOUSE; UNLAWFUL ORGANISATION.

**private prosecution.** Colloquial term referring to the prosecution by a member of the public as a *common informer* of another person in respect of an alleged criminal offence by that other. Any party with a bona fide concern and interest in the protection of a constitutional right (in this case the right to life of the unborn) has sufficient standing to invoke the jurisdiction of the courts to take such measures as would defend and vindicate that right: SPUC v Coogan & Ors (1989 SC) IR 734. See O'Donnell v DPP (1988) HC. See COMMON INFORMER.

**private treaty.** A sale of land by agreement between vendor and purchaser, as distinct from a sale by auction (qv). See SALE OF LAND.

**private trust.** See TRUST.

**privatisation.** The sales of shares in a company owned by the State to the private sector. The partial privatisation of the Irish sugar industry was provided for by the Sugar Act 1991 and of Irish Life Assurance plc by the Insurance Act 1990. The B & I Line was prepared for sale to the Irish Continental Group plc by the B & I Line Act 1991. See COMPANY, STATUTORY.

**privatorum conventio juri publico non derogat.** [An agreement between private persons does not derogate from the public right]. See ILLEGAL CONTRACTS.

**privatum commodum publico cedit.** [Private good yields to public good]. See PUBLIC POLICY, EVIDENCE EXCLUDED BY.

**privatum in commodum publico bono pensatur.** [Private loss is compensated by public good]. See PRIVATE PROPERTY, RIGHT TO.

**privilege.** A special right or immunity. In defamation (qv), privilege is the immunity from liability conferred by law for statements made in certain circumstances. The privilege is either *absolute* or *qualified*.

*Absolute* privilege, which is a complete defence to a defamation action, applies even where the words complained of are published even with knowledge of their falsehood and with the intention of injuring another. It applies to: (a) judical proceedings: Macauley Co Ltd v Wyse Power (1943) 77 ILTR 61; (b) parliamentary proceedings, which includes all official reports and publications of the Oireachtas and utterances made in either House wherever published: 1937 Constitution art.15; (c) discussions at meetings of the government: AG v The Sole Member of the Beef Tribunal (1993 SC) ILRM 81.

*Qualified* privilege, arises where a communication is made upon an *occasion of qualified privilege* and is fairly warranted by it; it is a good defence in the absence of malice. An *occasion of qualified privilege* arises where a person who makes a communication has a duty (legal, social or moral) or an interest to make it to the person to whom it is made, and the person to whom it is made has a corresponding duty to receive it. See Kirkwood Hackett v Tierney (1952) IR 185; Hynes-O'Sullivan v O'Driscoll (1989 SC) ILRM 619. See DISCOVERY OF DOCUMENTS; FAIR AND ACCURATE REPORT; MALICE; UTTERANCE.

**privilege, communications to another.** The privilege to refrain from giving evidence which attaches to a communication made by one person to another. Four conditions must be present — (a) the communication must originate in a confidence that it would not be disclosed, (b) the element of confidentiality must be essential to the full and satisfactory maintenance of the relation between the two persons, (c) the relation must be one which, in the opinion of the community, must be sedulously fostered, and (d) the injury by the disclosure must be greater than the benefit gained: Cook v Carroll (1945) IR 515. Privilege attaches to a communication by a parishioner to his parish priest in confidence in private consultation: ibid Cook v Carroll; Forristal v Forristal (1966) 100 ILTR 182. Privilege also applies to communications from a constituent to a member of the Oireachtas (see McHugh in 11 ILT & SJ (1993) 119). It would appear that for the privilege to be waived, it must be waived clearly and unequivocally by both: E R v J R (1981) ILRM 125. See UTTERANCE.

**privilege, evidential.** The right or immunity conferred on a person or body which justify their refusal to produce a document or to answer a question. The following matters are generally protected from disclosure on the grounds of privilege: (a) criminating questions — a witness need not answer any question which exposes the witness to any criminal charge, penalty or forfeiture; (b) professional communications between counsel or solicitor and client; (c) matrimonial communications; (d) private consultation with parish priest; (e) title deeds of a stranger to an action.

The privilege may be waived by the person entitled to it, whereas even a willing witness will not be allowed to give evidence of a matter required to be excluded by reason of public policy. See PUBLIC POLICY, EVIDENCE EXCLUDED BY; GOVERNMENT; INCEST; INCRIMINATE; JOURNALIST, COMMUNICATIONS WITH; WITNESS, COMPETENCE OF.

**privilege, legal professional.** The right whereby evidence of communications between counsel or solicitor and a client may not be given without the client's consent. The privilege applies to communications made within the ordinary scope of professional employment for contemplated or existing litigation; it extends to confidential communications only and not to, say a letter written on the client's instructions: Bord na gCon v Murphy (1970) IR 301.

Before the privilege can be properly claimed for a particular document, the dominant purpose of its existence must be preparation for apprehended litigation: Silver Hill Duckling v Minister for Agriculture Attorney General (1987) ILRM 516.

Communications between a lawyer and his client for the purpose of seeking or obtaining legal assistance other than legal advice are not privileged from disclosure, as they could not be said to contain any real relationship with the area of potential litigation: Smurfit Paribas Bank Ltd v AAB Export Finance Ltd (1990 SC) ILRM 588. See also Tromso Sparebank v Beirne & Ors (1989) 7ILT Dig 83. See Companies Act 1990 s.23(1); Building Societies Act 1989 ss.31(5), 41(7), 46(5); Patents Act 1992 s.94. [Text: Clark (2)]. See PERSONAL DATA; WITHOUT PREJUDICE.

**privilege, matrimonial communications.** The right whereby evidence of communications between husband and wife during marriage may not be given. However, the privilege does not prevent evidence of such communications being given by other admissible evidence. See Criminal Justice (Evidence) Act 1924 ss.1 and 4 as amended by Criminal Evidence Act 1992. See however INCEST. See also EVIDENCE TENDING TO BASTARDISE CHILDREN; WITNESS, COMPETENCE OF.

**privileged wills.** Informal documents which did not require signatures or oral declarations before witnesses, previously provided for by statute, but not re-enacted by the Succession Act 1965. See NUNCUPATIVE WILL.

**privilegium non valet contra rempublicam.** [A privilege avails not against the state]. See PUBLIC POLICY, EVIDENCE EXCLUDED BY.

**privity of contract.** The relationship which exists between parties to a contract. Generally privity of contract is necessary to enable one person to sue another in contract. No one can sue on, or be sued on, a contract to which he is not a party eg a contract cannot impose liability on a stranger.

There are exceptions eg: (a) restrictive covenants running with land will bind a subsequent purchaser with notice of the covenant: Tulk v Moxhay (1848) 13 Jur 89; (b) transactions within the scope of the authority created by agency will bind the principal: Pattison v Institute for Industrial Research Standards (1979) HC; (c) inducement by a third party of a party to a contract to breach the contract will render the third party liable for damages in tort: Lumley v Gye (1853) 1 WR 432; (d) where a stranger acquires rights by way of a trust: In re Schebsman (1944) Ch; (e) statutory exceptions eg the Married Womens' Status Act 1957, ss.7-8 confer a right of action to the spouse or child of a contracting party. See also SGSS Act 1980 ss.13(2) and (7); 14. See Quill in 9ILT & SJ (1991) 211. See FINANCE HOUSE; NEXT FRIEND.

**privy.** A person who is a party to, or has a share or interest in something.

**prize bond.** A scheme whereby redeemable bonds purchased for £5 participate in periodic draws for prizes: Finance (Miscellaneous Provisions) Act 1956. See Heaney v Minister for Finance (1986)

ILRM 164.

**pro.** [For].

**pro confesso.** [As if conceded].

**pro forma.** [As a matter of form].

**pro hac vice.** [For this occasion]. Eg an appointment for a particular occasion.

**pro indiviso.** [As undivided].

**pro interesse suo.** [As to his interest].

**pro rata.** [In proportion].

**pro tanto.** [For so much; to that extent].

**probability.** See PRESUMPTION OF REGULARITY.

**probability, balance of.** See BALANCE OF PROBABILITY.

**probate.** A grant of representation issued from the Probate Office, or from a District Probate Registry, both of which are part of the High Court, to the effect that the will of a testator has been proved and registered in court and that administration of his effects has been granted to the executor proving the will, *he having been first sworn faithfully to administer the same* (RSC App Q Form 6). The executor undertakes to exhibit a true inventory of the estate and to render a true account thereof (RSC App Q Form 3).

Where a grant of probate has been made and the proving executor has died and all other executors have either died or renounced, *administration with the will annexed de bonis non* will be given to the next person entitled. See also Status of Children Act 1987 s.30. See ADMINISTRATION OF ESTATES; DOUBLE PROBATE; INSOLVENT ESTATE; LETTERS OF ADMINISTRATION; OFFENSIVE WORDS; SUPPLEMENTAL PROBATE; UNADMINISTERED PROBATE.

**probate, revocation of.** The revoking, cancelling or recalling of a grant of probate which the High Court and Circuit Court are empowered to do. See Succession Act 1965 ss.26 and 35. See RSC O.125 r.1; RCC O.34 r.4.

**probate action.** Any proceedings in the High Court commenced by originating summons and seeking the grant or recall of probate, or letters of administration or similar relief: RSC O.125 r.1. The Circuit Court has jurisdiction in certain specified probate matters but requires the consent of the parties in writing where the estate of the deceased includes personal estate in excess of £30,000 value or real estate with rateable valuation in excess of £200. See Succession Act

1965 s.6; Courts Acts 1981 s.4 and 1991 s.2; RCC O.34.

**probate office.** The central probate registry located at the Four Courts in Dublin, which is attached to the High Court and which has jurisdiction for the whole State. See Court (Supplemental Provisions) Act 1961 s.55(1). See DIS-TRICT PROBATE REGISTRY; SIDE BAR ORDERS.

**probate tax.** A tax of 2 per cent of the taxable value of estates of persons dying on or after 18th June 1993: Finance Act 1993 ss.109-119. There is an index-linked threshold of £10,000 before tax is payable and there is an exemption from a second charge of tax where spouses die in quick succession. Debts owing at the time of death (including funeral expenses) are allowed in arriving at the taxable value. Where the deceased was domiciled in the State, all assets wherever situate are liable to the tax, except where specifically exempted. Where the deceased was not domiciled in the State, only assets situate in the State are liable to the tax.

The personal representative is primarily accountable for payment of the tax, which in effect is borne proportionately by the beneficiaries, who may claim the tax as an expense in calculating any inheritance tax (qv).

**probation and welfare officer.** An officer who carries out social inquiry and pre-sentence assessments for the courts; supervises in the community, offenders who are referred by the courts; supervises offenders under community service orders or who have been conditionally released from custody; and provides a counselling service to offenders and their families. See COMMUNITY SERVICE ORDER; PROBATION OF OFFENDERS.

**probation in employment.** The period during which an employee is being assessed to determine his suitability for employment. The Unfair Dismissals Act 1977 does not apply to dismissal of an employee on probation where the duration of probation is one year or less (ibid s.3(1)). An office holder on probation is in an insecure position: Hynes v Garvey (1978) IR 174.

However, it has been held that the power of termination of employment during, or at the end of, a probationary period is not a power which can be exercised arbitrarily; a person's rights to fair procedures are not affected by being in a probationary position: The State (Daly) v Minister for Agriculture (1988) ILRM 173.

In a particular case it was held that termination of employment required a decision of the hospital board; they were not expected to emulate the conduct of a judge who must distance himself from any prior knowledge of the matters in issue: O'Neill v Beaumont Hospital Board (1990 SC) ILRM 419. As regards a civil servant, it has been held that the Minister must, during the employee's probationary period, have been satisfied that the person had failed to fulfil his conditions of probation: Whelan v Minister for Justice (1991 HC) 2 IR 241. See CIVIL SERVANT; GARDA SIOCHANA.

**probation of offenders.** An order of the District Court releasing an offender having (a) dismissed an information or charge or having (b) discharged the offender conditionally on his entering into a recognizance (qv), with or without securities, to be of good behaviour and to appear for conviction and sentence when called on at any time during such period, not exceeding three years, as may be specified in the order: Probation of Offenders Act 1907 s.1(1).

Such an order may be made where any person is charged before a court of summary jurisdiction (qv) with an offence punishable by that court, and the court considers that the charge is proved, but is of opinion that it is inexpedient to inflict any punishment: ibid s.1(1) and Criminal Law Amendment Act 1935 s.16(2). This however does not prevent the court making a *compensation order* (qv) against the offender in favour of the injured party: Criminal Justice Act 1993 ss.6(12)(b) and 8(6).

The order placing a person on probation may include requirements so as to lessen the likelihood of further involvement in crime eg avoiding certain people or places, undergoing a course of treatment (eg for alcohol or drug dependence), residing in a probation hostel, or attending a workshop or training centre.

An order of probation dismissing a charge should specify the particular ground relied upon: Gilroy v Brennan (1926) IR 482. Also as regards offences by an employer involving social welfare contributions, a probation order must not be made until the court is satisfied that all arrears in respect of contributions by the offending employer of an employed contributor, have been paid by the employer: Social Welfare (Consolidation) Act 1981 s.118. Similar provisions now apply to any person charged with an offence in relation to any social welfare benefit, pension, assistance or allowance: Social Welfare Act 1988 s.19. See also Social Welfare Act 1993 ss.27 and 30.

The Probation of Offenders Act is generally not applicable to revenue, customs or excise duty offences — see Finance Act 1984 s.78. There is provision for the fingerprinting of persons dealt with under the Probation of Offenders Act in respect of indictable offences: Criminal Justice Act 1984 s.28. See APOLOGY; COMMUNITY SERVICE ORDER; COSTS AND CRIMINAL PROCEEDINGS.

**procedure.** The formal manner of conducting judicial proceedings. [Text: Gannon]. See PRACTICE; RULES OF COURT.

**proceedings, stay of.** See STAY OF PROCEEDINGS.

**process.** Any operation or series of operations being an activity of more than a minimal duration: SI No 283 of 1972 and Dunleary v Glen Abbey Ltd (1992 HC) ILRM 1. See WEIGHTS, MAXIMUM.

**process, abuse of.** See ABUSE OF PROCESS.

**process, civil.** See CIVIL PROCESS.

**proclamation.** A formal public announcement (eg the dissolution of the Dail by the Presidential Commission) usually notified in Iris Oifigiuil eg see Iris Oifigiuil 10th November 1992.

**procreate.** See BEGET.

**procuration.** Agency. See PER PRO.

**procurement.** The offence committed by a person who procures any girl or woman, who is not a common prostitute or of known immoral character, to have unlawful carnal knowledge with any other person or persons. There is no offence where it is shown that the girl needed no procuring at all and acted of her own free will: R v Christian 23 Cox 540. To *procure* is to obtain, cause or bring about a connection: R v Jones (1896) 1 QB 4. See Criminal Law Amendment Act 1885 ss.2-3 as amended by the Criminal Law Amendment Act

1935 ss.7-8. See Attorney General (Supt Shaughnessy) v Ryan (1960) IR 181. *Procurement* of rape (qv) is also an offence: Criminal Law (Rape) Act 1981.

**procuring breach of contract.** See INDUCING BREACH OF CONTRACT.

**product liability.** (1) The liability which arises by way of contract or tort for a defective product. A person who suffers loss as a result of a defective product may be able to recover damages for breach of an express or implied term of contract. In tort, the plaintiff may succeed in an action based on negligence where he is able to establish the existence of a duty of care and the breach thereof by the manufacturer, assembler, subcontractor, packager, bottler, distributor, repairer or retailer. See Donoghue v Stevenson (1932) AC 562; Kirby v Burke and Holloway (1944) IR 207; Power v Bedford Motor Co Ltd (1959) IR 391; Bolands Ltd v Trouw Ireland Ltd (1978) HC; Cole v Webb Caravans Ltd (1983) ILRM 595. [Text: Forde (5)]. See CONDITION; QUALITY OF GOODS; SAMPLE, SALE BY.

(2) Under the EC Products Liability Directive (85/374) a *producer* of a *product* is liable to pay compensation for death or personal injuries caused by a *defect* in his product (ibid art.1): Liability for Defective Products Act 1991 s.2. Compensation may also be claimed in respect of loss, damage, or destruction of property used for private use or consumption. A product is said to be defective when it does not provide the safety a person is entitled to expect having regard to the presentation, expected uses and time it was put into circulation (ibid s.5).

A *product* is defined as all movables, including electricity, with the exception of *primary agricultural products* which have not undergone initial processing (ibid s.1(1)). A *producer* is defined as (a) the manufacturer or producer of a finished product; or (b) the manufacturer or producer of any raw material or of a component part; or (c) the person who carried out processing of the products of soil, stockfarming, fisheries and game; or (d) any person who by putting his name, trade mark or other distinguishing feature on the product thereby identifies himself as its producer; or (e) the importer of goods into the EC; or (f) any person who supplied the product where the producer cannot be identified (ibid s.2).

A producer has six defences: (1) he did not put the product into circulation; or (2) it is probable that at the time of putting the product into circulation it did not have the defect; or (3) the product was not manufactured by him for sale or distribution for an economic purpose nor in the course of business; or (4) the defect was due to compliance with EC law; or (5) that given the state of technical knowledge, it was not possible at the time of distribution to discover the defect; or (6) if the product is a manufactured component the defect is the result of a design defect in the product into which the component has been fitted (ibid s.6).

Liability is limited to the period of three years following the date the plaintiff became aware, actual or constructive, of the damage, defect or identity of the producer (ibid s.7).

A right of action expires after 10 years from when the product was put into circulation, except where proceedings have already commenced (ibid s.7(2)). No damages for property will be awarded where the damage does not exceed £350; for damage greater than £350, only the amount in excess of £350 will be awarded (ibid s.3). The Act came into operation on 16 December 1991. See Bird in 10 ILT & SJ (1992) 188. [Text: Schuster].

**production of documents.** See DISCOVERY OF DOCUMENTS.

**professional disciplinary bodies, appeals.** For rules governing appeals against the decisions of disciplinary bodies dealing with nurses, dentists, medical practitioners, or veterinary surgeons, see RSC O.95. In relation to solicitors, see RSC O.53. See Phillips v Medical Council (1992 HC) ILRM 469. See DISCIPLINARY PROCEEDINGS.

**professional indemnity policy.** A policy of insurance (qv) generally providing an indemnity to professional persons in respect of claims in negligence (qv) against them. The cover provided is often for breach of professional duty by reason of any negligent act, error or omission by the assured or any person employed by him. Generally such policies exclude any claim against the assured

brought about by any dishonest, fraudulent, criminal or malicious act of the assured or of any person employed by him. Insurers are not enabled to avoid liability under a professional indemnity policy on the basis that the same act amounts to both a tort (qv) and a breach of contract (qv): Rohan Construction v Insurance Corporation of Ireland (1988) ILRM 373. See PROFESSIONAL NEGLIGENCE.

**professional negligence.** A person who professes to exercise any profession or trade is guilty of negligence if he fails to exercise the skill and knowledge reasonably to be expected of an ordinary member of that profession or trade, as the case may be. See Somers v Erskine (1944) IR 368 and Roche v Peilow (1986) ILRM 189 (*solicitor*); Boyle v Martin (1932) 66 ILTR 187 (*general practitioner*); O'Donovan v Cork County Council (1967) IR 173 (*anaesthetist*); Dunne v National Maternity Hospital (1989) ITLR (24 Apr) (*obstetrician*); Chariot Inns Ltd v Assicurazioni Generali SPA (1981) ILRM 173 (*insurance broker*); Colgan v Connolly Construction Co (Ireland) Ltd (1980) HC (*builder*); Western Meats Ltd v National Ice & Cold Storage Co Ltd (1982) ILRM 99 (*meat processor*); Crowley v Allied Irish Banks (1988) ILRM 225 (*architect*); Golden Vale Co-Operative v Barrett (1987) HC (*accountant*); Moran v Duleek Developments Ltd & Hanley (1991 HC) ITLR (14 Oct) (*engineer*). [Text: Jackson & Powell UK]. See BARRISTER; ENGINEER, PROFESSIONAL NEGLIGENCE; MEDICAL NEGLIGENCE; NO FAULT COMPENSATION; PROFESSIONAL INDEMNITY INSURANCE; SOLICITOR, PROFESSIONAL NEGLIGENCE; PROFESSIONAL WITNESS; SURGICAL OPERATION.

**professional services tax.** See WITHHOLDING TAX.

**professional witness .** It is the practice of the courts to have evidence of professional witnesses, particularly medical witnesses, taken out of turn or by specially fixing a date for an action, since their inconvenience may be accompanied by hardship to other people. See Aspell v O'Brien (1992 HC) 10 ILT Dig 267.

A High Court judge has said that when professional witnesses are called in a case of professional negligence and there is no challenge to their integrity or their professional qualifications, the practice of attacking them merely on the basis that they had appeared in similar cases is deplorable: O'Hanlon J in Doherty v Whelan (1993 HC) ITLR (26 Apr). See EXPERT OPINION; STANDBY FEE.

**profit a prendre.** The right of a person to take the produce or part of the soil from the land of another person eg sporting and fishing rights, sand from the soil, turbury (qv), pasturage (qv). The right may be acquired by grant or by prescription. See Prescription Act 1832 (extended to Ireland 1859). See COMMON; PISCARY; PRESCRIPTION.

**profit and loss.** The form of account required to be prepared by a company showing its income and expenditure during the previous accounting period: Companies Act 1963, sixth schedule, reg 12-14. In a company not trading for profit, it is called an *income and expenditure* account. Banks, discount houses and assurance companies are exempted from many of the requirements (ibid reg 23-26). The profit and loss account must give a true and fair view of the profit or loss of the company for the financial year: Companies Amendment Act 1986 s.3(1).

While *profits* are not defined in the Income Tax Acts, the courts have consistently interpreted profits as being the difference between receipts in a given period and the expenditure laid out to earn those receipts in that same period, consequently the *current cost accounting* method was not an appropriate one for revenue purposes: Carroll Industries plc v O'Culachain (1989 HC) ILRM 552.

Gains realised by a bank from compulsorily held government stocks are part of the bank's trading profits for corporation tax purposes: Browne v Bank of Ireland Finance Ltd (1991 SC) ITLR (18 Mar). See ACCOUNTS; CURRENT COST ACCOUNTING CONVENTION.

**prohibited degrees.** The degrees of relationship within which parties cannot marry: any such marriage is void: Marriage Act 1835.

A man cannot marry his grandmother; grandfather's wife; wife's grandmother; father's sister; mother's sister; father's brother's wife; mother's brother's wife; wife's father's sister; wife's mother's sister; mother; stepmother; wife's mother; daughter; wife's daughter; son's wife; sister; son's daughter; daughter's daughter; son's son's wife; daughter's son's wife; wife's son's daughter; wife's daughter's daughter; brother's daughter; sister's daughter; brother's son's wife; sister's son's wife; wife's brother's daughter; wife's sister's daughter. Analogous prohibitions apply to a woman.

A man however is permitted to marry his deceased wife's sister and a woman may marry her deceased husband's brother: Deceased Wife's Sister's Act 1907; Deceased Brother's Widow's Act 1921. See MARRIAGE.

**prohibited weapon.** Any weapon of whatever description designed for the discharge of any noxious liquid, noxious gas, other noxious thing, and also any ammunition which contains or is designed or adapted to contain any noxious liquid, noxious gas, or other noxious thing: Firearms Act 1925 s.1(1) and Firearms and Offensive Weapons Act 1990 s.4(e). See FIREARM.

**prohibition.** An order of the High Court preventing or prohibiting a body or person from exercising a power it does not legally possess. Relief by way of prohibition will be refused where the matter raised is properly one of defence: Minister for Agriculture v Norgo Ltd (1980) IR 155; McGrail v Ruane (1989) ILRM 498. See R (Kelly) v Maguire (1923) 2 IR 58; The State (Williams) v Kelleher (1983) ILRM 285. See JUDICIAL REVIEW; STATE SIDE ORDERS.

**prohibition notice, work.** A notice, signed by an inspector, stating his opinion regarding an activity which involves, or is likely to involve, a risk of serious personal injury to persons at work and directing that the activity cease until the matters giving rise to the risk are rectified: Safety, Health and Welfare at Work Act 1989 s.37. A prohibition notice takes effect immediately on receipt if it so declares. There is a right of appeal against a prohibition notice to the District Court. If activities are carried on in contravention of a prohibition notice, the inspector may apply with the High Court, by motion, for an order prohibiting the continuation of the activities (ibid s.37(9)). Contrast with IMPROVEMENT NOTICE, WORK; WORK, PROHIBITION OF.

**prohibition notice, data.** The notice by which the Data Protection Commissioner (qv) may prohibit the transfer of personal data (qv) from the State to a place outside the State: Data Protection Act 1988 s.11. The notice is served on the person proposing to transfer the data and it must prohibit the transfer concerned either absolutely or conditionally, specifying the time when it is to take effect and the grounds for the prohibition (ibid ss.11(5) and (6)).

In considering whether to issue a prohibition notice, the Commissioner must consider whether the transfer would be likely to cause damage or distress to any person and also must have regard for article 12 of the Data Protection Convention (qv), which article is designed to reconcile the requirements of effective data protection with the desirability of facilitating international transfers of data. See DATA PROTECTION; TRANSBORDER DATA FLOWS.

**prohibition of trade.** See TRADE, PROHIBITION OF.

**prohibition of work.** See WORK, PROHIBITION OF.

**prolixity.** Unnecessary length in summons, pleadings or affidavit, the cost of which may have to be borne by the responsible party. See RSC O.1 r.5; O.19 r.1; O.40 r.3; RCC O.22 r.16.

**promise.** An undertaking to do or to forbear from some act. It has no legal effect, unless it complies with the requirements of a contract or unless it is made under seal. The person making the promise is the *promissor* and to whom it is made is the *promisee*. See BREACH OF PROMISE.

**promissory estoppel.** See EQUITABLE ESTOPPEL.

**promissory note.** An unconditional promise in writing, made by one person to another, signed by the maker, engaging to pay, on demand or at a fixed or determinable future time, a sum certain in money to, or to the order of, a specified person or to bearer: Bills of Exchange Act 1882 s.83.

Most of the rules applicable to bills of exchange (qv) also apply to promissory notes; the main distinction between them being that a note is a *promise* to pay, whereas a bill is an *order* to pay; a promissory note must be presented for payment (ibid s.87) although it need not be presented for acceptance as must a

bill. See Creation Press Ltd v Harman (1973) IR 313; Tromso Sparebank v Beirne & Ors (1990 SC) ITLR (5 Mar). [Text: Paget UK; Richardson UK].

**promoter.** A person who undertakes to form a company with reference to a given project, and to set it going, and who takes the necessary steps to accomplish that purpose: Twycross v Grant (1877) 36 LT 812. A promoter may incur civil and criminal liability for mis-statements in a prospectus: Companies Act 1963 ss.49-52. Rules to protect a plc from promoter fraud were introduced by s.32 of the Companies Amendment Act 1983.

New rules have been introduced to prevent persons from being involved in the promotion or formation of a company if they have been involved previously with a company which is insolvent on its winding up or receivership, unless the first named company meets certain capital and other requirements: Companies Act 1990 ss.159. See DIRECTOR; DISQUALIFICATION ORDER, COMPANY.

**pro-mutuum.** A quasi-contract which arises when a person, acting under a mistake of fact, delivers to another a chattel which cannot be restored in specie; the recipient is required to restore its equivalent under the quasi-contract. See MUTUUM.

**proof.** (1) The evidence by which a court is satisfied as to the truth of a fact. The *burden of proof* generally rests on the party who asserts the affirmative of the issue or question in dispute. Proof is not required for matters which are *judicially noticed*, matters which are *presumed* by law, and matters which are formally admitted.

(2) The standard of strength of spirituous liquors.

(3) To *prove* a will is to obtain probate of it.

(4) To *prove* a debt in bankruptcy is to establish the existence of the debt.

See BURDEN OF PROOF; STANDARD OF PROOF; JUDICIAL NOTICE; PRESUMPTIONS; ADMIT, NOTICE TO; INTERROGATORIES; STATEMENT.

**proof of will.** See WILL, PROOF OF.

**proper law of a contract.** The phrase used in private international law to denote the system of law by which a contract is to be interpreted. The proper law of a contract is the law which the parties intended to apply: Vita Foods v Unus Shipping (1939) AC 277. If there is no express choice of applicable law, the court will determine whether there is an implied choice of law in the contract. See Contractual Obligations (Applicable Law) Act 1991. See Quinn in 10 ILT & SJ 244. See CONTRACT; PRIVATE INTERNATIONAL LAW.

**proper look out.** The failure of a driver or a pedestrian to keep a proper look out may amount to negligence or contributory negligence: Stapleton v O'Regan (1956 SC). The test is whether the area he observed was in the circumstances reasonably sufficient: Nolan v Jennings (1964 SC). See also O'Connell v Shield Insurance Co Ltd (1954) IR 286; McEleney v McCarron (1993 SC) 11 ILT Dig 188.

**properties.** Attributes, inherent qualities, characteristics, abilities; it has been held that sodium chlorate is specially dangerous by reason of its explosive *properties*: Hardy v Special Criminal Court & AG (1992 HC) ITLR (6 Apr). See EXPLOSIVE.

**property.** That which can be owned; *real* property (realty) and *personal* property (personalty). As regards bankruptcy (qv), *property* includes money, goods, things in action, land and every description of property, whether real or personal and whether situate in the State or elsewhere; also obligations, easements, and every description of estate, interest, and profit, present or future, vested or contingent, arising out of or incident to property as defined: Bankruptcy Act 1988 s.3. See LICENCE; PRIVATE PROPERTY, RIGHT TO.

**property adjustment order.** An order which the court may make in respect of property on granting a decree of judicial separation (qv) eg transferring the property to the other spouse or to a child; or making a settlement of the property; or varying any ante-nuptial or post-nuptial settlement; or extinguishing or reducing the interest of either spouse under such settlement: Judicial Separation and Family Reform Act 1989 s.15. See MATRIMONIAL PROPERTY.

**property, damage to.** See DAMAGE TO PROPERTY; MALICIOUS INJURIES SCHEME.

**property, matrimonial.** See MATRIMONIAL PROPERTY.

**property, right to.** See LICENCE; PRIVATE PROPERTY, RIGHT TO.

**property, taxation of.** It has been held that a taxation based on the occupation of property does not infringe any personal rights to equality: Madigan v AG & Ors (1986) ILRM 136.

**property in goods.** See GOODS, PROPERTY IN.

**property in possession of garda.** Property in the possession of the gardai may by order of the court be delivered to the person appearing to the court to be the owner thereof, or, if the owner cannot be ascertained, as the court considers just; this applies to property possessed in connection with a criminal offence even though no person has been charged: Police Property Act 1897 s.1; Criminal Justice Act 1951 s.25. See also Offences Against the State Act 1939 s.29; Official Secrets Act 1963 s.16; Criminal Law Act 1976 s.9; Criminal Damage Act 1991 s.13(3). See Quinn v Pratt (1908) 2 IR 69.

**proportional representation.** An election system based on the principle that the distribution of seats in a representative assembly should reflect as nearly as possible the distribution of the electors' votes among the competing parties or contending candidates. Voting in the elections to Dail Eireann, Seanad Eireann and for the President of Ireland are required to be by the system of proportional representation by means of the *single transferable vote*: 1937 Constitution, arts.12(2((3), 16(2)(5) and 18(5).

Under this system, voters number the candidates on the ballot paper in the order of their preference. A *quota* is established by dividing the total number of valid votes cast by the number of seats to be filled plus one and by adding one to this result. Candidates who reach the quota are declared elected and their surplus is divided among the other candidates in accordance with their second preferences; also candidates who are eliminated have their second preferences distributed in similar manner. A referendum to amend the Constitution to remove this voting system was defeated both in 1959 and 1968. See CONSTITUENCY; EUROPEAN PARLIAMENT; QUOTA; SPOILT VOTE; TRANSFERABLE VOTE.

**proportionality.** (1) The principle in administrative law which requires that there be a balance between the injury to an individual's interest by an administrative measure and the consequential gain to the polity. It has been held that the principle of *proportionality*, even if it were to be adopted in this jurisdiction, could apply only to the exercise of administrative powers and not to the imposing of a sanction by the Oireachtas: Hand v Dublin Corporation (1991 SC) ILRM 556. See also Balkan Tours v Minister for Communications (1988) ILRM 101 at 108.

(2) As regards EC law, in order to establish whether a provision is consonant with the principle of proportionality it is necessary to establish whether the means it employs to achieve its aim correspond to the importance of the aim and whether they are necessary for its achievement: Fromoncais SA v FORMA (Case 66/82) (1983) ECR 395.

(3) The test applied in criminal law on the reasonableness of the relationship between the amount of force used by an accused and the provocation involved. See The People v MacEoin (1978 CCA) IR 27. As regards sentences, see PUNISHMENT. See SELF-DEFENCE; SUBSIDIARITY.

**proposal form.** A form completed by or for a person seeking insurance (qv). Until it is accepted by the insurer there is no contract and generally the insurer does not come on risk in respect of the event insured until the first premium has been paid. See INSURANCE, CONTRACT OF; INSURANCE AGENT; PREMIUM.

**proprietary lease.** A sub-lease, mediate or immediate, under a building lease (qv), where the term of the former was either not less than 99 years or, if less, was equal to or greater than 20 years, or, if this was the lesser period, two thirds of the term of the building lease, and which expired at the same time as, or not more than 15 years before, the expiration of the building lease: Landlord and Tenant (Reversionary Leases) Act 1958. A proprietary lease (although not now referred to as such), entitled to acquire the fee simple, is entitled to a reversionary lease (qv): Landlord and Tenant (Amendment) Act 1980 s.30.

**proprietary right.** Rights of property; rights of ownership.

**proprietor.** A person who has title to property eg the proprietor of a trade mark (qv). The proprietor of a patent is the person to whom the patent was granted or the person whose title is subsequently registered: Patents Act 1992 s.2(1).

**proprietor of new or original design.** Either (a) the person for whom a design is executed, where the author of the design, for good consideration executes the design for such person; (b) the person by whom the design or the right to apply the design to any article is acquired either exclusively or otherwise, or on whom it has devolved; or (c) in any other case, the author of the design: Industrial Commercial Property (Protection) Act 1927 s.3. The proprietor of such a design may apply to be registered as the registered proprietor thereof. See DESIGN.

**proprietory estoppel.** See EQUITABLE ESTOPPEL.

**prosecution.** The institution of criminal proceedings in the courts. See DIRECTOR OF PUBLIC PROSECUTIONS; COMMON INFORMER; PROSECUTOR.

**prosecutor.** A person who institutes legal proceedings against another eg the Director of Public Prosecutions (DPP). A garda siochana may institute proceedings in courts of summary jurisdiction as a *common informer* (qv) and the DPP has no power to compel the withdrawal of the complaint: State (Collins) v Ruane (1984) IR 106. See also Courtney v Well-Woman Centre (1985 HC). Costs cannot be awarded against a garda prosecuting a case: DCR r.67(b) and Dillane v Ireland (1980) ILRM 167. A garda is entitled to have another garda act as advocate in his behalf: DCR r.7. A garda or private citizen can institute proceedings in the name of the DPP: People v Roddy (1977) IR 177; however, after a return for trial on indictment, only the DPP may prosecute. See INDICTMENT.

**prospecting.** See Mineral Development Act 1940; Petroleum and Other Minerals Development Act 1960. See PETROLEUM, EXPLORATION FOR.

**prospective damages.** See GENERAL DAMAGES.

**prospectus.** Any document, notice, circular, advertisement or other invitation, offering to the public for subscription or purchase, any shares or debentures of a company: Companies Act 1963 s.2(1). It must specify, inter alia, the nominal capital of the company, the names and addresses and descriptions of the directors, the *minimum amount* required to be raised, the time of opening of the subscription lists, the amount payable on application and allotment of each share, and details of *material contracts* (ibid third schedule). The directors and promoters may incur civil and criminal liability for mis-statements in the prospectus (ibid ss.49-52). See also ibid ss.43-52.

In relation to companies on the Stock Exchange, persons who are responsible for listing particulars are required to provide information set out in the EC Directive on Listing Particulars: SI No 282 of 1984. See Companies Act 1990 s.238. See Components Tube Co v Naylor (1900) 2 IR 1; Aarons Reefs Ltd v Twiss (1895) 2 IR 207 and (1896) AC 273. See MATERIAL CONTRACTS; PROMOTER; UNDERSUBSCRIBED.

**prostitute.** A woman who hires herself or is hired to a man for sexual intercourse. A reference to a prostitute now includes a reference to a male person who is a prostitute and a reference to prostitution is to be construed accordingly: Criminal Law (Sexual Offences) Act 1993 s.1(4). It is an offence for a person in a street or public place to solicit or importune another person for the purposes of prostitution (ibid s.7).

A person *solicits or importunes* where the person (a) offers his or her services as a prostitute to another person, (b) solicits or importunes another person for that other person's services as a prostitute, or (c) solicits or importunes another person on behalf of a person for the purposes of prostitution (ibid s.1(2)). This includes soliciting or importuning from or in a motor vehicle (ibid s.1(1)).

It is an offence for a person for gain to control or direct the activities of a prostitute, to organise prostitution, or to compel or coerce a person to be prostitute (ibid s.9). It is also an offence for a person to live in whole or in part on the earnings of prostitution where the person aids and abets that prostitution (ibid s.10). See also Childrens Act 1908 s.17 as amended by 1935 Act s.11. See BROTHEL; LOITERING; PROCUREMENT.

**protected road.** A public road (qv) or proposed public road specified to be a protected road in a *protected roadway scheme* approved by the Minister: Roads Act 1993 ss.2(1) and 45. A protected road is intended to be a type of road subject to some limitation of access and some limitation on traffic, somewhat between (a) an ordinary public road to which there is widespread access and very few traffic restrictions, and (b) a motorway (qv) which is restricted to certain type of traffic and to which all access from adjoining land is prohibited.

A road authority may submit a protected roadway scheme to the Minister having first notified the public and affected landowners/occupiers (ibid s.48). The Minister, before approving a scheme, must cause a public local inquiry to be held, must consider any objections, and the report and recommendations of the person conducting the inquiry (ibid s.49). Planning permission must not be granted which would contravene the provisions of a protected roadway scheme (ibid s.46). The National Roads Authority is empowered to direct a road authority to make a protected road scheme (ibid s.20(1)(c)).

Similar provisions apply regarding compulsory purchase, compensation for disturbance and loss, and alternative access for adjoining landowners/occupiers as for a motorway scheme. See MOTORWAY; SERVICE AREA.

**protection of animals.** See ANIMALS; HOUSEHOLD CHATTELS.

**protection of company.** See COURT PROTECTION OF COMPANY.

**protection of debtor.** See ARRANGING DEBTOR.

**protective equipment, personal.** All equipment designed to be worn or held by an employee for protection against one or more hazards likely to endanger the employee's safety and health at work: SI No 44 of 1993, reg.2(1). It is the duty of every employer to provide *personal protective equipment* free of charge where the use of the equipment is exclusive to the place of work (ibid reg.7). It is the duty of every employee to make full and proper use of such equipment (ibid reg.14(b)). The personal protective equipment must be appropriate for the risks involved (ibid regs.21-26).

**protective trust.** A trust for the life of the beneficiary, or any lesser period, which is to be determined on the occurrence of certain events eg the bankruptcy of the beneficiary, upon which the trust income is to be applied at the absolute discretion of the trustees for the benefit of the beneficiary and his family. See BANKRUPTCY, ACT OF; TRUST.

**protector of the settlement.** The person without whose consent a tenant in tail cannot *bar* the entail except as against his own issue. The consent of the *protector* is also required by the tenant in base fee who wishes to enlarge his estate into a fee simple. The office of protector was established by the Fines and Recoveries Act 1833. See BARRING THE ENTAIL.

**protest.** (1) Payment under protest is a payment of money made by a person who denies that the money is due from him, with a view to its later recovery. (2) A certificate under seal made by a notary public (qv) attesting the dishonour of a bill of exchange (qv) ie a formal written statement made and signed by the notary public that the bill was duly presented for acceptance or payment, as the case may be, and that it was refused. Such a certificate is accepted as proof that a bill has been dishonoured. See Bills of Exchange Act 1882 s.51. See NOTARY; NOTING AND PROTESTING; TENDER.

**protest, right to.** See ASSEMBLY, FREEDOM OF; EXPRESSION, FREEDOM OF.

**protocol.** (1) The minutes of a meeting setting out matters of agreement. (2) An original draft or preliminary memorandum. (3) A code of procedure. Often associated with international agreements eg see Abortion Protocol to the Maastricht Treaty.

**prove.** See PROOF.

**provident society.** See INDUSTRIAL AND PROVIDENT SOCIETY.

**proving a will.** Obtaining probate (qv) of a will.

**provision.** In a company's accounts, a *provision* is an amount written off or retained in order to provide for an asset's depreciation, renewal or diminution in value, or to provide for a known or unquantifiable liability: Companies Act 1963, sixth schedule, reg 27(1)(a).

**provisional conviction.** A conviction of an accused which is subject to revision at the same trial; there is no such thing in law. If a district court judge has concluded that an offence is fit to be tried summarily and the accused then pleads guilty, once the judge embarks upon an enquiry as to the penalty appropriate to the offence, he is precluded from changing his mind, there being no such thing in law as a provisional conviction: Feeney v Clifford (1990 SC) ITLR (14 May).

**provisional liquidator.** The liquidator appointed to a company by a court before any winding up order is made, usually when the company's assets are in danger. He can be appointed without advertisement or notice to any party unless the court directs otherwise. See RSC O.74 r 14. See LIQUIDATOR; STATEMENT OF AFFAIRS; WINDING UP.

**provisional specification.** See COMPLETE SPECIFICATION.

**proviso.** A clause in a deed or statute which usually begins — *provided always that*. In a deed, it usually provides a condition upon which the validity of something is based. In a statute, it usually qualifies or exempts something which, but for the proviso, would have been included.

**provocation.** Some act or series of acts, done by a deceased to the person accused of his killing, which would cause in any reasonable man, and certainly caused in the accused, a sudden and temporary loss of self-control, which rendered the accused so subject to passion as to make him for the moment not the master of his own mind: The People (Director of Public Prosecutions) v MacEoin (1978) IR 27. When successfully pleaded it reduces a murder (qv) to manslaughter (qv).

**proximity.** There is a duty of care owed by a person to those in proximity to him. The duty is to take reasonable care that they are not injured by his acts or that they do not suffer loss as a result of his action or inaction. Racing authorities have been found to have a duty of care to persons wagering on horse races: Madden v Irish Turf Club (1993 HC) ITLR (26 Jul). See Purtill v Athlone Urban District Council (1968) IR 205: McNamara v ESB (1975) IR 1; Nolan v Kilkenny Co Council (1990 CC) in 8ILT & SJ (1990) 210.

**proxy.** A person deputed to vote for another; the instrument appointing such a person. Any member of a company who is entitled to attend and vote at a meeting of the company, may appoint someone else as his proxy to attend and vote instead of him. The proxy so appointed has the same rights as the member to speak at the meeting and to vote on a show of hands and on a poll: Companies Act 1963 s.136.

A person who is both a member and a proxy can vote only once on a show of hands: *Ernest v Loma Gold Mines* (1897) 1 Ch 1. Partial distribution of proxy invitations to some members only is prohibited (ibid s.136(5)). Under the Rules of the Stock Exchange, every company's articles of association must allow for *two way* forms of proxy ie forms which enable the shareholder to direct the proxy to vote for or against a resolution (Listing Agreement s.9 ch12.1). Similar but more stringent provisions regarding proxy forms apply to building societies: Building Societies Act 1989 s.72. See POLL; VOTING AT MEETINGS.

**psychiatric centre.** A district or registered psychiatric centre; a *district psychiatric centre* is one designated as such by the Minister at the request of a health board (qv) or every district mental hospital or psychiatric unit in any hospital maintained by a health board immediately before commencement of this section; a *registered psychiatric centre* is one which is registered by the Minister in acccordance with regulations or deemed to be so registered: Health (Mental Services) Act 1981 ss.9-10. The Minister may refuse to register or may cancel the registration of a psychiatric centre (ibid s.11).

It is an offence for any person, other than a health board, to operate any premises for the detention of persons requiring care and treatment for mental disorder, or to describe or hold out any place as such, unless it is approved and registered (ibid ss.8 and 10(1)). The 1981 Act had not been brought into force by 1993. See MENTAL TREATMENT; RECEPTION ORDER; SPECIAL PSYCHIATRIC CENTRE.

**psychiatric disorder.** A mental illness; it may be a ground for the *nullity* of marriage. It has been held in a particular case that a person suffering from paranoid schizophrenia was at the time of the marriage ceremony, suffering from a psychiatric disorder of such a character that it prevented him from giving his full and informed consent to the marriage and rendered him incapable of sustaining a normal married relationship with the petitioner: *E v E* (1987 HC) IR 147. In the UK, the House of Lords has held that liability for a psychiatric illness depended on foreseeability and the relationship of proximity between the claimant and the defendant: *Alcock & Ors v Chief Constable of South Yorkshire Police* (1991) 4 All ER 907. See MARRIAGE, NULLITY OF; MENTAL DISORDER; MENTAL TREATMENT; PERSONALITY DISORDER.

**public.** The *public* means the public generally and not a particular or special class of members of the public: *Stanbridge v Healy* (1985) ILRM 290.

**Public Accounts, Committee of.** A committee of members of Dail Eireann (qv) which (a) examines and reports to the Dail upon the public accounts showing the appropriation of the sums granted by the Dail to meet public expenditure and which (b) suggests alterations and improvements in the form of the Estimates submitted to the Dail. The committee can enquire into allegations of criminal misconduct: *In re Haughey* (1971) IR 217. Accounting officers of Departments are required to give evidence to the committee on the economy and efficiency of their Departments, and the systems, procedures and practices employed: Comptroller and Auditor General (Amdt) Act 1993 s.19.

**public Act.** A statute which has a general application as compared with a *private Act* (qv). See BILL.

**public appeal, money collected in.** The procedure for disposing of funds, gathered in a public appeal, which becomes impossible to apply for the purpose for which it was collected, or where a surplus remains, is provided for by the Charities Act 1961 s.48. See COLLECTION.

**public authority.** For the purposes of environmental protection, a Minister, a local authority, harbour authority, health board, a body established by statute, a company in which all the shares are held by a minister, the Commissioners of Public Works in Ireland: Environmental Protection Agency Act 1992 s.3(1). See also Local Government Act 1991 s.2(1). See ENVIRONMENTAL PROTECTION AGENCY.

**public bill.** See BILL.

**public company.** See COMPANY, PUBLIC.

**public dance licence.** A licence granted under the Public Dance Hall Act 1935 s.6. See FUNCTUS OFFICIO.

**public documents, evidence of.** Statements appearing in public or official documents are admissible in proof of the facts recorded therein. Statements in public registers are admissible in proof of the facts recorded where the document is one required by law to be kept for public information, and the entry has been made promptly and by the proper officer. See BANKERS' BOOKS; DOCUMENTARY EVIDENCE; NATIONAL ARCHIVES.

**public execution.** The carrying out in public of the court's sentence of death. Public executions were abolished by the Capital Punishment Amendment Act 1868. See DEATH PENALTY.

**public health.** The EC is required to contribute towards ensuring a high level of human health protection by encouraging cooperation between the member States and, if necessary, lending support to their action: Treaty of Rome 1957 art.129 as replaced by Maastricht Treaty 1992 art.G(D)(38). Community action must be directed towards the prevention of diseases, in particular the major health scourges, including drug dependence, by promoting research into their causes and their transmission, as well as health information and education. See COMMITTEE OF THE REGIONS.

**public holidays.** Days on which an employee is entitled to a paid day off work, or an extra day's annual leave (qv) or an extra day's pay, as the employer may decide. Public holidays are 1st January (New Year's Day: SI No 341 of 1974), St Patrick's Day, Easter Monday, Christmas Day, St Stephen's Day, the first Monday in June and August, the last Monday in October (SI No 193 of 1977), and the first Monday in May with effect from 1994 (SI No 91 of 1993). Certain *Church holidays* (qv) may be substituted for certain public holidays. See Holiday (Employees) Act 1973; Public Holidays Act 1924; Worker

Protection (Regular Part-time Employees) Act 1991 s.4(3)(e). See BANK HOLIDAYS.

**public indecency.** See INDECENCY.

**public inquiry.** See COMPULSORY PURCHASE ORDER; TRIBUNALS OF INQUIRY.

**public international law.** See INTERNATIONAL LAW.

**public justice.** Justice must be administered in courts in public save in such special and limited cases as may be prescribed by law: 1937 Constitution, art.34(1). The law prescribes that the general public may be excluded if a criminal offence is of an indecent or obscene nature: Criminal Justice Act 1951; or in cases involving matrimonial matters or lunacy or infancy matters; or urgent applications for habeas corpus, bail, injunctions; or involving the disclosure of a secret manufacturing process: Courts (Supplemental Provisions) Act 1961 s.45(1).

In addition, in certain cases the press may report a case but have limitations placed on disclosure of the identity of the parties eg the identity of children accused of crimes must not be disclosed: Childrens Act 1908; the identity of the complainant, and of the accused until convicted, is prohibited in rape cases: Criminal Law (Rape) Act 1980 ss.7-8. See Beamish & Crawford Ltd v Crowley (1969) IR 142. See IN CAMERA.

**public law.** The area of domestic law dealing primarily with the relations between the State and the individual eg constitutional law and criminal law. See PRIVATE LAW.

**public lighting.** The maintenance of a public road (qv) includes the provision and maintenance of public lighting: Roads Act 1993 s.2(4).

**public limited company.** See COMPANY, PUBLIC LIMITED.

**public mischief.** An offence committed by a person who wilfully interferes with the course of justice or with the police, by an act or attempt, which tends to the prejudice of the community eg false statements to the police with the objective of wasting their time. The common law offence still subsists despite a similar offence created by statute: The People (DPP) v Carew (1981) ILRM 91 and Criminal Law Act 1976 s.12. See O'Malley in 7 ILT & SJ (1989) 243.

**public morals.** Any practice which tends to injure public morals is a common law offence: R v Rogier 2 D & R 435. Conspiracy to corrupt public morals is a misdemeanour indictable in common law: AG (SPUC) v Open Door Counselling Ltd (1987) ILRM 447. See O'Malley in 7ILT & SJ (1989) 243. [Text: Daly CB]. See also PATENT, REVOCATION OF.

**public music licence.** A licence granted under the Public Health Acts Amendment Act 1890 s.51. See FUNCTUS OFFICIO.

**public nuisance.** See NUISANCE, PUBLIC.

**public order and morality.** The term used to describe an overriding condition, subject to which many rights, both constitutional and statutory, may be limited, eg see ASSEMBLY, FREEDOM OF; EXPRESSION, FREEDOM OF; PATENT, REVOCATION OF.

**public place.** Any street, road or other place to which the public have access with vehicles whether as of right or by permission and whether subject to or free of charge: Road Traffic Act 1961 s.3(1). It is an essential ingredient of many road traffic offences that they be committed in a public place. A street or place to which access with vehicles is prohibited is not a public place eg a street which has been pedestrianised and closed to traffic: DPP v Molloy (1993 HC) ILRM 573. See Stanbridge v Healy (1985) ILRM 290; DPP v Joyce (1985) ILRM 206; Montgomery v Loney (1959) NI 171. See also Environmental Protection Act 1992 s.3(1); Criminal Law (Sexual Offences) Act 1993 s.1(1); draft Criminal Justice (Public Order) Bill 1993 s.3(1).

**public policy.** The principle in law that a person will not be permitted to do that which has a tendency to be injurious to the public, or against the public good. Certain acts are said to be contrary to public policy when the law refuses to enforce or recognise them on the grounds that they are injurious to the interest of the State or the community eg the law will not enforce an illegal contract, or permit evidence to be given which would affect the security of the State. See Egerton v Brownlow (1853) 4HL Cas 1; Stanhope v Hospitals Trust Ltd (1936) Ir Jur Rep 25. See also Contractual Obligations (Applicable Law) Act 1991,

first schedule, art.16.

**public policy, evidence excluded by.** Evidence of matters which may not be given on the grounds that disclosure would affect the security of the State or the administration of justice eg

(a) affairs of state — however, a refusal by a Minister to withhold production of a document on public interest grounds is capable of review by the courts: Murphy v Dublin Corporation & Minister for Local Government (1972) IR 215; Geraghty v Minister for Local Government (1975) IR 300; see also Cully v NBFC Ltd (1984) ILRM 683; Incorporated Law Society v Minister for Justice (1987) ILRM 42; Director of Consumer Affairs v Sugar Distributors Ltd (1991 HC) ILRM 395; Ambiorix Ltd v Minister for the Environment (1992 SC) ILRM 209.

(b) information which would disclose channels through which information is obtained for the detection of crimes: Attorney General v Simpson (1959) IR 105; but see DPP v Holly (1984) ILRM 149;

(c) previously at common law, statements by parents tending to bastardise their offspring, known as the rule in Russell v Russell (1924) AC 687, which rule no longer applies; the evidence of a husband or wife is now admissible in any proceedings to prove that marital intercourse did or did not take place between them during any period: Status of Children Act 1987 s.47; S v S (1983) IR 68; AS v RB (1984) ILRM 66;

(d) judicial disclosures eg matters which arise before judges or between jurors.

A willing witness will not be permitted to give evidence on matters if public policy requires its exclusion; also secondary evidence of the matter is not permitted.

**public prosecutor.** See DIRECTOR OF PUBLIC PROSECUTIONS.

**public records.** See NATIONAL ARCHIVES.

**public right.** A right conferred on the public eg the right of owners and occupiers of premises to cause drains to empty into a public sewer without charge: Ballybay Meat Exports Ltd v Monaghan Co Council (1990 HC) ILRM 864. See however SEWER.

**public road.** A road over which a public right of way exists and the responsibility for the maintenance of which lies on a road authority: Roads Act 1993 s.2(1). A road authority may, by order, declare any road over which a public right of way exists to be a public road, having satisfied itself that the road is of general public utility, having considered the financial implications and any objections to a public advertisement of its proposed declaration (ibid s.11).

A public road is a national road, regional road, or a local road; it may also be motorway, busway, or protected road (ibid ss.2(1), 10, 43, 44, 45). Only a local road requires a formal declaration (ibid s.11(4)). A road constructed in future by a road authority is a public road without declaration unless the authority decides otherwise (ibid s.11(7)). See Concorde (Roadhouse) Ltd v Dublin County Council (1978) HC.

The public has the right to pass and re-pass on a public road, over the whole surface including the *via trita* (qv). The owner of land beside a public road is presumed to be the owner of the soil up to one half of the road and has the right of access to and from the road: Holland v Dublin County Council (1979) 113 ILTR 1. This right of access is subject to the public right of passage. However, these rights are restricted in terms of access or traffic in the case of a motorway and a busway, and may be restricted on a protected road.

A person who causes damage to a public road by *excessive* weight or *extraordinary traffic* is liable to pay the extraordinary expenses incurred by the local authority in the repair thereof: Road Traffic Act 1961 s.17; Hill v Thomas (1893) 2 QB 333. It is an offence for any person without lawful authority or consent of a road authority to deface a public road, damage it, excavate it, permit dung or urine from an animal to be left on a public road (ibid 1993 Act s.13(10)).

Local authorities and other public authorities are authorised by statute to interfere with public roads, but they must use reasonable care and skill eg Johnson v Dublin Corporation (1961) IR 24. They must also obtain the appropriate consent (ibid 1993 Act s.53). See Giant's Causeway Company Ltd v AG and Ors 5 NI JR 301; Merriman v Dublin Corporation (1993 HC) ILRM

58. See CARAVAN; CYCLEWAY; MISFEASANCE; NONFEASANCE; MOTORWAY; ROAD RACE; ROAD USER'S DUTY; SIGN; TREE.

**public road, abandonment of.** A road authority is empowered to abandon a public road, by order, following notice to the public and consideration of objections: Roads Act 1993 s.12. Ministerial approval is required in respect of a national or regional road (ibid s.12(4)). Following abandonment, the road authority ceases to be responsible for the maintenance of the road, but this does not affect any public right of way over such road (ibid s.12(5)) unless that right of way is itself extinguished (ibid s.73).

A public road may be extinguished by natural causes, such as the encroachment of the sea or by landslips, or if public access to it is cut off by the destruction, or lawful extinction, of the only public roads leading into it: R v Greenhow (Inhabitants) 1 QBD 703; Bailey v Jamieson 1 CPD 329. See WAY, RIGHT OF.

**public service vehicle.** A mechanically propelled vehicle (qv) used for the carriage of persons for reward: Road Traffic Act 1961 s.3. A large public service vehicle is one having seating passenger accommodation for more than eight persons exclusive of the driver. For licensing of public service vehicles see Road Traffic (Public Service Vehicles) (Licensing) Regulations 1978 (SI No 292 of 1978) as amended by SI No 272 of 1991. Licences may be granted for wheelchair accessible public hire vehicles (SI No 172 of 1992).

**public trust.** A charitable trust. See CHARITIES.

**public waste collector.** A local or other sanitary authority (qv) for the purposes of the Local Government (Sanitary Services) Acts 1878 to 1964. See WASTE OPERATION.

**public worship, disturbance of.** The offence of disturbing public worship in a riotous, violent, or indecent manner which is being held in any church, churchyard or burial ground. See Ecclesiastic Courts Jurisdiction Act 1860 s.2; Offences Against the Person Act 1861 s.36. See WORSHIP, PUBLIC.

**publication.** (1) For the purposes of copyright, *publication* of a work means the issue of reproductions of the work to the public: Copyright Act 1963 s.3(2)(c). See BOOK; COPYRIGHT.

(2) In relation to defamation (qv), *publication* is the making known of the defamatory matter to some person other than the person of whom it is made. Any person who makes the defamatory words, who repeats them, who distributes them, or who disseminates them, publishes them. An *innocent publication*, which is a ground for making an *offer of amends* (qv), means (a) that the publisher did not intend to publish the words about the party aggrieved, and that he did not know of circumstances under which they might be understood to refer to the party aggrieved; or (b) that the words were not defamatory on the face of them and the publisher did not know of circumstances under which the words might be understood to be defamatory of the party aggrieved: Defamation Act 1961 s.21(5). In either case the publisher must have exercised all reasonable care in relation to the publication. See RSC O.36 r.36.

(3)As regard inventions, prior publication can destroy the *novelty* required for the grant of a patent. An invention must be new ie not forming part of the *state of the art*: Patents Act 1992 s.11. *State of the art* comprises everything made available to the public (whether in the State or elsewhere) by means of a written or oral description, by use or in any other way, before the date of filing of the patent application. See SOUND RECORD-ING.

**publication, right of.** There is a constitutional right to publish information which is not a breach of copyright: The AG for England and Wales v Brandon Books (1987) ILRM 135. However, certain statutes prohibit publication or broadcast of certain matters eg matters likely to lead members of the public to identify (a) the complainant (or the accused until convicted) in rape cases: Criminal Law (Rape) Act 1980 ss.7-8 and Criminal Law (Rape) Amdt Act 1990 s.14; or (b) a child in care proceedings: Child Care Act 1991 s.31(1). Additionally, no person may publish any information as to any particular *preliminary examination* of an accused in the District Court, which is conducted to determine if there is sufficient evidence to return the defendant for trial to a higher court, other than a statement of the fact that such examination in relation to a named person on a specified charge had been held and of the decision thereon: Criminal Proceedure Act 1967 s.17. See DISTRICT COURT, PRELIMINARY EXAMINATION. See also IN CAMERA; PUBLIC JUSTICE.

**publicci juris.** [Of public right].

**publicity.** It was held in a particular case that improper publicity coupled with prosecution counsel's remarks that the accused was "patently guilty" deprived the accused of the prospect of a fair trial: Doherty v DPP (1993 HC) ITLR (5 Apr).

**publish.** See PUBLICATION.

**puffer.** See AUCTION SALES.

**puisne.** [Later born; younger].

**puisne mortgage.** An equitable mortgage created out of the mortgagor's equity of redemption (qv): Antrim County Land, Building and Investment Co Ltd v Stewart (1904) 2 IR 357. Where a redemption suit is brought by a puisne mortgagee, the costs of each prior mortgage are added to his security, and the total is paid, with interest, according to the respective priority of each mortgage. See Hilliard v Moriarty (1894) 1 IR 316. See REDEMPTION.

**punctuation.** The division of words in a document by stops and commas etc. The sense of a document is to be collected from the words and the context and not from the punctuation: Sandford v Raikes (1916) 1 Mer 646.

**punishment.** Sentence; the penalty inflicted by a court on a convicted offender. It is the primary sanction of the criminal law. The penalty may be: (a) formerly, the death penalty for capital murder or treason; now, imprisonment for life, of not less than 40 years, for aggravated murder and treason: Criminal Justice Act 1990 s.4; (b) imprisonment with hard labour (The People v Giles (1974) IR 422); (c) penal servitude (The State (Jones) v O'Donovan (1973) IR 329); (d) simple imprisonment without hard labour; (e) a money fine; (f) an order to pay compensation; (g) a community service order (qv); (h) a probation order. It appears that in practice there is now no distinction in the treatment of prisoners sentenced to penal servitude or imprisonment, or between imprisonment with or without hard labour.

The object of passing sentence is not merely to deter the criminal from committing a crime again but to induce the criminal, in so far as possible, to turn to an honest life: The People v O'Driscoll (1972 CCA) Frewen 351. The particular punishment is subject to the principle of proportionality; the sentence must match the circumstances of the offence and the relevant personal circumstances of the defendant: DPP v Conry (1993 CCC) — Irish Times 15/7/1993.

A court is required to take into account in determining the sentence, the effect of certain offences on the victim; the offences concerned are sexual offences and offences involving violence or threat of violence to the person: Criminal Justice Act 1993 s.5. The Court of Criminal Appeal is now empowered to review unduly lenient sentences (ibid s.2). In Northern Ireland it has been held that if the existing level of sentences for a particular offence is failing to deter, then the level of sentencing may well have to rise: Queen v Gregory & Carroll (1993 C of A in NI) ITLR (10 May).

In relation to *parole,* a sentence of imprisonment may be reactivated after its original currency has expired, but there must be fairness of procedure in relation to such re-activation: Cunningham v Governor of Mountjoy Prison (1987) ILRM 34. A District Court is empowered to impose consecutive sentences up to a maximum of two years imprisonment: Criminal Justice Act 1984 s.12. See Law Reform Commission Consultation Paper on Sentencing (No 45 of 1993). See Ni Raifeartaigh in 11 ILT & SJ (1993) 101. See CHARACTER; CONCURRENT SENTENCES; COMPENSATION ORDER; CONSECUTIVE SENTENCES; CONVICTION, EVIDENCE OF; CORPORAL PUNISHMENT; HANGING; LIFE IMPRISONMENT; PARDON; PROBATION OF OFFENDERS; RAPE; RELEASE, TEMPORARY; REMISSION OF SENTENCE; REVIEW OF SENTENCE; SUCCEED, UNWORTHINESS TO; VICTIM IMPACT REPORT; WHIPPING; YOUNG PERSON.

**punitive damages.** Synonymous with exemplary damages (qv): McIntyre v Lewis & Dolan (1991 SC) ITLR (22 Apr). See also Civil Liability Act 1961 ss.7(2) and 14(4). See EXEMPLARY DAMAGES.

**pupil.** See Dawson v Hamill (1990 HC) ILRM 257. See BARRISTER; CORPORAL PUNISHMENT; SCHOOL AUTHORITY'S DUTY; SUSPEND.

**pur autre vie.** [For the life of another]. See LIFE ESTATE.

**purchase.** To acquire land by a lawful act eg by a conveyance, as opposed to a title acquired by act of law.

**purchase, compulsory.** See COMPULSORY PURCHASE ORDER.

**purchase, words of.** See WORDS OF PURCHASE.

**purchase notice.** The notice whereby the owner of land may require the planning authority to purchase his interest in the land; it arises only where planning permission is refused on an appeal to An Bord Pleanala (qv) and where as a result of that decision, the land has become *incapable of reasonably beneficial use in its existing state*: LG(P&D) Act 1963 s.29. It has been held in England that this does not mean merely that the land has become less valuable: R v Minister of Housing and Local Government, ex parte Chicester RDC (1960) 2 All ER 407. An appeal to confirm or annul a purchase notice lies to An Bord Pleanala. See also Portland Estates Ltd v Limerick Corporation (1980) SC. See LG (P&D) Act 1990 s.12(4). See COMPENSATION AND PLANNING PERMISSION.

**purchaser.** (1) A person who acquires land by purchase (qv). (2) In a transaction of sale, the opposite party to the vendor.

**purchaser for value without notice.** A person who purchases property bona fides for valuable consideration without notice of any prior right or title; he is generally entitled to priority. See NOTICE.

**purchaser's equity.** The equitable interest which the purchaser of land acquires; he acquires an *equity* proportionate to the amount of the purchase price paid: Tempany v Hynes (1976) IR 101. See Lyall in 7ILT & SJ 270.

**putative father.** Formerly the person alleged to be the father of an illegitimate child in proceedings for an affiliation order (qv). See PARENTAGE, DECLARATION OF; PATERNITY, PRESUMPTION OF.

**pyramid of titles.** The series of titles which may exist, particularly in respect of urban land, where a particular piece of land may have been the subject of a series of successive fee farm grants (qv), long leases and sub-leases. See TITLE.

**pyramid selling.** A trading scheme under which goods and services are to be provided by a promoter to be supplied to or for others under transactions effected by participants, where the prospect is held out to participants of receiving payments or other benefits in respect of persons who become participants and which provides for payments by a participant to the promoter: Pyramid Selling Act 1980. It is an offence to induce or attempt to induce a person to become a participant in a pyramid selling scheme (ibid s.2). There is a prohibition on certain payments to promoters of such schemes and provision is made for the return to participants of payments for goods in certain instances (ibid ss.3–4).

# Q

**qua.** [In the capacity of; as].

**quae non valeant singula, juncta juvant.** [Words which are of no effect by themselves are effective when combined].

**quaelibet concessio fortissime contra donatorem interpretanda est.** [Every grant is to be construed as strongly as possible against the grantor].

**quaere.** Question. See SED QUAERE.

**qualification shares.** The specified number of shares required by the articles of association (qv) of a company to be held by a director; in which event the director must obtain the specified shares within two months of his appointment or within such shorter time as the articles provide: Companies Act 1963 s.180. If the articles do not provide for qualifying shares, a director does not have to own shares in the company.

**qualified acceptance.** The acceptance of an offer to create a contract must generally be unqualified. There can be a conditional acceptance of a bill of exchange. See ACCEPTANCE OF BILL.

**qualified privilege.** See PRIVILEGE.

**qualified property.** A limited right to property eg the right of a bailee to possession. See BAILMENT.

**qualified title.** The registration of an interest in land in the Land Registry where the title can be established only for a limited period or only subject to specified reservations: Registration of Title Act 1964 ss.33, 39, 40, 48. Registration with a *qualified title* has the same effect as if the registration were absolute, save that it will not prejudice the enforcement of any right appearing on the register as excepted.

**qualifying patent.** A patent in relation to which the research, planning, processing, experimenting, testing, devising, designing, developing or similar activity leading to the invention, that is the subject of the patent, was carried out in the State: Finance Act 1973 s.34 as amended by Finance Act 1992 s.19. There is an exemption from tax for income from *qualifying patents* when earned by any person who is resident in the State and not resident in any other country.

**quality of goods.** Includes their state or condition: Sale of Goods Act 1893 s.62. Where a seller sells goods in the course of a business, there is an implied condition that the goods supplied are of *merchantable quality* (qv), except that there is no such condition (a) as regards defects specifically drawn to the buyer's attention before the contract is made, or (b) if the buyer examines the goods before the contract is made, as regards defects which that examination ought to have revealed.

Where a seller sells goods in the *course of a business* and the buyer, expressly or by implication, makes known to the seller any particular purpose for which the goods are being bought, there is an implied condition that the goods are reasonably fit for that purpose, whether or not that is a purpose for which such goods are commonly supplied, except where the circumstances show that the buyer does not rely, or that it is unreasonable for him to rely, on the seller's skill or judgement. See Sale of Goods Act 1893 s.14; SGSS Act 1980 s.10.

Any term in a contract which exempts a seller from these implied conditions is void where the buyer *deals as a consumer* (qv) and in any other case, is not enforceable unless it is shown to be fair and reasonable (ibid 1893 Act s.55; 1980 Act s.22). There are similar provisions governing the quality of goods let under a hire-purchase agreement (ibid 1980 Act s.28). See Draper v Rubenstein (1925) 87 ILTR 198; Egan v MSweeney (1956) 90 ILTR 40; T O'Regan Sons Ltd v Micro-Bio (Ireland) Ltd (1980) HC; McCullagh Sales Ltd v Chetham Timber Co (Ireland) Ltd (1983) HC. See FAIR AND REASONABLE TERMS; PRODUCT LIABILITY.

**quamdiu se bene gesserit.** [During good behaviour].

**quando acciderint.** [When it happens].

**quando aliquid mandatur, mandatur et omne per quod perrenitur ad illud.** [When anything is commanded, everything by which it can be accomplished is also commanded].

**quando aliquid prohibetur fieri, prohibetur ex directo et per obliquum.** [When the doing of anything is forbidden, then the doing of it either directly or indirectly is forbidden].

**quando lex aliquid alicui concedit, concedere videtur id sine quo res ipsa esse non potest.** [When the law gives anything to anyone, it gives also all those things without which the thing itself could not exist]. Eg the right of way to a *close*, see WAY, RIGHT OF.

**quando plus fit quam fieri debet, videtur etiam illud fieri quod faciendum est.** [When more is done than ought to be done, then that is considered to have been done which ought to have been done].

**quantity, wrong.** See WRONG QUANTITY.

**quantum.** [How much; amount]. A *book of quantum* is a legal publication with details of damages awarded in legal actions. [Text: White]. See DAMAGES; JURY, ABOLITION OF.

**quantum meruit.** [As much as he has earned]. Where work is done or services performed by one person for another in circumstances which imply that the work done or services performed will be paid for, there is an implied promise to pay *quantum meruit*, ie as much as he deserves.

A claim for quantum meruit may arise from contract eg from an implied agreement to pay a reasonable sum or where there is acceptance of partial performance of a contract: Planche v Colburn (1831) 8 Bing 14. It can also arise from quasi-contract eg (a) for work

done where a contract has been discharged by the breach of the defendant; or (b) in respect of work done under a void contract, believed to be valid: O'Connor v Listowel UDC (1957) Ir Jur Rep 43 applying Craven-Ellis v Canons Ltd (1936) 2 KB 403; or (c) for preparatory work requested by the defendant who received no benefit: Folens & Co v Minister for Education (1984) ILRM 265 applying Brewer Street Investments Ltd v Barclay's Woolen Co (1953) 3 WLR 869; or (d) as a result of agency: Chaieb v Carter (1987) SC.

An action in quantum meruit may be brought to recover the value of benefits conferred on a defendant on foot of an unenforceable contract eg where there is a failure to satisfy the writing requirement of the Statute of Frauds (Ireland) 1695. [Text: Goff & Jones UK]. See PART PERFORMANCE.

**quantum ramifactus.** [The amount of damage suffered].

**quantum valebrant.** [As much as they were worth]. An action for payment for goods supplied, similar to quantum meruit (qv), but in respect of goods.

**quarry.** See MINE.

**quash.** To discharge; to annul; to set aside; to make void.

**quasi.** [As if it were].

**quasi ex contractu.** [As if arising out of contract].

**quasi-estoppel.** A voluntary promise to forego a right (ie a promise without *consideration*) does not give a cause of action but may operate as a quasi-estoppel as the court will not allow a promisor to act inconsistently with a promise. See Central London Property Trust v High Trees House (1946) KB 130; Cullen v Cullen (1962) IR 268.

**quasi-contracts.** Contracts implied by law, giving a right to a person to recover money from another: Moses v Macferlan (1760) 1 W Bl 219. These can arise by: (a) *money had and received* (qv) by the defendant to the use of the plaintiff; (b) money paid by the plaintiff to the defendant's use: Brewer St. Investments v Barclay's Woolen Co (1954) 2 All ER 1330; (c) quantum meruit (qv); (d) contribution from a concurrent wrongdoer (qv): Civil Liability Act 1961 s.30.

**quasi-judicial.** Having a character which is partly judicial eg where there is an exercise of discretion following the hearing of evidence, as in the case of proceedings before an arbitrator. See ARBITRATION.

**quasi-loan.** A transaction under which one party (the creditor) agrees to pay, or pays otherwise than in pursuance of an agreement, a sum for another (the borrower) or agrees to reimburse, or reimburses otherwise than in pursuance of an agreement, expenditure incurred by another party for another (the borrower) — (i) on terms that the borrower (or a person on his behalf) will reimburse the creditor or (ii) in circumstances giving rise to a liability on the borrower to reimburse the creditor: Companies Act 1990 s.25(2). See LOAN TO DIRECTOR.

**quasi-tail.** An estate *pur autre vie* which is limited to a person and the heirs of his body eg *to B and the heirs of his body for the life of A.* See Ex p Sterne (1801) 6 Ves 156. See FEE TAIL; LIFE ESTATE.

**question, leading.** See LEADING QUESTION.

**questioning.** See INTERROGATION; JUDGES' RULES.

**qui approbat non reprobat.** [He who accepts cannot reject]. See ELECTION.

**qui facit per alium facit per se.** [He who does something through another does it through himself]. A principal is liable for the acts of his agent. Generally an employer is liable for the acts of his employee. See AGENT; EMPLOYER, DUTY OF; VICARIOUS LIABILITY.

**qui jure suo utitur neminem laedit.** [He who exercises his legal right inflicts upon no one any injury].

**qui omne dicit nihil excludit.** [He who says everything excludes nothing].

**qui prior est temptore potier est jure.** [He who is first in time has the strongest claim in law]. The equitable maxim that where there are two equal equitable claims made to the same property, the first in time prevails. See EQUITY, MAXIMS OF; NOTICE; PRIORITY.

**qui sentit commodum sentire debet et onus; et e contra.** [He who enjoys the benefit ought also to bear the burden]. See ELECTION.

**qui tacet consentire videtur.** [He who is silent is deemed to consent]. See SILENCE, RIGHT TO.

**quia timet.** [Because he fears]. An action by a person for an *injunction* to prevent or restrain some act, feared or threatened, which if done, would cause the person substantial damage, for which money would be no adequate or sufficient remedy. The plaintiff must show a very strong possibility of grave damage; the cost to the defendant must also be considered. See Attorney General v Rathmines and Pembroke Hospital Board (1904) 1 IR 161; Independent Newspapers v Irish Press (1932) IR 615; C & A Modes v C & A (Waterford) Ltd (1976) IR 148.

**quicquid plantatur solo, solo cedit.** [Whatever is fixed to the soil, belongs to the soil]. See FIXTURES.

**quid pro quo.** [Something for something]. An essential of a valid contract ie consideration (qv).

**quiet enjoyment, covenant for.** The usual covenant (qv) in a lease (qv) that the lessee will have quiet enjoyment eg *And the Lessor doth hereby covenant with the Lessee that the Lessee performing and observing his covenants may quietly hold and enjoy the said premises during the said term without interruption by the Lessor or any person claiming through him.* A covenant for quiet enjoyment is implied in every lease on behalf of the landlord: Deasy's Act 1860 s.41.

**quit, notice to.** See NOTICE TO QUIT.

**quit rent.** Perpetual rents on land reserved to the Crown (now the State) under the Settlement of Ireland Acts 1662 and 1665. They have largely disappeared as the Land Purchase Acts provided that if land was subject to a quit rent, the rent could be redeemed by the tenant purchasing the land. Where not redeemed and where the land is registered, a quit rent remains a burden which affects the land without registration: Registration of Title Act 1964 s.72(1)(a). See also Statute of Limitations 1957 s.2(1).

**quittance.** A discharge from an obligation.

**quo ligatur, eo dissolvitur.** [Whatsoever binds can also release].

**quo warranto.** [By what authority]. A proceeding by which inquiry is made as to the authority of a person who has claimed or usurped any office or franchise. The proceeding is now by way of judicial review (qv). See RSC O.84 r.18.

**quoad hoc.** [As to this].

**quod ab initio non valet, in tractu**

**temporis non convalescit.** [That which is bad from the beginning does not improve by length of time]. For example, see *void marriage* under MARRIAGE, NULLITY OF.

**quod aedificatur in area legata cedit legato.** [That which is built on ground that is devised passes to the devisee].

**quod per me non possum, nec per alium.** [What I cannot do in person, I cannot do by proxy]. See PROXY.

**quorum.** [Of whom]. The minimum number of persons who constitute a valid formal meeting. Unless the articles of association provide otherwise, the quorum for a private company is two and for a public company is three members present in person: Companies Act 1963 s.134(c).

**quota.** The number of votes sufficient to secure the election of a candidate: the number is obtained by dividing the number of all valid ballot papers by a number exceeding by one the number of vacancies to be filled, and by adding one to the result, any fractional remainder being disregarded: Electoral Act 1992 s.120. Where at the end of any count the number of votes credited to a candidate is greater than the quota, the surplus is transferred to the continuing candidate or candidates (ibid s.121). A candidate may be deemed to be elected without reaching the quota (ibid s.124). See also draft Presidential Elections Bill 1993 s.50.

**quoties in verbis nulla est ambiguitas ibi nulla expositio contra verba expressa fienda est.** [When in the words there is no ambiguity then no interpretation contrary to the actual words is to be adopted].

**quousque.** [Until].

**qv, quod vide.** [Which see].

# R

**race.** A dismissal from employment is deemed to be unfair where it results wholly or mainly from the race or colour of the employee: Unfair Dismissal Act 1977 s.6(2) as amended by Unfair Dismissals (Amdt) Act 1993 s.5(a). See HATRED, INCITEMENT TO; ROAD RACE; VIDEO RECORDING.

**racketering.** See EXTORTION WITH MENACES.

**radio and television commission.** The independent commission, appointed by the government, with the function to arrange for the provision of sound broadcasting services (including a national sound broadcasting service) and one television programme service additional to any broadcasting services provided by Radio Telefis Eireann: Radio and Television Act 1988 ss.3-4.

The Commission is required to enter into: (a) sound broadcasting contracts under which the contractors will have the right and duty to establish, maintain and operate sound broadcasting transmitters serving the areas specified in the contract and to provide a sound broadcasting service and (b) a television programme service contract under which the contractor will have the right and duty to provide a television programme service (ibid s.4(2)). See TV3 Television Co Ltd v IRTC (1993 HC) 11 ILT Dig 187. See ADVERTISEMENT, RADIO; SOUND BROADCASTING SERVICE; TELEVISION PROGRAMME SERVICE.

**radioactive substance.** Any substance capable of emitting ionising radiation and includes any radio-nuclide, whether natural or artificial: Radiological Protection Act 1991. This Act gives effect to the 1986 Convention on Assistance in the Case of a Nuclear Accident or Radiological Emergency, and the 1979 Convention on the Physical Protection of Nuclear Material. It also provides for the establishment of the Radiological Protection Institute of Ireland and for radiological protection measures generally.

**random crime check.** See ROAD TRAFFIC CHECK.

**rape.** The offence committed by a man if he has unlawful sexual intercourse with a woman who at the time of the intercourse does not consent to it, and at that time he knows that she does not consent to the intercourse or he is reckless as to whether she does or does not consent to it: Criminal Law (Rape) Act 1981 s.2.

At a trial of a rape offence, no evidence may be adduced and no question may be asked in cross-examination about any sexual experience of the complainant with any person, including the accused, unless the judge so allows where he is satisfied it would otherwise be unfair to the accused (ibid 1981 Act s.3(1) as amended by the Criminal Law (Rape) Amdt Act 1990 s.13). An application to so question should be made as early as possible in a trial and if unsuccessful may be repeated at further stages of the trial: DPP v McDonagh & Cawley (1991 CCA) 9ILT Dig 171.

There are provisions governing the anonymity of the complainant and of the accused, by restricting publication and broadcasts which could lead members of the public to identify them (ibid 1981 Act ss.7-8). The restriction on the identity of the accused does not apply after he has been convicted of the offence; except where it might lead to the identification of the complainant (ibid 1990 Act s.14).

It has been held that, except in wholly exceptional circumstances, the appropriate sentence for rape is immediate and substantial terms of imprisonment or detention; a plea of guilty is a relevant factor to be considered in the imposition of sentence and may constitute a mitigating circumstance: The People (DPP) v Tiernan (1988 SC) IR 250. However, in a case in which an accused was sentenced to seven years, suspended on conditions, it was held that the sentence must match the circumstances of the offence and the relevant personal circumstances of the defendant: DPP v Conry (1993 HC) — Irish Times 15/7/1993.

The trial of a person indicted for a rape offence is by the Central Criminal Court (ibid 1990 Act s.10). See also The People (Attorney General) v Dermody (1956) IR 307. See LRC 24 of 1988. [Text: O'Malley (2)]. See CARNAL KNOWLEDGE, UNLAWFUL; CONSENT; COMPLAINT; CORROBORATION; MARITAL RAPE; PROCUREMENT OF RAPE; PUNISHMENT; SEXUAL ASSAULT; SEXUAL OFFENCES.

**rate of exchange.** The numerical proportion between the currencies of two states in relation to an exchange of one currency for the other. The Minister is empowered to vary the general exchange rate for the Irish pound in respect of other monetary units: Central Bank Act 1989 s.24(2). As regards VAT payable on intra-Community acquisitions, the VAT rate is the rate applicable to the supply of similar goods in the State and where the invoice is in a foreign currency, the *rate of exchange* is the latest selling rate recorded by the Central Bank for the currency at the time the tax becomes due, unless an alternative arrangement is agreed with the Revenue Commissioners. In relation to legal proceedings, and the rate of exchange to be used to determine the Irish currency equivalent of amounts expressed in foreign currencies, see CURRENCY, FOREIGN.

**rateable hereditament.** All land, buildings and opened mines; all commons (qv), and rights of common, and all other profits (qv) to be had, received or taken out of land; all rights of fishery; and canals, navigations and rights of navigations, and rights of way (qv) and other tolls levied in respect of such rights and easements, and all other tolls: Poor Relief (Ireland) Act 1838 s.63. Parts of a building held under separate titles are properly regarded as separate rating units; structural severance of the parts is not essential: Carlile Trust Ltd v Dublin Corporation (1965) IR 456. See RATES.

**rateable occupier.** The occupier who must pay the rate levied on the property occupied: Poor Relief (Ireland) Act 1838 s.71. To be such an occupier: (a) the occupation must be exclusive: Carroll v Mayo County Council (1967) IR 364; (b) the occupation must be of value or benefit to the occupier: Sinnott v Neale (1948) Ir Jur Rep 10; and (c) the occupation must not be for too transient a period: Dublin Corporation v Dublin Port and Docks Board (1978) IR 266. See RATES.

**rates.** A form of taxation on property based on a valuation (qv) which is used to finance expenditure by local authorities: Poor Relief (Ireland) Act 1838. The making and levying of such rates as may be necessary is provided for (ibid s.61) and must be paid *by the person in the actual occupation of the rateable property at the time of the rate made* (ibid s.71). An occupier includes every person in the immediate use of any hereditament rateable under the Act, whether corporeal or incorporeal.

Where a hereditament is unoccupied at the making of the rate, the rate is made on the owner, who is defined as the person for the time being entitled to occupy the hereditament: Local Government Act 1946 ss.14 and 23. Rates levied by county councils are known as the *county* rate and by urban authorities as the *municipal* rate.

Each year the local authority determines the rate having received the final lists of valuations for its area; the *rate book* is then compiled in the light of the appropriate poundage and valuations, is signed and sealed and demand notes are issued to the rate collectors: Public Bodies Order 1946, arts. 61-63, 68, form RA1. See Butterly v Corporation of Dublin (1986) HC.

An appeal against the rate may be brought on the ground (a) that the rate as determined is wholly illegal: Kettle v Dublin County Council 57 ILTR 113 or (b) the ratepayer is aggrieved by the rate, or has material objection to any persons being included or excluded from the rate or has material objection to the sum charged on any person: 1838 Act ss.106-112 as modified by the Valuation (Ireland) Act 1852 s.28; Poor Relief (Ireland) Act 1849 ss.22-23 and 29-30. See also Local Government (Financial Provisions) Act 1983. See also Stevenson v Orr (1916) 2 IR 619. See ESTIMATES MEETING; MARINA; RATES, RECOVERY OF; RATE-ABLE HEREDITAMENT; RATEABLE OCCUPIER; RATES, EXEMPTION FROM; RECLAIMED LAND; VALUATION.

**rates, exemption from.** Relief from rates has been provided in respect of dwellings: Local Government (Financial Provisions) Act 1978 s.3. It has been held that, apart from specific exceptions to be found in other statutes, the grounds for exemption from rates are to be found in the proviso to s.63 of the Poor Relief (Ireland) Act 1838 dealing with churches, chapels, burial grounds, infirmaries, hospitals, charity schools and buildings exclusively used for charitable purposes or for the education of the poor and buildings dedicated to or *used for public purposes*: McGahon and Ryan v Commissioner of Valuations (1934) IR 736; Barrington's Hospital v Commissioner of Valuations (1957) IR 299.

Property is *used for public purposes* where, and only where it belongs to the government or each member of the

public has an interest in the property: Guardians of the Londonderry Union v Londonderry Bridge Commissioners IR 2 CL 577; Maynooth College v Commissioner of Valuations (1958) IR 189. See also St Macartan's Diocesan Trust v Commissioner of Valuations (1990) 1 IR 508.

Societies established exclusively for the purpose of science, literature or fine arts may be entitled to exemption from local rates: Scientific Societies Act 1843; Valuation (Ireland) Amdt Act 1854. See Quinn in 8ILT & SJ (1990) 286. See SCIENTIFIC SOCIETIES.

**rates, mesne.** See MESNE RATES.

**rates, recovery of.** The payment of arrears of county or municipal rates is normally enforced by summons in the District Court, on failure to pay on foot of a notice in the name of the rate collector damanding payment within six days thereof: Poor Relief (Ireland) Act 1838 s.73.

The court may order the payment of the sum found due with costs, and in default, may issue a warrant to levy the sum by distress (qv) and sale of the goods and chattels of the defendant. There is no monetary limit on the jurisdiction of the District Court in respect of summary proceedings by summons for recovery of arrears of rates. See also County Council of Clare v McInerney (1902) 2 IR 536.

**ratification.** The act of adopting a contract or other transaction by a person who was not bound by it originally. The ratification of a contract by a minor on reaching *full age* (qv) is itself void: Infants Relief Act 1874 s.2. A minor may enter into a fresh contract on reaching full age: Holmes v Brierley (1888) 4 TLR. However, a new contract to pay a *debt* contracted during infancy is unenforceable (ibid s.2). See Leslie v Sheill (1914) 3 KB 607.

A contract made by an agent with no or insufficient authority may be ratified by his principal only if (a) the agent expressly contracted as agent; (b) the principal was named or ascertained when the contract was made; (c) the principal had contractual capacity at the date of the contract and at the date of ratification and (d) the principal at the time of ratification has full knowledge of the material facts or intends to ratify the contract whatever the facts may be. Ratification dates back to the original making of the contract. See Barclay's Bank v Breen (1962) 96 ILTR 179; Brennan v O'Connell (1980) IR 13. See AGENT.

**ratification of treaty.** The formal approval of a treaty after it has been signed. See CHARGE ON PUBLIC FUNDS.

**rating authority.** The council of a county, the corporation of a county or other borough, or the council of an urban district: Valuation Act 1987 s.1.

**ratio decidendi.** The reason for a judicial decision. It is the ratio decidendi which forms the precedent for other similar cases. Contrast with OBITER DICTUM. See PRECEDENT.

**ratio legis.** [The reason for the law].

**ratione soli.** [By reason only].

**re.** [In the matter of].

**reading the Riot Act.** See RIOTOUS ASSEMBLY.

**real estate.** Real property; realty; land, tenements, and hereditaments.

**real security.** A security charged on land.

**realty.** Real property; generally freehold interest in land.

**re-arrest.** See DETENTION

**reason, rule of.** The method used in the USA to determine whether a restraint of trade was illegal pursuant to the wide-sweeping Sherman Act 1890; only undue and unreasonable restraints would be condemned: Standard Oil v US (1911) 221 US 1. The *rule of reason* approach was adopted in Master Foods Ltd t/a Mars v HB Ice Cream (1992 HC) ITLR (5 Oct) and has been adopted in judgments of the European Court of Justice eg Procureur du Roi v Dassonville (1974) ECR 852(6).

**reasonable doubt.** See BEYOND REASONABLE DOUBT.

**reasonable expectation.** See EXPECTATION, LEGITIMATE.

**reasonable man.** A careful man; a man of ordinary prudence: Murphy v Hurley (1929) SC; Curry v Foster (1960) Ir Jur Rep 33. *The law of negligence lays down that the standard of care is that which is expected from a reasonably careful man in the circumstances*: McComiskey v McDermott (1974) IR 75.

**reasonable time.** A reasonable time is a question of fact: Sale of Goods Act 1893 s.56. See OFFER.

**reasonableness.** In a particular case it was held that when forming a decision to dismiss an employee, the effect of the dismissal on the employee is relevant to its reasonableness: Lundy v Airmotive Ireland Ltd (1992 CC) ELR 211 (under appeal).

**reasonably practicable.** Phrase used in some statutory provisions which impose a duty eg *so far as is reasonably practicable* in relation to safety at work legislation: Safety, Health and Welfare at Work Act 1989 s.6. *Practicable* has been interpreted as to mean in effect technologically possible; *reasonably practicable* has been interpreted to mean a level of precaution which takes account of the balance between the risk involved in a particular hazard and the cost involved in remedying it. See Edwards v National Coal Board (1949) 1 KB 704; Kirwan v Bray UDC (1969 SC); Bradley v CIE (1976) IR 217; Brady v Beckmann Instruments Inc (1986) ILRM 361; Keane v ESB (1981) IR 44.

**rebate.** A refund; a credit; a discount.

**rebus sic stantibus.** [In these circumstances].

**rebut.** To contradict; to disprove; to oppose; eg to disprove a presumption.

**rebuttal, evidence in.** Evidence to answer or defeat his opponent's evidence which the party *beginning* in the trial of an action may be allowed to adduce. Generally rebuttal evidence is not allowed, as the party beginning is normally expected to anticipate his opponent's evidence. However, in criminal trials, the trial judge has a discretion to allow the prosecution to call evidence in relation to some new matter introduced by the defence, which the prosecution could not have foreseen.

In civil cases, the party beginning may be allowed to call rebuttal evidence to answer evidence on a matter the proof of which lay with his opponents, and also where he has been taken by surprise. See Riordan v O'Shea (1926) 60 ILTR 61; Attorney General v Gleeson (1930) 64 ILTR 225.

**recaption.** The lawful retaking by a person, without causing a breach of the peace, of his chattels from another, which other had wrongfully taken and detained them.

**receipt.** Written acknowledgement of money paid or of goods received. A receipt under seal is conclusive whereas a receipt under hand is but prima facie evidence of same which can be rebutted. A receipt is not a written offer; hence its acceptance does not make its terms binding on the person who receives it. See Chapelton v Barry RDC (1940) 1 KB 532. See PAYMENT; VOUCHER.

**receiver, company.** A person appointed by the court or by creditors of a company to manage the company's business until satisfaction of a debt. Often a debenture will authorise the appointment of a receiver on certain conditions being satisfied. The court has an inherent jurisdiction to appoint a receiver over charged assets. A body corporate cannot be a receiver of the property of a company, nor may an undischarged bankrupt or an officer, or servant, or auditor of a company, or their close relatives: Companies Act 1963 ss.314 and 315 as amended by the Companies Act 1990 s.170.

The appointment of a receiver operates to *crystallise* floating charges which then become fixed; it also operates to suspend the company's powers and the directors' authority in relation to the assets covered by the receivership. Appointment of a receiver by the court operates to dismiss the company's existing employees, although they may become employed by the receiver. The appointment of a receiver out of court, however, does not of itself automatically terminate employment contracts with the company.

The receiver has power to do everything necessary to realise the security and he may apply to the court for directions: ibid 1963 Act s.316(1), as amended by the 1990 Act s.171; Industrial Development Authority v Moran (1978) IR 159. The following may also apply to the court for directions in connection with the performance by the receiver of his functions:- an officer, member, contributory, liquidator or employees. A receiver is not bound by the company's contractual obligations: Airlines Airspares v Handley Page (1970) 1 Ch 193; Ardmore Studios (Ireland) Ltd v Lynch (1965) IR 1.

Receivers are *fiduciaries* for those who appointed them and owe those persons duties of good faith, including a duty of care to the company: McGowan v Gannon (1983) ILRM 516. A receiver, in selling property of a company, must exercise all reasonable care to obtain the best price reasonably obtainable for the property as at the time of sale: 1963 Act s.316A as inserted by 1990 Act s.172. He must give notice to the creditors if he intends to sell by private contract a non-cash asset of *requisite value* to an officer of the company (ibid s.316A(3)). See also McCarter v Roughan and McLaughlin (1984) ILRM 447.

Every business letter, order for goods or invoices issued by or for the company or the receiver, must state that a receiver has been appointed (ibid 1963 Act s.317). The directors and secretary and such other officers and employees of the company as the receiver directs, must draw up a statement of the company's affairs at the date of the receiver's appointment (ibid 1963 Act s.320 as amended by 1990 Act ss.173-174). The receiver must make certain information and accounts available to the company and to the Registrar of Companies (ibid ss.319(1) and 321).

The court may, on cause shown, remove a receiver and appoint another (ibid 1963 Act s.322A as inserted by s.175 of 1990 Act) and may determine or limit a receivership on the application of a receiver (ibid 1963 Act s.322B as inserted by 1990 Act s.176). The court may also order the return of assets of a company in receivership which have been improperly transferred (1990 Act s.178).

While there are no qualifications specified for receivers, the Minister is empowered to add to the list of persons who are not qualified for appointment (1990 Act s.237). See also Building Societies Act 1989 s.40(5). [Text: Forde (1) and (9); Keane (1); Ussher; Kerr (UK); Picardu (UK)]. See DISQUALIFICATION ORDER.

**receiver by way of equitable execution.** See EQUITABLE EXECUTION.

**receiver of bankrupt's property.** The receiver or manager of a bankrupt's property, or of the property of an *arranging debtor* (qv), who the High Court is empowered to appoint; the court may direct the receiver to take immediate possession of such property or any part thereof: Bankruptcy Act 1988 s.73. See BANKRUPTCY.

**receiver of mortgaged property.** A receiver appointed by the mortgagee (lender) under an express power in the mortgage deed or under statutory power given by the Conveyancing Act 1881 s.19. The statutory power arises when the mortgage is by deed and after the redemption date has passed; it becomes exercisable where there is default of three months after notice is given to the mortgagor demanding payment of the principal outstanding, or interest is in arrears for two months, or there has been a breach of covenant, other than for payment of money.

The receiver is deemed in law to be the *agent of the mortgagor* and consequently the mortgagee is not liable to the mortgagor for the receiver's default. Monies received by the receiver must be applied: to discharge the outgoings; to meet annual payments which have priority to the mortgage; to discharge his commission, insurance and repairs; to discharge interest on the mortgage and, if directed by the mortgagee in writing, to discharge the principal; and to pay the residue to the mortgagor.

It has been held that the powers of s.24(3) of the 1881 Act do not entitle the receiver to appropriate any part of the proceeds of sale of the dairy produce or the cattle on land subject to a mortgage: Donohue v Agricultural Credit Corporation (1986) IR 165.

**receiving stolen goods.** Formerly, the offence committed by a person who received stolen goods knowing them, at the time he received them, to have been stolen: Larceny Act 1916 s.33. The offence has now been abolished and replaced by the wider offence of *handling stolen property* (qv), which includes receiving: Larceny Act 1990 s.3 which substitutes a new s.33 in the 1916 Act.

In the former offence of receiving, the original act of dishonesty included not only a stealing of the goods but also the obtaining of them in circumstances which amounted to a felony (qv) or misdemeanour. It had to be shown that the accused took the goods into his possession, actual or constructive. The goods had also to be stolen by a person other than the accused. It had to be shown that the accused at the time he received them, knew they were stolen; this guilty knowledge could be shown by *inference* eg the price, place or time when he received them.

In the absence of a reasonable explanation from the possessor of recently stolen goods, a jury was entitled to conclude that he was either the thief or the guilty receiver. Evidence that (a) other property, stolen within one year previously, has been found in the accused's possession, or that (b) the accused was convicted, within five years previously, of any offence involving fraud or dishonesty, was admissible to prove guilty knowledge on the part of the accused (ibid 1916 Act s.43 repealed by 1990 Act). See Attorney General v Farnan (1933) 67 ILTR 208; The People (Attorney General) v Berber and Levey (1944) IR 405; The People v Carney and Mulcahy (1955) IR 324. See also LRC 23 of 1987. See HANDLING STOLEN PROPERTY; UNLAWFUL POSSESSION OF GOODS.

**reception order.** An order in prescribed form which provides for the reception, detention and treatment of a person for a period not exceeding 28 days from the date of his admission to a specified psychiatric centre; the period of validity of a reception order may be extended from time to time by order, signed by two authorised medical practitioners each of whom has separately examined the person: Health (Mental Services) Act 1981 s.24. A reception order is made by an authorised medical practitioner of the psychiatric centre within a period not exceeding 48 hours after the arrival of the person on foot of a *recommendation for reception* containing the written recommendation of two registered medical practitioners (or one where prescribed by regulation) (ibid s.19).

Where a reception order is extended, the person must be informed of the reason for the extension and of the right to a *review* under s.38 (ibid s.24(4)); also the applicant for, and the medical practitioners who signed, the recommendation for the reception, must also be so informed. There are safeguards for patients, including inspection of centres, psychiatric review boards, and a requirement that letters from such patients are to be delivered or posted unopened (ibid s.35 and Part IV). The 1981 Act had not come into force by 1993; for existing reception orders, see MENTAL TREATMENT. See also PSYCHIATRIC CENTRE.

**reciprocity.** The term used in international law to describe the agreement of states to bestow privileges on each others' subjects. See Government of Canada v Employment Appeals Tribunal (1992) ELR 29. See FRANCHISE.

**recitals.** Statements in an instrument, commencing *whereas...*, which explain or lead up to the operative part of the instrument. In a conveyance (qv), they may be *narrative recitals* which set out the facts and instruments necessary to show title, or *introductory recitals* which explain the motive for the execution of the deed. They are not necessary to the validity of the deed (qv), but they are useful from the purchaser's standpoint because: they may act as an estoppel (qv) against the vendor; they explain the operative part of the deed; they are evidence of their truth after 20 years: Vendor & Purchaser Act 1874 s.2(2). An erroneous and unnecessary reference to a repealed statute in a recital to a mortgage deed will not invalidate the mortgage: Bray UDC v Coughlan (1989) ITLR (24 Jul).

**reckless trading.** Includes (a) the carrying on of a business by an officer of a company who ought to have known that his actions or those of the company would cause loss to the creditors of the company or (b) being a party to the contracting of a debt by the company where the officer did not honestly believe on reasonable grounds that the company would be able to pay the debt as it fell due for payment: Companies Act 1963 s.297A(2) as inserted by s.138 of the Companies Act 1990.

If in the course of the winding up of a company or in the course of examinership (under the Companies Amendment Act 1990), it appears that any person was, while an officer of the company, knowingly a party to the carrying on of any business of the company, in a reckless manner, he can be declared by the court to be personally responsible for all or any part of the debts or other liabilities of the company, without limitation (ibid 1963 Act s.297A(1)(a)).

There is not a collective responsibility on the board of directors of a company as regards reckless trading; reckless trading must be proved against each individual defendant officer of the company ie that his conduct fell within the ambit of conduct prohibited or liable to be penalised: In re Hefferon Kearns Ltd (No 2), Dublin Heating Co Ltd v Hefferon & Ors (1993 HC) as reported by MacCann in 11 ILT & SJ (1993) 31.

If the court considers that the person has acted honestly and responsibly, it may relieve him wholly or partly from personal liability, on whatever terms it deems fit (ibid 1963 Act s.297A(6)). See Flynn in 9ILT & SJ (1991) 186 and MacCann in 10 ILT & SJ (1991) 31 and 61. See FRAUDULENT TRADING.

**recklessness.** Intentional creation of unjustifiable risk. As regards a trespasser, an occupier must not do an act which is intended to injure, or is so *reckless* as to be likely to injure the trespasser, whose presence was known or ought to have been known: Coffey v McEvoy (1912) 2 IR 95. The higher the likelihood of trespassers being present, the greater the likelihood that the conduct of the occupier was reckless: Donovan v Landy's Ltd (1963) IR 441. See also Tiernan v O'Callaghan (1944) 78 ILTR 36. See OCCUPIER'S LIABILITY TO TRESPASSERS.

**reclaimed land.** Newly reclaimed land is capable of being valued for rates: Valuation (Ireland) Act 1854 s.4; Coal Distributors Ltd v Commissioner of Valuation (1990) ILRM 172.

**recognisance.** An obligation or bond made before a court of record (qv) binding a person (called the *recognisor*) to perform some act eg to appear before a court or to keep the peace or to be of good behaviour. See RSC O.84 rr.16-17; RCC O.46; DCR rr.60, 80, 81. See ESTREAT.

**recommendations of EC.** See COMMUNITY LAW.

**recommended price.** The price of goods recommended by the manufacturer, producer or other supplier and the recommended price generally for supply by retail in the area where the goods are offered: Consumer Information Act 1978 s.7(2)(b). See PRICE, FALSE OR MISLEADING INDICATION OF; RESALE PRICE MAINTENANCE.

**reconcilation.** The act of settling disputes

and harmonising differences. See INDUS-TRIAL RELATIONS OFFICER; JUDICIAL SEPARA-TION; LABOUR COURT.

**reconstruction of company.** A capital reorganisation of a company arising from a *compromise* or *arrangement* between shareholders or creditors, or between any class of them: Companies Act 1963 ss.201-203. On application, the court will stay or restrain all further proceedings against the company, thereby allowing it to continue in business.

The court will summon meetings of each class of shareholder and creditor affected to consider the arrangement, which will be sanctioned by the court only if the scheme is supported by at least three fourths in value of each class affected by it who vote, either in person or by proxy. If the scheme involves *reconstruction* of one or more companies or an *amalgamation* of two or more companies, the court possesses extensive powers that facilitate making the scheme effective.

There is provision for a compromise or a scheme of arrangement in respect of a company which is subject to the protection of the court: Companies (Amendment) Act 1990 ss.17(4)(e) and 24. Also reconstruction orders made by courts outside the State may be enforced by the High Court (ibid s.36). See In re Pye (Ireland) Ltd (1985) HC; In re John Power Son Ltd (1934) IR 412; In re Van Dyk Models Ltd 100 ILTR 177 (1966). [Text: Forde (7)]. See MERGER; COURT PROTECTION OF COMPANY.

**reconversion.** The notional restoration of previously notionally converted property to its original character in contemplation of equity. Reconversion may take place by act of the party for whose benefit the conversion was directed or by operation of law. An absolute owner who is *sui juris* may elect to take the property in whatever form he chooses; if he wishes to take it in its unconverted form, a reconversion takes place. Reconversion also takes place by law in certain conditions where property, though subject to an inoperative trust for conversion, has not actually been converted, and the property is *at home*. See McDonagh v Nolan (1882) 9 LR IR 262. See CONVERSION IN EQUITY.

**reconveyance.** The revesting in the mortgagor of the legal estate on redemption of the mortgage. A reconveyance is not necessary in specified circumstances. See REDEMPTION.

**record.** (1) A memorial of an action in a court of record (qv). (2) An authentic account of some event. (3) To make a written account. (4) Any disc, tape, perforated roll or other device in which sounds are embodied so as to be capable of being automatically reproduced therefrom: Copyright Act 1963 s.2(1). It is an offence to supply a record with the intent that it may be comprised in an illegal broadcast: Broadcasting and Wireless Telegraphy Act 1988 s.5(2)(a). See also SOUND RECORDING; COURT OF RECORD.

**recount.** In an election, the returning officer (qv) must re-examine and recount ballot papers at the conclusion of any count at the request of any candidate or his election agent; he is not required to do so more than once: Electoral Act 1992 s.125(1). Each candidate has a right to demand one complete re-examination and recount (ibid s.125(3)). See also draft Presidential Elections Bill 1993 s.52. See ELECTION AGENT; SPOILT VOTE.

**recourse, right of.** The right which the *holder in due course* (qv) has as against every person who signed a negotiable instrument (qv), if the party primarily liable on it fails to meet his obligation.

**recovery.** A collusive action, called *common recovery*, first recognised in Taltarum's case 1472, which was used to *bar an entail* until its abolition by the Fines and Recoveries Act 1833, which substituted a simple disentailing assurance. See BARRING THE ENTAIL.

**recovery of goods.** As regards goods the subject of a hire-purchase agreement, the owner has no authority to enter on the hirer's premises for the purpose of taking back the goods: Hire-Purchase Act 1946 sch. Where one third of the *hire-purchase price* (qv) has been paid, the owner cannot enforce any right to recover possession of the goods otherwise than by action (ibid s.12). There are special provisions governing motor vehicles. See Capital Finance Co Ltd v Bray (1963) 1 All ER 604; Mercantile Credit Company of Ireland Ltd v O'Malley (1957) IR 22; Irish Buyway Ltd v Ivory 86 ILTR 83; United Dominions Trust (Commercial) Ltd v

Jeremiah Byrne (1957) IR 77; McDonald v Bowmaker (Ireland) Ltd (1949) IR 317. See RSC O.27 rr.2 and 16. See RECOVERY OF MOTOR VEHICLE.

**recovery of land.** See EJECTMENT; MORTGAGEE, RIGHTS OF.

**recovery of motor vehicle.** As regards a motor vehicle the subject of a hire-purchase agreement, the owner is entitled to enforce any right he may have to enter any premises of the hirer for the purpose of taking back the vehicle; this does not include, however, a house used as a dwelling or any building within the curtilage thereof: Hire-Purchase Act 1946 sch. Where one third of the *hire-purchase price* (qv) has been paid, the owner cannot enforce any right to recover possession of the vehicle otherwise than by action (ibid s.12).

However, where the owner has commenced an action to recover possession of the vehicle and one third of the hire-purchase price has been paid (or if it is a *further* hire-purchase agreement) and the vehicle has been abandoned or has been left unattended in circumstances likely to result in damage or more than the normal depreciation to the vehicle, the owner is entitled to recover possession of the vehicle: Hire-Purchase Act 1960 s.16. *Motor vehicle* means any mechanically propelled vehicle constructed for use on roads for the carriage of persons and goods and includes a tractor. See McDonald v Bowmaker (Ireland) Ltd (1949) IR 317. See RSC O.27 rr.2 and 16.

**recrimination.** Formerly, a defence plea in a suit for *divorce a mensa et thoro* (qv) by the respondent, whereby in answer to the petitioner's allegations of adultery (qv) on the part of the respondent, the respondent alleged that the petitioner had also committed adultery. It could be a complete defence to such a petition. However, recrimination on the part of an applicant is not now a bar to the grant of a decree of judicial separation (qv): Judicial Separation and Family Law Reform Act 1989 s.44. See Chettle v Chettle (1821) 161 ER 1399. See CONDONATION; CONNIVANCE.

**rectification.** (1) The correction of an error in a register, or instrument or judgment eg due to a clerical error or an error of draftmanship. (2) Where parties have reduced a contract between them to writing which does not accurately express their agreement, it may be rectified under the *doctrine of rectification*. The doctrine is invoked where the consent of the parties is real and undoubted, but it has by mistake been inaccurately expressed in a later written agreement. The onus of proof on the plaintiff is heavy; oral evidence to justify rectification must be conclusive rather than on the balance of probability.

It has been held that rectification can be granted where there was prior accord on a term of the proposed agreement, outwardly expressed and communicated between the parties; the common intention of the parties must be continuous and must have the necessary precision; the onus of proof on the plaintiff is heavy: Irish Life Assurance Co Ltd v Dublin Land Securities Ltd (1989 SC) IR 253. See Ferguson v Merchant Banking Ltd (1993 HC) ILRM 136. See O'Ceidigh in 8ILT & SJ (1990) 186. See DATA PROTECTION; MISTAKE; REGISTER OF TRADE MARKS; SLIP RULE.

**recycling.** See WASTE OPERATION.

**reddendo singula singulis.** [Giving each to each].

**reddendum.** That which is to be paid; the clause in a lease which specifies the rent which is payable and the time when payable eg *Yielding therefor during the said term, the yearly rent of £... clear of all deductions by equal half yearly payments on..., the first payment to be made on... .*

**redeemable shares.** Includes shares which are liable at the option of the company or the shareholder to be redeemed: Companies Act 1990 s.206. A company may now issue redeemable shares and redeem them, except where the nominal value of the issued share capital which is not redeemable is less than one tenth of the nominal value of the total issued share capital of the company; also no such shares can be redeemed unless they are fully paid (ibid s.207). There is provision for cancelling of shares on redemption or for holding them as *treasury shares* (qv) instead of cancellation (ibid ss.208-209). Previously, a limited company could, if authorised by its articles of association, issue preference shares which could be redeemed at the option of the company, without going through the cumbersome capital reduction procedure: Companies Act 1963 ss.64-65 as amended by Companies Act 1983, first schedule, para 12. See also 1990 Act ss.220-221. See RSC O.75 r 19. See Nolan in 9 ILT & SJ (1991) 9. See PREFERENCE SHARES.

**redemption.** The repayment of a mortgage debt whereby the equitable and legal estates merge in the mortgagor (qv). A mortgagor may bring a *redemption suit* to compel the mortgagee to reconvey the land on payment of debt and interest and to return his title deeds: RSC O.18 r.2; O.54 r.3; RCC O.8 r.2.

The rules of a building society must provide for the conditions on which a borrower of a housing loan (qv) can redeem the amount due from him before the end of the period for which such a loan was made: Building Societies Act 1989, second schedule, part II, para 5(e).

Where all moneys secured by a mortgage have been fully paid or discharged, a building society may issue a receipt under the seal of the society; this receipt operates to vacate the mortgage and, without any reconveyance or re-surrender, vests the estate or interest in the property in the person for the time being entitled to the *equity of redemption* (qv) (ibid s.27).

A simplified procedure for discharging mortgages of housing authorities and other specified cases is provided for in the Housing Act 1988 s.18. See also PAWN.

**redemption, equity of.** See EQUITY OF REDEMPTION.

**redemption fee.** In relation to a loan, any sum in addition to principal and any interest due on such principal (without regard to the fact of the redemption of the loan) at the time of redemption of the whole or part of the loan: Building Societies Act 1986 s.6; SI No 27 of 1987, first schedule; SI No 339 of 1987. A member of a building society may at any time before the time agreed, repay the society the whole or any part of a loan, and is not liable to pay any redemption fee in relation to the loan or any part of the loan.

Notwithstanding the repeal of the 1986 Act, this provision is continued in force as regards existing and future housing

loans; however the ban on redemption fees does not apply to fixed rate interest loans as it restricts the making of such loans: Building Societies Act 1989 s.6. The 1989 Act provides that the ban does not apply to a *housing loan* (qv) in respect of which the mortgage or loan agreement provides that the rate of interest may not be changed or may only be changed at intervals of not less than one year (ibid s.6(3)).

The Central Bank is empowered to prescribe, by regulation, rules prohibiting or restricting the charging of redemption fees (ibid s.11(2)(b)(i)). No such rules had been prescribed by 1993 and none were planned.

**redress.** See RELIEF; REMEDY.

**reduction of capital.** The reduction of capital of a company which must be approved by special resolution of the members, by creditors and by the court eg reduction in share capital of the exploration company Oliver Resources plc approved by the High Court — Irish Times 17th November 1992. See Companies Act 1963 ss.72-77 as amended; RSC 0.75 r.17. See CAPITAL RECONSTRUCTION.

**redundancy.** Includes dismissal of an employee where the dismissal is due to the complete or partial closing down of his place of employment or due to a decrease in his employer's requirements for employees of his kind and qualifications: Redundancy Payments Act 1967 s.7(2) as amended by the Redundancy Payments Act 1971. An employee who is dismissed by his employer is presumed to have been dismissed by reason of redundancy, unless the contrary is proved (ibid 1971 Act s.10(b)).

Redundancy is a substantial ground justifying dismissal; however selection for dismissal in contravention of an agreed or established procedure is an unfair dismissal: Unfair Dismissals Act 1977 s.6. In the absence of such procedure, there is no provision in s.6 to enable the Employment Appeals Tribunal to consider the fairness of the procedure used: Roche v Sealink Stena Line Ltd (1993 EAT) ELR 89. An employer has an obligation to look at alternatives to redundancy and to consider all employees as candidates for redundancy: Mulcahy v Kelly & Barry,

Architects (1993 EAT) ELR 35.

Reorganisation of a company by replacement of an employee by an outside contract worker comes within the definition of a redundancy situation: McCafferty v Nostex Properties Ltd (1990 EAT) ELR 87. There is no general right to a hearing prior to dismissal involving redundancy even for an officer: Hickey v Eastern Health Board (1991 SC) 9ILT Dig 24. In a particular case, an employer was estopped from using alleged misconduct as a reason for selection for redundancy, since the employment of the employee continued after the alleged misconduct: Fox v Des Kelly Carpets Ltd (1992 EAT) ELR 182.

An employee is entitled to a redundancy lump-sum payment provided he has had 104 weeks continuous employment with the dismissing employer (ibid 1967 Act s.7(5) as amended by the 1971 Act). The lump-sum is related to the employee's age, length of service and his normal earnings. There are safeguards where there are changes in the ownership of the company or business (ibid 1967 Act s.20). Acceptance and retention by an employee of a redundancy payment, where a business is transferred to another owner, breaks that employee's continuity of service: Minimum Notice and Terms of Employment Act 1973, first schedule, para 7, as amended by Unfair Dismissals (Amdt) Act 1993 s.15.

Redundancy now applies to regular part-time workers: Worker Protection (Regular Part-time Employees) Act 1991 s.1.

The first £6,000 of non-statutory redundancy payment is exempt from tax; this may be increased by up to £4,000 in certain circumstances; as an alternative the taxpayer may claim an amount known as SCSB — *standard capital superannuation benefit*: Finance Act 1993 s.8. See also Kelly v Tokus Grass Products 196/1981; McSorely v Mogul of Ireland Ltd 992/1982; Irish Shipping v Adams (1987) HC. [Text: Forde (8)]. See ACQUIRED RIGHTS; ALTERNATIVE EMPLOYMENT; INSOL-VENCY OF EMPLOYER; REDUNDANCY, COLLEC-TIVE; TIME OFF; UNFAIR DISMISSAL.

**redundancy, collective.** Occurs where in the same establishment a number of employees are dismissed for redundancy in a period of 30 days. The number varies with the size of the workforce. Where an employer proposes to create *collective redundancies,* he has a statutory obligation to notify the Minister before the first dismissal takes effect and to enter into consultation with employees' representatives with a view to reaching an agreement: Protection of Employment Act 1977.

**redundancy and employers' insolvency fund.** See REDUNDANCY; INSOL-VENCY OF EMPLOYER.

**re-engagement.** The redress which may be available to a successful applicant in a claim alleging unfair dismissal from employment. The *re-engagement* can be to his former position or to another reasonably suitable position (Holden v Bank of Ireland (1993 CC) — Irish Times 6/7/1993) and it may be awarded from the date of dismissal (Harrison v Gateau Ltd UD 158/1981) or can be subject to a prior period of suspension (Healy v O'Neill UD 82/1982). See Unfair Dismissals Act 1977 s.7(1)(b). See also The State (IPU) v EAT (1987) ILRM 36. Contrast with RE-INSTATEMENT. See also EMPLOYMENT APPEALS TRIBUNAL.

**re-entry, proviso for.** See LEASE, DETER-MINATION OF.

**re-examination.** See EXAMINATION.

**refer to drawer.** The words written on a cheque by a banker which indicate that the cheque is being dishonoured for want of funds. It has been held that the return of cheques by a bank marked *refer to drawer — present again* and *return to drawer* are reasonably capable of a defamatory meaning: Pyke v Hibernian Bank (1950) IR 105. See also Grealy v Bank of Nova Scotia (1975) HC. See DEFAMATION.

**referee.** (1) A person to whom a question is referred for an opinion; an arbitrator. (2) A person who provides a character reference for another. See ARBITRATION; REFERENCE.

**reference.** (1) The submission of a matter to an arbitrator for his decision. (2) The submission of a Bill by the President of Ireland to the Supreme Court for a decision as to its constitutionality. (3) As regards employment, a statement made concerning an employee usually made by his employer or former employer. It has been held that no action lies against an employer for refusing to furnish a certificate of character in respect of an employee leaving the employment: Lint v Johnston (1894) 28 ILTR 16. An employer who gives a reference which he knows to be untrue to a prospective employer, may be liable in deceit (qv) or in negligence for a mis-statement (qv) or in defamation (qv). See ARBITRATION; PRESIDENT OF IRELAND.

**referendum.** The submission to the decision of the people of the State (a) of an amendment of the Constitution or (b) of a Bill which is the subject of a petition to the President of Ireland: 1937 Constitution arts.27 and 47. A statement in relation to the proposal which is the subject of the referendum may be prescribed for the information of voters by resolution of each House of the Oireachtas: Referendum (Amendment) Act 1992 s.2. Every citizen who has the right to vote at an election for members of Dail Eireann has the right to vote at a referendum: ibid Constitution art.47(3).

Applications to the courts failed to stop the referendum on the Maastricht Treaty 1992 eg Slattery & Ors v An Taoiseach (1993 SC) 11 ILT Dig 67; Price v An Taoiseach (1992 SC); McKenna v An Taoiseach (1993 HC) 11 ILT Dig 67. A petition questioning a referendum cannot be presented to the High Court now unless the court grants leave to the person to do so: Referendum Act 1942 s.34A inserted by Electoral Act 1992 s.168.

Three referenda were held on the one day in 1992; in order to avoid confusion, provision was made for different coloured ballot papers: Referendum (Amendment) (No 2) Act 1992. See CONSTITUTION; PETITION; PROPORTIONAL REPRESENTATION; TRANSFERABLE VOTE.

**reformatory schools.** Institutions for young offenders which have as their objective the teaching of a trade and the imparting of the principles of good citizenship. See Jenkins v Delap (1989) 7ILT Dig 259.

There are three forms of school provided for by law: (a) *industrial schools* for persons up to 12 years of age and in certain circumstances up to 15 years of age; (b) *reformatory schools* for persons between 12 and 17 years of age; and (c) *St Patrick's Institution* (formerly known as borstal institutions) for persons be-

tween 16 and 19 years of age.

The District Court is not prohibited by statute from imposing consecutive periods of detention in St Patrick's Institution exceeding twelve months: The State (Clinch) v D J Connellan (1986) ILRM 455. See Childrens Act 1908 ss.57-58; Childrens Act 1941 ss.9-10, 12; Childrens (Amendment) Act 1949 s.4; Criminal Justice Act 1914 s.11(1); Criminal Justice Act 1960 ss.12-13; Child Care Act 1991 s.79. [Text: Barnes; Osborough]. See CHILDRENS RESIDENTIAL CENTRE; YOUNG PERSON.

**refresher fee.** A fee payable to counsel in addition to that originally marked on the brief (qv).

**refreshing memory.** A witness in court may refresh his memory while under examination about an event, by referring to a writing made by himself at the time of the event or so soon after that the judge considers it likely that the event was fixed in his memory. A witness may also refresh his memory from a writing made by another person, if when the witness read it, he knew it to be correct. The writing does not itself become evidence although it must be handed to the opposite party who may cross-examine on it. An expert may refresh his memory by reference to professional treatises. See Jones v Stroud (1825) 2 C P 196; Talbot de Malahide (lord) v Cusack (1864) 17 ICLR 213; Northern Bank Company v Carpenter (1931) IR 268.

**refuge.** Land which is designated by the Minister by order that it be a refuge for fauna, where the Minister considers that a particular species of fauna should be specially protected: Wildlife Act 1976 s.17. For example, see Refuge for Fauna (Cliffs of Moher) Designation Order 1988 (SI No 98 of 1988). See NATURE RESERVE.

**refugee.** A person, who owing to well-founded fear of being persecuted for reasons of race, religion, nationality, membership of a particular social group or political opinion, is outside the country of his nationality and is unable, or owing to such fear, is unwilling to avail himself of the protection of that country; or who, not having a nationality and being outside the country of his former habitual residence is unable or, owing to such fear, is unwilling to return to it: United

Nations Convention relating to the Status of Refugees of 28 July 1951, art.1, as amended by the Protocol of 31 January 1967 art.1. While not incorporated into domestic law, the Minister has undertaken to apply the principles of the convention in deciding applications for refugee status and the Minister is bound by that undertaking: Gustrani v Governor of Mountjoy Prison (1993 SC) 11 ILT Dig 88. See Ji Yoa Lau v Minister for Justice (1993 HC) ILRM 64; Fakih v Minister for Justice (1993 HC) ILRM 274. See Irish Nationality and Citizenship Act 1986 s.5. See ASYLUM; NATURALISATION; STATELESS PERSON.

**refuse disposal.** See HOUSEHOLD REFUSE; NATIONAL MONUMENT; TRADE REFUSE; WASTE OPERATION.

**regional authority.** See LOCAL AUTHORITY.

**regional road.** A public road or a proposed public road which is classified as a regional road: Roads Act 1993 s.2(1) and 10. See PUBLIC ROAD; WAY, RIGHT OF.

**register.** Formal written record.

**register of electors.** The register of persons which is required to be published in each year of persons who were entitled to be registered as electors on the *qualifying date* (ie the 1st day of September in the year in which the register comes into force): Electoral Act 1992 ss.13 and 20, and second schedule r.1. Persons may be entitled to be registered as presidential electors, Dail electors, European electors and/or local government electors (qqv). The register must be prepared by reference to registration areas and a person must not be registered more than once or in more than one such area (ibid ss.11(1) and 13(1)). A *special voters list* must also be prepared without removing the names of these voters from the register (ibid s.17). Also certain electors are entitled to have their names entered in a *postal voters* list (ibid s.14).

**register of members.** Every company must keep a register of its members, which must not be kept outside the State: Companies Act 1963 s.116. It must be open to the inspection of any member (ibid s.119). Often the real ownership of shares is disguised by having them registered in the names of *nominees*. A company may by its articles of association require that information

be furnished to it as to the beneficial ownership of its shares.

The beneficial ownership of a notifiable percentage (5%) of shares in a public limited company must be declared; and in the case of a private company, a person with a financial interest in the company may obtain a *disclosure order* from the court in relation to share ownership: Companies Act 1990 ss.67-88 and 97-104.

A building society is required to keep a register of its members; unlike a company however, there is no requirement to make the register available to be consulted by other members or by the public: Building Societies Act 1989 s.65. See DISCLOSURE ORDER; SHARES, DISCLOSURE OF.

**register of patents.** The register kept at the Patents Office in Dublin in which is entered particulars of published patent applications, of patents in force, of assignments and transmission of patents and of licences: Patents Act 1992 s.84. It is open to inspection by the public and certified copies, sealed with the seal of the Controller of Patents, must be given to any person requiring them, on payment of the prescribed fee. Notice of a trust must not be entered in the register but an equitable interest can be recorded: ibid s.84(5); Kakkar v Szelke (1989) FSR 225. See PATENT.

**register of trade marks.** The register which is required to be kept under the control and management of the Controller of Trade Marks, open to inspection by the public, in which is entered all registered trade marks (qv) with the names, addresses and descriptions of their proprietors, notification of assignments and transmissions, and of all registered users, disclaimers, conditions, limitations, and such other matters as may be prescribed: Trade Marks Act 1963 s.9. It is divided into two parts, Part A (qv) and Part B (qv). There are provisions governing the rectification of any entry made in the register (ibid ss.40-44).

The Controller is required to state in writing the reasons for his decision to refuse an application for the removal of a mark from the register: Anheuser Busch v Controller of Trade Marks (1988 HC) ILRM 247. See TRADE MARK,

REGISTERED.

**registered agreement.** See EMPLOYMENT AGREEMENT.

**registered charge.** See CHARGE, REGISTERED.

**registered company.** See COMPANY, REGISTERED.

**registered design.** See DESIGN.

**registered land.** See LAND REGISTRATION.

**registered office.** A company must have a registered office in the State to which all communications and notices may be addressed; notice of any change in its situation must be given to the Registrar of Companies within 14 days of the change: Companies (Amendment) Act 1982 s.4. The company's name must be displayed outside its registered office conspicuously and legibly: Companies Act 1963 s.114(a). The registered office of a building society is known as its Chief Office: Building Societies Act 1989 s.15. See FOREIGN COMPANY; SEAT OF CORPORATION.

**registered trade mark.** See TRADE MARK, REGISTERED.

**registered trade union.** See TRADE UNION, REGISTERED.

**registered user.** As regards a trade mark, the person other than the proprietor of a trade mark who is registered as the user thereof: Trade Marks Act 1963 s.36(1). There must however subsist a *prescribed relationship* between the proprietor and the proposed registered user.

**registrar.** An official responsible for compiling and keeping records. In many cases, he is also empowered with important decision making functions eg Registrar of Companies, Registrar of Friendly Societies.

**registrar of companies.** The officer, appointed by the Minister, with responsibility for administering the registry of companies, which is located at Dublin Castle: Companies Act 1963 s.368. The Registrar must be satisfied that all statutory prerequisites have been met before he issues the certificate of incorporation (ibid s.17-18 and 20; Companies Amendment Act 1983 Part II). The Registrar may refuse to register a company where the objects are unlawful: R v Registrar of Companies (1931) 2 KB 197.

Every registered company must deliver an annual return to the Registrar each year and he can strike off the register, companies which are no longer carrying on business or who fail to make returns (1963 Act ss.125-129 as amended by 1990 Act s.244; Companies Amendment Act 1982 ss.11-12 as amended by 1990 Act s.245). He has authority to institute prosecutions in respect of numerous provisions of the Companies Acts eg concerning annual accounts and returns, and liquidations and receiverships (1982 Act s.16).

The Registrar is required to keep a register of persons subject to *disqualification orders* (1990 Act s.168), a register of *restricted persons* (ibid s.153) and a register of auditors (ibid s.198). The Registrar is also required to register a building society as a public limited company following a *conversion* procedure completed by the society: Building Societies Act 1989 s.106(1)-(2).

Any person is entitled to inspect the documents kept at the registry and to have certified copies made of them (1963 Act s.370). See COMPANY; STRIKE OFF.

**registrar of friendly societies.** The officer with powers and functions mainly relating to the registration, regulation and supervision of friendly societies, credit unions, trade unions, and industrial and provident societies (qqv). See Friendly Societies Act 1896, Registrar of Friendly Societies (Adaptation) Order 1926; Registry of Friendly Societies Act 1936; Friendly Societies (Amendment) Act 1977.

The Registrar is obliged to consider whether the rules proposed for registration of an industrial and provident society conflict with Industrial and Provident Societies Act 1893; even when they do so conflict, the registrar does not commit an actionable wrong in registering them: Kerry Co-operative Creameries Ltd v An Bord Bainne (1990 HC) ILRM 664. See also McMahon v Ireland (1988) ILRM 610. See CREDIT UNION; FRIENDLY SOCIETY; INDUSTRIAL & PROVIDENT SOCIETY; PERPETUAL FUND; SCIENTIFIC SOCIETIES.

**registration of births.** See BIRTH, REGISTRATION OF.

**registration of business names.** See BUSINESS NAME.

**registration of charge.** See CHARGE, REGISTRATION OF.

**registration of deeds.** See DEEDS, REGISTRATION OF.

**registration of electors.** See REGISTER OF ELECTORS.

**registration of judgment.** See JUDGMENT.

**registration of land.** See LAND REGISTRATION.

**registration of title.** See LAND REGISTRATION.

**registry of deeds.** See DEEDS, REGISTRATION OF.

**regularity, presumption of.** See PRESUMPTION OF REGULARITY.

**regulation.** A formal order made by a designated Minister exercising his power to make sub-ordinate legislation, usually in the form of a statutory instrument (qv). Ministers have been given a general power to implement EC law by regulation, including provisions repealing, amending or applying, with or without modification, other law: European Communities Act 1972 s.3.

However, s.3(2) of the 1972 Act has been found to be unconstitutional as it allowed a Minister to amend the substantive law of Ireland by regulation, without there being a proven necessity under EC law for it, whereas the Constitution provides that the sole and exclusive power of making laws for the State is vested in the Oireachtas: 1937 Constitution arts.15(2) and 29(4)(5); Meagher v Minister for Agriculture (1993 HC) ITLR (5 Jul) — under appeal. To remove any doubt regarding existing regulations, and to ensure that the State could comply with its obligations to EFTA contracting states under the European Economic Area Agreement, these regulations have been confirmed with retrospective effect: European Communities (Amendment) Act 1993 s.5. See EEA AGREEMENT; IRRATIONALITY, TEST OF; STATUTORY INSTRUMENT.

**regulation of EC.** Legislation of the European Community which has a general application and is binding in its entirety and *directly applicable* in all member States. See Lawlor v Minister for Agriculture (1987) HC. See DIRECT APPLICABILITY; COMMUNITY LAW.

**rehabilitation.** Health boards are required to make available a service for the training of disabled persons (whether mentally or physically handicapped) for employment and for making arrangements with employers for placing disabled persons in suitable employment: Health Act 1970 s.68. The National Rehabilitation Board, established under the Health (Corporate Bodies) Act 1961, advises the Minister on rehabilitation services, co-ordinates the work of other bodies engaged in rehabilitation and provides direct services itself eg vocational assessment. See DISABLED DRIVER.

**re-hearing.** A re-arguing of a case which has already been adjudicated upon eg an appeal from conviction in the District Court results in a complete re-hearing in the Circuit Court. Also an appeal lies to the High Court from an order of the Circuit Court in a civil action by way of re-hearing: Courts of Justice Act 1936 s.38. While appeals to the Supreme Court are by way of re-hearing, this is interpreted as involving a re-hearing of the legal issues arising in the court of trial and not a re-hearing of the oral evidence: RSC O.58 and Hay v O'Grady (1993 SC) 11 ILT Dig 27. See DE NOVO; FRESH EVIDENCE.

**re-instatement.** (1) The redress which may be available to a successful applicant in a claim alleging unfair dismissal from employment. The re-instated employee is treated in all respects as if he had not been dismissed and he returns to his former position on the terms and conditions on which he was employed immediately before the dismissal: Unfair Dismissals Act 1977 s.7(1)(a). Re-instatement entitles the employee to benefit from any improvement in terms and conditions which may have occurred between the dates of dismissal and reinstatement (ibid s.1 as amended by Unfair Dismissals (Amdt) Act 1993 s.2(b)). See Groves v Aer Lingus Teo UD 265/79; Lundy v Airmotive Ireland Ltd (1992 CC) ELR 211. Contrast with RE-ENGAGEMENT. See also EMPLOYMENT APPEALS TRIBUNAL.

(2) Replacement or repair of damaged property under an insurance policy; many such policies have a *re-instatement clause* therein giving to the insurer the right to re-instate the property, at the option of the insurer, rather than paying an amount in respect of damage to the property. If the insurer chooses this option, he has a duty to replace it

substantially to the same condition prior to the damage and may be liable in negligence if he fails to do so properly. See St. Alban's Investments Co v Sun Alliance & London Insurance Co Ltd (1984) ILRM 501.

**reinstatement notice.** See HABITABLE HOUSE.

**re-insurance.** The act of an insurer in relieving himself of part or of the whole of the liability he has undertaken, by insuring the subject matter himself with other insurers. Re-insurance was formerly illegal. Re-insurance can take the form of *facultative re-insurance* ie re-insurance against liability on a stated policy, or *treaty re-insurance* ie re-insurance against liabilities on policies in general.

Direct insurers authorised in the State are not permitted to accept re-insurance business in classes of insurance for which they do not hold a direct authorisation: Insurance Act 1989 s.22. Where an insurance company agrees to re-insure a secured risk which turns out to be unsecured, then the re-insurer is not bound to indemnify the insurer for any loss incurred on such risk: International Commercial Bank plc v Insurance Corp of Ireland (1990 HC) ITLR (3 Dec) and (1992 SC) ITLR (9 Nov). See Winterthur Swiss Insurance v Insurance Corporation of Ireland (1989) ILRM 13. See also Marine Insurance Act 1906 s.9.

**rejected goods.** Unless otherwise agreed, where goods are delivered to a buyer and he refuses to accept them having the right so to do, he is not bound to return them to the seller, but it is sufficient if he intimates to the seller that he refuses to accept them: Sale of Goods Act 1893 s.36.

**rejection of offer.** An offer is rejected if the rejection is communicated to the offeror, or if the offer is accepted subject to conditions, or if the offeree makes a counter offer. See Hyde v Wrench (1840) 3 Beav 334. See OFFER.

**related company.** A company related to another company. There are a number of definitions of what constitutes a *related* company for the purposes of the Companies Acts eg where the other company is its holding company or subsidiary: Companies Act 1990 s.140. There are provisions whereby (a) the assets of related companies can be ordered to be pooled in the case of the winding up of both or (b) one can be required to contribute to the debts of the other where only one is being wound up (ibid ss.140-141).

**relation back.** The doctrine whereby an act is referred back to an earlier date and made effective from that date eg a person who enters land with lawful authority but who, by a wrongful act, becomes a trespasser *ab initio,* his wrongful act relates back to his initial entry. Probate when granted relates back to the testator's death. An adjudication of bankruptcy is no longer related back to the act of bankruptcy; the vesting of the bankrupt's property in the Official Assignee (qv), does not now, subject to some exceptions, commence at an earlier date than the date of adjudication: Bankruptcy Act 1988 s.44(2). See BANKRUPTCY, ADJUDICATION OF.

**relations.** Next-of-kin (qv).

**relations, prohibited degrees of.** See PROHIBITED DEGREES; MARRIAGE.

**relatives.** Relations (qv). The term includes those connected to a person by marriage. As regards adoption, relatives mean a grandparent, brother, sister, uncle or aunt, whether of the whole blood, of the half-blood or by affinity: Adoption Act 1952 s.3. See ADOPTION, APPLICATION FOR.

**relator.** A person at whose suggestion or information an action is instituted by the Attorney General (qv) in a matter of public interest eg in the case of an act which is unlawful having regard to the Constitution. See RSC O.15 r.20. It has been held in England that if the Attorney General does not consent to relator proceedings, his decision is final and is not subject to review: Gouriet v Union of Post Office Workers (1977) 3 WLR 300. See also Attorney General at the Relation of the Society for the Protection of Unborn Children (Ireland) Ltd v Open Door Counselling Ltd and Dublin Wellwoman Centre Ltd (1989 SC) ILRM 19. [Text: Collins & O'Reilly].

**release.** The renunciation, discharge or giving up of rights or claims against another. A release of an obligation under a contract may be obtained by a deed, whether or not the release is based on consideration. As regards the administration of estates, the executors normally require a release from those beneficially entitled before handing over the property eg in the form of a covenant not to sue.

A mortgagee is not entitled to refuse to release his security in the sale by a liquidator of mortgaged land, merely because the liquidator is disputing his claim and the matter is awaiting adjudication: McCairns (PMPA) (In Liquidation) (1989 HC) ILRM 501. See ACCORD AND SATISFACTION.

**release, temporary.** The Minister is empowered to make rules for the temporary release of persons serving penal servitude, imprisonment, or in detention centres: Criminal Justice Act 1960 s.2; Prisons Act 1970 ss.2 and 4. The temporary release of a person in custody is a privilege or concession to which the person has no right: Ryan v Governor of Limerick Prison (1989) 7 ILT Dig 84. However, a prisoner who has been granted regular periods of temporary release is entitled to be given an explanation if his temporary release is not renewed: Sherlock v Governor of Mountjoy Prison (1991 HC) 1 IR 451. For restrictions on powers to grant temporary release in cases of treason and aggravated murder, see Criminal Justice Act 1990 s.5.

**relevancy test.** The test which must be complied with in order to support an application for the discovery of documents (qv); discovery may be ordered of any documents which might reasonably be supposed to contain information which would advance the case of one party or damage that of the other: Sterling Winthrop v Farbenfabriken Bayer AG (1967) IR 97 as cited in Dunne v National Maternity Hospital (1989 SC) ITLR (27 Nov). See RETRIAL.

**relevant.** A fact which is so connected directly or indirectly with a *fact in issue* in a case that it tends to prove or disprove the fact in issue. Only *relevant* evidence is admissible in any proceedings. See ADMISSIBILITY OF EVIDENCE; FACT IN ISSUE.

**relief.** The remedy which a plaintiff seeks or obtains in an action.

**relief of poverty.** See CHARITIES; POVERTY.

**religion, advancement of.** A trust which has as its object the advancement of religion may meet the legal requirements

of a charity. See CHARITIES; RELIGIOUS FREEDOM.

**religious employer.** The nature of the relationship between a religious superior and a subordinate is unlikely to be that of an employer/employee. See Reverend Fr Buckley v Bishop Cathal Daly 112/85 UD (Northern Ireland). See Barry in 10 ILT & SJ (1992) 222. See INCARDINATION; VOW.

**religious freedom.** Freedom of conscience and the free profession and practice of religion are, subject to public order and morality, guaranteed to every citizen: 1937 Constitution, art.44(2)(1). The State is required to respect and honour religion and further guarantees not to endow any religion or to impose any disability or make any discrimination on the ground of religious profession, belief or status (ibid arts.44(1), 44(2)(2) and 44(2)(3)). The recognition by the State of the special position of the Roman Catholic Church and the recognition of other specified churches in arts.44(1)(2) and 44(1)(3) was deleted by referendum (qv) of the people in 1972: Fifth Amendment to the Constitution.

Parents have a constitutional right to decide the religion of their children and the State cannot interfere with this right; in the case of disagreement between parents, the courts will endeavour to supply the place of the parents: In re Tilson infants (1951) IR 1; Guardianship of Infants Act 1964.

See also Quinn's Supermarket Ltd v Attorney General (1972) IR 1; McGee v Attorney General (1974) IR 284; Mulloy v Minister for Education (1975) IR 88. See ADOPTION, CONSENT TO; FOSTER-PARENTS; HATRED, INCITEMENT TO; WORSHIP, PUBLIC; VOW.

**remainder.** A grant to take effect in possession on the natural determination of a *particular* (qv) estate of freehold created by the same instrument eg *to A for life, remainder to B for life, remainder to C in tail*; B and C take remainders and the grantor retains the reversion (qv) in fee simple. See CONTINGENT REMAINDER.

**remand.** The sending back of a person charged with a crime, pending the hearing of the charge at a future date. The court is empowered to remand an accused from time to time as the occasion requires: Criminal Procedure Act 1967 ss.21-33. Where the District Court remands a person or sends him forward for trial or sentence, the court may either (a) commit him to prison or other lawful custody or (b) release him conditionally on his entering into a recognisance (qv) with or without security (ibid s.22). See Maguire v O'Hanrahan (1988) ILRM 243. See BAIL.

**remanent pro defectu emptorum.** [They are left in my hands for want of buyers].

**remarriage.** See FATAL INJURIES.

**remedial statute.** Legislation which is intended to remedy a defect in existing law.

**remedy.** The means provided by the law whereby the violation of a right is prevented, redressed or compensated. A remedy may be provided by: (a) a judicial or quasi-judicial process eg by court action or arbitration; (b) by agreement between the parties eg accord and satisfaction; or (c) by the act of the injured party eg abatement or distress (qv). See ACCORD AND SATISFACTION.

**remise.** To release or surrender.

**remission.** The pardoning of an offence or the cancelling in whole or in part of an obligation. A prisoner may obtain a remission of up to one quarter of the total sentence on account of good behaviour during imprisonment; the remission may be lost in whole or in part. See Rules for the Government of Prisons 1947 r.38(1) (S R & O No.320 of 1947). In relation to restrictions on the power to remit punishment for treason and aggravated murder, see Criminal Justice Act 1990 s.5. See PARDON.

**remittal of action.** Transfer of an action from one level of court to another. Any action which is pending in the High or Circuit Court may be remitted or transferred to a lower court, on application to the court in which it is pending by any party to the action before commencement of the trial, if the court so orders: Courts Act 1991 s.15; Courts of Justice Act 1924 s.25. Where an action claiming *unliquidated* damages is remitted from the High Court to the Circuit Court, the latter court has jurisdiction to award damages without limit: Courts of Justice Act 1936 s.20 as amended by

the Courts Act 1991 s.2(3)(a). Where remitted to the District Court, that court is limited to awarding between £5,000 and £10,000 in an action for unliquidated damages (ibid 1991 Act s.15(2)). See RSC O.49 r.7; RCC O.32.

**remoteness.** A disposition of a future interest in property is void for *remoteness* where it is not to take effect within the period allowed by the rule against perpetuities (qv), or where it offends against the rules against inalienability (qv) or accumulations (qv) or the rule in Whitby v Mitchell. This latter rule states that if an interest in realty is given to an unborn person, any remainder (qv) to that unborn person's issue is void together with all subsequent limitations.

**remoteness of damage.** (1) In contract (qv), the general rule is that damages for breach of contract will apply only to the loss flowing naturally from the breach, such that a reasonable man could foresee, or such as may reasonably be supposed to have been in the contemplation of the parties, at the time they made the contract, as the probable result of the breach of it; otherwise, the loss will be too remote: Hadley v Baxendale (1854) 9 Exch 341; French v West Clare Railway Co (1897) 31 ILT & SJ 140; Victoria Laundry v Newman Industries (1949) 2 KB 528; Stock v Urey (1955) NI 71; Wagon Mound Case (1961) AC 388; McGrath v Kiely (1965) IR 497; Lee Donoghue v Rowan (1981) HC.

(2) In tort (qv), a defendant is liable only for the damage of such a kind as a reasonable man would have foreseen: Burke v John Paul Ltd (1967) IR 277. See DAMAGES; ECONOMIC LOSS; NOVUS ACTUS INTERVENIENS.

**remuneration.** See EQUAL PAY; WAGE.

**remuneration of directors.** A director of a company is not entitled to remuneration for acting as a director except by express agreement; the articles of association (qv) usually provide for such remuneration to be determined by the company in general meeting. Remuneration of directors and loans to them must be disclosed in the company's accounts: Companies Act 1963 ss.191; Companies Act 1986, schedule, para 49(a). See GOLDEN UMBRELLA; LOAN TO DIRECTOR.

**remuneration of trustees.** Generally, a

trustee is not entitled to remuneration for his work as a trustee no matter how onerous it may be: In re Ormsby (1809) 1 Ball & B 189. This is based on the principle that a trustee should not obtain a material benefit from his position. There are exceptions eg where remuneration is provided for expressly in the trust instrument; or where so ordered by the court; or where the trustee's work has generated a profit for the beneficiary which the trustee is not allowed to retain. See Boardman v Phipps (1967) 2 AC 46. See TRUSTEE, DUTY OF.

**render.** To yield or to pay.

**rendition.** The backing of warrants; the term *extradition* is often used to embrace the term *rendition*. It is similar to extradition except that the handing over of fugitives is not based on a formal agreement between States but on the enactment by these States of virtually identical legislation which provides for the handing over of fugitives to each other State eg Extradition Act 1965, Part III in this State and the Backing of Warrants (Ireland) Act 1965 in the UK. [Text: Forde (3)]. See EXTRADITION; JUDICIAL AUTHORITY.

**renewable fine.** See LEASE FOR LIVES RENEWABLE FOR EVER.

**renewal of insurance.** See PREMIUM.

**renewal of summons.** See SUMMONS, RENEWAL OF.

**renouncing probate.** See RENUNCIATION.

**rent.** A periodic payment payable by a tenant to the landlord for the possession and use of land. It includes any *sum or return* and consequently may include money or services and goods: Deasy's Act 1860 s.1. A *peppercorn* rent is a nominal rent which serves as an acknowledgement of the tenancy. A landlord may bring an action for *ejectment* for non-payment of rent. See McQuaid v Lynam (1965) IR 564. See THIRD PARTY INFORMATION.

**rent book.** The Minister is empowered to make regulations requiring the landlord of a rented house to provide the tenant with a rent book or other document that would serve the same purpose: Housing (Miscellaneous Provisions) Act 1992 s.17. House includes any building or part of a building used as a dwelling eg house, flat, or maisonette (ibid s.1(1)). There is provision for

inspection by a person authorised by the housing authority (ibid s.17(3)). Under regulations made in 1993, the rent book must contain, inter alia, the address of the rented dwelling, name and address of landlord or agent, tenant's name, term of tenancy, amount of rent and when and how to be paid, particulars of any payments other than rent, amount of deposit and conditions for refund, and statement of tenant's basic statutory rights: Housing (Rent Books) Regulations 1993 (SI No 146 of 1993). Tenants of controlled dwellings (qv) are already entitled to rent books.

**rent control.** The control of rents in respect of *controlled dwellings*: Housing (Private Rented Dwellings) Act 1982. The terms of the tenancy of a controlled dwelling are fixed by a Rent Tribunal: Housing (Private Rented Dwellings) (Amendment) Act 1983. See de Blacam in 7ILT & SJ (1989) 62 and 209. See CONTROLLED DWELLING.

**rent review clause.** A clause in a lease which provides for a periodic review of the rent payable under the lease, provided the property is not subject to some statutory rent control. The clause may provide for a pre-determined increase, or an increase based on an escalator clause, or it may be subject to agreement or arbitration. For review of rents payable under sporting leases and reversionary leases (qv), see Landlord and Tenant (Amendment) Act 1984 ss.3 and 5. See also Landlord and Tenant (Amendment) Act 1980 s.24. See Hynes v O'Malley Property Ltd (1989) ILT Dig 204; Erin Executor and Trustee Co v Farmer (1987) HC. See DISREGARD CLAUSE; TENANT STATUTORY.

**rent seck.** [Dry rent] A rent payable in respect of land to a person who has no reversion in it (eg a fee farm grant) and with no power of distress. Distress and other remedies however are provided by Deasy's Act 1860 and the Conveyancing Act 1881 s.44. See FEE FARM GRANT.

**rent tribunal.** See RENT CONTROL.

**rentcharges.** Charges relating to land which do not arise from the relationship of landlord and tenant eg tithe rentcharges (qv); perpetual rentcharges sometimes created by a fee farm grant (qv); payment of advances under the Landed Property Improvement (Ireland) Act

1847; and an annuity charged on land: Revenue Commissioners v Malone (1951) IR 269. See also the definition of rentcharges in the Statute of Limitations 1957 s.2(1).

**rented house, registration of.** The Minister is empowered to make regulations requiring a landlord of a house let for rent or other valuable consideration to register the tenancy with the housing authority and to furnish such particulars as the regulations require: Housing (Miscellaneous Provisions) Act 1992 s.20. House includes any building or part of a building used as a dwelling eg house, flat, or maisonette (ibid s.1(1)). There is provision for a register to be kept by the housing authority, for inspection of the register by any person, and for inspection of the house by a person authorised by the housing authority.

**rented house, standard of.** The Minister is empowered to prescribe standards for houses let for rent or other valuable consideration and it is the duty of the landlord of such house to ensure that the house complies with the standards prescribed: Housing (Miscellaneous Provisions) Act 1992 s.18. House includes any building or part of a building used as a dwelling eg house, flat, or maisonette (ibid s.1(1)). The regulations may make provision for such matters as, classes of houses or tenancies, maintenance, quality and condition of accommodation, ventilation and lighting, facilities for heating, cooking and storage of food, water supplies, sanitary facilities and drainage (ibid s.18(7)). There is provision for inspection by a person authorised by the housing authority (ibid s.18(2)). Regulations were made in 1993 which come into force on 1st January 1994 in respect of private rented dwellings, and on 1st January 1998 in respect of dwellings let by housing authorities: Housing (Standards for Rented Houses) Regulations 1993 (SI No 147 of 1993). See UNFIT HOUSE.

**rented residential accommodation relief.** See SECTION 23 RELIEF.

**renunciation.** A disclaimer. A renunciation by a person appointed by a testator as his executor, giving up his right to extract probate, must be in writing; the person is known as a *renunciant*. A renunciation by a spouse to her legal right (qv) in an estate must be in writing: Succession Act 1965 s.113. See RSC O.79 r.38; O.80 r.43.

**renvoi.** [To send back]. The doctrine in private international law (qv) regarding the choice of law where the law of more than one country may be applicable. See In re Adams deceased (1967) IR 424; In re Interview Ltd (1975) IR 382; Kutchera v Buckingman International Holdings Ltd (1988) IR 61. See Contractual Obligations (Applicable Law) Act 1991, first schedule, art.15. [Text: Binchy]. See CONTRACT.

**re-open case.** See FRESH EVIDENCE.

**reorganisation of company.** See RECONSTRUCTION OF COMPANY; COURT PROTECTION OF COMPANY.

**repairs notice.** See UNFIT HOUSE.

**repatriation.** Resumption by a person of his former nationality; sending back a person to his own country. See ALIEN; NATIONALITY; REFUGEE.

**repeal.** The cancellation or annulment of a statute or part of a statute. It may be express eg *the enactments mentioned in the second schedule are hereby repealed to the extent specified in the third column*. It may be implied ie the necessary result of the subsequent enactment. The repeal of a repealing enactment does not revive the enactment originally repealed.

Where an Act repeals in whole or in part a previous statute, then, unless the contrary intention appears, such repeal does not prejudice any legal proceedings pending at the time of such repeal: Interpretation Act 1937 s.21. Where an Act repeals the whole or a portion of a previous statute and substitutes other provisions for the statute or portion repealed, the statute or portion so repealed shall, unless the contrary is expressly provided in the repealing Act, continue in force until the substituted provisions come into operation (ibid s.19(1)). The substitution of one section in an Act by another may have the effect of the repeal of the previous section and its replacement by the new section eg section 3 of the Larceny Act 1990 amends s.33 of the Larceny Act 1916 by substitution: People (DPP) v Gilligan (1992 CCA) ILRM 769.

It would appear that an enactment may be *de facto* repealed without any legislation having been adopted for the purposes of such repeal: Farm Tax Act 1985 and Purcell v AG (1989 HC) ITLR (18 Dec). What remains of such legislation is unenforceable both retrospectively and prospectively. See GENERALIA SPECIALIBUS NON DEROGANT; LEGISLATION, INTERPRETATION OF.

**repetitive legal work.** A solicitor's remuneration should reflect the amount of work performed by him; regard should be had for the repetitive nature of work where it involves the preparation of instructions in respect of second and subsequent motions involving identical factors: Ormond v Ireland (1988 HC) ILRM 490.

**replevin.** A means whereby a person from whom goods or chattels have been allegedly unlawfully taken can have them judicially restored to him pending an action for their return, upon giving security to prosecute the action and return the goods if so directed by the court. See RSC, appendix B, part II. [Text: Dixon & Gilliland]. See CONVERSION.

**replication.** Reply (qv).

**reply.** The answer of a plaintiff to a defence or counterclaim; in High Court proceedings a reply must be delivered within fourteen days from delivery of the defence; a reply is not necessary in any case where all the material statements of fact in the relevant pleading are merely to be denied and put in issue: RSC O.23. In the Circuit Court, no pleadings subsequent to defence, or defence and counterclaim, is allowed: RCC O.12 r.17.

**reply, right of.** The right of a party or his legal representatives to re-address the Court.

**report, law.** See LAW REPORT.

**representation.** (1) Taking the place of another eg an agent for his principal. (2) Being represented in a legislative body eg the Houses of the Oireachtas. (3) A statement or assertion of fact made by one party to another which induces a course of action eg entering into a contract. A representation may amount to a condition (qv) or a warranty (qv); it may create an estoppel (qv) or it may be an expression of opinion or mere *puffing* and thereby have no legal effect. See MISREPRESENTATION.

**representative.** A person who stands in

the place of another eg an agent for his principal; a personal representative for a testator. The dismissal of an employee may be unfair where the employee is not offered the opportunity to have a representative present at any meeting which led to his dismissal: McEvoy v Avery Dennison Ltd (1992 EAT) ELR 172. See LEGAL REPRESENTATION.

**representative action.** An action brought by a member of a class of persons on behalf of himself and the other members of the class. Where there are numerous persons having the same interest in one cause or matter, one or more such persons may sue or be sued, or may be authorised by the Court to defend, on behalf of or for the benefit, of all persons so interested: RSC O.15 r.9. See Moore and Others v Attorney General for Saorstat Eireann (No 2) [1930] IR 471.

**reprieve.** The formal suspension of the execution of a sentence. See PARDON.

**Republic of Ireland.** The description of the State: Republic of Ireland Act 1948. See STATE.

**republication of will.** The re-execution by a testator of a will or codicil previously revoked: Succession Act 1965 s.87. See WILL.

**repudiation.** Words or conduct indicating that a person does not intend to be or does not regard himself as being bound by an obligation eg repudiation of a contract. A company, under the protection of the court, may repudiate contracts made by it where proposals for a compromise or a scheme of arrangement are to be formulated: Companies (Amendment) Act 1990 s.20. See BREACH OF CONTRACT; COURT PROTECTION OF COMPANY; ONEROUS PROPERTY; REPUDIATORY BREACH; STRIKE.

**repudiatory breach.** The decision by a party to a contract not to perform his contractual obligations. The other party may treat the contract as terminated and sue for damages. See Athlone Rural District Council v A G Campbell Son (No 2) 1912 47 ILTR 142; Woodar Investments v Wimpey Construction (1980) 1 All ER 571; House of Spring Gardens Ltd v Point Blank (1985) FSR 327.

**repugnant.** Contrary to, or inconsistent with. The Oireachtas (qv) must not enact any law which is in any respect repugnant to the Constitution and any law which is so repugnant is invalid to the extent of the repugnancy: 1937 Constitution, art.15(4).

**reputation.** The estimation in which a person is generally held. Disparagement of a person's reputation may constitute the tort of defamation. See CHARACTER, EVIDENCE OF; DEFAMATION.

**reputed ownership, doctrine of.** The doctrine whereby a bankrupt trader was deemed to be the reputed owner, with the true owner's consent, of goods which at the time the trader became bankrupt were in his possession, order or disposition; under the doctrine these goods became available for distribution to his creditors. The doctrine has not been re-enacted in the consolidating Bankruptcy Act 1988 which repeals the Hire-Purchase Act 1946 s.17(1) and Agricultural Credit Act 1947 s.32(3).

**request, letter of.** See LETTER OF REQUEST.

**requisition.** A request to a judge in a criminal trial, when the jury has retired, to correct matters in the judge's summing up and charge to the jury. The judge may, if he thinks fit, recall the jury and direct them further.

**requisitions on title.** The questions in writing which are put by the purchaser to the vendor of real property, having received from the vendor the *abstract of title* (qv). The vendor is bound to answer all relevant questions put to him. Compliance with the questions usually requires the production of originals of documents, the furnishing of searches (qv) and statutory declarations (qv), the proving of performance of covenants (qv) and of compliance with planning permission (qv). See Hanafin v Gaynor (1991 HC) 9ILT Dig 76.

**res.** [Things].

**res accessoria sequitur rem principalem.** [Accessory things follow principal things].

**res extincta.** [Things extinct]. There can be no contract in relation to a matter which is non-existent. See Couturier v Hastie (1856) 5 HL Cas 673. See FRUSTRATION.

**res furtivae.** [Stolen goods].

**res gestae.** [Things done; the events which happened]. Facts which are parts of the same *transaction* as the fact in issue are admissible as forming parts of the res gestae. A transaction is any physical act, or series of connected acts, together with the accompanying words. See The People (Attorney General) v Crosbie & Meehan (1966) IR 490. See FACT IN ISSUE.

**res integra.** [A whole thing; an unopened thing]. Refers to where a point has to be decided on principle as there is no rule or decision of court governing it. See In re United Bars Ltd (1989) 7ILT Dig 259.

**res inter alios acta alteri nocere non debet.** [A transaction between others does not prejudice a person who was not a party to it]. An admission generally is admissible only against the party making it. See ADMISSION.

**res ipsa loquitur.** [The thing speaks for itself]. In negligence actions, the plaintiff must prove negligence (qv) on the part of the defendant; however under the maxim *res ipsa loquitur*, there is a presumption of negligence on the part of the defendant where (a) the cause of an accident is shown to have been under the control of the defendant or his servants at the time of the accident, and (b) the accident is such as in the ordinary course of events would not have happened, if those in control of the cause of the damage had used proper care: Maitland v Swan & Sligo Co Council (1992 SC) ITLR (6 Jul).

When the maxim is properly invoked, the onus will be on the defendant to show that he was not negligent.

In a *medical negligence* (qv) action where no evidence of the defendant's lack of care is adduced by the plaintiff then, before the principle of res ipsa loquitur becomes applicable, the onus is on the plaintiff to establish that the accident was such that, in the ordinary course of things, did not happen with the use of care: Duffy v North Eastern Health Board (1989) ITLR (13 Feb). Where a person goes in for a routine medical procedure, is subject to an anaesthetic without any special features, and there is a failure to return the patient to consciousness, res ipsa loquitur applies: Lindsay v Mid Western Health Board (1993 SC) ILRM 550.

Res ipsa loquitur does not have to be specifically pleaded before a plaintiff may rely on it, if the facts pleaded and proved show that the doctrine is applicable to the case: O'Reilly v Lavelle (1990) 2 IR 372; Mullen v Quinnsworth Ltd (1990 SC) ITLR (28 May). See also Scott v London & St Katherine Docks Co (1865) 3 H & C 596; Collen Bros v Scaffolding Ltd (1959) IR 245. See ANIMALS; BURDEN OF PROOF; SURGICAL OPERATION.

**res judicata pro veritate acciptur.** [A thing adjudicated is received as the truth]. Parties and their privies are estopped from denying not only the state of affairs established by a judgment but also the grounds upon which that judgment was based. Such estoppel may be (a) *cause of action estoppel* eg where one party brings an action against another and judgment is given on it, there is a strict rule of law that he cannot bring another action against the same party for the same cause or (b) *issue estoppel* eg where the degree or proportion of liability in a negligence action has already been fixed by a court in a separate action between the parties: Murphy v Hennessy (1985) ILRM 100.

The doctrine of res judicata applies to certificates issued by a local government auditor: The State (Dowling) v Leonard (1960) IR 381. See also Cassidy v O'Rourke (1983) ILRM 332; McCarthy Construction v Waterford County Council (1987) HC; Dublin Co Council v Taylor (1989) 7 ILT Dig 150. See ISSUE ESTOPPEL; FINALITY IN LITIGATION.

**res nova.** [A new thing]. A matter which has not yet been decided.

**res nullius.** [A thing belonging to no one]. See BONO VACANTIA.

**res perit domino.** [The loss falls on the owner].

**res sic stantibus.** [Things standing so or remaining the same].

**res sua.** [A person's own goods].

**res sua nemini servit.** [No one can have an easement over his own property]. See EASEMENT.

**resale price maintenance.** An agreement for the maintenance of minimum prices at which goods are to be resold. Such an agreement (eg between producers and retailers) is not invalid at common law, unless the person challenging the agreement is able to show that the price level maintained is unreasonable or is designed to produce a monopoly:

Cade v Daly (1910) 1 IR 306. Many prices are now controlled by the Prices Act 1958 and regulations thereunder. Also, such resale price maintenance agreements may amount to a distortion of competition and be prohibited and void: Competition Act 1991 s.4(1). See also COMPETITION, DISTORTION OF; RESTRICTIVE PRACTICES.

**rescission.** Abrogation or revocation, particularly of a contract. A contract may be rescinded where there has been some mistake, mutual or unilateral. Where *mutual,* the mistake must have been fundamental; where *unilateral* there must have been some element of unfairness or sharp practice involved to justify the equitable remedy: Cooper v Phibbs (1867) 2 HL 149; Solle v Butcher (1950) 1 KB 671.

The court will not grant an order rescinding a contract where the mistake by one of the parties is not shared or contributed to by the other party who is unaware that the contract does not give effect to the intention of that party: Ferguson v Merchant Banking Ltd (1993 HC) ILRM 136.

A contract to subscribe for shares may be rescinded if it is induced by a material allegation which was not true, even if there was no fraud in the matter: Components Tube Co v Naylor (1900) 2 IR 1. Rescission will not be ordered where *restitutio in integrum* (qv) is no longer possible or where it would disrupt third party rights: Northern Bank Finance Corp v Charlton (1979) IR 149. See MISTAKE; ORAL AGREEMENT, MODIFICATION OF CONTRACT BY.

**rescous.** Rescue of distrained goods which are being taken to the pound (qv).

**rescue of company.** See COURT PROTECTION OF COMPANY.

**rescuer.** A person who sustains injuries during rescue operations arising from the negligence of another, may have a good cause of action, provided that that other by his negligence brought about the peril situation which prompted the rescue. The principle of rescue is essentially a doctrine of foreseeability and it cannot come into operation without an initial negligence; where a person by his fault creates a situation of peril, he must answer for it to any person who attempts to rescue the person who was thereby placed in danger: *Phillips v Durgan* (1991 SC) ILRM 321. See also *Wagner v International Railroad Company* (1921) 133 NE 437; *Chadwick v British Transport Commission* (1963) 2 QB 650. See Delaney: *The Duty of Care to Rescuers* (1959) 25 Ir Jur 7. See also CRIMINAL INJURIES COMPENSATION TRIBUNAL.

**reservation.** A clause in a deed whereby the donor, lessor or grantor reserves to himself some new thing out of that which he has granted eg a rent in a lease, a wayleave (qv).

**reservation of title.** See RETENTION OF TITLE.

**reserve.** In a company's accounts, a *reserve* must not normally include amounts written off or retained in order to provide for an asset's depreciation, renewal or diminution in value or to provide for a known and unquantifiable liability: Companies Act 1963, sixth schedule, reg 27(1)(b). A *revenue reserve* is an amount regarded as free for distribution through the profit and loss account; a *capital reserve* must not include any amount so regarded (ibid reg 27(1)(c)). See CAPITAL.

**reserve price.** See AUCTION SALES.

**reserved functions.** The functions of a county council which are exercisable only by the elected members: County Management Act 1940 s.16 and second schedule and later enactments. It is the general function of members of a local authority to determine by resolution the policy of the authority: Local Government Act 1991 s.41. The Minister is empowered to declare by order that certain specified functions are reserved functions for the purposes of the 1940 Act (ibid s.41(2) and (3)). See Local Government Act 1991 (Reserved Functions) Order 1993 (SI No 37 of 1993). See also Environmental Protection Agency Act 1992 s.45(5). See COUNTY MANAGER.

**reserved judgment.** The formal decision of a court made following consideration by the judge or judges, at a date subsequent to the otherwise conclusion of the trial of an action. Contrast with EXTEMPORE JUDGMENT. See JUDGMENT.

**residence.** The place of a person's home; the place where he abides. Formerly, a person could be ordinarily resident in more than one electoral constituency: *Quinn v Mayor of City of Waterford* (1991 SC) ILRM 433; now, a person is deemed not to have given up ordinary residence if he intends to resume residence within 18 months after giving it up: Electoral Act 1992 s.11(3). There are provisions for determining the residence of members of the defence forces, prisoners, patients or inmates in hospitals or homes (ibid s.11(4)-(6)). Also certain persons are deemed to be resident in the State eg civil servant members of missions abroad (ibid s.12). See EC (Right of Residence for Non-Economically Active Persons) Regulations 1993 (SI No 109 of 1993). See Travers in 11 ILT & SJ (1993) 152 on right of residence of non-Community nationals. See ABODE; DOMICILE.

**residence, right of.** A right given to a person to live on property and, in some cases, to receive support in the form of food, fuel and other material benefits. The right is often created where land is conveyed *inter vivos* or devised to another subject to the right eg where a farmer devises the farm to his children with a right of residence reserved for his widow. The right is registrable as a burden on registered land and is a lien for money's worth: Registration of Title Act 1964 ss.69(1) and 81. Of less importance now due to legal right of spouses: Succession Act 1965 ss.111–115. See *National Bank v Keegan* (1931) IR 344; *Johnston v Horace* (1993 HC) reported by Coughlan in 11 ILT Dig (1993) 168.

**residential property tax.** The tax charged in respect of all *relevant residential property* owned by an assessable person where the *market value* exceeds an exemption limit and the income of the assessable person exceeds an income limit: Finance Act 1983 s.96. *Relevant residential property* is any residential property to which the assessable person is the owner and which is occupied by him as a dwelling or dwellings (ibid s.97). *Market value* is the price which the unencumbered fee simple (qv) of the property would fetch on the open market (ibid s.98).

There is inflation relief in respect of the income limit and exemption limit (ibid ss.100-101). There is also relief in respect of qualifying children residing with the taxpayer and simplification in respect of the inflation relief: Finance Act 1990 ss.121-125. See also Finance Acts 1991 s.112 and 1992 ss.218-221. An assessable person who does not lodge a return or fails to comply with a notice is liable to penalty (ibid 1983 Act s.112). See Madigan v Attorney General Ors (1986) ILRM 136.

With effect from 1st August 1993, any person selling a residential property valued in excess of the market value threshold must provide the purchaser with a certificate from the Revenue Commissioners indicating that all residential property tax has been paid: Finance Act 1993 s.107. If such certificate is not forthcoming, the purchaser is required to deduct an amount from the purchase price and remit it to the Commissioners. The amount is 1.5 per cent of the difference between the sale price and the market value exemption limit, multiplied by the number of years that the vendor has owned the property up to a maximum of 5 years.

**residuary devisee.** The person named in a will who is to take the *real* property remaining after satisfying specific gifts of real property in the will. The residuary devise includes any lapsed or void devises: Succession Act 1965 s.91.

**residuary legatee.** The person entitled under a will to the balance of the *personal* estate remaining after paying the debts, expenses and legacies bequeathed by the will. The residuary legacy includes any lapsed or void legacies.

**residue.** That which remains of a deceased's estate after payment of debts, funeral and testamentary expenses, legacies and annuities. Where a testator does not effectually dispose of the residue of his property, he dies intestate as to it eg if a share of residue lapses, it does not fall into residue, but goes to the next-of-kin (qv) on intestate succession (qv).

**resignation, employment.** Termination by an employee of a contract of employment in accordance with its terms. Failure by an employer to accept the withdrawal of a letter of resignation, where the resignation has been made in ignorance of a grievance procedure, amounts to a *constructive dismissal* (qv): Keane v Western Health Board (1990

EAT) ELR 108.

**resile.** To withdraw from.

**resisting arrest.** See ARREST, RESISTING.

**resolution.** A formal expression of opinion or intention by a meeting.

Decisions of a company are made by the resolution of its members. The articles of association provide who is entitled to vote and in what circumstances. Resolutions are either *ordinary* or *special*. An *ordinary* resolution is one which needs a simple majority of the votes cast to pass. A *special resolution* is one which has been passed by not less than three-fourths of the votes cast by such members as being entitled so to do, vote in person or (where proxies are allowed) by proxy at a general meeting of which at least 21 days notice has been given specifying the intention to propose the resolution as a special resolution has been duly given: Companies Act 1963 s.141.

All *special business* must be transacted by special resolution. *Special business* is defined as all business transacted at an extraordinary general meeting and also at an annual general meeting other than the principal business of an agm: ibid Table A, art 53.

Notices of ordinary and special resolutions must sufficiently describe what is being proposed so as to permit shareholders to form a reasoned judgement, and in particular, must not be misleading: Kaye v Croydon Tramways Co (1898) 1 Ch 358; Jackson v Munster Bank (1884) 13 LR Ir 118.

As regards resolutions of the Houses of the Oireachtas, they enjoy the presumption of constitutional validity: Goodman International v Mr Justice Hamilton (1992 HC & SC) ILRM 145. The passing of such resolutions may be evidenced by producing a copy of the Journal of the relevant House: Criminal Evidence Act 1992 s.11. As regards a *rescinding resolution* of a local authority, see Cartmill v Donegal County Council (1987 HC) IR 192. See also Building Societies Act 1989 ss.50(17), 74, and second schedule, part 11, para 5(n). See PROXY; STATUTORY INSTRUMENT; VOTING AT MEETINGS.

**resoluto jure concedentis resolvitur jus concessum.** [The grant of a right comes to an end on the termination of the right of the grantor].

**respite.** To discharge or dispense with.

**respondeat superior.** [Let the principal answer]. Refers to the liability of an employer generally for the acts of an employee. See VICARIOUS LIABILITY.

**respondent.** A person against whom a petition is sought, a summons issued, or an appeal brought.

**respondentia.** The securing of repayment of a loan by cargo on board a ship. See BOTTOMRY.

**responsibility.** Care and consideration for the outcome of one's own actions. See DUTY OF CARE; COLLECTIVE RESPONSIBIL-ITY; MINISTERIAL RESPONSIBILITY.

**restaurant.** See INTOXICATING LIQUOR.

**restitutio in integrum.** [Restoration to the original position]. The remedy by which a court orders that a contract be rescinded or otherwise that the parties be placed in the position they occupied before entering into a transaction. See DAMAGES.

**restitution.** Restoration to the rightful owner. See MONEY HAD AND RECEIVED; UNJUST ENRICHMENT.

**restitution of possession.** An order for restitution of stolen property may be made by the criminal court before which any person is convicted of larceny, embezzlement, conversion, or false accounting: Larceny Act 1916 s.45.

A person who gives a thief valuable consideration for the stolen property, acquires a good title to it only where the property is money or a negotiable instrument (qv) or it was transferred to him in market overt (qv), except that in the case of market overt, the property will be revested in the original owner if the thief, or receiver, is convicted of the stealing or receiving. See also Probation of Offenders Act 1907 s.1(4). See PROPERTY IN POSSESSION OF GARDA.

**restraint of trade, contract in.** Contractual interference with individual liberty of action in trading, which as a general rule is void as being contrary to public policy. *A contract in which a party (the covenantor) agrees with any other party (the covenantee) to restrict his liberty in the future to carry on trade with other persons not parties to the contract in such manner as he chooses*: Esso Petroleum Co Ltd v Harpers Garage (Stourport) Ltd 1968 AC 269.

The tests to be applied to determine whether the contract is void are: (a) does the restraint go further than to afford adequate protection to the party in whose favour it has been granted; if so, the covenant is prima facia void; (b) can the covenant be justified as being in the interests of the party restrained; (c) is the covenant contrary to the public interest.

The onus of showing that the restraint is reasonable rests with the party seeking to uphold the transaction. See House of Spring Gardens Ltd v Point Blank Ltd (1985) FSR 327; Macken v O'Reilly (1978) SC.

Covenants in employment contracts that restrict or deter an employee from freely exercising his trade, profession or calling are generally void. An employee who solicits orders from his employer's customers, intending to meet the orders personally rather than *qua* employee, breaches an implied term in an employment contract.

The Competition Authority does not consider employees to be *undertakings* within the meaning of the Competition Act 1991; however, if an employee leaves his employment, and the former employer seeks to enforce a non-competition clause in the employment contract, the Authority would regard this as a restriction on competition within the meaning of s.4(1) of the 1991 Act:- Iris Oifigiuil (18 September 1992). See Notification No CA/1011/92E — Peter Mark / Majella Stapleton in Iris Oifigiuil (26 Feb 1993). See also Stanford Supply Co Ltd v O'Toole 1972 HC; Faccenda Chicken Ltd v Fowler (1985) ICR 589; ECI European Chemical Industries Ltd v Bell (1981) ILRM 345; Orr Ltd v Orr (1987) ILRM 702; Time Manager International v O'Donovan & McCabe (1990) in 8ILT & SJ (1990) 164. See COMPETITION, DISTORTION OF; INJUNCTION; SEVERANCE; TRADE UNION; UNFAIR PRACTICES.

**restriction order.** The order which a court may make restricting a person from acting as a director of a company: Companies Act 1990 ss.150-158. A register of such persons must be kept by the Registrar of Companies (ibid s.153). See DIRECTORS.

**restrictive covenant.** See COVENANT.

**Restrictive Practices Commission.**

Originally known as the Fair Trade Commission (qv), a name to which it reverted as a result of the Restrictive Practices (Amendment) Act 1987 s.5(1); SI No 2 of 1988. It no longer exists: Competition Act 1991 s.22. See COMPE-TITION AUTHORITY.

**restrictive practice, orders relating to.** The orders which the Minister could make, if he considered that the exigencies of the common good warranted, prohibiting restrictive practices, unfair practices or unfair methods of competition: Restrictive Practices Acts 1972 and 1987 s.8 — since repealed; however certain orders may be retained. See Competition Act 1991 s.2(2) and 22. See Director of Fair Trade and Consumer Affairs v Sugar Distributors Ltd (1991 HC) ILRM 395. See BELOW COST SELLING; BOYCOTT; COMPETITION; DISTORTION OF; HELLO MONEY; LOTTERY.

**resulting trust.** A trust (qv) which arises in circumstances where the beneficial interest comes back to the settlor/transferror or to the person who provided the purchase money. A resulting trust arises where (a) the trust fails, or does not exhaust the whole of the fund, in which case the whole fund or the residue, as the case may be, results back to the settlor; or (b) where a purchase is made in the name of a stranger who provides no consideration, he holds in trust for the provider of the purchase money, unless there is clear evidence of intention to bestow the beneficial interest or the presumption of *advancement* arises: Heavey v Heavey (1977) ILTR 1; Baines v McLean (1934) ILTR 197; or (c) where a voluntary transfer of property is made but no intention of a gift can be inferred: Owens v Green (1932) IR 225. See also Daniels & O'Shea v Dunne (1990) 8ILT & SJ 35. See Leahy on "Indirect contributions and the law of trusts" in ISLR (1993) 65. See JOINT ACCOUNT.

**retail price.** It is an offence to prevent, without reasonable cause, a person from reading retail prices of goods or to interfere or obstruct that person. See Consumer Information Act 1978 s.15.

**retail price display order.** See PRICE CONTROL.

**retainer.** The right of the personal representative of a deceased person to retain out of the assets sufficient to pay any debt due to him from the deceased in priority to other creditors whose debts are of equal degree. It is restricted where the estate is insolvent or where the personal representative is not entitled to the debt in his own right: Succession Act 1965 s.46. See also Bankruptcy Act 1988 s.122.

**retention of mortgaged property.** A building society may retain a mortgaged property on the default of the mortgagor (borrower), in exercise of a power given by the mortgage and in exercise of an *adopted* power to develop land which it may also have: Building Societies Act 1989 ss.26(2) and 21.

The *value* of the mortgaged property must be determined by an independent competent person, appointed by the society and agreed to by the mortgagor and any other mortgagee, and the value so determined is to be treated as if it were money received by the mortgagee (ibid s.26(2)). Particulars of the value must be sent by registered post to the mortgagor and any other mortgagee (ibid s.26(5)). In the event of failure to agree a valuer, there is provision for the court to appoint one (ibid s.26(3)).

**retention of title clause.** Also known as a *reservation of title* clause. A term in a contract for sale of goods by which title in the goods remains with the seller until the goods are paid for; if the original buyer sells the goods, he holds the proceeds of that sale as fiduciary for the original seller and the latter is entitled to trace the proceeds of that sale. Difficulties concerning the effectiveness of a retention of title clause often arise where the goods sold are altered physically or are admixed with other goods.

It has been held that a retention of title clause which gave the buyer an express right to sell the goods and to hold in trust all moneys so received, created a *charge* on the proceeds of sale which required registration under the Companies Act 1963 s.99: Carroll Group Distributors Ltd v J F Bourke Ltd (1990 HC) ILRM 285.

See In re Interview Ltd (1975) IR 382; Aluminium Industrie Vaassen BV v Romalpa Aluminium Ltd (1976) 2 All ER 552; In re Stokes McKiernan Ltd (1978) HC; Frigosccondia (Contracting)

Ltd v Continental Irish Meats Ltd (1982) ILRM 396; Sugar Distribution Ltd v Monaghan Cash & Carry Ltd (1982) ILRM 399; In re Galway Concrete Ltd (1983) ILRM 493; Somers v Allen (1984) ILRM 437; Uniake v Cassidy Electrical Supply Co Ltd (1987) HC. See Report on Debt Collection: (2) Retention of Title (LRC 28 of 1989). See McCormack in 8ILT & SJ (1990) 248; de Lacy in 8ILT & SJ (1990) 279. [Text: Forde (5); Maguire; Parris UK]. See CHARGE, REGISTRATION OF.

**retention tax.** See DEPOSIT INTEREST RETENTION TAX; WITHHOLDING TAX.

**retirement, early.** It has been held that early retirement by an officer of the Defence Forces is not a right, but a statutory concession; the Minister has a right to refuse an application for such early retirement: Defence Act 1954 ss.42 and 47; Egan v Minister for Defence and Ors (1989) 7ILT Dig 81. In a particular case, an employee, who applied for early retirement and then endeavoured to retract his application, was ordered to be reinstated to his job: Griffin v Telecom Eireann (1992 CC) — Irish Times 4/5/92.

**retirement relief.** Generally understood to mean the relief from capital gains tax when an individual, aged over 55, disposes of business assets, or farm, or shares in a family company, as defined, by way of sale or gift: Capital Gains Tax 1975 s.26 as amended by Finance Acts 1990 s.84 and 1991 s.42.

**retours sans protet.** [Return without protest]. A direction by the drawer that a bill of exchange (qv) should not be protested. See PROTEST.

**retraction.** The withdrawal of a renunciation (qv).

**retrial.** A new trial.

The various aspects of a criminal trial are not severable; where there is to be a retrial, the High Court has no jurisdiction to issue an order of prohibition in respect of a matter which may or may not arise in the retrial: Ryan V DPP (1989) 7ILT Dig 104. The Court of Criminal Appeal in quashing a conviction is entitled to exercise its discretion and refuse to order a retrial: DPP v Brophy (1992 CCA) ITLR (9 Mar).

In civil matters, documents created after a trial may be relevant at a retrial where they contain matters which would advance the case of one party or damage that of the other: Dunne v National Maternity Hospital (1989 SC) ITLR (27 Nov). Where the Supreme Court on appeal finds for a plaintiff on the issue of liability, it may order that a retrial be on the issue of damages only: Mullen v Quinnsworth Ltd (1991 SC) ITLR (17 Jun). In a defamation action, the judge will order a retrial where the jury is inconclusive as to whether the words complained of were defamatory, even where they assessed the damages as zero: Kenna v McKinney (1992 HC).

**retroactive legislation.** See RETROSPECTIVE LEGISLATION.

**retrospective legislation.** Legislation which takes away or impairs any vested right acquired under existing laws or creates a new obligation, or imposes a new duty, or attaches a new disability in respect to transactions or considerations already past: Craies on Statute Law — cited with approval in many Irish cases. The Oireachtas (qv) cannot declare acts to be infringements of the law, which were not so at the date of their commission: 1937 Constitution art.15(5). However, the retrospective operation of criminal *procedural rules* is not an infringement of the Constitution: In re McGrath and Harte (1941) IR 68; nor is the retrospective application of the Garda Siochana (Discipline) Regulations 1989: McGrath v Commissioner of Garda Siochana (1993 HC) ILRM 38. However, see Healy v Garda Commissioner (1993 HC) — Irish Times 14/7/1993. See GARDA, DISCIPLINE OF.

It has been held that the Constitution did not contain any general prohibition on retrospection of legislation, nor could it be interpreted as a general prohibition: Magee v Culligan (1992 SC) ILRM 186. However, unless a contrary intention appears, a statute is presumed to be prospective and not retrospective: Hamilton v Hamilton (1982) IR 471.

Whether a statute is to have retrospective affect or not is a matter of construction of the provision concerned; there is a presumption against retrospective construction: O'H v O'H (1990 HC) 2 IR 558 reported in 9ILT & SJ (1991) 28 and 50. An inspector appointed under the Companies Act 1990 can procure documents predating the commencement of the Act: Chestvale Properties Ltd & Hoddle Investments Ltd v Glackin & Ors (1992 HC) ILRM 221.

Generally the courts lean against injurious retrospection of legislation, holding that the position in which a person already finds himself at the time when the new law is actually passed should not be affected for the worse: Fitzpatrick v Minister for Industry and Commerce (1931) IR 457. It has been held that the Employment Equality Act 1977 does not have retrospective effect: Aer Lingus Teo v Labour Court (1990 SC) ILRM 485. It has also been held that the invalidity of conviction by an improperly re-appointed District Court judge is not cured by retrospective legislation: Shelly v DJ Mahon & DPP (1990) ITLR (23 Jul); Courts (No 2) Act 1988.

Retrospective legislation may be drafted in such a manner as to help prevent it being found to be unconstitutional — by providing that in so far as any provisions in the legislation conflict with the constitutional right of any person, the provisions will be subject to such limitations as are necessary to secure that they do not so conflict eg legislation giving the Commissioners of Public Works retrospective power to carry out developments on in or under land, has such a provision: State Authorities (Development and Management) Act 1993 s.2(3).

Examples of other legislation intended to have retrospective effect:Income Tax (Amendment) Act 1986 retrospectively to 1973 to close a loophole in the law of taxation on the grounds that otherwise the loss of income to the Exchequer would be considerable; Mental Treatment Act 1961 to validate detentions for which no lawful authority existed; Garda Siochana Act 1979 to validate the appointment of the then Garda Commissioner when the previous occupant had been found to have been unfairly dismissed (Garvey v Ireland (1980) IR 75); LG (P & D) Act 1982 s.6 to validate planning permissions following the decision in The State (Pine Valley) v Dublin Co Co (1984) IR 407; the abolition of the death penalty: Criminal Justice Act 1990; judges' pensions: Courts (Supplemental Provisions)

(Amdt) Act 1991; the Presidential Establishment (Amendment) Act 1991; the Statute of Limitations (Amdt) Act 1991; validation of certain payments already made: Housing (Miscellaneous Provisions) Act 1992 s.35; planning permission deemed not to have been required for certain developments commenced or completed: LG (P&D) Act 1993 s.4(1); and validation of regulations already made to implement EC law: European Commuties (Amdt) Act 1993 s.5. See Condon v Minister for Labour (1980) HC; Doyle v An Taoiseach (1986) ILRM 693; Lawlor v Minister for Agriculture (1988) ILRM 400. See Delaney in 10 ILT & SJ (1992) 133. See EUROPEAN COURT; ULTRA VIRES.

**return.** A report. Execution orders (qv) and other orders are returnable ie the person to whom they are directed is bound or may be required to make a return or report on them. The term *return* is mostly used with reference to the time when an order is returnable. Some orders are returnable on the date named in them; others are returnable as soon as they are executed. A summons is said to be returnable on the day appointed for hearing it.

**return for trial.** The order returning an accused for trial. There is no requirement in the Criminal Procedure Act 1967 that the date of trial be specified in the return for trial; all that is required is that the return for trial indicate the sitting of the court to which the accused is returned: AG v Sheehy (1990) 1 IR 434. See INDICTABLE OFFENCE.

**returning officer.** The officer with the general duty to do such acts and things as may be necessary for effectually conducting an election, to ascertain and declare the results and to furnish a return of the persons elected: Electoral Act 1992 s.31. In Cork and Dublin, the sheriffs are the returning officers for their areas while in the rest of the country, county registrars are the returning officers (ibid 1992 Act s.30; European Assembly Elections Act 1977 s.14, as amended by the Electoral (Amendment) Act 1986 s.2).

The decision of the returning officer is final subject only to reversal on a petition questioning the election (ibid 1992 Act s.128). There is provision for the appointment of deputy returning officers in Dail elections (ibid 1992 Act s.30(3)). Also provision is proposed to be made for the appointment of a presidential returning officer and local returning officers for presidential elections: draft Presidential Elections Bill 1993 ss.9-10. See COUNTY REGISTRAR; ISLAND, POLLING ON; SHERIFF.

**revaluation.** See ASSET VALUATION.

**revenue.** Income; yield of taxes. It is a principle and practice that the Irish Courts do not aid the collection by another country of its revenue; a passport fee is not capable of being a revenue raising device: McDonald v McMahon (1990) 8ILT Dig 60.

**revenue offence.** In relation to extradition (qv), means an offence in connection with taxes and duties in relation to any country or place outside the State: Extradition Act 1965 s.50. In relation to betting offences, the power of the Revenue Commissioners to arrest and imprison a person for failure to pay fines for revenue offences is unconstitutional: Murphy v DJ Wallace (1990 HC) ITLR (24 Dec). It was held that there was an absence of due process of law in the trial and sentencing to prison of a person who had failed to make a return of income: Finance Act 1983 s.94(2); O'Callaghan v DJ Clifford (1993 SC) — Irish Times 3/4/1993.

**revenue penalty.** A penalty which the Revenue is entitled to impose for failure by a taxpayer to comply with some statutory requirement; it does not amount to a criminal penalty requiring a trial: McLoughlin v Tuite (1989) 7ILT Dig 321. See TAX, FALSE STATEMENT.

**revenue statute.** Legislation dealing with the raising of revenue eg taxation. Words or expressions which create a taxation liability should be construed strictly: Inspector of Taxes v Kiernan (1981) IR 117.

**reversal.** The setting aside of a judgment on appeal. See APPEAL; SET ASIDE.

**reversing.** Before reversing, a driver of a vehicle is required to ensure that he can do so without endangering other traffic or pedestrians: Road Traffic General Bye-Laws 1964 art.25 (SI No 294 of 1964).

**reversion.** The residue of ownership which continues in the person who makes a grant of an estate eg when a fee simple owner makes a grant of a life estate, the fee simple (qv) which he retains is a reversion. See LEASEHOLD, MORTGAGE OF.

**reversionary lease.** The lease to which *building lessees* and *proprietary lessees* were entitled to on termination of their leases: Landlord and Tenant (Reversionary Leases) Act 1958. The right to a reversionary lease is now linked to the right to purchase the fee simple under the Landlord and Tenant (Ground Rents) (No 2) Act 1978: Landlord and Tenant (Amendment) Act 1980 s.30.

In the absence of agreement, the court will fix the terms of the reversionary lease according to the provisions of the 1980 Act s.34 ie for a term of 99 years at a rent not lower than the old rent, unless a new covenant or condition is included, with the rent being calculated at one-eighth of the open market value of the land. The reversionary lease is deemed to be a *graft* on the previous lease.

**revesting.** The vesting of property again in its original owner eg stolen property. See Sale of Goods Act 1893 s.24. See PROPERTY IN POSSESSION OF GARDA; RESTITUTION OF POSSESSION.

**review.** See APPEAL; JUDICIAL REVIEW.

**review of sentence.** If it appears to the Director of Public Prosecutions that a sentence imposed by a court on conviction of a person on indictment was unduly lenient, he may apply to the Court of Criminal Appeal (qv) to review the sentence: Criminal Justice Act 1993 s.2(1). That Court may refuse the application or it may impose such sentence as could have been imposed on the convicted person by the sentencing court concerned (ibid s.2(3)). There is an appeal to the Supreme Court on a point of law of exceptional public importance (ibid s.3). Provision is made for legal aid to be granted to a person whose sentence is the subject of an application or appeal (ibid s.4). See O'Malley in 11 ILT & SJ (1993) 121.

**revival.** The renewal of rights which were at an end or in abeyance by subsequent acts or events eg a will once revoked may be revived by republication (qv).

**revocation.** Recalling, revoking or cancelling.

(1) Revocation by act of a party is an intentional or voluntary revocation eg revocation of a will: Succession Act 1965 s.85. There is no general presumption that a subsequent will revokes a former one.

(2) Revocation can operate by a rule of law irrespective of the intention of the parties eg the power of attorney or authority of an agent is generally revoked by the death of the principal.

(3) Many statutes provide for the revocation of a right already bestowed eg the revocation of a patent (qv) or of planning permission (qv). See DEPENDENT RELATIVE REVOCATION; WILL, REVOCATION OF.

**revocation of offer.** An offer may be revoked at any time before acceptance; once accepted an offer is irrevocable. Revocation does not take effect until it is actually communicated to the offeree. If the offeree agrees to keep his offer open for a specified time, he may nevertheless revoke it before the expiration of that time, unless it has been acccepted before notice of revocation has reached the offeree, or there is consideration for keeping the offer open. See Dickinson v Dodds (1876) 2 Ch D 463; Byrne v Van Tienhoven (1880) 5 CPD 349. See OFFER; OPTION.

**reward.** It is an offence to advertise publicly a reward, with or without an offer to pay compensation, for the return of any property which has been stolen or lost, *no questions asked* or enquiry made: Larceny Act 1861 s.102. See also Larceny Act 1916 s.34. See BRIBERY AND CORRUPTION; SALVAGE.

**RIAI contract.** The standard form of building contracts of the Royal Institute of the Architects of Ireland. [Text: Keane D]. See FINAL CERTIFICATE.

**rider.** A statement eg added to a jury's verdict. See INQUEST.

**right.** An interest recognised and protected by the law, respect for which is a duty, and disregard for which is a wrong.

**right of entry.** See ENTRY, RIGHT OF.

**right of first refusal.** See FIRST REFUSAL.

**right of way.** See WAY, RIGHT OF.

**right to begin.** The right to begin in the trial of an issue generally belongs to the party on whom the burden of proof (qv) rests. In criminal cases, the prosecution begins except if the accused raises some special *plea in bar* eg autrefois acquit

(qv). In civil cases, where the onus of proving at least one of the issues rests with the plaintiff or if he claims unliquidated damages, he is entitled to begin.

**right to bodily integrity.** See BODILY INTEGRITY, RIGHT TO.

**right to emblements.** See EMBLEMENTS.

**right to fixtures.** See FIXTURES.

**right to life.** See LIFE, RIGHT TO.

**right to light.** See LIGHT, RIGHT TO.

**right to private property.** See PRIVATE PROPERTY, RIGHT TO.

**right to support.** See SUPPORT, RIGHT TO.

**right to work.** See WORK, RIGHT TO.

**rights, natural.** See NATURAL RIGHTS.

**Rights Commissioner.** A person appointed by the Minister under the Industrial Relations Act 1969 to investigate and issue recommendations to resolve certain types of trade disputes, usually relating to individual grievances, and to make recommendations on disputes under the Unfair Dismissals Act 1977 and the Maternity Protection of Employees Act 1981, which either party may appeal to the Employment Appeals Tribunal (qv).

The Rights Commissioner is independent in the performance of his function, while also operating as a service of the Labour Relations Commission: Industrial Relations Act 1990 s.35. He cannot investigate a dispute if a party to the dispute objects (ibid 1969 Act s.13(3)(b)(ii) and 1990 Act s.36).

A Rights Commissioner is precluded from dealing with a dispute in relation to unfair dismissal if brought in reliance on s.13(2) of the Industrial Relations Act 1969: Unfair Dismissals Act 1977 s.8(1O); Sutcliffe v McCarthy & Ors (1993 HC) ELR 53. He can only deal with such a claim under s.8(1) of the 1977 Act using the procedure prescribed by s.8(2). See now Unfair Dismissals (Amdt) Act 1993 s.7 amending s.8 of the 1977 Act.

The High Court has declared a Rights Commissioner's recommendation to be without efficacy and ultra vires even though the recommendation was not binding on the parties: An Taoiseach v Colin Walker (1992 HC) reported by Barry in 11 ILT & SJ (1993) 30. See Walker in (1986) 5 JISLL 67.

**rights issue.** Issue of shares in a company

whereby existing shareholders are given a prior right to take part of the new issue at a price below the market value of the shares. Often the rights are renounceable in favour of any other person, enabling the shareholder to sell them to such other person. While there is an element of *bonus* in a rights issue, they are not bonus shares. In a rights issue, new funds are raised whereas an issue of bonus shares involves a distribution of profits hitherto undistributed. See In re Afric Sive (1988) HC. See BONUS SHARES.

**riot.** A tumultous disturbance of the peace which is a common law misdemeanour, comprising the following essential elements: at least three persons; with a common purpose; involved in the execution of the common purpose; an intent to help one another by force if necessary against anyone who might oppose them in the execution of their common purpose; the display of force or violence in such a manner as to alarm at least one person of reasonable firmness and courage: Field v Receiver of Metropolitan Police (1907) 2 KB 859.

Under draft legislation, it is proposed that the offence of *riot* will be committed where (a) 12 or more persons who are present together at any place, use or threaten to use unlawful violence for a common purpose, and (b) the conduct of those persons, taken together, is such as would cause a person of reasonable firmness present at that place to fear for his or another person's safety; each of the persons using unlawful violence for the common purpose will commit the offence of riot: Criminal Justice (Public Order) Bill 1993 s.15. The place may be a public place, a private place or both. It is proposed that the common law offence of riot will be abolished (ibid s.15(4)), and that every reference to the common law offences of "riot" or "riot and to tumult" in previous enactments are to be construed as a reference to the proposed offence of "violent disorder" (ibid s.16(5)). See MALICIOUS INJURIES SCHEME; RIOTOUS ASSEMBLY; UNLAWFUL AS-SEMBLY; VIOLENT DISORDER.

**riotous assembly.** The statutory offence committed whenever an unlawful assembly (qv) of twelve or more persons do not disperse within an hour after a justice of the peace (qv) has read, or attempted to read, them a proclamation as prescribed, calling on them to disperse: Riot Act 1787 s.1. From this comes the popular expression *reading the Riot Act*. Force may be used to quell a riotous assembly but only so much force as is reasonable to protect lives and property. See Lynch v Fitzgerald (1938) IR 382.

**riparian.** Property bounded by a river or stream. Riparian owners, or owners of land on the banks of a river or stream, have a right to water flowing in a defined channel; they may sue to protect their natural rights if the river or stream is dammed or diverted: McClone v Smith (1888) 22 LR Ir 559. The owners of the bed and soil of waters, and the corporeal fishing rights in them, are entitled to an order restraining interference with the said waters: Tennant v Clancy (1988) ILRM 214. See also Uyettewaal v Commissioners of Public Works (1987 HC) IR 439.

**risk, transfer of.** As regards the sale of goods, the principle by which risk generally passes with the property, unless the parties agree otherwise: Sale of Goods Act 1893 ss.20 and 33. See GOODS, PROPERTY IN.

**road.** Includes (a) any street, lane, footpath, square, court, alley or passage, (b) any bridge, viaduct, underpass, subway, tunnel, overpass, flyover, carriageway (whether single or multiple), pavement or footway, (c) any weighbridge, toll plaza, service area, emergency telephone, margin, hard shoulder, island, roundabout, ...... and (d) any other necessary or prescribed structure or thing forming part of the road: Roads Act 1993 s.2(1).

A *public road* is a road over which a public right of way exists and the responsibility for the maintenance of which lies on a road authority (ibid s.2(1)). A public road may be classified by Ministerial order as a *national* road, a *regional* road, or a *local* road (ibid s.10). A public road is a *motorway* when so specified in a motorway scheme (ibid s.43) or a *busway* when so specified in a busway scheme (ibid s.44), or a *protected road* when so specified in a protected road scheme (ibid s.45). See HIGHWAY; MOTORWAY; PUBLIC ROAD.

**road authority.** The council of a county,

the corporation of a county or other borough, or the council of an urban district: Roads Act 1993 s.2(1). As regards toll roads, a road authority means (a) in the case of the national road, the National Roads Authority, (b) in the case of a regional road or a local road, a road authority as defined above (ibid s.56). See DANGEROUS STRUCTURE; DRAIN; ROAD, CLOSURE OF; SIGN; SKIP; TOLL ROAD.

**road, closure of.** A road authority is empowered to close a public road (qv) to traffic, by order, for a specified period to facilitate a road race or any other event, for carrying out works, or for any other purpose, as it thinks fit: Roads Act 1993 s.75.

**road development, proposed.** Any *proposed road development* in respect of which an environmental impact statement is required: Roads Act 1993 s.2(1). It is such a development if it consists of the construction of a motorway or busway, or any prescribed type of development consisting of the construction of a proposed public road or the improvement of an existing public road (ibid s.50(1)). A proposed road development must not be carried out unless the Minister has approved it or approved it with modifications (ibid s.51(1)). The Minister must, prior to such approval, consider the environment impact statement submitted to him by the road authority, and consider the report and any recommendation of the person who conducted a public inquiry in relation to the proposed development (ibid s.51(5)). See EC Directive No 337/85. See NORTHERN IRELAND.

**road freight licence.** See CARRIER'S LICENCE.

**road maintenance.** A local authority has been held to be equally responsible with the driver for an accident on a road which had been recently resurfaced with tar and loose chippings: Tobin v Tipperary (NR) County Council (1992 CC) reported in 11 ILT & SJ (1993) 139. See MISFEASANCE; NONFEASANCE; PUBLIC ROAD.

**road race.** A prescribed class of race, time trial or speed trial on a public road (qv) involving persons, vehicles or animals: Roads Act 1993 s.74(1). A person who intends to hold a road race must give notice in writing to the road authority and to the Superintendent of the Garda Siochana and must comply with the written notice from the road authority (ibid s.74(2) and (3)). See ROAD, CLOSURE OF.

**road traffic accidents.** Accidents which often have legal consequences, whether in respect of prosecution for a road traffic offence or an action for damages arising from eg negligence (qv) or breach of statutory duty. Such an action for damages for *personal injuries* is no longer heard by a jury, as formerly in the High Court.

There is provision for the payment of damages by the Motor Insurer's Bureau of Ireland in the case of an uninsured driver. Damages may also be recoverable by dependants in respect of a death from fatal injuries. See ACCIDENT, REPORTING OF; FATAL INJURIES; JURY, ABOLITION OF; MOTOR INSURERS' BUREAU OF IRELAND; MOTOR VEHICLE, NEGLIGENT DRIVING OF; PATIENT CHARGES.

**road traffic check.** A garda has a common law power to operate random or spot road traffic checks, including checks in relation to drunken driving which involve the stopping of vehicles, even though there is no immediate suspicion that an offence has been committed; this includes saturation roadblocks mounted by the gardai especially at Christmas time: DPP v Fagan (1993 HC) ITLR (8 Mar). The power of a garda to stop a vehicle and make enquiries does not carry with it the power to detain or arrest, and if the member of the public refuses to answer the garda's questions, he cannot be detained unless the garda has grounds for arresting him. See STOP, OBLIGATION TO

**road traffic offences.** The wide range of offences connected with the ownership, driving or control of mechanical propelled vehicles in public places, including drunken, dangerous, and careless driving (qqv). Provision has been made to increase penalties in respect of many offences under the Road Traffic Acts 1961 to 1978: Road Traffic Amendment Act 1984. The first ever reported road traffic case is believed to be Gibbons v Pepper (1695) 1 Ld Raym 38. Over 90% of prosecutions in District Courts are road related: Dail Debates vol 347 vol 2680. [Text: Pierce; Woods (4)].

**road user's duty.** A person using a public road (qv) has a duty to take reasonable care for his own safety and for that of any other person using the public road: Roads Act 1993 s.67.

**roadway.** That portion of a road which is provided primarily for the use of vehicles: Roads Act 1993 s.2(1). See FOOTWAY.

**robbery.** Stealing by force or fear of force; the offence committed by a person who steals, and immediately before or at the time of doing so, and in order to do so, he uses force on any person or puts or seeks to put any person in fear of being then and there subjected to force: Criminal Law (Jurisdiction) Act 1976 s.5. The ingredients of larceny (qv) must be present together with some element of force, or fear of force. If actual stealing does not take place, the offence of *assault with intent to rob* is committed.

**robes.** See DRESS IN COURT.

**rod licence.** See FISHING LICENCE

**rogatory letter.** See LETTER OF REQUEST.

**rolled-up plea.** The plea used in the defence of fair comment in an action for defamation (qv) which usually states *"in so far as the words complained of consist of facts, they are true in substance and in fact, and in so far as they consist of expressions of opinion they are fair comment made in good faith and without malice upon the said facts which are a matter of public interest."* The court will not order the defendant to specify which words are statement of facts and which are statements of opinions, this being a question to be decided by the jury. See also Defamation Act 1961 s.23.

**root of title.** The conveyance or other document with which the title to land commences. A *good root* of title is some instrument dealing with the ownership of the whole legal and equitable estate, containing a description by which the property can be identified and showing nothing to cast any doubt on the title eg a conveyance for value, a settlement for value, a legal mortgage of a fee simple.

The conditions of sale of land may provide for any document to be a satisfactory root of title; in the absence of such a provision the purchaser can ask for: (a) 40 years title where the freehold is being sold; (b) in the case of the sale of leasehold, the lease itself, however old, in addition to assignments during the forty years prior to the purchase date; (c) in the sale of a reversionary interest, the document creating the reversionary interest, however old, in addition to the 40 years prior to the purchase date. See Vendor and Purchasers Act 1874 ss.1-2; Conveyancing Act 1881 s.13. See ABSTRACT OF TITLE; MARKETABLE TITLE.

**roundabout.** A road junction so constructed that traffic which enters it must proceed slowly in a circular direction: Road Traffic (Signs) Regulations 1962 art.2 (SI No 171 of 1962).

**rout.** See UNLAWFUL ASSEMBLY.

**Royal Irish Constabulary.** Every mention of or reference to the Royal Irish Constabulary contained in any statute or statutory rule, order, or regulation in force in Saorstat Eireann (qv) is to be construed and take effect as a mention of or reference to the Garda Siochana (qv): Garda Siochana Act 1924 s.19.

**royal prerogative.** *The residue of discretionary or arbitrary authority which at any given time is legally left in the hands of the Crown*: Dicey on the Law of the Constitution. It has been held that no royal prerogative in existence prior to the 1922 Constitution was vested in the State by virtue of that Constitution: Byrne v Ireland (1972) IR 241; Webb & Webb v Ireland Attorney General (1988 SC) IR 353. See TREASURE TROVE.

**royalty.** Share of the sales or profits arising from a product paid to the owner thereof eg payments to an author by a publisher, or by a licensee to a patentee. The person making a payment in respect of any royalty, or other sum, paid in respect of a patent, is entitled to deduct income tax at source but is not obliged to so do: Income Tax Act 1967 s.433. The recipient of such income is entitled to have his tax liability computed as if such royalty income had been spread over a number of years (ibid s.291). Advance royalties may qualify as income from a *qualifying patent* (qv): Finance Act 1973 s.34; Pandion Haliaetus v Revenue Commissioners (1988) ILRM 419.

There are special statutory provisions regarding royalty in respect of records of musical works: Copyright Act 1963 s.13. The Controller of Patents, Designs and Trade Marks may determine disputes referred to him in relation to copyright royalties (ibid s.31).

Where a bankrupt's property includes the copyright in any work and he is liable to pay royalties to the author, the author will be entitled to receive royalties in full where the Official Assignee (qv) sells any copies of the work or authorises it to be performed: Bankruptcy Act 1988 s.48.

**rule against perpetuities.** See PERPETU-ITIES, RULE AGAINST.

**rule of law.** (1) A legal rule. (2) The government of the State based on the general acceptance of the law.

**rule of reason.** See REASON, RULE OF.

**rules of court.** The rules governing the practice and procedure in the courts. See Rules of the Superior Courts 1986 (RSC) as amended; Rules of the Circuit Court 1950 (RCC) as amended; District Court Rules 1948 (DCR) as amended.

Where there is no rule given to govern practice and procedure in the Circuit Court, the practice and procedure of the High Court may be followed: RCC O.59 r.14. For example of a refusal by the Circuit Court to import a High Court rule, see Aerospan Board Centre (Dublin) Ltd v Dean Furniture Ltd (1987 CC) as reported in 7ILT & SJ (1989) 79. [Text: Gannon]. See LANGUAGE; PRACTICE DIREC-TIONS; SEPARATION AGREEMENT.

**rules of the road.** The publication issued under that title by the Minister, being the edition thereof which at the relevant time, is the latest edition: Road Traffic Act 1961 s.3(4). Failure to observe the Rules of the Road is only evidential in its effect.

**run with the land.** See COVENANT.

**rundale system.** A system of frequent redistribution of land, prevalent in the western counties of Ireland, whereby rights of pasturage continue to be owned in common by many landowners, particularly of mountain land, and whereby rights to arable land are periodically redistributed amongst the farmers of a neighbourhood. The Land Commission is empowered to purchase land where it requires it to facilitate re-arrangement of lands held in rundale or intermixed plots: Land Act 1950 s.27(1)(c).

**rural district councils.** Formerly, the bodies established to exercise the func-tions previously exercised by the boards of guardians (qv): Local Government (Ireland) Act 1898. These councils were later abolished and their functions trans-ferred to the county councils. See Local Government Act 1925 ss.3 and 9-10; Local Government (Dublin) Act 1930 s.82; County Management Act 1940 s.36.

**Rylands v Fletcher, Rule in.** An occupier of land or buildings, who brings or keeps on it anything, though perhaps harmless while it remains there, will do damage if it escapes, is bound to prevent its escape and is liable for all the damage if it does escape. The rule is one of strict liability independent of wrongful intent or negligence.

Defences include: Act of God; act of a stranger; consent or default of the plaintiff; statutory authority; and acci-dental fire which occurs on land or in buildings and escapes without negligence (Accidental Fires Act 1943). See Noonan v Hartnett (1950) 84 ILTR 41; McKenzie v O'Neill & Roe Ltd (1977) HC. See also Healy v Bray UDC (1962) Ir Jur Rep 9; Berkery v Flynn (1982) HC. See FIRE, LIABILITY FOR; POLLUTION, CIVIL LIABIL-ITY FOR.

# S

**sacrilege.** The offence which consisted of breaking and entering and committing a felony in, or entering, committing a felony in and then breaking out of, any place of divine worship: Larceny Act 1916 s.24 repealed by the Criminal Law (Jurisdiction) Act 1976 s.21. The offence remains as the common law felony of burglary as redefined in the 1976 Act ss.6-7.

**safety at work.** At common law, an employer is under a duty to provide a safe system of work for his employees. By statute, a general duty is placed on all employers to ensure so far as is *reasonably practicable*, the safety, health and welfare at work of all their employees, which includes those undergoing training for employment or receiving work ex-perience: Safety, Health and Welfare at Work Act 1989 s.6. There is also a general duty in respect of persons who are not employees to ensure that they are not exposed to risks to their safety and health (ibid s.7).

Every place at which any person has at any time to work must be kept in a safe condition: Safety in Industry Act 1980 s.12(1). Every dangerous part of any machinery, other than prime movers and transmission machinery, must be securely fenced: Factories Act 1955 s.23(1). The Mines and Quarries Act 1965 contains specific provisions regarding safety at places of work to which it relates.

An employee has a duty to take reasonable care for his own safety and health and that of any other persons who might be affected by his acts or omissions at work: Safety in Industry Act 1980 s.8(1)(a); Kennedy v East Cork Foods Ltd (1973) IR 244; ibid 1989 Act s.9).

The first comprehensive reform of occupational safety and health law since the foundation of the State culminated in the 1989 Act which extended protection legislation to all employers and employees; it also provided for the establishment of the National Authority for Occupational Safety and Health. It imposed general duties on designers and manufacturers regarding articles and substances for use at work, and on persons who design or construct places of work (ibid ss.10-11). The National Authority has extensive enforcement powers through: improvement plans (qv), improvement notices (qv), prohibition notices (qv), and in extreme cases *ex parte* application to the High Court.

See also Close v Steel Company of Wales (1962) AC 367; Daly v Avonmore Creameries Ltd (1984) IR 131; Johnson v Gresham Hotel Company (1986) HC. See Office Premises Act 1958; Shops (Conditions of Employment) Acts 1938 1942; SI No 279 of 1960 (docks); SI No 282 of 1975 (construction); SI No 423 of 1981 (unfenced machinery); Safety, Health and Welfare at Work (General Application) Regulations 1993 (SI No 44 of 1993). [Text: Byrne R (2)]. See ACCESS; CARCINOGENS; OFFSHORE INSTALLATION; REASONABLY PRACTICABLE; SAFETY STATEMENT; WORK ACTIVITY; WORK, PROHIBITION OF.

**safety belt.** A person driving and a person occupying a front seat of passenger vehicles and station wagons, having passenger accommodation of not more than eight persons exclusive of the driver, must wear a safety belt, unless the person is exempted, or produces a certificate of a registered medical practitioner that because of physical or mental disability or for medical or psychological reasons, it was undesireable or inadvisable for the person to wear a safety belt on the occasion in question: Road Traffic (Construction, Equipment and Use of Vehicles) Amendment No 2 Regulations 1978 (SI No 360 of 1978).

In a negligence action involving the collision of motor vehicles, failure of a plaintiff to wear a safety belt has been held to amount to *contributory negligence* (qv), resulting in a reduction of fifteen percent in the damages which would otherwise have been awarded: Sinnott v Quinnsworth Ltd (1984) ILRM 523. A reduction of fourteen percent was made in Conley v Strain (1989 HC) 7 ILT Dig 149 and twenty percent in Ward v Walsh (1992 SC) 10 ILT Dig 74.

**safety representative.** The person whom employees have a right to appoint to represent them in relation to consultations with their employer regarding the development and promotion of measures for their safety, health and welfare at work and the ascertaining of the effectiveness of such measures: Safety, Health and Welfare at Work Act 1989 s.13. [Text: Byrne R (2)].

**safety statement.** The statement which must be prepared by every employer specifying (i) the arrangements made for safe-guarding safety, health and welfare at work; (ii) the resources provided for this; (iii) the co-operation required from employees; (iv) the names of persons responsible for performance of the tasks in the statement: Safety, Health and Welfare at Work Act 1989 s.12. In preparing the safety statement, the employer must be in possession of an assessment in writing of the risks to safety and health at the place of work: SI No 44 of 1993, reg.10. [Text: Byrne R (2)].

**sale.** (1) The act of selling. (2) A contract for a sale of goods. See SALE OF GOODS.

**sale, bill of.** See BILL OF SALE.

**sale and return.** See APPROVAL, SALE ON.

**sale of goods.** A contract for the sale of goods is a contract whereby the seller transfers or agrees to transfer the property in the goods to the buyer for a money consideration called the price: Sale of Goods Act 1893 s.1. A contract of sale may be made in writing, or by word of mouth, or partly in writing and partly by word of mouth, or may be implied by the conduct of the parties (ibid s.3). However the Minister may by order require certain contracts to be in writing: SGSS Act 1980 s.54.

Where under a contract of sale, the property in the goods is transferred from the seller to the buyer, the contract is called a *sale*. But where the transfer of the property is to take place at a future time or subject to some condition thereafter to be fulfilled, the contract is called an *agreement to sell* (ibid 1893 Act s.1(3)). An agreement to sell becomes a sale when the time elapses or the conditions are fulfilled subject to which the property in the goods is to be transferred (ibid s.1(4)).

A contract for the sale of any goods of the value of ten pounds or upwards is not enforceable by action unless the buyer accepts part of the goods so sold, and actually receives the same, or gives something in earnest to bind the contract, or in part-payment, or unless some note or memorandum in writing of the contract be made and signed by the party to be charged or his agent in that behalf (ibid s.4). See Uniacke v Cassidy Electrical Supply Company (1987) HC. The Law Reform Commission has recommended that the State should ratify the United Nations Vienna Convention for the International Sale of Goods: see Kaczorowska in 9ILT & SJ (1991) 281 and LRC 42 of 1992. [Text: Forde (5); Grogan, King & Donelan; Benjamin UK]. See PRICE.

**sale of land.** The usual practice in the sale of land by *private treaty* (qv) is for the purchaser to sign the contract for the sale of land which is then returned to the vendor for his acceptance and signing, whereupon a binding agreement is in force. There is no provision, as in the UK, for an exchange of contracts with the contract being binding only on such exchange.

In a sale by *auction* (qv) of land, an agreement is in force when the property is knocked down to the highest bidder,

the necessary memorandum to that agreement being signed by the bidder while still in the auctioneer's premises and signed by the auctioneer on behalf of the vendor. See CONVEYANCE; CONDITIONS OF SALE; EJECTMENT; MORTGAGEE, RIGHT OF; SETTLEMENT; STATUTE OF FRAUDS; TRUSTEE, POWER OF.

**salmon dealer's licence.** It is not lawful for any person, other than the Electricity Supply Board, to sell, expose for sale or keep for sale at any place salmon or trout unless, such person is the holder of a salmon dealer's licence, and such place is a place at which he is authorised by that licence to sell salmon or trout: Fisheries Act 1959 s.156 and 1980 s.50. It is an offence for any person to buy salmon or trout from a person whom he knows or has reason to believe is selling in breach of the licensing provision. A licence is similarly required for the export for sale of salmon or trout (ibid 1959 Act s.157 and 1980 Act s.50).

**salmon rod licence.** A licence which authorises the person named therein to use during the period and in the fishing district specified therein, a salmon rod: Fisheries (Amendment) Act 1991 s.16.

**salus populi est suprema lex.** [The welfare of the people is the paramount law].

**salvage.** (1) The voluntary saving of maritime property from danger at sea.

(2) The compensation allowed to salvors by whose assistance a ship or cargo or the lives of persons belonging to her are saved from danger or loss at sea. Salvage includes "a reference to such claims for services rendered in saving life from a ship or in preserving cargo, apparel or wreck as, under sections 544 to 546 of the Merchant Shipping Act 1894, are authorised to be made in connection with a ship (including in the case of cargo or wreck salvage claims in respect of cargo or wreck found on land)": Jurisdiction of Courts (Maritime Conventions) Act 1989 s.2.

To confirm and validate a salvage service: (a) the service must have been rendered to a legally-recognised subject of salvage ie to vessels, their apparel, cargo and merchandise, bunkers, wreck and *freight at risk*; (b) the service must have been voluntary; (c) the subject of the salvage must have been in danger;

472

and (d) the service must be successful. Where salvage services are rendered by any State ship, the Minister is entitled to claim salvage; his consent is required to salvage proceedings instituted by the commander or crew of such State ship: Defence Act 1954 ss.315-316.

(3) The damaged property to which a marine insurer is entitled, where the cost of repairs will exceed the repaired value, and where the doctrine of *constructive total loss* (qv) comes into play; in which event, the insured is entitled to give notice of abandonment and the insurer is bound to pay the full value as for a total loss and becomes entitled to the subject matter insured. There is no such doctrine in non-marine insurance law and the insured is, strictly speaking, only entitled to the difference between the value of the undamaged property and the value of what remains. In practice, however, insurers often pay as for a total loss of goods which are seriously damaged and when they do so they are entitled to the damaged goods as salvage, or their value. [Text: Hill UK]. See INEQUALITY OF POSITION; RE-INSTATEMENT.

**salvage payments.** Payments made in respect of property which will be repaid before all other prior charges on the property, provided (a) the payments had the effect of saving the property from loss, (b) the payments were made by a person with an interest in the property, and (c) the payments were made voluntarily and not under any duty or obligation, or as agent for someone else: In re Powers' Policies (1899) 1 IR 6; In re Kavanagh (1952) Ir Jur Rep 38.

**salvo jure.** [Without prejudice].

**sample.** Specimen presented for examination as evidence of the composition or quality of the whole. See Murdoch: (1981) 44 MLR 388. See SAMPLE, SALE BY.

**sample, sale by.** In a contract for sale by sample there is an implied condition that the bulk will correspond with the sample in quality, that the buyer will have a reasonable opportunity of comparing the bulk with the sample, and that the goods will be free from any defect rendering them unmerchantable, which would not be apparent on reasonable examination of the sample: SGSS Act 1980 s.10. There are similar provisions governing goods which are let

under a hire-purchase agreement (ibid s.29). See MERCHANTABLE QUALITY.

**sanction.** A penalty or punishment as a means of enforcing obedience to the law.

**sanctuary.** Formerly, consecrated places where execution of the law could not take place. It has been held that there was no form of sanctuary which could be availed of by a person who had been requested to submit to a breath test, on the basis that at the time of the request, his vehicle was in the car park of a hotel: Dougal v Mahon (1989) 7ILT Dig 229.

**sanitary authorities.** Sanitary authorities comprise all the country boroughs and borough corporations, county councils and urban district councils (qqv). See Public Health Act 1878. See SANITARY SERVICES.

**sanitary authorities and nuisances.** Sanitary authorities (qv) have a duty to inspect their districts from time to time and take steps to abate nuisances (qv): Public Health (Ireland) Act 1878. Nuisances include any accumulation or deposit which is a *nuisance or injurious to health*. A *summary* (qv) procedure is provided for, which involves serving a notice on the person by whose act, default or sufferance the nuisance arises or continues (ibid s.110). Certain matters are deemed to be nuisances liable to be dealt with in a summary manner (ibid 1878 Act s.107 as amended by the Factories Act 1955 and the Office Premises Act 1958).

*Nuisance or injurious to health* include not only things which are injurious to health, but also anything which, though not injurious to health, really diminishes the comfort of life: Bishop Auckland Local Board v Bishop Auckland Iron Co (1882) 10 QBD 138.

**sanitary conveniences.** Urinals, water closets, privies and ashpits and other similar conveniences for public accommodation which a local authority is empowered to provide: Public Health (Ireland) Act 1878 s.49. A local authority is not authorised to construct such a convenience in such a location as to be a nuisance (qv): Sellors v Matlock Bath Local Board (1884-85) 14 QBD 928. See also Public Health Acts Amendment Act 1890 ss.20-21; Public Health Acts Amendment Act 1907 ss.39 and 47.

**sanitary facilities.** Every employer is

required to provide and maintain suitable and sufficient sanitary and washing facilities available for the use of employees; more stringent requirements are laid down for places of work which are used for the first time after 1992 or which undergo modification after 1992 or where required by the features of the place of work: SI No 44 of 1993, reg.17, second to fourth schedules.

**sanitary services.** The services which *sanitary authorities* have a duty or are empowered to provide eg the provision and maintenance of sewers and of water supplies, the abatement of nuisances, the control of building standards, the prevention of buildings becoming dangerous, refuse collection, street cleaning and lighting, and the provision of burial grounds: Local Government (Sanitary Services) Act 1878 to 1964.

**sanity, presumption of.** See INSANITY; McNAGHTEN RULES.

**sans frais.** [Without expense]. An endorsement of a bill of exchange *sans frais* indicates that the endorser accepts liability for the value of the bill but not for the expenses involved in enforcing it. See Bills of Exchange Act 1882 s.16. See ENDORSEMENT.

**sans recours.** [Without recourse (to me)]. An endorsement on a bill of exchange such that the endorser (eg an agent endorsing for his principal) is not personally liable: Bills of Exchange Act 1882 s.16.

**Saorstat Eireann.** The Irish Free State; the previous name of the territory of Ireland: Constitution of the Irish Free State (Saorstat Eireann) 1922; Articles of Agreement for a Treaty between Great Britain and Ireland (6th December 1921). The laws in force in Saorstat Eireann continue to have full force and effect until repealed or amended, provided they are not repugnant to the 1937 Constitution (ibid art.50). See LEGISLATION, CONSTITUTIONALITY OF.

**satisfaction.** (1) The extinguishment of an obligation or a claim by performance. See Murphy & Murphy (infants) v O'Dononue Ltd & Ors (1992 SC) ILRM 378.

(2) The equitable doctrine by which the donation of property, if accepted by the donee, operates as a complete or pro tanto discharge of a prior claim of the donee: Lord Chichester v Coventry (1867) 36 LJ Ch 673. A prior debt may be satisfied by a legacy, where the legacy is a sum of money equal to or greater than the debt: Talbot v Duke of Shrewsbury (1714) Prec Ch 394. Equity presumes a person is just before he is generous. A portion (qv) may be satisfied by a legacy eg where a father or person *in loco parentis* covenants to provide a portion and subsequently gives a legacy, the court will presume that the covenant is satisfied by the legacy in toto or pro tanto depending on the amount of the legacy. See Ellard v Phelan (1914) 1 IR 76.

**satisfaction, certificate of.** The certificate which issues from the judgments office of the courts to authenticate that a judgment has been paid. Lodgement of this certificate (a) in the Registry of Deeds will operate as a reconveyance of the land so as to vacate a judgment mortgage in the case of unregistered land or (b) to cancel a judgment mortgage as a burden on registered land: Judgment Mortgage Act 1850 s.9; Judgment Mortgage Act 1858; Registration of Title Act 1964.

**satisfaction piece.** A creditor's document which shows that a debt has been paid.

**satisfied.** The use of the word *satisfied* in the Mental Treatment Act 1945 (s.260) indicates that the Oireachtas had in mind a higher standard of proof than that which a plaintiff ordinarily would be required to discharge in a civil case: O'Dowd v North Western Health Board (1983 SC) ILRM 186.

**savings protection scheme.** A scheme of protection for depositors with licensed banks whereby a depositor may be compensated for 80 per cent of a deposit up to £5,000 (or the first £5,000 of a larger deposit), 70 per cent in respect of the next £5,000 of a deposit and 50 per cent in respect of the next £5,000, thereby providing maximum compensation of £10,000 for a qualifying deposit of £15,000 or more: Central Bank Act 1989, Chapter V, ss.53-73.

The Minister is empowered to provide, by regulations, for the application to shareholdings in and deposits with building societies of the provision of any enactment for the protection of deposits with banks (*the savings protection scheme*):

Building Societies Act 1989 s.94. Although a shareholding ranks behind a deposit in a winding up, the regulations may provide for the treatment of shareholdings as deposits for the purpose of the scheme or for the exclusion of certain shareholders and depositors eg these could be persons involved in the management of the society (ibid s.94(2)(b) and (2)(c)). The regulations may also provide for the transfer of deposits maintained by societies with the Central Bank to an account maintained by the Central Bank for the purposes of the savings protection scheme (ibid s.94(2)(a)).

The savings protection scheme was provided for, as regards most deposits with and shareholdings in building societies, in 1990: Building Societies (Savings Protection) Regulations 1990 (SI No 108 of 1990).

**SC.** Senior counsel (qv).

**sc; scil; scilicet.** [That is to say].

**scandalising the court.** The offence of contempt of court which arises when what is said or done by the accused is of such a nature as to be calculated to endanger public confidence in the court and thereby interfere with the administration of justice: State (DPP) v Walsh (1981) IR 412 cited in Desmond & Dedeir v Glackin & Minister for Industry & Commerce (1992 HC) ILRM 489.

**scandalous matter.** The court may at any stage of proceedings, order to be struck out or amended any matter in any endorsement or pleading which is scandalous or which may tend to prejudice, embarrass or delay the fair trial of the action: RSC O.19 r.27. See OFFENSIVE WORDS.

**schedule.** An appendix to an Act of the Oireachtas or to a Statutory Instrument (qv).

**scheduled offence.** An offence declared to be a *scheduled offence* by order of the government when Part V of the Offences Against the State Act 1939 is in force. Part V provides for the establishment of *Special Criminal Courts* and is brought into force by proclamation whenever the government is satisfied that the ordinary courts are inadequate to secure the effective administration of justice and the preservation of public peace and order: SI No 142 of 1972.

Conviction of a scheduled offence in a Special Criminal Court previously resulted in forfeiture of any office or employment which was renumerated out of public funds: 1939 Act s.34; this section however has been found to be unconstitutional as it amounted to an unreasonable and unjustified interference with personal rights; Cox v Ireland (1991 HC) 9ILT Dig 170; the section was impermissibly wide and discriminate (ibid 1992 SC) 10 ILT Dig 55.

There is no requirement that an arrest under the 1939 Act s.30 must be predominantly motivated by a desire to investigate a scheduled offence: The People (DPP) v Howley (1989 SC) ILRM 629. Scheduled offences are heard by the Special Criminal Court (qv). Scheduled offences have been declared to be offences under the Malicious Damage Act 1861 (now largely repealed), Explosive Substances Act 1883, Firearms Act 1925 to 1971, Offences Against the State Act 1939 and the Conspiracy and Protection of Property Act 1875 (SI No 282 of 1972).

**scheme of arrangement.** An agreement between a debtor and his creditors allowing his debts to be paid in accordance with that agreement, rather than by his being adjudged a bankrupt. In bankruptcy, the court has power to approve a *scheme of arrangement*. For provisions regarding an arrangement with creditors, see ARRANGING DEBTOR. See also COMPOSITION; BANKRUPTCY; RECONSTRUCTION OF COMPANY.

**school attendance.** It is an offence for a parent not to comply with a warning issued to him for failing to send a child below the school leaving age (qv), to school: School Attendance Act 1926 s.17; SI No 105 of 1972. Where a parent fails to send a child to school, a *care order* may be made, committing the child to the care of the health board (qv): Child Care Act 1991 s.75 amending the 1926 Act s.17.

**school authority's duty.** The duty of care owed by a school authority to pupils while on its premises in course of normal school activities is to take reasonable care to protect them from foreseeable risks of personal injury or harm: Mapp (an infant) v Gilhooley (1990 HC) ITLR (5 Mar). In measuring that duty, the court must take into account all relevant factors, including the age of the children, the activities in which they may be engaged, the degree of supervision and the opportunity which those in charge had to prevent or minimise the mischief complained of. The school authority's duty to supervise pupils does not extend to pupils waiting to be collected outside school grounds after school hours: Dolan v Keohane (1992 HC) ITLR (27 Apr). See CORPORAL PUNISHMENT; PRE-SCHOOL SERVICE.

**school discipline.** See DISCIPLINE IN SCHOOL; CORPORAL PUNISHMENT.

**school leaving age.** The age at which the School Attendance Act 1926 ceases to apply. It is currently 15 years of age: School Attendance Act 1926 (Extension of Application) Order 1972 (SI No 105 of 1972). The government has proposed to increase the school leaving age to 16: Green Paper on Education 1992.

**scienter.** Knowledge. The common law rule that an animal must be kept securely by its owner from causing damage where he knows or is presumed to know of its mischievous disposition. The requirement of *scienter* is not that the dog *will* bite somebody but that, having displayed a vicious propensity, it *may* do so: McCarthy N in Duggan v Armstrong (1993 SC) ILRM 222. The owner of a dog is now liable for damage caused in an attack on any person by the dog and for injury done by it to any livestock; it is no longer necessary to show a previous mischievous propensity in the dog: Control of Dogs Act 1986 s.21. The *scienter* action however has not been abolished; there is now a statutory remedy under s.21 and the common law remedy. A circuit court judge is reported as having said "the days when a dog is entitled to a first bite are gone": Martin F in O'Sullivan v Delahunty (1988 CC) — Irish Times 19/9/1988. See also Kavanagh v Centreline Ltd (1987) IRLM 306. See ANIMALS; DOGS.

**scientific evidence.** The courts must not take on the role of a determining scientific authority resolving disputes between scientists; the court should apply common sense and an understanding of the logic and likelyhood of events to conflicting opinions and theories: Best v Wellcome Foundation Ltd (1992 SC)

ILRM 609.

**scientific societies.** Societies established exclusively for the promotion of science, literature or the fine arts may under a certificate granted by the Registrar of Friendly Societies, obtain an exemption from local rates in respect of lands and buildings occupied by them: Scientific Societies Act 1843.

**scintilla juris.** [A spark or fragment of a right].

**scribere est agere.** [To write is to act].

**scrip.** A memorandum or certificate of shares (qv) in a company; it is generally a negotiable instrument (qv).

**scrip dividend.** The allocation to a member of a company of ordinary shares in the company in lieu of a cash dividend; the shares are treated as fully paid up. Often called *bonus shares* or *scrip issue*. A scrip issue enables a company to increase its equity while avoiding the transaction costs normally associated with share issues. Formerly, a scrip issue was treated for tax purposes as income to the value of the cash dividend foregone: Finance Act 1974 s.56. Now, no tax charge arises from the acquisition; in the event of a subsequent disposal, the additional shares are treated as acquired, at no additional cost, at the same time as the earlier shareholding was acquired by the shareholder: Finance Act 1993 s.36. See BONUS SHARES.

**script.** A draft of a will (qv) or codicil (qv) or written instructions relating thereto. See RCC Form 27.

**scrutiny.** An inquiry into the validity of votes recorded in an election.

**sculpture.** See ARTISTIC WORK; ARTIST, TAX EXEMPTION OF.

**scuttling.** The deliberate sinking of a ship for the purpose of recovering insurance money.

**S E.** [Societas Europaea]. See EUROPEAN COMPANY.

**se defendendo.** [In self-defence (qv)].

**sea, carriage by.** See CARRIAGE BY SEA.

**sea pollution.** Local authorities have responsibility for the protection of the coastline from pollution arising from an incident at sea. Ships are required to have certain oil pollution equipment on board and to follow specified procedures to reduce the discharge of oil into the sea; similar requirements apply to chemical tankers to prevent pollutant discharges: Sea Pollution Act 1991 (Annexes I & II of MARPOL). When regulations are made there will be requirements to prevent pollution by sewage, garbage or by harmful substances (Annexes III, IV and V). See also Oil Pollution of the Sea Act 1977. See also DUMPING AT SEA; OIL POLLUTION.

**seal.** Wax impressed and attached to a document so as to authenticate it. Sealing is a solemn mode of expressing consent to a written instrument. "To constitute a sealing neither wax nor wafer nor a piece of paper, not even an impression is necessary": Re Sandilands (1871) LR 6CP 411. Every company must have a seal with its name engraved on it: Companies Act 1963 s.114(b). Contracts which require the company seal for their execution include conveyancing of property, granting a power of attorney, issuing share certificates and warrants (ibid ss.40 and 87 as amended by Companies Amendment Act 1977 s.5). See In re Hussey (1987) HC. See also Presidential Seal Act 1937. See RSC O.116. See DEED.

**Seanad Eireann.** The upper house of the Oireachtas, established by the 1937 Constitution, composed of sixty members, of whom eleven are *nominated* members and forty-nine are *elected* members (ibid art.18). The nominated members, are nominated, with their prior consent, by the Taoiseach. Six of the forty-nine elected members are elected by university graduates who have reached the age of eighteen years and are Irish citizens; at present Dublin University graduates elect three members, and the National University of Ireland graduates also elect three members: Seanad Electoral (University Members) Act 1937 as amended by Electoral Act 1992 s.166. In 1979, the seventh amendment to the Constitution was passed which permitted a redistribution by law of these six seats among the existing universities and other institutions of higher education; no such legislation has been enacted as of 1993.

The remaining forty-three members are elected from panels: 1937 Constitution, art.18(7). The electorate is confined to members of the new Dail, members of the outgoing Seanad, and the elected members of the county and borough councils. Voting is by secret postal ballot.

See Seanad Electoral (Panel Members) Acts 1947 and 1954; Iris Oifigiuil — 19th March 1993. See DISSOLUTION; UTTERANCE.

**search warrant.** A written order giving authority to the person named therein to enter specified premises and to search for and seize specified property. Certain statutes empower the issuing of a warrant which permits not only the searching of premises but also any persons found on the premises eg Offences Against the State Act 1939 s.29 and Misuse of Drugs Act 1977 s.26(2). The gardai have wide powers of search and seizure for which they do not require the protection of a search warrant: Jennings v Quinn (1968) IR 305.

Some statutes require that the information grounding an application for a search warrant is to be laid by a particular person eg a member of the Garda Siochana not below the rank of inspector. A search warrant may be issued by someone who is not a judge eg a peace commissioner (qv): Ryan v O'Callaghan (1987) HC; Larceny Act 1916 s.42. For power of a garda to seize any property during a search which he believes to be evidence of an offence, see Criminal Law Act 1976 s.9. See also Criminal Justice Act 1984 s.6; Criminal Damage Act 1991 s.13; Child Care Act 1991 s.35; Criminal Justice (Sexual Offences) Act 1993 ss.10(1) and 12. See FORCIBLE ENTRY; STOP AND SEARCH; WARRANT.

**searches.** Investigations made by or on behalf of a purchaser for the purpose of finding any incumbrances affecting the title to property. Searches in the Registry of Deeds comprise: (a) *hand search* which may be made by any member of the public; (b) *official search* with the issue of an official certificate of the result.

Official searches comprise a *common search* and a *negative search*, the latter rendering the officials, signing the certificate issued therein, liable to damages to the party aggrieved by any fraud, collusion or neglect in making the search. The search is directed at ascertaining whether any acts are disclosed by the Registry which are inconsistent with the title as disclosed by the *abstract of title* (qv).

It may be necessary to conduct a search in the Companies Office in respect of charges registered pursuant to the Companies Act 1963: Roche v Peilow (1986) ILRM 189. The Controller of Patents will on request cause a search to be made as regards any product, process or apparatus: Patents Act 1992 s.89. A search report is an essential pre-requisite to any action for infringement of a *short-term* patent (qv) (ibid s.66). See CHARGE, REGISTRATION OF; LAND REGISTRATION.

**seashore.** The foreshore (qv) and every beach, bank, and cliff contiguous thereto and includes all sands and rocks contiguous to the foreshore; the removal of beach material (qv) from the seashore in contravention of a *prohibitory order* is an offence: Foreshore Act 1933 ss.1 and 6.

**season, open.** See OPEN SEASON.

**seat belt.** See SAFETY BELT.

**seat of corporation.** The domicile of a corporation; a corporation has its seat in the State if, but only if (a) it was incorporated or formed under the law of the State, or (b) its central management and control is exercised in the State: Jurisdiction of Courts and Enforcement of Judgments (European Communities) Act 1988 s.13(2).

**seaweed.** It has been held that the general public has no right to enter on the foreshore (qv) to take away seaweed: Mahoney v Neenan (1966) IR 559. However, seaweed driven above high water mark belongs to the owner of the land upon which it is driven and seaweed floating in the sea may be recovered by the general public in exercise of the public right to fish in the sea: Brew v Haren (1877) IR 11 CL 198.

**seaworthiness of ship.** In a voyage policy (qv) of insurance there is an implied warranty that at the commencement of the voyage the ship shall be seaworthy for the purposes of the particular adventure insured: Marine Insurance Act 1906 s.39(1). See PASSENGER BOAT; PASSENGER SHIP.

**second mortgage.** A mortgage subsequent to a prior mortgage. See PRIOR MORTGAGE.

**secondary facts.** Inferred facts; facts which do not follow directly from an assessment or evaluation of the credibility of the witnesses by the trial judge, or the weight to be attached to their evidence, but derive from inferences drawn from the *primary* facts. The Supreme Court will draw its own inferences on an appeal where it considers that the inferences drawn by the trial judge were not correct: JM and GM v An Bord Uchtala (1988) ILRM 203; Hanrahan v Merck Sharpe & Dohme (Irl) Ltd (1988 SC) ILRM 629. See also Pernod Ricard v FII (Fyffes) 7 ILT Dig (1989) 53. Contrast with PRIMARY FACT. See FACT.

**secondary picketing.** Picketing of an employer who is not a party to a trade dispute. It is lawful if it is reasonable for the picketers to believe at the commencement of their attendance and throughout the continuance of their attendance that the employer being picketed has directly *assisted* the employer in dispute for the purposes of frustrating the strike or other industrial action: Industrial Relations Act 1990 s.11. Any action taken by an employer in the health services to maintain life-preserving services, during the strike or industrial action, does not constitute assistance (ibid s.11(3)). See PICKETING; STRIKE.

**secondment.** Temporary removal from employment. There is generally a provision in Acts establishing state-sponsored organisations that an employee stands seconded from employment with the organisation immediately upon election to either House of the Oireachtas or of the Assembly of the European Communities until he ceases to be a member eg see Industrial Development Act 1986 s.40(2); Environmental Protection Agency Act 1992 s.35(2).

**secret, official.** See OFFICIAL SECRET.

**secret ballot.** See BALLOT; STRIKE.

**secret manufacturing process.** See PUBLIC JUSTICE.

**secret prior use.** Acts carried out before the date of filing or priority of a patent by a person in the State which would have constituted an infringement of the patent if it were in force: Patents Act 1992 s.55(1). Such a person is allowed to continue to carry out such acts and to assign his rights without infringing the patent (ibid s.55(2)).

**secret profit.** It is a breach of duty for an agent to make a secret profit, (or accept a bribe), beyond the commission agreed with the principal, in which event the principal: may recover the amount of the secret profit from the agent; may refuse to pay the agent commission; may dismiss the agent without notice; may repudiate the contract the subject of the secret payment whether or not the secret payment had had any effect on the contract; and may sue the agent receiving and the third party giving the secret payment for any loss he may have sustained by entering the contract. An agent receiving and a person paying a bribe commit a criminal offence: Prevention of Corruption Act 1906. See BRIBERY AND CORRUPTION.

**secret societies.** The promotion of secret societies within the army or Garda Siochana is an offence: Offences Against the State Act 1939 s.16.

**secret trust.** An express trust (qv) based on the expressed intention of the settlor communicated to and acquiesced in by the secret trustee. A secret trust may be a *fully secret* one where the existence of the trust or its terms are not disclosed in the will or other instrument creating it: Revenue Commissioners v Stapleton (1937) IR 225; or a *half secret* trust where property is given on trust to trustees but the particulars of the trust are not disclosed in the will or instrument itself: In re Browne (1944) IR 90.

A secret trust by will must be communicated to the legatee in the testator's lifetime before or after the execution of the will; the legatee must accept the trust, or at least must not object; the terms of the trust must not be vague or uncertain; and the trust must not be illegal: In re Kings Estate (1888) 21 LR Ir 273.

**secretary.** The person in a company whose principal function is regarded as being to ensure that the company's affairs are conducted in accordance with the law and with its own regulations. Every company must have a secretary, who may be one of the directors: Companies Act 1963 s.175.

There are no professional qualifications required of a secretary; the position may be occupied by a body corporate. However, the directors of a *public limited company* must take all reasonable steps to ensure that the secretary is a person who appears to them to have the requisite knowledge and experience to discharge the functions of secretary: Companies

Act 1990 s.236. A register must be kept by a company of the name and address of its secretary: 1963 Act s.195 as substituted by the 1990 Act s.51. The secretary must also be named in the statement required to be delivered to the Registrar of Companies: Companies Amendment Act 1982 s.3.

The duties of the secretary are, inter alia, to sign the annual return which is made to the Registrar; to issue share and debenture certificates; to deliver to the Registrar a return of all allotments of shares; to keep and make available for inspection the minutes of general meetings and the various registers concerning shareholders, debenture holders, charges, director and secretaries; to send out copies of the balance sheet and the auditors' and directors' reports; and to ensure that the company's name is published on its business letters. For secretary of building society, see Building Societies Act 1989 ss.14(2) and 49. [Text: Doyle; McCann (4)]. See REGISTRAR OF COMPANIES.

**section 4 resolution.** Generally understood to mean a resolution of the elected members of a local authority requiring the manager to do any particular act, matter or thing: City and County Management (Amendment) Act 1955 s.4. Under the section, a local authority may by resolution require any particular act, matter or thing specifically mentioned in the resolution and which the local authority or the manager can lawfully do or effect, to be done or effected in performance of the executive functions of the local authority.

The intention to propose such a resolution must be given in writing to the county manager and, except for planning matters, must be signed by at least three members of the council; the resolution must be passed by a majority of members present but in circumstances where the number of members voting in favour exceeds one-third of the total number of the members (ibid s.4(6)).

There are limitations, however, in that such a resolution does not extend to the performance or any function or duty of a local authority *generally*, or to the *executive* functions of the manager in relation to officers and servants of the local authority, or to matters which he cannot lawfully do.

In addition such a resolution can only be put into effect if and when and so far as money for the purpose is or has been provided. Once such a resolution is validly passed, the elected members are *functus officii* and it is likely that it cannot be rescinded, revoked or varied: Interpretation Act 1937 s.15(3). A council resolution which is not in exercise of a reserved function of a power derived from s.4 is not binding on the manager; he is free to act on it as he thinks fit: Browne v Dundalk UDC (1993 HC) ILRM 328.

Section 4 resolutions have been frequently used to require the manager to decide an application for planning permission (qv) in a particular manner. Since 1991, the notice required for a Section 4 resolution in planning matters must be signed by not less than three-quarters of the total members and the resolution requires not less than three-quarters of the total members voting in favour to be passed: Local Government Act 1991 ss.44-45. It has been held that a planning authority exercising its powers under s.4 of the 1955 Act must do so in a judicial manner, without taking into consideration irrelevant considerations, and that once such a resolution is made the Manager was bound to carry out the decision as a mere executive duty: Sharpe Ltd v Dublin City & County Manager (1989) ILRM 545; Flanagan v Galway City & County Manager (1990) 2 IR 66. See also Griffin v Galway City & Co Mgr (1991 HC) 9ILT Dig 226; Kenny Homes v Galway Corporation (1992 HC). See COUNTY MANAGER; SURCHARGE.

**section 23 relief.** Generally understood to mean the tax relief obtained by a person incurring expenditure on the construction of certain residential premises for letting, whereby he can deduct the qualifying expenditure from the resulting rental income: Finance Act 1981 s.23 and 24. The qualifying period of this scheme was originally extended to 31st March 1987: Finance Act 1983 s.29-30. The qualifying period of the restored scheme was 27th January 1988 to 31st March 1991: Finance Act 1988 s.27. There was also a scheme of tax relief applicable to expenditure incurred on the *refurbishment* of *specified buildings*:

Finance Act 1985 s.21 which was similarly restored: Finance Act 1988 s.28. There was a further extension of the time limits in areas designated under the urban renewal scheme ie to end November 1993 in respect of laying foundations for new-building developments, while the final deadline for relief is extended to 31st July 1994: Finance Act 1993 s.32. [Text: Judge].

**section 31.** Popularly understood to refer to the power given to the Minister to direct Radio Telefis Eireann by order to refrain from broadcasting any matter or any matter of a particular class, where the Minister is of the opinion that the broadcast of such matter would be likely to promote, or incite to, crime or would tend to undermine the authority of the State: Broadcasting Authority Act 1960 s.31(1) as amended by the Broadcasting Authority Act 1976 s.16. Any such order may remain in force for not greater than twelve months, which period may be extended (ibid s.31(1)A and (1)B). Any such order also applies to independent radio and television broadcasts: Radio and Television Act 1988 ss.12 and 18. For example, see SI No 1 of 1993.

The European Commission of Human Rights has held that the restrictions imposed by Section 31 were legitimate: Purcell, O'Cuaig & Ors v Ireland (1991) — Irish Times 11/6/1991. The Supreme Court has held that while RTE has a legal duty to obey a ministerial order made pursuant to section 31 prohibiting the broadcast of reports of interviews with spokesmen for Sinn Fein, such a duty did not extend to prohibiting the broadcasting on any subject or under any circumstances of a person who was a member of Sinn Fein: O'Toole v RTE (No 2) (1993 SC) ILRM 458. See also The State (Lynch) v Cooney (1983) ILRM 89; O'Toole v RTE (1993) ILRM 454.

**secundum legem.** [According to law].

**secured creditor.** See CREDITOR.

**securities.** (1) Things deposited or pledged to ensure the fulfilling of an obligation. (2) Written evidence of ownership eg certificates. (3) *Securities* are also defined as shares in the share capital of any body corporate or stock of any body corporate, or debentures, debenture stock or bonds of any body corporate: Central Bank Act 1971 s.2. See also Building Societies Act 1989 s.29(2)(c). See DEBENTURE; PRE-EMPTION; STOCK EXCHANGE; UNIT TRUST SCHEME.

**securitisation of mortgage.** The transfer, sale or assignment of mortgages often to a company or body which specialises in the management of such mortgages. The Minister is empowered to make regulations governing the securitisation of mortgages of residential property: Housing (Miscellaneous Provisions) Act 1992 s.13. These regulations may deal generally with the protection of the interests of mortgagors and may prescribe such matters as eg information to be given to mortgagors, the obtaining of their consent to the disposal, and undertakings to be given by the body acquiring the mortgage. The management of these *qualifying assets*, which the body acquires from the original lender, is subject to tax on the profit or gains: Finance Act 1991 s.31.

**security for costs.** The security, by way of lodgment into court of money or by a bond, which the court may order the plaintiff in an action to provide, on the application of the defendant: RSC O.29. Security may be ordered eg (a) where the plaintiff resides outside the jurisdiction and the defendant has a defence upon the merits; (b) where an insolvent person sues as nominal plaintiff for another; (c) where the plaintiff is a company without realisable assets. See Thalle v Soares (1957) IR 182.

The amount of such security and the time and manner in which it is given is determined by the Master of the High Court and is usually fixed at one third of the estimated costs involved; the court must bear in mind that no litigant should be denied access to the courts because of poverty: ibid RSC O.29 rr.6-7 and Fallon v An Bord Pleanala (1991 SC) ILRM 799.

The court may refuse to order security if a prima facie case has been made by the plaintiff that his inability to give security flows from the wrong committed by the defendant: Collins v Doyle (1982) ILRM 495; Jack O'Toole Ltd v MacEoin Kelly (1987) ILRM 269. The court has a discretion as regards a company's security for costs pursuant to an application under the Companies Act 1963

s.390 (ie where there is reason to believe that the company will be unable to pay the defendant's costs if successful in his defence): SPUC v Grogan (1990 HC) ITLR (12 Feb). Security for costs will not be ordered where a plaintiff insolvent company has sufficient funds available to pay the costs, as these costs would rank in priority to all other claims: Companies Act 1963 ss.281 and 285; Comhlucht Paipear Riomhaireachta Teo v Udaras na Gaeltachta (1990 SC) ILRM 266.

Security for costs of a respondent (qv) will be ordered only in special circumstances eg the appellant's lack of means to pay the costs of the appeal if it is unsuccessful and the absence of good grounds of appeal.

For provisions dealing with security for costs in the Circuit and District Courts, see RCC O.13; DCR r.152. See also Arbitration Act 1954 s.22(1)(a); Building Societies Act 1989 s.64(6). See SEE Co Ltd v Public Lighting Services (1987) ILRM 255; Salih v General Accident Fire Life Assurance Corporation (1987 HC) IR 628; Irish Commercial Society v Plunkett (1987) ILRM 504; Performing Rights Society Ltd v Casey (1990) 8ILT Dig 105. See Patents Act 1992 s.91. See NORTHERN IRELAND.

**security of tenure.** See TENURE, SECURITY OF.

**secus.** [Otherwise].

**sed quaere.** [But question]. Enquire further.

**sedition.** The publication, orally or in writing, of words intended to bring into hatred or contempt, or to excite disaffection against the government and parliament, or to raise discontent or disaffection among the people of the State or to promote ill will and hostility between different classes of people: R v Burns (1886) 16 Cox CC 335. *Sedition* must be punishable in accordance with law: 1937 Constitution, art.40(6)(1)(i). [Text: Larkin]. See also LIBEL.

**seduction.** The tort of undue persuasion of a person whereby the services of the party seduced are lost to another, where the relationship of master and servant existed between the party seduced and that other. No action now lies for inducing a spouse to leave or remain apart from the other spouse: Family Law

Act 1981 s.1(1).

A parent however, continues to have a right of action against a person who entices, harbours or seduces his child. The action is now regarded as anacronistic. See Hamilton v Long (1903) 2 IR 407; Murray v Fitzgerald (1906) 2 IR 254; Brennan v Kearns (1943) 77 ILTR 194. See also LRC Working Papers 6 and 7 of 1979 and Report No 1 of 1981. See PER QUOD SERVITIUM AMISIT.

**segregation.** A housing authority is required to draw up and adopt a written statement of their policy to counteract undue segregation in housing between people of different social backgrounds: Housing Act 1988 s.20(1A) as inserted by Housing (Miscellaneous Provisions) Act 1992 s.28. This is a *reserved function* (qv) of the authority.

**seised.** Feudal term referring to one possessed of a freehold (qv).

**seisin.** Feudal concept of possession.

**self assessment.** Provision for the assessment and collection of income tax from the self-employed and certain other persons is provided for by the Finance Act 1988 ss.9-21. Self assessment in respect of gifts and inheritance taxes was introduced by the Finance Act 1989 s.74. Companies were brought within the self-assessment procedure by the Taxation of Companies (Self-Assessment) Regulations 1989, SI 178 of 1989. [Text: Cassells, Clayton & Moore]. See PRELIMINARY TAX.

**self defence.** Acting so as to defend one's person, the person of another, or one's own or another's property against feloneous attack. A person so acting may be excused from doing an act which would otherwise be an offence.

In relation to a charge of murder (qv), if the accused used more force than may objectively be considered to be necessary for his own protection, then the killing is unlawful; in such circumstances, the act will be murder if the accused has *malice aforethought* (qv). If the accused used more force than was reasonably necessary but no more than he honestly believed to be necessary in the circumstances, then there is no malice aforethought and the unlawful act is manslaughter: The People (Attorney General) v Dwyer (1972) IR 416.

A person who is attacked is entitled to use *proportionate* force in retaliation to protect himself; he is entitled to defend not only himself and his family but anyone else who is attacked in his presence: People v Keatley (1954) IR 12. The killing of a trespasser of property will only be justified where the interference involves a felony of violence (eg robbery, arson or burglary) and only where the interference is used so as to endanger life. See also The People (Attorney General) v Commane (1975) CCA.

**self-employed.** Safety health and welfare at work regulations apply to a self-employed person as they apply to an employer and as if that self-employed person was an employer and his own employee: SI No 44 of 1993, reg.4(1). See also SELF ASSESSMENT.

**self-help.** An extra-judicial remedy eg in the case of trespass where the person in possession may eject the trespasser using no more force than is necesssary: Green v Goddard (1798) 2 Salk 641. The removal of persons from an aircraft who have committed or are about to commit an offence is authorised: Air Navigation and Transport Act 1975 s.4(4)(a). See DISTRESS.

**self-service.** Commonly understood to mean where a buyer selects goods which are exposed for sale. A sale of goods in this manner does not prevent the sale from being a sale by description: Sale of Goods Act 1893 s.13; SGSS Act 1980 s.10. See DESCRIPTION, SALE BY.

**seller.** A person who sells or agrees to sell goods: Sale of Goods Act 1893 s.62. A seller may maintain an action against the buyer for the price of the goods, where the property in the goods has passed to the buyer, and the buyer wrongfully neglects and refuses to pay for the goods (ibid s.49). A seller also may maintain an action for non-acceptance of goods by the buyer (ibid s.50). See RSC O.4 r.13; O.13 r.15; O.27 rr.2 and 16. See See Spicer-Cowan Ireland Ltd v Play Print Ltd (1980) HC. See UNPAID SELLER.

**semble.** [It appears]. Term used in law reports and text books where a proposition of law is introduced which cannot be stated too definitely as there may be doubt about it. For example, see Murphy v Asahi Synthetic Fibres (1986) ILRM

24.

**semi-state company.** See COMPANY, STATUTORY.

**semper in dubiis benigniora praeferenda.** [In doubtful matters the more liberal construction should always be preferred].

**semper praesumitur pro legitimatione puerorum.** [It is always to be presumed that children are legitimate]. See LEGITIMACY, PRESUMPTION OF.

**senator.** A member of Seanad Eireann (qv). See SEVERANCE PAY; UTTERANCE.

**senior counsel.** A senior barrister, called to the inner bar by the Chief Justice in the Supreme Court, on the approval of the government. He takes precedence over junior counsel in court and he wears a silk gown (hence the phrase *to take silk*). See BARRISTER.

**sentence.** See Law Reform Commission Consultation Paper on Sentencing (No 45 of 1993). See PUNISHMENT; REVIEW OF SENTENCE; VICTIM IMPACT REPORT.

**separation, judicial.** See JUDICIAL SEPARATION; DIVORCE A MENSA ET THORO.

**separation agreement.** An agreement made between a husband and wife which usually contains terms relating to: the living apart of the parties; the custody of any children; the maintenance by one spouse of the other; the manner in which the family property is to be dealt with; an undertaking by each not to molest the other; an indemnification clause; and a covenant not to bring *judicial separation* proceedings for matrimonial misbehaviour prior to the agreement (see Courtney v Courtney (1923) 2 IR 31).

Such an agreement is void if it excludes or limits the operation of the Family Law (Maintenance of Spouses and Children) Act 1976 which has as its objective the protection of economically vulnerable spouses.

A separation agreement may be made a *rule of court* if the court is satisfied that it is fair and reasonable and protects the interests of both spouses and dependent children (ibid s.8). Having the agreement a rule of court enables a spouse to have *maintenance* paid through the District Court and to have it enforced by an attachment (qv) of earnings order. See Dalton v Dalton (1982) ILRM 418; PJ v JJ (1992 HC) ILRM 273. The Dublin Solicitors' Bar Association has drafted a

deed of separation: ILSI Gazette (May 1993) 139. See DIVORCE A MENSA ET THORO; DUM CASTA CLAUSE; JUDICIAL SEPARATION; MAINTENANCE AGREEMENT; MOLESTATION.

**separation of powers.** The division of the functions of government ie legislative, executive, and judicial, between independent separate institutions. The *legislative* power, which is the power to make laws for the State, is reserved to the Oireachtas: 1937 Constitution, art.15(2)(1). The *executive* power, which is the power to carry laws into effect, is vested in the government (ibid art.28(2)). The *judicial* power, which is the power to administer justice, is reserved to the Courts (ibid art.34(1)). See Buckley v Attorney General (1950) IR 67; In re Haughey (1971) IR 217; Murphy v Dublin Corporation (1972) IR 215; Boland v An Taoiseach (1974) IR 338; Crotty v An Taoiseach (1987) ILRM 400; The State (Calcul International) v Appeal Commissioners (1987) HC. See BYE-ELECTION; COMMUNITY LAW; COURTS; GOVERNMENT; OIREACHTAS.

**sequestration.** The legal process whereby a person is temporarily deprived of his property until he clears his contempt, arising from his refusal or his neglect to obey a direction to pay money into court or do any other act in a limited time, after due service of such judgment or order: RSC O.43 rr.2-4; appendix F, form 17. See also RSC O.42 rr.4 and 6. See Building Societies Act 1989 s.40(5).

**seriatim.** [In order]. Serially.

**series trade mark.** A composite mark registered as a whole and the parts as separate trade marks; each part must satisfy the conditions of an independent trade mark: Trade Marks Act 1963 s.29(1). See TRADE MARK, REGISTERED.

**serious loss of capital.** See CAPITAL, SERIOUS LOSS OF.

**serjeants-at-law.** Formerly senior barristers of the Order of the Coif who had an exclusive audience in the Court of Common Pleas. Judges were chosen from their ranks but the order died out with the abolition of this rule by the Judicature Act 1873 s.8. The last serjeant-at-law was A.M. Sullivan (1871–1959) who was called to the Irish Bar in 1892 and retained the curtesy title after the establishment of the Irish Free State (qv). [Text: Hogan & Osborough; Sullivan].

**servant.** See EMPLOYEE; OFFICE HOLDER.

**service.** The relationship of a servant to his master. See EMPLOYEE.

**service area.** A motorway scheme or a protected road scheme may include provision for a service area; facilities or services may be provided in a service area for persons and vehicles using the motorway (qv) or protected road (qv), either directly by the road authority or by agreement with the authority or jointly: Roads Act 1993 s.54.

**service, aftersale.** See SPARE PARTS.

**service, contract for and of.** See CONTRACT FOR SERVICES; CONTRACT OF SERV-ICES.

**service, supply of.** Includes the rendering or provision of a service or facility and an offer to supply: SGSS Act 1980 s.2.

In every contract for the supply of a service where the supplier is acting *in the course of a business*, the following terms are implied — (a) that the supplier has the necessary skill to render the service; (b) that he will supply the service with due skill, care and diligence; (c) that where materials are used, they will be sound and reasonably fit for the purpose for which they are required; and (d) that where goods are supplied under the contract, they will be of *merchantable quality* (qv): SGSS Act s.39. *In the course of a business* includes the professions and the activities of any State authority or local authority (ibid s.2).

The implied terms may be excluded by agreement between the parties but where the recipient of the service *deals as consumer*(qv), the exclusion must be shown to be *fair and reasonable* (qv) and that it has been specifically brought to his attention (ibid s.40). There is provision for exclusions in respect of the supply of electricity and the international carriage of passengers or goods by land, sea or air.

Certain statements purporting to restrict the rights of recipients of a service can amount to an offence (ibid s.41). See Brown v Norton (1954) IR 34; Hollier v Rambler Motors (1972) 1 All ER 399; Thornton v Shoe Lane Parking Ltd (1971) 1 All ER 686. [Text: Grogan, King & Donelan]. See VALUE ADDED TAX.

**service by post.** Where a document is required to be served by post, then, unless a contrary intention appears, it is deemed to have been effected at the time such letter would be delivered in the ordinary course of post, unless the contrary is proved: Interpretation Act 1937 s.18.See FAX; PRESUMPTION OF REGU-LARITY.

**service of summons.** See CASE STATED; FAX; SUMMONS, SERVICE OF; SUMMONS, SERV-ICE OUT OF JURISDICTION.

**service out of jurisdiction.** See LRC 22 of 1987. See SUMMONS, SERVICE OUT OF JURISDICTION.

**services, false or misleading statement as to.** It is an offence for a person in the course or for the purposes of a trade, business or profession, to make a statement which he knows to be false or to make recklessly a statement which is false to a material degree as to a number of matters relating to a service, eg provision, nature, effect, fitness, time, manner, examination, approval, use, evaluation, or place: Consumer Information Act 1978 s.6. See Director of Consumer Affairs v Sunshine Holidays Ltd (1984) ILRM 551.

**services, loss of.** See PER QUOD SERVITIUM AMISIT.

**services, provision of.** Natural and legal persons in the EC have the freedom to provide services within the EC: Treaty of Rome 1957 arts.55-66. The freedom concerns in particular activities of an industrial or commercial character and activities of craftsmen and the professions (ibid art. 50(2)). Freedom to *provide* services implies the right to *receive* services: Luisi & Carbone v Ministero del Tesoro (1984) ECR 377. Medical termination of pregnancy, performed in accordance with the law of the state in which it is carried out, constitutes a service: SPUC v Grogan 3 CMLR 1991, 849. See Council Directive 73/148 EEC. See AG v X (1992) ILRM 401.

**servient tenement.** A tenement subject to a servitude or easement (qv).

**servitium.** Services.

**servitude.** An easement (qv).

**session.** The period when the Houses of the Oireachtas are sitting.

**set aside.** To cancel; to make void. The courts have wide powers to *set aside* previous decisions on appeal eg where judgment has been entered in default of appearance of the defendant, the court is empowered to set aside or vary the judgment upon such terms as may be just: RSC O.13 r.11.

A judgment of a court may be set aside on the grounds of fraud; the complainant is required to produce evidence of new facts discovered since the judgment which would in all probability have had a significant effect on the judgment: Dennis v Leinster Paper Co (1901) 2 IR 337. Fraud must be pleaded with particularity and established on the balance of probability: Tassan Din v Banco Ambrosiano SPA (1991 HC) 1 IR 569. See also Waite v House of Spring Gardens (1985) HC; Albans Investment Company v Sun Alliance (1990) HC.

A foreign judgement may not in general be re-examined on the merits: La Societe Anonyme La Chemo-Serotherapie Belge v Dolan & Co Ltd (1961) IR 281. For discussion on whether fraud could be a ground for setting aside a foreign judgment, see Gill in 7ILT & SJ (1989) 29. See AQUACULTURE; CANCELLATION; FINALITY IN LITIGATION; RES JUDICATA.

**set down.** The request that a case be listed for hearing. See RSC O.36 r.18; RSC O.30 rr.1-4. See NOTICE OF TRIAL.

**set off.** (1) Counterbalancing of mutual debts between parties; where there is mutuality there can be set off eg Freaney v Bank of Ireland (1975) IR 376. See Barrington v Bank of Ireland (1993 HC) ITLR (19 Apr).

(2) A pleading by way of defence to the whole or part of a plaintiff's claim, whereby the defendant claims a liquidated amount; it has the same effect as a cross action and may be used as a shield as well as a sword: RSC O.19 r.2.

(3) Statutory arrangements are sometimes made to *set off* payments due by a party to an authority or person (eg a Minister) against payments due to that party from the authority or person eg Housing Acts 1966 s.10 and 1988 s.19. See In re Casey, a bankrupt (1986 HC). See also RSC O.21 r.16; O.99 r.37(14); District Court (Set-off or Counterclaim) Rules 1992 (SI No 317 of 1992). See COUNTERCLAIM.

**settle.** (1) To compromise (qv) a case. (2) To create a settlement (qv). (3) To draw up a document and decide upon its terms eg where counsel *settles* a document.

**settled account.** See ACCOUNT SETTLED.

**settled land.** Land which is the subject of a settlement (qv). See also [Text: Arnold].

**settlement.** (1) A compromise of a case. A pre-hearing settlement precludes the Employment Appeals Tribunal from hearing a claim for unfair dismissal: Duffy-Finn v Lundbeck Ltd (1990) ELR 224. *Structured* settlements are settlements whereby the plaintiff is paid an annual monetary amount, usually index-linked and paid for life with a minimum payment period; they are becoming more common in the UK. See COMPROMISE.

(2) A deed, will or other instrument under which any land stands for the time being limited to, or in trust for, any persons by way of succession: Settled Land Acts 1882 and 1890. Extensive powers are given by these Acts to the *tenant for life* or other limited owner in possession of the settled land, including the power of sale at the best price; the power to lease the land, or to exchange settled land for other land and take money for equality of exchange; the power to concur in partition of the land and to raise money by mortgage of the land.

*Capital money,* which is money raised by a tenant for life through the exercise of the powers under the Acts, must be paid to *trustees of the settlement* or into the court to be invested in authorised securities or to be applied for specified purposes, the object being the benefit of the tenant for life and all others who would have been entitled to the property in succession. See Landy v Power (1962-63) Ir Jur Rep 45; Northern Bank Ltd v Allen (1984) HC. See also Conveyancing Act 1881 s.60; Landlord and Tenant (Reversionary Leases) Act 1958. See COMPOUND SETTLEMENT; PROPERTY ADJUSTMENT ORDER; STRICT SETTLEMENT; TRUST FOR SALE.

**settlement, EC.** A settlement which has been approved by a court of a *contracting* State in the EC in the course of proceedings and which is enforceable in the State in which it was concluded, is enforceable in the State in which enforcement is sought under the same conditions as *authentic instruments* (qv):

Jurisdiction of Courts and Enforcement of Judgments (European Communities) Act 1988, first schedule, art.51. For enforcement of settlements in EC and EFTA countries, see Jurisdiction of Courts and Enforcement of Judgments Act 1993, sixth schedule, art.51. See COMPROMISE.

**settlor.** A person who makes a settlement (qv) of his property.

**several.** Separate, in contrast to *joint*. See JOINT AND SEVERAL OBLIGATION

**severalty.** Separate and exclusive possession. Property is said to belong to persons in *severalty* when the share of each is sole and exclusive, as contrasted with concurrent or co-ownership. See JOINT TENANCY

**severance.** Where a contract is made up of several parts, and it is possible to divide it up so as to preserve some part and to disregard the other part, the contract is said to be severable. There can be no severance where the contract is illegal involving immoral or prohibited acts or otherwise against public policy: Miller v Karlinski (1945) TLR 85. However, severance may be possible where the illegal promise forms a collateral or incidental part of the transaction and no compelling social, economic or moral imperative would be subverted by enforcement of the rest of the transaction: Carney v Herbert (1985) AC 301.

Where any provisions of an Act (eg section, sub-section or part thereof) is found to be unconstitutional, the remaining provisions in the Act may continue with full effect, if found by the court to be severable from the repugnant provisions; the court may hold that consequential deletions be made to other provisions of the Act: 1937 Constitution art.15(4)(2); Companies Act 1990; Desmond & Dedeir Ltd v Minister for Industry and Commerce (1992 SC) ITLR (7 Dec).

Severance may also be possible in relation to a *covenant* in restraint of trade which is too wide, if severance leaves a covenant remaining which is not too wide: Mulligan v Corr (1925) IR 169: European Chemical Industries Ltd v Bell (1981) ILRM 345. See also Lewis v Squash (Ireland) Ltd (1983) ILRM 363; Greene v Minister for Agriculture

(1990 HC) ILRM 364.

**severance, words of.** Words in a grant which denote that tenants are to take a distinct share in a property eg *in equal shares* or *equally*. See JOINT TENANCY; TENANCY IN COMMON.

**severance and injurious affection.** In assessing compensation to an owner of land in respect of its compulsory purchase (qv) by a local authority, regard must be had not only to the value of the land, but also to the damage, if any, to be sustained by the owner of the land by reason of the *severing* of the land taken from other land of such owner or otherwise *injuriously affecting* that other land by the exercise of the statutory power of acquisition: Land Clauses Consolidation Act 1845 s.63. See COMPENSATION AND COMPULSORY PURCHASE.

**severance pay.** Payment to an employee whose contract of employment is terminated. A scheme of *severance payments* for former holders of ministerial office and a scheme of *termination allowances* for defeated members of both Houses of the Oireachtas, has been provided for: Ministerial and Parliamentary Offices (Amdt) Act 1992 ss.5 and 10; Finance Act 1993 s.7. See DISABILITY AND SEVERANCE.

**sewage effluent.** As regards water pollution (qv), means effluent from any works, apparatus, plant or drainage pipe used for the disposal to waters of sewage, whether treated or untreated: Local Government (Water Pollution) Act 1977 s.1.

The Minister is empowered to make regulations for the collection, treatment, discharge or disposal of sewage or other effluents from — (a) any plant or drainage pipe vested in or controlled or used by a sanitary authority for the treatment of drinking water, or (b) any plant, sewer or drainage pipe vested in or controlled or used by a sanitary authority for the treatment and disposal of sewage or other effluents: Environmental Protection Agency Act 1992 s.59. This is to enable implementation of Council Directive on urban waste water treatment (91/271/EEC). See also INTEGRATED POLLUTION CONTROL.

**sewer.** As regards water pollution legislation, means a sewer within the meaning of the LG (Sanitary Services) Acts 1878 to 1964 that is vested in or controlled by a sanitary authority, and includes a sewage treatment works, and a sewage disposal works, that is vested in or controlled by a sanitary authority: LG (Water Pollution) Act 1990 s.2.

There is an obligation on sanitary authorities to cause to be made and to maintain such sewers as may be necessary for effectually draining their district: Public Health (Ireland) Act 1878 s.17. Sewer includes sewers and drains of every description, except drains serving one premises only or *combined drains* (ibid 1878 Act s.2; Local Government (Sanitary Services) Act 1948 ss.10-11).

A *combined drain* is deemed to be a drain and not a sewer and comprises a single private drain used for the drainage of two or more separate premises (ibid 1948 Act ss.10-11). It is not necessary for a pipe to carry sewage in order for it to be a sewer: Ferrand v Halles Land and Building Company (1893) 2 QB 135. A grid or grating to drain off surface water is a sewer within the meaning of the 1878 Act s.2: Merriman v Dublin Corporation (1993 HC) ILRM 58.

Machinery exists to compel a sanitary authority to provide sewers for its district: Public Health (Ireland) Act 1896 s.15. Owners and occupiers are entitled to connect their drains to existing sewers (ibid 1878 Act s.23 and Ballybay Meat Exports Ltd v Monaghan Co Council (1990 HC) ILRM 864) and can be compelled so to connect: Local Government (Sanitary Services) Act 1962 s.8. However, the consent of the sanitary authority to such a connection is now required: LG (P&D) Act 1990 s.25(3). That consent is deemed to have been given where planning permission or building bye-law approval has been granted in relation to a structure (ibid s.25(7)). See also St Annes Estate Ltd v Dublin County Council (1978) HC; Merriman v Dublin Corporation (1992 HC) 10 ILT Dig 200. See COMBINED DRAIN; INTEGRATED POLLUTION CONTROL; PUBLIC RIGHT; TRADE EFFLUENT; WAYLEAVE.

**sex discrimination.** See DISCRIMINATION; EQUAL PAY.

**sexual assault.** The offence of *indecent assault* is now known as *sexual assault*: Criminal Law (Rape) (Amendment) Act 1990 s.2. The offence of *aggravated sexual assault* is a sexual assault that involves serious violence or the threat of serious violence or is such as to cause injury, humiliation or degradation of a grave nature to the person assaulted (ibid s.3). It is a felony (qv) carrying a sentence of imprisonment for life.

A sexual assault that includes (a) penetration (however slight) of the anus or mouth by the penis, or (b) penetration (however slight) of the vagina by any object held or manipulated by another person is the offence of *rape under section 4* (ibid s.4). It is also a felony carrying a sentence of life imprisonment. [Text: O'Malley T (2)]. See ASSAULT, INDECENT; DOLI INCAPAX.

**sexual abuse.** See CHILD AT RISK.

**sexual harassment.** "Verbal or physical conduct of a sexual nature which the perpetrator knows or should have known was offensive to the victim": The Dignity of Women at Work by Michael Lobenstein — see 8 ILT & SJ (1990) 243. "The unwanted, real, implied, or perceived request for, or threat of extracting, sexual favours": Labour Court 1991.

While sexual harassment is not specifically mentioned in the Employment Equality Act 1977, the Labour Court has held that freedom from sexual harassment is a condition of work which an employee of either sex is entitled to expect and that the Court would treat any denial of that freedom as discrimination within the terms of the 1977 Act: A Worker v A Garage Proprietor EE02/ 1985.

The Labour Court has also held that the initiating, pursuit and fulfilment by an employer of a sexual interest in a female employee without or outside that employee's consent is a breach of the 1977 Act; in considering consent the Court must have regard for the employer's dominant position in the employment relationship: A Worker v A Company EEO2/90 in 8ILT & SJ (1990) 244 & (1990) ELR 187.

Where two persons of the same sex are involved, particular circumstances must be established to justify the claim that the conduct of one constitutes sexual harassment of the other: A Worker v A Company (1992 LC) ELR 40. It is irrelevant that the perpetrator of the harassment is not an employee of the company if the employer was in a position to protect the worker. An employee is entitled to a work environment which is free from the fear of sexual harassment: An Employee v An Employer (1993) ELR 76.

In the UK it has been held that sexual harassment is a particularly degrading and unacceptable form of treatment which it must have been the intention of parliament to restrain: Strathclyde Regional Council v Porcelli (1986) IRLR 134 as considered in A Limited Company v One Female Employee EE10/1988. See also A Worker v A Company (1992 LC) ELR 73; A Worker v A Company (1993 LC) ELR 6. See Barry in 10 ILT & SJ (1992) 102; Flynn in 10 ILT & SJ (1992) 205. See DISCRIMINATION.

**sexual intercourse.** Sexual intercourse is proven in cases of sexual offences (qv) by proof of *penetration*. It has been held that if the male organ entered the opening of the vagina, this amounts to penetration even if there is no emission: The People (Attorney General) v Dermody (1956) IR 307. References to *sexual intercourse* in the Criminal Law (Sexual Offences) Act 1993 must be construed as references to *carnal knowledge* as defined in section 63 of the Offences against the Person Act 1861: ibid 1993 Act s.1(3). See BUGGERY; CARNAL KNOWLEDGE; EVIDENCE TENDING TO BASTARDISE CHILDREN.

**sexual offences.** These offences include: (a) bestiality (qv): Offences against the Person Act 1861 ss.61-62; (b) buggery (qv) with a person under 17 years of age or a mentally impaired person of any age: Criminal Law (Sexual Offences) Act 1993 ss.3 and 5; (c) gross indecency by a male with a male under 17 years of age (ibid 1993 Act s.4); (d) soliciting or importuning for the purposes of commission of a sexual offence (ibid s.6); (e) the felony of unlawful carnal knowledge of a girl under 15 years: Criminal Law Amendment Act 1935 s.1; (f) the misdemeanour of unlawful carnal knowledge of a girl between 15 and 17 years (ibid ss.2-3); (g) rape (qv): Criminal Law (Rape) Acts 1981 s.2 and 1990; (h) indecent assault of a female (ibid 1981 Act s.10)- now called sexual assault (qv); (i) aggravated sexual assault: Criminal Law (Rape) (Amendment) Act 1990 s.3;

(j) rape under section 4 (ibid 1990 Act s.4). See also Mental Treatment Act 1945 s.254. See COMPLAINT; CONSENT; PROCUREMENT; TELEVISION LINK; VICTIM IMPACT STATEMENT.

**sexual orientation.** See HATRED, INCITEMENT TO; HOMOSEXUAL CONDUCT; LESBIANISM; UNFAIR DISMISSAL; VIDEO RECORDING.

**shadow director.** A person in accordance with whose directions or instructions the directors of a company are accustomed to act; he is deemed generally to be a director. There is an exemption for persons who give advice in a professional capacity. See Companies Act 1990 s.27. See DIRECTOR.

**Shannon Navigation.** The river Shannon, the lakes from or through which it flows and certain other rivers which flow into it or into those lakes: Shannon Navigation Act 1990 s.1. This act enables the Commissioners of Public Works to undertake the care, management, control and improvement of the Shannon navigation. It also extends the powers of the Commissioners to the Ballinamore and Ballyconnell navigation and the section of the River Erne navigation which is within the State. The Commissioners have power to acquire land compulsorily (ibid 1990 Act, schedule). See also Act for the Improvement of the Navigation of the River Shannon 1839 (2 & 3 Vict, c.61) and also 5 & 6 Vict, c.89. See NAVIGATION, RIGHT OF.

**share certificate.** An instrument under the seal of a company, which certifies that the person named therein is entitled to a stated number of shares. It is not a negotiable instrument nor a document of title and it is only prima facie evidence of its contents: Companies Act 1963 s.80-87; Companies Amendment Act 1977 s.5. The true evidence of title is the holder's name registered in the register of members.

A *share warrant to bearer* is a certificate under the seal of a company stating that the bearer of the warrant is entitled to the shares therein specified; it is a negotiable instrument in that the shares can be transferred by delivery of the warrant: Companies Act 1963 ss.88 and 118; Listing Agreement s.9, ch 4.2. Provision is often made in such warrants for detaching coupons in order to claim future dividends. See SHARES; SHARES,

EQUITABLE MORTGAGE OF.

**share premium account.** The account in which is placed the aggregate amount or value of the premium received on the issue of shares of a company. A reduction of the share premium account requires approval by special resolution of the members of a company and by the High Court eg cancellation of £40m of the share premium account of Aran Energy plc in 1993 by effectively setting against it the debit balance of £40m in the company's profit and loss account: Iris Oifigiuil 9th July 1993 p.518. See PREMIUM.

**share price, movement of.** A company with a quotation on the Stock Exchange is obliged to make a public announcement as soon as possible regarding any major new developments in its sphere of activity which may have the effect of moving the share price: Companies Act 1990 s.119. The objective is to prevent *insider dealing* (qv) from taking place.

**share transfer.** See TRANSFER OF SHARES.

**share, value of.** For valuation of shares in private companies, see [Text: Giblin].

**share warrant.** See SHARE CERTIFICATE.

**shared ownership lease.** A lease granted for a term of between 20 and 100 years on payment to the lessor of between 25 and 75 per cent of the market value of the house and which gives to the lessee the right to buy out the interest of the lessor, in one or more transactions and on the terms specified in the lease: Housing (Miscellaneous Provisions) Act 1992 s.2(1). Shared ownership is a means of enabling a person to purchase a portion of the equity in a house and to pay a rent to the owner of the remaining equity for the right of occupation. A housing authority may grant shared ownership leases and charge rent for occupation of the leased house, the maintenance of which is the responsibility of the lessee (ibid s.3). See GROUND RENT; PERPETUITIES, RULE AGAINST.

**shareholder.** One who owns shares as a member of a company. See DERIVATIVE ACTION; SHARES; VOTING AT MEETINGS.

**shareholder, oppression of.** See OPPRESSION OF SHAREHOLDER.

**shareholding, building society.** The value of a person's shares in a building society is taken as the amount standing to his credit in respect of the payments made by him on the shares and interest credited to the shares by way of capitalisation: Building Societies Act 1989 s.2(2). Where a society becomes converted into a public limited company, every shareholding in the society becomes a deposit of the same amount with the successor company (ibid s.107(1)(a)).

**shares, building society.** A share in a building society is entirely different from a share in a limited liability company. "A share in a limited liability company is part of the capital and is something which cannot be got rid of. It may be transferred to someone else, but it cannot be put out of existence. A share in this building society represented no proportionate quota of the company's capital. There might be as many shares in this society as people like to apply for ...": Irvine & Fullarton Building Society v Cuthbertson (1905) 45 SLR 17.

A building society with an *authorisation* may raise funds to be used for the objects of the society, by the issue of shares of one or more than one denomination, either with or without accumulating interest, and may repay such funds: Building Societies Act 1989 s.18(1). A repayment of such funds to a shareholder however is not permitted, other than at the shareholder's request, at particular times eg between the date the member indicated his intention to propose a resolution at a meeting and the date of the meeting (ibid s.18(2)). Also shares must not be issued without voting rights (ibid s.18(4)).

A society is required to keep at least 50 per cent of its funding liabilities in the form of members' shareholdings, although the Central Bank may grant a dispensation from this requirement (ibid s.18(3)).

The rules of a society must state the manner of determination of the terms on which shares are to be issued and repaid, and the manner in which shareholders are to be informed of changes in the terms on which their shares are held (ibid s.10(2)(b), and second schedule, part II, para 5(c)). The rules must also state whether any preferential or deferred shares (qv) are to be issued and, if so, within what limits and on what terms.

Every person holding one or more shares in a society is a *member* (qv) of the society (ibid s.16(1)) and two or more persons may jointly hold shares in a society (ibid s.16(3)). The Central Bank may impose as a condition to an *authorisation* granted to a society, limitations on the issue of shares or debt instruments (ibid s.17(6)(a)).

**shares, company.** A definite portion of the capital of a company. A share means a share in the share capital of a company and includes *stock* except where a distinction between stock and shares is expressed or implied: Companies Act 1963 s.2(1). A share is *personal* property (ibid s.79). Shares may be divided into different classes eg *preference, ordinary, deferred,* or *founders'* shares. The ownership of a share entitles the owner to receive a proportionate part of the profits of the company and to take part in the control of the company in accordance with the *articles of association*, which also regulate the mode in which the shares may be transferred.

Most articles of association give the board the exclusive power and a wide discretion over allocating further shares. Existing shareholders are not in common law entitled to be given the opportunity to subscribe for additional shares before those shares are offered to others; however a proposed allotment can be enjoined which has as its purpose to convert a minority into a majority: Nash v Lancegage Safety Glass (Ireland) Ltd (1958) 90 ILTR 11. However, since 1983 *pre-emption* (qv) is now compulsory for every company with certain exceptions.

Shares may not be issued at a discount (qv). However, shares may be allotted for a consideration other than cash. Shares allotted by a company and any premium (qv) payable on them may be paid up in money or in money's worth, including goodwill and expertise: Companies Amendment Act 1983 s.26(1). However, in a public limited company (plc), every subscriber to its memorandum of association must pay for his shares in cash (ibid s.35). A plc is prohibited from accepting as payment for shares an undertaking to do work or perform services (ibid s.26(2)), or to an undertaking which is to be or may be performed more than five years after the date of the allotment (ibid s.29).

Where a plc proposes to allot shares in exchange wholly or partly for something other than cash, the consideration must be valued by someone who would be eligible to be the company's auditor (ibid s.30).

Contrast with *debentures* which can resemble shares in various respects but are fundamentally different. See Eddison v Allied Irish Banks (1987) HC; Lombard Ulster Banking v Bank of Ireland (1987) HC; In re PMPS (1988) HC; Pernod Richard and Comrie plc v FII (Fyffes) plc 7 ILT Dig (1989) 53. See CAPITAL; CAPITAL RECONSTRUCTION; CONTRACTS FOR DIFFERENCES; DEBENTURES; DISTRINGAS NOTICE; DIVIDEND ; FORFEITURE OF SHARES; FRAUD; MATERIAL CONTRACTS; OFFER FOR SALE; OPTION; PROSPECTUS; SURRENDER OF SHARES; TAKE OUT MERGER; TRANSFER OF SHARES.

**shares, compulsory purchase of.** Where a company makes a takeover bid for all the shares of another company, and the offer is accepted by the holders of 80% in value of the shares, the offeror can upon the same terms acquire the shares of the members who had not accepted the offer, unless such persons obtain an order of the court preventing this compulsory acquisition: Companies Act 1963 s.204. However, see European Communities (Mergers and Divisions) Regulations 1987 (SI No 137 of 1987) in respect of relevant mergers and divisions. Also, the court can order the purchase of the shares of a minority shareholder in proceedings alleging *oppression of the shareholder* (qv); the court has a wide discretion in valuing these shares: 1963 Act s.205(3) and In re Clubman Shirts Ltd (1991 HC) ILRM 43. See Linnane in 8ILT & SJ (1990) 253. See GOING CONCERN; MERGER OF COMPANY; DIVISION OF COMPANY.

**shares, disclosure of.** The Minister is empowered to obtain information on the ownership of shares and debentures of a company and to impose restrictions on them: Companies Act 1990 ss.15-16 eg restriction imposed by the Minister on the shares in UPH Ltd registered in the name of Aurum Nominees (Iris Oifigiuil — 18 August 1992).

A director or secretary of a company (public and private) is required to notify the company of the extent of his interest in shares or debentures of the company or another *related* company and of any changes; the company must keep a register of these interests and disclose them in the directors' report and report them to the Stock Exchange where dealing facilities are provided for such shares or debentures (ibid ss.53-65).

The beneficial owner of a notifiable percentage (5%) of the issued share capital of a public limited company (plc) is required to declare that fact to the company and this information must be available to directors, shareholders, employees and creditors of the company (ibid ss.67-88). There is provision for dealing with *concert parties*. (qv): ibid ss.73-75. There are also disclosure requirements in respect of large acquisitions or disposals of shares in plcs: see COVERT TAKE-OVER.

A general regime of disclosure of share ownership for private companies is not provided for, but a person with a financial interest in such a company may be able to obtain a *disclosure order* from the court, compelling disclosure in certain circumstances (ibid ss.97-104). See CONCERT PARTY; DISCLOSURE ORDER; REGISTER OF MEMBERS.

**shares, equitable mortgage of.** An equitable mortgage of shares in a company is normally created by the deposit of the share certificate, with or without delivery of a *blank transfer* to the lender. The borrower remains on the register of members and retains all the rights of a member unless other arrangements are made as between himself and the lender. It is common practice for the transferor to sign and hand over a blank transfer ie a transfer signed by the transferor, but with a blank for the name of the transferee. An equitable mortgage of shares can be defeated if the transferor obtains a second share certificate from the company and sells the shares to a bona fide purchaser.

**shares, investigation of.** The Minister is empowered to appoint inspectors to investigate suspected contraventions of the requirements to disclose ownership of shares by directors or secretaries of companies or of their spouses or children or of the prohibition on the dealing in options (qv) by a director: Companies Act 1990 s.64.

**shares, purchase of own.** A company may, if so authorised by its articles, purchase its own shares, including any redeemable shares (qv): Companies Act 1990 s.211. Such a purchase cannot be made if as a result the nominal value of the issued share capital which is not redeemable would be less than one tenth of the nominal value of the total issued share capital of the company.

There are many advantages eg (a) the purchase of shares of employees, acquired through an employee share scheme, on their ceasing to be employed by the company; (b) buying out a dissident shareholder; and (c) providing a market for unlisted shares. There are provisions to prevent abuse eg market rigging of listed shares (ibid s.215). The Stock Exchange is given a role in effecting compliance (ibid s.230). The Minister is empowered to make regulations governing the purchase by companies of their own shares (ibid s.228). No such regulations had been made by 1993 and none were planned. For taxation of the acquisition by a company of its own shares, see Finance Act 1991 ss.59-72.

**Shelley's case, rule in.** It is a rule of law that when a person by any deed or will takes an estate of freehold (qv) and by the same deed or will an estate is limited either mediately or immediately *to his heirs* or *to the heirs of his body,* these words are words of limitation and confer no estate to his heirs: Shelley's Case 1581. See Finch v Foley (1949) Ir Jur Rep 30. See WORDS OF LIMITATION.

**sheriff.** The office holder with wide powers, eg to execute an order of fieri facias (qv), originally appointed by the Lord Lieutenant, whose appointment is now governed by the Court Officers Act 1945 s.12; Court Officers Act 1951 s.6; Electoral Act 1963 s.3, first schedule; Juries Act 1976 s.33. Special tax collection sheriffs were appointed in 1986; legislation was introduced to ensure that they would not be required by virtue of their office to act as returning officers at elections or referenda: Electoral (Amendment) Act 1986 ss.1-2.

An *order for protection* issued by the court will protect a debtor against execution unless the sheriff has made a seizure or has gone into possession: Bankruptcy Act 1988 s.89. See Kennedy v Hearne (1988) ILRM 52 and (1988) SC. See Report on Debt Collection: (i) The Law relating to Sheriffs (LRC 27 of 1988). [Text: Dixon & Gilliland]. See COUNTY REGISTRAR; ENTRY, RIGHT OF; PEACE OFFICER; POUNDAGE; RETURNING OFFICER.

**sheriff's interpleader.** See INTERPLEADER.

**ship.** Includes every description of vessel used in navigation not propelled by oars: Merchant Shipping Act 1894 s.742. In marine insurance, a ship includes the hull, materials and outfit, stores and provisions for the officers and crew and, in the case of vessels engaged in a special trade, the ordinary fittings requisite for the trade: Marine Insurance Act 1906, first schedule, art.15. [Text: Power UK]. See ADMIRALTY ACTION; CHARGE ON SHIP; DETENTION OF SHIP; PASSENGER SHIP; VESSEL.

**ship protest.** A formal declaration, made by a ship's master or a member of its crew, before a notary public or other competent person, describing some event or happening relating to a ship, its cargo or crew, which the declarant desires to be formally recorded for subsequent evidential use. See DEPOSITION; NOTARY PUBLIC.

**shipping grants.** Grants up to 25% of approved capital expenditure on certain new or second-hand ships may be made by the Minister: Shipping Investment Grants Act 1987.

**shock, nervous.** See NERVOUS SHOCK.

**shop.** See SAFE SYSTEM OF WORK; WORKING HOURS.

**shore.** See FORESHORE.

**short-term patent.** A patent for a term of 10 years which is less costly and simpler to obtain; it is intended to be more appropriate for less technologically complex inventions which do not have a long life cycle. An invention is patentable as a *short-term* patent if it is new and susceptible of industrial application provided it is not clearly lacking an inventive step: Patents Act 1992 s.63. An application for a short-term patent must contain (a) a request for a grant of a short-term patent; (b) a specification (i) which describes the invention and the best method of performing it known to the applicant, (ii) incorporates one or more claims, not exceeding five, (iii) accompanied by drawings and an abstract (ibid s.63(7)).

As short-term patent applications are not subject to a novelty check or to detailed examination, an action for infringement of a short-term patent must not be instituted by the proprietor unless he has requested and obtained a *Search Report* from the Controller of Patents, which report will be published and be made available to the Court and to the party against whom proceedings are contemplated (ibid s.66).

In addition to the normal grounds for revocation of a patent, a further special ground is provided in the case of short-term patents ie that the claims of the specification of the short-term patent are not supported by the description (ibid s.67). A short-term patent and a normal patent cannot co-exist in respect of the same invention (ibid s.64). See PATENT.

**short title.** The title by which an Act may be cited eg *Succession Act 1965*. See PREAMBLE.

**short weight and measure.** A person who sells or exposes for sale or offers for sale any goods by weight, measure or number, is guilty of an offence if the quantity of such goods is less than that purported or less than corresponds with the price charged on the basis of the total price to be paid for the goods or the stated price per number or unit of measurement used to determine the total price: Restrictive Practices (Amendment) Act 1987 s.39. See also Weights & Measures Act 1878 and 1889.

**shorthand reporting.** See TRANSCRIPT.

**short-time.** A reduction in remuneration or hours of work by 50% in any week caused by diminished requirements for the work the employee performs under his contract of employment, provided that this is temporary and the employer gives notice to that effect prior to the reduction: Redundancy Payments Act 1967 s.11(2) as amended by the Redundancy Payments Act 1979. See LAY-OFF.

**show cause.** See NISI.

**S.I.** Statutory Instrument (qv).

**sic.** [So; thus]. Used to indicate that a word or statement is intended as written, despite the fact that there is an obvious error or it results in an absurdity.

**sic utere tuo ut alienum non laedas.** [So use your own property as not to injure your neighbours].

**sick pay.** Payment to an employee during periods of sickness may arise as a result of the employment contract or as a result of the State welfare insurance schemes. *Disability benefit* from the State scheme is payable to insured workers during periods of incapacity for work. To be eligible, the person must be unfit for work due to illness and must satisfy the contribution conditions. In addition *pay related benefit* may be payable. However where the incapacity is the result of a prescribed industrial disease, *injury benefit* may be payable instead. An *invalidity pension* is payable, instead of disability benefit, to insured persons who are permanently incapable of working and who satisfy the contribution conditions. See SOCIAL WELFARE LAW.

**sickness.** The ill-health of an employee may render him incapable of performing his duties; this incapacity may be a good cause to justify dismissal: Unfair Dismissal Act 1977 s.6(4). A single medical report is not sufficient: Lawless v Dublin Co Council (1990 EAT) ELR 101.

For a dismissal on grounds of incapacity to be deemed fair, the onus is on the employer to show that (a) it was the incapacity which was the reason for the dismissal: (b) the reason was substantial; (c) the employee received fair notice that the question of his dismissal for incapacity was being considered; and (d) the employee was afforded an opportunity of being heard: Bolger v Showerings (Ireland) Ltd (1990 HC) ELR 184. The court has refused to intervene in a decision to place a civil servant on compulsory sick leave with pay: Ahern v Minister for Industry & Commerce 9ILT Dig (1991 HC) 127.

The Advocate General of the European Court has given an opinion that the dismissal of a female worker outside her periods of maternity leave because of absence due to illness originating in pregnancy or childbirth does not constitute discrimination based on sex: see 8ILT & SJ (1990) 279. See also Duff v Dun Laoghaire Corp (1991 EAT) ELR 82; Gavin v Bus Eireann (1990 EAT) ELR 103; Mulhern v An Post (1990 CC) ELR 131; Molloy v Irish Glass Bottle Co Ltd UD 693/1983. See UNFAIR DISMISSAL.

**side-bar orders.** Particular types of order made by a court: RSC O.30. Known as a *side-bar* due to their origin to Westminister Hall where at a bar or partition, which came to be known as the side-bar, attorneys would move judges on their way to their respective courts. An example of a side-bar order is an order to proceed, notwithstanding the death of a party, his right surviving, which order is made in the High Court by the Master and in the Circuit Court by the County Registrar: RSC O.30; O.63 r.1(1); RCC O.16. A side-bar order may also be made by a Probate Officer directing a party cited to extract a grant of probate or to renounce his rights: RSC O.79 rr.57-58.

**sign.** Any sign, hoarding or other structure used for the purpose of advertising: Roads Act 1993 s.71(8). It is an offence to erect, place or retain a sign on a public road (qv) without lawful authority or the consent of the road authority; the sign may be removed by an authorised person (ibid s.71(1)(a)). This provision does not apply to a sign which relates to an election or referendum unless it is in place for seven days or longer after the poll (ibid s.71(10)). The National Roads Authority is empowered to prepare, or arrange the preparation of, schemes for the provision of traffic signs (ibid s.19(1)(c)).

**sign manual.** Formerly a document signed at the head by the Sovereign in his own hand. Where the cy-pres (qv) doctrine is applied by the government and where there are no trustees, it is done by *letters missive* under the present sign manual procedure; in the procedure the plaintiff submits a memorial to the government, which replies with the letters missive to the Attorney General to be issued to the court which makes the appropriate order: Merrins v AG (1945) 79 ILTR 121.

**signals.** It is an offence to signal smuggling vessels; proof that such signal was not for the purpose of giving notice to the vessel, lies on the defendant: Customs Consolidation Act 1876 ss.190-191. See also MALICIOUS DAMAGE.

**signature.** A person's name written in his own hand or a sign or other such mark to signify his name. A person signs a document as a token of his intention to be bound by its contents. Illiterate persons commonly sign by making a cross; companies sign by their corporate seal. A rubber stamp or typed words may be interpreted as a signature. See Casey v Irish Intercontinental Bank (1979) IR 364; Kelly v Ross & Ross (1980) HC. See ACKNOWLEDGEMENT; NON EST FACTUM; TRADE MARK, REGISTERED.

**silence, right to.** The right in general which an accused person has to remain silent. However there are some occasions where the right to silence is excluded by statute eg it is an offence for a person to fail to give an account of his movement and actions during a specified period when so demanded by a garda: Offences Against the State Act 1939 s.52. Also an inference may be drawn in the trial of an arrested person if he fails (a) to account to the garda for marks on clothing or footwear; or (b) to explain his presence at the scene of a crime: Criminal Justice Act 1984 s.18-19. See ADMISSION; CONFESSION; INCRIMINATE; UNLAWFUL POSSESSION OF GOODS.

**silk, to take.** See SENIOR COUNSEL.

**silver.** See GOLDSMITHS OF DUBLIN, COMPANY OF.

**similiter.** [In like manner].

**simple contracts.** All contracts which are not under seal; they require consideration (qv) to support them. Some simple contracts are required to be in writing eg bills of exchange and promissory notes: Bills of Exchange Act 1882 s.3(1); contracts of marine insurance: Marine Insurance Act 1906 s.22; moneylending contracts: Moneylenders Act 1933 s.11; hire-purchase contracts: Hire Purchase Acts 1946-1960.

Certain other contracts are unenforceable unless they are *evidenced* by some memorandum in writing signed by the party to be charged or his agent: (a) contracts specified in the Statute of Frauds 1695 s.2 and (b) contracts specified in the Sale of Goods Act 1893 s.4 ie in the absence of acceptance and receipt of the goods or of part payment. See STATUTE OF FRAUDS; SALE OF GOODS; SALE OF LAND.

**simplex commendatio non obligat.** [A mere recommendation does not impose a liability]. See PRECATORY TRUST.

**simpliciter.** [Simply]. Absolutely; without qualification.

**simultaneous invention.** Understood to be where two or more persons have made the same invention independently of each other at or about the same time. The right to a patent belongs to the person whose patent application has the earlier or earliest date: Patents Act 1992 s.16(2). See PRIORITY DATE.

**sine die.** [Without a day]. Indefinitely. See ADJOURNMENT.

**sine qua non.** [Without which not]. An indispensable condition.

**Single European Act; SEA.** The Act done at Luxembourg on the 17th February 1986 and at The Hague on the 28th February 1986 which brought about many amendments to the constitutional treaties of the European Community. Its most important provision is in relation to the establishment of an *internal market* (qv) by 31st December 1992. Its other provisions are (a) to establish a tribunal to hear certain classes of action, (b) to extend the role of the European Parliament in the decision making process, (c) to permit further delegations of power from the Council to the Commission and (d) various measures on monetary capacity, social policy, economic and social cohesion, research and development, the environment and European political cooperation.

Certain portions of the SEA were incorporated into our domestic law by the European Communities (Amendment) Act 1986; however it was held that it would be unconstitutional for the State to ratify the SEA: Crotty v An Taoiseach (1987) ILRM 400. This Supreme Court decision necessitated an amendment to the Constitution which was carried by a substantial majority. See Tenth Amendment to the Constitution Act 1987; Referendum (Amendment) Act 1987. The Government ratified the SEA on 25th June 1987 by depositing the instrument of ratification with the Government of the Italian Republic and it came into force on 1st July 1987. See 1937 Constitution art.29(4)(5). [Text: EC Pub (1)]. See BORDER; COMMUNITY LAW; FIRST INSTANCE, COURT OF; MAASTRICHT TREATY.

**single trader.** See ONE MAN COMPANY; SOLE TRADER.

**singular.** The use of a singular noun in an Act imports the plural (unless the contrary intention appears): Interpretation Act 1937 s.11(a). This interpretation also applies to nouns in instruments made wholly or partly under an Act. See The People v Kelly (No 2) (1983) IR 1.

**site value, cleared.** See CLEARED SITE VALUE.

**sit-in.** Occupation of premises usually in pursuance of a trade dispute. There is no immunity to a union or its members for unlawful occupation of premises despite the existence of a bona fide trade dispute. The occupation may amount to trespass (qv) or to a criminal offence under the Prohibition of Forcible Entry and Occupation Act 1971, the Conspiracy and Protection of Property Act 1875 or the Criminal Law (Jurisdiction) Act 1976. See F W Woolworth Ltd v Haynes (1984) HC; Galt v Philp (1982) SLT 28. See FORCIBLE ENTRY AND OCCUPATION.

**sittings of court.** The sittings of the Supreme Court and in Dublin the High Court are four in every year: the *Michaelmas* sittings begin on the first Monday of October and end on the 21st December; the *Hilary* sittings begin on the 11th January and end on the Friday of the week preceding the Easter vacation; the *Easter* sittings begin on the Monday of the week following the Easter vacation and end on the Thursday preceding Whit Sunday; and the *Trinity* sittings begin on the Wednesday following Whitsun week and end on the 31st July. See RSC O.118 r 1. See STATUTORY SITTING; VACATION.

**skip.** A container used for the storage or removal of builder's materials, rubble, waste, rubbish or other materials and which is designed to be transported by means of a mechanically propelled vehicle: Roads Act 1993 s.72(13). A road authority (qv) may, after consultation with the Garda Commissioner, make bye-laws to regulate and control skips on public roads (ibid s.72(1)). A person who contravenes a bye-law is guilty of an offence (ibid s.72(6)).

**skipper.** In relation to a fishing vessel (qv), means the person having for the time being the command or charge of the vessel: Merchant Shipping Act 1992 s.2(1).

**slander.** Defamation by means of spoken *words*. *Words* include visual images, gestures and other methods of signifying meaning: Defamation Act 1961 s.14(2). Slander is a tort and not a crime and is not actionable without proof of *special*

*damage* (ie some real or actual loss, such as the loss of friendship, or the loss of a contractual or other tangible business advantage) and the damage must flow directly from the words complained of.

However, slander is actionable without proof of special damage in the case of words imputing: (a) a criminal offence punishable by imprisonment; (b) a contagious venerial disease; (c) unfitness of the plaintiff for his office or business: McMullan v Mulhall (1929) IR 420; Bennett v Quane (1948) Ir Jur Rep 28; (d) unchastity or adultery of a woman: Defamation Act 1961 s.16. See RSC O.36 r.36. [Text: McDonald; Duncan & O'Neill UK; Gatley UK]. See DEFAMATION; LESBIANISM; LODGMENT IN COURT; MITIGATION OF DAMAGES; NAME, RIGHT TO GOOD; OFFER OF AMENDS; PUBLICATION; VULGAR ABUSE.

**slander of goods.** A tort (qv) consisting of a false and malicious statement on merchandise sold. See White v Mellin (1895) AC 154. See Civil Liability Act 1961 s.20(1). See INJURIOUS FALSEHOOD.

**slander of title.** A tort (qv) consisting of a false and malicious statement of fact, written or spoken, which denies or casts doubts over the plaintiff's title to property, thereby causing damage to him. See Riding v Smith (1876) 1 Ex D 91. See Civil Liability Act 1961 s.20(1). See INJURIOUS FALSEHOOD.

**slaughter.** A person is not permitted to slaughter an animal in a *slaughter-house*, unless he is a registered veterinary surgeon or the holder of a slaughter licence for the time being in force: Slaughter of Animals Act 1935 s.19. See also Abattoirs Act 1988 s.47. See ABATTOIR.

**sleeping partner.** See LIMITED PARTNERSHIP.

**slip rule.** The rule which provides that clerical mistakes in judgments or orders, or errors arising therein from any accidental slip or omission, may be corrected at any time by the court on motion without appeal: RSC O.28 r.11. However, in a particular case, the High Court has held that it could not correct an error in an order drawn up by a district court clerk and subsequently signed by the district court judge: DPP v Anthony Coyne (1991 HC). See also Arbitration Act 1954 s.28; Patents Act

1992 s.110. See CLERICAL ERROR; ORDER; SUMMONS, AMENDMENT OF; TYPOGRAPHICAL ERROR.

**slot machine.** A machine which is operated by the insertion of a coin in a slot — Oxford Dictionary as quoted in DPP v Cafolla (1992 SC) ITLR (22 Jun). See GAMING.

**small claims.** A civil proceeding instituted by a consumer against a vendor in relation to any goods or services in which the amount of the claim does not exceed the sum of £500. It is intended to be consumer orientated and to relate to claims in respect of faulty goods, goods and services not supplied, and bad workmanship. It is an alternative simpler and less expensive method of commencing and dealing with a civil proceeding in respect of a small claim (known as the *Small Claims Procedure*) which was introduced as a pilot scheme in Dublin, Cork and Sligo in December 1991. It does not apply to claims arising from an agreement under the Hire Purchase Acts 1946 and 1960 or arising from a breach of a leasing arrangement, but it does apply to goods bought on hire purchase which prove unfit for their purpose. See District Court (Small Claim Procedure) Rules 1992 (SI No 119 of 1992). See Bird in 10 ILT & SJ (1992) 35.

**small company.** A private company which satisfies at least two of the following conditions: (a) balance sheet total does not exceed £1.25 million, (b) turnover does not exceed £2.5 million, (c) the average number of employees does not exceed 50: Companies Amendment Act 1986 s.8. A small company is exempted from the necessity of preparing and publishing a full set of accounts (ibid s.10). It need only draw up an abridged balance sheet and is not obliged to annex the profit and loss account or the report of the directors to the Registrar of Companies. It must however satisfy the overriding requirement that the accounts give a *true and fair view* of the company's affairs. See ACCOUNTS.

**smoke.** Includes soot, ash, grit and any other particle emitted in smoke: Air Pollution Act 1987 s.7(1).

**smoking.** See TOBACCO PRODUCT.

**smuggling.** A variety of offences created by the Customs Consolidation Act 1876 as amended. See SIGNALS.

**snuff.** Tobacco in powder or grain form specially prepared to be taken as snuff but not to be smoked, but does not include offal snuff: Finance (Excise Duty on Tobacco Products) 1977 s.1(1). See TOBACCO PRODUCT.

**social employment scheme.** A scheme designed to provide unemployed persons with work for an average of 2 1/2 days per week for up to one year on projects intended to benefit the community. The eligibility requirements that a person must be receiving either unemployment benefit or unemployment assistance did not discriminate against a married woman ineligible for either: Vavasour v Northside Centre for the Unemployed & FAS (1993 HC) ELR 112.

**social policy.** The policy of the EC whereby the member States agree to promote improved working conditions and an improved standard of living: Treaty of Rome 1957 arts.117-122 as amended by the Single European Act 1987.

Important changes to increase the Community's capacity to act on social matters were agreed by eleven of the twelve EC member States (excluding the UK): Maastricht Treaty 1992, Protocol and Annexed Agreement. The main changes are: (a) revised policy objectives including the promotion of employment and the integration of persons excluded from the labour market; (b) qualified majority voting procedures in relation to decisions on working conditions, information and consultation of workers, and on equality between men and women; (c) unanimous decision in the area of social security, and representation and collective defence of the interests of workers and employers; and (d) increased role for the social partners.

The Protocol reconfirms the commitment to *equal pay* and extends it to include piece rate and part-time pay. Also member States will be permitted to maintain or bring in measures to make it easier for women to pursue a vocational activity or to prevent or compensate for disadvantages in their professional careers.

**social welfare law.** The body of law dealing with financial and other support from the State to a wide range of persons eg the sick, disabled, unemployed, the elderly and the family. Over one million persons are in receipt of social welfare payments from the State. The law is contained in the Social Welfare (Consolidation) Act 1981 together with amending statutes and over 200 statutory instruments. Provision for social welfare for the self-employed is contained in the Social Welfare Act 1988, part III; SI No 62 of 1988.

Decisions relating to entitlement to social welfare payments and to insurability of employment are made by *deciding officers* appointed by the Minister (ibid 1981 Act s.296). These decisions may be appealed to an *Appeals Officer*. A further appeal on a point of law lies to the High Court: Kingham v Minister for Social Welfare (1985 HC). See Cousins in 10 ILT & SJ (1992) 114 & 159.

The Social Welfare (Consolidation) Bill 1993, initiated in 1993, is intended to replace the 1981 Consolidation Act and 19 subsequent amending Acts; it also incorporates certain provisions currently contained in Statutory Instruments. [Text: Whyte]. See CONSOLIDATION ACT; EURO-JUS; INFLATION.

**social welfare tribunal.** See STRIKE.

**societas Europaea; SE.** [European Company (qv)].

**societies, secret.** See SECRET SOCIETIES.

**society, friendly.** See FRIENDLY SOCIETY.

**sodomy.** Anal intercourse between a man and another man or a woman. See BUGGERY.

**solatium.** An additional amount awarded by a court for injured feeling or mental distress. See FATAL INJURIES; MENTAL DISTRESS.

**sole.** Single, unmarried; separate.

**sole, corporation.** See CORPORATION SOLE.

**sole agent.** See COMMISSION; AGENT.

**sole licence.** See EXCLUSIVE LICENCE.

**sole trader.** A person carrying on business in his own name. A sole trader's business is part of his property and its obligation and debts are the trader's own personal liability. Contrast with a registered company which exists in law entirely separate from its owners; its business is not necessarily disrupted with the death of the principal owner; and ownership is easily transferred by selling of shares. See PARTNERSHIP; COMPANY; ONE MAN COMPANY.

**solemn declaration.** A declaration made by each member State of the EC. It may clarify the intention of a Treaty entered into by the members but it is not legally binding, although it would be taken into account by the EC Court of Justice. For example, see *solemn declaration* on the Abortion Protocol in the Maastricht Treaty.

**solemn form.** See WILL, PROOF OF.

**solicit.** It is an offence to solicit or importune (a) a girl under 17 years of age or a mentally impaired woman of any age to commit buggery or to have sexual intercourse or (b) a boy under 17 years of age or a mentally impaired man of any age to commit buggery or for the purposes of gross indecency: Criminal Law (Sexual Offences) Act 1993 s.6. Soliciting or importuning by a prostitute, or by a client or by a third party on behalf of a prostitute or client is an offence (ibid s.7). See BUGGERY; GROSS INDECENCY; LOITERING; MENTALLY IMPAIRED; PROSTITUTE.

**solicitor.** A person who advises on legal matters and conducts legal proceedings. He has a right of audience before all courts: Courts Act 1971 s.17. A person may not practice as a solicitor unless he has been admitted as a solicitor, unless he has his name on the roll of solicitors, and unless he has a current *practising certificate* issued by the Incorporated Law Society of Ireland (qv). A solicitor is an officer of the court.

A solicitor owes a duty of care to his client and he also is in a fiduciary relationship to him. He has a lien (qv) on documents in his possession for his costs; this arises by operation of law and not by unilateral act of the solicitor: In re Gandan Properties Ltd (1988 SC) ILRM 559.

It has been held that the duty of a solicitor with regard to the conduct of a case in court where counsel has been briefed is first, to brief appropriate and competent counsel and secondly, to instruct them properly in relation to the facts of the case which he has obtained from his client, and to make provision for the attendance of appropriate witnesses and other proofs; a solicitor has not got any vicarious liability for the individual conduct of counsel: Fallon v Gannon (1988) ILRM 193. The jurisdiction of the High Court to discipline solicitors as officers of the court continues to exist: Judicature (Ireland) Act 1877 s.78; In re IPLG Ltd (1992 HC) ILSI Gazette (Oct 1992) 317.

A solicitor who instructs himself in litigation is entitled to recover costs which are awarded: Bourke v W G Bradley & Sons (1990 HC) 1 IR 379. See also In re O'Farrell (1960) IR 239; Roche v Peilow (1986) ILRM 189; Park Hall School v Overend (1987) ILRM 345. See Solicitors Acts 1954-1960.

Under draft legislation, which lapsed with the 26th Dail, it was proposed to give greater protection to clients of solicitors, to increase the Law Society's powers to intervene in solicitors' practices, to increase the High Court's supervisory powers over the profession, to update the Law Society's function in relation to the education and training of solicitors and to promote competition in the provision of certain legal services: Solicitors (Amdt) Bill 1992. The Bill had not been restored to the Dail Order paper by September 1993. [Text: Hogan; Horne UK]. See COMPANY, REGISTERED; COMPENSATION FUND; LAW AGENT; PARTNERSHIP, NUMBER TO FORM; UNCONSCIONABLE BARGAIN; UNDUE INFLUENCE.

**solicitor, access to.** The right of reasonable access to a solicitor of a detained person is constitutional in origin; it is directed towards the vital function of ensuring that the detained person is aware of his rights and has independent advice to permit him to reach a truly free decision as to his attitude to interrogation or to making any statement, whether exculpatory or inculpatory, and must be seen as a contribution towards a measure of equality in the position of him and his interrogators: DPP v Healy (1990 SC) ILRM 313; 1937 Constitution, art.40(3). An incriminating statement will be inadmissible if obtained when the accused's constitutional right is being deliberately and consciously violated (ibid Healy case). See also Criminal Justice Act 1984 s.5. See BLOOD SPECIMEN; LEGAL AID; LEGAL REPRESENTATION.

**solicitor, change of.** A party suing or defending by a solicitor in the High Court is entitled, without the order of the court except in matrimonial matters, to change or discharge his solicitor, provided notice is given to the other side and the change or discharge is filed in the Central Office (qv): RSC O.7 r.2. See also RSC O.7 r.3. See OFF RECORD.

**solicitor, professional negligence.** Where a solicitor is guilty of such failure as no other solicitor of equal status and skill would be guilty of if acting with ordinary care; this does not mean that a solicitor following a practice which was general and which was approved of by colleagues of similar skill would escape liability, if it were established that such practice had inherent defects which ought to be obvious to any person giving the matter due consideration: Hanafin v Gaynor (1991) 9ILT Dig 76 applying Dunne v National Maternity Hospital (1989) ILRM 735. A solicitor has a prima facie duty to advise a purchaser of a house to have an independent inspection by a suitably qualified person: O'Connor v First National Building Society (1991 HC) ILRM 208. See also Kehoe v CJ Louth & Son (1992 SC) ILRM 283. See LITIGATION.

**solicitor and client costs.** The costs incurred in non-contentious legal matters which a solicitor claims from a client; they also include costs incurred in contentious matters which a party to an action is not entitled to recover from the other party; they are only *taxed* when the client so requests.

A solicitor cannot lawfully sue for his costs for one month after delivery of the costs; a client has twelve months within which to demand and obtain taxation of the costs: Attorney and Solicitors (Ireland) Act 1849 ss.2 and 6; The State (Gallagher Shatter & Co) v de Valera (1986) ILRM 3. See COSTS IN CIVIL PROCEEDINGS; TAXATION OF COSTS; LEGAL COSTS.

**solus agreement.** Generally a promise given by a petrol wholesaler who undertakes to keep a retailer supplied with petrol if the retailer in turn agrees to take all the petrol he will require only from that wholesaler; the retailer may also undertake to keep the petrol station open at all reasonable hours and to take a minimum quantity.

*Solus* agreements have been restricted so that they could run for a maximum period of 10 years only; a wholesaler has been prohibited from discriminating between *solus* and *non-solus* retailers, although the wholesaler could charge a lower price to solus retailers provided the differential was *reasonable and justifiable*; there was a restriction on wholesaler-owned retail outlets: SI No 294 of 1961; SI No 70 of 1981. See also Continental Oil Company of Ireland Ltd v Moynihan (1977) lll ILTR 5; Irish Shell Ltd v Dan Ryan Ltd (1985) HC.

In 1993, the Competition Authority granted a *category licence* under the Competitions Act 1991 s.4(2) in respect of certain motor fuel agreements ie agreements whereby one party, the reseller, agrees with the other party, the supplier, in consideration for the according of special commercial or financial advantages, to purchase only from the supplier — Iris Oifigiuil 9th July 1993 p.513. See COMPETITION, DISTORTION OF.

**solvency, declaration of.** A statutory declaration made by the directors of a company in a *voluntary winding up* that they are of the opinion that the company will be able to pay its debts in full within a period not exceeding 12 months from when the winding up commences: Companies Act 1963 s.256 as amended by the Companies Act 1990 s.128. The declaration of solvency must be accompanied by a report by an independent person ie a person qualified to be the company's auditor: ibid s.256(2)(c).

If a declaration of solvency is made and shortly afterwards the company is wound up and cannot pay its debts in full, then any director who made the declaration is deemed not to have had reasonable grounds for his opinion until the contrary is shown: ibid s.256(9). As regards the position where a declaration of solvency has not been made by the directors, see Walsh v Registrar of Companies (1987) HC. See PERSONAL LIABILITY; WINDING UP.

**solvency margin.** In life insurance, the solvency margins which are required are specified in arts.17-18 of the European Communities (Life Assurance) Regulations 1984 (SI No 57 of 1984).

**solvent.** In a position to pay debts as they fall due. See FLOATING CHARGE; INSOLVENT.

**solvents, sale of.** It is an offence for a person to sell, offer or make available a substance to a person under the age of eighteen years, or to a person acting on behalf of that person, if he knows or has reasonable cause to believe that the substance is, or its fumes are, likely to be inhaled by the person under the age of eighteen years for the purpose of causing intoxication: Child Care Act 1991 s.74. This offence is intended to tackle the problem of *glue-sniffing* among children.

**solvitur in modum solventis.** [Money paid is to be applied according to the wish of the person paying it].

**sound broadcasting service.** A broadcasting service which transmits, relays or distributes by wireless telegraphy, communications, sounds, signs, or signals intended for direct reception by the general public whether such communications, sounds, signs or signals are received or not: Radio and Television Act 1988 s.2(1).

This Act provides for the Independent Radio and Television Commission to arrange for the provision of sound broadcasting services additional to those provided by RTE (ibid s.4). The Minister is empowered, following a report from the Commission, to specify the areas in relation to which applications for a sound broadcasting contract are to be invited by the Commission; the Minister is required to have regard to the availability of radio frequencies for sound broadcasting (ibid s.5).

The Commission in awarding contracts is required to have regard to a wide range of specified matters eg the quality, range and type of programmes proposed to be provided; the extent to which the proposed service serves recognisable local communities and is supported by various interests in the community, or serves communities of interest (ibid s.6). See ADVERTISEMENT, RADIO; BROADCASTING; RADIO AND TELEVISION COMMISSION.

**sound disposing mind.** An essential requirement for a valid will: Succession Act 1965 s.77. *It is essential that the testator shall understand the nature of the act and its effect; shall understand the extent of the property of which he is disposing, and shall be able to comprehend and appreciate the claims to which he ought to give effect; and with a view to the latter object, that no disorder of the mind shall poison his affections; pervert his sense of right; or prevent the exercise* *of his natural faculties; that no insane delusions shall influence his will in disposing of his property and bring about a disposal of it which, if the mind had been sound, would not have been made*: Banks v Goodfellow (1870) LR 5 QB 549. See also Parker v Felgate (1883) 8 PD 171; In bonis Glynn dec'd (1990) 2 IR 326. See TESTAMENTARY CAPACITY.

**sound recording.** The aggregate of the sounds embodied in, and capable of being produced by means of, a record of any description, other than a sound track associated with a cinematograph film: Copyright Act 1963 s.17(14). Copyright subsists in a sound recording for fifty years from the end of the year in which the recording is first *published* (ibid s.17(2)). *Published* means the issue to the public of *records* (qv) embodying the recording or any part thereof (ibid s.17(14)).

A person who reproduces a sound recording to be heard in public, or broadcasts or transmits it, must pay equitable remuneration to the owner of the copyright (ibid s.17(4)). A body which has gathered copyrights in sound recordings for the purpose of exploitation, is supplying a service within the meaning of the VAT Act 1972: Phonographic Performance (Ireland) Ltd v Somers, Inspector of Taxes (1992 HC) ILRM 657. See Coughlan in 10 ILT & SJ (1992) 180. See DOCUMENTARY EVIDENCE.

**soundtrack.** See CINEMATOGRAPH FILM.

**sovereign state.** Ireland is declared to be a *sovereign* independent, democratic state: 1937 Constitution, art.5. This declaration of sovereignty means that the State is not subject to any power of government save those designated by the People in the Constitution itself, and the State is not amenable to any external authority: Byrne v Ireland (1972) IR 241. See, however, COMMUNITY LAW.

**spare parts.** In a contract for the sale of goods there is an implied warranty that spare parts and an adequate aftersale service will be made available by the seller for a reasonable period. The Minister may by order define, in relation to any class of goods, what shall be a reasonable period. See SGSS Act 1980 s.12.

**special agent.** See AGENT.

**special amenity order.** The order which a planning authority (qv) has power to make which declares any particular area to be an area of *special amenity* by reason of its outstanding natural beauty, its special recreational value or a need for future conservation: LG(P&D) Act 1963 s.42(1) as substituted by the LG(P&D) Act 1976 s.40(a). The making of such an order is a *reserved function* (qv) and must be confirmed by the Minister to be effective; there are also provisions regarding public notice of such an order, objections thereto, a public local inquiry, and the laying of such an order before each House of the Oireachtas (qv).

Exempted developments (qv) are not exempted in a special amenity area and compensation (qv) is not payable in respect of a refusal of permission for development in such an area: LG (P&D) Act 1990 s.12(1)(a), second schedule para 6.

**special case.** The stating by the parties to any cause or matter, of questions of law arising therein, for the opinion of the court: RSC O.34 rr.1-8. See also RSC O.56 r.4(d). See PRELIMINARY ISSUE.

**special control area.** An area in relation to which a *special control area order* is in operation: Air Pollution Act 1987 ss.7(1) and 39.

**special courts.** The courts which may be established by law for the trial of offences in cases where it may be determined in accordance with such law that the ordinary courts are inadequate to secure the effective administration of justice, and the preservation of public peace and order: 1937 Constitution, art.38(3)(1).

The Special Criminal Court was established under the Offences Against the State Act 1939, Part V. Members of this court must be either a judge of the High, Circuit or District Court, a barrister or solicitor of not less than 7 years standing, or an army officer not below the rank of commandant; they are appointed and removable at the will of the government (ibid s.39). The court consists of three persons without a jury and its decision is that of the majority. An appeal lies to the Court of Criminal Appeal.

A person may be sent for trial to the Special Criminal Court if charged with a *scheduled offence* (qv), which is a list of particular offences (ibid s.45), or if charged with a non-scheduled offence where the Director of Public Prosecutions (qv) so requests and certifies as required (ibid s.46). Such certification by the DPP is not reviewable by the Courts unless the applicant can establish a prima facia case of some irregularity of a serious nature such as to amount to some impropriety: Foley v DPP (1989 HC) ITLR (25 Sep).

Also a person lawfully before the Special Criminal Court in respect of a scheduled offence, may be tried by the court in respect of a non-scheduled offence: McElhinney v Special Criminal Court (1989 SC) ILRM 411. See also Criminal Justice (Verdicts) Act 1976. See Eccles v Ireland (1986) ILRM 343.

**special damages.** The damages which the law does not presume to flow from the defendant's act and which must be expressly pleaded and proved eg loss of earnings, medical expenses. Slander is not actionable without proof of *special damage*, although there are some exceptions. The term *special damages* is also used to denote damages which are capable of substantially exact calculation, as distinct from those not capable of such calculation which are known as *general damages*. See Doran v Dublin Plant Hire Ltd (1990) 1 IR 488. See DAMAGES; GENERAL DAMAGES; PLEADINGS; SLANDER.

**special investment scheme.** An authorised unit trust scheme where a substantial part of the investment is in Irish equities; the effective rate of tax charged is 10 % on the income and capital gains accruing to the scheme, no tax being payable by the holder: Finance Act 1993 s.13. Holdings are subject to limits similar to *special savings accounts* (qv).

**special pleading.** Sometimes refers to the essential requirement in pleadings (qv) which if not raised would likely take the opposite party by surprise or would raise issues of fact not arising out of the pleadings eg fraud, release, payment, performance, Statute of Limitations, Statute of Frauds, or facts showing illegality, either by statute or at common law: RSC O.19 r.15.

**special psychiatric centre.** A district psychiatric centre or part of any such centre so designated by the Minister; the Central Mental Hospital is specified to be a special psychiatric centre: Health (Mental Services) Act 1981 s.30. A person who is detained in a district or registered psychiatric centre may be transferred to a special psychiatric centre if a *review board* think fit, on the recommendation to them for such transfer from the medical officer of the district or registered centre (ibid s.31). The 1981 Act had not been brought into force by 1993. See MENTAL TREATMENT.

**special resolution.** See RESOLUTION.

**special savings account.** An account in which a relevant deposit made by an individual is held, which meets certain conditions and in respect of which a declaration has been made; the interest on such a deposit is taxed at 10%: Finance Act 1992 s.22. All moneys held in a special savings account must be subject to the same terms: Finance Act 1993 s.15. An investment limit of £50,000 per individual has been established, which reduces to £25,000 where the individual also invests in another special investment product eg a *special investment scheme* (qv) (ibid s.16).

**special summons.** See SUMMONS, HIGH COURT.

**special trading house.** See TRADING HOUSE, SPECIAL.

**special verdict.** (1) A verdict by which the facts alone of the case are found by the jury and the legal inferences therefrom are drawn by the court; such verdicts are exceptionally rare eg R v Dudley and Stevens 14 QBD 273; Defamation Act 1961 s.3.

(2) A verdict of *guilty but insane* which is brought in when the accused at the time of commission of the alleged crime was insane in the legal sense: Trial of Lunatics Act 1883. The special verdict is a verdict of acquittal; the only order which the court can make is an order that the accused person be kept in custody as a criminal lunatic; it is a matter for the Executive (the Government or the Minister, as the case may be) to order the accused person's release when it is satisfied, having regard to his mental health, that it is safe to release him: DPP v John Gallagher (1991 SC) ILRM 339. See INSANITY; VERDICT.

**special voter.** See VOTERS, SPECIAL.

**special waste.** See TOXIC AND DANGEROUS WASTE.

**specialia generalibus derogant.** [Special words derogate from general ones]. See GENERALIA SPECIALIBUS NON DEROGANT.

**specialty contract.** A contract under seal; a deed. See DEED.

**specialty debt.** A debt due under a deed. See DEED.

**specialty rule.** The rule in international law which requires that a person who has been extradited will not be proceeded against, sentenced or detained for any offence committed prior to his surrender other than that for which he was extradited: European Convention on Extradition 1957 art.14; Extradition Act 1965 s.20. Specialty does not apply where the Minister consents to extradition or once the fugitive has left the requesting State. See The State (Jennings) v Furlong (1966) IR 183; Shannon v Fanning (1985) ILRM 385; Ellis v O'Dea & Shields (1990) 8ILT Dig 159.

**specific goods.** See GOODS.

**specific performance.** The equitable discretionary remedy by which a party to an agreement is compelled by order of the court to perform his obligations according to the terms of that agreement eg in contracts for the sale, purchase or lease of land, or the sale of unique chattels not readily available on the market.

In any action for breach of contract to deliver specific or ascertained goods, the court may, if it thinks fit, on the application of the plaintiff, direct that the contract be performed specifically, without giving the defendant the option of retaining the goods on payment of damages: Sale of Goods Act 1893 s.52.

Specific performance will not be granted (a) where damages are an adequate remedy; or (b) where the court cannot supervise the execution of the contract (eg a building contract); or (c) where one of the parties is a minor (qv); or (d) where the contract is for personal services, although express negative stipulations therein may be enforced by injunction (qv). However, an interim injunction has been ordered by the High Court restraining the purported termination of a plaintiff's service: McCann v Irish Medical Organisation (1990) 8ILT & SJ 67. See also Robb v London Borough of Hammersmith & Fulham (1991) IRLR 72.

Specific performance may be refused also where the party against whom it is sought would not have entered the contract but for a misrepresentation (qv). It may also be refused where there has been delay in seeking the remedy. See Murphy v Harrington (1927) IR 339; Smelter Corporation of Ireland v O'Driscoll (1977) IR 305; McCarter v Roughan and McLaughlin (1986) ILRM 447; O'Neill v Ryan (1991 HC) ITLR (2 Sep). See Companies Act 1963 s.97; Arbitration Act 1954 s.26.

**specificatio.** The making of a new article out of the chattel of one person by the work of another.

**specification.** The form of information required to be supplied in the application for a patent (qv). See COMPLETE SPECIFICATION.

**speech, freedom of.** See EXPRESSION, FREEDOM OF.

**speed limit.** The *general* speed limit for motor vehicles is 60 mph, the *motorway* speed limit is 70 mph, and the *ordinary* speed limit (applying to all goods vehicles with a gross design vehicle weight in excess of 3,500 kilograms and to all vehicles drawing a trailer) is 50 mph. The speed limit for single deck buses/coaches is 50 mph and the limit for double deck buses and single deck buses with standing passengers is 40 mph. Special speed limits apply to built-up areas eg 30 mph. See Road Traffic Acts 1961 ss.5, 45 and 46 as amended by 1968 Act s.25. See Road Traffic (General & Ordinary Speed Limits) Regulations 1992; SIs No 194, 195, 196 and 197 of 1992.

Under recent legislation, speed limits are classified as ordinary, general, built-up area, special and motorway (ibid 1961 Act s.47(3) amended by Road Traffic Act 1993 s.34). Responsibility for certain speed limits are transferred to local authorities (ibid 1993 Act s.33), and the motorway speed limit is given a specific statutory basis in primary legislation (ibid 1993 Act s.31).

**sperm bank.** See ARTIFICIAL INSEMINATION.

**spes successionis.** A mere hope of succeeding to property. *Administration with will annexed* under spes successionis may be granted to the child of a universal legatee or devisee on such person's renunciation and consent. *Administration* *intestate* may be granted to the child of a person who is entitled to all the estate on the renunciation and consent of such person. See RSC O.79 rr.5(12) and 5(13); O.80 rr.6(11) and 6(12). See In re Simpson (1904) 1 Ch 1.

**splitting of action.** The division of an , action to be made the ground of two or more different proceedings in order to bring the cases within the jurisdiction of a court. Such splitting in the District Court will lead to a dismissal of such proceedings with costs: DCR r.141. A plaintiff is similarly prohibited from dividing his cause of action into two or more different actions to bring them within the jurisdiction of the Circuit Court: Courts Act 1991 s.2(3)(b) amending the Courts of Justice Act 1936 s.23.

**spoilt vote.** A ballot paper in an election which is deemed to be invalid and is not to be counted eg where it does not bear the official stamp, or where (under proportional representation) the number one preference is not indicated definitely, or where there is included some writing calculated to identify the elector: Electoral Act 1992 s.118(2). It is normal practice for a returning officer to discuss with all candidates, or their agents, in relation to ballot papers whose validity is in doubt before deciding on their validity.

He must endorse *rejected* on any ballot paper which is not to be counted (ibid s.118(3)). Where he adjudicates on a doubtful ballot paper and rules it valid, he may record on the paper an indication of his decision, thus ensuring that the same paper will not come up again for adjudication later in the count or on a recount (ibid s.118(4)). A voter who inadvertently spoils his ballot paper may be given another ballot paper (ibid s.102).

**sponsalia per verba de praesenti.** The declaration by parties in the present tense, agreeing to take each other as husband or wife, which previously constituted a valid marriage under common law. *Sponsillia per verba de futuro et copula* was a promise to marry in the future, the parties becoming husband and wife on a subsequent consummation. See MARRIAGE.

**sponsors' mark.** The distinctive mark of a maker, worker of, or dealer in, an article of precious metal struck on such article, a register of which must be kept by the Company of Goldsmiths of Dublin, which registration is valid for a period of ten years and may be renewed every ten years: Hallmarking Act 1981 ss.1 and 9. See GOLDSMITHS OF DUBLIN, COMPANY OF.

**sporting lease.** A lease to which a sports club is entitled which carries on some outdoor sport, game or recreation and which holds land in accordance with specified conditions: Landlord & Tenant (Amendment) Act 1971 s.2(1). A claim to enlarge an interest in property from a *sporting lease* to a *fee simple* may only be made in respect of land comprised of permanent buildings and such ground as is ancillary and subsidiary thereto: Fitzgerald v Corcoran (1991 SC) ILRM 545. See GROUND RENT; RENT REVIEW CLAUSE.

**spot check.** See ROAD TRAFFIC CHECK.

**spouse.** Husband or wife. In respect of certain social welfare provisions and higher education grants, a spouse means each person of a married couple who are living together or a man and a woman who are not married to each other but are cohabiting as man and wife: Social Welfare Act 1992 s.17(a); Local Authorities (Higher Education Grants) Act 1992 s.2. See EVIDENCE TENDING TO BASTARDISE CHILDREN; PRIVILEGE, MATRIMONIAL COMMUNICATIONS; MATRIMONIAL PROPERTY.

**spouse, legal right of.** Prior to the Succession Act 1965, a testator could disinherit his spouse. However this Act introduced an important new provision which gives the surviving spouse a *legal right* to a share in his estate; to one-third of the estate where the testator leaves a spouse and children; to one-half of the estate where there are no children. This legal right has priority over devises, bequests and shares on intestacy; it may be renounced by a spouse in writing by ante-nuptial contract or during marriage.

A devise or bequest to a spouse is deemed to have been intended to be in *satisfaction* of the spouse's legal right, unless it is expressed in the will to be in addition to the legal right. The spouse may *elect* between her legal rights and rights under the will. See Succession Act 1965 ss.111 to 115.

Following grant of a decree of *judicial*

*separation,* the court may make an order extinguishing the share that either spouse would otherwise be entitled to in the estate of the other spouse as a legal right or on an intestacy under the Succession Act 1965 where it is satisfied that adequate and reasonable provision has been made for the future security of the spouse: Judicial Separation and Family Law Reform Act 1989 s.17. See also ibid s.42. See also Bank of Ireland v Caffin (1971) IR 123; Reilly v McEntee (1984) ILRM 572. See ELECTION; DISIN-HERITANCE; JUDICIAL SEPARATION; RENUNCIA-TION; UNWORTHINESS TO SUCCEED.

**spring board.** A person who has obtained information in confidence is not allowed to use it as a *spring board* for activities detrimental to the person who has made the confidential information, and spring board it remains even when all the features have been published or can be ascertained by actual inspection by members of the public: Terrapin Builders Ltd v Builders Supply Co Ltd (1960) RPC 128 as adopted by House of Spring Gardens v Point Blank (1984) IR 611. See CONFIDENCE, BREACH OF.

**spying.** Colloquial term to describe the offence committed by a person who, in any manner prejudicial to the safety or preservation of the State, obtains, records, communicates or publishes certain specified information: Official Secrets Act 1963 s.9(1). The fact that a person charged had been in communication with or attempted to communicate with a foreign agent or with a member of an unlawful organisation is evidence that the act in respect of which he is charged has been done in a manner prejudicial to the safety or preservation of the State (ibid s.10).

The specified information includes information relating to: (a) the number, description, armament, equipment, disposition, movement or condition of the Defence Forces or of any vessel or aircraft belonging to the State; (b) any operation of any of the Defence Forces or of the Garda Siochana; (c) any measures for the defence or fortification of any place on behalf of the State; or (d) munitions of war. See also OFFICIAL SECRET.

**squatter.** A person who wrongfully enters upon land; he may acquire a title to it by *adverse* or *long possession.* Where a squatter bars the right of action and title of the dispossessed owner of land, he acquires a title good against anyone other than a person with a better title to the land. See O'Connor v Foley (1906) 1 IR 20; Perry v Woodfarm Homes Ltd (1975) IR 104. [Text: Wiley (1)]. See LONG POSSESSION, TITLE BY.

**S. R. & O.** Statutory Rules and Orders. See STATUTORY INSTRUMENTS.

**stabit praesumptio donec probetur in contrarium.** [A presumption will stand good until the contrary is proved]. See PRESUMPTION.

**staff.** "A member of a body of persons employed in a business": An Foras Aiseanna Saothair v Minister for Social Welfare & Ryan (1991 HC No 653 Sp). Many state sponsored bodies have power to appoint such staff as they may determine but with the consent of the Minister eg Labour Services Act 1987 s.7(1)(a).

**stag.** A person who subscribes to an issue of shares with no intention of keeping those allotted to him, but in the speculative hope that he can sell them at a profit. The process is called *stagging.* See R v Greenstein (1975) 1 WLR 1353.

**stake.** Any payment for the right to take part in a game and any other form of payment required to be made as a condition of taking part in a game: Gaming and Lotteries Act 1956 s.2. See GAMING; STAKEHOLDER.

**stakeholder.** (1) A person with whom money is deposited pending the decision of a bet or wager. Money paid to a stakeholder to abide the result of a wager can be recovered from him at any time before it has been paid away; this applies even if the person demanding the return of his stake has lost the wager, as in effect he is revoking the stakeholders' authority as an agent for him: Grehane v Thompson (1867) IR 2 CL 64.

(2) A stakeholder may also be a person who holds money or property which is claimed by rival claimants but in which he himself claims no interest eg an auctioneer in relation to a deposit in the sale of land by auction. See Desmond v Brophy (1986) ILRM 547. See DEPOSIT; INTERPLEADER.

**stakeholder's interpleader.** See INTERPLEADER.

**stale.** Ineffective, usually because of lapse of time. See CHEQUE, STALE; LACHES; LIMITATION OF ACTIONS.

**stamp duties.** Revenue raised by means of stamps affixed to written instruments eg to conveyances and leases: Stamp Duty Act 1891 as amended. Stamp duties are either fixed in amount or *ad valorem* ie proportionate to the value of the property on which the instrument is based.

Stamp duty was a voluntary tax; however unstamped documents could not be used as evidence in court proceedings and were ineffective for such purposes as registration of title; the tax is now a compulsory tax: Finance Act 1991 ss.94 and 96-110. No stamp duty is payable on any instrument whereby property is transferred between spouses: Family Home Protection Act 1976 s.14 and Finance Act 1990 s.114. Substantial changes to the rates applying to covenants, mortgages, stock transfers, leases, conveyances, collateral and counterpart instruments were made in the Finance Act 1990. The government is empowered to impose, vary or terminate stamp duties by order: Imposition of Duties Act 1957; McDaid v Judge Sheehy (1991 SC) ILRM 250. Building Societies Act 1989 s.118. [Text: O'Connor & Cahill]. See UNSTAMPED DOCUMENT.

**standard form of contract.** It has been held that where the terms of a contract have been completely agreed between the parties thereto, a jurisdiction clause in a subsequent standard form of order is not part of the contract: Unidare plc v James Scott Ltd (1991 SC) 2 IR 88. The Minister may by order require a person who uses a standard form of contract in the course of a business to give notice to the public whether he is or is not willing to contract on other terms: SGSS Act 1980 s.52. See CONTRACT OF ADHESION.

**standard of care.** See DUTY OF CARE; MEDICAL NEGLIGENCE; OCCUPIERS' LIABILITY.

**standard of proof.** In civil cases, the standard of proof normally required is on the *balance of probability* (qv). However, see RECTIFICATION.

In criminal cases, where the burden of proof (qv) rests with the prosecution, the guilt of the accused must be proved *beyond reasonable doubt*; the accused is entitled to acquittal if his evidence does no more than raise a doubt in the jury's mind. In criminal cases, where the burden of proof on any issue rests with the accused, the standard of proof is on the balance of probability. See The People (Attorney General) v Byrne (1974) IR 1. See INFERENCE.

**standard specification.** A *specification* declared to be a standard specification for the commodity, process or practice to which it relates: Industrial Research and Standards Act 1961 ss.2 and 20(3); Science and Technology Act 1987. A *specification* includes description of any commodity, process or practice by reference to any one or more of the following, namely, nature, quality, strength, purity, composition, quantity, dimensions, weight, grade, durability, origin, age and any other characteristic (ibid 1961 Act s.2). It is an offence to make a false representation that a commodity, process or practice is of standard specification (ibid s.23).

As regards EC law, a *standard* is a *technical specification* approved by a recognised standardizing body for repeated or continuous application, with which compliance is not compulsory: Council Directive 83/189/EEC art.1. In recognition that technical regulations may act as barriers to the free movement of goods, there is provision for: (a) standards institutions in member States to keep each other advised on national standards and (b) the drawing up of European standards (ibid art.6(3)). See Travers in 11 ILT & SJ (1993) 35.

**standard time.** The time for general purposes in the State which is one hour in advance of Greenwich mean time throughout the year (Standard Time Act 1968 s.1(1)) and which during a period of winter time is Greenwich mean time (Standard Time [Amendment] Act 1971 s.1(1)(a)). Any reference to a specified point in time in any enactment or any legal document shall be construed accordingly. See WINTER TIME.

**standby fee.** A fee paid to a witness, usually a professional witness, for being available to testify in legal proceedings, in addition to a fee paid for actual attendance. A standby fee will be allowed in taxation of costs to secure the attendance of witnesses: Aspell v O'Brien

(1993 SC) ITLR (6 Sept). See also RSC O.99 r.37(18); Aspell v O'Brien (1991 HC) 2 IR 416; ILSI Gazette (June 1993) 188.

**standing mute.** See MUTE.

**standing orders.** The rules governing the formal manner of proceedings of a body. The Houses of the Oireachtas (qv) have the power to make their own rules and standing orders, with power to attach penalties for their infringement: 1937 Constitution, art.15(10).

**stare decisis.** The doctrine by which previous judicial decisions must be followed. *It is a policy and not a binding, unalterable rule*: The State (Quinn) v Ryan (1965) IR 70. The Supreme Court has refused to follow its own previous decisions but will only do so for the most compelling reasons. See also McNamara v ESB (1975) IR 1; Costello v Director of Public Prosecutions (1984) ILRM 413; Doyle v Hearne (1988) ILRM 318. See PRECEDENT.

**state.** A self-governing political community; the central political authority. Ireland is declared to be a sovereign, independent state: 1937 Constitution, art.5. The name of the State is *Eire*, or in the English language, *Ireland* (ibid art.4). The description of the State is the *Republic of Ireland*: Republic of Ireland Act 1948. It is impermissible for requesting courts to refer to the State as anything other than "Ireland" when referring to it in the English language: per Walsh J and McCarthy J in Ellis v O'Dea & Shields (1990) 8ILT Dig 159. The State, like any individual, is a juristic person and is capable of holding property and being sued for the wrongful acts of its servants: Byrne v Ireland (1972) IR 241. See also Crotty v An Taoiseach (1987) ILRM 400. For practice and procedure where the State is a party, see [Text: Collins & O'Reilly].

**State authority.** (1) As regards planning matters, means any authority being (a) a Minister of the Government, or (b) the Commissioners of Public Works in Ireland: LG (P&D) Act 1993 s.1(1). The Minister is empowered to provide by regulations that planning permission will not be required in respect of specified categories of development by or on behalf of State authorities (eg development in connection with or for the purpose of public safety or order, the administration of justice, national security or defence, or if the development has to be authorised under another enactment (ibid s.2(1)(a)). The Minister is empowered to establish alternative procedures of public notice and consultation for any such development (ibid s.2(1)(b)).

Previously, a State authority was held to be exempted from the necessity of applying for planning permission; the State authority was required however to consult with the planning authority to such extent as determined by the Minister: LG (P&D) Act 1963 s.84; Byrne & Ors v Commissioners of Public Works (1992 HC) — "Luggala" interpretive centre case. However, in a later case, it was held that section 84 did not exempt a State authority from the necessity to apply for planning permission: Howard & Ors v Commissioners of Public Works (1993 HC) — "Mullaghmore" interpretive centre case. In 1993, on appeal of both these cases, the Supreme Court held that a State authority was required to apply for planning permission — Irish Times 27/5/1993 — hence necessitating the 1993 Act which repeals s.84 of the 1963 Act (ibid 1993 Act s.5).

A State authority is also any authority being — (a) a Minister of the Government, or (b) the Commissioners of Public Works; such a State authority has, and is deemed always to have had, power to carry out, or procure the carrying out of any *development* ie the carrying out of any works on, in or under land or the making of any material change in the use of any structures or land: State Authorities (Development and Management) Act 1993.

(2) As regards the limitation of actions, a *State authority* means any authority being (a) a Minister of State, or (b) the Commissioners of Public Works in Ireland, or (c) the Irish Land Commission, or (d) the Revenue Commissioners, or (e) the Attorney General: Statute of Limitations 1957 s.2(1).

(3) As regards roads, a *State authority* means any authority being a Minister of the Government or the Commissioners of Public Works: Roads Act 1993 s.2(1).

**State guarantee.** See GUARANTEE.

**state of emergency.** See NATIONAL EMERGENCY.

**state of the art.** See PUBLICATION.

**state side orders.** The orders of the High Court by which it exercises supervisory jurisdiction over inferior courts, administrative bodies and individuals. The orders are of *certiorari, prohibition, mandamus* and *habeas corpus* (qqv). These orders are now obtained by the procedure of *judicial review*. The orders are used to check bodies or persons who have exceeded their legal powers; or to prevent bodies or persons from exercising a power which they do not possess; or to compel bodies or persons to perform a legally imposed duty; or to compel a person in whose custody another person is detained to produce the body of that other person before the court and certify in writing the grounds of his detention and if not satisfied to order his release. See JUDICIAL REVIEW.

**state-sponsored company.** See COMPANY, STATUTORY; EQUALITY BEFORE THE LAW.

**stateless person.** A person who is not considered as a national by any state under the operation of its law: United Nations Convention relating to the Status of Stateless Persons of September 28, 1954 art.1. See Irish Nationality and Citizenship Act 1986 s.5. See NATURALISATION; REFUGEE.

**statement.** Provision has been made for the admission in criminal proceedings of written statements of matters which are not in dispute between the parties; previously such statements had to be proved by oral evidence: Criminal Justice Act 1984 s.21. See CONFESSION; JUDGES' RULES; PREVIOUS STATEMENT, INCONSISTENT; SOLICITOR, ACCESS TO; UNSWORN STATEMENT.

**statement, liability for false.** See DECEIT.

**statement of affairs.** (1) The statement required to be filed in court of a company's affairs following a winding up order or the appointment of a provisional liquidator by the court. It must be in a prescribed form and verified by affidavit. See Companies Act 1963 s.224; RSC O.74 rr 24-28. The statement may be used in evidence against any person making or concurring in making it: Companies Act 1990 s.18.

(2) The statement required to be made by a bankrupt and by an arranging debtor (qv): Bankruptcy Act 1988 ss.19 and 91. See BANKRUPT, DUTIES OF.

**statement of claim.** A written or printed statement by a plaintiff in an action by *plenary* summons in the High Court, stating the facts on which he relies to support his claim against the defendant, and the relief which he claims: RSC O.20. The plaintiff may amend his statement of claim once without leave (ibid O.28 r.2). The statement of claim must be served within twenty one days after service of the summons (ibid O.20 r.2) in default of which the defendant may apply to dismiss the action for want of prosecution (ibid O.27 r.1; McGowan v Doherty (1986) HC). The court may, at any stage in the proceedings, allow a plaintiff to alter or amend his pleadings for the purpose of determining the real questions in controversy between the parties (ibid O.28 r.1). The statement of claim may be amended to introduce a new and hitherto unpleaded claim (ibid O.28 r.6 and Rubotham v M & B Bakeries Ltd and Irish National Insurance Co plc (1993 HC) ILRM 219.

In arbitration, *points of claim* are the equivalent to the statement of claim. See INDORSEMENT OF CLAIM; PLEADINGS.

**station bail.** The setting at liberty of a person on a recognisance (qv), the person having been charged with an offence in a garda station: Criminal Procedure Act 1967 s.31(1). The District Court does not receive seisin of the matter until the charge is laid before a judge: The State (Lynch) v Ballagh (1987) ILRM 65. See also The State (DPP) v Ruane (1987) HC.

**statistics.** Includes, in addition to numerical data, information not expressible numerically which is necessary for the collection, compilation, analysis or interpretation of data: Statistics Act 1993 s.3(1). This Act (a) establishes the Central Statistics Office (CSO) as a statutory body with responsibility for the compilation of official statistics, (b) establishes a National Statistics Board to guide the strategic direction of the CSO, (c) provides for the confidentiality of all information collected by the CSO and for its use for statistical purposes only, (d) provides that the Taoiseach may prescribe by order a statutory requirement on persons and undertakings to provide statistical information.

Statistics are collected on many matters eg population; vital, social and educational matters; local government; employment and unemployment; emigration and immigration; agriculture; sea and inland fisheries; industry; commerce; banking, insurance and finance; transport; and ancient monuments. See, for example, Statistics (Census of Production) Order 1988 (SI No 167 of 1988).

A CSO publication or a document signed by the Director General of the CSO must be accepted in legal proceedings as prima facie evidence of any official statistic (ibid 1993 Act s.45). See also Vital Statistics and Births, Deaths and Marriages Registration Act 1952; SI No 280 of 1954; SI No 302 of 1956; EC (Intrastat) Regulations 1993 (SI No 136 of 1993). See CENSUS; CONSUMER PRICE INDEX.

**status.** The legal position or condition of a person eg a minor, a married woman, a dependent child, a child whose parents are not married to each other, an adopted child, a person of full age, an alien, an Irish citizen, a citizen of the EC, a bankrupt, a person of unsound mind, a ward of court (qv). The legal rights and duties, powers and disabilities, of a person depend on the legal status of that person. See CHILD, STATUS OF.

**status quo ante.** [The same state as before]. See Curust Financial Services Ltd v Loewe-Lack-Werk Otto Loewe GmbH & Co KG (1993 SC) ITLR (11 Jan).

**statute-barred.** Term used to indicate that proceedings in a cause of action have not been commenced within the time allowed by statute. See Sheehan v Amond (1982) IR 235. See CAUSE OF ACTION; LIMITATION OF ACTIONS.

**statute, citation of.** Legislation can be cited by reference to the short title (qv) therein specified eg *Companies (Amendment) Act 1983.*

**statute, interpretation of.** See LEGISLATION, INTERPRETATION OF.

**statute law.** The body of law enacted by the parliamentary process. A *statute* includes, in addition to Acts of the Oireachtas (qv), Acts of the Oireachtas of Saorstat Eireann (qv), Acts of the Parliament of the former United Kingdom of Great Britain and Ireland, and Acts of a Parliament sitting in Ireland at any time before the coming into force of the Union with Ireland Act 1800: Interpretation Act 1937 s.3. See ACT; BILL; STATUTORY INSTRUMENT.

**Statute of Frauds (Ireland).** The Statute passed in 1695 to prevent fraud and perjury. It required certain contracts to be *evidenced* by some memorandum in writing signed by the party to be charged or his agent. These contracts are: (a) any special promise by an executor to answer damages out of his own estate; (b) any special promise to answer for the debt, default or miscarriage of another person (a *contract of guarantee*): Dunville & Co v Quinn (1908) 42 ILTR 49; (c) an agreement in consideration of marriage: Saunders v Cramer (1842) 5 I Eq 12; (d) any contract for the sale of land or any interest in land; (e) any agreement not to be performed within the space of one year from the making thereof: Naughton v Limestone Land Co Ltd (1952) Ir Jur Rep 19; Hynes v Hynes (1984) HC. See also Guardian Builders v Sleecon & Berville (1989) 7 ILT Dig 22. See MEMORANDUM, STATUTE OF FRAUDS; ORAL AGREEMENT, MODIFICATION OF CONTRACT BY; PART-PERFORMANCE; QUANTUM MERUIT; TRUST, EXPRESS.

**Statute of Limitations.** See LIMITATION OF ACTIONS; TIME.

**statutory company.** See COMPANY, STATUTORY.

**statutory declaration.** A written statement of facts which the person making it, the *declarant*, signs and solemnly declares conscientiously believing it to be true, before a notary public (qv), a commissioner of oaths (qv), or a peace commissioner (qv): Statutory Declarations Act 1938. A statutory declaration in connection with an application for a grant, loan, subsidy, or assistance under the Housing Acts, may be made by a person before a clergyman or a member of the garda siochana: Housing (Miscellaneous Provisions) Act 1992 s.21.

It is an offence for a person to make a statutory declaration knowing it to be false or misleading in any material respect (ibid 1938 Act s.6). Declarations were substituted for oaths in many cases by the Statutory Declarations Act 1835 and are now required by many statutes eg Companies (Amendment) Act 1983 s.5(5). See Interpretation Act 1937 s.12 sch.

**statutory duty.** A duty or liability, imposed by some statutes. A failure to carry out a statutory duty may amount to a tort (qv) depending on the construction of the statute. A breach of a statutory duty may give rise to a private right of action where the absence of such a right would infringe the constitutional right of the plaintiff eg the right to earns one's livelihood: Parsons v Kavanagh (1990) ILRM 560.

Failure to comply with the provisions of the Building Control Act 1990 does not entitle a person to bring any civil proceedings by reason only of that contravention (ibid s.21). Failure to comply with general statutory duties imposed on employers, employees, designers and manufacturers in relation to safety, health and welfare at work cannot confer a right of action in civil proceedings; however breach of a duty imposed by regulations may do so: Safety, Health and Welfare at Work Act 1989 s.60. See also Dunleary v Glen Abbey Ltd (1992 HC) ILRM 1.

**statutory instrument.** An order, regulation, rule, scheme or bye-law made in exercise of a power conferred by statute: Statutory Instruments Act 1947. They are often formal documents by which designated Ministers exercise their power to make sub-ordinate legislation, which power is given to them by various statutes.

Statutory instruments may be cited by number and year and also by their title eg SI No 46 of 1987; Courts Martial (Legal Aid) Regulations 1987. Many statutory instruments are required to be placed before the Houses of the Oireachtas (qv) and only become effective after a specified period if they are not annulled by a resolution of either House. [Text: Humphreys]. See BYE-LAW; REGULATION; STATUTORY RULES AND ORDERS.

**statutory interpretation.** The interpretation of statutes is said to be by the *mischief* approach and the *literal* approach. Under the former, the judge is concerned primarily with ascertaining the policy or goals which the provision in question was adopted to promote, and the provision will be applied in the light of that purpose.

Under the *literal* approach, the judge will give effect to the literal meaning of the provision even if that is inconsistent with what the legislature was endeavouring to achieve. Words in a statute are to be considered in their context and surrounding circumstances: Dillon v Minister for Posts Telegraphs (1981) ILRM 477. See LEGISLATION, INTERPRETATION OF.

**statutory power, restraint of.** No special principle governs the grant of an interlocutory injunction restraining the exercise of a statutory power: Pesca Valentia Ltd v Minister for Fisheries (1986) ILRM 68. See INJUNCTION.

**statutory rape.** See CARNAL KNOWLEDGE, UNLAWFUL; SEXUAL ASSAULT; RAPE.

**statutory rules and orders.** [SR & O]. The former name given to statutory instruments (qv). [Text: Humphreys].

**statutory sitting.** The sitting of the court at which a bankrupt must make a full disclosure of his property and at which the creditors may prove their debts and choose and appoint a *creditors' assignee*: Bankruptcy Act 1988 s.17. A statutory sitting is held within three weeks of the publication of the notice of the adjudication of the debtor as a bankrupt in Iris Oifigiuil (qv) and in at least one daily newspaper in circulation in the area where the bankrupt resides. For procedure, see SI No 79 of 1989, Part VII. The second sitting, formerly held, was abolished by the 1988 Act. See BANKRUPTCY.

**statutory tenant.** See TENANT, STATUTORY.

**statutory undertaker.** A person authorised by statute to construct, work, or carry on a railway, canal, inland navigation, dock, harbour, gas, electricity, or other public undertaking: LG (P&D) Act 1963 s.2(1); Environmental Protection Agency Act 1992 s.3. A statutory undertaker who wishes to carry out works on roads must obtain consent: Roads Act 1993 s.53.

**stay of execution.** The suspension of the operation of a judgment or order of a court. The court may, at or after the time of giving judgment or making an order, stay execution until such time as it thinks fit; also any party against whom judgment has been given, may apply to the court for a stay of execution or other relief against the judgment, upon the grounds of facts which have arisen too late to be pleaded: RSC O.42 rr.17 and 28.

While the Court has discretion to grant a stay, special reasons must exist to enable that discretion to be exercised: Rohan Construction Ltd v Antigen Ltd (1989) ITLR (8 May). An appeal of a judgment does not automatically operate as a stay on execution: RSC O.58 r.18; O.61 r.6. An appellant is not generally entitled to an unconditional stay of execution: Corish v Hogan (1990 SC) ITLR (21 May).

When deciding whether to grant a stay of execution on an award of damages (qv), the Court must balance conflicting considerations so that the justice will not be denied to either party: Redmond v Ireland and AG (1992 SC) ILRM 291. A stay which has been granted without objection from the plaintiff may be later removed where the justice of the case lay in such removal: Emerald Meats Ltd v Minister for Agriculture (No 2) (1993 SC) 11 ILT Dig 116. A stay will be granted on an order of discovery (qv) where a refusal to grant the stay would determine the action: Magaleasing UK Ltd v Barrett (1991 SC) ITLR (29 Jul).

It has been held that the Supreme Court has not the power to grant a stay of execution of an order of the High Court to release a person: The State (Trimbole) v Governor of Mountjoy Prison (1985) IR 567.

See also RCC O.30 r.14; O.35 r.7; DCR r.142 and r.192 (as amended by DCR 1955 r.16). See also Enforcement of Court Orders Act 1926 ss.21 and 51. See O'Toole v RTE (1993 SC) ILRM 454. See EXECUTION OF JUDGMENT; STOP ORDER.

**stay of proceedings.** The suspension of proceedings by a court eg (a) where the proceedings are vexatious or frivolous, or (b) where legal proceedings are instituted contrary to an arbitration agreement; or (c) where no reasonable cause of action is shown; or (d) on acceptance of lodgment; or (e) where a preliminary issue of law is to be decided.

As regards a company, when a winding-up order has been made or a provisional liquidator appointed, no action or proceeding may be proceeded with or commenced against the company except by leave of the court and subject to such terms as the court may impose: Companies Act 1963 s.222. This does not apply to proceedings before the Employment Appeals Tribunal: Companies (Amdt) Act 1986 s.23. The court may allow secured creditors to proceed to enforce their security in such company cases and also proceedings in respect of fatal accidents under the Civil Liabilities Act 1961. See RSC O.19 r.28; O.22 r.4(2); O.34 r.2; O.56 r.2; RCC O.14 r.4; O.18 r.4; O.31 r.1; O.12 r.11; DCR r.131. See also Murphy v Hennessy (1985) ILRM 100. See ABUSE OF PROCESS; ARBITRATION; OPPRESSIVE PROCEEDINGS; STEP IN PROCEEDINGS.

**stealing.** See LARCENY.

**step in proceedings.** Delivery of pleadings or taking any other steps in court proceedings is fatal to an application by a party to an arbitration agreement to have the court proceedings *stayed* in respect of any matter agreed to be referred to arbitration: Arbitration Act 1980 s.5.

The court will only refuse to *stay* proceedings if satisfied that the party seeking such order has instituted some process in the action which involves costs which are lost when the matter is referred to arbitration; seeking an extension of time from the other party within which to lodge a defence is not a step in the proceedings: O'Flynn v An Bord Gais Eireann (1982) ILRM 324. See also MacCormack Products Ltd v Town of Monaghan Co-op Ltd (1988) IR 304. See ARBITRATION.

**sterile transaction.** In a company, a transaction which has no tangible economic benefit to the company. Sterile transactions which fall within the terms of a particular objects clause of a company's memorandum of association are not ultra vires. See Parke v Daily News Ltd (1962) Ch 927; In re Horsley Weight Ltd (1982) 1 Ch 442.

**stet.** [Let it stand].

**stet processus.** [Stay of proceedings].

**still born.** See FOETAL DEATH.

**stirpes.** Stocks or families. See PER STIRPES.

**stock.** (1) A family or line of descent. (2) The capital of a company consisting of fully paid shares which have been converted and combined into one unit eg 1000 shares of £1 each becoming stock of £1000; formerly called its joint-stock, signifying that it was a common or joint fund contributed by its members. See SUCCESSION; COMPANY; SHARES.

**stock exchange.** A place appointed for the purchase and sale of stocks and shares and other securities. The Irish stock exchange merged with the London stock exchange in 1973. The rules of the exchange must be complied with in order for a company to secure and retain a quotation for its securities. A *recognised stock exchange* for the purposes of any provision of the Companies Acts is an exchange prescribed by the Minister: Companies Act 1990 s.3(2).

The Irish stock exchange is largely self regulating. It is a *competent authority* for the purposes of EC Directives concerning stock exchanges: SI No 282 of 1984. Take-over bids between companies quoted on the exchange must comply with the City Code on Take-Overs and Mergers.

The practice of an exchange may amount to a custom which is incorporated as an implied term into contracts between buyers and sellers of securities.

Companies which seek a stock exchange quotation for their securities must satisfy the rules for admission of securities for listing (Listing Agreement) which are contained in the *Yellow Book*. In 1981 an unlisted securities market (USM) was opened to cater for companies which cannot satisfy these stringent rules.

It is planned that the Irish stock exchange will be independent of the London stock exchange in 1994, implementing the EC Investment Services Directive. See 39 Geo 111 ch 40 (Ir) for the original establishment of the Dublin stock exchange. See STOCKBROKER.

**stock transfer.** The Stock Transfer Act 1963 provides for a simplified transfer of securities. See TRANSFER OF SHARES.

**stolen property.** See HANDLING STOLEN PROPERTY; RESTITUTION OF POSSESSION; REVESTING; WITHHOLDING INFORMATION.

**stop and search.** A garda has power to stop and search a person where he suspects that the person has *anything stolen or unlawfully obtained*: Dublin Police Act 1842 s.29. The suspect may be stopped for the purpose of exercising the power of search and need not be formally placed under arrest prior to the search; the garda must tell the suspect of his suspicion and his power under s.29: DPP v Rooney (1993 HC) ILRM 61.

**stop, obligation to.** The obligation of a person driving a vehicle in a public place to stop the vehicle on being so required by a garda: Road Traffic Act 1961 s.109. A garda is authorised to stop a motor vehicle without having a particular reason to do so in order to ascertain if the vehicle was being driven by a drunken driver: DPP v Fagan (1993 HC) ITLR (8 Mar).

**stop order.** An order of the court made on the application of a person having any derivative interest in any funds or securities standing in court, to stay the transfer, sale, payment out or other disposition of the funds or securities, without notice to the applicant, which application is made ex-parte and grounded on an affidavit of facts: RSC O.46 rr.14-18. The derivative interest which the applicant must have, may be by way of assignment, or charge or lien or otherwise eg a judgment creditor. See CHARGING ORDER; DISTRINGAS NOTICE.

**stoppage in transitu.** The right which an unpaid seller has to resume possession of goods and to retain them until payment or tender of the price, where the buyer has become insolvent. The right exists only as long as the goods are in transit; if the buyer or his agent obtains delivery of the goods before their arrival at the appointed destination, the transit is at an end. The seller's right is not affected by any sale or disposition of the goods by the buyer, unless the seller has assented thereto, or unless the documents of title to the goods have been transferred to a person who takes them in good faith and for valuable consideration. See Sale of Goods Act 1893 ss.44-48.

**stopping of cheque.** See CHEQUE, COUNTERMAND OF PAYMENT.

**stranger.** One who is not privy or party to an act or transaction.

**stranger to the consideration.** A phrase used where a person may be a party to a contract, but cannot sue for its performance because he is a *stranger to the consideration* eg A, B and C enter into a contract under which A promises both B and C that if B will perform an act, A will give £200 to C; B can compel A to pay C, but C cannot sue as he is a stranger to the consideration.

There is an exception as regards a bill of exchange where an antecedent debt or liability suffices as consideration (ie *past* consideration), in addition to consideration sufficient to support a simple contract: Bills of Exchange Act 1882 s.27. See Roscorla v Thomas (1842) 3 QB 234: Dunlop Tyre Co v Selfridge & Co (1915) AC 847; Shadwell v Shadwell (1860) 9 CB(NS) 159. See CONSIDERATION; PRIVITY OF CONTRACT.

**stray dog.** Includes any dog which appears to be unaccompanied by a person unless such dog is in the premises of its owner or of some other person who has the dog in his charge or of any other person with that person's consent: Control of Dogs Act 1986 s.11(11). Stray dogs may be seized by dog wardens or the garda siochana and disposed of or destroyed. A person claiming a stray dog must produce a current dog licence in respect of that dog (ibid s.11(5)(b) as substituted by Control of Dogs (Amdt) Act 1992 s.5).

**street lighting.** The lighting of streets, markets and public buildings which local authorities are empowered to supply or to contract with others to supply by means of gas or other means: Public Health (Ireland) Act 1878 s.80; Public Health (Ireland) Act 1896 s.1; Town Improvements (Ireland) Act 1854 s.51 now repealed by Roads Act 1993 s.4. See PUBLIC LIGHTING.

**street trading.** Selling of goods by retail in a street to passers-by which was regulated by the Street Trading Act 1926, which now stands repealed as it applies to casual trading (qv) or occasional trading (qv). Note however the transitional provisions under s.19(2) of the Casual Trading Act 1980. See CASUAL TRADING.

**strict liability.** Legal obligation or duty which is independent of wrongful intent or negligence. See Mullen v Quinnsworth Ltd (1991 SC) ITLR (17 Jun). See also O'Higgins in 9ILT & SJ (1991) 134. Contrast with *fault liability* which is dependent on proof of negligence. See ACT OF GOD; OIL POLLUTION; PRODUCT LIABIL-ITY; RYLANDS V FLETCHER, RULE IN.

**strict liability in criminal law.** If a matter is made a criminal offence, it is essential that there should be something in the nature of *mens rea* ... But there are exceptions to this rule... and *the reason for this is, that the legislature has thought it so important to prevent the particular act from being committed that it absolutely forbids it to be done; and if it is done the offender is liable to a penalty whether he has any mens rea or not, and whether or not he intended to commit a breach of the law*: Pearks, Gunston & Tee Ltd v Ward (1902) 2 KB 1. See MENS REA.

**strict settlement.** A settlement which was designed to keep land in the family. The usual settlement gave a life interest to the husband and a fee tail (qv) to the children. Provision was made for the wife by giving her a *jointure* (qv) and for the children, who did not obtain the land under the entails, by giving them *portions* (qv). The difficulties which such a settlement created were overcome by the Settled Land Acts 1882 and 1890, which gave extensive powers to the *tenant for life* and protected the interests of those entitled in succession. See SETTLEMENT.

**stricti juris.** [According to strict right or law].

**strike.** Cessation of work by any number or body of workers acting in combination, or a concerted refusal or a refusal under common understanding of any number of workers to continue to work for their employer, done as a means of compelling their employer, or to aid other workers in compelling their employer, to accept or not to accept terms or conditions of or affecting employment: Industrial Relations Act 1990 s.8. See also Unfair Dismissals Act 1977 s.1; Redundancy Payments Act 1967 s.6. Such action can expose the participants to liability unless it is *in contemplation or furtherance of a trade dispute* (qv).

As from 18 July 1992 the rules of every trade union must contain certain provisions relating to the holding of a *secret ballot* in respect of strikes and other industrial action (ibid 1990 Act s.14). Action taken in disregard of or contrary to the outcome of a secret ballot does not enjoy the immunity conferred on members and trade unions by ss.10-12 of the 1990 Act (ibid s.17). Supportive action by another trade union must not be taken without the approval of the Irish Congress of Trade Unions (ibid s.14 (3)).

An employee going on strike does not necessarily frustrate or repudiate his contract of employment: Becton Dickinson Ltd v Lee (1973) IR 1; Bates v Model Bakery Ltd (1992 SC) ELR 193.

Dismissal of an employee for taking part in a strike will be deemed an unfair dismissal if one or more of the striking employees were not dismissed, or were dismissed but subsequently permitted to resume employment: Unfair Dismissals Act 1977 s.5(2) as amended by Unfair Dismissals (Amdt) Act 1993 s.4.

Unemployment resulting directly from a trade dispute in which the claimant is involved, disqualifies him from receiving social welfare benefit or assistance: Social Welfare (Consolidation) Act 1981 ss.35(1), 142(3), 203(1) and Social Welfare (Family Income Supplement) Regulations 1984, art 20(1). However, unemployment benefit or assistance may be paid to a person on strike if the Social Welfare Tribunal considers it reasonable in all the circumstances: Social Welfare (No 2) Act 1982. See also Social Welfare (No 2) Act 1987 ss.13-14. See Twomey in ISLR (1993) 131. See LABOUR INJUNCTION; TRADE DISPUTE; PICKETING; UNLAWFUL INTERFERENCE WITH CONSTITUTIONAL RIGHTS.

**strike off.** The Registrar of Companies is empowered to strike defunct companies off the register: Companies Act 1963 s.311. Notice is given in Iris Oifigiuil (qv) of the intention to *strike off* the name of a stated company unless cause is shown to the contrary: Companies (Amdt) Act 1982 s.12 as amended by Companies Act 1990 s.245. The Registrar may restore a company to the register, in which case the company is deemed to have continued in existence as if its name had not been struck off: 1990 Act s.246 inserting s.311A in the 1963 Act.

**strike out.** An order of a court to withdraw an action or a claim or part of a claim or a defence eg a defence may be struck out where a defendant fails to comply with an order of discovery (qv): RSC O.31 r.21; RCC O.29 r.6.

A district court judge may strike out any case brought in his court which the court has not jurisdiction to hear: DCR r.14. The district court may also strike out a case where there is excessive delay in bringing a case, (the onus being on the State to justify the delay) or where the defendant would be prejudiced by the delay (the onus being on the defendant to prove prejudice): DPP v Carlton (1992 HC) 10 ILT Dig 73.

The court may order any pleading to be struck out on the ground that it discloses no reasonable cause of action or where it appears from the pleadings that the action is frivolous or vexatious the court may order the action to be stayed or to be dismissed: RSC O.19 r.28. A court has jurisdiction to strike out any claim which is an *abuse of process* of court: Kelly v Ireland (1986) ILRM 318. However, it should only exercise this inherent jurisdiction where it is clearly established that the plaintiff's claim is unsustainable; where there are questions of fact and of controversial legal arguments to be resolved, the matter cannot be said to be so clear and unassailable that the plaintiff's claim should be struck out: DK v AK and Governors of Rotunda Hospital (1992 HC) ITLR (14 Dec). See also Olympia Productions Ltd v Cameron Mackintosh (1992 HC) ITLR (3 Feb).

**sub colore juris.** [Under colour of the law].

**sub contractors, payment of.** Any person who receives from a *principal contractor* any payment in relation to the performance of the whole or any part of a *construction contract*: Finance Act 1970 s.17 as amended by Finance Acts 1991 s.128 and 1992 s.28. Every principal contractor is required to deduct tax from that payment. No such deduction of tax is required where a subcontractor has a *certificate of authorisation* from the Revenue Commissioners.

**sub judice.** [In course of trial]. Not yet decided; under judicial consideration. When a matter is before a court and is sub judice, any words or action which have a tendency to interfere with the fair administration of justice may amount to a *contempt of court*. See Desmond v Minister for Industry & Commerce (1992 HC) ILRM 489. The courts may act to prevent the publication in the media of anything which may prejudice the fair trial of an action and impose a punishment for such publication. The rules of the Houses of the Oireachtas prohibit debate on a matter which is sub judice. See CONTEMPT OF COURT.

**sub-letting.** A grant to another by a *lessee* of a letting for a period less than the period held by the lessee under his lease. The lessee retains a reversion (qv) on the sub-letting or sub-lease and remains subject to all the rights and liabilities under the lease. See Deasy's Act 1860 ss.9,12,13; Landlord and Tenant (Amendment) Act 1980 s.66. See LEASE; LEASE, CREATION OF.

**sub modo.** [Under consideration or restriction].

**sub nom; sub monine.** [Under the name].

**sub-ordinate legislation.** See DELEGATED LEGISLATION.

**sub rosa.** [Under the rose]. Confidentially.

**sub silentio.** [Under silence].

**sub tit; sub titulo.** [Under the title of].

**sub voce.** [Under the title].

**subinfeudation.** See FEUDAL SYSTEM.

**subject to contract.** Generally, an offer or acceptance made *subject to contract* means that no legally binding agreement or contract will exist until the formal contract has been completed by the parties. There may be a binding contract if the court can conclude that all the terms of a bargain have been agreed and set down in writing and signed. See Lowis v Wilson (1949) IR 347; O'Flaherty v Arran Property (1976) SC; Kelly v Park Hall Schools (1979) 113 ILTR 9 ; Casey v Irish Intercontinental Bank (1979) IR 364; Mulhall v Haren (1981) IR 364; Carthy v O'Neill (1981) ILRM 443; Cunningham v Maher 9ILT & SJ (1991 CC) 168; Boyle & Boyle v Lee & Goyns (1992 SC) ILRM 65. See ACCEPTANCE; GAZUMPING; MEMORANDUM, STATUTE OF FRAUDS.

**submission.** The instrument by which a dispute or question is referred to arbitration pursuant to an agreement between the parties.

**subordination of debt.** A process whereby one creditor, secured or unsecured, agrees to rank after another eg subordinated bond issues, particularly by banks and other financial institutions.

There is statutory recognition of *subordination of debts* in the winding up of a company: Companies Act 1963 s.275 as amended by Companies Act 1990 s.132. [Text: Wood (UK)].

**subornation of perjury.** The offence of procuring a person to commit a perjury (qv) which he actually commits in consequence of such procurement.

**subpoena.** [Under penalty]. An order issued in an action or arbitration requiring the person to whom it is directed to be present at a specified place and time and for a specified purpose under penalty. A *subpoena ad testificandum* commands a witness to attend and give evidence. A *subpoena duces tecum* commands a witness to attend and give evidence and to bring with him and to produce certain documents specified in the subpoena.

In High Court proceedings a *praecipe* in a particular form is delivered and filed at the Central Office when it is intended to apply for the issue of a subpoena; in Circuit Court proceedings, a *witness summons* is issued by the county registrar or by the court (in case of difficulty); and in the District Court it is issued by the judge or by the clerk of the court: RSC O.61 rr.18-19; RSC O.39 r.25-34, Appendix D; RCC O.21; DCR r.148. An order of the Master of the High Court must be obtained before a *subpoena duces tecum* may be served on a public official to produce any record in his custody: RSC O.39 rr.30-31.

A District Court judge may order the arrest of a person who fails to appear to a witness summons and no just excuse is offered for such failure; the judge can set aside or disregard the summons if reasonable expenses have not been paid or offered to the witness. A Circuit Court judge may attach a witness who fails without lawful excuse to attend or he may impose a fine: RCC O.21. In the High Court, any person wilfully disobeying an order requiring his attendance will be deemed guilty of *contempt of court* (qv) and may be dealt with accordingly: RSC O.39 r.7. If he attends but refuses to be sworn, or to answer any lawful question, he may be ordered to pay any costs occasioned by his refusal or objection (ibid rr.12-14).

A subpoena may be issued against a

person having custody of a will in order to compel lodgment of the will in the probate office: RSC O.79 r.59. See also Criminal Procedure Act 1967 s.9; Criminal Justice Act 1993 s.11(b).

**subrogation.** Substitution. Subrogation is a convenient way of describing a transfer of rights from one person to another, without assignment or assent of the person from whom the rights are transferred and which takes place by operation of law in a whole variety of circumstances eg arising from contract as in insurance or to prevent an unjust enrichment (qv): Orakpo v Manson Investments Ltd (1977) 3 WLR 229 cited in Highland Finance v Sacred Heart College (1993 HC) ILRM 263.

In subrogation, a person or thing is substituted for an other, so that the same rights and duties which attach to the original person or thing, attach to the substituted one. If one person is substituted for another, he is said *to stand in the other's shoes.*

In insurance, the insurer can be subrogated to the rights of the insured and can maintain an action against a third party who caused the loss suffered by the insured, but only when the insured has been paid. The insurer can enforce a remedy which the insured could have enforced against a third party. Also, a person paying the premium on a policy of insurance belonging to another may be subrogated to that other. See Driscoll v Driscoll (1918) 1 IR 152; Orakpo v Manson Investments (1978) AC 95; Hibernian Insurance v Eagle Star Insurance (1987) HC; Zurich Insurance v Shield Insurance (1988 SC) IR 174; Incorporated Law Society v Owens (1990) 8ILT Dig 64.

Where moneys are advanced for the purchase of property by the borrower, the lender is entitled to be subrogated to the rights of the vendor unless the bargain between the lender and the borrower is inconsistent with the retention of a right of subrogation: Bank of Ireland Finance Ltd v Daly (1978) IR 79. See also Marine Insurance Act 1906 s.79.

For subrogation in international contract law, see Contractual Obligations (Applicable Law) Act 1991, first schedule, art.13.

**subscribe.** To sign or attest; to write under. To apply for shares in a company.

**subscribing witness.** A person who signs a document as an attesting witness. See ATTESTATION.

**subscription.** An application for shares. See PROSPECTUS.

**subsequent bankruptcy.** Where an *undischarged bankrupt* (qv) is again adjudicated a bankrupt. Formerly, the Official Assignee (qv) claimed the assets of the second bankruptcy for the benefit of the first bankruptcy. Now, creditors of second and subsequent bankruptcies have priority in those bankruptcies: Bankruptcy Act 1988 s.43.

All *after-acquired property* (qv) in the possession of or unclaimed by the Official Assignee at the date of the subsequent bankruptcy transfers or vests to the credit of the subsequent bankruptcy. Any surplus arising on a subsequent bankruptcy is transferred to the credit of the former bankruptcy.

**subsidiarity, principle of.** The principle enshrined in European Community law whereby in areas which do not fall within its exclusive competence, the Community is to take action only if and in so far as the objectives of the proposed action cannot be sufficiently achieved by the member States and can therefore, by reason of the scale or effects of the proposed action, be better achieved by the Community: Treaty of Rome 1957 art.3b inserted by Maastricht Treaty 1992 art.G(B)(5). Also any action by the Community must not go beyond what is necessary to achieve the objectives of the Treaty. The Edinburgh European Council (Dec 1992) agreed guidelines to be used in examining whether a proposal for a Community measure conforms with art.3b.

An example of subsidiarity is the new EC policy on *education*, wherein national governments are fully responsible for the content of education and the organisation of educational systems and the EC role is to support and supplement the actions of the member States. See PROPORTIONALITY.

**subsidiary company.** See HOLDING COMPANY.

**subsidy.** A subvention.

**substantial grounds.** Where the court is required by statute to be satisfied that there are *substantial grounds* for a particular view, substantial means something more than *reasonable grounds*: Richardson v London County Council (1957) 1 WLR 751 cited with approval in O'Dowd v North Western Health Board (1983 SC) ILRM 186. Substantial grounds has also been held to mean more than probable or prima facie grounds: Murphy v Greene (1991 SC) ILRM 404. See SATISFIED.

**substantive law.** The actual law, as opposed to adjectival or procedural law. See ADJECTIVE LAW.

**substitute.** See REPEAL.

**substituted service.** See SUMMONS, SERVICE OF.

**substratum.** [Bottom or basis].

**succeed, unworthiness to.** The preclusion of certain specified persons from taking any share in the estate of another eg a sane person who has been guilty of the murder, attempted murder or manslaughter of another; a spouse against whom the deceased obtained a decree of divorce a *mensa et thoro;* a spouse guilty of desertion for at least two years; a person found guilty of an offence against the deceased (or against his spouse or child) punishable by imprisonment for at least two years: Succession Act 1965 s.120. See also Judicial Separation and Family Law Reform Act 1989 s.17. See SPOUSE, LEGAL RIGHT OF.

**succession.** The devolution of property on the death of its owner; where property passes on the death of a corporation sole to his successor.

**succession, law of.** The branch of law governing the devolution of property on the death of its owner. Property devolves on death to *personal representatives,* known as *executors* where the deceased left a will (testate succession) and *administrators* where there is no will (intestate succession). Executors are usually appointed by the will and administrators by the court. The personal representatives transfer the property to the *beneficiaries.*

The State guarantees to pass no law attempting to abolish the general right to bequeath or inherit property, subject to regulation of that right by the principles of social justice: 1937 Constitution, art.43. The Succession Act 1965 changed the previous law significantly;

inter alia, it gives the surviving spouse a *legal right* to a share in the estate and provides protection for the interest of children. There is provision for the extinguishing of succession rights where a decree of *judicial separation* has been granted: Judicial Separation and Family Law Reform Act 1989 s.17. See Report on the Hague Convention on Succession to the Estates of Deceased Persons (LRC 36 of 1991). [Text: Brady; Maguire; Maxwell; Mongey; Theobald UK]. See WILL; INTESTATE SUCCESSION; PROBATE; LETTERS OF ADMINISTRATION; ADMINISTRATION OF ESTATES.

**successor.** For capital acquisitions tax purposes, a person who takes an inheritance: Capital Acquisitions Tax Act 1976 s.2.

**successor company.** The public company, limited by shares, into which a building society converts itself: Building Societies Act 1989 s.100. Such a company's independence is protected for a period of 5 years after conversion against any one person gaining control. See CONVERSION.

**sue.** To bring an action against a person.

**sufference, tenancy by.** See TENANCY BY SUFFERENCE.

**suffrage.** Right to vote in an election. See FRANCHISE.

**suggestio falsi.** [Suggestion of falsehood]. An active misrepresentation (qv) as opposed to a *suppresio veri* (qv) or passive misrepresentation.

**sui generis.** [Of its own right]. Constituting a class of its own; the only one of its kind.

**sui juris.** [Of one's own right]. A person of full legal capacity. A person who can validly contract and bind himself by legal obligation uncontrolled by any other person.

**suicide.** Formerly, the common law felony (qv) of self-murder. The crime of suicide or attemped suicide has been abolished: Criminal Law (Suicide) Act 1993 s.2(1). However, a person who aids, abets, counsels or procures the suicide of another, or an attempt by another to commit suicide is guilty of an offence (ibid s.2(2)). A person who assists another in suicide by killing that other is guilty of murder. A *suicide pact* survivor may be guilty of an offence as encouraging the suicide of another (ibid s.2(3)). See

Verrier v DPP (1966) 3 AER 568.

In insurance law, there is a rebuttable presumption against suicide and in favour of an accident: Harvey v Ocean Accident & Guarantee Corporation (1905) 2 IR 1; The State (McKeown) v Scully (1986) ILRM 133; Kelleher v Irish Life Assurance Co Ltd (1989) 7 ILT Dig 229. See Report of the Department of Justice's Advisory Group on Prison Deaths (1991). See O'Mahony in 10 ILT & SJ (1992) 258. See INQUEST.

**suit.** A legal proceeding; an action.

**suitor.** A person who is a party to a suit.

**suitors, funds of.** The cash and securities belonging to suitors and other persons which have been transferred to or paid into and deposited with the High Court. In the ordinary way these funds may be used only for the benefit of those entitled to them. A small proportion of the funds is represented by unclaimed balances and dividends which have accumulated over a long period, as long as two centuries, and these funds are being used principally for renovation work on the King's Inns (qv) building. See Funds of Suitors Act 1984. See also RCC O.15 r.3 — Iris Oifigiuil 10th November 1992.

**sum assured.** Often refers to the maximum sum which is payable under a policy of insurance. The sum payable may be less if there is an average clause (qv). Where a fixed sum is payable irrespective of loss the policy is called a *valued policy*. The sum payable may also be affected by the operation of a *reinstatement clause* (qv).

In marine insurance (qv) a valued policy is one which specifies the agreed value of the subject matter insured; in the absence of fraud, the value fixed by the policy is, as between the insurer and the assured, conclusive of the insurable value whether the loss be total or partial: Marine Insurance Act 1906 s.27. See INSURANCE, CONTRACT OF.

**summary conviction.** See SUMMARY OFFENCE; SUMMARY PROCEEDINGS.

**summary dismissal.** Dismissal of an employee without the notice to which the employee is entitled by statute or by virtue of his contract of employment. It may be justified by reason of the employee's misconduct eg theft, fighting. See McCarthy v O'Sullivan Brothers Ltd (1991 EAT) ELR 44; Caffrey v

Avonmore Creameries Ltd (1991 EAT) ELR 51; O'Mahony v Whelan (1992 EAT) ELR 117. See NOTICE, EMPLOYMENT; UNFAIR DISMISSAL.

**summary judgment.** The judgment in the Circuit Court for which a plaintiff may apply in certain circumstances eg where the plaintiff's claim is for a debt or liquidated sum in money, and the plaintiff proves by affidavit that the defendant has no bona fides defence to the claim and that the appearance or defence (if any) has been entered solely for the purpose of delay: RCC O.25. See also Circuit Court Rules (No 1) 1983 (SI No 267 of 1983). For summary judgment procedure in the District Court, see District Court (Summary Judgment) Rules 1963 (SI No 213 of 1963). As regards the High Court, see SUMMARY SUMMONS.

**summary offence.** An offence heard by the District Court (qv), without a jury and for which the maximum punishment is generally six months imprisonment and/or a fine. An accused is not entitled to trial by jury in such cases either because the offence is *minor* (qv) or because the accused has waived his right to a jury trial, which he can do in certain cases. See INDICTABLE OFFENCE.

**summary proceedings.** Proceedings, without a jury, in the District Court of summary offences (qv) and those indictable offences (qv) which may be heard by the District Court on the consent of the accused and, in certain instances, the agreement of the Director of Public Prosecutions (qv): Criminal Justice Act 1951 s.2.

An accused is entitled to copies of all statements of witnesses whose evidence is crucial to the prosecution case against him: Cowzer v Kirby (1992 HC) 10 ILT Dig 54. Summary proceedings for an offence must be instituted within 6 months of the offence unless otherwise provided for by statute: Petty Sessions (Ireland) Act 1851 s.10(4); many statutes permit one year from the offence eg Industrial Relations Act 1990 s.5.

*Minor* offences may be tried by courts of summary jurisdiction: 1937 Constitution, art.38(2). See MINOR OFFENCE.

**summary summons.** A summons by which specified civil proceedings are commenced in the High Court and where the proceedings are heard on affidavit (qv) without pleadings and with or without oral evidence: RSC O.1 r.3; O.2.

A summary summons indorsed with a claim, other than for an account, is set down before the Master by the plaintiff, following entrance of an appearance by the defendant, on motion for *liberty to enter final judgment* for the amount claimed (or for the recovery of land) supported by an affidavit showing that the plaintiff is entitled to the relief claimed and stating that in the belief of the deponent, there is no defence to the action: RSC O.37. In uncontested actions, the Master may deal with the matter summarily; in contested actions, or where *pre-judgment interest* (qv) is claimed, the Master must transfer the case, when in order, to the court (ibid rr.4-6).

It has been held that where the court decides that the defendant has an arguable case, he is entitled to exercise his right to defend and it cannot be a condition precedent to his defence that he should lodge a particular sum of money in court: Calor Teoranta v Colgan (1990 SC) — see Doyle in 8ILT & SJ (1990) 255.

**summer time.** The period which was prescribed by the Summer Time Act 1925 and the Summer Time Order 1926, which now stand repealed. Any enactment expressed to apply or operate during a period of summer time shall be construed as operating or applying during the period previously prescribed: Standard Time Act 1968 s.1(2). See STANDARD TIME.

**summing-up.** The address by a judge to a jury after the closing speeches by the parties in which he summarizes the evidence and gives directions in relation to the law eg burden and onus of proof, effect of presumptions of law. A defective summing-up or charge to the jury can be a good ground for an appeal. See The People v Byrne (1974) IR 1. See ACCOMPLICE; CHILD, EVIDENCE OF; CORROBORATION; PREVIOUS STATEMENT, INCONSISTENT; REQUISITION; VISUAL IDENTIFICATION.

**summons.** A written command issued to a defendant for the purpose of getting him to attend court on a specified date to answer a specified complaint (qv): DPP v Clein (1983) ILRM 76. Generally,

a summons may be issued by a district court judge, a peace commissioner (qv) or a district court clerk: DCR rr.30(1)-31(1). A summons must be signed (ibid r.45; The State (Attorney General) v Judge Roe (1951) IR 172).

Provision has been made for a district court office to issue a summons *as a matter of administrative procedure*: Courts (No 3) Act 1986. This provision is designed to overcome the objection of the case [The State (Clarke) v D J Roche and Senezio (1987) ILRM 309] by creating a new method of issuing a summons which does not involve the administration of justice in criminal matters by non-judicial personages.

The actual attendance of an accused in court can cure a defect in a summons where the defect related to the process for procuring such attendance: Joyce v CC Judge for Western Circuit (1987) ILRM 316. See also DPP v Hennessy (1990) 8ILT & SJ 102.

The time limit applicable to summonses issued pursuant to the 1986 Act is a limit of six months from the date of the alleged offence to the date of the application pursuant to s.1(4) for the issue of a summons; no other time limit arises except in the case of certain statutory offences where shorter time limits may apply: DPP v D J Roche and Paul Kelly and DPP v Arthur Nolan (1988) SC. See also McGrail v Ruane (1989) ILRM 498; DPP v Howard (1990 HC) ITLR (26 Feb).

**summons, amendment of.** The district court has a discretion to amend a summons on application to it (eg amending the date of the alleged offence), provided that this is not prejudicial to the defendant: District Court Rules 1948 rr.21 & 88. See DPP v Corbett (1992 HC) ILRM 674.

**summons, Dail Eireann.** The Dail is summoned and dissolved by the President of Ireland on the advice of the Taoiseach: 1937 Constitution, art.13(2)(1).

**summons, High Court.** Civil proceedings are commenced in the High Court (qv) by originating summons, except those cases commenced by petition (qv). A summons may be plenary, summary or special.

A *plenary* summons (form 1) is used

for cases requiring pleadings (qv) and oral evidence; it must be used for some claims eg for unliquidated damages: RSC O.1 r.2. A *summary* summons (form 2) is used for proceedings to be heard on affidavit (qv) without pleadings eg for liquidated sums or for the recovery of possession of land; it may be supplemented by oral evidence in certain circumstances: RSC O.1 r.3; O.2; O.37; RG v BG (1993 HC) ITLR (1 Feb). A *special* summons (form 3) is used mainly for equity claims eg in relation to probate matters or the administration of trusts: RSC O.1 r.4; O.3; O.38. See APPEARANCE; CIVIL PROCEEDINGS.

**summons, renewal of.** A High Court summons remains in full force and effect for twelve months from the date of issue: RSC O.8. A summons may be renewed by order of the court after the expiration of 12 months (or by the Master before such expiration) on showing by affidavit that the summons has not been served and the reasons therefor, showing that reasonable efforts have been made to serve it, and that the claim is still unsatisfied. The renewal may be for a period of six months from the date of renewal and from time to time during the currency of the renewed summons. A defendant is at liberty before entering an appearance to serve a *notice of motion* to set aside such an order, where it has been obtained on an *ex parte* application.

In the district court a second summons may be issued, on application to the court (eg due to difficulty in serving the first summons within the time limit): Petty Sessions (Ireland) Act 1851 s.10; Courts (No 3) Act 1986 s.1; DPP v McKillen (1992 HC) 10 ILT Dig 73.

**summons, service of.** A High Court summons may be served: (a) by *personal service* by delivery to the defendant in person of a copy, showing him the original or duplicate original at the same time; (b) by *non-personal service* by delivery of a copy summons to the spouse, child, parent, brother, sister, or to any clerk or servant (over 16 years of age) of the defendant, and, at the same time showing the original or duplicate original summons; (c) by *service on a solicitor* who accepts service on behalf of the defendant and undertakes in writing to enter an appearance; (d) by *service*

*deemed good* by the court where the service actually effected does not comply with all the requirements but does so substantially; (e) by *substituted service* by order of the court in particular cases eg by post, by advertisement, by delivery to an agent, or otherwise as the court deems fit; (f) by *service out of the jurisdiction.* See RSC O.9.

Similar provisions apply to the service of a *civil bill* in Circuit Court proceedings: RCC O.10; O.11. Service of a *civil process* in District Court proceedings is effected by summons server or by registered post: DCR rr.47 and 127 as amended by DCR (1962); Courts Act 1964 s.7 as amended by Courts Act 1971 s.22.

Provision has been made for the service of summonses in summary criminal proceedings also by registered pre-paid post to the last known residence or most usual place of abode or last place of business of the person to whom it is addressed: Courts Act 1991 s.22. See AFFIDAVIT OF SERVICE.

**summons, service out of jurisdiction.** Subject to the exceptions below, a summons may be served out of the jurisdiction *with the leave of the court,* which will be given only in particular circumstances eg if the action is in respect of land within the jurisdiction; or to enforce foreign arbitration awards under the Arbitration Act 1980; or in respect of a contract which is to be governed by Irish law; or in respect of a tort committed within the jurisdiction. See Grehan v Medical Incorporated (1986) ILRM 627; Kutchera v Buckingham International Holdings (1988) ILRM 1 and 501; Mitchelstown Co-op Ltd v Nestle (1989 SC) ILRM 582. See RSC O.9; O.11 r.1(f).

However, a summons may now be served out of the jurisdiction *without the leave of the court,* if the summons complies with the following conditions: (a) each claim made by the summons is one which by virtue of the Jurisdiction of Courts and Enforcement of Judgments (European Communities) Act 1988, the court has power to hear and determine and (b) the summons is endorsed before it is issued with a statement that the court has power to hear and determine the claim and that no proceedings involving the same cause of action are pending in another *contracting* state: Practice Direction from the President of the High Court 1st June 1988. See also SI No 91 of 1988; District Court Rules 1988 (SI No 173 of 1988). See Campbell v Holland Dredging Co (Ire) Ltd (1990) 8ILT Dig 63.

**summum jus summa injuria.** [Extreme law is extreme injury]. See EQUITY.

**Sunday trading.** Prohibition on Sunday trading was repealed by the Statute Law Revision (Pre-Union Irish Statutes) Act 1962.

**super altum mare.** [Upon the high seas].

**super visum corporis.** [Upon view of the body]. See CORONER; INQUEST.

**superficies solo cedit.** [Whatever is attached to the land forms part of it]. See FIXTURES.

**superior courts.** The courts above the inferior courts (qv) in the hierarchy of courts eg High Court, Central Criminal Court, Court of Criminal Appeal, Supreme Court.

**supermarket.** See OCCUPIERS' LIABILITY TO INVITEES.

**superior orders, obedience to.** See OBEDIENCE TO ORDERS, DEFENCE OF.

**supervision order.** An order which the District Court is empowered to make, authorising a health board (qv) to have a child visited on such periodic occasions as the board may consider necessary to satisfy itself as to the welfare of the child and to give to his parents, or to a person acting *in loco parentis*, any necessary advice as to the care of the child: Child Care Act 1991 s.19(2).

The court may make a supervision order on being satisfied on similar grounds as apply to a *care order* (qv) but not so serious as would justify the latter order but yet desirable that the child be visited periodically (ibid s.19(1)). A supervision order remains in force for not more than 12 months but a further order may be made with effect from the expiration of the previous order (ibid s.19(5) and (6)). The court may give directions for the care of the child eg to attend medical or psychiatric examination, treatment or assessment at a hospital, clinic or other place specified by the court (ibid s.19(4)). A health board has a duty to apply for a care order or a supervision order in respect of a child who requires care or protection (ibid s.16). See CARE ORDER.

**supplemental probate, grant of.** A grant of representation given to a proving executor where subsequently a codicil (qv) is discovered.

**supply of services.** See SERVICES, SUPPLY OF.

**support, right to.** The natural right of support is a right not to have support removed by a neighbour, and is confined to support for land in its natural state: Latimer v Official Co-operative Society (1885) 16 LR Ir 305. No natural right to support exists in respect of buildings on land although such a right may be acquired by easement (qv): Gatelly v Martin (1900) 2 IR 269. A local authority which exercises its power to demolish a dangerous building must protect an existing easement of support enjoyed by an adjoining terraced building and its weather-proofing: Treacy v Dublin Corporation (1992 SC) ILRM 650. See FLAT.

**suppressio veri, suggestio falsi.** [The suppression of truth is the suggestion of falsehood]. Misrepresentation (qv). See Delaney v Keogh (1905) 2 IR 267.

**suppression order.** See UNLAWFUL ORGANISATION.

**supra.** [Above].

**supra protest.** See ACCEPTANCE OF BILL.

**Supreme Court.** The court of final appeal in the State: 1937 Constitution art.34(4)(1). It consists of the Chief Justice (qv) and other judges. In constitutional cases, the court consists of five judges and in other cases three suffice. The decision of the court is that of the majority although each judge may deliver a separate judgment except in a decision on a question as to the validity of a law having regard to the Constitution, when one decision only may be delivered (ibid arts.26(2)(2) and 34(4)(5)). Separate judgments may be given when the constitutionality of a pre-1937 law is in issue eg see AG v X (1992 SC) ILRM 401.

The Supreme Court hears appeals from the High Court and from the Central Criminal Court; it considers references to it from the President of Ireland on the constitutionality of certain Bills (ibid art.26(1); it is consulted by the Circuit Court and the High Court by way of *case stated* (qv); it considers questions of law referred to it by the Director of Public Prosecutions, without prejudice to a verdict by a trial judge in favour of a defendant, on a point of law. An appeal lies also to the Supreme Court from an *acquittal by direction* of a trial judge in the Central Criminal Court: The People (DPP) v O'Shea (1982) IR 384.

The Supreme Court is a court of appeal and has no originating jurisdiction except as outlined above; it cannot therefore consider a question of the interpretation of the Constitution which had never arisen in or been decided in the High Court: AG v Dublin Well Woman Centre (1993 SC) — Irish Times 21/7/ 1993.

In relation to the jurisdiction of the Supreme Court to review the findings of a trial judge on facts rather than on law, see FACT; SECONDARY FACTS. See also APPEAL; LEGISLATION, CONSTITUTIONALITY OF; RE- VIEW OF SENTENCE.

**sur.** [Upon].

**surcharge.** The function of a local authority auditor in *charging* or *surcharg- ing* (a) the person who has made, or authorised the making of an illegal payment by the local authority or (b) any member or officer of a local authority in respect of the amount of any deficiency or loss incurred by his negligence or misconduct: Local Government (Ireland) Act 1871 ss.12 and 20. In relation to a *section 4 resolution* (qv), elected members who vote for a proposal in consequence of which an illegal payment is to be made out of the funds of the local authority, must be surcharged on any surcharge which may subsequently be made: City and County Management (Amendment) Act 1955 s.16(1). Sur- charging also applied to health boards (qv): Health Act 1970 s.28(2) now repealed by Comptroller and Auditor General (Amdt) Act 1933 s.20, fourth schedule. A *surcharge* may also be imposed on a taxable person who fails to pay tax by its due date eg see Finance Act 1993 s.92(c) in relation to VAT. See AUDITOR, LOCAL GOVERNMENT.

**surcharge, classification of.** Surcharges have been judicially classified in respect of payments which are (a) unfounded in whole or in part: The State (Raftis) v Leonard (1960) IR 408; (b) illegal eg where ultra vires (qv): R (Jephson) v

Roscommon JJ 12 LR (Ir) 331; (c) incurred through negligence or miscon- duct: R (Kennedy) v Browne (1907) 2 IR 505; and (d) sums which ought to have been, but were not brought into the accounts by accounting persons. See R (Drury) v Dublin Corporation and Campbell 41 ILTR 97.

**surety.** A guarantor; a person who binds himself, usually by deed, to satisfy the obligations of another person, if the latter fails to do so. A surety to an *administration bond* must swear he is worth at least half of the penal sum (qv) in the bond. [Text: Rowlatt UK]. See GUARANTEE; MARSHALLING; STATUTE OF FRAUDS.

**surgical operation.** A medical practi- tioner is under a greater duty of care to explain the consequences of *elective* surgery than would be the case in *non- elective* surgery, so that the patient can give an informed consent to the medical procedure; the mere following of an accepted practice could not be regarded as meeting the standard of care required: Walsh v Family Planning Services Ltd (1993 SC) 11 ILT Dig 90.

In a case concerning a surgical opera- tion, prior to the Statute of Limitations (Amendment) Act 1991, it had been held that the three year period of limitation began to run when a provable personal injury, capable of attracting compensa- tion, occurred to a person; it did not begin to run from the date of the occurrence of the wrongful act nor could it be postponed until the time when the person could have discovered, by reason- able diligence, that such damage was caused by the wrongful act complained of: Hegarty v O'Loughran & Edwards (1990 SC) ITLR (2 Apr). The three year limitation period now runs from the date of accrual of the cause of action or from the date of knowledge, if later (ibid 1991 Statute).

In a particular case involving a person who went into a coma after an appendix operation, it was held that it would be an unjustifiable extension of the law to say that negligence on the part of the defendants must be inferred in the absence of an explanation that must be proved on the balance of probability; the defendants had established that there was no negligence in the anaesthetic procedure and thus rebutted the burden of proof that rested on them: Lindsay v Mid-Western Health Board (1993 SC) ILRM 550. See also Dunleavy v McDevitt & North Western Health Board 10 ILT Dig (1992 SC) 296. See CAUSE OF ACTION; LIMITATION OF ACTIONS; MEDICAL NEGLIGENCE; RES IPSA LOQUITUR.

**surname.** Family as distinct from Christian or first name. See Registration of Business Names Act 1963 s.2; Companies Act 1963 s.195(15) as substituted by Companies Act 1990 s.51. See NAME, CHANGE OF.

**surplus assets.** The assets remaining on the winding-up (qv) of a company after its debts have been paid and capital returned to ordinary and preference shareholders. The question as to whether preference shareholders have a right to participate in the distribution of these surplus assets is a question of construction of any clause in the *articles of association* delimiting their rights exhaustively and exclusively: Cork Electric Supply Co Ltd v Concannon and Others (1932) IR 314.

**surplus in bankruptcy.** Any surplus remaining in a bankrupt's estate after the payment of one pound in the pound, with interest at the rate currently paid on judgment debts. The High Court will order the surplus to be paid or delivered to or vested in the bankrupt, his personal representatives (qv) or assigns, which order is deemed to be a conveyance, assignment or transfer of the property: Bankruptcy Act 1988 s.86. See also ibid ss.102 and 121. See BANKRUPTCY.

**surprise.** The Circuit Court will review a judgment made in default of appearance or defence where the defendant has been taken by surprise: RCC O.27. For High Court provision, see SET ASIDE See also REBUTTAL, EVIDENCE IN; SPECIAL PLEADING.

**surrender.** The yielding up of the residue of a term of interest in land: Wallis v Heads (1893) 2 Ch 75. See LEASE, DETERMINATION OF; TENANCY, TERMINATION OF. See also ABANDONMENT.

**surrender of shares.** The yielding up of the shares of a company where the *articles of association* so permit and the circumstances are such as to justify their forfeiture: Bellerby v Rowland Marwood's SS Co Ltd (1902) 2 Ch 14. Where a valid surrender of shares in a

plc brings the allotted share capital below the authorised minimum, the company is required to re-register as another form of company: Companies (Amendment) Act 1983 ss.19 and 43 (as amended by Companies Act 1990 s.232(b)). See FORFEITURE OF SHARES.

**surrender value.** The amount which an insurer will pay to an insured on termination before the maturity date of a policy of insurance.

**surrogate.** A person appointed to act in the place of another.

**surrogate mother.** A woman who agrees with another to conceive and give birth to a child for that other by means of artificial insemination by the semen of that other. Payment to a surrogate mother could be in contravention of the prohibition of any payment or other reward in consideration of the adoption (qv) of a child: Adoption Act 1952 s.42(1). See ARTIFICIAL INSEMINATION.

**surveillance.** A watch kept on a suspected offender. Surveillance of a suspect can be justified and may not be illegal: The State (Kane) v Governor of Mountjoy Prison (1987) HC. Where a person who is entitled to liberty is placed under continuous garda surveillance and challenges that surveillance, the onus is on the garda authorities to provide adequate justification for the surveillance: DPP v Kane, McCaughey and Carlin (1988) HC & SC.

**survival of causes of action.** See DEATH, EFFECT OF.

**survivorship, presumption of.** See DEATH, SIMULTANEOUS.

**survivorship, right of.** See JOINT TENANCY.

**sus per coll; suspendatur per collum.** [Let him be hanged by the neck]. See DEATH PENALTY; HANGING.

**suspend.** To debar temporarily from the exercise of an office or occupation. The suspension of a person can be rendered invalid by an unjustified delay in holding an enquiry into matters alleged against the person: Flynn v An Post (1987 SC) IR 68. See also Farrell v Minister for Justice (1991 HC). An injunction to lift the suspension of a person will not be granted, even if a strong prima facie case has been made, where damages would be an adequate remedy and where the balance of convenience does not warrant the lifting of the suspension: Sweeney v Sligo Vocational Educational Committee (1988) HC.

A three day suspension of a pupil from a national school was not a matter for judicial review: Murtagh v St Emer's National School (1991 SC) ILRM 549. An injunction to lift the suspension of a GAA chairman was granted because the management committee had acted contrary to natural justice: O'Murchu v Waterford Gaelic Athletic Association County Board (1991 HC). Indefinite suspension of an employee may amount to a dismissal: Deegan & Ors v Dunnes Stores (1992 EAT) ELR 184. See also The State (Co Donegal VEC) v Minister for Education (1986) ILRM 399.

**suspended sentence.** A sentence which is ordered not to take place immediately, usually on conditions eg upon the offender entering into a recognisance (qv) with or without securities, to keep the peace and to be of good behaviour for a specified period. See R v Spratling (1911) 1 KB 77; The State (Woods) v Governor of Portlaoise Prison 108 ILTR 54.

**swabs.** A garda was empowered to take swabs from an arrested person's skin or samples of his hair for the purpose of making any test designed to see if the person had been in contact with firearms or explosives: Criminal Law Act 1976 s.7. See also Criminal Justice Act 1984 s.6. This power has been repealed and replaced by a wider power to take bodily samples, which includes swabs. See Criminal Justice (Forensic Evidence) Act 1990. See BODILY SAMPLE.

**swap transaction.** Generally understood to mean the exchange of debt with fixed interest rates for debt with floating rates, or in one currency for another. Swap transactions enable a borrower to convert a floating interest loan into a fixed rate loan, or in the case of a foreign currency loan to purchase the foreign currency on a forward-contract basis. Swaps are a common method of hedging against movement in interest and exchange rates.

Power has been given to certain State companies to effect such transactions: Financial Transactions of Certain Companies and Other Bodies Act 1992. The legislation was introduced because the UK House of Lords had held that such transactions entered into by a UK local authority was ultra vires its powers (Hazell v Hammersmith and Fulham London Borough Council (1991) 2WLR 372) and there was concern that this decision might lead to doubt as to the legality of such transactions by Irish bodies which did not have express statutory power to enter into them. See also Finance Act 1993 s.137.

**sweepstake.** Formerly was a drawing or distribution of prizes by lot or chance whether with or without reference to the result of a future uncertain event: Public Charitable Hospitals (Temporary Provisions) Act 1930 s.1(1). The famous Irish Hospital Sweepstakes ran its last sweepstake in January 1986. Provision has been made for the disposal of prize monies left unclaimed: Public Hospitals (Amendment) Act 1990.

**syndicate.** A type of association which is neither a partnership nor an unincorporated company, sometimes found in insurance and banking. Syndicates of underwriters at and outside Lloyd's and banks providing finance by means of *syndicated loans* fall into this category. A member of a syndicate is not liable to a party contracting with the syndicate for a defaulting member's share. A syndicate which has the object of *acquisition of gain* must be registered as a company if the number of its members exceeds 20 persons; or in the case of a bank if its members exceeds 10 persons: Companies Act 1963 ss.372 and 376.

# T

**tabula in naufragio.** [Plank in the shipwreck].

**tacking.** The equitable doctrine by which a third mortgagee, with no notice of a second mortgage at the time his mortgage was made, can squeeze out the second mortgage, by acquiring the first mortgage and the legal estate therein. He could tack on his third mortgage to the legal estate; the doctrine is based on the maxim of *where the equities are equal, the law prevails*. However the doctrine of tacking has no application to registered instruments, where the priority of mortgages is based on their time of registration: Registration of Deeds (Ireland) Act 1707 and Registration of Title Act 1964.

**tail.** See FEE TAIL.

**take-out merger.** The provision by which a company, which acquires at least 80 per cent in value of another company's shares, is entitled to acquire for itself the remaining 20 per cent or less, on the same terms: Companies Act 1963 s.204. Because of the significance of this power, the court must be satisfied that the requirements of s.204 have been strictly complied with. A take-out of dissident shareholders is possible also using powers to change a company's constitution or capital structures, provided 75 per cent in value of each class affected who vote, agree and the court consents (ibid ss.201-204). See In re National Bank Ltd (1966) 1 All ER 1006. See MERGER.

**take-over of company.** See MERGER/ TAKEOVER, DOMESTIC STATUTORY PROVISION; MERGER OF COMPANY; MERGER OF COMPANY, EC REGULATIONS.

**Tanaiste.** A member of the government nominated by the Taoiseach; he acts for all purposes for the Taoiseach if the Taoiseach should be temporarily absent or if he should die or become permanently incapacitated: 1937 Constitution art.28(6).

**tangible property.** *Corporeal* property eg goods, compared with intangible property eg choses in action (qv).

**Taoiseach.** [Prime Minister]. The head of government appointed by the President of Ireland, on the nomination of Dail Eireann: 1937 Constitution, art.13(1)(1). The Taoiseach is required to resign from office on ceasing to retain the support of a majority in Dail Eireann, unless on his advice the President dissolves the Dail and on the reassembly after the dissolution the Taoiseach secures the support of a majority in the Dail (ibid art.28(10)). The office of Taoiseach has been held by: Albert Reynolds (1992 to present); Charles J Haughey (1979-1981; 1982-1982; 1987-1992); Garrett Fitzgerald (1981-1982; 1982-1987); John M Lynch (1966-1973; 1977-1979); Liam Cosgrave (1973-1977); Sean F Lemass (1959-1966); John A Costello (1948-1951; 1954-1957); Eamonn de Valera (1932-1948; 1951-1954;

1957- 1959); W T Cosgrove (1922-1932).

**tax and patents.** See QUALIFYING PATENT.

**tax and the courts.** The traditional approach to tax liability is that the courts do not look at the substance or financial results of a transaction, but rather at the legal effects and legal rights of the parties according to legal ideas and concepts; and an exemption from tax is governed by the same considerations as a liability to tax: McGrath v McDermott (Inspector of Taxes) (1988) ILRM 181. It is an established rule of law that a citizen is not to be taxed unless the language of the relevant section of the taxing statute clearly imposes an obligation: Texaco (Ireland) Ltd v Murphy, Inspector of Taxes (1992 SC) ILRM 304. See DOUBLE TAXATION AGREEMENT; TAX AVOIDANCE.

**tax avoidance.** Formerly, where a transaction resulted in the avoidance of a tax liability, the taxpayer was entitled to the benefit of the relevant statutory provision: McGrath v McDermott (Inspector of Taxes) (1988) ILRM 181; it was not for the courts to intervene; taxation should be according to the strict wording of the legislation: McDertmott v McGrath (1989) IR 258. However, since 1989, if a transaction is a *tax avoidance transaction* as defined, it is ineffective to avoid tax: Finance Act 1989 s.86. It is such a transaction if it gives rise to a tax advantage and was not undertaken primarily for purposes other than to give rise to the tax advantage. For a transaction to be struck down, the Revenue Commissioners must first form an opinion that it is such a transaction and notify the taxpayer, who may appeal to the Appeal Commissioners. See also 1989 Act ss.87-90. See BOND WASHING.

**tax clearance certificate.** A certificate issued by the Collector-General to a person where that person has complied with all the obligations imposed on him in relation to the payment of taxes, interest and penalties, and the delivery of returns: Finance Act 1992 s.242(2). A tax clearance certificate is required in many cases eg before a person can obtain a grant from many State schemes or as a precondition for the issue of a liquor licence (ibid s.156). The requirement of a tax clearance certificate was extended in 1993 as a precondition to the granting of an excise licence for a wholesale dealer in spirits beer or wine, a bookmaker's licence, a gaming licence, an auctioneer's licence, or a licence for a vendor of hydrocarbon oil or liquid petroleum gas: Finance Act 1993 ss.79 and 140.

**tax defaulters.** The Revenue Commissioners are empowered to publish the names and addresses and occupations or descriptions of tax defaulters: Finance Act 1983 s.23 as amended by Finance Act 1992 s.240. See AMNESTY.

**tax, false statement.** A taxpayer who makes a false return or makes a false claim for allowances (or a person who assists him to do so) is liable to specified penalties (financial or at the discretion of the court, imprisonment or both) on a graduated scale: Income Tax Act 1967 s.516 as amended by Waiver of Certain Tax, Interest and Penalties Act 1993 s.11. See REVENUE PENALTY.

**tax, prior opinion.** An inspector of taxes is not bound by a prior opinion of the Revenue Commissioners on the prospective liability of a taxpayer: Pandion Haliaetus v Revenue Commissioners (1988) ILRM 419.

**tax year.** The twelve months beginning on the 6th April.

**taxation law.** The body of law dealing with the raising of revenue by the State by compulsory contribution by individuals and by companies, levied on goods and services, income and wealth. *Direct* taxes are those imposed on the individual, usually in accordance with his ability to pay eg income tax. *Indirect* taxes are those applied to goods and services eg value-added taxes. Local taxes which are imposed by local authorities include rates (qv).

Other taxes include capital gains tax, corporation tax, capital acquisitions tax on gifts and inheritances, probate tax, pay related social insurance contributions, customs and excise duties, capital duty on the contribution of assets to companies, stamp duty on conveyances and other documents for the transfer or assignment of property and for certain other purposes, and residential property tax. Taxation statutes enjoy an especially strong presumption of constitutionality: Madigan v Attorney General & Ors (1986) ILRM 136. [Text: Cooney McLaughlin & Taggart; Judge; Butterworth Ireland (2); Institute of Taxation of Ireland; O'Hare & Judge; O'Reilly & Carroll; Gov Pub (1); Cremin; Harrison UK]. See DOUBLE TAXATION AGREEMENT; REVENUE PENALTY; SELF ASSESSMENT; TAX AND THE COURTS; TAX AVOIDANCE; TAX, PRIOR OPINION; THIRD PARTY INFORMATION; UNLAWFUL ORGANISATION.

**taxation of costs.** The procedure whereby a solicitor's bill of costs is examined by a Taxing Master and allowed or reduced. Where *party and party* costs (qv) are awarded by a court, the court also orders that they be taxed: RSC O.99. In the case of *solicitor and client* costs (qv), they are not taxed unless the client demands that they be taxed; in such taxation, all costs are allowed except in so far as they are of an unreasonable amount or have been unreasonably incurred; all amounts incurred with the express or implied approval of the client are conclusively presumed to have been reasonably incurred (ibid r.11). If these costs are reduced by one-sixth or more, the solicitor claiming the costs, must pay for the costs of taxation (ibid r.29(13)).

Costs which have been taxed and a certificate therefor issued by the taxing master for the amount due, may be recovered (a) in the case of party and party costs by having the amount entered in the judgment and by executing the judgment and (b) in the case of solicitor and client costs, by issuing separate proceedings for their recovery. An application may be made to the High Court for an order requiring the Taxing Master to review the taxation and the court may give directions to the Taxing Master or it may itself settle the matter. See O'Sullivan v Hughes (1986) ILRM 555; The State (Shatter & Co) v de Valera (1987) ILRM 599 & (1990 SC) 8ILT Dig 240.

Costs in Circuit Court proceedings are taxed by the County Registrar: RCC O.58 r.6. A scale of costs is provided for in District Court proceedings, to which value-added tax may be added where such tax is not otherwise recoverable: District Court (Costs) Rules 1982 (SI No 218 of 1982) and District Court (Costs) (Amendment) Rules 1983 (SI No 173 of 1983). See also BARRISTER; BRIEF; INSTRUCTION FEE; STANDBY FEE.

**taxidermy.** See WILDLIFE DEALING.

**taxing master.** See TAXATION OF COSTS.

**TD.** [Teachta Dala]. A member of Dail Eireann (qv). A TD who is returned in an election as a member for two or more constituencies, must declare for one: Electoral Act 1992 s.35. A TD may voluntarily resign his membership by notice in writing to the Chairman of the Dail; it takes effect on receipt by the Chairman (ibid s.34). A person is disqualified from membership of the Dail unless he is a citizen and has reached 21 years of age, or where he is of unsound mind or an undischarged bankrupt or where he is undergoing a sentence of imprisonment as specified (ibid s.41). See SEVERANCE PAY; UTTERANCE.

**teacher, language qualification.** The compulsory requirement of an Irish language qualification for a vocational teacher was upheld by the European Court of Justice, which decided that the nature of the post justified a linguistic requirement and consequently there was no discrimination: Groeher v Minister for Education (ECJ) (1990) ILRM 335. See CORPORAL PUNISHMENT; SCHOOL AUTHORITY'S DUTY.

**telegraph.** It is an offence to damage telegraphs or prevent or obstruct telegraphic communications: Malicious Damage Act 1861 s.37 as amended by Criminal Damage Act 1991 s.14(2)(a).

**telephone services.** See LIABILITY, STATUTORY EXEMPTIONS FROM.

**telephone tapping.** It is an offence without lawful authority to intercept a telephone message, or to disclose the substance of a message which has been intercepted: Postal and Telecommunications Act 1983 s.98 as amended by Interception of Postal Packets and Telecommunications Messages (Regulations) Act 1993 s.13. *Intercept* means listen to, or record by any means, in the course of its transmission, a telecommunications message; it does not include listening or recording which is consented to by either the person making the telephone call or by the person intended to receive the message (ibid 1983 Act s.98(5) as amended by 1993 Act s.13(3); see also 1993 Act s.1).

The Minister may give an authorisation of interceptions but only for the purpose of criminal investigation or in the interests of the security of the State (ibid

1993 Act ss.2, 4 and 5) and only in response to an application for an authorisation from the Commissioner of the Garda Siochana or the Chief of Staff of the Defence Forces, as appropriate (ibid s.6).

There is provision for a Complaints Referee to investigate an alleged interception and to quash an authorisation, to direct the destruction of any copy of the communication intercepted, and/or to make a recommendation on compensation (ibid s.9). There is provision also for a review from time to time of the operation of the 1993 Act by a judge of the High Court (ibid s.8). See also PRIVACY.

**television broadcast.** Copyright in a television broadcast subsists in Radio Telefis Eireann for fifty years from the end of the year in which the broadcast was first made by RTE: Copyright Act 1963 s.19. See TELEVISION PROGRAMME SERVICE.

**television dealer.** A person who by trade or business, sells television sets by wholesale or retail, lets such sets on hire or hire-purchase: Wireless Telegraphy Act 1972 s.1(1). Such dealers are required to make returns to the Minister on sales and lettings: Broadcasting and Wireless Telegraphy Act 1988 s.10. It is an offence for a person to have an unlicensed television set (ibid s.12).

**television link.** Provision has been made to enable witnesses to give evidence by live television link in criminal cases involving physical or sexual abuse: Criminal Evidence Act 1992 ss.12-13. A witness may give evidence in this manner if the court permits; however, if the witness is under 17 years of age (or is mentally handicapped) the witness is entitled to give such evidence unless the court sees good reason to the contrary (ibid s.13(1)).

The purpose of the 1992 Act is to make it easier for victims and vulnerable witnesses to give evidence; the witness gives evidence from a witness room and does not have to be in the presence of the accused when recounting the facts of the offence. Wigs and gowns are not worn by judges and lawyers when the tv link is being used.

An intermediary may be used to convey questions to the witness (ibid s.14).

There are special provisions governing a preliminary examination in the district court (ibid ss.15-16) There is also provision in any criminal proceeding for the giving of evidence by a person who is outside the State through a live television link with the permission of the court (ibid s.29). See also Criminal Justice Act 1993 s.11. See DISTRICT COURT, PRELIMINARY EXAMINATION; LEGAL AID; IDENTIFICATION PARADE; VIDEO RECORDING; VISUAL IDENTIFICATION.

**television programme service.** A service which comprises a compilation of audio-visual programme material of any description and is transmitted or relayed by means of wireless telegraphy directly or indirectly for reception by the general public: Radio and Television Act 1988 s.2(1). This Act provides for the Independent Radio and Television Commission to arrange for the provision of one television programme service additional to that provided by RTE (ibid s.4).

The Commission is required to ensure that the service in its programming is responsive to the interests and concerns of the whole community; upholds the democratic values enshrined in the 1937 Constitution; includes a reasonable proportion of news and current affairs programmes; and has regard to the formation of public awareness and understanding of the values and traditions of other countries, particularly those of the EC (ibid s.18(3)). See also Broadcasting Act 1990 s.6. See RADIO AND TELEVISION COMMISSION.

**temperamental incompatibility.** Not a ground for granting a nullity decree in marriage; however a purported marriage may be null and void from the outset by reason of elements of immaturity in the character and temperament of both parties and an inability to form and sustain a normal marriage relationship: PC v VC (1990) 2 IR 91.

**temporary dwellings.** A sanitary authority is empowered to make bye-laws regulating the use of *temporary dwellings* and to prohibit the erection or retention of such dwellings on any land or water of their district if they are of opinion that such erection or retention would be prejudicial to public health or the amenities of the locality or would interfere to an unreasonable extent with traffic on any road: Local Government (Sanitary Services) Act 1948 ss.30-31. See Listowel UDC v McDonagh 105 ILTR 99; Gammell v Dublin Co Council (1983) ILRM 413.

It is an offence to erect, place, or retain, without lawful authority a temporary dwelling on a national road, motorway, busway or protected road: Roads Act 1993 s.69. See TRAVELLER.

**tenancy.** The relationship of a tenant (qv) to that land which he holds from another. See LEASE.

**tenancy, controlled.** See CONTROLLED DWELLING.

**tenancy, termination of.** Previously, many tenancies could, under comman law, be terminated on one week's notice ie by a *notice to quit* served on a tenant by a landlord, or a *notice of surrender* served on a landlord by a tenant. Now a notice terminating certain tenancies must be in writing and served not less than 4 weeks before the date on which the notice is to take effect: Housing (Miscellaneous Provisions) Act 1992 s.16. The new requirement applies to lettings of residential accommodation, whether by private landlords, local authorities or voluntary bodies; it does not apply to holiday lettings, tenancies tied to employment, or tenancies made bona fide for the temporary convenience of a landlord or tenant. See also LEASE, DETERMINATION OF.

**tenancy at will.** A lease where the lessor lets land to another to hold at the will of the lessor; the lessee is known as a *tenant at will.* Either party may terminate the tenancy at any time. See Bellew v Bellew (1982) IR 447. [Text: Wylie (4)]. See LEASE.

**tenancy by sufference.** Arises where a tenant holds on after the lawful title under which he previously held the tenancy has expired; he has no estate in the land and is just not a trespasser. See LEASE.

**tenancy in common.** The ownership of land by two or more persons where they have undivided possession but where there is no right of survivorship; the interest of a tenant in common passes on death as part of his estate. Tenants in common need not have an equal share; they need not claim under the same interest, and their interests need not have been created at the same time. Equity favoured tenancy in common as it regarded the right of survivorship of *joint tenancies* to be unfair. See JOINT TENANCY.

**tenant.** Lessee; a person who holds land. A tenant is obliged to pay the rent as it becomes due, and not to damage the premises over and above normal wear and tear. He must permit the landlord to enter the premises from time to time to inspect them. He must observe the covenants (qv) in the lease. [Text: Deale]. See LEASE; COVENANT; RENT BOOK; RENTED HOUSE, REGISTRATION OF; RENTED HOUSE, STANDARD OF; TENANCY, TERMINATION OF.

**tenant, business.** See BUSINESS TENANT.

**tenant, statutory.** A tenant who is given statutory protection eg security of tenure is given in business leases by providing for a renewal of such a lease at a marketable rent: Landlord and Tenant (Amendment) Act 1980. In a particular case, the use of a multiplier rent review clause was held to be invalid as it was designed as an ingenious method of circumventing the right of a tenant to a renewal of the lease: Bank of Ireland v Fitzmaurice (1989) ILRM 452. The statutory protection given to certain tenants by the Rent Restrictions Act 1960 was declared unconstitutional as an unjust attack on the landlord's property rights: Blake v Attorney General (1982) IR 117. See CONTROLLED DWELLING.

**tenant for life.** See SETTLEMENT.

**tenant in tail.** See FEE TAIL.

**tenant pur autre vie.** [Tenant for the life of another]. See LIFE ESTATE.

**tenant purchase scheme.** A scheme since 1966 whereby the tenant of a dwelling could purchase the dwelling from a local authority; the sale is effected by a *transfer order*, which may be subject to *special conditions*, and since 1978 was required to vest in the tenant the fee simple: Housing Act 1966 s.90; Landlord and Tenant (Ground Rents) Acts 1978 s.4 and 1987.

A *transfer order* normally provides for payment of the purchase money by instalments and may be secured by way of mortgage (qv) or charge (qv). The *special conditions* may include (a) a requirement that the dwelling be occupied as a normal place of residence by the purchaser and (b) a prohibition on the sale of the dwelling without the consent of the housing authority (ibid 1966 Act s.89). Since 1988 tenant purchase schemes did not require a housing authority to put the dwelling into good structural condition before selling it to a tenant: Housing Act 1988 s.23.

From 1992, where a dwelling is occupied by a tenant, the housing authority may sell it, in the state of repair and condition existing at the date of sale, to (a) the tenant in accordance with a *purchase scheme*, or (b) to another housing authority, or (c) to a voluntary housing body: Housing (Miscellaneous Provisions) Act 1992 s.26(1) substituting a new s.90 in the Housing Act 1966. Where the dwelling is not occupied by a tenant, the housing authority may sell the dwelling to any person (ibid s.90(1)(b)).

There is no warranty given as the state of repair or condition or its fitness for human habitation (ibid s.90(8)). Generally the sale of a house to tenants must continue to grant freehold title but, where appropriate, a leasehold interest may be conveyed in the case of a transfer to an approved voluntary body or a disposal by means of a *shared ownership lease*. Special conditions may be attached by the housing authority on the sale of a house including restrictions on resale or mortgaging. See FLAT.

**tender.** (1) An offer of performance in accordance with the terms of a contract eg an offer by a debtor to his creditor of the exact amount of the debt. If such a tender is made but the other party refuses to accept it, the party tendering is freed from liability under the contract if the tender was made under such circumstances that the other party had a reasonable opportunity of examining the goods or the money tendered. However a tender of money does not discharge the debt unless it is followed by payment of the sum tendered into court on action being brought. A tender of money must be unconditional although it may be made *under protest* (qv) so as to reserve the right of the payer to dispute the amount. The debtor must meet any contractual terms set as to the place, time and manner of payment: Morrow v Carty (1957) NI 174. See LEGAL TENDER.

(2) An offer for sale by tender eg an offer of shares in a company by tender or an invitation by tender to supply a local authority with goods; in the latter case, the tender document sets out the terms of the contract and there is no obligation on the local authority to accept any of the tenders unless it has undertaken in the statement inviting tenders to accept the lowest.

(3) Payment into court of a sum of money, offered before action, in satisfaction of a claim, which acts as a defence to the action. See RSC O.27 r.3 and 9. See LODGMENT IN COURT.

**tenement.** A thing which could be held by common law tenure, ie land. For the purposes of statutory protection of business tenants (qv), a *tenement* means a premises consisting of a defined portion of a building, or of land covered wholly or partly by buildings where the land not covered by buildings is subsidiary and ancillary to the buildings; such premises must be held by the occupier on a tenancy and the letting must not have been made either for the temporary convenience of either party or be dependent on the continuance in any office, or employment, or appointment of the tenant: Landlord and Tenant (Amendment) Act 1980 s.5. A tenement in this context, excludes agricultural lettings.

**tenendum.** [To be held].

**tenor.** The general import of a document or submission; the substance of some matter.

**tenor, executor according to.** See EXECUTOR ACCORDING TO THE TENOR.

**tenure.** The relationship between a tenant and his reversioner or landlord.

**tenure, security of.** A landlord cannot recover possession of a *controlled dwelling* without a court order; such an order will not be made unless the court considers it reasonable and one of the specified grounds for such an order is proved by the landlord: Housing (Private Rented Dwellings) Act 1982 s.16. These restrictions do not apply to service or employment lettings, or to lettings bona fide for the temporary convenience or to meet a temporary necessity of the landlord or the tenant, or to recovery by a local authority in exercise of their statutory powers (ibid ss.9 and 16;

Housing Act 1966 ss.62(6), 66(17) and 118(1)). See also BUSINESS TENANT; CONTROLLED DWELLING; LEASE, DETERMINATION OF; TENANCY, TERMINATION OF.

**teoranta, teo.** [Limited]. See LIMITED COMPANY.

**term.** (1) A fixed period of time for which a right is to be enjoyed or an obligation borne. (2) The period for which an estate is granted. (3) A provision, condition or limitation. (4) A provision in a contract which creates legal obligations.

**term of patent.** Formerly, the term of a patent ran for 16 years from the date of filing of a complete specification: Patents Act 1964 s.26. The term could be extended on the application of the patentee for a further term of five, or in exceptional cases for ten years, on the grounds that the patentee has been inadequately remunerated for his patent (ibid s.27). See John Hilton v Controller of Patents (1932) HC; In re Smithkline Beckman Corp (1984) HC; In re Fisons Pharmaceuticals Ltd (1984) ILRM 393; In re Technobiotic Ltd (1990 HC) 2 IR 499; In re Sandoz Ltd (1990) HC & (1991) HC. See RSC O.94 rr.26-44.

Since 1992, a patent takes effect from the date on which notice of its grant is published in the Patents Office Journal and, subject to renewal fees being paid, remains in force for a period of 20 years beginning with the date of filing of the patent application: Patents Act 1992 s.36. There is no provision for an extension of the term. The term of a *short-term* patent (qv) is 10 years. Patents granted under the 1964 Act are extended to 20 years unless they have already been extended pursuant to s.27 (ibid 1992 Act s.5, first schedule para.2(2)). See Patent Rules 1992 r.34 (SI No 179 of 1992).

**terminating society.** Originally was a building society which by its rules was to terminate at a fixed date or when a result specified in its rules was attained eg Cork Mutual Benefit Terminating Society (1893): Building Societies Act 1874 s.5; since repealed and only of historical importance now. [Text: Murdoch (2)]. Contrast with PERMANENT SOCIETY.

**termination of employment.** In a particular case it was held that the date of termination of employment was the date the employee received his last pay package: Reilly v An Post (1992 CC) ELR 129. See DISMISSAL OF EMPLOYEE; INJUNCTION.

**termination of tenancy.** See TENANCY, TERMINATION OF.

**terminus a quo.** [The starting point].

**terminus ad quem.** [The finishing point].

**terms of employment.** The written statement which an employer is required to give to an employee, setting out the conditions under which he is employed. See Minimum Notice and Terms of Employment Act 1973 s.9. See CONTRACT OF EMPLOYMENT; EQUALITY CLAUSE.

**terra.** [Land].

**territorial jurisdiction.** See JURISDICTION.

**territorial sea.** See MARITIME JURISDICTION.

**territorial waters.** See MARITIME JURISDICTION.

**terrorism.** See Extradition (European Convention on Suppression of Terrorism) Act 1987. For prevention of terrorism in the UK, see [Text: Walker UK]. See EXTRADITION; POLICE COOPERATION.

**test case.** An action, the result of which will affect other similar cases which are not litigated. Contrast with REPRESENTATIVE ACTION.

**test tube fertilisation.** See EMBRYO EMPLANTATION.

**testament.** A will. A distinction is sometimes drawn between a *will* (a disposition of real property) and a *testament* (relating to personal property).

**testamentary capacity.** The ability in law to make a valid will eg having attained 18 years of age or having been married, being of *sound disposing mind* and having the animus testandi (qv): Succession Act 1965 s.77. In legal proceedings where it is alleged that a testator was not of sound mind, it is necessary to give particulars of any specific instance of delusion or mental incapacity: RSC O.19 r.6(1). As a matter of public policy there is a presumption of testamentary capacity: In bonis Glynn dec'd (1990) 2 IR 326. See MINOR; SOUND DISPOSING MIND.

**testamentary disposition.** See DISPOSITION.

**testamentary expenses.** The expenses incurred in the proper performance of an executor's duties. Priority in payment out of a deceased's estate is given to funeral and testamentary expenses. See ADMINISTRATION OF ESTATES; EXECUTOR; INSOLVENT ESTATE.

**testamentary freedom.** The right of a person to dispose of his property by will according to his wishes. The State guarantees to pass no law attempting to abolish the general right to transfer, bequeath and inherit property: 1939 Constitution, art.43(1)(2). Testamentary freedom is now limited by the Succession Act 1965. See SPOUSE, LEGAL RIGHT OF; CHILD, PROVISION FOR.

**testamentary guardian.** A guardian appointed by a deed or will: Status of Children Act 1987 s.9. A person who is entitled to appoint a guardian of an infant may make the appointment by will notwithstanding that he has not the capacity to make a will ie notwithstanding that he has not attained the age of eighteen years or is or has not been married: Succession Act 1965 s.77(2).

**testate.** Having made a will. Contrast with INTESTACY.

**testate succession.** Devolution of property where the deceased left a will. See WILL; PROBATE.

**testator/testatrix.** A person, male/ female, who makes a will. A person may be a testator notwithstanding that he might fall within the statutory definition of an intestate: G(R) v PSG (1981) HC.

**testatum.** The start of the operative part of a deed which usually begins *Now this Indenture witnesseth that, in pursuance of said Agreement, and in consideration of the sum of £....*

**teste meipso.** [Witness myself].

**testimonium.** The concluding clause in a deed or will by which the parties have signed their names *in witness* of what it contains eg *In witness whereof the parties hereto have hereunto set their respective hands and seals the day and year first above written.*

**testimony.** The evidence of a witness given *viva voce* in court and offered as evidence of the truth of that which he asserts. There is provision for *perpetuating* testimony (qv). See OATH.

**theft.** See DISHONESTY; LARCENY.

**third party information.** Persons, companies and government departments are required to make a return to the Revenue Commissioners of payments made to third parties for services rendered, including payments for copyright: Finance Act 1992, Part VII. Particulars must also be given where payment is given in a form other than money. Returns must also be made by persons or companies who receive income belonging to others, by persons who are nominee holders of securities, by persons who act as intermediaries in relation to UCITS or who, as agents, receive rents or other payments arising from premises. Excluded are payments from which income tax has been deducted, payments which do not exceed £3,000 in a year, and payments where the value of goods provided as part of the service exceeds two thirds of the total charge.

**third party notice.** A notice issued and served in an action, by leave of the court, on a person who is not already a party to the action, following an application by a defendant, where he claims to be entitled to contribution (qv) or indemnity (qv) from that person: RSC O.16. The application is made by motion on notice to the plaintiff made within twenty eight days from the time limited for delivery of the defence (ibid rr.1(2) and 1(3)).

As regards a claim for personal injuries arising from an accident, facts must be alleged by the defendant which would support his claim that the proposed third party had contributed to the accident: Johnston (a minor) v Fitzpatrick (1991 SC) ILRM 269. There is no inflexible rule that an application for liberty to issue and serve a third party notice must be based on a *direct* affidavit (qv) of the facts, rather than on an *information and belief* affidavit, although in certain circumstances, the former will be necessary: ibid Johnston case.

When the third party is served with the notice he becomes a party to the action and has the same rights in respect of defence as if he had been duly sued in the ordinary way by the defendant (ibid RSC O.16 r.3). The third party procedure in the District Court is governed by the District Court (Third Party Procedure) Rules 1984 (SI No 3 of 1985). See International Commercial Bank plc v Insurance Corp of Ireland plc (1989) 7ILT Dig 326. See NEXT FRIEND; O'BYRNE LETTER.

**threat.** A mere oral threat to commit a crime generally does not constitute a crime; however it is a crime when the threat is in language which causes or might cause a *breach of the peace* (qv) or is threatening or abusive language within the provisions of the Dublin Police Act 1842 s.14(13). Also a threat to kill or murder any person which is contained in any letter or writing, maliciously sent, with knowledge of its contents, is a felony (qv); Offences Against the Person Act 1861 s.16. It is an offence to make a threat (a) to damage property of another or (b) to damage one's own property in a way likely to endanger the life of another: Criminal Damage Act 1991 s.3. See CONFESSION; DURESS; EXTORTION BY MENACES; TRESPASS TO PERSON.

**ticket.** Where a ticket contains a written offer subject to printed conditions, those conditions are incorporated into the contract formed by acceptance of the offer, if adequate *notice* of the conditions are given to the offeree. See Richardson v Rowntree (1894) AC 217.

**tied insurance agent.** A person who enters into an agreement or arrangement with an insurer, whereby he undertakes to refer all proposals of insurance to such insurer, or which restricts his freedom to refer proposals of insurance to other insurers: Insurance Act 1989 s.51(3). An insurer is responsible for any act or omission of its tied insurance agent in respect of contracts of insurance offered or issued by the insurer, as if the tied insurance agent was an employee of the insurer (ibid s.51(2)). See INSURANCE OMBUDSMAN.

**tiered interest rate.** The rate of interest on a loan where the rate (a) is determined by reference to the amount of the loan made, or to the amount outstanding at any time on foot of the loan, or to the income of the member to whom the loan is made, as the case may be, and (b) is greater than the lowest rate of interest applicable at the time to loans of the same type made by a building society to members generally: Building Societies Act 1989 s.24(2).

Under the Building Societies (Amendment) Act 1986 it was prohibited to charge tiered interest rates on loans made by a society on or after 23rd October 1986 or on loans made before 1st August 1986 on which a tiered rate was not being charged on that date (ibid ss.4(1) and 4(2)).

Notwithstanding the repeal of the 1986 Act by the 1989 Act, a society must not charge a tiered interest rate on a loan made under the *repealed enactments* in respect of a *house*, unless a tiered rate was lawfully charged on the date of the repeal: 1989 Act ss.24(1)(a) and 24(2)(b). Furthermore, a society must not charge a tiered interest rate on a *housing loan* (qv), unless the tiered rate is charged from the day on which the mortgage securing the loan is created, and the charging of a tiered rate is specifically mentioned in the mortgage, and is acknowledged in writing by the member in a form to be specified by the Central Bank (ibid s.24(1)(b)).

A member who is wrongly charged a tiered interest rate is not in breach of his mortgage agreement if he does not pay the additional sum involved (ibid 1986 Act s.5).

**timber.** See ESTOVERS.

**time.** In statutory provisions, where a period of time is expressed to begin on or to be reckoned from a particular day that day shall, unless the contrary intention appears, be deemed to be included in such period: Interpretation Act 1937 s.11(h). Time limits up to six days do not include a Saturday, Sunday or public holiday (qv) and where the time expires on any such day, the time is extended to the first following day which is not a Saturday, Sunday or public holiday: Companies Act 1990 s.4. See also LG (P&D) Act 1992 s.17.

As regards the Statute of Limitations 1957, the statutory period of time is construed as ending on the last day of the period; however, if the act required (eg issuing a summons) is impossible to do on the last day because the offices of the court are closed, the period will be construed as ending on the next day the offices are open: Poole v O'Sullivan (1993 HC) ILRM 55. In personal injuries actions arising from an accident, the date on which the accident occurs is deemed to be included in the limitation period: McGuinness v Armstrong Patents Ltd (1980) IR 289.

Time limits in statutory provisions may be either mandatory or discretionary; in deciding into which category a provision falls, the court must seek to interpret the meaning, intention and objective of the legislation at issue: Irish Refining plc v Commissioner of Valuation (1990 SC) 1 IR 568. See also Cork County Council v Whillock (1993 SC) 11 ILT Dig 144.

*Universal Co-ordinated Time* replaces Greenwich Mean Time for navigational warnings from 1st February 1993: Merchant Shipping (Navigation Warnings) (Amdt) Rules 1992. See STANDARD TIME; MONTH; WEEK; YEAR.

**time, court rules.** The court has power to enlarge or abridge the time for doing any act or taking any proceedings. The time for delivering amending or filing any pleadings, answer or other document may be enlarged by consent. Where time is limited by months, such time is to be computed by calendar months.

Where any limited time less than six days is allowed, certain days are not reckoned in the computation of such limited time (Saturday, Sunday, Christmas Day, Good Friday). Where any particular number of days is not expressed to be *clear days,* the same is reckoned exclusively of the first day and inclusive of the last day. The time of the *long vacation* (qv) is not to be reckoned in computing time.

It has been held that a plaintiff seeking an extension of time within which to appeal would need to establish (a) that she had formed an intention to appeal within the limited time; (b) that failure to file a notice of appeal within time was due to mistake on her part or on the part of her legal advisors; and (c) that she had an arguable case on appeal: Clonmel Foods Ltd v Eire Continental Trading Co Ltd (1955) IR 170 considered in Dalton v Minister for Finance (1989 SC) ILRM 519. There is a desirability of adhering to time limits prescribed by court rules: Bord na Mona v Sisk (1990 SC) 1 IR 85. See RSC O.122. See VACATION.

**time limits, statutory.** See TIME.

**time immemorial.** A term used to denote a time before legal memory. Fixed by the Statute of Westminster 1275 as 1189, the first year of the reign of Richard 1.

**time of essence of a contract.** Time is of the essence of a contract when the parties have expressly provided for it to be so in the contract or when the circumstances show that the parties intended it to be so. Where a conditional contract of sale fixes the date by which a condition must be met, the date so fixed must be strictly adhered to: Aberfoyle Plantations v Cheng (1960) AC 115: Crean v Drinan (1983) ILRM 82; Hynes v Independent Newspapers (1980) IR 204.

If a contract does not originally make time of the essence, one party may subsequently serve notice that from a stated date, time will be of the essence: Nolan v Driscoll (1978) HC. See also Sale of Goods Act 1893 s.10(1) and Judicature Act 1877 s.28(7). See also PRICE; VOIDABLE.

**time off.** An employee who has been given notice of dismissal for redundancy may take reasonable time off during working hours on full pay to seek or be trained for future employment: Redundancy Payments Act 1967 s.7. See REDUNDANCY.

**time policy.** A contract of insurance to insure the subject-matter for a definite period of time: Marine Insurance Act 1906 s.25(1).

**tipping of waste.** See WASTE OPERATION.

**tithe rentcharges.** Originally a rentcharge on land, payable previously in kind, and later in money. Any such tithe rentcharges which subsisted on 28th September 1975 were extinguished by the Land Act 1984 s.7(3).

**title.** (1) An appellation of office or distinction eg lord mayor (qv). (2) A description or heading eg of an action at law or the description of an Act of parliament: Vacher v London Society of Compositors (1913) AC 107. (3) The right to ownership of property or evidence of such right. Such a title may be (a) *original*, where the person entitled does not take from any predecessor eg in the case of copyright, and (b) *derivative*, where the person takes the place of a predecessor, by act of parties or by operation of law. For a checklist on title-parties relating to estates, see Stynes in 7ILT & SJ (1989) 92. See Criminal Damage Act 1991 s.8. See

ABSTRACT OF TITLE; LODGMENT IN COURT; MARKETABLE TITLE; ROOT OF TITLE; TITLE OF NOBILITY.

**title, long.** See PREAMBLE.

**title, short.** See SHORT TITLE.

**title by long possession.** See LONG POSSESSION, TITLE BY.

**title deeds.** The documents and instruments conferring or evidencing the title to land. In the case of *unregistered* land, they consist of deeds and conveyances, eg conveyances of freehold, fee farm grants and sub-grants, leases and sub-leases and mortgages. In the case of *registered* land, they consist of the entries in the Land Registry on the folio relating to the land, the charges registered thereon, the land certificate and charge certificates. See also Building Societies Act 1989 s.76(11). See DEPOSIT OF TITLE DEEDS; DOCUMENTS, EVIDENCE OF.

**title of nobility.** A title of nobility cannot be conferred by the State and government approval is required prior to any citizen accepting a title of nobility or honour: 1937 Constitution, art.40(2). See CIVIC HONOUR; HONOUR.

**title to goods.** In contracts for the sale of goods and hire-purchase of goods there are implied terms as to title: SGSS Act ss.10 and 26. Where goods are sold by a person who is not the owner thereof, and who does not sell them under the authority or with the consent of the owner, the buyer acquires no better title to the goods than the seller had, unless the owner of the goods is by his conduct precluded from denying the seller's authority to sell: Sale of Goods Act s.21. See FACTOR; MARKET OVERT; NEMO DAT QUI NON HABET; RETENTION OF TITLE; VOIDABLE TITLE, SALE UNDER.

**tobacco product.** Cigarettes cigars, cavendish or negrohead, hard pressed tobacco, other pipe tobacco, other smoking or chewing tobacco, manufactured wholly or partly from tobacco: Finance (Excise Duty on Tobacco Products) Act 1977 s.1(1) first schedule.

The Minister has power to prohibit or restrict the consumption of tobacco products in a designated area or a designated facility, which includes, but is not limited to: aircraft, trains, public service vehicles, health premises, schools, cinemas, theatres, concert halls, and buildings to which the public have access and which belong to or are in the occupation of the State or a body established by or under an Act of the Oireachtas: Tobacco (Health Promotion and Protection) Act 1988 s.2 and Regulations 1990 (SI No 39 of 1990).

It is now an offence to sell tobacco products to a person under the age of 16 years (ibid s.3) or to sell cigarettes otherwise then in packets of ten or more (ibid s.4). See also Tobacco Products (Control of Advertising, Sponsorship and Sales Promotion) Act 1978 and the 1988 Act s.9. See ORAL SMOKELESS TOBACCO PRODUCT.

**toll.** A tax paid for some privilege or compensation paid for some service provided eg a payment for passing over a road, bridge or ferry. The right to demand a toll may arise by way of franchise (qv) or by statute. See TOLL ROAD.

**toll road.** A public road or proposed public road in respect of which a *toll scheme* is in force: Roads Act 1993 s.56. A toll scheme, the decision on which is a reserved function (qv) of a road authority, must be approved by the Minister (ibid s.57). Road authorities are empowered to charge and collect tolls in respect of toll roads (ibid s.59) and to enter into agreements with other persons in relation to the financing, maintenance, construction and operation of toll roads (ibid s.63). A road authority as regards tolls on regional and local roads is the local authority, and on national roads is the National Roads Authority (ibid s.56).

**tontine.** An insurance scheme whereby contributors to the scheme pay into a fund which is divided at the end of a specified period among the survivors by way of repayment of capital or by annuity.

**topography right.** A right which exists in its creator where the topography of a semiconductor product is the result of the creator's own intellectual effort: European Communities (Protection of Topographics of Semiconductor Products) Regulations 1988 (SI No 101 of 1988) as amended by SI No 318 of 1991. Protection is given which consists of the exclusive right to reproduce and commercially exploit the topographics; the right commences at the time of creation and lasts for ten years from first commercial exploitation or fifteen years after creation. The Regulations implement Council Directive 87/54/EEC and Council Decisions 90/510-511/EEC. See INTELLECTUAL PROPERTY.

**tort.** [Crooked; twisted; distorted; a wrong]. A civil wrong, independent of contract, which arises from a breach of a duty imposed by law, the main remedy for which is an action for unliquidated damages (qv). The principal torts are trespass, nuisance, defamation and negligence (qqv).

The remedies for tort are either *extra-judicial* or *judicial*. The *extra-judicial* remedies are: distress damage feasant; re-entry on land; expulsion of a trespasser; abatement of nuisance (qqv). The *judicial* remedies are: damages, injunction; restitution of property (qqv). The defences in tort include: necessity; statutory authority; volenti non fit injuria; inevitable accident; statute-barred (qqv).

Action for damages in tort is commenced, in the Circuit Court by *civil bill*, and in the High Court by *summons*.

A person domiciled in a *contracting* state of the EC may, in another contracting state, be sued in matters relating to tort, delict or quasi-delict, in the courts for the place where the harmful event occurred: Jurisdiction of Courts and Enforcement of Judgments (European Communities) Act 1988, first schedule, art.5. It has been held that jurisdiction lies in either the courts for the place (a) where the event ultimately causing the harm occurred or (b) where the actual harm occurred: Bier v Mines de Potasse — Case 21/76 (1976) ECR 1735. It has also been held that the phrase "*tort, delict or quasi-delict*" must be independently interpreted and not by reference to national law: Kalfelis v Banque Schroder — Case 189/87 ECR — see 7ILT & SJ (1989) 2. As regards tort and EFTA States, see Jurisdiction of Courts and Enforcement of Judgments Act 1993, sixth schedule, art.5. [Text: McMahon & Binchy; Clerk & Lindsell UK; Salmond UK]. See IMMUNITY.

**tortfeasor.** A person who commits a tort. See JOINT TORTFEASORS.

**tortious.** Wrongful.

**torture.** Any act by which severe pain or suffering, whether physical or mental, is intentionally inflicted on a person for a number of stated purposes : United Nations Convention Against Torture, Art 1. Torture constitutes an aggravated and deliberate form of cruel, inhuman or degrading treatment or punishment: UN General Assembly Resolution 3452 (XXX) 9/12/75. "No one shall be subject to torture or to inhuman or degrading treatment or punishment": European Convention on Human Rights. Torture includes the infliction of mental suffering by creating a state of anguish and stress by means other than bodily assault: Greek Case — Yearbook of European Convention on Human Rights Vol 12, 1986 p.461.

Provision for the establishment of a European Committee for the prevention of torture is made by the European Convention for the prevention of Torture and Inhuman or Degrading Treatment or Punishment which came into force as regards Ireland on 1st February 1989. See also Ireland v United Kingdom in 8ILT & SJ (1990) 216. See VIDEO RECORDING.

**total loss.** In marine insurance, the total loss of the subject matter insured may be either actual or constructive. Actual loss arises where the ship or cargo is totally destroyed or so damaged that it can never arrive in specie (qv) at its destination. See Marine Insurance Act 1906 s.60. See CONSTRUCTIVE TOTAL LOSS.

**tote.** See WAGERING CONTRACT.

**toties quoties.** [As often as something happens]. Repeatedly.

**tour operator.** A person other than a carrier who arranges for the purpose of selling or offering for sale to the public, accommodation for travel by air, sea or land transport to destinations outside Ireland, or who holds himself out by advertising or otherwise as one who may make available such accommodation, either solely or in association with other accommodation, facilities or services: Transport (Tour Operators and Travel Agents) Act 1982 s.2.

A person may not carry on business as a tour operator without a licence granted by the Minister. A *bond* is a prerequisite to the granting of a licence, being an arrangement for the protection of persons, during the validity of the licence, who enter into contracts with tour operators relating to overseas travel. See

SI No 175 of 1987; RSC O.102. See Balkan Tours Ltd v Minister for Communications (1988) ILRM 101. See TRANSPORT AUXILIARY; TRAVEL AGENT; TRAVELLERS' PROTECTION FUND.

**town.** The area comprised in a town (not being an urban district) in which the Towns Improvement (Ireland) Act 1854, is in operation: Interpretation Act 1937, schedule, para 32. The *boundaries* of a town may be extended: ibid 1854 Act s.5 as amended by the Local Government Act 1991 s.4. As there is no definition of *town* in the Judgments (Ireland) Act 1850, its meaning must be ascertained by reference to the law as it was and the English language as used in 1850: Irish Bank of Commerce v O'Hara (1992 SC) ITLR (10 Aug). See BOUNDARY ALTERATION.

**town commissioners.** The bodies which, as corporations aggregate, exercise functions in relation to the paving, lighting, draining, cleansing and supplying with water of a number of towns: Town Improvements (Ireland) Act 1854; Lighting of Towns (Ireland) Act 1828. Some towns became urban district councils: Public Health (Ireland) Act 1878 s.4; Local Government (Ireland) Act 1898 s.22. Town commissioners are not sanitary, planning or fire authorities, but they are housing authorities, except in respect of grants under the Housing Act 1966 and of certain functions (eg the homeless) under the Housing Act 1988 s.21.

A county council is deemed to have, and always to have had, a power to provide dwellings or building sites in a town commissioners' area without withdrawing that power from the commissioners: Housing Act 1988 s.20(2).

**toxic and dangerous waste.** Waste containing or contaminated by specified substances of such a nature, in such quantities or in such concentration, as to constitute a risk to health or to the environment: European Communities (Toxic and Dangerous Waste) Regulations 1982 (SI No 33 of 1982). A total of 27 substances are specified, including eg asbestos, arsenic, mercury, and cyanides.

Local authorities are responsible for the planning, organisation and supervision of operations for the disposal of toxic and dangerous waste in their areas, including the preparation of a *special waste plan*, and for the authorisation of the storage, treatment and depositing of such waste (ibid arts.3-4). Any person, other than a local authority acting in its own area, who stores, treats or deposits toxic and dangerous waste, may do so only in accordance with a *permit* issued by the local authority in whose area the operation is carried out (ibid art.5).

A permit is not required for the transport of toxic and dangerous waste. A system of *consignment notes* is specified to regulate the manner in which such wastes are transported (art.8). See also Hanrahan v Merck Sharpe & Dohme (Irl) Ltd (1988 SC) ILRM 629. See Asbestos Waste Regulations — SI No 28, 30 and 31 of 1990. See INCINERATION; WASTE OILS; TRANSFRONTIER SHIPMENT; POLYCHLORINATED BIPHENYLS.

**tracing.** The equitable right of beneficiaries or creditors to follow assets to which they are entitled (or other assets into which they have been converted) into the hands of those who hold them. Thus beneficiaries and creditors have the right to follow the property of a deceased person into the hands of anybody other than a purchaser. Also where money which has been borrowed, can be traced, the lender may be entitled to a *tracing order*. The right to trace ends with a purchaser for value who has no notice of the circumstances which have given rise to the right to trace: Incorporated Law Society v Owens (1990) 8ILT Dig 64. See Shanahan's Stamp Auctions v Farrelly (1962) IR 386; In re Irish Shipping Ltd (1986) ILRM 518. See Succession Act 1965 s.59.

**trade.** For the purpose of taxation, means every trade, manufacture, adventure or concern in the nature of trade: Income Tax Act 1967 s.1(1). Since 1983, the profits of any trade consisting of or involving illegal activities are taxable, reversing the decision in Collins v Mulvey 31 TC 151: Finance Act 1983 s.19. See LIVELIHOOD.

**trade, course of.** See COURSE OF TRADE.

**trade, prohibition of.** The Minister may by regulation prohibit trade with other States eg the prohibition imposed in 1990, with penalities for infringement,

of trade with Iraq pursuant to EC Regulation 2340/90 of 8 August 1990: SI No 215 of 1990.

**trade description.** Any description, statement or other indication, direct or indirect, concerning goods, as to their number, quantity, measure, guage, capacity, weight; mode of manufacturing or producing, etc; material composition; person by whom manufactured; place and time of manufacture; fitness for purpose and physical characteristics; other history etc. See Consumer Information Act 1978 s.2(1); Merchandise Marks Act 1887 s.3(1) for full definition.

A trade description also concerns the contents of books and their authors, films and producers, and recordings and performers. See [Text: Grogan, King & Donelan; O'Keeffe UK]. FALSE TRADE DESCRIPTION; DEFINITION ORDER; MILEOMETER READING.

**trade dispute.** Any dispute between employers and workers which is connected with the employment or non-employment, or the terms or conditions of or affecting the employment, of any person: Industrial Relations Act 1990 s.8. *Worker* in this context means a person who is or was employed whether or not in the employment of the employer with whom a trade dispute arises (ibid s.8). The term *non-employment* cannot have an unrestricted meaning: Bradbury Ltd v Duffy (1984) 3 JISLL 86.

There is statutory protection to *authorised* trade unions, their members and officials, in respect of acts done in contemplation or furtherance of a trade dispute: Industrial Relations Act 1990 ss.9-13. For example, actions in respect of tortious acts cannot be entertained by any court (ibid s.13), or acts by a person which induce or threaten to induce another person to break a contract of employment, or a threat to break his own contract of employment (ibid s.12), or acts which are an interference with the trade, business or employment of some other person (ibid s.12). There is no immunity for a trade union in respect of actions taken against them for restitution, for breach of constitutional rights or for breach of contract. See Universe Tankships v ITWF (1989) IRLR 363; Hayes v Ireland (1987) ILRM 651. See also Esplanade Pharmacy Ltd v Larkin

(1957) IR 285; Becton Dickinson & Co Ltd v Lee (1973) IR 1. See CONSPIRACY; INDUSTRIAL ACTION; IMMUNITY; LABOUR INJUNCTION; LABOUR RELATIONS COMMISSION; PICKETING; SECRET BALLOT; STRIKE; TRADE UNION.

**trade effluent.** As regards water pollution (qv), means effluent from any works, apparatus, plant or drainage pipe used for the disposal of waters or to a sewer of any liquid (whether treated or untreated), either with or without particles of matter in suspension therein, which is discharged from premises used for carrying on any trade or industry, including mining, but does not include domestic sewage or storm water: Local Government (Water Pollution) Act 1977 s.1. The powers of local authorities to carry out reviews of trade effluent discharge licences have been extended: LG (Water Pollution) (Amendment) Act 1990 s.5. See INTEGRATED POLLUTION CONTROL

**trade mark.** A mark used or proposed to be used in relation to *goods* for the purpose of indicating, or so as to indicate, a connection *in the course of trade* between the goods and some person having the right either as proprietor or as registered user to use the mark, whether with or without any indication of the identity of that person: Trade Marks Act 1963 s.2.

A *mark* includes a device, brand, heading, label, ticket, name, signature, word, letter, numeral, or any combination thereof (ibid s.2). As to *goods* and *in the course of trade*, see ITT World Directories Inc v Controller of Patents, Designs and Trade Marks (1985) ILRM 30; Bank of Ireland v Controller of Trade Marks (1987) HC. A trade mark must be registered (qv) to obtain statutory rights against infringement (ibid s.10).

The vendor of goods to which a trade mark, or mark, or trade description has been applied, is deemed to warrant that the mark is a genuine trade mark and that the trade description is not a false trade description: Merchandise Marks Act 1887 s.17.

The fact that a trade description is a trade mark, or part of a trade mark, within the meaning of the Trade Marks Act 1963, does not prevent it from being a false trade description when applied to goods; there is an exception however for some previous trade marks: Consumer Information Act 1978 s.24. See T O Regan & Sons Ltd v Micro-Bio (Ireland) Ltd (1980) HC. See EC Directive on Trademarks 89/104/EEC. [Text: Tierney; Kerly (UK)]. See COMMUNITY TRADE MARK; TRADE MARK, REGISTERED.

**trade mark, assignment of.** At common law, trade marks could only be assigned with the *goodwill* of the business in the goods in relation to which they were used. *Registered* trade marks (qv) are assignable and transmissible, and deemed always to have been, either in connection with the goodwill of a business or not, despite any rule of law or equity to the contrary: Trade Marks Act 1963 s.30. Unregistered trade marks cannot be assigned without the goodwill of the business unless the assignment or transfer can be brought within the terms of s.30(3).

**trade mark, associated.** See ASSOCIATE TRADE MARK.

**trade mark, certification.** See CERTIFICATION TRADE MARK.

**trade mark, community.** See COMMUNITY TRADE MARK.

**trade mark, infringement of.** See INFRINGEMENT OF TRADE MARK.

**trade mark, registered.** A trade mark registered in the register of trade marks kept in the Patents Office in Dublin; the register is divided into two parts, Part A (qv) and Part B (qv), which give the registered proprietor different rights: Trade Marks Act 1963 ss.9 and 13.

A trade mark may only be registered in respect of particular goods or classes of goods (ibid s.11) and the rights arising from registration relate only to the goods in respect of which it is registered (ibid s.12).

In order for a trade mark to be registered in Part A it must contain or consist of at least one of the following essential particulars: (a) the name of a company, individual, or firm, represented in a special or particular manner; (b) the signature of the applicant for registration or some predecessor in business; (c) an invented word (qv) or invented words; (d) a word or words having no direct reference to the character or quality of the goods, and not being according to its ordinary signification a geographical name (qv) or a surname; (e) any other *distinctive mark* (qv), but a name, signature, word or words, other than such as fall within the descriptions in (a), (b), (c) and (d) is not registrable except upon evidence of its distinctiveness (ibid s.17(1)).

In order for a trade mark to be registered in Part B, it must be *capable* of distinguishing goods with which the proprietor of the trade mark is or may be connected in the course of trade, from goods in the case of which no such connection subsists, in relation to use within the extent of the registration (ibid s.18 (1)). See Miller Brewing Company v The Controller of Patents (1988) ILRM 259; Seven-Up Co v Bubble-Up Co Inc (1990 HC) ILRM 204.

In order to register a trade mark, an *intention to use* the trade mark is necessary (ibid ss.25(1) and 37(1)). In addition, it is not lawful to register as a trade mark any matter the use of which would, by reason of its being likely to deceive or cause confusion, be disentitled to protection in a court of law, or would be contrary to law or morality, or any scandalous design (ibid s.19). No mark may be registered in respect of any goods or description of goods that is identical with a trade mark belonging to a different proprietor and already on the register, or that so nearly resembles such a trade mark as to be likely to deceive or cause confusion (ibid s.20). [Text: Tierney; Kerly (UK)]. See COURSE OF TRADE; EXCLUSIVE JURISDICTION; INFRINGEMENT OF TRADE MARK; PART A; PART B; REGISTER OF TRADE MARKS; TRAFFICKING IN TRADE MARKS; TRADING STAMP; VARIETAL NAMES.

**trade mark, registration period.** The registration of a trade mark is for a period of seven years, but it may be renewed from time to time for successive periods of fourteen years thereafter, subject to prescribed renewal fees: Trade Marks Act 1963 s.28; Trade Mark Rules 1963 (SI No 268 of 1963) and 1992 (SI No 313 of 1992).

**trade mark agent.** A person who carries on the business of acting as agent for others for the purpose, inter alia, of applying for trade marks. A person acting for gain must not, either alone or in partnership with any other person,

practise, describe himself, or hold himself out as a trade mark agent, unless he is registered as a trade mark agent in the register of trade mark agents and similarly in the case of a partnership unless all the partners are so registered: Trade Marks Act 1963 s.69; SI No 35 of 1964; SI No 371 of 1985.

**trade mark at common law.** A mark used so widely in connection with a group or class of goods that the public recognise goods carrying that mark as associated with the owner of the mark. Use of that mark by another could be grounds for an action of *passing-off* (qv).

**trade refuse.** A local authority is required to remove trade refuse if it is requested so to do by the owner or occupier of a premises: Public Health (Amendment) Act 1907 s.48. The owner or occupier must however pay a reasonable sum to them for so doing, the amount of which is to be settled in the case of dispute by the District Court, whose decision is final. See LITTER; HOUSEHOLD REFUSE.

**trade regulation.** See BELOW COST SELLING; COMPETITION AUTHORITY; COMPETITION, DISTORTION OF; HELLO MONEY; MERGER OF COMPANY; PRICE CONTROL; WITHHOLDING OF SUPPLIES.

**trade, right to.** See LIVELIHOOD.

**trade secret.** Information concerning commercial, manufacturing or production processes of a firm where the disclosure of such information would be a breach of confidence or breach of contract. Such disclosure can be prevented by injunction (qv).

Breach of confidence can arise: (a) where the information has the necessary confidence about it ie it must not be something which is public knowledge; (b) the information must have been imparted to the defendant in circumstances imposing an obligation of confidence; (c) the unauthorised use of the information would be to the detriment of the plaintiff. Breach of contract could arise in the case of the relationship of employer and employee. See Cranleigh Precision Engineering v Bryant (1965) I WLR 1293; Aksjeselskapet Jutul v Waterford Iron Founders Ltd (1977) HC. See CONFIDENCE, BREACH OF; EMPLOYEE; PUBLIC JUSTICE.

**trade union.** Any combination, whether temporary or permanent, the principal object of which are under its constitution the regulation of the relations between workmen and masters, or between workmen and workmen, or between masters and masters, or the imposing of restrictive conditions on the conduct of any trade or business, and also the provision of benefits to members: Trade Union Act 1913 s.2; National Union of Journalists (NUJ) and IPU v Sisk (1992 SC) ILRM 96; Barry in 9ILT & SJ (1991) 271.

A trade union may be unregistered (qv), certified (qv), registered (qv) or authorised (qv). The statutory immunities conferred on trade unions by the Industrial Relations Act 1990 are restricted to *authorised* trade unions only (ibid ss.9-13). See Riordan v Butler (1940) IR 347; Sherriff v McMullen (1952) IR 236. [Text: Kerr; Kerr & Whyte]. See IMMUNITY; TRADE DISPUTE; PICKETING; UNFAIR DISMISSAL; UNLAWFUL INTERFERENCE WITH CONSTITUTIONAL RIGHTS; WORK, RIGHT TO.

**trade union, authorised.** A body of persons entitled to be granted or to hold a *negotiation licence:* Trade Union Act 1941 s.7 as amended by the Trade Union Acts of 1971 and 1975. It is an offence for any body of persons to carry on negotiations for the fixing of wages or other conditions of employment unless such body is the holder of a negotiation licence or is an excepted body: Trade Union Act 1941 s.6. Excepted bodies include teachers' organisations, civil service staff associations, bodies exempted by the Minister and a body carrying on negotiations with its own employees: ibid s.6(3). Generally, to obtain a negotiation licence, a union must be registered with the Registrar of Friendly Societies, have not less than 500 members, and maintain a deposit in the High Court depending on the size of the union. For new trade unions, the minimum number of members must be 1,000: Industrial Relations Act 1990 s.21(2).

Authorised trade unions, their members and officials are entitled to the protection of the Industrial Relations Act 1990 ss.9-13. This protection, originally confined to those in trade and industry by the Trade Disputes Act 1906, was extended to all employees, except members of the Defence Forces and the Gardai by the Trade Disputes (Amendment) Act 1982.

Certain advantages under employment protection legislation accrue to authorised trade unions and their members eg dismissal for trade union membership or activity is deemed to be unfair only if the union is an authorised or excepted one. See Irish Aviation Executive Staff Association v Minister for Labour (1981) ILRM 350; Post Office Workers Union v Minister for Labour (1981) ILRM 355; O'Riordan v Clune (1991 EAT) ELR 89. See RSC O.107. See TRADE UNION.

**trade union, certified.** A body which has been certified by the Registrar of Friendly Societies that it is a union within the meaning of the Trade Union Acts 1871-1982. A body must apply to the Registrar in compliance with the Trade Union Act 1913 s.2(3). The only advantage of being a certified trade union is that the certificate issued is conclusive evidence that the body is a trade union. The immunities conferred by the Industrial Relations Act 1990 and the advantages conferred by the employment legislation of the 1970's do not apply to a certified trade union. See TRADE UNION.

**trade union, registered.** A body of seven or more members of a trade union which has been registered with the Registrar of Friendly Societies in accordance with the Trade Union Act 1871. The certificate of registration is conclusive evidence that the holder is a trade union within the meaning of the Trade Union Acts.

There are a number of advantages in registration eg exemption from income tax (Income Tax Act 1967 s.336), property vesting in succeeding trustees without need of conveyance or assignment. However, the immunities conferred by the Industrial Relations Act 1990 are restricted to *authorised* trade unions only as are the advantages conferred by the employment legislation of the 1970's.

It has been held that an Irish registered trade union is entitled to transfer its engagements to a UK registered trade union which has members within the State and an Irish negotiation licence: Trade Union Act 1975; National Union of Journalists (NUJ) & Irish Print Union v Sisk (1992 SC) ILRM 96. See

NEGOTIATION LICENCE; TRADE UNION.

**trade union, unregistered.** A trade union which is an unincorporated voluntary association of individuals similar in legal status to a social club. It has no legal personality itself and consequently any action concerning the union, its property or activities, must be brought or defended by way of representative action (qv). See Nolan v Fagan 1985 HC; RSC O.15 r.9.

**trade-in.** Generally understood to mean a part payment by way of exchange in a contract for the sale of goods where the consideration (qv) is partly goods and partly money. See Clarke v Reilly (1962) 96 ILTR 96. See HIRE-PURCHASE PRICE; MOTOR VEHICLE, SALE OF.

**trading house, special.** A company which exists solely for the purpose of carrying on a trade which consists solely of the selling of export goods manufactured by a firm which employs less than 200 persons: Finance Act 1987 s.29 as amended by SI No 61 of 1988. A special trading house, to benefit from the special 10% rate of corporation tax (ibid s.29) must have a licence which may be granted by the Minister: Export Promotion (Amendment) Act 1987 s.2. An appeal against a refusal to grant such a licence lies to the Circuit Court (ibid s.2).

The requirements to qualify as a special trading house have been set out by the Minister:- it must be a registered company; its business must be solely the sale abroad of Irish *goods* to which it has title; it must not be the manufacturer of those goods or of any other goods; it must *sell only by wholesale. Goods* means goods manufactured in Ireland, and includes data processing equipment and computer software services. *Selling by wholesale* means selling to a person who carries on a business of selling such goods or who uses the goods for the purpose of a trade or undertaking.

**trading stamp.** Any stamp, coupon, voucher, token or similar device which is, or is intended to be, delivered to any person upon, or in connection with, the purchase of goods or the provision of services and is, or is intended to be, *redeemable* by that or some other person: Trading Stamps Act 1980 s.1. *Redeemable* means exchanged for money, goods or

services. It does not include a newspaper or periodical of which the stamp forms part or in which it is contained. It also excludes a stamp which is redeemable only from the seller of the goods, or his supplier, or the person who provides the service.

A trading stamp must bear on its face in clear and legible characters a value expressed in the currency of the State and the name or registered trade mark (qv) of the issuing company (ibid s.4). See TRADING STAMP SCHEME.

**trading stamp scheme.** Any arrangement for making trading stamps (qv) available for use in shops or elsewhere, including arrangements for their redemption: Trading Stamps Act 1980 s.1. There are restrictions on persons who may carry on business as promoters of trading stamps (ibid s.2) and provision for the redemption of trading stamps for cash (ibid s.5). An exchange of goods or services for trading stamps is to be regarded as a monetary consideration for the purposes of the Sale of Goods Act 1893 and the SGSS Act 1980 (ibid s.8).

**traffic refuge.** A refuge for pedestrians on a roadway provided by a raised pavement, guard posts or similar means: Road Traffic (Signs) Regulations 1962 art.2 (SI No 171 of 1962).

**traffic management.** The Commissioner of the Garda Siochana is empowered to carry out various functions regarding the management of road traffic pursuant to the Road Traffic Acts 1961 to 1987. The Commissioner is required to have regard to any recommendations made to him by the National Roads Authority in relation to the performance of his function: Roads Act 1993 s.23(1). See CROWD CONTROL.

**traffic regulation.** Under recent legislation, the Minister is empowered to make traffic and parking regulations in a single code to replace (a) the existing general regulations made by the Minister (Road Traffic Act 1968 s.60) and (b) the local traffic and parking bye-laws or temporary rules on a county basis made by the Garda Commissioner (Road Traffic Act 1961 ss.89-90): Road Traffic Act 1993 s.35. Road authorities are given power to make bye-laws governing the type of parking controls in their area and to apply traffic management measures eg traffic signs (ibid 1993 Act s.36-37).

**traffic sign.** See TRAFFIC REGULATION; SIGN.

**traffic wardens.** Persons employed by a local authority (qv) to carry out functions in respect of offences (a) under the Road Traffic Acts which relate to the prohibition or restriction of the stopping or parking of mechanical propelled vehicles and (b) under the Finance Act 1976 s.73 for failing to display a current licence disc: Local Authority (Traffic Wardens) Act 1975 s.2.

**trafficking in trade marks.** It has been held that *trafficking* in a trade mark conveyed the notion of dealing in a trade mark primarily as a commodity in its own right and not for the purpose of identifying or promoting merchandise with which the proprietor of the mark was connected: Holly Hobbie trade mark (1984) RPC 329. The Controller of Trade Marks is required to refuse an application to register a person as the registered user of a trade mark if it appears to him that the grant thereof would tend to facilitate *trafficking* in a trade mark: Trade Marks Act 1963 s.36(6).

**trainee garda.** See GARDA SIOCHANA.

**training.** The imparting of skill, knowledge and attitudes to another. An employer has a duty at common law to provide adequate training and instruction to his employee. There is a statutory duty on all employers in providing training to ensure that his employees receive, during time off from their duties and without loss of remuneration, adequate safety and health training: SI No 44 of 1993, regs.13 and 26(d). There is also a statutory duty on every employee, taking into account training and instructions, given by his employer, to make correct use of machinery, apparatus, tools, dangerous substances, transport equipment and other means of production (ibid reg.14).

The Unfair Dismissals Act 1977 does not apply to dismissal of an employee while undergoing training which is one year or less from commencement of employment. The Act does not apply also to dismissals during training for specified qualifications eg nurse, health inspector, social worker (ibid s.3).

Training levies may be imposed on employers in designated industrial activ-ities by way of *levy orders* and may be appealed to a Levy Appeals Tribunal: Industrial Training Act 1967 ss.21-22. Rules may be made on the employment and training of certain industrial apprentices (ibid ss.27-36). The Youth Employment Levy imposed by the Youth Employment Agency Act 1981 s.15 became the Employment and Training Levy from 1st January 1988: Labour Services Act 1987 s.25.

An Foras Aiseanna Saothair (FAS), took over the functions and powers of An Chomhairle Oiliuna (AnCO), the National Manpower Service and the Youth Employment Agency on 1st January 1988: Labour Services Act 1987. See Cityview Press Ltd v An Chomhairle Oiliuna (1980) IR 381.

Refusal or failure to avail of any reasonable opportunity of receiving training provided by or approved of by FAS, without just cause, can lead to disqualification of unemployment assistance: Social Welfare (Consolidation) Act 1981 s.140(5)(c) substituted by Social Welfare Act 1992 s.27. See APPRENTICESHIP; SAFETY AT WORK; VOCATIONAL EDUCATION COMMITTEE; VOCATIONAL TRAINING; WEIGHTS, MAXIMUM; WITHHOLDING TAX.

**training grants.** Training grants may be made by An Foras Aiseanna Saothair (FAS) or by the Industrial Development Authority, following consultation with FAS: Industrial Training Act 1967 ss.19-20; Labour Services Act 1987; Industrial Development Act 1986 s.28. It has been held that training grants received by a company from the Industrial Development Authority, were not part of the company's profits or gains arising or accruing to the company from a trade within the meaning of s.52 of the Income Tax Act 1967: Jacobs International v O'Cleirigh (1985) ILRM 651.

**transborder data flows.** The transfer across national borders, by whatever medium, of *personal data* undergoing automatic processing or collected with a view to being automatically processed: Data Protection Convention 1981 art.12(1). A party to the Convention may not, for the sole purpose of privacy, prohibit or subject to special authorisation transborder flows of personal data going to the territory of another party (ibid art.12(2)). Nevertheless, a party may derogate from this requirement in specific circumstances. See Data Protection Act 1988 s.11. See PROHIBITION NOTICE, DATA.

**transcript.** The reproduction in longhand of the notes taken, usually in shorthand, of the proceedings at a hearing. Where a transcript records that a question was asked in a trial, an applicant would have difficulty in convincing an appellate court that the question was not asked, even though transcripts cannot be completely accurate: DPP v McKeever (1992 CCA) ITLR (24 Aug) and 11 ILT Dig (1993) 186. The court disapproves of trawling through the transcript of a trial for errors and omissions and including as a ground of appeal such errors or omissions not thought worthy of mention or objection during the course of the trial: People (DPP) v James Ryan (1993 CCA) ITLR (19 Apr) and 11 ILT Dig (1993) 185.

In a personal injuries action, it was held that the defendant should not be required to bear the cost of a daily transcript of the evidence, as there were instructing solicitor, one junior and two senior counsel, and there was no detailed scientific evidence in the case: Ward v Walsh (1992 SC) 10 ILT Dig 74. See RSC O.123; O.86 r.14; O.96 r.36.

**trans-European networks.** The EC is required to contribute to the establishment and development of trans-European networks in the areas of transport, telecommunications and energy infrastructures; there is a requirement to take account in particular of the need to link island, landlocked and peripheral regions with the central regions of the Community: Treaty of Rome 1957 art.129b as replaced by Maastricht Treaty 1992 art.G(D)(38). The funding of such infrastructures in the less prosperous regions of the EC is provided for, as is the financing of specific projects through the Cohesion Fund (qv). See COMMITTEE OF THE REGIONS.

**transfer.** The passage of a right from one person to another either (a) by act of the parties eg in a conveyance of land or (b) by operation of law eg forfeiture, bankruptcy, succession (qqv).

**transfer of action.** See REMIT OF ACTION.

**transfer of employment.** Protection for employees where the identity of their employer changes is provided for in the European Communities (Safeguarding of Employees' Rights on Transfer of Undertakings) Regulations 1980: SI No 306 of 1980.

Protection is not lost by the transfer of the undertaking to a paying agent: O'Beirne v Fox (1990) ELR 151. Protection is not lost either in the contracting out of a business if the business retains its identity or if there is a change in the legal or natural person who is responsible for carrying on the business regardless of whether or not ownership of the business is transferred: Bannon v Employment Appeals Tribunal (1992 HC) ELR 203 — reported by Barry in 10 ILT & SJ (1992) 242. Reversion of the lease of a business premises to the original lessor constitutes a transfer of undertakings: Guidon v Farrington (1992 EAT) ELR 146. Acceptance of a redundancy payment in respect of employment with the first employer did not break continuity of service: Yorke & Tuite v Teenoso Ltd (1992 EAT) ELR 161; it now does — see REDUNDANCY.

See also Nova Colour Graphic Supplies v Employment Appeals Tribunal (1987 HC) IR 426; Ennis & Bonney v Coffey & Ryan — UD 132/88 and 133/88 — 7ILT & SJ (1989) 5; Westman Holdings Ltd v McCormack & Ors (1991 SC) ILRM 833; Mythan v Employment Appeals Tribunal (1990 HC) ELR 1; Purcell & McHugh v Bewley's Manufacturing Ltd (1990 CC) ELR 68; Sweeney v Deantus Alfa Teo (1993 EAT) ELR 22; Guidon v Farrington (1993 EAT) ELR 98. See also Barry in 7ILT & SJ (1989) 262 & 294 and in 11 ILT & SJ (1993) 166. See ACQUIRED RIGHTS, EMPLOYEES.

**transfer of engagements.** A building society may transfer its engagements to another society to any extent, and that other society may undertake to fulfil the engagements, provided each resolves to do so by special resolution, or, if the Central Bank consents, by resolution of the board of directors: Building Societies Act 1989 ss.96(1)-(2) and 99(2).

**transfer of shares.** The change in ownership of shares which takes place when they are transferred under a proper instrument of transfer, or when vested in another person by operation of law, the name of the new owner being entered in the register of members: Companies Act 1963 ss.81 and 31(2). The standard form of transfer for fully paid transferable shares in most limited companies is set out in the Stock Transfer Act 1963, first schedule. *Share warrants* to bearer are transferred by mere delivery (ibid s.88).

In a private company, its *articles of association* must impose restrictions on the transferability of its shares, whereas in other companies a member has an unfettered right to transfer shares unless the articles provide otherwise. Some articles give directors the right to decline to register a transfer, but such a refusal must be exercised bona fide and in the best interest of the company. See also Casey v Bentley (1902) 1 IR 376; Lee & Co (Dublin) Ltd v Egan (Wholesale) Ltd 1978 HC; Pernod Ricard and Comrie plc v FII Fyffes plc (1989 HC) 7 ILT Dig 53.

The Official Assignee (qv) in bankruptcy, is empowered, without court order, to transfer stocks and shares of the bankrupt (qv) to the same extent as the bankrupt could have: Bankruptcy Act 1988 s.67. See CAPITAL GAINS TAX; DISTRINGAS NOTICE; SHARES; SHARES, EQUITABLE MORTGAGE OF; SHARES, COMPULSORY PURCHASE; TRANSMISSION OF SHARES.

**transfer order.** See TENANT PURCHASE SCHEME.

**transferable vote.** A vote in an election which is (a) capable of being given so as to indicate the voter's preference for the candidates in order, and (b) capable of being transferred to the next choice when the vote is not required to give a prior choice the necessary quota of votes, or when, owing to the deficiency in the number of votes given for a prior choice, that choice is excluded from the list of candidates: Electoral Act 1992 s.37. A *transferable paper* is a ballot paper on which, following a first preference, a second or subsequent preference is recorded in consecutive numerical order for a continuing candidate (ibid s.118(1)). See also draft Presidential Elections Bill 1993 s.45. See PROPORTIONAL REPRESENTATION; QUOTA.

**transfrontier shipment of hazardous waste.** An inter-country system of monitoring and supervision of the ship-

ment of toxic and dangerous waste within the European Community, including such wastes trans-shipped for use, recycling or recovery, is contained in Directives 84/631/EEC and 86/279/EEC. It is given effect in the State by the European Communities (Transfrontier Shipment of Hazardous Waste) Regulations 1988 (SI No 248 of 1988). See TOXIC AND DANGEROUS WASTE.

**transit in rem judicatem.** [It passes into a *res judicata* (qv)]. A cause of action is merged into a judgment; further proceedings cannot be taken on the same cause of action other than to enforce the judgment already obtained.

**transitu, stoppage in.** See STOPPAGE IN TRANSITU.

**translation.** See LANGUAGE.

**transmission of shares.** The automatic vesting of shares of a company in another person by operation of law eg on the death of a shareholder, the automatic vesting in favour of the personal representative takes place. The personal representative may be entitled to be registered as shareholder himself; in any event, he has power to transfer the shares even though he is not registered as a member of the company. In the case of bankruptcy of a shareholder, the Official Assignee (qv) is entitled to disclaim the bankrupt's shares within 12 months of the date of adjudication of bankruptcy. See Companies Act 1963 ss.81(2), 82, and 87 as amended by Companies Act 1977 s.5(1); Bankruptcy Act 1988 s.56.

**transparency.** The concept in the European Community whereby its decision making processes and its laws are better understood. The European Council at Edinburgh (Dec 1992) decided that *transparency* would be improved by (a) improving access to the work of the Council (eg by open debates and publication of voting records); (b) by improved information on the role of the Council (eg better information on the decisions of Council); (c) simplification of and easier access to Community legislation (eg unofficial and official codification of Community legislation).

**transport policy.** The EC Council is empowered to lay down (a) common rules applicable to international transport to and from the territory of a member State or passing across the territory of one or more member States; (b) the conditions under which non-resident carriers may operate transport services within a member State; (c) measures to improve transport safely; and (d) any other appropriate provisions: Treaty of Rome 1957 art.75 as replaced by Maastricht Treaty 1992 art.G(D)(16).

**transport auxiliary.** Self employed persons or employees who are either a forwarding agent, freight agent, airfreight agent, road haulage broker, tour operator (qv), travel agent (qv), air broker, air travel organiser: (all category A); a shipping and forwarding agent, shipping agent, shipbroker: (category B); a market or lairage operator: (category C): European Communities (Transport Auxiliaries) Regulations 1988 (SI No 18 of 1988). These Regulations provide for a grant of a *certificate of experience* to any appropriately experienced person who wishes to operate as a transport auxiliary in any other EC Member State, implementing Council Directive 82/47O/EEC.

**transportation.** Formerly, the penalty for felons who were transported overseas to a penal colony; it was abolished and replaced by *penal servitude* (qv) under the Penal Servitude Act 1853.

**transposing of words.** The alteration of the order of words in a document which the court may make in order to give effect to the intention of the parties. See Parkhurst v Smith (1742) Willes 327.

**travel, right to.** There is a constitutional right to travel outside the State: The State (KM) v Minister for Foreign Affairs (1979) IR 73; Lennon v Ganley (1981) ILRM 84. It is an unenumerated right under the Constitution. In 1992, an amendment to the Constitution provided that art.40(3)(3) — the right to life of the unborn — shall not limit freedom to travel between the State and another state: Thirteenth Amendment to the Constitution Act 1992. In a particular case, two persons from Northern Ireland were banned from travelling south of the border during the period of a three year suspended sentence: DPP v Warnock & Morton (1993 CCC) — Irish Times 24/3/1993. See also AG v X (1992 SC) ILRM 401; Kingston & Whelan in 10 ILT & SJ (1992) 95. See ABORTION; NE EXEAT REGNO; PASSPORT.

**travel agent.** A person other than a carrier who, as agent, sells or offers to sell to, or purchases or offers to purchase on behalf of the public, accommodation on air, sea or land transport to destinations outside Ireland or who holds himself out by advertising or otherwise as one who may make available such accommodation, either solely or in association with other accommodation, facilities or services: Transport (Tour Operators and Travel Agents) Act 1982 s.2. Similar requirements concerning a *bond* and a *licence* apply as in the case of a tour operator (qv). See Balkan Tours v Minister for Communications (1988) ILRM 101; Minister for Tourism Transport v Grimes (1988) HC. See SI No 176 of 1987; RSC O.102. See TOUR OPERATOR; TRANSPORT AUXILIARY; TRAVELLERS' PROTECTION FUND.

**traveller.** Colloquial expression to describe a person belonging to the class of persons who traditionally pursue or have pursued a nomadic way of life. Provision is made for a housing authority to provide manage or control halting sites for travellers: Housing Act 1988 s.13. In a particular case it was held that the nature and size of a proposed halting site for travellers was one which no reasonable planning authority could consider was consistent with proper planning and development of an area: Wilkinson v Dublin County Council (1991 HC) ILRM 605.

Where a temporary dwelling (eg a caravan) is parked in a public place within 5 miles of a housing authority halting site in which the dwelling could be appropriately accommodated, the authority may require the owner to remove it to the site: Housing (Miscellaneous Provisions) Act 1992 s.10. See Housing Act 1988 s.13(1). See Casey v Cork Corporation (1993 HC). See CARAVAN; HATRED, INCITEMENT TO; HOUSING; TEMPORARY DWELLING; UNFAIR DISMISSAL; VIDEO RECORDING.

**travellers' protection fund.** A fund established by the Minister from which payments may be made in respect of losses or liabilities incurred by customers of tour operators (qv) or travel agents (qv) in consequence of the inability or failure of the tour operators or travel agents to meet their financial or contractual obligations in respect of overseas travel contracts. A tour operator is obligated to make contributions to the fund as specified. See Transport (Tour Operators and Travel Agents) Act 1982 ss 15-19.

**traverse.** An express and specific denial of a fact in pleadings (qv). Where a defence traverses the plaintiff's claim and the plaintiff has sufficient information of all matters arising out of the defence, the court will not order the defendant to furnish particulars of his traverse: Behan v Medical Council (1993 HC) ILRM 240. See PARTICULARS, PLEADINGS.

**treason.** "Treason shall consist only in levying war against the State, or assisting any State or person or inciting or conspiring with any person to levy war against the State, or attempting by force of arms or other violent means to overthrow the organs of government established by this Constitution, or taking part or being concerned in or inciting or conspiring with any person to make or to take part or be concerned in any such attempt:" 1937 Constitution, art.39.

Treason may be committed by every person within the State and by Irish citizens (or persons ordinarily resident within the State) outside the State: Treason Act 1939 s.1. There can be no conviction for treason on the uncorroborated evidence of one witness. A person convicted of treason must be sentenced to imprisonment for life (of not less than 40 years); previously the mandatory sentence was death: Criminal Justice Act 1990 ss.2-5. See also Criminal Justice Act 1964. See also COMMUTE; MISPRISION OF TREASON; RELEASE, TEMPORARY; REMISSION; UNLAWFUL ORGANISATION.

**treasure trove.** Any money, coin, gold, silver, plate or bullion found in the earth, or other private place, which contains a substantial amount of gold or silver. If the owner is unknown, it belongs to the State. It was held in Webb & Webb v Ireland & Attorney General (1988 SC) ILRM 565 that treasure trove is a royalty or franchise vested in the State by virtue of its sovereign nature and not by royal prerogative, as no royal prerogative in existence prior to the 1922 Constitution was vested in the State by virtue of that Constitution (Byrne v Ireland [1972] IR 241 approved). The right of the State to

treasure trove has the characteristics of the prerogative at common law, which included the practice of rewarding a diligent and honest finder. A coroner (qv) has jurisdiction to inquire into the finding of treasure trove: Coroners Act 1962 s.49.

**treasury management, national.** The borrowing of moneys for the Exchequer and the management of the national debt. An agency to which is delegated the functions in this regard of the Minister for Finance has been established: National Treasury Management Agency Act 1990. The national debt amounted to £25 billion in 1990. See EXCHEQUER BILLS.

**treasury shares.** When a company acquires its own shares, it may cancel them or hold them; those held by the company are known as *treasury shares*: Companies Act 1990 s.209. See also Finance Act 1991 s.70. See Nolan in 9ILT & SJ (1991) 9.

**treat, notice to.** See NOTICE TO TREAT.

**treaty.** An agreement between the governments of two or more states. Approval by the Dail may be required before this State is bound by any such agreement. The treaty-making powers of the government are judicially reviewable: McGimpsey v Attorney General and Ireland (1989) ILRM 209; (1990) ILRM 440. See CHARGE ON PUBLIC FUNDS; INTERNATIONAL AGREEMENTS.

**Treaty, the.** Popularly refers to the Articles for a Treaty between Great Britain and Ireland, signed in London on 6th December 1921, under which Ireland was to have Dominion status within the British Empire and was to be styled and known as the Irish Free State.

**Treaty of Rome 1957.** See EUROPEAN COMMUNITY.

**Treaty of European Union.** See MAASTRICHT TREATY.

**tree.** An occupier of land must take reasonable and prudent care that a tree is not a danger to persons using an adjoining public highway: Lynch v Hetherton (1990 HC) ILRM 857. The owner or occupier of land must take all reasonable steps to ensure that a tree, shrub, hedge or other vegetation on land is not a hazard or potential hazard to persons using a public road (qv): Roads Act 1993 s.70(2)(a). Where there is such a hazard, a road authority is empowered to serve notice on the owner or occupier of the land requiring corrective action; the authority may take immediate action itself to reduce or remove the hazard where it presents an immediate and serious hazard (ibid s.70(2)(b) and (9)).

It is an offence to uproot any tree over ten years old or to cut down trees other than specified ones, without first giving notice to the Gardai: Forestry Act 1946 s.37. It is often a condition of a planning permission (qv) that specified trees on the site are preserved. A planning authority (qv) has power to plant trees, shrubs or other plants on any land and to make tree preservation orders in the interest of amenity: LG(P&D) Act 1963 ss.45 and 50. Compensation may be payable in respect of the reduction in the value of a person's interest in land as a result of a tree preservation order: LG (P&D) Act 1990 s.21 as amended by LG (P&D) Act 1992 s.21.

A number of bodies are given power by statute to lop, cut or remove trees or shrubs or plant without payment of compensation eg in the vicinity of a service aerodrome: Defence (Amendment) Act 1987 s.7. This has been held not to be unconstitutional: Electricity Supply Act 1927 s.98; ESB v Gormley (1985) IR 129. See ESTOVERS; FORESTRY.

**tree preservation order.** The order which a planning authority (qv) is empowered to make to preserve any tree, trees, groups of trees or woodlands in the interests of amenity: LG(P&D) Act 1963 s.45. No appeal lays to An Bord Pleanala in respect of the granting or witholding of a consent under a tree preservation order: Wicklow Co Council v An Bord Pleanala (1990) 8ILT Dig 107.

**trespass.** [To pass beyond]. A tort (qv) consisting of the unlawful direct interference with the person, land or goods of another. It is actionable *per se* without proof of actual damage. See MESNE RATES; TRESPASS AB INITIO; TRESPASS TO GOODS; TREPASS TO LAND; TRESPASS TO THE PERSON.

**trespass, offence of.** The offence which is committed by a person who wilfully trespasses on land and refuses to leave after a warning to leave is given: Summary Jurisdiction (Ireland) Act 1851. A warning given by posting a *warning off* notice is not sufficient. Under draft legislation, it is proposed to be an offence for a person without lawful excuse, to trespass on any dwelling or the curtilage thereof in such a manner as causes or is likely to cause fear in another person: Criminal Justice (Public Order) Bill 1993 s.14. It will also be an offence to enter a building as a trespasser with intent to commit an offence (ibid s.12). See also ASSAULT; FORCIBLE ENTRY AND OCCUPATION.

**trespass to goods.** The direct unlawful interference with the goods of another. It can consist of (a) the trespass to goods *per se:* ESB v Hastings Co (1965) Ir Jur Rep 51; (b) conversion (qv) and (c) detinue (qv). The defences include: consent of the owner, lawful justification and self-defence.

**trespass to land.** A tort (qv) consisting of entering or remaining on land or premises in the possession of another without lawful justification. Trespass is actionable *per se* ie the plaintiff does not have to show damage to succeed. The owner of premises may re-enter his own property and expel a trespasser using reasonable force: Beattie v Mair (1882) 10 Lr Ir 208; however the use of *ejectment proceedings* is preferable. Defences to trespass include: consent (eg licence (qv)), legal authority, and necessity (qv). See O'Brien v McNamee (1953) IR 86. See EJECTMENT; JUS TERTII; MESNE RATES; OCCUPIER'S LIABILITY TO TRESPASSERS.

**trespass to the person.** The tort of unlawful direct interference with a person, being either *assault, battery* or *false imprisonment. Assault* is the threat of, or attempt to apply, force to another which puts that other in reasonable apprehension that immediate violence will befall him: Dullaghan v Hillen (1957) Ir Jur Rep 10.

*Battery* is the touching of the person of another, either directly or indirectly, however slightly, with either hostile intention or against the other person's will: R v Day (1845) 9 JP 212.

*False imprisonment* is the unlawful and total restraint of the personal liberty of another whether by constraining him or compelling him to a particular place or confining him to a prison or police station or private place or by detaining him against his will in a public place:

Dullaghan v Hillen (1957) Ir Jur Rep 10.

The defences to the tort of trespass to the person include: consent; self-defence; lawful authority; reasonable chastisement by a parent or some other in *loco parentis*. See Ross v Curtis (1990) 8ILT Dig 64. See CORPORAL PUNISHMENT; JURY, ABOLITION OF.

**trespasser ab initio.** A person who abuses a right, authority or licence which he has to enter the land or premises of another; he becomes a trespasser *ab initio*, and becomes liable for trespass from the time of entry and not from the time he abused the right.

**trial.** The formal examination and determination of a matter of law or fact by a court of law. In civil actions, such trial is by a judge sitting alone, except in the High Court where, since the abolition of juries for *personal injury* actions, a trial is with a judge and jury only in a limited number of actions. In criminal matters, the trial is before a judge and jury, except in the District Court, the Special Criminal Court, and military courts. The essential ingredient of a trial of a criminal offence is that it is before a court or judge which has the power to punish in the event of a verdict of guilty: Goodman International v Mr Justice Hamilton (1992 HC & SC) ILRM 145. For the right to trial by jury in criminal matters, see TRIAL BY JURY, CRIMINAL OFFENCES. See also TRIAL BY JURY, CIVIL MATTERS; JURY, ABOLITION OF; NOTICE OF TRIAL.

**trial, separate.** See DEFENDANT, JOINT.

**trial by jury, criminal offences.** No person may be tried on any criminal charge without a jury, except for minor offences (qv) or in the case of trial in special courts (qv) or by military courts: 1937 Constitution, art.38. It is a personal right under the Constitution: People (DPP) v O'Shea (1982) IR 384. In a trial by jury, the functions of the judge is to decide questions of law and to direct the jury accordingly, to ensure that the rules of evidence are observed in the conduct of the case, and in cases of conviction to impose punishment (qv). The role of the jury is to decide on the guilt or innocence of the accused.

A *majority verdict* of ten from a minimum of eleven jurors is now sufficient; formerly the jury had to be unanimous in its verdict: Criminal Justice Act 1984 s.25. However, before the court may accept a majority verdict, the jury must have had at least two hours for deliberation; and where the accused is acquitted, the fact that it was a majority verdict, cannot be disclosed. Before the two hours has expired the trial judge may inform the jury that he will accept a majority verdict after two hours: DPP v O'Callaghan 9ILT Dig (1991 CCA) 170; DPP v Brophy (1992 CCA) ILRM 709. During the two hour period, the jury must be able to talk to one another when deliberating and the deliberations must be in secret; the period does not include any time the jury spend in the courtroom: DPP v Jackie Kelly (1988) CCA. These provisions regarding majority verdicts are not unconstitutional: O'Callaghan v AG & DPP (1993 HC) ILRM 267 and (1993 SC) ITLR (9 Aug). See also DPP v McKeever (1993 CCA) 11 ILT Dig 186. See RSC O.36 rr.5, 10, 34. See JURY; MILITARY TRIBUNAL; SUMMARY OFFENCE; SUMMING UP; VERDICT.

**trial by jury, civil matters.** Trial by jury in civil matters is now restricted to certain causes of action within the jurisdiction of the High Court, since the abolition of juries in respect of actions for the recovery of damages for *personal injuries*: Courts Act 1988 s.2(1). A person is still entitled to a jury trial in certain actions eg defamation, false imprisonment. In such actions, a majority verdict of the jury suffices. Otherwise, the function of the judge is similar to that of a judge in a criminal trial. See TRIAL BY JURY, CRIMINAL OFFENCES; SUMMING UP.

**trial within a trial.** See VOIRE DIRE.

**tribunals.** Bodies with quasi-judicial or administrative functions established by statute and being outside the hierarchy of the court system eg the Employment Appeals Tribunal (qv) established by the Redundancy Payments Act 1967. Such bodies must comply with the principles of natural justice (qv); they are subject to judicial review (qv), and where provided for, an appeal may lie from the findings of these bodies to the courts. It appears that tribunals should furnish unequivocal findings of fact referable to the evidence which supports their findings: *semble* in North Western Health Board v Martyn (1987 SC) IR 565. See

ADMINISTRATIVE TRIBUNAL; TRIBUNALS OF INQUIRY.

**tribunals of inquiry.** Tribunals established for inquiring into a definite matter of urgent public importance and with power to enforce the attendance and examination of witnesses and the production of documents: Tribunal of Inquiry (Evidence) Act 1921. A tribunal of inquiry may consist of one or more persons, sitting with or without an assessor or assessors; an assessor is not a *member* of the tribunal: Tribunals of Inquiry (Evidence) (Amendment) Act 1979 s.2.

A tribunal may make such orders as it considers necessary for the purpose of its functions and in that respect has the powers, rights and privileges which are vested in the High Court (ibid s.4). A statement or admission by a person before a tribunal of inquiry is not admissible as evidence against that person in any criminal proceedings (ibid s.5).

A tribunal which has been appointed to enquire into matters of public interest pursuant to resolutions of the Oireachtas, may enquire into all matters within its terms of reference, including matters which are the subject of current civil proceedings or allegations of breaches of the criminal law or matters which involve allegations attacking the good name of a citizen: Goodman International v Mr Justice Hamilton (HC & SC) (1992) ILRM 145.

The National Authority for Occupational Safety and Health is empowered, with Ministerial consent, to direct that an inquiry be held into any accident, disease or occurrence: Safety, Health and Welfare Act 1989 s.47.

Tribunals of inquiry have been held in recent times into moneylending in Dublin (1970); the Betelguese tanker disaster in Bantry Bay – Whiddy inquiry (1979); the Stardust fire (1981); the Kerry Babies inquiry (1985) and the inquiry into the Beef Processing Industry (1991-1993). See also Boyhan & Ors v Tribunal of Inquiry into the Beef Industry (1992 HC) ILRM 545; Kiberd v Tribunal of Inquiry into the Beef Industry (1992 HC) ILRM 574. See also ADMINISTRATIVE TRIBUNAL; ACCIDENT; MARINE INCIDENT; UTTERANCE.

**trick, larceny by.** See LARCENY BY TRICK.

**Trinity.** A sitting of the court. See SITTINGS OF COURT.

**tripartite contract.** A contract to which there are three parties. It is a matter of construction as to whether such a transaction binds all the parties equally or whether the relationship subsists in a series of separate transactions. See Fox v Higgins (1912) 46 ILTR 22; Henley Forklift (Ireland) Ltd v Lansing Bagnall & Co Ltd (1979) SC. See also FINANCE HOUSES; NOVATION.

**trout.** A licence is not required for angling for trout and coarse fish: Fisheries (Amendment) Act 1991 s.3. Provision has been made for the establishment of Fisheries Co-Operative Societies to raise and disburse for the public benefit funds for the development of trout and coarse fisheries in specified areas (ibid s.4). A person may not be entitled to angle for trout or coarse fish unless he is the holder of a share certificate in such a society (ibid s.9). Exempted are persons 66 years of age and over or under 18, or unemployed, or in receipt of an invalidity pension. See FISHERY SOCIETY; SALMON DEALER'S LICENCE.

**truck system.** The practice by which employers paid their employees in tokens exchangeable for goods, which was prohibited by the Truck Acts 1831, 1887 and 1896. These Acts were repealed by the Payment of Wages Act 1991. See WAGES.

**true person.** The expression "true person" in the Companies Act 1990 s.14(1) means the real individuals who are financilly interested in the success or failure of a company; if an inspector appointed by the Minister to determine the true persons so interested finds a company as a shareholder of the company he is investigating, he must go further and seek to determine the persons who are the beneficial owners of the company: Lyons v Curran (1993 HC) ILRM 375. See INVESTIGATION OF COMPANY.

**trust.** An equitable obligation binding a person (called the *trustee*) to deal with property over which he has control (called the *trust property*) for the benefit of persons (called *beneficiaries* or *cestuis que trust*) of whom he may himself be one, and any one of whom may enforce the obligation. The person creating the trust is called the *settlor* or *donor*. A trust is either a *private* trust, for the benefit of an individual or class but not for the benefit of the public at large; or a *public* or *charitable* trust for the benefit of the public at large, although it may confer a benefit on an individual or class (qqv).

A trust may be either an express, an implied, a resulting, or a constructive trust (qqv). In a will, an *executed* trust is one which is finally declared by the instrument creating it, where the executor may be said to be his own conveyancer. An *executory* trust is one created by a direction to make a settlement upon trusts which are indicated in, but are not finally declared by, the instrument containing the direction; some further act is required to give effect to it.

No special form of words are necessary to create a trust, but the words must be imperative, the subject-matter of the trust must be certain, and the objects or persons intended to benefit under the trust must be certain: Chambers v Fahy (1931) IR 17. See also Brown v Gregg (1945) IR 224. [Text: Keane (2); Kiely; O'Callaghan; Wylie (3); Snell UK]. See FOREIGN TRUST; TRUSTEE; TRUSTEE INVESTMENTS; USE.

**trust, breach of.** See BREACH OF TRUST.
**trust, charitable.** See CHARITABLE TRUST.
**trust, discretionary.** See DISCRETIONARY TRUST.
**trust, express.** A trust in which the settlor has declared the terms of the trust. A trust to take effect on the death of the settlor must be created by will (qv) duly executed by the settlor. A trust to take effect in the lifetime of the settlor must comply with the evidence requirements of the Statute of Frauds (Ireland) 1695 and the Statute of Uses 1634 in respect of freehold land. The courts however never allowed these statutes to be used as *engines of fraud* and have recognised trusts, not created in accordance with the statutes, called *secret* trusts (qv). A *resulting* trust (qv) arises when an express trust fails, the trustee holding the property in trust for the donor. See FRAUDULENT CONVERSION.
**trust, future.** See FUTURE TRUST.
**trust, illusory.** See ILLUSORY TRUST.
**trust, implied.** A trust which the court infers from the presumed intention of the parties eg where property is held in the name of a person, an *implied trust* will be implied in favour of the person who supplied the purchase money. See RESULTING TRUST.
**trust, protective.** See PROTECTIVE TRUST.
**trust, resulting.** See RESULTING TRUST.
**trust, secret.** See SECRET TRUST.
**trust, void.** A trust which, because it is illegal, unconstitutional or contrary to public policy, will not be enforced eg a trust which is to take effect on the future separation of husband and wife: Westmeath v Westmeath (1831) 1 Dow & Cl 519; a trust conditional on children being reared as Roman Catholics: In re Blake (1955) IR 89.
**trust, voidable.** A trust, the creation of which was induced by mistake, fraud, or duress, and which may be set aside or rectified by the court. The assignment of property to trustees with the intention of defeating creditors is voidable at the instance of the party prejudiced, although there is protection for the bona fide purchaser for value with no notice of the intention to defraud: Conveyancing (Ireland) Act 1634; Bankruptcy Act 1988 ss.7(1)(a) and 57. See ILLUSORY TRUST.
**trust corporation.** A corporation to which the High Court may grant *probate* or *administration* which (a) is appointed by the court or (b) is empowered by its constitution to undertake trust business (being established by Act or Charter or a Bank under the Central Bank Act 1942 or a company having an issued capital of at least £250,000 of which at least £100,000 has been paid up in cash) or (c) satisfies the President of the High Court that it undertakes the administration of any charitable ecclesiastical or public trust without remuneration: Succession Act 1965 s.30. See RSC O.79 rr.17-19; O.80 rr.21-23.
**trust for sale.** A trust created by the vesting of the legal estate of land in trustees on trust to sell the land and to hold the income until sale and the proceeds thereafter for the beneficiaries. Under the doctrine of conversion (qv), the rights of the beneficiaries are deemed to be rights in personalty. In a trust for sale, the trustees have an obligation to sell the land although they have a discretion to postpone the sale.

Land which is held on trust for sale,

where the proceeds are to be applied for any person for life or other limited period, is deemed to be *settled land;* the *tenant for life* in such case cannot exercise the statutory powers without the consent of the court: Settled Land Acts 1882 and 1890. See SETTLED LAND.

**trust property.** All property, realty or personalty, whether a legal estate or an equitable one, or whether in possession, reversion (qv) or remainder (qv), can be made the object of a trust. On the death of one trustee the trust property devolves on the other trustees as they hold as joint tenants (qv); on the death of a sole or surviving trustee, the legal estate, still subject to the trust, vests on his personal representative (qv): Succession Act 1965 s.10.

The usual way of vesting trust property in new trustees is by a *vesting declaration* in a deed appointing new trustees: Trustee Act 1893 s.12. In any case of difficulty the court will make a vesting order.

**trustee.** A person who holds property on trust (qv) for another. A sane adult person who is capable of taking and holding property is capable of being a trustee; a registered company may be a trustee. The trust instrument usually appoints the original trustees, and when they die, or refuse to accept trusteeship, new ones are appointed either by a person nominated to so appoint, or by the surviving trustee, or by the personal representative (qv) of the last trustee, or by the court, or by the Commissioners of Charitable Donations and Bequests (qv): Trustee Act 1893 ss.10 and 25; Trustee Act 1931; Charities Act 1961 s.43; Charities Act 1973 s.2; Succession Act 1965 s.57. See BENEFICIARY, REMEDIES OF; BREACH OF TRUST.

**trustee, bankrupt.** The court is empowered to substitute a new trustee in place of one who becomes bankrupt: Trustee Act 1893 s.25(1). See In re Barker's Trusts (1875) 1 Ch D 43. A sole trustee who is bankrupt or an *arranging debtor* (qv), will be permitted, without the leave of the court, to prove in his own bankruptcy or arrangement for a debt due from him to the trust estate: Bankruptcy Act 1988, first schedule, para 12, reversing In re Howard and Gibbs, Ex p Shaw (1822) 1 Gl and J

127. See BANKRUPTCY.

**trustee, duty of.** The primary duty of a trustee is to get in and preserve the property subject to the trust. He must administer the trust in accordance with the trust instrument. He must keep accounts and produce them to any beneficiary when required. He must pay over the trust property and income to the parties entitled. Unless the trust instrument directs the trustee to retain the trust in its present state, he must invest it in securities named by law: Trustee (Authorised Investments) Act 1958. See TRUSTEE INVESTMENTS.

A trustee must not make a profit for himself; he is not allowed to put himself in a position where his interest and his duty conflict: Bray v Ford (1896) AC 44. However, the trust instrument may provide for remuneration of a trustee and the court has an inherent jurisdiction so to do. A trustee cannot purchase the trust property from himself and his co-trustees, unless there is an express power in the trust instrument or the court orders such a sale. Also a trustee cannot delegate his powers — the maxim *delegatus non potest delegare* (qv) — unless expressly authorised or delegation is usual in the ordinary course of the business; a trustee however may appoint a solicitor to be his agent to receive and give a discharge for any money receivable under the trust: Trustee Act 1893 s.17.

The trustees of an occupational pension scheme are required to provide for the proper investment of the resources of the scheme: Pensions Act 1990 s.59. See REMUNERATION OF TRUSTEE; UNDUE INFLUENCE.

**trustee, power of.** A trustee has a wide range of powers, unless prohibited in the trust instrument eg power of sale, power to insure, to renew leaseholds, to give receipts, to compromise, to use income for a minor's maintenance: Trustee Act 1893 ss.13-14 and 18-21; Conveyancing Act 1911 ss.9-10 and 43; Succession Act 1965 s.58.

**trustee, removal of.** A trustee may be removed by a power in the trust instrument, or by the court, or by the provisions of the Trustee Act 1893 ss.10 and 25 where a trustee is unfit or incapable of acting or remains outside the jurisdiction for more than 12 months, or becomes a bankrupt (qv) or is guilty of a felony (qv). The court places the welfare of the beneficiaries above all else. See Arnott v Arnott (1924) 58 ILTR 145. See also Pensions Act 1990 s.63 as amended by Social Welfare Act 1993 s.49. See BREACH OF TRUST.

**trustee, retirement of.** A trustee may retire in accordance with a provision in the trust instrument, or with the consent of the beneficiaries who are entitled to the whole beneficial interest, or when new trustees are lawfully appointed to replace him. He may also retire by *deed of retirement* or exceptionally, by payment of the trust money into court: Trustee Act 1893 ss.11 and 42.

**trustee de son tort.** [Trustee of his own wrongdoing]. A person who intermeddles in a trust without authority; he is held liable to account as a trustee. See In re Barney (1891) 2 Ch 265.

**trustee in bankruptcy.** See WINDING UP BY TRUSTEE.

**trustee investments.** Investment of trust property which is permitted by law. These include securities of the government, of the ESB, ACC, Bord na Mona, and county councils, county borough corporations; debentures (qv) of any industrial or commercial company registered in the State, provided a dividend of not less than 5% has been paid on the ordinary shares in each of the five previous years; securities guaranteed by the Minister for Finance; loan stock of the Bank of Ireland and Allied Irish Banks; bank deposit accounts including the Post Office Savings Bank and the Trustee Savings Banks; real securities in the State: Trustee (Authorised Investments) Act 1958 s.1.

The Minister may vary the list of investments by order, which he has done on a number of occasions eg to include building societies (qv) (ibid s.2). A simpler method of amending the list of authorised trustee investments has been provided for: Central Bank Act 1989 s.138. Also, interest bearing deposits with the Central Bank have been made authorised investments for trustees (ibid s.137).

In relation to the power to invest in real securities in the State, this does not entitle the trustee to buy land, but merely empowers him to invest funds in mortgages of realty: see Trustee Act 1893 ss.3, 5, 8, 9.

**trustee savings bank; TSB.** A society formed for the purpose of establishing and maintaining an institution in the nature of a bank, whose business is under the supervision of trustees: Trustee Savings Bank Act 1989 s.9(1). A trustee savings bank requires a licence to operate and may operate abroad with the consent of the Central Bank (qv) which is the supervisory and licensing authority. Such banks are required to invest a proportion of their funds with the Exchequer and are paid interest thereon (ibid s.32). There is also provision to convert from trustee to company status (ibid s.57) and to amalgamate with another TSB (ibid ss.47-48).

The assets of a bankrupt officer of a trustee savings bank must be charged with all moneys received by him by virtue of his office and remaining due by him to the bank: Bankruptcy Act 1988 s.81(10). See also Finance Acts 1990 ss.59-61; 1993 ss.42-43. See CREDIT INSTITUTION.

**tumultuously.** Involving a type of mob out of control, agitated and heavily imbued with some emotion, whether of wantonness, anger, indignation or some other strong motivating force: Malicious Injuries Act 1981 s.6(1); Duggan v Dublin Corporation (1991 SC) ILRM 330. There is a right to compensation for the unlawful taking of property during a riot ie where more than two persons are tumultuously and riotously assembled together (ibid s.6(1) and 6(2) of 1981 Act as amended by Malicious Injuries (Amdt) Act 1986 s.4). See MALICIOUS INJURIES SCHEME.

**turbary, common of.** The right of digging and taking away of turf as fuel from the land of another. See PROFIT A PRENDRE.

**turpi causa.** [Bad cause]. See EX TURPI CAUSA.

**twinning.** The linking for social and cultural reasons of two areas, usually between two towns or cities in different countries. Local authorities are empowered to enter into arrangements for twinning: Local Government Act 1991 s.49.

**type approval, motor vehicles.** Application may be made by manufacturers who wish to have their products type-approved under the relevant EC Directives: SI Nos 13 of 1990, 35 of 1989; 305 of 1978. The Framework Directive (92/53/EEC) which puts in place the European Whole Vehicle Type Approval System (ECWVTA) for motor vehicles, is given effect in Irish law by SI No 345 of 1992.

**type, size of.** The Minister may by order prohibit the seller of goods or supplier of services from making use of any printed contract, guarantee, or other specified class of document unless it is printed in type of at least such size as the order prescribes: SGSS Act 1980 s.53.

**typographical error.** An obvious typographical error does not affect a certificate, where there is no inherent defect in the certificate: DPP v Flahive (1988) ILRM 133. See SLIP RULE.

# U

**Uachtaran na hEireann.** [President of Ireland (qv)].

**uberrimae fidei.** [Of the utmost good faith]. A contract is said to be *uberrimae fidei* when the promisee is under an obligation to inform the promisor of all those facts and surrounding circumstances which may influence the promisor in deciding whether or not to enter the contract. All contracts of insurance fall into this class. In insurance contracts, the insured must also disclose those *material facts* which would affect the premium the insurer should impose, if he does accept the risk.

The consequences of non-disclosure is to allow the insurer to avoid the policy. Before renewing a policy of insurance, it is necessary for the insured to disclose material facts which could affect the renewal or the premium. Also a fraudulent claim by an insured may allow an insurer to avoid liability even though he was on risk when the loss occured. See Superwood Holdings v Sun Alliance (1991 HC).

The common law obligation to disclose material information continues notwithstanding a waiver by an insurance company of the normal obligation to have a medical examination: Kelleher v Irish Life Assurance Co Ltd (1989) 7ILT Dig 229. Also non-disclosure can only be relevant to some fact of which the person has knowledge at the relevant time: Keating v New Ireland Assurance Co plc (1989) 7ILT Dig 321 and (1990 SC) ILRM 110. See Ellis in 8ILT & SJ (1990) 45.

See also Furey v Eagle, Star & British Dominions Insurance Co (1922) 56 ILTR 109; Irish National Assurance v O'Callaghan (1934) 68 ILTR 248; Griffin v Royal Liver Friendly Society (1942) Ir Jur Rep 29; Chariot Inns Ltd v Assicurazioni Generali SPA (1981) ILRM 173; Harney v Century Insurance Co Ltd (1983) HC; Aro Road & Land Vehicles v Insurance Corporation of Ireland (1986) SC; Keenan v Shield Insurance Co Ltd (1987 HC) IR 113; Curran v Norwich Union Life Insurance Society (1987) HC. See also Marine Insurance Act 1906 s.17. See CONTRA PROFERENTEM; INSURANCE; PROSPECTUS.

**ubi aliquid, conceditur, conceditur et id sine quo res ipsa esse non potest.** [Where anything is granted, that is also granted without which the thing itself is not able to exist] eg the right of way presumed to be given by the grantor of land to a *close* surrounded by the grantor's land. See WAY, RIGHT OF.

**ubi easem ratio ibi idem jus.** [Like reasons make like law].

**ubi jus ibi remedium.** [Where there is a right, there is a remedy]. See EQUITY, MAXIMS OF.

**ubi remedium ibi jus.** [Where there is a remedy, there is a right].

**ubi supra.** [At the place above].

**UCITS.** See UNDERTAKINGS FOR COLLECTIVE INVESTMENT IN TRANSFERABLE SECURITIES.

**ultima voluntas testatoris est perimplenda secundum veram intentionem suam.** [Effect is to be given to the last will of a testator according to his true intention]. See ARMCHAIR PRINCIPLE.

**ultra.** [Beyond].

**ultra vires.** [Beyond the power]. An act in excess of the authority conferred by law and therefore invalid. A company's powers are limited to carrying out of its objects as set out in its *memorandum of association;* an act in excess of that power, eg in a contract, is ultra vires and void. It has been held that an ultra vires transaction cannot be rendered effective by all the company's members attempting to ratify it or by extending the objects clause with retrospective effect: Ashbury Railway Carriage Co v Riche (1875) LR 7 HL 653.

However, ultra vires acts are effective in favour of a person relying on such acts, if he was not aware at the time that the company was acting beyond its powers: Companies Act 1963 s.8(1). In addition, any transaction entered into by the board of directors of a company is deemed to be within the capacity of the company in favour of a person dealing with the company in good faith and any limitation imposed by the company's articles or memorandum of association cannot be relied upon by the company against such person: European Communities (Companies) Regulations 1973 (SI No 163 of 1973). These provisions do not apply to statutory companies unless they are incorporated under the Companies Acts.

A member or debenture holder may on application to the court restrain a company from acting beyond its power: Companies Act 1963 s.8(2)).

The general competence of local authorities has been widened considerably thereby reducing the possibility that they will engage in activities which are ultra vires their powers: Local Government Act 1991 s.6. Premiums paid to an insurance company on ultra vires policies are recoverable as money paid without consideration: Flood v Irish Provident Assur Co (1912) 2 Ch 597n.

Damages will not be awarded for an ultra vires action or decision, unless it involved the commission of a tort, or was activated by malice, or was carried out in the knowledge that it was ultra vires: O'Donnell v Corp of Dun Laoghaire (1991 HC) ILRM 301. See In re Bansha Woolen Mill Co (1887) 21 LR Ir 181; In re Cummins (1939) IR 60; Hennessy v National Agricultural Industrial Development Association (1947) IR 159; Northern Bank Finance Corporation v Quinn (1979 HC). See also Building Societies Act 1989 s.12(1), 12(2) and 18(7). See CERTIORARI; STERILE TRANSACTIONS.

**umpire.** See ARBITRATION.

**UN.** United Nations (qv).

**unadministered probate, grant of.** A grant of representation to another executor, whose rights had been reserved by the first executor who had extracted a grant but has since died.

**unambiguous.** It has been held that if a term in a lease has an *unambiguous* meaning, that meaning ought to be given full effect: Hynes Ltd v O'Malley Property Ltd (1989 SC) ITLR (27 Feb).

**unascertained goods.** Goods defined by description only eg 5 kilos of coal. Property in unascertained goods is not transferred to the buyer until the goods are ascertained: Sale of Goods Act 1893 s.16. See GOODS, PROPERTY IN.

**unborn, injuries to the.** The laws relating to wrongs apply to an unborn child for his protection in like manner as if the child were born, provided that the child is subsequently born alive: Civil Liability Act 1961 s.58. Consequently, a child may sue for all injuries sustained before birth as a result of another person's tort (qv). See Dunne v National Maternity Hospital (1989) ILRM 735.

**unborn, right to life of the.** The State acknowledges the right to life of the unborn and, with due regard to the equal right to life of the mother, guarantees in its laws to respect, and, as far as practicable, by its laws to defend and vindicate that right: 1937 Constitution, art.40.3.3, inserted by referendum. See AG v X (1992) ILRM 401.

The Maastricht Treaty 1992 provides that "Nothing in the Treaty on European Union, or in the Treaties establishing the European Communities, or in the Treaties or Acts modifying or supplementing those Treaties, shall affect the application in Ireland of Article 40.3.3 of the Constitution of Ireland": Protocol No 17. The member States, by Solemn Declaration, have agreed that this Protocol shall not limit freedom either to travel between member States or to obtain or make available in Ireland, information relating to services lawfully available in member States. They also declared that they will be favourably disposed to amending the Protocol so as to extend its application to a future constitutional amendment concerning the subject matter of Article 40.3.3 if Ireland so requests. See Kingston & Whelan in 10 ILT & SJ (1992) 93, 104, 166 and 279. See ABORTION; LIFE, RIGHT TO; TRAVEL, RIGHT TO.

**uncalled capital.** The amount remaining unpaid on partly paid shares in a company. See CAPITAL.

**uncertainty.** Failure to define or limit with sufficient exactitude. A gift by will or trust may be void for uncertainty. There is a presumption of simultaneous death in cases of uncertainty: Succession Act 1965 s.5. See also AMBIGUITY.

**unchastity.** Words spoken and published which impute unchastity to any woman or girl do not require proof of *special damage* to render them actionable. See SLANDER; LESBIANISM.

**unclaimed funds in court.** See SUITORS, FUNDS OF.

**unconscionable bargain.** A contract which is harsh in its terms and where one party is clearly in a stronger bargaining position or where the bargain is so improvident that no reasonable man would enter it. In a suitable case, the court will intervene and set aside the transaction or amend the terms in order to produce what the court sees as a fairer transaction. It is an exception to the general rule that consideration need not be adequate to the promise.

In cases where a sale is at gross undervalue and between persons not on equal footing, and the transaction is thus improvident, it is not necessary to show improper behaviour. See Slator v Nolan (1876) IR 11 Eq 367; Grealish v Murphy (1946) IR 35; Smyth v Smyth (1978) HC; JH v WJH (1979) HC; Rooney v Conway (1982) NI Ch; McCoy v Greene Cole (1984) HC. See INEQUALITY OF POSITION; MONEYLENDER; PENALTY.

**unconscionable use.** See WASTE.

**unconstitutional contract.** A contract the formation or performance of which is in breach of the Constitution of the State. The question as to whether a person can contract out of a constitutional right was raised but no opinion was given in Becton Dickinson Ltd v Lee (1973) IR 1.

**uncontrollable impulse.** See IRRESISTIBLE IMPULSE.

**undefended case.** Where a defendant to a proceedings fails to enter an appearance

(qv) or a defence (qv), the plaintiff may obtain judgment. See JUDGMENT IN DEFAULT OF APPEARANCE; JUDGMENT IN DEFAULT OF DEFENCE.

**under lease.** A sub-lease. See LEASE.

**undersubscribed.** Where shares in a company are offered for subscription but the entire offer is not taken up. In the case of shares offered to the public for the first time, no allotment may be made until at least the *minimum amount* is raised: Companies Act 1963 s.53(1). By minimum amount is meant the sum stated in the prospectus and which in the directors' opinion it is necessary to raise in order to pay for the company's preliminary expenses, any commissions, the purchase price to be paid for any property it is intended to buy with the proceeds of the issue, and any working capital.

Where a public limited company (plc) offers its shares and the offer is undersubscribed, it is prohibited to allot the shares which are subscribed unless the offer stated that the allotments would be made in such circumstances: Companies (Amendment) Act 1983 s.22. See also 1983 Act, first schedule, para 7. See PROSPECTUS; UNDERWRITER.

**undertaking.** (1) A promise which involves an obligation to act in accordance with the promise, which obligation may be enforced in law eg an undertaking by a defendant to a court. Undertakings given by a foreign state in relation to extradition (qv) matters cannot be relied upon: Sloan v Culligan (1992 SC) ILRM 194.

(2) A business enterprise or a project. A person, being an individual, a body corporate or an unincorporated body of persons engaged for gain in the production, supply or distribution of goods or the provision of a service: Competition Act 1991 s.3(1). See GAIN.

**Undertakings for Collective Investment in Transferable Securities; UCITS.** An undertaking, whether established as a company or as a unit trust, the sole object of which is the collective investment in transferable securities of capital raised from the public and which operates on the principle of risk spreading, and the units of which are, at the request of the holders, re-purchased or redeemed, directly or indirectly out of those undertaking's assets: EC UCITS Regulations 1989 (SI No 78 of 1989). The Central Bank (qv) is the supervisory authority for entities establishing in Ireland as a UCITS. The provisions of the Unit Trusts Act 1990 do not apply to a UCITS that is authorised under the UCITS Regulations (ibid 1990 Act s.2). For taxation of UCITS, see Finance Acts 1991 s.19; 1993 ss.17-18. See INVESTMENT COMPANY; THIRD PARTY INFORMATION.

**underwater heritage order.** See WRECK.

**underwriter.** (1) A person, as insurer, who joins with others in entering into a policy of insurance; he subscribes his name to the policy against the sum for which he accepts liability.

(2) In a public issue of shares in a company, a person who offers to take up shares and debentures not taken up by the public, in consideration of a commission at a rate disclosed in the prospectus. A *sub-underwriting agreement* is a contract between an underwriter and another person which, in exchange for a commission, relieves the underwriter of liability. See FLOATATION; SHARES.

**undesireable administrative practice.** See OMBUDSMAN.

**undischarged bankrupt.** A bankrupt who has not obtained a discharge by way of a *certificate of conformity* (prior to 1989); or an order or certificate of *discharge* (since 1989): Bankruptcy Act 1988 s.85. An undischarged bankrupt cannot own property, be a director of a company, be a member of the Oireachtas, a county councillor or a member of a local authority or be a solicitor or auctioneer. See Electoral Act 1992 s.41; Debtors Ireland Act 1872 s.20; Local Government (Ireland) Act 1898 s.104(1); Local Government (Application of Enactments) Order 1898; Companies Act 1990 s.169 amending Companies Act 1963 s.183; Building Societies Act 1989 s.64(1).

An insurance agent (qv) and insurance broker (qv) are disqualified from acting as such if adjudged bankrupt: Insurance Act 1989 s.55. See BANKRUPTCY; BANKRUPTCY, DISCHARGE OF.

**undisclosed principal.** A principal whose existence and identity is not disclosed at the time of making a contract. When an agent (qv) conceals the fact that he is merely the agent of another (the principal) and has authority at the time of the contract to act on behalf of that other, either the agent or the principal (when discovered) can be sued by the third party and the third party may be sued by either.

The option of the third party is subject to two considerations: (a) the option is alternative, so that if the third party unequivocally indicates either principal or agent as liable to him, he cannot afterwards sue the other; (b) if the third party by his words or conduct induces the principal to believe that a settlement has been agreed between the third party and his agent, in consequence of which the principal settles with his agent, the third party cannot sue the principal on the contract.

The undisclosed principal's right to sue is limited where the agent has contracted in terms which import that the agent was the real and only principal. Also the third party may use any defence or counter claim against a suit by the principal, which he would have in relation to the agent. See O'Keefe v Horgan (1897) ILT 429; Keighley Maxsted & Co v Durant (1901) AC 240. See AGENT.

**undue influence.** The equitable doctrine under which a court will set aside an agreement or a disposition of property made by a person under circumstances which show, or give rise to the presumption, that the person has not been allowed to exercise a free and deliberate judgement in the matter.

A presumption of undue influence arises in transactions between parent and child, solicitor and client, trustee and beneficiary, guardian and ward, physician and patient, but not husband and wife. The presumption may be rebutted by evidence eg that the other party had independent legal advice and took it; it may also be rebutted by proof that the transaction was the result of the free exercise of independent will by the other party: Provincial Bank v McKeever (1941) IR 471.

A contract induced by undue influence is voidable at the option of the party influenced; however, conduct by that person after the undue influence has ceased may amount to an *affirmation* of the contract: Allcard v Skinner (1887) 36 Ch D 145. See also Morley v Loughnan (1893) Ch 736; Noonan v O'Connell (1987) HC; Leonard v Leonard (1988) ILRM 245; McGonigle v Black (1989) 7ILT Dig 103. See also Electoral Act 1992 s.136. See DURESS; INEQUALITY OF POSITION.

**undue influence in pleadings.** In any legal proceedings where undue influence is pleaded, the party making the plea, before the case is set down for trial, must give particulars of the persons against whom the charge of undue influence is preferred, the nature of the conduct alleged to constitute the undue influence and the dates upon which the acts alleged to constitute undue influence were exercised: RSC O.19 rr.5(2) and 6(1). See PLEADINGS.

**unenforceable.** That which cannot be proceeded for, or sued upon, in the courts. An unenforceable contract is a contact which cannot be enforced by action because of some technical defect eg where there is an absence of writing as required by the Statute of Frauds in the case of a contract for the sale of land. However, under the doctrine of *part performance,* an otherwise unenforceable contract may be enforceable eg in the sale of land where there is entry into possession of land with the agreement or acquiesence of the defendant: Kennedy v Kennedy (1983) HC. See also Hope v Lord Cloncurry (1874) IR 8 Eq 555; Lowry v Reid (1927 NI 142. See MEMORANDUM, STATUTE OF FRAUDS; PART PERFORMANCE; QUANTUM MERUIT.

**unfair and oppressive procedure.** See FAIR PROCEDURES.

**unfair dismissal.** The dismissal of an employee is deemed to be an unfair dismissal unless, having regard for all the circumstances, there were substantial grounds justifying the dismissal: Unfair Dismissal Act 1977 s.6. The onus of proof is on the employer to show that there were substantial grounds, which include: the capability, competence or qualifications of the employee for the work he was employed to do; the employee's conduct; redundancy; or the fact that continuation of the employment would contravene another statutory requirement; however, regard must be had to the reasonableness or otherwise of the

conduct of the employer and to compliance with dismissal procedures and codes of practice (ibid ss. 6(6) and 6(7) as amended by Unfair Dismissals (Amdt) Act 1993 s.5(b)).

A dismissal is deemed to be an unfair dismissal if it results wholly or mainly from trade union membership; or religious or political opinions; or race, colour or sexual orientation; or age; or the employee's membership of the travelling community; or legal proceedings against the employer where the employee is a party or a witness; or unfair selection for redundancy; or pregnancy (ibid 1977 Act s.6(2) as amended by 1993 Act s.5(a)). See White v Betson (1992 EAT) ELR 120.

A dismissal is deemed to have taken place (a) if the employer terminates the contract of employment with or without notice or (b) if the contract is for a *fixed term* (qv) and is not renewed or (c) if the employee, with or without notice, terminates the employment because of the conduct of the employer (known as *constructive dismissal*) (ibid 1977 Act s.1). An employee may request from the employer a written statement of the reasons for the dismissal, which must be supplied within fourteen days (ibid 1977 Act s.14(4) as amended by 1993 Act s.9).

Redress for an employee for unfair dismissal includes (a) *re-instatement* to his former position or (b) *re-engagement* in the former or a suitable alternative position or (c) *financial compensation* not exceeding 104 weeks remuneration; compensation may be paid even if no financial loss has been incurred by the employee; also payments under the social welfare and income tax codes are to be disregarded (ibid 1977 Act s.7 as amended by 1993 Act s.6).

A claim for redress is heard by a Rights Commissioner (qv) or the Employment Appeals Tribunal (qv); notice of the claim with a copy to the employer must be given within 6 months of the dismissal or within 12 months in exceptional circumstances (ibid 1977 Act s.8(2) as amended by 1993 Act s.7(a); Devereux v McInerney & Co Ltd UD 39/89; Kavanagh v PARK UD 1130/88 as reported in 7ILT & SJ (1989) 179).

This statutory dismissal protection applies to employees who have at least one year's continuous service with the same employer and are normally expected to work a minimum of 8 hours per week (reduced from 18 hours by the Worker Protection (Regular Part-Time Employees) Act 1991). One year's service is not required where dismissal is for pregnancy or trade union membership or activity (ibid 1993 Act s.14). Employees who have reached normal retirement age or who work for close relatives in a private house or farm or who work in specified employments are not covered by this dismissal legislation, nor are parties to an illegal contract.

However, where a term or condition of the employment contract contravened the Income Tax Acts or the Social Welfare Acts, the employee, notwithstanding the contravention, is entitled to redress for unfair dismissal (ibid 1977 Act ss.8(11) and 8(12) inserted by 1993 Act s.7(d)). See Lewis v Squash Ireland Ltd (1983) ILRM 363; Locke v Southern Health Board (1987) HC; Loftus v Bord Telecom (1987) HC; O'Riordan Jnr & Ors v Clune (1991 EAT) ELR 89. See also SI No 66 of 1979; SI No 316 of 1981. [Text: Madden & Kerr]. See BALANCE OF PROBABILITY; EMPLOYMENT AGENCY; FIXED TERM CONTRACT; MISCON-DUCT; PREGNANCY; SICKNESS; WRONGFUL DIS-MISSAL; RE-INSTATMENT; RE-ENGAGEMENT.

**unfair practices.** Formerly, practices so defined in the third schedule to the Restrictive Practices Act 1972, since repealed. See Competition Act 1991 s.22. See COMPETITION, DISTORTION OF.

**unfit.** Has a more limited meaning than "incapable": DPP v Fanagan (1991 HC). See INCAPABLE.

**unfit food.** See FOOD UNFIT FOR HUMAN CONSUMPTION; FOOD BUSINESS, SUSPENSION OF.

**unfit house.** A house which a housing authority is of opinion is unfit for human habitation in any respect: Housing Act 1966 s.55 and second schedule. The housing authority must serve on the owner a *repairs notice* giving particulars of the unfitness and requiring the owner to execute the works specified in the notice; or if the housing authority is of opinion that the house is not capable of being rendered fit at a reasonable expense, they must give the owner the opportunity of making an offer to carry

out works or to use the house in a particular manner. If an undertaking is not accepted or accepted and contravened, the authority must make a *closing order* or a *demolition order*. It is an offence to make use of a house for human habitation where a repairs notice, closing order or a demolition order has not been complied with or which is contrary to an undertaking (ibid s.68).

It has been held that lettings by a housing authority under the provisions of the 1966 Act are subject to an implied warranty that the premises let are fit for human habitation: Siney v Dublin Corporation (1979) SC. See CLEARED SITE VALUE; RENTED HOUSE, STANDARD OF.

**unfit to plead.** The question as to whether a person is fit to plead is determined by a jury specially empanelled for the purpose: Criminal Procedure (Insanity) Act 1964. The test is whether the person is of sufficient intellect to comprehend the course of the proceedings so as to make a proper defence, to challenge a juror to whom he might wish to object, and to understand the detail of the evidence. If the jury find the accused unfit to plead, he must be detained in the Central Mental Hospital at the pleasure of the government. See The State (Coughlan) v Minister for Justice (1968) ILTR 177. See INSANITY; OATH, FORM OF.

**unfitness for office.** Words spoken and published which impute that a person is unfit for his office or business do not require proof of *special damage* to render them actionable. See SLANDER.

**uniform, wearing of.** It is an offence to put on or wear the uniform of the Garda Siochana: Garda Siochana Act 1924 s.15; Police Force Amalgamation Act 1925 s.19. It is also an offence to wear without permission the uniform of the Defence Forces: Defence Act 1954 s.264 as amended by Defence (Amendment) Act 1987 s.14. A member of the garda siochana or of the defence forces is not permitted to wear his uniform in a civil court when he is a defendant in a criminal matter.

**unilateral.** One-sided. See MISTAKE.

**unincorporated body.** A body which has no legal existence separate from its members, who are individually liable for its debts without limit eg a partnership.

See INCORPORATION; COMPANY.

**uninsured driver.** See MOTOR INSURER'S BUREAU OF IRELAND.

**unintentional defamation.** See OFFER OF AMENDS.

**union, trade.** See TRADE UNION.

**unit trust scheme.** Any arrangement made for the purpose, or having the effect, of providing facilities for the participation by the public, as beneficiaries under a trust, in profits or income arising from the acquisition, holding, management or disposal of securities or any other property whatsoever: Unit Trusts Act 1990 s.1.

The 1990 Act provides, in the public interest and in the interests of holders of units of unit trust schemes, for the control and regulation of such schemes, and to prohibit in certain circumstances, the advertising of, and the purchase or sale of units of such schemes. The 1990 Act also provides for developments in accepted international practice with regard to the supervision and operation of unit trusts, repealing the initial Unit Trusts Act 1972. The Central Bank (qv) is given statutory responsibility for the supervision of unit trust schemes eg the authorisation of schemes and the establishment and maintenance of a register of authorised schemes. See UNDERTAKINGS FOR COLLECTIVE INVESTMENT.

**United Ireland.** The governments of Ireland and the United Kingdom have declared that, if in the future a majority of the people of Northern Ireland (qv) clearly wish for and formally consent to the establishment of a United Ireland, they will introduce and support in their respective parliaments, legislation to give effect to that wish: Anglo-Irish Agreement 1985; Crotty v An Taoiseach (1987) ILRM 400. See also 1937 Constitution arts.1-3; McGimpsey v Attorney General Ireland (1989 HC) ILRM 209; (1990 SC) ILRM 440. See ANGLO-IRISH AGREEMENT; NATION.

**United Nations.** The international organisation established by Charter at San Francisco on 26th June 1945 with the objective of helping to secure international peace and to encourage international co-operation in the solution of economic, social and humanitarian problems. Ireland became a member in 1955. Service with the United Nations does not equate with war: Defence Act 1960 s.4 and Ryan v Ireland (1989) 7ILT & SJ 118. See DEFENCE FORCES; GARDA SIOCHANA; HUMAN RIGHTS COVENANTS; INTERNATIONAL COURT OF JUSTICE; MILITARY LAW.

**United States.** See PREINSPECTION; PRECEDENT; RULE OF REASON; UTTERANCE.

**unities, four.** See JOINT TENANCY.

**universal agent.** See AGENT.

**Universal Copyright Convention.** This Convention was signed in Geneva on September 6, 1952 and revised in Paris in 1971. Each contracting state undertakes to give the published or unpublished works of all other contracting states the same protection as it gives to similar works of its own nationals, as well as the protection specially granted by the Convention. The Convention provides for a minimum term of protection of the life of the author and 25 years after his death.

Under the UCC the only formality to secure protection is the use of the symbol © on all published copies of the work, accompanied by the name of the copyright owner and the year of first publication, placed in such a manner and such location as to give reasonable notice of the claim to protection. Ireland is a member of the Convention. Works published in any country of the Convention or of the Berne Copyright Union are given the same protection in Ireland as if the works were first published within the State: Copyright (Foreign Countries) Order 1978. [Text: Copinger UK; Laddie UK]. See BERNE COPYRIGHT CONVENTION.

**Universal Declaration of Human Rights; UDHR.** The catalogue of fundamental human rights, adopted by the United Nations General Assembly on 10 December 1948, which is a common standard of achievement for all societies to aspire to and which promises an era of "universal respect for and observance of human rights and fundamental freedoms": Preamble to UDHR. See HUMAN RIGHTS COVENANTS.

**universal succession.** Succession to the property of another in its entirety. See SPES SUCCESSIONIS.

**unjust enrichment.** The profit or gain unjustly obtained by a wrongdoer. A person who deliberately breaks a contract because he calculates that he will make a profit from so doing, even after calculating damages payable for loss suffered by the other party, will have the profit or gain unjustly obtained by him considered by the court, in addition to the injury suffered by his victim: Hickey & Co Ltd v Roches Stores (Dublin) Ltd (No 1) 1976 HC and (No 2) (1980) ILRM 107. See also Thurstan v Nottingham Permanent Benefit Building Society (1903) AC 6 cited in Highland Finance v Sacred Heart College (1993 HC) ILRM 263. [Text: Goff & Jones UK]. See SUBROGATION.

**unlawful arrest.** An arrest which does not comply with the law. If an arresting garda is in a person's dwelling unlawfully as a trespasser, the arrest of the person by the garda is unlawful: DPP v Gaffney (1988) ILRM 39 applying Morris v Beardmore (1981) AC 446. See also The People (DPP) v Coffey (1987) ILRM 727. See ARREST WITHOUT WARRANT.

**unlawful assembly.** The common law misdemeanour consisting of the assembly of three or more persons (a) with intent to commit a crime by open force or (b) in such a manner as to give ground in the mind of their neighbours any reasonable apprehension of violence: Barrett v Tipperary County Council (1964) IR 22.

An unlawful assembly becomes a *rout* as soon as the assembled persons do any act towards carrying out their illegal purpose. It becomes a *riot* (qv) as soon as the illegal purpose is put into effect by persons mutually intending to resist any opposition. An unlawful assembly may be dispersed forceably, even by private persons acting on their own initiative, but only with so much force as is reasonable to protect lives and property. See Lynch v Fitzgerald (1938) IR 382.

Under draft legislation, it is proposed that the common law offences of "rout" and of "unlawful assembly" will be abolished: Criminal Law (Public Order) Bill 1993 s.16(6). New offences of "riot" and "violent disorder" are proposed. See RIOT; VIOLENT DISORDER.

**unlawful carnal knowledge.** See CARNAL KNOWLEDGE, UNLAWFUL.

**unlawful interference in economic relations.** The tort of interference by unlawful means in the trade or activities

or economic, commercial activities of another. It is necessary for the plaintiff to prove, conjunctively, that the defendant (a) used unlawful means to intefere in the plaintiff's business interest, (b) that the unlawful means were used with the intention of injuring the plaintiff, and (c) that the plaintiff suffered actual damage: O'Neill & Co Ltd v Adidas Sportschuhfabriken & Ors (1992 SC) ITLR (17 Aug). The tort is not established where the defendant used unlawful means with the sole intention of promoting his own economic interests in contrast to intending to injure those of the plaintiff (ibid O'Neill case).

**unlawful interference with constitutional rights.** An action lies for damages for unlawful interference by a person with the constitutional rights of another; a trade union does not have immunity under the Trade Disputes Act 1906 s.4 (now the Industrial Relations Act 1990 ss.9-13) in respect of such action: Hayes v Ireland & INTO & Ors (1987) ILRM 651.

It has been held that exemplary damages (qv) are properly awardable in the case of a breach of a constitutional right even where the defendants are neither servants nor agents of the government or the executive: Conway v INTO (1991 SC) ILRM 497. See EVIDENCE AND CONSTITUTIONAL RIGHTS; PRIVATE PROSECUTION; SOLICITOR, ACCESS TO.

**unlawful oath.** It is an offence to administer an unlawful oath: Offences Against the State Act 1939 s.17(1). See also Riot Act 1787 s.6. See OATH.

**unlawful organisation.** An organisation which: encourages treason; or advocates by force an alteration of the Constitution; or raises an armed force without lawful authority; or encourages the commission of crimes; or encourages the attainment of any object, lawful or unlawful, by unlawful means; or encourages the non-payment of taxes: Offences Against the State Act 1939 s.18.

It is an offence to be a member of an unlawful organisation (ibid s.18). Evidence of the belief of a Chief Superintendent of the Garda Siochana that the accused was a member on the date specified in the indictment (qv) is evidence that the accused was then such a member; however this does not require the court to convict on the evidence of that belief; ibid s.3(2) and O'Leary v AG (1991 HC) ILRM 455.

The government (qv) may make a *suppression order* against an unlawful organisation and thereby all the property of the organisation becomes forfeited to the Minister (ibid s.19).

The Minister is empowered to require any bank to pay into the High Court moneys which in his opinion stand forfeited under expanded forfeiture powers in respect of the property of organisations in respect of which a *suppression order* has been issued: Offences Against the State (Amendment) Act 1985; Clancy v Ireland (1989 HC) ILRM 670. See MALICIOUS INJURIES SCHEME; SPYING.

**unlawful possession of goods.** The summary offence committed by a person who is charged with having in his possession or conveying anything which may be reasonably suspected of being stolen or unlawfully obtained and who does not give an account to the satisfaction of the court how he came by it: Criminal Justice Act 1951 s.13. See HANDLING STOLEN PROPERTY; RECEIVING STOLEN GOODS.

**unlimited company.** See COMPANY, UNLIMITED.

**unliquidated damages.** Unascertained damages to be determined by the court. The Circuit Court has jurisdiction to award unlimited damages where an action for unliquidated damages is remitted to it by the High Court: Courts Act 1991 s.2(3)(a). See DAMAGES; PENALTY; REMITTAL OF ACTION.

**unlisted securities market; usm.** See STOCK EXCHANGE.

**unnamed persons, insurance of.** There is a general requirement in insurance law that each individual be named on a policy of insurance. In order to remove any obstacles that may have existed in relation to the issue of certain *group insurance* policies, the law was amended to provide that nothing in the Life Assurance Act 1774 s.2 (as applied by the Life Assurance [Ireland] Act 1866), shall invalidate a policy of insurance for the benefit of *unnamed persons* from time to time falling within a specified class or description, if the class or description is stated in the policy with sufficient

particularity, to make it possible to establish the identity of all persons who, at any given time, are entitled to benefit under the policy: Insurance Act 1989 s.26.

**unnatural offence.** Buggery (qv).

**uno flato.** [With one breath]. On a single occasion; in a short space of time.

**unofficial action.** Commonly means industrial action taken or a strike by members of a trade union which is contrary to union policy or union rules. A strike or industrial action which is contrary to the outcome of a secret ballot does not enjoy the immunity conferred by ss.10-12 of the Industrial Relations Act 1990 (ibid s.17). Also, unofficial work stoppages can justify the dismissal of the employees involved: Barry & Ors v Gardeur (Ireland) Ltd (1991 EAT) ELR 31. See STRIKE.

**unpaid seller.** A seller of goods in circumstances in which the whole of the price has not been paid or tendered, or, in which a negotiable instrument (qv) received as a conditional payment has been dishonoured: Sale of Goods Act 1893 s.38. An unpaid seller, notwithstanding that the property in the goods may have passed to the buyer, has (1) a lien on the goods or right to retain them for the price while he is in possession of them; (2) a right of stopping the goods *in transitu* if the buyer is insolvent; (3) a right of resale (ibid ss.39-48). See LIEN.

**unreasonableness.** See IRRATIONALITY, TEST OF.

**unregistered rights.** See BURDENS; INHIBITIONS.

**unreported judgments.** The written judgments of the Superior Courts which have not been published in the law reports. They may be and are frequently cited in court.

**unsafe premises.** See OCCUPIER'S LIABILITY.

**unsecured loans.** A building society may provide unsecured or partly secured loans, provided it has *adopted* the power so to do: Building Societies Act 1989 s.23. See BRIDGING LOAN.

**unsolicited goods.** Goods sent to a person that are sent without any prior request by him or on his behalf: SGSS Act 1980 s.47. Where *unsolicited goods* are sent to a person with a view to his acquiring them and are received by him and the recipient has neither agreed to acquire nor agreed to return them, the recipient may treat the goods as if they were an unconditional gift to him and any right of the sender to the goods is extinguished, provided the sender does not take possession of them within six months of their receipt, or earlier if the recipient gives notice to the sender.

It is an offence to demand payment for unsolicited goods where the person making the demand has no reasonable cause to believe that there is a right to payment. In relation to *invoices* see SGSS Act s.49.

**unsound mind.** A grant of administration of an estate may be made to the *committee* of a person of unsound mind: RSC O.79 rr.26-27. For provisions governing the appointment of a guardian to a person of unsound mind, see RSC O.67; RCC O.49. An extension of the limitation period within which an action must be commenced is permitted where the claimant is of unsound mind at any time on the date the cause of action accrued: Rohan v Bord na Mona (1991 HC) ILRM 123. See LIMITATION OF ACTIONS. See also WARD OF COURT; INSANITY; MENTAL DISORDER; TESTAMENTARY CAPACITY; UNFIT TO PLEAD.

**unstamped document.** An unstamped or insufficiently stamped document, which is required to be stamped, will not be admitted as evidence in any civil proceedings, even for a collateral purpose, nor will secondary evidence thereof: Stamps Act 1891 s.14. The practice of the courts is to allow an unstamped document to be admitted on the personal undertaking by a solicitor to produce it, when stamped, to an officer of the court. An unstamped document is admissible in criminal cases (ibid s.14(4)). See STAMP DUTY.

**unsworn statement.** (1) The statement which an accused formerly had a right to make in criminal proceedings without being sworn; the right has been abolished: Criminal Justice Act 1984 s.23. An accused, if giving evidence, must now do so on oath and be liable to cross-examination. However, this provision does not affect the right of an accused (a) to make an unsworn statement if he makes it by way of mitigation before the court passes sentence on him, or (b) if

unrepresented, to address the court or jury in like manner as his counsel or solicitor would have been so entitled if he has been represented.

(2) As regards the unsworn evidence of a child or of a person with a mental handicap, see CHILD, EVIDENCE OF; MENTAL HANDICAP.

**untraced driver.** Prior to 1989, an *ex gratia* payment could be made by the Motor Insurers' Bureau of Ireland (qv) in respect of certain injuries resulting from the use of a motor vehicle, the owner or driver of which could not be traced. Where a person had sustained serious and permanent disablement or had died as a result of injury and there was, in the view of the Bureau, reasonable certainty that the disablement or death was caused by the negligent use of a mechanically propelled vehicle the owner or driver of which could not be traced, then the Bureau would at their discretion, give sympathetic consideration to making some *ex gratia* payment.

Under a new Agreement between the Minister and the Bureau, victims of road accidents involving unidentified or untraced drivers are now entitled, as of right, to compensation for all personal injuries arising from road accidents occurring on or after 31st December 1988. Compensation for property damage caused by unidentified or untraced drivers is not available because of the risk of fraudulent claims by persons who could crash their own vehicles and falsely attribute the damage to an untraced driver. See also MOTOR INSURERS' BUREAU OF IRELAND.

**unvalued policy.** A policy of insurance which does not specify the value of the subject-matter insured, but, subject to the limit of the sum insured, leaves the insurable value to be subsequently ascertained: Marine Insurance Act 1906 s.28.

**unworthiness to succeed.** See SUCCEED, UNWORTHINESS TO.

**upset price.** See AUCTION SALES.

**urban district councils.** The bodies which were formerly *urban sanitary authorities*: Local Government (Ireland) Act 1898 s.22; Public Health (Ireland) Act 1878 ss.4-7. Urban district councils are sanitary, housing, planning and fire authorities. See BOUNDARY ALTERATION.

**urban renewal.** Statutory provision for the designation by the Minister of *urban renewal areas* and for the remission of rates in such areas, is contained in the Urban Renewal Act 1986. This Act also provides for the establishment of the Custom House Docks Development Authority (ibid ss.8-22). This authority is given the power to acquire land compulsorily within a specified area and to have the same authority as a housing authority under the Housing Act 1966 Part V: Urban Renewal (Amendment) Act 1987.

Tax incentives to promote the redevelopment of certain inner city *designated areas* is provided for: Finance Acts 1986 ss. 41-45; 1987 s.27; 1991 s.54; 1992 ss.29-30; 1993 ss.30-32. The tax incentives include capital allowances in respect of construction; deduction from rental income of construction expenditure and from the income of the individual owner occupier; and *double rent* deduction where occupied for the purpose of trade or profession. See also Temple Bar Area (Renewal & Development) Act 1991.[Text: Judge].

**urine specimen.** The specimen of urine which a garda may require certain persons in a garda station to provide for a designated registered medical practitioner; it is an offence to refuse or fail to so provide: Road Traffic (Amendment) Act 1978 ss.13(1), 14(1), 17(5); Medical Practitioners (Amdt) Act 1993 ss.4-5. When such a person is required to provide a blood specimen, he has the *option* to provide a urine specimen instead (ibid 1978 Act s.16(5)). A quantity of the specimen must be offered to the person (ibid s.21(2)). Where a person declares that he wishes to avail of the option to provide a urine sample and is unable to do so, the obligation to provide a blood specimen is revived and any refusal to permit the taking of blood is the offence with which the person should be charged: DPP v Swan (1993 HC) — Irish Times 12/5/1993. See Connolly v Salinger (1982) ILRM 482; DPP v Regan (1993 HC) ILRM 336.

Under draft legislation, it is proposed that the category of persons who will be obliged to give a blood specimen will be extended to include those arrested for dangerous driving or for taking a vehicle

without authority: Road Traffic Bill 1993 s.13.

For power of garda to have a urine sample taken in relation to other offences, see BODILY SAMPLE. See BLOOD SPECIMEN; DESIGNATED; DRUNKEN DRIVING.

**usage.** See CUSTOM AND PRACTICE.

**use.** Before the Statute of Uses (1634), if A conveyed land to B with the intention that B was to hold it for the benefit of C, B was said to hold the land *to the use* of C. At common law B, as the *feoffee to uses*, was the legal owner of the land while in the Court of Chancery he was regarded as the nominal owner, bound to allow C, the *cestui que use*, to have the profits and benefit of the land.

The Statute of Uses 1634 (1536 in England) sought to abolish *uses* by providing that where a person was seized of an estate of freehold to the use of another, the *use* should be converted to a legal estate and the cestui que use should become the legal owner. The Statute failed to abolish uses, as in Jane Tyrrel's Case (1557) Dyer 155a, it was held that if there was a *use* upon a *use*, the Statute executed the first *use* and was then exhausted, so that the first cestui que use held on behalf of the second cestui que use, who still had an equitable estate. The second *use* became known as a trust (qv). The formula developed to *unto and to the use of B and his heirs in trust for C and his heirs* which vests the legal estate in B and the equitable estate in C.

**user.** The enjoyment, benefit or use of a thing. See CUSTOM AND PRACTICE.

**usm.** [Unlisted securities market]. See STOCK EXCHANGE.

**usque ad medium filum aquae (viae).** [As far as the middle of the stream (road)]. See PUBLIC ROAD; RIPARIAN.

**usurpation.** Unauthorised or illegal assumption of rights.

**usurpation of government.** The offence which may be commited by (a) setting up, maintaining, or taking part in any body purporting to be a government or legislature not authorised by the Constitution; or (b) establishing, maintaining or taking part in any court or tribunal not constitutionally based; or (c) partaking in any army or police force not authorised by law: Offences Against the State Act 1939 s.6 as amended by the

Criminal Law Act 1976 s.2.

**usury.** Illegal or excessive interest; under the Usury Laws, repealed in 1854, interest above certain rates was prohibited. Protection is now given to borrowers against excessive interest charged by moneylenders by the Moneylenders Act 1933. See MONEYLENDERS.

**ut infra.** [As (mentioned) below].

**ut res magis valeat quam pereat.** [It is better for a thing to have effect than to be made void]. See Curtis v Stovin (1889) 22 QBD 512; An Foras Aiseanna Saothair v Minister for Social Welfare & Ryan (1991 HC No 653 Sp).

**ut supra.** [As (mentioned) above].

**uterine.** Born of the same mother but not of the same father.

**utter.** The offence committed by a person who uses, offers, publishes, delivers, disposes of, tenders or puts off a forgery (qv), knowing it to be forged and having the same intent (whether to defraud or deceive) that the law requires for the corresponding forgery.

**utterance.** Utterances made in either House of the Oireachtas are privileged; members of each House are not, in respect of any such utterances, amenable to any court or any authority other than the House itself: 1937 Constitution art.15(12) and (13). A Dail deputy cannot be made to explain his utterances or to give the information upon which the utterances are based, the nature of such information or its source: Attorney General v The Sole Member of the Tribunal of Inquiry (1992 SC) ITLR (23 Nov). The Chairman of the Beef Tribunal in 1992 ruled that the privilege and immunity enjoyed by members of the Houses of the Oireactas prevents the disclosure of such sources of information when privilege in respect thereof is claimed by a member: Mr Justice Hamilton on 10th December 1992.

This absolute privilege was held by the High Court to apply only to utterances in the Houses of the Oireachtas and not to statements submitted to the Beef Tribunal which went beyond mere re-publication of Dail allegations: AG v The Sole Member of the Beef Tribunal (1993 HC) — Irish Times 19/2/1993. However, the Chairman of the Beef Tribunal held that members of the Oireachtas had a common law privilege

to refuse to reveal their sources; he based his ruling on an essay by Thomas Jefferson in 1797 approved of in Gravel v The US 408 US — Irish Times 6/3/1993. This view was upheld by the High Court: Goodman v The Sole Member of the Beef Tribunal (1993 HC) — Irish Times 28/5/1993.

The matter was finally disposed of by the Supreme Court which held that TDs had a constitutional right to refuse to disclose the identity of informants who gave them information on which they based allegations made in the Dail and which were included in the book of evidence of the tribunal: AG v The Sole Member of the Beef Tribunal (1993 SC) — Irish Times 29/7/1993. See also In re Haughey (1971) IR 216. See McHugh in 11 ILT & SJ (1993) 119. See EXPRESSION, FREEDOM OF; PRIVILEGE, COMMUNICATION TO ANOTHER.

# V

**v.** versus (qv)

**vacantia bona.** See BONA VACANTIA.

**vacation.** The periods in the year during which the Supreme and High Courts are not normally sitting. There are four vacations in every year. One of the judges of the High Court is selected to hear in Dublin all such applications as may require to be heard immediately or promptly (eg injunctions, habeas corpus) See RSC O.118. See LONG VACATION; SITTINGS.

**vaccine, care involving.** The Supreme Court has held that the legal duty of the manufacturer of a vaccine to exercise sufficient care is not discharged by merely complying with mandatory or minimum requirements imposed by national health authorities where the vaccine was manufactured or by merely relying on one particular point of view concerning the risks involved: Kenneth Best v Wellcome Foundation Ltd (1992 SC) ITLR (28 Sep). See IMMUNISATION SCHEMES.

**vadium.** See BAILMENT; PAWNBROKER; PLEDGE.

**vagrancy.** See WANDERING ABROAD.

**valuable consideration.** Money or money's worth. Consideration in money or money's worth: Succession Act 1965 s.3(1).

The title of a purchaser of land for valuable consideration in good faith and without notice of an adjudication of bankruptcy, whereby the land became vested in the Official Assignee (qv), will not be affected by the adjudication, provided the purchaser has registered his conveyance before registration of the Official Assignee's vesting certificate (if according to law any conveyance of the land is required to be registered), unless the vesting certificate is registered within two months after the adjudication: Bankruptcy Act 1988 s.46. See CONSIDERATION; GOOD CONSIDERATION; HOLDER FOR VALUE; NOTICE; PRIORITY; INTERPRETATION CLAUSE.

**valuation.** (1) The estimate of the net annual value of every tenement or rateable hereditament which formerly had to be made annually: Valuation (Ireland) Act 1852. The Commissioner of Valuations sent a list of valuations in each area to the local authorities, which lists were published, and any person aggrieved by reason of the valuation was entitled to complain by notice in writing (ibid ss.17-18) and the hereditament was then valued again by a different valuer: Armstrong v Commissioner of Valuations (1905) 2 IR 448. An appeal lay to the Circuit Court and on a point of law to the High Court: Courts of Justice Act 1936 s.31(3). See also Davey v Commissioner of Valuations (1956) IR 295. For re-valuation see 1852 Act s.34 and Local Government (Ireland) Act 1898 s.65.

The annual revision was abolished in 1988 and new proceedings were adopted for the continuous revision of rateable properties: Valuation Act 1988 s.3. Revisions may be requested by the local authority, the ratepayer or an officer of the Commisioner. Provision was also made for global valuation (qv) of public utilities. A Valuation Tribunal to hear valuation appeals was established; the decision of the tribunal is final, subject to the right of appeal to the High Court on a point of law (ibid ss.2 and 5). The form of *case stated* by the Tribunal to the Court was specified in Mitchelstown Co-Op Society Ltd v Commissioner of Valuation (1989 SC) ILRM 582. The

members of the tribunal are appointed by the Minister (ibid 1988 Act first schedule).

The application of the poor law valuation system to agricultural land has been held to be unconstitutional: Brennan v Attorney General (1984) ILRM 355. It has also been held that the profit-earning ability of a business is an essential element in determining the net annual value of a hereditament: Rosses Point Hotel v Commissioner of Valuation (1987) ILRM 512. The courts have wide powers when dealing with valuation matters: Siuicre Eireann v Commissioner of Valuation (1992 SC) ITLR (27 Jul). See ASSET VALUATION; GRIFFITH'S VALUATION; RATES.

(2) Where there is agreement to sell goods on terms that the price is to be fixed by the valuation of a third party, and such third party cannot or does not make such valuation, the agreement is avoided: Sale of Goods Act 1893 s.9.

(3) As regards capital gains tax (qv), it has been held that the High Court was entitled, on a case stated, to examine whether there was evidence to support a valuation decision made in the Circuit Court: McMahon v Murphy (1989) 7ILT Dig 151.

**valuation, industrial plant.** Statutory provision has been made to continue the rating of industrial plant which had traditionally been considered rateable, prior to court decisions which had decided otherwise: Valuation Act 1986.

**valuation report.** (1) As regards a building society, the written report which must be available, dealing with the adequacy of the security to be taken by a building society in respect of a loan to be made by the society: Building Society Act 1976 s.79. The report must be furnished to the member of the society at the same time as he is notified of the society's approval of the loan: Building Societies Act 1986 s.6(1)(b); SI No 27 of 1987, first schedule; SI No 339 of 1987, art.6. Notwithstanding the repeal of the 1976 and 1986 Acts, this provision, that the valuation report must be furnished to the member, continues in force as if made by the Central Bank: Building Societies Act 1989 s.6(2). See also Housing Act 1966 s.90(10) as inserted by Housing (Miscellaneous Provisions) Act 1992 s.26(1).

(2) As regards a public limited company, the report which the company must have prepared by an independent person whenever it proposes to allot fully or partly paid-up shares on a non-cash consideration: Companies (Amendment) Act 1983 ss.30-33. The report must be sent to the proposed allottee. The report must contain a note that the assets valued, together with any cash that is being paid, are worth not less than the nominal value of the shares to be allotted plus any premium on them (ibid s.30(8)(d)). See ALLOTMENT; ASSET VALUATION; HOUSING; PREMIUM.

**value.** Valuable consideration, as in *purchaser for value*.

**valued policy.** See SUM ASSURED.

**value-added tax.** A tax charged, levied and paid (a) on the supply of goods and services effected within the State for consideration by a *taxable person* in the course or furtherance of any business carried on by him, and (b) on goods imported into the State: Value-Added Tax 1972 s.2(1) as amended by Value-Added Tax (Amendment) Act 1978 s.30 and annual Finance Acts.

With the completion of the Single Market, significant changes have been made in respect of VAT on goods purchased from other EC member states from 1st January 1993. Generally goods supplied by a VAT registered trader in Ireland to a VAT registered trader in other EC states are zero rated. Also VAT is not payable at the point of entry in Ireland in respect of goods purchased from other member states.

However, private individuals buying goods in another member state for their own personal use, pay VAT in that member state and there is no Irish VAT liability, except (a) in respect of new motor vehicles, boats and planes, which are subject to Irish VAT when brought into Ireland by traders or private individuals and (b) goods purchased through "distance selling" arrangements (eg mail order sales and tele-shopping) in excess of £27,000 annual value.

Irish traders are required to have the prefix IE before their VAT number. The identifying prefix for other member states are: BE — Belgium, DE — Germany, DK — Denmark, EL —

Greece, ES — Spain, FR — France, GB — United Kingdom, IT — Italy, LU — Luxembourg, NL — Netherlands and PT — Portugal.

A legal mechanism has been provided for a supplier who has invoiced out VAT at a higher rate than should have applied, to give a refund and issue a new invoice: Finance Act 1993 s.91(b). [Text: Gov Pub (1); O'Reilly & Carroll; Cremin; Hoskins UK]. See EXCHANGE RATE; SOUND RECORDING.

**variation.** Change in a contractual term. Consideration must be present if a contractual term is deleted or altered, leaving the rest of the contract untouched, unless the change is by deed: Fenner v Blake (1900) 1 QB 427. A variation may require to be evidenced in writing: McQuaid v Lynam (1965) IR 564. See MEMORANDUM, STATUTE OF FRAUDS; MEMORANDUM, SALE OF GOODS; ORAL AGREEMENT, MODIFICATION OF CONTRACT BY; WAIVER.

**varietal names.** The names for plant varieties which are the subject of applications for plant breeders' rights under the Plant Varieties (Proprietary Rights) Act 1980. The Minister may by regulation provide for the selection of names and for the entry in a register of the names so selected. See SI No 369 of 1992.

Where a plant variety is entered in the register every person who sells the reproductive material of that plant variety is required to use that name as the name of the variety. Failure to do so constitutes an actionable wrong in proceedings at the suit of the relevant holder of the plant breeders' rights. It is not permitted to register varietal names under the Trade Marks Act 1963. See Wheatcroft Bros TMs 71 RPC 43.

**vastum.** [Waste].

**VAT.** Value-added tax (qv).

**VEC.** See VOCATIONAL EDUCATION COMMITTEE.

**vehicle.** Ordinarily means a carriage or other conveyance on land. The term *vehicle* is not defined per se in the Road Traffic Acts. See MECHANICAL PROPELLED VEHICLE; PUBLIC SERVICE VEHICLE; INSURANCE, VEHICLE; FUEL; TYPE APPROVAL, MOTOR VEHICLES.

**vehicle insurer, proceedings against.** For leave of the court to institute and prosecute proceedings or to execute judgment against a vehicle insurer, see Road Traffic Act 1961 s.76. See Stanbridge v Healy (1985) ILRM 290; Boyce v McBride (1987) ILRM 95. See RSC 0.91.

**vehicle, registration of.** Only *authorised* dealers are permitted to hold unregistered vehicles on their premises as from 1st January 1993. Such vehicles must be registered before the dealer releases them to unauthorised traders or to retail customers. A private individual or an unauthorised trader who imports a vehicle must register the vehicle and pay the *Vehicle Registration Tax* by the next working day. Authorisation of dealers is by the Revenue Commissioners. See Finance Act 1992 ss.130-144; Finance (No 2) Act 1992 ss.4-23; Finance Act 1993 ss.52-56.

**veil, lifting the.** See LIFTING THE CORPORATE VEIL.

**vendee.** A purchaser, usually of land.

**venditioni exponas.** [That you expose for sale]. When an order of fieri facias (qv) has been issued and the sheriff returns that he has taken goods but that they remain in his hands unsold, this order may be sued out to compel a sale of goods for any price they may fetch. See RSC O.43 r.1; O.42 r.35.

**vendor.** A seller, usually of land.

**vendor's rights.** Until completion of the sale of land, the vendor has a lien on the property for the unpaid purchase money; if he is still in possession and still unpaid he can refuse to give up possession. A vendor has a right to keep the rent and profits accruing before the time fixed for completion. See In re Aluminium Shopfronts (1987 HC) IR 419.

**venerial disease.** There is a prohibition on the advertisement of cures for venerial disease: Venerial Diseases Act 1917.

**venia aetatis.** [Privilege of age].

**venue of trial.** Proceedings in the High Court are tried at the Four Courts Dublin, unless application is made by any party to a judge for trial elsewhere than in Dublin; however where parties were entitled as of right to a trial with a jury, notice of trial could be served without prior application to the court, for the following venues — Cork, Limerick, Galway, Sligo, Dundalk and Kilkenny: RSC O.36 rr.1-2. However,

since the abolition of juries in cases for personal injuries, jury actions may not be set down for trial at those venues without a prior order of the court; non-jury actions may be set down for trial without the order of the court: Practice Direction (July 1988).

**verba accipienda sunt secundum subjectam materiem.** [Words are to be interpreted in accordance with the subject-matter].

**verba chartarum fortuis accipiuntur contra proferentem.** [The words of a deed are to be interpreted most strongly against him who uses them]. This maxim is to be interpreted in the context that the interpretation works no wrong. See CONTRA PROFERENTEM.

**verba cum effectu accipienda sunt.** [Words are to be interpreted in such a way as to give them some effect].

**verba intentioni, non e contra, debent inservire.** [Words ought to be made subservient to the intent, and not the other way about].

**verba ita sunt intelligenda ut res magis valeat quam pereat.** [Words are to be understood that the object may be carried out and not fail].

**verba relata hoc maxime operantur per referentiam ut in eis inesse videntur.** [Words to which reference is made in an instrument have the same operation as if they were inserted in the instrument referring to them].

**verbatim.** Exactly; word for word; precisely.

**verdict.** The answer of a jury (qv) to a question put to them for their decision. The verdict is usually announced by the foreman, who is chosen by the jurors to speak for them.

Where the jury disagree and are unable to agree, they are discharged and a new jury is called to try the case. It is more desireable that a jury be urged to agree if possible rather than that they be told that they are entitled to disagree: McIntyre v Lewis & Dolan (1991 SC) 1 IR 121. In civil cases, a simple majority verdict is sufficient; in criminal cases, a majority verdict of ten from a minimum of eleven jurors is sufficient: Criminal Justice Act 1984 s.25. Such a majority verdict is not repugnant to the Constitution: O'Callaghan v Governor of Mountjoy Prison (1992 HC & SC).

It has been held that the introduction of further issues by a judge to a jury after the jury has delivered its verdict, is of doubtful propriety: The People (DPP) v Mulvey (1987 CCA) IR 502. The finding of a coroner's jury is also called a verdict. See ALTERNATIVE VERDICT; INQUEST; JURY; SPECIAL VERDICT; TRIAL BY JURY.

**versus.** Against, abbreviated to *v* eg Attorney General v O'Reilly.

**vessel.** Includes any ship (qv) or boat and any other vessel used in navigation: Merchant Shipping Act 1992 s.2(1). A waterborne craft of any type, whether self propelled or not, and includes an air cushion craft and any structure in or on water: Environmental Protection Agency Act 1992 s.3(1). See Southport Corporation v Morris (1893) 1 QB 359. See FISHING VESSEL; PASSENGER BOAT; PASSENGER SHIP.

**vest.** To clothe with legal rights.

**vested.** An estate is said to be vested when there is a present right to its ownership. See OWNERSHIP.

**vesting before completion.** The right of a local authority to vest the title in lands, the subject of a compulsory purchase order (qv), in themselves before the assessment or payment of compensation: Housing Act 1966 s.81. See NOTICE TO TREAT.

**vesting by deed poll.** The right of a local authority to vest the title in lands, the subject of a compulsory purchase order (qv), in themselves, by deed poll in specified circumstances by paying the purchase money agreed or assessed into court eg where the owner refuses to convey the land: Land Clauses Act 1845 ss.69-70.

**vesting declaration.** See TRUST PROPERTY.

**vesting order.** The order which a local authority has power to make to acquire a derelict site (qv), having followed a specified procedure of giving notice to the occupier and the owner, publishing a notice in a newspaper circulating in the area, obtaining the consent of the Minister if any objection is not withdrawn: Derelict Sites Act 1990 s.17.

Any person who had an estate or interest in the land immediately prior to the making of the vesting order is entitled to obtain compensation (ibid s.19). Vesting orders may also be obtained under the LG(P&D) Act 1976 in relation to open spaces and under the Forestry Act 1946. The Minister may revoke any vesting order made under the Land Purchase Acts where the Land Commission has not entered into actual possession of the land: Irish Land Commission (Dissolution) Act 1992 s.7.

**veterinary surgery.** The art and science of veterinary surgery and medicine: Veterinary Surgeons Act 1881 s.2. It is an offence for a person to practise or to hold himself out as practising veterinary surgery or veterinary medicine unless he is a registered veterinary surgeon: Veterinary Surgeons Act 1931 s.46.

The register of veterinary surgeons is maintained by the Veterinary Council which has the responsibility also of inquiring into the conduct of registered veterinary surgeons for alleged professional misconduct (ibid 1931 Act). It also is required to satisfy itself as to the adequacy of veterinary education and training in Ireland. See also Veterinary Surgeons Acts 1900, 1920, 1952, 1960; SI Nos 85 of 1954 and 66 of 1988.

Regulations and directives have been made with a view to the mutual recognition of qualifications in veterinary medicine across the EC eg see SI Nos 391 of 1980, 323 of 1982, 159 of 1987, 253 of 1992, 150 of 1993; EEC — 78/1026, 78/1027, 78/1029; 81/1057. See ABATTOIR; SLAUGHTER.

**vexata quaestio.** [A vexed question]. A problem which has not been settled despite having been discussed repeatedly.

**vexatious proceedings.** See ABUSE OF PROCESS.

**vi et armis.** [With force and arms]. See TRESPASS.

**via trita.** The strips of land alongside the metalled tracks of a public road (qv). The public has the right to pass and repass on the *via trita*, in the absence of clear evidence to the contrary. See Attorney General (Cork County Council) v Perry (1904) 1 IR 247.

**vibration.** Formerly, it was an offence to create noise or vibration in an area which was so loud, so continuous or so repeated or of such duration or pitch as to give reasonable cause for annoyance to persons in any premises in the neighbourhood or to persons lawfully using any public place: LG(P&D) Act 1976 s.51

repealed by Environmental Protection Agency Act 1992 s.18(1) and largely replaced by s.108 of 1992 Act. See NOISE; NUISANCE.

**vicarious liability.** The liability which falls on one person as a result of an action of another eg the liability generally of an employer for the acts and omissions of his employees. An employer is vicariously liable for wrongful acts done by a servant in the course of his employment: Poland v Parr (1927) 1 KB 240. However, the means employed by an employee may be so unreasonable and excessive as to take the act of the employee out of the class of acts which are impliedly authorised by the employer eg using a customer as a shield against an intruder: Reilly v Ryan (1991 HC) ILRM 449.

An employer may be found to be vicariously liable for a person who is not an employee but is an independent contractor (contract for services) where in practical terms the degree of control exercised by the employer was the same as one would expect a master to have over a servant: Phelan v Coillte Teo (1993 HC) ELR 57; see Barry in 11 ILT & SJ (1993) 2.

The State is vicariously liable for the negligence of its servants; the common law rule that the State was immune from action did not survive the enactment of the 1922 Constitution: Byrne v Ireland (1972) IR 241. See also Doyle v Fleming's Coal Mine Ltd (1953) 87 ILTR 198. See PRANK; TIED INSURANCE AGENT.

**vicious propensity.** See ANIMALS; SCIEN-TER.

**victim impact statement.** A statement, prepared by the gardai, on the physical or emotional harm, or any loss or damage to property, suffered by the victim of a crime through or by means of the offence, and any other effects of the offence on the victim. The statement is put before the judge after the accused has been found quilty but before sentencing.

Judges have generally requested such information before passing sentence, but in 1992 the formal practice was initiated in the Central Criminal Court by Mr Justice Declan Budd of requesting a Victim Impact Statement in DPP v Kiernan (a case involving the rape of a mentally retarded woman) and the practice has been followed in other courts since.

In New Zealand there is a statutory requirement for a Victim Impact Statement: Victim of Offences Act 1987. The Victim Impact Statement is usually in narrative form and covers (a) details on the victim eg age, occupation, relationship with offender; (b) physical injuries eg long/short term effects, medical/dental reports; (c) property damage or loss; (d) financial costs eg loss of wages; (e) emotional/psychological effects; (f) other effects on victim or victim's lifestyle.

In Ireland, there is now a statutory requirement on courts, in determining the sentence to be imposed on a person for certain offences, to take into account any effect (whether long-term or otherwise) of the offence on the victim: Criminal Justice Act 1993 s.5. The court may where necessary receive evidence or submissions concerning the effects on the victim, and must receive evidence of the victim when the victim so requests. The offences concerned are sexual offences and offences involving violence or the threat of violence to the person.

The voluntary organisation *Victim Support* provides support and assistance to individuals and their families who have been victims of crime, including a support service in the Four Courts for victims who are required to give evidence in court. [Irish Association for Victim Support, 29-30 Dame Street, Dublin 2. Tel: (01) 6798673]. See Law Reform Commission Consultative Paper on Sentencing (No 45 of 1993). See COMPENSA-TION ORDER.

**victimisation.** Selective or unfair punishment or discrimination; it may have a legal significance if prohibited eg unfair selection for redundancy. Where an employee is penalised for having taken action in good faith to protect his employment rights, this can amount to discrimination which is prohibited: Employment Equality Act 1977 s.2; SIPTU v Dunne (1993) ELR 65.

**videlicet; viz.** [Namely; that is to say].

**video.** A video cassette comes within the definition of a cinematograph film for the purpose of the Copyright Act 1963 s.18(10)). It is an offence to infringe the copyright which subsists in a video recording; seizure by a garda of infringing copies can be made without warrant on the authorisation of the District Court: Copyright (Amendment) Act 1987 s.2. See DPP v Irwin (1985 HC). See CINEMATOGRAPH FILM.

**video recording.** (1) Evidence by means of a video recording may be admissible in court proceedings eg DPP v McElhinney (1988 SCC). Also a video recording may be admissible in proceedings relating to sexual offences and offences involving violence as evidence of any fact stated therein (a) of any evidence given by a person under 17 years of age through a live *television link* (qv) at a preliminary examination and (b) of any statement made by a victim under 14 years of age during an interview with a garda: Criminal Evidence Act 1992 s.16.

(2) Any disc or magnetic tape containing information by the use of which the whole or part of a *video work* may be produced; a *video work* means any series of visual images (whether with or without sound), (a) produced, whether electronically or by other means, by the use of information contained on any disc or magnetic tape, and (b) showing a moving picture: Video Recordings Act 1989 s.1(1). A licence is required by persons who wish to sell or let on hire video recordings either by wholesale or by retail (ibid s.18).

The *supply* of video recordings requires the authorisation of the Official Censor of Films in the form of a *supply certificate* in respect of the video work contained in a video recording (ibid s.3). *Supply* includes supply in any manner, whether or not for reward and includes supply by way of sale, letting on hire, exchange or loan (ibid s.1(1)). A supply certificate contains a classification as to the suitability of the video work for different age groups (ibid s.4).

The Censor may refuse a certificate if he is of opinion that the video work is unfit for viewing on specified grounds eg (a) the viewing of the work would be likely to cause or encourage persons to commit crimes or would tend to deprave or corrupt persons, or would be likely to stir up hatred against a group of persons on account of their race, colour, nationality, religion, ethnic or national origins, membership of the travelling community, or sexual orientation, or (b) the work depicts acts of gross violence or cruelty towards humans or animals, including mutilation and torture (ibid s.3).

The Censor may issue *prohibition orders* in respect of video works (ibid ss.3(3) and 7); an appeal lies to the Censorship of Films Appeal Board (ibid s.10). Provision has been made for the appointment of assistant censors and for the refund of fees in the event of a successful appeal: Censorship of Films (Amdt) Act 1992. See DOCUMENTARY EVIDENCE; INFRINGEMENT OF COPYRIGHT; WITHHOLDING TAX.

**viduity.** Widowhood.

**vigilantibus non dormientibus, jura subveniunt.** [The laws give help to those who are watchful and not to those who sleep]. Equitable maxim that delay defeats equity. See LACHES; LIMITATIONS OF ACTIONS.

**vinculo matrimonii.** See DIVORCE A VINCULO MATRIMONII.

**vindictive damages.** Punitive or exemplary damages (qv).

**violent disorder.** Under proposed draft legislation, the offence committed where (a) three or more persons who are present together at any place, use or threaten to use unlawful violence, and (b) the conduct of those persons, taken together, is such as would cause a person of reasonable firmness present at that place to fear for his or another person's safety; each of the persons using or threatening to use unlawful violence commits the offence of violent disorder: draft Criminal Justice (Public Order) Bill 1993 s.16. The place may be a public place, a private place or both. It is proposed that the common law offence of riot will be abolished (ibid s.15(4)), and that every reference to the common law offences of "riot" or "riot and to tumult" in previous enactments are to be construed as a reference to the proposed offence of "violent disorder" (ibid s.16(5)). See AFFRAY; RIOT.

**vir et uxor consentur in lege una persona.** [Husband and wife are considered one person in law]. See HUSBAND AND WIFE.

**virgo intacta.** [Untouched virgin]. A

female whose hymen has not been broken. Evidence that a spouse is *virgo intacta* may be sufficient to obtain a decree of nullity of marriage on the grounds that the marriage has not been consummated: AMN v JPC (1988) ILRM 170. See MARRIAGE, NULLITY OF.

**vis et metus.** [Force and fear].

**vis major.** [Greater force]. Insuperable accident; irresistible force eg a storm; unforeseeable conditions beyond the charterer's control. [Text: Tiberg UK]. See ACT OF GOD; FORCE MAJEURE.

**visa.** An authority to enter and stay in the State according to its terms. An immigration officer can refuse leave to land to an alien who is not the holder of a valid Irish visa. See Alien's (Amendment) Order 1975 (SI No 128 of 1975); Alein's (Amendment) Order 1985 (SI No 154 of 1985). See The State (Kugan) v Fitzgibbon St Garda Station (1986) ILRM 95; The State (Bouzagon) v Fitzgibbon St Garda Station (1986) ILRM 98.

The EC Council will determine the third countries whose nationals must be in possession of a visa when crossing the external borders of the member States: Treaty of Rome 1957 art.100(c) as inserted by Maastricht Treaty 1992 art.G(D)(23). See also LAISSEZ-PASSER; PASSPORT.

**visual identification.** In cases where a verdict depends substantially on the correctness of the visual identification of an accused, the attention of the jury should be drawn in general terms to the fact that in a number of instances, visual identification of an accused person had been shown subsequently to be erroneous, and for the necessity to treat such evidence with caution: The People (Attorney General) v Casey (1963) IR 33. The trial judge must also relate the general warning to the particular facts in which the witness observed the accused: DPP v O'Reilly (1990) ITLR (9 Jul). See also DPP v McCarthy (1993 CCA) 11 ILT Dig 186.

Witnesses may be asked to identify persons in court: The State (Daly) v Ruane (1988) ILRM 117. However, where a witness gives evidence through a live *television link* (qv) in criminal cases of physical or sexual abuse, the witness may not be required to identify the

accused at the trial, if evidence is given that the accused was known to the witness before the offence is alleged to have been committed: Criminal Evidence Act 1992 s.18. See IDENTIFICATION PARADE.

**viva voce.** [By word of mouth]. Generally the evidence of witnesses at the trial of an action must be made *viva voce*, ie orally, in open court and subject to examination, although the court has power, for sufficient reason, to order that any particular fact may be proved by affidavit (qv). See RSC O.39 r.1. See also Patents Act 1992 s.92(1). See DECLARATION BY DECEASED; DEPOSITION; DOCUMENTARY EVIDENCE; OATH.

**viz.** Videlicet (qv).

**vocational educational committee.** A body corporate with perpetual succession which has a duty to supply or aid the supply of technical education in its area and to establish and maintain a suitable system of continuing education in its area. In 1993, the Dublin Institute of Technology and the Regional Technical Colleges became independent from the VEC. See Vocational Education Act 1930 as amended in 1936, 1944, 1947, 1950, 1953, 1962 and 1970. In relation to the power to appoint teachers, see Devitt v Minister for Education (1989) ILRM 639. See COMPTROLLER AND AUDITOR GENERAL; EDUCATION; SUSPEND.

**vocational training.** Any system of instruction which enables a person being instructed to acquire, maintain, bring up to date or perfect the knowledge or technical capacity required for the carrying on of an occupational activity: Employment Equality Act 1977 s.6. Discrimination (qv) in relation to vocational training is prohibited (ibid s.6(1)). See EEA v Football Association of Ireland (1991) ELR 12 and (1992 LC) ELR 57.

The EC is required to implement a vocational training policy which supports and supplements the actions of the member States, while fully respecting the responsibility of the member States for the content and organization of vocational training: Treaty of Rome 1957 art.127 as replaced by Maastricht Treaty 1992 art.G(D)(36). See TRAINING.

**void.** Empty; destitute of legal effect; of no force eg a contract which is contrary to public policy. See VOID CONTRACTS.

**void contracts.** A contract which is destitute of legal effect. A contract may be void on the face of it or evidence may be required to show that it is void. Property generally does not pass under a void contract, although it has been held in England that property in goods delivered in pursuance of an illegal contract may pass to the purchaser: Singh v Ali (1960) AC 167.

Some contracts are declared void by statute, eg wagering contracts. Contracts which are void at common law include: (a) contracts to oust the jurisdiction of the courts: Scott v Avery (1856) 5 HL Cas 811; (b) contracts which subvert the sanctity of marriage, eg marriage broker contracts, contracts for future separation: Williamson v Gihan (1805) 2 S & L 357; Marquess of Westmeath v Marquess of Salisbury (1830) 5 Bli (ns) 339; and (c) contracts in restraint of trade: Nordenfelt v Maxim Nordenfelt (1894) AC 535. See QUANTUM MERUIT.

**void marriage.** See MARRIAGE, NULLITY OF.

**voidable.** Capable of being voided or set aside eg a voidable contract is one which one of the parties can put an end to at his option, without reference to the other party, so that the contract is binding if he elects to treat it as binding and void if he elects to treat it as void eg in the case of a contract induced by fraud: Phillips v Brooks (1919) 2 KB 243.

If, however, the party entitled to rescind the contract affirms it, or fails to exercise his right within a reasonable time, so that the position of the parties becomes altered, or if he takes a benefit under the contract, or if third parties acquire rights under it, he will be bound by it.

**voidable marriage.** See MARRIAGE, NULL-ITY OF.

**voidable title, sale under.** When the seller of goods has a voidable title thereto, but his title has not been avoided at the time of sale, the buyer acquires a good title to the goods, provided he buys them *in good faith* and without notice of the seller's defect of title: Sale of Goods Act 1893 s.23. *In good faith* means done honestly, whether done negligently or not (ibid s.62(2)). See NEMO DAT QUI NON HABET.

**voire dire.** [To speak the truth]. A *trial within a trial* which is resorted to whenever before, or in the course of, a trial an issue arises involving a decision of law by the judge without the presence of the jury eg whether a child witness is capable of understanding an oath; whether a confession is voluntary; whether a witness is privileged from answering a specific question; or whether some point of law be argued, at the request of the defence, in the absence of the jury. See The People (Attorney General) v Ainscough (1960) IR 136; The People v O'Brien (1969) CCA; The People (DPP) v Conroy (1988) ILRM 4.

**volenti non fit injuria.** [That to which a man consents cannot be considered an injury]. The defence to an action in tort, that the plaintiff with full knowledge and appreciation of the danger, voluntarily accepted the risk and exposed himself to the danger eg by taking part in a boxing match. Mere knowledge of the risk, or *sciens*, is not sufficient. Volenti non fit injuria is a partial defence: Civil Liability Act 1961 s.34. See Flynn v Irish Sugar Mfg Co Ltd (1928) IR 525; Judge v Reape (1968) IR 226.

**voluntary.** (1) Free exercise of will involving an act of choice. (2) Without valuable consideration (qv).

**voluntary care.** See WELFARE OF CHILDREN.

**voluntary conveyance.** A disposition of an interest in land without valuable consideration or marriage to support it; it may be void if the grantor becomes bankrupt. Land conveyed to others by way of a *voluntary conveyance* can be recaptured by the Official Assignee; the conveyance is void if the grantor becomes bankrupt within two years of the conveyance, and it is voidable within five years unless it can be shown that at the time the conveyance was made, the bankrupt was solvent without the aid of the lands conveyed: Bankruptcy Act 1988 s.59. See OFFICIAL ASSIGNEE.

**voluntary health insurance.** A voluntary scheme of insurance for defraying the cost to persons, paying subscriptions to the Voluntary Health Insurance Board, of medical, surgical, hospital and other health services: Voluntary Health Insurance Act 1957 s.4(1). The Minister is empowered to specify the extent of the scheme and he also appoints the members of the board, which is a body corporate with perpetual succession with power to sue and to be sued in its corporate name and to acquire, hold and dispose of land.

The VHI is an *undertaking* within the meaning of the Competition Act 1991; while it is a non-profit making body it still operated *for gain*: Deane & Ors v VHI (1992 SC) ITLR (31 Aug). The VHI was held to have acted unreasonably and unfairly in deciding to withdraw all cover from the plaintiff's hospital: Deane & Ors v VHI (1993 HC). See also Ormiston v Gypsum Industries Ltd EE16/1992 (1993) ELR and as reported by Barry in 11 ILT & SJ (1993) 94. See WITHHOLDING TAX.

**voluntary trust.** A trust in favour of a volunteer (qv).

**voluntary waste.** See WASTE.

**voluntary winding up.** See WINDING UP, VOLUNTARY.

**voluntas in delictis non exitus spectatur.** [In crimes, the intention, and not the result, is looked at]. See MENS REA.

**volunteer.** (1) A person who takes under a disposition for which he, or anyone on his behalf, has not given valuable consideration (qv). Equity will not assist a volunteer; consequently an incompleted trust for the benefit of a volunteer will be unenforceable. See Plumptre's Marriage Settlement (1910) 1 Ch 609. See TRUST.

(2) A person who gives his services without any express or implied promise of remuneration. He may be liable in damages if he performs a voluntary act negligently, but not if he fails to perform it at all. See AGENT, GRATUITOUS; EQUITY, MAXIMS OF; NEIGHBOUR PRINCIPLE.

**vote, right to.** See FRANCHISE; PERSONATION; SPOILT VOTE.

**voters, special.** Persons whose names are included in the special voters list: Electoral Act 1992 s.2(1). An elector is entitled to be entered in this list if he satisfies the registration authority that he is unable to go in person to vote by reason of his physical illness or physical disability (ibid s.27 and second schedule rr.19-23). A first application must be accompanied by a certificate from a medical practitioner (ibid r.19(c)).

Special voters are entitled to cast their vote on a ballot paper delivered to the special voter by a special presiding officer accompanied by a member of the Garda

Siochana (ibid ss.81-82 — Dail elections; Electoral (Amendment) (No 2) Act 1986 s.9 — European, local elections, and referenda); draft Presidential Elections Bill 1993 s.41 — proposed for presidential elections). See Draper v Ireland (1984) IR 277. See DISABLED VOTER.

**voting at elections.** Voting in presidential, European, and Dail elections must be by the elector in person at the polling station allotted to him, except where permitted either at another polling station, or by postal vote, or in another manner for special voters eg see Electoral Act 1992 s.38. For rules governing the counting of votes, see 1992 Act ss.118-128. See SPOILT VOTE.

**voting at meetings.** All questions arising at a meeting of a company must be decided in the first place by a show of hands; however members are empowered to demand a poll except in respect of the election of chairman and voting on adjournments: Companies Act 1963 s.137; In re Horburg Co (1879) 11 Ch D 109.

When voting is by show of hand, each member has one vote only irrespective of the number of shares he holds; when voting is on a poll, every member has a vote for every share he has, which he can use to vote some for and some against a resolution as he so wishes (ibid s.138). A member can appoint another person, a *proxy*, who need not be a member, to attend, speak and vote for the member (ibid s.136). See Kinsella v Dublin Gas Consumers' Company (1982) HC. See also Building Societies Act 1989 s.69. See ARMS LENGTH, AT; CHAIRMAN; COUNCILLOR, DISCLOSURE OF INTEREST; POLL; PROXY; RESOLUTION.

**voting by post.** See POSTAL VOTER.

**vouch.** To bear witness; to summon; to answer for.

**voucher.** A document which evidences a transaction eg a receipt for money.

**vow.** Solemn promise. Members of religious communities usually bind themselves by agreement to vows eg vow of celibacy, vow of obedience. The power of a religious superior appears to be absolute or virtually absolute, the vow of obedience being a converse of that power; the making of an order by a religious superior is unlikely to be intended to be subject to review by any other tribunal: Sister O'Dea v O'Briain & Ors (1992 HC) ILRM 364. See Barry in 10 ILT & SJ (1992) 222. See FAIR PROCEDURE.

**voyage policy.** A contract of insurance to insure the subject matter at and from or from one place to another or others: Marine Insurance Act 1906 s.25(1).

**vulgar abuse.** The use of words in an abusive way or in anger about a person so that they injure only the pride of the person rather than his reputation, is unlikely to be defamatory. To call someone a "shithead" or a "gobshite" was vulgar abuse: Lardner J in Kenna v McKinney (1992 HC) — Irish Times 11th December 1992. See ABUSE; DEFAMATION.

# W

**wagering contract.** An agreement between two parties that upon the happening of some uncertain event, one party will pay a sum of money to the other, which party is to pay depending on the issue of the event. Neither party must have any other interest in the contract other than the sum he will win or lose. If either of the parties may win but cannot lose, or may lose but cannot win, it is not a wagering contract. Wagering contracts are not illegal but the courts will give no assistance in enforcing them; every contract by way of gaming (qv) or wagering is void and no action may lie for the recovery of any money won thereon: Gaming and Lotteries Act 1956 s.36(1) and (2).

A bet placed with *the Tote* is not a wager as the Racing Board is legally bound to pay the money received to successful ticket holders and consequently cannot win or lose: Duff v Racing Board (1971) HC. It was held that the defendants owed a duty of care, as regards the eligibility of a horse to take part in a race, to the holder of a jackpot ticket affected by that race at Punchestown: Madden v Irish Turf Club & Ors (1993 HC) ITLR (26 Jul).

A promise express, or implied (a) to pay any person any sum of money paid by him in respect of a gaming or wagering contract or (b) to pay any money by way of commission, fee, reward or otherwise, in respect of such contracts, is null and void and no action can be brought to recover any such money (ibid 1956 Act s.36(3)). This is an exception to the usual rule that an agent is liable to be indemnified for all lawful acts by his principal.

A contract of insurance is not a wager if the assured has an insurable interest (qv) in the subject matter insured. See Pujolus v Heaps (1938) 72 ILTR 96; McElwain v Mercer (1859) 9 ICLR 13. See GAMING.

**wages.** Any sums payable by an employer to his employee in connection with his employment, including — any fee, bonus or commission, or any holiday, sick or maternity pay: Payment of Wages Act 1991 s.1. Wages must be paid by one or more of specified modes eg cash, cheque, draft or other bill of exchange; a postal, money or paying order; a credit transfer to an account specified by the employee (ibid s.2).

Employees paid in cash before commencement of the 1991 Act (or who entered an agreement to be paid other than in cash under the Payment of Wages Act 1979) continue to be entitled to be paid in cash until another mode of payment is agreed with the employer (1991 Act s.3).

An employer must give each employee a written statement of wages and deductions (ibid s.4). Deductions must not be made unless required by statute, or authorised by the contract of employment, or authorised by the employee in writing (ibid s.5). See Payment of Wages (Appeals) Regulations 1991 (SI No 351 of 1991).

An employee is entitled to be paid his salary or wage during his absence in order to comply with a jury summons: Juries Act 1976 s.29. Employees may also be entitled to a mandatory injunction (qv) compelling their employer to pay their wages and salaries: Boyle & Ors v An Post (1992 HC) ELR 65. See Glasgow v Independent Printing (1901) 1 IR 278. See Barry in 10 ILT & SJ (1992) 78; Twomey in ISLR (1993) 131. See ATTACHMENT; CASH; EMOLUMENTS; MAINTENANCE ORDER; NOTICE, EMPLOYMENT.

**wages, minimum.** See JOINT LABOUR

COMMITTEE.

**waiver.** The relinquishing, renouncing, disclaiming, forebearance or abandonment of a claim to a right or benefit. A waiver may be express or implied. Waiver of a contractual right does not have to be evidenced in writing because, the right continues, although it may be unenforceable, unlike the case of a *variation* (qv) where the contractual right is extinguished.

Waiver may have the effect of affecting the range of remedies available to the party forebearing: Car & General Insurance Corporation v Munden (1936) IR 584. It is not an act of waiver to intimate that one may be prepared to waive some contractual right in certain circumstances: S.A. Fonderes Lion MV v International Factors (Ireland) Ltd (1984) ILRM 66. As regards waiver of constitutional rights, see Murphy v Stewart (1975) IR 97.

**wall.** See PARTY WALL.

**wandering abroad.** The offence contained in the Vagrancy Act 1824 (as applied in Ireland by the Prevention of Crimes Act 1871 s.15) which has been repealed: Housing Act 1988 s.28. See LRC 11 of 1985.

**want of prosecution.** See DISMISSAL FOR WANT OF PROSECUTION.

**war.** War must not be declared and the State must not participate in any war save with the assent of Dail Eireann: 1937 Constitution, art.28(3)(1). In the case of actual invasion, however, the government may take whatever steps they consider necessary for the protection of the State. See NATIONAL EMERGENCY; PRISONER OF WAR.

**war, time of.** See NATIONAL EMERGENCY.

**war crimes.** Offences created by the law governing the conduct of combatants during warfare. See Geneva Conventions Act 1962.

**ward.** A person under the care and protection of another; a person under the care of a guardian (qv) appointed by the court or a minor (qv) or person of unsound mind brought under the authority of the protection of the court.

**ward of court.** The protection by the court of persons, and their property, who are unable to look after themselves eg minors (qv): RSC O.65. A ward includes a person who has been declared to be of unsound mind and incapable of managing his person or property, and includes where the context so admits, a person in respect of whom or whose property an order has been made under the Lunacy Regulations (Ireland) Act 1871 ss.68 or 70: RSC O.67 r.1.

It has been held that the court has jurisdiction to take a minor into wardship when no property matter is involved, if to do so is in the minor's welfare: The State (Bruton) v Judge of Circuit Court and Bruton (1984) HC. The jurisdiction of the High Court to take persons of unsound mind into wardship whether they have property or not *is and must always remain a discretionary jurisdiction*: In re Midland Health Board (1988) ILRM 251.

When a person is made a ward of court, all matters affecting the ward's welfare become the responsibility of the court; failure to comply with an order of the court constitutes a contempt (qv) and may result in imprisonment of the person in contempt: In re McLorinan, a Minor (1935) IR 373.

The most usual circumstance in which a minor is made a ward of court is where it is thought desirable to obtain independent protection of the minor's property interests. See in the Matter of JS, an Infant (1977) 111 ILTR 146; Guardianship of Infants Act 1964 s.11(1). A minor may be made a ward of court by proceedings commenced by originating summons: RSC O.65, appendix K, form no 19. For general guideline on procedure, see Costello in ILSI Gazette (May 1993) 143. See LEGAL AID.

**warehouse.** It has been held that if a person through his negligence injures property in a warehouse, he must take responsibility for damaging whatever goods are there; because a warehouse is part of the world of commerce, it is foreseeable that there will be economic loss and possible loss of profits: Egan v Sisk (1986) ILRM 283.

**warning.** In relation to the administration of estates, a direction to a *caveator* to enter an appearance setting forth his interest and that in default of so doing, the caveat will cease to have effect: RSC O.79 rr.47-51; O.80 rr.48-55. See CAUTION; CAVEAT; CORROBORATION; INCRIMINATE.

**warning, employment.** It has been held

in a particular case that a written warning by an employer to an employee that failure to follow a set procedure would lead to dismissal is necessary to justify a dismissal of the employee: Carroll v Foxrock Inn (1990) ELR 236.

**warning notice.** The notice which a planning authority (qv) has power to serve where it appears to them that land is being or is likely to be developed without permission or any unauthorised use is being or is likely to be made of land: LG(P&D) Act 1976 s.26 as amended by LG (P&D) Act 1992 s.19(4). The warning notice may be served on the owner of the land and may also be given to any other person who, in their opinion, may be concerned with the matter to which the notice relates. The notice may require that the development or use be discontinued or not be commenced. It is an offence for a person knowingly to fail to comply with such a notice or to assist or permit the carrying out of a development or unauthorised use affected by it. See Dublin Co Council v Taylor (1989) 7 ILT Dig 150. See INJUNCTION, PLANNING.

**warrant.** (1) A document authorising some action eg a dividend warrant authorising the payment of money.

(2) An order in writing authorising the arrest of a specified person; arrest warrants are issued pursuant to the District Court Rules. A garda properly executing a warrant is protected against any irregularity or want of jurisdiction which may have occurred in the issue of the warrant: Constabulary (Ireland) Act 1836 s.50; Public Officers Protection (Ireland) Act 1803 s.6. See also Criminal Justice Act 1984 s.13(4) and (5). See McGirl v McArdle (1989) ILRM 495. See COMMITTAL WARRANT; DISTRESS; EXTRA-DITION; IDENTIFICATION; PENAL WARRANT; SEARCH WARRANT; WARRANT, ARREST WITH-OUT.

**warrant, search.** See SEARCH WARRANT.

**warrant, share.** See SHARE CERTIFICATE.

**warrantor.** A person who gives a warranty (qv).

**warranty.** (1) A term in a contract which gives rise to a right to recover damages in the event that it is breached but which does not entitle the injured party to repudiate the contract. (2) An agreement with reference to goods which are

the subject of a contract of sale, but collateral to the main purpose of such contract, the breach of which gives rise to a claim for damages, but not a right to reject the goods and treat the contract as repudiated: Sale of Goods Act 1893 s.62. See CONDITION; GUARANTEE; SERVICE, SUPPLY OF; SPARE PARTS; WARRANTY, BREACH OF.

**warranty, breach of.** Where there is a breach of warranty by a seller of goods, the buyer is not entitled to reject the goods, but he may maintain an action for damages for the breach, or set up the breach in diminution or extinction of the price. The measure of damages for breach of warranty is the estimated loss directly and naturally resulting, in the ordinary course of events, from the breach.

As regards quality, such loss is prima facie the difference between the value of the goods at delivery to the buyer and the value they would have had if they had answered the warranty on quality. The fact that the buyer has set up the breach in diminution or extinction of the price or that the seller has replaced goods or remedied a breach, does not of itself prevent the buyer from maintaining an action for the same breach if he has suffered further damage. A breach of warranty can amount to a total failure of consideration: Yeoman Credit Ltd v Apps (1962) QB 508.

See McAuley v Horgan (1925) IR 1; Egan v McSweeney (1956) 90 ILTR 40. See Sale of Goods Act 1893 s.53; SGSS Act 1980 s.21. See CONDITION.

**warranty of authority, breach of.** A person who professes to act as an agent, where in fact he has no authority from the alleged principal or has exceeded his authority, is liable to an action for a *breach of warranty of authority* at the suit of the party with whom he professed to contract. The action is based, not on the original contract, but on an implied promise by the agent that he had authority to make the original contract.

The action can be brought only by the third party and not by the principal. The agent is liable whether he acted fraudulently or innocently and even if his authority has been terminated without his knowledge, by the death, lunacy or bankruptcy of the principal: Yonge v

Townbee (1910) 1 KB 215. However, the agent is not liable if his lack of authority was known to the third party or if the contract excludes his liability. See also DECEIT; ULTRA VIRES.

**waste.** Acts or omissions of a tenant which does lasting damage to property or which alters the nature of the property. Waste may be voluntary, permissive, equitable or ameliorating. *Voluntary* waste is the doing of positive acts which makes the property less valuable to the person entitled after the life tenant eg opening mines or cutting the timber more than 20 years old; it is forbidden unless the life estate is made *without impeachment of waste*: Templemore v Moore (1862) 15 ICLR 14.

*Permissive* waste is omiting to do what ought to be done eg allowing buildings to go into disrepair; the life tenant is only liable if the grantor expressly put a duty to repair on him. *Equitable* waste is the doing of wanton acts by a life tenant who makes unconscionable use of his right to commit voluntary waste. *Ameliorating* waste is the doing of acts which though nominally waste are really for the benefit of the property: Craig v Greer (1899) 1 IR 258.

The remedy for waste is by way of an injunction (qv) and damages (qv). See DEVASTAVIT; LIFE TENANT.

**waste, toxic and dangerous.** See DISPOSAL; INCINERATION; LANDFILL SITE; TOXIC AND DANGEROUS WASTE.

**waste disposal.** See SKIP; WASTE OPERATION.

**waste management plan.** A waste plan prepared under the EC (Waste) Regulations 1979 art.4(2), or a special plan within the meaning assigned to it under the EC (Toxic and Dangerous Waste) Regulations 1982: Environmental Protection Agency Act 1992 s.3(1). A local authority is required to prepare a *waste management plan* indicating the type and quantity of waste for disposal, general technical requirements, suitable disposal sites and any special arrangements for particular wastes (ibid 1979 Regulations art.4(2)). A local authority is also required to prepare a *special waste plan* for the disposal of toxic and dangerous waste (ibid 1982 Regulations art.4(1)). See TOXIC AND DANGEROUS WASTE.

**waste oils.** Any mineral-based lubrication or industrial oils which have become unfit for the use for which they were originally intended: European Community (Waste Oil) Regulations 1992 (SI No 399 of 1992) reg.2(1). Local authorities are responsible for the planning, organisation and supervision of waste oil collection and disposal operations (ibid reg.3(1)). A local authority may grant a *permit* to a person to carry on the business of collecting or disposal of waste oil in its area (ibid reg.4(1)).

**waste operation.** The collection, sorting, transport and treatment of waste as well as its storage and tipping above and underground and the transformation operations necessary for its re-use, recovery or recycling: European Communities (Waste) Regulations 1979 (SI No 390 of 1979). Local authorities are responsible for the planning, organisation and supervision of *waste operations* in their area, excluding certain types of waste eg radioactive waste (ibid art.8).

A person other than a *public waste collector* (qv) may not carry out the treatment, storing or tipping of waste on behalf of another person without an appropriate *permit* issued by the local authority (ibid art.4). If a holder of waste does not himself dispose of the waste, he must not permit disposal by any person, other than a public waste collector or the holder of a permit. Persons collecting and transporting waste on behalf of others do not require a permit, but they are subject to the supervisory powers of the local authority. [Text: Cabot & Haigh]. See DISPOSAL; DUMPING AT SEA; ENVIRONMENT ASSESSMENT DIRECTIVE; TOXIC AND DANGEROUS WASTE; LITTER; HOUSEHOLD REFUSE; TRADE REFUSE.

**watching and besetting.** It is a criminal offence for a person, wrongfully and without legal authority, to watch and beset the house or other place where another person resides, or works, or carries on business or happens to be, or the approach to such house or place, with a view to compel such other person to abstain from doing or to do any act which such other person has a legal right to do or abstain from doing: Conspiracy and Protection of Property Act 1875 s.7. It is a *scheduled* offence under s.36 of the Offences against the State Act 1939: SI No 282 of 1972. See Barton v Harten (1925) 2 IR 37. See PICKETING; SIT-IN.

**water, right to.** A right exists to a supply of water for domestic purposes: Waterworks Clauses Act 1847 s.53. This right does not apply in relation to a dwelling house which contravenes planning law: LG (P&D) Act 1990 s.26. A sanitary authority is empowered to serve notice requiring connection to a public water supply system: LG (Sanitary Services) Act 1962 s.8(2). See DRINKING WATER; RIPARIAN; WATER SUPPLY.

**water charges.** A sanitary authority is empowered to make charges for water supplied by it; the power became a *reserved function* (qv) exercisable by elected members from 1 Jan 1985: SI No 341 of 1985; Public Health (Ireland) Act 1878 s.65A inserted by LG Financial Provisions (No 2) Act 1983. Disconnection can be made by the sanitary authority where the water charges remain unpaid after the expiration of two months from the due date. See O'Donnell v Corp of Dun Laoghaire (1991) ILRM 301. See INCONVENIENCE.

**water, drinking.** See DRINKING WATER.

**water pollution.** It is an offence for a person to cause or permit any *polluting matter* (qv) to enter waters: Local Government (Water Pollution) Act 1977 s.3(1). It is also an offence for a person to discharge or cause or permit the discharge of any *trade effluent* (qv) or *sewage effluent* (qv) to any waters except under and in accordance with a licence (ibid s.4(1) and SI No 16 of 1978).

Any person may apply to the appropriate court for an order directing the party responsible to mitigate or remedy any effects of such contraventions within such period and in such manner as may be specified in the order (ibid s.10 as substituted by the LG (Water Pollution) (Amendment) Act 1990 s.7). An appeal in relation to the granting or refusal of a licence lies to An Bord Pleanala (qv) (ibid 1977 Act s.21 as substituted by the 1990 Act s.16). More extensive powers are given to local authorities to prevent and abate pollution: 1990 Act s.10. See Ballybay Meat Exports Ltd v Monaghan Co Co (1990) ILRM 864; Clarke v Brady (1991 HC) 9ILT Dig 226. See also 1990 Act s.6 and SI No 96 of 1978. See Courts Act 1991 s.10. See RSC O.108.

**water supply.** Sanitary authorities are under a statutory duty to supply their districts with a supply of suitable water, proper and sufficient for public and private purposes: Public Health (Ireland) Act 1878 ss.61 and 65; Housing of the Working Classes Act 1885 s.7. Machinery exists to compel a sanitary authority to comply with this duty: Public Health (Ireland) Act 1896 s.15. A sanitary authority can require the owner of premises to connect the premises to the public water supply: Local Government (Sanitary Services) Act 1962 s.8. As regards water charges, see Athlone UDC v Gavin (1986) ILRM 277 and WATER CHARGES. See WAYLEAVE.

**watercourse.** A watercourse, even an artificial one, may be acquired as an easement (qv). See Hanna v Pollock (1900) 2 IR 644; Kelly v Dea (1966) 100 ILTR 1. See RIPARIAN.

**way, right of.** The right to pass over the lands of another. A right of way is either *public* or *private*. A public right of way is a highway (qv). A private right of way may arise by way of easement (qv) or by necessity eg the right of way presumed to be given by the grantor of land to a *close* surrounded by the grantor's lands. A private right of way may be lost by abandonment: O'Gara v Murray (1989) 7ILT Dig 82.

If it is proposed in the draft *development plan* (qv) of a planning authority, to preserve a public right of way, notice must be given to the owner and occupier of the land over which the right of way exists; any person may appeal to the Circuit Court against such a proposal: LG(P&D) Act 1963 s.21(3).

A public right of way over land may be created compulsorily by a local authority: LG (P&D) Act 1963 s.48. Compensation may be payable to the person with an interest in the land: LG (P&D) Act 1990 s.22.

It is the function of a local authority to protect the right of the public to use public rights of way in its administrative area: Roads Act 1993 s.73(11). A road authority is empowered to extinguish a public right of way over a public road by following a specified procedure; Ministerial approval is required where the order relates to a national or regional road (ibid s.73). In cases other than public roads, the planning authority is similarly empowered (ibid s.73(13)). Where the authority extinguishes the right of way to facilitate the development of land, reasonable costs can be recovered from the developer (ibid s.73(12)). See EASEMENT; PUBLIC ROAD; ZEBRA CROSSING.

**wayleave.** A right of way over or through land (eg for the carriage of goods, to carry gas in pipes; to carry wires on pylons, etc), created by express grant, by reservation (qv) or by statute. A sanitary authority is empowered to carry any sewer (qv) into, through, or under any lands whatsoever within their district after giving reasonable notice to the owner or occupier: Public Health (Ireland) Act 1878 s.18. Similar power is given in respect of the laying of pipes for the supply of water (ibid s.64). Compensation is payable for any damage sustained by the exercise of this power (ibid s.274).

**weapon, offensive.** See OFFENSIVE WEAPON.

**wedding presents.** See ENGAGED COUPLE.

**week.** When used without qualification, a week means the period between midnight on any Saturday and midnight on the next following Saturday: Interpretation Act 1937 s.12 sch. See MIDNIGHT; TIME.

**week-day.** A day which is not a Sunday: Interpretation Act 1937 s.12 sch.

**weighing facility.** The weighing scales or weighing machine which is required to be provided in a prominent position by any person who offers food for sale by retail by weight. See Consumer Information Act 1978 s.14.

**weight, short.** See SHORT WEIGHT.

**weights, maximum.** The statutory maximum weights which may be lifted or carried by employed persons eg not more than 55 kilograms in the case of adult males, 16 kilograms in the case of males between 16 and 18 years of age and adult females, 11 kilogrammes in the case of females between 16 and 18 years of age, and 8 kilogrammes in the case of 14 to 16 year olds. It is an offence to employ a person to lift, carry or move any load so heavy as to be likely to cause injury to him.

Persons employed in any *process* which is composed of the manual transport of loads must be given training on methods of lifting, carrying, putting down, loading and stacking different types of loads: Factories Act 1955 (Manual Labour) (Maximum Weights and Transport) Regulations 1972) (SI No 283 of 1972); Dunleavy v Glen Abbey Ltd (1990) ELR 121. It is understood that the Minister intends to repeal these 1972 Regulations following the more general but comprehensive 1993 Regulations (SI No 44 of 1993) — see MANUAL HANDLING OF LOADS. See also PROCESS.

**welfare.** In relation to a minor, comprises the religious and moral, intellectual, physical and social welfare of the minor: Status of Children Act 1987 s.9. See CHILD, CUSTODY OF; GUARDIAN; SAFETY AT WORK.

**welfare of children.** It is the function of health boards to promote the *welfare of children* up to 18 years of age who are not receiving adequate care and protection and to provide child care and family support services: Child Care Act 1991 s.3.

It is the duty of a health board to take into its care any child in its area who requires care or protection provided this is not against the wishes of a parent having custody *(voluntary care)* and where the child appears to be lost or deserted or abandoned, to endeavour to reunite him with his parent (ibid s.4). A health board may also take a child into care with a view to his adoption (ibid s.6). Child care advisory committees must be established and the health board must have regard to their advice (ibid s.7). A health board also has power to take a child into care against the wishes of his parents — see CARE ORDER. See also AFTERCARE; CHILD, EMERGENCY CARE OF; JUDICIAL SEPARATION; LEGAL AID.

**well charging order.** See MORTGAGE SUIT.

**welsh mortgage.** A mortgage whereby the mortgagor (qv) is under no obligation to repay the principal and whereby the mortgagee (qv) takes possession of the land and takes the rents and profits in lieu of interest or until payment of interest and principal; the mortgagee has no right to call in the principal whereas the mortgagor is entitled to redeem at any time on its payment. See Cassidy v Cassidy (1889) 24 LR Ir 577. See Statute of Limitations 1957 s.34.

**wet time.** Generally means hours of intermittent employment in respect of which supplementary benefit is payable under s.28 of the Insurance (Intermittent

Employment) Act 1942. See ANNUAL LEAVE.

**whipping.** The infliction of corporal punishment as a punishment is obsolete in practice; however it is still authorised in some statutes eg Offences Against the Persons Act 1861 s.21. The European Court of Human Rights (qv) has ruled that whipping of a 15 year old boy with birch twigs, ordered by an Isle of Man court, constituted degradating punishment under the European Convention on Human Rights (qv); it did not amount to torture or inhuman punishment: Tyrer v UK – Judgment of the Court – Series A, No 26. See CORPORAL PUNISHMENT; PUNISHMENT.

**whiskey, Irish.** Spirits which have been distilled in the State or Northern Ireland from a mash of cereals which has been saccharified by the diastase of malt contained therein, with or without other natural diastases, fermented by the action of yeast, and distilled at an alcoholic strength of less than 94.8% by volume, in such a way that the distillate has an aroma and flavour derived from the materials used, and the spirits have been matured in wooden casks in a warehouse in the State or in Northern Ireland for not less than three years: Irish Whiskey Act 1980. Irish whiskey is not to be regarded as corresponding to that description unless it complies with this definition. See Scotch Whisky Association v Cooley Distillery plc (1991 HC). See DESCRIPTION, SALE BY.

**white knight.** Popularly understood to mean a corporate hero of sorts which comes to the rescue of a company besieged by a take-over bid which it regards as unfriendly; the white knight makes an alternative take-over bid for the shares of the company at a price sufficient to stave off the unfriendly take-over. The white knight is initially regarded as friendly; whether this remains the case after the take-over battle is another matter. See MERGER.

**whole blood.** See BLOOD RELATIONSHIP.

**widow.** The words "widow, widower, married woman, married man, spinster or bachelor" indicate marital status and where a person holds an occupation, these words are not a title trade or profession as required by the Judgment Mortgage Act 1850; that Act requires that the title trade or profession of the plaintiff and the defendant be inserted in the affidavit registering a mortgage: AIB v Griffin (1992 HC) ILRM 590. See JUDGMENT MORTGAGE.

**widower.** A man who has lost his wife by death and has not married again. Restrictions are placed on the adoption of children by a widower which do not apply to a widow: Adoption Act 1974 s.5. However, a widower may now complete the adoption process and have an adoption order made in his favour, if he and his wife had applied for an adoption order but she had died before the adoption order had been made: T O'G v Attorney General (1985) ILRM 61. See also PROHIBITED DEGREES; WIDOW.

**wife.** See FAMILY HOME; HUSBAND AND WIFE; MATRIMONIAL PROPERTY; SPOUSE, LEGAL RIGHT OF.

**wig and gown.** See DRESS IN COURT.

**wild animal.** See ANIMALS.

**wild animals, protected.** Animals which are statutorily protected and listed: Wildlife Act 1976, fifth schedule. Hares and deer are listed as game which may be hunted with firearms during open season (qv).

**wild birds, protected.** All wild birds are statutorily protected, including game (qv), except species which are commonly regarded as pests and are listed: Wildlife Act 1976, third schedule. See SI No 254 of 1986.

**wildlife dealing.** It is an offence for a person to carry on *business as a wildlife dealer* except under and in accordance with a wildlife dealer's licence: Wildlife Act 1976 s.47. Wildlife dealing means buying for resale any protected wild birds or protected wild animals and includes engaging in taxidermy in respect of such birds or animals (ibid s.2(3)). Records must be kept in a form prescribed by the Minister: Wildlife Act 1976 (Wildlife Dealing) Regulations 1977 (SI No 253 of 1977).

It is an offence for a person who is the owner, manager or person otherwise in charge of any hotel, guest house, inn, restaurant, public eating house, registered club, or any other premises in which meals are provided for reward to purchase a protected wild bird (qv) or protected wild animal (qv) from anybody except a licensed wildlife dealer (ibid

1976 Act s.45(4)).

**wilful neglect.** The common law misdemeanour (qv) to refuse or neglect to provide sufficient food or other necessaries to life to any person, such as a child, apprentice, servant or aged or sick person unable to provide or take care of himself, or for the provision of which there is an obligation by duty or contract. See Offences Against the Person Act 1861 s.26; Conspiracy and Protection of Property Act 1875 s.6. See PLEADINGS.

**will.** A disposition by which the person making it (the *testator/testatrix*) provides for the distribution or administration of property after his/her death. A will is *ambulatory* in that it remains revocable until death.

Formerly the law did not allow land to be devised. However, the Wills Act 1837 allowed all land to be disposed of by a written will witnessed by two credible witnesses. This Act was repealed by the Succession Act 1965. Under the 1965 Act, which amended and consolidated the law of succession, *realty* and *personalty* devolve in the same way under new rules as to intestate succession (qv). Primogeniture and cannons of descent were abolished except in so far as they apply to the descent of an *estate tail*. The Act also made new provision (a) to give the surviving spouse a legal right (qv) to a share of the estate and (b) to allow the children of a testator to apply to the court to have just provision made for them out of the estate.

A valid will can be made by a person who has attained 18 years or has been married and is of sound disposing mind (ibid s.77). The will must be in writing; there is no longer any provision for privileged wills (qv). No particular form of words are required so long as the testator's intention can be ascertained. Extrinsic evidence (qv) is admissible to show the intention of the testator and to assist in the construction of or to explain any contradiction in a will (ibid s.90). A will is construed to speak and take effect as if it had been executed immediately before the testator's death, unless a contrary intention appears (ibid s.89). See In re Mitten (1934) 68 ILTR 38; In re Farrell (1954) 88 ILTR 57; In b Corboy (1969) IR 148.

A will must be signed at the foot or end thereof by the testator or by some person in his presence and by his direction and the signature must be made or acknowledged by the testator in the presence of at least two witnesses present at the same time and each witness must attest by his signature the signature of the testator in the presence of the testator (ibid s.78). No form of attestation (qv) is necessary and witnesses do not have to sign in each others presence. They do not need to know that they are witnessing a will; they only need to know that they are witnessing a signature. See In re Dowling (1933) IR 150; In re Kiernan (1933) IR 222; Clarke v Early (1980) IR 223.

A devise or bequest to an attesting witness or to the spouse of a witness is void but does not affect the validity of the will (ibid s.82). An executor may be a witness but then cannot benefit under the will. [Text: McGuire, Maxwell, Mongey, Theobald UK]. See ADMINISTRATION OF ESTATES; CONSTRUCTION SUIT; GIFT; LEGACY; LUCID INTERVAL; OFFENSIVE WORDS; PINHOLES; PROBATE; SUBPOENA; SUCCEED, UNWORTHINESS TO; SUCCESSION, LAW OF; TESTAMENTARY CAPACITY; WORDS OF LIMITATION.

**will, international.** A will made in accordance with the Hague Convention on the Conflict of Laws relating to the form of Testamentary Dispositions 1961. Such a disposition will be valid as regards form if it complies with the internal law (a) of the place where it was made, or (b) of the place of the testator's domicile or nationality or habitual residence or (c) insofar as immovable property is concerned, of the place where the property is situated: Succession Act 1965 s.102. See LEX SITUS.

**will, limited.** A will which deals with the estate of a testator in this country when another will exists which deals with his estate abroad. Only the will specifically limited to property in this State will be admitted to proof although all other wills must be produced to the Probate Officer.

**will, proof of.** A will is proved in *solemn form* when it is declared valid following court proceedings; it is proved in *common form* when it is admitted to proof in the Probate Office or District Probate Registry without litigation. Where a will is in any language other than Irish or English, it may be admitted to proof by the probate officer in terms of a translation in Irish or English: RSC O.79 r.5(10); O.80 r.6(9). See In re Corboy (1969) IR 148.

**will, revocation of.** A will may be revoked by: (a) another will or codicil duly executed; or (b) by some writing executed like a will declaring an intention to revoke the will; or (c) tearing or destruction by the testator or by someone in his presence and by his direction, with intent to revoke; or (d) by subsequent marriage of the testator, except a will made in contemplation of that marriage.

Revocation may be conditional in which case the will remains unrevoked until the condition is fulfilled. Also deletions made after execution of a will, initialled by a testatrix but not signed by witnesses in the manner required, do not effect revocation of a will or any part thereof: In the matter of the Estate of Margaret Ismay Myles, deceased (1993 HC) ILRM 34. See also In the Goods of Keenan (1946) 80 ILTR; In re Millar (1931) IR 364; In re Bentley (1930) IR 455; In re Fleming, deceased (1987) ILRM 638. Succession Act 1965 s.85. See ALTERATION; DEPENDENT RELATIVE REVOCATION.

**winding up.** The process whereby the end is put to the carrying on of the business of a company or partnership. The assets are collected and realised, the resulting proceeds are applied in discharge of all its debts and liabilities, and any balance (surplus) which remains after paying the costs and expenses of winding up is distributed among the members according to their rights and interests, or otherwise dealt with as the constitution of the company or partnership directs. Also called *liquidation*. A liquidator is appointed by the members or by the creditors or by the court to carry out the winding up.

The winding up of a partnership is either voluntary (ie by agreement between the partners) or by order of a court made in an action for the dissolution of the partnership.

Companies are wound up in three different ways (a) compulsory winding up by the court, (b) voluntary winding up by the members, or (c) voluntary

winding up by the creditors: Companies Act 1963 Part IV ss.206-313 as amended. Certain provisions of the Companies Acts also apply to insolvent companies which go out of business without formally going into liquidation: Companies Act 1990 s.251. Also a building society may, subject to certain modifications, be wound up under the Companies Acts as if the society were a company: Building Societies Act 1989 s.109. [Text: Forde (9)]. See LIQUIDATOR; PREFERENTIAL PAYMENTS; MALICIOUS PROSECUTION; ONEROUS PROPERTY; PHOENIX COMPANY.

**winding up, compulsory.** A compulsory winding up by the court may be imposed on a company at the instigation of any member, or contributory (qv), or creditor, or the Minister in particular circumstances. The court appoints the liquidator (known as the *official liquidator*) and determines his remuneration. The liquidator is an officer of the court and works under its supervision.

The grounds under which the court may order a company to be wound up are set out in s.213 of the Companies Act 1963. These include where the company has passed a special resolution for compulsory liquidation; or the company does not commence its business within a year of its incorporation, or suspends its business for a whole year; or the number of members is reduced below the minimum allowable; or the company is unable to pay its debts; or the court is of the opinion that it is just and equitable that the company should be wound up; or the court is satisfied that the affairs of the company are being conducted, or the powers of the directors are being exercised, in a manner oppressive to any member of the company.

The most frequent ground on which orders for a winding up are sought is that the company is unable to pay its debts (ibid s.213(e)). A company is deemed to be unable to pay its debts if either (a) a creditor proves that the company owes that creditor more than £1,000, that the demand for payment was made in writing and that the company has for three weeks failed to comply or (b) a judgment creditor of the company has levied execution and has remained unsatisfied: Companies Act 1963 ss.214 and 345 as amended by the

Companies Act 1990 s.123.

The procedure governing compulsory winding up is contained in the Companies Act 1963 ss.216-250; it involves the presentation of a petition to the High Court for a *winding up order*: RSC O.74 rr 7-23. The winding up dates from the presentation of the petition and not from the date of the winding up order: 1963 Act s.220(2). Any disposition of property made after commencement of the winding up is void, unless the court otherwise orders: 1963 Act s.218 and In re Ashmark Ltd (1990 HC) ILRM 330. A liquidator is prohibited from selling non-cash assets of a requisite value to an officer or former officer of the company unless he gives notice to the creditors of the company: 1990 Act s.124 amending the 1963 Act s.231.

The court will look at the justification presented in the petition to wind up a company in receivership; it may amount to an abuse of court: In re Bula Ltd (in receivership) (1988) SC. For winding up rules for companies, see SI No 28 of 1966.

A company which is under the protection of the court, can be wound up by order of the court, following receipt of the *examiner's* report: Companies (Amendment) Act 1990 s.17. The winding up is deemed to have commenced on the date of the making of the order (ibid s.17(6)). See COURT PROTECTION OF COMPANY. See also COSTS IN CIVIL PROCEEDINGS; LIQUIDATOR; PETITION FOR WINDING UP; STATEMENT OF AFFAIRS; STAY OF PROCEEDINGS.

**winding up, voluntary.** A voluntary winding up *by members* is accomplished by special resolution of the company to wind itself up and by preparation by the directors of a *declaration of solvency* ie a statutory declaration that they are of the opinion that the company will be able to pay its debts in full within a period not exceeding 12 months from when the winding up commences: Companies Act 1963 s.256 as amended by Companies Act 1990 s.128. A liquidator may be appointed by the shareholders who may fix his remuneration (ibid 1963 Act s.258(1)). A voluntary winding up dates from the passing of the special resolution (ibid s.220(1)).

A voluntary winding up *by creditors* is accomplished at a publicly advertised meeting of creditors, following the members' meeting at which the proposal to wind up the company has been put (ibid 1963 Act s.266 as amended by 1990 Act s.130). While the creditors may accept the liquidator nominated by the shareholders, they may appoint their own nominee to the office (ibid 1963 Act s.267). However, before the resolution is put, the fact that any creditor has a connection with the proposed liquidator must be disclosed to the meeting (ibid 1990 Act s.147 inserting new s.301A in 1963 Act). The Court may also, on application, appoint some other person as liquidator.

The creditors can appoint a *committee of inspection* whose function is to determine the liquidator's remuneration and monitor the winding up (ibid 1963 Act ss.268-269).

Where the liquidator forms the opinion that the company will not be able to pay its debts, the creditors may substitute their own liquidator and the winding up becomes a creditors' winding up (ibid 1963 Act s.261 as substituted by 1990 Act s.129). Also a failure to make a statutory declaration of solvency strictly in compliance with s.256 results in the ensuing liquidation being a creditors' winding up; the court cannot cure a defective declaration: In re Favon Investments Co Ltd (in liquidation) (1992 HC) ITLR (21 Dec). See CREDITORS' MEETING; LIQUIDATOR; SOLVENCY, DECLARATION OF.

**winding up by trustee.** A bankrupt's estate may be wound up by a trustee and *committee of inspection* as an alternative to its being administered by the Official Assignee (qv): Bankruptcy Act 1988 ss.110-114. The trustee and committee are appointed by the creditors following a resolution by them that the bankruptcy be wound up in that way. The trustee, who is subject to the control of the court, will in general have the same power and functions as are conferred on the Official Assignee (qv). See BANKRUPTCY.

**winter time.** The period during which for general purposes in the State the time is Greenwich meantime: Standard Time (Amendment) Act 1971. The period begins at two o'clock GMT in the morning of the Sunday following the fourth Saturday in October and ending either at two o'clock GMT in the morning of the Sunday following the third Saturday in the month of March in the following year or, if the last-mentioned Sunday is Easter Day, at two o'clock GMT in the morning of the Sunday following the second Saturday in the month of March in that year (ibid s.1(1)(c)). The Minister may vary by order the period of winter time (ibid s.2). See SI 371 of 1992. See SUMMER TIME.

**WIPO.** [World Intellectual Property Organisation (qv)].

**withdrawal from jury.** The procedure by which a judge withdraws an issue or a case from the jury eg when he decides that the plaintiff or the prosecution has failed to discharge the appropriate onus of proof. See Hynes-O'Sullivan v O'Driscoll (1989 SC) ILRM 619. See DIRECTION.

**withholding information.** It is an offence to withhold information concerning firearms and stolen goods: Criminal Justice Act 1984 s.15-16.

**withholding of supplies.** The withholding of grocery goods from a person by a supplier or wholesaler is prohibited in specified circumstances eg on the grounds that a person is or is not a member of a trade association: Restrictive Practices (Groceries) Order 1987 (SI No 142 of 1987).

**withholding tax.** A tax which must be deducted at source by *accountable persons* from payments for professional services: Finance Act 1987 s.15. Accountable persons include government departments, local authorities, health boards, and state-sponsored bodies (ibid s.14). *Professional services* include medical, dental, pharmaceutical, optical, aural, veterinary, architectural, engineering, quantity surveying, surveying, accountancy, finance, economic, marketing, legal, geological, and training services of An Foras Aiseanna Saothair (ibid s.13(1); Finance Act 1988 s.8(a)(ii)). *Professional services* do not include the work of a film or video maker: Iskra Productions Ltd v An Foras Aiseanna Saothair (1992 CC) — Irish Times 22nd October 1992. The tax has been extended to include payments made by health insurers in respect of fees for services provided by

practitioners to in-patients of hospitals in the State: Finance Act 1988 s.8. See CONTRACTORS, PAYMENT TO.

**without prejudice.** Where communications, written or oral, made by a party to a civil action, are stated to be *without prejudice*, they cannot be given in evidence against the party making them. A letter headed *without prejudice* protects from disclosure the whole of the correspondence of which it forms part. However, such correspondence may be produced in evidence where (a) the parties consent, or (b) the letter cloaks an illegality eg a threat, or (c) an offer to settle is accepted and the letters are proved to show the terms of the settlement.

**without recourse to me.** See SANS RECOURS.

**without reserve.** The phrase used in an auction (qv) where there is no reserve price.

**witness.** (1) To attest by signature. (2) A person who gives evidence, usually on oath (qv). The death of an alibi witness before a criminal trial takes place may unfairly prejudice an accused: People (DPP) v Quilligan & O'Reilly (No 3) (1993 SC) 11 ILT Dig 88. See ATTEST; PROFESSIONAL WITNESS; STANDBY FEE; UNFAIR DISMISSAL; VIVA VOCE.

**witness, competence of.** In general, all persons are *competent* to give evidence and may be *compelled* to attend to give evidence by subpoena (qv). Exceptions include any person who is prevented by disease of mind or by extreme youth or other cause from understanding the questions put to him. A spouse of a party to a civil action is competent to give evidence but is not compellable to disclose communications made one to the other during marriage.

In criminal proceedings, the spouse (or former spouse) of an accused is *competent* to give evidence at the instance of (a) the accused or any person charged with him, and (b) the prosecution except where the accused and spouse are charged in the same proceedings: Criminal Evidence Act 1992 ss.21 and 25. A spouse (or former spouse) of an accused is *compellable* to give evidence at the instance of the accused (ibid s.23). Also a spouse of an accused is *compellable* to give evidence at the instance of the prosecution where the offence (a) involves violence to the spouse, a child of either spouse, or any person under 17 or (b) is a sexual offence against a child of either spouse or of any person under 17 (ibid s.22). None of these provisions however affect any right of a spouse or former spouse in respect of marital privacy (qv) (ibid s.26). See DPP v T (1988) CCA — see O'Connor in 7ILT & SJ (1989) 95. See INCEST.

An accomplice is not a competent witness for the prosecution if he is jointly indicted and jointly tried. See Attorney General v O'Sullivan (1930) 552. See Criminal Justice (Evidence) Act 1924 ss.1 and 4 as amended by 1992 Act; Social Welfare Act 1952 s.59 as repealed and re-enacted by the Social Welfare (Consolidation) Act 1981 s.121; Married Women's Status Act 1957 s.2. See LRC 13 of 1985. See INCRIMINATE; PRIVILEGE, MATRIMONIAL COMMUNICATIONS.

**witness, credibility of.** See CREDIBILITY.

**witness, hostile.** See HOSTILE WITNESS.

**witness, recall of.** A witness may be recalled in a criminal trial at the discretion of the judge, on request of the jury: The People v O'Brien (1963) IR 65.

**witness summons.** See SUBPOENA.

**witnessing part.** See TESTATUM.

**woodcock.** See GAME.

**woodcut.** See ARTISTIC WORK.

**word, invented.** See INVENTED WORD; CHARACTER OR QUALITY OF GOODS.

**words, meaning of.** See DEFINITION ORDER; DICTIONARY, USE OF; LEGISLATION, INTERPRETATION OF; LITERAL RULE; STATUTORY INTERPRETATION; VERBA CHARTARUM.

**words, operative.** See OPERATIVE WORDS.

**words, precatory.** See PRECATORY TRUST.

**words of limitation.** The words in a conveyance (qv) or a will (qv) which have the effect of marking out the duration of the estate eg in a grant *to A and his heirs*, the words *and his heirs* are words of limitation and confer no estate on his heirs (Shelley's Case 1581) but create a *fee simple* in A. A fee simple may also be created by the words *to A in fee simple*: Conveyancing Act 1881 s.51.

A *fee tail* (qv) may be created by the words *to A and the heirs of his body* and a *life estate* (qv) by *to A for life* or by the use of expressions insufficient to create a fee simple or fee tail eg *to A* or *to A for ever*.

A devise of real estate in a will without words of limitation, is to be construed as passing the whole estate which the testator had power to dispose of, unless a contrary intention appears from the will: Succession Act 1965 s.94. See In re McIntyre, Crawford v Ruttledge (1970) HC. See WORDS OF PURCHASE; REMOTENESS; SHELLEY'S CASE, RULE IN.

**words of purchase.** The words in a conveyance (qv) or a will (qv) which denote the person who is to take an estate or interest in land eg in a grant *to A and his heirs*, the words *to A* are words of purchase and *and his heirs* are words of limitation. The words *heirs* when used as words of purchase are to be construed to mean those entitled under Part VI of the Succession Act 1965 (ibid s.15). See WORDS OF LIMITATION.

**words of severence.** See SEVERENCE, WORDS OF.

**work .** See ARTISTIC WORK; DRAMATIC WORK; LIKE WORK; MUSICAL WORK; LITERARY WORK.

**work activity.** A work activity may be prescribed by the Minister, for the purpose of protecting the safety, health or welfare of persons at work, which may then not be carried on except in accordance with the terms and conditions of a licence: Safety, Health and Welfare at Work Act 1989 s.59.

**work equipment.** Any machine, apparatus, tool or installation used at work: Safety Health and Welfare at Work (General Application) Regulations 1993 (SI No 44 of 1993) reg.2(1). Every employer has a duty to ensure that work equipment is suitable for the work to be carried out (ibid reg.19).

**work experience.** See SAFETY AT WORK.

**work in EC.** Each member state is required to provide a service for those seeking work in another member state: Treaty of Rome 1957 art. 49. A network of offices has been established throughout the EC; the offices in this State are the FAS Employment Services Offices which operate the EURES placement service.

**work, prohibition of.** The High Court is empowered to order that the use of a place of work, or part thereof, be restricted or prohibited on an *ex parte* application by the National Authority for Occupational Safety and Health; the

Authority may apply to the court when it considers that the risk to the safety and health of persons is so serious that the restriction or prohibition is necessary until specified measures have been taken to reduce the risk to a reasonable level: Safety, Health and Welfare at Work Act 1989 s.39. See PROHIBITION NOTICE.

**work, right to.** The Constitution recognises the right to work in that it requires that the State shall, in particular, direct its policy towards securing that the citizens (all of whom, men and women equally, have an adequate means of livelyhood) may through their occupations find the means of making reasonable provision for their domestic needs: art.45(2)(1).

It has been held that a compulsory retirement scheme does not infringe the right to work: Rodgers v ITGWU (1978) HC. However a union may not be able to refuse membership to a person if the refusal is to prevent that person exercising the right to work: Murphy v Stewart (1973) IR 97. See also Scally v Minister for the Environment (1988) HC.

**workstation.** An assembly comprising *display screen equipment* (qv) which may be provided with a keyboard or input device and/or software determining the operator and machine interface, and includes optional accessories: SI No 44 of 1993, reg.29. Every employer is required to evaluate the health and safety conditions to which workstations give rise for his employees, particularly as regards possible risks to eyesight, physical problems and problems of mental distress (ibid reg.31). Minimum requirements for display screen equipment and workstations have been specified (ibid tenth and eleventh schedules).

**work to rule.** A form of industrial action by employees which takes the form of working slower than usual and reducing output, by paying exaggerated attention to rules relating to that work. Also known as *go-slow*. See Secretary of State for Employment v ASLEF (1972) 2 QB 455.

**worker.** See INDUSTRIAL ACTION; TRADE DISPUTE.

**worker democracy.** See WORKER PARTIC-IPATION.

**worker participation.** The involvement of employees at board level in the company of their employment which is provided for by statute eg Worker Participation (State Enterprises) Act 1977 which provides for the election of worker representatives to one third of board places in single-tier boards of specified state enterprises. A lower percentage of worker directors is provided for in individual statutes eg Labour Services Act 1987 establishing FAS.

Worker participation at board level has been extended to further state enterprises and provision has been made to enable sub-board participative arrangements to be set up in a wide range of such organisations: Worker Participation (State Enterprises) Act 1988. A number of amendments to the 1977 Act are provided for, including giving power to the Minister to provide for worker representation less than one third of board size in certain State enterprises, subject to a minimum of two worker directors (ibid ss.9-23). See also Worker Participation (State Enterprises) Regulations 1988 (SI Nos 170, 171 and 172 of 1988).

Worker participation now extends to regular part-time workers: Worker Protection (Regular Part-time Employees) Act 1991 s.1. See Code of Practice on Employee Representatives (Declaration) Order 1993 (SI No 169 of 1993). See POSTAL VOTING RULES.

**workers, freedom of movement of.** There is a right to freedom of movement for workers within the EC under the Treaty of Rome 1957, art.48. Member States are required to abolish any discrimination based on nationality between workers of these states as regards employment, remuneration and other conditions of work and employment. See Cousins in 8ILT & SJ (1990) 258.See EURO-JUS; FREE MOVEMENT.

**working capital.** See CAPITAL; UNDERSUB-SCRIBED.

**working hours.** Generally the normal working day for employees must not be longer than 9 hours, the working week must not exceed 48 hours and work must not be continued after 8pm. Overtime must not exceed 2 hours per day, 12 hours per week, 240 hours per year or 36 hours in a period of four consecutive weeks. Shift work may be unlawful unless it is done on a continuous process; an employee may not work on two consecutive shifts. It is unlawful to permit a woman to do industrial work at any time between the hours of 10pm and 8am.

There are very many exceptions to these general rules by way of Ministerial regulations and licences, such as *shift work licences*. There are also restrictions on the hours which children and young persons can work. See Conditions of Employment Acts 1936 and 1944; Shops (Conditions of Employment) Acts 1938 and 1942; Mines and Quarries Act 1965; Night Work Bakeries Act 1936 and 1981; Road Traffic Act 1961 and 1968; EEC Regulations 543/69 and 1463/70; ILO Convention No 89 (Night Work for Women).

It has been contended that an employer has a duty to exercise reasonable care not to occasion injury to his employee by over-working him: Johnstone v Blomsbury Health Authority (1991) 2 All ER 293 (CA) as reported by White in 9ILT & SJ (1991) 240. See CHILD, EMPLOYMENT OF; OVERTIME; YOUNG PERSON; NIGHTWORK; OVERTIME; WORKING TIME DIRECTIVE.

**working-men's club.** See FRIENDLY SOCIETY.

**working time directive.** The EC Directive agreed on 1st June 1993 which limits working time to a maximum of 48 hours per week, inclusive of overtime, averaged over either 4 or 6 months, depending on job category. Night work must not exceed 8 hours per night on average. There must be a minimum rest period of 11 consecutive hours in each period of 24 consecutive hours, and a minimum weekly rest period of 35 consecutive hours, in principle to include a Sunday; a mandatory rest period when the working day exceeds 6 hours; and a minimum four weeks' annual paid leave. Individual member States have 3 years in which to implement the Directive, with the UK claiming it has 10 years to implement the 48 hour limit.

**World Court.** Term sometimes used to describe the International Court of Justice (qv) of the United Nations.

**World Intellectual Property Organisation; WIPO.** An inter-governmental organisation and successor since 1970 of the United International Bureaux for the Protection of Intellectual Property (BIRPI) which had been in existence for over 80 years. WIPO administers the Paris Convention (qv), which is an open convention, open to all states who have but to inform WIPO of their accession; WIPO then informs all other member states of that accession. WIPO is now an agency of the United Nations.

**worship, public.** The State acknowledges that the homage of public worship is due to Almighty God: 1937 Constitution, art.44(1)(1). See PUBLIC WORSHIP, DISTURBANCE OF; RELIGIOUS FREEDOM.

**worts.** The liquid which is fermented to produce beer: Finance Act 1992 s.89.

**wounding.** See BODILY HARM, GRIEVOUS.

**wound pension.** See PENSION.

**wreck.** A vessel, or part of a vessel, lying wrecked on, in or under the sea bed or on or in land covered by water, and any objects contained in or on the vessel and any objects that were formerly contained in or on a vessel and are lying on, in or under the sea bed or on or in land covered by water: National Monuments (Amendment) Act 1987 s.1(1). The Commissioners for Public Works may make an *underwater heritage order* designating as a restricted area, an area of the sea bed, or land covered by water, around and including a site where a wreck or an archaeological object lies or formerly lay (ibid s.3). There are further provisions to protect such sites.

**writ.** A document issued in the name of a court, or a duly appointed person, commanding the person to whom it is addressed to do or to forebear from doing some act eg a summons (qv); or a direction to hold an election: Electoral Act 1992, fourth schedule. See BYE-ELECTION; DISSOLUTION.

**writer.** See ARTIST, TAX EXEMPTION OF; AUTHOR.

**writing, contracts requiring.** Some contracts are required to be in writing eg contracts without consideration (qv); and some contracts are required to be evidenced in writing eg contracts for the sale of land. See DEED; ORAL AGREEMENT; MODIFICATION OF CONTRACT BY; SALE OF GOODS; SIMPLE CONTRACTS; STATUTE OF FRAUDS.

**wrong.** (1) An act contrary to law. (2) A tort (qv) involving the breach of a duty imposed by law or the violation of a right. (3) A tort, breach of contract or breach of trust whether the act is committed by the person to whom the wrong is attributed or by one for whose acts he is responsible, and whether or not the act is also a crime, and whether or not the wrong is intentional: Civil Liability Act 1961 s.2(1). See CONTRIBU-TORY NEGLIGENCE; PLEADINGS.

**wrong baby.** See BABY, WRONG.

**wrong quantity.** Where a seller delivers to a buyer a quantity of goods less than he contracted to sell, the buyer may reject them, but if the buyer accepts the goods so delivered, he must pay for them at the contract rate: Sale of Goods Act 1893 s.30. See Wilkinson v McCann Verdon Co (1901) 35 ILTR 115; Norwell v Black (1931) 65 ILTR 104.

**wrongdoer.** A person who commits or is otherwise responsible for a wrong: Civil Liability Act 1961 s.2(1). See CONCURRENT WRONGDOER; UNJUST ENRICHMENT.

**wrongful dismissal.** An employee has a claim for damages at common law for *wrongful* dismissal. Apart from loss of pension rights, a wrongfully dismissed employee is entitled to damages representing loss of earnings in kind, but bonus payments, overtime, incentive payments, or commission may be recovered only if the employee can show that the employer was contractually bound to allow him earn them.

An employee also has a statutory right of redress if he is *unfairly* dismissed. Formerly, in seeking redress he had to choose between an action at common law for wrongful dismissal or the statutory procedure under the Unfair Dismissal Act 1977 (ibid s.15). However, he now may pursue both the common law and statutory remedies at the same time, up until the point where a hearing in the courts under the common law has commenced, on the one hand, or a recommendation of a rights commissioner has issued (or a hearing of the Employment Appeals Tribunal has commenced) on the other hand (ibid 1977 Act s.15 as amended by Unfair Dismissals (Amdt) Act 1993 s.10). See Meskell v CIE (1973) IR 121; Carvill v Irish Industrial Bank Ltd (1968) IR 325. See UNFAIR DISMISSAL.

**wrongful interference with goods.** See CONVERSION; DETINUE; TRESPASS TO GOODS.

**yacht.** See CHARGE ON SHIP; VALUE ADDED TAX.

**year.** When used without qualification, means a period of twelve months beginning on the 1st day of the month of January in any year: Interpretation Act 1937 s.12 sch. The exchequer and local financial year is the calendar year: Exchequer and Local Financial Years Act 1974. The income tax year commences on the 6th day of April in one calendar year and ends on the 5th day of April in the following calendar year; it is also referred to as the *year of assessment*. In employment, the annual leave (qv) year begins on 1st April.

**year, executor's.** See EXECUTOR'S YEAR.

**yellow book.** See STOCK EXCHANGE.

**young offender.** See REFORMATORY SCHOOLS.

**young person.** (1) For the purposes of employment, a *young person* is a person who has reached the school leaving age (qv) but is less than 18 years of age: Protection of Young Persons (Employment) Act 1977 s.1. It is an offence for an employer (a) to employ a person under 18 years of age without first requiring production of a birth certificate or other satisfactory evidence of age or (b) to permit a young person to work more than specified maximum hours eg 40 hours in any week for a young person aged between 15 and 16, or (c) to permit a young person to work at any time between the hours of 10pm and 6am (ibid s.14) or between 8pm and 8am in respect of industrial work (Conditions of Employment Act 1936 s.3 and 1944 s.2). A person under the age of 18 cannot be employed on or in an offshore installation: Safety, Health and Welfare (Offshore Installations) Act 1987 s.14.

(2) A *young person* aged between 15 and 17 years, within the meaning of the Summary Jurisdiction Over Children (Ireland) Act 1884 as amended, tried in a court of summary jurisdiction on an indictable offence and found guilty thereof, can be sentenced to a maximum period of imprisonment of 3 months:

Hatch v Governor of Wheatfied Prison (1993 SC) ITLR (29 Mar) and 11 ILT Dig 142. See CHILD, EMPLOYMENT OF; IDENTITY CARD SCHEME.

# Z

**zebra crossing.** A portion of a roadway on which roadway markings have been provided and at which beacons have been provided: Road Traffic (Signs) Regulations 1962 art.9 (SI No 171 of 1962). A driver approaching a zebra crossing must yield the right of way to a pedestrian on the crossing (ibid art.22(9)). See PEDESTRIAN.

**zillmerizing.** The method of modifying the *net premium reserve method* of valuing a long term insurance policy, by increasing the part of the future premiums for which credit is taken so as to allow for initial expenses: European Communities (Life Assurance) Regulations 1984 (SI No 57 of 1984), arts.2(1) and 17(2)(e)(ii).

**zoning.** Generally understood to mean the designation by a planning authority (qv) in its development plan (qv) of permitted uses for land eg for residential, commercial, or agricultural purposes. The actual term *zoning* is not referred to in the planning legislation.

# Appendix 1

## LAW REPORTS

Note:

Reference to Irish Labour Court and other employment determinations are listed at the end of this Appendix. See also ELR.

| Abbreviation | Report | Period |
|---|---|---|
| AC | Appeal Cases | 1891 – present |
| A & E | Adolphus & Ellis | 1834 – 1840 |
| Aleyn | Aleyn | 1646 – 1648 |
| All ER | All England Law Reports | 1936 – present |
| Amb | Ambler | 1737 – 1784 |
| App Cas | Appeal Cases | 1875 – 1890 |
| Ball & B | Ball and Beatty, Chancery | 1807 – 1814 |
| B & Ad | Barnewall & Adolphus | 1830 – 1834 |
| B & Ald | Barnewall & Alderson | 1817 – 1822 |
| B & C | Barnewall & Cresswell | 1822 – 1830 |
| B & S | Best & Smith | 1861 – 1870 |
| Beav | Beaven | 1838 – 1866 |
| Bing | Bingham | 1822 – 1834 |
| Bli (ns) | Bligh, New Series | 1826 – 1837 |
| Burr | Burrow | 1756 – 1772 |
| Casey | Judgments of the Court of Criminal Appeal – Ireland (See Frewen for 1924-1983) | 1984 – 1989 |
| Camp | Campbell | 1807 – 1816 |
| CB (NS) | Common Bench, New Series | 1856 – 1865 |
| CC | Circuit Court – Ireland unreported | — |
| CCA | Court of Criminal Appeal Ireland – unreported | — |
| Ch D | Chancery Division | 1875 – 1890 |
| Ch | Chancery (UK) | 1891 – present |
| Cl & Fin | Clark & Finnelly | 1831 – 1846 |
| Co Rep | Coke | 1572 – 1616 |
| Cox | Cox's Equity | 1783 – 1796 |
| Cox CC | Cox's Criminal Cases | 1843 – 1941 |
| C & P | Carrington & Payne | 1823 – 1841 |
| CMLR | Common Market Law Reports | 1962 – present |
| CPD | Common Pleas Division | 1875 – 1880 |
| Cr App R | Criminal Appeal Reports | 1908 – present |
| Curt | Curteis | 1834 – 1844 |
| D & R | Dowling & Ryland | 1821 – 1827 |
| DC | District Court – Ireland unreported | — |
| Dow & Cl | Dow & Clark's Appeals | 1827 – 1832 |
| Dyer | Dyer | 1513 – 1582 |
| E & B | Ellis & Blackburn | 1851 – 1858 |
| ECR | European Court Reports | 1954 – present |
| EEC OJ | EEC Official Journal | 1952 – present |
| EHRR | European Court of Human Rights | 1979 – present |
| ELR | Employment Law Reports — Ireland | 1990 – present |
| ER | English Reports | 1220 – 1865 |

| | | |
|---|---|---|
| Ex | Exchequer Reports | 1847 – 1856 |
| Ex | Exchequer Cases | 1865 – 1875 |
| Exch | Exchequer Reports | 1847 – 1856 |
| Ex D | Exchequer Division | 1875 – 1880 |
| F & F | Foster & Finlayson | 1856 – 1867 |
| Fed Cas | Federal Cases (USA) | 1789 – 1880 |
| Frewen | Judgments of the Court of Criminal Appeal – Ireland (Casey) | 1924 – 1983 |
| | | 1984 – 1989 |
| FSR | Fleet Street Reports | 1963 – present |
| Gl and J | Glyn and Jameson | 1819 – 1828 |
| Hag | Haggard | 1789 – 1838 |
| Hare | Hare | 1841 – 1853 |
| H & C | Hurlstone & Coltman | 1862 – 1866 |
| HC | High Court – Ireland unreported | — |
| HL | House of Lords Appeals | 1866 – 1875 |
| HL Cass or HLC | House of Lords Cases | 1847 – 1866 |
| ICJ | International Court of Justice | — |
| ICLJ | Irish Criminal Law Journal | 1991 – present |
| ICLR | Irish Common Law Reports | 1849 – 1866 |
| I Eq R or IR Eq | Irish Equity Reports | 1838 – 1850 |
| IJEL | Irish Journal of European Law | 1992 – present |
| ILRM | Irish Law Reports Monthly Index 1976-90 (1992) | 1976 – present |
| ILSI or ILSI Gazette | Incorporated Law Society of Ireland Gazette | 1971 – present |
| ILTR | Irish Law Times Reports | 1867 – 1980 |
| ILT & SJ | Irish Law Times and Solicitor's Journal | 1980 – present |
| ILT Dig | Irish Law Times Digest (incorporated in ILT & SJ) | 1980 – present |
| IR | Irish Reports | 1838 – present |
| Ir Ch R | Irish Chancery Reports | 1850 – 1856 |
| IR CL | Irish Reports Common Law | 1867 – 1877 |
| IR Eq R | Irish Reports, Equity | 1866 – 1878 |
| Irish Digests | Maxwell | 1894 – 1918 |
| | Ryland | 1919 – 1928 |
| | Ryland | 1929 – 1938 |
| | Harrison | 1939 – 1948 |
| | Harrison | 1949 – 1958 |
| | Ryan | 1959 – 1970 |
| | De Blaghd | 1971 – 1983 |
| | – | 1984 – 1988 |
| Ir Jur Rep | Irish Jurist Reports (New Series) | 1935 – 1965 1966 – 1985 |
| IRLR | Industrial Relations Law Reports (UK) | 1972 – present |
| ISLR | Irish Student Law Review | 1991 – present |
| ITLR | Irish Times Law Reports | 1989 – present |
| JP | Justice of the Peace & Local Government Review | 1837 – present |
| Jur | Jurist Reports | 1837 – 1854 |
| KB (or QB) | King's or Queen's Bench | 1841 – present |
| Ld Ray | Raymond | 1694 – 1732 |

| | | |
|---|---|---|
| Leach | Leach | 1730 – 1815 |
| LJ Ch | Law Journal Chancery | 1831 – 1949 |
| LJ KB(QB) | Law Journal Reports King's (Queen's) | 1831 – 1949 |
| LJ CP | Law Journal Reports, Common Pleas | 1822 – 1880 |
| LRC | Law Reform Commission Reports | 1981 – present |
| LR CP | Law Reports, Common Pleas | 1865 – 1875 |
| LR Ex | Law Reports, Exchequer Cases | 1865 – 1875 |
| LR Eq | Law Reports, Equity Cases | 1865 – 1875 |
| LR HL | Law Reports, House of Lords | 1865 – 1875 |
| LR (Ir) or Lr Ir | Law Reports (Ireland) | 1878 – 1893 |
| LR P & D | Law Reports, Probate & Divorce | 1865 – 1875 |
| LR QB | Law Reports, Queen's Bench | 1865 – 1875 |
| LT | Law Times Reports | 1859 – 1947 |
| Mac & G | Macnaghten & Gorden | 1849 – 1851 |
| Madd | Maddock | 1815 – 1822 |
| Mer | Merivale | 1815 – 1817 |
| MLR | Modern Law Review | 1937 – present |
| M & W | Meeson & Welsby | 1836 – 1847 |
| NE | North Eastern Reporter (USA) | — |
| NI | Northern Ireland Law Reports | 1925 – present |
| NI JR | New Irish Jurist | 1900 – 1905 |
| NLJ | New Law Journal | 1965 – present |
| NSWSR | New South Wales Law Reports | 1901 – present |
| OJ | Official Journal of the European Communities | 1952 – present |
| P | Law Journal Reports (Probate) | 1831 – 1949 |
| PD | Probate Division | 1875 – 1890 |
| Peake | Peake | 1790 – 1794 |
| Prec Ch | Precedents in Chancery | 1689 – 1722 |
| P Wms | Peere Williams | 1695 – 1735 |
| QBD | Queen's Bench Division | 1875 – 1890 |
| QB | Queen's Bench | 1841 – present |
| RPC | Reports on Patent Cases | 1884 – present |
| RR | Russell & Ryan | 1799 – 1824 |
| RTR | Road Traffic Reports | 1970 – present |
| Russ | Russell | 1823 – 1829 |
| SC | Supreme Court – Ireland unreported | — |
| SCC | Special Criminal Court Ireland – unreported | — |
| Sel Cas Ch | Select Cases in Chancery | 1724 – 1733 |
| S & L | Schoales & Lefroy (Ir) | 1802 – 1806 |
| SLT | Scots Law Times | 1893 – present |
| Sm & Bat | Smith & Batty (Ir) | 1824 – 1825 |
| Stark | Starkie | 1814 – 1823 |
| Supp OJ | Supplement to the Official Journal of Industrial and Commercial Property (Irish) | 1928 – present |
| Taunt | Taunton | 1807 – 1819 |
| TR | Taxation Reports | 1939 – present |
| TR | Term Reports | 1785 – 1800 |
| TLR | Times Law Reports | 1884 – 1952 |
| USPQ | U S Patents Quarterly | 1929 – present |
| Ves | Vesey | 1789 – 1817 |

| W Bl | Blackstone | 1746 – 1780 |
| Willes | Willes | 1737 – 1760 |
| WLR | Weekly Law Reports | 1953 – present |
| WR | Weekly Reporter | 1853 – 1906 |

## Irish Labour Court and other employment determinations:
(See also ELR)

| DEE | Labour Court determination under the Employment Equality Act 1977 |
| DEP | Labour Court determination under the Anti-Discrimination (Pay) Act 1974 |
| EE or EP | Equality Officer determination |
| M | Employment Appeals Tribunal determination under the Minimum Notice & Terms of Employment Act 1973 |
| P | Employment Appeals Tribunal determination under the Maternity Protection of Employment Act 1981 |
| UD | Employment Appeals Tribunal determination under the Unfair Dismissals Act 1977 |

# Appendix 2

**LAW REFORM COMMISSION'S REPORTS**

LRC = Report of the Commission

WP = Working Paper

C = Consultation Paper

**Conflict of Laws**

| | |
|---|---|
| Domicile and Habitual Residence as connecting factors in the Conflict of Laws | WP 10 – 1981<br>LRC 7 – 1983 |
| Private International Law aspects of Capacity to Marry and choice of law in proceedings for Nullity of Marriage | LRC 19 – 1985 |

**Contract**

| | |
|---|---|
| Minors' Contracts | LRC 15 – 1985 |
| United Nations (Vienna) Convention Contracts for the International Sale of Goods 1980 | LRC 42 – 1992 |
| Research Paper on Retention of Title (Barbara Maguire) | 1989 |

**Crime**

| | |
|---|---|
| Child Sexual Abuse | C – 1989 |
| Child Sexual Abuse | LRC 32 – 1990 |
| Confiscation of the Proceeds of Crime | LRC 35 – 1991 |
| The Law relating to Dishonesty | LRC 43 – 1992 |
| Crime of Libel | C – 1991 |
| Crime of Libel | LRC 41 – 1991 |
| Offences under the Dublin Police Acts and related offences | LRC 14 – 1985 |
| Rape – Consultation Paper | C – 1987 |
| Rape and Allied Offences | LRC 24 – 1988 |
| Receiving Stolen Property | LRC 23 – 1987 |
| Sentencing – Consultation Paper | C – 1993 |
| Sexual Offences against the Mentally Handicapped | LRC 33 – 1990 |
| Malicious Damage | LRC 26 – 1988 |
| Vagrancy and Related Offences | LRC 11 – 1985 |

## Evidence

| | |
|---|---|
| Competence and Compellability of Spouses as Witnesses | LRC 13 – 1985 |
| Oaths and Affirmations | LRC 34 – 1990 |
| Taking of Evidence Abroad in Civil and Commercial Matters (Hague Convention) | LRC 16 – 1985 |
| The Rule against Hearsay | WP 9 – 1980 |
| The Rule against Hearsay in Civil Cases | LRC 25 – 1988 |

## Family (see also Conflict of Laws)

| | |
|---|---|
| Age of Majority, Age of Marriage, and some connected subjects | WP 2 – 1977<br>LRC 5 – 1983 |
| Breach of Promise of Marriage | WP 4 – 1978 |
| Criminal Conversation and the Enticement and Harbouring of a Spouse | WP 5 – 1978 |
| Civil Aspects of International Child Abduction and some related matters (Hague Convention) | LRC 12 – 1985 |
| Divorce a Mensa et Thoro and related matters | LRC 8 – 1983 |
| First Report on Family Law<br>— criminal conversation<br>— enticement of spouse or child<br>— loss of consortium<br>— personal injury to a child<br>— seduction of a child<br>— matrimonial property<br>— breach of promise of marriage | LRC 1 – 1981 |
| Illigitimacy | LRC 4 – 1982 |
| Jurisdiction in Proceedings for Nullity of Marriage, Recognition of Foreign Nullity Decrees, and the Hague Convention on the Celebration and Recognition of the Validity of Marriages | LRC 20 – 1985 |
| Loss of Consortium and Loss of Services of a Child | WP 7 – 1979 |
| Nullity of Marriage | LRC 9 – 1984 |
| Recognition of Foreign Adoption Decrees | LCR 29 – 1989 |
| Recognition of Foreign Divorces and Legal Separations | WP 11 – 1984<br>LCR 10 – 1985 |
| Restitution of Conjugal Rights, Jactitation of Marriage and related matters | LRC 6 – 1983 |
| Seduction and Enticement and Harbouring of a Child | WP 6 – 1979 |

## General

| | |
|---|---|
| Annual Reports of Commission | 1977 to date |

## Land

Land Law and Conveyancing Law
  (1) General Proposals — LRC 30 – 1989
  (2) Enduring Powers of Attorney — LRC 31 – 1989
  (3) Passing of Risk from Vendor to Purchaser — LRC 40 – 1991

  (4) Service of Completion Notices — LRC 44 – 1992
  (5) Further General Proposals

Liability of Builders, Vendors and Lessors for the Quality and Fitness of Premises — WP 1 – 1977

Defective Premises — LRC 3 – 1982

## Practice & Procedure

Contempt of Court — C – 1991

Debt Collection

  (1) The Law Relating to Sheriffs — LRC 27 – 1988

  (2) Retention of Title — LRC 28 – 1989

Indexation of Fines — LRC 37 – 1991

Judicial Review of Administrative Action: The Problem of Remedies — WP 8 – 1979

Sentencing – Consultation Paper — C – 1993

Service of Documents Abroad re Civil Proceedings (the Hague Convention) — LRC 22 – 1987

Statute of Limitations: Claims in respect of Latent Personal Injuries — LRC 21 – 1987

## Succession

Hague Convention on Succession to the Estates of Deceased Persons — LRC 36 – 1991

## Tort

Civil Law of Defamation — C – 1991
Civil Law of Defamation — LRC 38 – 1991

Civil Liability for Animals — WP 3 – 1977 / LRC 2 – 1982

## Appendix 2

# Appendix 3

**TEXT – BIBLIOGRAPHY**

**Books on Irish Law referred to in Dictionary**

Notes:

* Regular updating service
+ Not a legal text but of historical interest or helpful in understanding the law
F Forthcoming publication

| Author | Title and Edition |
|---|---|
| Appleby T & Roche J | Capital Gains Tax (1988) |
| Arnold L J | The Restoration Land Settlement in County Dublin (1660 – 1688) (1993 +) |
| Ashe M & Murphy Y | Insider Dealing (1992) |
| Babington A B | The Jurisdiction and Practice of County Courts in Ireland On Equity and Probate Matters (1910) |
| Bale N & Condon J | Capital Acquisitions Tax (1989) |
| Barnes J | Irish Industrial Schools 1868-1908 (1989 +) |
| Barron J & Ford M | Practice and Procedure in the Master's Court (1993 F) |
| Bell | Modern Law of Personal Property in England & Ireland (1991) |
| Berger V | The Case Law of the European Court of Human Rights: A Practical Guide <br> Vol 1 1960-87 (1989); <br> Vol 2 1988-90 (1992). |
| Binchy W (1) | Irish Conflict of Laws (1988) |
| Binchy W (2) | A Casebook of Irish Family Law (1984) (2nd Edition 1993 F) |
| de Blacam M (1) | The Control of Private Rented Dwellings (1992) |
| de Blacam M (2) | Drunken Driving and the Law (1986) |
| Brady J C | Succession Law in Ireland (1989) |
| Brady J C & Kerr T | The Limitation of Actions in the Republic of Ireland (1984) |
| Brennan F | A Company purchasing its own Shares (1992) |
| Brennan O | Laying down the Law (1991) |
| Browne D | Separation and Divorce Matters for Women (1989) |
| Brown J | Competition Law and Regulation in Ireland: the New Business Requirements (1992) |
| Butterworth Ireland (1) | Guide to the European Communities (1989) |
| Butterworth Ireland (2) | Tax Acts 1991/92 (1992) |
| Butterworth Ireland (3) | Tax Acts 1992/93 |
| Butterworth Ireland (4) | Tax Guide 1992/93 |
| Byrne P | The EEC Convention on Jurisdiction and the Enforcement of Judgments (1990) |
| Byrne R (1) | Irish Commercial Law (1988) – 2nd Edition |

| | |
|---|---|
| Byrne R (2) | The Safety, Health and Welfare at Work Act 1989 – a Guide (1992) |
| Byrne R & Binchy W | Annual Review of Irish Law (1987; 1988; 1989; 1990; 1991; 1992) |
| Byrne R & McCutcheon P | The Irish Legal System (1989) |
| Carroll P | The Garda Siochana Guide (1991) |
| Casey J | Constitutional Law in Ireland (1987) |
| Casey J P | The Office of the Attorney General in Ireland (1980) |
| Cassells F Clayton C & Moore P | Self Assessment (1988) |
| Central Bank of Ireland | Exchange Control Manual (1979*) |
| Charleton P (1) | Controlled Drugs and the Criminal Law (1986) |
| Charleton P (2) | Offences against the Person (1992) |
| Charleton P (3) | Criminal Law – Cases & Materials (1992) |
| Clark R (1) | Contract (1986) |
| Clark R (2) | Data Protection Law in Ireland (1990) |
| Cole J S R | Irish Cases on Evidence (1982) |
| Collins A M & O'Reilly J | Civil Proceedings and the State in Ireland: A Practitioner's Guide (1990) |
| Competition Authority | A Guide to Irish Legislation on Competition (1992) |
| Comyn Sir J | Summing it up – Memoirs of an Irishman at Law in England (1991 +) |
| Cooney, McLaughlin & Taggart | Summary of Taxation in the Republic of Ireland 1992/1993 (1992) |
| Cremins D | Value Added Tax (1983) Supplement (1986) New Edition (1988) |
| Curtin D | Irish Employment Equality Law (1989) |
| Curtin D & O'Keeffe D | Constitutional Adjudication in European Community and National Law (1992) |
| Daly B D | Handbook of Irish Case Law (1989) |
| Daly C B | Law and Morals (1993) |
| Deale K E L | The Law of Landlord and Tenant in the Republic of Ireland (1968) |
| Delaney H | The Courts Acts (Annotated) (1993 F) |
| Delaney V T H | The Law relating to Charities in Ireland (1962) |
| Dempsey B | Company Law on Computer (1992) |
| Dempsey F J | Handbook of Essential Law for the Irish Hotel and Catering Industry (1991) |
| Dixon G Y & Gilliland W L | The Law relating to Sheriffs in Ireland (1888) |
| Doolan B (1) | Principles of Irish Law (1986) |
| Doolan B (2) | A Casebook on Irish Company Law (1987) |
| Doolan B (3) | Constitutional Law (1984) |
| Doolan B (4) | Casebook of Irish Contract Law (1989) |
| Doolan B (5) | Casebook of Irish Business Law (1989) |
| Doyle C | Company Directors and the Law in Ireland (1992) |
| Doyle C | The Company Secretary (1994 F) |
| Duggan F | EEC Environment Legislation (Environment Research Unit) (1992) – A Handbook for Local Authorities |
| Duncan W & Scully P | Marriage Breakdown in Ireland: Law and Practice (1990) |

| | |
|---|---|
| EC Publications (1) | Treaties Establishing the European Communities (1987) |
| EC Publications (2) | The Rules Governing Medicaments in the European Community (1984) |
| Ellis E & Eustace PB | Registry of Deeds Dublin – Abstract of Wills – Vol III 1785 – 1832 (1984) |
| Ellis H | Insurance Brokers – Their Role and Regulation in the Republic of Ireland (1987) |
| Fennell C | The Law of Evidence in Ireland (1992) |
| FIE (IBEC) | Guide to Employment Legislation (1991) |
| Finlay T A (1) | The Constitution fifty years on (1988) |
| Finlay T A (2) | Advocacy: has it a future (1986) |
| Fitzgerald J B | Land Registry Practice (1989) |
| Forde M (1) | Company Law in Ireland (1985) |
| Forde M (2) | Constitution Law of Ireland (1987) |
| Forde M (3) | Extradition Law in Ireland (1988) |
| Forde M (4) | Bankruptcy Law in Ireland (1990) |
| Forde M (5) | Commercial Law in Ireland (1990) |
| Forde M (6) | Industrial Relations Law (1991) |
| Forde M (7) | Reorganising Failing Business (The Legal Framework) (1991). |
| Forde M (8) | Employment Law (1992) |
| Forde M (9) | The Law of Company Insolvency (1993) |
| Gannon Judge S | Practice and Procedure in the Superior Courts (1993 F) |
| Giblin H | Valuation of Shares in Private Companies (1987) |
| Ginnel L | The Brehon Laws (1894) |
| Government Publications | (1)  Law of Value-Added Tax (1987★) |
| | (2)  Bankruptcy Law Committee Report (1972) |
| | (3)  The Law of Nullity in Ireland (1976) |
| | (4)  Report on the Criminal Legal Aid Review Committee (1981) |
| | (5)  Scheme of Civil Legal Aid and Advice (1986) |
| Grogan V King T, Donelan E J | Sale of Goods and Supply of Services (1983) |
| Hadden T & Boyle K | The Anglo-Irish Agreement – Commentary Text and Official Review (1989) |
| Healy M | The Old Munster Circuit (1948 +) |
| Hensey B | The Health Services of Ireland (1988 +) |
| Hogan D | The Legal Profession in Ireland 1789-1922 (1986 +) |
| Hogan D & Osborough W N | Brehons, Sergeants and Attorneys (1990 +) |
| Hogan G & Morgan D | Administrative Law (1991) |
| Holohan B & Sanfey M | Bankruptcy Law & Practice in Ireland (1990) |
| Humphreys R F | Index to Irish Statutory Instruments (1988) Supplement (1990) |
| ICEL | Insider Dealing – Papers from Irish Centre for European Law Conference (1990) |
| | The New Competition Legislation (1991) |
| | The New Product Liability Regime (1992) |
| | Legal Aspects of Commercial Sea-Fishing in the EC (1992) |
| | European Initiatives in Intellectual Property (1993) |
| | Irish Competition Law and Practice in Ireland (1993) |
| | Legal Aspects of Doing Business in the EC (1993) |
| Institute of Taxation of Ireland | Taxation of International Financial Transactions in Ireland (1991) |
| Judge N E | Irish Income Tax (1987★) |
| Keane D | The RIAI Contracts – A Working Guide (1992) |

| | |
|---|---|
| Keane Judge R (1) | Company Law in the Republic of Ireland (1991) |
| Keane Judge R (2) | Equity and the Laws of Trusts in the Republic of Ireland (1988) |
| Keane Judge R (3) | The Law of Local Government in the Republic of Ireland (1982) |
| Kelleher S | Companies (Amendment) Act 1986. A Guide to the Accounting Reporting and Filing Requirements (1987) |
| Kelly F | A Guide to Early Irish Law (1989) |
| Kelly J M | The Irish Constitution (1987) (Supplement to 2nd edition) (3rd edition – Hogan G & Whyte G – 1993 F) |
| Kennedy & McWilliams | The Law on Compensation for Criminal Injuries in the Republic of Ireland (1977) |
| Kenny C | King's Inns and the Kingdom of Ireland (1991): The Irish "inn of court" 1541-1800 |
| Kerr A (1) | The Trade Union & Industrial Relations Acts of Ireland, Commentary (1991) |
| Kerr A (2) | The Civil Liability Act 1961 (Annotated) (1993 F) |
| Kerr A & Whyte G | Irish Trade Union Law (1985) |
| Kiely T O'Neill | The Principles of Equity as applied in Ireland (1936) |
| Kilty B J | Building and Civil Engineering Contracts in Ireland (1988) |
| Kotsonouris M | Talking to your Solicitor (1992) |
| Larkin J | The Trial of William Drennan (1991) |
| Laffoy M & Wheeler D | Irish Conveyancing Precedents (1992) |
| Lee G | A Memoir of the South Western Circuit (1990 +) |
| Linehan D | Irish Consumer Law (1980) |
| Linehan D M | Irish Land and Conveyancing Law (1989) |
| Lyden J & MacGrath M | Irish Building and Engineering Case Law (1989) |
| McAllister D L | Registration of Title (1973) |
| McAteer W & Reddin G | Income Tax (1987) |
| McAuley F | Insanity, Psychiatry and Criminal Responsibility (1993) |
| McCann L (1) | A Casebook on Company Law (1991) |
| McCann L (2) | Company Directors (1993 F) |
| McCann L (3) | Companies Acts 1963 – 1990 (1993 F) |
| McCann L (4) | Company Secretarial manual (1994 F) |
| Mackey N | Constitutional Rights: a practical guide for the layperson (1992) |
| Mackey R | Windward of the Law (1991 +) |
| McCormack G | The New Companies Legislation (1991) |
| McCutcheon J P | The Larceny Act 1916 (1988) |
| McDermott S & Woulfe R | Compulsory Purchase and Compensation in Ireland: Law and Practice (1992) |
| McDonald M (1) | Irish Law of Defamation (1987) |
| McDonald M (2) | Hotel, Restaurant & Public House Law (1992) |
| McGahon D | Irish Company Law Index (1991) |
| McGann J R | Cheques: The Paying and Collecting Banker (1973) |
| McGuire W J | The Succession Act 1965; A Commentary (Second Edition by Robert A Pearce) (1983) |
| McHugh D | Libel Law (1989) |
| MacKenzie P | Lawful Occasions: the Old Eastern Circuit (1991 +) |
| McMahon BME & Binchy W | Irish Law of Torts (1989); Casebook on the Irish Law of Torts (1992) |
| McMahon BME & Murphy F | European Community Law in Ireland (1989) |

| | |
|---|---|
| Madden D & Kerr T | Unfair Dismissal (1990) |
| Madden D H | Deeds, Conveyances and Judgment Mortgages (1901) |
| Maguire B | Research Paper on Retention of Title (for Law Reform Commission) (1989) |
| Mahon A P | Auctioneering and Estate Agency Law in Ireland (1990) |
| Mason Hayes & Curran | The Irish Mergers Act (A Guide) (1992) |
| Matheson Ormsby Prentice | A Guide for Business and Industry to Environmental Law in Ireland (1991) |
| Maxwell T H | Miller's Probate Practice (1900) |
| Mongey E G | Probate Practice in a Nutshell (1980) |
| Morgan D G | Constitutional Law of Ireland (1990) (2nd Edition) |
| Moore P & Brennan F | Corporation Tax (1987); Supplement (1988) |
| Moore A | Tax Acts 1991-92 (1992) |
| Murdoch H (1) | Invention and the Irish Patent System (1971 +) |
| Murdoch H (2) | Building Society Law in Ireland – A Guide (1989) |
| Murphy Y & Ashe M | Insider Dealing in Ireland (1992) |
| Nowlan K I | A Guide to the Planning Acts (1978); A Guide to Planning Legislation in the Republic of Ireland (1988) |
| O'Callaghan J M | Taxation of Estates: The Law in Ireland (1993) |
| O'Connor E R | The Irish Notary (1987) |
| O'Connor M & Cahill P S | The Law on Stamp Duties (1992) |
| O'Connor P A | Key Issues in Irish Family Law (1988) |
| O'Halloran K | Adoption Law and Practice (1993) |
| O'Hara J & Judge N | Finak (1992) – Finance Act 1992 with commentary |
| O'Higgins P | A Bibliography of Irish Trials and other Legal Proceedings (1986) |
| O'Higgins P & McEldowney J | The Common Law Tradition (1989) |
| O'Malley L | Business Law (1986) |
| O'Malley L & Courtney T | The Law of Business Association (1993 F) |
| O'Malley T (1) | Round Hall Press Guide to the Sources of Law (1993) |
| O'Malley T (2) | The Law of Rape and Sexual Assault in Ireland (1993) |
| O'Reilly & Redmond | Cases and Materials on the Irish Constitution (1980) |
| O'Reilly J | Human Rights and Constitutional Law (1992) |
| O'Reilly M F & Carroll B A | Colls' Tax Planning in Ireland (1986) |
| Osborough N | Borstal in Ireland (1975) |
| O'Siochain P A | The Criminal Law of Ireland (1981) |
| O'Sullivan P A & Shepherd K | Source Book on Planning Law in Ireland (1987) Planning Law & Practice (looseleaf) |
| Pearse R A | Land Law (1985) |
| Phelan M B | Guide to the Companies Act 1990 (1991) |
| Pierse R R | Road Traffic Law in the Republic of Ireland (1989) |
| Power B J | Accountancy Law and Practice for Limited Companies (1987) |
| Power V | Competition Law in Ireland (1994 F) |
| von Prondzynski F & McCarthy C | Employment Law (1989) |
| Redmond M (1) | Dismissal Law in the Republic of Ireland (1982) |

| | |
|---|---|
| Redmond M (2) | Guide to Irish Labour Law (1984) |
| Robb J H | The Law and Practice of Bankruptcy and Arrangements in Ireland (1907) |
| Roche D | Local Government in Ireland (1982 +) |
| Ryan E F & Magee P P | The Irish Criminal Process (1983) |
| Scannel Y | Environment Law (1994 F) |
| Scanlon J W | Practice and Procedure in Administration and Mortgage Suits in Ireland (1963) |
| Schuster A | The New Products Liability Regime and Annotation of the Liability for Defective Products Act 1991 (1992) |
| Shatter A J | Family Law in the Republic of Ireland (1986) |
| Sheeran N | Irish Business Law (1991) |
| Smyth A | Gender and the Law in Ireland (1993) |
| Stewart E | Arbitration Law in Ireland (1994 F) |
| Stout R | Administrative Law in Ireland (1986) |
| Sullivan A M | The Last Serjeant (1952 +) |
| Sweet & Maxwell | Irish Current Law Statutes Annotated (1984 *) |
| TCD | Law and Liberty in Ireland (1993) |
| Tierney M | Irish Trade Marks Law and Practice (1987) |
| Ussher P | Company Law in Ireland (1986) |
| Vanston G T B | The Law relating to Local Government in Ireland (1915) |
| Waldron J K | Rules of the Superior Courts 1986. Guide to Changes from the former Rules (Government Publications 1986) |
| Walsh E M & Keane R | Planning & Development Law (1984) |
| Whelan A | Law & Liberty in Ireland (1993) |
| White J P M | The Irish Law of Damages for Personal Injuries and Death (1989) Vol 1 Law and Practice Vol 2 Quantum for Non-pecuniary Loss |
| Whyte G | Social Welfare Law in Ireland (1987) |
| William Fry | The Company's Act 1990, A Commentary (1993). |
| Williams A G | Principles of Corporation Tax in the Republic of Ireland (1981) |
| Woods J V (1) | The District Court Practitioner — Remedies (1987) — Forms (1987) |
| Woods J V (2) | A District Court Guide in Offence Cases (1977) First Supplement (1981) |
| Woods J V (3) | Liquor Licensing Laws of Ireland (1992) |
| Woods J V (4) | A Guide to Road Traffic Offences (1990) |
| Wylie J C W (1) | Irish Land Law (1986); A Casebook on Irish Land Law (1984) |
| Wylie J C W (2) | Irish Conveyancing Law (1983) |
| Wylie J C W (3) | A Casebook on Equity and Trusts in Ireland (1985) |
| Wylie J C W (4) | Irish Landlord and Tenant Law (1990) |

## Books on UK or EC law, of relevance to Irish law, referred to in  Dictionary

| Author | Title and Edition |
|---|---|
| Abrahamson M W | Engineering Law and the Institution of Civil Engineers Contract (1975 UK) |
| Archbold | Pleadings, Evidence and Practice in Criminal Cases (1979 UK) |

| | |
|---|---|
| Bean D | Injunctions (1984 UK) |
| Benjamin | Sale of Goods (1987 UK) |
| Bennion F A R | Statutory Interpretation (1984 UK) |
| Bernstein R | Handbook of Arbitration Practice (1987 UK) |
| Blackstone | Criminal Practice (1993 UK) |
| Bowstead | Bowstead on Agency (1985 UK) |
| Bullen Leak & Jacob | Precedents of Pleadings (1975 UK) |
| Burgess R A | The Law of Borrowing (1990 UK) |
| Butterworths | Encyclopaedia of Forms and Precedents (1966 UK) |
| Byles | Bills of Exchange (1983 UK) |
| Cameron Markby Hewitt | EC Insurance Law (1991 UK) |
| Charlesworth & Percy | Charlesworth & Percy on Negligence (1990 UK) |
| Cheshire Fifoot & Furmston | Law of Contract (1986 UK) |
| Chitty | Chitty on Contracts (1989 UK) |
| Clarke L | Confidentiality and the Law (1990 UK) |
| Clarke M A | International Carriage of Goods by Road CMR (1982 UK) |
| Clerk & Lindsell | Clerk & Lindsell on Torts (1989 UK) |
| Copinger & Skone James | Copyright (1980 UK) |
| Cross Sir Rupert | Evidence (1985 UK) |
| Dicey A V | Law of the Constitution (1962 UK) |
| Dine J | EC Company Law (1991 UK) |
| Downes T A & Ellison J | The Legal Control of Mergers in the European Communities (1991 UK) |
| Duncan & Neill | Defamation (1983 UK) |
| Fisher & Lightwood | Law of Mortgage (1988 UK) |
| Gatley | Gatley on Libel and Slander (1981 UK) |
| Goff & Jones | The Law of Restitution (1986 UK) |
| Goode R M | Commercial Law (1982 UK) |
| Gough W J | Company Charges (1978 UK) |
| Gurry | Breach of Confidence (UK) |
| Harrison | Inland Revenue Index to Tax Cases (UK ⋆) |
| Hill C | Maritime Law (1985 UK) |
| Holden J | Law and Practice of Banking (1991 UK) |
| Horne F T | Cordery's Law relating to Solicitors (1988 UK) |
| Hoskin, E | VAT Case Digest – UK & Community Law (1991 UK) |
| Inglis-Jones N | The Law & Occupational Pension Schemes (1989 UK) |
| Ivamy H E R | Marine Insurance (1985 UK) |
| Jackson R M & Powell J L | Professional Negligence (1987 UK) |
| Jones C, van der Wonde M, Lewis X | EEC Competition Law (1990 UK) |
| Kerly | Law of Trade Marks and Trade Names (1986 UK) |
| Kerr | Kerr on the Law and Practice as to Receivers (1989 UK) |

| | |
|---|---|
| Laddie H, Prescott P & Victoria M | The Modern Law of Copyright (1980 UK) |
| Lindley | Lindley on the Law of Partnership (1984 UK) |
| Linell A | The Law of Names (1938 UK) |
| MacGillivray & Parkington | Insurance Law (1988 UK) |
| McGregor H | Damages (1988 UK) |
| McGuffie K C, Fugeman P A & Gray P V | British Shipping Laws (1964/70 UK) |
| Murdoch | Law of Estate Agency and Auctions (1984 UK) |
| Moore M | Managing Lawyers (1991 UK) |
| Napley, Sir D | The Technique of Persuasion (1991 UK) |
| Newbold W | Organising Lawyers (1991 UK) |
| Odgers | Principles of Pleading and Practice (1975 UK) |
| Ogus A I | The Law of Damages (1973 UK) |
| O'Keeffe | Law Relating to Trade Descriptions (1980 UK) |
| Ovey E & Waters M | Building Societies Act 1986 (1987) |
| Paget | Law of Banking (1982 UK) |
| Palmer | Palmer's Company Law (1987 UK) |
| Parris J | Retention of Title (1982 UK); Effective Retention of Title Clauses (1986 UK) |
| Parry & Clark | Law of Succession (1983 UK) |
| Phibson | Evidence (1982 UK) |
| Picardu | The Law relating to Receivers and Managers (1984 UK) |
| Powell-Smith V | Problems in Construction Claims (1990 UK) |
| Power V J G | European Shipping Law (1993 UK) |
| Richardson D | Negotiable Instruments (1983 UK) |
| Rowlatt, Marks & Moss | Law of Principal and Surety (1982 UK) |
| Russell | The Law of Arbitration (1982 UK) |
| Salmond & Heuston | The Law of Torts (1987 UK) |
| Shaw Sir S & Smith E D | Law of Meetings (1979 UK) |
| Shawcross & Beaumont | Air Law (1988 UK) |
| Snell | Snell's Principles of Equity (1982 UK) |
| Spenser J R & Flin R | The Evidence of Children (1990 UK) |
| Stroud | Stroud's Judicial Dictionary (1990 UK) |
| Terrell | Law of Patents (1982 UK) |
| Theobald | Theobald on Wills (1982 UK) |
| Tiberg H | The Law of Demurrage (1979 UK) |
| Wadlow C | The Law of Passing off (1989 UK) |
| Walker C | The Prevention of Terrorism in British Law (2nd Ed) |
| Weinberg & Blank | Take-overs and Mergers (1989 UK) |
| Whish R | Competition Law (1985 UK) |
| Williams & Muirhunter | The Law and Practice in Bankruptcy (1979 UK) |
| Wood P | The Law of Subordinated Debt (1990 UK) |
| Wurtzburg & Mills | Building Society Law (1989 UK) |